T0398968

Debt Restructuring

Debt Restructuring

Third Edition

RODRIGO OLIVARES-CAMINAL, RANDALL GUYNN,
ALAN W. KORNBERG, ERIC MCLAUGHLIN,
SARAH PATERSON, AND DALVINDER SINGH

OXFORD
UNIVERSITY PRESS

Great Clarendon Street, Oxford, OX2 6DP,
United Kingdom

Oxford University Press is a department of the University of Oxford.
It furthers the University's objective of excellence in research, scholarship,
and education by publishing worldwide. Oxford is a registered trade mark of
Oxford University Press in the UK and in certain other countries

First Edition published in 2011
Second Edition published in 2016
Third Edition published in 2022

Impression: 1

Published in the United States of America by Oxford University Press
198 Madison Avenue, New York, NY 10016, United States of America

British Library Cataloguing in Publication Data
Data available

Library of Congress Control Number: 2022938061

ISBN 978-0-19-284810-9

DOI: 10.1093/law/9780192848109.001.0001

Printed and bound by
CPI Group (UK) Ltd, Croydon, CR0 4YY

Foreword to the Third Edition

One would expect that the recent rapid developments in insolvency laws would exhibit a common philosophy. This is not so. The attitudes of the mosaic of jurisdictions point in all directions of the compass as legislators wave a legal wand in the hope of, by magic, conjuring up assets out of thin air.

This situation greatly complicates the international legal arena. This has already been intensified in its intricacy by other potent factors. These include the fact that all jurisdictions, except a handful, are now part of the world economy or seek to become a meaningful participant. They include the fact that financial crises exacerbate passions and hence drive the panicky search for some panacea. The result is that the world is immeasurably more daunting than it used to be from a legal point of view.

Law is the one universal ideology in which everybody believes. Our societies could not exist without it. The law expresses the credentials of a jurisdiction, its civilization. One of the fields of law, bankruptcy law, is the most powerful impulse behind commercial and financial law. Since there are not enough biscuits and brandy on the raft, it is the law which must ruthlessly decide who is to be paid, who is to be ahead of the others on the bankruptcy ladder of priorities to escape the swirling tide of debt, who wins and who loses, who is the victor and who is the victim. There is no question that bankruptcy is the most critical indicator of the culture of a legal system in its business law.

In addition, nowadays it is not possible to sidestep the interconnectedness of the world and hence the global impact of bankruptcy. No state is an island.

The strict black-letter rules of bankruptcy law are the backdrop against which the resolution of financial difficulties is negotiated. It is probably true that by far the majority of financial problems are resolved by a private restructuring, with or without a final judicial stamp.

The events of the first decades of the twenty-first century so far show conclusively the interrelationship between bank insolvencies, corporate insolvencies, and sovereign insolvencies. Each can have a contagion effect on the others. Hence the three areas have to be treated as a whole. It is a great merit of this book that all three are dealt with in one volume.

Yet it is astonishing that bank resolutions are now governed by prescriptive laws expressing the icy and iron hand of the state in response to the emergencies of the recent financial crisis, while sovereign bankruptcies largely rely on free contract, unfettered by an international bankruptcy statute. This is ironic, and perhaps part of the comedy of ideologies.

This book is a major contribution to the practice and the law on this fundamentally important topic. It is a work on the most useful aspect of law, namely applied law, the law in action, law in flight, what actually happens in the real world. The book is a real classic, produced by leading practitioners and academics in this field who possess an extraordinary depth of expertise and knowledge. It marks a huge step forward in the state of the art.

Philip R Wood, CBE, QC (Hon)
Head, Allen & Overy Global Law Intelligence Unit
Visiting Professor in International Financial Law, University of Oxford
Yorke Distinguished Visiting Fellow, University of Cambridge
Visiting Professor, Queen Mary, University of London
November 2021

Preface

Introduction

The first edition of this book went to press in the immediate aftermath of the 2007–09 financial crisis, when significant issues were being raised as to the appropriateness of restructuring mechanisms, in particular for addressing failures in a timely and speedy way. These concerns applied to corporate, banking, and sovereign debt restructuring, although of course the specific dynamics and objectives differed in each of them.

In the second edition, the authors were challenged by a significant volume of new case law, particularly as a result of the tragic events that we had recently experienced, marked mainly by the collapse of Lehman Brothers and the EU sovereign debt crisis. There were also new developments in English schemes of arrangement for foreign companies, policy change surrounding the rescue of Bear Sterns, and Argentina's sovereign litigation in New York. Many more examples come to mind, all of which were addressed in the second edition of the book and these examples were singled out merely by way of illustration.

Moreover, at the time of the second edition there were substantial regulatory, legislative, and policy changes to cover, including the recast EC Insolvency Regulation, the Bank Recovery and Resolution Directive, the changes implemented on the whole US financial regulatory landscape by the enactment of the Dodd-Frank Wall Street Reform and Consumer Protection Act, the model collective action clauses (CACs) of the International Capital Market Association (ICMA), the streamlined sovereign debt instruments or the European Stability Mechanism, and so on. This third edition comes at a turning point in the restructuring and insolvency landscape. This latest edition pivots on three seismic events. Probably the most important, due to its magnitude, length, and the fact that it affects all three sectors alike, that is, corporate, banking, and sovereign, is the COVID-19 pandemic.

We are witnessing the full effects of the pandemic, which has triggered a crisis that is having a major impact on economic activity around the globe and is still unfolding, producing some devastating consequences. As result of this crisis, many businesses will need to restructure, both operationally and financially. Regrettably, because of COVID-19, others will cease to be viable and will be liquidated. As has been evidenced, the crisis has already affected the corporate sector, especially small and medium-sized enterprises (SMEs), with losses of output, redundancies, and some closures. In turn, banks' loan portfolios have also been affected and it will unavoidably lead to higher levels of non-performing loans (NPLs) in the banking sector. This may be particularly challenging for economies that struggled with NPLs before the crisis and is expected to delay economic recovery. In addition, many economies are already in recession, a phenomenon that has affected both emerging and developed economies alike. In this crisis corporations and financial institutions have been affected, but also the central government. This sudden stop of cash flow and the resulting over-indebtedness have produced deep dents not only in the corporate and banking sectors but also in central governments, which have been badly hit by over-indebtedness to support the economy and by a loss in tax revenue. Moreover, the instability in all three sectors can lead to a 'doomed loop' (or vicious cycle).

There have been two main reactive policy responses to the crisis: (1) the use of emergency legislation to suspend enforcement and/or insolvency procedures (eg Turkey); or (2) a combination of emergency measures supporting businesses coupled with insolvency law reform to introduce a wider moratorium for businesses in support of restructuring (eg the UK and the US). This notwithstanding, corporations, banks, and sovereign nations are feeling the pressure and what we have witnessed so far is just the tip of the iceberg. Moreover, this unprecedented cross-sectoral crisis that does not distinguish between developed and emerging economies will require a widespread restructuring to try to keep alive economically sound businesses that have had to face a sudden stop in liquidity.

The other two significant game changers are region specific. The first one is the materialization of Brexit, and the implications that it has for the UK and its schemes of arrangements at the time that the EU is implementing the Restructuring Directive. In this vein, the Dutch seem to have taken the lead with the newly enacted Dutch Act on Wet homologatie onderhands akkoord (also referred to as the 'WHOA' or the 'Dutch Scheme') and the UK, in an attempt to counteract the effects of Brexit, has upped its game with the new Part 26A Restructuring Plans. The other important regional development which at the moment seems to be African-centred but would probably would soon have to expand beyond the African continent, is the adoption of the Debt Service Suspension Initiative, which was superseded by the Common Framework. These are two policy initiatives that the World Bank and the International Monetary Fund (IMF) urged the G20 countries to establish to assist less-developed economies to cope with the growing burden of accumulated debts, which has been exacerbated by the pandemic. These are two new building blocks of the international financial architecture.

Finally, the book once more aims to give an up-to-date international legal analysis of corporate, banking, and sovereign debt restructuring from the perspective of both creditors and debtors by setting out a practical guide to help practitioners, policymakers, and academics to understand current trends in debt restructuring and providing solutions for creditors holding distressed debt and options to debtors facing impending debt claims. As has been evidenced, there have been important and substantial developments in all three areas covered in the book, making this third edition a must read. The main aspects of each of the sections are highlighted below.

Corporate Restructuring

Corporate distress may be described both as a symptom and a cause of economic weakness. The capacity to resolve troubled corporations has become a priority, jointly with establishing appropriate rescue proceedings to protect the value of the company as a going concern and reassuring creditors that the value of their claim will not be diminished. Corporate distress is an unavoidable, and to certain extent a desired, outcome of market economies. Therefore, as a matter of policy, rescue processes may be regarded as an intervention aiming at reversing the distress scenario and averting the failure of the company by rescuing it, which is the main aim of modern insolvency laws. A properly structured corporate rescue process aims to obtain debt sustainability by reducing debt burden in an orderly manner while protecting the value of the assets and the rights of creditors to avoid litigation. These two important aspects (ie debt sustainability and creditor protection) need to be achieved over a short period of time in order to reduce possible disruptions and regain access to financing options.

A debtor may enter into negotiations with its creditors to reach a reorganization agreement, which most likely will imply less beneficial economic and financial terms for the latter. However, the counter side of this is that creditors may pursue remedies against the debtor in a court of law, trying to collect the full face value of the credit. It is in the interest of both parties to maintain a balanced approach that can successfully lead to an agreement: for the debtor to maintain the company as a going concern; for the creditor, because more often than not, a company being liquidated cannot face its liabilities and therefore a 'haircut' is imposed, and sometimes there is not even any prospect of recovery. In order to restore debt sustainability and revert the temporary distress scenario, a company can enter into a reorganization process. A reorganization process can be performed under the auspices of a court: a formal court-supervised (or judicial) reorganization. Another option is to proceed with an informal out-of-court (or non-judicial) reorganization plan, ie a private workout. The latter has been the focus of attention of policy makers and regulators around the world in an attempt to fast-track the rescue of corporations.

The principal objective in formal rescue processes is the protection of both the business as a going concern and the interests of the creditors of the company. By contrast, the key aspect in private workouts is the pursuit of self-interests by the relevant actors. The creditors of the troubled company tend to negotiate to maximize their own potential returns while the debtor tries to continue as a going concern. Sometimes, expedited corporate debt restructuring contemplates the use of rescue mechanisms that combine formal court-supervised judicial and non-judicial reorganization elements, which is the so-called 'hybrid approach'. These reorganization mechanisms use private (voluntary) contractual arrangements, which are supported by the intervention of the courts or an administrative authority. The support provided as a result of the intervention of the courts or an administrative authority is a cramming-down or binding effect. The courts or the administrative authority will ensure that the formal requirements and minimum thresholds have been met to assure that no fraud or deceit has taken place and that all creditors have been treated fairly and have had their right to express their will. These proceedings are generally referred to as pre-packaged deals and pre-negotiated arrangements, and both are directed to enhance the efficiency of the insolvency-related procedures by favouring a quick recovery from a situation that might otherwise lead to a collapse.

This third edition reflects, among other things, the impact of COVID-19 on US restructurings, including (i) potential grounds for investors/lenders to modify or terminate commitments to fund or to support restructurings by invoking material adverse effect or *force majeure* clauses, (ii) unprecedented forms of relief granted by bankruptcy courts to aid ailing retailers, and (iii) challenges facing bankruptcy courts in making the necessary confirmation findings regarding the feasibility of reorganization plans due to market instability.

The US section also reflects recent case law developments affecting the chapter 11 and chapter 15 process, including recent decisions regarding the 'safe harbour' provisions of the Bankruptcy Code, the impact of *Stern v Marshall* on bankruptcy court jurisdiction over third party releases in chapter 11 plans, and limitations on comity when not complying with chapter 15 procedures. The UK section, on the other hand, has incorporated the recent changes triggered by both Brexit and COVID-19, mainly changes regarding recognition in Europe and the changes introduced by the Corporate Insolvency and Governance Act 2020 (CIGA), most notably, the Part 26A Restructuring Plans. Also, reference is made to the new EU Restructuring Directive. Needless to say, relevant case law and transactional related updates are reflected throughout.

Bank Recovery and Resolution

In the Eurozone, the design of the Banking Union, which was successfully implemented due to the urgency triggered by the collapse of Lehman, has determined a transfer to the European level of the regulatory and institutional framework for safeguarding the robustness and stability of the banking and financial sector. In particular, the Banking Union introduced a common platform for regulation of (1) supervision; (2) resolution mechanisms; and (3) deposit insurance. The establishment of a single, unique safety net within the Banking Union addressed the 'vicious circle' between national governments and banks. A notable pillar of the new legislative structure is the resolvability system for bank crises. The Bank Recovery and Resolution Directive (BRRD) and the Single Resolution Mechanism (SRM) aim at ensuring that failing financial institutions can be resolved in an orderly and uniform manner in the Eurozone. Regrettably, the momentum gained in the aftermath of the great financial crisis and the collapse of Lehman was not sufficient to make the common deposit scheme a feature of the European Union.

In the UK, under the Banking Act 2009 (as amended), the Bank of England has the responsibility for the resolution of a failing bank, building society, or investment firm incorporated in the UK, as well as their group companies. It also deals with the subsidiaries of foreign firms and the BRRD has extended this scope to branches of firms from outside the European Economic Area.

In the US, the Dodd-Frank Act 2010 created a number of new agencies and merged or closed down others in an effort to streamline the regulatory process and increase the oversight of systemically important financial institutions, promoting greater transparency. Overall, the crisis has resulted in a complete overhaul of the US financial regulatory system.

This third edition digs deeper into these issues focusing on the fine tuning of a regime that was completely rebuilt in the aftermath of the great financial crisis and was overhauled with new common features such as the wide adoption of living wills or recovery and resolution plans, the emergence of bail-in and contingent convertibles (CoCos) aimed at ending taxpayer-funded bailouts, increased supervision, and greater macro-prudential oversight. Specific new sections include the maximization of the loss-absorbing capacity of banks, the experience gained after some successful resolution episodes, the contractual recognition of bail-in and, eventually, the usefulness, but at the same time, the challenges posed by bank insolvency procedures.

Sovereign Debt Restructuring

In the area of sovereign debt restructuring the challenges have been quite substantial, and the developments have been no less important. The last edition was completed after the EU sovereign debt crisis and once the 14-year Argentine *pari passu* litigation in New York came to an end. These gigantic episodes resulted in new developments from the official sector and the private sector alike, mainly the establishment of the European Stability Mechanism (ESM) in Europe, an intergovernmental organization under public international law. The function of the ESM is to mobilize funding and provide financial assistance (under strict conditionality) to Euro-area Member States and also to exceptionally intervene in debt markets. On the other hand, and because of the Greek crisis and more than 14 years of litigation in the Argentine *pari passu* saga, the ICMA proposed a menu of CACs and streamlined *pari passu* clauses.

The recent financial constraints triggered by the COVID-19 pandemic have given impetus to another revisiting of the status quo of the international architecture dealing with sovereign debt crises. In response to the impending difficulties being faced by certain economies which would be faced with additional massive fiscal spending to face the health crisis triggered by COVID-19, two initiatives were unveiled to avert instances where servicing existing debt would compound and constrain those countries' response to the crisis. The G20 devised the Debt Service Suspension Initiative (DSSI), by which bilateral official creditors suspended debt payment obligations from 73 low- and lower-middle-income economies. This initiative is being supported by the IMF and the World Bank, which help in monitoring the use of resources to address the pandemic shock. The aim of the DSSI is to temporarily free liquidity so that these countries can use available cash to mitigate the impact of the COVID-19 crisis on their population.

The shortcomings of the DSSI have been officially recognized by the G20, which endorsed the 'Common Framework for Debt Treatments beyond the DSSI' (the Common Framework). Under the Common Framework, eligibility is based on the IMF-World Bank Group (WBG) Debt Sustainability Analysis (DSA). The Common Framework requires the applicant to disclose the necessary public sector information on financial commitments (debt) but respecting commercially sensitive information (without clarifying what this is composed of). The Common Framework also requires the participating debtors to seek treatment on a comparable basis to other creditors, including the private sector, and brings on board official creditors previously unaffected, such as China.

This third edition has been faced with these substantive changes in the international financial architecture but also with an important challenge to the established tool of the trade, ie the CACs. The restructurings of Argentina and Ecuador in 2020 raised important questions around the extent of the comfort that these clauses provide. Therefore, two new techniques, the redesignation and the Pacman technique, that can undermine the value of CACs are analysed in detail.

Moreover, this third edition deals with several other issues such as the applicable interests to claims filed in the UK and US (both pre- and post-ruling), the use of domestic statutes to protect the debtor, transparency, and the ongoing Venezuelan litigation.

These changes have reshaped sovereign practices and enlarged the number of available restructuring tools in this ever-changing area of the law, all of which are reflected in this edition.

About the Book

This is a collaborative effort by some of the leading experts in the field who have pooled their resources to produce an ultimate guide to debt restructuring, covering corporate, banking, and sovereign debt. In this third edition, we were faced with a whole new landscape, with important developments in all three parts of this book.

The approach is theoretical and eminently practical since it is very closely related to different types of international financial transactions and their legal documentation. Wherever possible and appropriate, an actual case study is provided, the law and jurisprudence are discussed, and a draft of a relevant clause or example is provided. This book relies strongly upon English and US law. This notwithstanding, references to legal norms in other jurisdictions, as well as EU norms, are provided where necessary (particularly due to recent developments in continental Europe, mainly the BRRD II and the Restructuring Directive).

When a creditor is faced with a distressed debtor there are three possible options: to sue, to seek the aid of a court through a reorganization procedure (this option is not available in the case of a sovereign entity), or to enter into a voluntary restructuring. In addition, the latter envisages a whole array of alternatives. The core subject matter of the book is transactional restructuring. However, the requisites and feasibility of suing and the possibility of insolvency and liquidation of distressed entities will be part of the study to frame the subject and provide the full spectrum of possibilities.

The aim of this book is to provide an overview of the different techniques to achieve sustainable debt restructuring on an expedited basis. In summary, the book will provide (1) a practical guide for creditors holding distressed debt; (2) debtor options when facing impending obligations; and (3) the necessary steps to achieve their goals.

Professor Rodrigo Olivares-Caminal
Chair in Banking and Finance Law
Centre for Commercial Law Studies
Queen Mary University of London
London, January 2022

Contents

II. BANK RESOLUTION

III. SOVEREIGN DEBT RESTRUCTURING

Author Biographies

Rodrigo Olivares-Caminal is Professor in Banking and Finance Law at the Centre for Commercial Law Studies (CCLS) at Queen Mary University of London. Prior to joining CCLS, he was a senior lecturer in Financial Law and the Academic Director at the Centre for Financial and Management Studies (SOAS), University of London and the School of Law, University of Warwick. He has acted as a sovereign debt expert for the United Nations Conference on Trade and Development (UNCTAD), senior insolvency expert for the World Bank/International Finance Corporation, and as a consultant to multilateral institutions in Washington DC and Europe, central banks, and sovereign states. He specializes in international finance and insolvency law, and is the author/editor of seven books.

Randall D. Guynn is co-head of the Financial Institutions Group at Davis Polk & Wardwell. He is a leading bank regulatory and mergers and acquisitions (M&A) lawyer, and has been ranked a Star Individual in bank regulation by Chambers. He was named Banking Lawyer of the Year and Most Highly Regarded Banking Lawyer in the World by *Law Business Research* (2014 and 2017). He advises on financial services, including on critical transactions, business opportunities, and corporate governance issues.

Alan W. Kornberg is co-chair of the Restructuring Department at Paul, Weiss, Rifkind, Wharton & Garrison LLP. Alan has been ranked by *Chambers USA* for more than a decade, is recognized in the "Hall of Fame" by *The Legal 500* and has received the Lifetime Achievement Award by *New York Law Journal*. Alan is a conferee of the National Bankruptcy Conference, a non-profit, non-partisan organisation formed in the 1930s to assist Congress in the drafting of major bankruptcy law amendments. He is a fellow of the American College of Bankruptcy and a member of the International Insolvency Institute.

Sarah Paterson is Professor of Law at the London School of Economics, researching corporate insolvency and restructuring law. Previously, Sarah was a partner in the Restructuring and Insolvency Group of Slaughter and May, where she retains a senior consultancy. She is editor of *McKnight, Paterson and Zakrzewski on the Law of International Finance* and author of *Corporate Reorganization Law and Forces of Change* (Oxford University Press 2020). Sarah is a member of the Council of the Insolvency Lawyers' Association, the technical committee of the Insolvency Lawyers' Association, III, and the General Technical Committee of R3.

Eric McLaughlin is a partner in the Financial Institutions Group at Davis Polk & Wardwell. He provides bank regulatory advice to financial institutions. He has advised clients on the Bank Holding Company Act, the National Bank Act, the Home Owners' Loan Act, and other statutes and regulations applicable to financial institutions. He also advises on capital markets and M&A transactions, as well as on compliance, enforcement, corporate governance matters, and matters relating to digital assets and distributed ledger technology.

Dalvinder Singh is Professor of Law at the University of Warwick. He has been Adjunct Professor, Alma Mater Studiorum (Università di Bologna), Department of Management since 2019. His research interests are in the fields of banking supervision and cross-border banking. He is the editor of the *Journal of Banking Regulation* and a member of the Advisory Panel of the International Association of Deposit Insurers, Switzerland.

Table of Cases

Table of Legislation

NATIONAL LEGISLATION

Statutory Instruments

UNITED STATES OF AMERICA

Primary Legislation

List of Abbreviations

ABCP	Asset Backed Commercial Paper
APR	absolute priority rule
BAP	Bank Administration Procedure
BBR	Bank board resolution
BCBS	Basel Committee on Banking Supervision
BCCI	Bank of Credit and Commerce International
BCFP	Bureau of Consumer Financial Protection
BES	Banco Espírito Santo SA
BHC	Bank holding company
BIP	Bank Insolvency Procedure
BLMIS	Bernard L Madoff Investment Securities
BLP	Banking Liaison Panel
BRRD	Bank Recovery and Resolution Directive
BSIP	Building societies insolvency procedure
BSPA	Banking (Special Provisions) Act 2008
BSSAP	Building societies' special administration procedure
C&DO	Cease and desist order
CA	Court of Appeal
CAC	Collective action clause
CAIC	Comisión para la Auditoría Integral del Crédito Público
CASS	Client Assets Sourcebook
CBIR (UK)	Cross-Border Insolvency Regulations
CBRG	Cross- Border Bank Resolution Group at the Basel Committee
CCAA	Canadian Creditors Arrangement Act
CCAR	Comprehensive Capital Analysis and Review
CCP	Central counterparty
CCRT	Catastrophe Containment and Relief Trust
CDD	Claims Determination Deeds
CDO	Collateralized debt obligation
CDS	Credit default swap
CFR	Code of Federal Regulations
CIF	Co- investment funds
CIGA	Corporate Insolvency and Governance Act 2020
CJEU	Court of Justice of the European Union (also ECJ)
CMG	Crisis Management Group
CMP	Client Money Pool
CMU	Capital Markets Union
COD	Cancellation of debt
COMI	Centre of main interests
CPR	Civil Procedure Rules
CRA	Claims Resolution Agreement
CRD IV	Capital Requirements Directive
CRR	Capital Requirements Regulation

CVA	Company voluntary arrangement
D&O	directors and officers liability
DCF	discounted cash flow
DFAST	Dodd-Frank Act Stress Testing
DGS	deposit guarantee scheme
DIF	Deposit Insurance Fund
DIP	Debtor in possession
DOJ (US)	Department of Justice
DSA	Debt sustainability analysis
DSSI	Debt Service Suspension Initiative
EAMS	Euro-area Member States
EBA	European Banking Authority
EBITDA	Earnings, excluding interest, tax, depreciation, and amortization expense
ECA	European Court of Auditors
ECB	European Central Bank
ECJ	Court of Justice of the European Union (also CJEU)
EFC	Economic and Financial Committee
EFSF	European Financial Stability Facility
EFSM	European Financial Stabilization Mechanism
EIR	European Insolvency Regulation
EMCA	Emerging Markets Creditors Association
EMTA	Emerging Markets Trade Association
ERM II	exchange rate mechanism
ESCB	European System of Central Banks
ESM	European Stability Mechanism
ESMA	European Securities and Markets Authority
EU	European Union
FCA	Financial Conduct Authority
FDIA	Federal Deposit Insurance Act
FDIC	Federal Deposit Insurance Corporation
FFIEC	Federal Financial Institutions Examination Council
FHC	Financial holding company
FHFA	Federal Housing Finance Agency
FIBA	Financial Institutions Bankruptcy Act
FIRREA	Financial Institutions Reform, Recovery, and Enforcement Act of 1989
FMA	Financial Market Authority
FPC	Financial Policy Committee
FRAN	Floating Rate Accrual Note
FRB	Board of Governors of the Federal Reserve System
FRCP	Federal Rules of Civil Procedure
FSA	Financial Services Authority
FSB	Financial Stability Board
FSCS	Financial Services Compensation Scheme
FSIA	Foreign Sovereign Immunity Act 1976
FSMA	2000 Financial Services and Markets Act 2000
FSOC	Financial Stability Oversight Council
GAAP	generally accepted accounting principles
GDP	Gross domestic product
GSE	Government-sponsored enterprise

G-SIB	global systemically important banking groups
G-SII	global systemically important institutions
HBH	Hans Brochier Holdings
HERA	Housing and Economic Recovery Act of 2008
HIPC	Highly Indebted Poor Country
HUD	Housing and Urban Development
ICJ	International Court of Justice
ICMA	International Capital Market Association
IDA	International Development Association
IDI	Insured depository institution
IFC	International Finance Corporation
IFRS	International Financial Reporting Standards
IIF	Institute of International Finance
ILOLR	International lender of last resort
IMF	International Monetary Fund
IMFC	International Monetary and Financial Committee
IP	intellectual property
IPO	Initial public offering
IRS	Internal Revenue Service
ISDA	International Swaps and Derivatives Association
KSF	Kaupthing Singer & Friedlander
LBHI	Lehman Brothers Holdings Inc
LBIE	Lehman Brothers International Europe
LBO	leveraged buyout
LBSF	Lehman Brothers Special Financing
LDCs	least-developed countries
LICs	low-income countries
LMICs	low- and middle-income countries
LOLR	Lender of last resort
MAE	material adverse effect
MAR	Market Abuse Regulation
MBS	Mortgage-backed securities
MDRI	Multilateral Debt Relief Initiative
MOU	Memoranda of Understanding
MPE	Multiple-point-of-entry
MREL	minimum requirement for own funds and eligible liabilities
MSME	micro, small, and medium enterprise
NBC	National Bankruptcy Conference
NCWO	'no creditor worse off'
NCWOL	'no-creditor-worse-off-than-in-liquidation'
NPL	non-performing loans
NPV	net present value
NYSE	New York Stock Exchange
OCC	Office Comptroller of Currency
OFHEO	Office of Federal Housing Enterprise Oversight
O-SII	other systemically important institution
OTS	Office of Thrift Supervision
P&A	Purchase and assumption
PCA	Prompt corrective action
PE	private equity

PONV	point of non-viability
PPIP	Public-Private Investment Program
PPP	Paycheck Protection Program
PRA	Prudential Regulation Authority
PRC	Prudential Regulation Committee
PRGF	Poverty Reduction and Growth Facility
PSI	private sector involvement
QFC	Qualified financial contract
RAO	Financial Services and Markets Act 2000 (Regulated Activities) Order 2001
RPR	relative priority rule
RTC	Resolution Trust Corporation
RUFO	Rights upon future offers
SAR	special administration regime
SBRA (US)	Small Business Reorganization Act of 2019
SCB	stress capital buffer
SDRM	Sovereign Debt Restructuring Mechanism
SEC	Securities and Exchange Commission
SIA (UK)	State Immunity Act 1978
SICL	Saad Investments Company Limited
SIFI	Systemically important financial institution
SIPA	Securities Investor Protection Act
SIPC	Securities Investment Protection Corporation
SLHC	Savings and loan holding company
SMCR	Senior Management and Certification Regime
SME	small and medium-sized enterprise
SPOE	Single-point-of-entry
SPV	Special purpose vehicle
SRB	Single Resolution Body
SRM	Single Resolution Mechanism
SRR	Special Resolution Regime
SSM	Single Supervisory Mechanism
SSN	senior secured noteholders
StaRUG	Unternehmensstabilisierungs-und restrukturierungsgesetz (Germany)
TARP	Troubled Asset Relief Program
TIA	Trust Indenture Act of 1939
TLAC	Total loss-absorbing capacity
TLGP	Temporary Liquidity Guarantee Program
TPRRA	Taxpayer Protection and Responsible Resolution Act
UK	United Kingdom
UN	United Nations
UNCTAD	United Nations Conference on Trade and Development
US	United States
USC	United States Code
WACC	weighted average cost of capital
WBG	World Bank Group
WHOA	Wet homologatie onderhands akkoord Act on the Confirmation of Private Plans (Netherlands)

PART I
CORPORATE DEBT RESTRUCTURING

1

INSOLVENCY IN THE UK AND THE US

I. The Case for a Comparative Approach

The US and English models for restructuring the debts of companies in financial difficul- **1.01**
ties are fundamentally different.[1] The US chapter 11 regime is a statutory process under the
Bankruptcy Code, which allows a company to restructure under court protection and does
not require proof of insolvency.[2] By and large, chapter 11 acts as a single gateway to a variety
of insolvency and restructuring tools. The English corporate insolvency law regime might, in
contrast, be described as 'modular' in approach.[3] Modular, here, means that rather than having
a single gateway leading to a range of possible applications, English law offers a wide range of
restructuring tools that can be used individually, or in combination, and for different purposes.

---

[1] Alan Kornberg would like to acknowledge the invaluable assistance of his colleagues, Lawrence G Wee,
Sarah Harnett, Karen Zeituni, Caitlin Toto, Jorge Gonzalez-Corona, and Amanda Fell. Sarah Paterson would like
to acknowledge the similarly invaluable help of Lynda Elms, Sophy Lewin, Lois Deasey, Sarah Ellicott, Frances
Churchard, and Genevieve Kirk.

[2] Section 109(c) of title 11 of the United States Code, 11 USC §§ 101, et seq ('the Bankruptcy Code') provides
that a municipality must be 'insolvent' to be eligible to file for relief under chapter 9 (11 USC § 109(c)). Although
proof of insolvency is not required for relief under other chapters of the Bankruptcy Code, the issue of insolvency often arises in connection with whether creditors will receive post-petition interest and whether certain pre-
petition transactions may be set aside.

[3] The term 'modular' is inspired by Ronald Davis, Stephan Madaus, Alberto Mazzoni, Irit Mevorach,
Rizwaan Jameel Mokal, Barbara Romaine, Janis Sarra, and Ignacio Tirado, *Micro, Small, and Medium Enterprise
Insolvency: A Modular Approach* (Oxford University Press 2018).

1.02 The first edition of this book was written in the wave of restructurings precipitated by the credit crisis which brought into the spotlight arguments that the time had arrived for a single debt restructuring regime to be adopted in England. Commentators engaged in vigorous debate as to the extent to which the principles behind chapter 11 ought to be imported into a UK statutory scheme. In the meantime, junior creditors in complex capital structures increasingly sought to borrow ideas from chapter 11 in raising challenges to financial restructurings in the UK. A comparative review of the two systems could not, therefore, have been more timely. The second edition went to print after the American Bankruptcy Institute Commission to Study Reform of Chapter 11 reported,[4] and the European Commission issued a recommendation on a new approach to business failure and insolvency.[5] We noted, in the second edition, that creditors increasingly had security over all or substantially all of the debtor's assets in the US, exerting greater control over the direction of the case,[6] whilst the very nature of the finance market was changing in the UK.[7] At the same time, across much of Europe reform of restructuring procedures was under way or under consideration. The second edition was written against this backdrop of reflection and revision.

1.03 This third edition is written against a new, dramatic backdrop. Firms in both the UK and the US have suffered government-imposed shutdowns during the COVID-19 pandemic. As they reopen, they have had to cope with many COVID-19-related challenges, from reduced footfall in some sectors, to supply issues, and the costs of adopting revised health and safety protocols in others. In the UK this has resulted in the extremely rapid passage of the Corporate Insolvency and Governance Act 2020 (CIGA) through Parliament, so that this third edition analyses significant bodies of new legislation for the first time. Furthermore, in both the US and the UK multiple changes have occurred within case law and restructuring practice that necessitate discussion in this third edition. In particular, this edition discusses how investors have attempted to use the pandemic as grounds to successfully litigate material adverse effect or *force majeure* clauses, how bankruptcy courts have provided unprecedented forms of relief to debtors in industries hit hard by the pandemic, and how courts have addressed chapter 11's feasibility requirement in light of market instability. This edition also highlights noteworthy changes in chapter 15 bankruptcy practice, including eligibility requirements under section 109(a) of the Bankruptcy Code, third party releases, and limitations on comity without complying with chapter 15 procedures.

1.04 Notwithstanding the very significant bodies of new statute and case law which this third edition analyses, and the significant shifts in practice which it discusses, the fundamental aims of the corporate section of the book remain the same. First, insofar as the UK is concerned, they seek to identify a coherent body of restructuring law from the disparate sources which provide it. Secondly, they provide a comparative functional account of restructuring law in the US and the UK so that practitioners, scholars, and judges in each jurisdiction can learn

---

[4] ABI Commission to Study Reform of Chapter 11 2012–2014, Final Report and Recommendations, available at <http://commission.abi.org>.

[5] Commission Recommendation 2014/135/EU on a new approach to business failure and insolvency [2014] OJ L 74.

[6] For a description see Douglas G Baird and Robert K Rasmussen, 'Private Debt and the Missing Lever of Corporate Governance' (2006) 154 *University of Pennsylvania Law Review* 1209, 1288.

[7] See AFME Annual Review 2013 and 'Unlocking Funding for European Investment and Growth' commissioned by AFME from Oliver Wyman June 2013, both available at http://www.afme.eu (last accessed 20 August 2021).

a little from the other with a view to the development of an effective debt restructuring regime fit for the twenty-first century. Finally, they consider the different normative concerns and assumptions of fact which have contributed to the development of law on the books in both jurisdictions, the extent to which these require reconsideration in today's finance markets, and the implications for restructuring law and practice now and in the future.

II. Directors' Duties to Promote a Restructuring in the US

Directors in the United States generally owe fiduciary duties only to the company and its **1.05** stockholders, and not creditors of the company who are protected through contractual agreements and provisions of debtor/creditor law.[8] Accordingly, when a company is solvent, only its stockholders can sue the directors on behalf of the company in the event that the directors breach their fiduciary duties (or sue in their own right, if their injuries are distinct from any general injury to the company). But when the company becomes insolvent, creditors become part of the community of interests that have a stake in the company and the board must take into account their interests as well. As a result, if the directors of an insolvent company breach their fiduciary duties, a company's creditors may also seek to sue the directors on behalf of the company.[9]

Actual insolvency is the dividing line for when a company's board must take the interests of **1.06** creditors into account and when, in turn, the company's creditors may have the right to seek to sue the directors on behalf of the company. Prior to 2007, some courts had suggested that a board should begin to consider the interests of creditors prior to actual insolvency, during a period known as the 'zone of insolvency'. This was premised on the notion that '*the possibility of insolvency* can do curious things to incentives, exposing creditors to risks of opportunistic behavior and creating complexities for directors'.[10] But *Gheewalla* affirmed that '[w]hen a solvent corporation is navigating in the zone of insolvency, the focus for Delaware directors does not change: directors must continue to discharge their fiduciary duties to the corporation and its shareholders by exercising their business judgment in the best interests of the corporation for the benefit of its shareholder owners'.[11]

While courts sometimes describe insolvency as shifting the board's duties—from duties **1.07** owed to a company's stockholders when solvent, to duties owed to creditors when the company becomes insolvent—a board's fiduciary duties do not in fact change: a board always owes duties to the company and its 'residual claimants'. Insolvency merely causes creditors to join the class of residual claimants whose interests must be considered.[12] In other words, the interests of creditors do not in fact supplant the interests of stockholders; rather, they

---

[8] *North American Catholic Educational Programming Foundation, Inc v Gheewalla*, 930 A 2d 92, 99 (Del 2007).
[9] Ibid at 103. Unlike stockholders, however, creditors generally cannot assert direct claims for breach of fiduciary duties against directors. Ibid.
[10] *Credit Lyonnais Bank Nederland, NV v Pathe Communs Corp*, 1991 Del Ch LEXIS 215, 108 n 55 (Del Ch 30 Dec 1991).
[11] *Gheewalla*, 930 A 2d at 101; see also *Quadrant Structured Products Co. v Vertin*, 102 A 3d 155, 174 n 4 (Del Ch 2014) ('After *Gheewalla*, actual insolvency is the relevant transitional moment').
[12] *Quadrant* 102 A 3d at 173 (explaining that '[t]he stockholders remain residual claimants, but they can benefit from increases in the corporation's value only after the more senior claims of the corporation's creditors have been satisfied').

join them. This subtle difference can be important to the board of a struggling company. In *Quadrant*,[13] for example, creditors challenged a decision made by the board of an insolvent company to engage in riskier business strategies in an effort to save the business. The creditors argued that this strategy favoured the sole stockholder (who controlled the board) while disfavouring creditors, and thus was a breach of the fiduciary duties that the board owed to creditors. The Delaware Chancery Court rejected this challenge, concluding that the decision was intended to increase the value of the company as a whole, for the benefit of all residual claimants, and that it would not 'speculate about whether those decisions might benefit some residual claimants more than others'.[14]

1.08 The theory of 'deepening insolvency' as a separate cause of action has fallen out of favour. Under such theory, creditors could impose liability on directors and officers, among others, for the '"fraudulent prolongation of a corporation's life beyond insolvency", resulting in damage to the corporation caused by increased debt'.[15] But, in 2006, the Delaware Chancery Court rejected deepening insolvency as a cause of action,[16] and its decision was later affirmed by the Delaware Supreme Court in *Trenwick America Litig Trust v Billet*.[17] The Chancery Court explained that Delaware law imposes 'no absolute obligation on the board of a company that is unable to pay its bills to cease operations and to liquidate', but rather, the insolvent company's board may pursue, in good faith, strategies to maximize the value of the firm. The Chancery Court further explained that '[i]f the board of an insolvent corporation, acting with due diligence and good faith, pursues a business strategy that it believes will increase the corporation's value, but that also involves the incurrence of additional debt, it does not become a guarantor of that strategy's success' nor does it give rise to a cause of action.[18] Such rationale underpins the *Quadrant* decision noted above.[19]

1.09 Notwithstanding this ruling, subsequent cases have left open the possibility that deepening insolvency can be used as a measure of damages. *George L Miller v McCown De Leeuw & Co (In re The Brown Schools)*[20] is one example, where the Bankruptcy Court for the District of Delaware dismissed a deepening insolvency claim based on *Trenwick*, but held that deepening insolvency remained a viable damages theory for the trustee's remaining claims, including breach of fiduciary duty claims brought against the equity sponsor and board of an insolvent company.[21]

---

[13] 102 A 3d 155.

[14] Ibid at 187–188.

[15] *Kittay v Atlantic Bank of New York (In re Global Service Group, LLC)*, 316 BR 451, 456 (Bankr SDNY 2004 (quoting *Schacht v Brown*, 711 F 2d 1343, 1350 (7th Cir), cert denied, 464 US 1002, 104 S Ct 508, 78 L Ed 2d 698 (1983)).

[16] *Trenwick America Litig Trust v Ernst & Young, LLP*, 906 A 2d 168 (Del Ch 2006).

[17] 931 A 2d 438 (Del 2007).

[18] *Trenwick*, 906 A 2d at 205. See also *In re Bullitt Utilities, Inc.*, 614 B.R. 676, 683 (Bankr. W.D. Ky. 2020) (noting that 'the deepening insolvency theory [is] redundant of other causes of actions recognized under state law, inconsistent with principles of fiduciary responsibility, as well as the business judgment rule'.); *In re Sabine Oil & Gas Corp.*, 562 B.R. 211, 231 (S.D.N.Y. 2016) ('even when confronted with possible insolvency, fiduciaries of a corporation are not required to shutter the business and may, consistent with the business judgment rule, continue to operate the corporation's business … [a] manager's negligent but good faith decision to operate an insolvent business will not subject him to liability for deepening insolvency'.). However, not all jurisdictions reject deepening insolvency as an independent cause of action. See *In re Bruno*, 553 B.R. 280, 285 (Bankr. W.D. Pa. 2016) (recognizing deepening insolvency as an independent cause of action under Pennsylvania law).

[19] 102 A 3d at 186–187.

[20] 386 BR 37 (Bankr D Del 2008).

[21] See also *In re Hawaii Island Air, Inc.*, Case No. 17-01078, 2020 WL 2845411, *4 (Bankr. D. Haw. Jan. 3, 2020) (stating that while Delaware does not recognize deepening insolvency as an independent cause of action,

III. Directors' Duties to Promote a Restructuring in England

A. The Common Law

Traditionally, a restructuring has been triggered in England by breach of a financial main- **1.10**
tenance covenant in the company's debt documents.[22] If a financial maintenance covenant
is breached, the lender is entitled to accelerate its loan and demand immediate repayment
of all outstanding debts. If this right is exercised, it will render the company cash flow insolvent,[23] unless the company is able to repay the loan from its own resources or refinance it
from new borrowings.[24] As this third edition is being written, this landscape is increasingly
changing. There has been an increase in high yield bond issuance, and high yield bonds
ordinarily have incurrence, rather than maintenance, financial covenants: often a single leverage covenant which is only breached if the debtor incurs further debt. And increasingly
large leveraged loan agreements are on 'covenant-lite' terms, adopting the incurrence covenant approach.[25] This is an issue to which we will return.

When a company is trading solvently, the Companies Act 2006[26] provides that the primary **1.11**
duty of directors is to act in a way that they consider, in good faith, would be most likely
to promote the success of the company for the benefit of its members as a whole, as between whom they are required to act fairly, and in doing so to have regard to other factors including various specific factors (such as, for example, the interests of the company's
employees) listed in section 172(1). In the substantial reform of company law in 2006 the
decision was taken not to codify the duties of directors once the company is insolvent, but
rather to leave this to the courts.[27] Thus the duty in section 172(1) of the Companies Act
2006 is stated to be subject to any enactment or rule of law requiring directors, in certain

---

'the damages for a breach of the usual fiduciary duties of care, skill, or loyalty can be based on any decrease in the
company's net worth caused by the breaches [of fiduciary duties]').

[22] For a good overview of financial covenants see Rafal Zakrzewski, 'Loan Facilities' in Sarah Paterson and
Rafal Zakrzewski (eds), *Mcknight, Paterson, and Zakrzewski on the Law of International Finance* (2nd edn, Oxford
University Press 2017) 177–180.

[23] On cash flow insolvency, see further at section G.

[24] See Lord Walker's judgment in *BNY Corporate Trustee Services Ltd v Eurosail-UK 2007-3BL plc* [2013] UKSC
28, [2013] 1 WLR 1408 ('*Eurosail*'). On time to pay if a notice of acceleration and demand is served, see *Bank of
Baroda v Panessar* [1987] Ch 335. One of the first issues which the directors may encounter is determining whether
a breach of covenant is in prospect or whether it has already occurred. A difficult question arises if the directors
are already in possession of sufficient financial information to know beyond doubt that a default will occur, but it
is still some time before the testing regime in the covenant will be triggered. This gives rise to the question as to
whether a 'potential event of default' (sometimes referred to simply as a 'default') has occurred. A potential event of
default is normally defined as an event which 'with the giving of notice or lapse of time or both would constitute an
event of default'. It is suggested here that this does not mean the passage of time independent of the requirements
of the event of default itself. The words 'lapse of time' in the definition of 'potential event of default' are words of
description designed to refer to those parts of the relevant event of default dealing with the passage of time (such
as grace periods or a requirement to give notice) and do not impose a separate regime. Thus, it is suggested that
the potential event of default is only triggered once the grace period or notice regime in the event of default itself is
in play.

[25] McKnight, Paterson, and Zakrzewski (n 22) 180–181; Sarah Paterson, 'The Rise of Covenant-lite Lending and
Implications for the UK's Corporate Insolvency Toolbox' (2019) 39(3) *OJLS* 654

[26] Section 172.

[27] See, eg, The Rt Hon Lady Justice Arden DBE, 'Regulating the Conduct of Directors' (2010) *Journal of
Corporate Law Studies* 1 at 9. For a description of the history see Andrew R Keay, 'Directors' Duties and Creditors'
Interests' (2014) *LQR* 443 at 445–448.

circumstances, to consider or act in the interests of creditors of the company and the courts are left to develop guidance in this area.[28] This has not, however, led to the development of clearly articulated tests.

1.12 While a company is clearly solvent directors' duties are owed to the company, but the principal constituency is the shareholders. Unpacking this proposition a little, because the company is solvent, it is assumed that trading for profit is in the interests of both members and creditors and so there will not ordinarily be different interests between the two.[29] By contrast, when a company is clearly insolvent, directors must consider creditors' interests.[30] It is now considered reasonably settled that this duty to act in the interests of creditors is not a separate duty owed to creditors directly but an aspect of the duties which the directors owe to the company.[31] In other words, the content of the duty in section 172(1) of the Companies Act 2006 remains the same but the duty must be carried out with the interests of the creditors in mind. In a recent Privy Council case Sir Geoffrey Vos (Master of the Rolls) referred to the directors of a company owing 'a duty to its creditors'.[32] However, it is suggested here that Sir Geoffrey Vos was not making a substantive point and was merely using 'duty to creditors' as a shorthand.

1.13 Articulating the content of the duty to the company when the company is distressed is not straightforward. In an article in 2010 Lady Justice Arden noted that section 172 did not define success and suggested, 'It is usually taken to mean for commercial companies a long-term increase in value.'[33] This interpretation accords perhaps more readily with a company trading for profit than with a company attempting a debt restructuring to get back on its feet, but it is suggested here that it does roughly accord with the duty to maximize the value of the company found in the US jurisprudence. It is also tolerably clear that the directors must have the interests of creditors in mind when considering all of the relevant Companies Act duties.[34]

---

[28] Companies Act 2006, s 172(3).

[29] Thus, the suggestion in some of the cases that there may be some limited duty to have regard to the interests of creditors even when a company is solvent: *Winkworth v Baron Development Ltd* [1986] 1 WLR 1512; *Brady v Brady* (1987) 3 BCC 535.

[30] *West Mercia Safetywear Ltd (In Liquidation) v Dodd* (1988) 4 BCC 30, CA in which Dillon LJ approved the following statement of Street CJ in the New South Wales Court of Appeal case of *Kinsela v Russell Kinsela Pty Ltd (In Liquidation)* 4 NSWLR 722 at 730: 'In a solvent company the proprietary interests of the shareholders entitle them as a general body to be regarded as the company when questions of the duty of directors arise. If, as a general body, they authorise or ratify a particular action of the directors, there can be no challenge to the validity of what the directors have done. But where a company is insolvent the interests of the creditors intrude. They become prospectively entitled, through the mechanism of liquidation, to displace the power of the shareholders and directors to deal with the company's assets. It is in a practical sense their assets and not the shareholders' assets that, through the medium of the company, are under the management of the directors pending either liquidation, return to solvency, or the imposition of some alternative administration.'

[31] See, eg, *Lonrho Ltd v Shell Petroleum Co Ltd (No 2)* [1982] AC 173; *Yukong Lines Ltd of Korea v Rendsburg Investments Corporation* [1998] BCC 870.

[32] *Stanford International Bank Limited (in liquidation) v HSBC Bank Plc* [2021] EWCA Civ 535 at [32]

[33] The Rt Hon Lady Justice Arden DBE, 'Regulating the Conduct of Directors'(n 27).

[34] There are seven relevant duties. A duty to act in accordance with the company's constitution and to use powers only for the purposes for which they were conferred (Companies Act 2006, s 171b); a duty to promote the success of the company for the benefit of its members (Companies Act 2006, s 172(1)); a duty to exercise independent judgement (Companies Act 2006, s 173(1)); a duty to exercise reasonable care, skill, and diligence (Companies Act 2006, s 174(1)); a duty to avoid conflicts of interest (Companies Act 2006, s 175(1)); a duty not to accept benefits from third parties (Companies Act 2006, s 176); and a duty to declare interests in a proposed transaction or arrangement with the company (Companies Act 2006, s 177).

The duty is typically described as a duty to act in the interests of creditors as a whole.[35]   **1.14**
Much of the authority on the meaning of this phrase (which also appears in the statutory language for the purposes of administration) concerns circumstances in which the interests of a particular creditor are apparently pitted against the interests of the rest. But more difficult questions arise where different classes of creditor are implicated in a debt restructuring. Here it is suggested that the duty is to promote the success of the company in the interests of all creditors, but not to the extent that risks are taken which further impair the claims of one class of creditors in attempting to improve the claims of another class who do not have much prospect of a return. It is acknowledged, however, that these are extremely difficult judgments which are, in many ways, at the heart of this book.

A further question concerns the extent to which creditor interests are implicated. The obli-   **1.15**
gation to have regard to creditor interests has variously been described as an apparently exclusive obligation,[36] an obligation to 'include' the interests of creditors,[37] and as promoting creditor interests to become 'paramount'.[38] In an article in 2015, Arnold noted that the 'paramount' test appeared to be gaining the greatest traction, although he also noted that the decisions he was referring to were all first instance decisions, and concluded that 'the prevailing view seemed to be that the interests of creditors were to be treated as paramount when they fall to be taken into account, even (it appeared) if the company is not actually insolvent but is on the verge of insolvent'. He finished by concluding that 'Whether that is as it should be must, it seems, await consideration in due course by a higher court.'[39]

An Australian academic, David Wishart, alternatively suggested that there should be 'a con-   **1.16**
tinuum of regard for creditor interests from being one interest amongst many competing interests to being the prime consideration',[40] and the Australian authorities do appear to support a balancing of shareholder and creditor interests.[41] The practical consequence of the continuum approach is that the degree of consideration which the directors need to give to the creditors' interests will increase with the degree of financial difficulty.[42] But it does very little to tell directors how to balance risk, and seems to offer little by way of practical guidance for directors making real-world decisions in real time.

The Court of Appeal has recently undertaken a detailed review of many aspects of the   **1.17**
common law duties in the *Sequana* case.[43] As this book goes to press, the *Sequana* appeal

---

[35]   *Re Pantone 485 Ltd* [2002] 1 BCLC 266. See also *Oxford Fleet Management Ltd (In Liquidation) v Brown* [2014] EWHC 3065 (Ch); *Re HLC Environmental Projects Ltd* [2013] EWHC 2876 (Ch); *Re Kudos Business Solutions Ltd (In Liquidation)* [2011] EWHC 1436 (Ch); *Re Idessa (UK) Ltd (In Liquidation)* [2011] EWHC 804 (Ch).
[36]   *Brady v Brady* (1987) 3 BCC 535 at 552.
[37]   *Whalley v Doney* [2004] BPIR 75.
[38]   *Colin Gwyer & Associates Ltd v London Wharf (Limehouse) Ltd* [2003] BCC 885.
[39]   Mark Arnold, 'Directors' Duties in the Zone of Insolvency: Recent Developments' February 2015 *South Square Digest* 46 citing, in addition to *Colin Gwyer* (ibid), *GHLM Trading Ltd v Maroo* [2012] 2 BCLC 369; *Roberts v Frohlich* [2011] EWHC 257, [2012] BCC 407 at [85]; *Re HLC Environmental Projects Ltd* [2013] EWHC 2876 (Ch); *Hellard v Carcalho* [2014] BCC 337 at [92]; *Vivendi SA v Richards* [2013] BCC 771 at [149] and *Goldtrail Travel Ltd (In Liquidation) v Aydin* [2014] EWHC 1587. See also Keay (n 27).
[40]   David A Wishart, 'Models and Theories of Directors' Duties to Creditors' (1991) 14 New Zealand Universities Law Review 323, 331, cited in Andrew Keay, 'Directors' Duties to Creditors: Contractarian Concerns Relating to Efficiency and Over-Protection of Creditors' (2003) 66 *MLR* 665, 671. See also the discussion in Keay (n 27) 459–460.
[41]   Arnold (n 39).
[42]   For evidence of such a balancing approach in the Australian authorities see Arnold (n 39) 50–51
[43]   *BTI 2014 LLC v Sequana* [2019] All E R (D) 36.

has been heard by the Supreme Court, but no judgment has been handed down. In the Court of Appeal, Richards LJ declined to answer the question of whether, 'once the creditors' interests duty is engaged, their interests are paramount or to be considered without being decisive'.[44] It was not an issue which arose on the facts of the case and, in his view, it ought to be considered on the facts of cases where it is to be decided. However, Richards LJ did state, *obiter,* 'that where the directors know or ought to know that the company is presently and actually insolvent, it is hard to see that creditors' interests could be anything but paramount'.[45] This stands in contrast to the US decision in *Quadrant* discussed in section 1.07. And it brings us to the difficult question of the position when the company is neither clearly solvent nor clearly insolvent.

1.18   Until the *Sequana* decision it was very unclear when the directors' duty to act in the interests of creditors is triggered. The courts had described the point at which the duty arises in different terms referring variously to 'doubtfully solvent',[46] 'near-insolvent',[47] 'on the verge of insolvency',[48] in a 'very dangerous' or 'parlous' financial state,[49] or in a 'precarious' financial state.[50] Arnold and Haywood noted how imprecise these terms are,[51] and referred, with approval, to the test of whether the transaction is one which involves a 'real and not remote risk of prejudice to creditors' which originates in Australian authority and which, whilst not being cited directly, did seem to have been adopted in several English cases at the time they were writing.[52] However, this replaces one difficulty (determining the point at which the shift in duty arises) with another (how great does the prejudice need to be at any given point in time for the creditors' interests to intrude). After a thorough and careful review of the authorities, Richards LJ decided, 'the duty arises when the directors know or should know that the company is or is likely to become insolvent'.[53] He went on to say that 'In this context, "likely" means probable'.[54] Of course, the Supreme Court may disagree.

1.19   As discussed above, the US approach has been to provide that creditor interests are implicated only on insolvency, and that at that point the directors' duty is still to maximize the value of the company, with creditor interests joining, rather than replacing, shareholder interests. This is known as the entity maximization approach, and Andrew Keay has argued persuasively that it should be adopted in the UK.[55] Certainly it would seem to be the best test when we are considering directors' duties in preparing the company's business plan for the purposes of a debt restructuring, and in choosing which transaction to pursue. In this case, we do want the directors to seek to maximize the value of the company for the widest range of stakeholders, recognizing that the plan must be feasible and sustainable.

---

[44] Ibid at [222].

[45] Ibid.

[46] *Re HLC Environmental Projects Ltd* [2013] EWHC 2876 (Ch).

[47] *The Liquidator of Wendy Fair (Heritage) Ltd v Hobday* [2006] EWHC 5803 at [66].

[48] *Colin Gwyer & Associates Ltd v London Wharf (Limehouse) Ltd* [2003] BCC 885 at [74].

[49] *Facia Footwear v Hinchcliffe* [1998] BCLC 218 at 228.

[50] *Re MDA Investment Management Ltd* [2004] 1 BCLC 217 at [75].

[51] Mark Arnold and Marcus Haywood, 'Duty to Promote the Success of the Company' in Simon Mortimore QC (ed), *Company Directors Duties, Liabilities and Remedies* (3rd edn, Oxford University Press 2017) 306; Arnold (n 39) 46–51. See also Keay, 'Directors' Duties and Creditors' Interests' (n 27) 447.

[52] Ibid 281 citing *Roberts v Frohlich* [2011] EWHC 257, [2012] BCC 407. See also *Re HLC Environmental Projects Ltd* [2013] EWHC 2876 (Ch).

[53] *Sequana* (n 43) at [220].

[54] Ibid.

[55] Andrew Keay, 'Formulating a Framework for Directors' Duties to Creditors: An Entity Maximisation Approach' (2005) 64(3) *CLJ* 614; Keay, 'Directors' Duties and Creditors' Interests' (n 27).

B. Wrongful Trading

Potential wrongful trading liability will also be relevant. A court, on an application by a **1.20** liquidator in a winding up, can order that a director of a company which has gone into insolvent liquidation is liable to make such contribution to the company's assets as the court thinks proper if: (i) before the commencement of a winding up, a director knew or ought to have concluded that there was no real prospect that the company would avoid going into insolvent liquidation; and (ii) thereafter the director failed to take every step to minimize the potential loss to the company's creditors which he ought to have taken (section 214 of the Insolvency Act 1986, known as the 'wrongful trading' test). Following the Small Business, Enterprise and Employment Act 2015 this power was extended to administrators with effect from 1 October 2015.[56] The standard required as to what a director ought to know, the conclusions he ought to reach, and the steps he ought to take are those which would be known, reached, or taken by a reasonably diligent person with *both* the general knowledge, skill, and experience that may reasonably be expected of a person carrying out the same functions as those of the director in relation to the company, *and* the general knowledge, skill, and experience that the relevant director actually has. The test to be applied is therefore both objective and subjective. Once the lenders' powerful rights of acceleration are in the contemplation of the directors, they will need some comfort from the lenders that a negotiated restructuring is a possibility in order to draw the conclusion that there is a reasonable prospect of avoiding insolvent liquidation or, following the Small Business, Enterprise and Employment Act amendments, insolvent administration and continuing to trade.[57] The directors do not need to be certain and the courts are reluctant to judge with the benefit of hindsight.[58] The practical point for directors is that regular board meetings should be held and the minutes should evidence the state of play with financial and other creditors and the basis on which the directors are concluding that there is still a reasonable prospect of avoiding insolvent liquidation or (following the Small Business, Enterprise and Employment Act amendments) insolvent administration.[59]

---

[56] Section 117 of the Small Business, Enterprise and Employment Act 2015 inserted new ss 246ZA and 246ZB into the Insolvency Act 1986.

[57] See *Roberts v Frohlich* [2011] EWHC 257, [2012] BCC 407 for the position where the bank had demonstrated that it would adhere to its funding conditions in advancing funds and the directors knew the bank was proceeding on a false premise as to the extent to which those conditions were met; *Re Brian D Pierson (Contractors) Ltd* [1999] BCC 26 and *Re Bangla Television (In Liquidation); Valentine v Bangla Television Ltd (In Liquidation)* [2009] EWHC 1632, [2010] BCC 143 for failure to adequately assess the company's financial position; *The Official Receiver, Neil Francis Hickling v Dhiren Doshi* 2001 WL 172017 for lack of working capital; *Rubin v Gunner & Anor* [2004] EWHC 316 where none of the proposed methods of raising funds could provide any reasonable basis for the directors to conclude that the company would avoid insolvent liquidation.

[58] See, in particular, *Re Sherborne Associates Ltd* [1995] BCC 40 at 54 '... there is always the danger of *hindsight*, the danger of assuming that what has in fact happened was always bound to happen and was apparent'; *The Continental Assurance Company of London plc (In Liquidation)* 2001 WL 720239 [109], 'I think that Mr Atherton accepts on behalf of the liquidators that the directors did do their best to behave responsibly and properly from June 1991 onwards. He says that, although they tried their best, they got it wrong, and it was their fault that they got it wrong. This is an austere attitude. In the written closing submissions of Mr Davis and Mr Ritchie they wrote this sentence, with which I am in sympathy: 'The liquidators' complaints are infested with hindsight and wholly ignore the realities of being a company director facing the situation faced by the non-executives at the material time.' Mr Davies and Mr Ritchie refer specifically to the non-executive directors, because their clients were non-executives, but the remark is in my view equally applicable to Mr Burrows'; and *Re Langreen Ltd (In Liquidation) (Also referred to as Mond v Bowles)* unreported, 21 October 2011.

[59] See (n 56).

1.21   In Chapter 3, we will consider the use of the pre-packaged administration as a restructuring tool. In this case, the distressed company may trade for a period of time while the restructuring is worked out, appointing an administrator and filing for administration to implement the restructuring once it has been agreed. This gives rise to the question of whether the directors could be liable for wrongful trading liability on the basis that they 'knew or ought to have concluded that there was no reasonable prospect that the company would avoid going into insolvent administration'.[60] In many cases, the pre-packaged administration will be a contingency plan if a quasi-consensual restructuring cannot be agreed. In this event, the directors may well consider that there is still a reasonable prospect of avoiding insolvent administration. Even where this is not the case, the directors will only be liable to contribute if the assets of the company are depleted during the relevant period of trading.[61] In *Ralls Builders* no contribution order was made because the measure of loss for contribution was the company's loss (not the loss to individual creditors) and the company had traded at a profit, albeit for the benefit of the (secured) bank and to the detriment of some of the trade creditors.[62]

C. Alleging Breach of Duty

1.22   A question has arisen as to how these duties should be interpreted where it is clear that the senior lenders prefer a debt restructuring to an enforcement and sale. In *Re Bluebrook Ltd* (commonly known as *IMO Carwash*),[63] the mezzanine creditors contended (albeit rather late in proceedings) that the directors had failed to act in the interests of all creditors, but rather had favoured the senior creditors at the expense of the mezzanine creditors, and that the group had sufficient cash and cash flow to keep trading. Although a financial maintenance covenant had been triggered, the mezzanine lenders maintained that the senior creditors had no intention of accelerating their loan and selling the business and assets and that this effectively gave the junior creditors a negotiating position which the directors should have exploited. Mann J disagreed:

> This seems to me to be somewhat unreal. The group was, on any footing, technically insolvent. That does not of itself inevitably require any course of action, but it is a starting point for considering the impropriety of continued trading ... The directors realised that there were problems, and set about addressing them by engaging in discussions with the lenders. There were, as the directors recognised, events of default under the major credit agreements. They had valuations, none of which suggested that the Mezzanine Lenders had an economic interest in the group ... for them to threaten to carry on trading in those circumstances, when they had quite properly recognised a problem about that, would arguably have been to threaten to engage in wrongful trading.[64]

1.23   It is thus clear that for junior lenders to argue that they should receive value in a debt restructuring they will need to provide evidence of real, as opposed to nuisance, value in

---

[60] Insolvency Act 1986, s 214(2).
[61] *Ralls Builders Ltd* [2016] EWHC 243.
[62] Ibid.
[63] [2009] EWHC 2114 (Ch), [2010] BCC 209.
[64] Ibid at [60].

alleging that directors have proceeded against their interests. This point is reinforced by the *Stabilus* case,[65] in which, notwithstanding findings that the security agent had acted in breach of duty to the mezzanine lenders, the mezzanine lenders made no recovery because they were unable to demonstrate that they had value to protect. In other words, junior creditors or equity seeking to challenge a debt restructuring in which they are to receive nothing must demonstrate an economic case for the allocation of value.

The details of valuation are dealt with in Chapter 3 but, for the moment, it is important to note   **1.24**
that management wields significant power in supporting the creditors' case or not. In a US context Lopucki and Whitford have put the point thus:

> … if management must choose between the immediate liquidation or continuation of the business, placing a value on either option may involve a good deal of guesswork. A management secretly allied with one interest or another could bias valuation judgments in their favour with little fear that their bias could be proven.[66]

If, having reviewed the budget, business plan, and valuations provided to them, the directors   **1.25**
conclude that a restructuring is necessary they would not be fulfilling their duties to the company in taking no action purely on the basis that the senior lenders are unlikely to take matters into their own hands. If, on the other hand, the budget, business plan, and valuations available to the board indicate that there is no immediate cash need and that there may be value for other creditors, then they may be equally justified in resisting attempts by senior creditors to drive a particular restructuring opportunistically. The US courts have been alert to the suggestion that the directors are acting not in the interests of the company, but in their own self-interest, because they stand to gain from the restructuring.[67] In contrast, and as described above, the English courts have been reluctant to second guess directors' decision making with the benefit of hindsight.[68] Thus, provided the directors take professional advice and properly minute their decision-making process it may be difficult to challenge the decisions which they reach, notwithstanding that fact that they may stand to receive an equity allocation in the new structure and may have every incentive for it to rank behind as little debt as possible.

In *Stabilus* great weight was put behind the fact that the valuer for the senior debt had taken   **1.26**
part in detailed discussions with management whilst the valuer for the mezzanine lenders had not, but it is, of course, entirely possible that management will be more sympathetic to assisting one valuer than the other. Moreover, the English courts have shown great reluctance to assess whether or not the directors' decisions have been motivated by a conflict of interest and claimants, fearing perhaps an adverse reaction from the bench in making allegations of bad faith, have proved extremely reluctant to put their claim in this way.[69]

---

[65] *Saltri III Ltd v MD Mezzanine SA SICAR (t/a Mezzanine Facility Agent)* [2012] EWHC 3025 (Comm).

[66] Lynn M LoPucki and William C Whitford, 'Corporate Governance in the Bankruptcy Reorganization of Large, Publicly Held Companies' (1993) 141(3) *University of Pennsylvania Law Review* 692, 782.

[67] Stemming from the heightened standard of review where directorial self-interest is in view *Revlon, Inc v MacAndrews & Forbes Holdings, Inc*, 506 A 2d 173 (Del 1986).

[68] *Re Sherborne Associates Ltd* [1995] BCC 40 and *The Continental Assurance Company of London plc (In Liquidation)* 2001 WL 720239.

[69] Chris Howard and Bob Hedger, Restructuring Law & Practice (LexisNexis 2014) 275: 'In the Stabilus case Eder J rejected outright any claims that certain senior bankers within JPMEL had given 'a pretty clear steer' on the independent valuation by American Appraisal, had tried to deliberately influence its outcome, or more seriously had acted in bad faith by dangling the prospect of future work to American Appraisal. This was considered by Eder J to be a serious allegation which had not even been pleaded (as it should have been, if it were to be advanced),

The position is even more stark because, in determining whether directors have complied with the core duty to promote the success of the company, their decision-making process will be judged by what the directors, and not what the court, considers to have been in the best interests of the company.[70] Only if the director failed to turn his mind to the interests of creditors at all will an objective standard be imposed. This means that, where the written record shows that the directors did consider the interests of creditors at the relevant point in time, junior classes will need to challenge the honesty of the directors.[71] This is clearly an extremely serious allegation which poses an equally serious evidentiary burden and brings into play rules of conduct for English barristers in pleading fraud.

1.27   Alert to this issue, English law has also placed great reliance on the role of the independent director—a director who does not stand to gain from the restructuring but nonetheless approves it.[72] But there may be practical limitations to this gatekeeper role. Individuals taking appointments as independent directors are often specialists in distressed situations (often former insolvency and restructuring lawyers, financial advisers, or insolvency practitioners). They are unlikely to interact with a particular company more than once, but they are likely to come into repeated interaction with the creditor body.[73] Thus, there is a risk that they wish to prioritize a restructuring which is in the interests of part of the stakeholder body with an eye to winning future work. For all these reasons it may be that junior creditors and equity become braver in making straightforward allegations of bad behaviour and that the English court will become more astute in determining whether strategic behaviour has crossed a line or not, but the evidential burden may still prove insurmountable. Ultimately, it is important that directors feel able to do what they can in the 'zone of insolvency' to maximize value for all the stakeholders in the company.

D. Other Miscellaneous Provisions

1.28   For completeness, there are a number of other relevant provisions which should be mentioned here. Under section 212 of the Insolvency Act 1986, if in the course of a winding up anyone who has been involved with the promotion, formation, or management of the company is found to have misapplied, retained, or become accountable for any money or other property of the company, or been guilty of misfeasance or breach of a fiduciary or other duty in relation to the company, a court may on application by the official receiver, liquidator, or a creditor compel him to:

---

but which was never properly put squarely to any of JPMEL's witnesses and, on the contrary, flies in the face of counsel for mezzanine lender's express repeated disavowal of any allegation of bad faith or dishonesty on the part of JPMEL' and Mann J's reaction to allegations of breach of duty which were not foreshadowed in the evidence in *In re Bluebrook Ltd* [2009] EWHC 2114 (Ch).

[70]   See, eg, *Re HLC Environmental Projects Ltd* [2013] EWHC 2876 (Ch) citing Jonathan Parker J in *Re Regentcrest plc v Cohen* [2001] 2 BCLC 80 at [120].

[71]   See Jonathan Parker J in *Re Regentcrest plc v Cohen* [2001] 2 BCLC 80 at [120]: 'No doubt, where it is clear that the act or omission under challenge resulted in substantial detriment to the company, the director will have a harder task persuading the court that he honestly believed it to be in the company's interest.'

[72]   *In re Bluebrook Ltd* [2009] EWHC 2114 (Ch).

[73]   See, eg, Douglas Baird's and Robert Rasmussen's description of a well-known independent director in the US: '... the banks have as their wartime general someone whose loyalties are not tied to the existing managers' and noting that he 'does not plan on staying with companies long'. Baird and Rasmussen (n 6) 1235.

(1) repay, restore, or account for the money or property of the company with interest; or

(2) contribute such sum to the company's assets by way of compensation in respect of the misfeasance or breach of fiduciary duty or other duty as the court thinks just.[74]

Section 212 is a procedural section and does not provide any additional causes of action, although it may be useful in terms of the remedies which are available.[75]

The Insolvency Act 1986 also contains a test for fraudulent trading in section 213. A fraudulent trading claim can be brought by a liquidator or administrator against 'any persons who were knowingly parties' to the fraudulent trading.[76] And it may be a ground for fraudulent trading that credit was incurred when there was no good reason to think that funds would be available to pay the debt when due.[77] This suggests that fraudulent trading may be relevant where the company has traded in anticipation of a pre-packaged administration to implement a debt restructuring. However, the threshold requirement for fraudulent trading is high: the business of the company must have been 'carried on with intent to defraud creditors of the company or creditors of any other person, or for any fraudulent purpose.'[78] Thus, where credit has been incurred with no good reason for thinking it would be repaid, the creditor must be misled, or the directors must have intended to defraud the creditor, or the carrying on of the business must have actually defrauded the creditor.[79]   **1.29**

Apart from these risks of incurring personal liability, where a director engages in fraudulent or wrongful trading or has been found guilty of other misconduct in connection with a company and is held to be unfit by the court, he may also be disqualified by court order or have a disqualification undertaking accepted by the Secretary of State under the Company Directors Disqualification Act 1986. The Small Business, Enterprise and Employment Act 2015 also introduced a new compensation regime.[80]   **1.30**

E. Groups

As each member of the group is a distinct legal entity, directors of a company have duties to the separate creditors of that company alone, irrespective of the interests of the group.   **1.31**

In the words of Owen J in the New South Wales Court of Appeal case of *The Bell Group Ltd (In Liquidation) v Westpac Banking Corporation (No 9)*:[81]   **1.32**

> When looking at a group of companies there is a tendency to slip into language that suggests the focus of attention is the solvency of 'the group'. But solvency is a concept that

---

[74] Insolvency Act 1986, s 212(3)

[75] *The Continental Assurance Company of London plc (In Liq)* 2001 WL 720239 at [393]: 'It has long been settled in relation to predecessor sections that what is now section 212 does not create liabilities and obligations which did not exist apart from it. The section might, however, give the court a measure of discretion as to the remedy for misfeasance, being a discretion which would not exist, or at least would not be so extensive, at common law. That is the result of the word "may" in subsection (3).'

[76] Insolvency Act 1986, s 213(2).

[77] *Morphitis v Bernasconi* [2003] Ch 552.

[78] Insolvency Act 1986, s 213(1).

[79] *Morphitis* (n 77) at [3].

[80] Small Business, Enterprise and Employment Act 2015, s 110.

[81] [2008] WASC 239 (Supreme Court of Western Australia).

applies to individual entities, not to the group ... Material disclosing the financial position of the group is relevant. It is a necessary starting point but the ultimate enquiry must focus on the state of individual companies. If from time to time I use language that smacks of the group insolvency heresy, it will be inadvertent or made necessary by the context. The reader should be in no doubt that I am aware of the need to look at the financial position of individual companies.[82]

1.33   In brief, financing had been provided by two different groups of lenders to certain companies in the Bell Group. At the time the financings were initially put in place, they were unsecured. Following the stock market crash of October 1987 and the Bell Group's financial difficulties, the financings were restructured and, among other matters, certain Bell Group companies who were not party to the original financing arrangements provided security over all of their assets in favour of the lenders. Approximately one year after the restructuring occurred, most companies in the Bell Group were placed into insolvency administration of some form or another. The case was commenced by the liquidator of the Bell Group companies, to recover for the benefit of unsecured creditors some $283 million received by the lenders from enforcement of the security. The judgment ran to over 2,500 pages, but of particular note for present purposes is that the judge found that the directors of the Australian companies were in breach of their duties by looking at the problem 'solely from a group perspective' approaching the issue effectively as: 'We all survive or we all go down.'[83] He noted that:

> They did not look at the circumstances of each individual company that was to enter into a Transaction. They did not identify what, if any, creditors (external and internal) the individual companies had or might have and what, if any, effect a Transaction would have on the creditors or shareholders of an individual company.[84]

1.34   The directors of the UK companies, however, 'did everything right—up until the last hurdle', when they improperly relied on assurances from the Australian directors, some of whom were conflicted, without seeking independent verification of financial matters consistent with advice received.

1.35   There are complicating factors where the group is international, as both insolvency triggers and directors' duties can vary between jurisdictions. Such issues can hamper restructurings, for example by requiring directors to file voluntarily for insolvency at a stage earlier than their director colleagues in England are so required. Indeed, in many EU Member States directors are required to file for insolvency in the courts when the company becomes insolvent.[85]

---

[82]   Ibid at 809.
[83]   Ibid at 6040.
[84]   Ibid.
[85]   Gerard McCormack, Andrew Keay, Sarah Brown, and Judith Dahlgreen, 'Study on a new Approach to Business Failure and Insolvency: Comparative Legal Analysis of the Member States' Relevant Provisions and Practices' 48 <https://op.europa.eu/en/publication-detail/-/publication/3eb2f832-47f3-11e6-9c64-01aa75ed7 1a1/language-en> (last accessed 31 July 2021).

F. Particular Issues for Directors of Listed Companies

A particular issue for the directors of listed companies and for the issuers of listed (publicly traded) securities is the reporting requirements relating to disclosure and control of inside information. The purpose of the rules is to promote a fair and transparent market for securities and, in order to achieve this, the rules require the prompt and fair disclosure of relevant information to the market as soon as possible. This, of course, presents a serious issue for directors in the course of a restructuring where the focus is likely to be on discretion in order to secure the transaction without damaging the underlying business. **1.36**

The UK has retained the European Market Abuse Regulation (MAR) following the end of the Brexit transition period.[86] The European Securities and Markets Authority (ESMA) has issued guidelines under Article 17(1) of MAR, which contain a non-exhaustive list of when it may be in the legitimate interest of issuers to delay disclosure of inside information. Two of these are particularly relevant for our purposes. First, paragraph 5(1)(8)(a) identifies a situation in which 'the issuer is conducting negotiations, where the outcome of such negotiations would likely by jeopardised by immediate public disclosure' and specifically refers to negotiations related to restructurings and reorganizations.[87] Paragraph 5(1)(8)(b) identifies a situation in which: **1.37**

> the financial viability of the issuer is in grave and imminent danger, although not within the scope of the applicable insolvency law, and immediate public disclosure of the inside information would seriously prejudice the interests of existing and potential shareholders by jeopardizing the conclusion of the negotiations designed to ensure the financial recovery of the issuer.[88]

The UK Financial Conduct Authority (FCA) has made clear that, in its opinion, paragraph 5(1)(8)(a) of MAR does not envisage that an issuer will delay 'public disclosure of the fact that it is in financial difficulty or of its worsening financial condition'.[89] Instead, the latitude given to issuers only relates to the 'fact or substance of the negotiations to deal with such a situation'.[90] Moreover, an issuer is not permitted to delay disclosure of inside information 'on the basis that its position in subsequent negotiations will be jeopardized by the disclosure of its financial condition'.[91] And paragraph 5(1)(8)(b) can be difficult to navigate, particularly given the focus on the interests of shareholders. Finally, even where it is in the legitimate interests of the issuer to delay disclosure, such delay must not mislead the public and a developing situation should be monitored so that 'if circumstances change an immediate disclosure can be made'.[92] Furthermore, the issuer has to be confident that

---

[86] Regulation (EU) No 596/2014 of the European Parliament and of the Council of 16 April 2014 on market abuse (market abuse regulation) and repealing Directive 2003/6/EC of the European Parliament and of the Council and Commission Directives 2003/124/EC, 2003/125/EC and 2004/72/EC.

[87] ESMA, 'MAR Guidelines: Delay in the Disclosure of Inside Information' 20 October 2016 <https://www.esma.europa.eu/sites/default/files/library/2016-1478_mar_guidelines_-_legitimate_interests.pdf> (last accessed 26 September 2021).

[88] Ibid.

[89] FCA, 'Disclosure Guidance and Transparency Sourcebook' r 2.5.4G, July 2021 handbook.fca.org.uk/handbook/DTR.pdf (last accessed 2 August 2021).

[90] Ibid.

[91] DTR 2.5.4 (1)(b).

[92] DTR 2.5.2(1).

the information can be kept confidential until an announcement can be made.[93] In short, navigating the triple requirements of not misleading the public, identifying that delay is in the issuer's legitimate interests, and maintaining confidentiality can be a challenging task.

1.38   As a result, a company that has issued listed securities will wish to stay in close contact with its advisers and its brokers to ensure that it meets its disclosure obligations. Furthermore, the restrictions around insider trading and market abuse will also affect the attitudes of creditors to receipt of price-sensitive information, given that they will wish to remain free to trade. This can lead to complex arrangements in which advisers for the creditors receive price-sensitive information but do not pass it on and the circumstances and terms on which the company will agree that price-sensitive information which it does disclose to creditors will be released to the market within a defined period of time, freeing the creditors to trade once again.

G. Implications of Changing Capital Structures and Relevance of the Tests for Inability to Pay Debts

1. Incurrence covenants and covenant-lite loans

1.39   We noted, earlier in the chapter, the increasing number of UK issuers accessing US high yield bond markets.[94] As we have also already noted, typically a high yield bond will not include financial covenants which are tested periodically or on an ongoing basis (known as 'maintenance covenants'). Instead, the high yield bond is likely to include only one financial covenant (the ratio of debt to equity), which is only tested if the company raises more debt (known as an 'incurrence covenant'). This means that the role of the financial covenant as a trigger for debt restructuring negotiations is much reduced. Nonetheless, the duties of directors discussed above will still be relevant if the company's solvency is in doubt and the creditors may be able to fall back on general concepts in pressing for debt restructuring negotiations to start. The position is the same for so-called 'covenant-lite loans' which adopt an incurrence covenant rather than a maintenance covenant structure. The question of whether the company has reached the point at which it is 'unable or reasonably likely to become unable to pay its debts' is likely to be particularly important in this context.

2. The tests of inability to pay debts

1.40   The various tests of inability to pay debts are set out in section 123(1) and (2) of the Insolvency Act 1986 and it is worth setting them out here in full:

> 123. Definition of inability to pay debts.
>
> (1) A company is deemed unable to pay its debts—
>   (a) if a creditor (by assignment or otherwise) to whom the company is indebted in a sum exceeding £750 then due has served on the company, by leaving it at

---

[93] DTR 2.5.2(2).

[94] For a description see Standard & Poor's Financial Services LLC, *High Yield Bond Primer* (2014) available at <https://www.spglobal.com/marketintelligence/en/pages/toc-primer/hyd-primer> (last accessed 20 August 2021).

the company's registered office, a written demand (in the prescribed form) requiring the company to pay the sum so due and the company has for 3 weeks thereafter neglected to pay the sum or to secure or compound for it to the reasonable satisfaction of the creditor, or

(b) if, in England and Wales, execution or other process issued on a judgment, decree or order of any court in favour of a creditor of the company is returned unsatisfied in whole or in part, or

(c) if, in Scotland, the induciae of a charge for payment on an extract decree, or an extract registered bond, or an extract registered protest, have expired without payment being made, or

(d) if, in Northern Ireland, a certificate of unenforceability has been granted in respect of a judgment against the company, or

(e) if it is proved to the satisfaction of the court that the company is unable to pay its debts as they fall due.

(2) A company is also deemed unable to pay its debts if it is proved to the satisfaction of the court that the value of the company's assets is less than the amount of its liabilities, taking into account its contingent and prospective liabilities.

Section 123 evidently lays down multiple tests for determining whether a company is to be deemed unable to pay its debts.[95] These tests can be summarized into two groups: **1.41**

- **Specific tests**: these comprise the statutory demand limb (section 123(1)(a)) and the jurisdiction specific tests in relation to enforcement of a court order (section 123(1) (b)–(d)).
- **General (principal) tests**: a company may also be regarded as unable to pay its debts if it is unable to pay its debts as they fall due (section 123(1)(e)) or if its liabilities exceed its assets (section 123(2)). The first meaning is sometimes referred to as 'cash flow insolvency'; the second meaning is commonly referred to as insolvency on a balance sheet basis, or 'balance sheet insolvency'.

The specific tests of inability to pay debts are satisfied by reference to irrefutable and easily established external facts or events. Under these tests, the court will decide the issue of solvency on the basis of a presumption; that is, the company will be presumed to be unable to pay its debts without it actually being proved, and the company has the burden of rebutting that presumption. By contrast, application of the principal tests requires detailed analysis of the debtor company's financial position. Evidence of solvency must be adduced and if the court is satisfied regarding the proof, the company is found unable to pay its debts as a matter of fact.   **1.42**

In considering whether a financial restructuring is necessary, the board of directors will ordinarily be focused on the general tests although a company in financial distress may also be experiencing creditor action based on the specific tests.   **1.43**

---

[95] A leading text notes that '[t]he reasons for selecting different tests for different provisions have never been clearly articulated': Kristin Van Zwieten (ed), *Goode on Principles of Corporate Insolvency Law* (5th edn, Sweet & Maxwell 2019) 136.

1.44 The distinction between cash flow insolvency on the one hand and balance sheet insolvency on the other is of quite recent origin. Section 80(4) of the Companies Act 1862 provided as follows:

> A company under this Act shall be deemed to be unable to pay its debts ... Whenever it is proved to the satisfaction of the court that the company is unable to pay its debts.

1.45 In *Re European Life Assurance Society*,[96] James VC held that the test in section 80 of the Companies Act 1862 referred to 'debts absolutely due' (thus excluding contingent and prospective liabilities), and that prospective creditors had no standing to petition for the winding up of a company.[97] This shortcoming was addressed by section 28 of the Companies Act 1907, which permitted prospective creditors to petition, and required the court to have regard to contingent and prospective liabilities when applying the Companies Act 1862.[98] The basic statutory formulation remained unchanged despite various re-enactments of the Companies Acts in 1929, 1948, and 1985, and the current division embodied in section 123(1)(e) and (2) only appeared in the short-lived Insolvency Act 1985, ultimately replaced by the Insolvency Act 1986.

3. The cash flow test

1.46 The English law cash flow test is embodied in section 123(1)(e) of the Insolvency Act 1986:

> 123. Definition of inability to pay debts.
>
> (1) A company is deemed unable to pay its debts—
>
> ...
>
> (e) if it is proved to the satisfaction of the court that the company is unable to pay its debts as they fall due.

1.47 Cash flow insolvency is sometimes referred to as 'commercial insolvency'. A leading text explains the rationale behind the cash flow insolvency test as follows:

> ... the fact that its assets exceed its liabilities is irrelevant; if it cannot pay its way in the conduct of its business it is insolvent, for there is no reason why creditors should be expected to wait while the company realises assets some of which may not be held in readily liquidated form.[99]

---

[96] (1869–70) LR 9 Eq 122.

[97] Ibid at 127. At 128, James VC observed: 'I take it that the Court has nothing whatever to do with any question of future liabilities, that it has nothing whatever to do with the question of the probability whether any business which the company may carry on tomorrow or hereafter will be profitable or unprofitable. That is a matter for those who may choose to be the customers of the company and for the shareholders to consider. I have to look at the case simply with reference to the solvency or insolvency of the company, and in doing that I have to deal with the company exactly as it stood on the day to which the evidence relates ...'

[98] The new provision was consolidated in the Companies (Consolidation) Act 1908 in s 130 in the following form: 'A company shall be deemed to be unable to pay its debts ... (iv) if it is proved to the satisfaction of the court that the company is unable to pay its debts, and, in determining whether a company is unable to pay its debts, the court shall take into account the contingent and prospective liabilities of the company.'

[99] *Goode* (n 95) 39.

In many cases, cash flow insolvency can readily be established by evidence showing persistent failure by a company to pay its debts as they fall due for payment. In this sense, application of the test is relatively straightforward insofar as the court will be looking at what the company is actually doing. However, in marginal cases, the vague and imprecise nature of the test makes the determination of a company's solvency on any particular day difficult.   **1.48**

However, the question of whether the company is facing cash flow insolvency is likely to be the real driver behind a decision that a financial restructuring is necessary. As we will discuss below, creditors who are 'out of the money' today are likely to argue for a 'wait and see' approach rather than radical surgery in a poor market. However, the company's ability to wait, or undertake only limited amendments, will be driven by whether or not it has a cash need. Even in the absence of an event of default, a company cannot continue to trade if it runs out of cash. Therefore, the question of whether and when the company faces a cash crisis can become the principal battle ground, with junior creditors arguing that the directors are not taking many of the actions available to them and that the cash need is not as real or immediate as the company is claiming.   **1.49**

In *Southern Cross Interiors Pty Ltd v Deputy Commissioner of Taxation*,[100] Palmer J in the New South Wales Supreme Court usefully set out the general principles guiding a court in applying the applicable Australian insolvency test (emphasis added, citations omitted):[101]   **1.50**

- (i) [w]hether or not a company is insolvent for the purposes of [relevant Australian statutory provisions] is a *question of fact to be ascertained from a consideration of the company's financial position taken as a whole* ...;
- (ii) *in considering the company's financial position as a whole, the Court must have regard to commercial realities.* Commercial realities will be relevant in considering what resources are available to the company to meet its liabilities as they fall due, whether resources other than cash are realisable by sale or borrowing upon security, and when such realisations are achievable ...;
- (iii) in assessing whether a company's position as a whole reveals surmountable temporary illiquidity or insurmountable endemic illiquidity resulting in insolvency, *it is proper to have regard to the commercial reality that, in normal circumstances, creditors will not always insist on payment strictly in accordance with their terms of trade* but that does not result in the company thereby having a cash or credit resource which can be taken into account in determining solvency ...;
- (iv) the commercial reality that creditors will normally allow some latitude in time for payment of their debts does not, in itself, warrant a conclusion that the debts are not payable at the times contractually stipulated and have become debts payable only upon demand ...;
- (v) in assessing solvency, the Court acts upon the basis that a contract debt is payable at the time stipulated for payment in the contract unless there is evidence, proving to the Court's satisfaction, that:
  - there has been an express or implied agreement between the company and the creditor for an extension of the time stipulated for payment; or

---

[100] 188 ALR 114 (Supreme Court of New South Wales).
[101] Ibid at 54.

- there is a course of conduct between the company and the creditor sufficient to give rise to an estoppel preventing the creditor from relying upon the stipulated time for payment; or
- there has been a well established and recognised course of conduct in the industry in which the company operates, or as between the company and its creditors as a body, whereby debts are payable at a time other than that stipulated in the creditors' terms of trade or are payable only on demand ...[102]

1.51 This highlights one of the challenges faced by the directors if they decide that they need to commence debt restructuring negotiations. During this time the company may well face a 'cash squeeze'. As news that the company is entering into debt restructuring negotiations leaks out, the company may face increasing pressure from suppliers for prompt payment, particularly if there is concern from the credit insurance industry. As a result, it may become necessary to 'stretch' suppliers, seeking to pay them as late as possible in order to reduce cash flow pressure. It will be clear from the above that the extent to which such action leads to a conclusion that the company is cash flow insolvent will be finely judged, and the directors will need to take care that their decisions are properly recorded.

1.52 It is also clear that in considering the company's solvency position the directors may have regard to other actions available to them. Asset sales may not be viewed as a source of liquidity where the debtor company is forced to accept large discounts in order to affect the sale in time to meet its debts. Keay points out that expert evidence could be heard as to the likelihood of any of the assets yielding ready cash in sufficient time to satisfy the debts as they fall due.[103] In the context of a complex capital structure, the board will not be expected to take action that may damage long-term value for short-term expediency unless that is part of a wider plan.

1.53 It is also legitimate to take into account any loan that the company might be able to obtain, either on the strength of its assets[104] or on an unsecured basis.[105] However, in order for borrowed funds to be a factor in the assessment of cash flow insolvency, either the funds must be available or there must be a significant probability that they would be available in time to enable the company's debts to be paid.[106]

1.54 The introduction of a distinction between cash flow insolvency and balance sheet insolvency in the Insolvency Act 1985 created uncertainty as to the degree to which 'future' debts could be taken into account when determining cash flow insolvency under section 123(1)(e). In particular, while at the worst 'as they fall due' would appear to extend the test to

---

[102] See, however, subsequent Australian case law, eg *White ACT (In Liquidation) v White GB & ors* [2004] NSWSC 71 at 291–293 (Supreme Court of New South Wales); *Iso Lilodw' Aliphumeleli Pty Ltd (In Liquidation) v Commissioner of Taxation* [2002] NSWSC 644 at 14 (Supreme Court of New South Wales); *Re New World Alliance Pty Ltd (receiver and manager appointed), Sycotex Pty Ltd v Baseler* (1994) 51 FCR 425 at 434 (Federal Court of Australia); *Tru Floor Service Pty Ltd v Jenkins (No 2)* (2006) 232 ALR 532 at 45–48 (Federal Court of Australia); *ASIC v Plymin, Elliott & Harrison* [2003] VSC 123 at 380 (Supreme Court of Victoria); and *Shakespeares Pie Co v Multipye* [2006] NSWSC 930 at 89 (Supreme Court of New South Wales).

[103] Andrew Keay, 'The Insolvency Factor in the Avoidance of Antecedent Transactions in Corporate Liquidations' (1995) 21(2) *Monash University Law Review* 322–323.

[104] *Sandell v Porter* (1966) 115 CLR 666 (High Court of Australia); (or those of a third party) *Lewis v Doran* 219 ALR 555 (Supreme Court of New South Wales).

[105] *Lewis v Doran* 219 ALR 555; *Re a Company (No 006794 of 1983)* [1986] BCLC 261.

[106] *MacPlant Services Ltd v Contract Lifting Services (Scotland) Ltd* 2009 SC 125, per Lord Hodge at 76.

obligations falling due in the near future, it was not clear whether the omission of the words 'contingent and prospective liabilities' (appearing in section 123(2)) from section 123(1)(e) was of any significance. This is of particular importance to the question of when the board concludes that it has a cash flow issue and when creditors may be able to take action on that basis.

Highberry Limited v Colt Telecom Group plc[107] involved the application for administration by **1.55** certain of Colt Telecom Group plc's noteholders (collectively called 'Highberry'). The petition was unusual in that Colt was both cash flow solvent and, according to a report prepared for Colt by one of the 'big four' accounting firms which the noteholders contested, balance sheet solvent at the time. The company was a member of the FTSE mid-250 index, had a market capitalization in excess of £550 million and net assets of £977 million. There was no default under the notes. The noteholders, keen to force Colt into administration in order to implement a debt for equity exchange and thereby gain full value from the notes they had recently purchased, argued that Colt would be unable to repay a substantial amount of the capital due on the notes when it became payable four years later. Highberry, largely relying on the dramatic fall in Colt's share price over the two preceding years, contended that it was unclear that Colt would be generating enough cash flow from its assets and that anyone would refinance. Jacob J gave short shrift to speculation over the future health of the company, criticizing any 'shaky, tentative, and speculative peering into the middle-distance'[108] when seeking to establish cash flow insolvency. The judge considered any allegation of insolvency to be a serious matter and one that requires a solid foundation.[109] He noted factors such as the company's ability to refinance and the volatility of the telecoms market being such that anything could happen prior to the time at which the noteholders claimed the company's cash would run out.[110]

However, the decision of Jacob J in the *Colt* case stands in contrast to the decision of Briggs **1.56** J in *Re Cheyne Finance Plc (In Receivership)*.[111] In the *Re Cheyne* case, receivers were appointed in respect of a structured investment vehicle by the security trustee pursuant to a security trust deed. Under the deed, 'Insolvency Event' was defined as follows:

> Insolvency Event means a determination by the manager or any receiver that the issuer [the Company] is, or is about to become, unable to pay its debts as they fall due to senior creditors and any other persons whose claims against the issuer are required to be paid in priority thereto, as contemplated by section 123(1) of the Insolvency Act 1986 …

The receivers sought guidance from the court as to whether, on the facts, Cheyne was or was **1.57** about to become unable to pay its debts; in particular, whether, and to what extent, regard could be had to senior debts falling due in the future. The senior creditors argued that the parties had agreed to a deliberate omission of section 123(2) of the Insolvency Act 1986 and that the receivers had to apply the commercial or cash flow insolvency test found in section 123(1)(e) which omits, and therefore requires to be ignored, all contingent and prospective liabilities.

---

[107] [2002] EWHC 2815.
[108] Ibid at [87].
[109] Ibid.
[110] Ibid at [27].
[111] [2008] BCC 182.

1.58   Briggs J rejected this argument, pointing out that, until recently, the question of inability to pay debts had been framed without any rigid distinction between commercial and cash flow insolvency on the one hand and balance sheet insolvency on the other.[112] He found that there was no English authority on the question of whether the introduction of a mandatory requirement to consider contingent and prospective liabilities in section 123(2) prevented reference to future debts under section 123(1)(e).[113] However, in the Australian context, Briggs J recognized that there was a wealth of authority indicating that a cash flow or commercial insolvency test permitted references to debts which would fall due in the future.[114] Furthermore, it was critical to note that when separating out balance sheet insolvency from commercial insolvency in 1985, the legislature added what in Australia had always been regarded as the key words of futurity, the phrase 'as they fall due'.[115] Briggs J concluded:[116]

> In my judgment, the effect of the alterations to the insolvency test made in 1985 and now found in s.123 of the 1986 Act was to replace in the commercial solvency test now in s.123(1)(e), one futurity requirement, namely to include contingent and prospective liabilities, with another more flexible and fact-sensitive requirement encapsulated in the new phrase 'as they fall due'.

1.59   In *Eurosail*,[117] Lord Walker in the Supreme Court approved the decision in *Re Cheyne Finance plc* that the cash flow test is concerned not only with the debts that are immediately due and payable but also those falling due in the reasonably near future,[118] and further support for this interpretation is provided by the approach of the Court of Appeal in *re Casa Estates*.[119]

1.60   To what extent, then, is a company to be regarded as currently insolvent on a cash flow basis when its forecasts show that, having regard to its contingent and future debts, it will run out of cash at some point in the future? The answer probably lies somewhere between the decision in the *Colt* case and the decision in the *Cheyne* case. While the adoption of 'reasonably near future' in the *Eurosail* judgment indicates that the English court is unlikely to support the view that a company is currently insolvent on a cash flow basis, and therefore required to take immediate action to adopt a restructuring, when forecasts look as far forward

---

[112] Ibid at [34].

[113] Ibid at [36].

[114] Ibid at [41]. In particular, Briggs J cites *Bank of Australasia v Hall* (1907) 4 CLR 1514 (High Court of Australia); *Cuthbertson v Thomas* (1998) 28 ACSR 310 (Supreme Court of the Australian Capital Territory); *Hymix Concrete Pty Ltd v Garrity* (1977) 13 ALR 321 (High Court of Australia); *Lewis v Doran* 219 ALR 555 (Supreme Court of New South Wales); *Sandell v Porter* (1966) 115 CLR 666 (High Court of Australia); *Southern Cross Interiors Pty Ltd v Deputy Commissioner for Taxation* (2001) 39 ACSR 305 (Supreme Court of New South Wales); and *Taylor v ANZ Banking Group Ltd* (1988) 6 ACLC 808 (Supreme Court of Victoria).

[115] *Re Cheyne Finance Plc (In Receivership)* [2008] BCC 182 at [53].

[116] Ibid at [56].

[117] (n 24).

[118] Ibid at [37]: '... the "cash-flow" test is concerned, not simply with the petitioner's own presently-due debt, nor only with other presently-due debt owed by the company, but also with debts falling due from time to time in the reasonably near future. What is the reasonably near future, for this purpose, will depend on all the circumstances, but especially the nature of the company's business ... The express reference to assets and liabilities is in my view a practical recognition that once the court has to move beyond the reasonably near future (the length of which depends, again, on all the circumstances) any attempt to apply a cash-flow test will become completely speculative, and a comparison of present assets with present and future liabilities (discounted for contingencies and deferment) becomes the only sensible test. But it is still very far from an exact test, and the burden of proof must be on the party which asserts balance-sheet insolvency ...'

[119] *Re Casa Estates (UK) Limited (In Liquidation) Carman v Bucci* [2014] EWCA Civ 383, CA.

as the *Colt* decision, equally matters are unlikely to be as clear-cut as in the *Cheyne* case for a trading company suffering the ebbs and flows of day-to-day trading compared with a 'closed' structured investment vehicle. The board of a company which has sufficient cash to meet its current liabilities and is forecasting a cash shortfall some way in the future for which it can see no other remedial action may be perfectly justified in moving for a restructuring sooner rather than later. A board is not expected to trade the business without taking any action until the eve of a cash flow crisis nor is it expected to trade the business for junior creditors whom it considers to be 'out of the money' at the expense of senior creditors who have clear value to preserve. This difficult area is discussed in greater detail in Chapter 3.

4. The balance sheet test

The balance sheet test is embodied in section 123(2) of the Insolvency Act 1986:   **1.61**

> 123. Definition of inability to pay debts.
>
> …
>
> (2) A company is also deemed unable to pay its debts if it is proved to the satisfaction of the court that the value of the company's assets is less than the amount of its liabilities, taking into account its contingent and prospective liabilities.

The essential difference between the balance sheet test and the cash flow test is that the focus   **1.62** of the former is on 'liabilities' (including contingent and prospective liabilities), which is a much broader concept than 'debts'.[120] As a leading text explains, the rationale behind the test is that 'it is not sufficient for the company to be able to meet its current obligations if its total liabilities can ultimately be met only by the realisation of its assets and these are insufficient'.[121]

The requirement in section 123(2) to take into account a company's contingent and pro-   **1.63** spective liabilities was considered for the first time in *Eurosail*.[122] In that case the debtor, Eurosail, issued notes as part of a securitization transaction in relation to a portfolio of UK residential non-conforming mortgage loans. Security for the notes was provided by a fixed charge over Eurosail's interests in the underlying mortgages entered into with the Trustee. Its risk in relation to changes in interest and exchange rates was hedged by means of interest and currency swaps with Lehman Brothers Special Financing Inc (LBSF), whose obligations were guaranteed by Lehman Brothers Holdings Inc (LBHI). The collapse of the Lehman Brothers Group in 2008 caused LBSF to default under the swap agreements and LBHI to default under the guarantee. Eurosail terminated the swap agreements which resulted in it having substantial claims against LBSF and LBHI but no protection against currency and interest rate changes. This led to concerns among certain of the noteholders that their notes would not be redeemed as early as initially projected, as the transaction structure did not allow for the absorption of such losses, and that there would be a significant shortfall if the

---

[120] There is of course a direct relationship between cash flow and balance sheet solvency, as the assets of a company that can be sold as a going concern will have a higher value than assets sold on a break-up basis.
[121] *Goode* (n 95) 159.
[122] (n 24).

principal amount of the foreign currency notes had to be paid back immediately.[123] They argued that the security trustee should therefore call an event of default under the notes and enforce the security on the basis that Eurosail should be deemed unable to pay its debts within the meaning of section 123(2). The security trustee sought a determination from the court on whether Eurosail should be deemed unable to pay its debts.[124]

1.64   The case was to proceed all the way to the Supreme Court where the court held that:

  (i) the expression 'balance sheet insolvency' is not to be taken literally;[125]

 (ii) the test applied in the Court of Appeal that the company had 'reached the point of no return because of an incurable deficiency in its assets' should not pass into common usage;[126]

(iii) the court must be satisfied, on the balance of probabilities, that a company has insufficient assets to be able to meet all its liabilities, including prospective and contingent liabilities (discounted for contingencies and deferment);[127]

 (iv) whether the test is satisfied will depend on the evidence as to the circumstances of the particular case; and

  (v) the burden of proof will be on the party asserting insolvency.

1.65   The court concluded that the factual evidence in *Eurosail* indicated that the debtor was well able to pay its debts as they fell due. The decision provides some clarification as to the interpretation of section 123(2) although it lacks clear guidance on how contingent and prospective liabilities should be taken into account in practice.[128]

1.66   Clearly there are differences between the legal and accounting definitions of assets and liabilities, with the general law focusing more on legal form, and the accounting treatment on economic substance. Accounting concepts will therefore often be wider than legal concepts. A leading text points out that:

> … differences between the legal and accounting concepts of what constitutes an asset and what constitutes a liability do not normally matter for the purpose of the balance sheet test

---

[123] In effect, the noteholders were arguing that the balance sheet test had to take into account Eurosail's prospective and contingent liabilities and that Eurosail should therefore be treated as liable for the full amount of those liabilities if converted into sterling at the exchange rates at that time.

[124] A second issue for consideration was whether, in the event that Eurosail was deemed unable to pay its debts, a post enforcement call option (PECO) which was exercisable by an associate of Eurosail to take the benefit of the notes at a nominal price if the security on enforcement was insufficient to pay all amounts due, had the effect that Eurosail was not unable to pay its debts. In the event, this issue did not require consideration as Eurosail had been deemed able to pay its debts. However, Morritt C, aware that the case might go further, expressed the view that, had it been found that the value of Eurosail's assets was less than the amount of its liabilities, taking into account its contingent and prospective liabilities, the PECO would have had no effect on those liabilities. Eurosail's liabilities remained the same, whether or not there was a PECO or, if there was, whether or not it had been exercised. It was to be assumed that the option company would release Eurosail from all further liability but it was under no obligation to do so and, until it did, Eurosail's liability was unaffected. The Court of Appeal came to the same decision but the point did not need to be decided when the case reached the Supreme Court. Nonetheless Lord Hope considered that both the Chancellor and the Court of Appeal had reached the right answer.

[125] *Eurosail* (n 24) at [1].

[126] Ibid at [42] and [48].

[127] Ibid at [48].

[128] See David Allison, 'The Continuing Search for the Meaning of Section 123(2) of the Insolvency Act 1986: the Supreme Court Decision in Eurosail' (2013) 8 *JIBFL* 492. The Supreme Court cited a useful article by Professor Peter Walton on the legislative history of the section; Peter Walton, 'Inability to Pay Debts: Beyond the Point of No Return?' [2013] *Journal of Business Law* 212.

of insolvency so long as the company is able to maintain the payments needed to preserve its right to retain assets which in law do not belong to it ... In most cases, therefore, the court is likely to follow generally accepted accounting principles in deciding what constitutes a balance sheet asset or liability, but may decline to do so where for any reason it considers this would be inappropriate.[129]

At first instance Morritt C said of the exercise required by section 123(2) that it was 'not   **1.67** the production of an annual balance sheet but a comparison of the value of assets with the amount of liabilities in order to ascertain solvency'.[130] In considering the liabilities shown on the financial statements in relation to currency conversion, Morritt C held that 'this part of the liabilities shown on the financial statements is entirely speculative ... I do not consider this element of the liabilities shown in the financial statements is a liability at all ... I do not think that at this stage, account should be taken of it for the purposes of s 123(2) at any material value'.[131] The Supreme Court confirmed that the label 'balance sheet test' was not to be taken literally. In *HLC Environmental Products* Jonathan Randall QC (sitting as a deputy high court judge) held that the starting point for the assessment of balance sheet insolvency was the company's accounts.[132] However, the question of whether, under accountancy standards, good or best practice would have required the inclusion of a contingent liability in the company's accounts and, if so, the value to be attributed to the liability, was not a central consideration in valuing a contingent liability for the purpose of section 123(2). Instead, the court looked at the commercial reality of the situation in concluding that the contingent liability should be taken into account. In a later case, Sir William Blackburn declined to take a putative restructuring into account in determining whether or not the company was balance sheet insolvent.[133]

It is also apparent that the line between cash flow insolvency and balance sheet insolvency   **1.68** is becoming somewhat blurred. Indeed, in *Re Casa Estates* the Court of Appeal agreed with Warren J at first instance that the two tests form part of the single exercise of establishing whether the company is unable to pay its debts.[134] In that case the Court of Appeal was prepared to ask not only whether the company was continuing to pay its debts but also how it was able to do so. Where it was only paying old debts by taking on new ones, the company was neither cash flow nor balance sheet solvent.

These cases have emerged after a fallow period of almost 30 years. However, as Lord Walker   **1.69** noted in *Eurosail* this is likely to be due, in part, to the role of financial covenants in effectively rendering debate about the technical tests redundant. In the next restructuring cycle

---

[129] *Goode* (n 95) 163.
[130] *Eurosail* [2010] All ER (D) 351 (Jul), [2010] EWHC 2005 (Ch) at [34].
[131] Ibid at [35].
[132] *Re HLC Environmental Projects Ltd* [2013] EWHC 2876 (Ch).
[133] *Myers v Kestrel Acquisitions Limited & Ors* [2015] EWHC 916 (Ch) at [92]: 'Kestrel's liabilities currently greatly exceed its assets. On the evidence the likelihood is that the deficiency will increase as each month passes up to the maturity date of the VLNs. It is conceded that a restructuring of some kind will be needed to restore Kestrel to solvency. The form and details of the restructuring are unknown. All that seems likely is the readiness of the main creditors to support it. I am not willing on that evidence to say that Kestrel is solvent. Similarly with Kestrel Holdings. In my judgment the Myers have discharged the onus which is upon them to demonstrate balance-sheet insolvency.'
[134] *Re Casa Estates (UK) Limited (In Liquidation); Carman v Bucci* [2014] EWCA Civ 383.

the tests may well assume a far greater importance if a significant number of 'incurrence covenant'-style financings become distressed.

H. The Relevance of the Accounts

1.70   The health of the balance sheet can also be significant if it prevents a company obtaining a clean going concern statement from its auditors in its accounts. In preparing the company's accounts, management will make an assessment of the company's ability to continue as a going concern. Accounting standards require management to take into account all available information in the future which is at least, but not limited to, 12 months from the balance sheet date. The auditors' responsibility is to consider the appropriateness of management's use of the going concern assumption and to consider whether there are any material uncertainties about the company's ability to continue as a going concern that need to be disclosed. If there are, the auditors consider whether the financial statements adequately describe the principal events or conditions and, assuming that they do, the auditors will express an unqualified opinion but add to their report a 'material uncertainty' statement which draws attention to the particular event or circumstance giving rise to the concern about continued going concern status.

1.71   There has been a proliferation of material uncertainty statements in company accounts in recent years (applying both UK generally accepted accounting principles (GAAP) and International Financial Reporting Standards (IFRS)), and this is expected to continue as auditors become increasingly conservative in their going concern sign-offs in the uncertain environment of the COVID-19 pandemic. This has, to some extent, meant that in many sectors companies have been less concerned about carrying a material uncertainty statement, as they do not perceive it to create such a competitive disadvantage as it might if others in the sector were not carrying the same sorts of statements in their accounts. However, in some businesses such as those heavily reliant on tendering, it can be a very real issue. It is worth noting that, in considering the need for a material uncertainty statement, the auditors are looking at least 12 months ahead and so this issue may cause discussions with lenders to start before there has been a financial covenant breach but where one is forecast such that reference can be made to ongoing discussions in the accounts.[135] It is also worth noting that a material uncertainty statement does not result in qualified accounts, so it will not cause an event of default relating to qualified accounts to be triggered. Particular accounting issues may arise for listed companies requiring a working capital statement in connection with a resolution to shareholders to approve a restructuring proposal. Where the clean working capital statement from the auditors is dependent on the passing of the shareholder resolutions in support of which it is issued it is possible for the circular to shareholders to make that inter-dependence clear, whilst any financial statements delivered at the same time are likely to contain a material uncertainty paragraph drawing attention to the material uncertainty as to whether the necessary support will be secured.

---

[135] Accounting standards also dictate that where there is a breach of covenant entitling lenders to accelerate on or before the end of a relevant accounting period any waiver of that breach after the end of the accounting period will not remove the need to show the liability for the loan as current at the balance sheet date. As a result, the directors will need to think about resolution to the problem some time ahead of breach.

IV. Avoidance Actions in the US

A. Fraudulent Conveyances

1. Overview

In the US, there are two basic types of fraudulent conveyances: intentional and constructive, **1.72**
which, when taken together, provide that the debtor may not dispose of its property with
the *intent* (actual fraud) or the *effect* (constructive fraud) of placing it beyond the reach of
creditors.[136] Under section 548 of the Bankruptcy Code, the trustee (or debtor in possession) may avoid: (1) any transfer of the debtor's property, or any obligation incurred by the
debtor, that was made with 'actual intent to hinder, delay, or defraud' present and future
creditors (intentional fraudulent conveyance); or (2) any transfer made for less than reasonably equivalent value and made while the transferor was insolvent, thereby rendered insolvent, had unreasonably small capital to operate the business, or intended or believed that
it would incur debts beyond its ability to pay as they matured (constructive fraudulent conveyance).[137] To recover property (or its value) or avoid an obligation as a fraudulent conveyance, the transfer must have been made or obligation incurred on or within two years before
the date of the filing of the bankruptcy petition.[138]

Section 544(b) of the Bankruptcy Code is commonly referred to as the 'strong arm' provi- **1.73**
sion because it permits a bankruptcy trustee (or debtor in possession) to exercise the same
rights an unsecured creditor would have under applicable state law.[139] Specifically, section
544(b) of the Bankruptcy Code permits a trustee to 'avoid any transfer of an interest of the
debtor in property or any obligation incurred by the debtor that is voidable under applicable law'.[140] Generally, state law look-back periods are longer than the two years provided by
the Bankruptcy Code, often four years.[141] Notably, a handful of bankruptcy courts have allowed trustees to challenge fraudulent transfers that would otherwise be time barred under
state statutes by taking advantage of the 10-year look-back period available to the Internal
Revenue Service (IRS) under the Internal Revenue Code for the collection of taxes.[142] These
courts have concluded that the IRS is a viable 'triggering creditor' under section 544(b) if the
IRS could theoretically assert the underlying fraudulent transfer claim against the debtor.[143]

---

[136] *United States v Green*, 201 F. 3d 251, 254 (3d Cir 2000) (internal citations omitted).
[137] 11 USC § 548(a)(1)(A) and (B).
[138] 11 USC §§ 548(a)(1), 550(a).
[139] See *In re LSC Wind Down, LLC*, 610 B.R. 779 (Bankr. D. Del. 2020) ('[The] strong-arm provision permits a
trustee or debtor-in-possession to step into the shoes of a debtor's unsecured creditor holding a state law avoidance
claim and pursue such claim on behalf of the bankruptcy estate ... for the benefit of the creditors.') Section 544(b)
(1) of the Bankruptcy Code allows the trustee (or a creditor, acting derivatively on its behalf) to succeed only to the
rights of an actual unsecured creditor with an allowable claim as of the commencement of a case (a so-called 'triggering creditor'). See 11 USC § 544(b)(1).
[140] 11 USC § 544(b).
[141] New York used to have a look-back period of six years. However, in December 2019, New York enacted a
law that brought the look-back period more in line with that of other states, reducing the look-back period to four
years. N.Y. Debt. & Cred. Law § 278 (McKinney). (Transfers made before 4 April 2020, the effective date of the new
law, will still be governed by the six-year look-back period. NY LEGIS 580 (2019), 2019 Sess. Law News of N.Y. Ch.
580, § 7 (A. 5622) (McKinney).)
[142] 26 U.S.C. § 6502(a).
[143] See, e.g., *In re Zagaroli*, Case No. 18-50508, 2020 WL 6495156, at *3 (Bankr. W.D.N.C. Nov. 3, 2020); *In re
Gaither*, 595 B.R. 201, 209–10 (Bankr. D. S.C. 2018).

The 'strong arm' provision, however, does not permit the trustee to exercise *greater* rights than a creditor would have under state law.[144] As a 1920 district court decision explained:

> It is well established that the effect of this section is to clothe the trustee with no new or additional right in the premises over that possessed by a creditor, but simply puts him in the shoes of the latter, and subject to the same limitations and disabilities that would have beset the creditor in the prosecution of the action on his own behalf; and the rights of the parties are to be determined, not by any provision of the [former] Bankruptcy Act, but by the applicable principles of the common law, or the laws of the state in which the right of action may arise.[145]

1.74   Thus, section 544(b) of the Bankruptcy Code permits a trustee to step into the shoes of an unsatisfied creditor to bring an avoidance action under state fraudulent transfer law.[146]

2. Elements of an intentional fraudulent conveyance

1.75   Avoiding a transfer as an actual fraudulent conveyance is not often successful in corporate transactions because it requires proof of actual intent on the part of the transferor to hinder, delay, or defraud creditors.[147] However, because there is rarely direct evidence of such intent courts look to circumstantial evidence, referred to as the 'badges of fraud', in determining whether a transfer was intended to hinder, delay, or defraud creditors. 'Badges of fraud' include the following:

(1) a close relationship among the parties to the transaction;

(2) a secret and hasty transfer not in the usual course of business;

(3) inadequacy of consideration;

(4) the transferor's knowledge of the creditor's claim and the transferor's inability to pay it;

(5) the use of dummies or fictitious parties; and

(6) retention of control of property by the transferor after the conveyance.[148]

1.76   While the existence of a single badge of fraud is not enough to demonstrate fraudulent intent, where there is a confluence of several 'badges of fraud', the trustee or debtor in

---

[144]   See *In re Jackson*, 318 BR 5, 26 (Bankr DNH 2004), aff'd *In re Jackson*, 459 F 3d 117 (1st Cir 2006).

[145]   *Davis v Willey*, 263 F 588, 589 (ND Cal 1920).

[146]   It is important to note that s 544(a) of the Bankruptcy Code grants trustees additional avoidance powers under the strong arm provision. Specifically, under s 544(a)(1) of the Bankruptcy Code, a trustee can avoid transfers or obligations of a debtor that are avoidable by a hypothetical creditor on a simple contract with a judicial lien on the property as of the petition date. Section 544(a)(2) permits trustees to avoid transfers or obligations of a debtor that are avoidable by a hypothetical creditor with an unsatisfied writ of execution as of the commencement of the case. Finally, under s 544(a)(3) trustees can avoid unperfected liens that a bona fide hypothetical purchaser of real property could also avoid as of the commencement of the case.

[147]   See *In re Sharp Intern Corp*, 403 F 3d 43, 56 (2nd Cir 2005) ('To prove actual fraud under [New York law], a creditor must show intent to defraud on the part of the transferor') (internal citations omitted). To determine whether a debtor corporation had the intent to hinder, delay, or defraud its creditors, courts must examine the intent of the corporate actors who effectuated the transaction on behalf of the corporation. *Kirschner v FitzSimons (In re Tribune Co. Fraudulent Conveyance Litig.)*, 2017 U.S. Dist. LEXIS 3039 (S.D.N.Y. Jan. 6, 2017). Additionally, the intent of a debtor corporation's officers can only be imputed to the debtor if the officers were in a position to control the disposition of the debtor's property. Ibid. See also *In re Lyondell Chemical Co.*, 554 B.R. 635, 649-50 (Bankr. S.D.N.Y. 2016) (holding that the allegations in the trustee's complaint stated a cause of action for intentional fraudulent conveyance to avoid a leveraged buyout, as the knowledge possessed by the CEO as to the inflated financial projections could be imputed to the corporation.).

[148]   *OODC, LLC v Majestic Mgmt, Inc (In re OODC, LLC)*, 321 BR 128, 140 (Bankr D Del 2005).

possession is entitled to a presumption of fraudulent intent.[149] The burden then shifts to the transferee to prove some 'legitimate supervening purpose' for the transfers at issue.[150]

3. Elements of a constructive fraudulent conveyance

Constructive fraudulent conveyance actions are typically more successful than actual fraudu-   **1.77**
lent transfer claims because the debtor's intent is not an element. Rather, there are two prongs to a constructive fraudulent conveyance analysis: the threshold question is whether the debtor received 'reasonably equivalent value'. Once it is established that the debtor did not receive 'reasonably equivalent value', the party challenging the transfer/incurrence of an obligation must also show that the debtor was insolvent at the time of the transfer or incurrence, rendered insolvent by such transfer, or had unreasonably small capital.

In determining whether fair value was exchanged, courts focus on the value exchanged at the   **1.78**
time of the transfer, taking a totality-of-the-circumstances approach. Such approach considers, among other facts, the fair market value of the assets or benefits received by the debtor and the arm's length nature of the transaction, giving significant weight to the sophistication of the parties. Significantly, it is the value received by the debtor, not the value given by the creditor, that is determinative.

Moreover, in the fraudulent conveyance context, a transfer of security on account of ante-   **1.79**
cedent debt is most often reasonably equivalent value.[151] For example, in *In re Applied Theory Corp*,[152] the debtor granted its lenders a security interest to secure antecedent debt, which included $30 million in unsecured debentures.[153] The trustee argued that the grant of such security interest constituted a fraudulent conveyance under section 548(a)(1) of the Bankruptcy Code.[154] The Bankruptcy Court, however, found that '[t]he security interest did not provide the [l]enders with a right to receive anything more than the amount of money they had provided, and the debtor's liability did not increase due to the security interest'.[155] Following the

---

[149] See *Kelly v Armstrong*, 141 F 3d 799, 802 (8th Cir 1998) (stating that '[o]nce a trustee establishes a confluence of several badges of fraud, the trustee is entitled to a presumption of fraudulent intent'). It is important to note, however, that as a matter of law, a finding of fraudulent intent cannot properly be inferred from the existence of just one 'badge of fraud'. See, eg, *Brown v Third Nat'l Bank (In re Sherman)*, 67 F 3d 1348, 1354 (8th Cir 1995) (holding that the presence of a single badge of fraud is not sufficient to constitute conclusive evidence of actual intent); *Diamant v Sheldon L Pollack Corp*, 216 BR 589, 591 (Bankr SD Tex 1995) (stating that '[w]hile one badge of fraud standing alone may amount to little more than a suspicious circumstance, insufficient in itself to constitute a fraud per se, several of them when considered together may afford a basis from which its existence is properly inferable'). Proving all of the badges of fraud is not necessary. *In Ritchie Capital Mgmt, LLC v Stoebner*, 779 F.3d 857, 866 (8th Cir 2015) ('The law does not require the trustee to prove *all* of the badges [because] [o]nce a trustee establishes a confluence of *several* badges of fraud, the trustee is entitled to the presumption of fraudulent intent.')

[150] See *In re Acequia*, 34 F 3d 800, 806 (9th Cir 1994) (stating that '[o]nce a trustee establishes indicia of fraud in an action under section 548(a)(1), the burden shifts to the transferee to prove some "legitimate supervening purpose" for the transferee at issue').

[151] See *Rubin v Manufacturers Hanover Trust Co*, 661 F 2d 979, 991 (2d Cir 1981) (stating that 'if the debtor receives property or discharges or secures an antecedent debt that is substantially equivalent in value to the property given or obligation incurred by him in exchange, then the transaction has not significantly affected his estate and his creditors have no cause to complain'); *Rebein v Cornerstone Creek Partners, LLC (In re Expert South Tulsa, LLC)*, 842 F.3d 1293, 1297 (10th Cir 2016) ('Because fraudulent-transfer statutes are for the protection of unsecured creditors, [courts] measure the value received in terms of the effect on those creditors.').

[152] 323 BR 838 (Bankr SDNY 2005).

[153] Ibid at 841.

[154] Ibid at 840.

[155] Ibid at 841.

'uniform'[156] view of federal case law on this issue, the Bankruptcy Court held that the grant of the security interest did not constitute a fraudulent transfer.[157]

4. Solvency and related tests

1.80 In the context of a constructive fraudulent conveyance analysis, there are three statutory tests: the 'balance sheet' solvency test (section 548(a)(1)(B)(ii)(I)); the 'unreasonably small capital' test (section 548(a)(1)(B)(ii)(II)); and the 'inability to pay debts as they come due' test (section 548(a)(1)(B)(ii)(III)). The party challenging the transfer must prove one of these circumstances.

(a) Balance sheet solvency test

1.81 A company is insolvent if 'the sum of [its] debts is greater than all of [its] property, at a fair valuation'.[158] Under the balance sheet test, the court compares the amount of the debtor's liabilities to the fair value of the debtor's assets. The analysis is not, however, literally limited to or constrained by the debtor's balance sheet.[159] Instead, it is appropriate to adjust items on the balance sheet that are shown at a higher or lower value than their going concern value and to examine whether assets of a company that are not found on its balance sheet should be included.[160] The debtor's assets should therefore be valued on a 'going concern' basis, unless the business is 'on its deathbed'.[161]

1.82 To determine the value of a debtor's assets, some courts look to the price of a debtor's publicly traded securities. As the *Iridium* court stated, 'a company's stock price is an "ideal datapoint" for determining value' as 'market price is a more reliable measure of the stock's value than the subjective estimates of one or two expert witnesses'.[162] In *Iridium*, the Official Committee of Unsecured Creditors challenged certain transfers and had to prove that the debtors were either insolvent or inadequately capitalized at the time of the challenged transfers, relying on expert witnesses. The court held that the Committee had not sustained its burden, in part because the Committee's expert witness' opinion was 'entitled to less weight because of his conscious disregard of ... contemporaneous market evidence, including Iridium's stock price'.[163]

(b) Unreasonably small capital test

1.83 An allegedly fraudulent transfer may also be avoided if, among other things, at the time of the transfer the debtor 'was engaged in business or a transaction, or was about to engage in

---

[156] See *In re Marketxt Holdings Corp*, 361 BR 369, 398 (Bankr SDNY 2007) (stating that '[t]he cases are uniform that the grant of collateral for a legitimate antecedent debt is not, without more, a constructive fraudulent conveyance').

[157] *Applied Theory*, 323 BR at 841.

[158] 11 USC § 101(32)(A); see also *In re 45 John Lofts, LLC*, 599 B.R. 730, 745 (Bankr. S.D.N.Y. 2019) ('a debtor is insolvent under the Bankruptcy Code where its assets exceed its liabilities at the time of the transfer').

[159] See *In re Iridium Operating LLC*, 373 BR 283, 344 (Bankr SDNY 2007) (stating that courts should adopt a flexible approach to the insolvency analysis).

[160] *In re Waccamaw's Homeplace*, 325 BR 524, 529 (Bankr D Del 2005).

[161] *Matter of Taxman Clothing Co*, 905 F 2d 166, 170 (7th Cir 1990).

[162] *In re Iridium Operating LLC*, 373 B.R. at 346–347; see also *VFB LLC v Campbell Soup Co.*, 482 F.3d 624, 631 (3d Cir 2007) ('Equity markets allow participants to voluntarily take on or transfer among themselves the risk that their projections will be inaccurate; fraudulent transfer law cannot be rationally invoked to undermine that function.'); see also *In re Lyondell Chemical Company*, 567 B.R. at 112 (recognizing that the 'valuation principles regarding professional investors and stock prices are applicable to [the] Court's balance-sheet insolvency analysis').

[163] *In re Iridium Operating LLC*, 373 B.R. at 351.

business or a transaction, for which any property remaining with the debtor was an unreasonably small capital'.[164] Unreasonably small capital generally 'refer[s] to the inability to generate sufficient profits to sustain operations'.[165] Courts have held that the 'unreasonably small capital test' is a test of 'reasonable foreseeability', which is 'an objective standard anchored in projections of cash flow, sales, profit margins, and net profits and losses, including difficulties that are likely to arise'.[166] The question is 'not whether the projection was correct ... but whether it was reasonable and prudent when made'.[167] Accordingly, '[t]he test is aimed at [transfers] that leave the transferor technically solvent, but doomed to fail'.[168]

Adequacy of capital is a question of fact in each case.[169] The test for unreasonably small cap-   **1.84**
ital is flexible and may depend on the industry or business at issue:

> Adequate capitalization is ... a variable concept according to which specific industry
> or business is involved. The nature of the enterprise, normal turnover of inventory rate,
> method of payment by customers, etc., from the standpoint of what is normal and cus-
> tomary for other similar businesses in the industry, are all relevant factors in determining
> whether the amount of capital was unreasonably small at the time of, or immediately after,
> the transfer.[170]

The unreasonably small capital test is prospective—the inquiry is whether it was reason-   **1.85**
ably foreseeable on the transfer date that the debtor would have unreasonably small capital
to carry on its business.[171] This analysis, however, is not necessarily static. For instance, a
debtor's projections may not reflect sufficient cash to pay off principal balances on loans or
notes when due. Loans and notes, however, often can be refinanced before they become due,
even by companies that are experiencing financial or operating difficulties.[172] Accordingly,
courts examining the question of adequate capital 'place great weight on the ability of the
debtor to obtain financing'[173] and take into account 'all reasonably anticipated sources of
operating funds, which may include new equity infusions, cash from operations, or cash

---

[164] 11 USC § 548(a)(1)(B)(ii)(II).

[165] *Moody v Sec Pac Bus Credit, Inc*, 971 F 2d 1056, 1070 (3d Cir 1992).

[166] *In re Bergman*, 293 BR 580, 584 (Bankr WDNY 2003) (citations omitted).

[167] *MFS/Sun Life Trust-High Yield Series v Van Dusen Airport Serv Co*, 910 F Supp 913, 943 (SDNY 1995) (internal quotations omitted).

[168] Ibid at 944.

[169] See *WRT Creditors Liquidation Trust v WRT Bankr Litig Master File Defendants (In re WRT Energy Corp)*, 282 BR 343, 441 (Bankr WD La 2001) ('Whether the amount of capital remaining in the hands of the debtor is unreasonably small for running the business is a factual question to be determined on a case-by-case basis'); see also *In re Suburban Motor Freight, Inc*, 124 BR 984, 994 (Bankr SD Ohio 1990) ('Whether the amount of capital remaining in the hands of the debtor is unreasonably small is a question of fact').

[170] 5 *Collier on Bankruptcy*, para 548.05[3][b] (16th edn, 2021).

[171] See *White v SemGroup Litigation Trust (In re SemCrude L.P.)*, 648 Fed. Appx. 205, 210 (3d Cir 2016) ('case law ... teaches as a general proposition, hindsight should not be used to answer the question of unreasonably small capital'); *Peltz v Hatten*, 279 BR 710, 744 (D Del 2002).

[172] *Peltz*, 279 BR at 747 (stating that 'the fact that a company may have operating difficulties at a point in time does not mean that it cannot reasonably expect to have access to traditional banking sources at the time of difficulty or at a later point in time').

[173] *Statutory Comm of Unsecured Creditors v Motorola Inc (In re Iridium Operating LLC)*, 373 BR 283, 345 (Bankr SDNY 2007) (to determine the adequacy of capital, courts compare 'a company's projected cash inflows (also referred to as 'working capital' or 'operating funds') with the company's capital needs throughout a reasonable period of time after the questioned transfer'); see also *In re SemCrude*, 648 Fed. Appx. at 211 (failure to satisfy the unreasonably small capital test where it was not reasonably foreseeable that debtor 'was likely to be denied access to a credit facility that had been in place').

from secured or unsecured loans over the relevant time period.[174] Also, at least one court has found that the transfer at issue must cause the condition of unreasonably small capital; if the debtor had unreasonably small capital before the alleged fraudulent transfer, the transfer will not be avoided.[175]

(c) Inability to pay debts as they come due test

1.86   Section 548 of the Bankruptcy Code also provides that an allegedly fraudulent transfer may be avoided if, among other things, the debtor was unable to pay its debts as they came due. This test is highly subjective, requiring the debtor or trustee to demonstrate that, at the time of the transfer, the debtor 'intended to incur, or believed it would incur, debts that would be beyond its ability to pay as such debts matured'.[176] This 'forward looking' test requires assessing the debtor's reasonable prediction about its ability to repay a debt as it is incurred.[177] Since this test requires a subjective inquiry into the debtor's intent, section 548 (a)(1)(b)(ii) (III) is rarely litigated to conclusion.[178]

B.   Preferences

1. Generally

1.87   Section 547(b) of the Bankruptcy Code grants a trustee (or a debtor in possession) the power to recover certain payments or transfers made to creditors within 90 days before the bankruptcy filing.[179] Such payments/transfers qualify as voidable 'preferences'. There is no intent aspect to a preference; a transfer is avoidable as a preferential transfer to the extent that it fits within the statutory requirements.[180]

1.88   The debtor must prove five elements to establish a preference: (1) a transfer of an interest of the debtor in property to or for the benefit of a creditor; (2) for or on account of an antecedent debt owed by the debtor before such transfer was made; (3) made while the debtor was insolvent; (4) made within a specified period before the filing of the bankruptcy petition (90 days, unless the transferee is an insider, in which case, one year); and (5) that

---

[174] *Peltz v Hatten*, 279 BR at 744–745.

[175] *In re Pioneer Home Builders, Inc v Int'l Bank of Commerce (In re Pioneer Home Builders, Inc)*, 147 BR 889, 894 (Bankr WD Tex 1992) ('Where a debtor has unreasonably small capital, that the debtor subsequently engaged in transfers which worsened, but did not cause, its financial infirmities, will not subject those transfers to avoidance as fraudulent conveyances').

[176] 11 USC § 548(a)(1)(B)(ii)(III).

[177] *In re Opus E. LLC*, 698 Fed. Appx 711, 715 (3d Cir 2017).

[178] See, eg, *In re Suburban Motor Freight, Inc*, 124 BR 984, 1000, n 14 ('There are few rulings on this particular prong … and it is rarely used by parties seeking to avoid a transfer as it appears to require the courts to undergo a subjective, rather than objective, inquiry into a party's intent'). But see *In re 45 John Lofts, LLC*, 599 B.R. 730, 746 (Bankr. S.D.N.Y. 2019) ('A complaint need not specifically state, verbatim, that the transferor made a transfer with the intent or belief that the transferor would be unable to pay debts as they become due. Rather, this element of a cause of action can be inferred by the facts and circumstances alleged in a complaint').

[179] The Bankruptcy Code's preference section serves two main goals: (1) preventing companies from racing to the courthouse to dismember the debtor during its slide into bankruptcy; and (2) protecting equality of distribution among creditors of the debtor. *United Rental, Inc v Angell*, 592 F 3d 525, 528 (4th Cir 2010).

[180] *Barash v Public Finance Cor*, 658 F 2d 504, 510 (7th Cir 1981) (stating that '[t]he creditor's knowledge or state of mind is no longer relevant [as] Congress eliminated this requirement in favor of the objective criteria under the new Code').

permits the creditor to receive a greater amount than it would get in a chapter 7 liquidation of the debtor if the transfer had not been made. Unless shielded by section 547(c)[181] or another exception, a transfer meeting these requirements can be 'avoided' and, under section 550 of the Bankruptcy Code, the trustee can recover the property transferred (or its value) from parties liable. Potential liable parties include 'the initial transferee of such transfer', 'the entity for whose benefit such transfer was made', or 'any immediate or mediate transferee of such initial transferee'.[182]

2. Trustees' rights to bring preference actions under section 544 of the Bankruptcy Code

The 'strong arm' provision of the Bankruptcy Code, as described above in relation to fraudulent transfers, also applies to preferential transfers. Specifically, section 544(b) of the Bankruptcy Code gives the trustee the ability to bring actions under state preferential transfer laws. Currently, however, only five of the 50 states in the US have preferential transfer statutes available to trustees under this 'strong arm' power.[183]   **1.89**

3. A transfer is broadly defined

A 'transfer' includes every mode, direct or indirect, absolute or conditional, voluntary or involuntary, of disposing of or parting with property or an interest in property. As stated in the House Report with respect to section 101(54), Congress intended '[t]he definition of transfer [to be] as broad as possible'.[184] The Supreme Court in *Nat'l Bank of Newport v Nat'l Herkimer County Bank of Little Falls*[185] observed: **1.90**

> To constitute a preference, it is not necessary that the transfer be made directly to the creditor. It may be made to another for his benefit. If the bankrupt has made a transfer of his property, the effect of which is to enable one of his creditors to obtain a greater percentage of his debt than another creditor of the same class, circuitry of arrangement will not avail to save it.[186]

Because the definition of 'transfer' is comprehensive, every conceivable type of transfer may be avoided if the other requirements of section 547(b) are met. This includes granting a security interest in the property of the debtor to secure a pre-existing obligation.[187]   **1.91**

---

[181] Section 547(c)(1) excepts a transfer intended as a contemporaneous exchange for new value (rather than in satisfaction of an antecedent debt) if the exchange was 'in fact' substantially contemporaneous. Section 547(c)(2) excepts payments made in the ordinary course of a debtor's business or financial affairs and according to ordinary business terms, if the obligation paid was incurred in the ordinary course of the debtor's business or financial affairs. The statutory exceptions in ss 547(c)(3)–(6) concern transfers of consensual security interests and statutory liens. Section 547(c)(7) excepts domestic support obligations, and section 547(c)(8) and (9) except *de minimis* transfers.

[182] 11 USC S 550(a). To qualify as a 'transferee' under the Bankruptcy Code s 550, a party must have received the actual transferred property. *Rajala v Spencer Fane LLP (Generation Resources Holding Company, LLC)*, 964 F.3d 958 (10th Cir 2020).

[183] 5 *Collier on Bankruptcy*, para 544.06[2]. These states include Ohio, Kentucky, New Mexico, Minnesota, and Maryland. See ibid.

[184] HR Rep No 95-595, 95th Cong, 1st Sess 314 (1977), reprinted in 1978 USCCAN 5963, 6271.

[185] 225 US 178, 184 (1912).

[186] Ibid at 184.

[187] See *Hughes v Lawson (In re Lawson)*, 122 F 3d 1237, 1240 (9th Cir 1997) ('Granting of security for a debt is a transfer under the Bankruptcy Code').

4. Antecedent debt

1.92   Although 'antecedent debt' is not defined by the Bankruptcy Code, a debt is 'antecedent' if it is incurred before the transfer. Thus, if the transaction at issue constitutes a debt incurred prior to the transfer, it is antecedent; if it becomes a debt contemporaneously with, or after the transfer, then it is not antecedent and does not give rise to a preference claim. The timing of certain transfers may, however, depend on perfection. Thus, if security is transferred for contemporaneous consideration, but is not perfected until a later point in time, the transfer will be considered made for or on account of antecedent debt, and, 'if the other statutory elements exist, will be an avoidable preference'.[188] Any pre-existing debt which is reduced or discharged as a result of payment within 90 days of bankruptcy is, therefore, an antecedent debt within the meaning of section 547(b)(2).

5. Insolvency presumed for 90-day preference period

1.93   For a transfer to be avoidable under section 547, it must be made while the debtor was insolvent.[189] Under section 547(f) of the Bankruptcy Code, there is a rebuttable presumption that the debtor was insolvent within the 90-day preference period. To overcome the presumption, the transferee must introduce some evidence showing that the debtor was solvent at the time of the transfer. The effect of this presumption is to shift the burden of going forward with the evidence, not the burden of proof, which remains on the party seeking to avoid the transfer. This presumption, however, does not exist for transfers made to insiders between 90 days and one year prior to the bankruptcy. Unlike a constructive fraudulent transfer claim, insolvency here is measured only by a balance sheet test, and not a capital adequacy or liquidity test.

6. Creditor must benefit from transfer

1.94   The trustee or debtor must also establish that the creditor received a quantifiable 'benefit' from the challenged transfer for purposes of section 547(b) and that any 'benefit' received exceeded the amount the creditor would have received in a hypothetical chapter 7 liquidation. The bankruptcy court is required to compare the monetary benefit the creditor in fact received from the alleged preferential transfer with the projected amount of any distribution to the same creditor in the event there were an order for relief under chapter 7 and the preferential transfer had never occurred. In other words, whether a specific transfer is a preference is determined 'not by what the situation would have been if the debtor's assets had been liquidated and distributed among his creditors at the time the alleged preferential payment was made, but by the actual effect of the payment as determined when bankruptcy results'.[190]

7. The SBRA's new preference claim requirement

1.95   The Small Business Reorganization Act of 2019 (the SBRA) went into effect in February 2020.[191] Significantly, the SBRA amended section 547(b) of the Bankruptcy Code requiring

---

[188] 5 *Collier on Bankruptcy*, para 547.03[4] (discussing 11 USC § 547(e)).
[189] 11 USC § 547(e)(2b)(3); see also *In re Bayonne Medical Center*, 429 BR 152, 192 (Bankr DNJ 2010) ('Insolvency is a necessary element . . . to establish a voidable preference').
[190] *Palmer Clay Prods Co v Brown*, 297 US 227, 229 (1936).
[191] Small Business Reorganization Act of 2019, Pub. L. No. 116-54, §3, 133 Stat. 1079, 1085.

the debtor or trustee to undertake reasonable due diligence before commencing a preference action. Such diligence requires taking into consideration a preference defendant's
'known or reasonably knowable affirmative defenses' before pursuing a preference claim.[192]
This change to section 547(b) may benefit potential preference defendants as it increases
the diligence a debtor or trustee must undertake before instituting a preference claim. Such
increased burden may indeed dissuade the pursuit of certain, more frivolous, preference
claims.

8. Defences to a preference action

Once the elements of a preference are established, the preference defendant may attempt   **1.96**
to prove that the transfer fits within one of the exceptions set forth under section 547(c) of
the Bankruptcy Code.[193] Examples of such exceptions include, among others, transfers in
which the parties intend for the transfer to be a contemporaneous exchange for new value
and payments made in the ordinary course of business, according to ordinary business
terms. Additionally, common law exceptions to preferences have developed, such as the
'earmarking defence', in which funds that that are specifically earmarked by a creditor for
payment to a designated creditor do not constitute a transfer of property—even if the funds
pass through the debtor's hands in reaching the specified creditor.

C. 'Safe Harbors' for Certain Financial Transactions

1. Generally

The Bankruptcy Code protects certain types of financial transactions from the statutory   **1.97**
avoiding powers discussed herein.[194] These so-called 'safe harbor' provisions are intended
to protect the US financial markets as a whole from instability that may result from dis-
turbing settled securities transactions. Accordingly, these provisions ensure that payments
or transfers received by a debtor's 'safe harbor' contract counterparties cannot be avoided
either as a fraudulent conveyance or as a preference in the debtor's subsequent bankruptcy
filing.[195] The sole exception to this protection is where the transaction is challenged as an
actual (as opposed to constructive fraud) fraudulent conveyance under section 548(a) of
the Bankruptcy Code.[196]

---

[192] Taking into account the SBRA's amendment, section 547(b) of the Bankruptcy Code now reads, in part:

Except as provided in subsections (c) and (i) of this section, the trustee may, *based on reasonable due diligence in the circumstances of the case and taking into account a party's known or reasonably knowable affirmative defenses under subsection (c)*, avoid any transfer of an interest of the debtor in property . . .

[193] Pursuant to s 547(g) of the Bankruptcy Code, 'the creditor or party in interest against whom recovery or avoidance is sought has the burden of proving the nonavoidability of a transfer under [section 547(c)]'.

[194] 11 USC § 546(e)–(g).

[195] In addition to protecting these parties from the trustee's avoiding powers, the Bankruptcy Code grants them other protections, including exemptions from the automatic stay and the prohibition on exercising a right of setoff. See 11 USC §§ 362(b)(6), 362(b)(7), 362(b)(17), 362(b)(27), 555, 556, 559, 560, 561.

[196] See 11 USC § 546(e)–(g) (prohibiting avoidance of 'safe harbored' transactions, except under section 548(a)(1)(A)).

2. The 'safe harbors' are broad in scope

1.98   The 'safe harbor' provisions are extremely broad in scope. They protect any payment or transfer from avoidance, so long as it is:

- a 'margin payment' or a 'settlement payment' made by or to (or for the benefit of) a commodity broker, forward contract merchant, stockbroker, financial institution, financial participant, or securities clearing agency;[197]
- a transfer made by or to (or for the benefit of) one of these protected financial parties or institutions in connection with a securities contract, … commodity contract, … or forward contract;[198]
- a transfer made by or to (or for the benefit of) a repo participant or financial institution, in connection with a repurchase agreement;[199] or
- a transfer made by or to (or for the benefit of) a swap participant or financial institution, under or in connection with a swap agreement.[200]

Each of the terms used in these provisions is itself broadly defined, substantially expanding the protections these provisions afford.[201]

1.99   Prior to the Supreme Court's ruling in *Merit Management Group, LP v FTI Consulting, Inc.*,[202] most appellate courts had adopted a plain reading of section 546 and its relevant definitions, resulting in a wide range of transactions being protected from avoidance as either a fraudulent conveyance or as a preference. The 'safe harbors' had been applied to payments made in private leveraged buy-out transactions that do not involve the broader financial markets, to transactions where the necessary financial participant has served only as a conduit for the flow of funds, and to payments made as part of fraudulent Ponzi schemes.[203] Some courts, and many commentators, had acknowledged that, by protecting private transactions that arguably could be unwound (or avoided) without impacting the financial markets, the 'safe harbor' provisions, as drafted, had gone beyond their intended purpose to protect the public markets.

---

[197]   11 USC § 546(e).
[198]   Ibid.
[199]   11 USC § 546(f).
[200]   11 USC § 546(g).
[201]   For example, the Bankruptcy Code defines 'securities contract' as, among other things, 'a contract for the purchase, sale or loan of a security, a certificate of deposit, a mortgage loan, any interest in a mortgage loan, a group or index of securities, certificates of deposit, or mortgage loans or interests therein (including an interest therein or based on the value thereof), or option on any of the foregoing, … including any repurchase or reverse repurchase transaction on any such security, certificate of deposit, mortgage loan, interest, group or index, or option (whether or not such repurchase or reverse repurchase transaction is a "repurchase agreement," as defined in section 101)'. 11 USC § 741(7)(A)(i).
[202]   138 S. Ct. 883 (2018).
[203]   See, e.g., *Official Comm of Unsecured Creditors of Quebecor World (USA), Inc v Am United Life Ins Co (In re Quebecor World (USA) Inc)*, 719 F 3d 94 (2d Cir 2013) (private leveraged buy-out payments protected, even though the financial institution involved served merely as a conduit for funds); *Peterson v Somers Dublin Ltd*, 729 F 3d 741 (7th Cir 2013) (payments made as part of a fraudulent Ponzi scheme protected); *In re Derivium Capital, LLC*, 716 F 3d 355 (4th Cir 2013) (same); *Enron Creditors Recovery Corp v ALFA, SAB de CV (In re Enron Creditors Recovery Corp)*, 651 F 3d 329 (2d Cir 2011) (voluntary redemption payments protected, even though not common in the securities industry); *QSI Holdings, Inc v Alford (In re QSI Holdings, Inc)*, 571 F 3d 545 (6th Cir 2009) (private leveraged buy-out payments protected, even though the financial institution involved served merely as a conduit); *Contemporary Indus Corp v Frost*, 564 F 3d 981 (8th Cir 2009) (same); *Brandt v BA Capital Co (In re Plassein Int'l Corp)*, 590 F 3d 252 (3d Cir 2009) (same).

3. The Supreme Court's ruling in *Merit Management Group*

In 2018, the Supreme Court clarified and limited the scope of the safe harbor provision in *Merit Management Group*, holding that the only relevant transfer for purposes of section 546(e) is the transfer that the trustee seeks to avoid rather than any sub-components of such transfer.[204] In particular, transferor Valley View Downs, LP and Bedford Downs Management entered into an agreement pursuant to which Valley View agreed to acquire Bedford's stock for $55 million. To consummate the sale, Valley View arranged for the transfer of $55 million from lender Credit Suisse to third-party escrow agent Citizens Bank.[205] Citizens Bank then disbursed the funds to the various shareholders, including $16.5 million to Merit Management Group. **1.100**

Shortly after the transaction was completed, Valley View and its parent filed for chapter 11 relief and a litigation trust was created under its chapter 11 plan.[206] The litigation trustee sought to avoid the $16.5 million transfer from Valley View to Merit Management arguing that the transfer was a constructive fraudulent transfer.[207] Merit Management, however, contended that the section 546(e) safe harbor applied because the transfer was a ' "settlement payment … made by or to (or for the benefit of)" two "financial institutions" ', that is, between Credit Suisse and Citizens Bank.[208] The trustee countered that the Court should not look to the various sub-components of the transaction—rather, the only relevant transfer for purposes of the safe harbor exception was the overarching transfer between Valley View and Merit.[209] **1.101**

The Supreme Court agreed with the trustee, holding that the relevant transfer for the purposes of the safe harbor defence was the end-to-end transfer between Valley View and Merit Management rather than component parts of the transfer, such as the transactions between Credit Suisse to Citizens Bank, and Citizens Bank to Merit Management.[210] In coming to this conclusion, the Supreme Court engaged in a statutory analysis, and found that the plain language of section 546(e) and the context in which it was used 'all point to the transfer that the trustee seeks to avoid as the relevant transfer for consideration of the § 546(e) safe harbor criteria'.[211] **1.102**

Applying the analysis above, the Supreme Court explained that the case 'yield[ed] a straightforward result'.[212] Because the trustee sought to avoid the overall transfer between Valley View and Merit Management, and not the intermediate transfers involving the financial institutions, the entire transfer fell outside the safe harbor provision. **1.103**

4. The debtor as a 'financial institution' following *Merit Management Group*

The Supreme Court's ruling in *Merit Management Group* ran contrary to rulings from various appellate courts, including in both the Second and Third Circuits.[213] Despite this **1.104**

---

[204] *Merit Management Group, LP*, 138 S.Ct. at 891.
[205] Ibid.
[206] Ibid.
[207] Ibid; 11 U.S.C. § 548(a)(1)(B).
[208] *Merit Management Group, LP* at 891–892.
[209] Ibid at 893.
[210] Ibid at 893–894.
[211] See ibid at 894–895.
[212] Ibid at 897.
[213] See, e.g., *In re Quebecor World (USA) Inc.*, 719 F.3d 94 (2d Cir 2013); *In re QSI Holdings, Inc.*, 571 F.3d 545 (6th Cir 2009); *Contemporary Indus. Corp. v Frost*, 564 F.3d 981 (8th Cir 2009); *In re Resorts Int'l Inc.*, 181 F.3d 505 (3d Cir 1999); and *In re Kaiser Steel Corp.*, 952 F.2d 1230 (10th Cir 1991).

ruling, the law is not entirely settled as both the Second Circuit and the Bankruptcy Court for the District of Delaware, among others, have narrowed the scope of *Merit Management* by holding that a debtor can be considered a 'financial institution' for the purposes of section 546(e).

1.105 For example, in *In re Tribune Company Fraudulent Conveyance Litigation*, the Second Circuit held that safe harbor provisions applied to a debtor who was in an agency relationship with a financial institution.[214] In that case, Tribune Media Company, borrowed over $11 billion, which was used to refinance some of Tribune's pre-existing bank debt and to cash out Tribune's shareholders.[215] Upon Tribune's bankruptcy, certain unsecured creditors sought to avoid the payment by Tribune to its shareholders. The Second Circuit held that Tribune was an entity covered by the safe harbor as it was a customer of Computershare Trust Company, N.A. (which was Tribune's agent), and the transaction documents established that Tribune was a covered entity due to its agency and customer relationship with Computershare.[216] Accordingly, the Second Circuit determined that the debtors were 'financial institutions' and were covered by the safe harbor provisions.[217] Following the Second Circuit's ruling, several courts adopted the *Tribune* reasoning in holding that the debtor was a 'financial institution' due to its use of an agent in a transaction, thus protecting the transaction from avoidance.[218] However, at least one court has criticized *Tribune's* reasoning narrowly interpreting *Merit Management Group*.[219]

1.106 Thus, the impact of the Supreme Court's decision in *Merit Management Group* is not entirely clear. Until further guidance from the Supreme Court, courts are likely to continue to diverge on certain aspects of the safe harbor analysis, such as when the debtor may be deemed a 'financial institution'.[220]

V. Vulnerable Transactions in England

1.107 Directors in England should also be aware that if the company enters into certain types of transaction within specified periods before its insolvency, an administrator or liquidator may be able to apply to the court for an order that the parties be put back into the position

---

[214] 946 F.3d. 66 (2019).

[215] Ibid at 72.

[216] Ibid at 80.

[217] In *Merit Management Group*, the Supreme Court did not address whether debtors qualified as financial institutions, noting that the parties did not contend that a debtor qualifies as such by 'virtue of its status as customer', which paved the way for the Second Circuit's ruling.

[218] See, e.g., *In re Nine W. LBO Sec. Litig.*, 2020 WL 5049621 (S.D.N.Y. Aug. 27, 2020); *Holliday v K Road Power Management, LLC (In re Boston Generating LLC)*, 617 B.R. 442 (Bankr. S.D.N.Y. 2020); *SunEdison Litigation Trust v Seller Note, LLC (In re SunEdison, Inc.)*, 2020 WL 6395497 (Bankr. S.D.N.Y. Nov. 2, 2020); *Fairfield Sentry Limited (In Liquidation) v Theodoor GGC Amsterdam (In re Fairfield Sentry Ltd.)*, 2020 WL 7345988 (Bankr. S.D.N.Y. Dec. 14, 2020); *In re Samson Res. Corp.*, 625 B.R. 291, 301 (Bankr. D. Del. 2020); *Kelley v Safe Harbor Managed Acct. 101, Ltd.*, 2020 WL 5913523, *4 (D. Minn. Oct. 6, 2020).

[219] See *In re Greektown Holdings, LLC*, 621 B.R. 797 (Bankr. E.D. Mich. 2020). (Bankruptcy court finding that the overarching transaction was the relevant transaction for purposes of the section 546(e) analysis in accordance with *Merit Management Group*, rather than the component parts of the transfer involving Merrill Lynch and other banks. The bankruptcy court then held that the debtor was not a 'financial institution' as the underwriter in the transaction was not an agent or custodian of the debtor.)

[220] In 2021, the Supreme Court denied a petition for certiorari from *In re Tribune. Deutsche Bank Tr. Co. v Robert R. McCormick Found.*, No. 20-8, 2021 WL 1521009 (U.S. Apr. 19, 2021).

they would have been in if the transaction had not been entered into, or require some other appropriate remedy. With regard to certain of these matters, entering into such a transaction could be treated as a breach of duty by the directors, in particular if a transaction is at an undervalue or is a preference. During the period in which the company is attempting to put together a financial restructuring, both directors and third parties dealing with the company will wish to be alive to the risk of a transaction being subsequently set aside if an insolvency proceeding follows (and if a chapter 11 proceeding or an administration is used to implement the restructuring). For example:

(1) the company may be working hard to preserve cash during the restructuring period, paying some critical creditors early and others as late as possible;
(2) lenders to the company, or pension fund trustees, may press for further guarantees or security for existing liabilities;
(3) the company may seek to realize assets for cash; and
(4) assignments of intra-group liabilities may need to be made to restructure the group going forward.

Moreover, because most of the statutory claims considered in this section are only available to a liquidator or administrator, transactions which could be potentially vulnerable to challenge should be disclosed in proposals for a debt restructuring by way of a scheme of arrangement, Part 26A restructuring plan, or CVA (all of which are discussed in Chapter 3). This is because 'creditors are entitled to know whether there are any potential causes of action which would be lost to them' upon approval of the relevant restructuring procedure.[221]

A. Transactions at an Undervalue (Section 238 of the Insolvency Act 1986)

A transaction is at an undervalue if a company makes a gift to a person or enters into a **1.108** transaction on terms where the company receives no consideration or one which has a value which is significantly less than the value of the consideration provided by the company. Section 238(5) provides a defence that the transaction is entered into in good faith for the purpose of carrying on the company's business and that there are reasonable grounds for believing that it will benefit the company. The burden of proof in establishing this defence is with the party seeking to avoid the application of section 238, so that it will be critical for counterparties to transactions which they suspect may be vulnerable to undertake sufficient enquiry and to obtain sufficient supporting evidence to defend a claim if it should be raised in the future.[222] To be vulnerable, a transaction at an undervalue must have been entered into during the period of two years before the onset of insolvency (broadly, the commencement of the winding up or administration procedure) and the company must have been insolvent at the time it entered into the transaction or become insolvent by entering

---

[221] *Carraway Guildford (Nominee A) Limited and 18 others v Regis UK Limited, Edward Williams (as joint supervisor of Regis UK Ltd) and Christine Mary Laverty (as joint supervisor of Regis UK Ltd)* [2021] EWHC 1294 (Ch) at [77].
[222] See, e.g., *Re Barton Manufacturing Co Ltd* [1998] BCC 827.

into it. There is a presumption of insolvency if the parties to the transaction are connected, for instance if it is an intra-group transaction or a transaction with a director.

1.109   One of the most common transactions which directors will need to consider in a restructuring scenario is the grant of security. Sometimes this is security for new money and creates no specific issues. But sometimes the directors may be pressed to provide security for outstanding indebtedness as a condition of continued support. In *Re MC Bacon Ltd*[223] Millett J held that the creation of security will not typically amount to a transaction at an undervalue as the security itself does not deplete the assets of the company or diminish their value. In that case, a company granted security for an existing overdraft at the time when it was insolvent. The company subsequently went into liquidation and the liquidator commenced proceedings under sections 238 and 239 of the Insolvency Act 1986 to have the security set aside. The court held that a transaction of this type could not be a transaction at an undervalue, as the mere creation of a security over a company's assets does not deplete them and the company retains the right to redeem, sell, or remortgage the charged assets.

1.110   However, as mentioned above, a transaction can be a transaction at an undervalue if:

(1) it is a gift or otherwise on terms that provide for the company to receive no consideration; or

(2) the value of the transaction, in money or money's worth, is significantly less than the value, in money or money's worth, of the consideration provided by the company.

1.111   In *MC Bacon* Millett J found that there was consideration consisting of 'the bank's forbearance from calling in the overdraft and its honouring of the cheques and making of fresh advances to the company during the continuance of the facility'.[224] He was therefore concerned with limb (2), and it was in this context that he considered the grant of security could not come within the paragraph as the mere creation of security over the assets does not deplete them.

1.112   In *Hill v Spread Trustee Company*,[225] Arden LJ doubted that it was the case that the grant of security could never constitute a transaction at an undervalue. In that case, Arden LJ found that charges which had been granted in favour of certain trustees had been granted notwithstanding that 'the trustees were not pressing for repayment of the sums due to them and did not give any consideration in the form of forbearance for the grant of the later charges and the assignment'. Arden LJ could see no reason why the value of the right to have recourse to security and to take priority over other creditors, which the debtor creates upon granting the security, should be left out of account when assessing whether a chargor has given any consideration (when granting security) for the purposes of the transaction at an undervalue provisions. It is worth noting that *Hill v Spread Trustees* was a case concerning claims by a trustee in bankruptcy to obtain relief under section 423 of the Insolvency Act 1986. Although it is applicable to corporate debtors, as will be seen from the discussion of section 423 that follows, the good faith defence available in section 238 would not have been applicable. Furthermore, it remains to be seen whether subsequent courts will be prepared

---

223 [1990] BCC 78.
224 Ibid at 92.
225 [2007] 1 WLR 2404, CA.

to distinguish *Hill* on the basis that it was a case involving no consideration, such that *MC Bacon* remains good law where the evidence shows that the grant of security was a condition of further forbearance or whether Millett J's analysis in *MC Bacon* will be comprehensively reopened.[226] Another possible ground of distinction is that *Hill* involved a legal mortgage (and thus a transfer of title to the chargee) whilst *MC Bacon* involved a 'mere charge'—that is, an encumbrance on the asset. However, it seems unlikely that Arden LJ had this distinction in mind in her judgment because she referred to the decision of the House of Lords in *Buchler v Talbot*,[227] which, as has been noted (and criticized) in another context, treated the 'ownership' of the assets by the secured creditors as substantively the same for both a charge and a mortgage.[228] In its response to the Insolvency and Governance Consultation in 2018, the UK Government indicated that it intended to work with stakeholders to consider whether any clarification of uncertainty is required about whether the granting of security can be challenged as a transaction at an undervalue.[229] However, at the time of writing there have been no further developments.

Thus, for the moment, directors of a company asked to grant security for existing indebtedness as a condition of forbearance are in a difficult position. We will see, shortly, that a specific regime governs the grant of floating charges but does not cover fixed security. Of course, general duties will be implicated, and the particular situation will turn on its facts. Where the directors have no alternative, it is suggested that the board should document the fact that the bank is forbearing and that the transaction is therefore within limb (b) such that the analysis in *MC Bacon* continues to apply but, if that is wrong, the company nonetheless is granting the security in good faith for the purposes of carrying on its business where there are reasonable grounds for believing it will benefit the company, such that the section 238(5) defence remains available if Millet J's reasoning does not withstand later scrutiny.   **1.113**

Lenders who receive new security as part of a restructuring should also always ensure that there are board minutes or other board papers, reflecting the necessary consideration, which may, for example, be the grant of new facilities or forbearance, and that the transaction is of benefit to the company. If the company is disposing of assets as part of its restructuring plan, a detailed minute or board paper addressing the decision-making process ought to be prepared. This should address the financial condition of the company and the reasons why the board considers that the value of the consideration received for the transaction is not significantly less than the consideration that the company has given. This may be evidenced by professional advice and, in some circumstances, by efforts to auction the asset more widely. The minute or paper ought also to address the reasons for entering into the transaction and the reasons why the directors consider that it is likely to benefit the company. The counterparty to the transaction who is aware of a possible solvency question would also be well advised to obtain a copy of these supporting papers.   **1.114**

---

[226] For suggestions that perhaps it should be see Reinhard Bork, 'Transactions at an Undervalue—A Comparison of English and German Law' 14(2) *JCLS* 453, 473.

[227] [2004] UKHL 9.

[228] Rizwaan Jameel Mokal, 'Liquidation Expenses and Floating Charges—The Separate Funds Fallacy' (2005) 21(2) *Insolvency Law and Practice* 46.

[229] Department for Business, Energy & Industrial Strategy, 'Insolvency and Corporate Governance: Government Response' 26 August 2018, para 3.8 <https://assets.publishing.service.gov.uk/government/uploads/system/uploads/attachment_data/file/736163/ICG_-_Government_response_doc_-_24_Aug_clean_version__with_Minister_s_photo_and_signature__AC.pdf> (last accessed 3 August 2021).

B. Transactions Defrauding Creditors (Section 423 of the Insolvency Act 1986)

1.115 The same undervalue definition applies in respect of transactions defrauding creditors, although there is no time limit between the transaction and the onset of insolvency for the transaction to be attacked. However, the transaction must have been entered into for the purpose of putting the assets beyond the reach of a creditor (current or prospective) or of otherwise prejudicing the interests of the claimant. The difficulties in establishing such intent have made this a difficult section to apply. In the *Hill v Spread Trustee*[230] case, Arden LJ commented:

> The test whether Mr Nurkowski had the necessary intention is a subjective test: the judge had to be satisfied that he actually had the purpose, not that a reasonable person in his position would have it. On the other hand, the judge could infer that such a purpose existed even if Mr Nurkowski himself denied it.[231]

1.116 Where a company enters into a transaction at an undervalue for the purpose of putting its assets beyond the reach of current or future creditors, the transaction is vulnerable to being unwound at any time, whether or not the company is insolvent.[232] This was important in the *Sequana* case in the Court of Appeal, in which the transaction was successfully challenged using section 423, notwithstanding that the company had not reached the point where its directors knew or should have concluded that the company was or was likely to become unable to pay its debts, so that the duty-shift towards creditors could be said to have been engaged.[233]

1.117 A challenge under section 423 can be brought by an administrator or liquidator or (with leave of the court) a victim of the transaction.[234] However, in order for a victim to be able to bring proceedings, they will need to show a good reason why they should be able to bring them where the liquidator or administrator does not.[235]

C. Preferences (Section 239 of the Insolvency Act 1986)

1.118 A preference is given to a creditor or a guarantor or a surety of its debts if the company does anything or allows anything to be done which has the effect of putting that person in a position which, if the company were to go into insolvent liquidation, would be better than the position he would have been in if the thing had not been done. The repayment of an unsecured debt by a customer to its bank on the due date could be within this wide definition. The company must have been influenced in deciding to give the preference by a desire to produce the preferential effect, in order for the preferential transaction to be vulnerable.

---

[230] [2007] 1 WLR 2404, CA.

[231] Ibid at 86.

[232] It should be noted that the Court has very wide jurisdiction as to the order which it makes. In *Watchorn v Jupiter Industries Limited* [2014] EWHC 3003 (Ch), Purle QC (sitting as a high court judge) awarded the liquidator the full going concern value of the assets as at the date at which they had been improperly assigned.

[233] *Sequana* (n 43).

[234] Insolvency Act 1986, s 424.

[235] *Re Simon Carves Limited; Carillion Construction Limited v Hussain* [2013] EWHC 685 at [22].

There is a presumption of such influence if the parties are connected. This is also the section which is classically implicated where security is granted for an outstanding debt.

Millett J first considered the requirement in the 1986 Act for the company to be 'influenced by a desire' to produce the preferential effect in *MC Bacon*.[236] He noted that it was not sufficient to establish a desire to make the payment or grant the security which it is sought to avoid. Rather, there must have been a desire to produce the preferential effect 'that is to say, to improve the creditor's position in the event of an insolvent liquidation'. He went on to say: **1.119**

> A man is not to be taken as *desiring* all the necessary consequences of his actions. Some consequences may be of advantage to him and be desired by him; others may not affect him and be matters of indifference to him; while still others may be positively disadvantageous to him and not be desired by him, but be regarded by him as the unavoidable price of obtaining the desired advantages. It will still be possible to provide assistance to a company in financial difficulties provided that the company is actuated by proper commercial considerations ... a transaction will not be set aside as a voidable preference unless the company positively wished to improve the creditor's position in the event of its own insolvent liquidation.[237]

Millett J then considered the requirement of 'influence'. It was not sufficient to show only that the desire to prefer was present. It was also necessary to show that it 'influenced' the decision to enter the transaction. It is not necessary, under the 1986 regime, to show that the desire to produce the preferential effect was the dominant factor but it must have been one of the factors that operated on the minds of those who made the decision. In *MC Bacon*, Millett J found that the directors knew that the company was probably insolvent and might not be able to avoid an insolvent liquidation, that its continuing to trade was entirely dependent on the support of the bank, that if the debenture that the bank had asked for was not forthcoming the bank would withdraw its support, and that if the bank were to withdraw its support the company would be forced into immediate liquidation. The decision to give the debenture was therefore a simple one: either it was given or the bank would call in its overdraft. Millett J found that there was no evidence that the directors had wanted to improve the position of the bank and there was no reason why they should have wanted to do so. **1.120**

In *Mark John Wilson, Oxford Pharmaceuticals Limited v Masters International Limited*,[238] Mark Cawson QC, sitting as deputy judge, considered whether the parties had satisfied him that: **1.121**

> ... on the balance of probabilities [they] were acting solely by reference to proper commercial considerations in making the payments and that a desire (i.e. a subjective wish) to better the position of [X] in the event of an insolvent liquidation did not operate on the directing mind or minds of the company.[239]

---

[236] (n 223) at 87–88.
[237] Ibid.
[238] [2009] EWHC 1753.
[239] Ibid at [76].

In that case, Mark Cawson QC did find the necessary elements of influence and desire but it is worth noting that this was a case concerning connected parties.

1.122   *Oxford Pharmaceuticals* is also interesting in touching upon the capacity in which a person or company must be preferred. Cawson QC held that section 239 is concerned with creditors and guarantors, and about setting aside preferences where a company has done something or caused something to be done which puts one of the company's creditors or a surety or guarantor for any of the company's debts or liabilities in a better position as creditor or surety/guarantor. It does not, however, operate to require a person 'to disgorge a benefit obtained in some other capacity from the mere accident of them being a surety or guarantor, and even though the benefit obtained has nothing to do with their status as surety or guarantor and they have not been benefitted in that latter capacity'.[240]

1.123   A transaction amounting to a preference will be set aside if, in the case of a non-connected person, it was entered into in the six-month period before the commencement of the winding up of the company or its entry into administration. This period extends to two years in the case of a connected person. Further, for the transaction to be set aside, the company must be insolvent at the time of the transaction or as a result of entering into the transaction. In the case of transactions at an undervalue, there is a presumption of insolvency where the parties are connected but this is not reflected in section 239. In its response to the Insolvency and Corporate Governance Consultation, the UK Government stated that it intended to align the position with transactions at an undervalue so that insolvency is presumed where the parties are connected. However, at the time of writing nothing appears to have been taken forward on this issue.[241]

1.124   We discussed above, in the context of the grant of security for an existing debt, the relationship between transactions at an undervalue and the preference regime. The courts have continued to struggle with the interrelationship between the two in other contexts. In *CI Ltd v The Joint Liquidators of Sonatacus Ltd*[242] the Court of Appeal considered the earlier case of *Phillips v Brewin Dolphin Bell Lawrie Ltd*[243] in which the court held that, as a matter of law, a preferential payment which was susceptible to challenge could not amount to consideration for the making of that payment and, therefore, that the transaction was liable to be set aside as a transaction at an undervalue if the consideration for the transaction was precarious because it was liable to be set aside as a preferential payment. The Court of Appeal referred to a case report[244] that was highly critical of this decision and its failure to recognize the distinct functions performed by sections 238 and 239. The report also expressed some doubt as to whether the approach in *Brewin Dolphin* was the right one. In practice, directors considering whether a particular transaction could be vulnerable (and counterparties to the transaction) would be well advised to analyse the transaction under all relevant heads of liability.

1.125   Section 239 provides that a company gives a preference to a person if it does anything or 'suffers anything to be done' which (in either case) has the effect of putting that person into a

---

[240]   Ibid at [70].
[241]   Government Response (n 229) para 3.7.
[242]   [2007] BCC 186, CA.
[243]   [2001] 1 WLR 143, HL.
[244]   [2007] BCC 186 at [19]. The case report is Look Chan Ho, 'Barber v CI—Judgment of the High Court of Justice' (2006) 22 *Insolvency Law and Practice* 183.

better position in an insolvent liquidation. The question of when the company suffers something to be done has been considered in *Parkside International Limited*.[245] Anthony Elleray QC, sitting as a deputy judge, considered the situation in which B and C assign a debt owed by A and the question of whether A 'suffers' the making of the assignment. The contention in the case was that A had deliberately delayed asking its bank to appoint an administrator in order for the assignment to complete. Elleray QC carried out a thorough review of the texts which had considered this question (in the absence of any direct authority) and concluded that in order for the company to suffer something to be done it must allow something to happen over which it exercises some element of control. He did not therefore consider that A had suffered the assignment of the debt to be done (for which its consent was not needed) so as to amount to a preference given by it being susceptible to challenge under section 239.

Parkside International concerned the assignment of debts between group companies in **1.126** order to ensure the survival of other group companies should one of them enter insolvency proceedings. Elleray QC considered whether this desire to improve the position of the residual group was the same thing as a desire to prefer one set of creditors over the other. He noted that it might be impossible to ensure group survival, if dealings by other group companies to help ensure their survival might be impugned as preferences on behalf of the insolvent companies. However, ultimately Elleray QC did not need to take his analysis any further given his conclusion that the insolvent company had not suffered anything to be done to produce the preferential effect and his findings on advice which had been given that the assignment was not susceptible to challenge.

A further question which has arisen in the scholarship is whether it is possible to bring a **1.127** claim for breach of directors' duties which is 'preference-like' but where the conditions for a section 239 claim have not been fulfilled.[246] Andrew Keay has argued persuasively that it is possible.[247] One particularly controversial question is whether it matters, for a section 172(3) claim, if the company has suffered no loss: in a preference-like claim ordinarily the company's liabilities will have been reduced by the payment made to the preferred creditor, and its balance sheet will be unaffected. In the recent case of *Stanford International*, Sir Geoffrey Vos appeared to reflect this concern, deciding, albeit in a different context, that a company suffers no loss if it makes a payment while trading, even if it is trading insolvently, where the payment reduces its liabilities so that its balance sheet remains unchanged.[248]

D. Jurisdiction of the Court

If a transaction is established as being at an undervalue or a preference, the court has very **1.128** wide powers to put the parties back into the position they were in before the transaction was entered into. Counterparties may therefore seek to derive some comfort from the fact that the overall scheme of the sections is restitutionary and that they might therefore expect that

---

[245] [2008] EWHC 3654.
[246] Kristin Van Zwieten, 'Director Liability in Insolvency and its Vicinity' (2018) 38(2) *OJLS* 382; Andrew Keay, 'Financially Distressed Companies, Preferential Payments and the Director's Duty to Take Account of Creditors' Interests' (2020) 136 *LQR* 52.
[247] Keay (n 246).
[248] *Stanford International Bank Limited (in Liquidation) v HSBC Bank Plc* [2021] EWCA Civ 535.

any property or benefits that they have provided ought properly to be restored to them if the transaction were to be subsequently unwound. While it is the case that the sections do not seek to enrich the insolvent company at the expense of the counterparty by putting the insolvent company in a better position than it would have been in if the transaction had never occurred, it should be noted that the court will only restore the position between the parties so far as it is possible to do so. Furthermore, it would be open to the court, for example, to charge interest on the company's assets which had been in the hands of the counterparty before the transaction is unwound.

E. Avoidance of Floating Charges (Section 245 of the Insolvency Act 1986)

1.129   A floating charge may be invalid if it is created within two years of the onset of insolvency if the parties are connected or one year if they are not. The charge is not invalid unless the company was unable to pay its debts when the charge was created or became unable to do so in consequence of the transaction, but this solvency test will not apply if the parties are connected. The charge will also be valid to the extent of the value of so much of the consideration for the charge as consists of money paid or goods or services supplied to the company at the same time as or after and in consideration of the creation of the charge, together with interest, if any, payable under the relevant agreement. In *Peak Hotels*, the court found that where services were supplied pursuant to a fixed fee agreement, the value of the services actually supplied needed to be objectively assessed with the benefit of hindsight.[249] The money must be paid to the company and not, for example, to the bank to reduce an overdraft which a third party has guaranteed (*Re Fairway Magazines Ltd* [1993] 1 BCLC 643). It is also worth noting that section 245 refers to value 'at the same time as, or after, the creating of the charge'. In *Shoe Lace*, the court held that these temporal requirements could not be ignored, so that for payments made before the execution of the charge to be treated as consideration the interval between payment and execution should be sufficiently short to be regarded as minimal (with the example of a coffee break offered).[250]

1.130   A floating charge given as security for an existing debt will be vulnerable to attack under this section. A lender seeking a floating charge for purposes other than credit support (for example, in order to be in a position to exercise the right of a qualifying floating charge holder to appoint an administrator or to select the identity of the administrator) may wish to provide a limited amount of new borrowing in order to ensure that at least some proportion of the floating charge cannot be vulnerable to attack. A question arises as to whether the directors can ever be justified in granting a floating charge with respect to existing indebtedness, given section 245. In many circumstances they may conclude that they cannot. Where, however, the borrower has borrowed a revolving facility, the effect of the grant of security may be to permit the borrower to repay and reborrow advances which may constitute new money.

---

[249] *Crumpler & Anor (Liquidators of Peak Hotels and Resorts Ltd) v Candey Ltd* [2019] EWCA Civ 345.
[250] *Re Shoe Lace Ltd* [1993] BCC 609.

2

THE EUROPEAN
RESTRUCTURING DIRECTIVE

This chapter is concerned with the new European Restructuring Directive. Following the end of the Brexit transition period on 31 December 2020, the UK is no longer within the scope of the Directive. However, we will occasionally refer to UK case law in this chapter where it may have informed, or been informed by, the Directive before the UK's departure from the EU was finalized. Reference will also be made to the new Dutch Act on Wet homologatie onderhands akkoord (WHOA)[1] and the new German scheme (StaRUG),[2] which both represent new preventive restructuring procedures of the type envisaged by the Directive. In Part III of the chapter, we will consider the recognition of restructuring plans developed partially in response to the Directive throughout the EU. This section is limited to the recognition of plans confirmed in an EU Member State, although there will be one context in which English experience may still have something to tell us about the future direction of travel. The chapter will only deal with the parts of the European Restructuring Directive which address financially distressed corporates.   **2.01**

I. The Case for a Restructuring Directive

The European Restructuring Directive came into force in 2019.[3] The Directive forms part of the European Commission's Capital Markets Union (CMU) project, which aims to increase   **2.02**

---

[1] Wet Homolgatie Obderhands Akoord—WHOA.

[2] Unternehmensstabilisierungs-und restrukturierungsgesetz—StaRUG.

[3] Directive (EU) 2019/1023 of the European Parliament and of the Council of 20 June 2019 on preventive restructuring frameworks, on discharge of debt and disqualifications, and on measures to increase the efficiency of procedures concerning restructuring, insolvency and discharge of debt, and amending Directive (EU) 2017/1132 (Directive on restructuring and insolvency) [2019] OJ L 172.

the flow of capital in the European Union (EU).[4] In 2014 the Commission had published a Recommendation on a new approach to business failure and insolvency, which aimed to encourage Member States to, 'implement early restructuring procedures and give a "second chance" to entrepreneurs'.[5] However, in the CMU Action Plan the Commission reported:

> While it is clear that the Recommendation has provided a useful focus for those Member States undertaking reforms in the area of insolvency, an assessment undertaken by the Commission shows that it has only been implemented partially, including in those Member States that have launched reforms.[6]

Thus, the Commission announced its intention to legislate, drawing on the experience of the Recommendation. The European Restructuring Directive is the result of that process.

2.03 The Directive aims to address two principal concerns with the relationship between insolvency law and the flow of capital in the EU. The first concern is that, where European Member States have insolvency procedures which are considered costly, unpredictable, slow, and biased towards liquidation rather than reorganization, the risk premiums of loan and bond debt are increased.[7] The contention is that there is a direct relationship between the availability and cost of finance and the returns which creditors anticipate in an insolvency. The second concern is that, where a Member State does not have an effective reorganization procedure, banks are hampered in efforts to deal with non-performing loans (NPLs) on their balance sheets. This may arise because banks have little incentive to engage early with the debtor if there is no procedure to assist in resolving the NPL problem. It may also arise because there is unlikely to be a secondary market for NPLs if they cannot subsequently be restructured. In many jurisdictions, banks have sought to address NPLs by selling them to specialist distressed debt investors but the concern is that distressed debt investors are unlikely to buy NPLs in the absence of tools to restructure them. Thus, the Directive aims to promote the introduction of cost-effective reorganization procedures for viable companies across the EU, with the aim of increasing the availability, and reducing the cost, of finance for healthy firms and facilitating resolution of NPLs on bank balance sheets, freeing up capital for new investment.

2.04 The European Restructuring Directive thus sets out certain principles which all Member States should reflect in a reorganization procedure available within the jurisdiction. As we shall see, the approach is one of minimum harmonization: there is significant optionality for Member States throughout the Directive and ample capacity to go beyond its limited mandatory requirements. Horst Eidenmüller is fiercely critical of this approach, arguing that what is created is inefficient, preventing Member States from experimenting with their own, potentially more efficient, approaches. The result, he suggests, will be more written-off loans.[8] Overall, Eidenmüller prefers the benefits of competition in promoting the

---

[4] European Commission, 'Action Plan on Building a Capital Markets Union' COM (2015) 468 final.
[5] Ibid at para 6.2.
[6] n 4.
[7] Bruegel blog post, 'Will Better Insolvency Standards Help Europe's Debt Deleveraging?' (23 January 2017) <https://www.bruegel.org/2017/01/will-better-insolvency-standards-help-europes-debt-deleveraging/> (last accessed 19 July 2021).
[8] Horst Eidenmüller, 'Contracting for a European Insolvency Regime' (2017) 18 *European Business Organization Law Review* 273.

development of reorganization procedures over the minimum harmonization approach adopted in the Directive.

The Directive focuses on what it calls 'preventive restructuring frameworks', the idea being **2.05** that by resorting to a restructuring procedure the debtor avoids the need to file for an insolvency procedure. Many commentators have struggled with this concept of a 'preventive' procedure—after all, the procedure should be accessed by companies in financial difficulties to address those financial difficulties, and not simply to wash off liabilities for the benefit of the remaining stakeholders. As Tollenaar puts it, 'in terms of its consequences, the procedure is nothing but an insolvency procedure ("if it's not called a duck, but looks like a duck, swims like a duck and quacks like a duck, it probably is a duck")'.[9]

The more useful distinction may be between an insolvency procedure, which facilitates the **2.06** sale of the business and assets as a going concern (or the assets on a break-up basis) and the distribution of the proceeds, and a reorganization procedure, in which the debtor negotiates a restructuring of its liabilities with some or all of its creditors (what Eidenmüller calls a 'structured bargaining procedure').[10] This distinction was preserved in the original Recommendation, which contemplated restructuring procedures but not sale transactions. However, this led to concerns in the scholarship that restructuring would be pursued even where a business sale ought to be preferred.[11] Scholars thus suggested an exit route needed to be built into the restructuring procedure, to facilitate the use of other procedures to achieve an auction of the business where that was the more appropriate solution to the company's financial difficulties.[12] However, in the Directive the definition of 'restructuring' is simply extended to include, 'sales of assets or parts of the business and, where so provided under national law, the sale of the business and assets as a going concern, as well as any necessary operational changes, or a combination of those elements'.[13] Thus, it is clear in the final version of the Directive that a going concern sale of the business is permitted, but the boundary between restructuring procedures (which naturally seem to fall within the Directive) and insolvency sale and distribution procedures (which would seem to more naturally fall outside it) is somewhat blurred.

Instead, Article 4 of the Directive makes clear that debtors should have access to the pre- **2.07** ventive restructuring framework if there is a 'likelihood' of insolvency falling short of actual insolvency as understood by national law. In other words, it is the financial condition of the debtor which determines the 'preventive' nature of the framework. Yet, there is a real balance to be struck here. Debtors with cash in hand and a runway in which they can agree a restructuring are more likely to succeed. Once liquidity problems become acute and customers start to desert the sinking ship, a restructuring may no longer be achievable with the very best will in the world. And yet, we also do not want debtors to use restructuring tools opportunistically, to wash off specific liabilities which it could have afforded to pay, for the

---

[9] Nicolaes WA Tollenaar, 'The European Commission's Proposal for a Directive on Preventive Restructuring' (2017) 30(5) *Insolvency Intelligence* 65.
[10] Eidenmüller (n 8) 274.
[11] Horst Eidenmüller and Kristin Van Zwieten, 'Restructuring the European Business Enterprise: The European Commission's Recommendation on a New Approach to Business Failure and Insolvency' (2015) 16 *European Business Organization Law Review* 625 at 653.
[12] Ibid.
[13] Article 2(1)(1).

benefit of its remaining stakeholders. We will see, in Chapter 3, that this was the concern of the Irish courts in *New Look*'s application for examinership, and the same concern recently led Zacaroli J to decline to sanction the *Hurricane Energy* Part 26A restructuring plan in England.[14] Irit Mevorach and Adrian Walters discuss the need for different procedures for the various stages of 'what accountants sometimes refer to as the demise curve of the corporate life cycle'.[15] The Directive attempts to locate itself at a Goldilocks point on the demise curve: not too insolvent and not too solvent, but just right. And yet, this is an exercise fraught with difficulty. It may be more challenging, but nonetheless entirely possible, that a company which has fallen further down the demise curve may be able to restructure using restructuring law's liquidity-creating and stabilization tools.[16] Thus, it is suggested here that the 'preventive' framing of the Directive is fraught with challenges.

2.08   The German StaRUG attempts to navigate this problem to some extent. It is still the case that in order to access the procedure, the debtor must be 'threatened to become illiquid (imminent illiquidity) without yet being insolvent'.[17] Milbank tells us that a debtor is imminently illiquid if 'it is more likely than not (>50%) that the debtor will be unable to honor all of its payment obligations which are due from time to time within the applicable forecast period' and that 'the applicable forecast period will generally be 24 months'.[18] However, crucially, if the debtor becomes insolvent before the restructuring is completed, the German court is entitled to keep the StaRUG proceedings on track if (i) taking account of progress achieved, insolvency proceedings would clearly not be in the interests of creditors as a whole; or (ii) the insolvency has been caused by acceleration of a debt which would be compromised in the restructuring plan, provided that achievement of the restructuring objective is predominantly likely.[19]

2.09   It is also worth noting that certain financial institutions are excluded from the scope of the Directive.[20] Gerard McCormack suggests that this is because they are subject to 'different, and possibly conflicting legal regimes'.[21]

II. The Substantive Approach

A. Incentivizing Early Action

2.10   Consistent with the 'preventive' goal of the Directive, Article 3 focuses on incentivizing debtors to take early action. And consistent with the minimum harmonization approach, the Directive merely suggests certain early warning systems: alert mechanisms which

---

[14]   *Re Hurricane Energy Plc* [2021] EWHC 1759 (Ch).

[15]   Irit Mevorach and Adrian Walters, 'The Characterisation of Pre-Insolvency Proceedings in Private International Law' (2020) 21 *European Business Organization Law Review* 855 at 857.

[16]   Kenneth Ayotte and David A Skeel Jr, 'Bankruptcy Law as a Liquidity Provider' (2013) 80 *University of Chicago Law Review* 1557.

[17]   Milbank, 'The New German Restructuring Regime ("German Scheme") Will Enter into Force on 1 January 2021' (30 December 2020) 5 <https://www.milbank.com/en/news/the-new-german-restructuring-regime-german-scheme-will-enter-into-force-on-1-january-2021.html> (last accessed 23 July 2021).

[18]   Ibid.

[19]   Ibid.

[20]   Article 1(2).

[21]   Gerard McCormack, *The European Restructuring Directive* (Edward Elgar 2021) 5.

are triggered where debtors have not made a certain type of payment; advisory services by public or private organizations; and incentives for third parties with relevant information to flag negative developments.[22] A recent IMF working paper notes this minimal detail and suggests that Member States will need considerably more detail to provide an effective early warning mechanism.[23] The focus on whistleblowing calls to mind John Armour and Sandra Frisby's work on concentrated creditor theory.[24] In their work, Armour and Frisby analysed the (now largely abolished) administrative receivership procedure in the UK in which secured creditors were afforded significant control rights over the assets, preventing junior creditors from taking action and avoiding the 'race to collect'.[25] In the Directive, whistleblowing incentivizes the debtor to seek the protection of the preventive restructuring framework, getting under way negotiations towards a solution. All of this assumes, of course, that the preventive restructuring framework offers effective tools to stabilize the situation, as other creditors and stakeholders of the debtor react to the whistleblower's warning. We shall consider this in more detail as we progress through the analysis.

The CMU is aimed not only at large corporates but also at the vast number of SMEs which make up the bulk of European companies. Thus, Article 3 focuses on making early warning tools accessible and user-friendly for SMEs. Jonathan McCarthy has expressed a good deal of scepticism about the utility of what he calls 'predictive resources' for SMEs.[26]   **2.11**

B. Who Can Apply

The US Chapter 11 procedure (analysed in Chapter 3) is built around the concept of the 'debtor in possession' (DIP). At its heart, the DIP concept is seen to promote the corporate reorganization objective: debtors will be willing to take early action if they know that they retain control of the procedure and will prefer a corporate reorganization over other options as it is most likely to preserve management's jobs. Thus, the DIP orientation is seen to promote the corporate reorganization objective. In other work, the author has suggested that this may be a somewhat dated view of debtor incentives in the twenty-first century, querying, particularly, the relationship between DIP and early action.[27] Nonetheless, if a principal objective of the preventive restructuring framework is to facilitate a restructuring of liabilities, there is a good deal of sense in a DIP orientation. Management will need to win the hearts and minds of creditors during the negotiation for a sustainable restructuring to be agreed and, in many cases, will know the business, and the creditors, best. Above all, the DIP orientation signals to the debtor's creditors and other stakeholders that a restructuring (as opposed to a sale and distribution of proceeds) is envisaged. Once again, the fact that the preventive restructuring framework can be used to sell all or part of the business as a going   **2.12**

---

[22] Article 3(2).

[23] José Garrido, Chanda DeLong, Amira Rasekh, and Anjum Rosha, 'Restructuring and Insolvency in Europe: Policy Options in the Implementation of the EU Directive' IMF Working Paper May 2021, 5–7 <https://www.imf.org/en/Publications/WP/Issues/2021/05/27/Restructuring-and-Insolvency-in-Europe-Policy-Options-in-the-Implementation-of-the-EU-50235> (last accessed 30 July 2021).

[24] John Armour and Sandra Frisby, 'Rethinking Receivership' (2001) 21 *Oxford Journal of Legal Studies* 73 at 87.

[25] Ibid.

[26] Jonathan McCarthy, 'A Class Apart: The Relevance of the EU Preventive Restructuring Directive for Small and Medium Enterprises' (2020) 21 *European Business Organization Law Review* 895.

[27] Sarah Paterson, *Corporate Reorganization Law and Forces of Change* (Oxford University Press 2020) 139–162.

concern perhaps blurs this boundary. Yet, overall, the preventive restructuring framework is heavily structured around a renegotiation of liabilities and a DIP orientation offers many benefits in this context.

2.13   Thus, Article 4(1) of the Directive provides the general rule that only the debtor can apply for the preventive restructuring framework. Article 4(8) also provides that Member States may permit creditors' and employees' representatives to apply with the agreement of the debtor, although Member States are permitted to limit the requirement for debtor agreement to cases where the debtor is an SME.[28] Article 9(1) provides that the debtor has the right to submit the restructuring plan but then states that Member States may decide 'whether, and when, creditors and restructuring professionals have the right to propose a plan'. Once again, a good deal of design flexibility is afforded to the individual Member States, and this is already reflected in the different approaches adopted in the Dutch WHOA and the German StaRUG.

2.14   In their excellent guide to the WHOA, the Dutch law firm De Brauw Blackstone Westbroek tells us that it permits individual creditors, shareholders, and employees (through the works council or other representatives) to initiate the debtor's restructuring by requesting the court to appoint a plan expert to design, negotiate, and file a restructuring plan on behalf of the debtor. However, if the debtor is an SME the plan expert requires the debtor's consent to propose a plan, provided that the plan expert can seek a court order in place of the debtor's consent where 'consent is withheld by the debtor without good reasons'.[29] Thus, the WHOA enables a wide number of parties to propose a plan. In contrast, only the debtor is entitled to propose a restructuring plan under the German StaRUG.[30]

2.15   Nicolaes Tollenaar expresses the fear that:

> A system that grants the right to propose a plan exclusively to the debtor, in effect gives controlling shareholders a hold-out position which they can use to delay or frustrate the process and extract value from creditors.[31]

This was a familiar concern with the chapter 11 system in the 1980s and 1990s, when scholars cited the celebrated case of Eastern Airlines in which Frank Lorenzo was said to have used the cover of chapter 11 to run down the business until there was virtually nothing left.[32] Recent scholarship has shown that creditors may have other control rights which tilt the balance of power away from the debtor, making this a less pressing concern.[33] However, the balance of power between the debtor and the creditors will be heavily dependent on the interaction between secured transactions law and wider corporate insolvency law within the jurisdiction, so that the impact of debtor exclusivity may vary significantly from

---

[28]   McCormack suggests that 'applying a standard principle of interpretation that the greater includes the smaller' Member States could also limit the requirement for debtor agreement to certain types of SME, e.g. medium-sized companies rather than small or micro enterprises—see McCormack (n 21) 5

[29]   De Brauw Blackstone Westbroek, 'Court Confirmation of Extrajudicial Restructuring Plans: What you Need to Know About the New Act' (July 2021) 11 <https://dwbxnuhxoazve.cloudfront.net/20210713-WHOA-Booklet-July-2021.pdf> (last accessed 23 July 2021).

[30]   Milbank (n 17).

[31]   Tollenaar (n 9).

[32]   Robert K Rasmussen, 'The Efficiency of Chapter 11' (1991) 8 *Bankruptcy Developments Journal* 319 at 319–321.

[33]   Paterson, *Forces of Change* (n 27) 109–137.

jurisdiction to jurisdiction.[34] Moreover, Article 5 and Recital 30 make clear that, while the general principle is that the debtor is left in control of the assets and the day-to-day business of the firm, the appointment of a 'restructuring professional' on a case-by-case basis is permitted. Indeed, appointment of a restructuring professional is mandatory where (i) there is a general stay on enforcement; (ii) cross-class cramdown is envisaged; or (iii) the debtor or a majority of its creditors request such an appointment (albeit, in the latter case, the creditors must bear the cost). McCormack notes that where mandatory appointment is prescribed, the role of the restructuring practitioner appears to be limited to assisting 'the debtor and creditors in negotiating and drafting the plan'.[35] He contrasts this with the definition of 'practitioner in the field of restructuring' in Article 2(12):

> any person or body appointed by a judicial or administrative authority to carry out, in particular, one or more of the following tasks:
> (a) assisting the debtor or the creditors in drafting or negotiating a restructuring plan;
> (b) supervising the activity of the debtor during the negotiations on a restructuring plan, and reporting to a judicial or administrative authority;
> (c) taking partial control over the assets or affairs of the debtor during negotiations.

McCormack concludes that 'there is not one conception of the restructuring practitioner who may be variously a manager, monitor or supervisor'.[36] Yet, the precise role which a restructuring practitioner plays in a case can be of some importance. On the one hand, creditors may hope for a neutral, independent party who can monitor and supervise the actions of the debtor. On the other hand, the debtor may need the benefit of the experience and advice of the restructuring practitioner in developing and implementing a restructuring strategy. Where restructuring practitioners are appointed, Member States will need to pay careful attention to the role which they are to fulfil.

De Brauw Blackstone Westbroek highlights two roles (and accordingly two different **2.16** titles: *herstructureringsdeskundige* and *observator*) for a restructuring professional in the Dutch WHOA. We have already seen that the Dutch WHOA envisages appointment of a plan expert to negotiate and propose a restructuring plan where the restructuring is initiated by individual creditors, shareholders, or employees acting through the works council or other representatives. The debtor can also request the appointment of a plan expert for the same purpose,[37] and a plan expert may be required in certain circumstances in order for a stay to be granted.[38] In addition, De Brauw Blackstone Westbroek identifies that an observer may (and in the case of a general stay must) be appointed if the court deems it necessary to protect creditors or shareholders,[39] and that the court will appoint an observer if a restructuring plan has not been accepted by all classes and a plan expert has not been appointed.[40] Thus, the Dutch WHOA reflects the different capacities in which a professional may act, identified by McCormack. The professional may have a relatively hands-on role in

---

[34] Sarah Paterson, 'Finding Our Way: Secured Transactions and Corporate Bankruptcy Law and Policy in America and England' (2018) 18(2) *Journal of Corporate Law Studies* 247.
[35] Article 5(3).
[36] McCormack (n 21) 6.
[37] WHOA Article 371(1).
[38] De Brauw (n 29) 16.
[39] Ibid.
[40] Ibid at 17.

developing, and attempting to negotiate, a plan, or they may have more of a supervisory and monitoring role. It is worth noting that the German StaRUG provides for the establishment of a creditors' committee to supervise the debtor where the proceedings involve all of the debtor's eligible liabilities and that, while the appointment of a restructuring officer is mandatory in a cross-class cramdown, it is not mandatory in the case of a cramdown of financial creditors.[41]

C. The Stay

2.17   Article 6 of the Directive sets out provisions for a stay on individual enforcement action, the purpose of which is 'to support the negotiations of a restructuring plan in a preventive restructuring framework'.[42] McCormack highlights the focus on 'individual enforcement action' and notes that this may not capture many other types of legal action—albeit there is nothing to prevent Member States from adopting a broader stay.[43] As we have already seen, a stay may be necessary to stabilize the business while negotiations are in course. Yet, debtors may also wish to avoid announcing a stay on creditor action if they consider that that may make creditors more suspicious of the restructuring effort or, indeed, may have longer-term consequences for the relationship between the debtor and the creditors if a restructuring is successfully agreed. Thus, the stay in the Directive is discretionary, not automatic. Article 6(1) provides that Member States may provide that judicial or administrative authorities can refuse to grant a stay in certain circumstances. This implies that the stay is only available on application to a judicial or administrative authority—reflected in the Dutch WHOA in which a stay can be granted on application to court by the debtor or the plan expert.[44]

2.18   Article 6 goes on to provide that the stay could be general (affecting all creditors) or limited towards individual creditors (while outstanding claims of workers cannot be stayed unless alternative protection is in place).[45] McCormack concludes that there is nothing in the Directive which would prevent a Member State from stipulating a mandatory stay, nor in having a stay covering all claims (other than employee claims, unless payment of those claims is guaranteed for the duration of the preventive proceedings).[46] Yet, the flexibility for a discretionary, general, or limited stay is a particularly useful aspect of the Directive. We touched, earlier, on the fact that a restructuring may be agreed with all, or with only some, of the debtor's creditors. It has been common, in the last decade, for a debt restructuring to be limited to the debtor's financial creditors.[47] A principal objective of this type of restructuring is to send a 'business as usual' message to the debtor's other creditors. Thus, the last thing a debtor would want to do in this case is to impose a general stay catching all creditors. At the same time, it may wish to stay the enforcement rights of certain of its financial creditors. Even where a debt restructuring includes other types of creditor, besides financial

---

[41]   Milbank (n 17) 9.
[42]   Article 6(1).
[43]   McCormack (n 21) 117.
[44]   De Brauw (n 29) 16.
[45]   Article 6(3).
[46]   McCormack (n 21) 7.
[47]   Paterson, *Forces of Change* (n 27).

creditors, it is now rare for it to include all of the debtors' creditors.[48] The debtor may well wish to leave creditors who are excluded from the plan outside any stay, while imposing restrictions on certain creditors who are included within it. And, as the IMF working paper has noted, the Directive appears to enable Member States to choose to keep the stay confidential from those creditors who are not included within it.[49] Thus, the flexibility which the Directive provides in this context is extremely useful. It should also be noted that Member States may provide that the stay does not apply to netting arrangements.[50]

The duration of the stay is initially no more than four months.[51] Renewal can be granted by **2.19** a judicial or administrative authority 'if well-defined circumstances show such extension or new stay is duly justified'.[52] Examples of when extension may be justified are offered in Article 6: relevant progress has been made on the restructuring plan; the continuation does not unfairly prejudice the rights or interests of any affected parties; or insolvency proceedings which could end in liquidation have not been opened.[53] The total period of the stay is limited to 12 months, although Member States are free to choose a shorter duration. Both the Dutch WHOA and the German StaRUG can be extended up to a maximum of eight months.[54] The judicial or administrative authority may lift the stay: (i) where the stay no longer fulfils the objective; (ii) at the request of the debtor or the insolvency practitioner; (iii) if provided by national law where one or more creditors or one or more classes or creditors are, or would be, unfairly prejudiced by a stay of individual enforcement actions; or (iv) if the stay gives rise to the insolvency of a creditor. Recital 36 provides a limited discussion of the concept of 'unfair prejudice'. First, the question is whether the stay would preserve the overall value of the estate and, secondly, whether the debtor acts in bad faith, or with the intention of causing prejudice or generally acts against the legitimate expectations of creditors. And Recital 37 states that a single creditor or class would be unfairly prejudiced if its claims would be made substantially worse off because of the stay, or if the creditor is put more at a disadvantage than other creditors in a similar position.

These design features around duration and the lifting of the stay all reflect the familiar ten- **2.20** sion between promoting the corporate reorganization objective, on the one hand, and interference with creditor rights, on the other. The concern is that, without a stay, creditors will rush to grab assets, making a restructuring impossible to achieve even if it is the most value-maximizing option.[55] Thus, the stay preserves the business while negotiations are in course. However, it does so at the cost of an individual creditor's ability to enforce its rights—as Jennifer Payne has put it, 'at the expense of party autonomy'.[56] Thus, as Payne notes, a balance needs to be struck. She argues that an integral part of any effective restructuring moratorium is 'a clear structure setting out a means to recognise and weigh these competing

---

[48] Sarah Paterson and Adrian Walters, 'Selective Corporate Restructuring Strategy' (15 September 2021) <https://papers.ssrn.com/sol3/papers.cfm?abstract_id=3924225> (last accessed 16 September 2021).
[49] IMF (n 23) 14.
[50] Article 7(6).
[51] Article 6(6).
[52] Article 6(7).
[53] Ibid.
[54] De Brauw (n 29) 16 and Milbank (n 17) 8.
[55] For the classic account see Thomas H Jackson, *The Logic and Limits of Bankruptcy Law* (Harvard University Press 1986).
[56] Jennifer Payne, 'An Assessment of the UK Restructuring Moratorium' (4 January 2021) 2 <https://ssrn.com/abstract=3759730> (last accessed 30 July 2021).

pressures'.[57] The European Restructuring Directive attempts to achieve this through the provisions on duration and extension and the provisions on the lifting of the stay but, in reality, each jurisdiction is likely to need to develop its own body of rules which articulates how the stay provisions are to work in practice.

2.21   Under Article 7, any requirement for the debtor to file for insolvency proceedings which could end in liquidation, and any right of creditors to request such insolvency proceedings, are suspended. However, Article 7(3) expressly provides that Member States may derogate from these provisions where a debtor is unable to pay its debts as they fall due. This is consistent with the 'preventive' nature of the framework and the core concept that debtors should access restructuring procedures to prevent insolvency, rather than once insolvency has occurred. The criticisms of this approach discussed in Part I are repeated here, and readers are referred to the discussion in that section.

D. Executory Contracts

2.22   In early work on the Recommendation, Horst Eidenmüller and Kristin Van Zwieten noted that it included no provisions on executory contracts.[58] US chapter 11 famously includes provision for the debtor to assign, assume, or reject an executory contract or unexpired lease.[59] No definition of executory contract is provided in chapter 11, but it will suffice for our purposes to define it as a contract in which some performance is outstanding from both parties. The ability to reject unprofitable executory contracts or unexpired leases or, indeed, to use the threat of rejection to negotiate modifications, is a vital tool which US debtors employ in restructuring their contractual arrangements. The power of assumption or rejection is coupled with the so-called ban on ipso facto clauses, preventing creditors from exercising contractual termination rights arising as a result of the debtor's chapter 11 filing. Thus, in theory at least, debtors can be assured of continued performance while controlling the decision to assume or reject, and bargaining power is shifted towards the debtor in attempting to agree modifications.

2.23   The final Directive does include some provisions on executory contracts, but they are somewhat skeletal, do not address assumption or rejection, and offer considerable design flexibility. The relevant provisions are to be found in Articles 7(4) and 7(5). Article 7(4) provides that:

> Member States shall provide for rules preventing creditors to which the stay applies from withholding performance or terminating, accelerating or, in any other way, modifying essential executory contracts to the detriment of the debtor, for debts that came into existence prior to the stay, solely by virtue of the fact that they were not paid by the debtor.

It goes on to state that essential executory contracts are those 'necessary for the continuation of the day-to-day operations of the business, including contracts concerning supplies, the suspension of which would lead to the debtor's activities coming to a standstill'. One can

---

[57] Ibid.
[58] Eidenmüller and Van Zwieten (n 11) 625.
[59] 11 USC § 365.

immediately foresee a good deal of dispute as to which contracts are 'essential'—indeed, in a recent reform effort the UK toyed with a similar construct and abandoned it because of the considerable uncertainty which it would attract. The Directive preserves the option for Member States to adopt a different approach, expressly providing that the restrictions can be extended to non-essential executory contracts.[60] It is also notable that Article 7(4) refers only to non-payment. The Dutch WHOA, on the other hand, applies this provision to all contracts and all defaults. However, the debtor must provide security for new obligations incurred during the stay.[61]

Article 7(5) goes on to provide: **2.24**

> Member States shall ensure that creditors are not allowed to withhold performance or terminate, accelerate, or, in any other way, modify executory contracts to the detriment of the debtor by virtue of a contractual clause providing for such measures, solely by reason of:
> (a) a request for the opening of preventive restructuring procedures
> (b) a request for a stay of individual enforcement action
> (c) the opening of preventive restructuring proceedings; or
> (d) the granting of a stay of individual enforcement actions as such.

It will be immediately apparent that Article 7(5) applies to all executory contracts and that it is mandatory. Yet, once again, the focus is on preventing the creditor from withholding performance, terminating, or modifying terms. The Directive is silent on the ability of the debtor to reject unprofitable executory contracts or to seek to modify their terms. And no reference is made to unexpired leases.

Thus, Member States may wish to pay close attention to the issue of executory contracts and   **2.25** unexpired leases in implementing reforms, perhaps going beyond the boundaries set by the Directive. This is particularly relevant as the third edition of this book is being written, as retailers, casual dining operators, and hospitality businesses grapple with restructuring leasehold liabilities in the wake of the COVID-19 crisis. There would appear to be suffi- cient flexibility in the Directive for Member States to take matters into their own hands on the wider issues surrounding executory contracts and unexpired leases. Yet, once again, there is a serious tension between the rights of individual counterparties and the debtor's desire to restructure its liabilities to ensure its long-term survival. Indeed, the Directive ex- pressly permits Member States to include 'appropriate safeguards' preventing 'unfair prej- udice' being caused to creditors by virtue of Article 7(4). This is reflected in the different approaches adopted in the Dutch WHOA and the German StaRUG. The Dutch WHOA provides that the debtor may seek to amend or terminate any contract with a contractual counterparty and, if the counterparty refuses, can apply to court for approval of unilat- eral termination.[62] In this event, De Brauw Blackstone Westbroek state that the court can only refuse termination if the 'light insolvency test is not met'[63]: where the debtor 'con- siders it reasonably plausible that it will be unable to pay its future debts as they fall due'.[64]

---

[60] Article 7(4).
[61] De Brauw (n 29) 16.
[62] De Brauw (n 29) 13.
[63] Ibid.
[64] Ibid at 9.

In Chapter 3 we will see that it is possible to impose modification of executory contracts without counterparty consent in a UK scheme of arrangement, Part 26 restructuring plan, or CVA. In US chapter 11, on the other hand, the debtor is statutorily permitted to assign, assume, or reject an executory contract but can only use the threat of rejection to reach agreement on modification of the contract with the counterparty. If the debtor does terminate the executory contract, then the counterparty has a claim in damages, but this damages claim can be compromised in the restructuring plan. The Dutch WHOA reflects the US approach in statutory terms. On the other hand, while the draft bill for the German StaRUG provided for the possibility to terminate executory contracts, the final law did not make such provision.[65]

E. Information

2.26   Another significant tension in the design of any restructuring regime is the tension between ensuring adequate disclosure for creditors to take an informed decision on the plan, on the one hand, and the direct and indirect costs of disclosure on the other. The direct costs are, of course, the costs of the professional advisers likely to be needed to assist the debtor in preparing the relevant disclosures. The indirect costs include the reaction of creditors, including creditors who are not affected by the restructuring, to the negative effects of published information. And the concern is not just with reactions during the restructuring negotiations but also after the restructuring has been completed. Moreover, another pressing concern is the use which competitors may be able to make of the granular information which is published. Indeed, the concern becomes that the restructuring is being conducted in a fishbowl.[66] In addition, if disclosure becomes too voluminous, there is a risk that the debtor will be able to hide the crucial wood within a forest of trees. As with so many things in corporate reorganization, there is a balance to be struck.

2.27   The Directive attempts to strike this balance by, on the one hand, setting out mandatory provisions about the minimum information which the restructuring plan must contain while, on the other hand, keeping these mandatory requirements relatively short. Article 8 includes the requirement to disclose:

> the debtor's assets and liabilities at the time of submission of the restructuring plan, including a value for the assets, a description of the economic situation of the debtor and the position of workers, and a description of the causes and the extent of the difficulties of the debtor.[67]

2.28   Strikingly, however, no detail is provided on how the assets are to be valued and Member States are presumably free to lay down further detail on this issue. Article 8 also provides that the restructuring plan must identify the 'affected parties', either individually or by category, together with their claims or interests covered by the restructuring plan.[68] The concept

---

[65] Milbank (n 17) 1.

[66] Mark D Bloom, 'Reorganizing in a Fish Bowl: Public Access vs Protecting Confidential Information' (1999) 73(4) *American Bankruptcy Law Journal* 775.

[67] Article 8(1)(b).

[68] Article 8(1)(c).

of an 'affected' party is surprisingly slippery. The core question is whether a party is 'affected' by the plan only if its legal rights are modified, or whether it can be 'affected' by the plan in a wider sense. In this context, the Directive provides the following definition:

> 'affected parties' means creditors, including, where applicable under national law, workers or classes of creditors and, where applicable, under national law, equity holders, whose claims or interests respectively, are directly affected by a restructuring plan.[69]

At first sight, this is not a particularly enlightening provision: the repetition of 'affected' is certainly somewhat unhelpful. However, it is suggested here that the reference to 'interests' suggests that the concept in the Directive is wider than creditors whose rights are modified by the plan. At the same time, as we have seen, the Directive is clear that the restructuring may be limited to certain creditors, and it seems unlikely that creditors who ride through the plan with their rights entirely untouched are 'affected' creditors. As we shall see in Chapter 3, the English courts have recently grappled with this concept of 'affected' stakeholders in the context of a Part 26A restructuring plan. In *Hurricane Energy* Zacaroli J concluded that shareholders were 'affected' by a plan where their shares remained untouched but their shareholding would be diluted to 5 per cent by a proposed debt for equity swap.[70] At the same time, it is common in English restructurings for ordinary, unsecured trade creditors to be left outside the plan and there is no suggestion in the case law that they are to be treated as 'affected' by it. It is suggested here that this is the balance the Directive is also trying to strike. This conclusion is reinforced by Article 8(1)(e), which requires a description of the parties who are not affected by the plan either individually or by category of debt 'together with a description of the reasons why it is not proposed to affect them'. It is further reinforced by Article 11 which draws a distinction between 'affected' parties and 'impaired parties'. Recital 54 provides that the 'impairment of creditors should be understood to mean that there is a reduction in the value of their claims'. This suggests a broader meaning of 'affected' than of 'impaired'. **2.29**

Article 8 contains other, specific disclosure requirements most of which appear relatively uncontroversial. There is a requirement, in Article 8(g)(v), to provide 'the estimated financial flows of the debtor, if provided by national law'. There is no elaboration as to how cash flows are to be reported—the detail is once again left to Member States. There is also a requirement to disclose any new financing anticipated as part of the restructuring plan together with 'the reasons why the new financing is necessary to implement the plan'.[71] This presumably reflects that fact that new financing may be provided on priority terms, potentially reducing returns to other creditors if the restructuring effort fails. This concern for the benefit of the restructuring to creditors as a whole is also reflected in Article 8(h), which requires the debtor to state why the plan has 'a reasonable prospect of preventing the insolvency of the debtor and ensuring the viability of the business'. Moreover, Member States may, if they choose, require this statement to be validated by an external expert or the restructuring practitioner, if one has been appointed. **2.30**

---

[69] Article 2(1)(2).
[70] *Re Hurricane Energy Plc* [2021] EWHC 1418 (Ch).
[71] Article 8(1)(g)(vi).

2.31   We have already noted the determination of the Commission that the preventive restructuring framework should also be accessible for SMEs. It is thus unsurprising to see a provision in Article 8 that Member States 'shall make available online a comprehensive check-list for restructuring plans, adapted to the needs of SMEs'.[72] The direct costs of a substantial disclosure exercise are particularly problematic for SMEs, who may simply not have the cash resources to pay for the necessary advisers to pull together the disclosures. Thus, in the US, the new sub-chapter V of chapter 11, specifically designed for SMEs, limits the disclosures the SME is required to make. There is no specific adaptation of the disclosure requirements in Article 8 of the Directive, and it is not entirely clear to what extent Member States are free to adapt them (in particular, whether the words 'adapted to the needs of SMEs' provide a mandate for specific adaptations). What is clear is that SMEs should be guided through the disclosure requirements which may, potentially, reduce the amount of adviser time which is needed to explain the debtor's information obligations.

F. Voting

2.32   One of the most challenging aspects of any restructuring regime is determining how creditors are to vote. In this regard, the Directive contains significantly more detail than the Recommendation. The Directive requires that all affected parties should have the right to vote on the restructuring plan. We have already seen, in section II.E above, that this concept of 'affected' is somewhat slippery. Readers are referred to the discussion in that section on the meaning of the term in the Directive. Specific reference was made in the earlier discussion to a recent English decision, in which shareholders were held to be 'affected' by the plan by virtue of dilution of their economic interest. Article 9 specifically provides that, even if they are affected by the plan, equity holders, creditors whose claims rank below the claims of ordinary unsecured creditors in the distributional order of priority in national insolvency law, and any related party with a conflict of interest can be excluded from the vote. Any further detail on when this would apply is left to the Member States themselves, but there is a hint of the English approach of leaving creditors outside the vote when they have 'no genuine economic interest' in the company, and of ensuring that the vote is not achieved by virtue of the votes of creditors who have their own, motivating agenda. Both issues are discussed in Chapter 3.

2.33   The Directive imposes a minimum requirement of placing unsecured and secured creditors into separate classes, although it also provides Member States with the option for SMEs to opt not to treat affected creditors in separate classes.[73] In the Dutch WHOA, secured creditors vote together in a class in respect of the amount of their debt which represents the expected value of their security in a bankruptcy liquidation. The secured creditors may be placed in separate classes to the extent the rights they have or will acquire pursuant to the plan substantially differ, so that financial creditors with mortgages and pledges may be placed in a different class from trade suppliers with the benefit of retention of title arrangements. The voting rights of secured creditors are also determined by reference to the

---

[72] Article 8(2).
[73] Article 9(4).

value of their security in the German StaRUG. As McCormack notes, it is not entirely clear whether SMEs are entitled to place secured and unsecured creditors in the same class, but he argues that 'Because of the general respect accorded property rights, the better view is that secured and unsecured creditors should not be put in the same class except for the unsecured portion of a secured claim.'[74] We will see, in Chapter 3, particular challenges which arise where creditors are placed in a single class for voting purposes. Jonathan McCarthy also calls on us to remember that many SMEs will be ordinary, unsecured creditors of the distressed debtor.[75] He highlights that single class voting in an SME debtor context may have the result that SME creditors are effectively outvoted by parties with more commercial power, and significantly different interests, such as tax authorities. At the same time, Article 4 also requires Member States to put in place 'appropriate measures to ensure that class formation is done with a view to protecting vulnerable creditors such as small suppliers'.[76] No further guidance is offered, although the intention would appear to be to deal directly with McCarthy's concern when class voting is permitted: ensuring that ordinary, unsecured creditors with weak bargaining power before the restructuring and weak bargaining power within it are not swamped in the vote by other unsecured creditors such as tax authorities who have very different interests. And this will not always be the result: in the Netherlands tax authorities have a statutory preference and for that reason are placed in a separate class. In the Dutch WHOA, a separate class is also mandatory for SME trade creditors and tort creditors in certain circumstances.[77] Furthermore, if the restructuring plan is not supported by the statutory majority in each class, the court may refuse confirmation in the Dutch WHOA if such SME trade creditors do not make at least a 20 per cent recovery (in money or the value equivalent) on their claims without compelling reasons.[78] Throughout the Directive there is a focus on workers' rights, presumably reflecting the priority afforded to employees in insolvency in many EU Member States. In a voting context, employees must be placed into a separate class. This is not the case in the Dutch WHOA, where the only rights which cannot be included in the restructuring plan are rights arising under employment contracts.[79] Similarly, employment-related rights, obligations, pension schemes, and pension obligations are excluded from the German StaRUG.[80] Milbank notes that, given the number of German industrial companies with underfunded pension schemes, the exclusion of pension schemes and obligations is a significant drawback in the new regime.[81]

Voting and issues relating to the formation of classes must be examined by a judicial or administrative authority if they are requested to confirm the plan, but Member States may choose to require judicial or administrative authority examination and confirmation of voting rights at an earlier stage.[82] We will see, in Chapter 3, that creditors vote in classes in the English scheme of arrangement procedure. Until 2002, the court did not consider class   **2.34**

---

[74] McCormack (n 21) 9.
[75] McCarthy (n 26).
[76] Article 9(4).
[77] De Brauw (n 29) 11.
[78] Ibid at 16.
[79] Ibid at 3.
[80] Milbank (n 17) 4.
[81] Ibid at 6.
[82] Article 9(5).

composition until after the scheme had been voted on, at the final, confirmation hearing. This meant that the debtor could discover, right at the end of the process, that the court was not happy with the classification of creditors for voting at the outset. As a result, as we shall see in more detail in Chapter 3, in 2002 a Practice Statement was issued in which it was stated that the court would consider issues relating to composition of class meetings at an initial hearing. Member States may thus wish to consider the chronology carefully. One attractive aspect of the Dutch WHOA is that an unappealable court order can be requested on any procedural or substantive matter at any time before the vote is held.[83]

2.35   Consistent with the minimum harmonization approach, the Directive leaves it to Member States to decide whether a successful vote should require a vote by a majority of claims or interests in the class, or whether it should also require a majority in number of the parties in the class.[84] We will see, in Chapter 3, that issues can arise with the majority in number formulation where the company has issued a bond, legal title is held by the trustee, and the numerous bondholders have only a beneficial interest. We will also see, in Chapter 3, that this challenge has caused England to require only a vote by a majority of claims and not a majority in number of parties in its new restructuring procedure. Interestingly, De Brauw Blackstone Westbroek report that in the context of the Dutch WHOA the beneficial owner will be invited to vote.[85] The minimum harmonization approach is also followed in the relevant statutory majority. The Directive sets down a maximum majority of 75 per cent of the amount of claims or interests in each class or, where appropriate, the number of affected parties, but Member States are free to make their own design choices within this framework. Interestingly, the new German restructuring plan procedure demands a vote of 75 per cent by value of all creditors within the class.[86] This may pose significant challenges in cases where it is difficult to engage rationally apathetic creditors or where creditors cannot be located and engaged. Thus, many jurisdictions prefer the option of limiting the requisite majority to those creditors who actually vote. This is the approach taken in the Dutch WHOA, where the majority is also lower: two-thirds of the total debt (or in the case of shareholders, subscribed capital) voting within a class.[87]

G. Confirmation of the Plan

2.36   A further, difficult issue in the design of any restructuring plan procedure is the extent of court involvement.[88] The Directive attempts to minimize court involvement, which brings obvious advantages in terms of speed, reducing costs, and the use of state resource. However, as Jennifer Payne has noted, the court can also play a vital role in protecting creditors in a restructuring context.[89] Payne identifies three specific contexts in which she sees a

---

[83] De Brauw (n 29) 3.
[84] Article 9(6).
[85] De Brauw (n 29) 11.
[86] Stephen Madaus, 'A Giant Leap for German Restructuring Law? The New Draft Law for Preventive Restructuring Procedures in Germany', *Oxford Business Law Blog* (26 October 2020) <https://www.law.ox.ac.uk/business-law-blog/blog/2020/10/giant-leap-german-restructuring-law-new-draft-law-preventive> (last accessed 22 July 2021).
[87] De Brauw (n 29) 11.
[88] Jennifer Payne, 'The Role of the Court in Debt Restructuring' (2018) 77(1) *Cambridge Law Journal* 124.
[89] Ibid at 125.

particular need for court review: the imposition of a restructuring on dissenting creditors; the imposition of a moratorium while a restructuring is negotiated; and circumstances in which new providers of finance may achieve a priority position which prefers them over existing creditors.[90] We have already seen, in section II.C, that a role does appear to be envisaged for the courts in the stay provisions. However, Article 10(1) also requires Member States to ensure review by a judicial or administrative authority where the restructuring plan affects the claims or interests of dissenting parties, where the plan provides for new financing, or where the plan involves the loss of 25 per cent or more of the workforce, if such loss is permitted under national law. It is striking that the review may be by an 'administrative authority' rather than a court. No further detail is provided on eligible administrative authorities in the Directive, and the IMF Working Paper highlights constitutional questions, including the extent to which administrative authorities can take decisions on private law issues and the ability for their actions to be reviewed by the courts.[91] Where the review is placed in the hands of the court, the circumstances described by the Directive map well onto Payne's particular concerns.

Article 10 then requires Member States to clearly specify the conditions for confirmation, **2.37** which must include certain minimum requirements. First, the relevant votes for the restructuring plan must have been achieved (subject to the cross-class cramdown power discussed below). Secondly, creditors with 'sufficient commonality of interest in the same class' must be treated equally and 'in a manner proportionate to their claim'. This is an interesting provision: the question of whether creditors of the same legal rank in corporate insolvency law's distributional order of priority can be treated differently in the restructuring plan is one of the most difficult questions in corporate reorganization.[92] There may be an element of the tail wagging the dog here. In a recent English restructuring, landlords were divided into separate classes according to the different lease modifications they were being offered in the plan.[93] However, as we have seen, both the Dutch WHOA and the German StaRUG limit the extent to which executory contracts and unexpired leases can be modified under the restructuring plan without counterparty consent. De Brauw Blackstone Westbroek tells us that under the Dutch WHOA:

> If creditors with equal rights (that is: belonging to the same ranking) are treated unequally in a restructuring plan, that plan can still be confirmed by the court if it has been approved with the majority consent of the creditors in the class that is worse off. If there is no majority, the plan can only be confirmed if there is a reasonable ground for unequal treatment, and this does not harm the interests of the creditors affected. If opposing creditors are worse off than they would be in bankruptcy liquidation, confirmation will be denied.[94]

The firm reports on a case in which a garden nursery was restructuring ordinary, unsecured **2.38** claims and secured bank financing in its restructuring plan. Ordinary, unsecured claims

---

[90] Ibid at 126.

[91] IMF (n 23) 9.

[92] For a detailed discussion of uneven treatment of otherwise equally ranking creditors, see Paterson and Walters (n 48).

[93] *Virgin Active Holdings Limited* [2021] EWHC 1246 (Ch).

[94] De Brauw Blackstone Westbroek, 'The WHOA in Practice: With Greater Clarity, Come Teething Problems' (17 March 2021) <https://www.debrauw.com/articles/the-whoa-in-practice-with-greater-clarity-come-teething-problems> (last accessed 23 July 2021).

incurred up to a cut-off date were to be compromised, together with the bank's secured debt. Ordinary, unsecured claims incurred after the cut-off date were to be paid in full out of new unsecured financing provided by the bank. Thus, there were two forms of unequal treatment of unsecured claims: unequal treatment of pre and post cut-off date claims and the fact that the new unsecured bank financing was not included in the compromise. The debtor justified these decisions on the basis that it would need to pay post cut-off claims in order to continue in business, and it required the bank financing to be able to make those payments. The Rotterdam District Court agreed. Furthermore, a draft valuation report showed no return to ordinary, unsecured creditors in a bankruptcy. Thus, pre cut-off date creditors were no worse off.[95]

2.39   Article 10 also requires notification of the restructuring plan to all affected parties, although it is left to national law to stipulate how this is to be achieved. It also requires that, where there are dissenting creditors, the plan meets the best interests of creditors test. This is defined in Article 2 and it is worth setting out the definition in full:

> a test that is satisfied if no dissenting creditors would be worse off under a restructuring plan than such a creditor would be if the normal ranking of liquidation priorities under national law were applied, either in the event of liquidation, whether piecemeal or by sale as a going concern, or in the event of the next-best-alternative scenario if the restructuring plan were not confirmed.

2.40   There appears to be something of a confluence here of the US chapter 11 'best interests of creditors' test, which requires that the dissenting creditor is not worse off than they would be in the event of a chapter 7 liquidation, and the UK counterfactual approach, which concentrates on what would happen if the restructuring plan were not confirmed. Both approaches are discussed in detail in Chapter 3, and readers are referred to the discussion in that chapter. However, a few further points are worthy of note. For an English corporate insolvency lawyer 'liquidation' refers to a break-up of the business and a sale of the assets, while in the US, unless it is specifically qualified, it is generally taken to refer to any sale transaction. The Directive adopts the US approach, so that liquidation refers to any sale transaction, whether piecemeal or of the business as a going concern, and Recital 49 makes clear that the relevant option depends on the specific circumstances of the debtor. Secondly, no detail is provided in the Directive as to how the next-best-alternative scenario is to be identified and, as the discussion in Chapter 3 reveals, this can be a particularly controversial question. Thirdly, as McCormack notes, even if the next-best-alternative can be readily identified, 'it may be difficult to calculate in practice what … dissentients would receive' in this event.[96] Finally, it is not entirely clear whether the approach is to consider only what the creditors would receive by virtue of the distribution of the proceeds of sale through the creditor priority waterfall or whether consideration is also to be given to what the creditor may receive in other ways in the event of the 'next-best-alternative'. Once again, readers are directed to the discussion of the 'relevant alternative' in the new English Part 26A restructuring plan context in Chapter 3. It will be immediately apparent that the application of the 'best-interests-of-creditors' test may be far from straightforward. And the discussion

---

[95]   Ibid, District Court Rotterdam 3 March 2021, ECLI:NL:RBROT:2021:1769.
[96]   McCormack (n 21) 10.

in Chapter 3 to which we have already referred demonstrates how complex court review of this issue can be. Consistent with the general approach of minimizing court involvement, the Directive specifically provides that the judicial or administrative authority will only review the application of the test if the restructuring plan is challenged on this ground.[97]

Particular focus is given to the provision of new financing and an explanation of why it is necessary to implement the plan and does not unfairly prejudice the interests of creditors, reflecting Payne's concern for the interests of existing creditors in this context.[98] Furthermore, Member States are required to ensure that judicial or administrative authorities are able to refuse to confirm the plan if it 'would not have a reasonable prospect of preventing the insolvency of the debtor or ensuring the viability of the business'.[99] Finally, the concern that involvement of a judicial or administrative authority may unduly slow down the process is reflected in an explicit requirement for Member States to ensure that 'the decision is taken in an efficient manner with a view to expeditious treatment of the matter'.[100]   **2.41**

Article 11 then deals with so-called cross-class cramdown. A restructuring plan may permit a majority to impose the plan on a minority within a class. More controversial is the question of whether the plan can be imposed on a dissenting class—generally known as a power of cross-class cramdown. The Directive mandates a cross-class cramdown power, upon the proposal of the debtor or with the debtor's agreement, where the plan complies with the relevant provisions of Article 10 and either the restructuring plan has been approved by a majority of the voting classes, at least one of which is either a secured creditor class or senior to the ordinary unsecured creditors, or: **2.42**

> at least one of the voting classes of affected parties or where so provided under national law, impaired parties, other than an equity-holder class or any other class which, upon a valuation of the debtor as a going concern, would not receive any payment or keep any interest, or, where so provided under national law, which could reasonably be presumed not to receive any payment or keep any interest, if the normal ranking of liquidation priorities were applied under national law.[101]

We have already touched on the distinction between 'affected' and 'impaired' parties in section II.E. We saw, in that section, that Recital 54 provides impairment of creditors 'should be understood to mean that there is a reduction in their claims'. McCormack notes, in the context of Article 11, that this is 'vague', given that the reference could be to a reduction of 'face value' or 'real economic value'.[102] As McCormack identifies, if repayment periods are extended or interest rates reduced, the real economic value of the claim decreases even though the face value is unaffected. Nonetheless, as suggested in section II.E, impairment implies real interference with the creditors' rights while a party may be 'affected' even if its   **2.43**

---

[97] See also Article 14(1). Article 14 provides that Member States shall ensure that judicial or administrative authorities may appoint or hear properly qualified experts on valuation issues.

[98] Payne (n 88) 131–132.

[99] Article 10(3).

[100] Article 10(4).

[101] Article 11(1)(b)(ii). Article 14(1) provides that a judicial or administrative authority shall only take a decision on valuation for the purposes of Article 11(1)(b)(ii) where a restructuring plan is challenged on that ground. See also n 97. This is also the case in the Dutch WHOA where only an opposing creditor in the opposing class who filed its claim on time may do so.

[102] McCormack (n 21) 11.

legal rights remain untouched. Article 11(1)(c) goes on to stipulate that dissenting classes must be treated at least as favourably as any other class of the same rank and more favourably than any junior class, although Article 11(2) permits a Member State to derogate from this requirement and provide that the claims of affected creditors in a dissenting voting class must be satisfied in full by the same or equivalent means where a more junior class is to receive any payment or keep any interest under the restructuring plan. A further derogation is permitted: Member States may limit the requirement to obtain the debtor's agreement to cases where the debtor is an SME. And Member States may increase the number of affected parties (or, where national law stipulates, impaired parties) required to approve the plan for the cross-class cramdown power to be engaged.

2.44   There is a great deal here that requires unpacking. First, there is some difficult drafting in Recital 49 which is worth setting out in full:

> ... where the plan is confirmed through a cross-class cram-down, reference should be made to the protection mechanism used in such scenario. Where Member States opt to carry out a valuation of the debtor as a going concern, the going-concern value should take into account the debtor's business in the longer term, as opposed to the liquidation value. The going-concern value is, as a rule, higher than the liquidation value because it is based on the assumption that the business continues its activity with the minimum of disruption, has the confidence of its financial creditors, shareholders and clients, continues to generate revenues, and limits the impact on workers.

It is extremely difficult to understand how Recital 49 and Article 11 fit together. First, it is not clear what is meant by 'the protection mechanism' used in the cross-class cramdown scenario. This could be the best-interests-of-creditors test in Article 10(d), or it could be the requirement for a vote in favour by an affected or impaired class in Article 11(1)(b)(ii). Furthermore, the reference to going-concern value taking account of the debtor's business in the longer term is a little curious. As we shall see in Chapter 3, the core dispute about the approach to valuation in a restructuring is whether value should be determined by reference to market prices in prevailing market conditions or whether that might undervalue the firm (if the industry in general is depressed or there is a lack of acquisition financing in the market), so that the search should rather be for the 'fundamental' or 'intrinsic' value of the firm without any discounts which a purchaser might be expected to apply. However, in both cases going-concern value takes account of future prospects: a purchaser of the business as a going concern is giving value for the future cash flows of the business, even if there is a concern that the purchaser is not giving enough value for them. And finally, the Directive typically uses liquidation in the US sense, to mean any sale whether piecemeal or as a going concern, so that the distinction between going-concern value and liquidation value in Recital 49 is confusing. Overall, it is suggested that the Directive is probably steering towards a valuation by a professional valuer, without any discount to bring value into line with current market prices in prevailing market conditions. It must be admitted, however, that the position is far from clear.

2.45   Moreover, the Directive offers Member States the option between what is commonly known as a 'relative priority' rule (RPR) and what is commonly known as an 'absolute priority' rule (APR). Relative priority requires only that a senior class must do better than a more junior class but provides no more colour than that. Absolute priority, on the other hand, requires that a senior class must recover in full before a junior class can recover but, as a corollary, the senior class must not recover more than it is owed.

This optionality between absolute and relative priority has provoked a furious debate in the   **2.46** literature. Jonathan Seymour and Steven Schwartz have argued that RPR risks undermining what they see as the incentives which the APR creates to reach a consensual, negotiated plan.[103] They note that APR is not mandatory in the US in a consensual plan, incentivizing junior creditors and shareholders to reach agreement while, presumably, the fear is that RPR incentivizes them to try their luck with the court. They note the difficulty of determining when RPR works fairly and of determining how it should work in practice. They fear that it enables senior creditors and shareholders to collaborate to exclude intermediate classes from recovery under a plan. And they note that while one of the arguments in favour of the RPR is that it may enable owner-managers to retain equity in the restructuring of small businesses, incentivizing them to seek a restructuring, the Directive in no way limits application of the RPR to SMEs. On the other hand, Riz Mokal and Ignacio Tirado have launched an equally spirited defence of the RPR.[104] And it is perhaps the case that Seymour and Schwartz somewhat overstate the lack of incentives which RPR creates for bargaining. Seymour and Schwartz pinpoint the consensus-motivating force of chapter 11 because cramdown in the US is expensive and uncertain. It seems likely that RPR creates the same conditions, albeit in a different way. As Seymour and Schwartz note, the Directive's provisions are extremely slim and leave much to be worked out. While RPR creates the conditions in which shareholders and junior creditors may retain an interest, even where senior creditors suffer a compromise, there would seem to be a great deal of uncertainty as to when the court will confirm such a plan. At the same time, RPR creates incentives for senior creditors to reach agreement to avoid the risk that the court permits shareholders and/or junior creditors to retain an even greater interest in a cramdown hearing.

In the Dutch WHOA, additional requirements are included for a restructuring plan to be   **2.47** confirmed over the objections of a dissenting class or a class which was unfairly not admitted to the vote and should have been placed in a dissenting class. We have already seen that SME trade creditors must receive at least a 20 per cent recovery on their claims, absent 'compelling reasons'. The Dutch WHOA also adopts the APR unless there is a justification for deviation from the APR and deviation is not detrimental to the interests of the relevant creditor class (what De Brauw Blackstone Westbroek term the 'reasonableness test').[105] Thirdly, the Dutch WHOA provides that cross-class cramdown can be withheld if the plan does not allow an unsecured creditor (other than a bank or other professional moneylender) to recover in cash the amount it would have been likely to receive in a liquidation of the debtor's assets.[106] And finally, it may also be withheld if the plan does not allow a professional money supplier to make a recovery other than in shares or cash.[107]

---

[103] Jonathan Seymour and Steven L Schwartz, 'Corporate Restructuring under Relative and Absolute Priority Default Rules: A Comparative Assessment' (4 December 2019) <https://ssrn.com/abstract=3498611> (last accessed 21 July 2021).

[104] Riz Mokal and Ignacio Tirado, 'Has Newton Had His Day? Relativity and Realism in European Insolvency' (2019) *Butterworths Journal of International Banking and Finance Law* 233.

[105] De Brauw (n 29) 16.

[106] Ibid.

[107] Ibid.

2.48   The IMF working paper supports the approach of an APR with what it calls 'targeted exceptions'.[108] The German StaRUG adopts what Milbank describes as a 'modified "absolute priority rule"', subject to a complex range of permissible deviations.[109] This approach is also supported by Recital 56, which provides:

> Member States should be able to derogate from the absolute priority rule, for example where it is considered fair that equity holders keep certain interests under the plan despite a more senior class being obliged to accept a reduction of its claims, or that essential suppliers covered by the provision on the stay of individual enforcement actions are paid before more senior classes of creditor. Member States should be able to choose which of the above-mentioned protection mechanisms they put in place.

2.49   McCormack notes that the Directive is silent on the situation in which the statutory majorities are achieved in every class, but no application is made to the judicial or administrative authority for confirmation.[110] However, he points to Recital 53, which states:

> While a restructuring plan should always be adopted if the required majority in each affected class supports the plan, it should still be possible for a restructuring plan which is not supported by the required majority in each class to be confirmed by a judicial or administrative authority, upon the proposal of the debtor or with the debtor's agreement.

This implies that if the statutory majority is achieved in each class, then the plan takes effect, without court review. It is not entirely clear how and if a minority creditor can challenge the plan in these circumstances. However, Article 10(1) provides that restructuring plans which affect the claims or interests of dissenting affected parties; restructuring plans which provide for new financing; and restructuring plans which involve the loss of 25 per cent of the workforce all require confirmation by a judicial or administrative authority. As the IMF Working Paper notes, it seems likely that almost all plans will fall under the first category.[111] Both the Dutch WHOA and the German StaRUG appear to require court confirmation of the extrajudicially negotiated plan to bind minority creditors within a class.[112]

H. Shareholders and Workers

2.50   We have already seen that Article 9 permits Member States to exclude equity holders from the vote on the restructuring plan. This is bolstered by Article 12, which provides that where Member States exclude equity holders from the application of Articles 9, 10, and 11, they 'shall ensure by other means that those equity holders are not allowed to unreasonably prevent or create obstacles to the adoption and confirmation of the restructuring plan'.[113]

---

[108] IMF (n 23) 23.
[109] Milbank (n 17) 6–7.
[110] McCormack (n 21) 12.
[111] IMF (n 23) 24.
[112] In the Netherlands a plan does not bind opposing or absent creditors/shareholders without court confirmation. However, if there are no opposing classes, opposing minority creditors within a class can only seek to prevent confirmation of the plan on the grounds that the best interests of creditors (or the 'no creditor worse off' (NCWO) principle) is not met and provided that they have made a timely complaint in the earlier phases of the restructuring. All other grounds for refusal discussed above cannot be invoked if there are no opposing classes.
[113] Article 12(1).

Recital 57 offers the examples of not making the adoption of a restructuring plan conditional on the agreement of equity holders that, upon valuation of the enterprise, would not receive any payment or other consideration if the normal ranking of liquidation priorities were applied or of ensuring that any approval rights shareholders have as a matter of company law are not subject to 'unreasonably high' majority requirements and that equity holders 'have no competence in terms of restructuring measures that do not directly affect their rights'. Article 12(3) provides that Member States may adapt what it means to unreasonably prevent or create obstacles to take account of, among other things, whether the debtor is an SME or a large enterprise, whether the debtor is a legal or natural person, or whether partners in a company have limited or unlimited liability. The reference to SMEs is particularly interesting, given the issue already touched on with owner-managers who may only be willing to contemplate a restructuring if they can retain equity in the firm.

We have also touched on the concern for workers' rights in the Directive, reflecting the priority consideration afforded to employees in the insolvency laws of many Member States. This is bolstered by Article 15 which mandates Member States to ensure that individual and collective workers' rights under EU and national labour law are not affected by the preventive restructuring framework, offering specific examples. Article 13(2) also provides that if the restructuring plan leads to changes in 'work organisation or in contractual relations with workers' those arrangements require workers' approval if national law or collective agreements provide for such approval.   **2.51**

I. Appeals, New and Interim Financing, Transaction Avoidance, Director's Duties, Judicial and Administrative Authorities and Practitioners

Article 16 provides that Member States must ensure any appeal right is to a higher authority. Appeals are to be 'resolved in an efficient manner with a view to expeditious treatment'. The starting point is that an appeal has no suspensory effect on the plan but Member States may derogate from this.[114] And the consequences of an appeal can be either revocation of the plan or confirmation of the plan with or without amendments.[115] Where the plan is confirmed on appeal, Member States may make provision for costs.[116] However, it appears that a Member State is free to provide no right of appeal, and this is the approach adopted in the Dutch WHOA.[117]   **2.52**

Certain Member States have robust transaction avoidance regimes. Article 17 sets out provisions to protect new or interim financing and Article 18 sets out protections for other restructuring-related transactions. Article 19 sets out certain duties of directors where there is a likelihood of insolvency. Finally, Articles 25 and 26 contain various stipulations around training judicial and administrative authorities dealing with restructuring procedures and the training and qualifications of restructuring professionals.   **2.53**

---

[114] Article 16(3).
[115] Article 16(4).
[116] Ibid.
[117] De Brauw (n 29) 3.

III. Recognition of Restructuring Plans

2.54   A further issue which arises in connection with the European preventive restructuring framework is the extent to which restructuring plans confirmed in one Member State will be recognized in other Member States where the debtor has assets or creditors may seek to bring claims. If the restructuring plan is not recognized in other Member States, it may be necessary to open parallel proceedings in those jurisdictions. This may make it considerably more difficult to achieve an overall restructuring plan: because of tensions between the restructuring procedures in the different jurisdictions; because creditors may be reluctant to agree to a plan if they are suspicious of uneven treatment with creditors located in another Member State; and because it may introduce unsustainable delays. Thus, the debtor is likely to wish to develop a single restructuring plan which can be confirmed in one Member State and recognized in others. At this point, a complex interaction between the Directive and other European insolvency legislation emerges.

A. The European Insolvency Regulation

2.55   The European Insolvency Regulation (EIR) is the foundational European legislation for recognition of insolvency proceedings throughout the EU.[118] The Regulation provides for the opening of main proceedings in the Member State where the debtor has its 'centre of main interests' (COMI).[119] Main proceedings have universal effect throughout the EU, although secondary proceedings can be opened in any Member State where the debtor has an establishment.[120] Thus, at first sight, it may appear attractive for the restructuring procedure to fall within the scope of the EIR, so that a restructuring plan can be confirmed as a main proceeding in the jurisdiction where the debtor has its COMI, benefiting from automatic recognition throughout the EU.

2.56   However, the EIR is also subject to detailed choice of law rules which can produce other effects. Notably, in the context of restructuring plans, Article 8(1) provides that:

> The opening of insolvency proceedings shall not affect the rights *in rem* of creditors or third parties in respect of tangible or intangible, moveable or immoveable assets ... which are situated within the territory of another Member State at the time of the opening of proceedings.

There is significant uncertainty as to the meaning of the statement in Article 8(1) that the law of the insolvency proceedings 'shall not affect' the rights *in rem* of creditors and third parties at the opening of such proceedings. One interpretation is that Article 8(1) merely protects the right *in rem* itself so that, in the context of secured debt, the security interest over the underlying asset would be protected but not the secured debt. If this is the correct interpretation, then any restructuring plan would erode the effectiveness of the security right by varying or discharging the debt it secures over assets that may be located in other Member

---

[118] Regulation (EU) 2015/848 of the European Parliament and of the Council of 20 May 2015 on insolvency proceedings (recast) [2015] OJ L 141.

[119] Ibid, Article 3(1).

[120] Ibid, Article 3(2).

States. An alternative interpretation is that the protection extends to the underlying debt so that there can be no variation or discharge of the debtor's secured indebtedness over any assets located in other Member States. In other words, the right of the secured debtor to enforce its security over those assets for its indebtedness would be preserved. Several distinguished commentators have preferred this second interpretation.[121] Of course, if this interpretation is right, it undermines the utility of the EIR in securing EU-wide recognition of any restructuring which seeks to compromise secured debt.

As a result, perhaps somewhat counterintuitively, there may be real benefit in a restruc-   **2.57** turing procedure that falls outside the EIR. Indeed, this may have contributed to the popularity of the English scheme of arrangement as a European restructuring tool in the years after the 2008 financial crisis: although England was still a member of the EU, the scheme of arrangement fell outside the EIR while, as we shall see shortly, there was a good argument that it fell within an alternative European recognition regime.

At the same time, there may be benefits in mobilizing the EIR in certain cases: for example,   **2.58** where secured debt is not compromised in the plan. This raises the question of whether the restructuring plan otherwise falls within the scope of the EIR. Since it was recast in 2015, Article 1(1) provides that the EIR applies to:

> public collective proceedings, including interim proceedings, which are based on laws relating to insolvency and in which, for the purpose of rescue, adjustment of debt, reorganisation or liquidation:
>
> (a) a debtor is totally or partially divested of its assets and an insolvency practitioner is appointed;
>
> (b) the assets and affairs of a debtor are subject to control or supervision by a court; or
>
> (c) a temporary stay of individual enforcement proceedings is granted by a court or by operation of law, in order to allow for negotiations between the debtor and its creditors, provided that the proceedings in which the stay is granted provide for suitable measures to protect the general body of creditors, and, where no agreement is reached, are preliminary to one of the proceedings referred in point (a) or (b).

Thus, restructuring proceedings are clearly contemplated. Article 1(1) goes on to provide that where proceedings are commenced in situations where there is only a likelihood of insolvency then 'their purpose shall be to avoid the debtor's insolvency or the cessation of the debtor's business activities'. Finally, Article 2(1) defines 'collective proceedings' as 'proceedings which include all or a significant part of a debtor's creditors, provided that, in the latter case, the proceedings do not affect the claims of creditors which are not involved in them'. As we will see in more detail in Chapter 3, modern restructuring cases frequently exclude ordinary, unsecured creditors or may be limited to financial creditors. Article 2(1) suggests that proceedings of this type can continue to be treated as 'collective' proceedings, provided they include 'a significant part of a debtor's creditors' and Recital 14 makes clear that proceedings including only financial creditors qualify as collective proceedings.

---

[121] Manfred Balz, 'The European Union Convention on Insolvency Proceedings' (1996) 70 *American Business Law Journal* 485 at 95; Miguel Virgos and Francisco Garcimartin, *The European Insolvency Regulation: Law and Practice* (Kluwer Law International 2004), 80; Philip Smart, 'Rights in Rem, Article 5 and the EC Insolvency Regulation' (2006) 15 *International Insolvency Review* 33.

2.59   Finally, Article 1(1) states that the proceedings referred to in it are listed in Annex A. As Eidenmüller and Van Zwieten note, the intention (also reflected in Recital 9) is that 'inclusion in Annex A will be determinative of the question of whether a national procedure falls within the scope of the EIR'.[122] Both Germany and the Netherlands have sought to preserve the benefits of the EIR by developing a public version of their new restructuring procedure to be included within Annex A,[123] while offering another, non-public version which falls outside the EIR, avoiding the Article 8 problem. In the Dutch WHOA a debtor with its COMI in an EU Member State has a choice between the public and non-public versions of the procedures. However, both the public and the non-public versions of the German StaRUG are only available to a debtor with its COMI in Germany.

B. The Brussels Regulation

2.60   If the restructuring plan does not fall within the scope of the EIR, a further question arises as to whether it can benefit from the scheme of recognition provided for in the Brussels Regulation.[124] The EIR is complementary to the Brussels Regulation, which deals with the recognition and enforcement of judgments in civil and commercial matters. Thus, while Recital 6 of the EIR provides that the Regulation should 'include provisions governing jurisdiction for opening insolvency proceedings and actions which are directly derived from insolvency proceedings and are closely linked with them', Article 1(2)(b) of the Brussels Regulation excludes 'bankruptcy, proceedings relating to the winding up of insolvent companies or other legal persons, judicial arrangements, compositions and analogous proceedings'. When England was still a member of the EU, judges considered whether creditor schemes of arrangement fell within the Brussels Regulation in a line of cases. While they never arrived at a clear conclusion on the issue, most judges proceeded by considering the analysis as if the Regulation did apply.

2.61   However, more difficult questions may arise as to whether non-public restructuring plans fall within the Brussels Regulation. In *Gategroup*, Zacaroli J was required to consider whether the new English Part 26A restructuring plan fell within the bankruptcy exception to the Lugano Convention, which mirrors the bankruptcy exception in the Brussels Regulation.[125] Zacaroli J concluded that Part 26A restructuring plans do fall within the bankruptcy exception, in part because of the financial conditions which are specified in Part 26A for access to the procedure. It remains to be seen what approach will be taken to restructuring procedures introduced in EU Member States, but designed to fall outside the EIR, insofar as the bankruptcy exception in the Brussels Regulation is concerned. De Brauw Blackstone Westbroek has expressed the opinion that the non-public version of the Dutch WHOA does not fall within the bankruptcy exception to the Brussels Regulation,

---

[122]   Eidenmüller and Van Zwieten (n 11) 646.
[123]   See Madaus (n 86).
[124]   Regulation (EU) No 1215/2012 of the European Parliament and of the Council of 12 December 2012 on jurisdiction and the recognition and enforcement of judgments in civil and commercial matters [2013] OJ L 79/4.
[125]   *In the matter of Gategroup Guarantee Limited* [2021] EWHC 304 (Ch).

meaning that it will be governed by that Regulation.[126] Milbank similarly suggests that the non-public version of the German StaRUG should fall within the Brussels regime.[127]

C. Rome I

Alternatively, it is possible that recognition could be sought in reliance on the Rome I **2.62** Regulation.[128] Rome I provides that contracting states should give effect to contracting parties' choice of the law governing their contractual relations. Article 12 provides that the law applicable to the contract shall govern the various ways of extinguishing obligations under the contract. Thus, if a restructuring plan is confirmed in a jurisdiction the law of which governs the debt claims that are extinguished under it, there is a good argument that Member States will give effect to the discharge in the restructuring plan. Sax and Berkner have noted that Rome I is not so much concerned with recognition as with identifying the applicable law to determine an issue. Thus, in their view, a Member State presented with a restructuring plan confirmed in the jurisdiction which matches the governing law of the debt will examine whether, as a matter of that governing law, the claims have been discharged.[129] It should also be noted that this analysis relates to the discharge of claims. A restructuring plan may, of course, contain many other terms besides discharge.

Even more fundamentally, Article 1(2)(f) excludes from the scope of Rome I: **2.63**

> questions governed by the law of companies and other bodies, corporate or unincorporated, such as the creation, by registration or otherwise, legal capacity, internal organisation or winding-up of companies and other bodies, corporate or unincorporated, and the personal liability of officers and members as such for the obligations of the company or body.

Thus, an alternative argument is that restructuring plans fall within this exclusion. Look Chan Ho has, indeed, argued that 'Rome I ... should not be read as saying that bankruptcy discharge is a contractual matter'.[130] In his view, both Article 1(2)(f) and Recital 7 of Rome I support the argument that such a discharge is excluded from the Regulation.

D. UNCITRAL Model Law on Cross-border Insolvency

We shall see, in Chapter 4, that the question of whether the UNCITRAL Model Law on **2.64** Cross-border Insolvency facilitates recognition of restructuring plans is likely to turn on the way in which it has been implemented and the particular jurisdiction which has adopted it.

---

[126] De Brauw (n 29) 7. see also Reinout Vriesendorp, Wies van Kesteren, Elena Vilarin-Seivane, and Sebastian Hinse, 'Automatic Recognition of the Dutch Undisclosed WHOA Procedure in the European Union' (2021) *Nederlands Internationaal Privaatrecht (NIPR)* 182.

[127] Milbank (n 17) 9.

[128] Regulation (EC) No 593/2008 of the European Parliament and of the Council of 17 June 2008 on the law applicable to contractual obligations [2008] OJ L 177.

[129] Stefan Sax and Marie Berkner, 'Roadmap to German Recognition' *LexisPSL*, 23 December 2020.

[130] Look Chan Ho, 'Recognising Foreign Insolvency Discharge and Stare Decisis' (2011) *Journal of International Banking Law and Regulation* 266.

In addition, only four EU countries have adopted the Model Law: Greece; Poland; Romania; and Slovenia.

E. Private International Law

2.65 Finally, it may be possible to obtain recognition under the private international law rules of another Member State. However, this will clearly require careful case-by-case analysis of applicable private international law rules.

3

OUT-OF-COURT VS
COURT-SUPERVISED RESTRUCTURINGS

I. Workouts and Other Restructurings in the US

A. Advantages and Disadvantages of Workouts

3.01 In the US, a voluntary court-supervised reorganization is commenced by filing a petition for relief under section 301 of title 11 of the United States Code, 11 USC §§ 101 et seq ('the Bankruptcy Code'). Companies seek reorganization relief for many reasons: to stave off foreclosure or obtain a breathing spell from debt-related lawsuits, to halt and manage other vexatious litigation, to reject burdensome contracts and leases,[1] to avoid and recover certain transfers,[2] to facilitate the sale of assets (if a prospective buyer is unwilling to proceed out-of-court),[2a] to obtain financing that would have been contractually prohibited or otherwise unavailable,[3] and generally to develop a rational basis for restructuring their liabilities in a forum which centralizes all of their assets and all of their creditors' claims.[4] Many of the same objectives apply to the commencement of a creditor-initiated involuntary reorganization case.

3.02 Although there are advantages to obtaining relief under the Bankruptcy Code, '[a] company confronted ... can choose to rearrange its finances out of court as an alternative to obtaining relief under the bankruptcy laws'.[5] In fact, the underlying policy of the Bankruptcy Code favours 'workouts' or 'private, negotiated adjustments of creditor-company relations'.[6] Indeed, the legislative history of the Bankruptcy Code contemplates that the bankruptcy laws would serve as an 'alternative' if a debtor and its creditors were unable to arrive at mutually acceptable agreements necessary to effectuate a workout.[7] This policy is embodied in the Bankruptcy Code in at least two ways: (i) the Bankruptcy Code itself ' "[l]ike a fleet-in-being ... may be a force towards mutual accommodation", and as such, sets parameters for negotiations preceding a workout',[8] and (ii) 'the Code, in several specific respects, contemplates that workouts will be a prelude to, yet [be] consummated in, bankruptcy' specifically through a 'pre-packaged'[9] plan of reorganization provided for in sections 1102(b)(1),

---

[1] 11 USC § 365.

[2] 11 USC § 547 (avoiding preferences); 11 USC § 548 (avoiding fraudulent transfers); 11 USC § 544 (trustee as lien creditor).

[2a] 11 USC § 363.

[3] 11 USC § 364.

[4] See 11 USC § 1129(a) (if a chapter 11 plan complies with the Bankruptcy Code, the court may confirm a plan if it has been accepted by at least two-thirds in dollar amount and one-half in number of claims actually voting in each class); 11 USC § 1129(b) (under certain circumstances, the court may 'cramdown' a plan even if a particular class has rejected it).

[5] *Texas Commerce Bank, NA v Seymour Licht*, 962 F 2d 543 (5th Cir 1992).

[6] *In re Colonial Ford, Inc*, 24 BR 1014, 1015 (Bankr D Utah 1982); see ibid *Texas Commerce Bank* 549 (stating that bankruptcy policy strongly favours the 'speedy, inexpensive, negotiated' adjustment of creditor-company relations afforded by out-of-court procedures).

[7] HR Rep No 95-595, at 220 (1977), reprinted in 1978 USCCAN 5963, 6368 (citing Hearings on HR 31 and HR 32 Before the Subcomm on Civil and Constitutional Rights of the House Comm on the Judiciary, 94th Cong, 1st Sess, Ser 27, pt 1, at 436–37 (1975–76)).

[8] *In re Colonial Ford, Inc* (n 6) 1017; see Thomas H Jackson, 'Bankruptcy, Non-Bankruptcy Entitlements, and the Creditors' Bargain' (1982) 91 *Yale LJ* 857, 867 ('formal bankruptcy process would presumably be used only when individualistic "advantage-taking" in the setting of multi-party negotiations makes a consensual deal too costly to strike ...').

[9] For a detailed discussion of 'pre-packaged' plans of reorganization, see section VI *infra*.

1121(a), and 1126(b) of the Bankruptcy Code.[10] Several bankruptcy court decisions have reinforced the general policy favouring out-of-court workouts.[11]

In many instances an out-of-court workout may be a more efficient method of debt restructuring **3.03** than a court-supervised bankruptcy proceeding. Pre-petition-negotiated agreements between a debtor and its creditors generally reflect a well-thought-out reorganization attempt. In addition, a chapter 11 filing does not come without its disadvantages. A debtor may encounter significant expenses associated with a chapter 11 filing in terms of administrative and professional costs. Management may be distracted by the additional responsibilities imposed on a debtor-in-possession, professional restructuring officers may be hired, or in rare cases management may be displaced by a court-appointed trustee. Management and shareholders may have to deal with the prospect of creditors filing their own reorganization plans that eliminate shareholder recoveries.[12] It is possible that a chapter 11 filing could be converted to a chapter 7 liquidation proceeding.[13] Finally, it is common for the debtor's business to experience some degree of backlash from a bankruptcy filing in the form of reputational harm and loss of business.

Determining whether a debtor should file for chapter 11 relief involves a delicate balancing **3.04** of the advantages and disadvantages discussed above. Implemented correctly, a successful out-of-court workout should convert a distressed company into one that is economically viable and comfortably sustainable. A summary of the principal advantages and disadvantages of out-of-court workouts are set forth below.

1. Advantages of a workout
The advantages of a workout include the following: **3.05**

- lower administrative costs;
- lower professional fees;
- increased control and flexibility;
- less management distraction;
- generally, no loss of management control;
- better preservation of going concern value;
- less negative publicity; and
- creditors not subject to potential subordination of claims or avoidance of pre-petition transfers.

2. Disadvantages of a workout
The disadvantages of a workout include the following: **3.06**

- limited ability to bind dissenting creditors or classes of creditors;
- no automatic stay protection;

---

[10] *In re Colonial Ford, Inc* (n 6) 1017.
[11] Ibid. (dismissing bankruptcy petition filed when debtor failed to get financing required by a workout agreement reached with its creditors because the court refused to abandon an out-of-court workout where it was clear that the debtor had agreed to compose its debts outside of the court system and then attempted to 'ambush' its creditors by filing a chapter 11 petition); *In re TS Industries, Inc,* 117 BR 682 (Bankr D Utah 1990) (holding that pre-petition workout agreements are assumable contracts under s 365(c)(2)).
[12] *In re Colonial Ford, Inc* (n 6) 1022.
[13] Debtors and creditors 'are familiar with the old saw that a "good" liquidation out of court is better than a "bad" reorganization in Chapter 11'. Ibid 1017.

- no ability to unilaterally reject executory contracts;
- no ability to pursue avoidance actions; and
- no ability to obtain contractually prohibited financing.

B. Considerations in Out-of-Court Workouts

3.07   Regardless of the restructuring process a debtor chooses, there are certain considerations that are fundamental to the workout process.

1. Moratorium

3.08   At the outset of out-of-court negotiations, a company will call a meeting of key creditors with 'impaired' claims and disclose its financial status and explain the difficulties it faces. Having explained the situation, the company should seek a moratorium, a temporary period during which the company can delay payment on obligations as they become due. This moratorium allows the company, in essence, a 'time-out' to negotiate restructuring agreements. If agreed upon, any payment defaults would be waived, which should prevent cross-acceleration of other debts as well as negative publicity and reactions based on news of a default.

3.09   It is important for the company to provide periodic progress reports on its financial dealings during a moratorium. Disclosure and transparency help foster a relationship of trust with creditors and encourage continued cooperation. Such cooperation will be needed in the potential negotiations that lie ahead.

2. Negotiations

3.10   A successful out-of-court workout requires negotiations and, ultimately, agreements between the company and its substantial creditors. Inevitably, the terms of each negotiation will be company and creditor-specific. Each agreement will be unique and will memorialize the specific contractual terms negotiated. As long as the company can reach agreement with each of its main creditors, it has a chance of consummating a successful out-of-court restructuring.

3. Ad hoc creditor's committee

3.11   Often, creditors of a company that expect to negotiate an out-of-court restructuring will facilitate formation of informal committees of creditors holding similar claims, such as bank, bond, or trade debt. The committee functions as the de facto representative of the larger creditor body and should further common interests and concerns. No rules exist as to who can be on the committee and committee members have no fiduciary duties to each other or to non-committee members.[14] Moreover, while the actions of the committee are not binding on any individual creditors, the committee process streamlines negotiations.

---

[14] But see *In re Washington Mutual, Inc*, 419 BR 271No 08-12229 (MFW), 2009 WL 4363539 (Bankr D Del, 2 Dec 2009).

It should be noted that section 1102(b) of the Bankruptcy Code permits the United States   **3.12**
Trustee to appoint a committee of unsecured creditors during a bankruptcy case that was
formed before commencement of the case.

4. Debt repayment

It is fundamental to a proper out-of-court workout to negotiate a debt repayment schedule   **3.13**
that is consistent with the debtor's current and predicted cash flows and anticipated financial condition. Typical arrangements include an extended repayment period, a debt-for-equity swap, or relief from interest or amortization payments.

5. Collateralization

The company may consider offering collateral to secure repayment of a currently unsecured   **3.14**
obligation. Collateralization affords the newly secured creditor substantial additional rights
and leverage against the company both in and out of court.

6. Management changes

Inadequate management or leadership may be a contributing cause to the financial hard-   **3.15**
ships a company is experiencing. If significant creditors do not have confidence in management, management should be changed or supplemented, often with the addition of a 'chief
restructuring officer'.

C. Typical Out-of-Court Approaches

When an out-of-court restructuring can effectively resolve the debtor's financial distress,   **3.16**
it generally is the preferred method of proceeding. Successful execution of an out-of-court
restructuring begins with an analysis of the debtor's business. As discussed above, such analysis should identify the specific problems that led to the necessity of a restructuring and
should address the company's financial prospects on a realistic basis.

However, an out-of-court restructuring only binds those creditors that agree to be so   **3.17**
bound. This is a principal disadvantage when compared to a confirmed chapter 11 plan
of reorganization that binds dissenting creditors and, in certain instances, classes of
creditors.

1. 'Down-round' financing

A down-round financing is an offering of securities at a price per share that is lower than   **3.18**
the price paid for shares in one or more prior financing rounds. This allows for an immediate profit and an incentive for existing investors, while simultaneously raising needed
capital. Down-round financings also may recruit new investors seeking to ensure an appropriate return on their investment. However, down-round financings often have a negative impact on existing investors trying to preserve their investment and on management
with pre-existing equity-based compensation arrangements. These directly opposing
interests must cooperate to ensure that the company is adequately capitalized and that
management has the proper incentives to aggressively develop the business for the new
funding to succeed.

2. 'Washout' or 'cramdown' venture financing

3.19   A 'washout' or 'cramdown' round of financing occurs when existing equity is either completely eliminated or severely impaired, and the new investors receive all or nearly all the equity in the restructured company enabling them to take control. Such investment generates new working capital which allows the company to remain functional and avoid a bankruptcy proceeding.

3. Debt conversion deals

3.20   Debt conversion deals involve the voluntary conversion or cancellation of existing debt in exchange for new obligations or different repayment terms. There are a range of common debt conversion mechanisms, including debt-for-debt swaps, debt-for-equity swaps, and debt buybacks. Such debt exchanges allow a potential debtor to alter the terms of its debt, while providing its creditors with a greater likelihood of some payment. In such a restructuring, the interests of a company and its creditors are aligned in achieving 'a successful restructuring of the [company's] financial obligations in order to avoid the uncertainties and daunting transaction costs of bankruptcy'.[15]

4. Assignment for the benefit of creditors (informal wind downs)

3.21   An assignment for the benefit of creditors occurs when the company conveys its assets to a creditor representative who is to use such assets to satisfy existing debt. Such an assignment allows the representative to hold the property in trust and to sell or liquidate the assets and then distribute the proceeds to creditors, returning any surplus to the debtor.

D.   Potential for Failure and a Subsequent Chapter 11 Filing

3.22   It should be noted that an out-of-court workout or restructuring may fail to resuscitate the business and revitalize the company. It is therefore vital to consider bankruptcy alternatives within the workout context. Most notably, the creditors who agree to a workout agreement should be wary of provisions in the Bankruptcy Code which allow the debtor to assume or reject executory contracts[16] and the provisions in the Bankruptcy Code that empower the debtor with a number of avoidance powers which may be used to void prior transfers or obligations.[17] In the event of a bankruptcy proceeding, these statutory provisions could be used to undermine agreed-upon terms of a workout or restructuring agreement and possibly require the creditor to forfeit payments or liens previously received. Therefore, each

---

[15]   *Texas Commerce Bank* (n 5) 547 (citing *In re Chateaugay Corp.*, 961 F.2d 378, 381 (2d Cir. 1992)).

[16]   11 USC § 365.

[17]   See 11 USC § 547 (the preference period extends to 90 days before the chapter 11 filing, unless the creditor is an insider, in which case the preference period is one year. There are a number of defences that can be raised, including the 'exchange for new value' defence, and the 'ordinary course of business' exception); 11 USC § 548 (a creditor in an out-of-court workout or restructuring also should be mindful of constructive fraudulent transfer risk. This would arise if the transfer occurred while the debtor was insolvent or the transfer rendered the debtor insolvent and the debtor did not receive reasonably equivalent value in return); s 238 of the Insolvency Act 1986 (transaction at an undervalue which occurs where the company is insolvent or becomes insolvent as a result of the transaction, the sale is at an undervalue and the company cannot benefit from the defence of acting in good faith, for the purpose of carrying on its business and with reasonable grounds that it would benefit the company. The challenge period is two years); s 239 of the Insolvency Act 1986 (grant of preference within six months or two years for connected persons where influenced by the desire to prefer); s 245 (vulnerable floating charges); s 423 (putting assets beyond the reach of creditors).).

creditor in workout negotiations should carefully analyse the potential bankruptcy ramifications of an out-of-court transaction.

II. Out-of-Court Restructurings in England

A. Advantages and Disadvantages of an Out-of-Court Restructuring in the UK

Until the early noughties, most large financial restructurings were conducted out-of-court **3.23** in England. The finance market at the time was dominated by a small number of deposit or 'clearing' banks and a set of principles was developed, initially by the Bank of England, known as the 'London Approach'. The London Approach set out how banks ought to behave when a debtor was distressed and much of it is carried over into INSOL's Statement of Principles for a Global Approach to Multi-Creditor Workouts II.[18] Crucially, however, in London Approach restructurings there was normally an expectation that all stakeholders would receive some allocation of consideration in the final restructuring.[19] This behaviour (which may have involved some creditors 'leaving something on the table' which they would have acquired in a court-led restructuring) was enforced precisely because the relatively homogeneous lending group of the time was able to threaten any lender who did not play by the rules of the game with exclusion from valuable deals in the primary market for healthy companies later.[20] Changes in the UK finance market were to make it far less effective as a code steering behaviour between the creditors.[21] In cases where creditors perceive there to be enough value to offer some equity to existing shareholders, in large listed companies where the listing rules provide shareholders with voting rights which may be difficult and costly to disapply, or in situations where the shareholder accepts that they no longer have a residual interest in the company and welcomes the discretion which an out-of-court restructuring may provide versus publicity around what may be seen as a bad initial credit decision, out-of-court restructurings do still occur. Similarly, many small and medium-sized companies with bilateral loan agreements with a single bank may seek to restructure out-of-court. But out-of-court restructurings are far from the ubiquitous affair which they once were in the UK and increasingly resort is needed to legal procedures to deliver a debt restructuring.

This somewhat generic reference to 'legal procedures' highlights an important distinction **3.24** between the analysis of out-of-court versus court supervised restructurings in a US context and the analysis in the UK. In the US, chapter 11 acts as a single gateway and, as we have seen in paragraph 3.01 above, debtors may turn to it for a variety of purposes: to create a

---

[18] Available at <https://www.insol.org/_files/Publications/StatementOfPrinciples/Statement%20of%20Principles%20II%2018%20April%202017%20BML.pdf> accessed 25 January 2021.
[19] John Armour and Simon Deakin, 'Norms in Private Insolvency Procedures: The "London Approach" to the Resolution of Financial Distress' (2001) 1 *Journal of Corporate Law Studies* 21, 36.
[20] Ibid 46.
[21] For a detailed account, see Sarah Paterson, 'Bargaining in Financial Restructuring: Market Norms, Legal Rights and Regulatory Standards' (2014) 14(2) *Journal of Corporate Law Studies* 333, 337–345.

breathing space from creditors or litigation; to reject burdensome contracts and leases; to avoid and recover certain transfers; or to obtain rescue financing which is otherwise contractually prohibited. The English corporate insolvency law regime might, in contrast, be described as 'modular' in approach.[22] Modular, here, means that rather than having a single gateway leading to a range of possible applications (*viz* chapter 11), English law offers a wide range of restructuring tools which can be used individually, or in combination, and for different purposes. We set out later in this chapter the distinctions between chapter 11 and administration (the principal insolvency procedure in England) and the reasons why schemes of arrangement and pre-packaged administrations have generally been used to implement large and larger mid-cap restructurings in the UK rather than a trading administration. In certain circumstances the advantages of an out-of-court restructuring when compared to a scheme of arrangement may not be as stark compared with the advantages of a workout compared with a chapter 11 case. The principal advantages of an out-of-court restructuring in the UK are speed, reduced cost, and discretion.

3.25   Since 2008, schemes of arrangement and pre-packaged administrations have generally been used as stand-alone procedures to implement large and larger mid-cap restructurings in the UK rather than being coupled with a trading administration proceeding. The Corporate Governance and Insolvency Act 2020 (CIGA) has now added two new tools to the toolbox: the Part A1 moratorium and the Part 26A restructuring plan,[23] and we will discuss both how the new tools might be expected to be used and the implications for the use of existing tools. The important point, for current purposes, is that the distinction between out-of-court and court restructuring is not as starkly drawn in the UK as it is in the US. As we shall see, it is possible for a restructuring to be implemented by contract without resort to any legal procedure (albeit resort to legal procedure may be developed as a contingency to encourage bargaining). And it is possible for a company to be placed into administration (or, following CIGA, a Part A1 moratorium) to stabilize the business and create liquidity while a restructuring is worked out. But some of the English law tools, such as the scheme of arrangement and the Part 26A restructuring plan procedure, may be used to implement a largely consensual deal in a way which is perhaps closer to an out-of-court negotiation in the US than a full chapter 11 case. For example, a scheme of arrangement or a Part 26A restructuring plan may be used where certain creditors have not engaged or cannot be traced, but where there is no explicit sign that they object to the debtor company's proposal. This insight will become clearer as Chapter 3 develops.

B. Considerations in Out-of-Court Restructurings in the UK

3.26   Where an out-of-court restructuring is attempted, minds will turn to approaching negotiations with the company's lenders.

---

[22] The term 'modular' is inspired by Ronald Davis, Stephan Madaus, Alberto Mazzoni, Irit Mevorach, Rizwaan Jameel Mokal, Barbara Romaine, Janis Sarra and Ignacio Tirado, *Micro, Small, and Medium Enterprise Insolvency: A Modular Approach* (OUP 2018).

[23] See CIGA, s 1, inserting new Part A1 into the Insolvency Act 1986 (Moratorium), and Sch 9, inserting new Part 26A into the Companies Act 2006.

1. Standstill

There may be circumstances where negotiations become protracted over many months **3.27** or where a formal standstill agreement cannot be agreed at all or can only be agreed in relation to the senior debt. This is becoming more common in today's multi-layered debt structures, as junior creditors are becoming increasingly reluctant to sign up and difficult to identify and organize. At this point, it is important to note another important distinction between restructuring in the US and restructuring in England. In the US, there is frequently no inter-creditor agreement between senior and junior lenders in the capital structure regulating priority and allocating control rights in distress. Instead, it is common for the financial creditors to rely on the mandatory provisions of chapter 11 to do this work for them. Indeed, an inter-creditor agreement is generally only put in place where the capital structure includes a second lien tranche of senior debt.[24] Moreover, US bankruptcy courts have shown some concern in enforcing the terms of inter-creditor agreements.[25] In England, in contrast, it is usual to have an inter-creditor agreement between all of the financial creditors, regulating priority and allocating control rights in distress. And the English courts have shown a general willingness to enforce inter-creditor agreements.[26] These inter-creditor contracts generally provide a junior standstill, which arguably reduces the need for a lengthy formal standstill agreement. At the same time, it may be possible to rely on the majority bank mechanism in the senior facility agreement to feel comfortable that senior lenders will not take action.[27] Nonetheless, standstill provisions within inter-creditor agreements may be subject to insolvency carve-outs and are likely to be time limited, which may give rise to concerns.[28] And it may be difficult to rely on majority bank provisions when loan participations are regularly traded in the secondary market. Thus, standstill agreements are still negotiated among senior and junior financial creditors, or among senior financial creditors, in English out-of-court debt restructuring. But there may be other ways to get comfortable that financial creditors cannot accelerate or take enforcement action without necessarily putting a standstill agreement in place.

The increasing prevalence of credit default swaps in the market has had a significant im- **3.28** pact on dynamics. Although 'Restructuring Event' may be specified in a credit default swap as an event entitling the protected party to call under its swap, counterparties are unenthusiastic about relying on it and prefer 'cleaner' triggers such as a failure to pay interest or principal or an insolvency filing.[29] An example of this occurred in the restructuring of LyondellBasell. The LyondellBasell group is one of the world's largest oil refiners and producers of petrochemicals and plastics. Faced with falling worldwide demand, Lyondell

---

[24] Danelle le Cren and Jeff Norton, 'Problems at the Border' (2015) 34(4) *International Financial Law Review* 52, 54.

[25] See, for example, *Beatrice Foods Co v Hart Ski Manufacturing Company* 5 BR 325 (Bankr ND Ill 2000); *In Contrarian Funds LLC v Westpoint Stevens, Inc* 333 BR 30 (SDNY 2005).

[26] See, for example, *HHY Luxembourg Sarl v Barclays Bank Plc* [2010] EWHC 2406 (Ch); [2010] 9 WLUK 401.

[27] Typically, in order to demand repayment of a syndicated loan on a financial covenant breach or other default a vote of lenders holding 66.6 per cent of the aggregate will be required. Thus, if the borrower is comfortable that there is a sufficient blocking minority it will not be concerned that the loan will be accelerated, even if some lenders might support that course of action.

[28] In many leveraged deals in the UK the intercreditor agreement will provide that upon a financial covenant or other default there will be a 90- to 150-day standstill before the junior lender can bring an action.

[29] See Frank Partnoy and David A Skeel Jr, 'The Promise and Perils of Credit Derivatives' (2007) 75 *University of Cincinnati Law Review* 1019, 1039; Daniel Hemel, 'Empty Creditors and Debt Exchanges' (2010) 27 *Yale Journal on Regulation* 159, 161.

Chemical Company and 78 of its subsidiaries and affiliates filed for protection under chapter 11 of the US Bankruptcy Code. At this stage, the Luxembourg-incorporated parent of Lyondell Chemical Company, LBIAF, did not file for chapter 11 protection or enter any other insolvency process. However, the chapter 11 filings made in respect of the US entities triggered an event of default under certain notes issued by LBIAF and, under their terms, holders of 25 per cent of the principal amount of the notes could accelerate amounts due under them. During January 2009, news services began to report that some of the holders of the notes held credit default swaps. These news services reported that noteholders who were also holders of credit default swaps were attempting to rally the requisite 25 per cent support needed to accelerate the notes and trigger a payout of the credit default swaps. This forced Lyondell to take some innovative steps to try to preserve the plan for its global restructuring.[30]

3.29   Recent high-profile newspaper reports have raised concerns about so-called 'net short' lenders who, it is argued, may be motivated to take aggressive action to push the company into corporate insolvency proceedings absent robust arrangements to neuter their power.[31] One response to this has been the development of 'net short disenfranchisement provisions'. The technology around these provisions is still evolving, but may include preventing a net short lender from voting on amendments or waivers or limiting the period of time following an event of default in which action can be taken.[32] In other cases, holders of credit default swap (CDS) protection may be nervous about taking proactive steps which may affect their ability to claim, if it can be demonstrated that they have triggered the very event which they subsequently come to rely on.[33] Thus, whilst CDS protection may affect holders' willingness to vote in favour of a debt restructuring and may affect the ability to get the deal done, disenfranchisement provisions may prevent them from taking proactively destructive steps and, even where this is not the case, it may be possible to conclude that holders will not take such action. This also applies to collateralized debt obligations or 'CDOs' which may be limited in their ability to vote for a debt restructuring but are likely to wish to continue to collect fees for as long as possible.[34] Other junior creditors and the shareholders have no incentive to enforce because the priority rights afforded to senior creditors mean that this will almost certainly result in a loss of value.[35]

---

[30] See Sarah Paterson, 'LyondellBasell: The Longer Arm of Chapter 11' (2009) *Corporate Rescue and Insolvency* 2.4.

[31] Sujeet Indap, 'Windstream Debt Battle Opens Up "Pandora's Box" for Hedge Funds' *Financial Times* (New York, 22 February 2019) and Elisabeth de Fontenay, 'Windstream and Contract Opportunism' (2020) *Capital Markets Law Journal* 1.

[32] Milbank Client Alert, 'Net Short Lender Disenfranchisement: is the New Anti-CDS Vaccine Safe and Effective?' (11 June 2019); Philip Stopford and Maria Cornilsen, 'Anti-Net Short Provisions: Emergence and Migration to the European Market' (2020) *Butterworths Journal of International Banking and Financial Law* 33.

[33] See cases from the insurance field where the insured is prevented from making a claim where he has deliberately caused the insured event. See, e.g., *Genesisuk.net Ltd v Allianz Insurance Ltd* [2014] EWHC 3676 (QB); *Bristol Alliance Ltd Partnership v Williams and another* [2012] EWCA Civ 1267; *CP (a child) v Royal London Mutual Insurance Society Ltd* [2006] EWCA Civ 421; *North Star Shipping Ltd & Ors v Sphere Drake Insurance plc & Ors* [2005] EWHC 665; *Kiriacoulis Lines SA v Compagnie d'Assurances Maritime Aeriennes et Terrestres (Camat) & Anor ('The 'Demetra K')* [2002] EWCA Civ 1070 and *O'Connell v Pearl Assurance Plc* [1995] 2 Lloyd's Rep 479.

[34] This is because CDOs may have reinvestment restrictions which prevent them from supporting the restructuring, see Douglas J Lucas, Laurie S Goodman, and Frank J Fabozzi, *Collateralised Debt Obligations: Structure and Analysis* (Wiley 2006) 17–23, 386.

[35] John Armour and Sandra Frisby, 'Rethinking Receivership' (2001) 21 *Oxford Journal of Legal Studies* 73, 87 citing Randal Picker, 'Security Interests, Misbehaviour and Common Pools' (1992) 59 *University of Chicago Law Review* 645, 699–675.

Whilst it may, therefore, require steady nerves the directors and their advisers may be able   **3.30**
to conclude that even if there is no legally enforceable standstill, there is a practical one.[36]

2. Negotiation

As with the US approach, the next stage is the negotiation stage during which the debtor   **3.31**
and its creditors work towards agreeing a restructuring agreement.

3. Coordinator and coordination committees

A specific problem in commencing negotiations with creditors in a large or larger mid-cap   **3.32**
modern case is identifying them. Whilst the facility agent will know the lender of record in
a syndicated loan, trading in the debt by way of equitable assignment or sub-participation
may mean that the institution with the real economic interest is a completely different entity.[37] Information on the identity of bondholders and noteholders will rest with the clearing
systems which will be reluctant to share it and, even then, the information will relate to the
participant in the clearing system and not necessarily the ultimate beneficial owner of the
bond.[38] Credit default swaps may be written in favour of holders who do not hold the underlying debt, so that the amount of credit default swap protection which has been written
may exceed the reference debt.[39]

It is common, during restructuring negotiations, for a coordinator to be appointed, usually   **3.33**
from a creditor with a significant exposure. Sometimes there will also be a need for one or
more coordinating committees to be appointed. There are several different possible models
for these committees. They may be ad hoc or relatively informal, appointed formally by
creditors but with a liaison role or (less usually) appointed formally with a mandate to bind
the creditors. The process of negotiating appointment terms for coordinators and coordinating committees can, itself, take some time, particularly if indemnities are demanded
either from the company or from the other creditors. Generally, the company will pay the
costs of advisers to coordinators and the committees, although these fee arrangements may
be capped and subject to detailed ongoing reporting requirements.

4. Debt repayment

Traditionally English bank lenders were reluctant to write off debt and restructuring agree-   **3.34**
ments would more usually involve non-core disposals (to pay down debt), covenant holidays, and revised amortization schedules (to create space for the company to get back on
its feet).[40] Agreeing a restructuring along these lines would require careful review of the financing documentation to establish the requisite majorities required. Sometimes it may be

---

[36] For a more detailed exploration of this point, see Sarah Paterson, 'Rethinking Corporate Bankruptcy Theory
in the Twenty-First Century' (2016) 36(4) *Oxford Journal of Legal Studies* 697. <http://ojls.oxfordjournals.org/cgi/
content/full/gqv038?ijkey=ESvFGKwAj6lTLDz&keytype=ref>.

[37] See Geoff Fuller, 'Loan Transfers, Securitisation, and Structured Finance' in Sarah Paterson and Rafal
Zakrzewski (eds) *McKnight, Paterson and Zakrzewski on The Law of International Finance* (2nd edn, OUP 2017)
para 12.5.3, 711 and para 12.8.5, 719.

[38] For a description of the private companies who will assist with identifying bondholders, see Chris Howard
and Bob Hedger, *Restructuring Law & Practice* (2nd edn, LexisNexis 2014) para 2.81, 50.

[39] The so-called 'empty creditor problem', see Hemel (n 29).

[40] Armour and Frisby (n 35) 93.

possible to structure the restructuring so that each element requires only a majority lender vote. Where this can be achieved, it increases the prospect of completing an out-of-court restructuring. However, even where it is possible the problem with these techniques may be that they do not sufficiently reshape the company's balance sheet. Thus, the company either suffers a dramatic fall in earnings without a commensurate fall in debt burden (in the case of non-core disposals) or continues to apply too much of its cash to service its debt burden, leaving it with insufficient cash to invest in its business. This gives rise to the so-called 'zombie company' problem,[41] and means that these deals, traditionally known as 'amend and extend' have acquired the somewhat pejorative tag 'amend and pretend'.

3.35   Instead, many in the market now recognize the value of a debt-for-equity swap as a debt restructuring technique. However, as discussed above, in order for a debt-for-equity swap to be implemented out-of-court it is likely to require the support of shareholders. This may limit the ability to agree a restructuring out-of-court unless shareholder support can be secured at a retained equity level acceptable to all the creditors.

5. Collateralization

3.36   As with the United States, lenders may also seek security for outstanding unsecured indebtedness. However, particular care will be needed here in case the out-of-court restructuring subsequently fails and the company seeks insolvency protection. This is because, as discussed in Chapter 1, the transaction avoidance provisions in English insolvency law may then come into play which could affect the ability of the lenders to rely on any security granted for outstanding indebtedness.

C. Typical Approaches in the UK

1. Rescue rights issue

3.37   As with the United States, an out-of-court restructuring may take the form of the raising of new equity, particularly where the lenders are not willing to undertake a debt-for-equity swap but the stakeholders recognize the need for the company to deleverage. In the UK, this is known as a rescue rights issue and involves persuading the existing shareholders to subscribe at a discount to the current market price. For a rescue rights issue to work, the shareholders need to be convinced of the 'equity story' or the case for the company trading out of its current difficulties, and that they will not simply be putting 'good money after bad'.

3.38   A rescue rights issue will also require production of a working capital statement. As described in Chapter 1, where the clean working capital statement from the auditors is dependent on the passing of the shareholder resolutions in support of which it is issued it is possible for the circular to shareholders to make that inter-dependence clear, whilst any financial statements delivered at the same time are likely to contain a 'material uncertainty'

---

[41] See 'The Zombie Business Phenomenon: An Update' (R3 Report January 2014); Tom Papworth, 'The Trading Dead. The Zombie Firms Plaguing Britain's Economy and What to Do About Them' (Adam Smith Institute Report 18 November 2013) https://www.adamsmith.org/blog/regulation-industry/the-trading-dead-the-zombie-firms-that-threaten-britain-s-recovery-and-what-to-do-about-them (last accessed 20 August 2021).

paragraph, drawing attention to the material uncertainty as to whether the necessary support will be secured.

2. Debt conversion

Ordinarily, in order for debt-for-debt exchanges to work, the finance documents need to **3.39**
provide a basket of permitted additional senior debt which converting lenders can swap
into. These baskets have commonly been included in US high-yield debt offerings,[42] but
were, until recently, less commonly a feature of the capital structures of UK corporates.

D. Subsequent Failure and Insolvency Filing

As discussed for the US, creditors will be mindful that if the restructuring subsequently fails, **3.40**
and an insolvency filing is made, its terms may be vulnerable to attack under the transaction
avoidance provisions of English law. These were discussed in detail in Chapter 1 but include,
in particular, the concern that any security granted for past indebtedness may be vulnerable
to attack as a preference,[43] transaction at an undervalue,[44] a transaction defrauding creditors,[45] or, in the case of a floating charge, as a vulnerable floating charge.[46]

III. US Exchange Offers

A. Introduction

Out-of-court debt exchange offers are a commonly used tool by US companies experiencing **3.41**
financial distress. Unusual events, such as the global financial crisis of 2007–2008 (and the
recession that followed) and the lockdowns and other social and economic repercussions of
the COVID-19 pandemic, often bring with them an increase in the number of companies
experiencing financial difficulties, resulting in an increase in the number of out-of-court
debt exchange offers.

1. Typical structure

Debt exchange offers are usually initiated by issuers of debt securities or borrowers of bank **3.42**
loans in an attempt to reduce leverage and debt service costs without going through an insolvency proceeding. The typical debt exchange offer will therefore involve an offer by the
borrower to holders of existing debt to issue new debt or equity interests in exchange for
their existing debt. The debt exchange offer will often be made pursuant to an exchange
offer document (which will contain information regarding the issuer, the exchange offer,

---

[42] See Proskauer, 2018 Global High-Yield Bond Study, available at: https://www.proskauer.com/release/proskauer-releases-2018-global-high-yield-bond-study (last accessed 26 January 2021).

[43] Insolvency Act 1986, s 239.

[44] Insolvency Act 1986, s 238; although note that the position here is unclear. Millet J has suggested in *MC Bacon* [1990] BCLC 324 that the grant of security always falls to be considered as a preference and not a transaction at an undervalue but see the comments of Arden J in *Hill v Spread Trustee* [1990] BCC 324.

[45] Insolvency Act 1986, s 423 and *Hill v Spread Trustee* (n 44).

[46] Insolvency Act 1986, s 245.

the new debt or other securities, and other material information) that is prepared by the borrower and disseminated to holders of the debt sought. Response deadlines are specified, and there may be a number of other conditions, such as minimum participation, maximum participation, the availability of associated financing, the completion of other transactions (such as acquisitions), or other customary conditions.[47] A solicitation of consents from holders of the existing debt to modify or strip away entirely the restrictive covenants (and sometimes the collateral, if the debt is secured) applicable to the existing debt is frequently coupled with the debt exchange offer. The economics and form of an offer will generally depend on the goals of the issuer, the ability of the issuer to access the capital markets at the time, the nature and characteristics of the debt holder base (including the prevalence of credit default swaps and other derivatives), and time constraints (which are often imposed by impending maturities).

2. Market trends

3.43   In the US, a wave of very large leveraged buyouts (LBOs) at very high valuations occurred from 2005 to early 2008, fuelled in large part by optimistic business projections, favourable economic conditions, very low interest rates, and a market that was awash in available capital.[48] A similar wave of LBOs occurred after 2009, after the economic recovery from the 2007–2008 financial crisis.[49] While the LBOs that occurred during 2007–2009 generated a wave of restructurings that occurred from 2010 to 2013, the continued low interest rate environment following the financial crisis also facilitated additional highly leveraged LBOs in the years that followed. A typical LBO is financed by a new secured credit facility (usually with a revolving portion and one or more tranches of term loans), new high-yield bonds of various levels of contractual or lien seniority and often existing debt that the equity sponsor was able to retain and 'roll over' into the new capital structure. Because capital has typically been plentiful in recent years, although LBO debt instruments are not rated investment grade and therefore typically have strong restrictive covenants, restrictive covenants in the debt instruments incurred in LBOs are usually very loose, as prominent equity sponsors have been largely able to dictate terms to the market, and debt investors are typically not able to request changes to the covenant packages. These same equity sponsors are often also able to negotiate for 'covenant-lite' credit agreements, which contain mostly 'incurrence-based' covenants (i.e. covenants that only restrict the company when it wishes to undertake some action) that are similar to those in the LBO high-yield debt securities and contain very few or even none of the traditional maintenance-based financial covenants that are typical

---

[47] In the case of a credit agreement debt that is the subject of a debt exchange offer, this information may be set forth in a 'lender presentation' that provides a high-level view of the business and the exchange offer and a 'marketing term sheet' that provides more detail with respect to the new debt or equity being offered.

[48] See Robert J Samuelson, 'The Private Equity Boom', *The Washington Post*, 15 March 2007, available at <http://www.washingtonpost.com/wp-dyn/content/article/2007/03/14/AR2007031402177.html>   ('[B]uyouts   are booming again ... Nine of the 10 largest buyouts have occurred in the past year'); 'Private Equity Fund Raising Up In 2007: Report', *Reuters*, 8 January 2008, available at <http://www.reuters.com/article/idUSBNG14655120080 108> (detailing ongoing increases in US private equity fundraising for buyouts).

[49] See Robert J Samuelson, 'The Private Equity Boom', *The Washington Post*, 15 March 2007, available at <http://www.washingtonpost.com/wp-dyn/content/article/2007/03/14/AR2007031402177.html>   ('[B]uyouts   are booming again ... Nine of the 10 largest buyouts have occurred in the past year'); 'Private Equity Fund Raising Up In 2007: Report', *Reuters*, 8 January 2008, available at <http://www.reuters.com/article/idUSBNG14655120080 108> (detailing ongoing increases in US private equity fundraising for buyouts).

Limitations on dividend-blocking provisions applicable to subsidiaries, limitations on asset sales, change of control provisions, financial reporting requirements, and merger/consolidation/asset sale covenants.

for senior credit facilities. Finally, because of the sheer size of some of the LBOs, the targets were often formerly investment-grade companies whose existing debt securities contained very few restrictive covenants. The relative lack of covenants in the existing debt securities often permit equity sponsors to retain the existing debt securities (which had the very attractive interest rates and long maturities that are common for investment-grade securities) rather than refinancing them, structuring the new LBO debt around the very limited covenants.

The US debt capital markets were very tight during the second half of 2008 through much **3.44** of the first quarter of 2009, so many of these 2005–2008 LBO companies found it difficult to refinance their existing debt, some of which was approaching scheduled maturities in 2010 or 2011. Simultaneously, as a result of the economic downturn that began in late 2007, a number of these companies became unable to service their LBO debt as their businesses suffered economically. Exacerbating this trend was the natural tendency of vendors and suppliers to tighten credit terms during periods of financial uncertainty, further reducing available liquidity. These factors, taken together with the relative laxity of the restrictive covenants and the nature of the capital structure of a number of the LBO companies (which made debt exchange offers easier to structure), contributed to a wave of very large debt exchange offers that were launched and closed during 2008 and 2009 as the debt capital markets were largely closed during that period.[50] There was a significant resurgence in the US debt capital markets during the second half of 2009, which continued fairly steadily into 2015 (albeit with some periodic interruptions brought on by economic setbacks and other similar events). As the economy improved between 2009 and 2015 and interest rates remained low, proceeds of new issuances of high-yield debt in US markets rose from US$146 billion to $311 billion,[51] although in certain periods (such as late 2011) there was considerable execution risk or issuances sometimes priced wide of the expected range due to market conditions. These trends continued between 2015 and early 2020, as a continued low interest rate environment, combined with the further expansion of the participation of alternative money managers in the debt markets, caused the demand for debt investments to often exceed supply.[52] During the time leading up to the COVID-19 pandemic, conventional refinancings of close-in maturities were often available, as investors reached for yield in a low interest rate environment. Nevertheless, while capital was generally available due to the low interest rate environment, companies in certain sectors did experience financial distress. For example, from 2014 through 2019, oil and gas industry companies with high-yield debt experienced significant financial distress as oil prices fluctuated and turned to increasingly aggressive tactics to address their capital structures.[53] 'Brick and mortar' retailers

---

[50] See, e.g., 'Realogy Announces Commencement of Exchange Offer', *Business Wire*, 9 January 2008, available at <http://www.businesswire.com/news/home/20080109006011/en/Realogy-Announces-Commencement-Excha nge-Offer>; Aleksandrs Rozens, 'GMAC Plans Exchange Offer, Prompting Downgrade', *Investment Dealers' Digest*, 31 October 2008, ('GMAC … said it plans to commence a "private offer to exchange a significant amount of its outstanding indebtedness for a reduced principal amount of new indebtedness"'); *Harrah's Finishes Debt Exchange Offer*—DealBook Blog—NYTimes.com, available at <http://dealbook.blogs.nytimes.com/2008/12/22/harrahs-finishes-debt-exchange-offer/> (22 December 2008, 16:22 EST).

[51] See, e.g., SIFMA Statistics, available at <http://www.sifma.org/research/statistics.aspx>.

[52] See Jim Baird, 'Alternatives for a yield-starved world', 17 June 2021, available at https://www.worth.com/alter natives-for-a-yield-starved-world/.

[53] See 'Number of financially distressed oil, gas companies increasing: S&P Ratings', *S&P Global*, 16 July 2019, available at <https://www.spglobal.com/platts/en/market-insights/latest-news/natural-gas/071619-num

(in the United States in particular) experienced sector-wide distress during the latter half of the 2010s, as changes in technology and cultural patterns caused a shift in the way customers purchased retail goods.[54] These changes led to a spate of both in-court and out-of-court restructurings, including those of Sears, Toys"R"Us, and Neiman Marcus, even before the pandemic occurred.[55]

3.45 A number of out-of-court debt restructuring transactions during the period from 2013 to 2018 involved what were arguably 'tailored' credit events for purposes of credit-default swaps. Certain companies and lenders entered into highly creative debt restructuring transactions that contemplated the intentional triggering of credit events (usually in the form of a failure-to-pay) under credit-default swaps referencing the company's debt instruments, often to the benefit of the lenders participating in the debt restructuring transactions. The resulting settlement of such credit-default swaps would then provide additional value to the lenders participating in the debt restructuring without requiring additional cash or other consideration to be paid by the company. In one instance, the transaction resulted in litigation (which was subsequently settled).[56] In response to market uncertainty engendered by these transactions, in July 2019, the International Swaps and Derivatives Association implemented amendments to the 2014 ISDA Credit Derivatives Definitions that were designed to address 'narrowly tailored credit events'.[57]

3.46 The COVID-19 pandemic has had a profound effect on the debt capital markets. The pandemic and the measures implemented to respond to it accelerated many of the trends (such as shopping online and working from home) that were already present in various sectors of the economy (not just retail but commercial real estate and energy in particular) and caused a number of otherwise healthy companies to experience financial distress (particularly in the restaurant and travel and leisure sectors).[58] Such financial distress usually took the form of liquidity concerns due to the disruptions to revenue that accompanied the lockdowns

ber-of-financially-distressed-oil-gas-companies-increasing-sampp-ratings>; see also Sridhar Natarajan, 'Venoco Bonds Drop as Driller Adds Secured Debt to Repay Revolver', *Bloomberg Business*, 6 April 2015, available at <http://www.bloomberg.com/news/articles/2015-04-06/venoco-bonds-drop-as-driller-adds-secured-debt-to-repay-revolver>.

[54] Suzanne Kapner, 'Brick-and-Mortar Stores Are Shuttering at a Record Pace', *Wall Street Journal*, 21 April 2017, available at <https://www.wsj.com/articles/brick-and-mortar-stores-are-shuttering-at-a-record-pace-1492818818>.

[55] See *In re Sears Holdings Corporation et al*, Case No. 18-23538-RDD (Bankr SDNY 2018); *In re Toys"R"Us, Inc., et al.*, Case 17-34665-KLP (Bankr ED Va 2017); Neiman Marcus Group LTD LLC (Form 8-k) (11 June 2019) (disclosing completion of recapitalization transaction which, among other things, extended the maturities of the company's existing debt obligations by three years).

[56] Complaint, *Solus Alternative Asset Management LP v GSO Capital Partners L.P. et al*, Case No. 18-cv-00232 (LTS) (SDNY Jan 11, 2018); see also Andrew Scurria, 'Blackstone Stands Down on Hovnanian Swaps Wager', *Wall Street Journal*, 30 May 2018, available at <https://www.wsj.com/articles/blackstone-stands-down-on-hovnanian-swaps-wager-1527722945>.

[57] '2019 Narrowly Tailored Credit Event Supplement to the 2014 ISDA Credit Derivatives Definitions', *International Swaps and Derivatives Association, Inc.*, 15 July 2019, available at <https://www.isda.org/a/KDqME/Final-NTCE-Supplement.pdf>.

[58] See 'The Travel Industry Turned Upside Down', *Skift Research*, September 2020, available at https://www.mckinsey.com/~/media/mckinsey/industries/travel%20logistics%20and%20infrastructure/our%20insights/the%20travel%20industry%20turned%20upside%20down%20insights%20analysis%20and%20actions%20for%20travel%20executives/the-travel-industry-turned-upside-down-insights-analysis-and-actions-for-travel-executives.pdf (discussing the pandemic's effect on the travel industry); Suzanne Kapner, 'Coronavirus Has Shut Stores, and Retailers Are Running Out of Time', 8 April 2020, *Wall Street Journal*, <https://www.wsj.com/articles/coronavirus-has-shut-stores-and-retailers-are-running-out-of-time-11586338200>.

and other pandemic-related responses or the spectre of financial maintenance covenant breaches that would likely result over time.[59]

As a result, in the early months of the COVID-19 pandemic, when uncertainty was great, **3.47** a number of companies entered into various transactions to respond to the threat posed. Some companies opted to issue additional equity or debt (often with government backing, such as was available under the US CARES Act, the UK Coronavirus Business Interruption Loan schemes, and similar legislation) to improve their liquidity while obtaining waivers of their financial maintenance covenants.[60] While not true in every case, there was a tendency for lenders to readily grant financial maintenance covenant waivers in the short to medium term, perhaps due to a general unwillingness by lenders to suddenly catapult large swaths of companies into insolvency proceedings as a result of circumstances that were unprecedented at the time.[61] Markets reacted accordingly, however, and investors in the new debt and equity issued by these companies appeared to evaluate the business risks of each company under the circumstances. They made what amounted to a 'bet', first as to whether the company would be able to eventually overcome the challenges posed by COVID-19 through operational changes and, second, as to whether (and when) a vaccine or cure would eventually emerge. A number of companies had to undergo out-of-court restructurings to obtain longer-term covenant relief and additional liquidity, often provided by existing lenders not wishing to put the borrower through a bankruptcy process that could materially and adversely affect the business of the company. Other companies (often because they were already distressed pre-COVID) were forced to undergo in-court insolvency proceedings.

This dynamic is illustrated in the behaviour of investors in travel companies. Investors in **3.48** the new debt and equity of leisure travel companies in the first few months of the pandemic generally made the calculation that people going on holiday would do whatever it took to go away, particularly if a vaccine or cure made holidays safer. As a result, a number of leisure travel companies that were issuing secured debt with very high rates of return and equity at significant discounts to their pre-COVID trading prices in April and May 2020 were issuing additional debt and equity on much more favourable terms after November 2020, when successful vaccines were announced, reflecting that the 'new post-COVID normal' would be not too different from the 'old pre-COVID normal'. The same dynamic was not prevalent for business travel companies, since, in many cases, business travellers want to avoid

---

[59] See, e.g., Declaration of Ramiro Alfonsin Balza in Support of First Day Motions and Applications in Compliance with Local Rule 1007-2 at 4, *In re LATAM Airlines Group S.A., et al*, Case No. 20-11254 (JLG) (Bankr SDNY May 26, 2020) (stating that chapter 11 filings were precipitated by COVID-19's impact on business operations and revenue); Declaration of Jamere Jackson in Support of Debtors' Petitions and Requests for First Day Relief, *In re The Hertz Corporation, et al*, Case No. 20-11218 (MFW) (Bankr D Del May 24, 2020) (discussing liquidity crisis brought on by a 73 per cent revenue decrease in April 2020 compared to April 2019, and default under debt documents that primarily arose as a result of the pandemic's effect on the company's operations).

[60] See David Caleb Mutua, 'Corporate America Hunkers Down After Pandemic-Fueled Debt Binge', *Bloomberg*, 31 July 2020, available at <https://www.bloomberg.com/news/articles/2020-07-31/corporate-america-hunkers-down-after-pandemic-fueled-debt-binge> (stating that '[b]lue-chip U.S. companies are slowing down on borrowing after months of massive bond sales' and investment grade companies 'sold more than $1.2 trillion of U.S. bonds this year [as of July 2020] … more than they sold for each of 2018 and 2019').

[61] See Matthew Schernecke and Kristen V. Campana, 'INSIGHT: Covid-19 Credit Concessions Rely on Give-and-Take', *Bloomberg Law*, 22 September 2020, available at <https://news.bloomberglaw.com/daily-labor-report/insight-covid-19-credit-concessions-rely-on-give-and-take> (stating that in light of the COVID-19 pandemic, lenders have been willing to make various concessions to borrowers including by 'modify[ing] the financial covenants by either loosening the actual required financial covenant levels or revising the terms of the core definitions.').

business travel whenever possible, and video conferencing services often provide acceptable substitutes, reflecting uncertainty as to what the 'new normal' would be for this sector. The same type of calculation often determined the path each company would be able to take to face the challenges posed by COVID-19.

3.49   A further trend that was accelerated by the COVID pandemic was that creditors of distressed companies more often proposed debt restructuring transactions that advantaged one group of creditors over another, a phenomenon often referred to as 'creditor-on-creditor violence'. Where most debt restructurings before 2019 and 2020 were made available to all holders of a series of debt, a number of 2020-vintage out-of-court restructurings involved restructuring transactions in which one group of creditors provided additional capital on a 'super-priority' basis that was senior to the existing debt and were thus able to 'roll-up' their existing debt to super-priority status.[62] The explicit calculation by such creditors was that by rolling-up their existing debt to super-priority status, the value of that rolled-up debt would increase, since not all holders of existing debt would be afforded the ability to roll up, and the rolled-up debt would be effectively senior to the remaining existing debt. This calculation created an incentive for participating creditors to exclude as many other creditors as possible from the deal while still obtaining the necessary majority consents for the deal, since the greater the amount of debt excluded from the deal, the better the value gain would be for the creditors that were included in the deal.

3.50   Furthermore, these transactions that pitted one group of creditors against another were often done at the behest of the company, which stood to benefit from the two groups of creditors actively bidding against each other. It appears that many companies and equity sponsors realized that if they engaged in an action that was potentially harmful to all creditors (or a large proportion of them), the creditors would tend to unite with one another (in spite of their potentially divergent interests) to confront the company and the equity sponsor.[63] The active encouragement of creditor-on-creditor violence has become a tool for companies and sponsors to obtain the results they want, as it may forestall the formation of a "united front" of creditors. Where there are multiple layers (e.g., first lien, second lien, unsecured, etc.) in a capital structure, the potential for creditor-on-creditor dynamics is increased, particularly if a number of large creditors have significant holdings in more than one layer of the capital structure and may seek favourable treatment in a restructuring

---

[62] See 'TriMark USA Enters Into Agreement with Lenders on Liquidity Enhancing Transaction', *TriMark USA*, 15 September 2020, available at <https://www.trimarkusa.com/news-room/news/trimark-usa-enters-into-agreement-with-lenders-on>; 'Serta Simmons Bedding Enters Into Agreement with Majority of Lenders on Deleveraging and Liquidity Enhancing Transaction', *PRNewswire*, 8 June 2020, available at <https://www.prnewswire.com/news-releases/serta-simmons-bedding-enters-into-agreement-with-majority-of-lenders-on-deleveraging-and-liquidity-enhancing-transaction-301072368.html>; 'Boardriders Discloses Recapitalization Negotiated Among Certain Term Lenders, French Government, Sponsor; Transaction Structure Includes Priming Term Loans With New Money, Rollup Components', *Reorg*, 1 September 2020, available at <https://app.reorg.com/v3#/items/intel/11373?item_id=116301>. See generally William Cohan, 'Lender civil warfare pierces credit euphoria', *Financial Times*, 18 November 2020, available at <https://www.ft.com/content/9be0794a-f107-449f-845c-edf07ae94fbf> (discussing TriMark, Serta, and Boardriders transactions).

[63] 'Neiman Marcus Group LTD LLC Reports Fourth Quarter and Fiscal Year 2018 Results', *Business Wire*, 18 September 2018, available at <https://www.sec.gov/Archives/edgar/data/1358651/000115752318001944/a51868055_ex991.htm> (disclosing organizational change whereby unrestricted, non-guarantor MyTheresa business was moved directly under company's ultimate parent, creating dispute with creditors); Reshmi Basu and Yifan Yu, 'PetSmart Moves Stake in Chewy.com, Loan Agent Hires Counsel', *Debtwire*, 4 June 2018, available at <https://www.debtwire.com/info/petsmart-moves-stake-chewycom-loan-agent-hires-counsel>.

for their more junior holdings in order for the company to gain their support for a restructuring of their more senior holdings.

A number of 2020 restructurings that pitted creditors against other creditors and the company or its equity sponsors resulted in litigation by the 'losing' creditor group against the company and the 'winning' creditor group.[64] The frequency of these litigations appeared to decrease through the first half of 2021, perhaps as a result of the deterrent effects such litigations have had on more aggressive transactions and perhaps as a result of market participants waiting to see the results of the ongoing litigations. It is also possible that the vaccine-related recovery of late 2020 made out-of-court restructurings of the type that would engender such litigation less necessary due to the increased availability of capital and improvements in companies' business operations, and once economic distress increases, additional similar transactions could occur, engendering additional litigations. **3.51**

B. Reasons for Doing a Debt Exchange Offer

The motivations of a company to do a debt exchange offer can vary. First, the company may wish to address an upcoming maturity in its capital structure by offering to issue new debt that matures later in exchange for the earlier-maturing existing debt. Second, the company may wish to deleverage itself by offering to issue the new debt in exchange for the existing debt at a discount to its face amount. Third, a company may be faced with impending financial maintenance covenant defaults and may need to obtain amendments from its lenders, offering a superior debt instrument in exchange for the existing one as an inducement to lenders to consent to the necessary amendments, often using an 'exit consent' mechanism.[65] Fourth, a company may need additional liquidity and may issue new debt for cash with a 'super' priority and, as an incentive to participate in the new money financing, offer to 'roll-up' the existing debt of lenders who agree to participate. **3.52**

A debt exchange offer is often an attractive possibility for a company that is unable to access the capital markets to refinance upcoming maturities. As noted above, a number of companies used debt exchange offers to address upcoming maturities without raising new funds and to take advantage of the fact that their debt was trading below its face amount, often at **3.53**

---

[64] Complaint, *Audax Credit Opportunities Offshore Ltd., et al v TMK Hawk Parent, Corp., et al* (Index No. 0565123/2020) (NY Sup Ct Nov 7, 2020); Complaint, *ICG Global Loan Fund 1 DAC, et al v Boardriders, Inc., et al* (Index No.: 655175/2020) (NY Sup Ct Oct 9, 2020); Complaint, *North Star Debt Holdings, L.P., et al v Serta Simmons Bedding, LLC et al.*, Index No. 652243/2020 (NY Sup Ct June 11, 2020).

[65] The availability of the 'exit consent' mechanism is well settled with respect to debt securities. See, e.g., *In re Loral Space and Communications Inc*, 2008 WL 4293781 (Del Ch 2008) (declining to prohibit what might have been deemed a non-pro rata consent payment to a holder of bonds that was a controlling stockholder, where the indenture was silent on the topic); *Katz v Oak Industries, Inc*, 508 A 2d 873 (Del Ch 1986) (upholding the legality of the consent payment against plaintiff bondholders' challenge that the offer of consideration for bondholder consents violated the implied covenant of good faith and fair dealing); *Kass v Eastern Airlines, Inc*, CA No 8700 (Del Ch 14 Nov 1986) ('[t]he fact that the offer in this case is one made publicly to all voters on the same terms ... precludes ... a conclusion that it disenfranchises any voter or group of voters ...'). Nevertheless, such a mechanism may be quite novel in the credit agreement context.

distressed levels,[66] and distressed companies continue to use these tactics to address their capital structures.[67]

3.54   Companies in financial distress often require high levels of lender participation in out-of-court debt exchange offers, in many cases requiring participation by lenders representing more than 90 or 95 per cent of the outstanding debt. As a result, relatively few 'hold-out' lenders who refuse to participate in the exchange offer could cause the exchange offer to fail. An out-of-court debt exchange offer may therefore be accompanied by a solicitation with respect to a prepackaged chapter 11 plan, in case the debt exchange offer fails to achieve the requisite level of support. In such cases, the exchange offer document will be accompanied by a disclosure statement with respect to the proposed prepackaged chapter 11 case.

C. US Securities Law Considerations

3.55   A number of US securities laws are applicable to debt exchange offers made into the United States or to US investors. The two principal regulations are the US Securities Exchange Act of 1934 ('the Exchange Act') (which generally governs the conduct of existing security holders and transactions in the US securities markets with respect to existing securities) and the US Securities Act of 1933 ('the Securities Act') (which generally governs the offer and sale of new securities by issuers and their affiliates into the US securities markets). To the extent a debt exchange offer involves a 'tender offer' (as discussed in more detail below) to US holders of debt securities, the Exchange Act and related rules and regulations will apply. To the extent that a debt exchange offer involves the issuance of new debt, equity, or other securities to holders of existing debt, the Securities Act and related rules and regulations will apply.

3.56   Bank loans are currently not considered 'securities' for the purposes of the Securities Act or the Exchange Act. As a result, an offer of securities to holders of bank loans would implicate the Securities Act but not the Exchange Act. Conversely, an offer of bank loans to holders of securities would implicate the Exchange Act but not the Securities Act. The anti-fraud rules under the various US securities laws (principally, Rule 10b-5) would apply to any transaction involving securities. Nevertheless, where only bank loans and no securities are involved in a transaction, common law and industry standard anti-fraud principles would apply.

---

[66]   See, e.g., 'Ford Distressed Debt Exchange Likely, Analyst Says', *Reuters*, 2 February 2009, available at <http://uk.reuters.com/article/idUK171977+02-Feb-2009+RTRS20090202> ('"We believe there is little chance that Ford's unsecured notes will be paid back at par and expect the company to announce a distressed debt exchange in the coming months, along with GM, in an effort to reduce its level of unsecured debt as it piles on secured debt", according to a report issued on Friday'); Rozens, *supra* n 51 ('Moody's warned that "there is a possibility that GMAC's offering will be a distressed exchange. Distressed exchanges have default-like implications for affected creditors because the changes to principal amount, tenor, coupon, and/or priority can cause debt holders to recognize economic loss"').

[67]   Natarajan (n 53); see also Matthew Fuller, 'Distressed Debt: Colt Defense Extends Bond Swap Deadline As Just 5% Join', *Forbes*, 12 May 2015, available at <http://www.forbes.com/sites/spleverage/2015/05/12/distressed-debt-colt-defense-extends-bond-swap-deadline-as-just-5-join>.

1. Considerations under the Securities Exchange Act of 1934—tender offer rules and anti-fraud provisions

(a) Regulation 14E

Because a debt exchange offer is typically made to most holders of a subject security for pre-set **3.57** consideration and is usually made publicly for a substantial portion of the outstanding securities and is subject to time limits for response, a debt exchange offer is generally viewed as a 'tender offer' for purposes of the Exchange Act. The test for the existence of a tender offer is set forth in Wellman v Dickinson as an eight-factor test:

(1) 'active and widespread solicitation of public shareholders for the shares of an issuer;

(2) solicitation made for a substantial percentage of the issuer's stock;

(3) offer to purchase made at a premium over the prevailing market price;

(4) terms of the offer are firm rather than negotiable;

(5) offer contingent on the tender of a fixed number of shares, often subject to a fixed maximum number to be purchased;

(6) offer open only a limited period of time;

(7) offeree subjected to pressure to sell his stock;' and

(8) 'whether the public announcements of a purchasing program concerning the target company precede or accompany rapid accumulation of large amounts of the target company's securities'.[68]

Under the Wellman analysis, 'the absence of one particular factor ... is not necessarily fatal' for a **3.58** purchase of securities to be found to be a tender offer.[69] However, market participants generally treat a debt exchange offer as a tender offer for purposes of the Wellman eight-factor test.

All tender offers (except certain tender offers conducted by foreign private issuers, as dis- **3.59** cussed below) are subject to Regulation 14E under the Exchange Act, whether initiated by the issuer or a third party.[70] In addition, if the debt security that is subject to the tender offer is a convertible security, the debt exchange offer will also be subject to the equity tender offer rules such as Regulation 14D or Rule 13e-4 under the Exchange Act, which govern tender offers for equity securities by issuers and third parties, respectively.[71] In addition, if the debt exchange offer is reasonably likely to result in the delisting or deregistration of a class of equity securities registered under the Exchange Act, Rule 13e-3 under the Exchange Act will also apply.[72]

---

[68] *Wellman v Dickinson*, 475 F Supp 783, 823–24 (SDNY 1979).

[69] Ibid.

[70] Section 14E of the Exchange Act prohibits untrue statements of material fact or material omissions in connection with any tender offer. Securities Exchange Act of 1934 § 14E, 15 USC § 78a, § 78n(e) (2009). SEC Rules 14e-1–14e-8 implement Regulation 14E, heavily regulating tender offers as 'a means reasonably designed to prevent fraudulent, deceptive or manipulative acts or practices'. Regulation 14E, 17 CFRCFR § 240.14e-1 et seq (Sec Exch Comm'n 2009).

[71] Rule 13e-4 will govern a tender offer conducted by the issuer. Tender offers by issuers, 17 CFR § 240.13e-4 (Sec Exch Comm'n 2009). Regulation 14D will govern a tender offer being conducted by a party other than the issuer. Regulation 14D, 17 CFR § 240.14d-1 et seq (Sec Exch Comm'n 2009). Certain tender offers for convertible securities may also need to consider the requirements of the proxy rules in Regulation 14A.

[72] See Going private transactions by certain issuers or their affiliates, 17 CFR § 240.13e-3 (Sec Exch Comm'n 2009) (bringing under the rubric of Rule 13E, inter alia, any solicitation 'of any proxy, consent or authorization of, or a distribution ... of information statements to [any equity holder] by the issuer ... in connection with: a merger, consolidation, reclassification, recapitalization, reorganization or similar corporate transaction ... [causing] any class of securities of the issuer which is ... listed on a national security exchange ... to be [delisted from] any national security exchange ...').

3.60   Certain foreign private issuers under US security laws may be exempt from some of the above requirements governing tender offers. The 'Tier I' exemption under Rule 14d-1(c) of the Exchange Act and Rule 802 of Regulation S of the Securities Act applies where US holders of a foreign private issuer hold 10 per cent or less of the issuer's securities. When the Tier I exemption applies, the tender offer is exempt from substantially all US tender offer regulation, including most of Regulation 14E, all of Regulation 14D, and in certain cases the Securities Act does not apply (such that securities offered as consideration in the exchange do not need to be registered). If US holders hold more than 10 per cent but less than 40 per cent of a foreign private issuer's securities, the 'Tier II' exemption applies, providing limited relief from Regulations 14E and 14D.

3.61   Generally, Regulation 14E governs the conduct of all equity and debt tender offers. The most significant portion of Regulation 14E is Rule 14e-1,[73] which, among other things:

- requires any tender offer to remain open at least 20 business days after the date the offer is first published or sent to security holders;
- requires that an offer remain open at least 10 business days after any increase or decrease in price or percentage of securities sought;[74]
- requires prompt payment for tendered securities after an offer expires; and
- requires that if an open tender offer is to be extended, it must be extended by press release or other public announcement prior to certain specified deadlines.[75]

3.62   As a result of the requirements of the Exchange Act, most debt exchange offers will remain open for at least 20 business days after commencement, although issuers may use various techniques to try to effectively shorten the amount of time necessary to complete the tender offer. The primary technique used by issuers is an 'early tender/early consent period' of 10 business days (as described further in para 3.65 below). In addition, under the Securities and Exchange Commission (SEC) no-action guidance published in January 2015,[76] for certain refinancing exchange offers, a five-business-day tender offer period may be used (as described further in para 3.70 below).

(b) The offer document and anti-fraud rules

3.63   In addition to Regulation 14E, because debt exchange offers involve the issuance and sale of a security in exchange for another security, they are subject to the anti-fraud provisions of the Exchange Act, including Rule 10b-5. Section 10(b) and Rule 10b-5 of the Exchange Act are the primary provisions under which injured parties seek in private actions to recover damages for fraud. Section 10(b) of the Exchange Act makes it unlawful to use or employ any 'manipulative or deceptive device or contrivance' in connection with the purchase or

---

[73]   Unlawful tender offer practices, 17 CFR § 240.14e-1 (Sec Exch Comm'n 2009).

[74]   Rule 14e-1(b) does, however, provide that the acceptance for payment of an additional amount of securities not to exceed 2 per cent of the class of securities that is the subject of the tender offer is not an 'increase' in the amount sought for purposes of this requirement. Ibid.

[75]   Rule 14e-1(d) requires that the press release or public announcement be issued not later than (i) 9.00 am Eastern time, on the next business day after the scheduled expiration date of the offer, or (ii) if the class of securities which is the subject of the tender offer is registered on one or more national securities exchanges, the first opening of any one of such exchanges on the next business day after the scheduled expiration date of the offer. Ibid.

[76]   See SEC release, 'Abbreviated Tender or Exchange Offers for Non-Convertible Debt Securities', 23 January 2015, available at <http://www.sec.gov/divisions/corpfin/cf-noaction/2015/abbreviated-offers-debt-securities012 315-sec14.pdf>.

sale of any security. Under Rule 10b-5, any documentation used in connection with an exchange offer must not contain any 'untrue statement of a material fact or omit to state a material fact necessary in order to make the statements made, in the light of the circumstances under which they were made, not misleading'.[77] Therefore, issuers will typically prepare some form of exchange offer document, which will contain all information deemed by the issuer to be material to a prospective participant in the exchange offer, including issuer business and financial disclosure, risk factors, the terms of the offer, the description of the securities being offered, and other material information. For issuers that file public reports with the US Securities and Exchange Commission (the 'SEC'), much of the issuer-related information will be 'incorporated by reference' to those reports. If an exchange offer is subject only to Regulation 14E and not the equity tender offer rules (because it is a tender offer for a non-convertible debt security), beyond the general anti-fraud requirements, Regulation 14E will not specify that the exchange offer document contain any particular items of disclosure, and the offer materials need not be filed with the SEC for review and comment.[78]

It is important to note that the standard for liability under Section 10(b) and Rule 10b-5 **3.64** is substantially higher than that under Section 11 of the Securities Act (described below). A Rule 10b-5 plaintiff must prove existence of the material fraudulent or misleading statement or omission as well as reliance on the fraudulent or misleading statement or omission[79] and resulting injury.[80] In addition to proving the substantive elements of fraud, reliance, and injury, a plaintiff claiming liability under Rule 10b-5 must 'state with particularity facts giving rise to a strong inference that the defendant acted with the required state of mind'.[81] Courts have defined scienter as the intent to defraud, deceive, or manipulate.[82] While scienter includes recklessness (i.e. conduct that involves an extreme departure from standards of ordinary care that presents a danger of misleading a buyer of securities), mere negligence is not sufficient in a cause of action under Rule 10b-5.[83] Those who control, directly or indirectly, persons subject to the Exchange Act are jointly and severally liable to the same extent as the issuer.[84]

---

[77] Employment of manipulative and deceptive devices, 17 CFR § 240.10b-5 (SEC 2009).

[78] Issuers that are public companies should evaluate whether the offer document contains material nonpublic information regarding the issuer. If so, the dissemination of the offer document may trigger simultaneous public disclosure requirements under Regulation FD.

[79] See *Basic Inc v Levinson*, 485 US 224, 243 (1988) (holding that 'reliance is an element of a Rule 10b-5 cause of action').

[80] See *Binder v Gillespie*, 184 F 3d 1059, 1065 (9th Cir 1999) ('The causation requirement in Rule 10b-5 securities fraud cases includes "both transaction causation, that the violations in question caused the plaintiff to engage in the transaction, and loss causation, that the misrepresentations or omissions caused the harm"' (citing *McGonigle v Combs*, 968 F 2d 810, 820 (9th Cir 1992)).

[81] Private Securities Litigation Reform Act of 1995 § 21D(b)(2), 15 USC § 78u-4(b)(2) (2009).

[82] See, e.g., *Ernst & Ernst v Hochfelder*, 425 US 185, 193 (1976) (holding that a private cause of action for damages will not lie under § 10(b) and Rule 10b-5 in the absence of any allegation of scienter, ie intent to deceive, manipulate, or defraud on the defendant's part).

[83] See *In re Vantive Corp Sec Litig*, 283 F 3d 1079, 1085 (9th Cir 2002) ('[T]he complaint must allege that the defendant made false or misleading statements either intentionally or with deliberate recklessness or, if the challenged representation is a forward looking statement, with actual knowledge ... that the statement was false or misleading' (internal citation omitted)).

[84] See Exchange Act, s 20(e), establishing liability for those who control persons subject to the Exchange Act, as amended by the Dodd-Frank Act in 2010 to expand the required state of mind from merely knowing acts to include reckless acts which aid or abet violations of the Exchange Act. However, a party that assists in the drafting and dissemination of a misleading statement has been held to not have 'made' the statement, and is not subject to primary liability under Rule 10b-5. *Janus Capital Group, Inc v First Derivative Traders*, 131 S Ct 2296 (2011).

(c) Early consent/early tender deadlines

3.65   As noted above, tender offers, including debt exchange offers, are generally required by Rule 14e-1 to remain open for at least 20 business days. Nevertheless, it is widely accepted market practice for issuers to set an 'early consent deadline' or an 'early tender deadline' of 10 business days after commencement followed by a final deadline after the full 20 business days.[85] For reference, we refer to these debt tender or exchange offers as '10/20 business day debt tender offers'. In the case of an exchange offer with respect to all of the outstanding bonds of a series that is coupled with a consent solicitation, the holder of a bond that is tendered is required to also consent to the removal of all or most of the restrictive covenants applicable to the bond. In the case of an exchange offer without a consent solicitation, the holder of the bond is asked to tender prior to the early tender deadline.

3.66   Holders who fail to tender into the 10/20 business day debt tender offer prior to the early deadline will receive an amount of total consideration that is somewhat less than the amount of total consideration that will be paid to holders who do tender into the offer prior to the early deadline. Usually, the difference in consideration, which the issuer will call a 'consent fee' (if there is a consent solicitation involved) or an 'early tender premium' (if not) will not be more than $50 per $1,000 principal amount of securities tendered.[86] Holders will not be permitted to withdraw tendered securities after the early deadline has passed. If a consent solicitation is involved, once the requisite level of consents has been received, the issuer and the indenture trustee will promptly enter into a supplemental indenture (which will contain the modifications consented to) that will become 'effective' immediately upon execution, although the actual modifications will not become 'operative' until the tendered bonds are accepted and paid for by the offeror.[87]

3.67   While there are no specific SEC rules permitting the 10/20 business day debt tender offer structure, such structure has become generally accepted as market practice on the basis of informal guidance by the SEC staff, and most debt tender and exchange offers use this structure. Issuers adopt the 10/20 business day debt tender offer structure for a number of reasons, including:

---

[85]   The same structure may be adopted in a cash tender offer for debt securities as well.

[86]   For example, the total exchange consideration per $1,000 of existing debt securities tendered may be $750 of new securities if the existing debt securities are tendered after the early consent period and $800 of new securities if they are tendered before the early consent period ($750 of tender consideration and a $50 consent fee). Consent fees or early tender premiums have generally ranged from $30 to $50 per $1,000 principal amount of securities tendered. See, e.g., 'McClatchy Announces Debt Tender Offer and Consent Solicitation', 27 January 2010, available at <http://www.mcclatchy.com/2010/01/27/2308/mcclatchy-announces-debt-tender.html>, 'Bank of America announces commencement of Cash Tender Offer for MBIA Notes', 13 November 2013, available at <http://newsr oom.bankofamerica.com/press-release/corporate-and-financial-news/bank-america-announces-commencem ent-cash-tender-offer-mbi>.

[87]   The reason for this mechanism is that most US indentures contain the following provision: 'Until an amendment, supplement or waiver becomes effective, a consent to it by a Holder of a Note is a continuing consent by the Holder of a Note and every subsequent Holder of a Note or portion of a Note that evidences the same debt as the consenting Holder's Note, even if notation of the consent is not made on any Note. However, any such Holder of a Note or subsequent Holder of a Note may revoke the consent as to its Note if the Trustee receives written notice of revocation before the date the waiver, supplement or amendment becomes effective. An amendment, supplement or waiver becomes effective in accordance with its terms and thereafter binds every Holder'. The mechanism is designed to prevent revocation of the consent of the bondholder after the supplemental indenture is executed and 'effective' (even though its provisions are not 'operative' until the tendered bonds are accepted and paid for).

- increasing the speed of the exchange offer, since most bondholders will tender prior to the early deadline in order to receive the maximum amount of consideration, thus facilitating the issuer's contemplated refinancing or restructuring;
- giving the issuer an earlier view of the certainty of the outcome, which may aid the completion of other transactions conditioned on completion of the exchange offer;
- if there is an associated consent solicitation, adding a coercive element to the exchange offer, since any securities that are not tendered will no longer have the benefit of restrictive covenants (or perhaps collateral) as a result of the successful consent solicitation; and
- significantly decreasing the amount of time bondholders have to organize themselves where the contemplated refinancing or restructuring may be contentious.

The significance of the last of the above-described motivations for the early deadline cannot **3.68** be underestimated. As a practical matter, for US bondholders, the very act of tendering bonds can be a significant administrative exercise. For many bondholders, because of administrative delays imposed by custodian banks,[88] the process can take several business days, effectively making the early deadline only seven to eight business days after commencement. Furthermore, the tender offer documents in 10/20 business day debt tender offers are often not available in readable form immediately at commencement, and effectively organizing bondholders can take several days. An issuer may have a large incentive to prevent organization of bondholder groups, particularly where speed is required and the issuer wishes to avoid negotiation of the terms of the new securities with bondholders.[89] In response, it has become common practice in the US for bondholders to take the precautionary step of having regular outside counsel review the debt documents of companies they believe may be 'ripe' for a debt restructuring and also preemptively contact other significant bondholders to organize an ad hoc bondholder committee in anticipation of a debt restructuring.

Certain exchange offers will be structured to permit early settlement of the exchange offer **3.69** soon after expiration of the 10-business-day early deadline. Under such a structure, bondholders who meet the early deadline for tenders will receive their new securities shortly after the early deadline, and the supplemental indenture to modify the existing debt covenants will go into effect at the time of such payment. In addition, recently, it has become accepted market practice that a tender offer for only a portion of a series of debt securities, commonly referred to as a 'partial tender offer', may be subject to early settlement at the 10 business day early deadline, and the proration of tenders in that partial tender offer can occur based on bonds tendered as of that early deadline. To the extent that bonds equalling or exceeding the amount sought in the partial tender offer have already been tendered as of the early deadline, any bonds tendered after the early deadline will not be accepted. In some cases, the issuer may choose to extend the deadline for early tenders beyond the 10 business

---

[88] These delays date from an earlier time period when instructions were given using signed paper forms and tenders were made using signed paper letters of transmittal. Currently, most tender or consent instructions are processed electronically through DTC.

[89] It should be noted, however, that notwithstanding the early deadlines, to the extent a sufficiently large group of bondholders manages to organize prior to the deadline, the group can often force the issuer to extend the deadline and negotiate, as was the case in the proposed exchange offer by GMAC LLC in November and December of 2008. See Caroline Salas, 'GMAC's Bondholders Want Debt Exchange Terms Amended', *Bloomberg*, 11 December 2008, available at <http://www.bloomberg.com/apps/news?pid=20601009&sid=aHSt6El3hZj4>.

days but may or may not permit withdrawals of tenders after the initial 10-business-day deadline. These structures may be used by issuers to further increase the incentives underlying the exchange offer or to facilitate other financing transactions that would otherwise be prohibited by the covenants being modified.

3.70   In 2015, an abbreviated five-business-day tender offer procedure[90] was authorized by the SEC. The five-business-day tender offer procedure was designed to permit issuers to quickly and efficiently refinance or retire indebtedness without having to wait for a 10- or 20-business-day tender offer period to lapse. In order to prevent the procedure from being used for coercive tender or exchange offers, the abbreviated procedure does not allow early settlement, partial tender offers, consent solicitations, or the issuance of new debt that ranks senior (as to contractual priority, security/lien priority, or structural priority) of the debt sought in the tender offer, and any exchange offer must be for securities with materially identical terms. The five-business-day tender offer procedure appears to have met its stated goals, as the abbreviated procedure has been used successfully by many issuers and has not engendered any significant litigation.

(d) Equity tender offer rules

3.71   If a debt exchange offer is subject to the equity tender offer rules, a number of additional requirements will apply in addition to Regulation 14E and Rule 10b-5, including the requirement for the issuer to file with the SEC a Statement on Schedule TO, which requires the issuer to provide certain rule-specified disclosures, exhibits, and other content relating to the proposed exchange offer and which will be subject to review and comment by the SEC after it is filed.[91] While the SEC has committed to provide comments as promptly as possible to avoid delaying the consummation of the tender offer,[92] the offer may not be consummated until the SEC review process is complete. Furthermore, if comments received from the SEC are deemed to be material, the issuer may be required to recirculate amendment materials or amended and restated offer materials once the comments have been cleared. In addition, the equity tender offer rules contain various limitations as to purchases outside the tender offer, requirements as to the price that may be offered to holders, requirements to make the offer to all holders and procedural rules as to proper commencement, withdrawal rights, reporting of results, amendments, and consummation of the offer.[93] The key disadvantages to being subject to the equity tender offer rules are:

- it is impossible to predict with certainty the duration or substance of an SEC review process, so the expected timing or structure of the offer may be disrupted;
- the equity tender offer rule requiring offers to be made to all holders of a security will preclude the offeror from limiting its offer only to certain classes of investors (such as accredited investors or qualified institutional buyers), and as a result, the exchange offer may be ineligible for exemptions from registration under the Securities Act;

---

[90] See *supra* n 76. For discussion, see, eg, 'SEC Grants No-Action Relief Permitting Five Business Day Debt Tender Offers', *Paul Weiss Client Memorandum*, 24 January 2015, available at <http://www.paulweiss.com/media/2779114/25jan15alert.pdf>.

[91] See Schedule TO, 17 CFR § 240.14d-100 (Sec Exch Comm'n 2009).

[92] See Regulation of Takeovers and Security Holder Communications, Release No 33-7760, 70 SEC Docket 2229 (22 October 1999) ('We are … committed to expediting staff review of exchange offers so that they may compete more effectively with cash tender offers').

[93] See generally Regulation 14D, 17 CFR § 240.14d-1 et seq (Sec Exch Comm'n 2009).

- it is not possible to use the early consent/early tender structure in connection with an equity tender offer (or the associated early settlement mechanic);
- purchases of securities outside the offer by the offeror will generally be prohibited; and
- if the tender offer is subject to a financing condition, the financing condition must be removed at least five business days prior to consummation.[94]

(e) Is there such a thing as a 'creeping tender offer'?

Market participants often ask whether there is such a thing as a 'creeping tender offer'. What they are referring to by this term is a series of related acquisitions of securities by a person or group in the open market that may eventually result in the person or group acquiring ownership over a 'substantial percentage' (as described in prong (3) of the eight-factor Wellman v Dickinson test for the existence of a tender offer) of the relevant securities. A number of market participants have taken the position that any such purchases aggregating more than 30 per cent of the outstanding class would be considered a tender offer. Nevertheless, such a position is perhaps too conservative and simplistic, since it focuses only on one of the eight factors to the exclusion of the others.   **3.72**

A more appropriate approach is to look to the entire eight-factor test, recognizing that while not all eight factors need to be present in order for a tender offer to exist, the presence of only a few factors (or any one factor) will also not necessarily be determinative. For example, a situation in which the issuer approaches privately (with no publicity) a handful of investors who own a substantial portion of the outstanding securities of the relevant class and makes purchases of more than 50 per cent of the outstanding securities of the class from those investors at varying prices, at different times and under differing terms and conditions has been found not to be engaged in a tender offer.[95] Therefore, the answer as to whether there is such a thing as a 'creeping tender offer' is both no and yes. The mere fact of accumulating a large position in a security does not constitute a tender offer, but it is possible that open market purchases of a substantial portion of the relevant security (particularly if a large number of holders are contacted and if other factors cited in the eight-factor test are satisfied) can constitute a tender offer. The inquiry is necessarily fact-specific.   **3.73**

2. Considerations under the US Securities Act of 1933—Issuance of new securities

Section 5 of the Securities Act prohibits an issuer from selling or offering to sell a security unless the offer and sale have been registered under the Securities Act or are otherwise   **3.74**

---

[94] This comment is often made by the SEC in equity tender offers. See, eg, Genentech, Inc, SEC Staff Comments, at 7 (2 March 2009) ('We note that this tender offer is conditioned on Roche obtaining financing to pay for the purchase of tendered shares, and that you had not obtained financing as of the date of the filing of this Schedule TO-T/13E-3. Please be aware that when financing is obtained, the offer must remain open for a sufficient time period (with withdrawal rights) from the date that information about the financing is disseminated to shareholders to allow them to react to this new information. We believe a minimum of five business days would be required under these circumstances'). See also Harrah's Operating Company, Inc, Issuer Response, at para 2 (22 July 2005) ('In response to the Staff's comment, the Company has revised the [offer] ... to specify that the only conditions to the offer are (1) the timely and proper delivery and tender of notes in accordance with the terms of the offer and (2) that the offer must comply with applicable law. The Company has also revised the [offer] to clarify that there is no financing condition to the offer'). Such a condition need not be removed at all in an offer that is subject only to Regulation 14E.

[95] See, e.g., *Corre Opportunities Fund, LP v Emmis Communications Corporation*, 892 F Supp 2d 1076, 1092–94 (SD Ind 31 August 2012).

exempt from registration under the Securities Act.[96] These prohibitions generally apply only to sales in the United States or to 'US Persons' (as defined in the relevant regulations).[97] Because a debt exchange offer involves the offer and sale by the issuer of a new security in exchange for an existing one, a debt exchange offer that is made in the United States or to US investors must either be registered under the Securities Act or exempt from such registration. Because the Securities Act registration process can be a time-consuming one, issuers often opt to make debt exchange offers that are exempt from registration under section 4(a)(2) or section 3(a)(9) of the Securities Act.[98] It should be noted, however, regardless of the issuer's chosen method of compliance with the Securities Act, it must also comply with the Exchange Act.

(a) Registration under the Securities Act

3.75   A debt exchange offer that is registered under the Securities Act will require the filing with the SEC of a registration statement on Form S-4 (or F-4, in the case of a foreign private issuer).[99] The registration statement is a lengthy document that is required to contain financial and other disclosures regarding the issuer, disclosures regarding the exchange offer, a description of the debt securities being offered, and any other information that may be material to an investor considering the exchange offer. Information relating to the issuer is ordinarily required to be set forth in full in the registration statement, but certain issuers that file periodic reports with the SEC may instead incorporate that information by reference to their existing public filings. Once filed, the registration statement is subject to review by the SEC. Although it is possible to commence the exchange offer prior to the time the relevant registration statement is declared effective, the exchange offer cannot be consummated before the review process is complete and the registration statement is declared effective by the SEC.[100] Furthermore, if the SEC review process results in material changes to the

---

[96] Securities Act of 1933 § 5, 15 USC § 77a, § 77e(c) (2009) ('It shall be unlawful ... to sell or offer to buy ... any security, unless a registration statement has been filed ...').

[97] US person, 17 CFR § 230.902(k) (Sec Exch Comm'n 2009). The provisions of Regulation S broadly define a US person to include, inter alia, natural persons resident in the United States, any partnership or corporation organized or incorporated in the United States, any trust whose trustee is a US person, and any agency or branch of a foreign entity located in the United States.

[98] See Securities Act of 1933 § 4(a)(2), 15 USC § 77a, § 77d(2) (2009) ('The provisions of section 77e of this title shall not apply to ... transactions by an issuer not involving any public offering'); Securities Act of 1933 § 3(a)(9), 15 USC § 77a, § 77c(a)(9) (2009) ('The provisions of this subchapter shall not apply to ... any security exchanged by the issuer with its existing security holders exclusively where no commission or other remuneration is paid or given directly or indirectly for soliciting such exchange ...').

[99] See Form S-4, for the registration of securities issued in business combination transactions, 17 CFR § 239.25 (Sec Exch Comm'n 2009); Form F-4, for registration of securities of foreign private issuers issued in certain business combination transactions, 17 CFR § 239.34 (Sec Exch Comm'n 2009).

[100] Prior to December 2008, a registered exchange offer for equity securities or convertible debt securities (which would be subject to the equity tender offer rules contained in Exchange Act Rule 13e-4 or Regulation 14D) could be 'early commenced' upon filing of the registration statement using a preliminary prospectus under Securities Act Rule 162 (17 CFR § 230.162), but a registered exchange offer for non-convertible debt securities could not be 'early commenced' until the applicable registration statement had been declared effective (since such an exchange offer would not be covered by Rule 13e-4 or Regulation 14D). Because of amendments to Rule 162 that were enacted in December 2008, under certain circumstances, the SEC will permit an issuer to early commence a registered exchange offer for non-convertible debt rather than being required to wait until the registration statement is declared effective. In order to do so, the issuer must: (i) provide the same withdrawal rights as it would be required to provide under the equity tender offer rules (Exchange Act Rule 13e-4 or Regulation 14D); (ii) if a material change in the offer materials occurs, disseminate the amended materials under the same conditions and in the same time periods as it would in an offer subject to Rule 13e-4 or Regulation 14D; and (iii) leave the offer open for the periods required for an offer that is subject to Rule 13e-4 and Regulation 14D. See Rule 162, 17 CFR § 230.162 (Sec Exch Comm'n 2009).

offer materials, a recirculation may be required, which could impose even further delay. Therefore, one primary disadvantage of a registered exchange offer is the potential delay and uncertainty associated with an SEC review, which can be a significant disadvantage for a company facing financial distress.

Another disadvantage of a registered exchange offer is the applicability of additional anti-fraud provisions in the Securities Act that would not otherwise be applicable to an exempt offering.[101] The most important of these provisions is Section 11 of the Securities Act, which provides that a person acquiring a security covered by a registration statement may recover damages if 'any part of the registration statement, when such part became effective, contained an untrue statement of a material fact or omitted to state a material fact required to be stated therein or necessary to make the statements therein not misleading'.[102] An unregistered offering would not be subject to Section 11 but would only be subject to Rule 10b-5. Unlike a Rule 10b-5 action, in a Section 11 action, subject to certain exceptions, plaintiffs do not have to prove that the material misstatement or omission caused the decline in value of the securities,[103] and they generally do not have to prove any scienter (i.e. fraudulent intent or recklessness) on the part of the defendant.[104] It is this feature of a Section 11 claim that is often referred to as 'strict liability' for misstatements or omissions. The issuer, each signatory to the registration statement (which will include at least the principal executive officer and the principal financial and accounting officers of the issuer), each director of the issuer, and each underwriter can be subject to Section 11 liability.[105] While there are affirmative defences (such as the 'due diligence' defence)[106] to Section 11 claims for all of the possible defendants aside from the issuer itself, a Section 11 claim can be much easier to establish than a Rule 10b-5 claim. **3.76**

The primary advantage of a registered debt exchange offer is the ability to make the offer to any investor, including retail investors. As discussed below, offers that are made pursuant to exemptions from registration under Section 4(a)(2) of the Securities Act may only be made to suitable investors (generally large institutions or sophisticated individual investors). Offers that are made under the Section 3(a)(9) exemption are subject to a number of other limitations. The ability to broadly disseminate the offer and include retail investors is often necessary for the success of a debt exchange offer, particularly for an issuer that is well known to the general public, since a significant portion of such an issuer's debt securities are often held by retail investors. For this reason, when General Motors Corp was considering **3.77**

---

[101] See, eg, s 12(a)(2) of the Securities Act which also imposes liability on sellers of securities for misstatements or omissions in prospectuses or oral communications made in the offer or sale of securities. Securities Act of 1933 § 12(a)(2), 15 USC § 77a, § 77k(a)(2) (2009).

[102] Securities Act of 1933 § 11, 15 USC § 77a, § 77k (2009).

[103] *Barnes v Osofsky*, 373 F 2d 269, 271–273 (2d Cir 1967).

[104] See *Fischman v Raytheon Mfg Co*, 188 F 2d 183, 186 (2d Cir 1951) ('A suit under Sec 11 of the 1933 Act requires no proof of fraud or deceit …'). Even statements of opinion in Securities Act filings may give rise to Section 11 liability if the registration statement omits facts about the issuer's inquiry into the statement of opinion or omits facts which conflict with the opinion. *Omnicare v Laborers Dist Council Constr Indus Pension Fund*, 2015 WL 1291916 (S Ct 2015).

[105] See, e.g., Section 15 of the Securities Act.

[106] See Securities Act of 1933 § 11(b)(3), 15 USC § 77a, § 77k(b)(3) (2009) (creating a safe harbour under certain conditions for anyone but the issuer who had reasonable grounds to believe the allegedly misleading statement was true, or who relied on an expert or official source in believing the statement to be true). See also Securities Act of 1933 § 11(c), 15 USC § 77a, § 77k(c) (2009) (stating that the standard of reasonableness for the § 10(b)(3) safe harbour is 'that required of a prudent man in the management of his own property').

an out-of-court debt exchange offer during the first and second quarters of 2009 (before it ultimately filed for chapter 11 relief in June 2009), it filed a registration statement on Form S-4[107] to register its proposed debt exchange offer, recognizing that a significant portion of its debt securities were held by retail investors. GM also simultaneously filed a Schedule TO[108] under Rule 13e-4 because a number of the securities subject to the proposed exchange offer were convertible into GM common stock. In contrast, one reason cited for the relatively low level of participation in the late 2008 debt exchange offer by GMAC LLC was that the exchange offer was structured as a private placement under Section 4(a)(2) of the Securities Act, which severely limited the ability of GMAC to appeal to retail bondholders.

(b) Exempt offerings—private placements under Section 4(a)(2) of the Securities Act

3.78   Section 4(a)(2) of the Securities Act provides an exemption from registration for 'transactions by an issuer not involving any public offering'.[109] Section 4(a)(2) permits 'private placements' of securities by issuers that are limited so as to only be available to investors who can 'fend for themselves' (and therefore do not need the protections of the registration process under the Securities Act) because they are sophisticated[110] and have access to the type of information that would be contained in a registration statement.[111] A retail investor would not likely be eligible to participate in a Section 4(a)(2) private placement, where an institutional investor (such as a hedge fund or mutual fund) would almost certainly be eligible.

3.79   The primary advantage of a Section 4(a)(2) private placement is speed. For this reason, a great majority of debt exchange offers are structured as such. The bondholders of most issuers tend to be large institutional investors who would be qualified institutional buyers (QIBs) under Rule 144A under the Securities Act, so they would clearly be sufficiently sophisticated not to require a Securities Act registration to protect them.[112] Furthermore, the offering document that would typically be used in a Section 4(a)(2) debt exchange offer would contain or incorporate by reference substantially all of the information that would be contained in a registration statement under the Securities Act, so the offerees would have the necessary access to information. In addition, debt securities issued in a Section 4(a)(2) debt exchange offer are exempt from the indenture qualification requirements under the

---

[107] See Gen Motors Corp, Registration Statement (Form S-4) (Apr 27, 2009), available at <http://www.sec.gov/Archives/edgar/data/40730/000119312509087739/ds4.htm>.

[108] See Gen Motors Corp, Tender Offer Statement (Schedule TO) (Apr 27, 2009), available at <http://www.sec.gov/Archives/edgar/data/40730/000119312509087775/dsctoi.htm>.

[109] Securities Act of 1933 § 4(a)(2), 15 USC § 77a, § 77d(2) (2009) (exempting transactions by an issuer not involving any public offering). Regulation D under the Securities Act was promulgated under section 4(a)(2) and provides specific requirements for private placements. See Regulation D—Rules Governing the Limited Offer and Sale of Securities Without Registration Under the Securities Act of 1933, 17 CFR § 230.501 et seq (2009). Issuers frequently structure their debt exchange offers to comply with Regulation D.

[110] *Sec Exch Comm'n v Ralston Purina*, 346 US 119, 125 (1953) ('An offering to those who are shown to be able to fend for themselves is a transaction "not involving any public offering"').

[111] Ibid at 125–26 (stating that an offering may not be public if the offerors or offerees as a class 'have access to the same kind of information that the act would make available in the form of a registration statement').

[112] 'Qualified Institutional Buyer' is defined in Rule 144A under the Securities Act. It includes, inter alia, any insurance company, investment company, state-owned employee plan, private employee plan, trust whose trustee is a bank or trust company, non-profit organization or corporation 'that in the aggregate owns and invests on a discretionary basis at least $100 million in securities of issuers that are not affiliated with the entity', or dealer acting on behalf of a QIB. See Private resales of securities to institutions, 17 CFR § 230.144A (Sec Exch Comm'n 2009).

Trust Indenture Act of 1939, so the indenture for such securities will not be required to incorporate the various mandatory provisions of the Trust Indenture Act.

As discussed above with respect to registered offerings, one primary disadvantage of a **3.80** Section 4(a)(2) private placement is that an issuer with a significant retail bondholder base will not be able to make the offer to those bondholders. While the Jumpstart Our Business Startups Act of 2012 (the 'JOBS Act') permits an issuer making a private placement (including a debt exchange offer) to 'accredited investors' under Regulation D under the Securities Act to make a 'general solicitation', many issuers will still avoid general solicitations in connection with debt exchange offers because under the JOBS Act, the investor eligibility verification requirements are more stringent if a general solicitation is made.[113] By effectively excluding the retail bondholder base from the offer:

- it may be more difficult for the issuer to obtain sufficient participation to achieve the issuer's economic goals (such as debt reduction or the fulfilment of regulatory requirements);
- it may be more difficult to complete an associated consent solicitation, which can be a serious problem if the consent solicitation is necessary either to complete the exchange offer itself or to permit some other required transaction;
- it may be easier for an individual significant bondholder or an ad hoc committee to form a blocking position against the exchange offer and negotiate with the issuer for better terms; and
- it may expose the issuer to lawsuits by retail bondholders who may feel that they are being treated unfairly at the expense of the bondholders who are eligible to participate.[114]

Therefore, it is essential that an issuer contemplating a private placement debt exchange **3.81** offer receive reliable information regarding the composition of its debtholder base prior to structuring the debt exchange offer. A dealer-manager that has been engaged to assist with the transaction may be able to provide this type of information.

It should be noted that certain investors who are receiving the new securities may not be **3.82** able to hold the securities being issued in exchange for the existing securities unless they are subject to 'registration rights', although this restriction has become much less prevalent in recent years.[115] Registration rights for debt securities usually allow the holder of the

---

[113] Under Rule 506(c)(2)(ii) under the Securities Act, if a general solicitation is being used in connection with a private placement exempt under Regulation D, the issuer or dealer manager must 'take reasonable steps' to verify the accredited investor status of those who eventually participate in the private placement, beyond merely receiving a questionnaire from the participant, where no such requirement would apply if no general solicitation were made. The non-exclusive verification methods noted by the SEC in this context include verification based on income through review of IRS forms reporting income, verification based on net worth through review of recent bank or brokerage statements, or written confirmation from a registered broker-dealer, registered investment advisor, licensed attorney, or certified public accountant that such investor is an accredited investor. Further, so long as the issuer is not aware of information to the contrary, an issuer that previously took reasonable steps to verify accredited investor status may meet the verification obligation over the next five years by obtaining a written representation at the time of sale that the person qualifies as an accredited investor. See 17 CFR § 230.506(c)(2)(ii)(E).

[114] Examples of such lawsuits include the suits filed against Harrah's Entertainment and Station Casinos, Inc. See Steve Green, 'Harrah's Hit With Class-Action Lawsuit Over Debt Plan', *Las Vegas Sun*, 16 February 2009, available at <http://www.lasvegassun.com/news/2009/feb/16/harrahs-hit-class-action-lawsuit-over-debt-plan/>.

[115] The constituent documents of certain funds prohibit them from receiving securities in a private placement that do not have 'registration rights'.

debt securities to compel the issuer either to: (i) issue a new series of debt securities (which have the same terms as the original privately placed securities) in exchange for the privately placed securities in an exchange offer that is registered under the Securities Act;[116] or (ii) register under the Securities Act for a specified period of time the resale of the privately placed securities by the holders of those securities.[117] Failure to comply with those requirements by certain specified deadlines will result in additional interest being paid on the debt securities. While the ostensible goal of registration rights is to maximize free transferability of the debt securities issued, in a number of cases, the registration rights are of little value, either because the securities issued in the debt exchange offer are already freely transferable under the US securities laws[118] or because the required holding period under the securities laws is fairly short.[119] Furthermore, for less well-known issuers whose retail bondholder base is small, the primary investors trading their bonds will be QIBs or other sophisticated investors, so no registration would be required to allow such investors to trade the bonds to other similarly sophisticated investors. Nevertheless, to maximize participation in an exchange offer, an issuer will sometimes offer registration rights.[120]

(c) Exchange offers under Section 3(a)(9) of the Securities Act

3.83   Section 3(a)(9) of the Securities Act exempts from registration 'except [for a security issued under chapter 11 of the Bankruptcy Code], any security exchanged by the issuer with its existing security holders exclusively where no commission or other remuneration is paid or given directly or indirectly for soliciting such exchange.'[121] The required elements of a Section 3(a)(9) exchange are:

- the issuer of the new securities is the same as the issuer of the securities being sought;[122]

---

[116] Such an offer is often referred to as an 'A/B exchange offer'.

[117] This type of registration is often referred to as a 'resale shelf registration'.

[118] So long as the issuers and guarantors of both the new security and the old security are the same, and no additional consideration is being paid by the offerees, the new security will be just as transferable as the old security. Conversions and exchanges, 17 CFR § 230.144(d)(3)(ii) (Sec Exch Comm'n 2009). See also Tech Squared Inc, SEC No-Action Letter, 1999 WL 288750 (4 May 1999) (SEC agreeing that a securityholder may tack the holding period of an option onto the holding period for shares received in exercise of that option).

[119] The holding period can be as short as six months for most public companies that are required to file periodic reports under the Exchange Act, and the typical deadlines in registration rights agreements can be in excess of six months.

[120] See, eg, the exchange offers by Tyco International Ltd and GMAC in 2008 and the exchange offers by Conn's, Inc and Tiffany & Co in 2015. See Tyco Int'l Ltd, Current Report (Form 8-k) (5 June 2008); GMAC LLC, Current Report (Form 8-k) (2 Jan 2009); Conn's, Inc, Current Report (Form 8-k) (27 April 2015); Tiffany & Co, Current Report (Form 8-k) (10 April 2015).

[121] Securities Act of 1933 § 3(a)(9), 17 USC § 77a, § 77c(a)(9) (2009).

[122] A guarantee by another entity (such as a parent or subsidiary) is generally viewed by the SEC as a 'security' that is separate from the security being guaranteed, so, in most instances, the guarantors of the old securities and the new securities being issued under s 3(a)(9) must be the same. There are a number of exceptions to this general policy. The SEC has previously taken a no-action position with respect to the issuance of a new parent security in a s 3(a)(9) exchange for a subsidiary's security that is guaranteed by the parent. See, eg, Kerr McGee Corporation, SEC No-Action Letter (31 July 2001), Nabors Industries, Inc, SEC No-Action Letter (29 April 2002), Weatherford International, Inc, SEC No-Action Letter (25 June 2002) and Duke Energy Corporation, SEC No-Action Letter (30 March 2006). In addition, in January 2010, the SEC took a no-action position with respect to the issuance of a new parent security (such as an equity security) that is not guaranteed by any subsidiaries in a s 3(a)(9) exchange for a security of the same parent entity that is guaranteed by one or more subsidiaries of the parent (including in the case of the issuance of non-guaranteed securities of the parent upon the conversion of a subsidiary-guaranteed convertible note). See Section 3(a)(9) Upstream Guarantees, SEC No-Action Letter (13 January 2010). The SEC in a number of instances has recognized the economic reality of a corporate group rather than its formal legal structure

- subject to limited exceptions, the offer is exclusively an exchange (although an issuer may pay cash in addition to issuing the new securities);[123] and
- no commission or other remuneration is paid or given directly or indirectly for soliciting such exchange.[124]

An issuer availing itself of the Section 3(a)(9) exemption would not be required to register **3.84** its debt exchange offer yet would be able to make the debt exchange offer to all holders of the relevant existing debt security without regard to investor suitability. Therefore, the issuer using Section 3(a)(9) would avoid the delay and Section 11 liability of a Securities Act registration while avoiding the offeree and private placement limitations of Section 4(a)(2).[125] Nevertheless, it should be noted that the issuance of debt securities under Section 3(a)(9) would require the filing with the SEC of a Form T-3 for the qualification of the indenture for the new debt securities under the Trust Indenture Act of 1939 prior to the time the solicitation for the 3(a)(9) exchange offer is commenced. The SEC may review and comment on the Form T-3.

Nevertheless, while the Section 3(a)(9) exemption seems on its face to provide a convenient **3.85** means of accomplishing a debt exchange offer without registration, Section 3(a)(9) is often not used where widespread participation is sought, because in many such cases, an issuer will find it necessary or advisable to engage a dealer-manager to ensure maximum participation. Because dealer-managers are usually paid to solicit debt exchange offers, most debt exchange offers involving dealer-managers are not able to be exempt under Section 3(a)(9). As a result, the Section 3(a)(9) exemption is often used by issuers in exchange offers that are not actively solicited, such as 'one-off' exchanges with individual holders of debt securities.

3. State securities law concerns

A debt exchange offer may be subject to the securities laws of the various states in which the **3.86** offerees reside (commonly referred to as 'Blue Sky' laws). State securities laws are preempted by US federal laws in the case of the issuance of a security that is equal in right of payment or senior in right of payment to a security that is listed on a national stock exchange under Section 18 of the Securities Act.[126] Furthermore, most private placements made to QIBs will require little or no state law compliance activity. Nevertheless, an issuer must consult with Blue Sky counsel prior to commencement of a debt exchange offer to ensure compliance with applicable state laws, particularly those relating to pre-commencement filing or registration requirements.

---

in confirming that a proposed exchange of securities issued by different issuers satisfied the 'identity of issuer' requirement of the s 3(a)(9) exemption. See, e.g., Bamboo.com, SEC No-Action Letter (20 December 1999), Ageas SA/NV and Ageas N.V., SEC No-Action Letter (20 March 2012) and H&R Real Estate Investment Trust and H&R Finance Trust, SEC No-Action Letter (29 March 2012).

[123] With limited exceptions, any cash consideration paid by the recipients of the new securities would make the s 3(a)(9) exemption unavailable. See definition of 'exchanged' in s 3(a)(9), for certain transactions, 17 CFR § 230.149 (Sec Exch Comm'n 2009).

[124] See definition of 'commission or other remuneration' in s 3(a)(9), for certain transactions, 17 CFR § 230.150 (Sec Exch Comm'n 2009). This prohibition applies both to employees of the issuer itself as well as to third parties.

[125] A s 3(a)(9) exchange offer would still be subject to Rule 10b-5 under the Exchange Act as well as the tender offer regulations of the Exchange Act.

[126] Securities Act of 1933 § 18, 15 USC § 77a, § 77r (2009) (exempting covered securities from state regulation).

4. Stock exchange rules

3.87   A common method used by companies experiencing financial distress is to deleverage themselves, issuing new equity securities in exchange for existing debt. The issuance of equity securities by a distressed company in a debt exchange offer can be very significant and may result in a change of control of the company. While the same US securities law concerns apply when equity securities are issued in exchange for debt, companies whose equity securities are listed on the New York Stock Exchange (NYSE) or NASDAQ are also subject to the rules of those stock exchanges regarding shareholder approvals required for certain issuances of stock.

3.88   Section 312.03 of the NYSE Listed Company Manual requires shareholder approval for certain issuances of stock by listed companies, including, among others:

- an issuance of securities that will result in a change of control;[127]
- an issuance of common stock (or securities convertible or exercisable for common stock) to a director, officer or substantial security holder of the company (each a 'Related Party') exceeding one percent of the number of shares of common stock outstanding or one percent of the voting power outstanding, unless the transaction is a cash sale at or above the 'Minimum Price';[128]
- certain issuances of common stock (or securities convertible or exercisable for common stock) in certain transactions involving a Related Party;[129] and
- an issuance of common stock, or of securities convertible into or exercisable for common stock, in any transaction or series of related transactions if:
    (1) the common stock has, or will have upon issuance, voting power equal to or in excess of 20 per cent of the voting power outstanding; or
    (2) the number of shares of common stock to be issued is, or will be upon issuance, equal to or in excess of 20 per cent of the number of shares of common stock outstanding; except that

such requirement does not apply to (i) a public offering for cash, or (ii) any other financing (that is not a public offering for cash) in which the company is selling securities for cash, if such financing involves a sale of common stock, or securities convertible into or exercisable for common stock, at a price at least as great as the Minimum Price.[130]

3.89   The NASDAQ Rules for listed companies also require shareholder approval for certain issuances of stock by listed companies, including, among others:

---

[127] NYSE Listed Company Manual, s 312.03(d).

[128] See ibid, s 312.03(b)(i). Per Section 312.04(h) of the NYSE Listed Company Manual, 'Minimum Price' means a price that is the lower of: (i) the Official Closing Price immediately preceding the signing of the binding agreement; or (ii) the average Official Closing Price for the five trading days immediately preceding the signing of the binding agreement.

Per Section 312.04(i) of the NYSE Listed Company Manual, 'Official Closing Price' of the issuer's common stock means the official closing price on the Exchange as reported to the Consolidated Tape immediately preceding the signing of a binding agreement to issue the securities. For example, if the transaction is signed after the close of the regular session at 4:00 pm Eastern Standard Time on a Tuesday, then Tuesday's official closing price is used. If the transaction is signed at any time between the close of the regular session on Monday and the close of the regular session on Tuesday, then Monday's official closing price is used.

[129] NYSE Listed Company Manual, s 312.03(b)(ii).

[130] See ibid, s 312.03(c).

- an issuance of securities that will result in a change of control;[131] and
- a transaction, other than a public offering (as defined in the NASDAQ Rules), involving the sale, issuance, or potential issuance by the listed company, at less than the 'Minimum Price',[132] of common stock (or securities convertible into or exercisable for common stock), which alone or together with sales by officers, directors, or substantial shareholders of the listed company, equals 20 per cent or more of the common stock or 20 per cent or more of the voting power outstanding before the issuance.[133]

A listed company experiencing financial distress should consider the shareholder approval **3.90** requirements under the NYSE and NASDAQ rules in structuring an out-of-court debt exchange offer where the issuance of a significant amount of equity securities is contemplated. Shareholder approval of such a transaction may not be possible to obtain in such a situation, particularly where the issuance of the new equity securities in the exchange offer significantly dilutes the existing equity. It is possible to apply to the relevant exchange for an exemption from the shareholder approval requirements.[134] In addition, the stock exchanges adopted temporary exemptions to the shareholder approval requirements (which are no longer applicable) related to the COVID-19 pandemic.[135] Nevertheless, a listed company experiencing financial distress may not have sufficient time to obtain the necessary exemption and may be forced to undergo an in-court restructuring.

D. Common Tactics in Debt Exchange Offers

Because a debt exchange offer is a voluntary transaction on the part of the holder of the **3.91** existing debt securities, an issuer may employ various tactics to encourage or even coerce participation. The holder of the existing debt securities either has to 'love' the offer enough to accept it or 'fear' the consequences of not accepting the offer (or some combination of both). Sometimes a debt restructuring tactic need not be seriously pursued by the issuer, but the possibility of the issuer consummating such a deal would be so damaging to holders of existing debt that they will agree to an alternative exchange offer on terms beneficial to the issuer.

As discussed above in paras 3.48–3.50, after the advent of the COVID-19 pandemic, cred- **3.92** itor groups proposed transactions that advantaged one creditor group over another and companies actively encouraged 'creditor-on-creditor violence' to secure better terms.

1. Exit consents and entrance consents
As discussed above, exit consents may be used to discourage debtholders from retaining **3.93** their existing debt because, if enough other holders tender, the existing debt will be stripped of covenants or even collateral as a result of a consent solicitation associated with the debt

---

[131] NASDAQ Rule 5635(b).
[132] NASDAQ Rule 5635(d)(1)(A) defines 'Minimum Price' as the lower of: (i) the NASDAQ Official Closing Price (as reflected on Nasdaq.com) immediately preceding the signing of the binding agreement; or (ii) the average NASDAQ Official Closing Price of the common stock (as reflected on Nasdaq.com) for the five trading days immediately preceding the signing of the binding agreement.
[133] NASDAQ, Rule 5635(d).
[134] See NYSE Listed Company Manual, s 312.05; NASDAQ, Rule 5635(f).
[135] See NYSE Listed Company Manual, s 312.03T; NASDAQ, Rule 5636T.

exchange offer, while consenting debtholders receive new debt under a different instrument, with new covenants and possibly new collateral. Often, the company may privately seek consents and agreements to participate from known significant holders of the existing debt in order either to ensure a successful exit consent solicitation or to increase the likelihood of success, thereby making the offer more coercive and likely to be accepted overall.

3.94 Many bond indentures contain a provision that requires consent payments, if offered to any holders of the bond, must be offered to all holders. Over the latter half of the 2010s, it became more common for bond indentures to omit that consent payment provision. If the consent payment provision is not included, a company could conceivably make a bond exchange offer available to only a select group of bondholders holding a sufficient amount of bonds to provide the necessary consent to strip out the protective covenants in an indenture or even to release collateral. Those bondholders could provide an exit consent to strip out covenants and possibly collateral as they exit to a new debt instrument with new covenants and new collateral, leaving the minority with a denuded debt instrument. Such an outcome is more difficult to achieve if the consent payment provision is present in the bond indenture, since it will be somewhat unclear what part of the total compensation to the participating bondholder is a consent payment (and is therefore required to be offered to all holders).

3.95 Indentures under which multiple series of debt securities are issued can present a number of issues with respect to consents and voting. If multiple series of debt securities with varying maturity dates and other varying terms and provisions vote together as a single class under an indenture, it may be possible for an issuer to make an exchange offer that is more attractive to certain holders than others yet will receive sufficient participation so an exit consent solicitation will be successful, thereby making the debt exchange offer more coercive. In particular, an indenture that governs both debt securities with a 'payment-in-kind' interest payment feature and other debt securities whose interest is payable in cash may be particularly susceptible to such an approach if all of the debt securities vote together as a single class for waiver and amendment purposes. Such indentures continue to be used at the time of writing.

3.96 In late 2017, a bondholder holding a majority of the 6.375 per cent Notes due 2023 of Windstream Holdings, Inc. claimed that a default had occurred under the covenants in the indenture governing the bonds (which were similar to those in all of Windstream's various series of bonds) resulting from a transaction that had occurred in 2015, bringing suit, claiming that the default had occurred and should result in the bonds being declared immediately due and payable.[136] In response, Windstream commenced a consent solicitation of all series of bonds that had the relevant covenant (including the 6.375 per cent Notes due 2023), seeking a waiver of any default thereunder. Because the bondholder holding the majority of the 6.375 per cent Notes due 2023 would not be expected to consent, in what was widely regarded as an innovative tactic at the time, Windstream also simultaneously offered to issue new 6.375 per cent Notes due 2023 under the same indenture in exchange for certain existing bonds of other series, asking the friendly holders of the newly-issued 6.375 per

---

[136] *U.S. Bank Nat'l Ass'n v Windstream Servs., LLC*, 2019 WL 948120, at *7–9 (S.D.N.Y. Feb. 15, 2019).

cent Notes due 2023 to consent to waivers of the purported defaults under that indenture. Such consents have become commonly known as 'entrance consents'. While this entrance consent tactic ultimately failed for various technical reasons,[137] the Windstream situation illustrates the danger that entrance consents pose to any bondholder that believes it can securely assert that a default has occurred under an indenture, and similar tactics may be able to be used under credit agreements via the 'incremental facility' mechanism.

2. Increased coupon or covenant enhancements

Because deleveraging is often a goal of a debt exchange offer, issuers may offer higher interest rates or more restrictive covenants in exchange for a reduction in principal amount to induce bondholders to participate. Alternatively, if holders of an existing debt security will not agree to covenant or maturity changes, the issuer may threaten to issue a new security with a greatly increased cash coupon or 'payment-in-kind' interest payment (often in exchange for another existing debt security) which will harm the existing debt security's holders. **3.97**

3. Threat of bankruptcy

Issuers that are experiencing financial distress may use the threat of bankruptcy to induce bondholders to tender into a deleveraging bond exchange offer, particularly when a bankruptcy could be disruptive to the business of the issuer and destroy enterprise value. **3.98**

As mentioned above in para 3.53, where a company seeks a very high level of participation in an out-of-court debt exchange offer, it may also solicit with respect to a prepackaged bankruptcy proceeding simultaneously with the exchange offer. Such a solicitation would accentuate the threat of bankruptcy to debtholders deciding whether or not to accept the offer and potentially deter 'hold-outs' from resisting the exchange offer. **3.99**

4. 'Leapfrog'

A number of companies have offered existing debtholders new debt that is in some way higher in priority than the existing debt, thus 'leapfrogging' over them. The purpose of this tactic is to make the new debt more attractive to debtholders while reducing the value of the existing debt to any holder that does not accept the exchange offer. The increase in priority may be accomplished in a number of different ways. **3.100**

(a) Increased contractual priority

The new debt may be contractually senior to the existing debt if the existing debt is subordinated in right of payment to 'senior debt' by issuing the new debt as senior debt. Companies using this method may need to comply with 'restricted payments' and similar covenants in existing debt instruments, which may prohibit the retirement of subordinated debt through the issuance of senior debt. Sometimes the retirement of subordinated debt may be accomplished using an accordion feature of a credit agreement to borrow additional loans which are offered in a debt-for-debt exchange to the holders of subordinated debt. **3.101**

---

[137] See ibid at 23–24.

(b) Increased structural priority

3.102   The company may make the new debt structurally senior by having subsidiaries that have significant assets or operations guarantee the new securities (and not guarantee the existing securities). This method is often used in exchange offers for debt that is rated investment grade (or was rated investment grade when it was originally issued), since such debt usually does not have stringent restrictive covenants and usually is not guaranteed by subsidiaries of the company. The company may also accomplish structural priority by interposing an intermediate holding company between the borrower of the existing debt and one or more subsidiaries holding valuable assets (but that do not guarantee the existing debt), and issuing the new debt from such intermediate holding company.

3.103   Often, a US company that issues debt is subject to 'high-yield' debt covenants, which usually include a covenant (the 'additional guarantor's covenant') to the effect that if the company forms a new subsidiary or acquires a new subsidiary, the new subsidiary must also guarantee the relevant debt. There are, however, notable exceptions from the additional guarantor's covenant, so certain subsidiaries may not be required to guarantee the existing debt. These subsidiaries may then issue the new debt or guarantee the new debt but not the existing debt, thereby structurally subordinating the existing debt to the new debt, since creditors of these subsidiaries will be able to have recourse to the subsidiaries' assets before holders of the original debt. Examples of subsidiaries that are often exempt from the additional guarantor's covenant include:

- 'Unrestricted subsidiaries': These are subsidiaries that are not subject to the debt covenants at all, so their debt incurrence is not restricted by the covenants. The amount of investment that may be made in Unrestricted Subsidiaries is, however, typically limited by 'high-yield' debt covenants (but, notably, not by 'investment-grade' debt covenants).
- 'Foreign subsidiaries': These are subsidiaries that are organized outside the home jurisdiction of the company. US debt documents have historically not required foreign subsidiaries to guarantee the debt (or pledge their assets to support the debt) because, prior to November 2018, US federal tax regulations treated a guarantee or other credit support by a foreign subsidiary for debt issued by a US taxpayer as a dividend by the foreign subsidiary.[138] Nevertheless, though the regulations changed in November 2018, US debt documents have not quite caught up with the change in regulations and still generally do not require foreign subsidiaries to guarantee the debt or pledge their equity or assets to support the debt. This mismatch between legal framework and the debt covenants can present an opportunity to use foreign subsidiaries for structurally priming debt issuances.
- Non-guarantor subsidiaries: Other categories of subsidiaries may be exempt from the additional guarantor's covenant, such as subsidiaries that are not wholly owned and subsidiaries that do not guarantee other debt of the 'credit family' (i.e. the borrower and the guarantors of the debt governed by the agreement).

3.104   In recent years, intellectual property (IP) has commonly been used for these structurally priming financings. Intellectual property is an identifiable asset the value of which is often

---

[138] Treas. Reg. § 1.956–1.

readily ascertainable, making it more able to be transferred to a new subsidiary for use in a financing. In contrast, a facility or assets that form part of a business may be more difficult to transfer or value. Typically, an IP-based financing involves the licensing of the IP to the business units in the company that uses it, then the transfer of the IP to a new subsidiary that is not required to guarantee the existing debt, which thereupon incurs the new structurally priming financing. As a result, a number of credit agreements and indentures have included covenants that prohibit transfers of IP to non-guarantor subsidiaries, foreign subsidiaries, and unrestricted subsidiaries.

In addition, a number of debt agreements contain an exception that permits unlimited receivables financings in subsidiaries that are not subject to the covenants, so companies may use those exceptions to make investments in receivables subsidiaries that guarantee the new debt being offered but not the existing debt. Such receivables financing exceptions may also be used for 'whole business' securitizations, in which an operating business that generates royalties or other regular revenue streams is placed in the new subsidiary to support newly issued debt using those royalties or revenue streams (which usually fall within the definition of 'receivables' or 'securitization assets' for purposes of the exception). **3.105**

(c) Increased priority as to security

The company may offer to secure the new debt with its assets, thereby effectively subordinating the existing debt to the extent of the value of the collateral. A number of indentures and credit agreements are relatively permissive with respect to liens that may be incurred. Often, those agreements have large 'baskets' permitting a significant amount of secured debt or other similar indebtedness and may also permit additional secured debt based on compliance with a ratio of secured debt to EBITDA.[139] Such debt agreements may also have definitions of EBITDA with various exceptions and adjustments that can be used to give the company significant additional secured debt incurrence capacity.[140] This method is often used by companies that have existing senior debt that is already guaranteed by the company's subsidiaries. Companies that have debt that is already secured by liens may also use this method by offering new debt that is secured by liens of higher priority. **3.106**

Exchange offers with short periods for tendering or which create uncertainty as to the actions of other securityholders can make it difficult for securityholders to coordinate to resist the exchange offer. In a so-called 'waterfall tender offer', an 'acceptance priority' structure is used to enhance competition among various groups of holders and create 'prisoner's dilemma' situations. In a waterfall tender offer the issuer typically makes an offer to several classes of debt securities but caps the amount the issuer is willing to accept in the offer at a maximum aggregate dollar amount or a maximum amount per class of debt. The issuer states that it will accept securities tendered in a certain priority, and securities with a lower acceptance priority will only be accepted if all or the stated maximum of a higher class are tendered.[141] Tendering into the exchange would generally put the securityholder in a worse **3.107**

---

[139] Generally, EBITDA is defined as earnings, excluding interest, tax, depreciation, and amortization expense. Indentures will also contain numerous adjustments to EBITDA that are negotiated by the issuer.

[140] For example, an indenture might permit the issuer to adjust EBITDA to take account of projected cost savings that are expected in good faith by management to result from operational improvements or other changes made to the business.

[141] See, eg, Sophia Pearson, 'Realogy Debt Exchange Violates Contracts, Judge Says', *Bloomberg*, 18 December 2008, available at <http://www.bloomberg.com/apps/news?pid=newsarchive&sid=aPOQodbPWD3M>.

position, but a securityholder who does not tender runs the risk that another group of holders who accept the exchange will leapfrog the holder in priority.

3.108   The 'creditor-on-creditor' transactions that are described above in paras 3.48 through 3.50 involved the issuance of new debt (for new cash proceeds), with a higher priority as to the collateral than existing debt. In addition, participating lenders were permitted by the company to exchange their existing debt for new debt with a higher priority as to the collateral than the existing debt (albeit lower in priority than the new money debt). In the case of Serta-Simmons, the exchange transaction was done in spite of 'pro-rata sharing' provisions in the credit agreement that would otherwise require proceeds (including the new superpriority debt issued in exchange for existing loans) received by each lender in respect of existing loans to be shared pro rata among all of the lenders. The company and participating lenders have taken the position that the exchange transaction fell into exceptions to the 'pro rata sharing' provisions, a position that has been disputed by a number of lenders that did not participate.[142]

5. Timing and mechanics

3.109   Exchange offers with short periods for tendering or that create uncertainty as to the actions of other debtholders can make it difficult for debtholders to coordinate to respond to the exchange offer. In a so-called 'waterfall tender offer', an 'acceptance priority' structure is used to enhance competition among various groups of holders and create 'prisoner's dilemma' situations. In a waterfall tender offer the issuer typically makes an offer to several classes of debt securities but caps the amount the issuer is willing to accept in the offer at a maximum aggregate dollar amount or a maximum amount per class of debt. The issuer states that it will accept securities tendered in a certain priority, and securities with a lower acceptance priority will only be accepted if all or the stated maximum of a higher class are tendered.[143] Tendering into the exchange would generally put the securityholder in a worse position, but a securityholder who does not tender runs the risk that another group of holders who accept the exchange will leapfrog the holder in priority.

6. Partial repayment and extension of maturity

3.110   A number of companies have offered, through a consent solicitation connected with a partial redemption or a credit agreement 'amend and extend' process, to repay a portion of their existing indebtedness in exchange for covenant relief (including of financial ratio compliance), permission to do a transaction, waiver of a change of control put in an acquisition, release of guarantors or security, or (for credit facilities, often in connection with a high-yield bond issuance) an extension of the maturity of the remaining debt. This method may be used to address an impending maturity by an issuer in a cyclical business experiencing a downturn the issuer believes to be temporary.

---

[142] See Complaint, *North Star Debt Holdings, L.P., et al v Serta Simmons Bedding, LLC et al*, Index No. 652243/2020 (NY Sup Ct June 11, 2020); Serta-Simmons Bedding LLC's Motion to Dismiss, *North Star Debt Holdings, L.P., et al v Serta Simmons Bedding, LLC et al.*, Index No. 652243/2020 (NY Sup Ct July 2, 2020); Lender Defendants' Motion to Dismiss, *North Star Debt Holdings, L.P., et al v Serta Simmons Bedding, LLC et al*, Index No. 652243/2020 (NY Sup Ct July 2, 2020).

[143] See, eg, Pearson (n 141).

E. Certain US Federal Income Tax Considerations and Accounting Considerations

In a deleveraging debt exchange offer, the issuer will generally realize income as a result **3.111** of the cancellation of debt (commonly referred to as 'COD income').[144] If debt is trading at a discount to its face amount, considerable COD income could result from any restructuring.[145] If either the existing bonds or the new bonds (or both) are 'publicly traded' for purposes of the relevant tax regulations, the amount of COD income from a debt exchange offer will generally be measured by the difference between (x) the adjusted issue price of the existing debt (which will in most cases be close to its face value if it was issued in a typical underwritten offering or private placement) minus (y) the fair market value of the publicly traded debt on the date of the new debt's issuance (which may or may not be its face value, depending on market conditions existing on the date the exchange offer is consummated).[146] The relevant regulations define 'publicly traded' broadly, requiring only an indicative, non-binding quote, which does not need to be publicly available, from a single broker, dealer, or pricing service.[147] The COD income may be offset somewhat by increased interest expense if a significant portion of the new debt immediately trades at a discount, and is therefore deemed to have been issued with original issue discount, which will be amortized over the remaining term of the debt.[148] With respect to transactions giving rise to COD income that occurred in 2009 and 2010, an issuer could elect to defer the recognition of the COD income until 2014, with the COD income included in the issuer's gross income ratably over the five-taxable-year period beginning in 2014.[149] In an out-of-court restructuring, an insolvent issuer may exclude the COD income from gross income to the extent of its insolvency, but the issuer is required to reduce its tax attributes by the amount of the excluded COD income.[150] In addition to the insolvency exception, other exceptions may be available to an issuer, which will permit the issuer to exclude the COD income from its gross income.[151] In sum, such tax matters require careful consideration.

Similarly, the extinguishment of the existing debt at a discount may result in income under **3.112** the accounting standards used by the issuer. Nevertheless, most modern debt covenant packages will exclude this sort of income from financial calculations. Still, the issuance of the new debt, if it is issued with original issue discount, may result in additional non-cash interest expense due to the amortization of the original issue discount over the life of the new debt. Therefore, if there are debt covenants based on consolidated net income or earnings (or similar measures),[152] an issuer should try to exclude such amortization from the calculation of consolidated net income or earnings for purposes of those debt covenants, since the income from the extinguishment of the existing debt is likely to be eliminated by

---

[144] IRC § 61(a)(12).
[145] See IRC § 108(e)(10); IRC § 1273(b).
[146] See IRC § 108(e)(10); IRC § 1273(b); Treas Reg § 1.1273-2(c); Treas Reg § 1.1273-2(f).
[147] See Treas Reg § 1.1273-2(f).
[148] See Treas Reg § 1.1273-1(1); Treas Reg § 1.1273-2; Treas Reg § 1.163-4(a)(1).
[149] IRC § 108(i).
[150] IRC § 108(a)(1)(B).
[151] IRC § 108(a)(1).
[152] Examples would include a 'Restricted Payments' limitation in a high-yield debt indenture, which would allow dividends and investments to be paid out of a growing 'basket' that increases by 50 per cent of cumulative consolidated net income.

the covenant calculations. The accounting effects of a debt exchange offer therefore need to be carefully considered.

IV. Exchange Offers in the UK

3.113 As discussed above, it has been less common for UK borrowers to have capital structures with the necessary senior capital facility baskets to enable a debt-for-debt exchange to be an attractive possibility and this may be why exchange offers have not been such a significant feature of the UK restructuring landscape. Moreover, private equity (PE) sponsors in the UK have tended to favour leveraged loan debt over high-yield bond issues. In recent years increasing numbers of UK PE-sponsored companies have accessed high-yield markets, and senior credit facility baskets have become a more common feature of the European high yield market.[153] This may result in a rise in exchange offers in the UK while there is comparatively little case law on the strategy. The *Assenagon*[154]case is an exception and introduces some important considerations in a UK context. *Assenagon* concerned the restructuring of the Anglo-Irish Bank during Ireland's financial difficulties in the depth of the 2008 Great Recession. The Anglo-Irish Bank proposed an exchange offer pursuant to which each accepting creditor would receive new €0.20 notes for every €1.00 note exchanged. The terms of the exchange offer also included a resolution by the majority that any notes which were not exchanged could be redeemed for a very small consideration. The timing of the offer was such that if the resolution were successfully passed, noteholders who did not participate would not subsequently be able to participate in it. The claimant did not participate, the resolution was passed, and the claimant received €170 in respect of €17 million of notes.

3.114 Briggs J held that the resolution was invalid. The *ratio* of the decision turned on the beneficial interest in the notes and a voting prohibition contained in the trust deed by which the notes were constituted. But Briggs J also found *obiter* that the resolution constituted an abuse of power by the majority. Advisers advising on exchange offers in the UK must therefore consider whether any exit consents constitute an abusive exercise of majority power. Briggs J commented:

> The exit consent is, quite simply, a coercive threat which the issuer invites the majority to levy against the minority, nothing more or less. Its only function is the intimidation of a potential minority, based upon the fear of any individual member of that class that, by rejecting the exchange and voting against the resolution, he (or it) will be left out in the cold.[155]

This leads to the concern that all exit consents will constitute an abuse of power in the English law context.

3.115 Several points can be made in this regard. The first is that *Assenagon* is a first instance judgment, not yet considered by an appeal court. The second is that it constitutes an extreme case; the bondholders lost all their value as a result of the majority resolution. The third,

---

[153] Proskauer (n 42).
[154] *Assenagon Asset Management SA v Irish Bank Resolution Corpn Ltd (formerly Anglo Irish Bank Corpn Ltd)* [2012] EWHC 2090 (Ch).
[155] Ibid [85].

important, point is that the timing of the offer in *Assenagon* meant that a minority bond-holder who did not vote in favour of the resolution had no subsequent right to participate. Advisers in an English law context may, therefore, wish to consider including 'follow on' rights in exchange offers so that those who do not participate have an opportunity to do so afterwards. This was implicitly approved by Briggs J in *Assenagon* and has received support from commentators subsequently.[156] Overall, it is suggested here that what is important is whether the terms of the exit consent are themselves likely to be determinative, so that no creditor would risk voting against the offer. In this circumstance, the court will be un-able to assess whether the offer was one which creditors genuinely supported or whether it was merely put on terms which no rational bondholder could accept. In this context, and in contrast to the decision in *Assenagon*, the payment of consent fees to bondholders voting in favour of restructuring resolutions has been upheld at both first instance and by the Court of Appeal.[157] It will be important, amongst other things, that the consent fee is clearly disclosed and available to all noteholders who vote in favour of the resolution but provided it is not so sizeable as to be determinative it is unlikely to be struck down.

It is perhaps surprising that *Assenagon* is framed in terms of the motivations of the cred- **3.116** itors voting for the resolutions rather than the duties of the directors proposing them. In *Redwood*,[158] the court recognized the limitations on an abuse of majority power doctrine in the context of classes of lenders voting on a commercial arrangement and it does indeed seem artificial to consider whether lenders are voting in their own self-interest when that is what they are bound to do. It is tentatively suggested here that a better approach in *Assenagon* and similar cases may be to focus on the duty of directors to exercise their powers only for the purpose for which they were conferred.[159] Where the directors' purpose is to coerce creditors into voting for an arrangement, then they will have exceeded their powers so that the reso-lution is invalid.[160] In determining whether the directors have exceeded their powers or not, the question is whether the terms in which the resolution are put are likely to be determina-tive so that a reasonable creditor is bound to vote in favour of it whether they support the resolution or not. An arrangement such as *Assegnagon* would fall foul of such a test, whilst a reasonably sized consent fee available to all would not. The advantage of such an approach is that it avoids rather artificial assessments of the motives of the creditors in voting.

V. Chapter 11 Plan Reorganizations

A. Introduction

As discussed above, there are certain advantages to pursuing an in-court restructuring pro- **3.117** cess under chapter 11 of the Bankruptcy Code.[161] An in-court restructuring is intended

---

[156] See, eg, Richard Nolan, 'Debt Restructurings: the Use and Abuse of Power' Case Comment (2013) 129 *Law Quarterly Review* 161; Paul Lenihan, 'Recent Decisions on Bond Consent Solicitations under English Law' (2015) 30(3) *Journal of International Banking Law & Regulation* 163.

[157] *Azevedo and Ors v Imcopa Importacao* [2013] EWCA Civ 364.

[158] *Redwood Master Fund Ltd v TBD Bank Europe Ltd* [2002] EWHC 2703 (Ch).

[159] Companies Act 2006, s 171(b).

[160] The creditors being aware of the directors' purpose in proposing the resolution.

[161] See section I.

to be accomplished through a plan of reorganization that must be approved by a federal bankruptcy court and satisfy the requirements of the Bankruptcy Code. Confirmation and consummation are the ultimate objectives of every plan of reorganization.[162] Below is an overview of certain aspects of the chapter 11 process, beginning with recent challenges to the appropriate scope of a bankruptcy court's jurisdiction, chapter 11 plan standards, and the trend towards chapter 11 plan mediation in significant cases.

B. Limitations on Bankruptcy Court Jurisdiction—*Stern v Marshall*

1. General

3.118   United States bankruptcy courts are 'Article I courts' created under Article I of the US Constitution, which governs and authorizes the legislative, rather than the judicial branch, of the federal government to establish a uniform system of federal bankruptcy laws.[163] They are to be distinguished from 'Article III courts' which exercise the 'judicial Power of the United States'.[164] Under principles of the separation of powers among the legislative, executive, and judicial powers of government, bankruptcy courts cannot, therefore, exercise the judicial power reserved for Article III courts.

3.119   Over 30 years ago, in *Northern Pipeline Constr Co v Marathon Pipe Line Co*,[165] the US Supreme Court struck down as unconstitutional the Bankruptcy Reform Act of 1978 that established bankruptcy courts because it conferred Article III power on bankruptcy judges. The Supreme Court held that 'while Congress ... could grant the bankruptcy courts the right to issue final orders in proceedings that were at the "core" of bankruptcy jurisdiction, primarily the restructuring of the debtor-creditor relationship, it could not give bankruptcy courts the right to issue such orders in "private right" claims (e.g., tort and contract) merely because those claims involved a debtor'.[166] To address the *Marathon* issue, Congress enacted the Bankruptcy Amendments and Federal Judgeship Act of 1984 by making bankruptcy judges judicial officers of the United States district court established under Article III of the US Constitution. To further resolve the concerns expressed by the Supreme Court, Congress reserved for the federal district courts jurisdiction over certain bankruptcy proceedings.

3.120   The scheme created under the 1984 legislation vests bankruptcy jurisdiction in the first instance in district courts, which may, but need not, refer cases and matters within the scope of that jurisdiction to the bankruptcy courts.[167] Bankruptcy jurisdiction is also divided into two types: 'core' and 'related to' jurisdiction.[168] 'Core' jurisdiction generally covers proceedings arising under title 11 of the United States Code—or the Bankruptcy Code, while 'related to' jurisdiction involves any non-core proceeding that is otherwise related to a title 11

---

[162] See *Bank of America Nat'l Trust and Sav Ass'n v 203 N LaSalle Street P'ship*, 526 US 434, 465 n 4 (1999) (quoting 7 Collier on Bankruptcy, para 1129.01, p 1129-10 (15th rev 1998)).

[163] See US Const art I, s 8.

[164] See US Const art III.

[165] 458 US 50 (1982).

[166] *Ben Cooper, Inc v Ins Co of Pennsylvania (In re Ben Cooper, Inc)*, 896 F 2d 1394, 1398 (2d Cir 1990) (citing *Marathon*, 458 US at 71).

[167] See 28 USC § 157(c), (d).

[168] Ibid § 157(b) (listing a non-exclusive list of matters considered 'core' including 'matters concerning the administration of the estate', 'allowance or disallowance of claims against the estate', 'counterclaims by the estate

case.[169] One distinguishing feature between the two types of jurisdictions is the ability to enter final orders. While bankruptcy courts may enter final orders with respect to matters within the scope of their core jurisdiction, which are subject to appellate review by the district courts or bankruptcy appellate panels,[170] they may only issue proposed findings of fact and conclusions of law when exercising related to jurisdiction, which are reviewed *de novo* by the district courts.[171]

2. *Stern v Marshall*

In *Stern v Marshall*, the Supreme Court found that Congress' grant of jurisdiction to bank-   **3.121**
ruptcy judges exceeded the limitations of Article III of the US Constitution.[172] The case involved a dispute between a wife and son of a wealthy businessman and their respective entitlements to the businessman's assets following his death. After the wife filed for relief under chapter 11 of the Bankruptcy Code, the son brought a claim for damages for defamation in the same proceeding, and the wife counterclaimed with a suit for tortious interference with a gift she expected from her late husband. The bankruptcy court entered what it called a final judgment in favour of the wife.[173] The decision was appealed up to the Supreme Court.

In a 5–4 decision, the Supreme Court held that the bankruptcy judge lacked the consti-   **3.122**
tutional authority to enter a final judgment on the wife-debtor's counterclaims that were based solely on state common law in spite of the fact that all of the Justices agreed that section 157 of the United States Code clearly gave the bankruptcy court the statutory authority to do so.[174] In short, in the Supreme Court's view, Congress' grant of jurisdiction to the bankruptcy courts under section 157(b) failed to comply with *Marathon* and was unconstitutional. Rather, the authority to enter final judgments in actions involving 'private rights' is vested in Article III courts, not bankruptcy courts, and the bankruptcy court lacked the constitutional authority to enter a final judgment on the wife's counterclaim.[175]

The dissenting Justices disagreed with the majority's conclusion that bankruptcy court   **3.123**
judges did not have constitutional authority to decide the counterclaim at issue. In the eyes of the minority, the Court's prior precedent mandated a more 'pragmatic approach' to Article III questions.[176] Applying such an approach, the dissenters concluded that bankruptcy courts could adjudicate on a final basis the counterclaim at issue without violating any constitutional principles of separation of powers.[177]

---

against persons filing claims against the estate', 'orders in respect to obtaining credit', 'orders to turn over property of the estate', 'proceedings to determine, avoid, or recover preferences', 'motions to terminate, annul, or modify the automatic stay', 'determinations as to the dischargeability of particular debts', 'objections to discharges', 'determinations of the validity, extent, or priority of liens', plan confirmation, orders approving the use or lease or sale of property, 'other proceedings affecting the liquidation of the assets of the estate', and 'recognition of foreign proceedings and other matters under chapter 15 of title 11').

[169] Ibid.
[170] Ibid § 157(b)(1).
[171] Ibid § 157(c)(1).
[172] 131 S Ct 2594 (2011).
[173] 253 BR 550 (Bankr CD Cal 2000).
[174] 131 S Ct at 25962594 (noting that 'counterclaims by the estate against persons filing claims against the estate' is clearly listed in the statute as part of the bankruptcy court's core jurisdiction).
[175] Ibid.
[176] 131 S Ct at 2624.
[177] Ibid at 2621–2622.

3. Post-*Stern* developments

3.124   Following the *Stern* decision, bankruptcy courts faced many challenges to their authority to rule on a broad range of bankruptcy matters and those related to the bankruptcy estate, particularly those statutory 'core' claims not explicitly addressed by the Supreme Court. In particular, with section 157 of the United States Code still in place, bankruptcy courts struggled to address claims over which they had 'core' jurisdiction based on the language of the statute, but which they lacked constitutional authority to hear and finally determine under *Stern*. After a few years, the Supreme Court responded in *Executive Benefits Insurance Agency v Arkison*,[178] by clarifying that such claims—or *Stern* claims—were not core proceedings because Article III did not permit such treatment, but were nonetheless within the purview of the bankruptcy court's 'related to' jurisdiction.[179] Thus, while a bankruptcy court cannot decide a *Stern* claim on a final basis, it may recommend a decision to the district court for *de novo* review.

3.125   Less than a year later, the Supreme Court in *Wellness Int'l Network, Ltd v Sharif*[180]then resolved whether Article III permits a bankruptcy court to enter a final judgment on a *Stern* claim with the consent of the parties, which is statutorily authorized under section 157(c)(2) of the United States Code.[181] The *Stern* claim in *Wellness* was a declaratory judgment from the Bankruptcy Court that a trust the debtor claimed to administer was in fact his alter ego, and that the trust's assets were his personal property and part of the estate. In *Stern*, the Supreme Court had held that Article III forbade bankruptcy courts to enter a final judgment on claims that seek only to augment the bankruptcy estate and which would otherwise exist without regard to any bankruptcy proceeding.[182]

3.126   Concluding in the affirmative by a 6–3 decision, the Supreme Court held that it is not unconstitutional for a bankruptcy court to adjudicate a *Stern* claim on a final basis when the parties knowingly and voluntarily consent to such adjudication. The Court explained that '[a]djudication by consent is nothing new. Indeed [d]uring the early years of the Republic, federal courts, with the consent of the litigants, regularly referred adjudication of entire disputes to non-Article III referees, master, or arbitrators, for entry of final judgment in accordance with the referee's report'.[183] The Court concluded that bankruptcy litigants may constitutionally waive the right to Article III adjudication of *Stern* claims.[184] Notably, the Court clarified that such consent need not be express to be valid.[185] Rather, regardless of whether the parties' consent is express or implied, a finding that the consent was knowing and voluntary is sufficient.[186] Courts post-*Wellness* have adopted this view of consent rather broadly and without issue. For example, a number of courts have found that a party impliedly consents to a bankruptcy court's jurisdiction where the party appears before

---

[178] 134 S Ct 2165 (2014).

[179] Ibid at 2167–2168.

[180] 135 S Ct 1932, 1939 (2015).

[181] 11 USC § 157(c)(2) states: 'the district court, with the consent of all the parties to the proceeding, may refer a proceeding related to a case under title 11 to a bankruptcy judge to hear and determine and to enter appropriate orders and judgments, subject to review under section 158 of this title'.

[182] 131 S Ct at 2618.

[183] 135 S Ct at 1942 (internal citations omitted).

[184] Ibid at 1944.

[185] Ibid at 1947.

[186] Ibid at 1948.

the court without objection[187], or even where a party fails to respond to a summons and complaint.[188]

Notwithstanding the above, parties in a bankruptcy proceeding involving a potential *Stern* claim should be aware of potential challenges to consent, and may find it useful to build a record of express consent.   **3.127**

C. Chapter 11 Plan Standards

1. General

Congress promulgated section 1129 of the Bankruptcy Code to establish the minimum requirements for plan confirmation, thus enabling an entity to discharge its debts and continue its operations.[189] Such a determination is made by the bankruptcy court at a statutorily required hearing.[190] The plan proponent has the burden,[191] by a preponderance of the evidence, to show that confirmation requirements have been satisfied.[192] This is true even in the face of overwhelming creditor support.[193]   **3.128**

The specific requirements that an entity must satisfy to confirm a plan of reorganization depend to some extent on whether this objective is sought consensually or not.[194] Confirmation is consensual if the plan is accepted by each class of impaired creditors and interest holders. For a consensual confirmation to be approved, the 13 enumerated paragraphs of section 1129(a) of the Bankruptcy Code also must be satisfied. If confirmation is non-consensual, however, section 1129(b) governs. While section 1129(b) removes the requirement that each class consent to the plan or be unimpaired, all other requirements of section 1129(a) must be satisfied as well as two additional requirements, commonly referred to as the 'cramdown provisions'.[195] Specifically, a non-consensual plan may be confirmed   **3.129**

---

[187] *Matter of Delta Produce, LP*, 845 F.3d 609, 617 (5th Cir 2016) (Party impliedly consented to bankruptcy jurisdiction when he raised 'no constitutional objection when joining the case'); see *In re Tribune Media Co.*, 902 F.3d 384, 395–396 (3d Cir 2018) (party provided implied consent to bankruptcy court jurisdiction where he filed a proof of claim and various responses to the debtor's claim objection without questioning the bankruptcy court's authority to decide the issue).

[188] *In re Fyre Festival LLC*, 611 BR 735 (Bankr SDNY 2020) ('[B]ankruptcy judges may enter default judgments based on implied consent resulting from a defendant's failure to respond to a summons and complaint.'); *Kravitz v Deacons (In re Advance Watch Co, Ltd)*, 587 BR 598 (Bankr SDNY 2018) (citing cases regarding same).

[189] See 11 USC § 1129. See *Bank of America Nat'l Trust and Sav Ass'n v 203 N LaSalle Street P'ship*, 526 US 465 n 4 (1999).

[190] See 11 USC § 1128(a).

[191] See *In re Hercules Offshore, Inc*, 565 BR 732, 766 (Bankr D Del 2016) ('The plan proponent bears the burden of establishing the plan's compliance with each of the requirements set forth in s 1129(a)') (internal citations omitted). See *In re Crowthers McCall Pattern, Inc*, 120 BR 279, 284 (Bankr SDNY 1990) (stating that to confirm a plan the court must find that the plan proponent has complied with all applicable provisions of s 1129).

[192] See *In re Cypresswood Land Partners, I*, 409 BR 396, 422 (Bankr SD Tex 2009) (the debtor has the burden of proving if a plan conforms with s 1129(b) of the Bankruptcy Code by a preponderance of the evidence).

[193] See *In re Union Meeting Partners*, 165 BR 553, 574 (Bankr ED Pa 1994) (providing that 'a plan proponent has the affirmative burden of proving that its plan satisfies the provisions of [section] 1129(a) by the preponderance of the evidence, even in the absence of an objection').

[194] See 11 USC § 1126(c).

[195] See *In re Journal Register Co*, 407 BR 520, 529 (Bankr SDNY 2009) ('[w]here [section] 1129(a)(8) cannot be satisfied because impaired classes fail to accept the plan or receive nothing and are deemed to reject the plan, confirmation of a chapter 11 plan requires compliance with all other requirements of [section] 1129(a) and also the "cramdown" provisions of [section] 1129(b)').

only if the plan does not discriminate unfairly and is fair and equitable with respect to each dissenting, impaired class.[196]

3.130 Once a plan is confirmed, the debtor is discharged from all pre-existing debts and all estate property is vested in the reorganized debtor, unless the plan provides otherwise.[197] A confirmed plan therefore essentially 'operates as a final judgment with res judicata effect'[198] on all issues not otherwise dealt with in the plan or confirmation order. Creditors who fail to timely object[199] to the plan or appeal a confirmation order are nevertheless bound by its terms and can sue only on the obligations created under the plan—even those that are inconsistent with the Bankruptcy Code.[200] It is therefore critical for a plan proponent to satisfy the applicable provisions of section 1129 and the court has an independent duty to determine that such proponent has done so. Below is a discussion of the most significant chapter 11 confirmation standards, including the 'best interests' test, the 'absolute priority rule', and feasibility.

2. Best interests test

3.131 The 'best interests' test of section 1129(a)(7) of the Bankruptcy Code protects creditors and equity holders who are impaired by the plan and who have not voted to accept it. The focus here is placed on individual dissenting parties rather than classes.[201] Specifically, the 'best interests' test requires that holders of impaired claims or interests who do not vote to accept the plan 'receive or retain under the plan on account of such claim or interest property of a value, as of the effective date of the plan, that is not less than the amount that such holder would so receive or retain if the debtor were liquidated under chapter 7 of ... title [11] on such date'.[202] If the court finds that each dissenting member of an impaired class will receive at least as much under the plan as it would receive in a chapter 7 liquidation, the plan satisfies the 'best interests' test.[203]

3.132 To prove that the plan satisfies the 'best interests' test, the plan proponent must submit sufficient evidence that the debtor's creditors will not receive less under the plan as compared to a chapter 7 liquidation.[204] Failure to provide such support—upon which the court

---

[196] See 11 USC § 1129(b)(1).

[197] See generally 11 USC § 1141.

[198] *In re Crown Vantage, Inc*, 421 F 3d 963, 972 (9th Cir 2005) (quoting *In re Robert L Helms Construction & Dev Co, Inc*, 139 F 3d 702, 704 (9th Cir 1998)).

[199] Under 11 USC § 1128(b) any 'party in interest' may object to plan confirmation. Specifically, a 'party in interest' includes 'the debtor, the trustee, a creditors' committee, an equity security holders' committee, a creditor, an equity security holder, or any indenture trustee ...' 11 USC § 1109(b). A 'party in interest', however, has standing only to assert an objection based on its *own* interests—not those of other parties. See *In re Congoleum Corp*, 414 BR 44, 56 (DNJ 2009) ('[t]he Bankruptcy Code affords standing to object to the confirmation of a reorganization plan to any "party in interest", which has been construed broadly to encompass anyone with a "practical stake in the outcome of the proceedings"') (internal citations omitted).

[200] See *Miller v US*, 363 F 3d 999, 1003 (9th Cir 2004).

[201] See *Bank of America Nat'l Trust and Sav Ass'n v 203 N LaSalle Street P'ship*, 526 US 434, 441 n 13 (1999).

[202] See 11 USC § 1129(a)(7)(A); see also *In re Journal Register Co*, 407 BR at 539 (the 'best interests test' 'requires that each holder of an impaired claim or interest receive at least as much in the chapter 11 reorganization as it would in a chapter 7 liquidation').

[203] See *In re Radco Properties, Inc*, 402 BR 666, 675 (Bankr EDNC 2009) ('for a plan to be confirmable, the plan must provide creditors with at least as much as the creditors would have received in a Chapter 7 liquidation').

[204] See *In re Piece Goods Shops Co, LP*, 188 BR 778, 791 (Bankr MDNC 1995) (finding the evidentiary burden on the plan proponents was satisfied by 'extensive evidence' presented at the confirmation hearing concerning debtor's current financial information including its assets and liabilities).

may undertake its own 'independent factual determination'[205]—will bar confirmation.[206] Most often, the plan proponent will provide expert testimony concerning a 'hypothetical chapter 7 liquidation' as of the 'effective date' of the plan, the time at which the plan will be implemented.[207] Consequently, a 'considerable degree of speculation' arises from an analysis based on 'hypothetical' fire-sale conditions.[208] Such conjecture, however, is tempered by the bankruptcy court's use of discretion in evaluating and weighing the relevant evidence presented during the confirmation hearing.[209]

3. Absolute priority rule

Section 1129(b) of the Bankruptcy Code contains a 'cramdown' provision, which applies **3.133** when confirmation is non-consensual. It provides that if all of the applicable confirmation requirements of section 1129(a)—other than subsection (8), which requires that all impaired classes accept the plan—are met, the court, on request of the plan proponent, shall confirm the plan if it does not 'discriminate unfairly' and is 'fair and equitable' with respect to each class of claims or interests that is impaired under, and has not accepted, the plan.[210] In the cramdown context, failure to comply with the 'absolute priority rule' will preclude confirmation of a plan of reorganization.[211]

(a) The plan must not unfairly discriminate

Under section 1129(b)(1), a non-consensual plan of reorganization can be confirmed only **3.134** if it does not 'unfairly discriminate' against impaired dissenting classes. While 'unfair'

---

[205] See *In re Produce Hawaii, Inc*, 41 BR 301, 303–04 (Bankr D Haw 1984).

[206] *In re Southern Pacific Transp Co v Voluntary Purchasing Groups, Inc*, 252 BR 373, 391 (ED Tex 2000) ('A plan obviously cannot be confirmed if there is an insufficient evidentiary basis to determine that it is in the best interests of creditors'). For example, confirmation was initially denied in *In re Ditech Holding Corp.* where the court found that the debtors' liquidation analysis did not value certain consumer claims retained against a hypothetical purchaser, and thus the debtors did not establish that those creditors fared better under the plan than in a hypothetical chapter 7 liquidation. 606 BR 544, 621 (Bankr SDNY 2019).

[207] But see *In re Lason, Inc*, 300 BR 227, 232–33233 (Bankr D Del 2003) (stating that a chapter 7 liquidation analysis can be conducted 'either under "forced sale" conditions or as a going concern').

[208] See ibid at 233. See also *In re Southern Pacific Transp Co v Voluntary Purchasing Groups, Inc*, 252 BR at 392 ('Because such matters as asset valuation and the estimation of liquidation recoveries can be drastically affected by the timing of one's calculations, a court must ensure that all financial projections incorporated into its analysis reflect the resources that are likely to be available to a debtor on a plan's effective date'); *In re Affiliated Foods, Inc*, 249 BR 770, 788 (Bankr WD Mo 2000) ('[t]he valuation of a hypothetical Chapter 7 for purposes of [section] 1129(a)(7)(ii) is not an exact science … [and] [t]he hypothetical liquidation entails a considerable degree of speculation about a situation that will not occur unless the case is actually converted to chapter 7') (internal quotations omitted).).

[209] See *In re Resorts Int'l Inc*, 145 BR 412, 477–78 (Bankr DNJ 1990) (finding sufficient evidence to hold that creditors would receive at least the same value under the proposed plan as they would under a liquidation analysis). But see *In re Southern Pacific Transp Co v Voluntary Purchasing Groups, Inc*, 252 BR at 390–91 (remanding the bankruptcy court's decision to confirm a plan on the grounds that the court engaged in a 'questionable liquidation' analysis using an 'apparently arbitrary' discount rate).

[210] 11 USC § 1129(b)(1); see also *Bank of America Nat'l Trust and Sav Ass'n v 203 N LaSalle Street P'ship*, 526 US 434, 441 (1999).

[211] In February 2020, subchapter V of chapter 11 of the Bankruptcy Code became effective, providing certain small business debtors an expedited chapter 11 process. One of the benefits afforded to debtors who elect to proceed under subchapter V is that the absolute priority rule does not apply, and thus equity holders may receive distributions under the plan even if dissenting unsecured creditors are not being paid in full (the debtor must show, however, that it has committed all of its projected disposable income to the plan for three years). See 11 USC § 1191(b)-(c). The debt limit for subchapter V cases is $2,725,625, but has been temporarily extended by Congress to $7.5 million as a result of the COVID-19 crisis. See COVID-19 Bankruptcy Relief Extension Act of 2021 § 2, 135 Stat 249 (2021).

discrimination is precluded, 'fair' discrimination is indeed permissible.[212] The Bankruptcy Code offers no description of 'unfair discrimination', however, it has been generally interpreted to mean that dissenting classes should receive relatively equal value under the plan as compared with other similarly situated classes.[213] While, bankruptcy courts have attempted to fashion a bright-light objective standard to evaluate 'unfair discrimination', such efforts have been met with little success.

3.135   For example, competing tests have arisen in *In re Aztec Company*[214] and *In re Dow Corning Corp.*[215] In *Aztec*, the court imported the underlying principles from section 1322(b)(1) of chapter 13 of the Bankruptcy Code, which concerns 'unfair discrimination' in the context of individual repayment plans, to develop a four-part test to evaluate 'unfair discrimination'.[216] These factors include: (1) whether the discrimination is supported by a reasonable basis; (2) whether the debtor can confirm and consummate a plan without the discrimination; (3) whether the discrimination is proposed in good faith; and (4) the treatment of classes discriminated against.[217] While some courts have adopted the test in *Aztec*,[218] others have criticized it.[219]

3.136   Other courts such as *Dow Corning*[220] have developed different criteria. There, the court held that a plan of reorganization will be rejected on the grounds of unfair discrimination where there is: (1) a dissenting class; (2) another class of the same priority; (3) a difference in the plan's treatment of the two classes that results in either: (a) a materially lower percentage recovery for the dissenting class—measured by the net present value of all payments; or (b) regardless of percentage recovery, an allocation under the plan of materially greater risk to the dissenting class in connection with its proposed distribution.[221] Unlike the *Aztec* factors, which focus on reasonableness, a presumption of unfair discrimination arises under *Dow Corning* only where the 'dissenting class [receives] a "materially lower" percentage recovery or will have a "materially greater risk" in connection with plan distributions'.[222] The US Court of Appeals for the Third Circuit recently adopted the *Dow Corning* test over the *Aztec* test in *In re Tribune Co.*, finding it better suited for the unfair discrimination analysis because it was 'developed for the Chapter 11 context ... tailored to the specific circumstances of cramdown, where only the interest of the dissenting class is at issue ... [and it]

---

[212] *Brinkley v Chase Manhattan Mortg & Realty Trust (In re LeBlanc)*, 622 F.2d 872, 879 (5th Cir 1980) ('A bankruptcy court can permit discrimination when the facts of the case justify it.'); *In re City of Detroit*, 524 BR 147, 255 (Bankr ED Mich 2014) ('The bankruptcy code permits discrimination in the treatment of classes of claims. It only prohibits unfair discrimination.').

[213] *In re Armstrong World Indus, Inc*, 348 BR 111, 122 (D Del 2006) (noting that '[a] finding that all classes of the same priority will receive the identical amount under the proposed [p]lan is not necessary to find that the [p]lan does not discriminate').

[214] 107 BR 585 (Bankr MD Tenn 1989).

[215] 244 BR 705 (Bankr ED Mich 1999).

[216] *Aztec*, 107 BR at 589–90.

[217] Ibid at 590.

[218] See *Mercury Capital Corp v Milford Connecticut Assocs, LP*, 354 BR 1, 10 (D Conn 2006); *In re Buttonwood Partners, Ltd*, 111 BR 57, 63 (Bankr SDNY 1990); *In re Creekstone Apartments Assocs, LP*, 168 BR 639, 644 (Bankr MD Tenn 1994).

[219] See *In re Tribune Co*, 972 F.3d 228, 241 n 15 (3d Cir. 2020); See *McCullough v Brown*, 162 BR 506, 516 (ND Ill 1993) ('This court ... cheerfully rejects any temptation to formulate a universal standard by which to measure all future class-discriminatory plans').

[220] 244 BR 705 (Bankr ED Mich 1999).

[221] Ibid at 710 (citing Bruce A Markell, 'A New Perspective on Unfair Discrimination in Chapter 11 ("A New Perspective")' 72 Am Bankr LJ 227, 228 (1998)).

[222] *Armstrong World Indus, Inc*, 348 BR at 121–122 (applying the *Dow Corning* test).

eschews concepts such as reasonableness, whether a plan can be confirmed without discrimination, and good faith.[223]

Accordingly, under either of the aforementioned approaches, as between two classes of **3.137** claims or two classes of equity interests, there is no unfair discrimination if the classes are comprised of dissimilar claims or interests, or taking into account the particular facts and circumstances of the case, there is a reasonable basis for such disparate treatment.[224] Thus, whether a plan of reorganization unfairly discriminates against an impaired class boils down to whether the proposed discrimination between classes has a reasonable basis and is necessary for successful reorganization of the debtor.[225]

(b) The plan must be fair and equitable
To confirm a plan under section 1129(b)(1) over the objection of dissenting classes of impaired **3.138** creditors or equity holders the plan must not only avoid 'unfair discrimination' but must also be 'fair and equitable'.[226] Justice Douglas labelled the words fair and equitable as a 'rule of full or absolute priority'[227] based on previous judicial interpretations in the field of equity receivership reorganizations. Such construction of the fair and equitable requirement continues to be correct.

To comply with the 'absolute priority rule' a plan must ensure that 'the holder of any claim **3.139** or interest that is junior to the claims of such [impaired][228] classes will not receive or retain under the plan on account of such junior claim or interest any property'.[229] An essential corollary of the 'absolute priority rule' holds that a senior class cannot receive more than full compensation for its claims or interests.[230] Thus, where the interests of former shareholders are eliminated in a cramdown plan, the court must ensure that the senior classes of claims do not receive more than they are owed.[231]

---

[223] *In re Tribune Co*, 972 F.3d at 241 n 15 (applying *Dow Corning* test to find that plan did not unfairly discriminate against dissenting class of creditors).

[224] See, eg, *In re Drexel Burnham Lambert Group*, 140 BR 347, 350 (SDNY 1992) ('where legal claims are sufficiently different as to justify a difference in treatment under a reorganization plan, reasonable differences in treatment are permissible') (internal citations omitted).

[225] *In re Leslie Fay Cos Inc*, 207 BR 764, 791 n 37 (Bankr SDNY 1997).

[226] 11 USC § 1129(b)(1).

[227] *Case v Los Angeles Lumber Prods Co*, 308 US 106, 117 (1939).

[228] The 'fair and equitable' requirement essentially codifies the 'absolute priority rule' but requires different treatment for different types of classes—depending whether the class is secured, unsecured, or a class of interests. See 11 USC § 1129(b)(2)(A) (stating the requirements for secured claims); 11 USC § 1129(b)(2)(B) (stating the requirements for unsecured claims); and 11 USC § 1129(b)(2)(C) (stating the requirements for a class of interests). Fair and equitable treatment of a class of secured creditors may be achieved in several ways, including where the class creditor receives deferred cash payments amounting to the full value of their claims: 11 USC § 1129(b)(2)(A) (i). To receive the full value of their claims, secured creditors will often need to be compensated for interest that has accrued on their claims. However, how this 'cramdown' interest rate is calculated is often hotly disputed. In *Till v SCS Credit Corp*, the Supreme Court held that the proper method of calculating cramdown interest in a chapter 13 bankruptcy case was the 'formula' approach, producing an interest rate that incorporates a base, risk-free interest rate plus compensation for credit risk and collateral risk: 541 US 465, 478–79, (2004). However, courts have moved away from this method in favour of a 'market test' approach. For example, in *Momentive Performance Materials Inc v BOKF, NA (In re MPM Silicones, LLC)*, the Court of Appeals for the Second Circuit held that where an efficient market exists, market testing the interest rate is the best determinant: 874 F.3d 787, 800–01 (2d Cir 2017).

[229] 11 USC § 1129(b)(2)(B)(ii).

[230] *In re Exide Techs*, 303 BR 48, 61 (Bankr D Del 2003) (internal citations omitted).

[231] *In re Trans Max Tech, Inc*, 349 BR 80, 89 (Bankr D Nev 2006) ('[o]ne component of fair and equitable treatment [required by section 1129(b) of the Bankruptcy Code] is that a plan may not pay a premium to a senior class'); see also *In re Future Energy Corp*, 83 BR 470, 495 n 39 (Bankr SD Ohio 1988) ('Clearly, overpayment of senior creditors is violative of the fair and equitable standard').

3.140   A key facet of the 'absolute priority rule' is the meaning of 'property'. Specifically, the legislative history refers to an expansive interpretation of 'property'—including both tangible and intangible interests.[232] This broad definition includes both property interests that may be received or retained by shareholders and creditors. As such, the method under which the property to be distributed or retained under the plan is valued plays a vital role in determining whether the 'absolute priority rule' is satisfied.

3.141   A significant 'exception' to the absolute priority rule concerns contribution of 'new value' under a plan. The new value exception has its origins in dicta from a 1939 Supreme Court decision, *Case v Los Angeles Lumber Products Co.*[233] In its decision, the Court stated that stockholders may participate in a plan of reorganization where 'the old stockholders make a fresh contribution and receive in return a participation reasonably equivalent to their contribution'.[234] Where such value is contributed by the stockholders, 'no objection can be made'.[235] The Supreme Court offered no guidance on whether or how the 'new value' exception applies under the current version of the Bankruptcy Code until its 1999 opinion in *Bank of America Nat'l Trust and Savings Ass v 203 North LaSalle Street P'ship.*[236]

3.142   Prior to *203 North LaSalle*, a split of authority existed as to whether the doctrine remained valid under the Bankruptcy Code.[237] Under the 'new value' exception, if old equity provides an infusion of 'new value', old equity holders are deemed not to have received property 'on account of' their old equity interests, thereby avoiding any violation of the 'absolute priority rule'.[238]

3.143   In *203 North LaSalle*, the Supreme Court held that even if the new value exception to the 'absolute priority rule' existed under the Bankruptcy Code it still would not have permitted the junior interest holders in that case to obtain an interest in the reorganized company.[239] Key to the Court's finding was the junior interest holders' *exclusive* opportunity to obtain such interest free of market competition.[240] Rather, the Court found that such 'exclusivity' was in fact a 'property interest' that the junior holders received 'on account' of their old equity position.[241] As a result of such exclusivity, replete with its 'protection against the market's scrutiny of the purchase price by means of competing bids or even competing plan proposals', the Court concluded that any value received by the junior interests was solely on the basis

---

[232]   See HR Rep No 95-595, at 413 (1977), reprinted in 1978 USCCAN 5963, 6368.

[233]   308 US 106 (1939).

[234]   Ibid at 121.

[235]   Ibid.

[236]   526 US 434 (1999).

[237]   Compare *In re Bonner Mall P'ship*, 2 F 3d 899, 910–16 (9th Cir 1993) (accepting the new value exception to the 'absolute priority rule'), with *In re Coltex Loop Central Three Partners, LP*, 138 F 3d 39, 44–45 (2d Cir 1998) (disfavouring the 'new value' exception without expressly rejecting it), and *In re Bryson Properties, XVIII*, 961 F 2d 496, 504 (4th Cir 1992) (same).

[238]   See *In re Bonner Mall P'ship*, 2 F 3d 899, 915–916. Here, the Ninth Circuit rejected the notion that the new value exception 'allows old equity to repurchase the business at a bargain price, while superior creditors go unpaid'. Ibid at 916. Rather, the court stated that, assuming proper application of the new value rule, its application will in fact 'enhance' the 'absolute priority rule' rather than contravene its principles. Ibid.

[239]   *203 North LaSalle*, 526 US at 458.

[240]   See ibid at 455–58. Moreover, the Court stated that 'there is no apparent reason for giving old equity a bargain ... unless the very purpose of the whole transaction is, at least in part, to do old equity a favor'. Ibid at 456.

[241]   Ibid. In evaluating the presence of the term 'on account of' in s 1129(b) the Court held that there 'could' be a new value corollary under the Code based on its inclusion in the statute. Ibid at 449.

of its old equity position rather than the new value provided.[242] As such, the Court emphasized 'market exposure' in determining the 'top dollar' for a particular interest—rather than
determination by a bankruptcy court.[243]

Following the Supreme Court's holding in *203 North LaSalle* and uncertainty as to its con-   **3.144**
tinuing viability, lower courts continue to walk a fine line in applying the contours of the
'new value' exception.[244] In doing so, courts have given special attention to the Court's creation of the so-called 'market test'[245] and its directive that any efforts by junior interests
to infuse new value into a debtor entity under a plan of reorganization first be exposed to
market competition, thus ensuring 'top dollar' is received.[246] The extent to which such 'exposure' is necessary, however, is an open question that bankruptcy courts will continue to
grapple with in the wake of *203 North LaSalle*.

In *In re Armstrong World Indus, Inc*,[247] the Third Circuit held that equity holders cannot re-   **3.145**
tain *any* interest if an impaired dissenting class of senior creditors does not receive full payment, including post-petition interest. In *Armstrong*, the company filed a chapter 11 case
principally to deal with its significant contingent asbestos-related liabilities. Three classes
were at the core of the *Armstrong* plan: Class 6 claimants—consisting of unsecured creditors, including bank lenders, that would receive a 59 per cent recovery; Class 7 claimants—
consisting of present and future asbestos-related claimants, who agreed to receive a 20 per
cent recovery, and Class 12—consisting of shareholders, whose equity interests would be
wiped out.[248] If Class 6 voted against the plan, then Class 7 asbestos claimants would receive
warrants, which they would automatically 'waive' in favour of Class 12, the equity class.[249]
The Third Circuit reversed the lower court's confirmation of the *Armstrong* plan on the basis
that this scheme violated the absolute priority rule:

> The absolute priority rule, as codified, ensures that 'the holder of any claim or interest that
> is junior to the claims of [an impaired dissenting] class will not receive or retain under the
> plan on account of such junior claim or interest any property'. The plain language of the

---

[242] Ibid. The Court further supported its conclusion that the new value exception did not apply because the
debtor's plan included a 'provision for vesting equity in the reorganized business in the Debtor's partners without
extending an opportunity to anyone else either to compete for that equity or to propose a competing reorganization plan'. Ibid at 436–545.

[243] See ibid at 456–457.

[244] See *Matter of Woodbrook Assocs*, 19 F 3d 312, 319–320 (7th Cir 1994). In *Woodbrook*, the Seventh Circuit
fashioned a three-pronged test to determine whether the new value exception applies to a particular case.
Specifically, the following inquiries are relevant: (1) whether the old equity owners made a new contribution in
money or money's worth; (2) that reasonably equivalent to the value of the new equity interests in the reorganized debtor, and (3) that is necessary for implementation of a feasible reorganization plan. Ibid at 320.

[245] See *In re Union Fin Servs Grp, Inc*, 303 BR 390, 423–426 (Bankr ED Mo 2003).

[246] See, eg, *In re Ameriflex Engineering LLC*, Case No. 17-60837 (TMR), 2018 WL 3701678, *4 (Bankr D Or 31
July 2018) (new value exception not satisfied where no market existed due to equity owner's control and exclusive opportunity to purchase assets); See, eg, *Cypresswood Land Partners, I*, 409 BR 396, 438–39 (Bankr SD Tex
2009) (applying the new value exception to permit approval of a plan of reorganization where there was sufficient
notice to the interested parties of the opportunity to offer competing plans); *In re PWS Holding Corp*, 228 F 3d 224,
238–240 (3d Cir 2000) (finding equity holders did not enjoy an exclusive opportunity under the plan to invest in
the reorganized entity thus avoiding violation of the 'absolute priority rule').

[247] 432 F 3d 507 (3d Cir 2005).

[248] Ibid at 509.

[249] Ibid.

statute makes it clear that a plan cannot give property to junior claimants over the objection of a more senior class if that class is impaired.[250]

3.146   The Court of Appeals rejected the argument that the asbestos claimants could do whatever they wanted with their plan distributions, observing that the absolute priority rule 'arose from the concern that because a debtor proposed its own reorganization plan, the plan could be "too good a deal" for the debtor's owners'.[251] Such value retention by the equity holders could otherwise result only from 'gifting' from the asbestos claims holders—an impermissible value transfer that was forbidden by *Armstrong*.

3.147   While *Armstrong* advocates a strict interpretation of the absolute priority rule, subsequent cases have indicated a more flexible approach to the concept of 'gifting' associated with proposed reorganizations plans.[252] For example, where the 'gift' does not reduce a more senior creditor's recovery,[253] courts have demonstrated a willingness to permit deviations from the absolute priority rule. The US Court of Appeals for the Second Circuit revisited this issue in 2011 in *In re DBSD North America Inc*, and held that the absolute priority rule per se prohibits all non-consensual 'gifting' plans. The Second Circuit left open the viability of gifting in limited circumstances—when the gift is part of a settlement outside a plan of reorganization.[254]

3.148   The Supreme Court's decision in *Czyzewski v Jevic Holding Corp.* has cast further doubt on 'gifting' plans.[255] In *Jevic*, the Supreme Court held that a structured dismissal cannot be approved if it 'provides for distributions that do not follow ordinary priority rules without the affected creditors' consent' and that even in 'rare cases' courts cannot disregard Bankruptcy Code priority.[256] Although the Supreme Court's decision was limited to the structured dismissal, rather than chapter 11 plan, context, there has been considerable speculation over whether its strict adherence to absolute priority represents the end of 'gift' plans.

3.149   However, notwithstanding *Jevic*, *Armstrong*, and *DBSD*, some courts have continued to approve such plans. For example, in *Hargreaves v Nuverra Environmental Solutions Inc*, the District Court for the District of Delaware upheld a bankruptcy court decision that approved a plan that 'horizontally' gifted money from senior creditors to two groups of

---

[250] Ibid at 513 (alteration in original) (quoting 11 USC § 1129(b)(2)(B)(ii)).

[251] Ibid at 512 (citing *203 North LaSalle*, 526 US at 444).

[252] See *In re Iridium LLC*, 478 F 3d 452, 464–465 (2d Cir 2007) ('[i]n the Chapter 11 context, whether a settlement's distribution plan complies with the Bankruptcy Code's priority scheme will often be the dispositive factor. However, where the remaining factors weigh heavily in favor of approving a settlement, the bankruptcy court, in its discretion, could endorse a settlement that does not comply in some minor respects with the priority rule if the parties to the settlement justify, and the reviewing court clearly articulates the reasons for approving, a settlement that deviates from the priority rule').

[253] See, eg, *In re TSIC, Inc*, 393 BR 71, 77 (Bankr D Del 2009) (holding that a settlement did not violate the absolute priority rule where the distributions to be paid to unsecured creditors—before more senior classes are paid in full—were derived from property that was not a part of the estate); *In re World Health Alternatives, Inc*, 344 BR 291, 297–298 (Bankr D Del 2006) (finding that a settlement does not violate the absolute priority rule where it allows general unsecured creditors to receive a recovery before priority creditors and the recovery is a 'carve out' of the secured creditors' lien and does not belong to the estate).

[254] *In re DBSD N Am, Inc*, 634 F 3d 79, 93–101 (2d Cir 2011) (holding that the plan violated the absolute priority rule because a junior class of interests (old equity) was receiving 'property' in the form of shares and warrants in the reorganized entity, 'under' the plan, 'on account of its junior interests' and noting that while Congress softened the absolute priority rule in some ways, 'it did not create any exceptions for "gifts" like the one at issue [in that particular case]' while avoiding overruling its prior decision in *Iridium*, 478 F 3d 452).

[255] 137 S. Ct. 973 (2017).

[256] Ibid. at 983, 986.

out-of-the-money unsecured creditors, consisting of noteholders and trade creditors, re-spectively.[257] The noteholders were to receive a 4–6 per cent recovery while the trade creditors were to recover in full.[258] The noteholders objected, arguing among other things that the payment to trade creditors was a prohibited gift under *Armstrong*. The *Nuverra* court disagreed, finding that *Armstrong* was not a per se rejection of gifting, especially in the circumstances before the court where a 'horizontal' gift was at issue (unequal gifting to two creditors with the same priority) rather than a 'vertical' gift (a gift that skips an intermediary junior class of dissenting creditors).[259] Interestingly, *Jevic* was not cited or otherwise discussed in *Nuverra*, indicating that the court did not find the decision of concern. Nonetheless, given that recent cases have signalled the end of the gifting doctrine, especially in the 'vertical' context, the utility of gifting as a tool for building consensus in connection with proposed reorganization plans may be limited.

4. Feasibility

A plan of reorganization must be feasible to be confirmed. Specifically, section 1129(a)(11)   **3.150**
of the Bankruptcy Code provides that a plan of reorganization may be confirmed only if '[c]onfirmation of the plan is not likely to be followed by the liquidation, or the need for further financial reorganization, of the debtor or any successor to the debtor under the plan, unless such liquidation or reorganization is proposed in the plan.'[260] To prove that a plan is feasible, the proponent must 'present proof through reasonable projections that there will be sufficient cash flow to fund the plan and maintain operations according to the plan.'[261] Thus, an inquiry into a plan's feasibility is essentially a 'question of fact', in which the debtor has the burden, by a preponderance of the evidence, to provide sufficient evidence.[262] The feasibility test of section 1129(a)(11) is intended to protect creditors against visionary or speculative plans.[263] The prospect of financial uncertainty, however, cannot defeat confirmation of a plan on feasibility grounds as only a 'reasonable assurance of success' rather than 'guaranteed success' is the standard.[264] Courts may consider several factors to determine whether a plan is feasible including: (1) adequacy of the capital structure; (2) the earning power of the business; (3) economic conditions; (4) the ability of management; (5) the probability of the continuation of the same management; and (6) any other related matter which affects the prospects of a sufficiently successful operation to enable performance of the plan's

---

[257] 590 BR 75 (D Del 2018).

[258] Ibid at 79–80.

[259] Ibid at 94.

[260] 11 USC § 1129(a)(11).

[261] *Pan Am Corp v Delta Air Lines, Inc*, 175 BR 438, 508 (SDNY 1994) (internal quotations omitted); see). See also *In re Christian Faith Assembly*, 402 BR 794, 799–800 (Bankr ND Ohio 2009) (denying confirmation of the debtor's plan on the grounds of feasibility because of the debtor's failure to obtain a firm financial commitment).

[262] *In re Radco Properties, Inc*, 402 BR at 678 (Bankr EDNC 2009)). See *Journal Register Co*, 407 BR at 539 (finding the plan was feasible based on testimony by an experienced restructuring professional, financial projections and an exit financing commitment letter).

[263] See *Bridgeport Jai Alai, Inc v Autotote Sys, Inc, (In re Bridgeport Jai Alai, Inc)*, 215 BR 651, 654 (Bankr D Conn 1997); see also *In re Biz As Usual, LLC*, No. 19-16476, 2021 Bankr LEXIS 1132, at *13 (Bankr ED Pa 28 Apr 2021) (denying confirmation where a plan was dependent on 'highly contested, undeveloped litigation' and a speculative sale of assets). See also *Christian Faith Assembly*, 402 BR at 799 ('Section 1129(a)(11) prevents confirmation of "visionary schemes" that promise creditors more than what the debtor can provide post-confirmation').

[264] *Kane v Johns-Manville Corp*, 843 F 2d 636, 649 (2d Cir 1988); see). See also *In re Biz As Usual, LLC*, 2021 Bankr LEXIS 1132, at *11 ('[T]he proposed plan must present a realistic and workable framework with a reasonable likelihood of succeeding on its own') (internal quotations omitted); *Crestar Bank v Walker (In re Walker)*, 165 BR 994, 1004 (ED Va 1994) (A plan must 'provide a realistic and workable framework for reorganization').

provisions.[265] Thus, to be confirmed, a plan proponent must meet a relatively low threshold of proof by demonstrating 'a realistic and workable framework for reorganization'.[266]

3.151   Despite this fairly flexible standard, the COVID-19 pandemic has created new obstacles for debtors seeking to meet the feasibility test, as market instability has at times called into question a debtor's ability to execute on its business plan and funding commitments. While courts have continued to apply the feasibility analysis thoroughly, they have also acknowledged that the pandemic cannot 'spell the end of attempts to reorganize' and 'it is especially important that debtors be given the opportunity to reorganize [during the pandemic] if they can find ways to adapt to [the] current circumstances'.[267] For example, in *In re Sanam Conyers Lodging, LLC*, the court found that a debtor's plan was feasible despite the uncertainty brought to its hotel business as a result of the pandemic. In particular, the court found the debtor's projections to be reasonably probable in light of the fact that the harsh market effects of the pandemic would likely subside sometime in 2021.[268] Thus, while debtors should be prepared for these types of challenge raised by creditors[269] and must still be able to prove that their financial projections are not speculative, debtors may take comfort in that courts have recognized that, even in industries harmed by the pandemic and where uncertainty still lies ahead, a plan may nonetheless be feasible.

5. Other plan confirmation standards

3.152   In addition to the 'best interests' test and feasibility, section 1129 of the Bankruptcy Code incorporates several additional standards that the plan proponent must satisfy.[270]

(a) The plan must comply with the applicable provisions of title 11 (section 1129(a)(1))

3.153   Under section 1129(a)(1) a plan must comply with the 'applicable provisions' of the Bankruptcy Code.[271] Despite its broad drafting, it is well established that section 1129(a)(1) is aimed at compliance with sections 1122 and 1123[272] of the Bankruptcy Code, which

---

[265] *In re Brice Road Developments, LLC*, 392 BR 274, 283 (6th Cir 2008).

[266] Ibid (internal quotations omitted); see also *In re The Prudential Energy Co*, 58 BR 857, 862 (Bankr SDNY 1986) ('Guaranteed success in the stiff winds of commerce without the protection of the Code is not the standard under [section] 1129(a) (11). … All that is required is that there be reasonable assurance of commercial viability'); see also *In re North Valley Mall, LLC*, 432 BR 825, 838 (Bankr CD Cal 2010)2010 WL 2632017, at *9 ('The Code does not require the debtor to prove that success is inevitable or assured, and a relatively low threshold of proof will satisfy [section] 1129 so long as adequate evidence supports a finding of feasibility').

[267] *In re Sanam Conyers Lodging, LLC*, 619 BR 784, 789 (Bankr ND Ga 2020); see *In re Velazquez*, No. 18-02209 (EAG), 2020 Bankr LEXIS 1387 (Bankr DPR 27 May 2020) (finding that a plan offered a reasonable likelihood of success although the debtors were not completely unharmed by the pandemic).

[268] *In re Sanam*, 619 BR at 789–790.

[269] See Emergency Motion of the Ad Hoc Noteholder Group for a Telephonic Status Conference 7, *In re Pioneer Energy Servs. Corp., et al*, No. 20-31425 (DRJ) (Bankr SD Tex 6 Apr 2020), ECF No. 179 (questioning whether debtor's plan could be consummated in light of updated projections showing that EBITDA would be 'approximately one-half of the 2020 EBITDA originally projected'). The parties ultimately settled and the issue was not litigated.

[270] 11 USC § 1129; see also *In re Cajun Elec Power Coop, Inc*, 230 BR 715, 728 (Bankr MD La 1999) ('for a plan to be confirmed, the plan proponent bears the burden of proof with respect to each and every element of section 1129(a)').

[271] 11 USC § 1129(a)(1).

[272] The plan must comply with each of the seven mandatory requirements of section 1123(a) of the Bankruptcy Code which include: (1) designating classes of claims and equity interests; (2) specifying any classes of claims or interests that are not impaired under the plan; (3) specifying the treatment of any class of claims or interests that is impaired under the plan; (4) providing the same treatment for claims or equity interests within each class; (5) providing adequate means for implementation of the plan; (6) containing certain provisions regarding the selection of

govern the classification of claims and the contents of a plan of reorganization, respectively, as well as section 510, which governs the subordination of claims.[273] To satisfy these provisions, classification must be based on the nature of the claim or interest. Specifically, a claim or interest should be included in a specific class only if it is substantially similar to other claims and interests in such class.[274] Classification, however, does not require that *all* substantially similar claims or interests be placed in the same class.[275] Thus, a proponent has significant flexibility in determining a classification structure so long as dissimilar claims are not classified together and similar claims are classified separately *only* for a legitimate reason.[276]

(b) The plan proponent must comply with the applicable provisions
    of title 11 (section 1129(a)(2))
While section 1129(a)(1) concerns the form and content of the plan itself, section 1129(a) **3.154**
(2) is concerned primarily with the actions of a plan proponent under the Bankruptcy Code.[277] Thus, the principal purpose of section 1129(a)(2) is to ensure that a plan proponent has complied with the disclosure and solicitation requirements set forth in sections 1125 and 1126 of the Bankruptcy Code.[278]

(c) The plan must be proposed in good faith (section 1129(a)(3))
Section 1129(a)(3) requires that a plan be 'proposed in good faith and not by any means **3.155**
forbidden by law'. Although not defined in the Bankruptcy Code, 'good faith' has been described to include a 'reasonable likelihood that the plan will achieve a result consistent with the objectives and purposes of the Bankruptcy Code'.[279] In evaluating 'good faith' courts will consider the 'the totality of the circumstances'.[280]

(d) Additional requirements under section 1129(a)
Several additional requirements must be satisfied for a plan of reorganization to be con- **3.156**
firmed. For example, section 1129(a)(4) requires that certain professional fees and expenses paid by a plan proponent, debtor, or by a person receiving distributions of property under

---

post-confirmation managers and officers; and (7) containing only provisions that are 'consistent with the interests of creditors and equity security holders and with public policy'. See 11 USC § 1123(a).

[273] See HR Rep No 95-595, 95th Cong, at 412 (1977), reprinted in 1978 USCCAN 5963, 6368; S Rep No 95-998, at 126 (1978), reprinted in 1978 USCCAN 5787, 5912.

[274] 11 USC § 1122(a).

[275] See *In re Sentinel Mgmt GrpManagement Group, Inc*, 398 BR 281, 296–297 (Bankr ND Ill 2008).

[276] See *In re Source Enters, Inc*, 392 BR 541, 555–56 (SDNY 2008). But see *In re New Midland Plaza Assocs*, 247 BR 877, 893 (Bankr SD Fla 2000); *In re Mid-State Raceway, Inc*, 343 BR 21 (Bankr NDNY 2006) ('[T]he one clear rule [that has] emerge[d] concerning [section] 1122 claims classification is that thou shalt not classify similar claims differently in order to gerrymander an affirmative vote on a reorganization plan') (internal citations omitted).

[277] See 7 Collier on Bankruptcy, para 1129.02[2] (16th edn, rev 2021).

[278] See *In re Cypresswood Land Partners, I*, 409 BR 396, 424 (Bankr SD Tex 2009) citing *In re Landing Assocs, Ltd*, 157 BR 791, 811 (Bankr WD Tex 1993). Moreover, the Court noted that '[s]ection 1129(a)(2) does not provide creditors with a "silver bullet" to defeat confirmation based on each and every minor infraction of Title 11 that a debtor may commit'. Ibid at 423–424.

[279] See *In re Sentinel Mgmt GrpManagement Group, Inc*, 398 BR at 281, 315 (Bankr ND Ill 2008) (internal citations omitted).

[280] *In re Madison Hotel Associates*, 749 F 2d 410, 425 (7th Cir 1984); see also *Todeschi v Juarez (In re Juarez)*, 603 BR 610, 626 (9th Cir BAP 2019).

a plan, be subject to court approval. This subsection requires that any and all post-petition professional fees promised or received in the bankruptcy case be disclosed and subject to the court's review and approval as to their reasonableness.[281]

3.157   Further, the plan proponent must disclose the identity and affiliations of any individual proposed to serve, after confirmation, as a director, officer, or voting trustee of the debtor or the debtor's successor.[282] Additionally, any regulatory commission having jurisdiction over the rates charged by the reorganized debtor in the operation of its business must approve any rate change provided for in the plan.[283]

3.158   At the 'heart' of consensual confirmation is section 1129(a)(8).[284] Specifically, it mandates that, subject to the cramdown exceptions contained in section 1129(b) of the Bankruptcy Code described above, each class of claims or interests must either have accepted the plan or be rendered unimpaired[285] under the plan.[286] Under section 1129(a)(10), however, if a plan impairs one or more classes of claims at least one such class must vote to accept the plan— not including acceptance of the plan by an insider.

3.159   Additionally, section 1129(a)(9) sets forth a number of requirements relating to the payment of priority claims. Among other things, this section provides that all administrative claims must be paid in full in cash upon the plan's effectiveness.[287] Other priority and non-tax claims must be paid as of the 'effective date' in a manner that depends on whether the class has accepted or rejected the plan.[288]

3.160   Furthermore, under section 1129(a)(12), certain fees listed in 28 USC § 1930, which relate primarily to quarterly amounts owed to the United States Trustee, must be paid or arranged to be paid under the plan as of its effective date.[289] Lastly, under section 1129(a)(13) of the Bankruptcy Code the plan must also provide for the continuation of retiree benefits for the duration of the period that the debtor has obligated itself to provide such benefits.[290]

---

[281] *Journal Register Co*, 407 BR at 537 (stating that the issue of reasonableness under s 1129(a)(4) will vary on a case-by-case basis and depend on the particular facts surrounding the payments).

[282] 11 USC § 1129(a)(5)(A)(i).

[283] 11 USC § 1129(a)(6).

[284] See *In re Middle Mountain 156, LLC*, No 208BK16119, 2009 WL 2493371 (Bkrtcy D Ariz March 10 Mar, 2009) (quoting 7 Collier on Bankruptcy at para 1129.03[8], pp 1129–1158 (15th edn)).

[285] See 11 USC § 1124; see also *In re Sentinel Mgmt GrpManagement Group, Inc*, 398 BR at 317 ('A class is impaired if there is any alteration of a creditor's rights, no matter how minor') (internal citations omitted).

[286] 11 USC § 1129(a)(8). A class of claims accepts a plan if the holders of at least two-thirds in dollar amount and more than one-half in the number of claims vote to accept the plan—counting only those claims whose holders actually vote. See 11 USC § 1126(c). A class of interests accepts a plan if holders of at least two-thirds of the amount of interests vote to accept the plan, counting only those interests whose holders actually vote. See 11 USC § 1126(d).

[287] 11 USC § 1129(a)(9)(A).

[288] 11 USC § 1129(a)(9)(B)–(D).

[289] While such fees must be paid to confirm a plan of reorganization, there is in fact no true need for this provision as the fees explicitly referred to are already classified as administrative (first priority claims) under section 507(a)(1) of the Bankruptcy Code and thus must be paid in full pursuant to the aforementioned section 1129(a) (9). See 7 Collier on Bankruptcy, para 1129.02[12] (16th edn, rev 2021).

[290] In addition to the requirements set forth under section 1129(a) of the Bankruptcy Code, two additional limitations on plan confirmation are set forth. Specifically, under section 1129(c) only one plan may be confirmed unless the confirmation order has been revoked under section 1144 of the Bankruptcy Code. Further, under section 1129(d) of the Bankruptcy Code, if the main objective of the plan is to avoid taxes or the application of federal securities laws, the plan cannot be confirmed.

D. Third-Party Releases

As noted paras 3.128 and 3.130, a confirmed plan will generally discharge the debtor from **3.161** all pre-existing debts and liabilities. However, a debtor's plan will often seek to extend re-leases to non-debtor third parties who participated in the reorganization process, such as officers, directors, lenders, and advisors. By virtue of a confirmed plan's binding effect, these releases may be binding on parties who have either rejected the plan or did not affirma-tively consent to the plan and thus the release contained therein. Courts have grappled with whether these nonconsensual third-party releases are proper on statutory and constitu-tional grounds.

A number of courts have found that nonconsensual third-party releases conflict with **3.162** section 524(e) of the Bankruptcy Code, which states that 'discharge of a debt of the debtor does not affect the liability of any other entity on, or the property of any other entity for, such debt'.[291] However, the majority of courts do not per se reject such releases, but rather require that certain factors be satisfied,[292] including whether:

(1) There is an identity of interests between the debtor and the third party, usually an indemnity relationship, such that a suit against the non-debtor is, in essence, a suit against the debtor or will deplete the assets of the estate;
(2) The non-debtor has contributed substantial assets to the reorganization;
(3) The injunction is essential to reorganization, namely, the reorganization hinges on the debtor being free from indirect suits against parties who would have indemnity or contribution claims against the debtor;
(4) The impacted class or classes have overwhelmingly voted to accept the plan;
(5) The plan provides a mechanism to pay for all, or substantially all, of the class or classes affected by the injunction;
(6) The plan provides an opportunity for those claimants who choose not to settle to re-cover in full and;
(7) The bankruptcy court made a record of specific factual findings that support its conclusions.[293]

Some have opined that nonconsensual third-party releases are unconstitutional in the **3.163** wake of *Stern v Marshall*, which, as discussed in section V.B, stands for the proposition

---

[291] The Fifth and Tenth Circuits have generally rejected nonconsensual third-party releases. See *In re Pac Lumber Co.*, 584 F.3d 229 (5th Cir 2009) (holding that nonconsensual third-party releases are precluded pursuant to § 524(e)); *In re W Real Estate Fund, Inc*, 922 F.2d 592 (10th Cir 1990) (same). But see Findings of Fact, Conclusions of Law, and Order Confirming the Second Amended Joint Chapter 11 Plan of Reorganization of Diamond Offshore Drilling, Inc. and Its Debtor Affiliates, *In re Diamond Offshore Drilling, Inc*, No. 20-32307 (DRJ) (Bankr SD Tex 8 Apr 2021) ECF 1231 (confirming chapter 11 plan containing nonconsensual third-party release over objection of United States Trustee). The Ninth Circuit has generally prohibited nonconsensual third-party releases, but has held that a chapter 11 plan may contain a 'narrow exculpation clause' releasing non-debtor claims related to the plan approval process. See *Blixseth v Credit Suisse*, 961 F.3d 1074 (9th Cir 2020).

[292] The Second, Fourth, Sixth, Seventh, and Eleventh Circuits generally permit nonconsensual third-party re-leases under certain circumstances. See *SE Prop. Holdings, LLC v Seaside Eng'g & Surveying, Inc (In re Seaside Eng'g & Surveying, Inc)*, 780 F.3d 1070 (11th Cir 2015); *Airadigm Commc'ns, Inc v Federal Commc'ns Comm'n*, 519 F.3d 640 (7th Cir 2008); *Class Five Nevada Claimants v Dow Corning Corp (In re Dow Corning Corp)*, 280 F.3d 648 (6th Cir 2002); *In re Munford, Inc*, 97 F.3d 449, 454 (11th Cir 1996); *In re Drexel Burnham Lambert Grp, Inc*, 960 F.2d 285, 293 (2d Cir 1992); *In re A.H. Robins Co*, 880 F.2d 694, 701 (4th Cir 1989).

[293] *In re Dow Corning Corp*, 280 F.3d at 658.

that a bankruptcy court cannot enter final judgments in actions involving 'private rights' but may adjudicate claims where the court 'resolves a matter that is integral to the restructuring of the debtor-creditor relationship'.[294] The US Court of Appeals for the Third Circuit recently addressed this issue in *In re Millennium Lab Holdings II, LLC*, holding that the bankruptcy court possessed the constitutional authority to confirm a plan that contained a nonconsensual third-party release benefiting certain equity holders.[295] In particular, the court was persuaded that the released equity holders were not willing to make their $325 million plan contribution without the release provision in the plan.[296] Absent the plan contribution, the debtor would have been unable to make payments pursuant to a crucial settlement agreement with the government, which likely would have led to the debtor's liquidation. The Third Circuit found that the '[r]estructuring in this case was possible only because of the release provisions', and accordingly, the claims were integral to the debtor–creditor relationship and thus permissible under *Stern*.[297] The court made clear, however, that it was not 'broadly sanctioning the permissibility of nonconsensual third-party releases' and that the holding was 'specific and limited'.[298] The Southern District of New York also addressed this question in *In re Kirwan Offices, S.á.r.l.*, and decided the issue on similar grounds.[299] Like the *Millennium* court, the *Kirwan* court found that it had constitutional authority to approve nonconsensual third-party releases where the release was 'absolutely necessary to the operation of [the debtor's] reorganization plan' and 'integral to the "restructuring of debtor-creditor relations" '.[300]

3.164   While these cases confirm the constitutionality of nonconsensual third-party releases post-*Stern*, the decisions make clear that courts will continue to thoroughly analyse releases under the facts of each case, and in particular, will examine whether the release was necessary to confirm the plan. Therefore, parties should remain prepared to defend the legality of such provisions on both constitutional and statutory grounds.

E. Plan Mediation

3.165   When successful, the use of mediation in bankruptcy can facilitate reaching a commercially reasonable outcome with certain advantages over the formal bankruptcy court process. Mediation, generally, has been a growing form of alternative dispute resolution to litigation in resolving key disputes in small to large cases, and involves an impartial third party with whom the parties seek to resolve their disputes consensually.[301] In the bankruptcy context, the use of mediation can help reduce time spent in a bankruptcy proceeding, reduce costs, remove sensitive issues from the court's discretion and the public's eye, increase control and

---

[294] *In re Millennium Lab Holdings II, LLC*, 945 F.3d 126, 135 (3d Cir 2019); *Stern v Marshall*, 564 US 462 (2011).
[295] 945 F.3d at 137–139.
[296] Ibid at 137.
[297] Ibid.
[298] Ibid at 139.
[299] 592 BR 489 (SDNY 2018).
[300] *In re Kirwan Offices, S.a.r.l.*, 592 BR at 511–512 ('The bankruptcy court thus possessed the inherent constitutional adjudicatory authority to include the exculpation and injunction clauses in [the debtor's] confirmed reorganization plan').
[301] See, e.g., NY State Unified Court System, *Resolving Your Case Through Mediation in Civil Court of the City of New York*, available at <https://www.nycourts.gov/courts/nyc/civil/pdfs/mediation.pdf> (last accessed 31 March 2021).

predictability, and eliminate the potential for appeal.[302] One key aspect of mediation is that it is non-binding unless, and until, a formal settlement agreement is executed by the parties involved.[303] This aspect of mediation encourages more open and consensual participation by parties who may be sceptical that any mutually acceptable agreement can be reached.[304] It can also be particularly beneficial in cases where the parties-in-interest expect or desire to maintain a relationship following the bankruptcy. Chief among the benefits of plan mediation is flexibility.[305]

Traditionally, mediation in the bankruptcy context has been used to resolve adversary proceedings, such as disputes over the valuation of assets, claims disputes, and preference claims.[306] More recently, however, mediation has become favoured in resolving issues critical to the reorganization itself, most notably, the plan of reorganization. Significantly, in recent years, plan mediation has been increasingly and successfully used not only in small cases, but in some larger chapter 11 cases involving complicated business issues and numerous stakeholders.   **3.166**

For example, in 2011, the Bankruptcy Court for the District of Delaware, in *In re Washington Mutual Inc* (*WaMu*), denied confirmation for a second time of the debtors' sixth amended plan of reorganization, and referred the parties to plan mediation almost three years after the debtors filed for chapter 11 relief.[307] The debtors were, prior to their bankruptcy filing, the United States' largest savings and loan association. Through court-ordered mediation, two key creditor groups were able to resolve certain disagreements, and the debtors were able to correspondingly revise their plan and clear significant obstacles with another group of dissident creditors. Four months after the order for mediation, the debtors submitted a final amended plan of reorganization, which was ultimately approved and confirmed by the Bankruptcy Court.   **3.167**

In re Residential Capital, LLC (*ResCap*)[308] represents another successful use of plan mediation. Also a complicated case, *ResCap* involved over 50 debtor entities that operated one of the largest residential mortgage loan servicing and mortgage loan origination businesses in the United States. The case involved federal and state governmental regulators, institutional investors asserting large claims arising out of the issuance of residential mortgage-backed securities, insurers, holders of secured and unsecured debt, and thousands of homeowners asserting claims under federal consumer protection laws. Seven months following their filing for bankruptcy protection, the debtors asked the court to appoint a mediator.[309] The court approved the debtors' motion, and appointed a fellow-sitting judge to act   **3.168**

---

[302] See, e.g., *FAQ on Bankruptcy Mediation*, Jams (1 April 2003), <http://www.jamsadr.com/publications/2003/faq-on-bankruptcy-mediation>.

[303] See, eg, NY State Unified Court System, *Resolving Your Case Through Mediation in Civil Court of the City of New York*, available at <https://www.nycourts.gov/courts/nyc/civil/pdfs/mediation.pdf>.

[304] See, eg, Marcus Stergio, *Mediation in Bankruptcy Cases*, MWI Bankruptcy & Finance ADR Blog (6 December 2012, 1:00 PM), <http://web.mwi.org/bankruptcy-blog/bid/249359/Mediation-in-Bankruptcy-Cases>.

[305] Ibid.

[306] See, e.g., *Mediation Provides Expediency, Certainty for Parties in Bankruptcy*, Sullivan Hazeltin Allinson LLC (4 February 2015), <http://www.sha-llc.com/bankruptcy-mediation-provides-expediency>.

[307] No 08-12229 (MFW) (Bankr D Del 13 Nov, 2011), ECF No. 8612 ('the Court will direct that the parties go to mediation on … the issues that remain an impediment to confirmation of any plan of reorganization in this case').

[308] No 12-12020 (MG) (Bankr SDNY 2012).

[309] Debtors' Motion for Appointment of a Mediator, *ResCap*, No 12-12020 (MG) (Bankr SDNY 6 Dec 2012), ECF No 2357.

as mediator.[310] An intense mediation process lasting for more than 10 months ultimately culminated in a global settlement embodied in the terms of a consensual chapter 11 plan.

3.169   Similarly, a bankruptcy judge in the Southern District of New York ordered the debtors and their creditors in *Excel Maritime Carriers Ltd* (*Excel*), to mediation before the same sitting judge who mediated *ResCap* to resolve disputes surrounding the debtors' pre-packaged plan of reorganization two months after the chapter 11 filing, with certain creditors seeking permission from the Bankruptcy Court to propose a rival plan.[311] Following mediation, the debtors proposed an amended plan of reorganization at the end of November 2013,[312] which was confirmed two months later.[313]

3.170   As the examples above reflect, there appears to be a strong trend towards chapter 11 plan mediation in significant cases. With an experienced and effective mediator and proper timing, plan mediation is an increasingly favoured and potentially effective alternative that debtors and creditors may consider as a path to improving the likelihood of successfully maximizing value and creditor recoveries.

VI. Pre-Packaged and Pre-Arranged Chapter 11 Plans

A. Pre-Petition Activities

1. General
(a) Pre-packaged chapter 11 plan

3.171   A pre-packaged chapter 11 case is one in which the debtor, *before* filing its chapter 11 petition, prepares, distributes, and solicits acceptances for a plan of reorganization from its creditors and shareholders.[314] Because the debtor already will have solicited acceptances of its plan, it will be able to file the plan on the petition date and immediately ask the bankruptcy court to schedule a hearing to confirm it.[315] In a few instances where there was virtually unanimous creditor support, parties have confirmed a pre-packaged chapter 11 plan on the first day of a bankruptcy case, although achieving such a feat requires months of pre-bankruptcy planning and may not be optimal for debtors seeking to use the bankruptcy process for benefits such as rejecting burdensome leases or avoiding pre-petition transfers.[316]

---

[310] Order Appointing Mediator, *ResCap*, No 12-12020 (MG) (Bankr SDNY 26 Dec 2012), ECF No 2519.

[311] Mediation Order, *Excel*, No 13-23060 (RDD) (Bankr SDNY 13 Sept 2013), ECF No 322.

[312] Amended Joint Chapter 11 Plan of Reorganization of Excel Maritime Carriers Ltd. and Certain of Its Affiliates, *Excel*, No 13-23060 (RDD) (Bankr SDNY 27 Nov 2013), ECF No 449.

[313] Findings of Fact, Conclusions of Law and Order Confirming Amended Joint Chapter 11 Plan of Reorganization of Excel Maritime Carriers Ltd. and Certain of Its Affiliates, *Excel*, No 13-23060 (RDD) (Bankr SDNY 27 Jan 2014), ECF No 562.

[314] Usually a debtor's chapter 11 reorganization plan must deal with two broad categories of individuals and entities that assert rights against the debtor's estate: (1) creditors who have claims against the debtor, and (2) equity security holders who have interests in the debtor. Equity security holders include not only shareholders, but others with similar equity or ownership interests in a debtor, such as a limited partner's interest in a limited partnership.

[315] Bankruptcy Code provisions specifically allow for pre-packaged bankruptcy cases. See 11 USC § 1102(b) (1) (allowing a committee of creditors chosen pre-petition to serve as the official committee of creditors in a chapter 11 case); 11 USC § 1121(a) (permitting a debtor to file a plan of reorganization with its petition); and 11 USC § 1126(b) (allowing pre-petition solicitation of plan acceptances).

[316] See *In re Belk, Inc, et al*, Case No. 21-30630 (MI) (Bankr SD Tex 2021); *In re Fullbeauty Brands Holdings Corp et al*, Case No. 19-22185 (RDD) (Bankr SDNY 2019).

(b) Pre-arranged chapter 11 plan

A pre-arranged bankruptcy case[317] is one in which the debtor negotiates with its creditors   **3.172**
and shareholders[318] the terms of a plan of reorganization before filing its chapter 11 bankruptcy petition, but waits to formally solicit acceptances until *after* the filing.[319] As with a
pre-packaged plan, because the terms of the plan of reorganization have been negotiated
pre-petition, the debtor will be able to file the plan on or close to the petition date and immediately ask the bankruptcy court to schedule hearings to approve the related disclosure
statement, solicitation procedures, and confirmation of the plan.[320]

2. Pre-petition disclosure and solicitation of a pre-packaged plan of reorganization

(a) Is court approval of the disclosure statement required?

A debtor is not required to seek court approval of its disclosure statement before soliciting   **3.173**
acceptances for a pre-packaged plan of reorganization.[321] As a result, the time between
commencement of the chapter 11 case and the reorganization plan's effective date is normally one to two months shorter in a pre-packaged case.[322] A two-month difference can be
significant when considering the public relations stigma associated with bankruptcy, the
distractions of dealing with committees and other interested parties, and the additional
costs associated with a bankruptcy case.

Although the bankruptcy court need not approve a disclosure statement for a debtor in a   **3.174**
pre-packaged chapter 11, the debtor is still obligated to distribute one, and it must comply
with applicable non-bankruptcy law standards or, if there are none, the Bankruptcy Code's
concept of 'adequate information'. Often, the debtor in a pre-packaged chapter 11 plan will
distribute a disclosure statement that is consistent with US securities laws requirements.[323]
Such requirements are more stringent and may be more costly than those required under
the Bankruptcy Code. For example, approval by the SEC may take two or three months,
which is time the debtor may not have to wait before filing its chapter 11 case.

(b) Sufficient disclosure

Irrespective of when a debtor solicits votes for a plan of reorganization, the Bankruptcy   **3.175**
Code requires that creditors and shareholders receive sufficient disclosure prior to voting.
When soliciting acceptances pre-petition, section 1126(b) of the Bankruptcy Code requires
that the debtor either: (a) comply with any applicable non-bankruptcy law, rule, or regulation (for example, federal securities laws and regulations) governing the adequacy of disclosure in connection with such solicitation; or (b) if no such law, rule, or regulation applies,
the debtor must provide, to each person it solicits, 'adequate information' as defined in the

---

[317] A pre-arranged bankruptcy case is also commonly referred to as a pre-negotiated case or a partial pre-
packaged case.

[318] The debtor need only negotiate with the most significant creditors who are expected to be impaired and
whose acceptances will be needed to confirm a plan.

[319] To provide the debtor with assurance that these creditors and shareholders will vote in favour of the pre-
negotiated plan, lockup or plan support agreements are typically used. Lockup agreements obligate the creditors
and shareholders (assuming certain conditions are met) to vote in favour of the pre-arranged plan.

[320] The process of post-petition disclosure and solicitation for a pre-arranged bankruptcy case is the same as in
any other chapter 11 case and is governed by s 1125 of the Bankruptcy Code.

[321] 11 USC § 1126(b).

[322] Norton Bankruptcy Law and Practice 3d § 97:36.

[323] See 11 USC § 1126(b)(1); *In re Zenith Electronics Corp*, 241 BR 92, 99 (Bankr D Del 1999).

Bankruptcy Code.[324] As a practical matter, the debtor should ensure that its pre-petition disclosure and solicitation comply both with any applicable non-bankruptcy law, rule, or regulation *and* with the Bankruptcy Code.

3.176   Prior to enactment of the Bankruptcy Abuse Prevention and Consumer Protection Act of 2005, a debtor was prohibited from continuing solicitation of votes for a pre-packaged plan if the pre-petition solicitation was interrupted by a bankruptcy filing by or against the debtor. The pre-petition solicitation was supposed to cease and post-petition solicitation was supposed to be accompanied by a court-approved disclosure statement. Section 1125(g) of the Bankruptcy Code now provides that notwithstanding the prohibition on post-petition solicitation of plan votes in the absence of a court-approved disclosure statement, acceptances of the plan may be solicited from a claim or interest holder if such solicitation complies with applicable non-bankruptcy law and if such holder was solicited prior to the commencement of the case in a manner that complied with applicable non-bankruptcy law.[325]

(c) The 'adequate information' standard

3.177   The debtor may not solicit post-petition acceptances of its reorganization plan before it transmits to those voting on the plan (a) a copy (or summary) of the plan and (b) a disclosure statement. The disclosure statement is designed to provide stakeholders with a detailed background and commentary on the debtor's reorganization and the plan's technical mechanics. The disclosure statement must contain 'adequate information', meaning 'information of a kind, and in sufficient detail, as far as is reasonably practicable in light of the nature and history of the debtor and the condition of the debtor's books and records, ... that would enable ... a hypothetical investor of the relevant class to make an informed judgment about the plan'.[326]

(d) Disclosure statement contents

3.178   The disclosure statement should include, or at least describe, the documents that the debtor expects to be executed in connection with the plan and other appropriate exhibits. In theory, the disclosure statement must clearly and succinctly inform the average creditor and shareholder what distribution it will receive under the plan, when it will receive it, and what contingencies there are to receipt. To that end, a disclosure statement usually includes descriptions of the following:

   (i)   the circumstances that gave rise to the filing of the debtor's bankruptcy petition;
   (ii)   the available assets and their value;
   (iii)   the anticipated future operations of the debtor;
   (iv)   the source(s) of the information provided in the disclosure statement;
   (v)   the condition and performance of the debtor while in chapter 11;
   (vi)   information regarding claims against the estate, including those allowed, disputed, or estimated;

---

[324] 'Adequate information' is the relevant standard for all post-petition disclosure statements. See 11 USC § 1125(a).
[325] 11 USC § 1125(g).
[326] 11 USC § 1125(a)(1).

(vii) a liquidation analysis describing the estimated return that creditors and shareholders would receive under a chapter 7 liquidation;[327]

(viii) the accounting and valuation methods used to produce the financial information in the disclosure statement;

(ix) information on the debtor's future management, including the amount of compensation to be paid to the debtor's directors, officers, and other insiders;

(x) a summary of the reorganization plan;

(xi) an estimate of all administrative expenses, including attorneys' and accountants' fees;

(xii) the collectibility of any accounts receivable;

(xiii) any financial information, valuations, or pro forma projections that would be relevant to creditors' and shareholders' decisions to accept or reject the plan;

(xiv) the risks being taken by the creditors and shareholders;

(xv) the actual or projected value that can be obtained from avoidable transfers;

(xvi) the existence, likelihood, and possible success of non-bankruptcy litigation; and

(xvii) the plan's tax consequences.

(e) Dissemination of the plan, disclosure statement, plan ballots, and voting notice to creditors and shareholders

The debtor must send to all 'impaired' creditors and shareholders copies of the plan, dis-   **3.179**
closure statement, plan ballot, and notice setting the time within which acceptances or rejections of the plan must be received. In general, a claim or interest is 'impaired' if the proposed plan alters the legal, equitable, or contractual rights of such claim or interest in any respect.[328] Significantly, the Bankruptcy Code provides that members of an 'unimpaired' class are conclusively presumed to have accepted the plan; the debtor need not solicit their acceptances.[329] On the other hand, a class that neither receives nor retains any property under the plan is deemed to have rejected the plan.[330] These presumptions, however, do not prevent creditors and shareholders from challenging their treatment under the plan.

(f) Deadline to vote on the plan

Neither the Bankruptcy Code nor the Federal Rules of Bankruptcy Procedure (the   **3.180**
'Bankruptcy Rules') prescribe a minimum period for soliciting votes in a pre-packaged bankruptcy case. However, the Bankruptcy Rules do provide that a bankruptcy court may disregard pre-petition votes if the court finds that creditors and shareholders were given an 'unreasonably short' period of time to vote on the plan.[331] What constitutes an 'unreasonably short' period depends on the circumstances of each particular case; nonetheless, guidance can be taken from the rules governing ordinary, non-pre-packaged bankruptcy cases. In such instances, the Bankruptcy Rules require that creditors and shareholders have at least

---

[327] See 11 USC §1129(a)(7) (requiring that each holder of a claim or interest of each impaired class of claims or interest must either accept the plan or receive or retain an amount not less than what that holder would receive under a chapter 7 liquidation); see also section V.C.2.

[328] 11 USC § 1124.

[329] 11 USC § 1126(f).

[330] 11 USC § 1126(g).

[331] Fed R Bankr P 3018(b).

28 days to consider, and object to the adequacy of, a proposed disclosure statement.[332] Thus, unless specific circumstances warrant otherwise, creditors and shareholders should be given at least 28 days to consider the debtor's pre-packaged plan and disclosure statement before casting their ballots.

3. The reorganization plan

3.181   The reorganization plan embodies the solution to the debtor's financial problems and provides for the transactions, distributions, and protections contemplated by such solution. It also defines and provides for (1) the classification and treatment of classes of creditor claims and shareholder interests and (2) the means of implementing the plan.

3.182   In a pre-packaged or pre-arranged case, this business solution usually results from extensive pre-petition negotiations between the debtor and its key creditors and shareholders along with their respective representatives and advisers. Such negotiations resemble typical non-bankruptcy workout negotiations, except that the goal of pre-packaged or pre-arranged plan negotiations is not the standard post-workout closing, but a bankruptcy 'closing', that is, confirmation and implementation of a court-approved reorganization plan, thereby allowing the debtor to take advantage of the benefits provided under the Bankruptcy Code.[333]

B. First-Day Filings

3.183   Once a debtor has obtained sufficient support for either its pre-packaged or pre-arranged plan of reorganization, it is ready to file its voluntary chapter 11 petition. Along with the petition, the debtor will need to file a number of 'first day' pleadings on or shortly after the petition date. First-day motions and applications can generally be grouped into two categories: (1) administrative—pleadings dealing with procedural and administrative matters; and (2) operational—those asking the court to ensure that the debtor's business and operations remain stabilized and allowing the debtor to continue to operate its business consistent with past practices.

1. Debtor's standard filings
(a) Administrative filings
3.184   As in any chapter 11 case, the debtor will, along with its bankruptcy petition, need to file a number of other Bankruptcy Code-prescribed documents including: schedules of assets

---

[332] Fed R Bankr P 2002(b).

[333] A pre-packaged plan allows the debtor to utilize many of the benefits available under chapter 11 including: (1) the ability to modify payment terms of debt owed to all members of a class of creditors thus eliminating the 'free rider' problem inherent in out-of-court restructurings; (2) the ability to define, liquidate, and, in some cases, disallow liabilities; (3) the ability to reject, assume, or assign contracts; (4) the ability to avoid certain pre-petition transactions; (5) the potential to receive more favourable tax treatment; (6) the ability to bind all creditor and equity holder classes, even those that do not consent to the plan; (7) the ability to resolve nearly all disputes with creditors in a single forum; (8) the ability to resolve contingent, unliquidated, and unmatured claims through estimation procedures; (9) the ability to complete expedited sales of encumbered assets free and clear of liens and other interests; (10) the ability to reject executory real estate leases while limiting lease termination damages; (11) the ability to reject collective bargaining agreements; (12) the ability to halt litigation and other creditor actions because of the automatic stay; and (13) the ability to eliminate balance sheet debt through less than full payment of claims while retaining control for existing management or owners. See Norton Bankruptcy Law and Practice 3d § 97:25.

and liabilities, schedules of income and current expenditures, a statement of financial affairs, a schedule of executory contracts and unexpired leases, lists of creditors and shareholders, and a list of the creditors holding at least the 20 largest unsecured claims. These administrative documents are typically prepared by the debtor's officers and professionals prior to filing for bankruptcy. In addition, the debtor will likely file applications to retain counsel and other professional advisers.

(b) Operational filings

Along with administrative pleadings, a debtor will usually file a number of motions asking **3.185** the court to approve procedures for allowing the debtor's operations to continue unimpeded. While the exact nature of the requests will depend on the specific circumstances, typical 'first day' operational pleadings include motions authorizing the debtor to: (i) continue to use its existing bank accounts, cash management system, and business forms; (ii) use cash collateral on an emergency basis; (iii) obtain post-petition financing; (iv) pay pre-petition wages and benefits; (v) pay its 'critical vendors'; and (vi) honour customers' pre-petition claims (i.e. returns, warranties, and deposits).

2. Additional filings for pre-packaged or pre-arranged plans

Since the debtor in a pre-arranged or pre-packaged chapter 11 case will have negotiated **3.186** the terms of the plan of reorganization or received sufficient votes in favour of its proposed plan prior to filing for bankruptcy, the debtor should be able to file the following additional documents on or close to the petition date—speeding up the normal plan confirmation process.

(a) Plan and disclosure statement

As noted, the goal of a pre-packaged or pre-arranged case is to minimize the debtor's stay **3.187** in bankruptcy by having the bankruptcy court promptly confirm its plan. The confirmation process begins with the filing of the plan of reorganization and the related disclosure statement. The Bankruptcy Rules also require the debtor to file, along with the plan and the disclosure statement, any other evidence of compliance with the pre-petition disclosure and solicitation requirements.

(b) Pleadings to establish date for plan confirmation hearing and date by which plan confirmation objections must be filed

Once the plan and disclosure statement are on file, the debtor will need to file requests for **3.188** the bankruptcy court to fix: (a) a date— usually on at least 28 days' notice to creditors, shareholders, and other parties-in-interest[334]—for the confirmation hearing, and (b) a date— usually a week or so before the confirmation hearing—by which interested parties must file objections to plan confirmation. The pleadings will also need to describe the proposed form, manner, and extent of notice the debtor plans on providing to creditors, shareholders, and other interested parties. Once the court enters the order, the debtor will have to mail the notice of the confirmation hearing and confirmation objection deadline to all creditors and shareholders.

---

[334] Under appropriate circumstances and for 'cause shown', the bankruptcy court may reduce the usualnormal 28-day notice period. Fed R Bankr P 9006(c).

(c) Pleadings to set bar date for filing proofs of claim or interest

3.189   A debtor cannot reasonably confirm and implement a plan without knowing the nature and amount of the claims and interests that creditors and shareholders assert against it. In most pre-packaged or pre-arranged plan cases, therefore, on the petition date the debtor should file a motion asking the bankruptcy court to set a date, usually on at least 20 days' notice (commonly referred to as the 'bar date'), by which all creditors and shareholders must file proof of the claims and interests they assert against the debtor or be forever barred from asserting those claims and interests in the debtor's bankruptcy case or otherwise. Once the bankruptcy court enters the 'bar date' order, the debtor will need to send creditors and shareholders notice of the bar date; the bankruptcy court may also order notice by publication.

(d) Pleadings to obtain court approval of pre-petition and post-petition documents and actions

3.190   As noted above, the bankruptcy court can, under certain circumstances, disregard votes obtained pre-petition. Therefore, it is imperative that the debtor request that the bankruptcy court approve the form, content, timing, and dissemination of the disclosure statement and all notices, ballots, and other documents transmitted pre-petition. Any order should expressly find that the documents are adequate and satisfy all legal requirements, including the notice requirements of the Bankruptcy Code, the Bankruptcy Rules, and any applicable non-bankruptcy law, rule, or regulation. In particular, the debtor should request an order expressly approving the debtor's pre-petition disclosure and solicitation; the order could be entered at the same time as, or as part of, the order confirming the debtor's plan.

C. Confirmation Hearing (Day 30–60)

3.191   At the confirmation hearing, the debtor will present evidence that its proposed plan complies with all the requirements of the Bankruptcy Code and Bankruptcy Rules and that it has followed the bankruptcy court's procedures for confirming the plan. The debtor will also present evidence that it has received the requisite votes to confirm the plan. Finally, the bankruptcy court will address any unresolved objections raised by parties-in-interest to the debtor's plan.

1. Determining plan acceptances and rejections

3.192   To confirm a plan, the debtor must receive the requisite approvals from its creditors and shareholders. Acceptance by a class of creditors requires the affirmative vote of creditors holding at least two-thirds in amount, and more than one-half in number, of the allowed claims of such class voting on the plan.[335] The plan acceptance standard for shareholders' interests has no 'numerosity' requirement and only requires the affirmative vote of shareholders holding at least two-thirds in amount of the allowed interests of such class voting on the plan. The bankruptcy court will calculate these numbers by (1) including *only* the creditors or shareholders that actually vote on the plan, and ignoring non-voting creditors and shareholders, and (2) in unusual circumstances, excluding votes that the court determines,

---

[335] 11 USC § 1126(c).

after notice and a hearing, were not cast or solicited in good faith or in accordance with the provisions of the Bankruptcy Code.

2. Confirmation when no impaired class rejects the plan

As discussed above, if the plan impairs no classes of claims or interests, or if all impaired classes vote to accept the plan, the bankruptcy court will confirm the plan if it satisfies the requirements of section 1129(a) of the Bankruptcy Code. At the confirmation hearing the debtor may have to present expert testimony or other evidence establishing, among other things, that (1) under the plan (and even if the class accepts the plan by the requisite majorities) any dissenting, impaired creditors or shareholders will receive or retain property of a value at least equal to what they would receive or retain if the debtor were liquidated under chapter 7 of the Bankruptcy Code and (2) the plan is feasible, that is, confirmation of the plan is not likely to be followed by the liquidation or other financial reorganization of the debtor, except as proposed in the plan.   **3.193**

3. Confirmation when an impaired class rejects the plan

If an impaired class rejects the plan, the debtor may nevertheless seek to confirm the plan under section 1129(b) of the Bankruptcy Code, the so-called 'cramdown' provision, as described above. To cramdown a plan, the debtor will need to show that: (1) the plan otherwise complies with the requirements of the Bankruptcy Code, and (2) the plan: (a) does not discriminate unfairly, and (b) is fair and equitable, with respect to each non-accepting class of impaired creditors and shareholders.[336] Practically speaking, this second requirement requires a showing that classes ranked below the objecting class(es) are not receiving any distribution under the plan. In general, the debtor should have little difficulty 'cramming-down' a plan over the opposition of shareholders, although particular plan provisions could make such a cramdown less likely.   **3.194**

D. COVID-19 Effects on Restructurings

1. Relief granted in bankruptcy

The extraordinary relief that courts have granted debtors as a result of the COVID-19 pandemic cannot be ignored. In light of the shutdowns and regulations that swept across the country, courts have granted relief that is not usually available under normal circumstances. For example, courts have extended the time by which debtor-retailers have had to pay their post-petition rent, relief rarely provided prior to COVID given the strong protections that landlords are afforded under the Bankruptcy Code.[337] Moreover, courts have also granted   **3.195**

---

[336] 11 USC § 1129(b)(1).

[337] Section 365(d)(3) requires that a debtor performs in a timely manner its post-petition obligations under an unexpired lease of nonresidential real property prior to the date the debtor assumes or rejects the lease. A court may extend the time for performance under the lease, but such extension cannot exceed sixty days. Ibid. In *In re Pier 1 Imports, Inc*, however, the court allowed deferral of rent payments beyond the 60 days, noting that 'COVID-19 presents a temporary, unforeseen, and unforeseeable glitch in the administration of the Debtors' Bankruptcy Cases ... There is no feasible alternative to the relief sought in the Motion', 615 BR 196, 203 (Bankr ED Va 2020). The court's legal basis for its decision was that section 365(d)(3) does not provide lessors the right to compel payment; rather 'to the extent that the Debtors are obligated to pay rent and fail to timely pay such rent, the Lessors are entitled to an administrative expense claim'. Ibid at 202.

motions to temporarily stay bankruptcy proceedings, such as in *In re Pier 1* where the court adjourned motions for relief from the automatic stay for no less than 45 days.[338] While it is unlikely that this type of relief will be available currently given that the shutdowns have eased and the industries harmed by the pandemic have begun to recover, debtors can take comfort that some courts have been liberally applying provisions of the Bankruptcy Code to achieve its fundamental reorganization objectives in these unprecedented times

2. Material adverse effect and *force majeure* clauses

3.196 The COVID-19 pandemic's dramatic impact on US markets, including but not limited to the travel, retail, and hospitality industries, transformed many would-be promising restructurings into unprofitable transactions for those involved. As a result, parties, both in and outside bankruptcy, have questioned whether they may act on rarely invoked contract terms: material adverse effect (MAE) and *force majeure* clauses.

3.197 An MAE clause determines when a party—usually a purchaser—may terminate a transaction if there has been a material adverse event prior to closing. While MAE clauses will vary, they typically protect purchasers against developments that would reasonably be expected to have a material adverse effect on the business, but typically exclude categories of broader market or industry risk.[339] With respect to debt financing, a third-party lender may also be able to make a determination that an MAE has or has not occurred, adding a level of complexity to the deal if the lender decides to walk away on those grounds.[340] For example, in the bankruptcy context, MAE clauses may be relevant where a debtor is selling assets pursuant to a plan or a section 363 sale.[341] A party seeking to excuse its performance 'faces a heavy burden' in proving that an MAE has occurred, and courts have found that the adverse change must be material 'when viewed from the longer-term perspective of a reasonable acquirer'.[342] Although challenges based on MAE grounds have been invoked by parties since the onset of the pandemic and sometimes litigated, the effects of COVID-19 have not generally created fresh grounds for successful invocation of MAE clauses.[343] Parties should carefully review the language of the relevant MAE clause as it may provide leverage to buyers and lenders in the negotiation process of a restructuring or refinancing. However, given the

---

[338] Order Granting (I) Relief Related to the Interim Budget, (II) Temporarily Adjourning Certain Motions and Applications for Payments, and (III) Granting Related Relief Motion to Approve, *In re Pier 1 Imports, Inc*, No. 20-30805 (KRH) (Bankr ED Va 6 Apr 2020) [ECF No 493]; see also Order Establishing Temporary Procedures and Granting Related Relief, *In re CraftWorks Parent, LLC*, No. 20-10475 (BLS) (Bankr D Del 30 Mar 2020) [ECF No 217] (granting temporary case procedures that limited available creditor relief, including that no stay relief hearing would be set for hearing for a certain time period).

[339] *Is the Coronavirus a Material Adverse Effect?* Paul Weiss, 6 March 2020, available at <https://www.paulweiss.com/practices/transactional/mergers-acquisitions/publications/is-the-coronavirus-a-material-adverse-effect?id=30800>

[340] Ibid.

[341] *In re Verity Health Sys of Cal, Inc*, Case No. 2:18-bk-20151 (ER), 2019 WL 9104240, at *1 (Bankr CD Cal 27 Nov 2019) (stalking horse bidder under an asset purchase agreement sought to excuse performance based on material adverse change clause).

[342] *Hexion Specialty Chems, Inc v Huntsman Corp*, 965 A.2d 715, 738 (Del Ch 2008) ('A buyer faces a heavy burden when it attempts to invoke a material adverse effect clause in order to avoid its obligation to close.... A short-term hiccup in earnings should not suffice.'); see *In re Verity Health Sys of Cal, Inc*, 2019 WL 9104240 at *4 (discussing case law that a party has a heavy burden in proving that an MAE has occurred and rejecting contention of stalking horse bidder that there had been a material adverse event).

[343] *AB Stable VIII LLC v MAPS Hotels and Resorts One LLC*, C.A. No. 2020-0310-JTL, 2020 Del. Ch. LEXIS 353 (Del Ch 30 Nov 2020) (MAE clause not triggered where COVID-19 pandemic fell within MAE exception).

heavy burden a party faces when invoking MAE clauses, proving that these provisions have been triggered due to COVID-19 is likely to be difficult, especially where an adverse effect created by the pandemic does not have durational significance.[344]

A *force majeure* clause excuses nonperformance of a contract if there has been an event be-   **3.198** yond the reasonable control of the contracting parties.[345] While these provisions are usually interpreted narrowly,[346] there has recently been debate as to whether COVID-19 consti- tutes a *force majeure*. While the outcome of such a challenge will depend on the language of the contract at issue, a few courts have found that the COVID-19 pandemic or government orders enacted as a result of the pandemic fall within *force majeure* provisions.[347] As with MAE clauses, parties should analyse whether they could bring, or may be subject to, a *force majeure* challenge if performance under the relevant contract may be hindered or even im- possible due to the COVID-19 pandemic.

E. Post-Confirmation Activities

1. Effectiveness of confirmation order

Confirmation of the debtor's plan is authorized by the court's entry of a confirmation order.   **3.199** Although generally such an order is effective 14 days after entry,[348] the bankruptcy court may, for cause shown, direct that it be effective sooner, or even immediately upon entry. The debtor and all other parties may rely on the confirmation order and, unless stayed, take all acts directed or contemplated by it, such as preparing and executing documents, transfer- ring property, issuing securities, and the like.

2. Effect of confirmation

Generally, confirmation of the debtor's reorganization plan (subject to certain limitations   **3.200** and exceptions): (1) discharges the debtor from its pre-confirmation debts and other obli- gations; and (2) binds the debtor, creditors, shareholders, and other parties within the bank- ruptcy court's jurisdiction to the terms of the plan.

3. Post-confirmation jurisdiction

The Bankruptcy Code and the Bankruptcy Rules give the bankruptcy court considerable   **3.201** authority to retain post-confirmation jurisdiction over the plan and its implementation, and to enter all orders necessary to: (1) administer the debtor's estate; and (2) ensure the

---

[344] See ibid.

[345] See *Harriscom Svenska, AB v Harris Corp*, 3 F.3d 576, 580 (2d Cir 1993) ('[A] *force majeure* clause in a con- tract excuses nonperformance when circumstances beyond the control of the parties prevent performance').

[346] *ARHC NVWELFL01, LLC v Chatsworth at Wellington Green, LLC*, No. 18-80712, 2019 WL 4694146 (SD Fla Feb 5, 2019).

[347] *JN Contemporary Art LLC v Phillips Auctioneers LLC*, No. 20-cv-4370 (DLC), 2020 WL 7405262 (SDNY 16 Dec 2020) (*force majeure* clause precluded breach of contract claim of art seller against auction house where auction house terminated consignment agreement to sell painting due to auction that was postponed for reasons beyond the auction house's reasonable control); *In re Hitz Restaurant Grp*, 616 BR 374, 378–379 (Bankr ND Ill 2020) (government order requiring restaurants to suspend on-premises service constituted a *force majeure* and debtor's obligation to pay rent would be reduced in proportion to its reduced ability to generate revenue). But see *In re CEC Entertainment Inc*, 625 B.R. 344 (Bankr SD Tex 2020) (finding that a *force majeure* clause did not excuse debtor's payment of timely rent payments despite the effects of the pandemic and government shutdown orders).

[348] See Federal Rules of Bankruptcy Procedure 3020(e).

performance of any act that is necessary for consummation of the plan. The plan itself also may provide that the bankruptcy court retain jurisdiction over particular matters. The bankruptcy court will close the case when the debtor's estate is 'fully administered'. Afterwards, the bankruptcy court may reopen the case to administer assets, to accord relief to the debtor, or for other cause.

F. Advantages and Disadvantages of a Pre-Packaged or Pre-Arranged Chapter 11 Plan

3.202   Along with the benefits[349] and costs of a traditional bankruptcy case, a debtor in a pre-packaged or pre-arranged case should remain mindful of some additional considerations, including the following.

1. Certainty

3.203   The debtor has a high degree of assurance that the plan of reorganization it negotiated will be implemented with minimal revisions and disruptions by third parties. Indeed, even before the debtor files its bankruptcy petition, it will know that its plan already has received the acceptances (or will receive the acceptances) required to confirm the plan.

2. Speed and control

3.204   Because most of the work is done pre-petition, a pre-packaged or pre-arranged bankruptcy case moves at a faster pace than a traditional chapter 11 case and can often go from filing the petition through plan confirmation in a few months. The speed of a pre-packaged or pre-arranged case greatly reduces the costs associated with the bankruptcy case and allows the debtor greater control over the bankruptcy process.[350] A drawback to the fast pace of the pre-packaged bankruptcy case is that it does not allow the debtor to take full advantage of the 'breathing spell' that normally accompanies a bankruptcy filing by application of the automatic stay. This 'breathing spell' can provide the debtor with ample time in which to thoroughly review its business operations, executory contracts, and manage any pending litigation. Thus, for a debtor that is facing significant operational difficulties, a pre-packaged bankruptcy, with its shortened lifespan, may not be optimal. Rather, such a debtor may be best served by filing a more traditional bankruptcy case.

3. Business deterioration

3.205   A pre-packaged bankruptcy case allows a debtor to avoid the stigma normally associated with bankruptcy and may provide comfort to both customers and suppliers that the debtor is working expeditiously and successfully to 'fix' its problems. This can help prevent deterioration of the debtor's business while in bankruptcy.

---

[349] These benefits include, among other things: (1) the ability to implement a plan without receiving unanimous consent of creditors and shareholders; (2) the ability to alter and/or modify the debtor's contractual obligations with third parties; (3) the ability to assume, reject, or assign executory contracts and unexpired leases and to issue securities; (4) the automatic stay; and (5) potentially favourable tax treatment.

[350] Note, however, that it is common for creditors to require a debtor to pay for their fees and expenses expended during the pre-petition negotiation period.

4. Pre-petition negotiation, solicitation, and voting

Navigating the pre-petition negotiation and solicitation period raises a number of additional considerations for the debtor. The key to a successful pre-packaged or pre-arranged bankruptcy case is the debtor's ability to negotiate a comprehensive plan of reorganization with its creditors. This requires the debtor to first identify the universe of creditors before it can begin. While a debtor may know the identity of some of its larger creditors (including debtholders) it may not know the identity of others. This is especially true if the debtor has a large amount of trade creditors, a group constantly in flux, or if its debt is largely held in 'street name'. The worst-case scenario for a debtor would be to find out that it spent significant time and resources negotiating with a group of creditors that could not deliver a confirmable plan.   **3.206**

In addition, during this pre-petition period, there is a heightened risk that a group of creditors may file an involuntary bankruptcy petition against the debtor pursuant to section 303(b) of the Bankruptcy Code. This risk is further heightened if the debtor is contemplating a 'cramdown' plan leaving shareholders and subordinated creditors with little or no recovery and nothing to lose by filing the involuntary petition.   **3.207**

VII. The Section 363 Sale Alternative

A. Relevant Standard: Sound Business Reason

Section 363 provides, in relevant part, that '[t]he trustee, after notice and hearing, may use, sell, or lease, other than in the ordinary course of business, property of the estate'.[351] In approving the sale of assets outside of the ordinary course of business and outside of a chapter 11 plan under section 363(b), courts generally have adopted the 'sound business reason' test established long ago by the Second Circuit Court of Appeals in *In re Lionel Corp.*[352] The *Lionel* ruling imposes a four-part test, requiring a debtor to demonstrate that: (1) there is a sound business purpose for the sale; (2) the proposed sale price is fair and reasonable; (3) the debtor has provided adequate and reasonable notice; and (4) the buyer has acted in good faith.[353]   **3.208**

As further described herein, the section 363 standard is deferential to the debtor's business judgment and such sales may be completed on an expedited timeline. As such, section 363 sales have become an attractive alternative to selling assets through the full-blown plan process, especially where the debtor's business may be rapidly deteriorating. Given the uncertainty that the COVID-19 pandemic has brought to the market and the dramatic and rapid decline in revenue that many companies with substantial secured debt burdens have faced, the section 363 alternative has been, and will likely remain, a popular restructuring tool.   **3.209**

---

[351]   11 USC § 363(b)(1).
[352]   *In re Lionel Corp*, 722 F 2d 1063 (2d Cir 1983).
[353]   See *In re Exaeris, Inc*, 380 BR 741, 744 (Bankr D Del 2008); *In re Delaware & Hudson Railway Co*, 124 BR 169, 175–76 (D Del 1991).

1. Sound business purpose

3.210   Under *Lionel* a bankruptcy court will approve a sale of all or substantially all of the debtor's assets under section 363 if there is some business justification, other than mere appeasement of major creditors, for the asset sale.[354] The *Lionel* court provided some guidance to bankruptcy courts in making such determination:

> [The] Bankruptcy judge must not blindly follow the hue and cry of the most vocal special interest groups; rather, he should consider all salient factors pertaining to the proceeding and, accordingly, act to further the diverse interests of the debtor, creditors and equity holders, alike.[355]

3.211   The *Lionel* court also provided a non-exhaustive list of factors courts should consider:

(i)   the proportionate value of the asset to the estate as a whole;

(ii)   the amount of time elapsed since filing;

(iii)   the likelihood that a plan of reorganization will be proposed and confirmed in the near future;

(iv)   the impact of the proposed disposition of assets on future plans of reorganization;

(v)   the value of consideration versus value of assets; and

(vi)   whether the value of the assets to be sold is decreasing or increasing.[356]

2. The sale must contemplate a fair and reasonable price

3.212   A fair and open sale process is crucial to a bankruptcy court's good faith finding.[357] In determining whether the sale price is fair and reasonable, courts should consider whether the assets have been marketed aggressively, what efforts were taken to maximize value to creditors, and whether the purchase agreement and auction process were designed to encourage and maximize competitive bidding to ensure the highest value.[358]

3. Notice must be given to creditors and interested parties

3.213   Section 363(b)(1) of the Bankruptcy Code provides that the trustee may use, sell, or lease estate property only 'after notice and a hearing'.[359] Section 102(1) provides that 'notice and a hearing' means 'after such notice as is appropriate in the particular circumstances, and such opportunity for a hearing as is appropriate in the particular circumstances'.[360] However, an actual hearing is not required if one is not timely requested or there is insufficient time for a hearing. Generally, Bankruptcy Rule 2002(a)(2) requires 21 days' notice by mail of a 'proposed use, sale, or lease of property of the estate other than in the ordinary course of business, unless the court for cause shown shortens the time or directs another method of giving notice'.[361]

---

[354]   *In re Lionel Corp*, 722 F 2d at 1070.
[355]   Ibid at 1071.
[356]   Ibid.
[357]   See *In re Summit Global Logistics*, No 08-11566, 2008 WL 819934, at *12 (Bankr DNJ 26 Mar 2008).
[358]   *In re Gulf Coast Oil Corp*, 404 BR 407, 424–427 (Bankr SD Tex 2009).
[359]   11 USC § 363(b)(1).
[360]   11 USC § 102(1).
[361]   Fed R Bankr P 2002(a)(2).

Most often, courts have shortened the notice period and permitted an expedited sale when a delay would cause substantial deterioration of a debtor's assets.[362]

In addition to the timing requirements, proper notice also requires that the content of the notice be sufficient, and courts may deny a sale where key sale terms are undisclosed in the motion.[363]   **3.214**

4. The purchaser is proceeding in good faith

The Bankruptcy Code does not define 'good faith'. Court-developed definitions include 'one who buys ... for value, without knowledge of adverse claims'.[364] The Third Circuit Court of Appeals has stated that 'the requirement that a purchaser act in good faith ... speaks to the integrity of his conduct in the course of the sale proceedings. Typically, the misconduct that would destroy a purchaser's good faith status at a judicial sale involves fraud, collusion between the purchaser and other bidders or the trustee, or an attempt to take grossly unfair advantage of other bidders'.[365] The good faith requirement prohibits fraudulent, collusive actions specifically intended to affect the sale price or control the outcome of the sale.[366]   **3.215**

The good faith analysis is focused on the purchaser's conduct in the course of the bankruptcy proceedings, including the purchaser's actions in preparation for and during the sale itself.[367] Two inquiries relevant to the question of good faith are: (1) whether the petition serves a valid bankruptcy purpose, i.e. by preserving the going concern value of a debtor or maximizing the value of the debtor's estate; and (2) whether the petition is filed merely to obtain a litigation advantage.[368]   **3.216**

B. Section 363 Sales Versus Plan Sales

A debtor may sell all or a portion of its assets to a purchaser through a chapter 11 plan, sometimes referred to as a 'plan sale' or a 'liquidating plan'. Under section 1123(a)(5), a plan must provide 'adequate means for the plan's implementation', which includes a 'sale of all or any part of the property of the estate'.[369] In some circumstances, for example, the plan may provide for the sale of either the entire business as a going concern or only a portion thereof, or the plan may propose a total shutdown of the debtor's operations and the orderly sale of   **3.217**

---

[362] See Order Under 11 USC §§ 105(A), 363, and 365 and Federal Rules of Bankruptcy Procedure 2002, 6004 and 6006 Authorizing and Approving (A) the Sale of Purchased Assets Free and Clear of Liens and Other Interests and (B) Assumption and Assignment of Executory Contracts and Unexpired Leases, *In re Lehman Brothers Holdings Inc*, No 08-13555 (Bankr SDNY 19 Sept 2008), ECF No 258 (the court approved a major sale transaction, free and clear of all liens, claims, encumbrances, obligations, liabilities, and contractual commitments and rights after only five days in bankruptcy).

[363] See *In re Flour Bagels, LLC*, 557 BR 53, 82–83 (Bankr WDNY 2016) (sale denied for reasons including that the motion did not disclose information regarding releases being offered as a condition of the sale).

[364] See *Matter of Youngstown Steel Tank Co*, 27 BR 596, 598 (WD Pa 1983).

[365] *In re Abbotts Dairies of Pennsylvania, Inc*, 788 F 2d 143, 147 (3d Cir 1986) quoting *In re Rock Indus Mach Corp*, 572 F 2d 1195, 1198 (7th Cir 1978); see *Licensing By Paolo, Inc v Sinatra (In re Gucci)*, 126 F 3d 380, 390 (2d Cir 1997) (adopting the same definition of good faith).

[366] *Abbotts Dairies of Pennsylvania, Inc*, 788 F 2d at 147.

[367] *Licensing By Paolo, Inc v Sinatra (In re Gucci)*, 126 F 3d at 390.

[368] *In re Integrated Telcom Express, Inc*, 384 F 3d 108, 120 (3d Cir 2004).

[369] 11 USC § 1123(a)(5)(D).

its remaining property. The plan may also provide for a variety of methods to effectuate such a sale. For example, the plan may incorporate bid procedures that direct the assets to be sold to the highest bidder at an auction. Alternatively, the plan may provide that the assets will be sold to a pre-petition or debtor-in-possession lender, or to another party that comes forward with a higher or better offer.

3.218　An important distinction between a section 363 sale and a plan sale is that any sale implemented through a chapter 11 plan is subject to all plan solicitation and confirmation requirements.[370] Thus, a debtor pursuing a sale under a plan must negotiate the plan with its key stakeholders, propose and seek approval of a disclosure statement, solicit acceptances of the plan from the debtor's stakeholders, and obtain confirmation of the plan. Unlike a plan sale, a section 363 sale does not require submission of a disclosure statement or a vote by stakeholders. Moreover, the legal standard of the 'business judgment rule' for approving a section 363 sale is far more lenient than the multiple legal standards required to be satisfied for confirmation of a plan which provides for a sale. As a result, a sale of assets under a plan is usually more complex, expensive, and time-consuming than a section 363 sale.

3.219　On the other hand, pursuing and administering a sale under a plan also has certain benefits. A plan sale may permit greater flexibility concerning the types of consideration that may be offered for the assets, for example securities issued by the purchaser which could be distributed under a plan. A plan sale may provide more favourable tax treatment than is available in a section 363 sale.[371] Additionally, a sale under a confirmed plan and a sale under section 363(b) may provide debtors and creditors with different liability protection[372] associated with the assets sold.[373] Relatedly, through a plan sale that conforms with the confirmation requirements of the Bankruptcy Code, a debtor can avoid the court's potential examination of whether a proposed section 363 sale amounts to a *sub rosa* chapter 11 plan.

C. Improper Section 363 *Sub Rosa* Plans

3.220　Courts first addressed the issue of a *sub rosa* plan in *Re Braniff Airways*.[374] The *Braniff* court held that the proposed 363 sale, which would have distributed travel coupons, promissory notes, and a share of profits to different groups of creditors, was a de facto plan of reorganization:

> The debtor and the Bankruptcy Court should not be able to short circuit the requirements of Chapter 11 for confirmation of a reorganization plan by establishing the terms of the plan *sub rosa* in connection with a sale of assets. ... Were this transaction approved, and

---

[370] See *supra* section V.C and section VI.

[371] See 11 USC § 1141(a).

[372] Section 1141(c) provides that property dealt with in a plan is sold 'free and clear' of all *claims and interests*, while section 363(f) provides for the sale of assets free and clear of any *liens or any interest* in such property.

[373] For example, in *In re Ditech Holding Corp, et al.*, the court found that a debtor need not comply with section 363(o) when selling assets through a plan, which allowed the debtor to free itself from certain consumer claims that would have been protected had the debtor been selling its assets under section 363. See *In re Ditech Holding Corp*, 606 BR 544 (Bankr SDNY 2019). Section 1141(c) provides that property dealt with in a plan is sold 'free and clear' of all claims and interests, while section 363(f) provides for the sale of assets free and clear of any liens or any interest in such property.

[374] *In re Braniff Airways*, 700 F 2d 935, 949 (5th Cir 1983).

considering the properties proposed to be transferred, little would remain save fixed based equipment and little prospect or occasion for further reorganization. These considerations reinforce our view that this is in fact a reorganization.[375]

A court should, therefore, find that a 363 sale is an impermissible *sub rosa* plan of reorganization when it 'short circuits' the protections set forth in section 1129 of the Bankruptcy Code.[376] These protections include:

3.221

- The Good Faith Requirement—section 1129(a)(3) of the Bankruptcy Code requires that a plan be proposed in good faith and not by any means forbidden by law. This generally means that there is a reasonable likelihood that the plan will fairly achieve a result consistent with the Bankruptcy Code, in light of the particular facts and circumstances.[377]
- Equal Treatment of Similarly Situated Creditors—section 1123(a)(4) requires the same treatment for each claim or interest in a particular class, unless the holder of a particular claim or interest agrees to a less favourable treatment of such claim or interest.
- Acceptance of Creditors—section 1129(a)(8) requires that each class of claims or interests accept the plan or such class is not impaired under the plan;[378] section 1129(a)(10) requires that if a class of claims is impaired under the plan, at least one class of claims that is impaired under the plan has accepted the plan, determined without including any acceptance of the plan by an insider.
- Cramdown Protection—under section 1129(b)(2)(B)(ii), the plan must satisfy the 'fair and equitable' requirement of section 1129(b), or the 'absolute priority rule', which ensures that a plan cannot give property to junior claimants over the objection of a more senior class of creditors if such dissenting class does not receive full value for its claims.
- The Best Interests of Creditors Test—section 1129(a)(7)(A)(ii) requires that an impaired claim holder who does not accept the proposed plan must receive property of a value that is not less than the amount that such holder would receive if the debtor were liquidated under chapter 7.
- The Feasibility Requirement—section 1129(a)(11) of the Bankruptcy Code requires that a plan be feasible in that confirmation of such plan is not likely to be followed by the liquidation, or the need for further financial reorganization, of the debtor or any successor to the debtor under the plan, unless such liquidation is proposed in the plan.

During the financial crisis that began in 2008, Chrysler LLC ('Chrysler') and General Motors Corporation ('GM') completed section 363 sales during 2009 that involved the transfer of massive, entire enterprises and courts were asked to scrutinize whether such

3.222

---

[375] Ibid at 940.

[376] Concerns regarding *sub rosa* plans are not limited to section 363 sales, but are 'germane to any transaction by a debtor that adversely impacts on interested parties' rights to participate in the restructuring process.' *In re LATAM Airlines Grp SA*, 620 BR 722, 813 (Bankr SDNY 2020). For example, in *In re LATAM Airlines Grp. S.A.*, the court initially denied a debtor's motion seeking debtor-in-possession financing on the grounds that the financing constituted a *sub rosa* plan. The financing facility included a provision that the debtor could elect to pay certain lenders through a discounted stock issuance, which the court found short circuited the chapter 11 plan review process. Ibid at 819.

[377] See *In re Madison Hotel Associates*, 749 F 2d 410 (7th Cir 1984), *In re PW Holdings Corp*, 228 F 3d 224, 242 (3d Cir 2000), *In re Leslie Fay Cos*, 207 BR 764, 781 (Bankr SDNY 1997).

[378] Acceptances of a plan may not be solicited post-petition unless a court-approved disclosure statement has been transmitted to the affected creditor or interest holder. 11 USC § 1125(b).

section 363 sales of all or substantially all of a debtor's assets should be permitted. The chapter 11 case of *In re Chrysler, LLC*,[379] although complex, proceeded swiftly. A reorganization that could have taken years to negotiate, was completed in a relatively short period of time. Chrysler filed for and 'emerged' from bankruptcy in 42 days. The Second Circuit affirmed the Bankruptcy Court's decision to approve a sale under section 363 of substantially all of Chrysler's assets without confirmation of a chapter 11 plan. It held that the asset sale transaction did not constitute a prohibited *sub rosa* plan, but served to 'maximize the value of the bankrupt estate'. On appeal, the US Supreme Court vacated the Second Circuit's decision and remanded the case with instructions to dismiss the appeal as moot,[380] but the Bankruptcy Court's judgment remains good law and the sale was left intact.

3.223   Following in Chrysler's footsteps, the disposition of GM's operating assets, which was expected to be extremely cumbersome and time-consuming, lasted only 40 days. Various objectors contended that allowing GM to dispose of so many of its assets in a single section 363 sale as a going concern was improper. Central to the objectors' case was the argument that a sale of all or substantially GM's assets could only be completed through a reorganization plan. Based on the *Chrysler* precedent, after filing a chapter 11 petition on 1 June 2009, GM immediately sought and won the Bankruptcy Court's approval of an asset sale under section 363 of the Bankruptcy Code.[381]

3.224   While section 363 sales have become common, especially during the COVID-19 pandemic due to the flexible and expedited process, such whole-company sales have generally not occurred on the highly expedited time frames seen in Chrysler and GM after the easing of the last financial crisis.

D. Secured Creditors' Right to Credit Bid

3.225   'Credit bidding' allows a secured creditor to purchase property sold in either a section 363 sale[382] or a plan sale[383] by using its secured claim against the debtor as consideration rather than cash. Credit bidding is statutorily permitted for a number of reasons, including, among other things, to avoid the incongruity of requiring a creditor to obtain new funds to pay itself, which consequently reduces borrowing and transaction costs. Credit bidding also protects the secured creditor against the risk that its collateral will be sold at an undervalued, depressed price by giving the creditor the opportunity to purchase the collateral for what it considers to be its fair market value.[384] Thus, a secured creditor can credit bid its

---

[379] *In re Chrysler LLC*, 576 F 3d 108 (2d Cir 2009) *vacated as moot*, 130 S Ct 1015 (2009).
[380] *Indiana State Police Pension Trust v Chrysler LLC*, 130 S Ct 1015 (2009).
[381] *In re General Motors Corp*, 407 BR 463 (Bankr SDNY 2009).
[382] 11 USC § 363(k) (providing that at a section 363 sale of assets subject to a 'lien that secures an allowed claim, unless the court for cause orders otherwise, the holder of such claim may bid at such sale, and, if the holder of such claim purchases such property, such holder may offset such claim against the purchase price of such property').
[383] While there had been a circuit split regarding whether a secured creditor had an absolute right to credit bid at a sale under a chapter 11 plan, the US Supreme Court affirmed such right for secured creditors in *RadLAX*. See *RadLAX Gateway Hotel v Amalgamated Bank*, 132 S Ct 2065 (2012) (holding that a debtor may not confirm a chapter 11 plan of reorganization contemplating a sale of a secured creditor's collateral free and clear of the creditor's lien without permitting the secured creditor to credit bid at the sale, even under an otherwise confirmable cramdown plan).
[384] See ibid at 2070 n 2 (Scalia J).

debt with the intent to either drive up other bids, or win the auction and take back its collateral in exchange for releasing the amount of debt equal to its winning bid.

Critics of credit bidding argue, among other things, that even the existence of the secured   **3.226**
creditor's right to credit bid chills competitive bidding for a debtor's property because other
potentially interested buyers recognize that the secured creditor will not need to make an
actual cash outlay. Other potential buyers may be deterred by the presence of what they
view as a strong bidder. This, in turn, may decrease the numbers of bidders, diminish the
debtor's expected proceeds from the sale, and minimize the estate's overall recovery. Critics
of credit bidding also argue that a secured creditor's interests as both a credit bidder and a
creditor with an interest in sale proceeds could lead the creditor to strategically over-bid on
its collateral in an aggressive effort to increase its cash recovery.

To submit a credit bid under section 363(k), the Bankruptcy Code imposes two require-   **3.227**
ments: (1) the creditor must have an allowed claim,[385] secured by a valid and perfected lien
on the asset being sold; and (2) the court must not have otherwise limited the credit bid 'for
cause'.[386] 'Cause' is not defined in the Bankruptcy Code but it is a flexible concept that allows
bankruptcy courts to address issues in credit bidding on a case-by-case basis. Typically,
'cause' to deny a credit bid may be found where: (i) there is a bona fide dispute as to the
allowed amount of the creditor's claim; (ii) there is a bona fide dispute as to the extent, validity, or priority of the creditor's lien in the property on which it seeks to credit bid; (iii) because of any of these disputes, determining the status of a creditor's lien would substantially
delay the sale process and diminish the value of the property sold; (iv) the secured creditor
fails to follow the proper bidding procedures; or (v) the sale is likely to leave the debtor administratively insolvent and unable to pay expenses incurred during the bankruptcy case
and other priority claims.

A series of rulings in 2014 examining the effect of a creditor's credit bid strategy on competi-   **3.228**
tive bidding appeared to chip away at a secured creditor's right to credit bid under the 'for
cause' requirement of the Bankruptcy Code. In *In re Fisker Automotive Holdings*,[387] debtors
that manufactured electric cars filed for chapter 11 relief for the purpose of selling substantially all of their assets to Hybrid Tech Holdings. Hybrid had acquired approximately
$168.5 million of the debtors' senior secured debt five weeks before the chapter 11 filing at
the deep discount price of $25 million. The debtors then negotiated a credit bid by Hybrid
for substantially all of the debtors' assets for $75 million. The official committee of unsecured creditors opposed Hybrid's right to credit bid on a number of grounds, notably that
'cause' existed to cap its credit bid 'because limiting the credit bid [would] facilitate an open
and fully competitive cash auction'.[388]

The Bankruptcy Court capped the amount of Hybrid's credit bid because otherwise 'there   **3.229**
[would] be *no* bidding—not just the chilling of bidding'.[389] Bidding would 'be frozen',

---

[385] A claim is deemed allowed if proof of such claim has been filed and there is no pending objection to such
proof of claim, or if the debtor listed the claim in its schedules filed with the bankruptcy court as non-contingent,
undisputed, and liquidated. Pursuant to s 506(a)(1) of the Bankruptcy Code, a creditor's claim is secured to the extent of the value of its collateral.
[386] 11 USC § 363(k).
[387] 510 BR 55 (Bankr D Del 2014).
[388] Ibid at 58.
[389] Ibid at 60 (emphasis in original).

and thus, the court found 'cause' to limit Hybrid's credit bid.[390] Further, the court capped Hybrid's credit bid at $25 million, the purchase price it paid for the debt, and so signalled that a purchaser of secured debt may only be permitted to credit bid an amount equal to the price paid for the debt, rather than the face amount of such debt, depending on the circumstances.[391]

3.230   A few months later, looking to *Fisker* as precedent, the Bankruptcy Court in *In re Free Lance-Star*[392] similarly decided to cap a secured creditor's credit bid because (1) the secured creditor's actions frustrated the competitive bidding process, and (2) capping the secured creditor's bid would restore a competitive bidding environment and reinvigorate interest in the sale. Notably, the court found that the secured creditor was 'overly zealous' and had engaged in 'inequitable conduct',[393] and further that the credit bid mechanism:

> does not always function properly when a party has bought the secured debt in a loan-to-own strategy in order to acquire the target company. In such a situation, the secured party may attempt to depress rather than to enhance market value. Credit bidding can be employed to chill bidding prior to or during an auction, or to keep prospective bidders from participating in the sales process. [The secured creditor's] motivation to own the [d]ebtors' business rather than to have the [l]oan repaid has interfered with the sales process. [The secured creditor] has tried to depress the sales price of the [d]ebtors' assets, not to maximize the value of those assets. A depressed value would benefit only [the secured creditor], and it would do so at the expense of the estate's other creditors. The deployment of [the secured creditor's] loan-to-own strategy has depressed enthusiasm for the bankruptcy sale in the marketplace.[394]

Although the face amount of the secured creditor's loan was $39 million, the court limited its credit bid to $13.9 million.[395]

3.231   *Fisker* and *Free Lance-Star* suggest antipathy by certain judges towards lenders pursuing 'loan-to-own' strategies. However, the 'for cause' challenge under section 363(k) of the Bankruptcy Code is necessarily fact-intensive and case-specific. While courts continue to cite *Fisker* and *Free Lance-Star* for the notion that the right to credit bid is not absolute, they have recognized that 'modification or denial of credit bid rights should be the extraordinary exception and not the norm'.[396] For example, in *In re Aéropostale*, the debtors sought to limit a secured creditor's right to credit bid under the *Fisker* and *Free Lance-Star* standards, primarily on the basis that the credit bid would chill bidding. However, the court rejected the debtors' contentions, stating that bid chilling alone is insufficient to justify a credit bid limit since 'all credit bidding chills an auction process to some extent'.[397] Further, the record

---

[390] Ibid.

[391] Ibid at 61.

[392] 512 BR 798, 806–07 (Bankr ED Va 2014).

[393] This case involved unusual facts, including the secured lender's unilateral filing of financing statements for unencumbered assets without giving any notice to the debtors. See ibid at 799–804.

[394] Ibid at 806.

[395] Ibid at 808.

[396] *In re Aeropostale, Inc*, 555 BR 369, 415 (Bankr SDNY 2016) (citing *In re RML Dev, Inc*, 528 BR 150, 156 (Bankr WD Tenn 2014)).

[397] Ibid at 417–418 (citing American Bankruptcy Institute Commission to Study the Reform of Chapter 11, 2012–2014 Final Report and Recommendations 147 (2014), available at http://commission.abi.org/full-report).

demonstrated an active interest in the debtors' assets, and there was no evidence of inappropriate behaviour by the secured creditors.

Debtors may continue to cite *Fisker* and *Free Lance-Star* as leverage for limiting credit bids, **3.232** and thus secured creditors seeking to credit bid should assess the wisdom of pressing for sales on aggressive time frames and the potential perception of abuse over the sale process.

VIII. English Law Tools to Stabilize the Business and Create Liquidity

As identified in paragraph 3.01, companies in the US file for chapter 11 protection for **3.233** multiple purposes: to stave off foreclosure or obtain a breathing space from debt-related lawsuits; to halt and manage other vexatious litigation; to reject burdensome contracts and leases; to avoid and recover certain transfers; to facilitate the sale of assets; to obtain financing that would have been contractually prohibited or otherwise unavailable; and generally to develop a rational basis for restructuring their liabilities in a forum which centralizes all of their assets and all of their creditors' claims. In other words, chapter 11 acts as a gateway to multiple tools which can be used to achieve a debt restructuring. English corporate insolvency law is, in contrast, modular.[398] Modular, in this context, means that England's corporate insolvency law toolbox provides a range of tools which can be used together, or alone, to achieve the numerous objectives which have been identified for a debtor filing for chapter 11 protection.

Of course, this considerably complicates the analysis of the English law tools, and the ex- **3.234** ercise of comparing the US and English debt restructuring regimes. For the purposes of facilitating both the analysis and the comparison, this section divides the English law procedures between the two broad objectives which a debtor may have in resorting to corporate insolvency law tools to achieve a debt restructuring. First, the debtor may need to stabilize its business and, second, create liquidity for a debt restructuring to be achieved. For these purposes, the following objectives are identified: staving off foreclosure; obtaining a breathing space from debt-related lawsuits; and halting and managing vexatious litigation. At the same time, rejecting burdensome contracts and leases; avoiding certain transfers; and obtaining finance are all tools which the debtor might use to create liquidity. As we shall see, English law offers two tools which can be used to stabilize the business and create liquidity: administration and the Part A1 moratorium procedure, and these are analysed first.

A. Administration

1. Introduction
Administration was first introduced into English law following a review by the committee **3.235** led by Sir Kenneth Cork.[399] At the time, the principal insolvency procedure in English

---

[398] The term 'modular' was inspired by Davis et al (n 22). Although the authors suggest the 'modular approach' specifically in the context of micro, small, and medium enterprise (MSME) corporate insolvency, it is apt to describe the English corporate insolvency law system.

[399] Kenneth Cork, *Insolvency Law and Practice: Report of the Review Committee* (Cmnd 8558, 1982).

law was receivership. Whenever a bank had security over all or substantially all of the debtor's assets (which has been comparatively easy to achieve in England since the Courts of Chancery embraced the idea of the floating charge in the nineteenth century) it could, where it was entitled to do so by the terms of the security document, appoint a receiver to sell the business and assets, or assets of the debtor. Critically, the receiver owed his duties primarily to the appointing creditor and the bank had a largely unfettered right to choose whether to agree to a restructuring or whether to appoint a receiver and sell the business and assets or, where that was not possible, the assets. The Cork Committee was largely satisfied with the way in which receivership operated.[400] However, where there was no creditor with security over all or substantially all of the assets of the debtor, the only available insolvency procedure in English law was liquidation. Liquidation is poorly designed to achieve a sale of the business and assets and the Cork Committee saw merit in being able to replicate what it regarded as the relative efficiency of the receivership procedure in achieving this where restructuring talks had broken down for companies which had not granted a floating charge.[401] It is important to note, however, that the Cork Committee also thought that administration might be used to 'enable a scheme of arrangement to be effected'.[402] As we shall see later, during this period debt restructuring was largely an out-of-court affair, and corporates did not petition for administration to stabilize the business and create liquidity while they sought to negotiate a scheme of arrangement with their creditors to restructure their debts. Yet, it is important that this application of administration was specifically contemplated in the report which inspired its enactment.

3.236   As Britain entered the noughties, receivership began to seem like a rather outmoded insolvency procedure for the modern world. Concerns emerged that banks might be incentivized simply to appoint a receiver and sell the business and assets rather than persevere with a restructuring, where a restructuring would have preserved value for other stakeholders, and that the banks had little incentive to maximize the sale price above the value of their security.[403] Dissatisfaction was also expressed with the administration procedure itself, which was seen as cumbersome and expensive, reducing returns for unsecured creditors and offering them very few participation rights.[404]

3.237   Part 10 of the Enterprise Act 2002 thus attempted to reform administration with a view to turning it into the 'go to' rescue procedure for companies in financial difficulties. First, the 2002 Act almost completely abolished administrative receivership.[405] Secondly, it looked to streamline the administration procedure by permitting the appointment of an

---

[400] Ibid paras 431–494.

[401] For example, whilst there is a stay on creditor action in a compulsory liquidation, because compulsory liquidation is primarily concerned with a realization of the assets it does not prohibit enforcement by a secured creditor, see *In re David Lloyd & Co* (1877) 6 Ch D 339.

[402] Cork Report (n 399) para 422.

[403] See 'A Review of Company Rescue and Business Reconstruction Mechanisms' Department of Trade and Industry and HM Treasury May 2000; Ian Fletcher, 'UK Corporate Rescue: Recent Developments—Changes to Administrative Receivership, Administration and Company Voluntary Arrangements—the Insolvency Act 2000, The White Paper 2001, and the Enterprise Act 2002' (2004) 5(1) *European Business Organisation Law Review* 119, 121–124; Rizwaan Mokal, 'Administrative Receivership and Administration—An Analysis' (2004) 57 *Current Legal Problems* 355.

[404] See 'Productivity and Enterprise—Insolvency—A Second Chance' The Insolvency Service and The Secretary of State for Trade and Industry July 2001, 9–12; Fletcher (n 403) 124–127.

[405] Insolvency Act 1986, s 72A (subject to eight specific exceptions).

administrator out of court by secured creditors and companies or their directors,[406] reducing the formalities for application to court by replacing the unpopular Rule 2.2 Report with a paper form and affidavit,[407] permitting an administrator to make distributions to secured and preferential creditors (and, with the leave of the court, unsecured creditors),[408] and clarifying the exit routes from administration.[409] In so doing, it sought to reduce costs, improve creditor returns, and incentivize resort to the procedure. It also sought to improve returns in more explicit ways, largely abolishing the preferential status which the Crown had previously enjoyed,[410] and ring-fencing a certain percentage of recoveries (designed to be a rough proxy for the amount which had previously been preferential) for unsecured creditors rather than secured creditors.[411] Perhaps most crucially of all, for the argument in this section, the primary objective of administration became rescue of the company as a going concern.[412] Only if the administrator thinks that this objective is not reasonably practicable to achieve may they proceed to the second objective of achieving a better result for the company's creditors as a whole than would be likely if the company were wound up,[413] (and only if they think it is not reasonably practicable to achieve either the first or second objective will the third objective apply, i.e. realizing the company's property to make a distribution to the company's secured or preferential creditors).[414] This might be seen as building on the concept of administration as a procedure to stabilize the business and create liquidity while a debt restructuring is worked out. In practice, matters have turned out rather differently.

Indeed, in practice, the success of the 2002 reforms in making administration a procedure   **3.238**
which debtors turn to proactively to stabilize the business and create liquidity has been extremely limited. Few companies have implemented any form of debt restructuring from within administration, the most notable examples being Olympia & York, the owners of Canary Wharf, and Railtrack. More commonly administration leads to the sale of the company's business and assets. The corporate rescue element has therefore transpired to be little more than a 'bolt-on' to what is fundamentally still regarded by the market as an insolvency procedure with the accompanying stigma which that entails. 'Pre-packs', discussed later, mitigate the stigma to some extent but have not been without criticism themselves. As we shall also see pre-packs have been adapted by enterprising commercial lawyers to achieve a debt restructuring but not in a way which was envisaged by the legislature when the Enterprise Act reforms were enacted.

As this book is being written, however, the landscape is shifting again. As a result of the   **3.239**
COVID-19 pandemic, many businesses have incurred liabilities during periods of economic lockdown, or reduced levels of operation, which they will inevitably need to restructure. Moreover, many of these businesses entered the crisis with relatively high levels of debt relative to their earnings, and many have incurred significant costs in meeting the health

---

[406] Ibid sch B1, paras 14–18 (secured creditors) and paras 22–30 (the company or its directors).
[407] Ibid sch B1, paras 18 and 29.
[408] Ibid sch B1, para 65.
[409] Ibid sch B1 paras 76–86.
[410] Enterprise Act 2002, s 251.
[411] Insolvency Act 1986, s 176A.
[412] Ibid sch B1, para 3(1)(a).
[413] Ibid sch B1, paras 3(1)(b) and 3(3).
[414] Ibid sch B1, paras 3(1)(c) and 3(4).

and safety demands of the pandemic. The UK Government has responded to the crisis with temporary legislative amendments which, in many cases, have created a breathing space for debtors and reduced liquidity pressures. These included: temporary provisions on winding-up petitions based on statutory demands and other restrictions on winding-up petitions and orders;[415] a temporary suspension of wrongful trading liability for directors;[416] and restrictions on the right of landlords to enforce their right of re-entry or forfeiture where a business tenant defaults on rent payments.[417] At the same time, many debtors and creditors have delayed commencing debt restructuring negotiations until there is some visibility on the scale of the overall restructuring required—which is likely to become apparent only when there is some sense that the worst of the crisis is over. Thus, as the temporary legislative provisions expire, and debtors look ahead to returning to business as normal, restructuring efforts may start in earnest. At this point, it may become necessary to use legal tools to stabilize and create liquidity while the debt restructuring is worked out. And the first tool which companies might turn to is the administration procedure. In analysing the capacity of administration to stabilize the business and create liquidity while a debt restructuring is worked out, it is necessary to start with perhaps the most striking difference between chapter 11 and administration: the debtor-in-possession versus practitioner-in-possession models.

2. Management of the debtor

3.240 The merits of debtor-in-possession processes versus practitioner-in-possession processes have been debated at length.[418] In summary, it is argued that where the shareholder base is narrow and consolidated, management are likely to be too sympathetic to fairly represent the creditors' interests during reorganization and should therefore be replaced. Absent a consolidated shareholder base, however, directors can be trusted to look after the creditors' interests and should be left in place as those best placed, by virtue of both qualification and information, to manage the debtor's day-to-day affairs.

3.241 The chapter 11 approach in theory conforms to this model. Shareholdings in large US corporates tend to be widely dispersed and the directors and officers of debtor companies are typically[419] expected as part of the chapter 11 proceedings to, in the words of the US Supreme Court, 'carry out the fiduciary responsibilities of a trustee'.[420] The management also enjoys an exclusive period to formulate and present to the court a plan of reorganization. In practice, the management of the debtor may change or become subject to additional

---

[415] CIGA 2020, sch 10.

[416] Ibid, s 12.

[417] Business Tenancies (Protection from Forfeiture: Relevant Period) (Coronavirus) (England) (No 2) Regulations 2020 (2020/SI 994).

[418] See, e.g., Nathalie Martin, 'Common Law Bankruptcy Systems: Similarities and Differences' 11 *American Bankruptcy Institute Law Review* 367, 390–391; David Hahn, 'Concentrated Ownership and Control of Corporate Reorganisations' (2004) *Journal of Corporate Law Studies* 117; Gerard McCormack, 'Super-Priority New Financing and Corporate Rescue' [2007] *Journal of Business Law* 701; Lijie Qi, 'Managerial Models During the Corporate Reorganisation Period and Their Governance Effects: the UK and US Perspective' (2008) 29(5) *Company Lawyer* 131; John Armour, Brian R Cheffins, and David A Skeel Jr, 'Corporate Ownership Structure and the Evolution of Bankruptcy Law: Lessons from the United Kingdom' (2002) 55 *Vanderbilt Law Review* 1699. See generally Vanessa Finch, *Corporate Insolvency Law: Principles and Perspectives* (2nd edn, 2009) Ch 9.

[419] In rare situations, an independent trustee may be appointed.

[420] *Commodity Futures Trade Commission v Weintroub*, 471 US 343, 355 (1985).

constraints during the course of chapter 11 proceedings, sometimes at the instigation of the creditors (and in particular those, if any, providing debtor-in-possession financing).[421]

By contrast, the administration regime in the UK does not conform to this model. Although **3.242** the shareholder base of publicly listed companies is also widely dispersed (although argu- ably not to the same extent as in the United States due to the larger stakes held by institu- tional investors), the management of the debtor company is invariably replaced with one or more qualified insolvency practitioners as administrators. From the day of his or her appointment, the administrator has wide powers to run the debtor's affairs.[422] Although still in office, the directors and secretary of the debtor cannot exercise *their* powers where to do so would interfere with the exercise by the administrator of *the administrator's* powers, unless the administrator consents. An administrator is also able to appoint additional dir- ectors,[423] although implementing such an appointment might prove complex in practice. Crucially, it is the administrators and not management who formulate proposals for the conduct and conclusion of the administration (including whether to sell assets and whether to enter liquidation). It had originally been envisaged that a court application would always be required in order to appoint an administrator.[424] However, as a result of fierce lobbying by the banks,[425] provisions were ultimately included which enabled the secured creditor to control the identity of the administrator.[426] Inevitably, administrators are mindful of this appointment power and the concern emerges that they remain as influenced to do the secured creditor's bidding as receivers before them.[427] Once appointed the administrator controls the decision to move from rescue of the company to a sale of the business and as- sets, or sale of the assets, and has a very wide margin of appreciation in doing so.[428] Two modern cases show how difficult it will be for a dissatisfied unsecured creditor to challenge the decision to move to the second purpose.[429]

Some commentators have attempted to attribute this differing approach to the differing his- **3.243** torical origins of administration and chapter 11,[430] some point to an alleged harsher atti- tude in the UK to failed businesses,[431] and some point to differences in the structure of the finance market.[432] Whatever the philosophical reasoning, the transfer of management re- sponsibilities in an administration remains a key point of distinction from chapter 11 pro- ceedings. And this is crucial to any analysis of the potential of administration as a procedure

---

[421] See Martin, (n 418) 390; McCormack, (n 418) 546.
[422] Insolvency Act 1986, sch B1, paras 59–69.
[423] ibid, sch B1, para 61.
[424] See 'Productivity and Enterprise' (n 404)
[425] For a description, see Fletcher (n 403)
[426] Insolvency Act 1986, sch B1, para 26 enables the floating charge holder to appoint his own nominee. Para 36 allows the fch to be able to apply to court to have their own nominee appointed.
[427] John Armour and Rizwaan Mokal, 'Reforming the Governance of Corporate Rescue: The Enterprise Act 2002' (2003) 1 *Lloyds Maritime and Commercial Law Quarterly* 28; Mokal, (n 403); Robert Stevens, 'Security After the Enterprise Act' in Joshua Getzler and Jennifer Payne (eds), *Company Charges: Spectrum and Beyond* (2006) 160; Finch (n 418) 298; Vanessa Finch, 'Insolvency Practitioners: The Avenues of Accountability' (2012) 8 *Journal of Business Law* 645.
[428] Armour and Mokal (n 427) 49–55.
[429] *Case Management Conference In the Matter of Coniston Hotel* [2014] EWHC 397; *Holgate and another v Reid and another* [2013] EWHC 4630 (Ch).
[430] See, e.g., Martin (n 418).
[431] See, e.g., Hahn, (n 418).
[432] See Armour, Cheffins, and Skeel (n 418).

to be used proactively to stabilize the business and create liquidity while a debt restructuring is worked out. Directors are unlikely to turn voluntarily to a tool which will inevitably result in their dismissal. Nonetheless, this aspect of administration may be more adaptable than is generally assumed.

3.244 In 2001, Railtrack plc, the company which owned the track in the UK's railway network, entered administration. Railtrack was subject to a 'special administration' regime which recognized its critical importance. One element of this regime was that the objectives were varied from those in a normal administration, crucially so that the administrator had to keep the railway running. For this and other reasons a 'Day One Order' was sought and obtained at the application hearing for the administration order pursuant to which day-to-day management powers were left with the directors. This approach was also adopted in the administration of Metronet, which operates part of London's underground rail network. It may be possible to use the Day One Order in an administration which is being sought to enable a financial restructuring to occur. The argument would be that it was important that a 'business as usual' message could be delivered—and as such that the directors continue to operate the business with the administrator in an oversight role.

3.245 In a paper early in the COVID-19 crisis, the Insolvency Lawyers' Association suggested that this adaptation could be more widely engaged to enable companies seeking to stabilize in the wake of the COVID-19 pandemic to adapt administration towards a debtor-in-possession model.[433] Some insolvency practitioners embraced this idea, while others worried a good deal about the liability implications. To this end, Mark Phillips QC, William Wilson, and Stephen Robins at South Square produced a consent protocol which was intended to act as a starting point for insolvency practitioners and their advisers in scoping out the role of management and the role of the insolvency practitioner when management were left to exercise a wider range of day-to-day powers in administration.[434]

3.246 Of course, an administration in which directors are left to exercise day-to-day management powers by the administrator is something different from a full debtor-in-possession procedure. As ICC Judge Jones put it in the *Dearing* case:

> Administrators may decide at any stage to involve a director(s) and permit that director to exercise management powers. There is also a myriad of possible circumstances when administrators may do so. At one end of the spectrum are cases where to best achieve the purpose of the administration, directors will be empowered to manage the day to day running of the business subject to the administrators' supervision. This may be because of their expertise and reliability and/or because it reduces the cost and expenses of the administration which may be unnecessary and/or may be detrimental to the purpose. It is this approach that has been mooted as a potential route for companies suffering the financial consequences of the Coronavirus (COVID-19). The extent of the supervision will depend upon the circumstances and the administrators' assessment of the need for supervision.[435]

---

[433] Insolvency Lawyers' Association, 'Changing the Narrative Around Administration' (2 April 2020) available at: <https://www.ilauk.com/docs/ILA.v_.1.ChangingtheNarrativeAfter260320Call_.pdf> (last accessed 29 January 2021).

[434] Mark Phillips QC, William Wilson, and Stephen Robins, 'Joint Administrators' Consent Under Paragraph 64 of Schedule B1 to the Insolvency Act 1986' available at: <https://www.ilauk.com/docs/ILA.consent_.protocol_.17.April_.2020.V2_.pdf> (last accessed 29 January 2021).

[435] *Dearing v Skelton* [2020] EWHC 1370.

This underlines that it is for the administrator to determine the extent to which management powers should be left with the directors and, indeed, an administrator who has consented to leave those powers with the directors can equally decide to remove them. As ICC Judge Jones puts it, 'Parliament has entrusted the administrators with the decision-making powers'.[436] Yet, as outlined in the earlier part of this chapter, in reality debtors in a modern chapter 11 case are unlikely to exercise untrammelled management rights, free from interference from creditors. And, as highlighted in other contexts, administrators are repeat players who will be conscious that, if they undermine the expectations of those who appoint them, they may face challenges in the market for appointments in the future. For all these reasons, the differences between an administration in which the administrator consents to leave day-to-day management powers with the directors and a chapter 11 case may not be as stark as they first appear.

3. Ability of third parties to terminate contracts with the debtor

Both chapter 11 and the administration regime provide a 'breathing space' for companies **3.247** who enter the process by protecting them, subject to certain exceptions, against claims and actions from third parties. The details of the application of the automatic stay provided for in chapter 11 and the moratorium provided for in the administration regime are set out below.

(a) Chapter 11 automatic stay

Section 362 of the Bankruptcy Code provides that a stay takes effect automatically upon the **3.248** filing of a petition for relief under the Bankruptcy Code without the need for a court order. The stay enjoins nearly all judicial and administrative proceedings, as well as most informal actions a creditor could take in an effort to collect a debt. As such, the automatic stay is one of the most significant features of the Bankruptcy Code as it preserves the debtor's going concern value and prevents creditors from a race to collect debts. The scope of the stay includes the following:

(i) **Judicial and administrative proceedings**   The automatic stay blocks the commencement or continuation of any judicial, administrative proceeding or other action against the debtor that was or could have been filed pre-petition.[437]

(ii) **Enforcement of judgments**   Section 362(a)(2) stays the enforcement of a judgment obtained before the commencement of the bankruptcy case either against the debtor or against the estate.

(iii) **Acts to obtain possession or control of estate property**   Section 362(a)(3) stays any act to obtain possession of property of the estate or of property from the estate or to exercise control over property of the estate. This section inhibits a creditor's right to self-help repossession of the debtor's property.[438]

(iv) **Acts to create, perfect, or enforce liens**   The automatic stay prohibits any act to create, perfect, or enforce any lien against property of the debtor. Therefore, once a debtor files a bankruptcy petition, a creditor who has not yet perfected a security interest generally is restrained from doing so.[439]

---

[436] Ibid.
[437] 11 USC § 362(a)(1).
[438] *In re Holman*, 92 BR 764 (Bankr SD Ohio 1988).
[439] 11 USC § 362(a)(4),(5).

(v) **Acts to collect**   Section 362(a)(6) stays any act to collect, assess, or recover a claim against the debtor that arose before the commencement of the case.

(vi) **Exercise of right to set-off**   Section 362(a)(7) stays the set-off of any debt owed to the debtor that arose before commencement of the case. Though a set-off right generally is preserved under section 553 of the Bankruptcy Code, section 362(a)(7) restricts the exercise of such right.

(vii) **Tax court proceedings**   Section 362(a)(8) stays the commencement or continuation of a proceeding before the United States Tax Court concerning a corporate debtor's tax liability for a taxable period the bankruptcy court may determine or concerning the tax liability of a debtor who is an individual for a taxable period ending before the date of the order for relief.

3.249   A bankruptcy court may, upon a creditor's request and after notice and a hearing, grant relief from the automatic stay.[440] The Bankruptcy Code provides two primary grounds for allowing relief from the automatic stay: (1) 'for cause, including the lack of adequate protection of an interest in property' held by such party in such interest, or (2) with respect to an action against property of the estate, if the debtor does not have any equity in such property (i.e. the claims against such property exceed its value) and such property is not necessary for an effective reorganization of the debtor.[441]

(b) Moratoria in administration

3.250   Schedule B1 to the Insolvency Act 1986 provides for both an interim moratorium in the period between either the filing of an application to appoint an administrator or the giving of notice of intention to appoint an administrator and the actual appointment, and a moratorium for the duration of the administration. Both moratoria have the same substantive scope,[442] set out in paragraphs 42 and 43 of Schedule B1, discussed below.

(i) **Moratorium on other insolvency processes**   This element of the moratoria's substantive scope is, and always has been, uncontroversial. Paragraph 42 provides for a moratorium on passing resolutions or granting orders for the winding up of a company; similarly paragraph 43(6A) provides for a moratorium on the appointment of an administrative receiver. Both these elements were present in much the same form prior to the coming into force of the Enterprise Act 2002 (in what was then section 11(3) of the Insolvency Act 1986).

(ii) **Moratorium on the enforcement of security**   Paragraph 43(2) provides for a moratorium on the enforcement of security over the company's property without the permission of either the administrator or the court. Again, this was present in substantially this form prior to the coming into force of the Enterprise Act 2002.

(iii) **Moratorium on the repossession of goods**   Paragraph 43(3) provides for a moratorium on the repossession of goods in the company's possession under a

---

[440] See 11 USC § 362(d). In addition, there are numerous exceptions to the automatic stay contained in s 362(b), including those relating to the exercise of certain police and regulatory authority and enforcement of rights under various designated securities contracts, repurchase agreements, commodity contracts, and the like.
[441] Ibid.
[442] Paragraph 44(5) provides that in the circumstances identified elsewhere in para 44 (i.e. where an interim moratorium arises) paras 42 and 43 apply.

hire-purchase agreement without the consent of either the administrator or the court. This was previously combined with the moratorium on the enforcement of security (as section 11(3)(c)) but it is not thought that the separation of these two elements is intended to make any substantive change to their scope.

(iv) **Moratorium on the exercise of a right of forfeiture by peaceable re-entry (or right of irritancy in Scotland)** Prior to the introduction of this specific element (paragraphs 43(4) and (5) of Schedule B1) as part of the Enterprise Act 2002 reforms, there had been some debate as to whether a landlord was able to exercise a right of peaceable re-entry against a company in administration without the leave of the administrator or the court.[443] This point has, however, now been clarified. The moratoria on claims set out above, and the moratorium on the institution of a legal process against the company or its property described below, can be lifted with the approval of the administrator or the consent of the court, with the exception of the moratorium on other insolvency processes which is absolute.

(v) **Moratorium on the institution of a legal process against the company or its property** The final limb of the administration moratorium is a prohibition on commencing or continuing any legal process (including legal proceedings, execution, distress and diligence) against the company without the consent of the administrator or the permission of the court. In *Re Olympia & York Canary Wharf Limited*[444] the court held that 'the taking of non-judicial steps such as the service of a contractual notice in order to crystallise the liability of the party on whom the notice is served' did not amount to instituting 'other proceedings ... execution ... or other legal process' within section 11(3)(d) of the Insolvency Act 1986 prior to its amendment by the Enterprise Act 2002. In other words, other parties were entitled to terminate contracts with the debtor during its administration. Other cases considered the application of the moratorium to specific self-help remedies, for example the forfeiture of a lease.

The Enterprise Act changed the wording of the moratorium on legal processes but it was not believed[445] that this change in wording was intended to in any way alter the position established in the *Re Olympia* case. Indeed, the European High Yield Association was vocal in its assertion that this constituted a missed opportunity to correct what it saw as a major flaw in the administration regime.[446] A limited regime existed in section 233 of the Insolvency Act 1986 to prevent utility suppliers demanding payment of pre-filing debts as a condition of further supply, subject only to their ability to demand a personal guarantee from the insolvency practitioner for those further supplies. And in 2015, this very limited regime was extended to certain IT suppliers and somewhat broadened.[447] Nonetheless, administration

3.251

---

[443] *Clarence Café Limited v Comchester Properties Limited* [1999] L&TR 303 held that the right of peaceable re-entry did not constitute security based on a previous decision in the personal bankruptcy area (*Razzaq v Pala* [1997] 1 WLR 1336), in the process disapproving of the decision in *Exchange Travel Agency Limited v Triton Property Trust* [1991] BCLC 396.

[444] [1993] BCC 154.

[445] See, e.g., Gavin Lightman and Gabriel Moss, *The Law of Administrators and Receivers of Companies* (4th edn, 2007), 22–2004 (although note that the theoretical possibility of a challenge to *Olympia* based on the changed wording is acknowledged at 22-030).

[446] The European High Yield Association's 2007 submission on insolvency law reform pp 3–4.

[447] The Insolvency (Protection of Essential Supplies) Order 2015 amending s 233 of the Insolvency Act 1986 and inserting s 233A.

provided no general moratorium on contract termination. Arguably, this severely restricted the attractiveness of administration as a procedure to stabilize the business and create liquidity while a debt restructuring was attempted. Indeed, far from creating stability, administration risked the loss of important contracts, potentially damaging the prospects for a successful debt restructuring. And, far from helping to create liquidity, it often created a ransom position for critical suppliers who were able to demand payment for outstanding supply as a condition of further supply and to seek to amend contractual terms. These effects were particularly significant in a modern economy where many companies were 'not much of anything except a good idea, a handful of people …, and a bunch of contracts'.[448]

3.252   Overall, the ability of other parties to terminate contracts with the debtor was a significant deterrent against proactively entering administration. Nonetheless, views were divided on the case for reform, with practitioners and scholars pointing out the potential unfairness to trade creditors in preventing them from terminating their contracts during the debtor's administration.[449]

3.253   All of this means that the introduction of a ban on so-called *ipso facto* clauses is perhaps one of the most radical of all the reforms ushered in by the Corporate Insolvency and Governance Act 2020 (CIGA).[450] The new ban not only applies in administration but, as we will see, in the new Part A1 moratorium, the new restructuring plan procedure, company voluntary arrangements, administrative receivership, and (perhaps controversially) winding up.[451] It applies to contracts for the supply of goods and services and provides that a provision that the contract or supply would terminate or any other thing would take place, or the supplier would be entitled to terminate the contract or the supply or do any other thing, in each case because the company becomes subject to administration, ceases to have effect.[452] Moreover, the counterparty is prevented from exercising any right of termination which arose before the administration filing—not just insolvency-related termination rights (although it appears that the counterparty is free to terminate for something arising after the administration provided it does not relate to the insolvency filing).[453] Crucially, the counterparty is expressly prohibited from demanding ransom payments.[454] It is possible for the office holder to consent to termination, and there is a limited ability for the court to consent to termination where 'continuation of the contract would cause the supplier hardship'.[455] Essential supplies falling within section 233 and section 233A of the Insolvency Act 1986 continue to be governed by that regime in administration or, as we shall see, in a company voluntary arrangement.[456] There are also exclusions for financial services firms.[457]

---

[448] John Micklewait and Adrian Wooldridge, *The Company: A Short History of a Revolutionary Idea* (2003) 183.
[449] Vanessa Finch, 'Corporate Rescue in a World of Debt' (2008) 8 *Journal of Business Law* 756.
[450] CIGA 2020, s 14 (Protection of supplies of goods and services: Great Britain) introducing a new s 233B (Protection of supplies) into the Insolvency Act 1986.
[451] Ibid, s 233B(2).
[452] Ibid, s 233B(3).
[453] Ibid, s 233B(4).
[454] Ibid, s 233B(7).
[455] Ibid, s 233B(5).
[456] CIGA 2020, sch 12 (Protection of Supplies of Goods and Services: Great Britain) inserting a new sch 4ZZA (Protection of Supplies under Section 233B: Exclusions) into the Insolvency Act 1986.
[457] Ibid.

Perhaps surprisingly, the new *ipso facto* ban has been introduced with retrospective effect. **3.254** This contrasts with the approach adopted in 2015, when the reforms only applied to contracts entered into after 1 October 2015. For present purposes, the question arises as to whether it makes administration more attractive as a procedure to stabilize the business and create liquidity. It is unlikely to be a magic bullet. Suppliers are still likely to offer commercial excuses for the failure to deliver (stock did not arrive; the van broke down) and will be only too aware of the company's need to litigate to enforce the ban. At the same time, the company is likely to be cautious about incurring the costs of litigation and aware of the need to secure supply while litigation is under way. Overall, then, it is suggested that the new ban does not signal the end of the ransom creditor.

Moreover, there are wider questions about how suppliers will react to the new provisions. **3.255** Concerns have been raised that they are likely to seek to terminate earlier than they might otherwise have done, potentially reducing, rather than enhancing, the prospects of a successful debt restructuring.[458] And numerous questions remain about the legislative drafting which will need some working out: the question of how continuing breaches are treated; the meaning of the prohibition on doing 'any other thing'; and the operation of the carve-outs.[459] Finally, questions have been raised about the impact of the ban on credit insurance and about whether the ban has extraterritorial effect.[460] Assuming the ban is intended to have extraterritorial effect, much will depend on the domestic private international law of the relevant overseas jurisdiction.[461] And overseas suppliers will be all too aware of the heightened problems of enforcement of the ban.

Thus, it is unlikely that the new ban on *ipso facto* clauses will revolutionize the approach to **3.256** administration overnight. Yet, it undoubtedly does shift bargaining power away from the creditor and towards the debtor company. Coupled with the argument about the potential for a more debtor-in-possession orientation outlined above, and some of the points made below, it may enhance the prospect of thinking about administration differently in the next decade. As we shall see, this may also depend on the success of the new Part A1 moratorium introduced by the Corporate Insolvency and Governance Act 2020 and on the adaptation of certain debt restructuring tools over the next decade. For the moment, the question is whether other aspects of the administration procedure undermine its adaptability as a stabilization and liquidity-creating process, starting with the ability of the debtor to raise new financing.

4. The ability of the debtor to raise new financing

Much has been made of the lack of a formal debtor-in-possession financing regime in the **3.257** English context. However, there are real questions as to how significant this has been in the failure of administration to develop as a restructuring regime. Any debt or liability on any contract entered into by the administrator in his role as the company's agent will be payable

---

[458] Felicity Toube QC and Georgina Peters, 'Ipso Facto Reform: Why Now and Does it Go Too Far (Or Not Far Enough?') (2020) *South Square Digest CIGA Special* 61.

[459] Ibid, 59-61.

[460] Ibid, 61.

[461] William Wilson and Paul Fradley, 'Ipso Facto Clauses: the International Dimension' (2021) 2 *Journal of International Banking & Financial Law* 103.

in priority to the administrator's fees and expenses and also in priority to floating charges, although after fixed charges: paragraph 99(4) of Schedule B1 to the Insolvency Act 1986. Thus, if the administrator raises rescue finance that finance ought to rank as an expense and there is some limited support for this proposition in case law.[462] There is a potential risk that the right of the administrator to repay rescue finance as an administration expense under paragraph 99 would breach negative pledge provisions given by the company to existing creditors. This gives rise to the concern that the administrator may be liable for the tort of inducing a breach of contract. In practice, however, charges arising by operation of law are commonly carved out from standard negative pledge provisions. Even without an express carve-out, a court is arguably likely to construe the provision so as to exclude charges arising by operation of law through no act on the part of the company. Furthermore, the courts have recently confirmed that in relation to the tort of inducing a breach of contract, the defence of justification would normally be open to administrators if it could be demonstrated that they acted in accordance with their powers, in good faith, and in a way that was necessary to further the objectives of the administration (and if they satisfied themselves that the performance of the contract would not be in the interests of the company's creditors).[463] The statutory moratorium would prevent a claim being brought against the company itself without either consent of the administrator or leave of the court and the court would be likely to apply a balance of fairness test (i.e. the counterparty's interests versus those of the estate) in deciding whether or not to uphold the negative pledge provision.[464]

3.258   As a result of developments in English case law,[465] the bar for the successful creation of a fixed charge has been significantly raised. As a result, in many companies a significant proportion of the assets will be subject to floating, rather than fixed, security and for the reasons outlined above finance raised to fund the administration ought to rank above those claims. Furthermore, the English investment grade market has typically been unsecured and so-called 'fallen angels' often have significant unencumbered assets. It may be that other aspects of the administration regime have made it cumulatively unattractive as a restructuring procedure and, as a result, there has been no need to test the boundaries on administration financing. Yet, it is suggested here that those boundaries do offer scope for rescue financing.

3.259   As a postscript, it may also be possible to provide rescue financing via a so-called *Quistclose* trust.[466] In a *Quistclose* trust arrangement, the financier advances monies to the company on the condition that the monies can only be applied for a specific purpose. If the monies are not so applied, then they are held on trust for the lender. *Quistclose* trusts do not protect the priority position of the lender if the monies are applied for the stated purpose and the company subsequently enters corporate insolvency proceedings. However, they are a useful device for ensuring that the company does not acquire the beneficial interest in the monies

---

[462] *Bibby Trade Finance Limited v McKay* [2006] EWHC 2836 (Ch). For analysis, see Vanessa Finch and David Milman, *Corporate Insolvency Law: Perspectives and Principles* (3rd edn, Cambridge University Press 2017) 336–338; McCormack (n 418) 728.

[463] *Lictor Anstalt v MIR Steel UK Limited and Libala Limited* [2014] EWHC 3316 (Ch).

[464] See, e.g., *Astor Chemicals Ltd v Synthetic Technology Ltd* [1990] BCC 97, and *Somerfield Stores Limited v Spring (Sutton Coldfield) Limited* [2010] L&TR 8; *Sunberry Properties Ltd v Innovate Logistics Ltd* [2009] BCC 164.

[465] *Re Brumark Investment Ltd* [2001] 2 AC 710, PC (sometimes reported as *Agnew v Commissioner for Inland Revenue*).

[466] Named after the case *Barclays Bank v Quistclose Investments Ltd* [1970] QC 657.

so that they can be applied for specific purposes. Thus, they can be used to ensure that payments vital to the restructuring effort are met. There is a good deal of uncertainty about the requirements for a *Quistclose* trust,[467] with the result that lenders may be cautious about relying upon the device, but it is a useful tool in the toolbox.

5. The ability to bind non-consenting creditors

In addition to offering the protection of an automatic stay (as discussed above), chapter 11 **3.260** includes a mechanism for implementing, with the courts' blessing, a plan of reorganization (typically formulated by the debtor's management) in the face of opposition from a dissenting minority of creditors (commonly referred to as a 'cramdown'). This mechanic is discussed in detail elsewhere but for present purposes it suffices to note that the statutory provisions also incorporate certain principles, such as the absolute priority rule, with which the plan must comply before creditors can be 'crammed down'. Of crucial importance to the application of these principles is the valuation of the debtor, to which end the chapter 11 process provides for valuation hearings where the court will approve a valuation in light of competing valuations from the debtor and dissenting creditors.

An administration offers no such opportunity of binding dissenting creditors. The admin- **3.261** istrator must formulate proposals to be put[468] to creditors for approval but such approval does not bind any of the creditors to a compromise of their rights. Where this is required as part of the restructuring of the debtor a combination of processes may be used, with the administrator including a company voluntary arrangement, scheme of arrangement, or the new Part 26A restructuring plan as part of their proposals. The question in these circumstances is whether it is necessary or desirable for the company to enter administration at all before the company voluntary arrangement, scheme of arrangement, or Part 26A restructuring plan is proposed. As we have seen, there has been little appetite for this approach to date. However, the combination of the reforms introduced by CIGA; the circumstances following the COVID-19 pandemic; and the creativity of English lawyers and insolvency practitioners may mean that administration might be mobilized and adapted in this way in the future. Perhaps the biggest challenge standing in the way of this new adaptation is the question of whether perceptions of participants in the corporate insolvency system towards administration can also adapt. This is the question to which we now turn.

6. Perceptions of administration and legislative intent

Although the legal differences between administration and chapter 11 are discussed above, **3.262** perhaps the most commercially significant distinction is how they are perceived. For an English company, administration is perceived as being a probable death-blow, whereas in the US filing for chapter 11 relief generally is perceived as taking advantage of a valid recovery technique. In part this may be because the finance market and the profession (after considerable political lobbying) managed to frame suitably broadly drawn revisions to the administration procedure which enabled them to interpret and implement it in much

---

[467] William Swadling (ed), *The Quistclose Trust: Critical Essays* (Bloomsbury 2004).
[468] Unless they state that (i) all creditors will be paid in full, (ii) that the debtor has insufficient property to make any distribution to unsecured creditors other than the prescribed part, or (iii) that the first and second purposes of administration cannot be achieved: Insolvency Act 1986, sch B1, para 52.

the same way as the receiverships which predated the reforms. Writing in 2004 Riz Mokal noted:

> There are reasons to believe that the Enterprise Act 2002 has revolutionised corporate insolvency law. But if that is the case, the revolution is a relatively quiet one. Many insolvency professionals—lawyers and accountants alike—have not even sensed that the existing order has been overthrown. They imagine that the new administration procedure introduced by the Act merely disguises administrative receivership so as to render it more generally acceptable. They think that while requiring them to jump through some additional but merely formal hoops, the statute benignly allows them to conduct business as usual under a new name.[469]

3.263 Two reasons may account for this. The first is the challenge in asking a profession to change a mindset fixed over many years for a new way of thinking.[470] But secondly, and perhaps more importantly, as Mokal notes the finance market in the UK at the time was highly concentrated in the hands of four big deposit or 'clearing' banks. These banks were quite happy with the way in which receivership had operated and the insolvency profession was dependent upon them for the referral of work. Thus, notwithstanding the potential to argue (as Mokal does) that the Enterprise Act 2002 fundamentally reformed the Insolvency Act 1986,[471] both banks and the insolvency profession sought ways to implement the new regime in the image of the old. Ironically, as the structure of the finance market has changed in Britain this has also led, to some extent, to the marginalization of the insolvency practitioner in restructuring and it is possible that if there were to be revolution today the profession would be more ready to embrace it.

3.264 Thus, although directly comparable figures are hard to come by, two separate empirical studies into the outcomes for companies which enter chapter 11 and administration suggest an interesting distinction. An analyst and assistant director of the Executive Office for Trustees published a study in May 2009 looking at the outcomes of all chapter 11 proceedings commenced after the Bankruptcy Abuse Prevention and Consumer Protection Act of 2005[472] came into force. Of those proceedings, 33.2 per cent were confirmed, which implies they had outcomes which might be classed as 'successful', i.e. where the same corporate entity continued to trade. A study looking at administrations in the period between September 2004 and May 2005,[473] however, concluded that 'less than 1 per cent [of the administrations in the study] result in a rescue of the company'. Although too much weight should not be given to the disparity (given, inter alia, the disparity in the length of periods looked at), the

---

[469] Mokal (n 403) 3.

[470] Robert C Clark, 'The Interdisciplinary Study of Legal Evolution' (1981) 90 *Yale Law Journal* 1238, 1253; Mokal (n 403) 26: 'The IPs who are appointed administrators would of course be the very individuals who have hitherto been acting as receivers. This means they would have socialised in a milieu where the interests of secured creditors—mainly banks—reigned supreme. There would therefore be a tendency for the professional judgements of those IPs to be shaped by those interests'.

[471] And see, e.g., academic comment on the ability to pre-pack in the new framework, Peter Walton, 'Pre-packaged Administrations: Trick or Treat?' (2006) 19(8) *Insolvency Intelligence* 113.

[472] Ed Flynn and Phil Crewson, 'Chapter 11 Filings Trends in History and Today' (2009) 28(4) *American Bankruptcy Institute Journal* 14. The Bankruptcy Abuse Prevention and Consumer Protection Act was passed on 17 October 2005.

[473] Sandra Frisby, 'The Pre-pack Progression: Latest Empirical Findings' (2008) 21(10) *Insolvency Intelligence* 154.

suggestion that as many as one-third of chapter 11 cases may result in the original company continuing to trade against no more than one per cent of administrations is noteworthy.

More anecdotally, one would be hard placed to name a UK listed company which had entered administration and successfully emerged to continue trading. In the United States, however, many household names have emerged from chapter 11 to continue trading in a recognizable form, such as United Airlines,[474] Continental Airlines (which has been through not one but two sets of chapter 11 proceedings),[475] Texaco,[476] Worldcom,[477] Marvel,[478] Greyhound,[479] CIT Group Inc,[480] and Macy's[481] (although Macy's emerged under new ownership).   **3.265**

The focus on the continuation of the original company does not take account of the impact of pre-packs, where a company is liquidated and its business sold to a new vehicle, leaving liabilities owed to junior creditors behind in the original company. However, in terms of public perception, such pre-packs may not be viewed as a 'success'. On the contrary, the press in the UK has typically had a very negative reaction to pre-pack administrations. Pre-packs are discussed in further detail later, in section X. Overall, for administration to be successfully mobilized as a procedure to stabilize the business and create liquidity, financial creditors, general, unsecured creditors, employees, and wider stakeholders have to accept that it can be used in this way. The Insolvency Lawyers' Association paper discussed above,[482] and the accompanying consent protocol drafted by Mark Phillips, William Willson, and Stephen Robins at South Square,[483] have certainly started a conversation about whether perceptions can be changed. Whether perceptions can ultimately be changed or not may also depend on the success of the new Part A1 Moratorium introduced by the CIGA, and that is where we turn next.   **3.266**

A final point should also be made about legislative intent. Given the long-term adaptation of administration as a tool to sell the business and assets of the company when efforts to rescue the company have failed, courts are likely to require some reassurance that Parliament intended administration to be used as a stabilization tool. Of course, identifying the first purpose of administration as rescue of the company provides powerful, supporting evidence.[484] But there is also other, compelling evidence including the fact that the decision to restrict the moratorium available to support Company Voluntary Arrangements to small companies in the Insolvency Act 2000 (discussed below) appears to have been motivated by a desire to encourage larger companies to use administration as a stabilization tool.[485]   **3.267**

---

[474] United Airlines filed for chapter 11 relief in December 2002 and exited chapter 11 in February 2006. Its stock resumed trading on 2 February 2006.

[475] Continental Airlines first filed for chapter 11 relief on 23 September 1983 and exited those proceedings on 30 June 1988. Subsequently, it filed for chapter 11 relief again on 3 December 1990 and exited those proceedings in May 1993.

[476] Texaco filed for chapter 11 Bankruptcy in April 1987 and emerged in May 1988.

[477] Worldcom filed for chapter 11 relief in July 2002 and emerged in April 2004.

[478] Marvel filed for chapter 11 relief in December 1996 and emerged in October 1998.

[479] Greyhound filed for chapter 11 relief in June 1990 and emerged in October 1991.

[480] CIT Group Inc filed for chapter 11 relief on 1 November 2009 and emerged on 10 December 2009.

[481] Macy's filed for bankruptcy in January 1992 and emerged approximately three years later.

[482] ILA (n 433).

[483] Phillips et al (n 434).

[484] Insolvency Act 1986, sch B1, para 3(1)(a).

[485] Fletcher (n 403) 131.

B. Part A1 Moratorium

1. Introduction

3.268 The Corporate Insolvency and Governance Act 2020 (CIGA) introduced the Part A1 moratorium into English corporate insolvency law.[486] As we shall see, this new moratorium appears to be explicitly designed as a tool to stabilize the business and create liquidity while a company rescue is worked out. In this section, we will analyse and evaluate how well suited it is to this task.

2. Eligibility

3.269 The legislation exempts a relatively wide range of companies from eligibility to apply for the new Part A1 moratorium.[487] In particular, a company is excluded if it is party to a capital market arrangement.[488] An arrangement is a capital market arrangement if any of the following apply:

(a) it involves a grant of security to a person holding it as trustee for a person who holds a capital market investment issued by a party to the arrangement;
(b) at least one party guarantees the performance of obligations of another party;
(c) at least one party provides security in respect of the performance of obligations of another party;
(d) the arrangement involves an investment of a kind described in articles 83 to 85 of the Financial Services and Markets Act 2000 (Regulated Activities) Order 2001.[489]

Overall, the effect is that many companies which have issued bonds to raise finance will not be eligible for the Part A1 moratorium at all. However, where the bonds are unsecured the Part A1 moratorium may still be available. For example, it appears that it would have been available to the Gategroup in their 2021 restructuring, given that Gategroup had issued unsecured bonds guaranteed by the group's parent alone.[490]

3.270 A company which is: eligible for the Part A1 moratorium; not subject to a winding up petition; and not an overseas company can apply for the moratorium out of court.[491] Otherwise, a company can apply to court for a Part A1 moratorium.[492] An insolvency practitioner, known as the monitor, is appointed in the Part A1 moratorium although, as we shall see, a relatively narrow role is envisaged for them. Indeed, at its heart the Part A1 moratorium has a debtor-in-possession orientation. Where an application is made to court for a Part A1 moratorium the monitor is required to confirm that the company is an eligible company and that, in their view, it is likely that a moratorium for the company would result in a rescue of

---

[486] CIGA 2020, s 1, inserting a new Part A1 (Moratorium) into the Insolvency Act 1986.
[487] CIGA 2020, sch 1, inserting a new sch ZA1 (Moratorium in Great Britain: Eligible Companies) into the Insolvency Act 1986.
[488] Ibid, para 13.
[489] Ibid, para 13(2).
[490] *Gategroup Guarantee Limited* [2021] EWHC 304 (Ch) [19], 'it might have been possible to mitigate the effect of [acceleration and enforcement action] by applying for a moratorium under Part A1 of the Insolvency Act 1986'.
[491] Part A1 (Moratorium) of CIGA 2020, inserting a new s A3 into the Insolvency Act 1986.
[492] Ibid, ss A4 and A5.

the company as a going concern. The directors of the company are required to confirm that, in their view, the company is, or is likely to become, unable to pay its debts.[493] As we shall see throughout our analysis of the Part A1 moratorium, the procedure can only be used if, and for so long as, the monitor thinks that a company rescue is likely. This contrasts with the position in administration. In an administration, the administrator is required to work through a hierarchy of purposes set out in paragraph 3 of Schedule B1 of the Insolvency Act 1986. The first purpose is a company rescue.[494] However, if the administrator thinks that a company rescue is not practicable, or that the purpose set out in paragraph 3(1)(b) would achieve a better result for creditors as a whole, they can move down the hierarchy to that purpose: achieving a better result for creditors as a whole than would be likely if the company were to be wound up (without first being in administration). Similarly, if the administrator thinks that it is not reasonably practicable to achieve either of the objectives specified in paragraphs 3(1)(a) and 3(1)(b) and the administrator does not unnecessarily harm the interests of the creditors as a whole, they can move to the purpose set out in paragraph 3(1)(c): realizing property in order to make a distribution to one or more secured creditors. Thus, administration offers the possibility of using the procedure to stabilize the business and create liquidity while options are explored. The administrator can start by exploring the possibility of a debt restructuring, but if it becomes clear that this is not practicable and that the paragraph 3(1)(b) option would achieve a better result for creditors as a whole, the administrator can move on to that purpose. The Part A1 moratorium does not offer this optionality: if the monitor is unable to confirm their view that a company rescue is likely, the moratorium is not available at all. And if the monitor comes to the view that a company rescue no longer remains likely, the monitor must terminate the Part A1 moratorium.[495]

It is also worth pausing to consider which companies would need to avail themselves of the Part A1 moratorium in order to stabilize a group business. As we shall discuss in more detail later, it is possible to release guarantees granted by group subsidiaries in a scheme of arrangement or a restructuring plan of the principal debtor. This means that, in England, it is common to seek to propose a scheme or a restructuring plan in the finance holding company, while keeping all of the operating subsidiaries outside the process. However, if resort is had to the Part A1 moratorium it may be necessary to consider placing a larger number of group subsidiaries into a process in order to achieve the necessary stabilization. This appears to have been the case in Gategroup and may be why the group chose not to turn to the Part A1 moratorium to address acceleration and enforcement risks. We are told, in the judgment, that the issuer of certain bonds in the Gategroup restructuring did not propose a Part 26A restructuring plan, 'because that would have constituted an event of default under condition 7(d) of the terms of the Bonds, leading to potential acceleration and enforcement action'.[496] We are further told that the Part A1 moratorium, 'would not have prevented cross-default occurring under contracts entered into by other Group entities, thus imperilling the Restructuring as a whole'.[497]

3.271

---

[493] Ibid, ss A4 and A6.
[494] Insolvency Act 1986, Sch B1, para 3(1)(a).
[495] (n 486) s A38.
[496] *Gategroup Guarantee Limited* (n 490) [19].
[497] Ibid.

3. Period of the moratorium

3.272   The initial period of the moratorium is 20 business days, beginning on the business day after the day on which the moratorium comes into force.[498] The moratorium can be extended once by the directors without creditor consent for a further 20 business days;[499] by the directors with creditor consent for up to one year (and multiple extensions are possible);[500] by the court on the application of the directors (and multiple extensions are, once again, possible);[501] where a proposal for a company voluntary arrangement is pending;[502] and by the court in the course of an application for a scheme or restructuring plan.[503] Once again, this contrasts with administration: an administrator has one year before he must vacate office and, at that point, the administration can be extended by the court but also by the creditors for a specified period not to exceed one year.[504] Moreover, in the case of the Part A1 moratorium an application to court for an extension must be accompanied by: a statement from the directors that moratorium debts and pre-moratorium debts without a payment holiday that have fallen due have been paid or discharged; a statement from the directors that the company is or is likely to become unable to pay its debts; a statement from the directors about whether pre-moratorium creditors have been consulted and if not, why not; and a statement from the monitor that, in the monitor's view, it is likely that the moratorium will result in a rescue of the company as a going concern.[505] This is perhaps unsurprising now that we understand the organizing principle that the Part A1 moratorium, and its interference with creditors' rights, should only be available if, and for so long as, a company rescue is likely. Yet it nonetheless requires the monitor to clear a relatively high hurdle and may limit the incentive to have resort to the procedure to stabilize the business and create liquidity. This brings us to the crucial concepts of pre-moratorium debts; pre-moratorium debts without a payment holiday; and moratorium debts.

4. Pre-moratorium and moratorium debts

3.273   A crucial role of the Part A1 moratorium is to create liquidity by suspending the obligation to pay pre-moratorium debts while negotiations are in course. This obviously provides an important incentive for resorting to the Part A1 moratorium while a debt restructuring is being worked out. However, the company is obliged to pay both moratorium debts and certain pre-moratorium debts which are not suspended by the Part A1 moratorium.[506] Unsurprisingly, the company must pay the monitor's remuneration and expenses and must pay for goods or services supplied during the moratorium. The company must also pay rent for the period of the moratorium. The meaning of this is not entirely clear but it does not seem immediately apparent that a company could close premises during the Part A1 moratorium and stop paying rent. Instead, rent on the company's entire rental estate would appear to be due during the Part A1 moratorium while it could not form part of any debt

---

[498] For the day on which the moratorium comes into force, see Part A1 Moratorium (n 486) s A7(1).
[499] Ibid, ss A11 and A12.
[500] Ibid.
[501] Ibid, s A13.
[502] Ibid, s A14.
[503] Ibid, s A15.
[504] Insolvency Act 1986, sch B1, para 76.
[505] Part A1 Moratorium (n 486) s A13.
[506] Ibid, s A18.

restructuring plan. As we will see later, if a company compromises rent through a Company Voluntary Arrangement (CVA) the debtor may seek to compromise rent accruing up to the date of the CVA. Thus, a company opting for the Part A1 moratorium would appear to restrict its ability to accrue and compromise rental liabilities when compared with a company which manages to agree a CVA outside the Part A1 moratorium process. A company which proactively files for administration to stabilize the business also restricts its ability to accrue unpaid rent during the administration proceeding which it compromises in any debt restructuring which is eventually agreed. This is because of the so-called *Lundy Granite* principle.[507] In *Lundy Granite* Lord Justice James said:

> if the company for its own purposes, and with a view to the realisation of the property to better advantage, remains in possession of the estate, which the lessor is therefore not able to obtain possession of, common sense and ordinary justice require the Court to see that the landlord receives the full value of the property.

The modern application of the *Lundy Granite* principle was set out by Lord Justice Lewison in *Jervis v Pillar Denton Ltd*:

> The true extent of the principle, in my judgment, is that the office holder must make payments at the rate of rent for the duration of any period during which he retains possession of the demised property for the benefit of the winding-up or administration (as the case may be). The rent will be treated as accruing from day to day. Those payments are payable as expenses of the winding up or administration. The duration of the period is a question of fact and is not determined merely by reference to which rent days occur before, during or after that period.[508]

Thus, it appears that it is open to an administrator to cease operating from leasehold premises during the administration and to stop accruing rent at that point. It is not readily apparent that this option is available in the new Part A1 moratorium, where the obligation is stated as the obligation to pay 'rent in respect of a period during the moratorium'. A further distinction between the new Part A1 moratorium and administration as procedures to create liquidity arises when we turn to consider employees. In administration, the administrator has 14 days to decide which employment contracts to adopt. At that point, the administrator is only liable for wages or salary (including holiday or sick pay) or contributions to occupational pension schemes in respect of the contracts of employment which they adopt for the period after adoption.[509] Crucially, neither redundancy and unfair dismissal payments nor protective awards are included in 'wages and salary'.[510] This contrasts starkly with the Part A1 moratorium, in which the company must pay both wages and salary under any contract of employment, and redundancy payments that accrue during the moratorium or which have accrued before the moratorium but remain unpaid. Finally, and perhaps most surprisingly of all, in the Part A1 moratorium the company must pay any debt or liability arising under a contract or other instrument involving financial services. At the very least, this means that the company cannot suspend debt service or principal repayments

---

[507] *Lundy Granite* (1871) LR 6 Ch App 462 (CA).
[508] [2014] EWCA Civ 180, [2015] Ch 87.
[509] Insolvency Act 1986, sch B1, para 99(4)–(5).
[510] *Allders Department Stores Ltd (in administration)* [2005] 2 All ER 122, [2005] BCC 289; *Huddersfield Fine Worsteds Ltd* [2005] BCC 915, [2005] 4 All ER 886.

falling due under loan and bond agreements. Moreover, the definition of financial services is relatively wide, and other financial services contracts may be implicated. This contrasts with the position in administration when it would be entirely usual to suspend debt service payments and debt repayments. Overall, the liquidity-creating potential of the Part A1 moratorium appears more limited than the liquidity-creating potential of administration. Moreover, a company which resorts to the Part A1 moratorium appears to impose limits on debts which can be restructured when compared with a company which manages to negotiate its debt restructuring without resorting to a Part A1 moratorium.

5. The scope of the moratorium

3.274   As we would expect, the Part A1 moratorium does provide reasonably extensive moratorium protection, so that while it may not deliver on creating liquidity it potentially offers more as a stabilization tool. Creditors are restricted from filing for insolvency proceedings;[511] from forfeiture proceedings;[512] and from enforcement and legal proceedings (subject to exceptions for collateral security and financial collateral arrangements and employment claims including employment tribunal proceedings).[513] Furthermore, floating charge holders are restricted from crystallizing their floating charges or imposing restrictions on disposals of property.[514] And the new *ipso facto* ban in section 233B of the Insolvency Act 1986, described in the section on administration above, is engaged. However, when compared with administration, the breathing space from creditors created by the Part A1 moratorium comes with relatively high burdens for the company. There are restrictions on obtaining credit of £500 or more without notifying the counterparty that the moratorium is in force; security can only be granted with the consent of the monitor (where the monitor thinks, relying on company information, that it will support a company rescue); and there are prohibitions on entering into market contracts, financial collateral arrangements, transfer orders, market or system charges, and collateral security.[515]

3.275   Furthermore, disposals of property must be in the ordinary course of business; or made with the consent of the monitor (where the monitor thinks it will support company rescue, relying on company information); or in pursuance of a court order.[516] Disposals of property subject to a hire purchase arrangement (which includes, for example, retention of title) must be made in accordance with the agreement or with the permission of the court, where the monitor thinks that disposal will support company rescue and where the net proceeds must be held for the counterparty and, if necessary, topped up to the open market value with a willing seller.[517] The requirement for disposals to be made 'in accordance with the agreement' may prove more difficult to navigate than at first appears. The difficulty arises because of the tendency for retention of title clauses to be drafted expansively and for the courts to subsequently read them down. Thus, it is not uncommon for a retention of title clause to state that the customer sells goods as fiduciary or agent for the supplier, and to purport to retain title for the supplier in proceeds of sale of the goods or manufactured goods,

---

[511] Part A1 Moratorium (n 486) s A20.
[512] Ibid, s A21.
[513] Ibid.
[514] Ibid, s A22.
[515] Ibid, ss A25–A27.
[516] Ibid, s A29.
[517] Ibid, ss A30 and A32.

or in products manufactured with the goods. In many modern cases, the courts have held that the substance of the relationship is not one of agent and principal, and have restricted the retention of title to the original goods in the hands of the customer but this approach has not been universal: in other cases the courts have upheld what they regard as a literal interpretation of the retention of title clause.[518] All of this can make it challenging for a company to know what the boundaries are to disposing of the property 'in accordance with the agreement'.

We are on somewhat more familiar ground with the procedure for obtaining the permission of the court, which reflects the procedure in administration.[519] However, it is not entirely clear whether the court is to specify the market price for the goods on the open market if sold to a willing vendor when it gives permission for the sale and, if it does, how it goes about fixing that price.[520] Moreover, as Gerard McCormack has noted in the context of the parallel provisions in administration, market conditions may have changed by the time of the sale in which case the insolvency practitioner might be expected to apply to court for directions.[521] Overall, resorting to court if there are doubts about the correct interpretation of the agreement would appear to be a relatively unattractive route. In administration, it would be usual for the administrator and the supplier to negotiate over the treatment of the goods subject to the retention of title clause and perhaps that will be the solution here.[522] However, rather than assisting continued trading in difficult circumstances, this would appear to add cost and challenge.   **3.276**

When we analysed the new ban on *ipso facto* clauses, we doubted that it would be the end of the ransom creditor. We noted considerable uncertainties in the legislative drafting; we noted that creditors would continue to be able to raise commercial excuses (the van broke down; the supply did not arrive); we noted that creditors would be aware of the company's need to litigate to enforce the ban; that the company may need to secure supply during any dispute. Against this background, the Part A1 moratorium provides an important provision which enables the company to pay pre-moratorium debts for which it has a payment holiday: up to the greater of £5,000 or 1 per cent of the value of debts and other liabilities owed by the company to unsecured creditors when the moratorium began; with monitor consent (where the monitor, relying on company information, thinks the payment will support company rescue); or in pursuance of a court order.[523] Thus, if a creditor retains a ransom position which cannot be ameliorated in practice through the operation of the new section 233B restrictions, ultimately the company can pay pre-moratorium debts. Incidentally, this reflects the position in administration where an administrator has a wide power to make payments which the administrator 'thinks ... likely to assist the achievement   **3.277**

---

[518] For an excellent analysis see Louise Gullifer, ' "Sales" on Retention of Title Terms: Is the English Law Analysis Broken?' (2017) 133(Apr) *Law Quarterly Review* 244.

[519] Insolvency Act 1986, sch B1, para 72.

[520] McCormack (n 418) 123.

[521] Ibid.

[522] Sally Wheeler, 'Capital Fractionalized: the Role of Insolvency Practitioners in Asset Distribution' in Maureen Cain and Christine B Harrington (eds), *Lawyers in a Postmodern World: Translation and Transgression* (Oxford University Press 1994) 85.

[523] Part A1 Moratorium (n 486) s A28.

of the purpose of administration'.[524] This means that an administrator who considers it essential to pay a ransom creditor, notwithstanding the operation of section 233B, should also be able to do so.

6. The role of the monitor

3.278   We have already noted that the role of the monitor appears to be relatively limited. As we have seen, the monitor is responsible for assessing the eligibility of the company at commencement and for sanctioning many of the transactions which the company completes during the Part A1 moratorium such as: the grant of security; disposals of property outside the ordinary course of business; and payment of pre-moratorium debts for which the company has a payment holiday. Yet, the principal role of the monitor is to monitor whether rescuing the company as a going concern remains likely and to bring the moratorium to an end where it is not.[525] Although the monitor must reach their own view on the tests for entry into, and extension of, the Part A1 moratorium, in many other cases they may rely on information from the company unless they have reason to doubt its accuracy. Indeed, they have power to require directors to provide information.[526] The monitor also has power to apply to court for directions.

3.279   A creditor, director, member, or any other person affected by the moratorium can bring a challenge against the monitor on the basis of unfair harm to the applicant.[527] The application may be made during the moratorium or after it has ended and the court may confirm, reverse, or modify the act or decision of the monitor; give the monitor directions; or make any other order but, notably, not an order for the monitor to pay compensation. Specific provisions also apply where the omission complained of is a failure to bring the moratorium to an end. Overall, the message appears to be that the monitor's role is limited to a strictly monitoring function and, accordingly, compensation orders would not be appropriate, and this is reinforced by separate provisions permitting a challenge to the directors' conduct.[528] This may have been intended to address one of the problems identified with the small company moratorium regime in CVAs (which is abolished by CIGA with the introduction of the Part A1 moratorium). The small company moratorium was only available for very small companies but research by Peter Walton, Chris Umfreville, and Lézelle Jacobs suggested that take-up was very slim, even by those companies eligible for it.[529] One reason for this may have been the liability risks for the insolvency practitioner in what were often small cases which did not attract large fees. Early indications suggested that insolvency practitioners were conscious that the limitations on liability in Part A1 are framed against a relatively limited role, and that they were anxious not to overstep the bounds of the monitor's role as conceived of in the legislation. Indeed, there has been some suggestion that the Regulated Professional Bodies who regulate insolvency practitioners take the view that a separate team would need to provide substantive advice, with a Chinese wall between

---

[524] Insolvency Act 1986, sch B1, para 66. For recent Court of Appeal authority on the breadth of para 66 see *Re Debenhams Retail Limited (in administration)* [2020] EWCA Civ 600.
[525] Part A1 Moratorium (n 486) s A38.
[526] Ibid, s A36.
[527] Ibid, s A42.
[528] Ibid, s A44.
[529] Peter Walton, Chris Umfreville, and Lézelle Jacobs, *Company Voluntary Arrangements: Evaluating Success and Failure* (R3 and ICAEW May 2018), 17–18.

the advisory team and the monitor. If this is the approach which is adopted there must be a risk that it will substantially increase costs while providing limited benefits. At the same time, presumably as part of the policy of balancing the risks of the Part A1 moratorium for creditors and the benefits of the Part A1 moratorium in promoting corporate rescue, the legislation contains a rather formidable range of offences for the directors; the monitor; and the company and its officers.[530]

7. Priority of debts in subsequent insolvency proceedings

Finally, the Part A1 moratorium contains important provisions about the ranking of mora-   **3.280**
torium debts and pre-moratorium debts for which the company did not have a payment holiday if efforts to rescue the company are unsuccessful and it is placed into an insolvency proceeding. Schedule 3 of CIGA inserts a new section 174A into the Insolvency Act 1986 which provides that, in any subsequent winding up proceedings, after the fees of the Official Receiver (in the event that the company is placed into compulsory liquidation), moratorium debts and certain pre-moratorium payment debts have priority over expenses of the insolvency case; preferential creditors; and floating charge holders. The relevant debts are debts in respect of: goods or services supplied during the moratorium; rent in respect of a period during the moratorium; wages or salaries, relating to a period of employment before or during the moratorium; any pre-moratorium debt that consists of liability to make a redundancy payment and that fell due before or during the moratorium; a pre-moratorium debt arising under a contract for financial services, falling due before or during the moratorium, and not 'relevant accelerated debt'; and the monitor's remuneration and expenses. A new paragraph 65 is also inserted into Schedule B1 of the Insolvency Act 1986 providing that in a subsequent administration the administrator must make a distribution to creditors in respect of these debts. Rule 3.51A of the Insolvency Rules 2016 now sets out how these liabilities are to rank among themselves. Notably, the legislation provides that an administrator *must* make a distribution in respect of moratorium debts and pre-moratorium debts for which the company did not have a payment holiday such that, if the company has insufficient cash to fund such a distribution, it would appear that the company must be placed into liquidation instead.

These new distributional rules have attracted considerable attention in the market, particu-   **3.281**
larly the risks posed to a floating charge holder by a potentially significant volume of priority debts.[531] At the same time, the now familiar policy objective of balancing the harm to creditors as a result of the Part A1 moratorium against the privileges it offers debtors is readily apparent. And, of course, financial creditors are likely to be well placed to monitor the progress of the Part A1 moratorium for themselves and to put pressure on the monitor to bring the procedure to a close if it becomes apparent that a company rescue is no longer likely. Indeed, while debt which is accelerated during the moratorium is expressly carved out of the priority debts in a subsequent insolvency procedure (out of fear that there would otherwise be incentives to 'game' the procedure), financial creditors nonetheless retain the

---

[530] Part A1 Moratorium (n 486) s A8(4) and (5); A17(6) and (7); A19(5); A24; A25(3); A26(4); A28(5); A29(6); A31(7) and (10); A32(4) and (5); A39(9); A45; A46 and A47.
[531] David Ereira and Crispin Daly, 'Rank Inequality: the Consequences of the Creation of "Super Priority" Debts under the Corporate Insolvency and Governance Act 2020 Moratorium' (February 2021) *Butterworths Journal of International Banking & Financial Law* 97.

power to accelerate their debt and to effectively bring the moratorium to an immediate termination (because the company would no longer be able to pay its debts). Thus, the concerns for subordination of the floating charge holder may not be as significant as they might at first appear. A further interesting question, for the purposes of this book, is whether the priority regime offers a new route by which to raise rescue financing.

C. Receivership

3.282 A receiver (or manager) is a person appointed pursuant to the terms of the relevant security document by a secured creditor as a means of enforcing his security. An administrative receiver is a receiver (or manager) of the whole or substantially the whole of a company's property who is appointed by or on behalf of holders of debentures secured by a floating charge or by such a charge and other forms of security.

3.283 An administrative receiver has similar management powers to those of an administrator and any additional powers conferred by the security document under which they are appointed. There is, however, no moratorium, although the appointment of an administrative receiver usually prevents the making of an administration order, unless the person appointing the administrative receiver consents.

3.284 The administrative receiver takes possession of the secured assets with a view to realizing their value and applying the proceeds to pay the amounts due to the secured creditor who appointed the receiver. Creditors with fixed charges and preferential debts must be paid before creditors with floating charges.

3.285 The Enterprise Act 2002 prohibits the appointment of an administrative receiver to most companies.[532] Administrative receivers appointed in respect of floating charges entered into before the prohibition came into force on 15 September 2003 are not subject to the prohibition. More importantly, where a charge is entered into on or after 15 September 2003 it is still possible to appoint an administrative receiver where the company granting the charge falls into an exception to the prohibition. The exceptions cover capital markets transactions, companies which trade on the financial markets, companies involved in public-private partnership and utilities projects, high value financed projects, companies subject to special administration regimes, companies involved in urban regeneration projects, and registered social landlord companies. The exceptions are complex and can be amended by statutory instrument. Whether a company has the benefit of an exception will fall to be determined on the date of appointment of an administrative receiver. In addition, for charges entered into on or after 15 September 2003, the receiver is required to set aside a proportion of the floating charge realizations for the benefit of unsecured creditors.[533]

3.286 As a result of these exceptions, administrative receivership remains an important corporate insolvency tool for whole business securitizations. A whole business securitization is a

---

[532] Insolvency Act 1986, s 72A.
[533] Insolvency Act 1986, s 176A. This provision will not apply if the company's net property is less than the prescribed minimum or the receiver thinks that the cost of making a distribution to unsecured creditors would be disproportionate to the benefits (s 176A(3)).

securitization in which the whole cashflow of the business is used to raise finance in bond markets via a special purpose vehicle. The originator of the securitization grants a fixed and floating charge over its assets to a security trustee but, crucially, the assets are not transferred to the special purpose vehicle and the company keeps control of them. This means that, in the event of a default, the security trustee may need to be able to gain control of the assets for the benefit of the bondholders.

At the time of the Enterprise Act reforms, the securitization industry lobbied for the ability to continue to appoint administrative receivers in these structures.[534] Retaining administrative receivership was regarded as crucial to the ongoing success of the whole business securitization. In the main, this is because administrative receivership is essentially a secured creditor remedy: provided the charge has become enforceable, the secured creditor can appoint the administrative receiver without any agreement from the directors, the shareholders or other creditors and unsecured creditors have very limited opportunities to participate in the case. It may be possible for unsecured creditors to appoint a liquidator to the company in administrative receivership and, if this happens, the administrative receiver loses their ability to exercise their powers as agent for the company. However, the administrative receiver can ordinarily rely on the power of attorney granted in the security agreement. Furthermore, although administrative receivership does not offer a moratorium, in practice the administrative receiver controls substantially all of the assets. And crucially, the administrative receiver's primary duty is to achieve repayment of the secured debt. An administrative receiver has very limited duties to the company. If the administrative receiver trades the business, they must make efforts to trade profitably, so that an administrative receiver who trades the business either to run off the securitization structure or while they seek a buyer for the assets must take steps to trade profitably.[535] And if the administrative receiver does sell the assets, they must take steps to obtain a proper price for them.[536] Yet, other than these very limited duties, the administrative receiver's duties are to achieve repayment of the secured debt, so that overall the bondholders, and the rating agencies which provide a rating for the structure, can be confident that the administrative receiver will have the bondholders' interests at heart.   **3.287**

In theory, an administrative receivership could be used to stabilize the business and create liquidity while a debt restructuring is worked out. However, administrative receivers cannot propose a CVA;[537] scheme of arrangement;[538] or a new Part 26A restructuring plan introduced by CIGA.[539] As a result, administrative receivership is more likely to be used when efforts to achieve a debt restructuring have failed, either to run off the book or (more likely) to realize the business and assets or the assets.   **3.288**

It may also still be possible for a secured creditor to appoint a receiver under a fixed charge. A receiver appointed under a fixed charge (usually called a fixed charge, or Law of Property   **3.289**

---

[534] Ian Field and Jennifer Marshall, 'Why UK Insolvency Bill Threatens Securitization' (2001) 20 *International Financial Law Review* 23.

[535] *Medforth v Blake & Ors* [1999] EWCA Civ 1482.

[536] Ibid.

[537] Insolvency Act 1986, s 1.

[538] Companies Act 2006, s 896(2).

[539] CIGA 2020, sch 9 inserting a new Part 26A (Arrangements and Reconstructions: Companies in Financial Difficulty) into the Companies Act 2006.

Act, receiver) has limited powers in respect of the property over which they are appointed. The fixed charge receiver pays the proceeds of the property to the holder of the fixed charge. If the company subsequently goes into administration, the fixed charge receiver must vacate office if required to do so by the administrator.[540] Thus, appointment of a fixed charge receiver may be appropriate where the debtor owns a single asset subject to a fixed charge which the chargee wishes to realize but is unlikely to be appointed where a debt restructuring is envisaged.

3.290   Overall, while receivership (administrative receivership or fixed charge receivership) still has a place in the corporate insolvency law toolbox, it is most likely to signal an acknowledgement that a debt restructuring cannot be achieved, and that the strategy is to maximize the proceeds of the sale of its assets or business.

IX. English Company Voluntary Arrangements and Corporate Debt Restructurings

A. The Company Voluntary Arrangement

1. Introduction

3.291   Part I of the Insolvency Act 1986 (sections 1–7B) looks to remedy a deficiency highlighted by the 1982 Cork Committee Report,[541] by introducing into English law a voluntary arrangement for companies which would be at the instigation of the debtor and be binding on creditors. A company voluntary arrangement (CVA) is a compromise between a company and its unsecured creditors enabling 'a composition in satisfaction of [the company's] debts or a scheme of arrangement of its affairs'.[542] It is not a prerequisite that the company should be technically 'insolvent' or 'unable to pay its debts'.

3.292   Initially, CVAs had very low levels of take up, remaining something of 'a backwater known only to a few very perceptive navigators'.[543] Even the introduction of a moratorium for small companies in the Insolvency Act 2000 (in force since 1 January 2003 but, as we shall see, abolished by CIGA 2020) did not cause any upsurge in its usage.[544] CVAs came into the spotlight in the government's 2009 consultation on insolvency law reform,[545] which flagged CVAs as the rescue procedure of choice for restructurings (given cost efficiencies and the fact that they can result in higher returns to creditors than administration).[546] However, in a report for R3, the trade association for the UK's insolvency professionals, Peter Walton, Chris Umfreville, and Lézelle Jacobs reported in May 2018 that, 'The frequency of CVAs is reasonably low compared with alternative corporate Insolvency Act 1986 procedures.'[547] A number of explanations have been advanced for this, considered in greater detail below.

---

[540] Insolvency Act 1986, sch B1, para 41(2).
[541] Cork Report (n 399).
[542] Insolvency Act 1986, s 1(1).
[543] David Milman and Francis Chittenden, *Corporate rescue: CVAs and the Challenge of Small Companies* (1995) ACCA Research paper, p i.
[544] John Tribe, 'Company Voluntary Arrangements and Rescue: A New Hope and a Tudor Orthodoxy' (2009) 5 *Journal of Business Law* 454.
[545] Insolvency Service, *Encouraging Company Rescue—a Consultation* (June 2009).
[546] Ibid, 'Background data: Impact Assessment'.
[547] Walton, Umfreville, and Jacobs (n 529) 5.

We shall also see, however, that a particular adaptation of the CVA has been used relatively frequently by some large operators in the retail, casual dining, and hospitality sectors to address rental liabilities. As we shall see, the adaptation of the CVA in this way has been controversial.

2. Process

The whole process is relatively quick and, subject to the risk of challenge (discussed later), can be implemented in around 45 days.   **3.293**

The legislation hands the initiative in proposing a CVA to the directors of the company (or, if the company is in administration or liquidation, the administrator or liquidator as the case may be). Indeed, unless the company is in administration or liquidation, the existing management typically continues to exercise management powers (although in certain circumstances management will be replaced, as was the case in the JJB Sports CVA). The proposal must provide for a nominee (a qualified insolvency practitioner) to act in relation to the CVA either as a trustee or otherwise to supervise its implementation.[548] The legislation provides that the nominee requires the person intending to make the proposal to provide them with the terms of the proposed CVA, and a statement of the company's affairs setting out, among other things, details of creditors, the company's debts and other liabilities, and its assets.[549] The directors' proposal of a CVA should provide a short explanation of why, in their opinion, a CVA is desirable and give reasons why the creditors may be expected to concur with such an arrangement.[550] The Insolvency Rules provide further details of the information that must be provided.[551]   **3.294**

In reality, the directors are likely to approach an insolvency practitioner to discuss their options and, if the insolvency practitioner considers that a CVA may be a viable option, they are likely to work with the directors to develop the proposal.[552] Statement of Insolvency Practice 3.2, which deals with practice guidance for CVAs, provides that 'An insolvency practitioner should differentiate clearly between the stages and roles that are associated with a CVA (these being, the provision of initial advice, assisting in the preparation of the proposal, acting as the nominee, and acting as the supervisor) and ensure that they are explained to the company's directors (where they are making the proposal), shareholders and creditors.' In other words, the regulatory structure acknowledges that the insolvency practitioner is likely to have an advisory role as well as the role of nominee (as we shall see, the nominee becomes the supervisor of the arrangement if the CVA is approved, until it is terminated). This provides an interesting counterpoint to the discussion about the role of the monitor in the new Part A1 moratorium. We have seen that a relatively limited role is envisaged for the monitor by the legislation; perhaps in part to keep the costs of the procedure down but maybe also to reinforce the independence of the monitor. A question has already been raised as to whether this is realistic, given the assistance directors are likely to need in navigating the moratorium period. In this context, it is interesting to note that the   **3.295**

---

[548] Insolvency Act 1986, s 1(2).
[549] Ibid, s 2(3).
[550] The Insolvency Rules 1986 (England and Wales) 2016, SI 1986/1925,2016/1024 r 2.2.
[551] Ibid, r 2.3.
[552] *Discovery (Northampton) Ltd v Debenhams Retail Ltd* [2019] EWHC 2441 (Ch); [2020] BCC 9 [119].

boundaries to the role envisaged for the CVA nominee in the legislation have been significantly expanded in practice to make the procedure a viable option, particularly for SMEs.

3.296   The nominee, within 28 days (or such longer period as the court may allow) of being given notice of the proposal for a CVA, is required to submit a report to court as to whether, in their opinion, the proposed arrangement has a reasonable prospect of being approved and implemented and whether, in their opinion, the proposal should be considered by a meeting of the company and by the company's creditors.[553] Court involvement is limited; the court has no role in approving the CVA or scrutinizing its terms unless a challenge is raised (as to which, see below) and the requirements are merely paper filing requirements. Company voluntary arrangements are consequently considered to be relatively quick and user-friendly when compared with more court-intensive restructuring tools such as schemes of arrangement. If the nominee considers that the proposed CVA should not be pursued, and submits a negative report, the company can seek another opinion from another nominee.

3.297   If the nominee believes the proposal should be considered, a meeting of shareholders is called to approve the proposal. The Small Business, Enterprise and Employment Act 2015 largely abolished compulsory creditor meetings in insolvency and provided a variety of decision-making procedures. A creditor decision to approve a proposed CVA cannot be made by deemed consent.[554] Instead, it must be made by a qualifying decision procedure: correspondence; electronic voting; a virtual meeting; or, if one is requisitioned, a physical meeting.[555] A physical meeting can be requisitioned within five business days of the notice of the decision-making procedure by 10 per cent of creditors by number; 10 per cent of creditors by value; or 10 individual creditors. Before the COVID-19 pandemic, insolvency practitioners frequently liaised with sufficient creditors to requisition a meeting. However, during the pandemic, it has been necessary to hold virtual meetings in many restructuring cases. It is possible, therefore, that virtual meetings will be a more regular feature of CVAs after the experience of the pandemic than they were before it. Notice of the qualifying decision procedure must be given to every creditor of the company of whose claim and address the person seeking the decision is aware.[556] The decision date for the creditors' decision procedure must be not less than 14 days from the date of delivery of the notice and not more than 28 days from the date the nominee's report is filed with the court.[557] The decision date may be on the same day as the shareholders' meeting but the creditors' decision must be made before the shareholders' meeting—and the shareholders' decision must be made no later than five business days after the creditors' decision.[558]

3.298   All creditors, secured and unsecured, receive notice of the vote on the CVA and are entitled to vote,[559]but secured creditors are only entitled to vote in relation to the unsecured

---

[553] Insolvency Act 1986, s 2(2).
[554] Insolvency Act 1986, s 3(3), which specifies that the decision must be sought by a qualifying decision procedure. The deemed consent procedure is not a qualifying decision procedure.
[555] The Insolvency (England and Wales) Rules 2016, SI 2016/1024, r 15.3.
[556] Ibid, r 2.27.
[557] Ibid, r 2.27.
[558] Ibid, r 2.28.
[559] Ibid, r 15.28(5).

(if any) part of their debt.[560] The author is not aware of any case law as to how the underlying security is to be valued for the purposes of establishing the allowed portion of the debt for voting purposes. Creditors are not divided into classes but vote as a single class (in contrast to the position under schemes of arrangement where creditors are divided into distinct classes, as discussed later). This may be because the Cork Committee, which originally conceived of the CVA and on whose recommendation it appears to have been introduced, envisaged that it was only likely to be used, 'where the scheme is a simple one involving a composition or moratorium or both for the general body of creditors which can be formulated and presented speedily', and that it would be of value for 'small companies urgently seeking a straightforward composition or moratorium'.[561] Against this background, it is hardly surprising that voting mechanics were relatively straightforward: little purpose would be served by dividing creditors into classes for voting on a 'simple composition or moratorium or both for the general body of creditors' and, indeed, such procedural complexity would add time and cost, which would undermine the role the committee saw for the CVA. However, there is nothing in the legislation which specifically restricts the type of proposal that can be made and, as we shall see, CVAs are regularly proposed in ways which differentiate between creditors rather than treating the 'general body of creditors' in the same way under the proposal. The courts have consistently upheld this approach,[562] and, after a careful review in the challenge to the *New Look* CVA, Zacaroli J decided that there is jurisdiction to use a single CVA to impose different deals on different creditors and that such a CVA is not automatically unfairly prejudicial.[563] One interesting point which was made in support of this contention in *New Look* is that the Insolvency Act 1986 and the Insolvency Rules 2016 both require that all creditors are given notice of the meeting and are permitted to vote, including preferential and secured creditors. As we have seen, secured creditors are only entitled to vote for the unsecured part of their claim (if any) but they are likely to be influenced in their decision to vote by the treatment of their secured debt. Preferential creditors cannot be compromised without their consent but are still included within the statutory majority. In *New Look*, Zacaroli J noted that it was unlikely that the vote of the preferential creditors would be determinative.[564] However, this may now change because, as we will see below, since the Finance Act 2020 the UK tax authorities once again have preferential status. Overall, the position does seem somewhat anomalous.

Although there is no formal need for separate class meetings, the fact that creditors may **3.299** have different rights which are to be varied or released by the CVA and may be granted different rights under it cannot be disregarded entirely (as discussed below in the context of the *Powerhouse* judgment). Votes are calculated according to the amount of the creditor's debt as at the date of the decision (or the date of the company's liquidation or administration).[565]

---

[560] Ibid, r 15.31(4) and (5).

[561] *Insolvency Law and Practice: Report of the Review Committee* (Cmnd 8552, 1981) para 430.

[562] *Inland Revenue Commissioners v Wimbledon Football Club Ltd & Ors* [2004] EWCA Civ 655 [18]; *Prudential Assurance Co Ltd v PRG Powerhouse Ltd and others* [2007] EWHC 1002 (Ch), [2007] Bus L R 1771; *Mourant & Co Trustees Ltd v Sixty UK Ltd* (in admin) [2010] EWHC 1890 (Ch), [2010] BCC 882; *Debenhams* (n 552).

[563] *Lazari Properties 2 Limited v New Look Retailers Limited* [2021] EWHC 1209 (Ch) [155]–[187].

[564] Ibid [121].

[565] Although the claim may be valued at a different level for the purposes of dividends see Geoffrey M Weisgard, Michael Griffiths, and Louis Doyle, *Company Voluntary Arrangements* (2nd edn, 2010) at 100 para 6.64. See also *Re Assisco Engineering Ltd* [2002] BPIR 15, [2002] BCC 481 where the directors were held to have demonstrated on the balance of probabilities that they were creditors for the purposes of voting, but the liquidator was to undertake investigations as to whether they were creditors for other purposes.

A creditor may vote in respect of a debt for an unliquidated amount or any debt whose value is not ascertained and for the purpose of voting (but not otherwise) such debt shall be valued at £1 unless the chairman of the meeting agrees to put a higher value on it.[566] The chairman should ordinarily attempt to put a fair value on the claim in order to avoid a subsequent successful challenge on the grounds of material irregularity or unfair prejudice (discussed in greater detail in section IX.A.3 below).[567] By way of example, as we shall see in greater detail when we discuss so-called landlord CVAs in section IX.B, claims for future rent are unliquidated and unascertained (because the landlord may exercise their right of re-entry in the future to bring the lease to an end) and so a discounted rent formula (i.e. a formula to work out a discounted rent for the remaining life of a lease) is typically used to create a mechanism for determining the level of voting rights for these unliquidated claims. The chairman ascertains the entitlement of persons wishing to vote and can admit or reject their claims accordingly, in whole or in part[568] (although the chairman's decision is subject to appeal to the court by any creditor or member of the company).[569]

3.300 Approval of the CVA requires a simple majority in value at the shareholders' meeting,[570] and a majority in excess of 75 per cent by value of creditors[571] (provided that the overall 75 per cent required to vote in favour must include more than 50 per cent of unconnected creditors).[572] There is no requirement to have a majority in number of those creditors who vote. Where there is a genuine dispute as to the amount of a claim, or the chairman is in doubt, then ordinarily the claim ought to be admitted at the amount claimed for the purposes of voting but marked as disputed.[573] In this way the vote can proceed but if it transpires that the admission of the disputed claim had a decisive effect on the outcome of the vote it can be brought before the court under section 6 of the Insolvency Act 1986. If the creditor has failed to provide details of their claim, but the chairman already has them (for example, in the company records), the chairman should proceed on the basis of the information which he has for the purposes of admitting claims for voting.[574]

3.301 Whilst the purpose of requiring a meeting of shareholders is arguably questionable (since the shareholders may no longer have a continuing economic interest in the company), the shareholders' vote cannot override the wishes of the creditors (although a disappointed shareholder may apply to the court).[575] Where a decision approving a CVA is made, under section 5 of the Insolvency Act 1986 it takes effect as if made by the company at the time the creditors decided to approve the CVA and binds every person who in accordance with the rules: (a) was entitled to vote in the qualifying decision procedure by which the creditors'

---

[566] The Insolvency (England and Wales) Rules 2016, SI 2016/1024 r 15.31(3).

[567] See, e.g., *Re Doorbar v Alltime Securities Ltd* [1995] BCC 1149 in which the Court of Appeal upheld the chairman's valuation of a landlord's claim at one year's rent after taking into account the possibility that the landlord would exercise his power of re-entry, finding that a genuine attempt had been made to put a fair value on the claim and *Re Sweatfield Ltd* [1997] BCC 744, both cited in Weisgard, Griffiths, and Doyle (n 565).

[568] The Insolvency Rules (n 568) r 15.33.

[569] Ibid, r 15.35.

[570] Ibid, r 2.36.

[571] Ibid, r 15.34.

[572] Ibid, r 15.34(4).

[573] Ibid, r 15.33(3).

[574] *Roberts v Pinnacle Entertainment Ltd* [2003] EWHC 2394.

[575] Insolvency Act 1986, s 4A(2).

decision to approve the voluntary arrangement was made, or (b) would have been so entitled if he had notice of it, as if he were a party to the voluntary arrangement.

However, as we have already touched on, a CVA cannot affect the rights of secured or prefer- **3.302** ential creditors without their consent,[576] thus giving secured creditors a veto on an arrangement if it affects their rights. This may prove particularly significant after the reintroduction of crown preference,[577] which will give HMRC a veto right in many CVAs.

As part of their 2018 report on CVAs, Walton, Umfreville, and Jacobs conducted a survey of **3.303** members of R3 (the trade association for the UK's insolvency practitioners) and conducted some semi-structured stakeholder interviews.[578] This revealed some interesting insights on the role of HMRC in the CVA process. The authors report that 'Over half of the IPs surveyed believe that a lack of support from HMRC is one of the main reasons which prevents a possible CVA being put to creditors' while, where a CVA failed to proceed 'nearly 60% of IPs' identified a lack of support from HMRC as a major factor.[579] HMRC was considered by 55 per cent of IPs as the most engaged creditor, and yet it was also seen by 71 per cent of IPs as 'the stakeholder most likely to oppose a CVA'.[580] Overall, more than 60 per cent of respondents thought that, 'more support from HMRC would increase the potential of CVAs as a rescue tool'.[581] These views were also reflected, and expanded on, by unsecured creditors in the semi-structured interviews. Unsecured creditors commented that HMRC often did not participate in early negotiations but instead appeared 'at the last moment with significant amendments'.[582] Others commented that HMRC was somewhat lax at enforcing breaches of its own Time to Pay scheme, thus allowing arrears to build up.[583] A running theme of the Walton, Umfreville, and Jacobs report is whether the time periods for CVAs are too long. In other words, in a typical trading CVA where creditors are to be paid a proportion of arrears out of trading profits over several years, a question arises as to how long the arrangement should last. The report is a rich source of information on the problems of trading in a CVA: the risk that creditors use the CVA period to move away from the company;[584] tendering problems;[585] and loss of credit insurance leading to pro forma invoicing, with the resulting detrimental consequences for cashflow; the general burden of dealing with the administrative side of the CVA; and potential tendering problems.[586] The report suggests that the longer the period of the CVA, the greater these challenges become. And unsecured creditors suggested that HMRC frequently insisted 'upon a duration of 5 years which often creates a slow lingering death for the company'.[587] The authors also highlight concerns over consistency and concerns that HMRC adopts a policy-based approach to voting rather than a commercial approach.[588]

---

[576] Ibid, s 4(3) and (4).
[577] Finance Act 2020, ss 98 and 99.
[578] Walton, Umfreville, and Jacobs (n 529).
[579] Ibid, 53.
[580] Ibid.
[581] Ibid, 54.
[582] Ibid, 63.
[583] Ibid.
[584] Ibid, 50.
[585] Ibid.
[586] Ibid, 62.
[587] Ibid, 63.
[588] Ibid, 64.

3.304   All of this suggests that the future of many CVAs may depend, to a great extent, on the approach which HMRC adopts now that it has been reinstated as a preferential creditor. It is clear that it has always been a powerful and influential creditor in the process, but the resumption of preferential status significantly strengthens its position. Thus, experience of HMRC's approach to CVAs following the change is likely to determine, to some extent, the future of the CVA as a restructuring tool.

3. Challenge

3.305   Section 6 of the Insolvency Act 1986 provides a right to challenge either the CVA itself or the manner by which its approval was obtained:

> (1) Subject to this section, an application to the court may be made ... on one or both of the following grounds, namely—
>   (a) that a voluntary arrangement ... unfairly prejudices the interests of a creditor, member or contributory of the company;
>   (b) that there has been some material irregularity at or in relation to the meeting of the company, or in relation to the relevant qualifying decision procedure.
>
>   ...
>
> (4) Where on such an application the court is satisfied as to either of the grounds mentioned in subsection (1) ... it may do one or both of the following, namely—
>   (a) revoke or suspend any decision approving the voluntary arrangement ... or, in a case falling within subsection (1)(b), any decision taken by the meeting of the company, or in the relevant qualifying decision procedure ...;
>   (b) give a direction to any person for the summoning of a further company meeting to consider any revised proposal the person who made the original proposal may make or, in a case falling within subsection 1(b) and relating to the company meeting, a further company meeting to reconsider the original proposal;
>   (c) direct any person—
>   (i) to seek a decision from the company's creditors (using a qualifying decision procedure) as to whether they approve any revised proposal the person who made the original proposal may make, or
>   (ii) in a case falling within subsection (1)(b) and relating to the relevant qualifying decision procedure, to seek a decision from the company's creditors (using a qualifying decision procedure) as to whether they approve the original proposal.

3.306   Any challenge must be brought within 28 days from the date of report to the court of the decisions, or if it is brought by someone without notice of the relevant qualifying decision procedure, 28 days from the first day they became aware that the relevant qualifying decision procedure has taken place.[589] There is thus an ongoing risk that an untraced creditor, who can demonstrate unfair prejudice or some material irregularity, may challenge the CVA many years after approval of the CVA. This is a distinct disadvantage given that it can often be difficult to identify precisely who all the creditors are, for example where

---

[589] Insolvency Act 1986, s 6(3).

there are contingent creditors, or where an SME's record keeping has not always been maintained. And it stands in stark contrast to the position in respect of schemes of arrangement where once the court gives its final sanction there is no risk of subsequent challenge, absent fraud.[590] At the same time, a creditor which raises a challenge to a CVA runs a serious risk of a costs order if their challenge is unsuccessful.[591] We will see later that the position on costs orders is relatively nuanced in the context of Part 26 schemes of arrangement. As we will see, this is because the role which a dissenting creditor plays at a sanction hearing for a Part 26 scheme of arrangement is not entirely on all fours with the role the applicant plays in litigation. In the *Debenhams* cost hearing Norris J saw no such distinction when a creditor challenges a CVA, and it is worth setting out his comments in full:

> In a CVA dissentient creditors are bound by the outcome of the statutory meetings (not by any order of the Court). They can seek a Court order overturning or varying that outcome within a limited time and only on the grounds specified in s.6 of the Insolvency Act 1986. That requires an application with respondents; and the need to establish one of the specified grounds creates a classic "*lis*". There will in the end be a 'successful party' and an 'unsuccessful party' and the 'general rule' is capable of application (though of course with the proviso that in all the circumstances a different order might be made). If the dissentient creditors' challenge is successful, then the company may expect to be viewed as the 'unsuccessful party' and under 'the general rule' to face the prospect of paying the dissentient creditors' costs. If the dissentient creditors' challenge is unsuccessful, then they may expect to be viewed as the 'unsuccessful party' under the 'general rule' and to face the prospect of paying the company's costs.[592]

The extent of the power to intervene under section 6 was considered by Warren J in the *Sisu Capital* case,[593] in which applicant creditors sought to revoke or suspend the approval given by creditors' meetings to CVAs relating to two companies in the TXU group. The creditors were challenging the CVAs on the basis that they contained releases for office holders in respect of claims that might have been brought against them. Warren J found that the speculative nature of the claims was not enough, by itself, to establish unfair prejudice for the purposes of revoking or suspending a CVA. The question of what constitutes 'unfair prejudice' for the purpose of a section 6 challenge was also considered by Etherton J in *Prudential Assurance Co Ltd v PRG Powerhouse Limited*[594] and Henderson J in *Mourant & Co Trustees Ltd and Anor v Sixty UK Ltd & Ors.*[595] In both those cases the challenges were successful.[596] **3.307**

In the *Powerhouse* case, which concerned the UK's third largest electrical retailer before it ran into financial difficulties, the directors proposed to close 35 underperforming stores and continue trading out of 53 more profitable sites. The claimants were landlords of closed stores who had the benefit of guarantees given by Powerhouse's parent company, PRG Group Limited, in respect of Powerhouse's obligations under the leases. When Powerhouse **3.308**

---

[590] *Fletcher v RAC* (1999) 96(11) LSG 69.
[591] *Discovery (Northampton) Ltd v Debenhams Retail Ltd* [2019] EWHC 1430 (Ch) [11]-[13].
[592] Ibid [13].
[593] *Sisu Capital Fund Ltd v Tucker* [2006] BPIR 154.
[594] [2007] BCC 500.
[595] *Sixty UK Ltd* (n 562).
[596] For more recent judicial consideration of what constitutes unfair prejudice and material irregularity see *HMRC v Portsmouth City Football Club Ltd & Ors* [2010] EWHC 2013 (Ch).

acquired the business as a going concern in 2003, the claimant landlords had required parent guarantees as a condition of their giving consent to the assignment of the leases. The guarantees were drafted in such a way that they were not affected by any subsequent insolvency of Powerhouse. The directors of Powerhouse proposed a CVA in 2007 under which the claims against it arising from the store closures would be compromised but all other claims would be settled in full. The creditors whose rights were to be affected by the CVA would receive a dividend of 28 pence in the pound. They included the claimant landlords, even though the proposed CVA also sought to release the parent company's guarantees in respect of the closed stores. The claimant landlords were to receive nothing extra for the loss of the benefit of the guarantees which (as acknowledged by the judge) had both real value in themselves and as a potential lever in negotiations. The majority of creditors were not affected at all as they stood to have their claims settled in full or obtain a dividend of 28 pence in the pound when they would have received nothing on liquidation. The landlord creditors with the benefit of the parent company guarantee were in the minority. The CVA was consequently approved by the requisite majority at a meeting of Powerhouse's creditors. The guaranteed landlords challenged the validity of the CVA, claiming that it was unfairly prejudicial to them as creditors of Powerhouse.

3.309   Etherton J acknowledged that it is common ground that the issue of 'unfair prejudice' should be judged on the information available at the time the CVA is approved.[597] He found that 'any CVA which leaves the creditor in a less advantageous position than before the CVA— looking at both the present and future—will be prejudicial'.[598] It is the additional need to show that the prejudice is 'unfair' which gives rise to difficulties.

3.310   It is common ground that there is no single and universal test for judging unfairness in this context. The cases show that it is necessary to consider all the circumstances including, in particular, the alternatives available and the practical consequences of a decision to confirm or reject the arrangement.[599]

3.311   The judge continued that unfairness may be assessed by a 'comparative analysis from a number of different angles', including both a vertical and horizontal comparison.

(a) Vertical comparison

3.312   Etherton J considered that '[i]t will often be a useful starting point, and will always be highly material, to compare the creditor's position under the CVA with what the creditor's position would have been on a winding up'. He referred[600] to the judgment of David Richards J in *Re T & N Ltd*:[601]

> I find it very difficult to envisage a case where the court would sanction a scheme of arrangement, or not interfere with a CVA, which was an alternative to a winding up but which was likely to result in creditors, or some of them, receiving less than they would in a winding up of the company, assuming that the return in a winding up would in reality

---

[597]   *Powerhouse* (n 594) [71].
[598]   Ibid [72].
[599]   ibid [74].
[600]   ibid [81].
[601]   [2005] 2 BCLC 488.

be achieved and within an acceptable time scale: see *Re English, Scottish and Australian Chartered Bank* [1893] 3 Ch 385.

Also, the Cork Committee Report had provided: 3.313

> Unless it can be shown that the treatment of the general body of creditors under the voluntary arrangement is likely to be at least as advantageous as that obtainable by Court proceedings, then a dissatisfied creditor will have reasonable grounds for complaint and will be normally entitled to have the debtor's affairs administered by the Court; otherwise he would be bound by the wishes of the majority voting in favour of the voluntary arrangement.[602]

Etherton J warned, however, that comparison with the position on a winding up is not always conclusive as to unfair prejudice.[603] He also noted that it is not for the court to speculate whether the terms of the proposed CVA are the best that could have been obtained, or whether it would have been better if it had not contained all the terms it did contain.[604] However, this issue is a complex one. Although a vertical comparison with the position on a winding up may establish that the creditor is no worse off, it does nothing to establish whether the CVA renders other creditors *too well off* at the expense of the applicant. In other cases, the courts have seemed content to consider all the circumstances, not just liquidation but also other, fairer schemes.[605] Zacaroli J reviewed the position in *New Look*.[606] He noted that in the cases on Part 26 schemes of arrangement (discussed in section XI below) the courts had resisted considering whether an alternative arrangement would have been fairer. Yet in the context of a CVA, in considering whether the allocation of assets among the creditors is fair, he considered it is necessary to modify the scheme principle. There is very little further discussion of this in the *New Look* judgment, but it appears that it is open to opposing creditors in a CVA to argue that an alternative arrangement would have been fairer. To date, opposing creditors have not tended to put forward alternative plans which they would accept. Yet this may be one way of bringing a 'fairer' scheme before the court. It would then be for the company to identify why that alternative plan was not capable of implementation.   3.314

(b) Horizontal comparison

This is a comparison with other creditors or classes of creditors. The fact that a CVA involves differential treatment of creditors will not necessarily be sufficient to establish unfair prejudice.[607] Indeed differential treatment may be required to ensure   3.315

---

[602] Report of the Review Committee into Insolvency Law and Practice (Cmnd 8558, 1982) para 364(4).

[603] Ferris J in *Re a Debtor* (No 101 of 1999) [2001] 1 BCLC 54.

[604] Warren J in *SISU Capital Fund Ltd* [2006] BCC 463 [73]; see also Chadwick LJ in *Re Greenhaven Motors Ltd* [1999] BCC 463, CA at 469.

[605] See *Inland Revenue Commissioners v Wimbledon Football Club* (n 564) [18] 'in determining whether or not there is unfairness, it is necessary to consider all the circumstances including, as alternatives to the arrangement proposed, not only liquidation but the possibility of a different fairer scheme' and *Re a Debtor (No 101 of 1999)* (n 603). A leading text, Edward Bailey, *Company Voluntary Arrangements* (2nd edn) 130, para 8.3 states 'The challenge should demonstrate that the scheme has been framed in a manner which prejudices a creditor or class of creditor in a way which is unfair compared to what would have been the position if the scheme had been framed in a different way'.

[606] *New Look* (n 563) [117]–[118], [147] and [196]

[607] *Powerhouse* (n 594) 88, referring to the judgment of Ferris J in *Re a Debtor (No 101 of 1999)* (n 605); *Inland Revenue Commissioners v Wimbledon Football Club* (n 562) [18]; and *New Look* (n 563) [155]–[199].

fairness,[608] or secure the continuation of the company's business for example where it is necessary to pay trade creditors.[609] Even where some general, unsecured creditors are clearly not essential to the business, it may not be practically possible to sift through them to bring certain creditors into the compromise. This may destabilize the business (as trade creditors can no longer be assured that everyone will be paid) so that the company experiences a tightening of credit terms, or the loss of orders, or limited or withheld supply, while customer confidence and brand image are damaged. At the same time, it may be costly to undertake the exercise and it may not improve the position of the impaired creditors materially. In short, the risks and costs may outweigh the benefits. This was the view of Norris J in the *Debenhams* case.[610] The company raised extensive evidence about the contagion risk of compromising trade creditors.[611] Counsel for the (impaired) landlords, responded by suggesting that certain unsecured creditors had been left out of the compromise which were in no way essential to the business: he identified, for example, a minicab firm; a firm of accountants; and a firm of solicitors.[612]It is worth quoting Norris J's response at length:

> in my judgment both the directors and the nominees were entitled to look at the matter in the round having regard to the likely reaction of the 1600 suppliers of goods and services, rather than to single out a small number of individual suppliers for separate treatment where such separate treatment would make a wholly immaterial contribution to the outcome. ... the question was not whether their supplies were critical to the business but whether their treatment was critical to the success of the CVA.[613]

3.316   In determining whether uneven treatment is unfairly prejudicial, the fact that all the creditors are to receive an equal dividend may not be decisive if the majority creditors are to receive some collateral benefit which is not available to the minority.[614]

3.317   Depending on the circumstances, Etherton J found that a helpful guide is comparison with the position if, instead of a CVA, there had been a formal scheme of arrangement under the Companies Act. Again, the judge quoted from the judgment of David Richards J in *Re T & N Ltd*:[615]

> There is no statutory guidance on the criteria for judging fairness either for a scheme of arrangement under section 425 of the Companies Act 1985 or for the CVA under section 6 of the 1986 Act. There is a difference in the onus. Under section 425, it is for the proponents to satisfy the court that it should be sanctioned, whereas under section 6 it is the objector who must establish unfair prejudice. I do not, however, consider that there is any difference in the substance of the underlying test of fairness which must be applied. It is deliberately a broad test to be applied on a case by case basis, and courts have struggled to do better than the approach adopted by the Court of Appeal in *Re Alabama, New Orleans, Texas and*

---

[608] *Sea Voyager Maritime Inc v Bielecki* [1999] 1 BCLC 133 at 149; *Inland Revenue Commissioners v Wimbledon Football Club Ltd* (n 562) 18.

[609] *Sea Assets Limited v Perusahaan Perseroan (Persero) PT Perusahaan Penerbangan Garuda Indonesia* [2001] EWCA Civ 1696 at 45–46; *Inland Revenue Commissioners v Wimbledon Football Club Ltd* [(n 562) 18.

[610] *Debenhams* (n 552) [107].

[611] Ibid [106].

[612] Ibid [107].

[613] Ibid.

[614] *Re a Debtor* (n 603).

[615] *Re T & N Ltd* (n 601) 81.

Pacific Junction Railway Co [1891] Ch 213 and summarized in the often cited passage from a leading textbook, Buckley on the Companies Acts (14th edn) vol 1, pp 473–474:

> 'In exercising its power of sanction the court will see, first, that the provisions of the statute have been complied with, second, that the class was fairly represented by those who attended the meeting and that the statutory majority are acting *bona fide* and are not coercing the minority in order to promote interests adverse to those of the class whom they purport to represent, and thirdly, that the arrangement is such as an intelligent and honest man, a member of the class concerned and acting in respect of his interest, might reasonably approve. The court does not sit merely to see that the majority are acting *bona fide* and thereupon to register the decision of the meeting, but, at the same time, the court will be slow to differ from the meeting, unless either the class has not been properly consulted or the meeting has not considered the matter with a view to the interests of the class which it is empowered to bind or some blot is found in the scheme.'

Etherton J accepted that, if a reasonable and honest man in the same position as the claimants might reasonably have approved the CVA, that would be a powerful, and probably conclusive, factor against the claimants on the issue of unfair prejudice. However, it was also the case that the fact that no reasonable and honest man in the same position as the claimants would have approved the CVA was not necessarily conclusive in favour of the claimants. **3.318**

Applying the vertical and horizontal tests, Etherton J held that the Powerhouse CVA unfairly prejudiced the interests of the guaranteed landlords as creditors of Powerhouse, within the meaning of section 6(1)(a) of the Insolvency Act 1986. The CVA left them in a worse position than without the CVA, having regard both to the present and also future possibilities. The guaranteed landlords would still have had the benefit of valuable guarantees on an insolvent liquidation of Powerhouse, whereas all the other unsecured creditors would have received nothing. The guaranteed landlords were thus the group of unsecured creditors that would suffer least, if at all, on an insolvent liquidation, but they were the group that was most prejudiced by the CVA.[616] Etherton J found that such an illogical and unfair result would not have occurred under a scheme of arrangement, as under a scheme the guaranteed landlords would have been in a class of their own and would have vetoed any scheme, and the scheme would not have needed to include creditors who were to be paid in full. The result was only different under the CVA because all the creditors formed a single class, including those creditors who were to be paid in full, the votes of the latter thus swamping the votes of the guaranteed landlords. **3.319**

After *Powerhouse*, CVAs were proposed in which additional voting conditions were imposed. Thus, the *Schefenacker* CVA was conditional not only on the statutory majority at the creditors' meeting but also required the support of in excess of 75 per cent of the bondholders.[617] Presumably, the concern was that Etherton's analysis might have been developed in subsequent cases so that the courts would pay close attention to whether creditors would have formed a separate class in a scheme of arrangement and, had they done so, whether the 75 per cent majority would have been secured in each class. However, in *Powerhouse* Ehterton J had clearly stated that, 'The fact that a particular class of creditors could and **3.320**

---

[616] A similar conclusion was reached in the *Miss Sixty* case (n 595).
[617] Ken Baird and Look Chan Ho, 'Company Voluntary Arrangement: the Restructuring Trends' (2007) 20(8) *Insolvency International* 124.

might have blocked a scheme ..., while relevant and potentially important, does not ne-cessarily mean that they have been unfairly prejudiced'.[618] Thus, following *Powerhouse* the courts have not regarded the question of whether a sub-group could have blocked a scheme as decisive. Thus, as we have seen, in *Debenhams* the fact that the statutory majority had been secured by including the votes of unimpaired creditors did not prove decisive. Instead, Norris J considered whether the substance of the differential treatment was justi-fied. Zacaroli J adopted a similar approach in *New Look*.[619]

3.321   The question of whether there has been substantive unfair prejudice is, therefore, decided on its facts. In *New Look*, Counsel for the company suggested that a CVA would not be unfairly prejudicial provided that (1) any differential treatment was objectively justified; (2) the vertical comparator was satisfied; and (3) a reasonably and honest person in the position of the application could have approved the CVA. However, Zacaroli J did not con-sider the position to be so straightforward. Where a sub-group of creditors is comprom-ised by the CVA and their vote is swamped by unimpaired creditors, Zacaroli J considered that whether unfair prejudice exists depends on all the circumstances, including those that would be taken into account in exercising discretion to sanction a Part 26 scheme of ar-rangement or to exercise discretion to cram down a class in a Part 26A restructuring plan procedure. In other words, the analysis is likely to be highly fact specific.

3.322   Before we turn to those developments, however, it is worth considering another case with very similar facts to those of *Powerhouse*: the *Miss Sixty* case.

3.323   Sixty UK Ltd was a retailer operating from several leasehold properties which ran into fi-nancial difficulties and decided to close its loss-making stores as part of its restructuring plan. Its attempts to negotiate the surrender of leases of those stores failed so it sought in-stead to compromise its liabilities in a CVA. Its liabilities to the landlord applicants related to two retail units which were guaranteed by its ultimate Italian parent company. The effect of the CVA was to release the parent from all guarantees upon payment to the landlords of a sum of £300,000 (said in the proposal to represent 100 per cent of the tenant's estimated liability to the landlords on a surrender of the leases). A lower level of compensation was offered to landlords in respect of leases which did not have the benefit of any guarantees.

3.324   The landlords' challenge to the CVA was advanced on a number of grounds but centred on the alleged inadequacy of the compensation payment and the compulsory deprivation of the benefit of the parent company guarantees (which would have been enforceable regard-less of whether the tenant went into liquidation or the leases were disclaimed). They argued that they had been unfairly treated, both in comparison with external unsecured creditors who had been paid in full and with at least one creditor whose claims related to one of the other closed stores.

3.325   On reviewing the evidence and the principles established in the *Powerhouse* case, Henderson J concluded that the landlords had been unfairly prejudiced as the CVA did not adequately compensate them for the loss of their rights under the guarantee, even though it purported to pay the full surrender value of the leases to the landlords. Accordingly, the

---

[618] *Powerhouse* (n 594) [95].
[619] *New Look* (n 563) [185]–[188].

CVA was revoked. Moreover, the CVA created no enforceable obligation upon the parent to make any of the compensation payments in return for which the applicants are obliged to give up their guarantees, nor did it make the release of the guarantees conditional upon the receipt of such payments.

Finally, Henderson J also expressed doubts as to the potential for a CVA to deprive a land-   **3.326**
lord of a third party guarantee, saying 'although the possibility of "guarantee-stripping" in a CVA was established in *Powerhouse*, and it has given rise to a good deal of debate among practitioners and academics, there is no subsequent reported case in which the court has had to consider whether and how a CVA might fairly effect a compromise of a landlord's claim against a guarantor of the tenant debtor'. Since *Miss Sixty* the question of guarantee stripping has been more thoroughly considered in the context of schemes of arrangement, where it is a frequent feature of restructurings of purely financial liabilities. However, guar-antee stripping has largely disappeared in the CVA space.

Nonetheless, CVAs continue to be implemented in which the majority of creditors voting   **3.327**
in favour are unaffected by the proposals, particularly where the objective of the CVA is to compromise leasehold liabilities.[620] We will return to some specific issues with these so-called 'landlord CVAs' later in this section. For the moment, it is suggested here that in order to mitigate the risks of subsequent challenge it will be important to show that at least some of the impaired creditors voted in favour of the plan. Where concerns arise that dir-ectors have advanced restructuring plans out of self-interest, the law has relied on the pres-ence of the 'independent director' who, whilst not constituting a majority, indicate that a disinterested bystander is still willing to support the contemplated transaction. In the same way, as a minimum it is likely to be necessary to show the court that at least some of the creditors who will be affected by the CVA are willing to support it. In this context, it is also worth noting that in the challenge to the *Regis* CVA Zacaroli J was of the view that the treat-ment of a connected creditor as a 'critical creditor' was 'not justified and that the preferential treatment that it received under the CVA was unfairly prejudicial to those creditors whose debts were impaired'.[621] Moreover, Zacaroli J found that, in failing to consider whether the connected creditor should have been treated in this way, one of the nominees had fallen below the standard required of him.[622] The applicants pressed for repayment of the nom-inees' fees but, while not ruling out the possibility in 'particularly egregious' cases, Zacaroli J did not consider that appropriate (in the absence of fraud or bad faith) unless the nom-inee could have been successfully sued in professional negligence.[623] And it was common ground that, in order to be sued in professional negligence, the nominee would need to have acted as no reasonable nominee would have done.[624] Nonetheless, the CVA was revoked.[625] And a finding by the court that a nominee has fallen short of the standards expected of them remains a serious issue for an insolvency practitioner.

---

[620] *Debenhams* (n 552).
[621] *Carroway Guildford (Nominee A Limited) and 18 others v Regis UK Limited, Edward Williams (as Joint Supervisor of Regis UK Ltd) and Christine Mary Laverty (as Joint Supervisor of Regis UK Ltd)* [2021] EWHC 1294 (Ch) [160].
[622] Ibid [207].
[623] Ibid [218].
[624] Ibid [211].
[625] Ibid [224].

4. Decision to implement a CVA

3.328   The first issue with the CVA process is the need to persuade the statutory majority of creditors to support it. In a trading CVA, where the objective is for the company to trade after approval and make contributions to the supervisor for a period of time on account of compromised pre-CVA liabilities, creditors may be highly suspicious that they are losing money whilst the directors retain their jobs and thus reluctant to support the company.[626] This may result in insufficient write-down of liabilities in the CVA so that it subsequently fails. Furthermore, this requirement to obtain the vote requires extensive engagement with creditors before the meetings to approve the CVA and this may destabilize the business as creditors react to news of financial distress. This may mean that the CVA is not an option where the creditors are too numerous, where it is not known whether they are supportive or not, or where their discretion cannot be relied upon.[627] The company must also have sufficient funding not only to meet the terms of the CVA itself but also to continue to trade during negotiations.[628] And, as touched on above, the CVA cannot bind secured or preferential creditors without their consent. A further problem with the CVA procedure before 2000 was the lack of a moratorium on creditor action. This meant that whilst the directors and the nominee worked to obtain creditor approval, creditors could, amongst other things, lodge winding-up petitions against the company. In reality, petitions can be dealt with as the court can generally be persuaded to adjourn until the CVA has been voted upon. Nonetheless, they have the potential to add further disruption, not least because of the impact of section 127 of the Insolvency Act 1986 pursuant to which any disposition of property made after the commencement of the winding up is, unless the court otherwise orders, void so that until the hearing of the petition the directors must make applications to court in order to make even ordinary course disposals.

5. Moratorium

3.329   Schedule A1 to the Insolvency Act 1986 therefore introduced an optional moratorium of up to 28 days[629] for certain small companies.[630] The effect of the moratorium was similar to the statutory moratorium which arises in administration, meaning that, among other things, security could not be enforced and proceedings could not be commenced or continued against the company or its property except with the consent of the court. However, data shows that the small company moratorium was infrequently used; Insolvency Service data showed that it was used in only 18 cases during 2007–08,[631] and Walton, Umfreville, and Jacobs also found low take-up.[632] The small companies moratorium has now been

---

[626] For a discussion of this issue see, e.g., John Flood, Robert Abbey, Eleni Skordaki, and Paul Aber, 'The Professional Restructuring of Corporate Rescue: Company Voluntary Arrangements and the London Approach' (1995) ACCA Research Report 45; Gary AS Cook, Naresh R Pandit, and David Milman, 'Formal Rehabilitation Procedures and Insolvent Firms: Empirical Evidence on British Company Voluntary Arrangement Procedure' (2001) *Small Business Economics* 255–271; Finch (n 418) 333; Walton, Umfreville, and Lézelle (n 529) 57, 62.

[627] Fletcher (n 403).

[628] John Tribe, 'The Extension of Small Company Voluntary Arrangements: A Response to the Conservative Party's Restructuring Proposals' in P Omar (ed), *Insolvency Law Issues, Themes and Perspectives* (2008) citing McCormack (n 418).

[629] Extendable up to a maximum of two months.

[630] Insolvency Act 1986, s 1A was enacted by the Insolvency Act 2000. Prior to then, there was no mechanism for a company to obtain a moratorium whilst a CVA was being put in place, unless an administrator was simultaneously appointed.

[631] Background data: Table 4 (n 546).

[632] Walton, Umfreville, and Jacobs (n 529) 15.

abolished by CIGA.[633] However, a company proposing a CVA can make use of the new Part A1 moratorium instead (see section VIII.B). This raises the question of whether the Part A1 moratorium is better adapted for the CVA than the old, small companies' moratorium and, therefore, whether we might expect to see greater enthusiasm for it. Interestingly, while the sample size was too small to draw firm conclusions, Walton, Umfreville, and Jacobs did detect more promising survival rates where companies had made use of the moratorium protection.[634] The point may, therefore, be of some importance.

Undoubtedly, one reason why take-up of the small companies moratorium was so low was   **3.330**
because so few companies were eligible for it. Eligibility was principally determined by reference to the definition of a small company under the Companies Act 2006.[635] A company will fall within the definition of being a small company if it satisfies two or more of the following requirements (in the year ending with the date the company files for the CVA moratorium or in the last financial year of the company ending before that date[636]):

- turnover of not more than £6.5 million;
- balance sheet total of no more than £3.26 million;
- no more than 50 employees.[637]

In practice, therefore, the number of companies eligible for the moratorium was extremely limited.

The new Part A1 moratorium does not have an eligibility threshold of this type. However, as discussed in section VIII.B, new eligibility requirements have been introduced, including the requirement that the company is not party to a capital markets arrangement. It may be that these eligibility requirements exclude companies which could have made good use of the Part A1 moratorium while proposing a CVA.

Moreover, the problems with the small companies moratorium were not limited to the eli-   **3.331**
gibility thresholds. Academic research showed that even amongst small companies eligible for the moratorium the take-up was very low.[638] Several reasons have been suggested for this and some of these appear to be applicable to the new Part A1 moratorium.

First, for a small company the steps to obtain a moratorium were not without cost and com-   **3.332**
plexity. Once it was established that the company was an eligible company the directors were required to submit a report to the insolvency practitioner setting out, among other things, the terms of the proposed voluntary arrangement and furnishing him with a statement of the company's affairs.[639] The insolvency practitioner was then required to provide his statement of opinion indicating whether he considered that the voluntary arrangement had a reasonable prospect of being approved and implemented, whether the company was likely

---

[633] CIGA 2020, sch 3, para 2.

[634] Walton, Umfreville, and Jacobs (n 529) 17.

[635] Companies Act 2006, s 382.

[636] Insolvency Act 1986, Sch A1, para 3.

[637] The Insolvency Act 1986 contains further exclusions from eligibility for certain companies (e.g., banks, building societies, insurance companies) as well as those involved in certain financial transactions.

[638] See Adrian Walters and Sandra Frisby, 'Preliminary Report to the Insolvency Service into Outcomes in Company Voluntary Arrangements' available at <http://papers.ssrn.com/sol3/papers.cfm?abstract_id=1792402>. Walton, Umfreville and Jacobs (n 529) 18.

[639] Insolvency Act 1986, sch A1, para 6(1).

to have sufficient funds to continue trading during the proposed moratorium, and whether meetings of creditors and the company should be summoned to consider the proposed voluntary arrangement.[640] In providing his opinion, the insolvency practitioner was entitled to rely on the information which had been provided to him by the directors.[641] These requirements, on the one hand, required money to be spent on compliance (including, rather oddly perhaps, a requirement to present the terms of the CVA when one might have thought that the point of the moratorium was to obtain a breathing space during which the terms could be hammered out with creditors), but, on the other hand, may have provided somewhat illusory protection for creditors. As Professor Fletcher noted:

> the fact that the directors are in a position to preselect the person whom they approach with a view to taking on the appointment, and the further fact that the nominee must perforce forego the possibility of earning the fees that would result from a positive opinion leading to appointment under the moratorium may come to be seen as a source of difficulties regarding the quality of the professional judgement exercised at the outset of the CVA process.[642]

No court approval was necessary: the moratorium came into effect once the requisite paper filings were made with the court.[643]

3.333   Arguably, the substance of many of these concerns is carried over into the new Part A1 moratorium. As already discussed, an insolvency practitioner, known as the monitor, is appointed in the Part A1 moratorium. The directors are required to confirm that, in their view, the company is, or is likely to become, unable to pay its debts;[644] at the same time, the insolvency practitioner is required to state that in their view it is likely that a moratorium for the company would result in the rescue of the company as a going concern.[645] Moreover, the moratorium can only be used if, and for so long as, the monitor thinks that a company rescue is likely. Thus, the monitor must clear a rather high hurdle in concluding that the Part A1 moratorium can properly be engaged. However, where a creditor, director, member, or any other person affected by the moratorium brings a challenge against the monitor, while the court may confirm, reverse, or modify the act or decision of the monitor; give the monitor directions; or make any other order, the court may not make an order for the monitor to pay compensation.[646] This may be an attempt to address a further reason given to explain low take-up of the small companies moratorium. In the small companies moratorium, the insolvency practitioner was required to express an opinion on it. Nominees appear to have been very reluctant to give opinions and to have been concerned that they may incur personal liability for a defective opinion.[647] Thus, the hope may be that removing the risk of a compensation order will render insolvency practitioners more willing to give the necessary confirmations for the Part A1 moratorium. However, it is also possible to

---

[640] Ibid, sch A1, para 6(2).
[641] Ibid, sch A1, para 6(3).
[642] Fletcher (n 403) 131.
[643] Insolvency Act 1986, sch A1, para 8.
[644] Ibid, s A6(1)(d).
[645] Insolvency Act 1986, s A6(1)(e).
[646] Ibid, s A44.
[647] Walton, Umfreville, and Jacobs (n 529) 8.

challenge the monitor's fees and a level of complexity is retained which may make the new moratorium unattractive, at least at the smaller end of the market.

This problem of complexity arose in the small companies moratorium once it was obtained. **3.334** The company's invoices were required to contain the nominee's name and a statement that the moratorium was in force in relation to the company;[648] the company could not obtain credit to the extent of £250 or more from a person who had not been informed that the moratorium was in place;[649] and restrictions were imposed on disposals and payments outside the ordinary course of business.[650] Not only were these complex provisions likely to increase cost and risk, they also heightened awareness of the company's situation. As discussed in section VIII.B, many of these problems of complexity are retained in the new Part A1 moratorium

This leads neatly to an overall disadvantage of any moratorium. Informing creditors of the **3.335** need for a moratorium may lead them to conclude that the company is facing cash flow difficulties and, therefore, to become more reluctant still to deal with the company, exercising termination rights where they are available or other 'self-help' remedies exercisable notwithstanding the moratorium. The CIGA attempts to deal with some of these concerns by providing that the new restrictions on terminating contracts or doing 'any other thing' by reason of insolvency, together with temporary restrictions on terminating on the grounds of pre-insolvency events of default, are engaged in the moratorium.[651] Nonetheless, the practical reality is that the support of creditors will be crucial, not only for approval of the CVA but also for the success of the CVA after it has been approved. Thus, it remains the case that companies may be anxious about alarming creditors early in the process by the announcement of moratorium protections.

The restrictions on termination or doing 'any other thing' by reason of insolvency are also **3.336** of wider application in the context of the CVA. The Walton, Umfreville, and Jacobs report noted that a challenge with the successful implementation of CVAs was that a creditor may seek to change credit terms during the CVA and may seek to 'take steps to ensure that it is not overly exposed should it ultimately lose the CVA's custom' in the period after the CVA has been approved.[652] The new section 233B may provide some protection against this although, as we have seen, there will need to be a good deal of working out of the provision in practice.

B. Landlord CVAs

As already noted, CVAs have been upheld which have differentiated between creditors. This **3.337** has been crucial in the adaptation of CVAs to compromise only leasehold liabilities: so-called landlord CVAs. This adaptation has been used, initially by retailers and latterly by

---

[648] Ibid, sch A1, para 16.
[649] Ibid, sch A1, para 17.
[650] Ibid, sch A1, paras 18 and 19.
[651] Insolvency Act 1986, s 233B(1).
[652] Walton, Umfreville, and Jacobs (n 529) 50.

other companies in the leisure industry such as hotels, restaurants, and gyms,[653] to deal with large, leased estates. It is not, however, without controversy.

3.338 Liabilities to landlords are typically unsecured and thus vulnerable to the CVA regime.[654] A company seeking to deal with rental liability via a CVA has a defined number of landlord creditors to approach to seek to reach agreement with and the CVA may offer several advantages over the alternative, most likely a pre-packaged administration of 'good' sites to a new holding company, discussed in more detail below. First, as we shall see in due course, it is likely to be necessary to market the business and assets for sale before concluding a pre-packaged sale, but this step is not necessary for a CVA. Second, the CVA may be a little less of a blunt instrument because it offers the ability to vary lease terms. The extent to which a CVA can vary rental terms, as opposed to compromising rent arrears, has been controversial.[655] Following the authorities on schemes of arrangement, although a CVA operates as a contract between the parties, it has been suggested that the CVA acquires its binding force by virtue of statute and, therefore, may validly affect a compromise of future liabilities.[656] In *Cancol*, Knox J was of the view that a CVA could validly compromise future rent.[657] He had already decided, in an earlier case, that future rent could be included in a voluntary arrangement for an individual.[658] He had based that decision on the breadth of the words 'scheme of arrangement of his affairs' in the relevant section of the Insolvency Act 1986 and on the fact that the statutory definition of 'creditor' was wide enough to include future payments of rents. Knox J went on to say that, in the context of a CVA, section 1(1) of the Insolvency Act provides that:

> The directors of a company ... may make a proposal under this Part to the company and its creditors for a composition or satisfaction of its debts or a scheme of arrangement of its affairs (from here on referred to, in either case, as a 'voluntary arrangement')

Given the breadth of this description, and the breadth of the definition of 'creditor' in the statute, Knox J considered that future rent could be included within a CVA. In *March Estates*, Lightman J agreed:

> A voluntary arrangement may postpone, modify or extinguish the lessor's right as a creditor of the company to the reserved rent whether past or future (see Re Cancol Ltd [1995] BCC 1133) and excuse the company (whether original lessee or assignee) personally from performance. The voluntary arrangement in such a case by operation of law absolves the lessee from, or limits or postpones, his personal liability.[659]

3.339 But in the Court of Appeal in *Thomas v Ken Thomas* Neuberger LJ, while doubting Lightman J's conclusion in *March Estates* that where the rent has been compromised the right against

---

[653] For retailers, see Focus DIY, Blacks Leisure, Suits You, JJB Sports, and Mamas & Papas; for hotels, see Travelodge; for restaurants, see La Tasca; and for gyms, see Fitness First.

[654] *Razzaq v Pala* [1998] BCC 66 and *Re Lomax Leisure Ltd* [1999] 2 BCLC 126

[655] See Barry Gross, 'Protecting the IP from Unfair Prejudice Claims in a CVA' *Recovery* Autumn 2014.

[656] See *Kempe v Ambassador Insurance Co* [1998] 1 BCLC 23, 1998 1 WLR 271 cited in Geoff O'dea, Julian Long, and Alexandra Smyth, *Schemes of Arrangement Law and Practice* (2012) 53 para 4.40.

[657] *Re Cancol Ltd* [1995] BCC 1133.

[658] *Doorbar v Alltime Securities Ltd* [1994] BCC 994.

[659] *March Estates plc v Gunmark* [1996] 2 BCLC 1.

forfeiture can continue to exist for the uncompromised rent, also doubted (*obiter*) whether the company can pay a reduced rate for rent falling due after the CVA has been approved.[660]

Nonetheless, *Cancol* was not overruled and many landlord CVAs continued to be proposed   **3.340** in which future rent was compromised in the years following *Thomas*. The position was finally reviewed by Norris J in *Debenhams* in 2019.[661] Norris J noted the *obiter* remarks in *Thomas*, but also noted that *Doorbar* and *Cancol* have 'not been overruled and have been followed' so that he 'should do the same unless persuaded they are wrong'.[662] He was not persuaded that they were wrong—indeed he positively considered that both decisions were right, concluding:

> 'Future rent' is a pecuniary liability (although not a presently provable debt) to which the company may become subject by reason of the covenant to pay rent in the existing lease: whilst the term endures the company is 'liable' for the rent, and the fact that in future the landlord may bring the term to an end by forfeiture does not mean that there is no present 'liability' ... As a matter of jurisdiction 'future rent' can be included in a CVA.[663]

In *New Look*, Counsel for the opposing landlords invited Zacaroli J to depart from this con-   **3.341** clusion but Zacaroli J was, 'not persuaded that Norris J was wrong to conclude that a CVA which provides for a reduction in future rent during a notice period before which a landlord can terminate the lease is necessarily unfairly prejudicial'.[664] Thus, future rent can be compromised within a CVA and this will not automatically render the proposal automatically unfair. It may, of course, be substantively unfair; and, as we can see, the fact that a landlord had a right to terminate if they did not consent to the lease modifications was crucial for Zacaroli J and it was also important in the *Debenhams* decision. This is an issue we shall return to in due course. But the important point is that the CVA offers a way to motivate bargaining around amended lease terms as opposed to the more binary choice between assuming the lease in the pre-packaged administration sale or leaving it behind in the old (and assetless) company.

Finally, although the CVA is to be found in the Insolvency Act, and undoubtedly has some   **3.342** negative connotations, it may nonetheless have some PR advantages compared with the pre-packaged administration. Perhaps counterintuitively, these advantages may be more pronounced for a large firm than for SMEs. As Cook, Pandit, and Milman observed in their 2001 research, stakeholders in large firms may be more likely to make decisions 'based on data rather than assumptions'.[665] As a result, large and larger mid-cap companies may actually be better able to take advantage of the CVA with significant institutional landlords than the small and smaller mid-cap companies for whom the procedure is primarily intended.

A further controversy has arisen in how landlords' claims are calculated for the purposes   **3.343** of voting. We have touched briefly on the concept that 'future rent' is an unliquidated and unascertained amount: this is because the landlord may terminate the lease at some point in

---

[660] *Thomas v Ken Thomas Ltd* [2006] EWCA Civ 1504 [39].
[661] *Debenhams* (n 552) [23]–[61]
[662] Ibid [60].
[663] Ibid [60]–[61].
[664] *New Look* (n 563) [212].
[665] Cook, Pandit, and Milman (n 626).

the future. There has been some debate in the CVA cases as to whether the claim is properly characterized as a contingent claim, or as a contingent claim which the Insolvency Rules require to be treated in a special way, or simply as a non-provable debt.[666] In *Debenhams*, Norris J settles for describing it as 'a pecuniary liability (although not a presently provable debt) to which the company may become subject by reason of the covenant to pay rent in the existing lease'.[667] This point is of some importance in calculating the landlords' entitlement to vote. As we have seen, the Insolvency Rules provide that a debt of an unliquidated or unascertained amount shall be valued at £1 for the purpose of voting unless the convener or chair puts a higher value on it.[668] As we have also seen, the chairperson should ordinarily attempt to put a fair value on the claim in order to avoid a subsequent successful challenge on the grounds of material irregularity or unfair prejudice,[669] so that a discounted rent formula (i.e. a formula to work out a discounted rent for the remaining life of a lease) is typically used to create a mechanism for determining the level of voting rights for future rent. However, the detail of how this is done is where the controversy lies. In *Re Park Air Services Plc*,[670] the House of Lords had been required to determine the value of a landlord's claim for loss following disclaimer of a lease. The House of Lords decided that the landlord's claim for loss should be discounted following a relatively complex formula. However, particularly in landlord CVAs between 2009 and 2019, it was common to apply a further, somewhat arbitrary, discount of 75 per cent to the *Re Park Air Services* calculation.[671] The loose justification appears to have been the uncertainty in calculating what the landlord's loss would be. Nonetheless, landlords, and the British Property Federation on their behalf, railed against the approach.[672] During the 2009–2019 period, as Inga West has shown, landlord CVA cases steadily increased as companies grappled with the shift to online shopping, increases in business rates, and Brexit.[673] In the early years, many landlords appear to have supported landlord CVAs. This may seem surprising because many of the landlord CVAs during this period subsequently failed, with the result that the company was placed into administration. However, Walton, Umfreville, and Jacobs have shown how difficult it is to decide what 'success' looks like in a CVA context.[674] It may be that landlords were able to use the period after the CVA to find new tenants for premises while collecting some rent and avoiding paying business rates on unoccupied premises. This would explain why, as conditions worsened on the high street and prospects for reletting premises diminished, their attitudes to landlord CVAs hardened. And, of course, this effect has only been magnified by the COVID-19 pandemic. Since the *Debenhams* challenge, multiple challenges to landlord CVAs have been launched. This appears to have made debtor companies more cautious, and recent CVAs

---

[666] *Debenhams* (n 552) [23]–[61].

[667] Ibid [60].

[668] The Insolvency (England and Wales) Rules 2016, SI 2016/1024 r 15.31(3).

[669] See, e.g., *Re Doorbar* (n 569) in which the Court of Appeal upheld the chairman's valuation of a landlord's claim at one year's rent after taking into account the possibility that the landlord would exercise his power of re-entry, finding that a genuine attempt had been made to put a fair value on the claim, and *Re Sweatfield Ltd* (n 567) both cited in Weisgard, Griffiths, and Doyle (n 565).

[670] *Re Park Air Services Plc* [1999] UKHL 2.

[671] British Property Federation CVA Briefing 2019 available at: https://bpf-stage.wearewattle.com/media/2630/bpf-cva-briefing-2019.pdf (last accessed 22 April 2021), paras 25–32.

[672] Ibid.

[673] Inga West, 'The Evolution of Landlord CVAs: at a Tipping Point?' Presentation at the Annual Insolvency Lawyers' Association Conference, 23 April 2021, on file with the author.

[674] Walton, Umfreville, and Jacobs (n 529) 57.

have seen lower discounts or, indeed, no discount at all for voting purposes. Indeed, in *New Look* a straightforward discount of 25 per cent was applied to the landlords' claims. Zacaroli J accepted that there was 'no particular science' to this discount but he declined to find that it amounted to a material irregularity for the purposes of section 6 of the Insolvency Act 1986.[675] In *New Look* the prospects of reletting and likely rent were estimated for each landlord and the 25 per cent discount was then applied to elicit 'a valuation at the lower end of the range'. As the values were provided as single numbers, rather than a potential range, this did not involve double counting. The formula for calculating claims had been provided to the landlords, together with a schedule of estimated minimum values. The evidence of the chairman of the meeting was that he would have considered any evidence supplied to support a different conclusion; thus, there was no fetter on his discretion. Yet no landlord provided any alternative evidence. The lesson for opposing landlords may be to challenge the evidence at the meeting, rather than waiting to bring a material irregularity claim. And the lesson for companies is that a more cautious approach to discounting may be appropriate.

As we have already seen, while both Norris J and Zacaroli J were not persuaded that a CVA **3.344** which compromised future rent was automatically unfair, both also considered that such a proposal may nonetheless be substantively unfair. In *Debenhams* one of the supervisors of the CVA, Mr Tucker, had given evidence that the valuation advice received was 'that all stores were over-rented'.[676] Thus, Norris J saw the purpose of the CVA as moving leases onto market rents. He contrasted this position with those of other suppliers: 'who provided goods under "one off" contracts or "short term" supply deals that would naturally reflect the current market price for such supplies'.[677] Norris J noted that all landlords had been offered an opportunity to break their leases if they did not consent to the amended lease terms proposed in the CVA.[678] The landlords had raised a specific challenge to the term of the CVA proposal which provided that, where notice to terminate the lease was served, the landlord would receive the compromised rent for the notice period. The difficulty is that the compromise is forced on the landlord, who has no ability to terminate the lease until the end of the notice period. In *Debenhams*, Norris J appeared to refer to the fact that the compromised rent was at a market rate and, perhaps implicitly, no more than was necessary to achieve the purpose of the CVA.[679] Notwithstanding that the applicants had not concentrated on it, Zacaroli J considered the same issue in *New Look*.[680] Zacaroli J did not consider Norris J to have laid down a rigid test that rent paid during this period must be a market rate. Instead, he focused on what would happen if the CVA were not approved and the company pursued a pre-packaged administration sale as the vertical comparator.

Norris J also turned to Etherton J's vertical comparator developed in the *Powerhouse* **3.345** case.[681] He referred to 'the unchallenged evidence of Mr Tucker that on the computation of KPMG the "vertical comparator" is satisfied'.[682] Norris J also used Etherton J's 'horizontal

---

[675] *New Look* (n 563) [287]–[298].
[676] *Debenhams* (n 552)[66].
[677] Ibid.
[678] Ibid [69]
[679] *Debenhams* (n 552) [71].
[680] *New Look* (n 563) [232]–[234].
[681] *Powerhouse* (n 594).
[682] *Debenhams* (n 552) [73].

comparator'.[683] As we have seen, this exercise involves comparing what a class of creditors is receiving under the CVA with what other creditors of equal legal rank in insolvency are receiving. In the *Debenhams* case, in common with most other landlord CVAs, trade creditors were unimpaired. Counsel for the company focused on the risk of 'contagion' if these trade creditors were compromised in the CVA. He argued that if trade creditors became concerned that they would be compromised, they would take steps to protect themselves such as refusing supply or tightening credit terms. This would lead, in turn, to poor customer experience and brand damage.[684] Counsel for the landlords argued that the company had excluded creditors from the compromise who could not possibly pose this risk: a minicab firm, a firm of accountants, and a firm of solicitors. It is worth setting out Norris J's response at length:

> in my judgment both the directors and the nominees were entitled to look at the matter in the round having regard to the likely reaction of the 1600 suppliers of goods and services, rather than to single out a small number of individual suppliers for separate treatment where such separate treatment would make a wholly immaterial contribution to the outcome. As Mr Haskell indicated in cross-examination, the question was not whether their supplies were critical to the business but whether their treatment was critical to the success of the CVA.[685]

Thus, overall, Norris J was content that there was no substantive unfairness in the proposal. Nonetheless, the market noted how crucial the landlords' break rights had been in the analysis and, following *Debenhams* and *New Look*, landlord CVAs generally provide a right for the landlord to break the lease if they do not consent to the amended lease terms proposed in the CVA. Of course, this does shift the bargaining power a little in favour of landlords: companies now have to consider carefully whether landlords would be likely to exercise the break right in formulating the proposals, and the consequences for the viability of the company if too many landlords did exercise the right. Yet, given the state of the market, particularly in the wake of the COVID-19 pandemic, the shift in bargaining power is scarcely dramatic. A landlord wishing to challenge the CVA terms would be well advised to submit evidence as to market rates and to show how another, fairer deal would still achieve the objective of the CVA or would have emerged in the event of the relevant comparator to the CVA.

3.346   As we have seen, in *Debenhams* there was focus on the differential treatment of creditors in the proposal. In *New Look* more attention was paid to the fact that the statutory majority had been achieved by the votes of creditors who receive substantially different treatment from the compromised landlords. Zacaroli J accepted that the fact that a statutory majority for a CVA is achieved by the votes of unimpaired or differentially treated creditors will be an important consideration in determining whether unfair prejudice exists.[686] However, in *New Look* the statutory majority had been achieved by including the vote of senior secured noteholders (SSNs) in respect of the unsecured part of their claim. The SSNs had received

---

[683] *Powerhouse* (n 594) [75] and [86]–[96].
[684] *Debenhams* (n 552) [106].
[685] Ibid [107].
[686] *New Look* (n 563) [186].

equity in exchange for releasing their secured debt in a separate scheme of arrangement, but Zacaroli J considered it right to bring that fact into the analysis. In his analysis, they had received nothing in exchange for the release of the unsecured portion of their debt—and it did not matter that a partially secured creditor had different incentives in voting from other unsecured creditors because that was embedded in the structure of the Insolvency Rules 2016. In Zacaroli J's judgment, there was no question that the SSNs had received a benefit from the assets of New Look which would or should have been available for unsecured creditors and it was because they had given up their security that the CVA compromise was possible.[687] Overall, Zacaroli J did not consider that the SSNs were materially better off than the landlords. Indeed, insofar as their equity participation following the scheme was concerned, he noted that 'At best, the value of their post-restructuring interest is speculative, as it is dependent on the performance of the restructured business in a trading environment that continues to be highly challenging'.[688] In *New Look* ordinary unsecured creditors, other than landlords, were kept whole. No distinction was drawn between creditors who were 'critical' to the business and others, in the way in which that issue was explored in *Debenhams*. But crucially the CVA would still have been approved even if the vote of the ordinary unsecured creditors had been discounted entirely.[689] Thus, this was not a case in which the statutory majority was secured by the votes of entirely unimpaired creditors. In an important paragraph, Zacaroli stated:

> if assets that would, in the relevant alternative, have been available to all unsecured creditors are allocated in a greater proportion to other creditors (eg where critical creditors are paid in full), then the fact that the requisite majority was reached by reason of the votes of those creditors may point towards the CVA being unfairly prejudicial, even if there was an objective justification to their payment in full.[690]

It will be interesting to see, following *New Look*, whether more emphasis is put on this point. It is also worth recalling that, in *Regis*, Zacaroli J did not consider that the treatment of a connected creditor as a critical creditor was justified and considered that it was unfairly prejudicial to the other impaired creditors.[691] It is suggested here that much will depend on how significant the vote of the unimpaired creditors is to the outcome, and whether, if they shared in the compromise, the landlords would be materially better off. This is reinforced by Zacaroli J's comment in *New Look* that 'where the creditors who were (justifiably) unimpaired, though sufficient on the numbers to tip the scales at the meeting, were small in number and value, then that is less likely to constitute unfair prejudice'.[692] We will see, later, that the new Part 26A restructuring plan provides an alternative mechanism for imposing a restructuring deal on landlords and it may be that, where the statutory majority for a CVA can only be achieved by including substantial votes from entirely unimpaired creditors, the Part 26A restructuring plan route is to be preferred. We will return to this issue later in the chapter.

---

[687] Ibid [240–[261].
[688] Ibid [261].
[689] Ibid [267]–[268].
[690] Ibid [193].
[691] *Regis UK Limited* (n 621) [160].
[692] *New Look* (n 563) [197].

3.347   The *Debenhams* judgment also established a further, important point which was relevant in *New Look*. We have seen that in *Thomas*, Neuberger LJ had been of the view that, where rent is compromised by a CVA, the landlord's right of forfeiture can only be exercised if the compromised rent is not paid, rather than the pre-CVA rent. Norris J agreed with this assessment in Debenhams, saying:

> The CVA can modify any pecuniary obligations upon breach of which the right of re-entry may be exercised; and the right will then be exercisable only in relation to the pecuniary obligation as so modified.[693]

But he also decided that the right of forfeiture was a property right and so could not be removed in its entirety by a CVA.[694] Before *Debenhams* this was what many CVAs had attempted to do. After *Debenhams* removal of forfeiture rights no longer became a regular feature of landlord CVAs. Given that Norris J had decided that the forfeiture right was only exercisable in relation to the compromised rent, this hardly struck a fatal blow to the development of landlord CVAs. Yet, like the break clause discussion earlier, it did tilt the balance a little away from the company, which now had to consider the possibility that a landlord would exercise the right and the implications for the business if they did. At around the same time, Zacaroli J decided, in the *Instant Cash* scheme of arrangement case, that it was not possible for the tenant to compel the landlord to accept a surrender.[695] We may wonder why a landlord would not wish to accept a surrender if a tenant ceased to pay rent, but the answer is, once again, that the landlord will not wish to be responsible for rates on the unoccupied premises if they are unable to relet them. Thus, the market found a relatively satisfactory workaround to the *Instant Cash* problem, by reducing rent to zero under the lease without surrendering it. Problems may persist where the CVA forms part of a wider transaction in which the company needs to be able to transfer the leases to a third party and the landlord cannot be traced or does not respond to negotiation efforts. In this case, creative solutions have been developed in the market, including arguments that in the absence to a response to a surrender by a landlord the lease has been surrendered by operation of law. In order for a lease to be surrendered by operation of law, there must have been conduct by both parties, 'unequivocally inconsistent with the continuance of the lease'.[696] The threshold is a high one and, crucially, mere inaction by the landlord is unlikely to be enough.[697] Thus, the route of reducing the rent to zero and accepting that there has been no surrender emerged, after *Debenhams*, as the more popular route. This is reinforced by the judgment in *New Look*. In that case, the landlords attempted to use the argument that there had been a surrender by operation of law against the company.[698] The argument was that by releasing the liability to pay rent and other sums under one category of lease the company had surrendered the lease by operation of law, in violation of the landlords' property rights—and that the cases had established that a CVA could not interfere with the landlords' property rights. Zacaroli J disagreed. He did not regard it as an essential requirement of a lease that the tenant is obliged to pay rent and he determined that the lease remains on foot

---

[693] *Debenhams* (n 552) [99].

[694] Ibid [91].

[695] *In the matter of Instant Cash Loans Limited* [2019] EWHC 2795 (Ch).

[696] *QFS Scaffolding Ltd v Sable* [2010] EWCA Civ 682, [2010] L&T 30.

[697] *Bellcourt Estates Ltd v Adesina* [2005] 2 EGLR 33, [2005] EWCA Civ 208. For a discussion see Nick Knapman and Stephen Dean, 'Property: No Surrender?' 160 *NLJ* 1213.

[698] *New Look* (n 563) [280].

with the consequence that New Look remained liable for rates.[699] This, then, would appear to be the technology to be used where the company wishes to cease paying rent, but the landlord wishes to avoid liability for rates.

A few other points which emerged from the substantial challenge in *New Look* are worthy of brief comment. First, the court declined to consider whether the absence of a rolling termination right made the proposal unfair: this was for the landlords to assess in deciding whether to exercise their break right.[700] And the fact that the exercise of the landlord's termination right was in full and final settlement of the compromised claims was answered by the fact that it achieved a better result for the landlords than the vertical comparator.[701] As we have seen, in *New Look* equity was allocated to the SSNs: indeed, the existing shareholders were wiped out entirely. In these circumstances, the absence of a profit share or other mitigating feature was not unfairly prejudicial. This suggests, however, that consideration should be given to such a feature where existing shareholders are keeping their shares. It was also understandable that an exit process had been designed for the SSNs, given that they were swapping debt for equity.[702] And, although non-disclosure did not render the *New Look* CVA unfair, creditors are entitled to be told about any management incentive plan and it would be wise to include details in any explanatory statement going forward.[703]   **3.348**

Foreign leases also remain problematic. In October 2020 five landlords to former Monsoon stores in Ireland successfully argued that their leases remained in force in Ireland notwithstanding a CVA in England which sought to compromise them.[704] At the time of the case, England was in the Brexit transition period and the European Insolvency Regulation (EIR) continued to apply.[705] Article 11 provides: **3.349**

1. The effects of insolvency proceedings on a contract conferring the right to acquire or make use of immoveable property shall be governed solely by the law of the Member State within the territory of which the immoveable property is situated.
2. The court which opened main insolvency proceedings shall have jurisdiction to approve the termination or modification of the contracts referred to in this Article where:
    (a) the law of the Member State applicable to those contracts requires that such a contract may only be terminated or modified with the approval of the court opening insolvency proceedings; and
    (b) no insolvency proceedings have been opened in the Member State.

The landlords successfully argued that Article 11(1) operated as an exception to the rule in the EIR that the law of the Member State which is opening the insolvency proceedings is to determine the effects of those insolvency proceedings. They further successfully argued that Article 11(2) conferred jurisdiction on the Irish court to approve the termination or modification of the leases, which fell within Article 11(1). The landlords also referred the

---

[699] Ibid [281]–[282].
[700] Ibid [227].
[701] Ibid [228].
[702] Ibid [324].
[703] Ibid [328]–[329].
[704] Gareth Steen, 'The Republic of Ireland as an Effective International Restructuring Jurisdiction' (2021) 1 *Corporate Rescue and Insolvency* 11
[705] Regulation (EU) 2015/848 of the European Parliament and of the Council of 20 May 2015 on insolvency proceedings (recast) [2015] OJ L 141 (the EIR).

Irish court to Article 33 of the EIR which permits a Member State to refuse recognition where the effects of recognition would be 'manifestly contrary to the State's public policy, in particular its fundamental principles or the constitutional rights and liberties of the individual'. Macdonald J determined that the landlords had not been provided with sufficient opportunity to make representations about the effects of the CVA and that this infringed their constitutional rights within the meaning of Article 33. However, as Steen has noted:

> While McDonald J found that the recognition of the CVA was contrary to public policy of the State in this particular case, he did state that the procedural unfairness which arose could have been avoided had the appropriate measure been taken in the course of the CVA process.[706]

Thus, one of the lessons of the Monsoon case would appear to be ensuring adequate transparency, disclosure, and participation for foreign creditors.

3.350   We have now, of course, reached the end of the Brexit transition period and so the EIR no longer applies. The question of whether a compromise of a foreign lease in an English CVA will be recognized in that jurisdiction will now need to be determined on a country-by-country analysis. It is possible that certain relevant jurisdictions will have implemented the UNCITRAL Model Law on Cross Border Insolvency, and readers are directed to Chapter 4 for an analysis of the Model Law.

X. English Pre-Packaged Administrations and Corporate Debt Restructurings

A. Introduction

3.351   A pre-packaged administration, commonly referred to as a 'pre-pack', is not a creation of law (it is not expressly contemplated by either the Insolvency Act 1986 or the Insolvency Rules 2016),[707] but is rather a practice which has evolved. It is an arrangement under which a sale of all or part of a company's business and/or assets is arranged before the formal appointment of an insolvency practitioner as administrator. The sale is then rapidly executed on the same day as, or shortly after, the appointment. The business may be sold to a third party, but more usually is sold back to the existing management or existing senior lenders.[708] In this section, we are primarily concerned with a sale to existing management, ordinarily financed by the existing lenders. Although this is functionally a sale of the business and assets, as we will see economically it achieves a debt restructuring in which existing trade debts are written off, but management remains able to continue to run the business. Pre-packs are not new. They were originally developed for use in the context of receiverships and were utilized in the administration regime which existed before the Enterprise Act amendments were introduced. Empirical research from the University of Wolverhampton reports that

---

[706] Steen (n 704) 13.

[707] SI 2016/1024.

[708] Insolvency Service data suggests that in the first half of 2009, 81 per cent of pre-pack sales reviewed were made to parties connected with the insolvent company: *Report on the First Six Months' Operation of Statement of Insolvency Practice 16* (20 July 2009), p 22. In the second half of 2009, 76 per cent of pre-packs reviewed were to connected parties: *Report on the Operation of Statement of Insolvency Practice 16* (July–December 2009), 14.

there are approximately 750 pre-packs per annum.[709] The key attraction is that the swift sale is more likely to preserve value, goodwill, and confidence than a protracted administration process, and therefore pre-packs with their 'business as usual' veneer are particularly attractive in 'people' businesses, those reliant on goodwill (such as retail, advertising, and financial services), or regulated businesses which generally cannot be traded in insolvency.

B. Criticisms of Pre-Packs

The procedure has been branded 'legalised robbery', 'shabby' and 'quickie bankruptcy'.
(Retail Week, 16 January 2009)

Despite their advantages in certain circumstances, pre-packs have been the subject of much media criticism and academic and public concern in the UK largely due to their perceived opaqueness—unsecured creditors (such as trade creditors and landlords) are presented with a 'done deal', only being informed of the pre-pack after the sale is completed.[710] (Secured creditors will usually be aware of the transaction as they will generally be required to release their security.) Concerns are magnified when the business is sold to an entity owned by secured creditors or existing management who may have been responsible for the company's demise in the first place. Robert Skildelsky has pointed to the challenges broader society will have with regarding an arrangement as 'fair' which rewards those who are seen to have done the harm in the first place. He says, 'In a rough and ready way, people expect to see a link between reward and benefit to themselves'.[711] The introduction of out-of-court administrations following the enactment of the Enterprise Act 2002 made these kinds of 'phoenix-style' pre-packs possible as it enabled management to appoint an administrator outside the glare of publicity. Robert Stevens has remarked, 'There is no other legal system anywhere in the world of which I am aware, and certainly none in either the common law world or the rest of Europe, which permits the opening of an insolvency proceeding by a security holder out of court'.[712] Out of court appointment, not only by the secured creditor but also by the directors, is the great benefit and the great curse of the pre-packaged arrangement and it lies at the heart of the controversy.

3.352

The following passage, taken from a report on pre-packs by Dr Sandra Frisby for the Association of Business Recovery Professionals,[713] succinctly summarizes a number of specific objections which are often raised in relation to pre-packs:

3.353

> A pre-packaged business has not, by definition, been exposed to the competitive forces of the market, which may lead to the business being disposed of for a consideration less than would have been obtained had it been marketed for an appropriate period.

---

[709] Peter Walton, Chris Umfreville, and Paul Wilson, 'Pre-pack Empirical Research: Characteristics and Outcome Analysis of Pre-pack Administration' Final Report to the Graham Review, April 2014.

[710] For scholarly comment see, e.g., Peter Walton, 'Pre-packaged Administrations: Trick or Treat?' (2006) 19(8) *Insolvency Intelligence* 113; Vanessa Finch, 'Pre-packaged Administrations and the Construction of Propriety' April 2011 *Journal of Corporate Law Studies*, and Sandra Frisby, 'The Second Chance Culture and Beyond: Some Observations on the Pre-pack Contribution' (2009) 3 *Law and Financial Markets Review* 242.

[711] Robert Skidelsky, *Keynes—The Return of the Master* (2nd edn, Penguin 2010) 145.

[712] Stevens (n 427) 163–164.

[713] Sandra Frisby, 'A Preliminary Analysis of Pre-packaged Administrations' (Report to The Association of Business Recovery Professionals, August 2007) 8.

Where a pre-pack is effected through administration, the rights of stakeholders to participate in the decision-making process, as envisaged by the Insolvency Act 1986, are frustrated.

The pre-pack process is insufficiently transparent: creditors, or at least certain classes of creditors, are not provided with information adequate to allow them to measure whether the practitioner has carried out his functions in a manner that has not improperly or unlawfully prejudiced their interests.

…a lack of transparency inevitably results in a want of accountability: creditors are entitled to challenge the practitioner's conduct but are disabled from doing so without the information necessary to mount a challenge.

Pre-packs may be unacceptably biased towards the interests of secured creditors, most notably floating charge holders. There may be no incentive to negotiate a consideration for the business much over the amount necessary to discharge the secured indebtedness …

Pre-packs may also be geared rather more towards achieving enough to satisfy the claims of the floating charge holder and practitioners' fees and expenses, with no effort at capturing any premium over and above these amounts

Where a pre-pack involves the sale of the business to a party previously connected with the company, usually as director, the process resembles the practice of 'phoenixing' …

… the opportunities for and appearances of collusion with the purchaser of the business are heavily amplified where a sale of the business is effected through a pre-pack.

C. SIP 16, the Graham Review, and New Regulations

3.354   In an attempt to alleviate such concerns and create greater confidence in the market, the Joint Insolvency Committee (a body made up of each of the recognized professional bodies and the Insolvency Service) issued 'Statement of Insolvency Practice 16: Pre-packaged Sales in Administrations' (SIP 16), which took effect from 1 January 2009. It sets out the standards required of practitioners who are involved in a pre-pack (as advisers or in the role of administrator), particularly concerning the disclosure of information to creditors. SIP 16 is not legally binding, although the Insolvency Service has indicated that it expects practitioners to comply with both the spirit and letter of the SIP and failure to comply could result in regulatory or disciplinary action. In October 2009 the Insolvency Service issued guidance to insolvency practitioners on completing SIP 16 reports (a so-called 'Dear IP letter') although, as we shall see, that guidance is no longer extant.[714] SIP 16 requires insolvency practitioners to make clear that their role is to advise the company as an entity and not individuals within it, encouraging directors to take independent advice—this will be particularly important where the directors have a stake in the acquisition vehicle.[715] It sets out a detailed list of information which administrators must disclose to creditors regarding the

---

[714] Dear IP, issue 42 October 2009.
[715] SIP 16, para 5.

sale in order to ensure that creditors are provided with a detailed explanation and justification of why a pre-pack was undertaken, and so that they can be satisfied that the administrator has acted with due regard for their interests.

Whilst the House of Commons Select Committee report published on 6 May 2009[716] wel- **3.355**
comed the introduction of SIP 16, it recognized that it was merely a step in the right direction and ongoing monitoring would be required:

> There must be a systematic monitoring of the situation by the Insolvency Service and the
> Department. If the new practice statement does not prove effective then it will be necessary
> to take more radical action, possibly by giving stronger powers to the creditors or the court.
> In the meantime, we urge anyone who suspects the abuse of pre-packs to contact either the
> Insolvency Service or the body that licenses the insolvency practitioner concerned. We
> also encourage large creditors, in particular Her Majesty's Revenue and Customs, to take
> an active role in rooting out abuse.[717]

Yet, in the Insolvency Service's first report on compliance with SIP 16 in its first six months of operation,[718] the Insolvency Service revealed that only 65 per cent of the 572 SIP 16 reports reviewed were fully compliant with the disclosure requirements of SIP 16. The main areas where reports fell down were statements being issued to creditors late; failure to provide full details of a valuation or marketing exercise; and failure to fully disclose a connection between the insolvent company and purchaser of its business. However, in a second report covering 2010, the Insolvency Service reported:

> Overall compliance during 2010 has increased to 75%, from 62% in 2009. Generally, the
> quality and timeliness of reports we have received during 2010 has been much improved in
> comparison to those received during 2009. In particular, overall compliance for the latter
> six months of 2010 increased to 84%.[719]

Nonetheless, the Insolvency Service recognized that pre-packs continued to attract criti- **3.356**
cism from creditors and the public. In 2010 the government launched the first consultation on a range of new measures to improve the transparency of, and boost confidence in, the pre-pack process.[720] This resulted in a Ministerial Statement in March 2011 that, amongst other things, administrators would be required to give notice to creditors when it was proposed to sell a significant proportion of the business and assets to a connected party where there had been no open marketing.[721] Something of an outcry followed, with insolvency practitioners, lawyers, and other advisers querying the benefits of a short period of notice against the potential detriment of publicity. As a result, on 26 January 2012 it was announced that the proposals had been withdrawn. In 2013, during a speech on trust and

---

[716] HC Business and Enterprise Committee *Sixth Report of Session 2008–09* (HC 198).
[717] Ibid, para 26.
[718] Insolvency Service (n 710).
[719] *Report on the Operation of Statement of Insolvency Practice 16* (1 January to 31 December 2010) available at <https://www.gov.uk/government/uploads/system/uploads/attachment_data/file/301179/final_sip_16_report_2 010.pdf> (last accessed 6 March 2015).
[720] Consultation/Call for evidence Improving the transparency of, and confidence in, pre-packaged sales in administration available at <http://webarchive.nationalarchives.gov.uk/20121212135622/http://www.bis.gov.uk/insolvency/consultations/prepack> (last accessed 6 March 2015).
[721] Written Ministerial Statement Thursday 31 March 2011 available at <http://www.publications.parliament.uk/pa/cm201011/cmhansrd/cm110331/wmstext/110331m0001.htm> (last accessed 6 March 2015).

transparency in business, the then Business Secretary Vince Cable referred to the pre-packaged administration issue and Teresa Graham was subsequently commissioned to undertake a new review.[722] With increasing focus on pre-packaged administrations generally, and ongoing reviews into their propriety, the Joint Insolvency Committee consulted on a new version of SIP 16 which was issued on 1 November 2013 (and the relevant 'Dear IP' guidance withdrawn).

3.357   SIP 16 (in its current form, as explained in greater detail below) requires insolvency practitioners, among other things, to provide details of the source of their initial introduction; the extent of the administrator's involvement prior to appointment; alternative courses of action that were considered with an explanation of possible financial outcomes and why it was not appropriate to trade the business and offer it for sale as a going concern during the administration; any marketing activities conducted by the company and/or the administrators; the names and professional qualifications of the valuers, confirmation that they have confirmed their independence, the valuations obtained, a summary of the basis of valuation and a rationale for it, and where no valuation has been obtained, the reason; the identity of the purchaser (including any connection with the directors, shareholders, or secured creditor); the price paid and certain breakdowns of the sale consideration. Other information required to be disclosed includes a detailed narrative explanation and justification of why a pre-packaged sale was undertaken.[723] If there are 'exceptional circumstances' (which are not further defined) which prevent the disclosure of any of the information, the administrator must state these. If the sale is to a connected party it is unlikely that considerations of commercial confidentiality would outweigh the need for creditors to be provided with the relevant information.[724] The information should be provided to creditors with the administrator's first notification to creditors and in any event within seven days of the transaction (or the delay explained).[725]

3.358   Teresa Graham's review, together with empirical research in support from Peter Walton and others at the University of Wolverhampton, was published in 2014.[726] Teresa Graham describes herself as 'a deregulator at heart',[727] and she expressed a preference for comply or explain regulation.[728] She found much that was good with pre-packaged administrations, concluding that they can save jobs, have benefits in terms of cost, are more likely to be successful than a trading administration, and have limited benefits in terms of overseas companies availing themselves of the procedure. But the Graham Review also reported some negatives in terms of continuing concerns around transparency, concerns around the adequacy of marketing, a lack of clarity around the valuation methodology which had been adopted, insufficient attention to continued viability after the pre-packaged sale had completed, and weaknesses in the regulatory structure.

---

[722] Available at <http://www.globalturnaround.com/cases/Pre-Pack_statement.pdf>.
[723] SIP 16 para 16.
[724] SIP 16 para 16.
[725] SIP 16 para 17.
[726] Available at <https://www.gov.uk/government/publications/graham-review-into-pre-pack-administration> (last accessed 6 March 2015) ('the Graham Review').
[727] ibid 5.
[728] In which the regulated entity is given the opportunity to explain and justify non-compliance and as opposed to command and control regulation in which failure to comply with regulatory standards will result in punitive sanction, see Robert Baldwin, Martin Cave, and Martin Lodge, *Understanding Regulation* (2nd edn, 2012) 106–110. For the principle of comply and explain in the Graham Review, 12.

To deal with these issues, the Graham Review proposed a new definition of 'connected **3.359** party'. The next (and perhaps most significant) recommendation was the establishment of the pre-pack pool, consisting of experienced businesspeople who would briefly review a proposed pre-packaged sale to a connected party and offer an opinion on it. An approach to the pool would be voluntary but the administrator would be required to disclose whether an approach had been made or not and the outcome. The report envisaged that the applicant to the pool would meet the costs of doing so. A connected party purchaser (not the administrator) would also be expected to express an opinion, which would be available to creditors, on how the purchaser would continue for 12 months after the purchase and, once again, if no review has been undertaken that would need to be disclosed. The Report also contained some recommendations which appeared to be intended for all pre-packaged administrations, including pre-packaged administration 'sales' used to implement large debt restructurings. The Graham Review recommended six principles of good marketing for inclusion in SIP 16, with any deviation explained to creditors. The six principles are: (i) marketing be 'broadcast rather than narrowcast'; (ii) the statement to creditors should 'justify the media used'; (iii) the insolvency practitioner should ensure his independence; (iv) marketing should be undertaken for the appropriate length of time commensurate with satisfying the insolvency practitioner that the best deal has been sought and creditors informed of the reason for length of time settled on; (v) online communication should be included by default and, where it is not, this should be justified; and (vi) a comply or explain procedure should be adopted, with the administrator satisfying all creditors by explaining the marketing strategy to achieve the best outcome for all creditors.

Consistent with the overall 'comply or explain' approach adopted in the Graham Review, **3.360** where marketing was not possible, or likely to harm creditors' interests, the administrator must explain why that is the case. And provision was included for valuations to be conducted by a valuer with professional indemnity insurance. The idea here was that the insurer will be concerned to control the valuer, acting as an indirect control on quality.

The government enthusiastically embraced the Graham Review, exhorting the profession to **3.361** adopt its recommendations and taking various legislative powers to intervene in the event that they did not consider that the profession has done so adequately.[729] A revised version of SIP 16 was published bringing it into line with the Graham recommendations,[730] and the pre-pack pool was launched. However, disquiet about the connected pre-packaged administration refused to go away. While the Corporate Insolvency and Governance Bill was proceeding through Parliament, the Government was pressed to renew its power to regulate or ban sales in administration to connected persons. Thus, the review power which had lapsed in May 2020 was renewed to the end of June 2021. And the Government published a new report into pre-pack sales.[731]

---

[729] Government response available at <https://www.gov.uk/government/consultations/insolvency-practitioner-regulation-and-fee-structure> last accessed 6 March 2015. The reserve legislative power is contained in s 129 of the Small Business, Enterprise and Employment Act 2015.

[730] See <http://www.ion.icaew.com/insolvencyblog/post/Joint-Insolvency-Committee-consults-on-SIP-16>.

[731] The Insolvency Service, *Pre-pack Sales in Administration Report* (8 October 2020) available at: <https://www.gov.uk/government/publications/pre-pack-sales-in-administration/pre-pack-sales-in-administration-report> (last accessed 16 June 2021).

3.362 The first issue which the report tackled was the extraordinarily low number of applications to the pre-pack pool: the report identified that in 2016 only 22 per cent of eligible transactions applied to the pool. The report suggested several explanations: that purchasers saw no benefit in making an application; cost; some concern (from a small number of respondents to inquiries) for a negative opinion; the fact that insolvency practitioners are not required to recommend an approach; and the fact that no consequences followed from failure to approach the pool. Similarly, there was very poor uptake of viability reviews with only 28 per cent of SIP 16 statements for eligible companies in 2016 stating that viability reviews or cash flow forecasts had been provided. More optimistically, there had been an increase in businesses marketed in 2016 from 49 per cent to 77 per cent and greater than 80 per cent compliance with the first three principles of marketing. Nonetheless, principles encouraging exposure to the market had been complied with in just over 50 per cent of cases. Of the 163 connected party pre-packs in 2016, 149 had obtained an independent valuation and 122 had complied with the requirements to use a valuer with professional indemnity insurance cover (27 cases did not report whether the valuer carried such insurance). And of these 163 cases, 142 had the necessary information to compare valuations to the purchase price, with 10 cases where the purchase price exactly matched the valuation and 54 where the business was sold for less than the market valuation. The report emphasized that greater consistency is still needed in SIP 16 reports and that there may be a need to strengthen regulatory requirements in SIP 16 to improve the quality of the information provided.

3.363 In many areas, relatively light touch suggestions were made. The Government indicated that it intends to work with stakeholders to encourage greater use of viability reviews and that it will work with stakeholders to improve adherence to the marketing principles and ensure that where no marketing is undertaken, the explanation provided by the administrator is interrogated by the regulator where necessary. However, the most significant response has been the introduction of new regulations which apply where there is a disposal in administration of all or a substantial part of the company's business to a person connected with the company within the first eight weeks of the administration. In this case, the sale can only proceed with either the approval of creditors or an independent written opinion from an 'evaluator'.[732]

3.364 First, and crucially for this book, the definition of connected person in the new Regulations does not expressly carve out secured lenders. Secured lenders had been carved out of Teresa Graham's recommendations, with the result that a relatively relaxed approach could be taken to the reforms where a pre-packaged administration was used to implement a financial restructuring. However, going forwards the new regulations may be engaged in this type of transaction, which we will consider a little later. Secondly, and somewhat surprisingly, very little detail is given of who can act as 'the evaluator'. The evaluator does not need to be an insolvency practitioner, or a member of the pre-pack pool, but beyond that the only requirement is that the person is satisfied that they have the relevant knowledge and experience, is independent, and holds professional indemnity insurance. There are some express exclusions, but these are also limited.[733]

---

[732] The Administration (Restrictions on Disposal etc to Connected Persons) Regulations 2021.
[733] Ibid, Regulation 13.

The principal statement which the evaluator is required to make is either: **3.365**

> The evaluator is satisfied that the consideration to be provided for the relevant property and the grounds for the substantial disposal are reasonable in the circumstances or, as the case may be,
>
> The evaluator is not satisfied that the consideration to be provided for the relevant property and the grounds for the substantial disposal are reasonable in the circumstances (a "case not made opinion").[734]

The evaluator must also set out their principal reasons for making the statement and a summary of the evidence relied on.[735] The focus on the price paid is consistent with previous reform efforts. However, in many cases the complaint will not be that the pre-pack occurred at an undervalue but rather that it should not have happened at all. The evaluator's opinion is presumably intended to give some confidence on this issue, given that the evaluator is expressly asked to opine, not only on the consideration for the sale, but also that the 'grounds for the substantial disposal are reasonable in the circumstances'. This is set in an overall context in which it is extremely difficult for an aggrieved creditor to challenge the administrator's decision-making process.

D. Challenging a Pre-pack

Paragraph 74 of Schedule B1 to the Insolvency Act provides that a creditor may apply to   **3.366** court claiming that the administrator is acting or has acted so as to unfairly harm his interests (either alone or in common with some, all or other members or creditors). As described above, paragraph 3 of Schedule B1 provides that the administrator may move from performing his functions with the objective of rescuing the company (the first purpose of administration) to a sale of the business and assets where he 'thinks' that it is not 'reasonably practicable' to achieve a rescue of the company as a going concern.[736] The administrator is, though, also under an obligation to act in the best interests of creditors as a whole and this is described in objective terms.[737]

Holgate concerned an application by two former owners claiming that the administrator   **3.367** was proposing to sell a business as a going concern in circumstances where the company could be rescued via a CVA. The secured creditor wished to pursue a sale, but the applicants argued that the debt to the bank arose out of an interest-rate hedging product in respect of which there was a mis-selling claim. The administrators had not held an initial creditors' meeting to approve their proposals because they considered that the company had insufficient property to enable a distribution to be made to unsecured creditors, other than out of the prescribed part. Accordingly, the deemed approval provisions of Insolvency Rule 2.33(5) applied. The administrators had required one of the applicants to meet the costs of a meeting if he requisitioned one and the applicant had withdrawn his request, having

---

[734] Ibid, Regulation 7(h).
[735] Ibid, Regulation 7(i).
[736] Insolvency Act 1986, sch B1, para 3(3).
[737] Ibid, Sch B1, para 3(2).

received an estimate of costs. The administration had been on foot for over a year and the applicants sought a creditors' meeting to consider the possibility for a CVA.[738]

3.368 Hodge QC (sitting as a judge of the High Court) was not prepared to conclude that the business was viable, or that the company could be rescued as a going concern. He found that descriptions of the position put to unsecured creditors to elicit support for a CVA had been misleading and thus it was impossible to predict how unsecured creditors would vote on the CVA proposal 'if the position were to be put to them fully and fairly'. Although he considered that the mis-selling claim had a real prospect of success, the quantum of the claim was less certain, and he did not consider it likely to be sufficient to cancel the bank's ongoing bank facility (although it may approach the level of the bank's pre-administration indebtedness).

3.369 He considered that the administrators had acted properly in requiring the applicant to meet the costs of the initial creditors' meeting and that although the estimate of costs may have been exaggerated, this was out of caution rather than to deter the creditor from pursuing requisitioning of a meeting. He did not consider that the applicant had acted reasonably in withdrawing his request, particularly as he would ultimately only have been liable for costs reasonably and properly incurred and that his liability would be subject to any contrary resolution passed at the meeting. Hodge QC also found that the restriction in paragraph 74(6)(c) of Schedule B1 to the Insolvency Act 1986 (which provides that an order may not be made under paragraph 74 which would impede or prevent the implementation of the administrators' proposals approved more than 28 days before the day on which the application for the order under paragraph 74 was made) applied to proposals deemed approved under the Insolvency Rules. He considered, looking at the statement of proposals as a whole, that it was implicit that the administrators would eventually dispose of the business and that the course which the applicants were advancing would impede or prevent implementation of these proposals which had been deemed approved more than 28 days before the day on which the application for an order under paragraph 74 was made.

3.370 It is perhaps not surprising that Hodge QC was reluctant to interfere in a sale to a third party, given that if the CVA then failed the purchaser would be likely either to not be there at all or to offer only at a reduced price. But, as discussed in greater detail below, sometimes the pre-packaged sale is to be used to implement a 'sale' to some of the creditors and the question arises as to whether the courts may be willing to take a more interventionist stance in this case.

3.371 Armour and Mokal argue that on some level a challenge to the administrator's decision-making under paragraph 3 requires a finding of irrationality given the use of the subjective 'thinks', thus involving a layering of the requirements of paragraph 74 and the requirements of paragraph 3.[739] Although in liquidation the courts have applied generally a rationality standard to all of the liquidator's decision-making,[740] it is submitted here that Le Poividin QC was right in *Hockin* to refuse to read such a standard into paragraph 74 which deals with

---

[738] *Holgate and another v Reid and another* (n 429).

[739] Armour and Mokal (n 427).

[740] *Re Edennote* [1996] 2 BCLC 389 where interference was held to be justified only if the office holder 'has done something so utterly unreasonable and absurd that no reasonable man would have done it'.

'unfair harm'.[741] However, if the paragraph 74 challenge implicates the decision-making process under paragraph 3 then the use of the word 'thinks' in paragraph 3(3) implicates a rationality standard.[742] In this case, Armour and Mokal draw a distinction between what they call 'limited irrationality' and 'comprehensive irrationality'.[743] 'Limited irrationality' requires the administrator, as a fiduciary, to act in good faith and not for a collateral purpose. The administrator must identify the right question to be asked and turn their mind to it. The administrator must take reasonable steps to gather and identify relevant information, but the courts will recognize the limitations in terms of time and money which are operating in the circumstances of the sale and are striving for the standard of the 'reasonable' administrator. 'Comprehensive rationality', on the other hand, requires the administrator to consider all relevant factors and to ignore irrelevant ones. This finds some support from the judgment of the court in *Bramston v Haut* which does indeed suggest a flexible rationality standard.[744] On the other hand, in *Unidare v Cohen* Lewison J said at [71]:

> Ms Agnello submitted that the administrator's conclusion must be based on reasonable grounds; or at least not be one which no reasonable administrator could have reached. I do not consider that paragraph 83 should be interpreted in this way. I accept that the process of thinking involves a rational thought process, and in that sense must be reasonable; but I do not accept that what the administrator thinks is subject to any form of test by reference to an objective standard.[745]

Armour and Mokal make a case for a higher standard given the objective language of paragraph 3(2) and the fact that the administrator must consider how best to balance the interests of competing creditors. It is suggested here that this higher standard is particularly appropriate where the administrator has been introduced to the insolvency by the company or the party benefiting from the pre-packaged administration as a means of ensuring independence of thought.

The elements of a claim under paragraph 74 are themselves the subject of some controversy. **3.372** Some judges have viewed 'unfair harm' as ordinarily meaning unequal or differential treatment to the disadvantage of the applicant (or applicant class) which cannot be justified by reference to the interests of the creditors as a whole or to achieving the objective of the administration.[746] However, in *Hockin*, Le Poidevin QC was not persuaded that paragraph 74 requires some element of unjustifiable discrimination to be shown, and in *Lehman Brothers Australia Limited* the Court of Appeal agreed that paragraph 74 can involve infliction of unfair harm on a particular creditor.[747] Nonetheless, for present purposes most situations are likely to involve some element of differential treatment between the creditors.

---

[741] *Hockin and others v Matsden and another* [2014] EWHC 763 (Ch).

[742] The same effect arose in *Unidare plc v Cohen and another* [2005] EWHC 1410 (Ch) which related to a challenge to the administrator's decision-making power in para 83 of Sch B1 to the Insolvency Act 1986 which similarly uses the word 'thinks'.

[743] Armour and Mokal (n 427) 49.

[744] *Bramston v Haut* [2012] EWCA Civ 1637.

[745] *Unidare plc* (n 742).

[746] *Re Coniston Hotel LLP* [2013] EWHC 93 (Ch) followed in *Marian Anne Curistan v Thomas Martin Keenan* [2013] NICh 13.

[747] *Hockin and others* (n 741); *Lehman Brothers Australia Limited (in liquidation) v Lomas* [2020] EWCA Civ 321.

3.373   If the creditor is unable to challenge the administrator's decision to move from paragraph 3(1)(a) to 3(1)(b) then he is most likely left with a claim that the administrator failed to obtain the best price reasonably obtainable.[748] The distinction between market value and market price is discussed in greater detail below and market value may be relevant to the question of the appropriate debt restructuring proposal for the purposes of 3(1)(a). But once a creditor is focusing solely on paragraph 3(1)(b), the court will be focused on price—that is what purchasers were willing to pay.[749] Accordingly, assuming that the administrator has acted in good faith, has properly marketed the business and assets, and has not unreasonably truncated the marketing period a creditor is unlikely to challenge successfully the price obtained.

3.374   In the end, the courts remain extremely reluctant to interfere in the administrator's commercial decision-making, particularly after the event, and the administrator is likely to be afforded a significant margin of appreciation by the courts.[750] Furthermore, where the administrator has been appointed, or at least has had his appointment blessed, by those who support the pre-packaged sale, and who often did have knowledge that it was about to take place, a sense of collusion can inevitably cloud the deal. In short, a disclosure approach does not improve trust because, even if the creditor believes that they have been provided with complete information, they have very little ability to take action even if they consider that there have been significant shortfalls in the process.[751]

3.375   The author of this chapter has argued elsewhere that this means a disclosure-based approach to SIPs is not the right method of regulation in this area.[752] Instead, the SIPs should take an expressly standard-setting approach in order to set and steer behaviour in the conduct of the pre-packaged administration itself. Whilst standard setting poses its own challenges in regulation,[753]it is suggested here that the informational requirements can be met by the market in this case so that appropriate standards which the market regards as legitimate could be laid down. The Graham Review proposals began this process with the recommendations on good marketing but the author has suggested that more could be done in the decision to move from rescue of the company to sale of the business and assets.[754] The new regulations take a somewhat different tack in seeking to insert a mandatory requirement to obtain an opinion from an independent party. Whether this allays the suspicions of those creditors who lose out remains to be seen.

E.   Courts' Approach to Pre-Packs

3.376   The English courts have confirmed that, where the circumstances require, an administrator is entitled to dispose of the business and assets of a company in advance of a creditors'

---

[748] *Re Charnley Davies Business Service Ltd* [1990] BCC 605.

[749] A similar point was made in the context of sales by a mortgagee in possession in *Aodhcon LLP v Bridgeco Ltd* [2014] EWHC 535 (Ch).

[750] See also the observations of Lewison J in *Re Trident Fashions plc (No 2)* [2004] EWHC 293 (Ch); [2004] 2 BCLC 35 at [39] and the observations of Blackburn J in *Four Private Investment Funds* [2009] BCC 632 at 646.

[751] On the problem of enforcement see, e.g., Ian Molho, *The Economics of Information: Lying and Cheating in Markets and Organisations* (1997).

[752] Sarah Paterson, 'Bargaining in Financial Restructuring: Market Norms, Legal Rights and Regulatory Standards' (2014) 14(2) *The Journal of Corporate Law Studies* 333.

[753] See, e.g., Baldwin, Cave, and Lodge (n 728) 296–302.

[754] Paterson (n 752).

meeting and without the need for direction from the court. Both pre- and post-Enterprise Act 2002, the courts have demonstrated themselves to be reluctant to become involved in the commercial decisions of administrators, in the absence of clear impropriety. Of course, it is only that relatively small proportion of pre-packs that are to be implemented by a court-appointed administrator which currently find themselves before the court (in the context of the court's approval of an administration order).

In *T&D Industries plc*,[755] a pre-Enterprise Act 2002 case involving the interpretation of **3.377** section 17 of the Insolvency Act 1986, Neuberger J held that an administrator could dispose of the assets of a company prior to the approval of his proposals by the company's creditors, without specific direction of the court. The administrators in that case decided some two weeks after the administration order that they wished to dispose of some of the assets of the relevant companies as a matter of some urgency. Neuberger J noted[756] that administration was meant to be a more flexible, cheaper, and comparatively informal alternative to liquidation. From the point of view of the court, it is undesirable to have a potential plethora of applications by administrators; save where the issue is whether the administrator has power to take the intended action as a matter of law, it will normally be an administrative or commercial decision for the administrator on which the court has nothing useful to say. A conclusion to the contrary, requiring the administrators to apply for directions whenever they wished to do something, would involve administrators in potential delay and expense. Neuberger J did however emphasize that the proposals should be put to the creditors 'as soon as reasonably possible'.[757]

The position does not appear to have changed radically post-Enterprise Act 2002 (a prime **3.378** purpose of which was, after all, to reduce court involvement in administrations) and the introduction by it of Schedule B1 to the Insolvency Act 1986, although of course an administrator must now always consider the hierarchy of objectives set out in paragraph 3 of Schedule B1 to the Insolvency Act 1986. In *Re Transbus International Ltd*,[758] Collins J determined that 'administrators are permitted to sell the assets of the company in advance of their proposals being approved by creditors'.[759] He reasoned that paragraph 68(2) of Schedule B1 to the Insolvency Act 1986 requires administrators to act in accordance with the directions of the court: '*if* the court gives [them]', considering this to be a deliberate choice by legislators to adopt wording which mirrors the interpretation which Neuberger J had put upon the earlier provisions.

There will be many cases where the administrators are justified in not laying any proposals **3.379** before creditors. This is so where they conclude that the unsecured creditors are either likely to be paid in full, or to receive no payment, or where neither of the first two objectives for the administration can be achieved: see paragraph 52 of the Schedule. If, in such administrations, administrators were prevented from acting without the direction of the court it would mean that they would have to seek the directions of the court before carrying out any function throughout the whole of the administration. The Enterprise Act 2002

---

[755] *Re T&D Industries plc (in administration)* [2000] 1 WLR 646.
[756] Ibid, 652.
[757] Ibid, 657.
[758] [2004] 1 WLR 2654.
[759] Ibid, 12.

reflects a conscious policy to reduce the involvement of the court in administrations, where possible.[760]

3.380   The first explicit judicial endorsement of the pre-pack administration as a legitimate technique is often considered to be *DKLL Solicitors v Revenue and Customs Commissioners*.[761] DKLL Solicitors applied for an administration order, following which it was intended that the proposed administrators would dispose immediately, and therefore prior to the holding of a creditors' meeting, of the business of the partnership to a newly formed LLP. Despite opposition from HMRC, the partnership's largest creditor, which argued that it would be wrong to make an administration order in circumstances where, had a meeting of creditors been held, HMRC as largest creditor would have voted against the proposed sale, the court made an administration order which allowed the pre-pack sale to go ahead. Andrew Simmonds QC, sitting as a judge of the High Court, held that even had there been a creditors' meeting at which HMRC voted down the proposal, even the majority creditor would not have had a right of veto of the administrator's proposals as there would still have been a real prospect of the court authorizing the proposed sale under paragraph 55 of Schedule B1 to the Insolvency Act 1986. Paragraph 55 provides that in circumstances where the creditors have failed to approve an administrator's proposals, the court may do a number of things, including making any order that the court thinks appropriate. There was no reason why DKLL should be in a worse position or HMRC in a better position simply because the matter involved a pre-pack.[762] The judge admitted that he was particularly influenced by the fact that the proposed sale seemed to be the only way of saving the jobs of DKLL's employees and was also likely to result in the affairs of DKLL's clients being handled with the minimum of disruption.[763]

3.381   The High Court judgment in *Re Kayley Vending*[764]—a post-SIP 16 case—appears to demonstrate a greater proactiveness by the courts to look beyond the proposed administrator's statement at the effect of the administration and proposed pre-pack. Provided the court is able to conclude, on the information submitted to it, that a pre-pack is in the best interests of the creditors as a whole, the courts can confer their *implicit* blessing on the pre-pack by making the administration order. Whilst it is primarily a matter for the applicant to identify what information is likely to be provided in an administration application to assist the court, and that information may not be limited to matters identified in SIP 16, the judge considered it likely that in most cases the information required by SIP 16, insofar as known or ascertainable at the date of the application, will fall within the requirement and be appropriate to enable the court to make its determination.[765]

3.382   Kayley Vending Limited supplied cigarette vending machines to public houses. Factors such as the ban on smoking in public houses had contributed to cash flow problems. HMRC applied for a winding-up petition, as a result of which the directors were unable to make an out-of-court appointment of an administrator. The directors applied for an

---

[760] Ibid, 14.
[761] [2008] 1 BCLC 112.
[762] Ibid 19.
[763] Ibid 20.
[764] [2009] BCC 578.
[765] Ibid 24.

administration order and filed evidence that showed that the directors and proposed administrator intended to conclude a pre-pack sale immediately upon their appointment. The evidence showed that directors and proposed administrators were negotiating with two potential purchasers, neither of which was connected to the directors. In fact, the potential purchasers were the two principal competitors of the company, supporting the opinion of the proposed administrator that they would be the most likely purchasers and would be prepared to pay the most for the assets. The administrator's opinion, supported by an asset valuer, was that if the company were to go into liquidation and the machines could not be serviced they could not be sold in their present locations and would have to be removed and sold separately, at a much lower value. The court was satisfied on the evidence before it that there was a reasonable prospect of achieving a better return to creditors as a whole through the administration and proposed pre-pack. There was nothing to suggest that the administration order should not be made as a matter of discretion.

In *Re Hellas Telecommunications*,[766] the court went one step further by expressly referring **3.383** to the proposed sale on the face of the order. The judgment concerned an administration application in relation to Hellas Telecommunications (Luxembourg) II SCA, made on behalf of the company and its directors on the grounds that it was unable to pay its debts and that administration would produce a better result for creditors than a winding up. The proposal by the potential administrators was to sell the company's key asset, namely its shareholding in Greek telecoms company WIND Hellas, by way of a pre-pack. The proposed buyer was Finance III Sàrl, a vehicle established by the incumbent sponsor, Weather Spa. As Lewison J highlighted in his judgment, there had been a lengthy bid process and an attempt by the company to attract bidders for its assets. Whilst complaints had been made about the method by which that bidding process had taken place and in particular that Weather had been given an advantage in terms of information provided to it, '[n]evertheless, the fact remains that the Weather bid is now the only bid on the table'. Furthermore, the senior creditors had made it clear that the only bid they were prepared to support was that of Weather; and in all cases it was envisaged that their debt would stay in place post-restructuring making their consent critical. 'Therefore on the evidence before the court there is no real alternative for the administrators other than to proceed with the pre-pack sale to Weather.' Lewison J was satisfied that SIP 16 had been 'fully complied with'. He further commented:

> It is not entirely easy to see precisely where in the statutory structure the court is concerned with the merits of a pre-pack sale. It seems to me that in general the merits of a pre-pack sale are for the administrator to deal with; and the creditors, if sufficiently aggrieved, have a remedy in the course of the administration to challenge an administrator's decision. It may on the evidence be obvious that a pre-pack sale is an abuse of the administrator's powers, in which event the court could refuse to make the administration order or could direct the administrators not to complete a pre-pack sale. At the other end of the spectrum it may be that it is obvious that a particular pre-pack is on the evidence the only real way forward, in which case the court could give the administrators liberty to enter into the pre-pack, leaving open the possibility that a sufficiently aggrieved creditor could nevertheless challenge the administrator's decision *ex post facto*. But in the majority of cases the position

---

[766] *Hellas Telecommunications (Luxembourg) II SCA* [2010] BCC 295.

may not be clear; in which event the making of an administration order, even in the context of a pre-pack should not be taken as the court's blessing on the pre-pack sale.[767]

3.384   Lewison J referred to three courses of action the court can take when faced with a proposed pre-pack. First, if the evidence before it suggests that the pre-pack would involve an abuse of process, the court can either refuse to grant the administration order or grant the administration order but order that the sale should not go ahead. Secondly, where the evidence before the court does not clearly point to the benefit of the pre-pack, the court can make the administration order but leave the pre-pack to the commercial judgment of the administrator. Thirdly, if the evidence before the court is compelling, the order can expressly permit the administrators to enter into the pre-pack. On the facts available to him, the judge felt confident that the pre-pack was the only legitimate option available to the company, and therefore felt able to endorse expressly the pre-pack on the face of the order. An express endorsement would not prevent a disgruntled creditor from challenging the pre-pack, but it is likely that such a creditor would be required to offer up some evidence which had not been originally put before the court at the time of the original application.

3.385   The case of *Clydesdale Financial Services Ltd v Smailes*[768] also warrants a mention as it highlights the importance of an administrator obtaining robust valuation evidence in support of any pre-pack sale, as well as emphasizing that SIP 16 is something which administrators need to consider from the outset. The case involved an insolvent firm of solicitors that specialized in personal injury claims. It sold its work in progress and retainers, together with its rights in respect of disbursements and other assets to another practitioner for a total price of £1.9 million. The sale agreement was executed immediately before the practice went into administration (therefore differing from the typical pre-pack administration which entails the sale being executed on or shortly after the appointment of the administrator), although the administrator in waiting in this case had been actively involved in the terms of the sale. The company's major creditors (the firm's two funders and its ATE insurers) applied for an order removing the administrator from office with a view to an investigation of the sale by an independent replacement office holder. In particular, the claimants alleged that the sale had occurred at a gross undervalue (they were particularly critical of the information provided to and methodology of the valuer), that they had not been adequately consulted prior to the sale, and that the letter sent to creditors informing them of the sale after the event did not contain the information required by SIP 16.

3.386   Richards J removed the administrator from office (under paragraph 88 of Schedule B1 to the Insolvency Act 1986). He found that the valuation evidence in support of the sale price was not thorough enough to prove that the sale was for the best price available and so a review of the sale was appropriate. The accountant who had conducted the valuation had merely carried out a 'desk-top review' of the practice's assets—he had not inspected the files or reviewed the assets of the firm, but rather based his valuation on the opinions of the practice partners on the value of the firm's work-in-progress. Whilst there was no clear evidence that a better deal would have been possible, in the absence of clear evidence that this deal was the best available, it was right for the transaction to be subject to review. The administrators'

---

[767] Ibid 8.
[768] [2009] BCC 810.

involvement in negotiating the deal meant they lacked the necessary independence to conduct such a review.

Whilst the judge agreed that the administrator had not complied with SIP 16, the failure **3.387** of the administrator in that respect was not in itself a ground to remove him from office. Keeping the creditors in the dark about the sale in order to prevent disruption to the sale was a legitimate tactic, provided it was done honestly and for the purpose of securing a better deal for creditors. Whilst the administrator had failed to appreciate that creditors had been entitled to receive, on request, a copy of the sale agreement and valuation (having forgotten 'that their sole task had been to act in the interests of creditors who were surely entitled, although perhaps not as a matter of enforceable right, to see the agreement made for their benefit and the valuation which was said to support it'), the delay in production to the creditors had not been sinister and did not provide a ground for removal.

In the *ATU* case Henderson J was entirely comfortable that a pre-packaged administration **3.388** was a 'court-approved process' for the purposes of the inter-creditor agreement where the proposed pre-packaged administration was put to the court notwithstanding that the administrators would be taking the decision to enter into the administration sale. In case he was wrong on this point, he expressly granted the administrators liberty to enter into the proposed sale.[769]

It is also worth pausing to consider a case which, while not expressly concerned with pre- **3.389** packaged administrations, may have consequences for them. In *Re System Building Services Group Ltd*, ICCJ Barber held that directors remain subject to their general statutory duties after the company has entered formal insolvency proceedings.[770] This was not a point frequently explored in the case law, where the focus has tended to be on proceeding against the office holder, and has led to some speculation that it would make it very difficult for administrators to enter into pre-packaged administration sales where the directors owned shares in the purchaser.[771] However, *System Building* suggests that this is to overstate the point. There is likely to be a particular focus on whether the director took account of the interests of creditors,[772] and, although not fiduciary in nature, there may also be a question over the exercise of reasonable care, skill, and diligence.[773] But *System Building* does not suggest it is the case that these duties can never be satisfied where the director owns shares in the purchaser.

Finally, it is worth mentioning the costs incurred by an administrator in waiting in **3.390** negotiating the terms of a pre-pack sale. A question arises as to whether such costs are recoverable as an administration expense. Prior to the coming into force of the Insolvency (Amendment) Rules 2010, an administrator could usually only recover costs incurred whilst in office as administrator, which precluded the recovery of costs incurred in

---

[769] *Re Christophorus 3 Limited* [2014] EWHC 1162 (Ch).

[770] *Re System Building Services Group Ltd; Hunt & System Building Services Group Ltd v Michie & System Building Services Ltd* [2020] EWHC 54 (Ch).

[771] Jamie Tilling and Rahim Hirji, 'Directors' Duties from Beyond the Corporate Grave', 5 February 2020, Charles Russell Speechlys.

[772] Companies Act 2006, s 172(3).

[773] Companies Act 2006, s 174.

negotiating a pre-pack sale before his appointment.[774] The only way of recovering such costs as an expense of the administration was if the appointment was made by court order and the court made a pre-appointment costs order under its discretion under paragraph 13(1)(f) of Schedule B1 to the Insolvency Act 1986 to make 'any other order which the court thinks appropriate'. This was the case in *Re Kayley Vending Limited*,[775] where the judge[776] considered that the incurring of such costs benefited the creditors as a whole more than it did any other stakeholders (such as management). By contrast, in *Re Johnson Machine and Tool Company Limited*,[777] again decided before the implementation of the Insolvency (Amendment) Rules 2010, the judge refused an administrator's application for permission to pay his pre-appointment costs in negotiating a pre-pack as an expense of the administration, because the pre-pack sale was to a company connected to the insolvent company's existing management. The judge could find no evidence that incurring the pre-appointment costs was plainly for the benefit of creditors as opposed to the benefit of management. In fact, he said it would rarely be possible to clearly establish the balance of advantage in the creditors' favour where the pre-pack is to a company connected with the existing management (even if the sale achieved a better return for creditors than would be the case in a winding up). Furthermore, the judge took the narrow view that the only costs and expenses recoverable are those relating directly to the appointment of administrators—'[i]f the costs occasioned by insolvency advice would have been incurred in any event, even if no decision to go down the administration route had been made, it will rarely (if ever) be appropriate to order those costs to be paid as an administration expense'.[778]

3.391   The position was altered by The Insolvency (Amendment) Rules 2010. The current position is set out in Insolvency Rule 3.52, which allows insolvency practitioners to recover certain pre-appointment costs and expenses from the insolvent estate, subject to the approval of the creditors committee, the creditors, or the court in accordance with the procedure in the rule.[779] In order to obtain that approval, administrators will need to justify why the pre-appointment work in question has assisted in achieving the objective of the administration.

XI. English Schemes of Arrangement and Corporate Debt Restructurings

A. Introduction

3.392   A scheme of arrangement is a statutory procedure for effecting a compromise or arrangement between a company and its members and/or creditors (or, importantly, any class of them), with the sanction of the court. A scheme of arrangement is a creature of corporate statute to be found in Part 26 (sections 895–899) of the Companies Act 2006.[780]

[774] Insolvency (Amendment) Rules 2010, SI 2010/686.
[775] (n 764).
[776] Following the earlier case of *Re SE Services Ltd* (High Court, 9 August 2006).
[777] [2010] BCC 382.
[778] Ibid 11.
[779] The Insolvency (England and Wales) Rules 2016 SI 2016/1024..
[780] Prior to 2008, the procedure was governed by Pt XIII (ss 425–430) of the Companies Act 1985, and before 1985 by various statutes.

An application for a scheme of arrangement may be made by the company, a creditor or member of the company, the liquidator, or the administrator.[781] Creditors are likely to face significant practical challenges in developing a scheme of arrangement without the support of the directors but it has also been held that if the company is not in liquidation or administration the court does not have jurisdiction to sanction the scheme without the consent of the company.[782] If the creditors do want to propose a scheme of arrangement without the support of the directors it is likely that they would need to place the company into administration first.[783]

'Compromise' and 'arrangement' have no fixed meaning; the scope for using a scheme of   **3.393** arrangement is therefore wide. Case law suggests that whilst the essence of a 'compromise' is that there must be some difficulty or dispute which the scheme seeks to resolve,[784] 'arrangement' is broad enough to encompass any transaction involving an element of 'give and take' between a company and its members or creditors.[785] In establishing the necessary element of 'give and take', the courts have been prepared to look beyond the scheme itself and to the terms of the wider restructuring.[786]

B. Meaning of 'Creditor'

The term 'creditor' for this purpose is not defined in the Companies Act 2006, but the courts   **3.394** have given the expression its ordinary meaning so as to include all persons having pecuniary claims against the company notwithstanding that claims are often difficult to quantify and irrespective of whether such claims are actual, contingent, unliquidated, or prospective.[787] Creditors are not limited to those who have a provable claim against a company, but will include those that do.[788]

Where bonds are held in global form through the clearing systems, a question arises as to   **3.395** whether it is possible to allow the ultimate beneficial holders of the bonds to vote on the scheme. Questions can arise as to whether the common depository or trustee is the creditor, or whether the ultimate beneficial holders may be able to vote as contingent creditors without the issue of definitive notes (as such issuance can be expensive and administratively burdensome). The point is of some significance because, as we shall see, a scheme must be passed not only by a 75 per cent majority in value of those creditors present and voting in a class but also by a majority in number.[789] Thus, if a single common depositary or trustee

---

[781] Companies Act 2006, s 896(2).

[782] *Re Savoy Hotel Ltd* [1981] Ch 351, 364-D, G-365B, H-366A.

[783] The identity of the insolvency practitioner is controlled by the holder of a qualifying floating charge who is either able to make his own appointment (Insolvency Act 1986, Sch B1, para 26) or to replace the company's nominee (para 36). Where there is no qualifying floating charge holder the unsecured creditors can control the identity of the appointee (Insolvency Act 1986, Sch B1, para 97).

[784] *Sneath v Valley Gold Ltd* [1893] 1 Ch 477; *Mercantile Investment and General Trust Co v International Co of Mexico* [1893] 1 Ch 484.

[785] *Re Alabama, New Orleans, Texas and Pacific Junction Railway Co Ltd* [1891] 1 Ch 213; *Re NFU Development Trust Ltd* [1972] 1 WLR 1548; *Re Savoy Hotel Ltd* (n 785).

[786] *Re Bluebrook Ltd* [2010] 1 BCLC 338 [72] to [74]; *In the Matter of Uniq plc v In the Matter of the Companies Act 2006* [2011] EWHC 749 (Ch).

[787] *Re Midland Coal, Coke and Iron Co* [1985] 1 Ch 267.

[788] *Re T&N and others (No 4)* [2007] Bus LR 1411.

[789] Companies Act 2006, s 899.

votes on behalf of all bondholders, they can be relatively easily outvoted by other creditors appearing to vote in person as a result of the majority in number requirement. In the past, for example in the Marconi scheme (2003), a process of 'attornment' was employed, whereby global bonds were exchanged for definitive bonds on the day before the creditors' scheme meetings. Each definitive bondholder identified in a duly completed account holder letter was then entitled to vote at the creditors' scheme meetings. In the Countrywide scheme (2009), the noteholders were able to vote directly without holding definitive notes. Under the terms of the Countrywide New York law bond indenture, the ultimate noteholders had the right to call for the issue of definitive bonds on an event of default. They were therefore contingent creditors with an entitlement to vote on the scheme. The relevant contingency was the potential issue of definitive notes—it did not require an actual request to issue definitive notes—the fact that there was power to do so was sufficient. The contingent creditor approach has been adopted many times since, including in the Energis plc, Ionica plc, Co-operative Bank, Obrascón, Noble, and Port Finance schemes. Where the bond terms do not provide ultimate noteholders with the right to call for definitive bonds it may be possible to amend the terms. Alternatively (although this is untested) it may be possible to persuade the court that it should 'look through' the legal owner to the person with the real economic interest. This would be consistent with the overall thrust of the scheme architecture which, as we are about to examine, is focused on identifying those with the real economic interest in the company.

3.396 As the Lehman Brothers administration shows, the concept of 'creditor' for this purpose does not encompass proprietary claims. The administrators of the European arm of Lehman Brothers had been hoping to return client assets which were held on trust pursuant to a scheme of arrangement. Lehman did not hold enough assets to satisfy the claims of all trust clients, and it was not clear which assets were held on trust for beneficiaries. The administrators, therefore, proposed a scheme of arrangement to compromise the claims of the trust clients and apportion the shortfall in the assets between them. Counsel for the administrators argued for the breadth afforded by case law to the definitions of 'creditor' and 'arrangement'. To be a Lehman scheme creditor one was required to have both a proprietary claim to a security which was held on a segregated basis at the time of administration *and* an associated pecuniary claim (however contingent) against Lehman. The pecuniary claim could be a claim for damages or equitable compensation for breach of trust or contract (for late delivery of the security for example). Counsel argued that the pecuniary claim arising out of the trust relationship is enough to take a party through the 'creditor gateway' and, once through, an arrangement under Part 26 can deal with the whole relationship of a client—i.e. once through the creditor gateway, the scheme jurisdiction is engaged and extends to all of a creditor's rights against the company and not merely those that give rise to a claim in debt. The significant practical difficulties in pursuing any alternative solution were emphasized.

3.397 The Court of Appeal unanimously affirmed[790] the earlier High Court decision[791] that the court does not have jurisdiction to sanction a scheme under Part 26 of the Companies Act 2006 which varies or extinguishes rights of clients whose property is held on trust. The court

---

[790] *In the matter of Lehman Brothers International (Europe) (In Administration) (No 2)* [2010] BCC 272, CA.
[791] *In the matter of Lehman Brothers International (Europe) (In Administration) (No 2)* [2009] All ER (D) 36.

ultimately considered the question to be one of statutory construction. The court's jurisdiction under Part 26 is circumscribed by the requirement that a scheme must be an arrangement between a company and its 'creditors' (or members). A 'creditor' consists of anyone who has a monetary claim (including contingent claims) against the company which, when payable, will constitute a debt. A proprietary claim to trust property is not a claim in respect of a debt or liability of the company. Whilst a trustee-beneficiary relationship may give rise to unsecured claims against the trustee for breach of trust or even negligence (and to that extent the beneficiary will be a creditor of the trustee), that is a consequence of the trust relationship and not a definition of it—it remains at core a different relationship. Neuberger MR considered that it would be surprising if a scheme could have been proposed and sanctioned in relation to trust property for over 100 years without anyone (including all the leading writers of company law and trust law textbooks) apparently being aware of such a feature. Furthermore, the judges considered it unlikely that the legislature would have intended beneficiaries' rights to be capable of being altered by a scheme if the trustee is a company when there is no such right if the trustee is an individual. The judges were sympathetic to the significant practical difficulties faced by the administrators but thought the wider impact at law of allowing the appeal would be positively undesirable. The trust mechanism has long been regarded as an important safeguard against insolvency and has been imported into commercial contracts for that very reason.

The Court of Appeal did, however, consider the ability of a scheme to release creditors' **3.398** claims not only against the company but also against third parties designed to recover the same loss. This is particularly important in the context of many complex debt structures where lenders have the benefit of a comprehensive guarantee package from group companies. A scheme of arrangement does not per se deal with these guarantees—and there is little to be gained if the creditor's claim has been released against the principal debtor, but the creditor is then able immediately to enforce a guarantee, as the guarantor would then be entitled to claim the entire amount back from the company pursuant to its right of indemnity.[792] In *ColourOz*,[793] Snowden J described this as a 'ricochet claim'.

Some authority already existed for the release of guarantees through the terms of an ar- **3.399** rangement in the context of CVAs in the *Powerhouse* case[794] and in the case of schemes in the *T&N (No 3)* judgment.[795] In *Lehman*, albeit that the comments are obiter, the Court of Appeal considered both the *T&N (No 3)* case and certain Australian authorities on the issue. Whilst noting that the point has not been without controversy in the Australian context, Patten LJ commented:[796]

> It seems to me entirely logical to regard the court's jurisdiction as extending to approving a scheme which varies or releases creditors' claims against the company on terms which require them to bring into account and release rights of action against third parties designed to recover the same loss. The release of such third party claims is merely ancillary to the arrangement between the company and its own creditors. Mr Snowden has not

---

[792] *Re ColourOz Investment 2 LLC* [2020] EWHC 1864 (Ch) [72].
[793] Ibid.
[794] *Powerhouse* (n 594).
[795] *T&N (No 3) Ltd* [2007] 1 BCLC 563.
[796] [2010] BCC 272 [63].

invited us to overrule *T&N Ltd (No 3)* and it would not be appropriate for us to do so without hearing full argument on the point.

3.400 Thus, releases of third party claims through the terms of the scheme are permitted, at least insofar as guarantees of the debt compromised by the scheme of arrangement are concerned. Interesting questions arise, however, where the 'ricochet claim' is somewhat artificially constructed. This has occurred in several cases where a newly formed English company has voluntarily assumed a liability to creditors of a different company in the group and entered into a co-obligor or contribution deed in favour of that other company.[797] These structures have been employed to engage the jurisdiction of the English court. In the convening hearing for the *Port Finance* scheme Snowden J noted that in cases such as these:

> the courts appear to have treated Patten LJ's comments in paragraph [65] of his judgment in Lehman Brothers that Part 26 can include releases of third parties that are 'necessary to give effect to the arrangement proposed for the disposition of the debts and liabilities of the company to its own creditors', to be satisfied simply by the existence, as a matter of law, of a contingent liability on the part of the scheme company that has been voluntarily undertaken to the third party. Questions of the degree of artificiality of the structure, the relative lack of benefit to the scheme company, and the commercial justification for the scheme from the perspective of the third party have been treated as matters going to the exercise of the court's discretion, together with questions such as whether the scheme is an example of 'good forum shopping', whether there is a high level of support for the scheme from the scheme creditors, and whether the scheme is likely to be recognised in other jurisdictions.[798]

Snowden J made these remarks at a convening hearing and did not consider it necessary to express his view on whether this was the correct approach. Thus, there may be more to come on the question of whether third party release technology works in these 'artificial' structures. Furthermore, Snowden J's comments in *Port Finance* focus on cases in which the artificial structure has been employed to engage the jurisdiction of the English courts. However, these structures may also be employed to avoid an event of default which would otherwise occur if the principal debtor were to enter into a scheme of arrangement. This was at least part of the motivation for the structure in the *AI Scheme*,[799] the *Gategroup plan*,[800] and *Swissport Fuelling*.[801] This use of artificial structures has not had a great deal of focus to date, and yet clearly raises different issues from the use of artificial structures to 'forum shop'.

3.401 A further question arises as to whether the effect of the release is to amend the rights as between the creditors and the third party, or whether it is rather to create a promise between the creditors and the company to release the third party which the company can enforce. Zacaroli J discussed this in detail in the *Gategroup* sanction judgment,[802] where the issue

---

[797] *Re AI Scheme Ltd* [2015] EWHC 1233 (Ch) and [2015] EWHC 2038 (Ch); *Re Codere Finance (UK) Ltd* [2015] EWHC 3778 (Ch); *Re Swissport Fuelling Ltd (No 2)* [2020] EWHC 3413 (Ch); *Gategroup Guarantee Limited* (n 492).

[798] *Port Finance Investment Limited* [2021] EWHC 378 (Ch) [73].

[799] *Re AI Scheme Ltd* [2015] EWHC 1233 (Ch).

[800] *Re Gategroup Guarantee Limited* (n 492) [19].

[801] *Re Swissport Fuelling Ltd* [2020] 12 WLUK 171.

[802] *Gategroup Guarantee Limited* [2021] EWHC 775 (Ch) [29]–[42]. *Gategroup* was a Part 26A restructuring plan proposal but the same analysis applies to Part 26 schemes of arrangement on this point.

was of some importance for the purposes of foreign recognition. Zacaroli J appears to conclude that the starting point is that the release is only enforceable between the creditors and the company. However, drawing on the analysis of Richards J (as he then was) in *Re T&N*,[803] he identified two mechanisms that can be used to bolster the enforceability of the release: appointing an attorney pursuant to the plan to sign a release by which the third party undertakes to be bound, or requiring the creditor to assign the benefit of any claim to an attorney.

It is clear that the relevant third party claims must be closely connected with the claims against the company compromised as part of the scheme. Longmore LJ commented:[804]   **3.402**

> the creditors' rights against the insurers in *T&N (No 3) Ltd* ... (a) were closely connected with their rights against the company as creditors, (b) were personal, not proprietary, rights and (c) if exercised and leading to a payment by the insurers, would have resulted in a reduction of the creditors' claims against the company. Bearing in mind these three factors, it seems to me, as it does to Patten LJ, that the decision of David Richards J was correct.

It has also become increasingly common for the scheme to release various persons, such as directors and officers, from liability arising in connection with the promotion of the scheme. Zaccaroli J has expressed the 'logic' for these releases to be that breaches of duty by persons in connection with the scheme may create a 'blot' on the scheme such that it should not be sanctioned, but that if no such argument is raised then the relevant persons should have certainty that no such claim can subsequently be sought.[805] However, it is not entirely clear whether such releases are permitted even where 'ricochet claims' would not otherwise arise. In *Far East Capital*, Snowden J said: **3.403**

> The possibility of a scheme including a mechanism for the release of claims against third parties that might otherwise give rise to 'ricochet' claims back against the scheme company is now well-established: see eg *re Lehman Brothers International Europe (No 2)* ... On the basis that such provisions simply grant a release in relation to (i) the guarantee and security obligations that support the Company's obligations under such notes, and (ii) any claims against the persons involved in the preparation, negotiation or implementation of the Scheme itself and their legal advisers, it seems to me that the inclusion of such provisions is well within the scope of the Companies Act 2006.[806]

This passage appears to suggest that the 'ricochet claim' is a requirement for both the release of guarantees and security and releases of those involved in preparing the scheme and their advisers. However, in *Noble*, Snowden J put the point more expansively, and in a way which suggests the presence of a ricochet claim is not required. In *Noble*, he described the basis of the granting of the releases as requiring scheme creditors 'to release claims against third parties where such a release is necessary in order to give effect to the arrangement between the company and the scheme creditors'.[807] Having identified that the jurisdiction is 'most

---

[803] *T&N* (n 795) [55].
[804] Ibid [83].
[805] *Re New Look Financing plc* [2020] EWHC 2793 (Ch) [27].
[806] *In the matter of Far East Capital Limited S.A* [2017] EWHC 2878 (Ch) [13]–[14].
[807] *Re Noble Group Limited* [2018] EWHC 3092 (Ch) [24].

clearly satisfied where the scheme compromises debts which are guaranteed and where, absent such a release, pursuit of the guarantor by a scheme creditor would undermine the compromise between the creditor and the company',[808] he went on to say that the jurisdiction is not limited to guarantees and claims closely connected to scheme claims. He expressed the justification for including releases against those who have prepared the scheme and their advisers in expansive terms, 'a need not to allow scheme creditors to undermine the terms of the scheme itself'.[809] This would appear to suggest that a finding of a ricochet claim is not required for a release of those who have prepared, negotiated, or implemented the scheme or their advisers, although it is suggested that the position is not free from doubt. Case law establishes that such releases should be explicitly drawn to the attention of creditors in the explanatory statement.[810] It is also worth noting, in passing, that it is a common feature of many schemes to include a bar date for claims.[811]

C. Stages of a Scheme and Related Issues

3.404   There are three distinct stages in the procedure for implementing a scheme: (i) the 'leave to convene' hearing; (ii) the scheme meetings; and (iii) the sanction hearing, each discussed more fully below. As Chadwick LJ explained in *Re Hawk Insurance*:[812]

> It can be seen that each of those stages serves a distinct purpose. At the first stage the court directs how the meeting or meetings are to be summoned. It is concerned, at that stage, to ensure that those who are to be affected by the compromise or arrangement proposed have a proper opportunity of being present (in person or by proxy) at the meeting or meetings at which they are to be considered and voted upon. The second stage ensures that the proposals are acceptable to at least a majority in number, representing three-fourths in value, of those who take the opportunity of being present (in person or by proxy) at the meeting or meetings. At the third stage the court is concerned (i) to ensure that the meeting or meetings have been summoned and held in accordance with its previous order, (ii) to ensure that the proposals have been approved by the requisite majority of those present at the meeting or meetings and (iii) to ensure that the views and interests of those who have not approved the proposals at the meeting or meetings (either because they were not present or, being present, did not vote in favour of the proposals) receive impartial consideration.

The process is court intensive (entailing not one but two court hearings) and from start to finish is likely to take at least six weeks. A scheme of arrangement can consequently be slower and more costly to implement than, for example, a CVA.

1. Leave to convene hearing

3.405   A company, any of its creditors or members, or a liquidator or administrator of the company, may apply to the court to sanction a compromise or arrangement, as well as providing

---

[808] ibid.
[809] ibid [25].
[810] *Re Indah Kiat International Finance Company BV* [2016] EWHC 246 (Ch).
[811] See, for example, *Re Card Protection Plan* [2014] EWHC 114 (Ch).
[812] *Re Hawk Insurance Co Ltd* [2001] 2 BCLC 480 [12].

for the convening of the relevant meetings by the court.[813] As discussed above, whilst a creditor (or class of them) may make an application, the company must still be a party to the application—i.e. a scheme of arrangement cannot be used as a mechanism to implement an arrangement between the creditors merely as between themselves.[814]

(a) Class issues

There is no requirement that all creditors and/or shareholders of the company be included in a scheme. In *Bluebrook* Mann J described the position in this way: **3.406**

> … in promoting and entering a scheme, it is not necessary for the company to consult any class of creditors (or contributories) who are not affected, either because their rights are untouched or because they have no economic interest in the company.[815]

It is useful, however, to 'unpack' this a little. The starting point is that the company is free to seek to reach a compromise or arrangement with only some classes of its creditors whilst leaving others outside the scheme and unaffected by it.[816] A creditor whose rights are affected by the scheme, but who considers that those left outside the scheme are treated too favourably, is free to vote against the scheme and, if the majority votes in favour, to argue at the sanction or fairness hearing that the scheme is unfair because those outside the scheme are treated too favourably compared with those within it.[817] Equally, a party who is left outside the scheme can appear at the sanction or fairness hearing to argue that the scheme is unfair because the class of creditor of which he is a member has been left out of it. However, if the court concludes that that class is not offered anything in the scheme because it has 'no economic interest' in the company, then the scheme will not be found to be unfair.

In the last edition of this book, we focused on the question of when the company can allocate no consideration in the scheme to a creditor on the grounds that it has 'no economic interest' in the company. And readers will find this discussed in more detail below. However, recent cases also reveal increasing focus on the creditors who are left out of the scheme in the sense of not being required to accept a compromise of their claims and being paid in full. In the *Sea Assets* case, the court assumes: **3.407**

> No company proposing a scheme will want to leave out of the scheme creditors other than those with whom they have reached agreement or those with whom agreement is impossible but who have to be paid in full if the company is to survive.[818]

Yet, the company may have far more prosaic reasons for excluding creditors, related to limiting the number of creditors it needs to engage with in order to save time and costs, rather than a laser-like focus on including everyone unless it is strictly necessary to exclude a particular creditor or class of creditors.[819] Thus, the English courts demand that the company

---

[813] Companies Act 2006, ss 895 and 896.
[814] *Re Savoy Hotel Ltd* (n 782).
[815] *In the matter of Bluebrook Ltd and Others* (n 786) [25].
[816] *Sea Assets Limited* (n 609).
[817] Ibid [45].
[818] Ibid [46].
[819] Sarah Paterson and Adrian Walters, 'Selective Corporate Reorganization', 15 September 2021 <https://ssrn.com/abstract=3924225> (last accessed 26 September 2021).

explain why it has excluded certain creditors who remain unimpaired.[820] This is likely to be particularly important where the counterfactual to the scheme is an insolvency in which shareholders would receive nothing, but where shareholders are retaining their shares in the scheme of arrangement.

3.408   Important issues arise in relation to costs where a creditor does choose to mount a challenge. In *Re Stronghold Insurance Company Limited* Hildyard J stated that he would wish to make clear:

> my understanding (and certainly my usual practice) that, unless the objections are wholly improper or irrelevant, obviously collaterally motivated, or sprung on the scheme company without offering a proper opportunity for their discussion, there is very little likelihood of any adverse order for costs …; and indeed there will usually be a real prospect of the relevant creditor recovering its reasonable costs of helpful and focused representation, fairly outlined in good time before the convening hearing to enable their proper consideration, on the class issues raised.[821]

This approach was endorsed by Snowden J as applicable in the context of a sanction hearing in *Ophir Energy Plc*,[822] and by Norris J in *Inmarsat*.[823] However, in *Inmarsat* Norris J underlined that this should not be seen as an encouragement to objection. The position remained as stated by Warren J in *Re Peninsular Orient*:

> I decline to elevate to some great principle of public policy the idea that, save in exceptional cases, objectors must, in order to ensure proper scrutiny of the scheme, always be immune from the normal costs rules provided that their objections are genuine and not frivolous. It seems to me that, as in any other litigation, the courts are perfectly capable of deciding on a case by case basis, what the justice of the case demands in relation to costs.[824]

Snowden J has also recently shown himself amenable to this more nuanced statement. *Virgin Active* was a case under the new Part 26A restructuring plan procedure but applicable to the scheme jurisprudence on the issue of costs.[825] Snowden J accepted that in the *Noble* case he appeared to have suggested that any creditor who attended a convening hearing could expect to have their reasonable costs paid, whatever the outcome.[826] In *Virgin Active* he readily admitted that this 'overstated the approach of the court',[827] and went on to set out a more nuanced position:

(i)   In all cases the issue of costs is in the discretion of the court.

(ii)   The general rule in relation to costs under CPR 44.2 will ordinarily have no application under Part 8 seeking an order convening scheme meetings or sanctioning a scheme, because the company seeks the approval of the court, not a remedy or relief against another party.

---

[820]   *In the matter of Sunbird Business Services Ltd* [2020] EWHC 2493 (Ch) [61].
[821]   [2019] EWHC 2909 (Ch) [145].
[822]   *In the matter of Ophir Energy Plc* [2019] EWHC 1278 (Ch) [39].
[823]   *Inmarsat plc* [2020] EWHC 776 (Ch).
[824]   *Re Peninsular and Orient* [2006] EWHC 3279 (Ch) [47].
[825]   *Re Virgin Active Holdings Ltd* [2021] EWHC 911 (Ch).
[826]   *Noble* (n 807).
[827]   Virgin Active (n 825) [28].

(iii) That is not necessarily the case (and hence the general rule under the Civil Procedure Rules (CPR) may apply) in respect of individual applications made within scheme proceedings.

(iv) In determining the appropriate order to make in relation to costs in scheme proceedings, relevant considerations may include:

    (a) that members or creditors should not be deterred from raising genuine issues relating to a scheme in a timely and appropriate manner by concerns over exposure to adverse costs orders;

    (b) that ordering the company to pay the reasonable costs of members or creditors who appear may enable matters of proper concern to be fully ventilated by the court, thereby assisting the court in its scrutiny of the proposals; and

    (c) that the court should not encourage members or creditors to object in the belief that the costs of objecting will be defrayed by someone else.

(v) The court does not generally make adverse costs orders against objecting members or creditors when their objections (though unsuccessful) are not frivolous and have been of assistance to the court in its scrutiny of the scheme. But the court may make an adverse costs order if the circumstances justify that order.

(vi) There is no principle or presumption that the court will order the scheme company to pay the costs of an opposing member or creditor whose objections to a scheme have been unsuccessful. It may do so if the objections have not been frivolous and have assisted the court, or it may make no order as to costs. The decision in each case will depend on all the circumstances.[828]

In *Inmarsat* Norris J declined to make any order as to costs. What mattered was not the **3.409** identity of the objector but the nature and substance of the objection: in *Inmarsat* 'very thin gruel'. Thus, this was not a case in which the company ought to meet the objectors' costs. But, at the same time, it was also not a case in which an adverse costs order ought to be made, as the company could have responded earlier to concerns by market announcements. In *Virgin Active*, Snowden J held the decision over to sanction.[829]

Overall, the lesson of the cases for the company appears to be to concentrate on consult- **3.410** ation and disclosure in advance of commencing the scheme process. The more the court can be persuaded that creditors were consulted and received adequate information, the less likely it is that the court will order the company to pay an objecting creditors' costs and there may even be a prospect of an adverse costs order against the objecting creditor. Merely pleading urgency without evidence is unlikely to persuade the court: the English courts are increasingly showing a scepticism of claims for urgency which are not made out in the evidence. And, as we shall see below, there is a growing focus on whether consultation was 'even' or whether some creditors were privileged over others in consultation and disclosure.

A court Practice Statement provides that any issues which may arise as to the constitution **3.411** of class meetings/class issues must be drawn to the court's attention at the first court hearing rather than leaving it to the final court hearing (i.e. the sanction hearing):

---

[828] Ibid [29].
[829] Ibid [32].

It is the responsibility of the applicant, by evidence in support of the application or otherwise, to draw to the attention of the court at the hearing for an order that meetings of creditors and/or members be held ('the convening hearing'): any issues which may arise as to the constitution of meetings of members or creditors or which otherwise affect the conduct of those meetings ...[830]

The purpose of the Practice Statement is to enable issues relating to the composition of the classes of creditors and the summoning of the relevant class meetings to be identified and resolved early in the proceedings to avoid the waste of time and costs associated with the court determining that the classes have not been properly identified at the hearing to sanction the scheme at the end of the process. Creditors who feel that they have been unfairly treated will still be able to raise objections at the hearing of the petition to sanction the scheme, but the court will expect them to show good reason why they did not raise their objections at an earlier stage. Thus, the Practice Statement goes on to provide that:

the applicant should, prior to the convening hearing, take all steps reasonably open to it to notify any person affected by the scheme of the following matters:
   a. that the scheme is being promoted,
   b. the purpose which the scheme is designed to achieve and its effect,
   c. the meetings of creditors and/or members which the applicant considers will be required and their composition,
   d. the other matters that are to be addressed at the convening hearing ...
   e. the date and place fixed for the convening hearing,
   f. that such persons are entitled to attend the convening and sanction hearings, and
   g. how such persons may make further enquiries about the scheme.[831]

3.412   The requirements of the Practice Statement are met by sending a letter to creditors giving notice of the convening hearing and setting out the background to the scheme and a summary of its terms. Until comparatively recently, it was usual practice to send this letter two weeks before the hearing. However, the courts have now made clear that there is no hard and fast rule as to the appropriate notice period and that in many cases the courts will expect longer notice to have been given. Snowden J has noted that, 'What is adequate notice will depend on all the circumstances. The more complex or novel the scheme, and the less consultation that has taken place with creditors as a whole before the scheme is launched, the longer the notice should generally be.'[832] Particular issues of timing arise where the notice is disseminated to bondholders via a clearing system, given that there will often be several intermediaries between the clearing system and the noteholders.[833] Indeed, it may be wise to adopt multiple methods of notification including on a scheme website page. In *ColourOz*, Snowden J appeared to imply that unless the company is in immediate financial distress, or there are other reasons for urgency, companies should generally give at least four

---

[830] *Practice Statement (Companies: Schemes of Arrangement under Part 26 and Part 26A of the Companies Act 2006)* 26 June 2020 at [6].
[831] Ibid [7].
[832] *Indah Kiat* (n 810) [29].
[833] Ibid [32].

weeks' notice of a convening hearing to scheme creditors.[834] For his part, Zacaroli J has focused on the following factors:

> … the urgency of the case as a result of the financial condition of the Company, not as a result of the delay in the Company getting to the point; the extent to which there has been prior engagement with the creditors; the likely degree of sophistication of the creditors; and the complexity of the scheme and of the issues raised for consideration at the convening hearing.[835]

In *MAB Leasing*, he noted, 'There is no particular time period prescribed, although in many recent cases a period of twenty-one days has been considered sufficient',[836] and around three weeks' notice does appear to have been regarded as acceptable in a number of cases. Where the court is not satisfied that adequate notice has been given, options are available to it besides adjourning the convening hearing. In *ColourOz*, Snowden J gave the scheme creditors liberty to apply to vary or set aside the convening order.[837] In *Swissport Fuelling Ltd*,[838] *Hema*,[839] and *Port Finance Investment*,[840] in contrast, scheme creditors were free to raise any relevant issue at sanction without explaining, where appropriate, why they had not raised it at the convening hearing.

Once again, it is possible to discern a growing preoccupation with the quality of consult- **3.413** ation and disclosure before the scheme is launched. In cases of real urgency, a short period of notice may be possible,[841] although, in this event, it may be that a creditor will be permitted to raise class issues at the sanction hearing. Yet, the court is increasingly likely to look behind the company's claim that the situation is urgent and to demand longer notice where it remains unconvinced.[842] In other words, the company must be able to justify the approach which it has adopted by careful and convincing evidence of the circumstances which it is facing. There is no commoditized answer to questions of how much notice must be given: as with many other aspects of the scheme process, a fact-sensitive approach should be adopted.

The Companies Act 2006 does not provide any guidance on the formulation of classes. **3.414** However, there is an extensive body of case law for guidance. The courts prefer to take a commonsense, practical approach to the classification of creditors; as Neuberger J remarked in *Re Anglo American Insurance*: 'Practical considerations are not irrelevant … if one gets too picky about potential different classes, one could end up with virtually as many classes as there are members of a particular group.'[843] The accepted starting point is that set out in *Re Hawk Insurance Co Ltd*,[844] namely a class 'must be confined to those persons whose

---

[834] *Re ColourOz Investment* (n 792).
[835] *Re ED&F Man Treasury Management plc* [2020] EWHC 2290 (Ch).
[836] *Re MAB Leasing* [2021] EWHC 152 (Ch) [15].
[837] *Re ColourOz Investment* (n 792).
[838] *Re Swissport Fuelling Ltd* [2020] EWHC 1499 (Ch).
[839] *Re Hema* [2020] EWHC 2219 (Ch).
[840] *Re Port Finance Investment* (n 798).
[841] *Re House of Fraser (Funding) Plc* [2018] EWHC 1906 (Ch).
[842] *Re Port Finance Investment* (n 798) [48].
[843] [2001] 1 BCLC 755, 764.
[844] (n 812).

rights are not so dissimilar as to make it impossible for them to consult together with a view to their common interest'.[845] When applying this test, the court held that it is necessary to consider both the rights which are to be released or varied under the proposed scheme, and the new rights (if any) granted under the scheme. In essence, the question is whether the rights of those who are to be affected by the scheme proposed are such that the scheme can be seen as a single arrangement; or whether the scheme ought to be regarded, on a true analysis, as a number of linked arrangements (in which case voting will take place in separate classes). And it is clear from case law that the governing factor in class composition is rights and not interests.[846] Nonetheless, difficult questions can arise.[847]

3.415   When considering the composition of classes, it is necessary to ensure not only that those whose rights really are so dissimilar that they cannot consult together with a view to a common interest should be treated as parties to distinct arrangements, but also that those whose rights are sufficiently similar to the rights of others that they can properly consult together should be required to do so; otherwise, by ordering separate meetings the court gives a veto to a minority group.[848]

3.416   When dealing with a scheme in complex capital structures, the operation of the test frequently results in creditors with differing levels of seniority constituting different classes of creditors. Senior secured creditors might form one class, senior unsecured lenders another class, and mezzanine or subordinated creditors will form a third class. Consider, by way of illustration, the classification of creditors in the *McCarthy and Stone* scheme.[849] The senior term loan holders formed one class of creditors. The senior term loan holders were all secured lenders under term loans. They each held guaranteed liabilities. They shared *pari passu* (by virtue of an inter-creditor agreement) in all realizations and recoveries. Under the proposed schemes they were each to acquire the same rights proportionate to their outstanding loans to the companies. Although there were minor differences in the rates of interest payable under the facilities, the schemes were to proceed by reference to the principal sums outstanding and not by reference to accrued interest. In any event, the judge in that case[850] viewed the interest differences to be so small in the context of the outstanding indebtedness that he took the view that the senior term loan holders could consult together with a view to a consideration of their common interests. The second class was made up of the senior revolving credit facility holders. They all had the same rights in respect of their respective advances to the company in each case and they were all to be treated identically under the scheme. They formed a class separate to the senior term loan holders because under the terms of the security documentation there was a pool of assets over which they had priority as against the senior term loan holders. The third class was that of the hedge counterparties, who had claims of a different nature against the companies. The scheme was not put to the second lien and mezzanine debt holders as they were considered to have no

---

[845] By reference to *Sovereign Life Assurance Company v Dodd* [1892] 2 QB 573.
[846] *UDL Argos Engineering & Heavy Industries & others v Li Oi Lin & others* [2001] HKEC 1440; *Re Hawk Insurance Co Ltd* (n 812) [30].
[847] Chadwick LJ in *Re Hawk Insurance Co Ltd* (n 812) [23].
[848] *Re Hawk Insurance Co Ltd* (n 812) [33].
[849] Discussed in further detail at para 3.450.
[850] *McCarthy & Stone Plc & McCarthy & Stone (Developments) Ltd* [2009] EWHC 712.

economic interest in the group: several valuations showed them to be out of the money. This is an issue we shall return to in a moment.

Where there are differences in, for example, termination dates, repayment, fees, or margin the question will be whether the differences are sufficiently significant to prevent the creditors consulting together as a class. In the *Cortefiel* scheme, both revolving and term facilities received a margin increase but in the case of the revolving facility it was cash pay whereas in the case of the term facility it was rolled up and paid at the end. Norris J was satisfied that the economic effect was the same for all the facilities and so there was no difficulty with the creditors consulting together.[851] In determining whether a separate class is required, the court may proceed by comparing the rights which the creditors would have if the scheme were not to be implemented with the rights which they will have if the scheme is implemented. This approach may create more latitude to disregard differences in interest rates and maturities in class composition where the relevant comparator is insolvent liquidation.

3.417

Thus, in *Apcoa* the differences in termination, repayment, fees, and margin were not such as to prevent them sensibly discussing 'what is best for them in the circumstances which have arisen',[852] and in *Hibu* there were minor differences which were not significant for the purposes of the comparison.[853] In *Stemcor* there were also differences in the guarantees which did not go to the question of class where the creditors were all unsecured and would have the same rights against the company in the event of insolvency.[854] In *House of Fraser* different repayment dates and different interest rates were not sufficient to fracture class where the creditors ranked *pari passu* on insolvency and shared a common security package,[855] and in *Swissport Fuelling* differences between lenders and noteholders as to interest rates and maturity dates did not fracture class,[856] Nonetheless, a company may pragmatically decide to propose separate meetings to avoid debate about the materiality of differences in rights. Thus, in *NN2,* the company proposed separate meetings for certain notes and bonds notwithstanding that both were unsecured claims against the issuer ranking *pari passu* on insolvency.[857]

3.418

Irrevocable undertakings to vote in favour of the proposed scheme are often sought from creditors in advance of the scheme meetings to give the applicant comfort as to the level of support for the proposed scheme. This was done, for example, in each of the *Telewest, Primacom, Countrywide, McCarthy and Stone, Cortefiel, Seat Pagine, Apcoa,* and *Privatbank* schemes.[858] As Lewison J noted in *Re British Aviation Insurance Company Limited*:[859] 'There

3.419

---

851 *Cortefiel, SA v MEP 11.S.a.r.l.* [2012] EWHC 2998 (Ch) [8].

852 *In re APCOA Parking (UK) Ltd and others* [2014] EWHC 997 (Ch) [29].

853 *In the Matter of Hibu Finance (UK) Ltd* [2014] EWHC 370 (Ch) [12].

854 *In the Matters of Stemcor (SEA) PTE Limited, Stemcor Trade Finance Limited* [2014] EWHC 1096 (Ch) [18].

855 *Re House of Fraser (Funding) Plc* (n 841).

856 *In re Swissport Fuelling Ltd* [2020] EWHC 3064 (Ch) [61]–[68].

857 *In the Matter of NN2 Newco Limited v In the matter of Politus BV* [2019] EWHC1917 (Ch) [45].

858 *Re Telewest Communications PLC* [2004] BCC 356; [2004] EWHC 924 (Ch) [52]–[54]; *Primacom Holding GmbH v A Group of the Senior Lenders & Credit Agricole* [2011] EWHC 3746 (Ch) [55]–[57]; *In the Matter of Castle Holdco 4 Limited* [2009] EWHC 3919 (Ch) [29]; *McCarthy & Stone* (n 752) [10]; *Cortefiel, SA v MEP 11.S.a.r.l.* [2012] EWHC 2998 (Ch) [11]; *In the Case of Seat Pagine Gialle Spa* [2012] EWHC 3686 (Ch) [14]–[22]; *In the Matters of Apcoa Parking Holdings GmbH* [2014] EWHC 3849 (Ch) [94]–[106]; *In the matter of Public Joint-Stock Company Commercial Bank 'Privatbank' v In the matter of the Companies Act 2006* [2015] EWHC 3299 (Ch) [25]–[26].

859 [2006] BCC 14 [103].

is nothing inherently objectionable about a company promoting a scheme from reaching agreement with some of its creditors under which they undertake to vote in favour of the scheme.' However, those who have given an irrevocable undertaking will be motivated to comply with their undertaking and, in that sense, it could be argued that there is a difference of rights between them and the other creditors. Most modern cases have arrived at the view that lock-up agreements do not fracture class but may be relevant at the sanctioning stage when the court was exercising its discretion as to whether to sanction the scheme. However, in *Sunbird*,[860] Snowden J was particularly concerned with the question of whether creditors who had locked up had had access to greater levels of information than other creditors.

3.420   Concerns also arise where creditors are to be paid a consent fee in consideration for voting in favour of the scheme. Several authorities suggest that a consent fee will not necessarily result in separate classes provided it is available to all creditors who vote in favour and it is of a sufficiently small size that it is unlikely to be determinative for creditors in deciding how to vote.[861] In *Primacom*, Hildyard J seems to have been particularly concerned to establish the second of these two elements and it is now tolerably clear that, in determining whether a consent fee fractures class, the court will ask both whether the fee was available to all creditors and whether it was sufficiently large that it may have materially influenced the decision of a reasonable creditor as to whether to support the scheme.[862] This then raises the question of how materiality is to be assessed. Snowden J has doubted that it is appropriate 'simply to look at the percentage which the fee bears to the face value of the debt'.[863] Instead, he considered that 'What would seem to be far more relevant is the size of the fee when compared to the predicted returns offered to all creditors under the scheme' and the returns which the creditors are predicted to make in the counterfactual.

3.421   A consent fee may also raise issues of fairness at the sanction hearing. In *Privatbank*, Richards J (as he then was) was content that no issue of unfairness arose because the fee was available to all creditors until a very late stage and there was no material change making the scheme less favourable between the date when the undertaking was given and the date of the scheme meeting. Thus, Richards J did not consider the materiality of the fee. However, he noted that if he had turned his mind to this question, it may have been more appropriate to assess materiality by reference to the price paid for the notes rather than the principal amount outstanding.[864] This observation does not appear to have been repeated in other cases and raises difficult issues, given that holders would not normally reveal the price paid for debt in the secondary market. It may be that Snowden J's suggestion of comparing the fee to the predicted returns provides a more practical way of addressing the problems of judging materiality by reference to nominal amounts.

3.422   The courts have also considered wider categories of fee and the extent to which these may fracture class or, alternatively, raise issues of fairness. In the *Noble Group* scheme, Snowden

[860] *Sunbird* (n 820) [116]–[123].
[861] *In the matter of DX Holdings Ltd and other companies* [2010] EWHC 1513 (Ch) [7] and [8]; *Primacom* (n 858) [56] and [57]; *In the Case of Seat Pagine Gialle Spa* [2012] EWHC 3686 (Ch) [14]–[22].
[862] *Primacom* (n 858) and [2012] EWHC 164 (Ch) [57]; *Re JSC Commercial Co Privatbank* (n 858); *KCA Deutag UK Finance plc* [2020] EWHC 2779 (Ch) [35]–[36]; *Re ColourOz Investment* (n 792) [98]; *Re Port Finance Investment* (n 798).
[863] *Noble* [2018] EWHC 2911 [149]–[151].
[864] *Privatbank* (n 858) [26].

J assessed fees amounting to $80.7 million (plus undisclosed legal fees): RCF waiver fees; a work fee for members of an ad hoc committee of creditors; an interim facility fee; and backstop lender fees.[865] He refused to discount the fees as *de minimis*. Indeed, referring to Nugee J in *Re Codere Finance (UK) Ltd*,[866] and his own judgment in *Global Garden Products*,[867] Snowden J made clear that it was necessary to analyse each fee and, crucially, to provide a 'statement of what, cumulatively, any particular creditor or creditors stands to get out of the scheme or wider restructuring that was different from that available to the general body of creditors'.[868] Where fees were paid in return for financial support, Snowden J's focus was on 'whether the fee includes an element of bounty or is in line with market rates'.[869] Snowden J was content that the work fee and RCF fee did not fracture class as there was a legitimate reason for the fees which were genuinely independent of the scheme: it was important for his conclusion that they were not a 'disguised part of the consideration offered under the scheme and restructuring'.[870] Similarly, the backstop fees did not fracture class as they were not material when assessed in the context of returns from the scheme as a whole and were in line with market underwriting rates. At sanction, Snowden J was content that the fees did not raise issues of fairness. He referred to the approach of Hildyard J in *Re Lehman Brothers International (Europe)(in admin)*[871] in which Hildyard suggested a fee could only give rise to an 'impermissible collateral interest' if it both created an interest adverse to the interests of the class as a whole and could be seen as a sufficiently motivating factor in the decision to vote in favour.[872] The backstop fee was at market rates but, more significantly, the majority of creditors who did not receive it voted in favour or the scheme. This latter point was also crucial to Snowden's conclusion that the total fees did not make the scheme unfair.[873] The reimbursement of creditors' legal fees was examined by Johnson J in *Re Selecta Finance*,[874] and *Re Obrascón Huarte Laín SA*.[875] This did not fracture class, as it did not make the creditors materially better off: they were simply not out of pocket. However, Johnson J underlined the importance of including details of the arrangements in the Practice Letter. In *Swissport Fuelling*, Trower J considered that reimbursement of advisers' fees did not fracture class because: (i) the fees were reimbursable come what may, so that it was difficult to see how the reimbursement obligation could influence the vote; (ii) the fees were reimbursable only to the extent they were reasonably incurred; and (iii) the agreement to reimburse the fees was entered into well in advance of the scheme itself.[876] In *Port Finance*,[877] Snowden J considered at length a success fee payable by the company to a financial adviser for a subgroup of noteholders. He appears to have had two concerns: the impact which the arrangement may have had on equality between noteholders and the effect which the terms may

---

[865] *Noble* (n 863).
[866] (n 797) [4].
[867] At [46]–[48]
[868] *Noble* (n 863) [129].
[869] Ibid [149]–[151].
[870] Ibid [132].
[871] *Re Lehman Brothers International (Europe)(in admin)* [2019] BCC 115.
[872] *Noble* (n 809) [56].
[873] Ibid [69].
[874] *Re Selecta Finance* [2020] 2689 Ch [65]–[67].
[875] *Re Obrascón Huarte Laín SA* [2021] EWHC 859 (Ch) [33].
[876] *Re Swissport* (n 856) [81].
[877] *Re Port Finance Investment* (n 798).

have had on noteholders' willingness to rely on the advice. As to the first, clarifications were made and, as to the second, further evidence was provided.[878]

3.423   Overall, the courts have been at pains in recent cases to note that the payment of fees to certain creditors *may* fracture class *and* may be relevant at sanction in determining whether the majority was representative of creditors as a whole. As a result, the company must observe the requirement for full and frank disclosure of fee arrangements and provide what Snowden J has described as 'absolute transparency and disclosure' to all creditors through the explanatory statement.[879]

3.424   In *Port Finance* the company launched a cash option via reverse Dutch Auction. Snowden J considered that this *could* fracture class because the cash option was required to be exercised two days before the scheme meeting. However, he did not divide the classes for essentially pragmatic reasons, noting:

> the question of who will actually be entitled to benefit, and in what amount, will not be known until the Scheme Company has gone through the exercise of the reverse Dutch auction to identify the Clearing Price and the particular Noteholders who have succeeded in the auction. Given the complexities of the exercise and the manner in which the Existing Notes are held through intermediaries, I do not see how I could define a separate class in a way which was practically workable on the timetable proposed for the Scheme meeting.[880]

Instead, he made clear that creditors could raise any concerns they had with the design of the scheme in this respect at the sanction hearing.

3.425   The *Noble* scheme contained an adjudication process by which the scheme administrators, KPMG, would determine whether to admit scheme claims using the same approach they would adopt in admitting claims in a winding up.[881] An appeals process was provided whereby, ultimately, disputes could be referred to an independent adjudicator. The question of whether this arrangement was sufficient to fracture class arose because the claims of financial creditors were unlikely to be disputed while the claims of certain non-financial creditors included within the scheme were more likely to be disputed. However, in Snowden J's view this was not a question of a difference in rights: all creditors were subject to the same adjudication process. To the extent the practical reality of the process led to differential treatment, the issue was one for fairness at the sanction hearing. The scheme also offered a proportionate right for creditors to participate in a senior, new money facility. In practice, financial creditors were more likely to take up the offer than non-financial creditors. Yet, once again, this was a question going to fairness and did not result in a difference in rights. Nonetheless, it is important to note that Snowden J arrived at this conclusion after some hesitation.[882] His hesitation arose out of a concern that the opportunity to participate in the new money facility was, for some creditors at least, an 'illusion' because of uneven consultation between the company and different groups of creditors. In *Noble*, the company dealt with this concern by extending the timetable for participation. This concern for uneven

---

[878] Ibid [41]–[42].
[879] *Re Port Finance Investment* (n 798) [111].
[880] *Re Port Finance Investment* (n 798) [93].
[881] *Noble* (n 863) [8].
[882] Ibid [107].

consultation has featured in other, recent cases; it is an issue which is actively concerning the courts.[883] Indeed, concern for uneven consultation appears to have been a significant factor in Snowden J's decision to refuse to sanction the first *Sunbird* scheme.[884] Companies proposing schemes should be at pains to spell out how they have consulted creditors and the information which has been provided to creditors ahead of distribution of the explanatory statement. Ideally, of course, all scheme creditors would have access to the same information, and the same rights of consultation, perhaps via a website. Where this is not practical, companies must be ready to explain and justify the approach which has been taken to consultation and disclosure, and to provide evidence as to why no issue of class constitution arises and how the court can get comfortable that the vote at the meeting is representative of the class as a whole.

Increasingly, there are likely to be within one class of creditors some creditors who also belong to another class of creditors or to the body of shareholders of the company. For example, a lender may hold both a senior and mezzanine piece. Creditors with different and potentially conflicting interests arising from circumstances unconnected with their interests as members of the class are not precluded from attending and voting at a meeting of the class. However, whilst their presence does not invalidate the result of the meeting, it may lead the court to decline to sanction the scheme.[885] It was held in *Re Alabama, New Orleans, Texas and Pacific Junction Railway Co*[886] that: **3.426**

> [i]t is perfectly fair for every man to do that which is best for himself, yet the Court, which has to see what is reasonable and just as regards the interest of the whole class, would certainly be very much influenced in its decision, if it turned out that the majority was composed of persons who had not really the interests of that class at stake.

In that case it had been objected that many of those who held first ranking debentures also held second ranking debentures or shares in the company, and that they ought not to have been allowed to vote at the meeting of first ranking debenture holders. The Court of Appeal held that this did not disqualify them from attending and voting at the meeting, but rather went to the discretion of the court to sanction the scheme. This was also the analysis in *Zodiac Pool Solutions SAS*,[887] and, at the time of writing, has been most recently summarized by Snowden J in *ColourOz*.[888] In *Re Heron*,[889] certain noteholders were also bank lenders to the Heron group, and in their capacity as bank lenders, entered into an agreement approving an overall restructuring of the group. Certain noteholders complained that the lenders should not vote at the meeting as they were in receipt of benefits under the restructuring proposals which were not available to all. It was held on the facts of the case that although the bank lenders did enjoy an element of benefit not available to the noteholders, this benefit was not sufficient to destroy the necessary degree of community of interest between the bank lenders and the other noteholders. **3.427**

---

[883] See, for example, *Re New Look Financing plc* (n 805).
[884] *Sunbird* (n 820).
[885] *Re UDL Holdings* [2002] 1 HKC 172 [16]–[20].
[886] [1891] 1 Ch 215.
[887] [2014] EWHC 2365 (Ch).
[888] *In re ColourOz Investment* (n 792) [88].
[889] [1994] 1 BCLC 667.

3.428   Other issues which have not been held to prevent the creditors consulting together as a class but which have been taken into account in determining whether or not the scheme should be sanctioned (in other words, which may affect the creditors' interests but do not affect their rights) include debts which are denominated in different currencies,[890] and arguments that some lenders have advanced funds only for the purposes of the scheme of arrangement or have entered into sub-participation arrangements with respect to their loans with third parties.[891] Governance rights attaching to majority holdings of shares to be issued in the scheme will not give rise to class issues where the governance rights arise as a function of the number of shares held and not any difference in rights as between the same class of shareholders.[892] Similarly, where particular creditors will have rights to nominate directors after the restructuring as a result of the size of their shareholdings, this will not ordinarily fracture class.[893] Certain schemes have contained provisions addressing the circumstances in which creditors are prevented from giving confirmations required by US securities laws or EU legislation in order to receive securities to be issued in the scheme. In these circumstances, the securities may be transferred to a holding trust and, after a period, sold with the proceeds being distributed to the relevant creditor. These arrangements will not generally fracture class.[894]

2. Convening and holding scheme meetings

3.429   Once the court has concluded that the scheme classes are properly constituted, the scheme proposal must be put to a meeting, or meetings, of creditors and voted on. An explanatory statement must be circulated to the members or creditors affected by the scheme, together with the scheme document. The explanatory statement must contain all the information necessary to enable such members or creditors to form a reasonable judgment on whether the scheme is in their interests or not and, therefore, how to vote.[895] It must also contain a statement of directors' interests.[896] It is not the role of the court at the convening hearing to approve the draft explanatory statement, although it may decline to convene scheme meetings until manifest deficiencies which are drawn to its attention are corrected.[897] At the meeting(s), the scheme would need to be approved by the relevant majority of each relevant class being a (i) majority in number; (ii) representing 75 per cent in value of those persons present and voting (in person or by proxy) in each relevant class of creditors.

3.430   The ability to amend the explanatory statement and the scheme document after the leave to convene hearing may be limited and so it is essential that the terms are thoroughly reviewed before launch. Nonetheless, it is wise to include an express right to modify the scheme which is drawn to creditors' attention in case the need should arise. In the *Co-operative Bank* scheme Hildyard J was asked to approve a modification to the scheme and it was

---

[890]   *Re Telewest Communications plc (No 2)* [2004] EWHC 1466 (Ch).
[891]   *Zodiac Pool Solutions SAS* (n 888) [19]–[20].
[892]   *Re Hibu Group Ltd* [2016] EWHC 1921 (Ch) [56]; *Re New Look Financing plc* (n 805) [40]; *Re Swissport* (n 856) [70]
[893]   *Re Stemcor* [2016] BCC 194 [21]–[22]; Re *PizzaExpress Financing 2 Ltd* [2020] EWHC 2873 (Ch) [44]; *Re Swissport* (n 856) [71].
[894]   *Re Lecta Paper UK Ltd* [2019] EWHC 3615 (Ch) [19]; *Re Swissport* (n 856) [82]–[83].
[895]   *Re Dorman Long & Co Limited* [1934] Ch 635, 657; *Re Heron* (n 889) 672.
[896]   Companies Act 2006, s 897(2)(b). For a case in which this was not done, see *Sunbird* (n 820).
[897]   Indah Kiat (n 810) [41]–[42].

important for his analysis that the account holder letter contained a provision which cross-referred to termination provisions in the lock-up agreement and which made clear that one possibility was that the scheme would be withdrawn or withdrawn and a new scheme on materially different terms proposed.[898] The ability to amend the scheme was also important in *Gategroup*.[899] In that case, a question arose as to whether further mechanics were needed in the scheme of arrangement to release third party rights in order to secure foreign recognition. It was important that if these mechanics did turn out to be needed, the scheme expressly contained a right for the company:

> to consent on behalf of all Plan Creditors to any modification of, or addition to, the Plan which the Court may think fit to impose and which is necessary for the purpose of implementing the Transaction, including those of a technical or administrative nature, which could not reasonably be expected directly or indirectly to have a material effect on the interests of any Plan Creditor.

The modification fell within this category and thus, if it did turn out to be necessary to bolster the mechanics for the release, this was possible within the terms of the scheme. It is worth noting that *Gategroup* involved a new Part 26A restructuring plan but, on this point, the analysis is the same for a Part 26 scheme of arrangement. In *Re Aon plc*,[900] a members' scheme, Trower J considered whether a modification would have caused a reasonable shareholder to take a different view in relation to the scheme if it had been put before them, alert to the note of caution in *Equitable Life* that 'it would be quite wrong to use the provision so as to foist on a class of creditors something substantially different to what has been approved at the relevant meeting'.[901] This approach was adopted by Miles J in the PGS scheme.[902] In the *Sunbird* scheme Snowden J helpfully considered it possible to update or supplement an explanatory statement after it has been circulated, but creditors must then have the amount of notice ordered in the convening hearings before the meetings in which to consider the new information, or further directions sought.[903]

During the COVID-19 pandemic, questions have arisen as to the ability to hold scheme meetings remotely. This was considered and approved in *Re Castle Trust plc*.[904] However, the judgment suggests that approval of remote meetings may be limited to exceptional circumstances such as the COVID-19 lockdown measures.   **3.431**

3. Sanction hearing

If approved at the meeting(s) there must be a further application to court to obtain the court's sanction to the arrangement. If the scheme is sanctioned by the court, a copy of the court order is delivered to the Registrar of Companies for registration, at which point the scheme of arrangement becomes effective. The sanctioning of the scheme by the court is no mere rubber stamping exercise—it is a genuine exercise of discretion. The court must   **3.432**

---

[898] *Co-operative Bank plc* [2013] EWHC 4072 (Ch) and *In the Matter of the Co-Operative Bank plc v In the Matter of the Companies Act 2006* [2013] EWHC 4074 (Ch).

[899] *In the matter of Gategroup Guarantee Limited* (n 802).

[900] *Re Aon plc* [2020] EWHC 1003 (Ch) [16]–[18].

[901] *Re Equitable Life Assurance Society* [2002] BCC 319 [102].

[902] *Re PGS ASA* [2021] EWHC 222 (Ch) [34]–[37].

[903] *Sunbird* (n 820).

[904] [2020] EWHC 969 (Ch).

be satisfied that:[905] (i) the provisions of the Companies Act 2006 and all other procedural requirements have been complied with; (ii) the class was fairly represented by those who attended the meeting and the majority are acting bona fide in supporting the scheme and not coercing the minority in order to promote interests adverse to those of the class whom they purport to represent; (iii) the scheme is such as an intelligent and honest man, who is a member of the class concerned and acting alone in respect of his interest as such member, might reasonably approve it; and (iv) there is no 'blot' or defect on the scheme. Thus, at sanction the court will consider whether any of the differences of interest, as opposed to rights, described above (such as the existence of lock-up arrangements, consent fees, cross holdings, currency differences, or sub-participation arrangements) mean that the court should decline to exercise its discretion to sanction. The position on sanction is nicely summarized by Hildyard J in *Primacom*, 'At the fairness hearing, the question whether any group of creditors even in properly constituted classes have been unfairly coerced by the majority within their class in terms of having been corralled by people whose rights appear similar but whose objectives and interests were poles apart will be taken into account at the hearing'.[906]

3.433   The court will recognize Lindley LJ's comment in *English, Scottish and Australian Chartered Bank* that:

> if the creditors are acting on sufficient information and with time to consider what they are about, and are acting honestly, they are, I apprehend, much better judges of what is to their commercial advantage than the court can be.[907]

Nonetheless, in determining whether the scheme is one which 'an intelligent and honest man, who is a member of the class concerned and acting alone in respect of his interest as such member might reasonably approve' the English courts will pay attention to the alternative to the scheme, particularly in the event of a challenge. In several recent cases the courts have emphasized the need for sufficient evidence supporting this counterfactual analysis. In *Re Van Gansewinkel Groep BV* Snowden J observed:

> I would, however, indicate for the future that companies that seek the consent of their creditors and the sanction of the court to a scheme of arrangement that is put forward as a more advantageous outcome for creditors than formal insolvency proceedings may be well advised to ensure that greater detail is provided, both in the explanatory statement and in the evidence before the court, as to the possible alternatives to the scheme and the basis for the predicted outcomes. The provision of such information is likely to be essential if there is a challenge to the scheme.[908]

Snowden J has subsequently found the evidence as to the counterfactual to be inadequate in *Indah Kiat*[909] and in the first attempt to sanction a scheme of arrangement for *Sunbird Business Services Ltd*.[910] And in *ALL Scheme*, Miles J refused sanction of a scheme proposed

---

905 *Re National Bank Ltd* [1966] 1 WLR 819; *Re Telewest Communications plc (No 2)* [2005] BCLC 36 [20]–[22]; *Noble* (n 807) [17].
906 *Primacom* (n 858) [57].
907 *Re English, Scottish and Australian Chartered Bank* [1893] 3 Ch 385.
908 [2015] EWHC 2151 (Ch); [2016] BCC 172 [24].
909 *Indah Kiat* (n 810).
910 *Sunbird* (n 820) is a comparatively rare example of a case where the court declined sanction, although the company went on to propose a second scheme on near identical terms which was sanction [2020] EWHC 3459 (Ch).

by a subprime lender group, following intervention by their regulator (the Financial Conduct Authority) in part because he considered that the company had provided insufficient evidence to support their claim that the alternative to the scheme was an insolvency proceeding.[911] A specific issue has arisen where expert evidence on the counterfactual has been provided on a non-reliance basis. In *House of Fraser* Briss J found that the court could not place any reliance on such evidence.[912] In order to solve this problem the expert, KPMG, agreed to extend reliance to the company solely for the purposes of advancing the scheme. Briss J was then satisfied that the company could put the evidence before the court and the court could rely on it. In *Sunbird*, the company had commissioned an independent review of its valuation methodology but on terms which prevented it from revealing the identity of the independent reviewer or the nature and precise outcome of their review.[913] In Snowden J's view, as a minimum the company should have been able to notify creditors that the third party accepted no responsibility to them, even to the extent of withholding its identity.

The courts are also likely to have regard to turnout at the scheme meetings, as low turnout may suggest equally low engagement with creditors—leading to the concern that the vote at the meeting cannot be taken to have been representative of the class.[914] The court should be provided with the chairperson's report of the meetings and, where turnout was low, this should be explained. In *Gategroup*, low turnout was explained by the fact that the relevant bonds were predominantly held by retail investors.[915] The court was satisfied that the vote was representative of the class, particularly in light of the extensive efforts the company had made to engage with bondholders. For similar reasons, the court will be keen to establish whether those voting in favour of the scheme were connected with the company, so that they may have had a collateral interest motivating their decision to support the scheme.[916] The important point is that the court may consider points beyond the statutory requirements in assessing fairness of the scheme and the decision to sanction. Thus, although there is no statutory requirement to discount the votes of connected parties in a scheme of arrangement, the court may be concerned if a significant proportion of creditors voting in favour of the scheme are connected with the company. Overall, the company should ensure that the chairperson's report of the meeting is sufficiently detailed so that the court can assess this type of issue, and that where concerns are foreseeable, they are explained, and evidence is provided for the explanation. **3.434**

The court must also consider whether there is a 'blot' or other defect on the scheme. Undisclosed side deals with creditors to motivate voting are likely to form just one such 'blot' and the company should seek to reassure the court that no such inducement was offered or provided, particularly where a creditor or class of creditor appears to have had a change of heart.[917] Similarly, elements of artificiality in the structure of the scheme may require explanation and evidence.[918] In the *Gategroup* judgment, Zacaroli J was content **3.435**

---

[911] *In the matter of ALL Scheme Limited* [2021] EWHC 1401 (Ch).
[912] *Re House of Fraser (Funding) Plc* (n 841).
[913] *Sunbird* (n 820) [87]–[89].
[914] *In the matter of Gategroup Guarantee Ltd* (n 490) [9].
[915] Ibid [9]–[10].
[916] *Sunbird* (n 820).
[917] *Privatbank* (n 858) [24].
[918] *Gategroup Guarantee Ltd* (n 490).

that an artificial co-obligor structure did not constitute such a blot, inter alia because the restructuring benefited all affected creditors and the alternative would be a value destructive liquidation.[919] However, it is worth noting that the artificial structure was adopted in the *Gategroup* scheme to prevent cross-defaults arising in operating contracts.[920] Notably, there is no specific discussion in the judgment of the impact of the artificial structure on these parties and whether they ought to have been free to exercise contractual termination rights arising as a result of the scheme. In *Swissport Fuelling*,[921] a similar structure was used, apparently to avoid obtaining a waiver from the holders of certain notes which would otherwise have been required. In the *Steinhoff* scheme, a creditor, whose rights were not affected by the scheme, appeared at sanction to object on the basis that the company proposed to pay monies in respect of a disputed claim to another creditor, which the objecting creditor argued separate litigation would reveal ought to be paid to it. The objecting creditor argued that this amounted to a 'blot on the scheme'.[922] Johnson J was unpersuaded: if it subsequently transpired that the monies ought to be paid to the objecting creditor, then the payment to the other creditor would not have discharged the company's liability. This perhaps contrasts with the position in *Gategroup*, where creditors were deprived of the opportunity to exercise termination rights through the artificial structure.

3.436   Difficult questions can arise at sanction if the scheme of arrangement is subject to a condition which is yet to be satisfied. In this case, the starting point is found in Henderson J's judgment in *Lombard Technologies*:

> I can see no reason in principle ... why the court may not in an appropriate case sanction a scheme where there is an outstanding condition which still needs to be satisfied and direct that the order should not be sealed (or, as in the present case, that the order should not be delivered to the Registrar) until the condition has been satisfied.[923]

However, Henderson J did not consider this an acceptable way forward where the outstanding condition confers on a third party the right to decide whether or when the scheme should come into operation, or which enables the scheme to be varied in some material respect. Trower followed this in initially declining to sanction the plan in *Smile Telecoms Holdings Limited*.[924] It is not always easy to connect these cases and those in which the scheme of arrangement is conditional on a wider restructuring taking effect. In *New Look Financing*, Zacaroli J was willing to sanction a scheme of arrangement which required that all the steps in the wider restructuring took place on the same day, including a CVA which was, itself, conditional on no challenge having been raised, in circumstances where there was an outstanding challenge.[925] A similar approach was adopted by Norris J in *PizzaExpress*.[926] Furthermore, while courts used to require the scheme order to remain unsealed or undelivered until chapter 15 recognition had been obtained in the US, where that

---

[919]   Ibid [12]–[22].
[920]   *In the matter of Gategroup Guarantee Ltd* (n 490) [19].
[921]   *Re Swissport* (n 856) [89].
[922]   *In the matter of Steinhoff International Holdings NV* [2021] EWHC 184 (Ch) [75].
[923]   *Re Lombard Technologies Plc* [2014] EWHC 2457 (Ch) [24]–[26].
[924]   [2021] EWHC 685 (Ch)–a Part 26A restructuring plan but applicable to Part 26 schemes of arrangement on this point.
[925]   *Re New Look Financing plc* (n 805).
[926]   *Re PizzaExpress Financing 2* (n 893).

was a condition to the scheme, this no longer appears to be the court's practice provided expert evidence is provided as to the likelihood of recognition.

As discussed above, at the sanction hearing it is open to disenfranchised creditors who were left outside the scheme to argue that the scheme is unfair because they have an economic interest in the company and, therefore, ought to be included within it. For a discussion of the ability of disenfranchised junior creditors to argue that they have an economic interest in the company and should be offered something within the scheme, see section XII below. **3.437**

It is possible for a scheme of arrangement to sanction what would otherwise amount to an unlawful return of capital or unlawful financial assistance, although it is important that it is drawn to the attention of the court at the sanction hearing.[927] **3.438**

In the *MAB Leasing* sanction hearing, Snowden J raised the question of whether a scheme could be an 'insolvency-related event' for the purposes of the Protocol to the Cape Town Convention on Matters Specific to Aircraft Equipment.[928] The point is of significance because the Protocol offers alternative consequences for an insolvency-related event and the UK has implemented Alternative A, which has the result that no obligation of the debtor under an agreement which falls within the Cape Town Convention can be modified without the consent of the creditor.[929] On the facts of the case Snowden J did not need to decide the point and so left it open for another day. It is worth noting that at the convening hearing in *MAB Leasing*, while similarly leaving the point open, Zacaroli J suggested that there were 'powerful arguments' that the scheme was not an insolvency-related event for the purposes of the Cape Town Convention.[930] Some commentators have supported this analysis, drawing a potential distinction between Part 26 schemes of arrangement and Part 26A restructuring plans, but others disagree.[931] **3.439**

A further issue which arose in the *MAB Leasing* case is whether the court is deprived of its jurisdiction where 100 per cent of creditors agree to the scheme. The point arose specifically because Snowden J had commented, in *Re Virgin Airways Limited*,[932] that 'it is not normal practice to include classes in a Part 26 scheme where 100% of the relevant creditors are known to be willing to consent'. However, in *MAB Leasing* he explained that the case was not the type of case he had in mind when making those comments, because in *MAB Leasing* it was not known until shortly before sanction that 100 per cent of creditors agreed. In this context he drew on the conclusions of Zacaroli J in *Dundee Pikco* that the requirement for creditor approval at scheme meetings is a minimum jurisdictional requirement and that, **3.440**

---

[927] *Barclays Bank plc v British and Commonwealth Holdings plc* [1996] 1 BCLC 1.

[928] *Re MAB Leasing Ltd* [2021] EWHC 379 (Ch).

[929] Regulation 37 of the International Interests in Aircraft Equipment (Cape Town Convention) Regulations 2015 (SI/ 2015/912).

[930] *Re MAB* (n 928).

[931] See, e.g., Barry Cosgrove, 'Airline Restructurings Under UK Schemes of Arrangement and Restructuring Plans' (Mayer Brown, February 2021) available at: <https://www.mayerbrown.com/en/perspectives-events/publications/2021/02/airline-restructurings-under-uk-schemes-of-arrangement-and-restructuring-plans> (last accessed 16 April 2021). But see also Louise Gullifer and Riz Mokal, 'UK Restructuring Plan and Scheme of Arrangement Proceedings Expert Opinion on Status Under the Cape Town Convention' available at: <http://awg.aero/wp-content/uploads/2021/04/CTC-status-of-RPs-and-Schemes-Expert-Report-Revised-29-Apr-2021.pdf> (last accessed 24 August 2021).

[932] [2020] EWHC 2376 (Ch); Kenneth Gray, 'Schemes of Arrangement and the Cape Town Convention' (Norton Rose Fulbright, February 2021) available at: <https://www.nortonrosefulbright.com/en-gb/knowledge/publications/dc0c0c34/schemes-of-arrangement-and-the-cape-town-convention> (last accessed 16 April 2021).

provided there is sufficient practical purpose in having a scheme, the court could consider whether to exercise its discretion in favour of sanction.[933] Thus, it appears that Snowden J's comments in *Virgin* may relate to efforts to construct classes for the purposes of engaging cross-class cramdown powers in Part 26A restructuring plan proposals and we will return to this below.

3.441 Once the scheme has been sanctioned by the court and registered, sections 899(3) and (4) of the Companies Act 2006 provide that the arrangements are binding on all persons affected by them, whether those persons voted in favour or not (even if they did not have notice of the meeting).

XII. 'Twinning' a Scheme of Arrangement with a Pre-Packaged Administration Sale

A. Introduction

3.442 Cramdown within schemes of arrangement is limited to the statutory majorities in each separate class cramming down the minorities within their own class—it is not possible for senior classes to cram down classes of junior creditors who have voted against the scheme (so-called cross-class cramdown). As we shall see, CIGA has introduced a new procedure offering the possibility of cross-class cramdown. Yet, before CIGA, the market had developed a 'workaround' to deal with the lack of a cross-class cramdown mechanic in schemes of arrangement. That workaround is covered here, first, because it has played an important part in the development of the new procedure and, second, because there may be circumstances in which it still remains the preferred option.

3.443 The workaround is to 'twin' the scheme of arrangement with a pre-packaged administration. The scheme is employed to novate all or a substantial amount of the debt owed to senior secured creditors to a newly incorporated company ('newco'). In this structure, the scheme is used to deal with the fact that the senior lenders may not, themselves, agree on how the restructuring ought to be implemented, particularly where there is a level of equitization or other reduction in senior debt which some lenders may find unacceptable, where some senior lenders are also holders of significant amounts of junior debt and are unhappy with the fate of the junior tranche, or where senior lenders consider that junior debtholders or shareholders are retaining too great an interest in the company. Once the scheme has been sanctioned, all or part of the company's assets and business are sold to newco via the pre-packaged administration sale, leaving the debt owed to junior creditors 'stranded' in the original company.

3.444 As discussed earlier, it is technically not necessary to call a meeting of junior creditors if their rights are unaffected by the scheme of arrangement and if assets can be transferred outside the scheme (although junior creditors will be able to appear at the sanction hearing to argue that the scheme is unfair because they have been left outside it). Advantages of such a structure include the transfer of the business and assets to a new company (which is clean

---

[933] *Re Dundee Pikco Limited* [2020] EWHC 1059 (Ch) [2]–[5].

of any prior trading and liabilities); avoiding the need to buy off 'crammed down' parties unjustifiably in cases where they are out of the money but might have 'nuisance value'; and circumventing the requirement for unanimous senior lender consent where it would otherwise be required, for example to effect a debt write-down of senior debt.

The terms of any existing inter-creditor agreement (ranking the senior and junior debt,   **3.445**
guarantees, and security inter se) will be critical to the ability to implement a transaction of this type. Senior creditors need the ability to bypass the junior creditors and dispose of the main operating companies free from junior borrowing and guarantee liabilities. If, under the terms of the inter-creditor agreement, the senior creditors have the ability to direct the security trustee on the enforcement of security and the release of existing guarantees and security in an enforcement or default context to allow assets to be sold free of existing security to newco then it is likely that, through a pre-pack, an administrator can transfer the assets underpinning the scheme and the security trustee can release the existing guarantees and security (which would also extend to supporting the junior debt).

In the *European Directories* case the Court of Appeal adopted a commercial and purposive   **3.446**
approach to drafting in the inter-creditor agreement which, on a strict reading, appeared not to extend to the release of obligations and security provided by the subsidiaries of the company whose shares were being transferred.[934] In *Stabilus* the court also adopted a commercial approach in interpreting the provisions of the inter-creditor agreement relating to consideration to include non-cash consideration.[935] In the *ATU* case detailed structure steps were implemented as a first stage in which a company was incorporated in England as a subsidiary of the main (German) operating entity in the group and then acceded to the inter-creditor agreement as an obligor. The company subsequently acquired the shares of one of the holding companies within the group, thus 'flipping' up the group structure. The proposed pre-pack involved a sale by the company of the shares in this holding company and it was proposed that the security trustee release the obligations of, and security provided by, the other entities within the group which would be effectively transferred. The security trustee was willing to do this in principle but required some comfort from the court before it would do so. Time did not permit definitive resolution of certain issues of construction. Instead, an application was made to court to appoint an administrator and the construction arguments were dealt with by the judge in that context. The judge found that the terms of the inter-creditor agreement allowed the security trustee to execute the releases.[936]

Notwithstanding the significant assistance lent by the courts, one of the most important   **3.447**
lessons of the 2008 financial crisis for English companies implementing a debt restructuring was the critical importance of the rights for the security agent to release security and guarantees in the inter-creditor agreement. As well as the reported cases, there was anecdotal evidence of other cases where narrowly framed inter-creditor provisions posed a real obstacle to the debt restructuring. As a result, the loan market association inter-creditor terms now provide very powerful rights for the security trustee to release security, release borrowing, guarantee and other claims on the sale of the shares in the main operating

---

[934] *Barclays Bank plc and Others v HHY Luxembourg SARL and Another* [2010] EWCA Civ 1248.
[935] *Saltri III Limited v MD Mezzanine SA Sicar (t/a Mezzanine Facility Agent)* [2012] EWHC 3025 [22] ('*Stabilus*').
[936] *Re Christophorus 3 Limited* [2014] EWHC 1162.

companies, and to dispose of lender or bondholder debt claims or transfer or novate intra group debt claims on a distressed disposal. But at the same time, junior creditors and equity have learnt lessons too. As we will see, the critical importance of valuation methodology has also become apparent and bondholders have sought to strengthen the conditions on which a release may be given, sometimes expressly mandating that consideration must be in cash, restricting the ability for a purchaser or its affiliates to assume secured claims, requiring that value is tested by public auction or supported by a fair value opinion from an investment bank, and requiring proceeds to be applied in accordance with a post-enforcement waterfall. Many of these new protections may give rise to new questions of interpretation. Furthermore, the *Stabilus* case emphasizes the importance of the security agent's duties to creditors and in certain circumstances these may have an impact notwithstanding the contractual provisions. It is unlikely, therefore, that all the challenges with the key provisions of the inter-creditor agreement have been solved.

B. The Courts' Approach

3.448   The structure of a scheme of arrangement followed by sale was first threatened in the *MyTravel* restructuring. MyTravel was a charter holiday business, heavily dependent on the operating licence granted to it by the Civil Aviation Authority. The business was adversely affected by a number of factors, not least 9/11, the SARS epidemic, the Iraq situation, and even the weather. The group had an unsupportable amount of debt: by March 2004 it had consolidated net liabilities of some £877.6 million. Efforts at a consensual deal failed, with the bondholders objecting to the equity allocation offered to them. Ultimately, the company proposed a scheme to its senior creditors but not its subordinated bondholders, pursuant to which, after restructuring the senior debt, the business and assets of MyTravel would be sold to a newco owned by its senior lenders leaving its junior creditors behind with effectively worthless claims against the legacy company. The alternative was liquidation under which bondholders would receive nothing. The subordinated bondholders challenged this structure at first instance and in the Court of Appeal.

3.449   A significant proportion of the High Court judgment[937] related to whether the scheme was a reconstruction scheme under section 427 of the Companies Act 1985. The judge held that it was not but, mindful of the accelerated timetable (the company was at risk of having its CAA licence revoked) and the risk of appeal, commented on the position of the bondholders. Given the judge's decision on section 427, the issue of whether the bondholders had an economic interest was strictly *obiter*. The company argued that as the alternative to the scheme was liquidation, where the assets would be insufficient to discharge even the unsubordinated creditors, the bondholders had no economic interest in the company. The judge concluded that insolvent liquidation was the appropriate comparison and concluded that the economic interest of the bondholders in the company was nil as there was no serious prospect that they would receive anything on a liquidation. The question was ultimately settled by the Court of Appeal[938] which held that it was not necessary to put a scheme

---

[937]   *MyTravel Group plc* [2004] EWHC 2741 (Ch).
[938]   *MyTravel Group plc* [2004] EWCA Civ 1734.

of arrangement to every class of a company's creditors if their rights were not affected by the scheme, and that the judge did not need to determine the question of whether the bondholders had an economic interest at the 'permission to convene' hearing. As such, at the initial court hearing the subordinated bondholders could not object to the convening of the class meetings. It may have been that they would subsequently have been able to raise challenges to the fairness of the scheme at the sanction hearing or have been able to challenge (as a transaction at an undervalue) the price at which the sale of the business and assets was concluded, but none of this was a relevant issue at the initial stages. In the event, the threat of the implementation of this structure caused the subordinated bondholders to agree to a consensual restructuring (and a much lower equity allocation than they had initially sought) outside a scheme of arrangement meaning that the scheme did not need to proceed.

The structure adopted in *MyTravel* was a variation on that used in *Re Tea Corporation*.[939] In   **3.450** that case, a scheme was proposed in a liquidation whereby the ordinary shareholders were to be given shares in a new company in place of their existing shares. The shareholders as a class voted against the scheme; the other stakeholders voted for it. As we have seen, under English law there is no inherent jurisdiction for the court to sanction a scheme which has been voted down by a class of creditors. In *Re Tea Corporation*, however, the court held that the shareholders' dissent could be disregarded when sanctioning the scheme as the financial state of the company was such that the ordinary shareholders had no economic interest in the company's assets. Two of the judges based their reasoning on treating the scheme as only an arrangement as between the company, the creditors, and the preference shareholders such that the new shares offered to the ordinary shareholders were in the nature of a gift, leaving the shareholders no avenue of complaint. According to the third judge, 'if you have the assent to the scheme of all those classes who have an interest in the matter, you ought not consider the votes of those classes who have really no interest at all'.

Re McCarthy and Stone plc[940] (a distressed company the business of which is the develop-   **3.451** ment of retirement homes), adopted a very similar 'cramdown' structure to that proposed in *MyTravel*, which completed in April 2009. McCarthy and Stone proposed a scheme of arrangement only to its senior debt, leaving its junior creditors to receive nothing, the justification being that multiple valuations demonstrated that the second lien and mezzanine lenders were out of the money. Once the scheme of arrangement had been approved, the company was placed into administration purely for the purposes of selling its business and assets to a newly incorporated company owned by the senior lenders. This left the mezzanine lenders and second lien lenders (valued at around £110 million and £40 million respectively) behind in the old rump, their debt claims being worthless. Objections to this structure were raised at the first court hearing (in relation to the constitution of classes) but, following the Court of Appeal in *MyTravel*, Norris J held that the purpose of that hearing was only to approve the convening of the class meetings; it was not a forum to address legal challenges or lender discontent.[941] Ultimately, the lenders did not choose to mount a challenge at the final sanction hearing.

---

[939] *Re Tea Corporation* [1904] 1 Ch 12, CA.
[940] [2009] EWHC 1116.
[941] [2009] EWHC 712.

3.452 It is notable that in *MyTravel* it was proposed that the subsequent sale was to be completed by the directors, whilst in *McCarthy and Stone* it was to be completed by an administrator. There are several reasons for this shift. First, it is likely that management is to have a stake in the new company, and a sale by the administrator avoids some of the issues of self-dealing and conflict of interest which would otherwise arise.[942] Secondly, an administrator cannot enter into a transaction at an undervalue[943] or a preference[944] and so the sale transaction will be seen as more robust. Thirdly, the directors avoid claims for breach of duty arising from the sale (including allegations of conflict of interest where they are to acquire equity in the new company). This issue was commented on by Mann J in *Re Bluebrook*,[945] who queried why it was that the directors proposed to implement the sale via a pre-packaged administration. Ultimately, however, nothing appears to have turned on the point.

C. Valuation

3.453 The fundamental issue in these cases is what method of valuation is appropriate to determine whether a class of creditors has a continuing economic interest. The English courts have traditionally adopted an approach we shall call the 'counterfactual' analysis. This approach holds that it is necessary to focus on what will happen if the scheme is not sanctioned. If the company is running out of cash, such that the directors can show that without the scheme they will have no choice but to place the company in administration, or there has been an event of default entitling the requisite majority of senior lenders to accelerate and take enforcement action, this approach focuses on the position of the various creditors at that point. In this sense, it is similar to the 'best interests' test in chapter 11, although ordinarily (unless there is a special factor such as a regulatory licence requirement) focused on a going concern value in current market conditions. However, whereas in the chapter 11 context this test is combined with other standards, in the English context many would argue that *only* the counterfactual analysis ought to be relevant. Proponents of this view argue that once there has been a 'crystallizing event' only current value should be taken into account. To do otherwise is to enfranchise those who ought properly not to be enfranchised.

3.454 The next question is how the amount which would be recovered in the counterfactual approach is established. In England market price is frequently established via an auction process in which, for a period normally ranging from six to eight weeks, the business is marketed.[946] Bids received in that process can then be used as evidence of the price which would be achieved if the business were to be sold to a third party instead of restructured. However, the concern arises that the auction process may undervalue the business. Very often the auction process will be taking place at a time when the market is generally depressed. This may mean that there is a lack of availability of credit so that potential bidders are unable to participate because they cannot raise financing for a bid. Other likely buyers

---

[942] Gavin Lightman and Gabriel Moss, *The Law of Administrators and Receivers of Companies* (6th edn, 2017).

[943] Insolvency Act 1986, s 238.

[944] Ibid, s 239.

[945] [2010] BCC 209 [7], 'The evidence when it came before me was somewhat coy as to the reason why the administrator, rather than the various boards of directors, were effecting the transfer'.

[946] Although it is not always necessary to run a marketing process if the evidence shows that the financial position of the company is such that it cannot sustain it see, eg, *Saltri III Limited* (n 935) [202]–[205].

may include competitors but if the market is generally depressed or the particular sector is depressed those bidders are likely to be preserving any cash which they have rather than launching on the acquisition trail. It is also possible that potential bidders will not be willing to commit time or money to the auction if they suspect that it is not a genuine process but rather merely a benchmarking exercise for the purposes of a debt restructuring. The sales contract itself is likely to include little or no warranty or indemnity protection. As such, it is not on the usual terms for an arm's length sale of the business and so will result in a depressed price. The comparatively rapid and certain timetable for the bid may also have an effect on price.

As a result of these concerns, US courts do not adopt a strict market price approach in chapter 11. Instead, investment bankers or financial advisers are retained to value the business using classic valuation techniques including comparable transaction pricing, discounted cash flow (DCF), and comparable companies analysis. This can lead to lengthy, complex, unpredictable, and costly valuation disputes between valuation experts for different classes of creditors or equity holders before the bankruptcy court. But the shadow of this dispute can itself incentivize the parties to reach a consensual solution. As a result, this approach is referred to in the US literature as the 'bargaining and litigation' approach.[947]   **3.455**

Questions of valuation are far less developed in English jurisprudence as compared to under chapter 11. Prior to the judgment in *Bluebrook Ltd* (commonly known as *IMO Carwash*),[948] there had been little direction from the English courts on the valuation standard to be used in valuation disputes and there is no guidance on how to approach the question in statute. Both the *Tea Corporation* and *MyTravel* cases involved unique sets of circumstances. Tea Corporation was already in liquidation, and for MyTravel the withdrawal of the Civil Aviation Authority licence would inevitably have resulted in liquidation. Consequently, a liquidation valuation was used in both cases. The *McCarthy and Stone* case offered a more 'typical' set of circumstances but the mezzanine creditors in that case ultimately chose not to mount a challenge at the sanction hearing.   **3.456**

Valuation was central to the submissions of the junior creditors in the *IMO Carwash* case. The business and assets of the existing group were to be transferred to a new group via a pre-packaged administration sale. A large portion of senior debt (approximately £185 million) was to be novated to the new group, with the remainder being exchanged by the senior lenders for the bulk of the equity in the new holdco (subject to a small interest in favour of management). The old group was to be released from the debt (other than £12 million which was to remain in the existing group in case some asset unforeseeably came in). It was necessary to implement the proposal via schemes of arrangement not to transfer the assets (which, although conditional on the schemes being sanctioned, was taking effect outside of the schemes), but rather to effect the release of the senior debt in the absence of all senior lender consent (a small percentage of the senior lenders were not in favour). The mezzanine lenders were to be left behind in the old rump group with worthless claims, the justification for this being that multiple valuation exercises indicated that the value broke well into the   **3.457**

---

[947] Lucian Ayre Bebchuk and Jesse M Fried, 'A New Approach to Valuing Secured Claims in Bankruptcy' (2001) 114 *Harvard Law Review* 2386, 2393.
[948] *Bluebrook* (n 786).

senior debt. As the mezzanine lenders were not party to the schemes, they were not summoned to vote at any class meeting. The mezzanine lenders challenged the schemes on the grounds of fairness. Their two main arguments (although not their only ones) centred on valuation and directors' duties.

3.458   The senior lenders had commissioned three valuation exercises. A valuation by the administrators in waiting valued the group using an income approach (based on discounted cash flow adjusted, by an alpha factor, for current market conditions), a market approach based on comparables, and a leveraged buyout analysis (assessing the level of equity investment a private equity investor would be prepared to make in the current market given a typical required equity rate of return). The maximum valuation was £265 million. Concurrently, a leading investment bank conducted a third-party sales process with a view to establishing whether a buyer for the existing group could be found. The sales process produced only one indicative offer which placed a value on the group of £150 million to £188 million on a cash and debt-free basis. (This was not considered by the board to be an appropriate level of interest to pursue.) A further exercise by property valuers valued a number of the group's sites, from which an overall value was extrapolated. This produced a valuation of £164 million on a swift sales basis and £208 million on a full market value basis. Each of the three valuations indicated that the value of the group fell significantly short of the £313 million of senior debt outstanding. Furthermore, the senior debt was trading in the secondary market significantly below par, at about 60 pence in the pound.

3.459   The mezzanine lenders, in contrast, relied on a report from a leading consulting firm to argue that the value of the group broke in the mezzanine debt. The report used a 'Monte Carlo simulation' to assess on a statistical basis the most likely valuation outcomes given a variety of inputs. It involved repeated calculation of a discounted cash flow valuation, using random sampling of input and assumptions, and then aggregated the result into a distribution of the probabilities of different valuation outcomes. The result indicated a range of £210 million to £700 million (as opposed to a single point valuation), with a significant majority of outcomes exceeding £320 million.

3.460   Mann J found the mezzanine's valuation 'unconvincing' and insufficiently robust. By giving more weight to the valuation reports prepared by the scheme companies, which were done on a present market value basis, and less weight to the mezzanine lenders' report which sought to demonstrate the 'intrinsic value' of the business, the court appeared to accept on the facts of the case that the appropriate benchmark for valuation is the present market value basis. Nonetheless, Mann J did 'pause for thought' over the question of whether the deal was too rich for the senior lenders.[949] In this context, he emphasized that even when the alpha factor was extracted from the senior lenders' DCF valuation (i.e. the adjustment for market conditions was removed) the mezzanine lenders were still shown to be out of the money. Furthermore, Mann J found the Monte Carlo simulation too mechanistic and devoid of any judgment and was critical of the late stage at which the mezzanine lenders had presented their valuation evidence.

---

[949] Ibid [49].

Given that Mann did 'pause for thought' over whether the auction approach was sufficient   **3.461**
to answer the charge that the senior lenders were receiving too good a deal,[950] and given
that the approach to questions of valuation in chapter 11 is now considerably better understood in the UK market, it is now perhaps unlikely that senior lenders would seek to rely
only on evidence from a market testing process.[951] However, this still leaves the question
of whether valuation should be conducted on a present market basis. And even if no discount is included to bring the valuation into line with current market conditions, there are
still challenges with seeking to establish the value of a business at a low point in the credit
cycle. For example, any discounted cash flow analysis will rely on a weighted average cost of
capital (WACC) and this may be high if there is a lack of credit in the economy.[952] Perhaps
even more fundamentally, the discounted cash flow will be based on an underlying business plan making projections for the business. Key questions will arise such as the nature of
the case advanced by the business plan[953] and how far into the future the directors should
speculate.[954] Classically, junior lenders will argue that as economic conditions improve the
business will see a rapid improvement in its fortunes and that if these were better reflected
in the company's projections a higher valuation would be achieved. In *Stabilus*, Eder J
strongly suggested that the valuation could be based only on the information available at the
time.[955] But the challenge with this approach is aptly illustrated by the account in Howard
and Hedger about what happened next:

> There has been a significant recovery in the business during the period since April 2010
> when the restructuring was completed. During the downturn EBITDA deteriorated to less
> than €30m per annum but according to the company is expected to recover to €75m for
> 2014/15. In addition the owners of the business were able to procure a refinancing of the
> restructured debt with a new senior secured note issue of €315m which refinanced €242m
> of debt and funded a distribution to shareholders of €81m and a distribution to holders of
> profit participating instruments of €12m.[956]

The real attraction of comparables pricing is that it avoids reliance on projected cash flows.   **3.462**
In comparables pricing, the valuation of the company is arrived at by a comparison with
other companies in the same sector or geography or which are 'comparable' for some other
reason. However, there is a good deal of subjectivity here and the question of whether there
is a genuinely comparable company or transaction can be a controversial one. Private equity
or leveraged buy-out valuations look instead at the amount a private equity firm might be
expected to pay having regard to assumptions about the rate of return it would require from

---

[950] Ibid [49].

[951] See, e.g., the subsequent *Stabilus* case—notwithstanding that in that process the marketing process was
somewhat stale and that the case concerned enforcement and sale by a security trustee introducing different questions of fiduciary duty and conflict of interest.

[952] In *Stabilus* the advisers for the mezzanine lenders used a WACC of 7.73 per cent compared with 11.9 per cent
used by the senior lenders, see (n 935) [68].

[953] Howard and Hedger (n 38) suggest that each of the valuation methodologies is applied to four cases downside, base, upside, and sensitized.

[954] A key point of dispute in the *Stabilus* case where the mezzanine lenders argued that management should have
looked further into the future where they would have identified possibilities for the company to grow back into its
capital structure.

[955] *Stabilus* (n 935) [157]–[163].

[956] Howard and Hedger (n 38) para 6.50, 306.

its investment. But these valuations are highly susceptible to debt financing capacity in the market. In *Stabilus* some considerable attention was paid to the discounted price at which the senior debt was trading in the market,[957] but this should be treated with great caution as there may be many extraneous reasons for the trading price of the debt. In short, each of the main valuation methodologies suffers from some disadvantage and none is immune from charges of subjectivity.

3.463 The challenges with both the auction approach and the bargaining and litigation approach have led some US scholars to suggest a different approach known as the options approach.[958] The options approach reflects the idea that a junior creditor or shareholder who is out of the money based on current valuations still has 'option' value equivalent to an option to acquire the entire firm at a value equal to all the senior claims ranking ahead of it. In other words, the junior creditors or equity will receive a return if it turns out to be possible to sell the company, list the shares, etc, at a price greater than the senior claims and some value attaches to this interest. The options approach enables junior stakeholders to argue for an option or warrant-like instrument which preserves what may admittedly be 'hope' value. One of the challenges, however, is that agreeing the terms of this warrant or option may be costly and time-consuming, reducing overall recovery where the prospect of junior or equity recovery is slight. The ABI Commission to Study Reform of Chapter 11 takes a different approach. It proposes a new concept of 'redemption option value (ROV)'. Having fixed the broad parameters against which the option would be *hyopthetically* issued,[959] it suggests that the option is then valued using traditional option pricing methodology.[960] If that pricing exercise determines that an option on the appropriate terms would have real value in the market, then the junior creditor receives whatever consideration the parties may agree in the restructuring including debt, equity, or cash. However, if the option pricing exercise indicates that the option would have no value, the junior creditor or shareholder receives nothing.

3.464 The ABI Commission concept of redemption option value is interesting in that it avoids the need to enter into costly negotiations over the terms of an option or warrant which may in fact have no real value and it is possible that junior creditors and shareholders will start to include options pricing methodology in their valuation evidence. The question, however, is whether the ROV introduces yet another layer of complexity and another area for dispute. It remains necessary to agree the enterprise value of the company in order to decide who is 'in the money' and who is 'out of the money' and therefore only entitled to option value. It then introduces a new layer of complexity in applying options pricing methodology to a distressed company—for example, picking the volatility rate. As the ABI have themselves

---

[957] *Stabilus* (n 935) [66], [73]–[78], [98], and [208].

[958] Lucian Bebchuk, 'A New Approach to Corporate Reorganizations' (1988) 101 *Harvard Law Review* 775; Philippe Aghion, Oliver Hart and John Moore, 'The Economics of Bankruptcy Reform' (1992) 8 *Journal of Law, Economics & Organization* 523; Oliver Hart, *Firms, Contracts and Financial Structure* (Oxford University Press, 1995); Lucian Bebchuk, 'Using Options to Divide Value in Corporate Bankruptcy' (2000) 44 *European Economic Review* 829.

[959] Very broadly, and without doing justice to the proposal, a redemption period of three years and a strike price equal to the claims ranking ahead of the option holder—see ABI Commission to Study Reform of Chapter 11 2012-2014 Final Report and Recommendations at 207–224.

[960] Building on the seminal work of Black and Scholes (Fischer Black and Myron Scholes, 'The Pricing of Options and Corporate Liabilities' (1973) 81 *Journal of Political Economy* 637), although the report admits that the proposal around redemption option value is only a first step, requires further development and may admit of the use of other options pricing methodology in certain circumstances including, notably, Monte Carlo methodology.

admitted, it is, therefore, an idea which will require more development in the market be-fore its utility can be properly tested, although in appropriate cases an option structure may prove the basis for agreement. Interestingly, in proposing the redemption option value con-cept, the ABI report makes very little of the question of whether senior creditors should re-cover only their original investment before the option holder makes a recovery or whether some risk premium should attach to the different credit risk of the company.[961]

As we shall see next, valuation disputes are perhaps more likely to arise in the context of Part 26A restructuring plans, and the development of valuation approaches to date is likely to be influential in that context. Specifically, we will suggest that the framing of the Part 26A restructuring plan leans firmly towards establishing value based on current market prices in prevailing market conditions. The benefit of an auction process, supported by a market valuation which takes account of current market conditions and is based only on informa-tion available at the time, is that it is the most objective of the various options and leaves least room for debate. It may result in allocative 'unfairness' in that it may result in some financial creditors receiving what might be objectively regarded as 'too good a deal' if the business recovers very quickly but as the route with the least scope for serious dispute it is also likely to minimize transaction costs and maximize the chances of an efficient outcome. Reasons for concern about allocative fairness in the past might be thought not to apply, for example, once the distribution is amongst financial creditors only.[962] This may be what has influenced the legislature in apparently preferring to avoid lengthy, costly valuation dis-putes in developing the Part 26A restructuring plan procedure. **3.465**

A further reason which has been advanced for preferring current market price in prevailing market conditions is that in general the junior creditors will have the right to buy out the se-nior creditors if they really believe in the value recovery story. Mann J put some weight be-hind this in *IMO Carwash* and the junior creditors exercised the right in the restructuring of Meridien Hotels.[963] But Eder J doubted that this point won the day in *Stabilus*, given the constrained liquidity environment in which the transaction occurred, and it is respectively submitted that this point alone cannot be a sound footing on which to build the English re-sponse to the problem. **3.466**

For the duties of the directors during the debt restructuring negotiations see Chapter 1. **3.467**

D. Pre-Packaged Administration and Section 363 Sales

It will be seen, from the descriptions of the *McCarthy and Stone* and *IMO Carwash* cases, that the scheme of arrangement has been used to implement the new capital structure in the senior debt rather than to compromise the junior debt. It is the 'pre-packaged' transfer of the assets to the newly capitalized group which effectively removes the junior debt. **3.468**

---

[961] ABI Commission Report (n 959) where only a passing reference is made in footnote 768 on p 210.
[962] For a sustained argument along these lines see Sarah Paterson, *Corporate Reorganization Law and Forces of Change* (Oxford University Press 2020).
[963] Howard and Hedger (n 38) 258.

3.469   The pre-packaged sale may not, however, always be coupled with a scheme of arrangement. WIND Hellas[964] is the second largest mobile and fixed-line telephony operator in Greece. Pre-restructuring it was owned indirectly by Weather Investments Limited, and it had a comprehensive financing package, including bank loans and senior notes in the operating group below WIND Hellas, and subordinated notes at the parent finance company level (Hellas Telecommunications (Luxembourg) II SCA).

3.470   Hellas II launched a competitive sale process for its assets, principally the shares in the main operating company and its subsidiaries. Two final bids were received: one from Weather Investments and one from a group of holders of subordinated notes. However, both bids assumed that a significant amount of senior debt would remain in place, and both required various consents from the senior lenders. Ultimately, the senior creditors supported the Weather bid over the subordinated noteholder bid. An administration order was made on 26 November 2009 and the sale of the assets of Hellas II was concluded on 27 November 2009.

3.471   The administrator needs to be satisfied that it is not practicable to achieve the rescue of the company as a going concern before effecting a pre-packaged sale.[965] The administrator's obligation is then to obtain the best price reasonably obtainable for the business and assets which are to be sold. In this context the focus is therefore very much on current value and, if there are similarities between the use of a scheme coupled with a pre-pack and a chapter 11 plan, there are also similarities between implementation solely through a pre-packaged administration and implementation via a section 363 sale. In this case, as in a section 363 sale, in order to preserve value the junior creditors (and, indeed, equity) may have to join in the bidding. Where the senior creditors are not prepared to support the bid, either because they prefer another bid or because they wish to take control themselves, the junior creditors may need to refinance the senior debt in order to maintain their interest. We should also remember that the new pre-packaged administration regulations may apply to a financial restructuring.[966]

XIII.   English Part 26A Restructuring Plans and Corporate Debt Restructurings

A.   Introduction

3.472   As we have seen, the Corporate Governance and Insolvency Act 2020 ushered in significant reforms to English corporate insolvency law. One of the most significant reforms was the introduction of a new restructuring plan procedure into Part 26A of the Companies Act 2006, closely modelled on the scheme of arrangement but with four significant differences.[967] These differences are:

---

[964]   *Hellas Telecommunications* (n 766).
[965]   Insolvency Act 1986, sch B1, para 3.
[966]   The Administration (Restrictions on Disposal etc to Connected Persons) Regulations 2021 SI 2021/427
[967]   CIGA, Sch 9, inserting new Part 26A into the Companies Act 2006. Henceforth, all references will be to the relevant sections of Part 26A.

(i) Specific eligibility requirements for a company to be able to take advantage of the Part 26A restructuring plan procedure.[968]

(ii) Express provision for who must be permitted to participate in a class meeting.[969]

(iv) A new voting threshold.[970]

(v) Provision for cross-class cramdown.[971]

The new Part 26A restructuring plan procedure follows that of the Part 26 scheme of ar-   **3.473**
rangement which we have already analysed in section XI above: a practice letter must be sent notifying creditors of the leave to convene hearing;[972] a hearing is held after notice has been given (usually at least 21–28 days unless the case is especially urgent) at which the court decides whether to convene meetings of creditors to vote on the plan;[973] assuming the court does convene the meetings, the meetings are held; and, if the statutory majorities are achieved at the meetings, or the company wishes to engage the cross-class cramdown provisions, a sanction hearing is held at which the court must decide whether to sanction the plan.[974] The Explanatory Notes which accompany the Corporate Insolvency and Governance Act specifically provide:

> While there are some differences between the new Part 26A and existing Part 26 (for example the ability to bind dissenting classes of creditors and members), the overall commonality between the two Parts is expected to enable the courts to draw on the existing body of Part 26 case law where appropriate.[975]

In this section, we will therefore focus on the four significant differences between the new   **3.474**
Part 26A restructuring plan procedure and the Part 26 scheme of arrangement. We will also draw out some other areas where there are early indications, in the emerging case law, that the court will not necessarily apply the same analysis to an issue under Part 26A as it has under Part 26. As Snowden J put it in the convening hearing for *Virgin Active*:

> it should be appreciated that a rigid application of the approach under Part 26 may not always be appropriate in the different context of a Part 26A plan. Under Part 26, the force of the procedure to bind dissentient creditors derives from their inclusion within a class where a majority votes in favour of the scheme. By contrast, in a Part 26A plan, the power to bind dissentient creditors may also derive from the court's cram down power under section 901G.[976]

Thus, while the court is likely to draw extensively on Part 26 case law in the areas of similarity between Part 26 and Part 26A, a different approach may also be warranted because of the different context. In Part 26 the court's inquiry focuses on whether there are reasons to doubt the motivation underpinning the majority vote. However, in a Part 26A plan,

---

[968] Companies Act 2006, Part 26A, s 901A.
[969] Ibid, s 901C.
[970] Ibid, s 901F.
[971] Ibid, s 901G.
[972] *Practice Statement (Schemes of Arrangement)* (n 830) para 7.
[973] Companies Act 2006, Part 26A, s 901C.
[974] Ibid, s 901F.
[975] Explanatory Notes to CIGA, para 16.
[976] *Re Virgin Active Holdings Limited, Virgin Active Limited, Virgin Active Health Clubs Limited* [2021] EWHC 814 (Ch) [62].

where the cross-class cramdown power is engaged, the court does not have a vote in favour by a statutory majority to guide it. As we shall see, this different context may result in a different approach, even where the Part 26 and Part 26A procedures appear substantially equivalent.

B. Threshold Conditions

3.475   The first significant difference between Part 26 and Part 26A is that Part 26A sets out two specific eligibility requirements which a company must meet to be able to take advantage of the Part 26A restructuring plan procedure. Condition A is that 'the company has encountered, or is likely to encounter, financial difficulties that are affecting, or will or may affect, its ability to carry on business as a going concern'.[977] Condition B is that:

> (a) a compromise or arrangement is proposed between the company and
>   (i) its creditors, or any class of them, or
>   (ii) its members, or any class of them, and
> (b) the purpose of the compromise or arrangement is to eliminate, reduce or prevent, or mitigate the effect of, any of the financial difficulties ... in [Condition A].[978]

Paragraph 6c of the Practice Statement provides that the ability of the company to meet these two conditions is to be considered at the convening hearing.[979] Paragraph 10 provides that shareholders and/or creditors may still raise objections based on the Conditions at sanction but, 'the court will expect them to show good reason why they did not raise the issue at an earlier stage'. In *Virgin Atlantic*, Trower J was of the view that the requirement, in a Part 26 scheme of arrangement, for there to be some element of 'give and take' applied to the first part of Condition B.[980] This point has been reiterated in a number of subsequent cases.[981] We shall return to this when we consider the ability to leave creditors out of the plan who have no genuine economic interest in the company.

3.476   In *DeepOcean* a question arose as to whether a restructuring plan designed to implement a more orderly wind down of a business, with a slightly enhanced dividend, met the requirements of Condition B that 'the purpose of the compromise or arrangement is to eliminate, reduce or prevent, or mitigate the effect of, any of the financial difficulties ... in [Condition A]'.[982] Trower J held that it did, stating:

> I can see no reason why a compromise or arrangement which provides for a slightly enhanced dividend on ... claims should not be treated as mitigating the effect of ...

---

[977] Companies Act 2006, Part 26A, s 901A(2).
[978] Ibid, 901(3).
[979] *Practice Statement (Schemes of Arrangement)* (n 830) para 6(c).
[980] *Virgin Atlantic Airways Limited* [2020] EWHC 2191 (Ch) [38].
[981] *Re PizzaExpress Financing 2 Ltd* [2020] EWHC 2873 (Ch); *Re DeepOcean 1 UK Limited* [2020] EWHC 3549 (Ch) [43].
[982] Ibid. *DeepOcean* [44]–[49].

financial difficulties, irrespective of whether or not there is any intention for the company to continue carrying on business as a going concern.[983]

A further, interesting question arose in the *Gategroup* convening hearing.[984] In that case, Counsel attempted to persuade the court that the effect of the Conditions was that a company could only propose a restructuring plan when the directors' duty to take account of the interests of creditors was engaged: at the time of the hearing, according to the Court of Appeal's decision in *Sequana*, when the directors know or should know that the company is or is likely to become insolvent.[985] The *Sequana* decision was discussed at length in Chapter 1, and readers are directed to that discussion for more detail on the implications of this argument. In *Gategroup*, Zacaroli J did not need to decide the point but he did comment: **3.477**

> I consider it doubtful that Parliament intended to equate the test within Conditions A and B with the duty at common law to take account of the interests of creditors (preserved by section 172(3) of the 2006 Act).[986]

It is suggested that this must be right: the alternative approach would seem to place an unjustifiable gloss on the statutory drafting. Nonetheless, we cannot rule out that there may be cases where the court is not content that the threshold tests have been met, and that the company is resorting to the restructuring plan opportunistically to shed liabilities which it can afford for the benefit of its other stakeholders. In October 2020, the Irish court refused New Look's application to appoint an examiner on the basis that New Look would not be unable to pay its debts until the early part of 2021 and that it was seeking to use examinership as an alternative to meaningfully engaging with the creditors it wished to compromise.[987] The author has also made the point, elsewhere, that courts will need to be mindful that companies do not turn to the Part 26A restructuring plan procedure as an alternative to bargaining.[988] In other words, courts will need to be mindful that companies are justified in using the powerful jurisdiction of Part 26A by their financial condition. Thus, notwithstanding the current direction of travel in the case law, we cannot rule out serious debate as to whether the threshold conditions have been met. As we shall see shortly, this issue effectively arose in the Part 26A restructuring plan proposed for *Hurricane Energy*.[989] In that case, the company argued that if the plan were not sanctioned it would face either an uncontrolled liquidation or a controlled wind down,[990] and proposed a plan in which the shareholders would be heavily diluted by a debt-for-equity swap. The shareholders objected to the financial information provided by the company. Nonetheless, Zacaroli J was content that the threshold conditions A and B were satisfied.[991] Instead, the focus of his attention was on the company's contention that insolvency would follow failure to sanction the scheme.[992] It may be, therefore, that courts will treat Conditions A and B as a relatively low

---

[983] Ibid [48].
[984] *Re Gategroup Guarantee Limited* (n 490).
[985] *BTI 2014 LLC v Sequana S.A.* [2019] EWCA Civ 112.
[986] *Gategroup* (n 490) [117].
[987] Steen (n 704).
[988] Paterson (n 962) 185–186.
[989] *In the matter of Hurricane Energy Plc* [2021] EWHC 1418 (Ch).
[990] Ibid [18].
[991] Ibid [24].
[992] *In the matter of Hurricane Energy Plc* [2021] EWHC 1759 (Ch).

hurdle, but will be alert to the company's claims as to what will happen if the restructuring plan is not sanctioned where the company is at a relatively early stage of what Irit Mevorach and Adrian Walters have called the 'demise curve'.[993]

C. Who Must Participate

3.478   As we have already seen, a company is free to decide who it includes within a scheme of arrangement. As Mann J put it in Bluebrook:

> in promoting and entering a scheme, it is not necessary for the company to consult any class of creditors (or contributories) who are not affected, either because their rights are untouched or because they have no economic interest in the company.[994]

As we have also seen, a creditor who is left out of the scheme is free to appear at sanction to argue that the scheme is unfair because it ought to have been granted rights in it. However, as the Court of Appeal made clear in *MyTravel*,[995] in a Part 26 scheme of arrangement this is a question for sanction. At the convening hearing the court determines only whether the classes which the company is proposing are correctly constituted.

3.479   Section 901C produces a different result for Part 26A restructuring plans. First, section 901C(3) expressly states that:

> Every creditor or member of the company whose rights are affected by the compromise or arrangement must be permitted to participate in a meeting ordered to be summoned under subsection (1).[996]

The first question is what is meant by 'affected' in this context. In *Hurricane Energy*, the proposed restructuring plan involved a debt-for-equity swap by the company's bond-holders, diluting existing shareholders to 5 per cent of their current value.[997] Moreover, by virtue of sections 549 (1) and 561(1) of the Companies Act 2006, the existing shareholders' pre-emption rights and rights to approve allotments of shares were both overridden. The company appeared at the leave to convene hearing to argue that this did not 'affect' the shareholders' rights, so that they could be left out of the vote. First, the company argued that dilution did not 'affect' the shareholders' rights. Secondly, it argued that it was statute, and not the restructuring plan, which affected the rights of pre-emption and approval. Zacaroli J disagreed with both arguments. He read 'affected' more broadly and he considered that the disapplication of pre-emption rights and approval rights was only engaged because of the plan. Thus, *Hurricane Energy* suggests a wider reading of 'affected' than impairing a creditor's legal rights.

The only exception to the requirement for all affected creditors and members to vote is **3.480** offered by section 901C(4), which provides that subsection (3) does not apply in relation to a class of creditors or members of the company if, on an application under the subsection, the court is satisfied that none of the members of that class has a genuine economic interest in the company. The 901C application is the application to convene meetings to vote on the plan. Thus, if a company wishes to exclude a class of creditor from the vote on the basis that they have 'no genuine economic interest in the company' this becomes a question for the leave to convene hearing.

The first important observation about this development is that it will potentially require **3.481** valuation evidence to be adduced at the leave to convene hearing, which has typically eschewed detailed consideration of evidence of this type. No definition of 'genuine economic interest' is offered, but it seems likely it was inspired by the comments of Mann J in *MyTravel*,[998] at first instance, and as follows in *Bluebrook*:

> the court is entitled to ascertain whether a purported class actually has an economic interest in a real, as opposed to a theoretical or merely fanciful, sense, and act accordingly ... Where things have to be proved, the normal civil standard applies. ... the mere fact that the possibility of establishing a negotiating position and extracting a benefit from a deal is not the same as having a real economic interest (though obversely a real economic interest may establish, or enhance, a negotiating position). The basis on which the assessment of that interest is to be carried out will vary from case to case.[999]

So far so good, but it is difficult to set subsection 901C in the context of the rest of section 901. As we shall see later in section XIII.E, the new cross-class cramdown power in section 901G engages centrally with what the dissenting class would receive in 'the relevant alternative' which is defined as 'whatever the court considers would be most likely to occur in relation to the company if the compromise or arrangement were not sanctioned'.[1000] As we shall see, in section 901G a distinction is drawn between a person 'who would receive a payment ... in the event of the relevant alternative' and a person who would 'have a genuine economic interest in the company' in the event of the relevant alternative.[1001] This suggests a distinction between receiving a payment in the relevant alternative and whether the enterprise value implied in the relevant alternative would suggest that the relevant class was 'in the money'. Section 901C does not refer to the relevant alternative at all.

Nonetheless, the approach which Mann J adopted to this question in *MyTravel Group plc*, **3.482** and which he referred to in *Bluebrook*, was essentially the exercise of establishing whether the relevant class of creditor would receive a payment in the relevant alternative to the scheme of arrangement. As he put it in *MyTravel*, the company:

> did not envisage consultation with the bondholders because the company came to the view that the bondholders had no economic interest in the company; the only alternative to the scheme was a liquidation and in a liquidation their subordinated status and the deficiency of the assets meant that they had no prospect at all of recovering any of the sums due under

[998] *Re MyTravel Group plc* (n 937).
[999] *Bluebrook* (n 786) [25].
[1000] Companies Act 2006, Part 26A, s 901G(4).
[1001] Ibid, s 901G(5).

the bonds. The factual question of whether that assessment is right is the factual question which lies at the heart of this aspect of the case.[1002]

In the sanction hearing for *Virgin Active*, Snowden J considered it, 'tolerably clear that this test of "genuine economic interest" reflects the observations of Mann J in Bluebrook ... and that it is to be applied to the plan company by reference to the relevant alternative for the company if the plan is not sanctioned'. Thus, notwithstanding that section 901C(4) does not refer explicitly to the 'the relevant alternative', Snowden J's (strictly *obiter*) comments suggest a company wishing to leave an affected class out of the vote would need to show, at the convening hearing, that the relevant class would not have a genuine economic interest in the event of the relevant alternative. It is suggested here that, in most cases, this will be the right approach. However, we discuss below limited circumstances in which another comparator may be more appropriate than the relevant alternative. We suggest here that the drafting in section 901C leaves open the possibility of establishing whether a creditor or member has a genuine economic interest by reference to that alternative comparator in relevant cases. The reader will find further detail on when that alternative comparator may apply when we discuss the cross-class cramdown power.

3.483   This is not, however, the only difficulty with section 901C. It is also not entirely clear what can be achieved in the restructuring plan if a class is excluded pursuant to section 901C(4). As we have seen, the *MyTravel* and *Bluebrook* cases were both cases in which a Part 26 scheme of arrangement was 'twinned' with a sale transaction to 'strand' the out of the money class (see section XII). As a result, the scheme did not purport to impair the creditors' legal rights at all. However, in many cases the debtor is likely to wish to cancel or vary the out of the money creditors' claim in the Part 26A restructuring plan. Thus, the question arises as to whether, if a class is excluded from the vote pursuant to section 901C(4) on the basis that it has 'no genuine economic interest' in the company, its rights can nonetheless be cancelled or varied in the plan.

3.484   The dominant view among practitioners, and in the emerging case law, appears to be that rights can be varied. In *DeepOcean* Trower J made the following, *obiter*, remarks:

> where the evidence is that the members of the dissenting class are out of the money in the relevant alternative, and that their exclusion would in any event have been achievable if a Part 26 scheme had been proposed, it seems to me that their receipt of any benefits under the terms of the proposed Restructuring Plan means that they are unlikely to have been treated in a manner that is not just and equitable.[1003]

In *Virgin Active*, having found the compromised landlords to be 'out of the money' in the event of the relevant alternative, Snowden J expressly stated that it would have been possible to implement the plan via section 901C rather than the cross-class cramdown powers in 901G—notwithstanding that the plan heavily amended the dissenting landlords' leasehold rights.[1004] Nonetheless, the legislative drafting is tortious. Court sanction is dealt with in section 901F. The difficulty is that sub-section 901F(1) provides:

[1002] *MyTravel* (n 937) [35].
[1003] *DeepOcean I UK Limited* [2021] EWHC 138 (Ch) [51].
[1004] *Virgin Active* [2021] EWHC 1246 (Ch) [312].

If a number representing 75% in value of the creditors or class of creditors or members or class of members (as the case may be), present and voting either in person or by proxy at the meeting summoned under section 901C, agree a compromise or arrangement, the court may, on an application under this section, sanction the compromise or arrangement.[1005]

Sub-section 2 tells us, explicitly, that this is subject to section 901G (the cross-class cramdown power) but does not mention the power to exclude a class of creditors from the vote pursuant to section 901C(4). The difficulty then arises in sub-section 901F(5), which provides that the compromise or arrangement is binding on 'all creditors or on the members or class of members (as the case may be)'.[1006] This would appear to refer back to the classes of creditors or members in section 901F(1), stated to be subject to exercise of the cross-class cramdown power but not section 901C. It is something of a muddle and two possible legislative interpretations are discernible. The first is to say that the intention is for the company to be able to vary the creditor's rights without giving them an opportunity to vote, and to bind the creditor to that result through the section 901C procedure. Certainly, the ability to offer an out of the money class nothing under the plan and to cancel or vary their rights within it would make the most commercial logic for the debtor company, although it would be a quite exorbitant jurisdiction at the leave to convene hearing if it meant that the excluded creditor could not appear at sanction to object when more detailed evidence is likely to be available. Indeed, it appears to undermine the characterization of the convening hearing which Richards J (as he then was) made in *Telewest* and which other judges have frequently referred to:

> This is an application by the companies for leave to convene meetings to consider the schemes. It is emphatically not a hearing to consider the merits and fairness of the scheme.[1007]

Alternatively, the section might have been intended to provide simply that the excluded class cannot complain that they are not being invited to vote on the plan but that the plan cannot cancel or vary their rights: that must be achieved in a different way, either by utilizing the cross-class cramdown mechanism in section 901G or twinning the restructuring plan with a sale transaction.

Overall, it is tentatively suggested that section 901C enables the company to offer nothing to a class under the plan if it can show that the class has no genuine economic interest in the event of the relevant alternative. This means that, where the relevant alternative is an insolvency sale of the business as a going concern, the question is whether the creditor would receive a payment or retain a claim in the event of the relevant alternative, subject to a limited ability to consider another comparator which we discuss in more detail below. However, in order to vary (in the sense of amend or alter) the creditor's rights under the plan, it is necessary to proceed via section 901G. It must be said, however, that the position is far from clear. **3.485**

A further difficulty arises in relation to cancellation. As we saw above, the courts have stated a number of times, in the early Part 26A restructuring plan cases, that a restructuring plan, **3.486**

[1005] Companies Act 2006, Part 26A, s 901F(1).
[1006] Ibid, s 901F(5).
[1007] *Re Telewest Communications plc* (n 858) [14].

like a scheme of arrangement, must provide some element of 'give or take'.[1008] This would appear to suggest that it is not possible to have a Part 26A restructuring plan which offers a wholly out of the money class nothing, but cancels its rights. If this is correct, then an out of the money class must always be offered a 'tip' under a restructuring plan, even if section 901C is engaged. This contrasts with the position in chapter 11. In chapter 11 a class which is offered nothing under the plan is deemed to reject it but can appear at the confirmation hearing to object. Crucially, the effect of confirmation is dealt with by statute which provides that, 'Except as otherwise provided ... in the plan, or in the order confirming the plan, the confirmation of a plan (A) discharges the debtor from any debt that arose before the date of such confirmation'.[1009] In England, in contrast, the effect of the plan depends on what the plan provides—and what it *can* provide is, in part, a question of statutory interpretation. Once again, the position is unclear.

3.487 Overall, then, section 901C appears fraught with difficulties and, at the time of writing, no Part 26A restructuring plan has attempted to engage with all aspects of it. At the same time, there may be advantages for the debtor company in establishing the 'no genuine economic interest' argument at the convening hearing, and the threat to do so may provide useful ammunition in restructuring negotiations. We will need to wait for a brave navigator to chart a path through these somewhat choppy waters.

D. The Vote

3.488 The third important distinction between a Part 26 scheme of arrangement and a Part 26A restructuring plan is the voting threshold. As we have seen, in a Part 26 scheme of arrangement this is a majority in number and 75 per cent in value of the creditors or members or class of creditors or members present and voting at the scheme meeting. However, the Part 26A restructuring plan procedure drops the requirement for a majority in number. This means that the particular issues with the bondholder vote discussed in the Part 26 scheme of arrangement context do not arise here.

E. The Cross-Class Cramdown Power

3.489 The most significant innovation introduced in the new Part 26A restructuring plan procedure is the ability to impose a plan on an entirely dissenting class. This power is provided by section 901G.[1010] In order to impose the plan on the dissenting class two conditions must be met: Conditions A and B.

3.490 Condition A is that the court is satisfied that, if the compromise or arrangement were to be sanctioned, none of the members of the dissenting class would be any worse off than they would be in the event of the relevant alternative.[1011] And, as we have already noted, the

---

[1008] See (n 980) and (n 981) with accompanying text.
[1009] 11 USC § 1141.
[1010] Companies Act 2006, Part 26A, s 901G.
[1011] Ibid, s 901G(3).

'relevant alternative' is 'whatever the court considers would be most likely to occur in relation to the company if the compromise or arrangement were not sanctioned under section 901F'.[1012]

Condition B is that the statutory majority has been achieved in at least one class 'who would receive a payment, or have a genuine economic interest in the company, in the event of the relevant alternative'.[1013] In the language of the market, at least one in the money class must have supported the plan. As Gerard McCormack has highlighted, the concern is that a vote by an out of the money class does not tell us very much about the reasonableness of the plan because the class would be expected to vote in favour of the plan if they stood to make no recovery in the alternative.[1014]   **3.491**

Even if the statutory requirements are met, the court still has a discretion to decline to sanction the plan. This is made clear in the Explanatory Notes which accompany the provisions, which state: **3.492**

> Drawing on well-established principles in schemes of arrangement, the court has absolute discretion over whether to refuse to sanction a plan even though the necessary procedural requirements have been met. This may be, for example, because a plan is not just and equitable.[1015]

No guidance is given on when a plan is 'just and equitable': the only hint is that the court is 'drawing on well-established principles in schemes of arrangement'. Yet, as we shall see, the context in which the court is asked to exercise its cross-class cramdown power is quite different from the context in a scheme of arrangement.

The first issue which section 901G demands to be tackled is whether the dissenting class would be better off in the 'relevant alternative'. Thus, the first question is what that relevant alternative would be. Guidance is to be found here in the approach in Part 26 scheme of arrangement cases. First, the courts have considered what the alternative to the scheme would be in determining class composition.[1016] Specifically, where the courts have determined that the alternative to the scheme would be an insolvent winding up, they have held that the rights to be compared in determining whether creditors can vote together are the rights to which they would be entitled in a winding up and the rights to which they are entitled under the scheme. Secondly, they have considered the alternative to the scheme in deciding whether creditors ought to have been consulted on the scheme. Thus, although Mann J erroneously tackled the question at the leave to convene hearing in *MyTravel*,[1017] in *MyTravel* he accepted the argument that the bondholders did not need to be consulted, even though their rights were affected by the wider arrangement of which the scheme formed part, because the only alternative to the scheme was a liquidation in which they stood no prospect of making any recovery. And, of course, the courts consider what the alternative is to a CVA in an unfair prejudice challenge. As Norris J put it in *Debenhams*:   **3.493**

[1012] Ibid, s 901G(4).
[1013] Ibid, s 901G(5).
[1014] Gerard McCormack, *The European Restructuring Directive* (Edward Elgar 2021) 186
[1015] Explanatory Notes to the CIGA 2020 para 190.
[1016] *Re Telewest Communications plc* (n 858) 351; *Re the British Aviation Insurance Co Ltd* [2006] BCC 14 [82] and [88]; and *Re ColourOz Investment* (n 792) [74].
[1017] *Re MyTravel Group plc* (n 937). The Court of Appeal determined that this was a question for sanction.

The authorities identify two useful heuristics for assessing whether a CVA is 'unfairly prejudicial' under s 6(1)(a). The first is commonly called 'the vertical comparator'. It compares
the projected outcome of the CVA with the projected outcome of a realistically available alternative process, and sets a 'lower bound' below which a CVA cannot go: see Re T&N Ltd
[2004] EWHC 2361 (Ch) at [82] per David Richards J and Prudential Assurance Co v PRG
Powerhouse Ltd [2007] EWHC 1002 (Ch); [2007] BCC 500 at [75]–[81] per Etherton J.[1018]

Thus, the requirement to establish the relevant alternative and what each class of creditor
would receive under it is not unfamiliar—although that does not mean that it will not be
susceptible to dispute. Indeed, there have been disputes, in the scheme context, where the
company has argued that the relevant alternative would be an insolvency proceeding.[1019]
The cases reveal that, in general, the courts are reluctant to second guess the directors on
this issue, and in *Virgin Active* Snowden J stated that the court is not required to satisfy itself that a particular alternative would definitely occur, nor to conclude that it is more likely
than not that a particular alternative would occur. As he put it, 'The critical words in the
section are what is "*most likely*" to occur.'[1020] Nor was it relevant to consider what might
have been if the directors had acted differently at an earlier stage: the question was what
the relevant alternative would be if, at the final hearing, the court declined to sanction the
plan.[1021] Nonetheless, the earlier the company is on the 'demise curve,'[1022] the more willing
the court may be to scrutinize the company's 'relevant alternative'. Thus, in *Hurricane
Energy* Zacaroli J did not accept the company's evidence that the relevant alternative would
be an uncontrolled liquidation or controlled wind down, so that he was unpersuaded that
the shareholders were no worse off under the restructuring plan than they would be in the
relevant alternative—leading him to decline to sanction the plan.[1023] Particular difficulties
may arise where the challenge is that what would occur would be a renegotiation, as it can
be difficult for the challenging creditor to provide solid evidence as to why a renegotiation
would be possible. The comments of Johnson J in the Part 26 *Steinhoff* case, in response to
the arguments of Counsel for the opposing creditor, bear this out nicely:

> I do not understand Mr Smith's submission to be made on the basis of any evidence, but
> rather based on general experience of how complex commercial negotiations tend to be
> conducted. It is no doubt correct that such negotiations involve a degree of brinksmanship.
> I do not however think it right for me to formulate an assessment of the possible
> counterfactual approach to the Scheme based on a general feeling about how commercial
> negotiations are sometimes (or perhaps even often) conducted. That seems to me to be
> straying too far into just the sort of commercial evaluation which the Courts should shy
> away from.[1024]

Thus, to call the company's bluff that an insolvency and not a renegotiation would follow
failure to approve the plan, something more than a 'general feeling' is needed. Plainly, the
longer negotiations have taken, and the more consultation which has taken place, the easier

---

[1018] *Debenhams* (n 552) ([12].
[1019] *Re APCOA Parking Holdings GmbH* [2015] Bus L R 375 [75].
[1020] *Virgin Active* (n 1004) [107].
[1021] Ibid [115].
[1022] Mevorach and Walters (n 993).
[1023] *Hurricane Energy* (n 992).
[1024] *Re Steinhoff International Holdings* (n 923) [134]–[135].

it will be for the debtor to persuade the court that the options are the plan which is before it or insolvency.

Notwithstanding these early demise curve cases, in many cases the company is likely to argue successfully that the relevant alternative would be an insolvent sale of the business as a going concern, or part of the business or the assets of the company. In *Virgin Active*, the company argued that the most likely alternative to the Part 26A restructuring plan was an administration, funded by secured creditors, with an accelerated sale of certain of the group's principal gym sites. In determining the value which such a sale would generate, a valuation report was commissioned from Grant Thornton which used discounted cash flow methodology (DCF methodology), cross-checked against other valuation methodologies, to arrive at a valuation. The company's advisers, Deloitte, then used this valuation to conclude what a purchaser would be likely to pay in the distressed sale.[1025] Notably, no auction or other market testing process was run. Snowden J noted 'that there is no absolute authority' for the proposition that a market testing process should be conducted, in the legislation or any other authority and he was 'not persuaded that it was unreasonable for the Plan Companies to follow the advice of their advisers, who did not recommend such a process'.[1026] Very little detail was provided on this issue in the judgment, although Virgin Active was a subscription business, dependent on membership renewals for its cash flows. It may be that marketing the business would have risked damaging customer confidence, while enabling competitors to go on something of a fishing trip. The short point is that there may be more of a case for conducting a market testing process in some situations than others.   **3.494**

A further important lesson from *Virgin Active* is that a creditor wishing to oppose the company's evidence would be well advised to submit their own, alternative evidence. In *Virgin Active* the opposing creditors' criticisms of the company's evidence were described as 'pot shots' and the suspicion must be that no one was willing to provide more robust valuation evidence. In addition to valuing the business, the company had commissioned valuations of the market value of its leasehold properties. The landlords, while criticizing this evidence, provided none of their own.[1027] Overall, the court was in possession of very little evidence to convincingly displace the company's evidence of the outcome for creditors in the event of the relevant alternative. Moreover, in *Virgin Active* experts for the opposing creditors were taken to other cases in which they had acted for the company and in which they had adopted positions similar to those which they sought to criticize.[1028] This is a salutary lesson for experts in Part 26A restructuring plan processes, particularly in the relatively small UK market where there is likely to be a high degree of familiarity with approaches adopted in other cases.   **3.495**

As discussed, even if the statutory requirements for cross-class cramdown are met, the court still has a general discretion to decline to sanction the plan. The Explanatory Notes suggest that the court should draw on well-established principles in schemes of arrangement in exercising its discretion. In *DeepOcean*, the first case in which the section 901G power was   **3.496**

[1025] *Virgin Active* (n 1004) [99].
[1026] Ibid [141].
[1027] Ibid [191].
[1028] Ibid [154].

engaged, Trower J therefore started by referring to the usual criteria applied in determining whether to sanction a Part 26 scheme of arrangement. He cited Snowden J's comments in *Virgin Atlantic* in which Snowden J referred to the classic formulation in Buckley on the Companies Act (as quoted in *National Bank* and *Telewest*):

> In exercising its power of sanction the court will see, first, that the provisions of the statute have been complied with; secondly, that the class was fairly represented by those who attended the meeting and that the statutory majority are acting bona fide and are not coercing the minority in order to promote interests adverse to those of the class whom they purport to represent, and, thirdly, that the arrangement is such as an intelligent and honest man, a member of the class concerned and acting in respect of his interest, might reasonably approve.

> The court does not sit merely to see that the majority are acting bona fide and thereupon to register the decision of the meeting: but at the same time the court will be slow to differ from the meeting, unless either the class has not been properly consulted, or the meeting has not considered the matter with a view to the interests of the class which it is empowered to bind, or some other blot is found in the scheme.[1029]

However, as Trower J noted in *DeepOcean*:

> It follows from the very nature of the court's powers under section 901G that, while a number of the matters which the court is required to consider are the same as the familiar questions which arise on any application to sanction a scheme of arrangement under Part 26 of the 2006 Act, additional questions arise where the cross-class cram down provisions are engaged and sought to be relied on. As I will explain, these differences include matters going to the court's discretion.[1030]

Indeed, cross-class cramdown raises radically different concerns. In a Part 26 scheme of arrangement the court is, at sanction, primarily conducting a final check to ensure that it does not have reason to doubt that the vote of the majority is representative of the class of which it is a part. The principle underlying scheme jurisdiction is one of majority rule, so that a minority should not be able to hold up a deal which the majority supports unless there is reason to doubt the *bona fides* of the majority. This is not all the court does but, as the passage underlines, 'the court will be slow to differ from the meeting, unless either the class has not been properly consulted, or the meeting has not considered the matter with a view to the interests of the class which it is empowered to bind, or some other blot is found on the scheme'.

3.497   In a cross-class cramdown the vote at the meeting may still be important. For example, if a specific creditor with a large holding and its own interest dissents, so that the statutory majority is not achieved, the court may still find guidance from the willingness of other creditors to support the vote. Nonetheless, there are limits on the extent to which the court must go. As Trower J put it in *DeepOcean* the Explanatory Notes to the Act suggest that:

[1029] *Re Virgin Atlantic Airways Ltd* [2020] EWHC 2376 (Ch) [51]–[52].
[1030] *DeepOcean* (n 981) [8].

an applicant company will have a fair wind behind it if it seeks an order sanctioning a restructuring plan notwithstanding a dissenting class where the section 901G conditions A and B are met. Paragraph 192 is drafted in a way which suggests that, where that is the case, the court will focus on the negative question of whether a refusal to sanction is appropriate on the grounds that the restructuring plan is not just and equitable. The draftsman's focus was not on the more positive question of why justice and equity point to the plan being sanctioned.[1031]

He went on to say:

On one view this is a small distinction, not least because no court will sanction a plan which it does not consider to be just and equitable. However, I think it reflects a recognition that, all other things being equal, satisfaction of conditions A and B is capable of justifying an override of the views of the dissenting class. This is not surprising in light of the fact that the court must have been satisfied already (a) that the purpose of the plan is to eliminate, reduce or prevent or mitigate the effect of financial difficulties that are affecting or may affect a company's ability to carry on business as a going concern (section 901A) and (b) that members of that class will be no worse off than they would be in the relevant alternative (section 901G(3)). So, to the extent their rights will have been varied by the plan in a manner which, objectively speaking, can only be neutral or better for them in its impact.[1032]

In *Virgin Active*, Snowden J did not consider Trower J to have decided that, 'provided that Conditions A and B were satisfied, the plans should be sanctioned unless the court thought the plans were not just and equitable'.[1033] He noted that the words 'just and equitable' do not appear in the section. He also noted that, contrary to the suggestion in the Explanatory Notes to section 901G, there has never been such a test in a Part 26 scheme of arrangement. He concluded, 'there is no more justification under Part 26A than in relation to Part 26 for the court simply to impose its own views of what is (or is not) "fair" or "just and equitable"'.[1034] Instead, the court would check that the creditors are likely to do better under the scheme than in the likely relevant alternative and will follow the rest of the approach set out by Richards J in *Telewest* in the scheme context, with appropriate modifications to reflect a Part 26A plan. In other words, the court will consider whether the scheme is one which 'an intelligent and honest man, a member of the class concerned, and acting in respect of his interest, might approve'.

3.498 The Part 26A restructuring plan does not contain any rules on how reorganization consideration should be distributed down the priority waterfall of the creditors. In particular, it contains no equivalent to the absolute priority rule in chapter 11 which provides that no junior class shall recover until a senior class has recovered in full and that, as a corollary, no senior class shall recover more than it is owed. In *Virgin Active* the existing shareholders retained their shares but made a financial contribution to the restructuring. The opposing

---

[1031] Ibid [48]–[49].
[1032] Ibid.
[1033] *Virgin Active* (n 1004) [218].
[1034] Ibid [221].

landlords argued that the equity in the business ought to have been divided between them and the existing shareholders. This appears to have been motivated, in part, by the idea of the 'restructuring surplus' referred to by a number of commentators and by Riz Mokal in two articles which appeared early in 2021.[1035] Here the idea appears to be that the restructuring will create a surplus over the value which would be achieved in a distressed insolvency sale, and that that surplus must be shared equitably among the creditors. Snowden J concludes, however, that this principle only applies to creditors who would be in the money in the case of the relevant alternative and that it is for those creditors to determine how the restructuring surplus is divided up. This appears to ignore the question of whether a class of creditors who would be 'in the money' in the relevant alternative gets too good a deal by virtue of the restructuring plan. Thus, if a senior, in the money class will recover significantly more than it is owed under the restructuring plan then it may be appropriate for some of that value to be shared with a class which is out of the money in the event of the relevant alternative. Or that, at least, is the question. That was not a relevant issue in *Virgin Active* because the senior class was not receiving equity or other instruments which implicated difficult valuation questions but in another case it might be.

3.499   Thus, it is suggested that the court may inquire as to whether the deal is too 'rich' for the senior class.[1036] However, it is suggested here that this emphatically does not implicate a full valuation fight as to the 'fundamental' or 'intrinsic' value of the firm. There is an extraordinary amount of uncertainty and crystal ball gazing in any such exercise, so that it has been described, in a chapter 11 context, as 'a guess compounded by an estimate',[1037] and if Parliament had wanted courts to value the insolvent company on this basis they would surely have said so. Instead, it is suggested that an opposing creditor would need compelling evidence as to why it is probable that the senior class will make such an outsized recovery that the court ought to decline to approve the plan.

3.500   A further issue arises as to whether existing shareholders can hold post-reorganization equity where junior creditors are compromised and recover less than they are owed. This was a significant issue in *Virgin Active*. In *Virgin Active* the company argued that the shareholders were not receiving anything on account of their existing equity (which was completely out of the money in the event of the relevant alternative) but rather that they were providing new junior facilities; a new equity injection; and a waiver of licence fees in exchange for the equity. Once again, the real difficulty which the opposing creditors faced was a lack of evidence as to whether better terms for the equity may have been available from another party.[1038] Interestingly, they may have been well advised to argue that a market testing process did need to be run for the shareholders to demonstrate that they were providing full value for the equity. In the US, where circuits are split over the ability for shareholders to bid for old equity, some circuits have insisted on some sort of market test to demonstrate that the shareholders are not simply retaining their old, out of the money equity in

---

[1035] Rizwaan Mokal, 'The Two Conditions for Part 26A Cram Down' (2020) 35(11) *Journal of International Banking & Financial Law* 730 and Rizwaan Mokal, 'The Court's Discretion in Relation to the Part 26A Cram Down' (2021) 36(1) *Journal of International Banking and Financial Law*.

[1036] *Bluebrook* (n 786).

[1037] Peter Coogan, 'Confirmation of a Plan Under the Bankruptcy Code' (1982) 32 *Case Western Reserve Law Review* 301, 313.

[1038] *Virgin Active* (n 1004) [297]

circumstances where junior creditors have been compromised and have lost the right to recover in the future.[1039] However, once again it is suggested that Parliament must have intended for existing equity to be able to provide new funding in exchange for shares as a matter of principle or it would have been relatively straightforward to prohibit this in the statutory drafting. Similarly, in *Virgin Active*, management are allocated equity to encourage their continued participation in the business to secure the success of the reorganization. There would seem to be nothing in section 901G to prohibit this, and every reason to suggest it should be permissible.

Next the court will consider whether the plan is fair and equitable as between the dissenting **3.501** class and other classes of equal priority in the distributional order of priority in insolvency. There are myriad, commercial reasons why classes of creditors of equal priority in the distributional order of priority may be treated differently in the plan. For example, unsecured bondholders may receive a longer-term payout than unsecured trade creditors or may be offered equity while unsecured trade creditors receive cash. Once again, it is suggested that an objecting creditor would need to demonstrate why this differential treatment provided the non-dissenting class with too good a deal without a reasonable basis necessary for the successful completion of the restructuring.

Finally, the court will consider whether any creditors who have been excluded and will **3.502** be paid in full ought to be brought within the plan. Two things are likely to be important here: (i) is there a good commercial reason for leaving the creditors in question outside the plan and unimpaired; and (ii) would it make a material difference to the dissenting class if the excluded creditors were brought within the plan?[1040] Frequently, creditors will be excluded and paid in full because their support is vital for the success of the restructuring.[1041] But the courts have also accepted that where there are multiple small claims, it may not be worth the cost and expense of bringing them into the plan, particularly where attempts to do so may further destabilize the business.[1042] It will be important that claims which are excluded from the plan are set out in the Explanatory Statement, together with an explanation of why they have been excluded.

[1039] Alexandra Wilde, 'Consideration for Private Equity Firms When Utilizing Chapter 11 New Value Deals' (2012) 1 *Michigan Business & Entrepreneurial Law Review* 197.

[1040] Paterson and Walters (n 819).

[1041] *Virgin Atlantic* (n 1029).

[1042] Ibid [65]–[67].

4

THE UNCITRAL MODEL LAW
ON CROSS-BORDER INSOLVENCY

I. The Impact of the UNCITRAL Model Law
on Cross-Border Insolvency

A. Introduction

The Model Law on Cross-Border Insolvency ('the Model Law') was adopted by the UN **4.01**
Commission on International Trade Law (UNCITRAL) in May 1997 and formally approved by the UN General Assembly in December 1997. It was drafted with the intention of
providing a template for use by countries seeking to put into place a cross-border insolvency

regime, or to strengthen one already in existence. The countries that enact the Model Law will then share a common set of cross-border insolvency laws providing an international network of cooperation and assistance. The Model Law has so far been adopted by 53 jurisdictions including the United States, under chapter 15 of the Bankruptcy Code, and Great Britain, under the Cross-Border Insolvency Regulations 2006 ('the Regulations').[1] Its usefulness as a tool in facilitating cross-border restructurings has already been demonstrated and a body of helpful jurisprudence has developed as its boundaries have been tested in the courts.

4.02 However, since the first edition of this book was written, it has become clear that the US and the UK, whilst each apparently seeking to adopt the same Model Law, have very different conceptions of how it is to work in practice. This chapter will start with a brief examination of the objectives and scope of the Model Law, which are common to both the US and English versions, before analysing in more detail key aspects of those two versions as enacted and the reasons why there appears to be a growing divergence in the way in which the Model Law is applied in practice.

B. Objectives

4.03 The Model Law seeks to provide effective mechanisms for dealing with cross-border insolvencies, including those where the debtor has assets in more than one jurisdiction or where creditors are located in a jurisdiction other than the jurisdiction where the insolvency proceeding is initiated. It does not attempt to unify substantive insolvency laws. Its stated objectives are to achieve:

- cooperation between the courts and other competent authorities of the enacting state and foreign states involved in cases of cross-border insolvency;
- greater legal certainty for trade and investment;
- fair and efficient administration of cross-border insolvencies that protects the interests of all creditors and other interested persons, including the debtor;
- protection and maximization of the value of the debtor's assets; and
- facilitation of the rescue of financially troubled businesses, thereby protecting investment and preserving employment.

---

[1] As of June 2021, the 53 jurisdictions which have adopted legislation based on the Model Law are: Australia (2008), Bahrain (2018), Benin (2015), Brazil (2020), Burkina Faso (2015), Cameroon (2015), Canada (2005), Central African Republic (2015), Chad (2015), Chile (2013), Colombia (2006), Comoros (2015), Congo (2015), Cote D'Ivoire (2015), Democratic Republic of Congo (2015), Dominican Republic (2015), Equatorial Guinea (2015), Gabon (2015), Greece (2010), Guinea (2015), Guinea-Bissau (2015), Israel (2018), Japan (2000), Kenya (2015), Malawi (2015), Mali (2015), Mauritius (2009), Mexico (2000), Montenegro (2002), Myanmar (2020), New Zealand (2006), Niger (2015), Panama (2016), Philippines (2010), Poland (2003), Republic of Korea (2006), Romania (2003), Senegal (2015), Serbia (2004), Seychelles (2013), Singapore (2017), Slovenia (2007), South Africa (2000), Togo (2015), Uganda (2011), United Arab Emirates (Abu Dhabi Global Market 2015, Dubai International Financial Centre 2019), United Kingdom of Great Britain and Northern Ireland (British Virgin Islands 2003, Great Britain 2006, Gibraltar 2014), the United States (2005), Vanuatu (2013), and Zimbabwe (2018). A list of the jurisdictions which have adopted legislation based on the Model Law is available at: <https://uncitral.un.org/en/texts/insolvency/modellaw/cross-border_insolvency/status>.

These objectives are replicated in both chapter 15[2] and the Regulations. Their value is apparent in the context of cross-border restructurings where, in the absence of a consensual agreement between the debtor and its creditors, the involvement of local courts is required in order to prevent creditors from taking action to enforce their rights in jurisdictions where the debtor's assets are located.   **4.04**

C. Scope of Application

The Model Law is intended to operate as an integral part of the existing insolvency law in the states in which it is enacted. Its scope is limited to procedural aspects of cross-border insolvency cases and, in both the US and the UK, may be applied where: **4.05**

- assistance is sought in an enacting state by a foreign court, or a foreign representative, in connection with a foreign proceeding; or
- assistance is sought in a foreign state in connection with a proceeding under the insolvency laws of the enacting state; or
- a foreign proceeding and a proceeding under the insolvency laws of the enacting state in respect of the same debtor are taking place concurrently; or
- creditors or other interested persons in a foreign state have an interest in requesting the commencement of, or participating in, a proceeding under the insolvency laws of the enacting state.

There is no requirement of reciprocity under the Model Law and in most instances it will be possible to apply for recognition of a foreign proceeding commenced in any foreign country, whether or not that foreign country is an enacting state.[3] An example of this can be found in *Re European Insurance Agency AS*.[4] In that case the Bristol District Registry recognized the Norwegian insolvency of the European Insurance Agency as a foreign main proceeding and the Norwegian trustee (who was seeking information from parties in the UK concerning the debtor's assets in England and Wales) as a foreign representative. The fact that Norway had not enacted the Model Law was not a bar to recognition by the English courts.[5]   **4.06**

D. Interpretation

UNCITRAL has produced background and explanatory information to assist in the interpretation of the Model Law, in the expectation of making it a more effective tool for legislators. The key work is the Guide to Enactment[6] which is based on the deliberations and decisions of the Commission and considerations of the Working Group on Insolvency Law, which carried out the preparatory work.   **4.07**

---

[2] Chapter 15 is the only chapter of the Bankruptcy Code that includes an express description of its purposes, goals, and scope. See 11 USC § 1501(a).

[3] A small number of countries, including Mexico, South Africa, Romania, and Mauritius, have included reciprocity requirements in their implementing legislation.

[4] High Court, 2006. This was the first recognition application to be heard in the English courts.

[5] Ian Fletcher, 'The UNCITRAL Model Law in the United Kingdom' (2007) 20(9) *Insolvency Intelligence* 138–141.

[6] UNCITRAL Model Law on Cross-Border Insolvency with Guide to Enactment, 15 December 1997.

4.08   The information was primarily directed at the relevant government departments and legislators preparing the necessary legislative revisions but was also expected to provide useful insight to other users of the text such as judges, practitioners, and academics. In particular, it was hoped that the information could be used by the courts to ascertain the meaning or effect of any of the provisions of the Model Law and to assist in achieving uniformity of interpretation.[7] We will see that courts in both the US and the UK have examined the Guide to Enactment but, nonetheless, have arrived at different interpretations of its provisions.

4.09   The Guide to Enactment recommends that, in order to achieve a satisfactory degree of harmonization and certainty, enacting states should make as few changes as possible in incorporating the Model Law into their legal systems. Both US and British legislators have attempted to respect this recommendation, although they necessarily depart from it in certain key provisions. We may pause to wonder, as we analyse the US and then the UK approach, whether implementing a necessarily generic piece of drafting as legislation has contributed to the scope for divergent interpretations.

II. The US Version—Chapter 15

A. Overview

4.10   On 20 April 2005, the Bankruptcy Code was amended substantially by the Bankruptcy Abuse Prevention and Consumer Protection Act of 2005 which, among other things, added chapter 15 to the Bankruptcy Code. Chapter 15 replaced section 304 as the mechanism for a representative in a foreign bankruptcy proceeding to obtain relief in a US bankruptcy court to facilitate a foreign insolvency proceeding. Under chapter 15, a foreign representative that obtains recognition of a foreign proceeding gains access to a wide variety of relief with respect to the foreign debtor's assets and operations in the US, including relief under the automatic stay and statutory provisions relating to the foreign debtor's US affairs.

B. History of Chapter 15

1. Section 304

4.11   Prior to the enactment of chapter 15, section 304 of the Bankruptcy Code permitted a foreign representative in a foreign proceeding to initiate an ancillary case in the US to obtain judicial assistance in administering US assets.[8] The filing of a petition by the foreign representative under section 304 commenced a limited proceeding, rather than a full-blown bankruptcy case, to administer the foreign debtor's US assets. Enacted as part of the Bankruptcy Reform Act of 1978, section 304 was Congress's first effort to provide specific procedures for dealing with issues related to foreign insolvency proceedings.[9] Section 304

---

[7]   Both the US and British versions state that, when interpreting the Model Law, regard will be had to its international origin and to the need to promote uniformity in its application (s 1508 of ch 15; art 8 of the Regulations).

[8]   Jay Lawrence Westbrook, 'Chapter 15 At Last' (2005) 79 *American Bankruptcy Law Journal* 713, 718–719.

[9]   *In re Iida*, 377 BR 243, 254 (9th Cir BAP 2007).

was a step towards achieving universalism in cross-border foreign proceedings[10] and it specifically codified principles of comity[11] and cooperation with foreign courts in bankruptcy matters.[12] The goal of section 304 was to afford deference to the country where the primary foreign insolvency case was pending, provide flexible cooperation in the administration of the debtor's US interests involved in that proceeding, and prevent the piecemeal distribution of assets in the US by local creditors.[13]

(a) Framework of section 304

Under section 304(b), a bankruptcy court had broad discretion to grant appropriate relief **4.12** to a foreign representative seeking judicial assistance in the administration of a foreign proceeding. The bankruptcy court could: (i) enjoin the commencement or continuation of any action against the debtor with respect to property involved in a foreign proceeding or any action against such property, including the enforcement of a judgment or the creation or enforcement of a lien; (ii) order turnover of such property to the foreign representative; or (iii) order other appropriate relief.[14]

In determining whether to grant relief under section 304(b), a bankruptcy court was re- **4.13** quired to consider six enumerated factors: (i) just treatment of all claim holders; (ii) protection of US claim holders against prejudice and inconvenience because of the foreign proceeding; (iii) prevention of preferential and fraudulent transfers; (iv) distribution of assets substantially in accordance with the Bankruptcy Code; (v) comity; and (vi) if applicable, the opportunity for a fresh start for the debtor.[15] Section 304 did not provide guidance as to the weight to be given to each factor, although several courts found that comity should be the primary consideration.[16] In addition, the statute itself did not provide any guidance as to how the factors should be applied.[17] This led

---

[10] *In re Treco*, 240 F 3d 148, 154 (2nd Cir 2001).

[11] The US Supreme Court has described comity as 'the recognition which one nation allows within its territory to the legislative, executive or judicial acts of another nation, having due regard both to international duty and convenience, and to the rights of its own citizens or of other persons who are under the protection of its laws'. See *Hilton v Guyot*, 159 US 113, 164 (1895). Under principles of international comity, state and federal courts in the US typically will refuse to review acts of foreign governments and defer to proceedings in foreign countries, allowing those acts and proceedings to have extraterritorial effect in the US. But, while state and federal courts 'may choose to give res judicata effect to foreign judgments on the basis of comity', they are 'not obliged to do so'. *Paramedics Electromedicina Commercial, Ltd v GE Med Sys Info Techs, Inc*, 369 F 3d 645, 654 (2nd Cir 2004) (internal quotation marks and citations omitted). As a general matter, courts will extend comity only if the following three conditions are met: (i) the foreign court had proper jurisdiction; (ii) the foreign proceeding adhered to fundamental standards of procedural fairness; and (iii) the judgment does not offend the public policy of the forum state. See *Cunard SS Co v Salen Reefer Serv AB*, 773 F 2d 452, 457 (2nd Cir 1985); see also *Pravin Banker Assocs, Ltd v Banco Popular Del Peru*, 109 F 3d 850, 854 (2nd Cir 1997) ('[F]rom the earliest times, authorities have recognized that the obligation of comity expires when the strong public policies of the forum are vitiated by the foreign act').

[12] Westbrook, *supra* n 8 at 718.

[13] See *In re Iida*, 377 BR at 254–255; *In re Atlas Shipping*, 404 BR 726, 733 (Bankr SDNY 2009).

[14] 11 USC § 304(b)(1)–(3) (repealed 2005). See also *In re Iida*, 377 BR at 255.

[15] 11 USC § 304(c) (repealed 2005).

[16] See *Universal Casualty & Surety Co v Gee (In re Gee)*, 53 BR 891, 901 (Bankr SDNY 1985); *In re Culmer*, 25 BR 621, 629 (Bankr SDNY 1982).

[17] Several commentators have noted that the factors were in direct tension with each other. For example, '[p]rotecting the claims and convenience for US creditors would conflict with a just outcome of all interested parties if at least some of those parties came from foreign jurisdictions or would benefit from the bankruptcy laws of a foreign jurisdiction rather than the U.S. Bankruptcy Code'. See Lesley Salafia, 'Note, Cross Border Insolvency Law in the United States and its Application to Multinational Corporate Groups' (2006) 21 *Connecticut Journal of International Law* 297, 309; see also Todd Kraft and Allison Aranson, 'Transnational Bankruptcies: Section 304 and Beyond' (1993) *Columbia Business Law Review* 329, 339–341.

to different courts, even within the same judicial district, reaching strikingly different results.[18]

4.14   Another challenge posed by section 304 was determining whether a particular foreign process constituted a 'foreign proceeding' under section 304. A 'foreign proceeding' was defined as a 'proceeding, whether judicial or administrative and whether or not under bankruptcy law, in a foreign country ... for the purpose of liquidating an estate, adjusting debts by composition, extension, or discharge, or effecting a reorganization'.[19] One of the first cases on this issue held that a voluntary winding up was not a 'foreign proceeding' because creditors had no voice in the proceeding and little right to notice, the debtor acted free from control or supervision of the local court, and the local court merely played a ministerial role.[20] Subsequent decisions appeared to limit the holding of *In re Tam* to whether the 'foreign proceeding' involved sufficient judicial oversight and creditor notice.[21] As the case law evolved, it became clear that a 'foreign proceeding' would be recognized if there was a sufficient amount of judicial involvement and supervision or creditors were given access to the proceeding to voice their objections.[22]

(b) Legislative history

4.15   As described above, chapter 15 generally implements the Model Law.[23] The US was an active participant in the drafting of the Model Law, and the Model Law was wholeheartedly accepted by the United States National Bankruptcy Review Commission.[24] The language of chapter 15 generally follows the form and substance of the Model Law with certain modifications designed to conform the Model Law to US law and terminology.[25]

4.16   Chapter 15 'was added to the Bankruptcy Code with the goal of promoting international comity and "to provide for the fair and efficient administration of cross-border insolvencies, which protects the interests of creditors and other interested parties, including the debtor"'.[26] Chapter 15 was not intended to change the basic approach of US law to multinational insolvencies, but is rather procedural in nature and designed to 'provide a common platform for cooperation with other countries around the world'.[27]

(c) Chapter 15 vs section 304

4.17   Chapter 15 was intended to streamline and simplify the ability of a foreign representative to obtain recognition of a foreign proceeding in the US compared to former section 304.[28]

---

[18] Kraft and Aranson, *supra* n 17 at 339–349.

[19] 11 USC § 101(23) (repealed 2005).

[20] *In re Tam*, 170 BR 838 (Bankr SDNY 1994).

[21] See *In re Ward*, 201 BR 357, 362 (Bankr SDNY 1996). In *Ward*, the court held that a Zambian voluntary winding up was a 'foreign proceeding' (though very similar to the Cayman winding up in *In re Tam*) because there was active court involvement and creditors had the right to be heard.

[22] See *In re Hopewell Int'l Insurance*, 238 BR 25, 50 (Bankr SDNY 1999), aff'd, 275 BR 699 (SDNY 2002). Interestingly, Hopewell was solvent, yet its scheme was nonetheless recognized as a 'foreign proceeding'. Ibid at 48.

[23] HR Rep No 109-31, at 105–107 (2005); *In re Tri-Continental Exchange Ltd,* 349 BR 627, 631–632 (Bankr ED Cal 2006).

[24] Westbrook, *supra* n 8 at 719.

[25] Westbrook, *supra* n 8 at 719–720; *In re Iida,* 377 BR at 256.

[26] *In re Steadman,* 410 BR 397, 402 (Bankr DNJ 2009) (quoting HR Rep No 109-31 at 106 (2005)).

[27] Westbrook, *supra* n 8 at 725–726.

[28] See Allan L Gropper, 'Current Developments in International Insolvency Law: A United States Perspective' (2006) 15 *Journal of Bankruptcy Law & Practice* 2, Art 3.

Section 304 did not specifically provide for recognition of a foreign bankruptcy proceeding, but rather gave courts the authority to open an ancillary proceeding and grant relief if the six statutorily enumerated factors were present. The enactment of chapter 15 'shifted from the subjective, comity-based process of section 304(c) to chapter 15's more rigid recognition standard'.[29] In its place, chapter 15 sets forth a procedure for recognition of a foreign proceeding. A foreign representative files a petition for recognition of the foreign proceeding and once recognition is granted, the foreign representative is entitled to relief.[30] As one court noted, '[r]equiring recognition to nearly all court access and consequently as a condition to granting comity distinguishes Chapter 15 from its predecessor section 304'.[31] Courts have adopted the approach that chapter 15 requires a factual determination with respect to recognition before principles of comity come into play, promoting predictability and reliability.[32]

4.18 While recognition turns on the strict application of objective criteria, relief is largely discretionary and turns on subjective factors that embody principles of comity.[33] However, the six section 304 criteria have limited application under chapter 15; they are used only when a bankruptcy court considers whether 'additional assistance' beyond that specifically provided for in chapter 15 is required *after* the court has recognized the foreign proceeding.[34] Moreover, comity has been elevated to an overarching principle.[35] Therefore, case law decided under section 304 is of limited use in chapter 15 cases and will generally only be applicable when courts consider whether to grant additional assistance.[36]

4.19 Chapter 15 is also designed to concentrate all issues dealing with foreign proceedings in the bankruptcy court. Under section 304, state or other federal courts could have granted comity to a foreign proceeding and deferred to the decisions of the foreign court. This left room for abuse as '[p]arties would be free to avoid the requirements of [chapter 15] and the expert scrutiny of the bankruptcy court by applying directly to a state or federal court unfamiliar with the statutory requirements'.[37] As a result, under section 1509(d), if a foreign representative is denied recognition under chapter 15, the court may prohibit the representative from seeking relief in another court. In addition, a foreign representative must include a copy of the recognition order when requesting comity or cooperation in any US court besides the court that granted recognition.[38]

---

[29] *In re Bear Stearns High-Grade Structured Credit Strategies Master Fund, Ltd*, 389 BR 325, 332 (SDNY 2008).

[30] Westbrook, *supra* n 8 at 721–722.

[31] *In re Bear Stearns High-Grade Structured Credit Strategies Master Fund, Ltd*, 389 BR at 333.

[32] Ibid. See also *In re Iida*, 377 BR at 257; *In re Basis Yield Alpha Fund (Master)*, 381 BR 37, 43–46 (Bankr SDNY 2008); *In re Loy*, 380 BR 154, 164–165 (Bankr ED Va 2007); *United States v JA Jones Construction Group, LLC*, 333 BR 637 (EDNY 2005) (holding that the court did not have authority to consider a foreign receiver's request for a stay of action in accordance with Canadian bankruptcy law because the foreign receiver had not sought recognition under chapter 15).

[33] *In re Bear Stearns High-Grade Structured Credit Strategies Master Fund, Ltd*, 389 BR at 333–334.

[34] See 11 USC § 1507(b).

[35] Ibid.

[36] Westbrook, *supra* n 8 at 720 ('Because § 304 has been repealed, the case law developed under that section is not directly controlling in Chapter 15 cases, but it remains relevant to a limited extent'). See also *In re Bear Stearns High Grade Structured Credit Strategies Master Fund*, 374 BR 122, 132 (Bankr SDNY 2007) ('the jurisprudence developed under section 304 is of no assistance in determining the issues relating to the presumption for recognition under chapter 15').

[37] HR Rep No 109-31, at 110 (2005).

[38] 11 USC § 1509(c); Notably, US courts will not extend comity to or recognize a foreign insolvency proceeding if the debtor has not sought and obtained such recognition in a US bankruptcy court under chapter 15. See *Halo Creative & Design Ltd v Comptoir Des Indes Inc*, WL 4742066 (ND Ill Oct. 2, 2018)(the District Court for the

4.20   Unlike section 304, chapter 15 also provides for provisional relief, contains specific provisions for cooperation with a foreign representative and provides for judicial cooperation between the courts and other authorities involved in a cross-border case.

C. Mechanics of Chapter 15

1. When does chapter 15 apply?

4.21   Chapter 15 only applies when: (i) US assistance is sought by a foreign court or a foreign representative in connection with a foreign proceeding; (ii) assistance is sought in a foreign country in connection with a case under the Bankruptcy Code; (iii) a foreign proceeding and a plenary case under the Bankruptcy Code are pending with respect to the same debtor; and (iv) creditors or other interested persons in a foreign country have an interest in requesting the commencement of, or participating in, a case or proceeding under the Bankruptcy Code.[39]

4.22   Chapter 15 does not apply to: (i) a proceeding concerning an entity, other than a foreign insurance company, that is ineligible to be a debtor under the Bankruptcy Code (eg a railroad, a domestic insurance company, or a domestic or foreign bank); (ii) an individual, or to an individual and such individual's spouse, who have debts within certain limits specified under section 109(e) and who are US citizens or permanent residents; (iii) an entity subject to a proceeding under the Securities Investor Protection Act of 1970, or a stock or commodity broker subject to the liquidation provisions of chapter 7; and (iv) any deposit, escrow, trust fund, or other security required or permitted under any applicable state's insurance law or regulation for the benefit of claim holders in the US.[40] In addition, as discussed in section IV below, certain foreign debtors may not be able to take advantage of the chapter 15 process based on recent case law concerning eligibility requirements under section 109(a) of the Bankruptcy Code.

4.23   Although chapter 15 appears to apply to all requests for assistance in the US by a foreign court or foreign representative in connection with a foreign proceeding, a foreign representative will be unable to obtain most types of relief from US courts if the underlying foreign proceeding does not qualify as either a main or non-main proceeding.[41]

4.24   There are certain circumstances in which a court cannot apply chapter 15. For example, if chapter 15 conflicts with a US obligation under a treaty or other agreement to which the US is a party with one or more countries, chapter 15 will not be available.[42] Courts, however, are instructed to read the Model Law and the US obligation so as not to conflict, especially if

---

Northern District of Illinois denied, and ruled that it had no authority to consider, a debtor in a Canadian bankruptcy case's motion to stay all proceedings in its ongoing US intellectual property litigation where the debtor had not complied with section 1509 and previously obtained a US Bankruptcy Court order recognizing the Canadian proceeding.)

[39]   11 USC § 1501(b).

[40]   11 USC § 1501(c)–(d).

[41]   Alesia Ranney-Marinelli, 'Overview of Chapter 15 Ancillary and Other Cross-Border Cases' (2008) 82 *American Bankruptcy Law Journal* 269, 272.

[42]   11 USC § 1503.

the subject matter of the international obligation 'is less directly related than the Model Law to a case before the court'.[43] In addition, a court has discretion to abstain from acting under chapter 15 if such action would be 'manifestly contrary' to US policy.[44]

2. Commencement of a chapter 15 case

A chapter 15 case begins when a foreign representative files a petition for recognition of a **4.25** foreign proceeding.[45] A 'foreign representative' is defined as a person or body, including an interim representative, 'authorized in a foreign proceeding to administer the reorganization or the liquidation of the debtor's assets or affairs or to act as a representative of such foreign proceeding'.[46]

A petition for recognition must be accompanied by a statement identifying all foreign pro- **4.26** ceedings involving the debtor that are known to the foreign representative, as well as one of the following three items: (i) a certified copy of the decision commencing the foreign proceeding and appointing the foreign representative; (ii) a certificate from the foreign court affirming the existence of the foreign proceeding and the appointment of the foreign representative; or (iii) in the absence of the evidence referred to above, any other evidence acceptable to the court of the existence of the foreign proceeding and of the appointment of the foreign representative.[47]

Because chapter 15 was 'designed to make recognition as simple and expedient as pos- **4.27** sible',[48] Congress adopted statutory presumptions regarding the petition and supporting documents. Specifically, a court is entitled to presume that documents submitted in support of a petition for recognition are authentic, regardless of whether they have been legalized.[49] There also is a presumption that a proceeding is a 'foreign proceeding' and the representative is a 'foreign representative' if the foreign decision or certificate indicates as much.[50] Such statutory presumptions are rebuttable and 'the court may hear proof on any element stated'.[51]

In practice, a foreign representative seeking recognition of a foreign proceeding under **4.28** chapter 15 typically should file the following documents with the bankruptcy court:

---

[43] HR Rep No 109-31, at 107 (2005).
[44] 11 USC § 1506.
[45] 11 USC §§ 1504, 1509(a).
[46] 11 USC § 101(24). At least one court has recognized an individual as a 'foreign representative' whose appointment occurred after a foreign proceeding had been closed. In *In re PT Bakrie Telecom TKB*, the debtors completed a financial restructuring pursuant to a 'PKPU' proceeding in Indonesia. 601 BR 707, 716-719 (Bankr SDNY 2019). Following the Indonesian court's approval of the restructuring, several of the debtors' noteholders sued in New York for breaches under their note documents and obtained several rulings in their favour. A director of the debtors then sought recognition of the PKPU proceeding in a chapter 15 case in the Southern District of New York. The noteholders argued that since the director had been appointed three years after the close of the foreign proceeding, the director was not a foreign representative under section 101(24) of the Bankruptcy Code. The Bankruptcy Court for the Southern District of New York held in the debtors' favour, ruling that section 101(24) should be read 'broadly' and that an individual properly appointed to administer the reorganization or the liquidation of a debtor's assets or affairs may serve as a foreign representative and that such appointment need not happen in a foreign proceeding necessarily.
[47] 11 USC § 1515(b).
[48] HR Rep No 109-31, at 112 (2005).
[49] 11 USC § 1516(b).
[50] 11 USC § 1516(a).
[51] HR Rep No 109-31, at 112 (2005); *In re Basis Yield Alpha Fund (Master)*, 381 BR at 53.

- *Voluntary Petition*: The voluntary petition is a standard document filed by all foreign representatives. A separate voluntary petition seeking chapter 15 recognition must be filed for each debtor.
- *Board Resolutions*: The board resolutions should, among other things, authorize the filing of the chapter 15 petition, designate an officer of the debtor to execute the chapter 15 petition and related documents, approve the retention of bankruptcy counsel and other professionals, and authorize further acts in support of the chapter 15 cases.
- *Verified Petition*: The verified petition is executed by the foreign representative. Among other things, it provides a factual background describing the debtor's business, the reasons for the chapter 15 filing, and the relief requested (e.g., providing that a scheme of arrangement be given full force and effect in the US). A variety of exhibits are attached to the verified petition, including but not limited to: (i) a certified copy of the decision (translated into English, if necessary) commencing the foreign proceeding and appointing the foreign representative; (ii) the proposed order granting recognition under chapter 15; (iii) the foreign order authorizing the foreign representative to convene a meeting to permit creditors to vote on a proposed scheme of arrangement; and (iv) the scheme of arrangement.
- *List Required Pursuant to Fed R Bankr P 1007(a)(4)*: Unless the bankruptcy court orders otherwise, rule 1007(a)(4) of the Bankruptcy Rules requires the foreign representative to file a list containing the name(s) and address(es) of all administrators in foreign proceedings of the debtor, all parties to any pending US litigation in which the debtor is a party, and all entities against whom provisional relief is sought under section 1519 of the Bankruptcy Code.
- *Statement Required Pursuant to Fed R Bankr P 7007.1(A)*: Rule 7007.1 of the Bankruptcy Rules requires a nongovernmental corporate party to list the corporations (as defined by section 101 of the Bankruptcy Code) owning more than a 10 per cent interest in such party or state that there are no such corporations.
- *Statement of Foreign Representative Pursuant to Section 1515(c)*: The statement pursuant to section 1515(c) of the Bankruptcy Code identifies all foreign proceedings with respect to the debtor that are known to the foreign representative.
- *Motion to Specify Form and Manner of Service of Notice of Filing of Chapter 15 Petition and to Schedule a Hearing on the Chapter 15 Petition*: By this motion, the foreign representative seeks the bankruptcy court's approval of the proposed notice to be sent to the debtor's creditors and other parties-in-interest notifying them of the filing of the debtor's chapter 15 petition. In an abundance of caution, the foreign representative also should seek the bankruptcy court's authorization to publish the notice in a national newspaper (e.g., *Wall Street Journal*). In addition, the motion requests that the bankruptcy court schedule a hearing on the chapter 15 petition. Bankruptcy Rule 2002(q)(1) provides that parties are to be given 21 days' notice of a hearing on a chapter 15 petition.
- *Memorandum of Law in Support of the Chapter 15 Petition and any* Ex Parte *Relief Requested*: The memorandum of law provides a factual background regarding the debtor's business, the reason(s) for seeking chapter 15 protection and arguments in support of the contention that the applicant is entitled to recognition under chapter 15. If the foreign representative requests *ex parte* provisional relief (see description below), the memorandum of law also explains why the bankruptcy court should grant such relief.

- *Declaration in Support of the Chapter 15 Petition and Related Motions*: A representative of the debtor will execute a declaration in support of the chapter 15 petition and any *ex parte* provisional relief requested by the debtor.
- *Motion Directing Joint Administration of Chapter 15 Cases (Optional)*: If two or more petitions are pending in the same court by related debtors, Bankruptcy Rule 1015(b) authorizes the bankruptcy court to order the joint administration of the cases for administrative purposes. Joint administration permits, among other things, the use of a single docket for all of the debtors' cases, and the ability to combine notices to creditors and other parties-in-interest. This is a typical motion that is routinely granted by the bankruptcy court.
- Ex Parte *Application for Order to Show Cause with Temporary Restraining Order and, After Notice and a Hearing, A Preliminary Injunction (Optional)*: Section 1519 of the Bankruptcy Code provides for the entry of relief that may be necessary during the gap period between the filing of the chapter 15 petition and a bankruptcy court's decision on recognition. A foreign representative sometimes requests that the bankruptcy court approve provisional injunctive relief, such as staying and restraining all persons and entities from: (a)(i) continuing any action or commencing any additional action involving the debtor or its assets; (ii) enforcing any judicial, quasi-judicial, administrative, or regulatory judgment, assessment, or order or arbitration award against the debtor; (iii) commencing or continuing any action to create, perfect, or enforce any lien, set-off, or other claim against the debtor or its property; or (iv) managing or exercising control over the debtor's assets located within the US except as expressly authorized by the foreign representative in writing; and/or (b) entrusting the administration or realization of all or part of the debtor's assets located in the US to the foreign representative; and/or (c) authorizing the foreign representative to operate the debtor's business and to exercise certain rights under the Bankruptcy Code; and/or (d) scheduling a hearing to consider the foreign representative's request for a preliminary injunction granting the same relief as set forth in items (a) to (c).

3. Recognition

'Recognition' is a central concept under chapter 15. A foreign representative initiates a **4.29** chapter 15 case by filing a petition for recognition of a 'foreign proceeding' in the bankruptcy court, but the foreign representative cannot obtain permanent (as opposed to provisional) relief under chapter 15 until the bankruptcy court recognizes the foreign proceeding. As described above, the petition must include certain evidentiary documents, such as a certified copy of the court order commencing the foreign proceeding and appointing the foreign representative. Absent contrary evidence, the bankruptcy court presumes the authenticity of these documents.

A 'foreign proceeding' is defined as 'a collective judicial or administrative proceeding in a **4.30** foreign country … under a law relating to insolvency or adjustment of debt in which proceeding the assets and affairs of the debtor are subject to control or supervision by a foreign court, for the purpose of reorganization, or liquidation'.[52] This definition clarifies that a 'foreign proceeding' need not be a bankruptcy proceeding; it may involve 'adjustment of debt' and be for the purpose of a reorganization. Specifically, the addition of 'adjustment

---

[52] 11 USC § 101(23). See also *In re Betcorp Limited*, 400 BR 266, 277 (Bankr D Nev 2009) (describing the seven elements of a foreign proceeding as '(i) a proceeding; (ii) that is either judicial or administrative; (iii) that is

of debt' 'emphasizes that the scope of ... chapter 15 is *not* limited to proceedings involving only debtors which are technically insolvent, but broadly includes *all* proceedings involving debtors in *severe financial distress*'.[53] In addition, the 'foreign proceeding' must be 'for the purpose of reorganization, or liquidation'. Although the term 'reorganization' is not defined in the Bankruptcy Code, courts have cited multiple legal treatises, encyclopedias, and dictionaries on this point.[54] The Legislative Guide on Insolvency Law defines 'reorganization' as 'the process by which the financial well-being and viability of a debtor's business can be restored and the business continue to operate, using various means possibly including debt forgiveness, debt rescheduling, debt-equity conversions and the sale of the business (or part of it) as a going concern'.[55]

4.31   Recognition involves classifying a foreign proceeding as main or non-main. A foreign main proceeding is a foreign proceeding pending in the country where the debtor has its 'center of its main interests' or 'COMI'.[56] A foreign non-main proceeding is any other proceeding 'pending in a country where the debtor has an establishment'.[57] An establishment is defined as 'any place of operations where the debtor carries out a nontransitory economic activity'.[58]

4.32   COMI is not defined in the Bankruptcy Code. The 'centre of main interests' concept is described in the EC Regulation[59] as 'the place where the debtor conducts the administration of his interests on a regular basis and is therefore ascertainable by third parties'.[60] Under chapter 15, there is a rebuttable presumption that absent evidence to the contrary, the location of the debtor's registered office, or the habitual residence of an individual, is presumed to be the debtor's COMI.[61]

4. Recognition timeline

4.33   Section 1517(c) of the Code provides that a petition for recognition of a chapter 15 case shall be 'decided upon at the earliest possible time'. However, Bankruptcy Rule 2002(q)(1) requires 21 days' notice of a hearing on a petition for recognition. Thus, an order granting foreign recognition should in most cases be entered within approximately one month after the chapter 15 petition and supporting documents are filed.

5. Relief under chapter 15

4.34   Unlike the filing of a chapter 7, 11, or 13 petition, filing a chapter 15 petition does not trigger automatic relief. Chapter 15 relief depends on whether the bankruptcy court recognizes the

---

collective in nature; (iv) that is in a foreign country; (v) that is authorized or conducted under a law related to insolvency or the adjustment of debts; (vi) in which the debtor's assets and affairs are subject to the control or supervision of a foreign court; and (vii) which proceeding is for the purpose of reorganization or liquidation').

[53]   HR Rep No 109-31, at 118 (2005) (emphasis added).

[54]   See *Paolini v Albertson's Inc*, 482 F 3d 1149, 1152 n 2 (9th Cir 2007) (citing 19 Am Jur 2d Corporations §§ 2306, 2306; (2006) 15 *Fletcher Cyclopedia of Law of Private Corporations* §§ 7201, 7202, 7205); *Lohnes v Level 3 Commc'n, Inc*, 272 F 3d 49, 56 (1st Cir 2001) (citing *Black's Law Dictionary* (6th edn, 1990), 1298).

[55]   UNCITRAL, Legislative Guide on Insolvency Law (UN 2005), p 7.

[56]   11 USC § 1502(4).

[57]   11 USC § 1502(5).

[58]   11 USC § 1502(2).

[59]   Council Regulation (EC) 1346/2000 on Insolvency Proceedings [2000] OJ L160/1 (hereinafter 'the EC Regulation').

[60]   EC Regulation, Recitals, para 13.

[61]   11 USC § 1516(c).

foreign proceedings as main or non-main. Only main proceedings trigger automatic relief, including application of the automatic stay under section 362. Relief in non-main proceedings is discretionary.

(a) Automatic relief

Recognition of a foreign main proceeding triggers the following relief automatically: **4.35**

- Sections 361 (adequate protection) and 362 (automatic stay) apply to the debtor and any of the debtor's property that is within the territorial jurisdiction of the US.
- Sections 363 (use, sale, and lease of property), 549 (post-petition transactions), and 552 (post-petition effect of security interests) apply to a transfer of an interest of the debtor in property that is within the territorial jurisdiction of the US to the same extent that such sections would apply to property of the estate.
- A foreign representative may operate the foreign debtor's business and may exercise the rights of a trustee under sections 363 and 552.[62]

(b) Discretionary relief

Upon recognition of a foreign proceeding as either a main or non-main proceeding, the   **4.36** court may grant discretionary relief 'where necessary to effectuate the purposes of [chapter 15] and to protect the assets of the debtor or the interests of the creditors'.[63] Only discretionary relief is available to a foreign representative of a non-main proceeding.

Discretionary relief includes: (i) staying the commencement or continuation of an indi-   **4.37** vidual action or proceeding concerning the debtor's assets, rights, obligations, or liabilities; (ii) staying execution against the debtor's assets; (iii) suspending the right to transfer, encumber, or otherwise dispose of any of the debtor's assets; (iv) providing for the examination of witnesses, the taking of evidence, or delivery of information concerning the debtor's assets, affairs, rights, obligations, or liabilities; (v) entrusting the administration, realization, and/or distribution of all or part of the debtor's assets within the US to the foreign representative or another person authorized by the court; (vi) extending any provisional relief granted under section 1519(a); and (vii) granting any additional relief available to a trustee under the Bankruptcy Code (but not authority to bring avoidance actions).[64] The court also may order turnover of assets located in the US to the foreign representative when 'the court is satisfied that the interests of the creditors in the United States are sufficiently protected'.[65]

There are various limitations on the grant of discretionary relief including the following: (i)   **4.38** the court may not enjoin a governmental unit's police or regulatory act, including a criminal action or proceeding;[66] (ii) with respect to a foreign non-main proceeding, the court must be satisfied that the relief relates to assets that, under US law, should be administered

---

[62] See 11 USC § 1520.
[63] 11 USC § 1521.
[64] 11 USC § 1521(a)(1)–(7).
[65] 11 USC § 1521(b). Note that additional protections of creditors and others are set forth in § 1522.
[66] See 11 USC § 1521(d). See also *US Intern Trade Com'n v Jaffe*, 433 BR 538 (Bankr ED Va 2010) (holding that the automatic stay, triggered upon entry of the recognition order, did not apply to a patent infringement action initiated by private entities pending before the International Trade Commission because the pending action was an enforcement of a governmental unit's police or regulatory power under s 364(b)(4) of the Bankruptcy Code).

in the foreign non-main proceeding or concerns information required in that proceeding;[67] (iii) discretionary relief that is injunctive must satisfy the standards, procedures, and limitations generally applicable to injunctions;[68] and (iv) avoidance actions are expressly not available.[69]

(c) Provisional relief

4.39   Although the filing of a chapter 15 petition does not trigger automatic relief unlike other chapters of the Bankruptcy Code, section 1519 allows a foreign representative to obtain provisional relief that may be necessary during the gap period between the filing of the chapter 15 petition and the bankruptcy court's decision on recognition. A bankruptcy court may grant provisional relief at the request of the foreign representative, but only 'where relief is urgently needed to protect the assets of the debtor or the interests of the creditors'.[70] A request for provisional relief is subject to the standards, procedures, and limitations applicable to an injunction.[71]

4.40   Upon such a finding, provisional relief includes, but is not limited to (i) staying execution against the debtor's assets;[72] (ii) entrusting the administration or realization of the debtor's assets that are perishable, susceptible to devaluation, or otherwise in jeopardy to the foreign representative or another court-authorized person;[73] (iii) suspending the right to transfer, encumber, or otherwise dispose of any of the debtor's assets;[74] (iv) providing for the examination of witnesses or the gathering of evidence regarding the debtor's assets, affairs, rights, obligations, or liabilities;[75] and (v) granting any additional relief available to a trustee under the Bankruptcy Code, excluding avoidance powers.[76] Unless extended, provisional relief terminates upon recognition of the chapter 15 petition.

4.41   Provisional relief is not unlimited and may be denied if it 'would interfere with the administration of a foreign main proceeding'.[77] In addition, a court may not order certain types of provisional relief, including enjoining a police or regulatory act of a governmental unit[78] or enjoining the exercise of set-off rights by non-debtor counterparties to financial contracts that otherwise are not 'automatically stayed'.[79]

---

[67]   See 11 USC § 1521(c).
[68]   See 11 USC § 1521(e).
[69]   11 USC § 1521(a)(7).
[70]   11 USC § 1519(a).
[71]   11 USC § 1519(e). A bankruptcy court considers the following factors in determining whether to grant an injunction: (i) whether there is a likelihood of successful reorganization; (ii) whether there is an imminent irreparable harm to the estate in the absence of an injunction; (iii) whether the balance of harm tips in favour of the moving party; and (iv) whether the public interest weighs in favour of an injunction. See *Calpine Corp v Nevada Power Co* (*In re Calpine Corp*), 354 BR 45 (Bankr SDNY 2006), *aff'd* 365 BR 401 (SDNY 2007).
[72]   11 USC § 1519(a)(1).
[73]   11 USC § 1519(a)(2).
[74]   11 USC §§ 1519(a)(3), 1521(a)(3).
[75]   11 USC §§ 1519(a)(3), 1521(a)(4).
[76]   11 USC §§ 1519(a)(3), 1521(a)(7).
[77]   11 USC § 1519(c).
[78]   11 USC § 1519(d).
[79]   11 USC § 1519(f).

(d) Additional assistance

Following recognition, a bankruptcy court may grant 'additional assistance'. Section 1507 **4.42**
authorizes the bankruptcy court to 'provide additional assistance to a foreign representative
under this title or under other laws of the United States'.[80] The grant of 'additional assistance' depends on evaluation of former section 304 factors: (i) just treatment of all holders of
claims against or interests in the debtor's property; (ii) protecting US claimholders against
prejudice and inconvenience in processing claims in the foreign proceeding; (iii) prevention of preferential or fraudulent dispositions of the debtor's property; (iv) distribution of
proceeds of the debtor's property substantially in accordance with the priority scheme set
forth in the Bankruptcy Code; and (v) if appropriate, the provision of an opportunity for
a fresh start for the individual that such foreign proceeding concerns.[81] Section 1507(b)
elevates 'comity' to utmost importance, essentially codifying section 304(c) case law that
emphasized its preeminence. Specifically, the introductory paragraph of section 1507(b)
provides that in determining whether to provide additional assistance the court must consider whether such additional assistance is consistent with the principles of comity.[82]

The scope of additional assistance provided for under this section is unclear. The legislative **4.43**
history states that additional relief is relief 'beyond that permitted under §§ 1519–1521'.[83]
Although the enactment of chapter 15 was intended to change the former approach to ancillary foreign proceedings, the legislative history notes that additional assistance does not
expand 'the scope of relief' currently available under section 304.[84] The legislative history
for section 1522, however, goes further and states that the bankruptcy court has 'broad latitude to mold relief to meet specific circumstances, including appropriate responses if it is
shown that the foreign proceeding is seriously and unjustifiably injuring United States creditors'.[85] There are express limits, however: section 1507 states that additional assistance is
subject to the specific limitations stated elsewhere in chapter 15.[86]

The 'additional assistance' section of chapter 15 departs from the Model Law in that recog- **4.44**
nition of the foreign proceeding is a prerequisite. The Model Law provides that '[n]othing in
the [Model] Law limits the power of a court ... to provide additional assistance to a foreign
representative under other laws of this State'.[87]

(e) Conditions to relief

A bankruptcy court may impose conditions to relief granted under section 1519 (provi- **4.45**
sional relief) or section 1521 (discretionary relief).[88] The bankruptcy court may also impose conditions on the ability of the foreign representative to operate the foreign debtor's
business upon recognition of a foreign main proceeding pursuant to section 1520(a)(3).[89]

---

[80] 11 USC § 1507(a).
[81] 11 USC § 1507(b).
[82] Ibid.
[83] Gropper, *supra* n 28 at 4 (citing HR Rep No 109-031, 109 (2005)).
[84] Ibid (quoting HR Rep No 109-031, 116 (2005)).
[85] Ibid.
[86] 11 USC § 1507(a).
[87] UNCITRAL Model Law on Cross-Border Insolvency, Art 7.
[88] 11 USC § 1522(b).
[89] Ibid.

The court may impose any conditions 'it considers appropriate, including the giving of security or the filing of a bond'.[90]

(f) Foreign representative

4.46   The foreign representative's ability to act in US courts changes following recognition. After recognition, the foreign representative gains the ability to sue and be sued in a US court and to apply directly to such US court for appropriate relief.[91] A US court also must grant comity or cooperation to the foreign representative[92] and a foreign representative may intervene in any proceeding in a US state or federal court in which the debtor is a party.[93]

4.47   Upon recognition of a foreign main proceeding, the foreign representative may operate the debtor's business and may exercise the rights and powers of a trustee under sections 363 and 552 of the Bankruptcy Code.[94]

6. Venue

4.48   A case under chapter 15 is commenced in the federal district in which the debtor has its principal place of business or principal assets in the US. If there is no such district, then a chapter 15 case may be commenced in the district in which a federal or state court action is pending against the debtor. Otherwise, a chapter 15 case may be commenced where venue 'will be consistent with the interests of justice and the convenience of the parties, having regard to the relief sought by the foreign representative'.[95]

4.49   The 'affiliate rule'[96] which normally permits the filing of related chapter 11 cases in the same district where an affiliate's chapter 11 case is pending does not appear on its face to apply to chapter 15 cases. However, in practice, corporate groups routinely file chapter 15 cases in the same jurisdiction.[97]

7. Cooperation and communication

4.50   The Guide to Enactment of the Model Law characterizes the articles on cooperation and communication as a 'core element' of the Model Law.[98] The objective of these provisions 'is to enable courts and insolvency administrators from two or more countries to be efficient and achieve optimal results'.[99] Chapter 15 closely tracks the Model Law provisions

---

[90] Ibid.
[91] 11 USC § 1509(b)(1).
[92] 11 USC § 1509(b)(3).
[93] 11 USC § 1524.
[94] 11 USC § 1520(a)(3).
[95] 28 USC § 1410.
[96] 28 USC § 1408. Venue of cases under title 11. Except as provided in section 1410 of this title, a case under title 11 may be commenced in the district court for the district— (1) in which the domicile, residence, principal place of business in the United States, or principal assets in the United States, of the person or entity that is the subject of such case has been located for the one hundred and eighty days immediately preceding such commencement, or for a longer portion of such one hundred-and-eighty-day period that the domicile, residence or principal place of business, in the United States, or principal assets in the United States, of such person were located in any other district; or (2) in which there is pending a case under title 11 concerning such person's affiliate, general partner or partnership. Section 1410 governs venue of chapter 15 cases and contains no language comparable to s 1408(2). See 28 USC § 1410.
[97] See, e.g., *In re Serviços de Petróleo Constellation S.A.* (Bankr SDNY Case No 18-13952) (order for joint administration of ten affiliate chapter 15 cases entered Dec 7 2018); *In re B.C.I Finances PTY Limited* (Bankr SDNY Case No 17-11266) (order for joint administration of four affiliate chapter 15 cases entered May 10 2017).
[98] Guide to Enactment of the Model Law, *supra* n 6 at para 173.
[99] Ibid.

on cooperation and communication between US and foreign courts or representatives. Sections 1525 and 1526 direct the bankruptcy court and the trustee, or other person, including an examiner, to 'cooperate to the maximum extent possible with a foreign court or foreign representative'. In addition, the bankruptcy court or trustee is authorized to communicate directly with, or to request information or assistance directly from, a foreign court or foreign representative.[100] Chapter 15 provides a non-exhaustive list of the types of cooperation that may occur between the US court or trustee and the foreign court, including: the appointment of a person or body to act at the direction of the court; communication of information by any appropriate method; coordination of the administration and supervision of the foreign debtor's assets and affairs; approval or implementation of agreements concerning the coordination of proceedings; and coordination of concurrent proceedings involving the same debtor.[101]

8. Multiple proceedings

Chapter 15 acknowledges the possibility of a concurrent plenary case under other chapters of the Bankruptcy Code. Following recognition, a foreign representative many commence (i) an involuntary case under section 303 or (ii) if the recognized proceeding is a foreign main proceeding, a voluntary case under section 301 or 302.[102] However, the debtor must have assets in the US to commence a plenary case under the Bankruptcy Code.[103]   **4.51**

If a plenary case is commenced after a foreign main proceeding has been recognized, the case will only affect (i) the assets of the debtor that are within the territorial jurisdiction of the US and (ii) to the extent necessary to implement cooperation and coordination with foreign courts and representatives, other assets of the debtor that are within the court's jurisdiction and not subject to the jurisdiction and control of a foreign proceeding that has been recognized under chapter 15.[104]   **4.52**

A foreign debtor may also have multiple non-main proceedings because a foreign debtor may have multiple establishments, as opposed to only one COMI.[105]   **4.53**

A court may dismiss or suspend a plenary bankruptcy case under section 305's abstention principles at the request of the foreign representative if doing so is consistent with the purposes of chapter 15.[106] Filing a motion under section 305 does not subject a foreign representative to the jurisdiction of any court in the US for any other purpose.[107]   **4.54**

9. Interpretation

Under section 1508, a bankruptcy court must consider non-US sources in addition to US case law and chapter 15 legislative history when interpreting chapter 15. Non-US sources that Congress described as 'persuasive' include decisions rendered by foreign courts construing the Model Law and the report of UNCITRAL and the Guide to Enactment of the   **4.55**

---

[100] 11 USC §§ 1525(b), 1526(b).
[101] 11 USC § 1527.
[102] 11 USC § 1511(a).
[103] 11 USC § 1528.
[104] Ibid.
[105] Ranney-Marinelli, *supra* n 41 at 298.
[106] 11 USC § 305.
[107] 11 USC § 306.

UNCITRAL Model Law on Cross-Border Insolvency.[108] Other sources that interpret provisions similar to the Model Law and may be useful include certain provisions of the EC Regulation, the Report on the Convention on Insolvency Proceedings by Miguel Virgos and Etienne Schmitt (which is the principal report on the EU convention on insolvency proceedings), decisions construing the EC Regulation, and reports and commentary on the EC Regulation prepared by various member states of the EU in connection with their adoption of the EC Regulation.[109]

III. Chapter 15 Recognition of English Schemes of Arrangement

4.56   Under chapter 15, bankruptcy courts generally recognize English proceedings involving schemes of arrangement under the UK Companies Act 2006,[110] as foreign proceedings.[111] A scheme of arrangement envisions expeditious court approval of consensual reorganization plans and is in some ways similar to a prepackaged chapter 11 plan of reorganization.[112] A scheme is a binding arrangement between a company and one or more classes of creditors to restructure the affairs of the company and creditors' rights and liabilities.[113] Schemes are only effective and binding on the company and its creditors after a requisite majority of creditors vote in favour of the scheme and the High Court, after a hearing, issues an order sanctioning the scheme.[114]

4.57   Prior to enactment of chapter 15, courts granted relief under section 304 when the foreign proceeding involved a scheme of arrangement.[115] Courts continue to recognize such schemes under chapter 15. In fact, a bankruptcy court in the Southern District of

---

[108]   HR Rep No 109-031, at 109–110 (2005).

[109]   Ranney-Marinelli, *supra* n 41 at 273–274.

[110]   Previously such schemes were made under the UK Companies Act 1985.

[111]   See, e.g., *In re Matalan Finance PLC* (Bankr SDNY Case No 20-11749) (chapter 15 and supporting documents filed on 29 July 2020; order granting recognition of scheme of arrangement entered on 2 September 2020) (no objections to requested relief); *In re Magyar Telecom BV* (Bankr SDNY Case No 13-13508) (chapter 15 and supporting documents filed on 29 October 2013; order granting recognition of foreign main proceeding and scheme of arrangement entered on 11 December 2013) (no objections filed to requested relief); *In re Hellas Telecom (Luxembourg) V* (Bankr D Del Case No 10-13651) (chapter 15 and supporting documents filed on 12 November 2010; order granting recognition of foreign main proceeding and scheme of arrangement entered on 13 December 2010) (no objections filed to requested relief); *In re The Meadows Indemnity Company Ltd* (Bankr MD Tenn Case No 09-08706) (chapter 15 petition and supporting documents filed on 31 July 2009; order granting recognition of proceeding implementing solvent scheme of arrangement pursuant to Part 26 of the Companies Act 2006 as a foreign proceeding entered 9 September 2009); *In re Petition of Philip Heitlinger, as foreign representative of AXA Insurance UK PLC, Ecclesiastical Insurance Office plc, Global General and Reinsurance Company Limited and MMA IARD Assurances Mutuelles* (Bankr SDNY Case No 07-12112) (chapter 15 petition and supporting documents filed on 9 July 2007; order granting recognition of foreign proceedings, permanent injunction, and related relief entered on 15 August 2007) (no objection filed to requested relief); *In re Europäische Rückversicherungs-Gesellschaft in Zürich* (Bankr SDNY Case No 06-13061) (chapter 15 petition filed on 21 December 2006; order granting recognition of foreign non-main proceeding entered on 14 January 2007) (no objection filed to requested relief); *In re Petition of Jeffrey John Lloyd*, Case No. 05-60100, 2005 Bankr Lexis 2794 (Bankr SDNY 2005) (chapter 15 petition and supporting documents filed on 11 November 2005; order granting recognition of foreign main proceeding entered on 7 December 2005) (no objection filed to requested relief).

[112]   See *In re Hopewell Int'l Insurance*, 238 BR 25, 50–52 (Bankr SDNY 1999).

[113]   Howard Seife and Francisco Vazquez, 'US Courts Should Continue to Grant Recognition to Schemes of Arrangement of Solvent Insurance Companies' (2008) 17 *Journal of Bankruptcy Law and Practice* 4 Art 4.

[114]   Ibid at 571–572.

[115]   See, e.g., *In re Hopewell Int'l Insurance*, 238 BR at 53.

New York recognized the schemes of arrangement for Countrywide plc, the UK's leading estate agency for residential properties, before such schemes were binding on the various parties-in-interest. The bankruptcy court issued an order recognizing the schemes of arrangement as foreign main proceedings before the required majority of creditors voted on such schemes.[116] After the English High Court issued an order sanctioning the schemes, the bankruptcy court entered an order recognizing and enforcing the English High Court's order.[117] This decision demonstrates that chapter 15 can be used as a tool to ensure 'uninterrupted promotion of the scheme' even prior to sanction by the English court.[118]

Both solvent and insolvent companies may make use of a scheme of arrangement. **4.58** Numerous solvent schemes of arrangement have been recognized under chapter 15 as foreign proceedings.[119] When Congress adopted chapter 15, the definition of foreign proceeding was changed to include proceedings involving 'adjustment of debt'. This addition was intended to 'capture solvent schemes of arrangement under Part 26 of the UK Companies Act 2006 or other equivalent legislation'.[120] Some commentators have suggested that bankruptcy courts should not recognize under chapter 15 schemes of arrangements implemented under English law by solvent insurance companies.[121] Some solvent insurance companies have used such schemes to shorten the period it takes to run off their business; the insurance company seeks to determine, settle, and pay all liquidated claims of its insureds on an expedited basis.[122] There is some debate as to whether solvent schemes for insurance companies fit the definition of foreign proceeding under section 101(23) of the Bankruptcy Code, are 'manifestly contrary' to US policy, including the sanctity of contracts and due process, and severely prejudice US claimholders. There has yet to be a published US decision that addresses this controversy.

In addition to schemes of arrangement, solvent insurance companies in the UK may use Part **4.59** VII insurance transfers, available under section 105 of the Financial Services and Markets Act 2000, to financially restructure their business. Unlike solvent schemes of arrangement that are generally recognized under chapter 15, there is no certainty that such a transfer

---

[116] See *In re Castle Holdco 4, Ltd*, Case No 09-11761 (REG) (Bankr SDNY, 22 April 2009).

[117] *In re Castle Holdco 4, Ltd*, Case No 09-11761 (REG) (Bankr SDNY, 7 May 2009).

[118] Look Chan Ho, 'Creative Uses of Chapter 15 of the US Bankruptcy Code to Smooth Cross-Border Restructurings' (2009) 9 *JIBLR* 485. The same article highlights the danger that bankruptcy courts will 'rubber stamp' recognition in the interests of comity or facilitating a coordinated settlement of all pending litigation at the expense of statutory recognition requirements. Ibid at 488. The article argues that in the *Grand Prix Associates* case, a New Jersey bankruptcy court recognized a British Virgin Islands plan of arrangement, which is different from an English scheme of arrangement, without fully considering whether the foreign proceeding should be entitled to recognition. Ibid at 487; see also *In re Grand Prix Associates Inc*, Case No 09-16545, 2009 WL 1850966 (Bankr DNJ, 26 June 2009).

[119] See, eg, *In re Petition of Jeffrey John Lloyd*, 2005 Bankr Lexis 2794 (Bankr SDNY 2005) (Lifland J); *Lion City Run-Off Private Limited*, Case No 06-B-10461 (Bankr SDNY 2006) (Bernstein J); *In re Gordian Runoff (UK) Limited*, Case No 06-11563 (Bankr SDNY 2006) (Drain J); *In re Petition of Philip Heitlinger*, 07-B-12110 (Bankr SDNY 2007) (Gerber J); *In re Petition of Clive Paul Thomas*, 07-B-12009 (Bankr SDNY 2007) (Glenn J); *In re Petition of PRO Insurance Solutions*, 07-B-12934 (Bankr SDNY 2007) (Peck J); *In re Virgin Atlantic Airways Limited*, Case No 20-11804 (Bankr SDNY 2020) (Wiles M). In each of these cases the court recognized an English scheme of arrangement as a foreign proceeding under chapter 15, however, such orders do not provide any reasoning or analysis to support the court's decision.

[120] Look Chan Ho, 'Recognising an Australian Solvent Liquidation under the UNCITRAL Model Law: In re Betcorp' (2009) 18 *Journal of Bankruptcy Law and Practice* 5 Art 3.

[121] See Susan Power Johnson, 'Why US Courts Should Deny or Severely Condition Recognition to Schemes of Arrangement for Solvent Insurance Companies' (2007) 16 *Journal of Bankruptcy Law and Practice* 6 Art 2; Seife and Vazquez, *supra* n 112.

[122] Seife and Vazquez, *supra* n 112.

would be recognized as a foreign proceeding under chapter 15. A Part VII transfer allows an insurance company to transfer all or a part of its business to another company to discharge it of the duties and obligations associated with the transferred business.[123] If a company decides to engage in such a transfer, the company must report the terms of the transfer and the potential impact of the transfer on policyholders and creditors to the Prudential Regulation Authority (PRA) and Financial Conduct Authority (FCA), as applicable.[124] While creditor approval of the proposed transfer is not required, the proposed transfer is subject to the approval of the English High Court.[125]

4.60   English insurance companies have sought recognition of such transfers in the US to bind US creditors or policyholders to the Part VII transfer; however, at least one bankruptcy court found that such a transfer was not a foreign proceeding under former section 304.[126] In *Rose*,[127] the bankruptcy court held that such a transfer was not a 'foreign proceeding' under section 304 because it did not effect a reorganization in the bankruptcy context. The court explained that section 304 does not cover any type of corporate restructuring within any type of foreign proceeding.[128] Again, there has been no published opinion analysing whether Part VII transfers qualify as foreign proceedings under chapter 15. Although Part VII transfers are in some ways analogous to chapter 11 cases of solvent debtors seeking to discharge burdensome obligations, there are several arguments against recognition of such transfers, in addition to the case law developed under section 304, including that (i) such transfers do not arise out of an insolvency-related law, (ii) they do not adjust debts because creditor liabilities are not determined on a final basis upon such a transfer, and (iii) the foreign debtor does not have to be in severe financial distress for such a transfer to occur.[129]

IV. Does Availability of Chapter 15 Relief Affect Willingness to Accept Jurisdiction in Chapter 11 Case Where Debtor's COMI is Outside the US?

A. Eligibility Requirements for Relief

4.61   A debtor must be eligible to file a petition for relief under the Bankruptcy Code. Specifically, section 109(a) provides that:

> Notwithstanding any other provision of this section, only a person that resides or has a domicile, a place of business or property in the United States, or a municipality, may be a debtor under this title.[130]

---

[123] Jennifer D Morton, Note, 'Recognition of Cross-Border Insolvency Proceedings: an Evaluation of Solvent Schemes of Arrangement and Part VII Transfers under U.S. Chapter 15' (2006) 29 *Fordham Int'l LJ* 1312, 1313.

[124] Ibid at 1325. Prior to 1 April 2013, the functions of the PRA and FCA were performed by the Financial Services Authority (FSA).

[125] Ibid.

[126] *In re Petition of Rose*, 318 BR 771 (Bankr SDNY 2004).

[127] Ibid.

[128] Ibid at 774–775. But see *In re Riverstone*, Case No 05-12678, 2005 Bankr WL 2138734 (Bankr SDNY, 26 July 2005) (order recognizing Part VII transfer under s 304). The order entered in *Riverstone* is not an opinion, and does not provide any discussion regarding whether Part VII transfers should be recognized as foreign proceedings under s 304. Ibid; see also Morton, *supra* n 122 at 1336.

[129] Morton, *supra* n 122 at 1354–1355.

[130] 11 USC § 109(a).

While a lack of property in the US generally did not prevent foreign debtors from obtaining   **4.62**
relief under chapter 15, a decision by the United States Court of Appeals for Second Circuit in
December 2013 holding that the eligibility requirements set forth in section 109(a) apply in
chapter 15 proceedings may limit foreign representatives' ability to obtain relief under chapter
15 of the Bankruptcy Code.[131]

In *Barnet*, Octaviar Administration Pty Ltd, an Australian company, was the subject of liquid-   **4.63**
ation proceedings in Australia.[132] Although the debtor had no operations or business in the
US, the foreign representatives filed for chapter 15 relief in the US Bankruptcy Court for the
Southern District of New York in connection with the potential prosecution of claims and
causes of action against entities located in the US. Drawbridge Special Opportunities Fund LP,
already subject to a lawsuit in the liquidation proceeding initiated by the Australian liquidators,
objected, arguing that the foreign debtor failed to meet the eligibility requirements of section
109(a). The bankruptcy court overruled the objection and entered an order recognizing the
liquidation proceeding as a foreign main proceeding.[133] Drawbridge appealed and the bankruptcy court certified the appeal directly to the Second Circuit. In the bankruptcy court's certification order, it explained that there was no controlling precedent governing its holding 'that a
debtor within the meaning of chapter 15 is not required to have a domicile, residence, place of
business or property in the United States', but that such ruling was consistent with law and practice under section 304 of the Bankruptcy Code, the predecessor to chapter 15.[134]

Taking up the question of whether section 109(a) of the Bankruptcy Code applies to a for-   **4.64**
eign debtor under chapter 15, the Second Circuit relied on a 'straightforward' interpretation of the Bankruptcy Code and held that section 109(a) does so apply.[135] Because section
103(a) of the Bankruptcy Code provides that chapter 1 of the Bankruptcy Code applies in a
case under chapter 15 and section 109(a) is within chapter 1, the Second Circuit concluded
that 'by the plain terms of the statute', section 109 applies to a case under chapter 15. The
Second Circuit held that the stated purposes of chapter 15 could be accomplished with or
without the imposition of section 109(a).[136] While acknowledging that the Model Law does
not contain an express requirement such as section 109(a), the Second Circuit reasoned
such omission does not outweigh the express language of sections 109(a) and 103.[137]

At least one bankruptcy court outside the Second Circuit has followed *Barnet* and held that   **4.65**
section 109(a) applies to cases under chapter 15.[138] Following his appointment in Australia,
the liquidator and foreign representative of Forge Group Power Pty Ltd. filed a petition for
recognition of the debtor's Australian proceeding under chapter 15 with the Bankruptcy
Court for the Northern District of California. In connection with the chapter 15 filing, the

---

[131] *Drawbridge Special Opportunities Fund LP v Barnet (In Re Barnet)*, 737 F 3d 238 (2d Cir 2013).
[132] Ibid at 241.
[133] Ibid.
[134] Ibid (citing Mem Op in Supp of Certification of Direct Appeal to the Court of Appeals for the Second Circuit at 6, 9, *In re Barnet*, No 12-13443, Dkt No 47 (Bankr SDNY 28 Nov 2012)).
[135] Ibid at 247.
[136] Ibid at 251.
[137] Ibid.
[138] *In re Forge Grp. Power Pty Ltd.*, 2018 WL 827913, at *8 (N.D. Cal. Feb. 12, 2018) ('[g]iven the plain, unam-
biguous language of §§ 103(a) and 109(a), a debtor that is the subject of a foreign proceeding seeking recognition
under Chapter 15 must satisfy the debtor eligibility requirement of residing or having a domicile, place of business
or property in the United States').

liquidator alleged that the debtor's $100,000 held as a retainer by a law firm in California satisfied the requirements of section 109(a).[139] Certain creditors objected to recognition, arguing that the retainer alone was insufficient to satisfy the debtor eligibility requirements under section 109(a). Bankruptcy Judge Montali agreed and denied the Debtor's petition as 'the retainer ... is property in a technical sense ... but it's illusory because there is a string attached to it if the lawyer ceases to represent[,] and as the lawyer does work, the retainer is consumed'.[140]

4.66   On appeal, the District Court for the Northern District of California, citing to *Barnet*, affirmed the Bankruptcy Court's conclusion that the debtor eligibility requirements under section 109(a) apply in Chapter 15 cases.[141] However, the District Court disagreed with the Bankruptcy Court and concluded that a debtor's retainer held by US counsel at the time of a chapter 15 filing satisfies section 109(a)'s eligibility requirements.[142]

4.67   Although *Barnet* and *Forge* do appear to raise the jurisdictional bar, at least in certain jurisdictions,[143] *Forge* confirmed that obtaining property for purposes of satisfying section 109(a) may not be an insurmountable hurdle for foreign debtors and foreign representatives. Other courts also have held in chapter 11 cases of foreign debtors that a minimal amount of property in the US will satisfy the requirements of section 109(a).[144]

4.68   The Bankruptcy Court for the Southern District of New York has held that a foreign debtor's claims located in the US constitute property of the debtor for the purposes of satisfying section 109(a).[145] On 24 April 2018, Bankruptcy Judge Lane, in the chapter 15 cases of Australian debtors B.C.I. Finances Pty Limited and affiliates, granted recognition of the Australian liquidation proceedings of these related debtors.[146] The chapter 15 cases were filed by the debtors' Australian liquidators because certain of the debtors' directors, who an

---

[139] Ibid at *4.

[140] Ibid.

[141] Ibid.

[142] Ibid at *12.

[143] On 17 December 2013 (and shortly after the *Barnet* opinion was issued by the Second Circuit), the bankruptcy court in Delaware held that s 109(a) does *not* apply in chapter 15 proceedings because s 109(a) of the Bankruptcy Code applies to debtors, and in chapter 15 proceedings, it is foreign representatives who petition the bankruptcy court for recognition, not debtors. The Delaware bankruptcy court further stated that it did 'not agree with the [*Barnet*] decision of the Second Circuit' regarding whether s 109(a) eligibility requirements apply to recognition under chapter 15. *In re Bemarmara Consulting as*, Case No 13-13037 (KG) (Bankr D Del 17 Dec 2013). No decision from a court in the Third Circuit has since been published on the issue, however.

[144] *In re McTague*, 198 BR 428, 431–432 (Bankr WDNY 1996) (holding that US$194 in a bank account was sufficient to satisfy eligibility requirements under s 109(a) and noting that s 109(a) 'seems to have such a plain meaning as to leave the Court no discretion to consider whether it was the intent of Congress to permit someone to obtain a bankruptcy discharge solely on the basis of having a dollar, a dime or a peppercorn located in the United States'); *In re Avanti Commc'ns Grp. PLC*, 582 BR 603, 613 (Bankr SDNY 2018) (holding while the chapter 15 debtor did not have a place of business or domicile in the United States, the debtor's retainer with a US law firm and an indenture governed by New York law satisfied the 'property in the United States' requirement for eligibility under section 109(a)); *In re Servicos de Petroleo Constellation S.A.*, 600 BR 237, 269 (Bankr SDNY 2019) (holding chapter 15 debtors satisfied section 109(a) as each debtor owned $1000 in a US bank account and were party to certain debt documents governed by New York law).

[145] *In re BCI Finances Pty Ltd*, 583 BR 288, 296-300 (Bankr SDNY 2018) (holding that foreign debtor's fiduciary duty claims were located in New York and constituted property in the United States sufficient to satisfy section 109(a)).

[146] Ibid.

Australian judge had found liable in Australia for statutory and fiduciary duty breaches, had fled to New York at some point during the proceedings, likely in an effort to avoid recovery by the liquidators.[147] The liquidators commenced chapter 15 cases seeking the Bankruptcy Court's assistance in pursuing discovery against the directors.[148] Certain parties, including one of the former directors, challenged the debtors' eligibility for Chapter 15 under section 109(a).[149]

The Bankruptcy Court overruled the objection based on section 109(a), and found that   **4.69** each debtor's $1,250 retainer deposited with US counsel and the existence of the fiduciary duty claims against the insiders who were located in the US constituted property sufficient to satisfy *Barnet* and section 109(a).[150] Judge Lane rejected the argument that the small retainers were provided to 'manufacture' statutory eligibility, holding that courts were bound to the 'plain meaning' of section 109(a).[151] Regarding the fiduciary duty claims, the Bankruptcy Court analysed the situs of the claims, holding that under New York's choice of law rules Australian law should determine situs, and under Australian law, the claims were located in New York because they were properly recoverable where the directors currently reside.[152] Thus, the claims constituted property in the US for purposes of section 109(a).

Relatedly, courts have held that chapter 15 may be used to assist foreign representatives   **4.70** seeking discovery from parties located in the US.[153] In *In re Platimum Partners*, Bankruptcy Judge Chapman held that the debtor's foreign representatives could use chapter 15 to obtain discovery against the company's auditors not otherwise available to them in the Cayman Islands main proceeding.[154] Judge Chapman reasoned, in part, that comity supported granting the requested relief under chapter 15, as Cayman discovery law neither prohibited nor was hostile to the discovery sought in the United States.[155] The District Court for the Southern District of New York affirmed the Bankruptcy Court's holding, dismissing the auditors' arguments that (i) the arbitration clause in the auditors' engagement letter prevented discovery, and (ii) the debtors were not able to obtain the auditors' work product under Cayman law.[156] The District Court held that '[e]ven if a Cayman Islands court would not itself order production of the documents, Cayman Islands courts are receptive to evidence obtained through US discovery law'.[157] Further, the District Court observed that '[t] he bankruptcy court is vested with broad discretion to grant access to discovery in order to fulfill the purposes of Chapter 15'.[158]

---

[147] Ibid at 290–291.
[148] Ibid.
[149] Ibid at 295–296.
[150] Ibid.
[151] Ibid.
[152] Ibid at 303.
[153] Ibid.
[154] *In re Platinum Partners Value Arbitrage Fund LP*, 583 BR 803 (Bankr SDNY 2018).
[155] Ibid at 816–817.
[156] *In re Platinum Partners Value Arbitrage Fund LP*, 2018 WL 3207119, at *5–6 (SDNY 29 June 2018).
[157] Ibid at *6.
[158] Ibid at *8.

B. Eligibility for Chapter 11 Relief when the Debtor's COMI is Outside the US

4.71   Chapter 15 contemplates that a foreign representative may commence a plenary bankruptcy case under chapter 11 after recognition of the foreign proceeding.[159] Furthermore, a foreign debtor can avoid chapter 15 altogether and file a chapter 11 petition in the first instance if it satisfies the eligibility requirements of section 109(a) of the Bankruptcy Code. That a debtor's COMI is located outside the US generally will not prevent a foreign debtor from filing for chapter 11 relief because plenary jurisdiction does not require a 'principal place of business', COMI, or meaningful assets in the US.

4.72   The requirements for eligibility are determined as of the date the bankruptcy petition is filed[160] and each related debtor individually must satisfy the test for eligibility.[161] The entity filing the bankruptcy petition carries the burden of establishing eligibility.[162] Under section 109(a), even if a debtor's COMI is not located in the US, there are other grounds that may form the jurisdictional basis for a chapter 11 petition. As discussed above, even a minimal amount of property in the US will do.

4.73   Courts generally are receptive to chapter 11 petitions filed by foreign debtors. LyondellBasell Industries used the chapter 11 process to protect its European parent, LyondellBasell Industries AF SCA, organized in Luxembourg with its principal place of business in the Netherlands, from the commencement of involuntary insolvency proceedings abroad.[163] Lyondell Chemical Co, its other US affiliates and one European affiliate, a subsidiary of LyondellBasell Industries AF SCA, filed for chapter 11 protection on 6 January 2009. There were no ongoing foreign insolvency proceedings to which the US bankruptcy court could consider granting comity.[164] Instead, in a decision that generated some controversy, the bankruptcy court granted the debtors' motion for an injunction to prevent creditors from acting against the foreign parent company for 60 days in an effort to protect LyondellBasell's European operations.[165] The parent company then filed for chapter 11 protection before the injunction expired even though its COMI was outside the US.

4.74   Although an extraordinary remedy,[166] a foreign debtor filing a chapter 11 petition should consider the risk that its chapter 11 case may be dismissed or suspended by a bankruptcy court.[167] Specifically, section 305(a) of the Bankruptcy Code provides that:

---

[159]   11 USC § 1511(a).

[160]   *Catholic School Employees Pension Trust*, 599 BR 634, 652 (BAP 1st Cir 2019); *In re Global Ocean Carriers Ltd*, 251 BR 31, 37 (Bankr D Del 2000); see also *In re Axona International Credit & Commerce, Ltd*, 88 BR 597, 614–615 (Bankr SDNY 1988).

[161]   *Bank of America v World of English*, 23 BR 1015, 1019–1020 (ND Ga 1982) (even where parent is eligible to file, subsidiary must be tested separately to see if it is eligible).

[162]   See *Global Ocean Carriers Ltd*, 251 BR at 37; *In re Secured Equipment Trust of Eastern Air Lines Inc*, 153 BR 409, 412 (Bankr SDNY 1993).

[163]   See Bench Decision on Motions for Preliminary Injunctions, *Lyondell Chemical Company v Centerpoint Energy Gas Services Inc (In re Lyondell Chemical Company)*, No 09-01039 (REG) (Bankr SDNY 26 Feb 2009).

[164]   Ibid.

[165]   Ibid.

[166]   11 USC § 305(a).

[167]   See *In re Paper I Partners, LP*, 283 BR 661, 678 (Bankr SDNY 2002).

(a) The court, after notice and a hearing, may dismiss a case under this title or may suspend all proceedings in a case under this title if—

  (1) the interests of creditors and the debtor would be better served by such dismissal
  or suspension; or

  (2) (A) a petition under section 1515 for recognition of a foreign proceeding has
  been granted; and

(B) the purposes of chapter 15 of this title would be best served by such dismissal or
suspension.[168]

A bankruptcy court considers several factors in determining whether to abstain by dis-   **4.75**
missal or suspension:

> (1) whether another forum is available to protect the interests of both parties or there is
> already a pending proceeding in state court; (2) economy and efficiency of administra-
> tion; (3) whether federal proceedings are necessary to reach a just and equitable solution;
> (4) whether there is an alternative means of achieving an equitable distribution of assets;
> (5) whether the debtor and the creditors are able to work out a less expensive out-of-court
> arrangement which better serves all interests in the case; (6) whether a non-federal insolv-
> ency has proceeded so far that it would be costly and time consuming to start afresh with
> the federal bankruptcy process; and (7) the purpose for which bankruptcy jurisdiction has
> been sought.[169]

If a foreign proceeding is pending, a bankruptcy court also must take comity considerations   **4.76**
into account and give deference to the foreign proceeding.[170] One court restated the factors
discussed above if a bankruptcy court is asked to abstain in favour of a foreign proceeding
as follows: (1) whether the foreign forum will determine and adjust the parties' rights in a
fair and equitable manner; (2) the relative benefits and burdens of exercising jurisdiction
over the US bankruptcy case, including the physical location of the parties-in-interest, the
existence of parallel actions, and the nature of the dispute; and (3) the reason for filing the
petition.[171] For example, the bankruptcy court in *Compañía de Alimentos Fargo* dismissed
an involuntary chapter 11 case against a foreign debtor initiated by creditors dissatisfied
with the progress of the foreign proceedings in Argentina. The court decided that even
though there were differences between Argentine and US law, including that Argentine law
did not provide for an automatic stay affecting secured creditors, the 'differences were not at
odds with our own *fundamental* notions of fairness'.[172]

In addition, a bankruptcy court may dismiss a foreign debtor's chapter 11 case if it has only   **4.77**
tenuous ties to the US and its COMI is located elsewhere. A bankruptcy court may decide
to dismiss a chapter 11 petition as a 'bad faith filing' if the foreign debtor's US property
had been specifically placed or left in the US for the 'sole purpose of creating eligibility
that would not otherwise exist'.[173] A bankruptcy court in the Southern District of Texas

---

[168] 11 USC § 305(a); see also *In re Compañía de Alimentos Fargo*, 376 BR 427, 433 (Bankr SDNY 2007) ('The decision to abstain, either by suspension or dismissal, is committed to the Court's discretion').
[169] *In re Compañía de Alimentos Fargo*, 376 BR at 434.
[170] Ibid.
[171] Ibid at 434–435.
[172] Ibid at 437.
[173] *In re McTague*, 198 BR at 432.

dismissed a chapter 11 case initiated by Yukos Oil Company after determining that the totality of the circumstances required a dismissal of the Russian oil company's chapter 11 case under section 1112(b) of the Bankruptcy Code.[174] There were several facts that contributed to the dismissal including, among others, that: (i) Yukos' plan of reorganization was a not a financial reorganization because the plan simply provided that the company's tax debts would be subordinated and causes of action held by the company would be transferred to a trust for continued litigation; (ii) the ability to effectuate its contemplated plan was unlikely without the cooperation of the Russian government; (iii) funds were transferred to banks in the US less than a week before the petition date and were transferred for the primary purpose of attempting to create jurisdiction in the US bankruptcy courts; (iv) several other forums were available to resolve the issues presented; (v) the vast majority of Yukos' business and financial activities occurred in Russia; and (vi) the size of Yukos and its impact on the Russian economy weighed in favour of allowing resolution in a forum in which participation of the Russian government was assured.[175]

V. Choosing Between Chapter 15 and Chapter 11 for Foreign Debtors

A. The Automatic Stay

4.78   One of the hallmarks of a chapter 11 case is a stay that goes into effect automatically upon the filing of the case without the necessity of any court action. The Bankruptcy Code provides that the commencement of a plenary case under any chapter automatically enjoins, without the need for a court order, all actions (with certain limited exceptions) to pursue or collect on a pre-bankruptcy claim against the debtor, obtain possession of property of the estate, or obtain a lien on property of the estate. This injunction is known as the 'automatic stay'. By its terms, the stay under section 362 of the Bankruptcy Code applies to protect the debtor and its property wherever located in the world.[176]

4.79   The automatic stay benefits the debtor by giving it relief from creditors' collection efforts and benefits the debtor's creditors by (a) preserving the debtor's going concern value and (b) maintaining the status quo, thereby preventing creditors from obtaining disproportionate recoveries in comparison with similarly situated creditors. As a corollary to the automatic stay, and consistent with its goal of promoting the equal treatment of similarly situated creditors, the Bankruptcy Code prohibits a debtor from paying any pre-bankruptcy, or 'pre-petition', claims (outside the context of a confirmed chapter 11 plan) without first having obtained bankruptcy court authorization to do so, and then, only upon giving notice to other creditors and parties-in-interest. A bankruptcy court may, upon a creditor's request and after notice and a hearing, grant relief from the automatic stay.[177] The Bankruptcy Code

---

[174] *In re Yukos Oil Company*, 321 BR 396, 410–411 (Bankr SD Tex 2005).

[175] Ibid.

[176] See also *In re McTague*, 198 BR at 430 ('Although it may be true that orders of this Court have "extraterritorial effect", it is fundamental that those orders can be enforced in a foreign nation only to the extent that the foreign nation grants those orders "full faith and credit" as a matter of comity, treaty or convention').

[177] 11 USC § 362(d).

provides two primary grounds for allowing relief from the automatic stay: (1) 'for cause, including the lack of adequate protection of an interest in property' held by such party in interest, or (2) with respect to an action against property of the estate, if the debtor does not have any equity in such property (ie the claims against such property exceed its value) and such property is not necessary for an effective reorganization of the debtor.[178]

The major difference between the automatic stay under chapter 11 and the automatic stay **4.80** under chapter 15 is scope. The effect of the stay under chapter 15 is limited to the territorial jurisdiction of the US.[179] The limited effect of the automatic stay under chapter 15 is in keeping with the general principle that the foreign main proceeding should ordinarily dominate the cross-border aspects of the debtor's insolvency proceedings because the 'foreign main proceeding is, by definition, pending in the center of the debtor's main interests'.[180] If a foreign main proceeding does not provide strong debtor protection from creditor actions, a foreign debtor may be more likely to file a petition under chapter 11 than chapter 15 to obtain the full benefit of the automatic stay.

A recent decision in Delaware discussed the application of the automatic stay in chapter 15 **4.81** cases. In *Irish Bank Resolution Corporation Limited*, the debtor bank was liquidated in a proceeding in Dublin and subsequently filed for chapter 15 relief.[181] Certain of the debtor's borrowers sued the debtor's foreign representatives in the chapter 15 case, asserting claims for breach of fiduciary duty, fraud, misrepresentation, negligent misrepresentation, and other misconduct, seeking damages for misusing the chapter 15 process and to terminate them as the foreign representatives.[182]

The Bankruptcy Court dismissed the suit and plaintiffs appealed. The District Court af- **4.82** firmed, addressing whether the *Barton* doctrine (a common law doctrine that bars suits against court-appointed trustees and other fiduciaries absent court permission) applies to actions against foreign representatives and whether the automatic stay applies to a suit against them.[183] District Judge Stark ruled that while application of the *Barton* doctrine in chapter 15 was an issue of first impression, the District Court need not decide 'whether the Barton doctrine may be applied extraterritorially'.[184] Judge Stark further clarified that the Bankruptcy Court 'did not commit legal error' by holding that for the purposes of *Barton* it was not the appointing court, and rather the appointing authority was Ireland.[185]

While the automatic stay bars lawsuits against debtors on claims that arose before bank- **4.83** ruptcy, the suit in *Irish Bank* was against the foreign representatives, not the debtor. The District Court found that the stay can be extended in 'unusual circumstances' to non-debtor parties where 'there is such an identity between the debtor and the third-party defendant that the debtor may be said to be the real party defendant and that a judgment against the third-party defendant will in effect be a judgment or finding against the debtor'.[186] Judge

---

[178] Ibid.
[179] 11 USC § 1520(a); Westbrook, *supra* n 8 at 722.
[180] See 8 *Collier on Bankruptcy*, para 1520.01 (16th edn, 2015).
[181] *In re Irish Bank Resolution Corp Ltd*, 2019 WL 4740249 (D Del 2019).
[182] Ibid at *2.
[183] Ibid at *3–5.
[184] Ibid at *4.
[185] Ibid.
[186] Ibid at *5.

Stark ruled that such circumstances existed in this case as there existed 'such an identity between the Debtor and these third-party defendants that a judgment against the [foreign representatives] individually [would] in effect be a judgment or finding against the Debtor'.[187]

4.84   While the automatic stay may be modified 'for cause', the Bankruptcy Court held that it would not lift the stay because the Bankruptcy Court would not have personal or subject matter jurisdiction because the conduct by the foreign representatives (i) occurred outside the US and (ii) 'in no way affect[ed]' the chapter 15 case.[188] The District Court added that '[b]ased on the facts asserted in the complaint, which would not support jurisdiction over the adversary proceeding, the Court finds no error in the Bankruptcy Court's determination that the likelihood of success ... [of the lawsuit] did not weigh in Appellants' favor'.[189]

B.   Debtor in Possession Financing

4.85   When a company files for chapter 11 protection, the existing management of the corporation generally remains in place as the 'debtor in possession' or 'DIP' and has all the rights and duties of the trustee.[190] These include serving as a fiduciary for the debtor's creditors and interest holders and operating the debtor's business. The debtor in possession also may seek post-petition financing under section 364 of the Bankruptcy Code,[191] commonly referred to as 'DIP Financing'. Under section 364, the trustee or debtor in possession can obtain financing: (i) on an unsecured basis with administrative expense status; (ii) on an unsecured basis with super-priority status; (iii) on a secured basis with a lien on unencumbered property and a junior lien on encumbered property; and (iv) on a secured basis with a senior or equal lien on encumbered property.

4.86   DIP financing is readily available under chapter 11 as compared to chapter 15, under which it is not automatically available. Under section 1521, a bankruptcy court may grant 'any additional relief that may be available to a trustee, except for relief available under sections 522, 544, 547, 548, 550, and 724(a)'. Such relief is entirely discretionary and only granted 'where necessary to effectuate the purpose of this chapter and to protect the assets of the debtor or the interests of creditors'.[192] Because there is no guarantee that a court would

---

[187]   Ibid at *6 (internal quotations omitted).
[188]   Ibid at *8.
[189]   Ibid.
[190]   11 USC § 1107.
[191]   Section 364 provides: (a) If the trustee is authorized to operate the business of a debtor ... unless the court orders otherwise, the trustee may obtain unsecured credit and incur unsecured debt in the ordinary course of business allowable under section 503(b)(1) of this title as an administrative expense. (b) The court, after notice and a hearing, may authorize the trustee to obtain unsecured credit or to incur unsecured debt other than under subsection (a) of this section, allowable under section 503(b)(1) of this title as an administrative expense. (c) If the trustee is unable to obtain unsecured credit allowable under section 503(b)(1) of this title as an administrative expense, the court, after notice and a hearing, may authorize the obtaining of credit or the incurring of debt: (1) with priority over any or all administrative expenses of the kind specified in section 503(b) or section 507(b) of this title; (2) secured by a lien on property of the estate that is not otherwise subject to a lien; or (3) secured by a junior lien on property of the estate that is subject to a lien. (d) (1) The court, after notice and a hearing, may authorize the obtaining of credit or the incurring of debt secured by a senior or equal lien on property of the estate that is subject to a lien only if (a) the trustee is unable to obtain such credit otherwise; and (b) there is adequate protection of the interest of the holder of the lien on the property of the estate on which such senior or equal lien is proposed to be granted. (2) In any hearing under this subsection, the trustee has the burden of proof on the issue of adequate protection. ***11 USC § 364(a)–(d).
[192]   11 USC § 1521.

permit a foreign debtor to incur post-petition financing under chapter 15, particularly over objection by a creditor or other party in interest, DIP lenders on the whole prefer that foreign debtors file for chapter 11 rather than chapter 15 relief.

C. Automatic Relief

In a voluntary chapter 11 case, the filing of the bankruptcy petition effectively constitutes **4.87** an order for relief under the Bankruptcy Code and commences the case. Specifically, upon the filing of the petition the automatic stay immediately goes into effect and there is no required proceeding to determine eligibility for relief unless an objection is raised. However, in a chapter 15 case, the filing of the petition does not automatically trigger relief; rather, it simply begins the recognition process. Relief is only available after notice of the petition has been sent, a hearing has been held before the bankruptcy court, and an order recognizing a foreign proceeding is entered. A foreign debtor may file a motion for provisional relief covering the period from filing the petition to when the recognition process is complete, but, as described above, such relief is discretionary. In addition, to obtain provisional relief the foreign representative must demonstrate that such relief is urgently needed to protect the assets of the foreign debtor or the interests of its creditors.

D. Additional Protections Under Chapter 11

Although a bankruptcy court has broad discretion to extend additional provisions of the **4.88** Bankruptcy Code that are not automatically triggered upon recognition to foreign debtors under chapter 15,[193] not all provisions of the Bankruptcy Code are available to chapter 15 debtors. A court may decline to extend certain provisions of the Bankruptcy Code if doing so would conflict with the insolvency laws of the foreign main proceeding, and foreign representatives are explicitly excluded from using avoidance powers available under other chapters of the Bankruptcy Code.

Bankruptcy courts have extended other sections of the Bankruptcy Code to foreign debtors **4.89** under chapter 15.[194] However, in *In Re Qimonda*,[195] the bankruptcy court, emphasizing the importance of comity and efficient administration of cross-border insolvencies, amended a supplemental order to exclude relief under section 365 because application of section 365 to this case would have substantially undermined provisions of German insolvency law, the location of the foreign main proceeding.[196] Patent licensees seeking to obtain the

---

[193] See 11 USC § 1521.

[194] See *In re MAAX Corporation*, Case No 08-11443 (CSS) (Bankr D Del 2008). The bankruptcy court entered an order for provisional relief that extended s 365(e)(1) of the Bankruptcy Code, which voids ipso facto clauses, to the real property leases of MAAX Corporation and its subsidiaries to prevent lease counterparties from terminating these leases based on the commencement of Canadian insolvency proceedings. A termination of such leases may have resulted in a failure to perform under an asset purchase agreement for the sale of all of the foreign debtors' assets that had already been approved by the Canadian court. See also *In re ROL Manufacturing (Canada) Ltd*, Case No 08-31022 (Bankr SD Ohio 17 April 2008) (allowing the debtors to obtain post-petition financing with super-priority claims and liens under s 364 of the Bankruptcy Code).

[195] 2009 WL 4060083 (Bankr ED Va 19 Nov 2009), *aff'd in part*, 2010 WL 2680286 (ED Va 2 July 2010).

[196] Ibid at *1.

protections of section 365(n) objected to the modification of the supplemental order arguing that section 365 should apply to the disposition of their patent licences.[197] The court held that all of the debtor's patents, which were issued under the laws of various countries, should be treated in the same manner to provide a coherent and efficient resolution to the debtor's patent portfolio.[198] The court explained that the German insolvency laws should govern because the 'principal idea behind chapter 15 is that the bankruptcy proceedings be governed in accordance with the bankruptcy laws of the nation in which the main case is pending'.[199]

4.90   On appeal, the district court affirmed the bankruptcy court's decision, but remanded the case to the lower court to articulate more fully how the court balanced the parties' respective interests as required by section 1522 and determine whether the relief granted violated fundamental US public policies under section 1506.[200] On remand, the bankruptcy court altered its ruling and held that the protections afforded under section 365(n) should apply to the debtor's US patent licences because (i) the licensee's interests were not 'sufficiently protected' under section 1522(a) given the risk to very substantial investments made the US licensees in research and manufacturing facilities in the US in reliance on certain cross-licences and (ii) the failure to apply section 365(n) would undermine a fundamental US public policy of promoting technological innovation, and thus be 'manifestly contrary to the public policy of the United States'.[201]

4.91   Despite the Bankruptcy Court's determination in *In Re Qimonda*, the public policy exception of section 1506 is narrow. It provides that a court may refuse 'to take an action governed by [chapter 15] if the action would be manifestly contrary to the public policy of the United States'.[202] Courts have construed this exception to be limited to the most fundamental public policies of the United States.[203]

4.92   In *Manley Toys Ltd*, the Bankruptcy Court for the District of New Jersey addressed this exception in connection with the debtor's Hong Kong liquidation and related chapter 15 case. Certain creditors of the debtor objected to the chapter 15 petition, arguing, among other things, that recognition of the Hong Kong proceeding would be manifestly contrary to US public policy.[204] In support, the creditors claimed that they had not received proper notice of the Hong Kong proceeding, recognition of the Hong Kong proceeding would permit the debtor to avoid US court orders, and creditors would not be able to pursue US law-based fraudulent transfer and other avoidance actions in Hong Kong.[205] The Bankruptcy Court granted recognition of the foreign proceeding finding that the creditors did, in fact, receive notice of the Hong Kong proceeding, pursuing a foreign liquidation, even with the goal to stay US litigation, was not contrary to US public policy, and the differences in Hong Kong

---

[197] Ibid.
[198] Ibid at *3.
[199] Ibid at *1.
[200] 2010 WL 2680286 (ED Va 2 July 2010).
[201] *In re Qimonda AG*, 462 BR 165, 182–186 (Bankr ED Va 2011), *aff'd by Jaffe v Samsung Elecs Co, Ltd*, 737 F 3d 14 (4th Cir 2013) (affirming the bankruptcy court's decision based on the balancing of the parties' interests as required by s 1522).
[202] See 11 USC § 1506.
[203] *In re Manley Toys Ltd*, 580 BR 632 (Bankr DNJ 2018).
[204] Ibid at 634.
[205] Ibid at 640, 648.

law were not manifestly contrary to US law.[206] That certain avoidance actions exist under US, but not under Hong Kong, law reflected 'a different way to achieve similar goals,' not conflicting public policies.[207]

The District Court affirmed the Bankruptcy Court's holding.[208] It held that the public policy exception applies '(i) where the procedural fairness of foreign proceedings is in doubt or cannot be cured by the adoption of additional protections, or (ii) where recognition would impinge severely on a US constitutional or statutory right.'[209] Regarding the creditors' lack of notice claim, the District Court emphasized that the liquidators had offered to place the objecting creditors on the 'Committee of Inspection' in the Hong Kong proceeding to cure any perceived prejudice, but that the creditors refused this offer.[210] As to the other public policy arguments, the District Court held that since there was no claim that any US statute had been violated, the 'high standard' of section 1506 had not been met.[211]   **4.93**

The avoidance powers under the Bankruptcy Code that give a chapter 7 or 11 trustee or debtor in possession the ability to set aside preferential and fraudulent transfers[212] are specifically excepted from the discretionary relief that a bankruptcy court may grant to a foreign representative under section 1521(a)(7) of the Bankruptcy Code.[213] In addition, section 1523 provides that upon recognition of a foreign proceeding, the foreign representative only has standing to assert avoidance actions in a case pending under another chapter of title 11.[214] Therefore, a foreign representative that wants to take advantage of the avoiding powers of a trustee or debtor in possession under the Bankruptcy Code must commence a full plenary chapter 11 case in the US under section 1509. This could put a foreign representative at risk of ceding control over such case to a trustee or debtor in possession.[215]   **4.94**

However, there may be other ways for a foreign representative to obtain certain avoiding powers. A foreign representative would likely be able to enforce an avoidance order from the foreign proceeding in a US court.[216] A foreign representative could also pursue an avoidance action based on foreign law in a US bankruptcy court. In *Re Condor Insurance Ltd*,[217] the Court of Appeals for the Fifth Circuit held that chapter 15 does not exclude avoidance actions under foreign law. In that case, the foreign representative of a Nevis-incorporated insurance company initiated an adversary proceeding seeking to avoid pre-chapter 15 petition fraudulent conveyances of assets located in the US.[218] The foreign representative argued that the fraudulent transfer action was based on Nevis law rather than section 548   **4.95**

---

[206] Ibid at 640, 649–650.
[207] Ibid at 650.
[208] *In re Manley Toys Ltd*, 597 BR 578, 581 (DNJ 2019).
[209] Ibid at 586.
[210] Ibid at 587.
[211] Ibid at 587–588.
[212] 11 USC §§ 544, 547, 548.
[213] 11 USC § 1521(a)(7).
[214] 11 USC § 1523(a); see 8 *Collier on Bankruptcy*, para 1523.01 (16th edn 2015).
[215] Ibid.
[216] See *In re Condor Insurance Ltd*, 411 BR 314, 318 n 6 (SD Miss 2009). The court mentioned in dicta that the foreign representative could seek avoidance of the fraudulent transfers in the foreign jurisdiction and then seek recognition of the foreign order in a US court. Ibid (citing *In re Ephedra Prods Liab Litig*, 349 BR 333 (SDNY 2006)).
[217] *Fogerty v Petroquest Resources Inc (In re Condor Insurance Ltd)*, 601 F 3d 319 (5th Cir 2010).
[218] Ibid at 320.

of the Bankruptcy Code, and, therefore, sections 1521(a)(7) and 1523 did not apply.[219] The bankruptcy court dismissed the adversary proceeding and the district court affirmed finding that sections 1521(a)(7) and 1523, when read together, 'are intended to exclude all of the avoidance powers specified under either United States or foreign law, unless a Chapter 7 or 11 bankruptcy proceeding is instituted.'[220] However, the Fifth Circuit Court of Appeals reversed the lower courts focusing on the legislative history and international origin of chapter 15.[221] The Fifth Circuit noted that while section 1521 specifically denies a foreign representative avoidance powers created by the Bankruptcy Code, the language of the statute does not suggest that other relief might be excepted.[222] Therefore, it does 'not necessarily follow that Congress intended to deny the foreign representative powers of avoidance supplied by applicable foreign law'.[223] In addition, the Fifth's Circuit's conclusion was bolstered by cases under section 304 that permitted avoidance actions under foreign law when foreign law applied and would provide for such relief.[224] The Fifth Circuit's decision has paved the way for foreign representatives to pursue avoidance actions under foreign law in US bankruptcy courts, with the potential for US bankruptcy courts to apply foreign law in other contexts under chapter 15.[225] It also provides foreign representatives with an important tool to protect a foreign debtor's assets in the US.

4.96   Certain limitations on avoidance actions in chapter 11 cases, discussed in more detail in Chapter 1, have been held to apply in chapter 15 cases. In *In re Fairfield Sentry Ltd*, the Bankruptcy Court for the Southern District of New York ruled that the safe harbour provided for in section 546(e) applied even though the plaintiffs were foreign liquidators in the chapter 15 case of a British Virgin Islands (BVI) company seeking to avoid, under BVI law, redemption overpayments made abroad to foreign funds by Bernard Madoff's Ponzi scheme.[226] As discussed above, section 546(e) provides that a pre-bankruptcy transfer may not be avoided if it 'is a margin payment or settlement payment ... made by or to (or for the benefit of) a commodity broker, forward contract merchant, stockbroker, financial institution, financial participant, or securities clearing agency, or that is a transfer made by or to (or for the benefit of) [any such parties] in connection with a securities contract ... commodity contract ... or forward contract,' unless such transfer was made with the actual intent to hinder, delay, or defraud creditors.[227] The Bankruptcy Court in *Fairfield Sentry* held that section 561(d) of the Bankruptcy Code extends the 546(e) safe harbour protections to

---

[219] Ibid at 320–321.

[220] *In re Condor Insurance Ltd*, 411 BR 314 at 319.

[221] *Fogerty v Petroquest Resources Inc (In re Condor Insurance Ltd)*, 601 F 3d 319 at 321. It should be noted that at least one other court was critical of the lower courts' conclusion that chapter 15 excludes all avoidance powers including those under foreign law. In *Atlas Shipping A/S*, although not deciding the issue, the Bankruptcy Court for the Southern District of New York found such conclusion unpersuasive based on the legislative history of chapter 15 and case law under s 304(c), which permitted a US bankruptcy court to act as a forum for the assertion of avoiding powers vested in the foreign representative under the law of the jurisdiction where the foreign proceeding was pending. *In re Atlas Shipping A/S*, 404 BR 726, 744 (Bankr SDNY 2009).

[222] *Fogerty v Petroquest Resources Inc (In re Condor Insurance Ltd)*, 601 F 3d 319 at 324.

[223] Ibid.

[224] Ibid at 328–329.

[225] See, e.g., *In re Gandi Innovations Holdings, LLC*, 2009 WL 2916908 (Bankr WD Tex, 5 June 2009) (in the order recognizing the debtors' Canadian insolvency proceedings as foreign main proceedings, the bankruptcy court gave full force and effect to the Initial Order, based on Canadian law, issued by the Canadian court that included extensive relief).

[226] *In re Fairfield Sentry Ltd*, 596 BR 275 (Bankr SDNY 2018).

[227] 11 U.S.C. §§ 548(e); 548(a)(1)(A).

proceedings brought by a foreign representative because section 561(d) provides that any provision in the Bankruptcy Code relating to securities contracts and the other contracts discussed in section 546(e) 'shall apply in a chapter 15 case ... to limit avoidance powers to the same extent as in a chapter 7 or chapter 11 case'.[228]

A foreign representative may also use other provisions of chapter 15 to avoid certain trans-   **4.97**
fers. In *Atlas Shipping A/S*, the foreign representative of two international shipping corporations, debtors in a bankruptcy proceeding in Denmark and petitioners under chapter 15, sought to vacate several Supplemental Rule B attachments in a US bankruptcy court.[229] The bankruptcy court permitted the post-recognition release of the previously garnished funds subject to the Supplemental Rule B attachments for administration in the Danish bankruptcy case under section 1521(a)(5) and (b), provisions that allow a court to turn over funds to a foreign representative for administration in the foreign bankruptcy proceeding.[230] The bankruptcy court further determined that the relief sought was not in the nature of an avoidance action. Although the court did not have to push the 'outer bounds of discretionary relief under chapter 15' because the relief requested by the foreign representative was expressly provided for in section 1521(a)(5) and (b), the court left open the possibility that a foreign representative may be able to pursue additional rights available under chapter 11 through the 'additional assistance' provision of chapter 15.[231]

VI. Notable Litigation Arising Under Chapter 15

A. Litigation Regarding COMI

Sparked by chapter 15 filings by offshore hedge funds, there have been some controversial   **4.98**
decisions analysing the determination of a foreign debtor's COMI. Several are described below.

1. *In re SPhinX, Ltd*
In re SPhinX, Ltd[232] involved the first chapter 15 case where a debtor's COMI was disputed.   **4.99**
In *SPhinX*, the District Court affirmed the Bankruptcy Court's decision to deny recognition of a Cayman Islands proceeding as a foreign main proceeding under chapter 15 of the Bankruptcy Code even though it was the only pending insolvency case involving the debtors.

---

[228] *Fairfield*, 596 BR at 308. However, in light of a recent Supreme Court ruling on the safe harbour provision, discussed in detail in Section IV.C of Chapter 1, the Bankruptcy Court denied safe harbour relief, giving the parties an opportunity to make subsequent arguments concerning whether the transferors were financial participants under section 546(e). Ibid; *Merit Management Group LP v FTI Consulting, Inc*, 138 S Ct. 883 (2018).

[229] *In re Atlas Shipping A/S*, 404 BR at 729 (Bankr SDNY 2009). Maritime attachment liens are governed by Rule B of the Supplemental Rules for Admiralty or Maritime Claims and Asset Forfeiture Actions to the Federal Rules of Civil Procedure and permit a plaintiff to obtain an order of attachment against a defendant's property that is in the hands of a garnishee. Ibid at 731–732.

[230] Ibid at 741–742.

[231] Ibid at 741.

[232] 371 BR 10 (SDNY 2007).

(a) Facts

4.100   In *SPhinX*, the debtors were a group of hedge funds organized and incorporated under the laws of the Cayman Islands.[233] With the exception of their corporate books and records and the retention of auditors who used a Cayman Islands address, the debtors held no assets in the Cayman Islands.[234] Their business was conducted under a management contract with a Delaware corporation and at least 90 per cent of the debtors' US$500 million in assets were located in US accounts.[235] Further, none of the directors resided in the Cayman Islands and no board meetings took place there.[236]

4.101   The debtors' largest client was Refco Capital Markets, Ltd (RCM), which was undergoing liquidation as a chapter 11 debtor. As part of its bankruptcy proceedings, the Refco creditors committee had brought an action against certain SPhinX debtors to recover a US$312 million preferential transfer made by RCM.[237] The parties ultimately entered into a settlement resolving the preference action, however, certain investors in the SPhinX funds objected to its terms.[238]

4.102   On 30 June 2006, the SPhinX companies were placed into a voluntary liquidation proceeding in the Cayman Islands.[239] Additionally, the Cayman Islands court-appointed joint official liquidators[240] who then filed chapter 15 petitions in the bankruptcy court to enjoin further litigation in the case, claiming additional time was needed to evaluate the proposed settlement.[241] The Bankruptcy Court denied such request.[242]

(b) The Bankruptcy Court's decision

4.103   On 6 September 2006, the Bankruptcy Court issued its opinion recognizing the Cayman Islands proceeding as a 'foreign nonmain proceeding' under chapter 15. In its opinion, the Court emphasized the 'maximum flexibility' given to courts under chapter 15.[243]

4.104   After making an initial determination that the Cayman Islands proceeding should be recognized as a foreign proceeding,[244] the Court then turned to the issue of whether the proceeding should be deemed 'main' or 'nonmain'. The Refco trustee objected to the proceeding being deemed a 'foreign main proceeding' as such a finding would trigger the automatic stay under section 362 of the Bankruptcy Code and thus prevent further adjudication of the settlement.[245] In discussing the differences between 'main' and 'nonmain' proceedings, the Bankruptcy Court explained that this distinction generally has 'limited specified consequences'.[246] Nevertheless, because a finding that the Cayman Islands case was a 'main'

---

[233] Ibid at 13.
[234] Ibid at 15.
[235] Ibid at 15–16.
[236] Ibid at 16.
[237] Ibid at 13.
[238] Ibid.
[239] Ibid.
[240] Ibid.
[241] Ibid at 15.
[242] Ibid.
[243] *In re SPhinX, Ltd*, 351 BR 103, 112 (Bankr SDNY 2006).
[244] Ibid at 116–117.
[245] Ibid at 115, 121.
[246] Ibid at 116. The Court also stated that 'chapter 15 ... minimiz[es] the practical differences between the recognition of a foreign proceeding as "main" or "nonmain" under [the Bankruptcy Code]'. Ibid at 114.

proceeding would trigger the automatic stay provision and prevent any final resolution of the settlement, the Court undertook a careful examination of whether the proceeding was 'main' or 'nonmain'.

The Bankruptcy Court acknowledged that the Bankruptcy Code 'provides considerable but **4.105** not complete direction' on the issue of whether a foreign proceeding should be deemed 'main' or 'nonmain'.[247] Specifically, under section 1502(4) of the Bankruptcy Code, a 'foreign main proceeding' is a 'foreign proceeding pending in the country where the debtor has its COMI'. Further, under section 1516(c) of the Bankruptcy Code, '[i]n the absence of evidence to the contrary, the debtor's registered office ... is presumed to be the [COMI]'.[248] The Court, however, noted that while the legislative history permits such presumption to be rebutted, the type of evidence required to rebut this presumption is unclear.[249] Nevertheless, the Bankruptcy Court stated that several factors could be used to make such a determination including: (i) the location of the debtor's headquarters; (ii) the location of those who manage the debtor; (iii) the location of the debtor's primary assets; (iv) the location of the majority of the debtor's creditors or of the majority of the creditors who would be affected by the case; and/or (v) the jurisdiction whose law would apply to most disputes.[250]

As this was a case of 'first impression', the Court considered the decision of *Bondi v Bank* **4.106** *of America NA (In re Eurofood IFSC Ltd)* by the European Court of Justice,[251] which interpreted the EC Regulation's provision concerning COMI. Specifically, the Court construed *Eurofood* as holding that COMI must be identified based on criteria that are (1) objective and (2) ascertainable by third parties.

Although the Bankruptcy Court acknowledged that 'in balancing all of the foregoing fac- **4.107** tors the Court might be inclined to find the debtors' COMI in the Cayman Islands and recognize the proceeding as a foreign main proceeding', the Court ultimately held that it was a 'foreign nonmain proceeding'.[252] The Court further stated that 'a primary basis for the [chapter 15] petition ... was improper [and] ha[d] the purpose of frustrating the [settlement] by obtaining a stay of the appeals upon the invocation of [the automatic stay provision]'.[253] Thus, 'staying the appeal would have the same effect as overturning the RCM settlement *without addressing or prevailing on the merits*'.[254]

In making its determination, the Court emphasized public policy concerns and the no- **4.108** tion that the liquidators' 'litigation strategy' was the 'only reason' they sought recognition as a 'foreign main proceeding'.[255] The Court viewed this strategy as 'taint[ing] the [liquidators'] request [and] giving the clear appearance of improper forum shopping'.[256] Thus, the Court held that 'where so many objective factors point to the Cayman Islands not being the

---

[247] Ibid at 117.
[248] Ibid.
[249] The Court referred to the legislative history as stating that '[t]he ultimate burden as to each element [of recognition] is on the foreign representative, although the court is entitled to shift the burden to the extent indicated in section 1516'. Ibid at 117.
[250] Ibid.
[251] Case 341/04, Slip op at 6, [2006] ECR I-3813, 2006 WL 1142304 (ECJ, 2 May 2006).
[252] *In re SPhinX, Ltd*, 351 BR at 120–122.
[253] Ibid at 121.
[254] Ibid (emphasis in original).
[255] Ibid.
[256] Ibid.

debtors' COMI, and no negative consequences would appear to result from recognizing the Cayman Islands proceedings as nonmain proceedings, that is the better choice'.[257]

(c) The District Court's opinion

4.109 On appeal, the District Court upheld the Bankruptcy Court's determination that the Cayman Islands proceeding should be deemed a 'foreign nonmain proceeding'. In referring to the Bankruptcy Court's finding that the chapter 15 filing was initiated solely on the bases of 'improper forum shopping' and 'frustration of an existing judgment' the District Court stated that '[s]uch circumstances as this support denial of recognition as a foreign main proceedings on the ground that the recognition is being sought for an improper purpose'.[258] Thus, the District Court held that 'it was appropriate for the bankruptcy court to consider the factors it considered, to retain its flexibility, and to reach a pragmatic resolution supported by the facts found'.[259]

2. In re Bear Stearns High-Grade Structured Credit Strategies Master Fund, Ltd

4.110 In a departure from prior decisions, Judge Lifland in *Re Bear Stearns High-Grade Structured Credit Strategies Master Fund, Ltd*[260] declined to recognize the Cayman Islands proceedings of Bear Stearns High-Grade Structured Credit Strategies Master Fund, Ltd and Bear Stearns High-Grade Structured Credit Strategies Enhanced Leverage Master Fund, Ltd as either foreign 'main' or 'nonmain' proceedings under chapter 15. This decision was later upheld by the District Court.[261]

(a) The Bankruptcy Court's decision

4.111 The *Bear Stearns* funds, which were organized under Cayman Islands law, invested in a wide array of securities. While registered in the Cayman Islands as exempt companies, the funds were administered by a Massachusetts corporation which provided day-to-day administrative services and acted as the funds' registrar and transfer agent.[262] Additionally, the funds' books and records were maintained in Delaware.[263]

4.112 In the wake of deteriorating economic conditions, the funds suffered a significant devaluation. As a result, their boards of directors filed winding-up petitions under Cayman Islands law and joint provisional liquidators were appointed.[264] The liquidators then filed petitions under chapter 15 seeking recognition of the Cayman Islands liquidation proceedings as 'foreign main' proceedings.[265] No objections to the chapter 15 petitions were filed.

4.113 In determining whether the funds deserved 'recognition', the Court stated that 'recognition is not to be rubber stamped by the courts'.[266] Instead, courts must make an 'independent

---

[257] Ibid at 122. Additionally, the Court stated that since 'nothing in chapter 15 provides that there cannot be a "nonmain" proceeding unless there is a "main" proceeding', the Court could recognize the Cayman Islands proceeding as 'nonmain' even though there was no other pending proceeding.
[258] 371 BR 10, 18 (SDNY 2007).
[259] Ibid at 19.
[260] 374 BR 122 (Bankr SDNY 2007).
[261] *In re Bear Stearns High-Grade Structured Credit Strategies Master Fund, Ltd*, 389 BR 325 (SDNY 2008).
[262] 374 BR at 124.
[263] Ibid.
[264] Ibid at 125.
[265] Ibid.
[266] Ibid at 126.

determination' as to whether 'recognition' is warranted—even where no party to the case objects to such a finding.[267] As such, the Court independently considered whether the Cayman Islands proceedings qualified for recognition.

First, the Bankruptcy Court held that the proceedings should not be recognized as foreign **4.114** 'main' proceedings under chapter 15. Indeed, the Court concluded that the funds' COMI was the United States—*not* the Cayman Islands, noting that '[t]he only adhesive connection with the Cayman Islands that the Funds have is the fact that they are registered there'.[268] Specifically, the funds maintained no employees or managers in the Cayman Islands, the investment manager for the funds was located in New York, a Massachusetts Administrator ran the funds' back-office operations, and its books and records also were located in the US. Thus, the Court found that 'the presumption that the [funds'] COMI is the place of [its] registered offices [was] rebutted by evidence to the contrary'.[269]

The Bankruptcy Court then considered whether the funds should be recognized as for- **4.115** eign 'nonmain' proceedings. To so qualify under section 1502(5) of the Bankruptcy Code, 'there must be an "establishment" in the Cayman Islands for the conduct of *nontransitory economic activity*, i.e., a local place of business'.[270] In this case, the Court found that the funds conducted 'no (pertinent) nontransitory economic activity' in the Cayman Islands but rather only those minimal activities necessary to maintain the funds' offshore business. While the Court acknowledged that its holding was 'at odds' with the District Court's earlier opinion in *SPhinX*, it explained this variance by stating that *SPhinX* did not address the issue of the 'establishment' requirement, thus no clear conflict resulted.[271]

It is important to note that the Bankruptcy Court did not foreclose all potential remedies to **4.116** the funds by denying recognition under chapter 15. Rather, Judge Lifland suggested that the funds would be eligible to commence cases under chapter 7 or chapter 11 of the Bankruptcy Code—especially since the court found that COMI was in the US.[272]

(b) The District Court's opinion
On appeal, District Judge Sweet upheld the Bankruptcy Court's refusal to recognize the **4.117** Cayman proceedings as either 'main' or 'nonmain'. Specifically, the District Court approved Judge Lifland's approach of evaluating 'recognition' under chapter 15 through an 'independent determination' of the facts.[273] The Court stated that 'Judge Lifland was right to reject' the notion that simply because no one objects to 'recognition' that it should automatically be granted. Rather, '[s]uch a rebuttable presumption [regarding a debtor's COMI] at no time relieves a petitioner of its burden of proof/risk of nonpersuasion'.[274]

---

[267] Ibid. Moreover, the Court stated that the liquidators' contention that 'this Court should accept the proposition that the Foreign Proceedings are main proceedings because [they] say so and because no [one] else says they aren't … must be rejected'. Ibid at 129.

[268] Ibid.

[269] Ibid at 130.

[270] Ibid at 131 (emphasis in original) (internal citations omitted).

[271] Ibid.

[272] Ibid at 132–133.

[273] *In re Bear Stearns High-Grade Structured Credit Strategies Master Fund, Ltd*, 389 BR at 335.

[274] Ibid.

4.118   Additionally, the District Court upheld the Bankruptcy Court's determination that 'the pleadings and facts elicited at hearings before the Bankruptcy Court place the conduct of the Funds' business, their assets, management company and sponsors in New York'.[275] Thus, there was no basis to find the Cayman Islands proceeding was a 'foreign main proceeding'.

4.119   Furthermore, the District Court upheld the Bankruptcy Court's interpretation of the meaning of 'establishment' within the context of 'recognition' as a 'foreign nonmain' proceeding.[276] Thus, the District Court affirmed that the funds 'ha[d] failed to put forward facts establishing that [they] had a "place of operations" that carried out "nontransitory economic activity" in the Cayman Islands'.[277]

3. *In re Basis Yield Alpha Fund (Master)*

4.120   In *Re Basis Yield Alpha Fund (Master)*, the Court took guidance from *Bear Stearns* on the issue of whether 'recognition' should be granted where the facts put forth are insufficient to warrant such a finding but no party in interest objects. The debtor was incorporated in the Cayman Islands and invested in various structured credit securities.[278] In addition to the debtor's books and records being located in the Cayman Islands, its administrator, pre-filing attorneys, and auditors also were located there.[279] Following the global economic downturn, the debtor suffered 'significant devaluation' of its assets causing its shareholders to ultimately file a petition to liquidate the fund under Cayman Islands law.[280] The Cayman Islands court then appointed joint provisional liquidators who sought recognition of the Cayman Islands proceeding under chapter 15 as a 'foreign main proceeding'. In finding the liquidators' petition silent as to the extent of the debtor's business operations in the Cayman Islands, the Bankruptcy Court ordered that additional evidence on the issue of the debtor's COMI be submitted.[281] Instead, the liquidators moved for summary judgment, claiming that since no party had objected, the presumption under section 1516 of the Bankruptcy Code that a debtor's COMI is the place where it is registered warranted a finding as a matter of law that the debtor's COMI was the Cayman Islands.[282]

4.121   In denying the liquidators' motion for summary judgment, Bankruptcy Judge Gerber relied on the 'recognition requirement' of section 1517[283] as well as the court's independent right to inquire under Rule 614 of the Federal Rules of Evidence.[284] Specifically, the Court held that the liquidators had failed to present evidence that the Cayman Islands proceeding qualified for 'recognition' as a 'foreign main proceeding'.[285]

---

[275] Ibid at 337.
[276] Ibid at 338–339.
[277] Ibid (internal citations omitted).
[278] 381 BR 37, 41 (Bankr SDNY 2008)
[279] Ibid at 41–42
[280] Ibid at 41.
[281] Ibid at 42.
[282] Ibid at 43.
[283] Under s 1517 of the Bankruptcy Code, 'an order recognizing a foreign proceeding shall be entered if: (1) such foreign proceeding for which recognition is sought is a foreign main proceeding or a foreign nonmain proceeding within the meaning of section 1502; (2) the foreign representative applying for recognition is a person or body; and (3) the petition meets the requirements of section 1515 [which concerns procedural requirements involved in submitting an application for recognition].'
[284] Under rule 614 the court is permitted to call witnesses, cross-examine witnesses, or interrogate witnesses on its own motion. See Fed R Evid 614.
[285] 381 BR at 48.

Indeed, the court found the liquidators' silence in putting forward relevant facts 'deafening'.[286]

The Bankruptcy Court then examined section 1516 of the Bankruptcy Code, which con-   **4.122** tains the presumption that a debtor's registered office is its COMI.[287] The Court held that summary judgment was not warranted on two grounds: (1) there was evidence that the debtor's COMI was not the Cayman Islands and (2) courts have the 'power to examine facts underlying a request for recognition under section 1517(c) and to inquire under [Rule] 614 [which] cannot be sidestepped'.[288]

Finally, the Court considered whether the absence of an objection by a party in interest pre-   **4.123** cluded it from undertaking its own examination of the record and making an independent determination on the issue of recognition. Relying on the Bankruptcy Court's decision in *Bear Stearns*,[289] the Court found that '[t]he absence of objections to recognition ... neither obviates the [liquidators'] evidentiary burden nor prevents the Court from concluding on the current record that genuine issues of material fact exist so as to prevent determination as a matter of law'.[290] Thus, the Court found that it was not bound by the presumption con-tained in section 1516 of the Bankruptcy Code and, therefore, that the debtor was not en-titled to recognition as a matter of law.[291]

4. *In re Saad Investments Finance Company (No 5) Limited*

In contrast to the decisions described above, in *Re Saad Investments Financing Company*   **4.124** *(No 5) Limited*, the Bankruptcy Court for the District of Delaware recognized a Cayman Islands liquidation proceeding of a privately owned investment company as a 'foreign main proceeding' under chapter 15 of the Bankruptcy Code.[292]

The debtor was organized as an exempted company under the laws of the Cayman Islands   **4.125** on 10 May 2006. Its principal assets were a portfolio of 57 private equity vehicles and one hedge fund.[293] Such funds were registered in several jurisdictions around the world, with the majority of funds, in terms of the percentage of the debtor's total assets by value, re-gistered in the Cayman Islands and the US.[294] The debtor had two classes of equity—one

---

[286] Ibid. Specifically, the Court referenced several factors mentioned in *SPhinX* which could be used to show a debtor's COMI including the location of the debtor's headquarters, the location of those who manage the debtor, the location of the debtor's primary assets, the location of the majority of the debtor's creditors or of the majority of the creditors who would be affected by the case, and/or the jurisdiction whose law would apply to most disputes. Ibid at 47 (quoting *In re SPhinX, Ltd*, 351 BR 103, 117 (Bankr SDNY 2006)).

[287] 11 USC § 1516(c).

[288] 381 BR 37 at 48.

[289] At the time this opinion was issued, the District Court had not yet ruled in *Bear Stearns*.

[290] 381 BR 37 at 52.

[291] Ibid at 52–54. In doing so, the Court referred to the Guide to Enactment of the UNCITRAL Model Law on Insolvency, promulgated in connection with the Model Act. Ibid at 53. The Guide states that the Model Act's presumption, embodied in s 1516, does 'not prevent, in accordance with applicable procedural law, *calling for* or assessing other evidence if the conclusion suggested by the presumption is called into question *by the court* or an interested party'. Thus, the Court highlighted the *Guide*'s favourable view on a court's ability to call for other evi-dence under s 1516.

[292] Order Recognizing Foreign Proceeding, *In re Saad Investments Financing Company (No 5) Limited*, Case No 09-13985 (KG) (Bankr D Del 4 Dec 2009).

[293] Declaration of Nicolas Paul Matthews in Support of Chapter 15 Petition for Recognition of Foreign Proceeding Pursuant to 11 USC §§ 1504, 1509, 1515, 1517, and 1520 at para 23, *In re Saad Investments Financing Company (No 5) Limited*, Case No 09-13985 (KG) (Bankr D Del 5 Nov 2009).

[294] Ibid at para 24.

class of shares held by Saad Investments Company Limited (SICL), an exempted company organized under the laws of the Cayman Islands that also acted as the debtor's investment manager, and the other class of shares held by Barclays Bank plc.[295]

4.126   On 24 July 2009, upon an *ex parte* application of a third party, the Cayman Grand Court appointed receivers over the assets, property, and business entities of the ultimate beneficial owner of SICL, including the debtor, and ordered a worldwide freeze on the assets of the various entities based on allegations that certain entities had breached their fiduciary duties and misappropriated funds.[296] The Cayman Grand Court eventually issued a winding-up order in respect of SICL on 18 September 2009.[297]

4.127   On 19 August 2009, Barclays petitioned the Cayman Grand Court for a winding-up order with respect to the debtor.[298] On 18 September 2009, the Cayman Grand Court issued the winding-up order appointing joint official liquidators who supplanted the receivers previously appointed.[299] On 11 November 2009, the joint official liquidators filed a petition for recognition of the Cayman winding-up proceedings under chapter 15 of the Bankruptcy Code to (i) protect the debtor's US assets from potential seizure or attachment by third parties through legal, equitable, or judicial action in connection with broad-based litigation efforts surrounding the beneficial owner of SICL, and (ii) take advantage of the breathing spell provided by the automatic stay to evaluate the debtor's investments in each of its US funds without triggering defaults under investment agreements of certain funds by failing to satisfy capital calls made by such funds' general partners.[300]

4.128   The debtor argued that recognition of the Cayman proceeding as a 'foreign main proceeding' was appropriate given the following facts that supported a finding that the debtor's COMI was located in the Cayman Islands: (i) all decisions regarding the debtor's assets and all other aspects of the debtor's business were made by the joint official liquidators from their headquarters in the Cayman Islands; (ii) the debtor's registered office was in the Cayman Islands; (iii) the joint official liquidators maintain the books and records of the debtor in the Cayman Islands and such books and records have always been maintained in the Cayman Islands; (iv) the estimated value of the debtor's assets in the Cayman Islands was greater than the estimated value of the debtor's assets in any other country; (v) SICL, one of the debtor's two equity holders and its former investment manager, was also in a liquidation and winding-up proceeding in the Cayman Islands; (vi) the debtor, SICL and other entities related to SICL were defendants in a litigation proceeding in the Cayman Islands; and (vii) Barclays, the debtor's other equity holder, commenced the winding-up proceeding in the Cayman Islands.[301] The debtor also emphasized that the relevant time for determining a debtor's COMI is the time that the chapter 15 case is commenced, without reference to the debtor's operational history.[302]

4.129   Without issuing a written opinion, Judge Gross of the Bankruptcy Court for the District of Delaware entered an order on 4 December 2009 recognizing the Cayman Islands

295   Ibid at paras 7–11.
296   Ibid at para 16.
297   Ibid at para 17.
298   Ibid at para 18.
299   Ibid at paras 19, 21.
300   Ibid at paras 28–29.
301   Memorandum of Law in Support of Chapter 15 Petition For Recognition of Foreign Proceeding Pursuant to 11 USC §§ 1504, 1509, 1515, 1517, and 1520 at para 48, *In re Saad Investments Financing Company (No 5) Limited*, Case No 09-13985 (KG) (Bankr D Del 11 Nov 2009).
302   Ibid at para 47.

winding-up proceeding of the debtor as a 'foreign main proceeding'. The Court found that the debtor had its COMI in the Cayman Islands.[303] Although the specific facts of this case appeared to require a finding that the debtor's COMI was in the Cayman Islands, this decision strengthens the possibility that hedge funds and investment firms may obtain relief under chapter 15 of the Bankruptcy Code.

5. *Lavie v Ran*

In *Lavie v Ran*,[304] the Bankruptcy Court considered the issue of COMI under chapter 15 with respect to an individual debtor. In this case, an involuntary bankruptcy proceeding was commenced against Yuval Ran in Israel on 16 June 1997 following a determination by an Israeli court that Ran had committed an act of bankruptcy under Israeli law and Zuriel Lavie was appointed as trustee of Ran's property in Israel.[305] At the time of Lavie's appointment, however, two and a half years had passed since Ran moved from Israel and established a residence in Houston, Texas.[306]   **4.130**

In 2006, Lavie sought an order from the Bankruptcy Court for the Southern District of Texas recognizing the Israeli proceeding as a foreign proceeding under chapter 15. The US Bankruptcy Court, however, found that the Israeli proceeding qualified as neither a foreign main nor non-main proceeding. Lavie appealed.   **4.131**

The District Court's decision set forth the standard for evaluating the COMI of an individual debtor under section 1516(c). Specifically, 'the debtor's habitual residence is presumed, in the absence of evidence to the contrary, to be the center of the debtor's main interests'.[307] Since Ran had lived and worked in Houston since 1997, the Bankruptcy Court held that his COMI was indeed Houston—*not* Israel—and that the pending proceeding in Israel was not a 'foreign main proceeding' under the Bankruptcy Code.[308] While the District Court held that the Bankruptcy Court had 'correctly' determined that Ran's habitual residence, Houston, was his presumed COMI, the Court remanded the case for further factual findings to determine if Lavie had met his burden of rebutting such presumption.[309]   **4.132**

On remand, the Bankruptcy Court reviewed objective factors used to determine 'habitual residence' by European courts,[310] US courts,[311] and Israeli courts.[312] Also, the Court conducted a more intensive factual inquiry into the circumstances   **4.133**

---

[303] Order Recognizing Foreign Proceeding at para H, *In re Saad Investments Financing Company (No 5) Limited*, Case No 09-13985 (KG) (Bankr D Del 4 Dec 2009).

[304] 390 BR 257 (Bankr SD Tex 2008).

[305] Ibid at 289 (Bankr SD Tex 2008). Specifically, it was alleged that Ran, CEO of a publicly traded Israeli company, owed certain personal debts to Bank Hapoalim that remain unpaid. Ibid at 285.

[306] Ibid at 289.

[307] *Lavie v Ran*, 384 BR 469, 471 (SD Tex 2008).

[308] Ibid at 471.

[309] Ibid at 472.

[310] *In re Ran*, 390 BR 257, 267–268 (Bankr SD Tex 2008). Such pertinent factors include the length and continuity of the person's residence before he moved, the length and purpose of his absence, the nature of his occupation in the other country, family situation, and the person's intentions. Ibid at 268.

[311] While no single factor is dispositive, courts generally review the following when determining domicile including 'the places where the litigant exercises civil and political rights, pays taxes, owns real and personal property, has driver's and other licenses, maintains bank accounts, belongs to clubs and churches, has places of business or employment, and maintains a home for his family'. Ibid at 282 (quoting *Coury v Prot*, 85 F 3d 244, 250–251 (5th Cir 1996)). While a person's state of mind is relevant it will receive less weight if it 'conflicts with the objective facts'.

[312] Israeli courts apply a 'centre of life' test to determine one's COMI. Specifically, courts there consider the following factors: (1) the possession of property abroad or the absence of property in Israel; (2) possession of US

surrounding Ran's residency. Significantly, the Bankruptcy Court credited Ran's testimony that he intended to leave Israel for the US because of death threats he and his wife had received as well as threats to kidnap his children.[313] Moreover, the Court found that Ran's concerns that returning to Israel would create a hardship on his family were 'legitimate', that he was not in fact a fugitive of Israeli law and had not violated any Israeli bankruptcy order[314] and that he had not continued to manage any companies located in Israel following his relocation to the US.[315] The Bankruptcy Court found additional facts which indicated that Ran's residency in Houston, Texas was intended to be permanent.[316]

4.134   Ultimately, the Bankruptcy Court found that evidence put forward by Lavie himself demonstrated that Ran's relocation to Houston was indeed permanent and that his COMI was the US.[317] Thus, the Court held that Lavie had failed 'to prove by a preponderance of the evidence that Israel is the location of Ran's [COMI]'.[318] The Court therefore held that '[h]aving failed to carry his burden of proof as the foreign representative, Lavie is not entitled to recognition of the Israeli bankruptcy', and denied his petition.[319]

4.135   The District Court for the Southern District of Texas[320] and the Court of Appeals for the Fifth Circuit[321] both affirmed the Bankruptcy Court's decision. The Fifth Circuit emphasized the timing of the COMI determination; courts should view the COMI determination at the time the petition for recognition is filed, rather than considering a debtor's operational history.[322]

6. In re Ocean Rig

4.136   The Bankruptcy Court for the Southern District of New York has determined that a debtor's 'COMI migration' may be justified if there exists no indicia of bad faith.[323] In 2017, Ocean Rig UDW Inc. and certain of its subsidiaries, owners of a fleet of deepwater oil drilling rigs leased to global oil and gas exploration companies, sought recognition under chapter 15 of foreign liquidation proceedings in the Cayman Islands.[324] Until sometime in 2016, each of the debtors' COMI was in the Republic of the Marshall Islands (RMI).[325] However, the debtors had never conducted operations or directed their affairs from RMI, maintained any

---

passports and 'green cards' indicating that one's centre of life is in the US; (3) possession of a permit for US residency and employment, and (4) the location of one's family abroad. Ibid at 283.

[313] Ibid at 293–294.

[314] Ibid at 295.

[315] Ibid at 299.

[316] Ibid at 300. The Court considered an array of pertinent facts that indicated Ran's relocation was permanent including, among others, Ran owned a home in the US where he resided with his wife and children, his children attended school in Texas, Ran worked in the US, Ran had not returned to Israel since he first left in April 1997, Ran maintained bank accounts in the US, both Ran and his wife were US citizens, Ran was a member of a local synagogue and he also was an assistant coach to a local little league team. Ibid at 295.

[317] Ibid at 300.

[318] Ibid at 301. The Court further stated that '[t]o the extent that Ran might be understood to have the burden of going forward with evidence to show that he had changed his COMI from Israel … to the U.S., Ran met that burden'.

[319] Ibid at 301–302.

[320] *Lavie v Ran*, 406 BR 277 (SD Tex 2009).

[321] *In re Ran*, 607 F 3d 1017 (5th Cir 2010).

[322] Ibid at 1024–1026.

[323] *In re Ocean Rig UDW Inc*, 570 BR 687, 695 (Bankr SDNY 2017).

[324] Ibid at 690–691.

[325] Ibid.

administrative, executive, or management offices in RMI, or had directors that were residents of RMI.[326] Due to the drop in oil and gas prices worldwide, the debtors contemplated the need for a restructuring, and quickly determined to change their COMIs because RMI laws only provide for corporate liquidations and not reorganizations.[327] To take advantage of the Cayman Islands Companies Law, which provides for reorganizations, in April 2016 the debtor parent-entity became a Cayman Islands-registered corporation, and in October 2016, the subsidiary debtors registered as foreign corporations in the Cayman Islands.[328] Each debtor then established its head office in the Cayman Islands.[329]

In addition to establishing head offices in the Cayman Islands, the debtors also provided notice to all of the agents under their debt documents, notice to their investment service providers, and public notice by filings with the Securities and Exchange Commission (SEC) of their relocation.[330] The debtors conducted board meetings in the Cayman Islands, had some officers and directors who resided in the Cayman Islands, opened bank accounts in the Cayman Islands, and hosted creditor discussions regarding the restructuring from the Cayman Islands.[331]In March 2017, the debtors commenced provisional liquidation proceedings and scheme of arrangement proceedings in the Cayman Islands and shortly thereafter, the liquidators sought recognition in New York of the Cayman proceedings under chapter 15 as either foreign main or nonmain proceedings, as well as the enforcement of schemes of arrangement sanctioned by the Cayman Court.[332] Certain parties objected due to the debtors' COMI migration from the RMI to the Cayman Islands.[333]   **4.137**

The Bankruptcy Court granted recognition of the foreign main proceedings and held that despite the debtors' previous contacts with RMI, each debtor's COMI was the Cayman Islands.[334] Engaging in a 'holistic analysis to ensure that the [debtors had] not manipulated COMI in bad faith,' Bankruptcy Judge Glenn found that the debtors' actions throughout 2016 and 2017 indicated that their shift of COMI to the Cayman Islands was 'done for proper purposes to facilitate a value-maximizing restructuring of the Foreign Debtors' financial debt.'[335] Because the debtors purposefully established their new COMI prior to their chapter 15 petitions, Judge Glenn found no evidence suggesting any 'insider exploitation, untoward manipulation, and overt thwarting of third party expectations that would support denying recognition' of the Cayman Islands proceedings.[336]   **4.138**

7. In re Ascot Fund Ltd

The Bankruptcy Court for the Southern District of New York recently took a flexible approach in determining a foreign debtor's COMI.[337] In *Ascot Fund*, the debtor was an investment fund organized in the Cayman Islands, which had invested nearly all of its assets in   **4.139**

---

[326] Ibid at 696.
[327] Ibid at 694.
[328] Ibid at 695.
[329] Ibid.
[330] Ibid at 697.
[331] Ibid at 705.
[332] Ibid at 690–691.
[333] Ibid.
[334] Ibid at 702.
[335] Ibid at 704.
[336] Ibid at 706–707.
[337] *In re Ascot Fund Ltd*, 603 B.R. 271 (Bankr SDNY 2019).

its Delaware affiliate, Ascot Partners, which had then invested such assets in the company Bernard Madoff had used to operate his infamous Ponzi scheme.[338] After nearly a decade of litigation between the Madoff estate and Ascot, the parties entered into a substantial settlement.[339] Thereafter, a shareholder of Ascot Fund voiced concerns to Ascot's board with the proposed distribution methodology for the settlement because, among other reasons, it was likely to favour Ascot's largest investors over its smaller ones.[340] Upon learning that Ascot was contemplating a Cayman Islands reorganization, the shareholder sued Ascot in New York state court seeking, among other things, an injunction against the distribution of the settlement funds.[341] Prompted by this litigation, Ascot commenced a voluntary liquidation in the Cayman Islands and its liquidators filed a petition for recognition of the foreign proceeding under chapter 15.[342] The shareholder objected, arguing that Ascot Fund's COMI was not the Cayman Islands, but the United States.[343] The shareholder argued that Ascot Fund had not been engaged in the investment business since the uncovering of Madoff's Ponzi scheme and that its only significant activity had been the subsequent litigation in New York.[344]

4.140 The Bankruptcy Court held that Ascot Fund's COMI was the Cayman Islands, citing numerous factors. First, it found that several Ascot Fund board members and directors were located in the Cayman Islands, that Ascot Fund's sole shareholder was a Cayman Islands-incorporated entity, that Ascot Fund regularly held board meetings in the Cayman Islands, and that this 'Cayman-centric management' did not change after the liquidation proceeding.[345] The Bankruptcy Court observed that 'COMI lies where the debtor conducts its regular business, so that the place is ascertainable by third parties', but emphasized that Ascot Fund had been 'dragged into' the New York litigations, and that such litigations did not define Ascot Fund's COMI.[346] The Bankruptcy Court also noted that Ascot did not manipulate its COMI as it had not engaged in investment activity *anywhere* over the past decade, and that, unlike the facts in *Sphinx* (cited by the shareholder), Ascot Fund had directors residing in the Cayman Islands since the fund's beginning.[347] Because the shareholder provided no support to rebut the presumption that Ascot Fund's COMI was in the Cayman Islands due to its registered office, the Bankruptcy Court recognized the Cayman Islands proceeding as a foreign main proceeding.[348]

B. Litigation Regarding Available Relief

1. *In re Metcalfe & Mansfield Alternative Investments*

4.141 In *Metcalfe & Mansfield Alternative Investments*,[349] the Bankruptcy Court for the Southern District of New York considered whether broad third-party releases included in a plan

---

338 Ibid at 273.
339 Ibid at 274–275.
340 Ibid at 275.
341 Ibid at 276.
342 Ibid.
343 Ibid at 284.
344 Ibid.
345 Ibid at 280–281.
346 Ibid 278, 281–282.
347 Ibid at 282–283.
348 Ibid at 283.
349 421 BR 685 (Bankr SDNY 2010).

implementation order issued in proceedings under Canada's Companies' Creditors Arrangement Act ('the CCAA') could be enforced in the US, even if such relief would not be available in a plenary chapter 11 case.

A committee of certain investors initiated the CCAA proceedings on 17 March 2008 **4.142** to restructure all of the outstanding third party (non-bank sponsored) Asset Backed Commercial Paper (ABCP) obligations of the debtors.[350] The investors paid money to acquire ABCP and in turn that money was used to purchase a portfolio of financial assets to support and collateralize each series of ABCP.[351] The ABCP market froze in 2007 triggered by the subprime mortgage crisis in the US and a perceived lack of transparency in the ABCP market.[352]

Considered to be the largest restructuring in Canadian history,[353] the Ontario Superior **4.143** Court of Justice entered an Amended Sanction Order and Plan Implementation Order ('the Canadian Orders') on 5 June 2008 sanctioning a plan that included releases for each participant in the Canadian ABCP market, including non-debtor third parties, from liability for any claims or causes of action in any way related to the ABCP market in Canada.[354] The releases were included at the insistence of those financial institutions that had sold the assets that 'backed' the ABCP to ensure their agreement to a plan that shifted the risks associated with the volatile credit markets to such financial institutions and away from investors.[355] In addition to the global release, the plan provided for an injunction against proceedings against the parties released under the plan.[356]

On appeal, the Ontario Court of Appeal decided that 'the CCAA permits the inclusion **4.144** of third-party releases in a plan of compromise or arrangement to be sanctioned by the court where those releases are reasonably connected to the proposed restructuring'.[357] The Ontario Court of Appeal affirmed the Canadian Orders and the Canada Supreme Court denied review.[358]

The court-appointed monitor sought recognition of the CCAA proceeding as a foreign **4.145** main proceeding in the US after the plan implementation order became effective in Canada. The monitor also moved for an order enforcing the Canadian Orders in the US on the basis that the release and injunction provisions would satisfy the applicable standard in a plenary case under chapter 11 or in the interests of comity.[359]

Rather than determining whether the significant limitations established by the Second **4.146** Circuit concerning non-debtor releases and injunctions in confirmed chapter 11 plans would be satisfied in this case, the Bankruptcy Court's inquiry focused on whether the foreign orders should be enforced in the US under chapter 15.[360] According to the Court, 'Chapter 15 specifically contemplates that the court should be guided by principles of comity

---

[350] Ibid at 687.
[351] Ibid at 688–689.
[352] Ibid at 690.
[353] Ibid at 687.
[354] Ibid at 692.
[355] Ibid.
[356] Ibid at 693.
[357] Ibid at 694.
[358] Ibid at 687.
[359] Ibid at 687, 694.
[360] Ibid at 696.

and cooperation with foreign courts in deciding whether to grant the foreign representative additional post-recognition relief'.[361] Under section 1507, courts may provide 'additional assistance', in this case an order enforcing the Canadian Orders in the US; however, such relief would not be available if manifestly contrary to US public policy.[362] The Bankruptcy Court explained that the public policy exception should be narrowly construed to only the most fundamental policies of the US, and the relief available in the foreign proceeding need not be identical as long as the procedures used in the foreign proceeding meet fundamental standards of fairness in the US.[363]

4.147   Even though the release and injunction provisions may have been unenforceable in a plenary chapter 11 case, US law did not preclude non-debtor third-party releases in all circumstances. In addition, the jurisdictional challenge to such releases and injunctions was fully and fairly litigated in Canadian courts that share common law traditions with US courts. Thus, the Bankruptcy Court found no basis to 'second guess' the Canadian courts' decisions and entered an order recognizing the case as a foreign main proceeding and enforcing the Canadian Orders.[364]

2. In re Vitro SAB de CV

4.148   In *In re Vitro, SAB de CV*, the United States Court of Appeals for the Fifth Circuit, considered whether the recognition and enforcement of a foreign reorganization plan that included, among other things, non-consensual third-party releases against non-debtor subsidiaries, was appropriate under chapter 15.[365]

4.149   Vitro SAB de CV was a holding company that, together with its subsidiaries, constituted the largest glass manufacturer in Mexico.[366] Vitro had manufacturing facilities in seven countries and distribution centres throughout the Americas and Europe and exported its products to more than 50 countries around the world.[367] Between 2003 through 2007, Vitro issued approximately US$1.2 billion of unsecured notes, which were predominantly held by US investors.[368] Substantially all of Vitro's indirect and direct subsidiaries guaranteed payment in full of the notes.[369] In February 2009, Vitro announced that it intended to engage in restructuring negotiations and stopped making interest payments on the notes. In December 2010, Vitro filed a voluntary judicial reorganization (or *concurso*) proceeding under the Mexican Business Reorganization Act.[370] While the Mexican insolvency proceeding was pending, certain bondholders dissatisfied with the reorganization process initiated litigation in New York state court for breach of contract to collect on the notes and the guarantees against Vitro's subsidiaries. In order to stay the litigation in the US, Vitro filed a chapter 15 proceeding in April 2011, and the Bankruptcy Court held that the Mexican reorganization proceeding was a foreign main proceeding. In February 2012, the Mexican

[361] Ibid.
[362] Ibid at 697; see 11 USC § 1506.
[363] Ibid at 697.
[364] See Ibid at 697–701.
[365] 701 F 3d 1031 (5th Cir 2012).
[366] Ibid at 1036–1037.
[367] Ibid at 1037.
[368] Ibid.
[369] Ibid.
[370] Ibid at 1038.

court approved Vitro's plan of reorganization, which included provisions releasing the bondholders' guarantee claims against Virtro's subsidiaries which were not debtors in the Mexican proceeding ('the *Concurso* Plan').[371] Notably, although the *Concurso* Plan received approval from 74.67 per cent of creditors, the required 50 per cent threshold could not have been reached without the votes of intercompany claims held by Vitro's subsidiaries.[372] Thereafter, Vitro's foreign representatives filed a motion in the chapter 15 proceeding for an order recognizing and enforcing the *Concurso* Plan in the US.[373] After a four-day trial, the Bankruptcy Court for the Northern District of Texas denied the motion because the *Concurso* Plan, which would extinguish the guarantee claims of the noteholders against non-debtor subsidiaries of Vitro, would 'manifestly contravene[] the public policy of the United States'.[374] Further, the *Concurso* Plan did 'not provide for the distribution of proceeds of the debtors' property substantially in accordance with the order prescribed' by the Bankruptcy Code.[375]

The Fifth Circuit upheld the Bankruptcy Court's decision relying on an analysis of sections **4.150** 1507 and 1521 of the Bankruptcy Code.[376] The Fifth Circuit applied the following framework to determine whether the *Concurso* Plan that discharged the bondholders' guarantee claims against the non-debtor Vitro subsidiaries should be enforced in the US: (i) the Fifth Circuit determined that the requested relief was not included in the specific forms of relief set forth in section 1521(a)(1)–(7) and (b); and (ii) since the requested relief was not explicitly set forth in section 1521(a)(1)–(7) and (b), the Fifth Circuit analysed whether the requested relief fell more generally under section 1521(a)'s grant of 'any appropriate relief' (which the Court considered to be relief previously available under chapter 15's predecessor, section 304).[377] The Fifth Circuit found that section 304 did not permit the non-consensual release of claims against non-debtors.[378] Finally, since the relief requested by Vitro did not fall under section 1521, the Fifth Circuit considered whether the relief would be appropriate as 'additional assistance' under section 1507.[379] The Fifth Circuit found that Vitro had failed to show 'exceptional circumstances' comparable to those that would make the releases in the *Concurso* Plan possible in the US as contemplated by section 1507(b) (4).[380] The Fifth Circuit also noted that distributions under the *Concurso* Plan were not substantially in accordance with the priority scheme of the Bankruptcy Code given that equity holders were to receive substantial value under the *Concurso* Plan, while the noteholder claims were significantly impaired and the noteholders would be enjoined from pursuing the guarantee by non-debtor subsidiaries.[381]

Rather than relying on the comity doctrine, the Fifth Circuit's decision suggests that bank- **4.151** ruptcy courts should not permit foreign insolvency law to circumvent US bankruptcy law through a chapter 15 proceeding.

---

[371] Ibid at 1039.
[372] Ibid.
[373] Ibid at 1041.
[374] Ibid at 1053 (citations omitted).
[375] Ibid at 1051.
[376] Ibid at 1069.
[377] Ibid.
[378] Ibid at 1059–1060.
[379] Ibid at 1054.
[380] Ibid at 1058, 1061–1062.
[381] Ibid at 1067.

3. *In re Sino-Forest Corp*

4.152   In a decision that was 'almost on all fours' with its decision in *In re Metcalfe* (discussed above), the Bankruptcy Court for the Southern District of New York in *In re Sino-Forest Corp* granted comity to a settlement order entered by a Canadian court.[382]

4.153   In February 2013, the foreign representative filed a petition for chapter 15 relief and the Bankruptcy Court recognized the debtor's Canadian proceeding under the Canadian Creditors Arrangement Act (CCAA) as a foreign main proceeding.[383] In the Canadian proceeding, the debtor sought approval of a settlement with Ernst & Young LLP (E&Y) under which E&Y would pay CAD$117 million to resolve claims asserted against it in class action litigations filed in Canada and the United States for alleged misrepresentations in the debtor's financial statements.[384] In the course of the Canadian proceeding, E&Y and the plaintiffs negotiated the terms of a settlement which was supported by substantially all of the constituents in the Canadian proceeding, including the lead plaintiffs in each of the class action suits.[385] The settlement provided, among other things, that E&Y would (i) pay CAD$117 million into a settlement trust for the benefit of the securities claimants; (ii) release all claims against the debtor and its subsidiaries; (iii) relinquish its rights to any distribution under the plan; and (iv) support approval of the plan.[386] In exchange, E&Y would obtain a global release, including third-party releases.[387] The Canadian court approved the E&Y settlement noting that outstanding litigation claims against third parties are regularly compromised and settled in CCAA proceedings and that 'third-party releases are not an uncommon feature of complex restructurings under the CCAA'.[388] Thereafter, E&Y filed a motion, in which the US class action plaintiffs and the foreign representatives joined, for an order recognizing and enforcing the Canadian order approving the settlement in the US.[389]

4.154   The Bankruptcy Court granted such relief, relying heavily on its decision in *Metcalfe*.[390] The Bankruptcy Court found that the parties to the Canadian proceedings had a 'full and fair' opportunity to litigate the issues consistent with US due process, the Canadian trial court had jurisdiction and it had reached a reasoned decision.[391] The Bankruptcy Court noted that, as in *Metcalfe*, the correct inquiry in a chapter 15 case was not whether a Canadian order (including an order approving a third-party non-debtor release) could be enforced under US law in a plenary chapter 11 case, but whether recognition of such a decision was a proper exercise of comity under chapter 15.[392]

4.155   The Bankruptcy Court also addressed any concern that the releases contained in the order approving the E&Y settlement were manifestly contrary to US public policy, citing *Metcalfe* for the proposition that the relief granted in a foreign proceeding and the relief available in

---

[382] 501 BR 655 (Bankr SDNY 2013).
[383] Ibid.
[384] Ibid.
[385] Ibid.
[386] Ibid.
[387] Ibid.
[388] Ibid at 660 (citations omitted).
[389] Ibid at 656–657.
[390] Ibid at 663–664.
[391] Ibid at 663.
[392] Ibid at 662 (citations omitted).

a US proceeding need not be identical.[393] Further, approval of such releases could not be 'manifestly contrary to public policy' since third-party releases are not categorically prohibited in the Second Circuit where the Bankruptcy Court sits. Finally, the Bankruptcy Court distinguished its decision from the Fifth Circuit's ruling in *Vitro*[394] (discussed above) in which the Fifth Circuit refused to extend comity to a foreign court order approving a reorganization plan providing non-consensual releases of non-debtor entities.[395] The Bankruptcy Court highlighted several distinguishing facts from *Vitro* noting that the plan of reorganization in the Canadian proceeding had 'near unanimous support', such support did not rely on votes by insiders, the Canadian court's decision to approve the non-debtor release reflected similar sensitivities that guide US courts, there were no objecting parties, and the relief did not run afoul of any of subsection 1507(b).[396]

4. *In re Avanti Communications Group PLC*

In 2018, the Bankruptcy Court for the Southern District of New York enforced under principles of comity a chapter 15 debtor's English scheme of arrangement which provided for certain third-party releases.[397] Facing financial difficulties, Avanti, an operator providing fixed satellite services to Europe, the Middle East, and Africa, proposed a restructuring of its 2023 notes to be implemented pursuant to a scheme of arrangement under Part 26 of the Companies Act of 2006.[398] The scheme contemplated that the 2023 notes would be exchanged for equity in Avanti, and that creditors would release the debtor and the non-debtor subsidiary guarantors of the 2023 notes from any claim or liability under the notes and related indenture.[399] Creditors representing over 98 per cent in value of the outstanding 2023 notes voted in favour of the restructuring and the English High Court sanctioned the scheme.[400]   **4.156**

Avanti's foreign representative filed a chapter 15 petition requesting an order 'granting comity to and giving full force and effect to' the UK proceeding, the scheme, and preventing any party from taking action inconsistent with the releases provided for in the scheme.[401] The Bankruptcy Court noted that third-party releases have been enforced under section 1507, which provides that a court may grant additional assistance 'consistent with the principles of comity' and 'if the just treatment of creditors is ensured'.[402] Similar to the holding in *Sino-Forest Corp*, the Bankruptcy Court noted further that while the Fifth Circuit in *Vitro* had declined to enforce the third-party releases in that case, the present situation was distinguishable as Avanti's scheme had near unanimous support from its creditors, and such support did not rely on votes from insiders.   **4.157**

In enforcing the scheme's releases, the Bankruptcy Court first emphasized that UK courts routinely sanction schemes of arrangement that contemplate third-party releases.[403] The   **4.158**

---

393 Ibid at 655.
394 *In re Vitro, SAB de CV*, 701 F 3d 1031 (5th Cir 2012).
395 501 BR 655 (Bankr SDNY 2013).
396 Ibid at 665–666.
397 *In re Avanti Communications Group PLC*, 582 BR 603 (Bankr SDNY 2018).
398 Ibid at 607.
399 Ibid at 609.
400 Ibid at 610.
401 Ibid at 607.
402 Ibid at 615–616.
403 Ibid at 618.

Bankruptcy Court then considered the fairness of the UK proceeding, finding that Avanti's creditors had a 'full and fair opportunity' to be heard on the scheme consistent with US due process standards and that a large majority of the creditors affected by the scheme voted in favour of it.[404] Finally, the Bankruptcy Court held that a failure to enforce the scheme and its contemplated third-party releases could prejudice Avanti's creditors and would 'prevent the fair and efficient administration' of the restructuring.[405]

5. *In re AJW Offshore, Ltd*

4.159 In *In re AJW Offshore, Ltd*, the US Bankruptcy Court for the Eastern District of New York held that a foreign representative was entitled to additional relief under section 1521(a), including the right to seek turnover of estate assets and records under sections 542 and 543, authority to conduct discovery and entrustment with the administration and realization of estate assets.[406]

4.160 AJW Offshore, Ltd and three affiliated funds were in liquidation proceedings before a court in the Cayman Islands.[407] In September 2011, the US Securities and Exchange Commission (SEC) filed an action against the funds' investment managers (and its principals) located in the US for various securities laws violations.[408] On 7 January 2013, the foreign representatives of the funds filed a petition for recognition of the Cayman Islands proceeding as a foreign main proceeding under chapter 15, primarily in an effort to obtain the books and records of the funds' pre-liquidation professionals in connection with the pending lawsuit by the SEC.[409] As part of their petition, the foreign representatives sought additional relief, including the authority to seek turnover under both sections 542 and 543 pursuant to section 1521(a)(7).[410] A law firm which had performed work for the offshore funds objected to such relief.[411]

4.161 In tackling the issue of whether foreign representatives were entitled to the relief provided in sections 542 and 543, the Bankruptcy Court explained that chapter 15 is 'silent' on the applicability of certain sections of the Bankruptcy Code, including sections 542 and 543 concerning turnover of property.[412] The Bankruptcy Court found that the plain language of section 1521(a)—which specifically excluded certain relief, but not sections 542 or 543—allows a foreign representative to utilize turnover subject to sufficient protections to creditors and other interested parties under section 1522 (which requires a balancing of the respective parties' interests).[413] In addition to its statutory analysis, the Bankruptcy Court also relied on cases under section 304 that permitted turnover and noted that the request for turnover was consistent with principles of international comity.[414]

---

[404] Ibid at 618–619.
[405] Ibid at 619.
[406] 488 BR 551 (Bankr EDNY 2013).
[407] Ibid at 554–555.
[408] Ibid at 555.
[409] Ibid.
[410] Ibid at 555–556.
[411] Ibid at 557.
[412] Ibid.
[413] Ibid at 558–559.
[414] Ibid at 561–564.

6. *In re ENNIA Caribe Holding NV*

While Chapter 15 allows foreign representatives access to various forms of relief under the   **4.162**
Bankruptcy Code and under principles of comity, the Bankruptcy Court for the Southern
District of New York recently discussed the limitations on such relief.[415] Section 1522 of the
Bankruptcy Code provides that '[t]he court may grant relief under section 1519 or 1521 …
only if the interests of the creditors and other interested entities, including the debtor, are
sufficiently protected', requiring courts to engage in an analysis balancing the relief's effect
on parties-in-interest.[416]

In *ENNIA*, following the Bankruptcy Court's recognition of a Curaçao proceeding as a for-   **4.163**
eign main proceeding, the debtor's foreign representative sought discretionary relief under
section 1521 to entrust the foreign representative with the administration, realization,
and distribution of all accounts in the names of the debtors at Merrill Lynch in the United
States.[417] The debtors were facing an immediate need for liquidity, which they believed they
could solve with the nearly $240 million held in the Merrill Lynch accounts.[418] The non-
debtor parent of the debtors objected to release of the funds, arguing it was an 'interested
entity' not given 'sufficient protection' under section 1522.[419]

The Bankruptcy Court addressed each of the non-debtor's arguments in turn, holding that   **4.164**
a determination of sufficient protection 'requires a balancing of the respective parties' interests' and that sufficient protection invokes three principles: 'the just treatment of all holders
of claims against the bankruptcy estate, the protection of U.S. claimants against prejudice
and inconvenience in the processing of claims in the foreign proceeding, and the distribution of proceeds of the foreign estate substantially in accordance with the order prescribed
by U.S. law'.[420] First, the Bankruptcy Court held that the non-debtor parent's interests in
certain of the accounts would not be prejudiced if the debtors were granted access because
the accounts were the property of the debtors and the debtors intended to use them to satisfy intercompany obligations.[421] Second, the Court found that the 1 per cent repatriation
fee which would be incurred once the Merrill Lynch funds were transferred to Curaçao
passed section 1522's balancing test as '[a] 1% repatriation fee is significantly outweighed
by the debtors' need to address their liquidity issues'.[422] Finally, the Bankruptcy Court rejected the argument that its ruling on the matter should be delayed until certain Curaçao
proceedings were completed. The non-debtor parent had cited to a case where a court had
conditioned the automatic stay on the resolution of certain foreign proceedings based on
the fact that certain debtor accounts contained non-debtor deposits.[423] Because the Merrill
Lynch funds were fully owned by the debtors, the Bankruptcy Court held it would not delay
its ruling and granted the foreign representative's motion.[424]

---

[415] *In re ENNIA Caribe Holding NV*, 596 BR 316 (Bankr SDNY 2019).
[416] 11 USC § 1520
[417] *ENNIA*, 596 at 319.
[418] Ibid.
[419] Ibid at 323.
[420] Ibid at 322.
[421] Ibid at 323–324.
[422] Ibid at 324.
[423] Ibid.
[424] Ibid.

7. *In re Energy Coal S.P.A.*

4.165 In *In re Energy Coal*, the Delaware Bankruptcy Court analysed whether a bankruptcy court may enjoin litigation in connection with an order enforcing a foreign proceeding not-withstanding a forum selection clause.[425] Energy Coal was the debtor in a 'Concordato Preventivo' under Italian Insolvency Law pending in Genoa, Italy.[426] The debtor's foreign representative sought recognition of the Concordato Preventivo as a foreign main pro-ceeding under chapter 15, which the Bankruptcy Court granted.[427] The Genoa court ap-proved Energy Coal's restructuring plan, which contemplated payment of administrative and secured claims in full, and a 1–7 per cent recovery to unsecured creditors, depending on the class.[428] Energy Coal's foreign representative subsequently filed a motion with the Bankruptcy Court seeking to enforce the Italian plan and an injunction enjoining US cred-itors from commencing lawsuits against Energy Coal in the US.[429]

4.166 Certain independent contractors objected to the injunction against their claims because the underlying contracts were governed by Florida law with any litigation under the contracts to be brought there.[430] The contractors argued they should be permitted to both liquidate their claims against Energy Coal in Florida and have a Florida court determine the priority of their claims because they should not be required to incur the substantial costs of ap-pearing in Genoa.[431] The foreign representative agreed that a Florida court could determine the amount of the claims, but not their priority.[432]

4.167 The Bankruptcy Court held that a contractual choice-of-law provision does not over-ride the important principle of affording comity to the priority scheme of a foreign main proceeding. While recognizing the extra cost for the contractors to appear in Genoa, the Bankruptcy Court emphasized that foreign creditors are required to file their claims in the US to recover from a US bankruptcy estate, and thus 'it is equally appropriate to expect U.S. creditors to file and litigate their claims in a foreign main bankruptcy case'.[433]

8. *In re Agrokor d.d.*

4.168 In *In re Agrokor d.d.*, the Bankruptcy Court for the Southern District of New York con-sidered whether it should recognize a foreign main proceeding that modified debt governed by laws of another jurisdiction, potentially in contravention to such foreign jurisdiction's laws.[434] In *Agrokor*, Agrokar Group, Croatia's largest private company, filed to effectuate a plan of reorganization under the Act on the Extraordinary Administration Proceedings in Companies of Systemic Importance of the Republic of Croatia (the 'Croatian Proceeding').[435] In accordance with Croatian law, the Agrokar Group's 'Settlement Agreement' (essen-tially a plan of reorganization) was successfully negotiated, accepted by the requisite vote

---

[425] *In re Energy Coal SPA*, 582 BR 619 (Bankr D Del 2018).
[426] Ibid at 621.
[427] Ibid.
[428] Ibid at 622.
[429] Ibid at 623.
[430] Ibid at 625.
[431] Ibid at 628.
[432] Ibid at 629 (internal citations omitted).
[433] Ibid.
[434] *In re Agrokor d.d.*, 591 BR 163, 167 (Bankr SDNY 2018).
[435] Ibid. at 166.

of creditors and approved by the Commercial Court of Zagreb (the 'Croatian Court').[436] Agrokar Group then sought recognition of its settlement agreement in a chapter 15 case in the Southern District of New York.[437]

Judge Glenn observed that the case presented 'challenging issues with very practical con-   **4.169** sequences', as the Agrokar Group had over €1,660 million of debt governed by English law which accounted for approximately 64 per cent of Agrokar Group's total debt to be restruc-tured.[438] The settlement agreement provided for a discharge of Agrokar Group's English debt which could potentially be in contravention of the English *Gibbs* rule, which provides that a foreign court may not change or discharge the substantive rights of creditors con-ferred by English law.[439] Despite the fact that an English court could hold the settlement agreement as unenforceable in the UK, Judge Glenn nevertheless recognized the settlement agreement under principles of comity.[440] '[S]ince no objections ha[d] been filed [and] that the Croatian Proceeding was procedurally fair, provided proper notice to all creditors and, through the Settlement Agreement, determined the rights of all creditors to property that was subject to the jurisdiction of the Croatian Court', there was no reason not to recognize the settlement agreement 'within the territorial jurisdiction of the United States'.[441]

C. Litigation Regarding Section 363

1. *In re Fairfield Sentry, Ltd*

In *Krys v Farnum Place, LLC (In re Fairfield Sentry Ltd)*,[442] the US Court of Appeals for the   **4.170** Second Circuit held section 363 review is mandatory for any 'transfer of an interest of the debtor in property that is within the territorial jurisdiction of the United States', overturning orders by the Bankruptcy Court and the District Court which had emphasized the role of comity in deciding not to review under section 363 the sale of a claim by the liquidator of Fairfield Sentry. To the contrary, the Second Circuit held that comity does not override 'plain' statutory language that dictates that a bankruptcy court is required to conduct a section 363 review when a debtor seeks to transfer an interest of property within the terri-torial jurisdiction of the United States.[443]

Fairfield Sentry, a British Virgin Islands investment fund, had invested approximately 95   **4.171** per cent of its assets with Bernard L Madoff Investment Securities LLC (BLMIS), a limited liability company owned by Bernard L Madoff.[444] In 2008, BLMIS collapsed and was placed into a liquidation proceeding in the US.[445] Fairfield Sentry and the trustee for the BLMIS estate settled Fairfield Sentry's claims against BLMIS for a substantial discount.[446] A few months later, Sentry itself was in trouble and was placed into liquidation in the British

---

[436] Ibid.
[437] Ibid.
[438] Ibid at 167.
[439] Ibid at 193.
[440] Ibid at 186.
[441] Ibid at 185.
[442] 768 F 3d 239 (2d Cir 2014).
[443] Ibid.
[444] Ibid at 241.
[445] Ibid.
[446] Ibid.

Virgin Islands.[447] The BVI liquidator subsequently filed a petition in the Bankruptcy Court of the Southern District of New York seeking recognition of the BVI liquidation proceeding as a 'foreign main proceeding' under chapter 15 and the Bankruptcy Court entered an order granting such relief.[448] One of Fairfield Sentry's assets in the BVI liquidation proceeding was the claim against BLMIS, which the BVI liquidator sold through an auction process to Farnum Place LLC.[449] The sale of the claim was conditioned upon approval of both the US Bankruptcy Court and the British Virgin Islands Court. Shortly after the parties agreed to the claim trade, the BLMIS estate entered into a multi-billion dollar settlement, causing the value of the claim to increase by approximately US$40 million.[450] The BVI liquidator requested that the British Virgin Islands court not approve the transaction given the sudden increase in value of Fairfield Sentry's claim.[451] The British Virgin Islands court, after a three-day evidentiary hearing, approved the terms and conditions of the sale.[452] Subsequently, the BVI liquidator filed an application with the Bankruptcy Court for the Southern District of New York seeking review of the sale under section 363.[453] The Bankruptcy Court denied the application, characterizing it as 'seller's remorse' and a 'last-ditch effort' to undo the transaction.[454] Moreover, the Bankruptcy Court held that section 363 review is not warranted under section 1520(a)(2) of the Bankruptcy Code because the sale did not involve a transfer of an interest in property within the United States.[455] Additionally, the Bankruptcy Court noted that 'comity dictates that this [c]ourt defer to the BVI judgement'.[456] On appeal, the District Court affirmed the Bankruptcy Court's decision.

4.172   The Second Circuit, however, determined that the sale of the claim involved a 'transfer of an interest of the debtor in property that is within the territorial jurisdiction of the United States'.[457] In reaching this conclusion, the Second Circuit relied on section 1502(8), which defines 'within the territorial jurisdiction of the United States' as '... intangible property deemed under nonbankruptcy law to be located within [the territory of the United States], including any property subject to attachment or garnishment that may be properly seized or garnished by an action in Federal or State Court in the United States'.[458] The Second Circuit cited New York state law for the proposition that, for attachment/garnishment purposes, the applicable situs is the location of the party who has a legal obligation to perform.[459] Since the trustee for the BLMIS estate was statutorily obligated to distribute to Fairfield Sentry its pro rata share of recovered assets, the Second Circuit reasoned that the situs of Fairfield Sentry's claim is the location of the trustee, which was New York.[460] Having concluded that the sale of the claim was a 'transfer' of an interest of the debtor in property within the United

---

447   Ibid.
448   Ibid.
449   Ibid at 242.
450   Ibid.
451   Ibid.
452   Ibid.
453   Ibid at 243.
454   *In re Fairfield Sentry Ltd*, 484 BR 615, 617 (Bankr SDNY 2013).
455   Ibid at 618.
456   Ibid at 628.
457   *In re Fairfield Sentry Ltd*, 768 F 3d at 245.
458   11 USC § 1502(8).
459   *In re Fairfield Sentry Ltd*, 768 BR at 244–245.
460   Ibid at 245.

States, the Second Circuit concluded that pursuant to section 1502(a)(2), the Bankruptcy Court was required to apply section 363.[461]

Second, the Second Circuit addressed whether principles of comity required the court to defer to the decision of the BVI court approving the sale.[462] While noting that Congress specifically directed courts in interpreting chapter 15 to consider comity, the Second Circuit explained that chapter 15 does impose certain requirements that limit comity.[463] In that vein, the Second Circuit further explained that the language of section 1520(a)(2) is 'plain' and requires a bankruptcy court to conduct a section 363 review when a debtor under chapter 15 seeks to transfer an interest in property within the United States to the same extent as the court world in a chapter 7 or 11 case, thus, an express limitation on comity.[464]   **4.173**

The Second Circuit remanded the case to the Bankruptcy Court so that it could apply section 363(b) to the proposed sale of the claim, which requires a finding that there was a good business reason to justify it.[465]   **4.174**

2. *In re Elpida Memory, Inc*

In *In re Elpida Memory, Inc*,[466] the US Bankruptcy Court for the District of Delaware held that section 363 standards related to transfers outside the ordinary course of business were applicable to the transfer of assets located in the US by a foreign debtor in a foreign main proceeding based on the plain meaning of section 1520(a) and its legislative history.[467] The Court also found that while comity is a general objective of chapter 15, in this case, principles of comity 'either do not apply or must defer to the plain meaning and legislative history' of section 1520(a).[468]   **4.175**

In February 2012, Elipda Memory, Inc, a manufacturer of dynamic random access (DRAM) products, filed a petition for commencement of corporate reorganization proceedings under the Japan Corporate and Reorganization Act.[469] Thereafter, the foreign representatives of Elipda filed for relief under chapter 15 and the Bankruptcy Court entered an order recognizing the Japanese proceeding as the foreign main proceeding.[470] In September 2012, the foreign representatives filed motions seeking Bankruptcy Court approval to sell certain patents (and grant licences in connection with the sale), including patents registered in the US.[471] These proposed transactions had already been approved by the Japanese court in the foreign proceeding.[472] A group of Elpida's bondholders objected to the motions.[473]   **4.176**

The issue before the Bankruptcy Court was the legal standard to be applied in a chapter 15 case to a transfer of assets located in the US pursuant to a transaction previously approved   **4.177**

---

[461] Ibid.
[462] Ibid.
[463] Ibid.
[464] Ibid at 246.
[465] Ibid.
[466] Case No 12-10947, 2012 WL 6090194 (Bankr D Del 20 Nov 2012).
[467] Ibid at 5–7.
[468] Ibid at 8–9.
[469] Ibid at 1.
[470] Ibid.
[471] Ibid at 2.
[472] Ibid at 1.
[473] Ibid.

by a foreign court in a foreign main proceeding.[474] In its decision, the Bankruptcy Court explained that section 1520(a)(2) of the Bankruptcy Code expressly provides that section 363 applies 'to a transfer of an interest of the debtor in property that is within the territorial jurisdiction of the United States to the same extent that the section would apply to property of the estate'.[475] The Bankruptcy Court found that the plain meaning of section 1520(a) clearly provides that section 363 is so applicable.[476] Further, the Bankruptcy Court noted that the section 363(b) standard is 'well-settled', and a debtor may sell assets outside of the ordinary course of business when it has demonstrated that the sale of such assets represents the sound exercise of business judgement.[477] Accordingly, the Court held that under the plain meaning of section 1520(a)(2), the sound business judgement test was applicable.[478]

4.178   The Bankruptcy Court also found that the legislative history of chapter 15 supported the conclusion that section 363 applies. The Bankruptcy Court noted that section 1520 is adopted from Article 20 of the Model Law, which in the court's view had two purposes: '(i) stopping all actions, proceedings and executions against the debtor's assets in all jurisdictions and (ii) stopping the debtor from transferring or disposing of any of its assets pending further court order'.[479] The Bankruptcy Court further explained that the Model Law tasks the domestic courts with responsibility for assets located in their jurisdiction, and thus, section 363 should apply to assets located in the US.[480]

4.179   Finally, the Bankruptcy Court considered the role of comity. The foreign representatives urged the court in the interest of comity to defer to the decision of the Japanese court and approve the transactions under section 363 because they were previously approved by the Japanese court.[481] While recognizing that promoting comity is a general objective of chapter 15, the Bankruptcy Court explained that 'it is not the end all and be all of the statute'.[482] The Bankruptcy Court noted that decisions relating to chapter 15 frequently invoke comity, but only two provisions of chapter 15 actually mention comity, sections 1507 ('additional assistance') and 1509(b)(3) (allowing the foreign representative access to and standing in US courts other than the chapter 15 court).[483] The Bankruptcy Court concluded that neither of these sections applied to the facts and circumstances of the case.[484] Accordingly, the Bankruptcy Court held that the business judgement test under section 363(b) controlled.[485]

---

[474] Ibid.
[475] Ibid at 4.
[476] Ibid at 5.
[477] Ibid. To satisfy such standard in the Third Circuit, requires that: (i) a sound business purpose exists for the sale; (ii) the sale price is fair; (iii) the debtor has proved adequate and reasonable notice; and (iv) the purchaser has acted in good faith.
[478] Ibid.
[479] Ibid at 6.
[480] Ibid.
[481] Ibid at 8.
[482] Ibid.
[483] Ibid.
[484] Ibid at 9.
[485] Ibid.

VII. Areas for Potential Improvement

The drafting of chapter 15 and subsequent case law interpreting it, as described above, have   **4.180**
hindered one of the ultimate goals of chapter 15: uniform application.[486]

In the US, it is clear that relief will be unavailable if a bankruptcy court does not recognize   **4.181**
the foreign proceeding as either a main or non-main proceeding. The exclusion of certain
non-qualifying foreign proceedings appears contrary to the purposes of chapter 15 and the
Model Law. Section 1501(b) makes chapter 15 applicable whenever assistance is sought in
the US by a foreign representative in connection with a foreign proceeding. However, relief under chapter 15, including comity and cooperation, is blocked unless the foreign proceeding is recognized as either a main or non-main proceeding.[487] The Model Law, on the
other hand, does not deny a foreign representative access to relief if the foreign proceeding
is not recognized. Article 7 of the Model Law, adopted verbatim in the UK, provides that
'[n]othing in this law limits the power of a court ... to provide additional assistance to a
foreign representative under other laws of this State'. Unlike the Model Law, section 1507
of chapter 15, which implements Article 7 of the Model Law, conditions 'additional assistance' on recognition. In addition, once a bankruptcy court refuses to recognize a foreign
proceeding, a foreign representative cannot seek relief in other courts of the US.[488] This
would seem to encourage foreign representatives in non-qualifying proceedings to avoid
chapter 15 and apply directly to non-bankruptcy courts for assistance either by arguing that
chapter 15 does not apply to non-qualifying foreign proceedings or that the requested relief
relates only to recovering a claim that is the property of the debtor.[489] This would defeat the
goal of having a centralized forum and procedures for requests for assistance in connection
with a foreign proceeding.

In addition to limiting the uniform application of the Model Law across all Model Law juris-   **4.182**
dictions, the denial of access to relief for certain foreign proceedings under chapter 15 narrows the circumstances under which courts will provide assistance from the prior section
304 and seems to be a step backward in the area of transnational insolvency.[490] To avoid
this outcome, US bankruptcy courts should interpret the concept of establishment broadly
to ensure that a foreign proceeding is not excluded from either the main or non-main
categories so that assistance can be granted.[491] Section 1507 could also be amended to

---

[486] For additional discussion regarding this issue see Ranney-Marinelli, *supra* n 41 at 298–304.
[487] One bankruptcy court dismissed an adversary proceeding by chapter 11 debtors against a foreign company
for turnover of assets that were transferred in a Netherlands bankruptcy proceeding based on principles of comity
and deferred to the appeal process in the Netherlands. In *In re Viking Offshore (USA) Inc*, 405 BR 434 (Bankr SD
Tex 2008), the foreign company asserted comity, among other things, as a basis for dismissal of the adversary
proceeding even though the Netherlands proceeding was not recognized under chapter 15 as required by s 1509.
Although this issue was not addressed in the bankruptcy court's decision, the bankruptcy court may have decided
to apply comity in this case because doing so did not undermine the purpose of s 1509—preventing foreign representatives from seeking relief by applying directly to non-bankruptcy courts without first obtaining recognition of
the foreign proceeding. In this case, the foreign company only invoked comity to defend allegations made against
it, rather than seeking ancillary assistance from the court.
[488] See 11 USC § 1509(d); Ranney-Marinelli, *supra* n 41 at 301–302.
[489] See Ranney-Marinelli, *supra* n 41 at 301–303.
[490] K Mayr and E Flaschen, 'Courts Issue Bearish Chapter 15 Rulings in Bear Stearns Cases' (2008) 25(10)
Bankruptcy Strategist 1, 2; Ranney-Marinelli, *supra* n 41 at 303.
[491] Ranney-Marinelli, *supra* n 41 at 303–304.

bring its language closer to the Model Law that does not condition additional assistance on recognition.

4.183 The Second Circuit's decision in *Barnet* also appears contrary to the Model Law's goal of making recognition a 'simple and easy' process.[492] While some foreign debtors may have property in the US, others may seek to obtain recognition for other purposes—for example, to invoke US discovery processes to investigate potential claims and causes of action—and the Second Circuit's decision may make such relief unavailable in such jurisdiction.[493] The decision also may lead to forum shopping given the Delaware bankruptcy court's express disagreement with *Barnet*, further hindering the Model Law's goal of uniform application.

4.184 The COMI presumptions embodied in the Model Law appear to be given more weight in other Model Law jurisdictions than in the US.[494] The foreign debtor's COMI is presumed to be the debtor's registered office 'in the absence of evidence to the contrary'. Courts in many jurisdictions accept that the place of incorporation will be the location of the main or principal insolvency proceedings unless such presumption is rebutted by objective evidence.[495] However, the 'US view seems to be that the presumption is only there for speed and convenience where there is no serious controversy'.[496]

4.185 Chapter 15 does not seem equipped to deal with different types of debtors.[497] The activities of a hedge fund consist of entering into contracts with managers and auditors, rather than producing goods or employing numerous people.[498] A hedge fund chooses a place of incorporation for tax and regulatory reasons, and may have no actual operations in such venue.[499] The court's decision in *Bear Stearns* undermines chapter 15 as a viable option for hedge funds and similar entities and may force such debtors to file full-blown chapter 11 or chapter 7 cases in the US in addition to insolvency proceedings they may be required to file in the jurisdictions where they are organized.[500] However, the 2010 decision in *Saad Investments Financing Company (No 5) Limited* indicates that at least some courts are more willing to open the door thought to be closed by *Bear Stearns* to hedge funds seeking recognition under chapter 15.

4.186 In addition, chapter 15 relief may not be available for corporate groups. Many international businesses are structured as enterprises with groups of related entities.[501] Such related entities may be incorporated, and thus may have their COMIs, in different countries.[502] Because a parent corporation and its subsidiaries are separate legal entities with COMIs/establishments in different countries, there is a risk that a subsidiary corporation's foreign

---

[492] Barbra R Parlin, 'Fairfield Sentry and the Second Circuit's Latest on Jurisdiction', *New York Law Journal* (8 Dec 2014).

[493] Ibid.

[494] Sandy Shandro, 'The International Scene: A Plea for the Amendment of Chapter 15' (2009) 28-MAR *Am Bankr Inst J* 48, 49.

[495] Ibid.

[496] Ibid.

[497] Ibid.

[498] Ibid.

[499] Ibid.

[500] Mayr and Flaschen, *supra* n 490 at 1.

[501] Samuel L Bufford, 'Tertiary and Other Excluded Foreign Proceedings Under Bankruptcy Code Chapter 15' (2009) 83 *Am Bankr LJ* 165, 176–177.

[502] Ibid.

proceeding may be ineligible for recognition as a main or non-main proceeding in con-nection with the parent corporation's foreign proceeding.[503] Even if a multi-tiered corpor-ation is recognized under chapter 15, the foreign representative at the parent level may have difficulty gaining control of the subsidiaries' assets because each corporation is a separate legal entity.[504] However, in 2019, UNCITRAL finalized and adopted legislation, along with a guide to states' enactment, to address the insolvency proceedings of multinational cor-porate groups.[505] The UNCITRAL Model Law on Enterprise Group Insolvency includes provisions on, among other things, (i) the coordination and cooperation between courts, insolvency representatives and a group representative, with respect to multiple insolvency proceedings concerning members of an enterprise group; (ii) the development of a group insolvency solution for an enterprise group through a single insolvency proceeding com-menced at the location where at least one group member has its COMI; (iii) the voluntary participation of multiple group members in that single insolvency proceeding for the pur-poses of coordinating a solution and access to foreign courts; (iv) the approval of finance arrangements post-commencement of the insolvency proceedings; (v) the cross-border recognition of a planning proceeding to facilitate the development of the group insolvency solution; (vi) measures designed to minimize the commencement of non-main insolvency proceedings, including measures to facilitate the treatment of claims of creditors of enter-prise group members, including foreign claims, in the main proceeding; and (vii) the for-mulation and recognition of a group insolvency solution.[506] As the UNCITRAL Model Law on Enterprise Group Insolvency is new, jurisdictions have yet to adopt it and there has yet to be any US case discussing its applicability to chapter 15.

VIII. The English Experience of the Model Law—The Cross-Border Insolvency Regulations 2006

A. Implementation

The Regulations, which implement the Model Law in Great Britain, came into force on 4 April 2006. They were made under powers conferred by section 14 of the Insolvency Act 1986 and have effect throughout England and Wales and Scotland.[507]   **4.187**

Prior to their enactment the Insolvency Service issued a consultation document[508] which provided information on how it proposed to implement the Model Law, while at the same time seeking the views of interested parties. Some of the modifications seen in the version implemented in Great Britain arise as a result of the responses to that consultation and are   **4.188**

---

[503] Ibid.

[504] See Salafia, *supra* n 17 at 330 (discussing treatment of corporate group insolvency by US courts before the enactment of chapter 15).

[505] See *UNCITRAL Model Law on Enterprise Group Insolvency with Guide to Enactment*, United Nations Commission on Trade Law Group V (Insolvency Law) February 2020.

[506] Ibid at 19–20.

[507] Northern Ireland implemented the Model Law by way of the Cross-border Insolvency Regulations (Northern Ireland) 2007, SR 2007/115 which came into force on 12 April 2007.

[508] *Implementation of UNCITRAL Model Law on Cross-Border Insolvency in Great Britain* (Insolvency Service, August 2005).

intended to provide sufficient protection for British creditors while remaining faithful to the underlying objectives of the Model Law.[509]

4.189   Unless otherwise indicated, all references in this section to 'articles' are references to the articles comprising the text in Schedule 1 to the Regulations which is the form of Model Law as enacted in Great Britain.

B.   Framework of the Regulations and Limitations on Application

4.190   The Regulations are divided into six main parts: the enacting provisions (Articles 1 to 8 inclusive) and five schedules. Schedule 1 contains the text of the Model Law in the form in which it has the force of law in Great Britain. Schedules 2 and 3 provide for procedural matters in England and Wales and Scotland, respectively; Schedule 4 makes provision for the delivery of notices to the registrar of companies; and Schedule 5 contains the forms that are to be used for applications and orders made pursuant to the Regulations.

4.191   A total of 13 entities are excluded from the scope of the Regulations (Article 1(2)). These are regulated industries which are generally subject to special insolvency regimes under national laws and, in some cases, these regimes are pursuant to harmonized provisions introduced through European directives. The exclusion prevents both assistance being sought in Great Britain in connection with a debtor from an excluded category and assistance being sought in a foreign state on the basis of the Model Law in connection with a proceeding under British insolvency law. Among the excluded entities are credit institutions and insurance undertakings.

4.192   The British courts may also refuse to provide assistance under the Regulations if it would be manifestly contrary to public policy (Article 6). The fact that foreign proceedings may differ from British proceedings, even in relation to creditors' rights in respect of priorities, would not without more be a reason to refuse relief.[510] In keeping with the Guide to Enactment, the comparable provision in the European Insolvency Regulation,[511] and the European Court of Justice guidance in *Re Eurofood IFSC Ltd*,[512] it seems likely that the use of this exception will be reserved for exceptional cases. This was Snowden J's view in *Nordic Trustee*.[513] However, he also considered it strongly arguable that the court would have a residual discretion to refuse recognition if it was satisfied that the applicant is abusing the recognition process for an illegitimate purpose.[514] In that case, Snowden J was of the view that seeking recognition in order to obtain a stay to prevent an arbitration which had nothing to do with protecting the foreign reorganization proceedings was such an abuse of the process for recognition of a foreign proceeding.[515]

---

[509]   Key differences include provisions relating to the range of entities falling outside the scope of the Regulations (art 1(2)), the transaction avoidance provisions (art 23) and the extent of cooperation with foreign courts and foreign representatives (arts 25–27).

[510]   *Re Stocznia Gdynia SA (Bud-Bank Leasing) Sp zo.o.* [2010] BCC 255, citing the decision of the House of Lords in *McGrath v Riddell* [2008] 1 WLR 852, HL.

[511]   Regulation (EU) 2015/848 of the European Parliament and of the Council of 20 May 210 on insolvency proceedings (recast) [2015] OJ L 141/19.

[512]   Case C-341/04 (2006) ECR I-3813.

[513]   *Nordic Trustee A.S.A & anr v OGX Petroleo e Gas SA* [2016] EWHC 25 (Ch).

[514]   Ibid at [60].

[515]   Ibid at [54].

The courts must also have regard to private international law when asked to grant assistance **4.193** (as implied in the definition of 'British insolvency law') and, where assistance is granted, they must be satisfied that the interests of creditors in Great Britain are adequately protected (regulation 21(2)).

C. Relationship Between the Regulations and Other Bases of Recognition and Assistance Under English Law

The Regulations operate in parallel with section 426 of the Insolvency Act 1986, which au- **4.194** thorizes international judicial cooperation between courts in the UK and courts in a designated list of mostly Commonwealth or ex-Commonwealth countries or territories.

Moreover, 'British insolvency law' (defined in the Regulations as the insolvency laws of **4.195** England and Wales, and Scotland) applies with such modifications as the context requires for the purpose of giving effect to the Regulations. In cases of conflict between the provisions of British insolvency law and the Regulations, the provisions of the Regulations will prevail (Article 3(2)).

The overlap in jurisdiction between the Regulations and section 426 of the Insolvency Act **4.196** 1986 is intentional: a decision was taken by the legislators to retain the jurisdiction conferred by section 426 so that the courts would have maximum flexibility when dealing with issues involving foreign insolvency proceedings.[516] This contrasts with the position in the US where chapter 15 appears to provide a single gateway.[517] In situations where both the Regulations and section 426 confer jurisdiction, it will be for the insolvency office holder who is seeking assistance to determine which of the two offer the most effective assistance. Section 426(5) expressly allows for the insolvency law of either jurisdiction to be applied in relation to comparable matters and, in this respect, it is potentially wider in scope than the Regulations.[518] However, the nature of the assistance given in response to the request from the foreign court remains at the discretion of the English courts.

It should be noted that the provisions in the Regulations also supplement the judicial assist- **4.197** ance available under English common law principles of recognition. Judicial confirmation of this can be found in *Re Stanford International Bank Limited*,[519] where Lewison J observed that the common law remains in being as regards corporations that are expressly excluded from the ambit of the Regulations and expressed the view that it should also continue to exist as regards entities that fail to satisfy the definition of 'foreign representative' and, more recently, in the decision of the Privy Council in *Singularis*.[520] The common law jurisdiction, which relies on the debtor having a 'presence of assets' or 'sufficient connection' with

---

[516] *Implementation of UNCITRAL Model Law on Cross-Border Insolvency in Great Britain—Summary of Responses and Government Reply* (March 2006), para 7.

[517] See Gabriel Moss, 'Beyond the Sphinx—is Chapter 15 the Sole Gateway?' (2007) 20 *Insolvency Intelligence* 55.

[518] Although it is arguable that foreign law should be applied under the Regulations: see Look Chan Ho, 'Applying Foreign Law under the UNCITRAL Model Law on Cross-Border Insolvency' (2009) 24(11) Butterworths J Intl Banking Financial L 655–659.

[519] [2009] BPIR 1157 at 100. The decision was upheld by the Court of Appeal in *Re Stanford International Bank* [2010] All ER (D) 219.

[520] *Singularis Holdings Ltd v PricewaterhouseCoopers* [2014] UKPC 36.

England, can also be used in cases where the debtor has neither its COMI nor an establishment in the state in question (or is an excluded entity) so cannot seek recognition under the Regulations. Thus, in the absence of recognition under the Regulations, a foreign representative is able to seek enforcement in England of orders and judgments of foreign courts in certain circumstances, on the grounds of international comity. And Snowden J undertook an excellent review of other common law principles in the case of *Kireeva & Anor v Bedzhamov*.[521] The Foreign Judgments (Reciprocal Enforcement) Act 1933, which facilitates the recognition of a judgment in an overseas jurisdiction once it is registered in a local jurisdiction, may also be relevant if (i) the local jurisdiction is listed in the Act and (ii) the judgment is one to which the Act applies.

D. Key Definitions

4.198   The key definitions which together play a significant part in the operation of the Regulations have been incorporated from the original Model Law text without amendments. These include 'foreign representative', 'foreign proceeding', 'foreign main proceeding', and 'foreign non-main proceeding'.

4.199   A 'foreign representative' is defined as a person or body, including one appointed on an interim basis, authorized in a foreign proceeding to administer the reorganization or the liquidation of the debtor's assets or affairs or to act as a representative of the foreign proceeding (Article 2(j)).

4.200   A 'foreign proceeding' is a collective judicial or administrative proceeding in a foreign state, including an interim proceeding, pursuant to a law relating to insolvency in which proceeding the assets and affairs of the debtor are subject to control or supervision by a foreign court, for the purpose of reorganization or liquidation (Article 2(i)).[522] The definition has not been extended to expressly state that it encompasses all proceedings involving debtors in financial distress. This may result in foreign proceedings which derive from a statute or code which is not expressly founded in insolvency law being denied recognition in the courts of Great Britain and other enacting states who have adopted the definition without amendment. In enacting states where the definition has been extended, as in the US, a corporate process such as an English scheme of arrangement will be recognized.[523] In *Carter v Bailey* Chief ICC Judge Briggs declined to recognize Bermudan winding-up proceedings as foreign main proceedings where the debtor was 'undoubtedly solvent'.[524] He considered it contrary to the stated purpose and object of the UNCITRAL Model Law to interpret foreign proceedings as including solvent debtors, particularly where the proceedings in question were intended to generate a return for members. Thus, proceedings will only be recognized as foreign proceedings in England if they relate to the resolution of the debtor's insolvency or financial distress.

---

[521]   *Kireeva & Anor v Bedzhamov* [2021] EWHC 2281 (Ch)

[522]   The ambit of this expression was considered in *Re Stanford International Bank* at 37–42 and 71–95, and subsequently approved by the Court of Appeal.

[523]   See section III above (Chapter 15 Recognition of English Schemes of Arrangement).

[524]   *Carter v Bailey and Hutchison* (as foreign representatives of Sturgeon Central Asia Balanced Fund Ltd) [2020] EWHC 123 (Ch).

A 'foreign proceeding' can be either a 'foreign main proceeding' or a 'foreign non-main proceeding'. A 'foreign main proceeding' is a proceeding taking place in the state where the debtor has its COMI (Article 2(g)). A foreign non-main proceeding is a proceeding, which is not a foreign main proceeding, taking place in a state where the debtor has an establishment (Article 2(h)). The former is akin to the concept of 'main proceedings' and the latter to 'secondary proceedings' under the European Insolvency Regulation.[525] COMI is not defined but is presumed to be where the debtor's registered office is located.[526] 'Establishment' is defined as any place of operations where the debtor carries out a non-transitory economic activity with human means and assets or services (Article 2(e)). The words 'assets or services' replace the word 'goods' in the original text thereby ensuring that both tangible and intangible assets fall within the definition.   **4.201**

The term debtor is not defined in the Regulations but is required for recognition purposes. It was considered at first instance in the decision in *Rubin and Lan v Eurofinance SA*.[527] In that case, a US trustee was seeking recognition of a form of US business trust which, according to English law, had no legal personality either as an individual or as a body corporate. Strauss QC considered it unrealistic to take the view that the term need be given its ordinary domestic meaning for the following reasons: **4.202**

(a) the drafting origins of the relevant definitions are international, not domestic;

(b) the definition which is principally relevant is the definition of 'foreign proceeding', where the word occurs in the phrase '*in which proceeding* the assets and affairs of the debtor are subject to control or supervision by a foreign court …'. It would therefore be perverse in that context to give the word 'debtor' any other meaning than that given to it by the foreign court in the foreign proceedings;

(c) Article 8 provides that, in interpreting the Model Law, regard is to be had to its international origin and to the need to promote uniformity in its application. Both these considerations would be disregarded if the court were to adopt a parochial interpretation of 'debtor' and as a result refuse to provide any assistance in relation to a bona fide insolvency proceeding taking place in a foreign jurisdiction. While the Guide to Enactment does not specifically address this issue, it is clear from many passages in it that its object is to promote communication, cooperation, and assistance in cross-border insolvencies of any kind; and

(d) while Article 20 imposes an automatic stay on the commencement or continuation of proceedings 'concerning *the debtor's* assets, rights, obligations or liabilities' and on 'execution against *the debtor's* assets', and suspends the right to transfer, encumber, or otherwise dispose of '*any assets of the debtor*'; the stay and suspension would apply to proceedings involving, or assets held by, the trustees in their capacity as trustees.

The conclusion drawn was that there should be no difficulty for the English courts in recognizing a debtor which is not a legal entity known to English law since the requirement to   **4.203**

---

[525] Regulation (EU) 2015/848 of the European Parliament and of the Council of 20 May 210 on insolvency proceedings (recast) [2015] OJ L 141/19. The European Insolvency Regulation no longer applies in the UK, following the UK's withdrawal from the European Union.

[526] See the discussion in section VIII.E.2 below (Presumptions concerning recognition).

[527] [2009] All ER (D) 102. The case was appealed (see section VIII.F.1) but not in respect of this part of the judgment.

cooperate is expressed in general terms and is mainly discretionary. However, as we shall see, the application of the Cross-Border Insolvency Regulations to the *Rubin* case was to run into far more profound obstacles by the time the case reached the UK Supreme Court.

E. Recognition of a Foreign Proceeding and Relief

1. Application for recognition

4.204   An application for recognition must be made to one of the Chancery's district registries or the High Court, for proceedings in England and Wales, or the Court of Session for proceedings in Scotland, as appropriate (Article 4). This will be the court in the area where the debtor has a place of business or assets. If the debtor does not meet these requirements the court can nonetheless assume jurisdiction if it considers that it is the appropriate forum. Article 4(3) adds flexibility where there are concurrent proceedings by allowing the court to take into account the location of other courts where insolvency proceedings are, or may in future be, taking place.

4.205   The foreign representative is entitled to apply to commence a proceeding under British insolvency law if the conditions for commencing such a proceeding are otherwise met (Article 11).[528] This provision confers procedural standing on the foreign representative to make the application and differs in this respect from the requirements of the Insolvency Act 1986, which specifically lists the office holders entitled to commence proceedings.

4.206   Article 15 sets out the key procedural requirements for an application for recognition of the foreign proceedings in respect of which the foreign representative has been appointed and lists the requisite supporting documentation. The foreign representative has a right of direct access to the courts under Article 9 so there is no requirement for him to engage in any form of diplomatic or consular communication prior to making the application. As noted in the *Millhouse Capital* case,[529] the right of direct access under Article 9 now enables the liquidator of a foreign debtor to commence proceedings on behalf of the debtor instead of having to resort to the court's winding-up jurisdiction.

4.207   The foreign representative is under an ongoing obligation to provide information identifying all foreign proceedings, proceedings under British insolvency law and section 426 requests relating to the debtor which are known to him (Articles 15(3) and (18)). This information will be used by the court in any decision it has to make when granting relief in favour of the foreign proceedings. Information on other relevant matters which might have an impact on the court's exercise of its discretion to grant relief, such as any move to reschedule the debtor's debts, must be provided in the supporting affidavit in accordance with Schedule 2 to the Regulations. However, the applicant should not simply 'tick the boxes' and make the disclosures specifically required by Article 15. Instead, the applicant has an obligation of full and frank disclosure to the court. Thus, in *Nordic Trustee* an applicant had not

---

[528] Foreign creditors do not have a right to apply for recognition but they do have a right under Art 13 to request the commencement of, and participation in, a proceeding under British insolvency law as creditors in Great Britain.

[529] *Millhouse Capital UK Ltd v Sibir Energy plc* [2008] EWHC 2614.

proceeded correctly in failing to bring to the attention of the court the purpose for which recognition was sought and the impact which recognition might have on third parties,[530] and in *Cherkasov* recognition granted at an *ex parte* hearing was set aside because the foreign representative was found to have failed in its duty of full and frank disclosure.[531]

In the hearing of the first application in the High Court under the Regulations,[532] in which **4.208** a US trustee sought recognition of US bankruptcy proceedings to facilitate the recovery of property situated in England, Registrar Nicholls made some observations concerning procedural matters, including as to the content of the supporting affidavit and filing and advertising requirements, which were intended to assist practitioners in future cases. These observations have since been made the subject of a practice direction.[533]

2. Presumptions concerning recognition and insolvency

Article 16 lays down presumptions that allow the court to expedite the process of gathering **4.209** evidence for the purposes of recognition of the foreign proceeding while retaining its ability to assess other evidence if the conclusion suggested by the presumptions is called into question by the court or an interested party.

Under Article 16(3) there is a presumption that, in the absence of proof to the contrary, a **4.210** debtor's COMI will be the place of its registered office. The burden of proof lies with the party trying to rebut the presumption. The wording is taken verbatim from the text of the Model Law. Chapter 15, in contrast, presumes the debtor's COMI to be the place of its registered office in the absence of 'evidence' (as opposed to 'proof') to the contrary. US jurisprudence thus holds that the burden of proof lies on the person who is asserting that particular proceedings are 'main proceedings' and that the burden of proof is never on the party opposing that contention. It has been suggested that the change in language of the enactment may explain why the jurisprudence of the US courts has diverged from that of the European Court of Justice.[534]

It is for the British court to decide whether the proceeding is a foreign main proceeding or a **4.211** foreign non-main proceeding for the purposes of recognition of that proceeding. In this regard, it is not bound by the opinion of the foreign court as to where the COMI of the debtor is located.

While the COMI presumption mirrors that found in Article 3(1) of the European Insolvency **4.212** Regulation, it should be borne in mind that the concept of COMI under the Regulations has a different function to that in the European Insolvency Regulation: the emphasis in the Regulations is on determining the nature of the foreign insolvency proceeding for recognition purposes only and not, as in the case of the European Insolvency Regulation, on determining which Member State has jurisdiction to open insolvency proceedings. For this reason, the law of the state of opening is largely irrelevant and those seeking assistance from the English courts will not be affected by where main proceedings are opened.

---

[530] *Nordic Trustee* (n 513).
[531] *Cherkasov & Ors v Olegovich* [2017] EWHC 3153 (Ch).
[532] *Re Rajapakse* (High Court, 23 November 2006).
[533] *Re Rajapakse* (Note) [2007] BPIR 99.
[534] Lewison J, *Re Stanford International Bank Limited* [2009] BPIR 1157 at [65].

4.213 Thus far, the determination of COMI has nonetheless been approached by applying similar principles to those used by the European Court of Justice in the *Eurofood* case.[535] In the *Stanford* case,[536] Lewison J expressed the view that 'the framers of the Model Law envisaged that the interpretation of COMI in the EC Regulation ... would be equally applicable to COMI in the Model Law'.[537] He too was guided by Recital 13 of the European Insolvency Regulation (notwithstanding the absence of equivalent clarification in the Model Law) which states that a company's COMI is where it conducts the administration of its interests on a regular basis and is therefore ascertainable by third parties. In his view, what is ascertainable by third parties is what is in the public domain and what third parties would learn in the ordinary course of business with the company. He emphasized that an important purpose of COMI is that it provides certainty and foreseeability for creditors of the company at the time they enter the transaction. The Court of Appeal upheld the decision. Morritt C examined the evolution of both the European Insolvency Regulation and the Model Law and laid stress on the Model Law's Guide to Interpretation, which states that the European Convention on Insolvency Proceedings,[538] as the forerunner to the European Insolvency Regulation, could be useful when interpreting the meaning of COMI under the Model Law. He found a 'clear correlation' between the words used and the purpose to which they are applied in the two instruments and considered that Lewison J was right to follow *Eurofood* (again emphasizing that the European Insolvency Regulation was successor to the European Convention). He could see nothing in the respective contexts of the Model Law and the European Insolvency Regulation to require different meanings to be given to the phrase COMI and concluded that the test was the same as in the *Eurofood* case.[539] Lewison J's approach was followed by Snowden J in *Videology*, in which the fact that strategic management decisions concerning the company were taken in the US was not sufficient evidence that the company's COMI was to be found there, so that chapter 11 proceedings were recognized as foreign non-main proceedings.[540]

4.214 The advantage of turning to the jurisprudence arising from the European Insolvency Regulation to set the standard for the way in which COMI is determined for the purposes of the Regulations is that it assists in promoting a uniform and consistent approach by the courts to establishing a debtor's COMI. Thus, by adopting this approach, the courts will be adhering to the statement of uniformity in Article 8. However, it remains to be seen how the English courts will approach this issue now that the European Insolvency Regulation no longer applies in the UK.

4.215 There is also a presumption as to insolvency in foreign main proceedings (Article 31). Thus, in the absence of evidence to the contrary, recognition of a foreign main proceeding is, for the purpose of commencing a proceeding under local insolvency law, proof that the

---

[535] Case C-341/04 *Re Eurofood IFSC Ltd* (2006) ECR I-3813.

[536] *Re Stanford International Bank Limited* [2009] BPIR 1157.

[537] Ibid at 46. This approach has not been without criticism: see Look Chan Ho, 'Cross-border Fraud and Cross-Border Insolvency: Proving COMI and Seeking Recognition under the UK Model Law' (2009) 24(9) *Butterworths J Intl Banking Financial L* 537–542.

[538] The Convention itself lapsed in 1995 for political reasons but was enacted in the form of the EC Regulation with very few changes: see Ian F Fletcher, *Insolvency in Private International Law* (2nd edn, 2005) at 339–358.

[539] See in particular paras [39] and [53]–[56] of the Court of Appeal's judgment: *Re Stanford International Bank Limited* [2010] EWCA Civ 137.

[540] *Re Videology Ltd* [2018] EWHC 2186; [2019] BCC 195.

debtor is insolvent. This may save time and expense by removing the need to prove that the debtor is insolvent. However, the wording is such that the local court may nonetheless seek to prove or disprove the insolvency. The decision of Chief ICC Judge Briggs in *Carter v Bailey*, that for recognition to be ordered in England and Wales the proceedings in question must be for the purpose of resolving insolvency or financial distress, raises the question of whether the English court will routinely make this investigation.[541] Chief ICC Judge Briggs was of the view that this would not be the result as, in the majority of cases, it would be readily apparent whether the debtor was solvent or not.

3. Decision to recognize a foreign proceeding

The critical determination to be made by the court is whether the foreign proceeding falls within the scope of the Regulations as defined in Article 1 and, if so, whether it is eligible for recognition as a foreign main proceeding or a foreign non-main proceeding.[542] The type of proceeding will determine the nature and extent of the relief available. Under Article 17(1), unless a foreign proceeding is contrary to public policy, it must be recognized by the British court if: **4.216**

(a) it is a foreign proceeding within the meaning of Article 2(i);
(b) the representative is a 'foreign representative' within the meaning of Article 2(j);
(c) the procedural and evidential requirements of Article 15(2) and (3) have been complied with (formal documents provided and statements about other existing foreign proceedings made in supporting documents); and
(d) the application has been made in the appropriate court.

Article 17(3) stipulates that the application must be decided upon 'at the earliest possible time'. In October 2008, recognition of winding-up proceedings taking place in Belize was granted seven days after application had been made to the English court.   **4.217**

If the foreign proceeding is recognized by the British court, the foreign representative will be entitled to participate in proceedings regarding the debtor under British insolvency law (Article 12). These proceedings include extra-judicial proceedings such as some forms of administration, company voluntary arrangements, and creditors' voluntary liquidation.   **4.218**

4. Interim relief pending recognition

Prior to recognition of foreign proceedings, the court may grant discretionary relief under Article 19 from the time of the filing of the application for recognition of a main or non-main foreign proceeding until the application is determined. Such relief must be required on an urgent basis to protect the assets of the debtor or the interests of the creditors. The relief granted is provisional and terminates when the application for recognition is decided upon. It can be extended, if necessary, under Article 21. Article 19(1) provides a non-exhaustive list of examples of the type of relief that may be granted. The Guide to Enactment suggests that it is the type of relief that is usually available in collective insolvency proceedings rather than that sought in respect of specific assets identified by a creditor. The court   **4.219**

---

[541] *Carter v Bailey* (n 524)
[542] The stay which comes into effect upon recognition of a foreign main proceeding will not prevent local creditors from initiating or continuing British proceedings in order to preserve a claim against the debtor (Art 20(4) and (5)).

must take into account the interests of creditors and third parties when exercising its discretion and may refuse to grant relief if it interferes with the administration of a foreign main proceeding.

F. Effects of Recognition

1. Automatic stay

4.220 Upon recognition of a foreign proceeding as a foreign main proceeding under the Regulations, a limited package of relief is automatically accorded pursuant to Article 20.[543] Key elements of that relief include a mandatory stay of actions of individual creditors against the debtor or a stay of enforcement proceedings concerning the assets of the debtor, and a suspension of the debtor's right to transfer or encumber its assets. Article 20(2) defines the automatic stay in such a way as to render its scope and effect comparable to that of a debtor made subject to a winding-up order under the Insolvency Act 1986. This suggests that the stay would not have extraterritorial effect.[544] Article 20(3) applies exceptions and limitations to its scope so that certain specified rights fall outside the stay. These include validly created security rights, rights to repossess goods subject to hire purchase agreements,[545] and set-off rights, insofar as these are exercisable in a British winding up. The exceptions, along with those relating to financial collateral arrangements under the Financial Collateral Arrangements (No 2) Regulations 2003[546] and certain financial markets transactions specified in Article 1(4), are intended to provide adequate protection to secured creditors and others and to enable them to have greater predictability on the likely returns and outcomes in a cross-border insolvency. In *Re Armada Shipping SA* Briggs J (as he then was) declined to consider whether arbitration proceedings were caught by the automatic stay, preferring instead to approach the question as one of judicial discretion in accordance with Article 22 of the Regulation discussed below.[547] However, in *Samsun Logix* Morgan J stated:

> I make it clear that the effect of my recognition of the Korean proceedings is that article 20 applies in this case. I mention that specifically because I have been told that there is a pending arbitration involving this company as respondent, with an intended hearing date of tomorrow in London, before an arbitrator. The consequence of my recognition decision under article 17 is that that proceeding, namely the arbitration against the company, is now immediately stayed.[548]

4.221 The automatic stay may go some way to providing a solution to the difficulties which arise under English common law in relation to debts incurred under English law contracts, but only a partial solution. The difficulties stem from the fact that, under English common law, a discharge of debt negotiated in a foreign jurisdiction will not be given effect in England in

---

[543] The automatic stay under art 20 does not arise in respect of foreign non-main proceedings. Instead, discretionary relief may be available under art 21.

[544] *Re Oriental Inland Steam Company* (1874) LR 9 Ch App 557; *Re Vocalion (Foreign)* [1932] 2 Ch 196; *Mitchell v Carter* [1997] 1 BCLC 673; *Harms Offshore AHT Taurus GmbH & Co KG v Bloom* [2010] 2 WLR 349, CA.

[545] See art 2(k) for the widely drafted definition of hire purchase agreement.

[546] SI 2003/3226.

[547] *Re Armada Shipping SA* [2011] EWHC 216 (Ch).

[548] *Samsun Logix Corporation v DEF* [2009] EWHC 576 (Ch).

respect of debts governed by English law (known as the rule in *Gibbs*).[549] Notwithstanding comment that the Regulations are drafted to permit sufficient variation in English private international law to permit recognition of a foreign judgment discharging an English law governed debt,[550] the English courts have declined to adopt that approach.[551] In the leading judgment in *Rubin*, Lord Collins found that notwithstanding that the chapter 11 proceedings in issue fell within the Regulations, the Regulations do not extend to enforcing judgments in the chapter 11 proceedings.[552] In determining what is meant by assistance and relief in the Regulations, Lord Collins concluded that we do not mean recognition of all judgments handed down in the foreign insolvency proceedings. For Lord Collins, Article 21 was concerned with procedural matters, not the recognition and enforcement of foreign judgments against third parties. Second, Lord Collins disapproved of Lord Hoffmann's analysis in *Cambridge Gas* that orders made in foreign insolvency proceedings are classified as neither judgments *in personam*, nor judgments *in rem*, for the purposes of recognition and that different principles govern recognition and enforcement of such orders.[553] Instead Lord Collins found that the usual conflicts of law principles apply. *Rubin* was subsequently followed in *Bank of Azerbaijan*, in which the Court of Appeal unanimously upheld Hildyard J's refusal, at first instance, to grant an indefinite moratorium which would have the effect of preventing the respondents from enforcing their English law rights pursuant to the rule in *Gibbs*.[554] Thus, for the moment at least, it appears that *Dicey and Morris* Rule 219 and *Gibbs* are alive and well.[555] This has serious implications in cases where the debtor is expected to continue trading since the debtor may be at risk of claims from creditors whose debts arise under English law notwithstanding their discharge under foreign law. It may be possible to apply for recognition of foreign proceedings while restructuring negotiations are in course, and to rely on either the Article 20 automatic stay or a discretionary stay (discussed below) to prevent enforcement action during this period. But the applicant may attempt to lift the stay and, in any event, the *Azerbaijan* case makes clear that once the restructuring has been concluded a moratorium is unlikely to be granted. Overall, the effect of Lord Collins' judgment in *Rubin* is that if any debts governed by English law are to be discharged as part of the restructuring plan, this will need to be done consensually or through an English process such as an English scheme of arrangement or a Part 26A restructuring plan coinciding with the foreign proceedings. This obviously has implications in terms of time and cost and leaves open the question of what we mean by assistance and relief in the context of the Regulations, which we will examine next.

---

[549] See *Antony Gibbs & Sons v La Société Industrielle et Commerciale des Métaux* (1890) 25 QBD 399 (CA); Albert Venn Dicey, JHC Morris and Lawrence Collins, *Dicey, Morris and Collins on the Conflict of Laws* (under the general editorship of Lord Collins of Mapesbury with specialist editors), Rule 219 '... a discharge from any debt or liability under the bankruptcy law of a foreign country outside the United Kingdom is a discharge therefrom in England if, and only if, it is a discharge under the law applicable to the contract'. For a detailed discussion, see Robin Dicker QC, 'Discharge of Debts by a Foreign Liquidation', 3–4 Digest July 2010, 2.

[550] See, in particular, Dicker (n 549) and Philip Smart, 'Cross-Border Restructurings and English Debts' (2009) 9(1) *International Corporate Rescue*.

[551] *Rubin v Eurofinance SA* [2013] 1 AC 236.

[552] See ibid at [24] and [133]–[144].

[553] *Cambridge Gas Transportation Corp v Official Committee of Unsecured Creditors of Navigator Holdings plc* [2006] UKPC 26, [2007] 1 AC 508 at [13]–[15].

[554] *Re OJSC International Bank of Azerbaijan: Bakhshiyeva v Sberbank of Russia & Ors* [2018] EWCA Civ 2802

[555] *Anthony Gibbs* and Dicey, Morris, and Collins (n 549).

4.222   The decision in *Rubin*, that the Regulations do not provide for the recognition of judgments handed down in foreign insolvency proceedings and that no special rules apply to the recognition of foreign insolvency judgments, also has important implications for the discharge of a foreign law governed debt by the laws of a jurisdiction other than the jurisdiction of incorporation of the debtor by way of debt for equity swap. This is because the ordinary conflict of laws rules for *in rem* and *in personam* judgments will continue to apply. If the shares in question are located in a jurisdiction other than the jurisdiction in which the debt is being discharged, then the courts in the jurisdiction in which the discharge proceedings are taking place will not have *in rem* jurisdiction over them. Furthermore, serious doubts may arise as to whether the existing shareholders have submitted to the jurisdiction in which the discharge is taking place. A number of specific difficulties arise in this regard as a result of the judgment in *Rubin*. *Rubin* concerned the recognition and enforcement of a foreign transaction avoidance provision and so detailed argument on *in personam* submission for the purposes of a discharge of debt by way of debt for equity swap was not heard. This means that the detailed scholarly argument that the shareholders would have submitted in these circumstances was not heard.[556] Nonetheless, in reaching his decision Lord Collins concluded, albeit *obiter*, that *Cambridge Gas* was wrongly decided on this point.[557] As a result, unless the shareholders have consented to the debt for equity swap it may not be possible to enforce the debt for equity swap in the jurisdiction of incorporation of the company so as to affect the cancellation of existing shares and the issue of new ones. This may give shareholders significant leverage and they may extract a heavy price for cooperation.

4.223   Two solutions are possible. The first may be to adapt the structure of the transaction to avoid the need to cancel existing shares and to issue new ones in much the same way as English law restructurings 'twin' schemes of arrangement and prepackaged arrangements.[558] However, there are concerns as to how the US courts would approach such a transaction and how an English court would approach recognition. The second (potentially safer) route would be to take advantage of the differences between the approach of the US courts and the UK courts to the Regulation, and to implement the discharge of the foreign law governed debt in English proceedings, seeking recognition in chapter 15.

---

[556] See, eg, KR Handley, 'Cambridge Gas Rejected' (2013) 129 (Apr) *Law Quart Rev* 144, arguing that the US order may have been binding on Cambridge Gas because it was aware of the proceedings and could therefore have intervened to protect its property; Adrian Briggs, 'Recognition of Foreign Judgments: A Matter of Obligation' (2013) 129 *Law Quart Rev* 87, n 75, suggesting that where the company had submitted 'it would not be altogether surprising if the submission were effective as against the shareholders and stockholders held to be affected as such'; and the arguments of Lord Hoffmann in *Cambridge Gas Transportation Corp v Official Committee of Unsecured Creditors of Navigator Holdings plc* [2006] UKPC 26, [2007] 1 AC 508 at [26] 'a share is the measure of the shareholder's interest in the company: a bundle of rights against the company and the other shareholders. As against the outside world, that bundle of rights is an item of property, a chose in action. But as between the shareholder and the company itself, the shareholder's rights may be varied or extinguished by the mechanisms provided by the articles of association or the Companies Act. ... As a shareholder Cambridge is bound by the transactions into which the company has entered, including a plan under Chapter 11'.

[557] *Rubin v Eurofinance SA* [2013] 1 AC 236 at [132]: 'The Privy Council accepted (in view of the conclusion that there had been no submission to the jurisdiction of the court in New York) that Cambridge Gas was not subject to the personal jurisdiction of the US bankruptcy court. The property in question, namely the shares in Navigator, was situated in the Isle of Man and therefore also not subject to the in rem jurisdiction of the US bankruptcy court. There was therefore no basis for the recognition of the order of the US bankruptcy court in the Isle of Man.'

[558] For one such adaptation see A Zacaroli QC and S Dickson, 'Recognition of Foreign Insolvency Restructuring Proceedings: Arcapita Bank' South Square Digest February 2014, suggesting a structure in which the assets of the company are sold to a newly incorporated company in exchange for fresh equity in the 'newco', leaving dissenters stranded in the old shell—a technique already used in the English market and discussed briefly below.

An automatic stay will not affect the right to request or otherwise initiate the commence- **4.224**
ment of a proceeding under British insolvency law (eg, to place a company into administration or into voluntary or compulsory liquidation) or the right to file claims in such a
proceeding (Article 20(5)). Additional text has been included in the Regulations to enable
the foreign representative or any person affected by the stay to have it modified, terminated,
or suspended at the court's discretion (Article 20(6)). The court may also do this of its own
accord.

2. Discretionary relief
(a) Stay and suspension

Article 21 empowers the court to grant, at the request of the foreign representative, 'any ap- **4.225**
propriate relief' for the benefit of any foreign proceeding, whether it is a main or non-main
proceeding.[559] We have already seen that this does not amount to recognition of judgments
handed down in the foreign insolvency proceeding. Instead, such discretionary relief may
consist of staying proceedings or suspending the right to encumber assets, staying execution against a debtor's assets, providing for the examination of witnesses, the taking of
evidence or the delivery of information concerning the debtor's assets, affairs, rights, obligations, or liabilities, and appointing the foreign representative or another person designated
by the court to administer all or part of those assets.[560] In *Re Chesterfield United Inc* Newey
J found that Article 21(1)(d) of the Model Law (providing for the examination of witnesses
and the provision of information) was intended to set a common minimum standard and
did not limit the 'additional' relief potentially available under Article 21(1)(g) (such as, eg,
the production/examination powers under section 236 of the Insolvency Act 1986). Thus, if
the local law provides for such 'additional' relief, a foreign representative can seek it under
Article 21(1)(g).[561]

The court must take account of the requirements in Article 22, relating to the protection of **4.226**
creditors and others, when exercising its jurisdiction. It can subject any relief granted under
Article 21 (and by way of interim relief under Article 19) to such conditions as it considers
appropriate, including the provision of security by the debtor or caution by the foreign representative to ensure the proper performance of his functions. As the provision of security
is not automatic, it will be for the interested party to bring any legitimate concerns about the
adequate protection of creditors' interests to the attention of the court.

Article 21(1)(g) specifically refers to relief provided under the administration moratorium **4.227**
provisions in paragraph 43 of Schedule B1 to the Insolvency Act 1986. In so doing it effectively extends the scope of the automatic stay in main proceedings beyond that which arises
on a winding up to that which arises in an administration. The court therefore has the discretion to override the rights conferred on creditors under paragraphs (2) and (3) of Article
20 so that, as in an administration, they are only exercisable with the consent of the office
holder or the permission of the court.

---

[559] Urgently needed relief may already have been granted upon filing an application for recognition—see section
VIII.E.4 above (Interim relief pending recognition).
[560] Article 21(1)(a)–(e).
[561] *Re Chesterfield United Inc; Akers v Deutsche Bank AG* [2012] EWHC 244 (Ch).

4.228 These additional restrictions on the exercise of a creditor's rights may provide considerable assistance when attempting to rescue or restructure a debtor with interests or assets in several jurisdictions. The need for these wider restrictions was recognized in the *Samsun Logix* case.[562] The case concerned a South Korean shipping conglomerate with global operations which filed for court receivership in Korea and was subsequently made subject to rehabilitation proceedings. Morgan J granted an order for the recognition of the Korean proceedings as foreign main proceedings under the Regulations and of the Korean receiver as a foreign representative. The automatic stay under Article 20(2) was consequently triggered which stayed arbitration proceedings due to be heard in London the following day. He also exercised his powers to grant discretionary relief under Article 21(1)(g) to provide for a moratorium so that no steps could be taken to enforce security over Samsun's property except with the consent of the receiver or the permission of the court.[563]

4.229 Similar relief was subsequently sought in *Re TPC Korea Co Ltd*.[564] The case is similar in a number of respects to the *Samsun Logix* case in that a Korean receiver was appointed to a global shipping company made subject to rehabilitation proceedings. Relief was again granted under Article 21(1)(g) in order to provide extra protection against creditor action. In both cases the wider moratorium was an appropriate form of relief, given that the aim of Korean rehabilitation proceedings (which combine elements of an English administration and a scheme of arrangement) is to rescue the debtor. Most recently, the approach has been followed in *NMC Healthcare Ltd*, in which Sir Alastair Norris stated, in an uncontested application, that in exercising the power to grant discretionary relief, 'where the foreign proceedings are more akin to an administration than to a liquidation it has become customary for the English court to align the moratorium arising automatically upon recognition with that under paragraph 43 of Schedule B1 to the Insolvency Act 1986'.[565]

4.230 A key question which has arisen in relation to Article 21 in both the US and the UK is whether 'appropriate relief' is relief in accordance with foreign or local law.[566] As we have already seen, the US courts have interpreted Article 21 as authorizing the application of foreign insolvency law. To date the UK has arrived at a different conclusion, although apparently starting with the same material in the form of the Model Law and the Guide to Enactment. The *Pan Ocean* case concerned rehabilitation proceedings in respect of a Korean company in Korea.[567] The proceedings were recognized by the English courts as 'foreign main proceedings' for the purposes of Article 17 of the Regulations and the administrator was recognized as the foreign representative. The Korean administrator argued that as a matter of Korean law where he elected to continue an executory contract in the Korean rehabilitation proceedings the counterparty to the contract could not exercise rights of termination and sought an order under Article 21(1) preventing a counterparty to

---

[562] *Samsun Logix* (n 548).

[563] Similar relief was requested in Australia, under the Cross-Border Insolvency Act 2008, and in the US under chapter 15.

[564] High Court, No 19984 of 2009.

[565] [2021] EWHC 1806 (Ch) at [19]

[566] It has been argued that the Model Law is intentionally neutral on this point so that it is for each enacting state to decide: e.g. J Clift, 'The UNCITRAL Model Law on Cross-Border Insolvency—a Legislative Framework to Facilitate Coordination and Cooperation in Cross-Border Insolvency' (2004) 12 *Tulane J Intl Comparative L* 307, 324 and Look Chan Ho, *Cross-Border Insolvency: A Commentary on the UNCITRAL Model Law* (2nd edn, 2009).

[567] *Re Pan Ocean Company Ltd* [2014] EWHC 2124 (Ch).

a highly profitable contract from walking away. The English courts did not start by examining Korean law to consider whether it entitled the administrator to raise this argument. Instead, Morgan J emphasized that the Regulations were concerned only with procedural relief and that procedural relief was limited to relief which the English courts could provide in a domestic insolvency.[568] Thus, instead of starting with a determination of which laws it ought to apply to the question before it, the English courts would start by asking themselves whether the relief sought by the foreign representative was consistent with the relief which would be available in a hypothetical English insolvency and, if the answer to that question was that it was not, then that would be the end of the inquiry.[569] In arriving at this conclusion Morgan J had a different reading of the UNCITRAL deliberations compared to the US courts. The decision is a first instance decision only but, at present, it appears that the position is that the English court will start by considering whether the relief which is sought is consistent with relief which the court would be able to provide under domestic insolvency law. It does also appear to be supported by the implementation of the Model Law in England, given the reference in Article 21(1)(g) to granting any additional relief 'that may be available to a British insolvency officeholder under the law of Great Britain'.

At the time *Pan Ocean* was decided a party was free to terminate a contract for insolvency in an English administration proceeding.[570] However, as we saw in Chapter 3, the Corporate Insolvency and Governance Act 2020 (CIGA) has introduced a significantly broader restriction on the exercise of contractual termination rights in insolvency.[571] Thus, the English courts will now have jurisdiction to grant relief in support of a foreign insolvency proceeding if the relevant termination right falls within the scope of the UK ban.[572] Nonetheless, this does not answer the question of whether English judges will exercise their discretion to do so. As we have also seen, since *Rubin* the courts have consistently underlined that the Regulations are concerned with procedural relief. Preventing a counterparty from exercising a right of contractual termination may, of course, have far-reaching substantive consequences. As we shall see, Article 21(2) of the Regulations provides an express power to remit assets located in Britain to the foreign representative and Article 23 of the Regulations provides the foreign representative with the ability to access English insolvency proceedings without a parallel insolvency proceeding. Both provisions clearly move beyond procedural relief. Hildyard J touched on this briefly at first instance in *Azerbaijan* but appears to consider that it is the explicit statutory permission which makes remittal possible.[573] In other words, perhaps Hildyard J is of the view that a narrow interpretation should be adopted for the rest of the Regulations precisely because these two statutory

4.231

---

[568] See also *Bernard L Madoff Investment Securities LLC; Picard v FIM Advisers LLC & ors* [2010] EWHC 1299 (Ch) and *Atlas Bulk Shipping A/S (in Bankruptcy) (and others) v Navios International Inc* [2011] EWHC (Ch) 878 (Norris J, 13 April 2011).

[569] Presumably, had Morgan J found that the relief sought was available as a matter of English law he would have considered expert evidence on whether the relief sought was also available as a matter of Korean law. See, e.g., *Singularis Holdings Ltd v PricewaterhouseCoopers* [2014] UKPC 36 which, whilst not a case on the Regulations, underlines that the court will not grant assistance as a matter of English law which goes beyond the relief which would be available to the liquidator in the foreign insolvency proceedings.

[570] *Re Olympia v York* [1993] BCC 154.

[571] CIGA, inserting new s 233B (Protection of Supplies of Goods and Services in Great Britain) into Insolvency Act 1986.

[572] William Watson and Paul Fradley, 'Ipso Facto Clauses: the International Dimension', *South Square Digest* (March 2021) 58

[573] *OJSC international Bank of Azerbaijan v Sberbank of Russia* [2019] EWHC 59 (Ch) at [142]

provisions which go beyond procedural relief have been included. The short point is that even if the judge has jurisdiction to grant the relief, we cannot be sure that the judge will exercise discretion to do so.

4.232   The US courts have also shown themselves from time to time predisposed to recognize the interests of local creditors over the universalist ideal of a single forum and the application of a single set of insolvency laws but they have arrived at this result not by starting their inquiry with the compatibility of the relief sought with the domestic position but rather by ending it with an examination of whether they ought to exercise their discretion either on public policy grounds (more usually at first instance) or on the grounds, discussed in greater detail below, that the interests of creditors ought to be sufficiently (in the US implementation) or adequately (in the UK implementation) protected. Whilst this approach also poses the risk that international efforts which should ultimately ensure that creditors in one jurisdiction do better than creditors in another do not achieve their objective,[574] it is at least more likely to result in protection of local creditors over the efficiencies of the case as the exception rather than the rule. In effect it provides the US courts with a safety valve rather than a stopcock.[575]

(b) Distribution of assets

4.233   Article 21(2) provides that the court may, at the request of the foreign representative in either type of proceeding, grant a turnover order, thereby entrusting the distribution of all or part of the debtor's assets located in Great Britain to the foreign representative or another designated person. The court will only grant such an order if it is satisfied that the interests of creditors in Great Britain are adequately protected.[576]

4.234   The court was seen to grant such an order in *Re Swissair*,[577] a case in which the debtor was subject to foreign main proceedings in Switzerland. During the course of its deliberations, the court considered its long-established power to order the remittal of assets realized in an English ancillary liquidation to the liquidators in the principal foreign liquidation, where the law of the principal proceedings provides for *pari passu* distribution.[578]

4.235   In *Re HIH Casualty*,[579] in contrast, the English courts had to decide whether it would be right for an English liquidator to remit assets and claims to principal proceedings in an Australian liquidation so that distribution could be implemented in accordance with Australian insolvency principles. The difficulty arising from this request was that distribution under Australian law did not at that time require strict *pari passu* distribution between all unsecured creditors so remittal would not be in accordance with the principles of English insolvency law and would therefore disadvantage some of the English creditors.

---

[574] See, eg, *In re Qimonda AG*, 462 BR 165 (Bankr ED Va 2011) and *In re Vitro, SAB de CV*, 701 F 3d 1031 (5th Cir 2012).

[575] For an excellent analysis of the difference in approach between the US and the UK see Adrian Walters, 'Modified Universalisms & the Role of Local Legal Culture in the Making of Cross-Border Insolvency Law' (2019) 93 *Am Bankr LJ* 47.

[576] Prior to the enactment of the Regulations any such application would have relied upon the court's inherent jurisdiction to remit assets.

[577] *Re Swissair Schweizerische Luftverkehr-Atkiengesellschaft* [2009] BPIR 1505.

[578] See, eg, *Re BCCI (No 10)* [1997] Ch 213.

[579] *Re HIH Casualty & General Insurance Ltd & Ors (otherwise known as McGrath v Riddell)* [2008] 1 WLR 852, HL. The case opened before the Regulations came into force.

The High Court refused the request on the basis of jurisdiction and the Court of Appeal refused the request on the basis of discretion. The House of Lords, however, overturned the decision by unanimous agreement although their lordships were divided as to whether jurisdiction lay with section 426 of the Insolvency Act 1986 or at common law, in accordance with the principle of universalism.[580] Under the common law approach, the foreign main proceedings would then be allowed to have universalist effect.

The subsequent case of *Stitching Shell* concerned the saga of Fairfield Sentry, a 'feeder fund' **4.236** to BLMIS which went into liquidation in the British Virgin Islands following the BLMIS collapse.[581] Prior to the making of the winding-up order, a Dutch pension fund had obtained a pre-judgment garnishing attachment from a Dutch court over approximately US$71 million in Fairfield Sentry's account in the Dublin branch of a Dutch bank. The liquidators applied for an anti-suit injunction from the BVI court to restrain the proceedings by the pension fund against Fairfield Sentry in the Netherlands. The Privy Council subsequently upheld the granting of the injunction.

The Privy Council found that the basis for the injunction is the need to uphold the effect-**4.237** iveness of insolvency proceedings, which applies to the debtor's assets worldwide. The law of the place of incorporation determined the distribution of assets among creditors and members and the court had equitable jurisdiction to restrain acts of persons which were contrary to the appropriate statutory scheme. It was not necessary to show that the creditors had acted vexatiously or oppressively by invoking the jurisdiction of the foreign court, but it was necessary to show that the court had personal jurisdiction over the defendant in order for it to be in a position to grant the injunction. In *Stitching Shell* it was sufficient for these purposes to demonstrate that a proof had been submitted in the insolvency—thus the defendant had submitted to the jurisdiction of the BVI court for the purposes of granting the injunction.

(c) Disclosure

Relief under Article 21(1)(d) (e.g., an order for the production of documents) will not be **4.238** granted if it results in a breach of confidence which amounts to an unjustified infringement of the rights of an interested third party under Article 8 of the European Convention on Human Rights.[582] The EU–UK Trade and Cooperation Agreement has a number of provisions requiring the UK to continue to observe the ECHR after its withdrawal from the European Union.[583]

3. Protection of creditors and interested third parties

The protection of creditors' interests is reinforced by Article 22 which seeks to ensure that **4.239** there is a balance between the relief that may be granted to the foreign representative and the interests of persons that may be affected by such relief. It stipulates that the courts must

---

[580] The court was also satisfied that the order for remittal was consistent with the ancillary liquidation in England, as required by art 29(a)(i).

[581] *Stitching Shell Pensioenfonds v Krys* [2014] UKPC 41.

[582] *Anthony John Warner (as trustee in bankruptcy of the estate of the late Rene Rivkin) v Verfides* [2009] Bus LR 500.

[583] Trade and Cooperation Agreement between the European Union and the European Atomic Energy Community, of the one part, and the United Kingdom of Great Britain and Northern Ireland, of the other part 19 April 2021 OJ 5198/2.

be satisfied that the interests of creditors 'and any other interested persons' are adequately protected when granting or denying relief (Article 22(1)). The text has been amended to include a specific reference to secured parties and parties to hire purchase agreements.[584]

4.240   Relief under Article 22(2) was provided in a case arising out of the *Samsun Logix* receivership.[585] In that case, Norden, a creditor of Samsun, applied to the English court to enforce a contractual lien in respect of unpaid sums relating to a ship charter, notwithstanding the stay which had been granted in response to a request for relief under Article 21(1)(g) made in the earlier recognition hearing of Samsun. The validity of Norden's lien was subject to litigation in Korea and Samsun's receiver had presented a petition to the Korean court to set aside the lien. Norden's concern was that a finding of invalidity by the Korean court would preclude it from attempting to enforce the lien in England. Newey QC, as deputy judge, recognized this to be a valid concern but refused to grant permission to enforce the lien on the basis that it would pre-empt the outcome of the Korean litigation.[586] He was, however, prepared to exercise his powers under Article 22(2) to make the stay conditional on Samsun and its receiver not arguing in subsequent English proceedings that, as a result of participating in the Korean proceedings, Norden was bound by the decision of the Korean court and estopped from challenging the decision in subsequent English proceedings.

4. Actions to avoid acts detrimental to creditors

4.241   As well as seeking judicial recognition of foreign proceedings, a foreign representative is granted certain rights of access to the courts to initiate proceedings to avoid or render ineffective actions taken which have been detrimental to creditors (Article 23). This enables an application to be made to the British courts under the anti-avoidance provisions of the Insolvency Act 1986. The provisions are listed in Article 23(1)[587] and are available to the foreign representative irrespective of whether the debtor is the subject of an insolvency proceeding under British law and where the foreign representative would not otherwise have standing to apply to the court. The revised text of Article 23(4) makes it clear that the law of the state where the proceeding is taking place shall determine the date of commencement of the foreign proceeding and that any doctrine of relation back[588] of the foreign law will apply.[589] It will be for the foreign representative to provide satisfactory evidence to the British court as to the effective date for the purpose of challenging any such transaction.

4.242   Article 23 does not confer any substantive rights on the foreign representative. It will therefore be necessary for the foreign representative to demonstrate to the court that there is a substantial connection between England and Wales or Scotland, as the case may be, and the transaction which is being called into question and that the court could hear the case under the applicable conflict of law rules. This requirement effectively prevents Article 23 from

---

[584] Defined in Art 2(k) to include conditional sale, chattel leasing, and retention of title agreements.

[585] *D/S Norden A/S v Samsun Logix Corporation* [2009] BPIR 1367.

[586] See also section VIII.H.1 below (Cooperation with foreign courts and foreign representatives).

[587] An order may be sought in the English courts in connection with ss 238, 239, 242, 243, 244, 245, 339, 340, 342A, 343, and 423 of the Insolvency Act 1986.

[588] Under this principle, insolvency proceedings are deemed as having started at the time of the filing of the petition rather than at the time of the hearing.

[589] This avoids the difficulties experienced in relation to the equivalent provision in the EU Insolvency Regulation which is ambiguous as to whether the relation back principle should be applied. The 2006 ECJ ruling in *Re Eurofood IFSC Ltd* (2006) ECR I-3813 confirmed that it should.

being used as a means of forum shopping by a party seeking to take advantage of British insolvency law and addresses similar concerns to those of the US courts in cases seeking the application of US avoidance provisions in Chapter 15.[590]

In instances where there might otherwise be an overlap between the rights of a foreign rep- **4.243**
resentative and a British insolvency office holder to bring an application under the anti-avoidance provisions, if the British proceedings commence after recognition then any existing Article 23 proceedings brought by a foreign representative must be reviewed by the court (Article 29(b)(iii)). If British proceedings have already been opened, the foreign representative must seek the consent of the court to bring proceedings under Article 23.

G. Foreign Creditors' Rights of Access to Proceedings Under British Insolvency Law

Although the Regulations are mainly concerned with the rights of access of foreign repre- **4.244**
sentatives to the courts, they also contain provisions which confer rights of access on foreign creditors. These rights to intervene or participate in insolvency proceedings in Great Britain are not dependent on the opening of foreign proceedings.

Foreign creditors have the same rights as local creditors to commence and participate in **4.245**
insolvency proceedings under British insolvency law (Article 13). This does not affect the ranking of claims under British insolvency law, except that a claim of a foreign creditor shall not be given a lower priority than that of general non-preferential claims solely because the holder of such claim is a foreign creditor (Article 13(2)). It may, however, be given a lower priority if an equivalent local claim would be so ranked, for example in respect of debts due to a person found liable for fraudulent trading under section 215(4) of the Insolvency Act 1986. Foreign revenue claims are now provable in Great Britain by virtue of Article 13(3) unless challenged as a penalty or rejected on other grounds.

Foreign creditors are also required to be notified of a proceeding under British insolvency **4.246**
law whenever notification is required to be given to creditors in an enacting state.

H. Cross-Border Cooperation

1. Cooperation with foreign courts and foreign representatives

The provisions in Articles 25–27 relating to cooperation between the courts of an enacting **4.247**
state and insolvency office holders may facilitate the cross-border disposal of a debtor's assets. Such cooperation is not conditional on recognition of, or application for recognition of, a foreign proceeding.[591] The possible forms of cooperation are listed in Article 27 and replicate those found in the Model Law template. They comprise:

---

[590] See *Hosking v TPG Capital Management, LP (In re Hellas Telecommunications (Luxembourg) II SCA)*, 524 BR 488 (Bankr SDNY 2015).
[591] In 2009 UNCITRAL adopted the Practice Guide on Cross-Border Insolvency which also aims to promote cross-border coordination and cooperation, particularly by the use of cross-border agreements, and is intended to complement the Model Law (see section J below (UNCITRAL Guidance)).

(a) appointment of a person to act at the direction of the court;

(b) communication of information by any means considered appropriate by the court;

(c) coordination of the administration and supervision of the debtor's assets and affairs;

(d) approval or implementation by courts of agreements concerning the coordination of proceedings;

(e) coordination of concurrent proceedings regarding the same debtor.

4.248 They were considered broad enough to allow the British courts to develop their own practices rather than allow themselves to be fettered by an exhaustive list of specific circumstances.[592]

4.249 Article 25 places cooperation on a discretionary basis by stating that British courts 'may' cooperate to the maximum extent possible with foreign courts or foreign representatives, either directly or through a British insolvency office holder. As such it departs from the original text which imposes on the courts of an enacting state an explicit duty to cooperate.[593] In the *Millhouse Capital* case Clarke J found that 'the intention of the Cross-Border Insolvency Regulations is to ensure that all proper assistance can be and is provided to a foreign office holder'.[594] He cited the text of Articles 25 and 27 in support of this analysis. In effect, these provisions can be viewed as reinforcing the position at common law, where the principles of cooperation and comity have long been recognized by the English courts, as is evidenced by the line of English cases which already emphasize the need to provide assistance.[595]

4.250 Article 26, on the other hand, places British insolvency office holders under an express obligation to cooperate. This is in keeping with the original text although additional wording has been added to make it clear that such cooperation is only to the extent consistent with their other duties, including duties towards British creditors, under the laws of Great Britain. The provision as amended will enable a British office holder to have regard to any perceived conflict of interest that might arise between his own position and that of a foreign representative without forcing him to seek directions from the court in order to safeguard his own legal position in the event of a subsequent challenge.

2. Extent of cooperation

4.251 The nature and extent of the duty to cooperate between a British court and foreign courts or foreign representatives has been considered in the landmark *Perpetual Trustee* case[596] which arose from the Lehman insolvencies and involves parallel proceedings in the English and US courts. The key issue to be decided was whether a clause in a trust deed, which altered the swap payment priorities in a structured finance transaction so that the claims of

---

[592] For a discussion of the interaction between the court's statutory jurisdiction to declare a foreign company insolvency under s 221 of the Insolvency Act 1986 and the cooperation inherent in arts 25–27: see PJ Omar, 'Cross-Border assistance in the common law and international insolvency texts: an update' (2009) 20(11) *International Company and Commercial Law Review* 379–386.

[593] The amendment was made in response to concerns raised in the course of the Insolvency Service consultation.

[594] *Millhouse Capital UK Ltd v Sibir Energy plc* [2008] EWHC 2614 at [52].

[595] See, e.g., *Banque Indosuez SA v Ferromet Resources Inc* [1993] BCLC 112 (per Hoffmann J at 117–118) and *Cambridge Gas Transportation Corp v Official Committee of Unsecured Creditors of Navigator Holdings plc* [2006] UKPC 26, [2007] 1 AC 508 at 158A.

[596] *Perpetual Trustee Company Limited v BNY Trustee Services Limited and Lehman Brothers Special Finance Inc* [2010] BCC 59, [2010] BPIR 228, CA.

noteholders would be payable in priority to the claims of the swap counterparty (Lehman Brothers Special Financing Inc or 'LBSF') in the event of a swap counterparty default, was valid. The documentation, other than that relating to the collateral, was governed by English law and the collateral was located in England. LBSF defaulted on the swap agreement when its parent, Lehman Brothers Holding Inc filed for chapter 11 protection. LBSF was itself then made subject to chapter 11 protection and the US bankruptcy court was asked to consider the validity of the clause as a matter of US bankruptcy law.

In the English proceedings, the Court of Appeal ruled that the clause was valid and enforceable under English law. It found that the operation of the clause did not violate the common law principle that a contractual provision is void if it provides for the transfer of an asset from the owner to a third party upon insolvency (known as the 'anti-deprivation principle'). However, the US bankruptcy court declined to recognize the judgment. Instead, it ruled that the provision constituted an unenforceable *ipso facto* clause that violated sections 365 and 542 of the US Bankruptcy Code and that any attempt to enforce the clause as a result of LBSF's bankruptcy would be contrary to the automatic stay under section 362(a) of the US Bankruptcy Code.   **4.252**

The case is instructive from the point of view of the duty to cooperate under Article 25. Mindful of this duty, the English court deliberately refrained from going beyond ruling on the validity of the clause. It chose not to make any further orders or declarations on the basis that it might be seen as precluding any request or other application to be made by a foreign representative of LBSF or the US court.[597] Both courts were conscious of the need for co-operation and, in accordance with Article 25, Judge Peck in the US proceedings invited the High Court to consider the US court's schedule of imminent hearings on the case and not to make any final disposition of the English proceedings until he was able to consider and rule on the US bankruptcy issues raised in the summary judgment briefing. He also stated that he intended to communicate further with the English court in an attempt to reach a coordinated result in light of each court's eventual ruling. Nonetheless, as Jo Braithwaite has noted, the efforts at cooperation did 'little to head off the eventual clash between the judgments'.[598]   **4.253**

Ward LJ noted obiter dicta in the Court of Appeal in *Rubin v Eurofinance* that it was troubling that the specific forms of cooperation provided under the Regulations did not include enforcement but considered that the Article 25 requirement for 'co-operation to the maximum extent possible' should include enforcement, especially since enforcement was available under the common law.[599] However, this was not endorsed by the Supreme Court which, as we have seen, took a more absolutist position, leading some commentators to wonder on the state of modified universalism in English law.[600]   **4.254**

---

[597] Recognition of the US proceedings as foreign main proceedings was subsequently granted.

[598] Jo Braithwaite, *The Financial Courts: Adjudicating Disputes in Derivatives Markets* (Cambridge University Press 2020), 307.

[599] But note that this interpretation does not lie comfortably with the fact that art 25 of the Regulations departs from the UNCITRAL template in that it gives the British courts a discretion (rather than imposing an obligation) to assist.

[600] See, e.g., B Isaacs, 'What's Left of the Golden Thread? Modified Universalism after Rubin and the New Cap' (2012) *Butterworths Journal of International Banking Financial Law* 675; Gerard McCormack, 'Universalism in Insolvency Proceedings and the Common Law' (2012) *Oxford Journal of Legal Studies* 325; F Toube, 'Isolationism Revived: Foreign Restructurings Still Do Not Discharge Debts under English Contracts' (2011) *Insolvency Intelligence* 77. For a different perspective see Walters (n 575)

4.255   Finally, Article 27 (in particular, Article 27(d)) is complemented by the UNCITRAL Practice Guide on Cross-Border Insolvency Cooperation which aims to further cooperation between courts and between insolvency office holders by the implementation of agreements concerning the coordination of proceedings.[601]

I. Commencement of Concurrent Proceedings and Coordination of Relief

4.256   Article 28 deals with the opening of British insolvency proceedings following recognition of a foreign main proceeding. It differs in one important aspect from the original text in that, by omitting the words 'may be commenced only if the debtor has assets in this State', jurisdiction to open proceedings can be exercised whether or not the debtor has assets in Great Britain. This amendment has preserved the position under British law for overseas cases, namely that a foreign company may be wound up as an unregistered company under section 221 of the Insolvency Act 1986 provided there is sufficient connection with Great Britain.[602] As in the original text, the effects of a local proceeding would, as far as the assets of the debtor are concerned, be limited to assets in Great Britain and, to the extent necessary to implement cooperation and coordination under Articles 25–28 inclusive to other assets of the debtor that, under the law of Great Britain, should be administered in that proceeding.

4.257   Restructuring plans may be assisted by provisions dealing with coordination of relief between local and foreign proceedings concerning the same debtor and between two or more foreign proceedings concerning the same debtor (Articles 29 and 30). The expectation here is that coordinated decisions will achieve a greater return when realizing the debtor's assets and a more advantageous restructuring of the debtor's undertaking. As discussed above, the British courts are expected (but not required) to cooperate with foreign courts and foreign representatives under Articles 25 and 30.

4.258   Where proceedings under the Insolvency Act 1986 are already underway at the time that recognition of a foreign proceeding is requested, any relief granted under Articles 19 and 21 for the benefit of the foreign proceeding must be consistent with the British proceeding. If the foreign proceeding is recognized as a foreign main proceeding the operation of Article 20 is disapplied (Article 29(a)).

4.259   When British proceedings are opened after the filing of an application for recognition of a foreign proceeding, the relief that has been granted for the benefit of the foreign proceeding must be reviewed and modified or terminated if inconsistent with the British proceeding. If the foreign proceeding is a main proceeding, the stay and suspension provisions of Article 20 must also be modified or terminated if inconsistent (Article 29(b)).

---

[601] See section J which discusses the UNCITRAL Practice Guide on Cross-border Insolvency Cooperation.

[602] For a discussion as to whether relief is better provided under s 221 of the Insolvency Act 1986 or by requiring the petitioner to request relief under the Regulations, see *Millhouse Capital UK Ltd v Sibir Energy plc* [2008] EWHC 2614.

In circumstances where the court is faced with more than one foreign proceeding, Article **4.260** 30 calls for tailoring relief in such a way that will facilitate coordination of the foreign proceedings; if one of the foreign proceedings is a main proceeding, any relief must be consistent with that main proceeding. If it is not consistent, it must be terminated.

The Regulations prescribe rules of payment in concurrent proceedings to ensure equality **4.261** of treatment among creditors (thereby codifying the hotchpot principle).[603] Thus if a creditor receives 10 pence in the pound in a foreign proceeding but the dividend in the local proceeding is 25 pence, he will receive only 15 pence in the local proceeding. Secured creditors and those with rights *in rem* will not be required to equalize if they receive priority payments.

J. UNCITRAL Guidance

Finally, this chapter would not be complete without reference to the Practice Guide on **4.262** Cross-Border Insolvency Cooperation, adopted on 1 July 2009, and the Legislative Guide on Insolvency Law.

The purpose of the Practice Guide on Cross-border Insolvency Cooperation is to provide **4.263** readily accessible information on current practice in insolvency proceedings with respect to cross-border coordination and cooperation for reference and use by practitioners and judges, as well as creditors and other stakeholders. Further information on cross-border insolvency agreements will be added as it becomes available.

The Guide places emphasis on the use and negotiation of cross-border insolvency agree- **4.264** ments. It provides an analysis of a number of agreements entered into since the late 1990s, which UNCITRAL intends to update as new cases emerge, and includes sample clauses based on provisions found in existing agreements. It is closely related and complementary to the promotion and use of the Model Law and, in particular, Article 27(d) which provides that the cooperation between courts and between insolvency office holders referred to in Articles 25 and 26 may be implemented by the courts' approval or by implementation of agreements concerning the coordination of proceedings. A summary of the cases where such agreements have been put to good effect, including *Federal Mogul, Daisytek,* and *Nortel Networks,* is also included.

The Legislative Guide on Insolvency Law seeks to provide a 'comprehensive statement of the **4.265** key objectives and principles that should be reflected in a State's insolvency laws'.[604] It is now divided into four parts. Part 1 discusses the key objectives of insolvency law; certain structural issues; types of mechanism available for resolving a debtor's financial difficulties; and questions relating to the institutional framework in which an insolvency regime operates. Part 2 deals with the features of 'an effective insolvency law'. Part 3 deals with the treatment

---

[603] Under the hotchpot principle, without prejudice to secured claims or rights *in rem*, any creditor who has received part payment in respect of claims abroad may not receive payment for the same claim in British insolvency proceedings in respect of the same debtor 'so long as the payment to the other creditors of the same class is proportionately less than the payment the creditor has already received'.

[604] Available at: <https://uncitral.un.org/en/texts/insolvency/legislativeguides/insolvency_law> (last accessed 16 June 2021).

of enterprise groups in insolvency. And Part 4 deals with the liabilities and responsibilities of officers and directors in insolvency. UNCITRAL has also published two further model laws: the Model Law on Recognition and Enforcement of Insolvency-Related Judgments and the UNCITRAL Model Law on Enterprise Group Insolvency. At the time of writing, neither of these model laws has been implemented in the UK.

PART II
BANK RESOLUTION

LEGAL ASPECTS OF BANKING REGULATION IN THE UK AND US

I. Introduction

The banking industry is one of the most regulated and supervised sectors in any economy in light of the real likelihood of collapse if their associated risks are not managed efficiently or regulated. The banking industry performs a number of services: it manages the distribution of savings and loans, which is essential for an economy to operate effectively, and banks are also a central vehicle for the exercise of a state's monetary policy due to their role in an economy's payment system. The susceptibility of banks to collapse or failure is all too clear as a result of the 'maturity mismatch' between their borrowing and lending: the former is usually short term and the latter is normally on a long-term basis. Banks function on a small asset reserve and hold a large proportion of illiquid assets in the form of loans, which makes them susceptible to failure. Their weakness is heightened by the fact that the inter-bank market is made up of a network of large unsecured creditor and debtor relationships, where the failure of one bank could lead to the collapse of others if confidence in this market was undermined in some way—like a bank not being able to meet its obligations on time. **5.01**

In an extreme scenario, the fallout from any failure may have wider systemic consequences, with a significant risk of contagion in the financial system where the collapse of a bank could spread to others in the sector. A systemic failure such as this can have wider repercussions on the performance of an economy. The economic costs of such failures can be considerable, and require huge amounts of public funds to stabilize the financial system. **5.02**

This requires specific focus on putting in place adequate legal preconditions and regulatory infrastructure to ensure the objectives of financial stability are achieved.

5.03   In light of the vulnerability of the banking system, a system of regulation and supervision is necessary. In general terms, bank regulation refers to the rules banks are required to comply with and supervision refers to the monitoring process undertaken by a regulator when an institution seeks entry into the banking industry; supervision also controls the exit of banks from the industry, so that this is as orderly as possible and does not disrupt the banking system. In order to ensure banking is undertaken with a degree of prudence, bank supervisors use a number of tools to regulate banks: capital adequacy, liquidity ratios, large exposure rules, consolidated supervision, and deposit insurance. These tools need to extend over the domestic and international operations of its business. As a result of this interdependency and interconnectedness, efforts have been made to improve the way countries regulate and supervise the operations of banks.

5.04   This chapter sets out the principal features of the regulation and supervision of UK and US bank regulation. The first part outlines the UK Financial Conduct Authority (FCA) and the Bank of England Prudential Regulation Authority (PRA)[1] supervisory regime. It will primarily focus on the PRA as the principal bank regulator and supervisor. The second part outlines the US federal bank regulatory system and the impact of the Dodd-Frank Wall Street Reform and Consumer Act 2010 ('the Dodd-Frank Act 2010') on the bank regulatory system as well as its impact on areas of the regulatory and supervisory regime. The chapter will focus on how supervision has undergone significant reform to improve the safety and soundness of banking and brings 'resolution' in to the forefront of supervision rather than at the tail-end.

II. The UK Model of Regulation and Supervision

5.05   The coalition government of 2010 initiated a major overhaul of the UK structure of financial regulation. The result of the reforms led to the abolition of the Financial Services Authority (FSA) as we know it to form the FCA, and the transfer of part of its responsibilities to the newly created Prudential Regulation Authority (PRA).[2] The reforms primarily transform the UK single microprudential regulatory regime into a so-called twin peaks model, but not simply on the basis of separating prudential and consumer regulation and supervision, as will be explained. The reforms mean that part of the financial services industry, the large systemically important institutions, are dual regulated and supervised by both the FCA and PRA, with the FCA designated as the conduct-of-business regulator and the PRA designated as the primary prudential regulator. The responsibility of overseeing the corporate governance of such institutions is divided between the FCA and PRA. The remainder of

---

[1]   As will be explained, the Bank of England and Financial Services Act 2016 amends the Financial Services and Markets Act 2000 s 2A(1)–2A(2) so that the PRA is the Bank of England and the Bank of England functions as the PRA. (Hereinafter reference will be made to the PRA in line with FSMA s 2A(7)).

[2]   Speech by the Chancellor of the Exchequer, Rt Hon George Osborne MP, at Mansion House, 16 June 2010, available at <https://www.gov.uk/government/speeches/speech-by-the-chancellor-of-the-exchequer-rt-hon-geo rge-osborne-mp-at-mansion-house>. Speech by Mervyn King, Governor of the Bank of England, at Mansion House, 16 June 2010, available at <http://www.bankofengland.co.uk/archive/Documents/historicpubs/speeches/2010/speech437.pdf>.

the financial services industry and the financial markets and exchanges are regulated and supervised by the FCA, inter alia, for the purposes of both conduct of business and prudential requirements. In addition to the role of the FCA and PRA on the microprudential level of oversight, the Financial Policy Committee (FPC) has a separate macroprudential responsibility to ensure the wider economy and financial system are overseen to ensure potential red flags at the higher level are acted upon at both the level of the Treasury and the regulator. These themes of microprudential and macroprudential oversight are difficult to divide with neat demarcation lines so it is inevitable the separate regulatory authorities will need to work extremely closely together to ensure matters of mutual importance do not fall between the gaps of the different regulators and are communicated to one another to improve their understanding of the financial institutions they oversee. In order to ensure efficient coordination and cooperation, a significant number of Memoranda of Understanding (MoU) have been entered into. The UK has implemented a myriad of other reforms and changes to the way financial services regulation and supervision is undertaken in addition to the regulatory architectural overhaul. The amended Financial Services and Markets Act (FSMA 2000) provides a legislative framework that also sets out the responsibilities of the FCA and Bank of England for the purposes of supervising Central Counterparties. The role and responsibilities of the regulators will be set out accordingly.

Reforms to prudential and conduct risk are analysed to provide context to the broad bank **5.06** and non-bank resolution reforms and insolvency measures that follow in subsequent chapters. The prudential and conduct threshold conditions have been expanded to cover areas that were rather implicitly addressed by regulators but have now been elevated to a threshold condition, so highlighting their importance most notably as they form the basis for determining whether a financial firm is likely to be placed in resolution or insolvency. The Bank Recovery and Resolution and Miscellaneous Provisions (Amendment) (EU Exit) Regulations 2018 has been introduced to ensure that the regime established by the Bank Recovery and Resolution Directive is recognized on a standalone basis to clarify how the EEA states are recognized and will be treated as Third Countries and how the responsibilities associated with resolution in the UK will be discharged after Brexit, in particular the recognition by the resolution authority of EEA proceedings as Third Countries.

The FCA and the PRA are designated competent authorities and the Bank of England is **5.07** designated the resolution authority in the UK official safety net arrangements.[3] The PRA will act as the competent authority, for the purposes of the new resolution reforms, for the banks and investment firms it solely regulates, as well as those firms that are dual regulated by both the PRA and FCA; for those, the PRA is designated the lead regulator for the purposes of prudential regulation and supervision. The FCA will be the designated competent authority for those firms for which it has sole responsibility for regulation and supervision. The Financial Services Act 2021 sets out a new prudential regime for investment firms (UK IFPR). It will not cover systemically important investment firms, which will continue to be regulated by the PRA. The IFPR's rules will predominantly by made and set out by the FCA. This provides a distinct set of newly designed prudential requirements to ensure the 'safety and soundness' of solo investment firms. A significant change of both regulators is

---

[3] The Bank of England's Approach to Resolution, October 2017 <https://www.bankofengland.co.uk/paper/2017/the-bank-of-england-approach-to-resolution>.

to move towards a more forward looking judgment-based approach which is translated by both regulators in accordance with their requisite objectives and principles of regulation and supervision.

5.08   The FCA[4] is conferred a range of responsibilities to exercise regulation and supervision in the UK financial system. Its primary role is to act as the conduct-of-business regulator and supervisor but it also plays the role of prudential regulator for those firms for which it is sole regulator and supervisor. The FCA is required to discharge its responsibilities in line with its objectives, divided into strategic and operational objectives.[5] The strategic objective is to ensure financial markets function well, which covers regulated institutions, individuals, and markets.[6] The operational objectives are consumer protection,[7] protecting and enhancing the integrity of the UK financial system,[8] and promoting competition in the financial markets from both a consumer and corporate perspective.[9] The second objective implicitly provides the FCA with a mandate to ensure the financial stability of financial markets and their orderly operation. The operational objectives of the FCA are not set in stone, like its predecessor the FSA, and the Treasury has the power to change its operational objectives.[10] The FCA is required to have in place arrangements for supervision and enforcement that essentially enable it to achieve its objectives.[11] More recently, the FCA has set out its approach to supervision by placing firms into four categories and designating how those respective firms will be supervised. Those in category C1 are deemed the largest financial services groups and providers from a retail consumer or wholesale markets point of view in the UK, and require the most intensive form of supervision of their business from the viewpoint of their conduct of business.

5.09   The FCA is required to assess whether the firms it is responsible for, for the purposes of the FSMA 2000 as the appropriate regulator, comply with their Principles of Businesses which are viewed as the 'fit and proper' criteria for firms. The principles not only apply to firms' UK operations but can also apply to their overseas activities as well in a number of areas, such as cooperating with regulators. In line with its Principles for Businesses, the FCA prescribes 10 supervision principles that explain how it will approach supervision of individual firms, which includes, inter alia, 'Ensuring fair outcomes for consumers and markets'; 'Being forward-looking and pre-emptive'; 'Being focused on the big issues and causes of problems'; 'Taking a judgement-based approach'; 'Ensuring firms act in the right spirit'; 'Examining business models and culture'; 'An emphasis on individual accountability'; 'Being robust when things go wrong'; 'Communicating openly'; and 'Having a joined-up approach'. The principles clearly indicate the new direction that the FCA is seeking to take, which is to decide whether firms have the appropriate corporate culture and strategic direction rather than solely focusing on technical operational and control failures, as in the past.

---

[4] FSMA 2000, s 1A, as amended by the Financial Services Act 2012. The Financial Services Act 2021 provides additional powers to the FCA. It allows them to cancel or vary a firm's authorization and issue a notice to firms who appear to no longer be carrying on regulated activities. The FCA may cancel the permission of unresponsive firms. FCA may also restore a firm's authorization or vary permissions when it considers it just and reasonable to.

[5] Ibid, s 1B.

[6] Ibid, ss 1B(2), 1F.

[7] Ibid, s 1C.

[8] Ibid, s 1D.

[9] Ibid, s 1E.

[10] Ibid, s 1J.

[11] Ibid, s 1L.

The Financial Services Act 2021 requires the FCA to consider international standards and the UK's standing as a financial centre for investment firms and the effect of any proposed rules on financial services. The PRA must consider similar matters, as well as the likely effect that the rules will have on firms' ability to sustainably provide finance to UK businesses and consumers.

The move to a judgement-based approach is also the approach taken by the PRA, as we will see later. The judgement-based approach will be interpreted in light of their respective responsibilities and will require the FCA and the PRA to exercise their functions in a coordinated manner.[12] The PRA and the FCA have entered into a variety of MoUs to explain how they will attempt to coordinate their responsibilities and formulate joint decisions.[13]   **5.10**

The PRA is a regulator and supervisor for banks, insurance companies, and systemically important investment firms. The PRA is required to exercise its responsibilities in accordance with its general objective to promote the safety and soundness of the firms it regulates.[14] The PRA is required to be mindful of the impact of the firms it regulates on the stability of the UK financial system. In order to discharge this responsibility, it needs to consider the potential impact of the firm on the continuity of the financial services it is permitted to undertake. The implication of this is that the PRA is particularly concerned about the continuity of financial services rather than the institutions that offer them.[15] The aim being to ensure that failure of the firm is as orderly as possible and so avoids a position that implies a zero failure regime.[16] The general objective is complemented by additional objectives for the insurance industry.[17] As with the FCA, the PRA also has the potential to widen its objectives, which it has done recently with the introduction of another secondary objective: to promote competition.[18]   **5.11**

The Bank of England is the resolution authority in the UK so therefore it is responsible for resolution planning and resolvability assessments and acts as the Treasury's agent where public funds are used in the execution of its stabilization powers. The Bank also serves as a critical part of the crisis management arrangements in the UK.[19] The Bank will have primary responsibility but HM Treasury has responsibility when decisions require public funds to assist in mitigating and/or resolving a crisis. The Bank has inter alia a number of designated responsibilities for the purposes of crisis management: **5.12**

(i) As the PRA, responsibility for the safety and soundness of individual firms it authorizes, which includes powers of early intervention when risks to viability materialize.

(ii) Oversight responsibilities for payment systems, settlement systems, and clearing houses.

---

[12] Ibid, s 3D.
[13] Ibid, s 3E.
[14] Ibid, s 2B.
[15] Ibid.
[16] Ibid, s 2G.
[17] Ibid, s 2C.
[18] s 2D Bank of England Act 1998.
[19] Memorandum of Understanding on resolution planning and financial crisis management October 2017 <https://www.bankofengland.co.uk/-/media/boe/files/memoranda-of-understanding/resolution-planning-and-financial-crisis-management.pdf?la=en&hash=57D8302D2AE09F004E67BEF19A554547CAD2D47B>.

(iii) Responsibility for Liquidity support via the Resolution Liquidity Framework and Emergency Liquidity Assistance outside its published frameworks. The Chancellor and Treasury would need to approve such decisions since they equate to the use of public funds.

(iv) Obligation to notify the Treasury when public funds are at material risk in a crisis and the options to reduce such risks.

5.13   The Bank of England and Financial Services Act 2016 amends the Bank of England Act 1998 to improve the accountability and governance of the Bank of England by making its Court of Directors a smaller, more focused unitary board with albeit a new Deputy Governor for markets and banking. As mentioned earlier, it brings the PRA within the Bank of England and establishes the Prudential Regulation Committee (PRC). Section 12(2A) states that the PRA is now the Bank of England, and the Bank's functions as the PRA are to be exercised through the PRC. It also brings changes to the Financial Policy Committee, making it a statutory committee of the bank. As a result of these changes the Oversight Committee is abolished and responsibilities for designated areas reside with the Financial Policy Committee, Monetary Policy Committee, and the PRC. The Treasury is set to make published recommendations at least once every Parliament regarding the government's economic policy matters that the PRC should address.[20] Issues related to the appointment of PRC members by the Chancellor,[21] the procedure to be followed in Committee meetings,[22] taking decisions in writing and dealing with potential conflicts of interest,[23] as well as delegating functions[24] and allocating a prudential regulation budget.[25]

5.14   In its role as the PRA, the Bank of England will be required to comply with Basel Core Principles on Supervision and specified EU directives. These call for the institution's supervision functions to be operationally independent from its resolution functions should it be responsible for both supervising and resolving financial institutions when they fail.[26] The Treasury may instruct the Bank not to take a proposed course of action or to take a different action that ensures compliance in case the former would not conform to the UK's obligations under the directives.[27] Financial Services Act 2021 acts as the UK's implementation of the final Basel III standards that were introduced into the EU Capital Requirements Regulation, but did not apply across the EU until after the UK transition period.

5.15   In the following discussion about the roles of the FCA and PRA, reference will be made to them both as the appropriate regulators to denote that the specific provisions apply to both of them in accordance with their specific responsibility in regulating financial services. The distinct approaches to exercising their roles will be highlighted.

---

[20]   s 30B Bank of England Act 1998.
[21]   Sch 6A Bank of England Act 1998.
[22]   Sch 6A Bank of England Act 1998.
[23]   Sch 6A Bank of England Act 1998.
[24]   Sch 6A Bank of England Act 1998.
[25]   Sch 6A Bank of England Act 1998.
[26]   s 30C Bank of England Act 1998.
[27]   s 30C Bank of England Act 1998.

A. The Scope of the Responsibilities of the FCA and PRA

1. Authorization and permission

The first facet of regulation is authorization to undertake a particular type of business. **5.16** Authorization serves two main purposes: it attempts to protect the marketplace from incompetent players, and encourages depositors and investors to do business confidently within a secure environment. A formal system of authorization acts as an effective way of limiting entry to and exit from a marketplace so that it can function in an orderly manner. The FCA and the PRA have the power to grant authorization to individual firms and individuals falling into their area of regulatory responsibility. This ensures that regulated activities are appropriately undertaken in accordance with the relevant prudential standards and conduct-of-business rules with which authorized firms are required to comply. The Financial Services Act 2021 contains new powers for the FCA, allowing the regulator to expedite cases where it appears that an authorized firm is no longer carrying on regulated activities, and cancel or vary their authorization as appropriate. This amends the FSMA 2000 by inserting section 55JA. Section 29 of the Financial Services Act 2021 also requires the FCA to carry out a consultation about whether it should make general rules providing that authorized persons owe a duty of care to consumers.

The FSMA 2000, section 19 prohibits any person from carrying on or purporting to carry **5.17** on a regulated activity unless they are authorized or exempt. The regulated activities highlighted in section 22(1) of the FSMA 2000 are set out and defined in secondary legislation: the Financial Services and Markets Act 2000 (Regulated Activities) Order 2001 (RAO) and the Financial Services and Markets Act 2000 (Carrying on Regulated Activities by Way of Business) Order 2001 ('the Business Order'). The original order has been amended on numerous occasions as the financial services business evolves and as new lines of financial services are classed as regulated activities governed by the FSMA 2000. Most notable is the Financial Services and Markets Act 2000 (PRA-regulated Activities) Order 2013, which sets out which financial services are specifically the responsibility of the PRA for the purposes of prudential supervision, such as accepting deposits, insurance business, and dealing in investments. In the case of accepting deposits, Article 5 of the RAO states that 'any money received by way of deposit is lent to others or the person accepting the deposit is financed wholly', or 'to a material extent, out of the capital of or interest on money received by way of deposit'. A deposit is defined as a sum of money 'which will be repaid with or without interest or premium, and either on demand or at a time or in circumstances agreed by or on behalf of the person'.[28] The accepting of deposits is further clarified by article 2(1) of the Business Order. This requires the person to hold themselves out as accepting deposits on a day-to-day basis or if they are only accepted on particular occasions, how frequent those occasions are.[29]

The FCA and PRA regime not only governs who can undertake regulated activities at an **5.18** institutional level but also those who are responsible for discharging a firm's responsibilities on its behalf.[30] An individual performing a controlled function is required to be a fit and

---

[28] RAO Art 5(2).
[29] For an analysis of this see *FSA v Anderson* [2010] EWHC 599 (Ch).
[30] AUTH 6 and exceptions, see AUTH 6.5.1G. See also TC 1 training and competency rules apply to employees responsible for regulated activities. SUP 10: Approved Persons.

proper person.[31] In recent years, as part of the reforms to deal with the gaps in the approach to regulation, supervision, and enforcement, how individuals are held responsible for their actions has come under close scrutiny due to the limited number of individuals held accountable for their part in the failure and government rescue of banks during the global financial crisis.

5.19 The appropriate regulator sets out a number of factors that need to be considered to decide whether an individual is fit and proper to undertake a role designed as a controlled function such as 'honesty', 'integrity', 'reputation', 'competence', 'knowledge', 'capability', and 'financial soundness'.[32] The reforms introduced post the Parliamentary Commission on Banking Standards by the Financial Services (Banking Reform) Act 2013 place specific attention on competency and knowledge, and on the way directors and senior management discharge their responsibilities. The Senior Management and Certification Regime (SMCR) has made significant reforms to improve individual accountability. Whether or not an individual requires approval by the appropriate regulator depends on the role they perform; that is, whether they perform a 'controlled function'.[33] The functions designated as controlled are those that 'add value' to the regulatory process and assist the appropriate regulator to fulfil its respective regulatory objectives and principles.[34] In this respect both the PRA and the FCA have responsibility for designated controlled functions to achieve either prudential and conduct-of-business objectives. Controlled functions are divided into PRA- and FCA-designated controlled functions and so individuals are required to apply to the regulator responsible for approval for such roles.[35] Therefore no person can exercise a controlled function unless the individual is approved by the appropriate regulator under sections 59 and 59ZA of the FSMA 2000.[36] Amendments to section 59 have been made under the Bank of England and Financial Services Act 2016. However, the general purpose of section 59 remains unchanged. In accordance with the FSMA 2000 those approved have to meet the appropriate regulators' 'fit and proper' criteria before they can take up their positions.[37] The appropriate regulator sets out a number of factors that need to be considered, such as 'honesty', 'integrity', 'reputation', 'competence', 'capability', and 'financial soundness'.[38] The emphasis on 'knowledge' and 'competence' has been specifically heightened in importance, and these factors appear on a statutory footing in the Financial Services (Banking Reform) Act 2013. In general terms, to be 'fit and proper' a person must be suitable to 'hold a licence' and undertake the business of the licence holder.[39] This requires an assessment of

---

[31] FIT 1.1.2G.

[32] FIT 1.3.1G.

[33] SUP 10.4.5R: Controlled Functions.

[34] APER 4.4.1G–4.4.9E.

[35] PRA, *PRA-designated Controlled Functions* (December 2014) <http://www.bankofengland.co.uk/pra/Documents/authorisations/approvedpersons/pracfs.pdf> FCA, 'Controlled Functions' (FCA, 27 August 2014) <http://www.fca.org.uk/firms/being-regulated/approved/approved-persons/functions>.

[36] SUP 10.2.1G.

[37] *The Fit and Proper Test for Approved Persons*, chs 1 and 2. For an analysis of the fit and proper criteria see: *Arch Financial Products LP (1) Robin Farrell (2) Robert Stephan Addison (3) v The Financial Conduct Authority* [2015] UKUT 0013 (TCC) (see <http://www.tribunals.gov.uk/financeandtax/Documents/decisions/Arch-v-FCA.pdf>); *Ghanshyam Batra v Financial Conduct Authority* [2014] UKUT 0214 (TCC) (see <http://www.tribunals.gov.uk/financeandtax/Documents/decisions/Batra-v-FCA.pdf>).

[38] FIT 1.3.1G.

[39] *R v Hyde JJ* (1912) *The Times Law Reports*, vol 106, 152, 158.

the individual's character and the nature and complexity of the business undertaken by the regulated firm. In this respect it is the responsibility of individuals to satisfy the 'appropriate regulator' that they are 'fit and proper' to undertake a controlled function rather than for the 'appropriate regulator' to show that they are not. The 'appropriate regulator' has the authority to withdraw approval of a person if it considers that person not to be fit and proper for the controlled function for which approval has been sought.[40] It is the responsibility of the regulated firm to exercise reasonable care when appointing individuals to undertake a controlled function to ensure they are appropriate for the position. The 'appropriate regulator' introduced an interview process for particular controlled functions, as part of its significant function review, to assess the person's competency to undertake the function that person is seeking approval for.[41]

The Senior Management Regime designates 'senior management functions' and other functions as 'prescribed responsibilities'. In respect of SMCR firms an individual will be designated a 'prescribed responsibility' for the recovery and resolution pack within the broader governance regime, which highlights the importance of effective resolution within the broader supervisory mandate. The individual firms will be required to designate as clearly as possible individual lines of responsibility to improve the ability of regulators to hold individuals accountable for their decisions rather than such decisions being hidden behind collective decision-making processes. Those at the board level of banks are specifically exposed to criminal prosecution if their individual decision causes a bank to fail.[42]   **5.20**

2. The threshold conditions

The FSMA 2000 provides minimum criteria for granting permission to carry out regulated activities under Part 4A. These are referred to as 'threshold conditions'.[43] The previous threshold conditions were considered narrow and did not capture appropriately other factors that a regulated firm would legitimately be expected to comply with on a continuous basis. Moreover, with the separation of responsibilities between the PRA and FCA it was considered necessary to allow the appropriate regulator to formulate their own threshold conditions to meet the requirements for their regulatory and supervisory purposes. With this in mind, the number of threshold conditions that apply to both FCA and PRA firms have been widened. These now relate to: location of offices, effective supervision, appropriate resources, suitability, business models, and business to be conducted prudently. In addition to those threshold conditions, another threshold condition added is for PRA-regulated firms to be effectively resolvable. The FCA and PRA are required to ensure that those seeking permission can satisfy these conditions. The concept of 'threshold' indicates that these requirements need to be met at the point of entry, although the actual requirement is to comply with them continuously.   **5.21**

The first threshold condition[44] is the requirement that the legal status of the entity seeking to authorize a person to accept deposits must be either a body corporate or a partnership.   **5.22**

---

[40] FIT 1.2.3G.

[41] FSA, *Approving and supervising significant influence functions—our more intrusive regulatory approach* (12 October 2009) <http://www.fsa.gov.uk/pubs/ceo/ceo_letter1009.pdf>.

[42] Financial Services (Banking Reform) Act 2013, s 36.

[43] FSMA 2000, Sch 6: these are explained in the The Financial Services and Markets Act 2000 (Regulated Activities) (Amendment) Order 2014.

[44] FSMA 2000 Sch 6.

The second condition[45] is the requirement that the head office and registered office both be located in the UK. This enables the appropriate regulator to focus its attention on the head office, where central management and control of the day-to-day activities of the authorized person are located. The requirement is designed to avoid another BCCI scenario[46] and complies with the 'Post-BCCI Directive' to adopt this policy within the EU. It was found that BCCI avoided effective supervision because its centre for management was in London and its place of incorporation was Luxembourg, which prevented effective supervision of its operations.[47] The third threshold condition[48] requires firms to carry on regulated activities to conduct their business in a prudent manner and require them to have appropriate financial and non-financial resources in place to be able to identify risks and manage their assets and liabilities appropriately. The fourth threshold condition is the suitability of the firm or the group, if it is part of a group, in terms of being fit and proper to be granted permission by the appropriate regulator to carry on regulated activities. The fifth threshold[49] requires firms to structure their business in a way that enables them to be effectively supervised. It incorporates another requirement of the 'Post-BCCI Directive': authorized persons must disclose close links with other persons so that the appropriate regulator can identify the location of possible risks to the authorized person. The appropriate regulator has the right to seek information about any close link it wishes to know about, even in cases where the close link is an exempted entity. The appropriate regulator can individually discuss its requirements of notification about close links, especially in the case of non-EEA-incorporated credit institutions and EEA-incorporated credit institutions following Brexit. The Bank of England has required all UK branches of EEA banks to apply for authorization as branches of international banks, as they are now treated the same way as other international banks. The close links materiality will be assessed, as will changes in links within the banking group. Extensive guidance is provided to supplement these conditions.[50]

5.23 The threshold conditions are broad and contain a large degree of discretion in their scope; they are complemented by a whole host of objectives, principles, and prudential rules and guides that flesh out and complement their application. For example, they are further complemented and elaborated in the FCA *Principles for Businesses*,[51] and the PRA high level 8 *Fundamental Rules*.[52] In respect of the PRA's *Fundamental Rules*, which are the equivalent to the FCA's *Principles for Businesses*, Fundamental Rule 8 requires firms to put in

---

[45] Ibid, FSMA 2000 Sch 6.

[46] The Bank of Credit and Commerce International (BCCI) was set up in the City of London in 1972. At the same time, it was incorporated in Luxembourg. It grew rapidly, opening 22 branches in the UK and totalling over 400 worldwide. Whilst there were reports about BCCI being badly run, the Bank of England was persuaded that regulatory responsibility lay in Luxembourg. When BCCI collapsed (owing more than £10 bn), the liquidators sued the Bank of England for misfeasance in public office. The claim was eventually dropped, with the BCCI creditors bearing the ultimate losses. See S Bowers, 'BCCI scandal: long legal wrangling over collapsed bank' (*The Guardian*, 17 May 2012) <http://www.theguardian.com/business/2012/may/17/bcci-scandal-long-legal-wranglings>.

[47] Bank of England, *United Kingdom Administrative Arrangements for the Implementation of the Close Links Provision of the Post-BCCI Directive*, No S&S/1996/9.

[48] FSMA 2000, s 5D.

[49] COND. 2.3. FSMA 2000, S 5F

[50] BIPRU 8.

[51] FCA, *Principles for businesses*.

[52] PRA, *The PRA Rulebook*, Policy Statement PS5/14 (June 2014) <http://www.bankofengland.co.uk/pra/Documents/publications/ps/2014/ps514.pdf>.

place plans for orderly resolution to minimize disruption to critical services.[53] As regards conduct rules for authorized persons, these are contained in the Senior Management Arrangements, Systems and Controls,[54] *Statements of Principles and Code of Practice for Approved Persons,*[55] and the General and Specialist *sourcebook for banks, building societies and investment firms.*[56] More recently, the introduction of the Capital Requirements Directive (CRD IV) and Capital Requirements Regulation (CRR) has led to the adoption of the CRR Rulebook.[57]The CRR has been onshored in the UK as part of the measures under the European Union (Withdrawal) Act 2018.

The PRA adopts a distinct departure from the approach adopted in the past; the current **5.24** handbook model combines rules and guidance into one Rulebook, which lacks the assistance to interpretation of regulatory expectations that used to be present before. This is possibly a move away from guidance curtailing the interpretation of the rule within specific parameters, and so curtailing the possible authority of the regulator. The PRA emphasizes that it interprets its powers and responsibilities with a purposive approach.[58] It is perhaps arguable the new Rulebook, once it is fully operational will confer a significant level of discretion on the PRA to allow it to exercise its statutory responsibilities to achieve the broad aims it intends to achieve in a given situation. In many respects this approach will allow the PRA to exercise its forward-looking judgement-based approach, where enforcement of essentially prudential requirements associated with the threshold conditions are enforced implicitly and explicitly, rather than the more transparent approach taken when conduct-of-business failures are found and acted upon by the FCA.[59] This is also a signal that the PRA is devising its own approach to regulation and supervision distinct from the FCA's approach of principles and guidance.[60] In this respect, the move by the Co-operative Bank to recapitalize to meet new capital adequacy requirements could be viewed as an enforcement decision so banks will be acutely aware of the enforcement role of the PRA but not in the explicit and transparent manner evident in the formal sense when banks are found to have mis-sold financial products, for instance. A formal decision to place a bank in administration or evidence of wrongdoing is an example where formal enforcement announcement is likely to be made.[61] In its short existence it has publicized some enforcement decisions most notably those linked to the problems experienced at the Co-operative Bank and its

[53] PRA, *The Prudential Regulation Authority's approach to banking supervision*, June 2014 <http://www.bankof england.co.uk/publications/Documents/praapproach/bankingappr1406.pdf>; See also PRA, *The Prudential Regulation Authority's approach to insurance supervision*, June 2014 <http://www.bankofengland.co.uk/publicati ons/Documents/praapproach/insuranceappr1406.pdf>.

[54] Senior Management Arrangements, Systems and Controls (SYSC): <https://www.handbook.fca.org.uk/ handbook/SYSC.pdf>.

[55] FCA, *Statements of Principles and Code of Practice for Approved Persons* <https://www.handbook.fca.org.uk/ handbook/APER.pdf>.

[56] GENPRU and BIPRU.

[57] PRA, *Prudential Regulation Authority Handbook—Rulebook CRR Firms* <http://fshandbook.info/FS/html/ PRA/D226>; PRA Rulebook: CRR Firms: Glossary Instrument 2017, which came into force 3 January 2018; PRA Rulebook: (EU Exit) Instrument 2019, which came into force 31 December 2020.

[58] PRA, *Interpretation* <http://media.fshandbook.info/Handbook/Interpretationv2_PRA_20150119.pdf>.

[59] FCA, 'Transparency', Discussion Paper DP13/1, March 2013 <http://www.fsa.gov.uk/static/pubs/discussion/ dp13-01.pdf> 5; FCA, 'How the Financial Conduct Authority will investigate and report on regulatory failure', April 2013 <https://www.fca.org.uk/static/fca/documents/how-fca-will-investigate-and-report-regulatory-fail ure.pdf> 4.

[60] Bank of England, PRA, *Statement of Policy—The Prudential Regulation Authority's approach to enforcement: statutory statements of policy and procedure*, January 2016.

[61] News Release—Co-operative Bank enforcement investigation, 06 January 2014.

management.[62] The most developed special resolution regime in place to date applies to banks and investment firms either solely regulated or dual regulated by the PRA; it is appropriate to focus on the PRA's approach to supervision and the prudential requirements applicable to those firms. Those matters are explored in the following sections.

B. Bank Supervision

5.25 The PRA and the FCA have adopted a different approach to overseeing the financial firms and markets from that which was adopted by the FSA prior to the global financial crisis.[63] The PRA describes its approach to achieving its objectives and principles and rules set out in the amended FSMA 2000 as adopting a 'judgement based' approach, 'forward looking', and 'focused'.[64] A significant move to one where it is more likely to exercise judgement about the strategic safety and soundness of firms rather than on operational failures—which was perhaps the case with previous regulators. In light of this, the PRA is likely to intervene in those strategic areas that are likely to expose the firm to risks—in particular, if those firm risks are considered to put at risk the stability of the financial system. It is likely that the PRA will take action at an early stage in respect of an issue which in its view could materialize into a serious risk to the firm. The PRA places firms into five categories, according to the level of risk they would pose if they were to fail or carry on their business in an unsafe manner.[65] The level of supervision designated to the individual category of firms is different, with those posing the highest potential impact in category 1 conferred the greatest intensity of supervision.[66]

1. Capital and liquidity requirements

5.26 The area of capital requirements has come under considerable scrutiny in light of the financial crisis and the limitations of the previous capital requirements.[67] A significant part of the reforms require banks to hold more capital in the good times rather than less to enable them to cushion them in the bad times. The implications of these reforms are far-reaching and controversial as they have an impact on the level of finance in the economy. The EU has incorporated the international Basel III standards in the CRD IV and the CRR.[68] The CRR was onshored in the UK under statutory instruments made under the European Union (Withdrawal) Act 2018. However, a number of the Basel III reforms were set out in the CRR2, which came into force after the Brexit transition period. The Financial Services Act

---

[62] Bank of England, PRA, The Co-operative Bank PLC, Final Notice, 10 August 2015; Bank of England, PRA, Barry Tootell, Final Notice, 14 January 2016; and Bank of England, PRA, Keith Brian Alderson, Final Notice, 14 January 2016.

[63] See, eg, HM Treasury, 'A New Approach to Financial Regulation: Building a Stronger System', February 2011   <https://www.gov.uk/government/uploads/system/uploads/attachment_data/file/81411/consult_newfin ancial_regulation170211.pdf> 15–16.

[64] See PRA, The Prudential Regulation Authority's approach to banking supervision, June 2014 <http://www. bankofengland.co.uk/publications/Documents/praapproach/bankingappr1406.pdf>.

[65] Ibid at 16.

[66] Ibid.

[67] See, eg, Jens Hagendorff and Francesco Vallascas, 'Capital Regulation After the Financial Crisis' Q Finance <http://www.financepractitioner.com/regulation-best-practice/capital-regulation-after-the-financial-crisis?full>.

[68] Basel Committee on Banking Supervision, Basel III: A global regulatory framework for more resilient banks and banking systems—revised version June 2011 available at <http://www.bis.org/publ/bcbs189.pdf>.

2021 gives the PRA the power to adopt the relevant rules. The PRA has used CRR2 as an initial basis for the UK framework, but does take a different approach to enhance proportionality of the UK regime and ensure consistency with the existing UK rules. The new prudential framework applies from 1 January 2022. The issue of capital requirements forms a critical threshold condition to decide whether or not a firm is failing or likely to fail and would so require resolution. The key areas that have had significant attention paid to them in the proposed reforms are: how the banking and trading books are managed, liquidity, leverage, the treatment of securitization, and the quality with which banks and regulators have managed their responsibilities relating to internal risk models.

CRD IV[69] and the CRR[70] implement Basel III requirements in Europe. In the case of CRD IV, the directive has been transposed in national law. In respect of CRR, the regulation does not require transposing so its rules are directly applicable and form part of a separate Rulebook of provisions that firms classed as CRR firms are required to comply with.[71] Another important factor in the interpretation of CRR is the technical compliance measures devised by the European Banking Authority (EBA) to explain and offer guidance on how CRR firms are expected to comply and how the appropriate regulator is required to ensure compliance.[72] The approach post Brexit is to transfer powers from EU bodies to the PRA and FCA, and EBA guidelines will be adopted by the PRA on a case-by-case basis.   **5.27**

The reforms require UK banks to hold appropriate levels of financial resources to cushion against financial shocks, such as those experienced during the financial crisis, so that banks can absorb a higher level of losses and thus minimize the possibility that they will need to proceed to resolution to address their solvency. A significant onus is on the firms to calculate on a prudent basis how much capital is adequate in terms of the risks they are exposed to. The PRA has the discretion to require a bank to change the composition of its capital to improve its loss absorbance. The major UK banks are required to comply with the CRR definition of capital, which primarily includes, inter alia, equity and subordinated debt, to form the basis of capital that is appropriately loss absorbing. Banks are expected to hold capital in two tiers, with Tier 1 including the highest quality capital in the form of common equity.   **5.28**

The framework builds on the three pillars model of minimum capital requirements, the supervisory review, and lastly the market discipline element. The first pillar sets out the technical requirements, setting out what constitutes capital in the form of equity and subordinated debt instruments. It also sets out, within the bank's Banking Book and Trading   **5.29**

---

[69] Directive 2013/36/EU of the European Parliament and of the Council of 26 June 2013 on access to the activity of credit institutions and the prudential supervision of credit institutions and investment firms, amending Directive 2002/87/EC and repealing Directives 2006/48/EC and 2006/49/EC Text with EEA relevance [2013] OJ L 176 (Capital Requirements Directive)(CRD).

[70] Regulation (EU) No 575/2013 of the European Parliament and of the Council of 26 June 2013 on prudential requirements for credit institutions and investment firms and amending Regulation (EU) No 648/2012 Text with EEA relevance [2013] OJ L 176 (Capital Requirements Regulation) (CRR).

[71] PRA, *PRA Rulebook* <http://fshandbook.info/FS/prarulebook.jsp>. The Capital Requirements (Amendment) (EU Exit) Regulations 2019 (CRR SI) 'onshores' CRR and related regulations. It is not intended to make policy changes other than to reflect the fact that the UK has left the EU.

[72] See, eg, EBA, *FINAL draft Regulatory Technical Standards, on prudent valuation under Art. 105(14) of Regulation (EU) No 575/2013 (Capital Requirements Regulation—CRR)* (23 January 2015) <https://www.eba.eur opa.eu/documents/10180/642449/EBA-RTS-2014-06+RTS+on+Prudent+Valuation.pdf>; EBA, 'EBA Publishes First Final Draft Technical Standards on Own Funds and Credit Risk Adjustment' (26 July 2013) <https://www. eba.europa.eu/-/eba-publishes-first-final-draft-technical-standards-on-own-funds-and-credit-risk-adjustment>.

Book, specific assets and price movements in the market according to designated risk weights to ensure that the level of risk is accounted for properly. In addition to setting out the appropriate parameters for what constitutes capital with higher levels of equity capital, the requirements in Pillar I also require banks to hold specific amounts of equity capital in reserve to counter particular risks at critical points in time. First, the 'Capital Conservation Buffer' requires banks to hold a minimum level of capital as a reserve to prevent them from distributing equity capital during periods of distress. Secondly, national authorities can require a 'Countercyclical Buffer', so that banks build up an amount of capital during good times to cushion against a period of distress. Thirdly, some banks in a particular sector are required to hold a 'Systemic Risk Buffer' as a whole to minimize the impact of market-wide risks to the bank's stability within the sector. The PRA requires firms to maintain adequate liquidity resources both in terms of amount and quality. The major UK banks are required, as a minimum, to comply with a 7 per cent common equity Tier 1 capital ratio and a 3 per cent end-point Tier 1 leverage ratio.[73]

5.30 Basel III reforms have also led to significant reforms to the other weak links revealed during the financial crisis, namely banks' poor level of liquid assets to meet financial obligations. The traditional perception of a liquidity problem was that it was a relatively short period of a matter of a few days. However, in light of the financial crisis, the need for liquidity was shown to be a crucial factor in safeguarding the viability of an institution, particularly if it holds a limited amount of liquidity and it relies on a narrow range of finance. In light of the position in which banks found themselves during the financial crisis, Basel III reforms require them now to comply with the liquidity coverage ratio which calculates the level of unencumbered liquid assets held to meet net cash outflows for a given stress period of 30 days. The firm is required to utilize this to ensure it can manage its liabilities as they fall due. The liquidity resources need to be available to the firm on a solo level and not simply be located in another part of the group, and they may not include emergency liquidity assistance from a central bank. For the purposes of identifying liquidity resources, a firm must ensure that they are marketable or realizable; that funds can be raised from those assets; that a range of assets with a range of maturities are held; and that they are able to generate unsecured funds. These resources will also need to be able to do so in a timely manner, and it is this which is crucial to deciding the range of resources it holds at any one time.[74] The liquidity resources held by a firm need to be managed properly, forming part of the corporate decision-making on a strategic level. Banks are required to build up the level of unencumbered assets in a phased approach; they were expected to hold at least 60 per cent by 2015 and should achieve 100 per cent of the required level by 2018. Moreover, the introduction of the Net Stable Funding Requirement means banks will also have to ensure that the sources of funds required to support their businesses are stable over the long term to assist with managing liquidity levels.

5.31 Managing liquidity risk requires the need to price liquidity risk and intra-day management of liquidity, but more importantly stress testing and contingency funding as well; the latter

---

[73] PRA, *Capital and Leverage Ratios for Major UK Banks and Building Societies*, November 2013 (last updated on 26 June 2014) Supervisory Statement | SS3/13 <http://www.bankofengland.co.uk/pra/Documents/publications/ss/2013/ss313.pdf>.

[74] BIPRU 12.2.5G.

being a principal gap in the previous regime.[75] The PRA requires firms to undertake stress testing for potential problems and reviewed at least once a year in the first instance, with the frequency increasing if circumstances such as periods of market volatility require a stress test to be carried out.[76] The PRA requires the stress test to factor in a variety of scenarios like institution and market stresses with underlying assumptions such as effectiveness of, inter alia, the correlations between funding markets, diversification of sources of funding,[77] and liquidity requirements off balance sheet.[78] A firm is also required to have a contingency funding plan to deal with a liquidity crisis which has got the approval of the board of directors.[79] The PRA requires a firm to have a contingency plan which forms part of its strategy for response as a liquidity crisis escalates in intensity.[80] A number of banks that operate in the UK may have some form of government or central bank assistance to support them, and a contingency plan needs to factor that into their assessment of the robustness of their planning. It also requires the firm to assess its contingency plans in light of the 'impact of stressed market conditions on its ability to sell or securitize assets'[81] which attempts to mitigate the problems experienced during the recent financial crisis.

The wider stress testing forms an important part of the process of gaining a better picture of the reliance of UK banks on pre-determined stress scenarios. The measures go a significant way to improve understanding of risks to financial stability in the UK financial system from domestic, regional, and international events. It also illustrates how the FPC, PRA, and FCA coordinate their discrete responsibilities to better understand how best to exercise macro-micro prudential regulation. The 2014 stress test required UK banks to stress test their capital ratios against a single stress scenario based on an adverse change to a combination of a slowdown in the housing market and subsequent drop in house prices leading to increased levels of negative equity and the impact of the level of indebtedness of households increasing on banks' capital ratios and the extent to which they could absorb the losses sustained. The stress test enabled the PRA to assess whether the banks required to improve their CET 1 ratio either through a revised capital plan or to improve it to increase its resilience to such shocks. In this round of assessments, only the Co-operative bank was required to submit a revised capital plan. The use of stress testing is an important component to improve supervisory understanding of the resilience of banks to shocks and provides valuable information about the viability of institutions and the risk of distress. The Bank of England has published the Solvency Stress Test 2021, the scenario is calibrated to robustly test and challenge business models and support firms in identifying key sensitivities and vulnerabilities within their balance sheets in the context of a severe downside outcome with an intensification of the macroeconomic shocks seen in 2020 as a result of COVID-19. The 2020 annual stress test was cancelled for the eight major UK banks and building societies. It was intended to help lenders focus on meeting the needs of businesses and households during the pandemic lockdown period. The 2019 stress test showed that the UK banking

5.32

---

[75] BIPRU 12.4.1R(1).
[76] BIPRU 12.4.2R.
[77] BIPRU 12.3.39R.
[78] BIPRU 12.4.5E.
[79] BIPRU 12.4.10R; 12.4.11R.
[80] BIPRU 12.4.13R.
[81] BIPRU 12.4.4E.

system was resilient to recessions worse than those in the UK and other economies during the 2008–9 financial crisis.

C. Ring-fencing

5.33 The depth of the financial crisis led to an extensive assessment of how banks, primarily retail banks, can be better protected from the threats of financial risk from the investment banking and securities trading side of the group's operations. The argument espoused is that the risks and culture of the latter ultimately place the UK retail depositors and ultimately taxpayers at a significant risk to bail out those riskier parts for their business failures. A move to safeguard the retail parts is one, albeit significant, part of the reforms to safeguard and ensure the retail parts can be resolved in as orderly a manner as possible, and ensure that the critical services it provides to the economy experience minimum disruption.

5.34 The move towards ring-fencing gives rise to a number of challenges due to the various intragroup connections that can exist from an ownership, governance, and product chain level. On a practical level, this amounts to concerns about: what should be left in and out of the ring-fenced entity in terms of business activities; the extent to which the ring-fenced entity is truly protected from risks from other parts of the group; and the disentangling of the governance arrangements within the group to ensure the ring-fenced entity is not at risk of being tainted by the management arrangements in place to direct the ring-fenced entity and non-ring-fenced parts. The ring-fence arrangements, as highlighted above, are a significant structural attempt to improve the safety and soundness of the retail operations. A significant requirement is to ensure the ring-fenced institution can ensure continuity of critical services which will require the bank to address critical facilities and services to achieve this objective. The latter cannot be underestimated in ensuring a smooth resolution, the objective of which is described by Andrew Bailey:[82]

> These proposals will allow customers to have continuous access to the money in their bank accounts—or receive payment from the FSCS if this is not possible. Additionally, the increase in FSCS limits for certain types of insurance will mean policyholders who may find it difficult to obtain alternative cover, or who are locked into a product, have greater protection if their insurer fails.[83]

5.35 The Financial Services (Banking Reform) Act 2013 requires the PRA and the FCA to implement the ring-fence measures on banks' activities. A practical challenge in such circumstances is many of the activities that are captured by ring-fencings are not necessarily undertaken within one legal entity but may be undertaken by a number of entities within the group. In this respect, the PRA appreciates that it will need to take a case-by-case approach to determine what are and are not permitted activities in the ring-fenced entity rather than taking a prescriptive approach at the outset and require all those designated to move ring-fenced activities to do so in a similar fashion. The PRA is required to assess these matters in light of their objective and assess the extent to which the legal structure poses

---

[82] Bank of England, 'News Release—Bank of England announces proposals to strengthen the financial system through structural reform' <http://www.bankofengland.co.uk/publications/Pages/news/2014/125.aspx>.
[83] Ibid.

risks to it achieving its objectives. The governance arrangement of the ring-fenced entity will remain part of the wider group the ring-fenced bank will be able to act independently and will not be influenced by decision-makers in other parts of the group. The restrictions do not prevent the formation of a subgroup of business activities within the perimeter of the ring-fence separate from the other parts of the wider group. The restructuring of the group activities due to regulatory requirements rather than commercial decisions is inevitably going to lead to some tensions within the structure. But it appears the PRA within the legislative and regulatory framework has provided a significant degree of discretion so that a one-size-fits-all approach is not taken. This is a further example of how supervision has reconfigured banking operations to ensure they are resilient to shocks from other parts of the financial group and to move towards improving the way such banks could be resolved in an orderly manner.

III. The US Approach to Bank Supervision

The US system of prudential regulation and supervision of banking is without doubt a complex structure; it is not centralized in a single regulator but is the responsibility of a number of separate and independent regulators.   **5.36**

In the early periods of the financial crisis of 2007, a number of proposals were put forward for wholesale reform of the US regulatory system. These proposals were to improve the effectiveness of the regulatory structure and to simplify the financial regulatory structure overseeing the US financial system in the post-Gramm-Leach-Bliley Act 1999 world of large complex financial conglomerates. These proposals took the form of either a twin peaks model or a single regulator model.[84] However, like other periods of financial crisis, the reforms introduced by the Dodd-Frank Act 2010 have not adopted the initial proposals for wholesale change to the regulatory structure (with the exception of one sacrificial lamb, in this case the scrapping of the Office of Thrift Supervision) but more specific changes to improve the regulatory and supervisory systems, and examination of the financial intermediaries and markets. The Dodd-Frank Act 2010 is very much a multi-faceted piece of legislation with specific changes to the regulatory system but also an attempt to allow the 'appropriate federal banking agencies' (§ 2(2)) the responsibility to work out how they will adopt some of the changes. In addition to this, it also initiates a number of studies on regulatory reform, so there is a considerable amount of work for both regulatory agencies and banks and non-banks ahead. The Dodd-Frank Act 2010 provides significant and wholesale changes in a host of other areas, namely the establishment of the Financial Stability Oversight Council, the Federal Insurance Office, and the Bureau of Consumer Financial Protection. Moreover, the Dodd-Frank Act also introduces a number of changes at the regulatory level in areas such as liquidation arrangements for bank holding companies and non-bank financial companies and derivatives and hedge funds. The Dodd-Frank Act does   **5.37**

---

[84] See the Department of the Treasury, *Blueprint for a Modernized Financial Regulatory Structure* (March 2008) <https://www.treasury.gov/press-center/press-releases/Documents/Blueprint.pdf> at 13–14 and HE Jackson, 'A Pragmatic Approach to the Phased Consolidation of Financial Regulation in the United States' (12 November 2008), Harvard Public Law Working Paper No 09–19. Available at SSRN: <http://ssrn.com/abstract= 1300431>.

not change the dual banking system of state and federal charters for depository institutions and indeed the core responsibilities of the FRB and FDIC.[85] One purpose of the legislation is to 'preserve and protect the dual system of Federal and State-chartered depository institutions'.[86] In other areas the Dodd-Frank Act maintains the status quo with the insurance industry for example, so it remains the responsibility of individual states. It does, however, create the Federal Insurance Office under the umbrella of the Treasury which will be primarily responsible for monitoring the insurance industry and reviewing regulation of the industry to assess the gaps which may exist.[87] This section of the chapter will also touch upon the reforms to improve the resilience and resolution of banks from a supervisory perspective. The US supervisory approach and regulation reform is also couched with a forward-looking perspective.

5.38   The Trump administration was harshly critical of the Dodd-Frank Act, describing it as a negative force which makes it impossible for bankers to function. In the 2016 Republican National Convention, the party voted to include a repeal of the Act in the party's election platform for that year. Trump in February 2017 issued an Executive Order (13772 Core Principles for Regulating the US Financial System), which tasked the Treasury with reviewing the Financial Stability Oversight Council established under Dodd-Frank and establish a set of 'core principles' of regulation for the Trump administration. This order was revoked by Biden in February 2021.

5.39   In May 2018, President Trump signed the Economic Growth, Regulatory Relief and Consumer Protection Act, which amended the Dodd-Frank Act to a degree, with the greatest impact on small banks and the Volcker Rule. Changes include limiting the Volcker Rule, exempting small banks from the Volcker Rule, and making changes to the capital rules and the Basel III liquidity coverage ratio. The biggest change is that the Act reduces the regulatory burden for all but the largest banks as companies with less than $250 billion in assets do not have to comply with the majority of the enhanced prudential standards, including stress testing and resolution planning.

A.   The Dual Banking System

5.40   The dual banking system consists of two formal methods of chartering commercial banks (authorizing them to undertake the business of banking): at the state level and at the federal level.[88] This is a consequence in many respects of the constitutional make-up of the US, based on both a state and a federal system of governance.[89] Historically, state-regulated

---

[85]   Dodd-Frank Act: Title III—Transfer of Powers to the Comptroller of the Currency, the Corporation, and the Board of Governors.

[86]   § 301(2).

[87]   § 502: see amendments § 313(a)–(c), in particular.

[88]   For an examination of the dual banking system see OCC, *National Banks and the Dual Banking System* (2003), in particular the limited powers of the state to intervene in the supervision of national banks, at p 16; HM Schooner, 'Recent Challenges to the Persistent Dual Banking System' (1996) 41 *Saint Louis University Law Journal* 263 at 267; HN Butler and JR Macey 'The Myth of Competition in the Dual Banking System' (1988) 73 *Cornell Law Review* 677. For a critique of the some of the limits of the dual banking system, in particular the utility of state involvement in banking regulation and supervision, see AE Wilmarth, 'The Expansion of State Bank Powers, the Federal Response, and the Case for Preserving the Dual Banking System' (1990) 58 *Fordham Law Review* 1113 at 1239–1255.

[89]   ES Redford, 'Dual Banking: A Case Study in Federalism' (1966) 31 *Law and Contemporary Problems* 749.

banks issued their own notes. This was before the federal government intervened to introduce, at a federal level, a national currency to support its war efforts at the time.[90] The Office Comptroller of Currency (OCC) was placed at the helm of the national currency to manage it.[91] The dual banking system was a by-product of the legislation to introduce the national currency, and put an end to states issuing their own banknotes. Indeed, the expectation was that state-chartered banks would abandon their state charter for a federal charter. But the introduction of the new federal charter did not result in a mass exodus from the state system, even when a subsequent punitive tax was imposed on state banknotes to force them to change.[92] The result was two formal systems of chartering: the bank regulator in the individual state charters the state banks, and the OCC charters national banks pursuant to the National Bank Act of 1864.[93] But the dual banking system is not rigidly divided into two parts—a state bank could convert its charter to a national charter and vice versa.[94] According to Kenneth Scott, 'the core of the dual banking system is the simultaneous existence of different regulatory options that are not alike in terms of statutory provisions, regulatory implementation and administrative policy'.[95]

In addition to these two chartering systems, membership of the Federal Reserve and the Federal Deposit Insurance Corporation (FDIC) also plays a significant role.[96] The FDIC and the Federal Reserve Board (FRB) have prudential responsibilities to oversee the activities of their members in addition to the primary regulators.[97] National banks are required to be members of the Federal Reserve and the FDIC.[98] There is a separate FDIC application process in order to become an insured depository institution.[99] State member banks have the option to choose to come under the jurisdiction of the Federal Reserve[100] and thus the FDIC. Membership means the banks are under the umbrella of their chartering authority, as well as the Federal Reserve and the FDIC, for the purposes of supervision and enforcement to a lesser or greater extent to fulfil their individual responsibilities.[101] For example, a national bank will be chartered by the OCC, which will have responsibility for its prudential supervision; the FDIC will have supervisory and enforcement responsibility to fulfil its obligations to the deposit insurance fund; and the Federal Reserve will have responsibility over its access to the discount window and reserve requirements.

5.41

---

[90] The National Currency Act of 1863 and subsequently modernized with the enactment of the National Bank Act of 1864.

[91] 12 USC § 1.

[92] HM Schooner and M Taylor, 'Convergence and Competition: The Case of Bank Regulation in Britain and the United States' (1999) 20 *Michigan Journal of International Law* 595 at 610.

[93] OCC, *National Banks and the Dual Banking System* (2003), in particular the limited powers of the state to intervene in the supervision of national banks, 16.

[94] For conversion from national banks to state banks see 12 USC § 214(a).

[95] KE Scott, 'The Dual Banking System: A Model of Competition in Regulation' (1977) 30 *Stanford Law Review* 1, 41, cited in OCC, *National Banks and the Dual Banking System, supra* n 106 at 3; HM Schooner, 'Recent Challenges to the Persistent Dual Banking System' (1996) 41 *Saint Louis University Law Journal* 263 at 272.

[96] 12 USC § 1813(d)–(e).

[97] 'Banking institutions and their regulators' previously available at <http://www.ny.frb.org/banking/regrept/BIATR.pdf> providing a matrix giving a 'simple' outline of the primary regulators and membership system in the US system of regulation and supervision, deposit insurance, and emergency liquidity support provided therein.

[98] 12 USC § 282; Board of Governors of the Federal Reserve System (1994) *The Federal Reserve System: Purposes and Functions*, Washington DC, available at <http://www.federalreserve.gov/pf/pf.htm>, 12.

[99] FDIC Forms, Interagency Charter and Federal Deposit Insurance Application, available at <http://www.fdic.gov/regulations/laws/forms/>.

[100] 12 USC § 321.

[101] See for instance 12 USC §§ 325–326.

B. The Individual Regulators

5.42   The primary regulators have the main responsibility for prudential regulation. The primary regulatory bodies are the Federal Reserve,[102] the OCC,[103] and the FDIC.[104] The Office of Thrift Supervision (OTS) was abolished on 19 October 2011 and its various responsibilities transferred to the Board of Governors of the Federal Reserve and the OCC.[105]

5.43   The regulation and supervision of the business of banking has evolved over a considerable period of time, most notably through legislative means codified in various places in Title 12 Banks and Banking of the United States Code (USC); this is divided into over 50 chapters, giving rise to a considerable level of complexity.[106] The responsibilities of the FDIC,[107] the OCC,[108] and the FRB[109] are broadly speaking set out in separate chapters; these make up the 'Appropriate Federal Banking Agency'.[110] In addition, a significant proportion of responsibility is conferred on the individual federal regulators as administrative bodies separately within the Code of Federal Regulations (CFR) designating administrative powers.[111] The primary regulators have devised their own styles of regulation, supervision, and enforcement which is reinforced by the Dodd-Frank Act. It also allows the federal regulatory agencies to interpret the various changes it requires them to adopt as well.

5.44   The OCC is responsible for chartering and supervision of national banks. Pursuant to § 27 of 12 USC,[112] it is authorized to grant national bank charters and is responsible on an administrative level, as provided in 12 CFR s 4.2, for overseeing national banks, with powers to regulate, supervise, and exercise enforcement actions in accordance with federal laws.[113] The OCC can appoint examiners to national banks 'as often as the [OCC] shall deem necessary',[114] and these banks are required to make reports about their 'condition', regarding their financial health in terms of assets and liabilities to the OCC.[115] The OCC is also responsible for ensuring that national banks operate in a safe and sound manner, which will be explored further on in this chapter. But it must be mindful that it achieves its other regulatory goals, which are to 'promote competitiveness for national banks' and 'improve efficiency of examinations and supervision, including reducing supervisory burden'.[116] It will also pursuant to § 312(b)(2)(B)(i)(I) take on responsibility for the regulation, supervision, and examination of federal savings associations that were previously under the jurisdiction of the OTS.[117] It is

---

[102] See <http://www.federalreserve.gov/>.
[103] See <http://www.occ.treas.gov/>.
[104] See <http://www.fdic.gov/>.
[105] §§ 312, 313.
[106] For a historical account of the evolution of bank regulation at both state and federal level see AK Davis, 'Banking Regulation Today: A Banker's View' (1966) 31 *Law and Contemporary Problems* 639.
[107] 12 USC, Chapter 16.
[108] 12 USC, Chapter 1.
[109] 12 USC, Chapter 3.
[110] Until 19 October 2011, 'Appropriate Federal Banking Agency' also included the OTS. 12 USC § 1813(q)(1)–(4).
[111] 12 CFR.
[112] 12 USC § 27.
[113] 12 CFR 4.2.
[114] 12 USC § 481.
[115] 12 USC § 161.
[116] OCC, *Bank Supervision Process* (1996) 1; OCC, Comptroller of the Currency Administrator of National Banks, *A Guide to the National Banking System* (2005) Washington DC, April, p 3.
[117] Until 19 October 2011, 'Appropriate Federal Banking Agency' will also include the OTS.

also required to designate a Deputy Comptroller who will have responsibility for the supervision and examination of federal savings associations.[118] Under the Comptroller of the Currency under the Trump administration (Joseph Otting) in 2018 the OCC published a bulletin promoting short-term, small-dollar installment loans to encourage national banks to help meet the credit needs of their customers. In 2019 it proposed to strengthen and modernize the CRA regulations, which were finalized in May 2020.

The Federal Reserve is at the helm of the banking system in its capacity as central bank to   **5.45**
manage monetary stability[119] and with a mandate for financial stability. It acts as a central source of liquidity and a single-note issuer.[120] The Federal Reserve puts emphasis on combining its responsibilities for monetary policy and bank supervision to gauge the prudential stability of the banking system.[121] The Dodd-Frank Act introduces changes to the way its credit lines can be sought by non-banks.[122] It seeks to limit such support to rescue the financial system rather than being any individual institution. Moreover, the decision to lend will, inter alia, require the Federal Reserve to consider whether the security for emergency loans is 'sufficient to protect taxpayers from losses'[123] and the facility is 'terminated in a timely and orderly fashion'.[124] If support is going to be provided then the individual institution needs to be experiencing liquidity rather than an insolvency problem. In this case insolvency is determined by whether the individual institution has sought bankruptcy protection.[125] This restricts the ability of the Federal Reserve to lend to institutions that are in distress; by providing the support to the financial system, it is essentially sending out a message that it is not willing to rescue individual institutions unless they pose a threat to the financial system. Providing liquidity to the financial system means it is primarily attempting to mitigate the impact on it rather than rescue an individual institution. The vexed issue of when a liquidity crisis is a systemic liquidity crisis so to speak, that warrants action by the authorities, is also given specific attention in the Dodd-Frank Act. The Federal Reserve is required to undertake consultation with the Treasury and FDIC 'to determine whether a liquidity event exists that warrants use of the guarantee program'.[126] In order to arrive at this, an evaluation of the evidence is required that such an event exists and 'failure to take action would have serious adverse effects on financial stability or economic conditions in the United States'; and action is needed to 'avoid or mitigate potential adverse effects'.[127]

The Federal Reserve has specific responsibility for supervising financial holding com-   **5.46**
panies, bank holding companies, state-chartered banks, and foreign bank operations.[128]
The Federal Reserve will also take over responsibility from the OTS for the supervision

---

[118] Revised Statutes of the United States, § 327B. Deputy Comptroller for the Supervision and Examination of Federal Savings Associations.

[119] Federal Reserve Act of 1913; Board of Governors of the Federal Reserve System, *supra* n 111 at 13.

[120] Ibid.

[121] Board of Governors of the Federal Reserve System, *supra* n 111 at 72.

[122] § 1101. Federal Reserve Act Amendments on Emergency Lending Authority.

[123] § 1101((a)6).

[124] Ibid.

[125] § 1101(a)(6).

[126] § 1104(a)(1).

[127] § 1104(a)(2)(A)(B).

[128] Board of Governors of the Federal Reserve System, *supra* n 111, Chapter 5, Supervision and Regulation. For bank holding companies see Bank Holding Company Act of 1956 as amended 12 USC § 1841 et seq; foreign banks, International Banking Act 1978 as amended 12 USC § 3101, et seq.

and rule-making powers for savings and loans holding companies and their subsidiaries.[129] The oversight that the Federal Reserve exercises over the respective holding companies is deemed necessary for the purposes of gauging the groups' safety and soundness. This gives rise to a necessity to cooperate and seek relevant information from the other primary regulators rather than making duplicate examinations of a bank and its subsidiaries.[130] The Federal Reserve reacted to the COVID-19 pandemic by lowering interest rates to zero in March 2020 and announcing measures to bolster markets, including a $700 billion of asset purchases to improve finance to the real economy. It launched a new programme to lend directly to businesses. $2.3 trillion in a separate support package to households, employers, financial markets, and state and local governments. The Federal Reserve lowered the Federal funds interest rates for banks to 0.25 per cent, lower than the Great Recession, extending the terms of their loans to 90 days—allows the banks to keep functioning and make new loans.

5.47   The FDIC was established in 1933 after the huge spate of bank failures in the 1920s and 1930s.[131] It was set up to insure 'the deposits of all banks and savings associations'.[132] FDIC membership gives rise to a further layer of prudential supervision for the purpose of safeguarding the deposit insurance fund.[133] The FDIC is the primary federal regulator and supervisor of state-chartered banks that have decided not to become members of the Federal Reserve System, which are categorized as non-member banks.[134] Furthermore, with the abolition of the OTS the FDIC will also take responsibility for state savings associations.[135] Its most important function is the administration of the deposit insurance fund. The level of protection afforded to depositors has been increased by the Dodd-Frank Act from $100,000 to $250,000 to an individual depositor.[136] The basis of calculating the deposit insurance premium will be changed as well—based on consolidated total assets rather than deposit liabilities. This move will mean the large complex institutions will contribute more towards deposit insurance than the less risky ones.[137] This will coincide with the reforms to the FDIC minimum reserve, which was planned to increase to 1.35 per cent by 30 September 2020.[138] According to the FDIC, since 2010, the reserve has increased steadily, reaching 1.35 per cent in 2018. However, as a result of the COVID-19 pandemic, the reserve ratio decreased from 1.41% to 1.30% at the end of the second quarter in 2020. The Federal Deposit Insurance Act requires the FDIC to establish a restoration plan any time the reserve ratio falls below 1.35 per cent, which must provide that it reaches 1.35 per cent within eight years.

5.48   The Federal Financial Institutions Examination Council (FFIEC) was set up in 1979 to assist the federal bank regulators to enhance the level of uniformity and consistency in their

---

[129] § 312(b)(1)(A).
[130] See, eg, FRB (2000) 'Framework for Financial Holding Company Supervision', Supervisory Letter SR 00-13, 15 August.
[131] Banking Act of 1933, Public Law 73–66.
[132] 12 USC § 1811(a).
[133] 12 USC § 1811 et seq.
[134] 12 USC § 1815.
[135] § 312(b)(2)(c).
[136] § 335(a).
[137] § 331(b) Deposit Insurance Reforms.
[138] § 334(d).

supervisory and examination practices.[139] The move towards creating a single body to co-ordinate and enhance consistency between the regulators should not come as a surprise: it is designed to reduce the potential inconsistency that might arise from the fact that a number of regulators have overlapping responsibilities to oversee the activities of federally regulated banks. In addition to enhancing the level of consistency, another concern is to reduce unnecessary regulatory burdens that might arise as a result of federal regulators' actions. The FFIEC periodically publishes interagency notices on, for example, the importance of notifying and coordinating information about possible enforcement decisions taken by a federal regulator with other regulators.[140]

The Dodd-Frank Act means a new level of coordination is required by the FFIEC on a federal bank agency level to ensure consistency in the way federal bank agencies apply the new reforms. Moreover, it could also be equally called into doubt whether it can sustain its current form given it is made up of federal bank agencies and does not include either securities or insurance regulators. The Dodd-Frank Act seems to better reflect the need for better coordination and consistency of treatment of banks and non-bank activities that undertake similar financial activities and so mitigates this with a host of new measures.   **5.49**

The Bureau of Consumer Financial Protection (BCFP) is a new body on the federal level to regulate consumer financial products and services.[141] The BCFP will form a part of the Federal Reserve rather than an independent body and so will be classed as an executive agency rather than a federal agency. The necessity for such an organization culminates primarily from the systemic failures to curb the 'mis-selling' of mortgages that formed part of the catalyst for the financial crisis. The BCFP will have regulatory, supervisory, and enforcement authority over those that provide financial products and services despite oversight of such banks and non-banks by the primary regulator. In order to execute its role effectively the BCFP will have the authority to request information and examination reports provided there are assurances about its confidentiality.[142] The introduction of the BCFP will mean that the federal agencies will lose a proportion of their responsibilities to the new agency with the mandate to enforce federal consumer financial law. More specifically, the Dodd-Frank legislation significantly curtails the ability of national banks and their respective regulators to exercise pre-emption rights. The Trump administration set in motion a policy of reducing bank supervision and regulation, which President Biden has begun to rescind. For example, The Consumer Financial Protection Bureau under President Biden is now introducing a stricter approach to banking supervision, as was seen in the Obama administration. In April the Consumer Financial Protection Bureau broadened the scope for what is considered to be abusive behaviour by providers of financial services to consumers, after the Trump administration under Kathy Kraninger narrowed the definition, leading to less monetary penalties. By their own calculations, the Bureau collected on average $650 million in fines or penalties a year under President Trump, compared to $1.84 billion per year under the Obama administration.   **5.50**

---

[139] 12 USC §§ 3301–3308, in particular § 3305; for information about the Federal Financial Institutions Examination Council see <http://www.ffiec.gov/>.

[140] FFIEC (1997) 'Interagency coordination of formal corrective action by the Federal Bank regulatory agencies', revised policy statement, February, available at <http://www.fdic.gov/regulations/laws/federal/rpsi.pdf>.

[141] § 1011(a).

[142] § 1022(c)(6)(B)(i).

1. The Gramm-Leach-Bliley Act of 1999

5.51 The move towards the dismantlement of barriers between banks, securities firms, and insurance businesses formally came about with the enactment of the Gramm-Leach-Bliley Act of 1999 (GLB).[143] The Act's remit is not to provide for a wholesale change to the regulatory structure for the dismantled financial services industry, but to take away the barriers that had prevented financial conglomeration between banks, securities, and insurance firms.[144] The objective of the 1999 Act is to encourage the growth of financial conglomeration to enhance the efficiency of the financial system in the US. However, it does not allow the commingling of investment and commercial banking under the same roof, as seen in a 'universal bank' model. The legislation in that respect is not a complete overhaul of the previous system, but only provides incremental change. It retains in part a functional system of regulation where financial businesses are overseen by their respective bodies: the Securities and Exchange Commission, the State Insurance Commissioner, and the state or federal regulators will respectively regulate the securities, insurance, and bank businesses.[145] But at the helm of this system is the Federal Reserve, with the responsibility of being 'lead regulator' to the financial system as a whole by acting as the consolidated supervisor of financial holding companies (FHCs). In particular the Federal Reserve is to act as the 'umbrella supervisor for financial holding companies, and the State insurance regulators' for the purposes of co-ordinating supervision of FHCs that have bank and insurance company subsidiaries.[146]

5.52 The 1999 Act extends a bank holding company's scope by giving it the right to form an FHC[147] which can engage in activities of a financial nature or 'incidental to such activities' or 'incidental' to a financial activity[148] provided 'it does not pose a substantial risk to the safety and soundness of depository institutions'. The FRB in consultation with the US Treasury is empowered to decide what activities are 'financial in nature' or may be 'complementary' to financial activities.[149] The provision and the long list of activities included indicate that the idea of 'financial in nature' is interpreted broadly.[150] The restrictions on banks' affiliation with commercial businesses have been relaxed somewhat: FHCs can in certain circumstances hold shares in commercial companies for a limited period, after which they need to be divested.[151] The significant premise for the decision to extend the scope of activities in which an FHC can engage is the safety and soundness of the deposit-taking institution.[152]

---

[143] Public Law 106-102, Gramm-Leach-Bliley Act of 1999: 'To enhance competition in the financial services industry by providing a prudential framework for the affiliation of banks, securities firms, insurance companies and other financial service providers, and for other purposes.'

[144] Ibid, §§ 101, 103, and 104.

[145] See Titles II and III, *supra* n 156. For a critical analysis of functional regulation of a financial services industry where barriers are closely eroding away giving rise to financial conglomeration, see HM Schooner, 'Regulating Risk Not Function' (1998) 66 *University of Cincinnati Law Review* 441.

[146] Public Law 106-102, § 307.

[147] It amends the Bank Holding Company Act 1956, § 4; Public Law 106-102, § 102.

[148] Public Law 106-102, § 103 (s 4(k)(1)(A) and (B)).

[149] Ibid, § 103 (s 4(k)(1)–(2)).

[150] Ibid, § 103 (s 4(k)(4)).

[151] Ibid, § 103 (s 4 (n)).

[152] In some instances a firewall is also allowed to be put in place; see Public Law 106-102, § 46, 'Safety and Soundness Firewalls for State Banks with Financial Subsidiaries' for insured state banks. In addition, to curb the risks associated with the title of 'too big to fail' for some financial holding companies the Federal Reserve and the Treasury are required to conduct a study into the 'feasibility' of financial holding companies holding 'a portion of their capital in the form of subordinated debt to enhance the discipline within such groups by such creditors: Public Law 106-102, § 108.

The Federal Reserve is conferred formal oversight of both bank holding companies (BHCs)   **5.53**
and FHCs for the purposes of consolidated supervision. The respective functional regulators are required to provide examination reports to the Federal Reserve.[153] It can, on the
findings of these reports or its own examination of the holding companies and their subsidiaries, take the necessary action to deal with their activities if they pose, inter alia, an adverse
risk to the deposit-taking institution or the deposit insurance fund. The Dodd-Frank Act
requires BHCs if they have consolidated assets of $50 billion or greater to be under a pro-
gramme of enhanced supervision and more stringent prudential standards to reduce the
risks they give to the stability of the financial system.[154] The Economic Growth, Regulatory
Relief and Consumer Protection Act of 2018 reduced the regulatory burdens for all but the
largest bank holding companies. This is expected to apply to 25 out of 38 of the largest banks
in the US. However, where it deems appropriate, the Federal Reserve may still apply the
standards to any financial institution with more than $100 billion in assets.

C. Financial Stability Oversight Council

The financial crisis highlighted the need to oversee macroprudential and micro-prudential   **5.54**
matters so as to reduce systemic risks in the financial system. This is by any stretch of the imagination a significant task so that financial intermediaries and markets are regulated more
effectively and consistently, to avoid gaps in the regulation of the whole financial system
which could materialize in possible systemic risks. The primary objective of the Financial
Stability Oversight Council (FSOC) is to undertake this huge task.[155] The FSOC is made
up of regulators responsible for the financial system.[156] The FSOC has three primary purposes, namely: to identify risks to the US financial system from both within the system or
outside for the purposes of financial stability by assessing risks that could arise from individual institutions or the activities of large interconnected banks or non-bank activities;[157]
to re-establish the constructive ambiguity associated with the expectation that counterparties have that the government will bail banks or non-banks out of trouble;[158] and to respond to emerging threats to the financial stability of the financial system.[159] In order to
achieve its purpose it will be able to obtain information and monitor the financial markets
both domestically and internationally in order to determine possible threats to the financial stability of the US financial system. It has the power to make recommendations to the
member agencies for the purposes of following up on its findings. More importantly, it has
the power to make recommendations to intensify the supervision undertaken by the primary federal agencies which includes, inter alia, the federal banking agencies, the Securities
and Exchange Commission, the Commodity Futures Trading Commission, State Insurance
Authority, and the Federal Housing Agency.[160] In exceptional circumstances the FSOC may
determine a non-bank financial company poses a threat to the financial stability of the US

---

[153] Public Law 106-102, § 111.
[154] § 165.
[155] § 111. Financial Stability Oversight Council Established.
[156] § 111(1)(A)–(J).
[157] § 112(1)(A).
[158] § 112(1)(B).
[159] § 112(1)(C).
[160] § 2(12).

and in such circumstances it could decide that the institution should be supervised by the Federal Reserve.[161] In order to decide whether to transfer a non-bank financial firm to the Federal Reserve the FSOC should take into account: its leverage, off balance sheet exposure, and interconnectedness, among other factors.[162] These primarily determine whether the non-banking financial firm is too-big-to-fail or too-interconnected-to-fail and so requires supervision by the Federal Reserve. Moreover, the FSOC has the authority to make recommendations to the Federal Reserve regarding how it exercised authority to require that a non-bank financial company or bank holding company report a plan for its rapid and orderly resolution in the event of material financial distress or failure.[163]

5.55   The decision in respect of non-bank financial institutions is open to judicial review to determine whether the decision is arbitrary and capricious.[164] The fact that it has such a broad mandate does mean it could potentially be a very influential player for both banks and non-bank activities to mitigate the risks of another systemic crisis, especially with its ability to influence the intensity of supervision. This will be primarily determined by its ability to develop an independent viewpoint on matters that can withstand the viewpoints of the primary regulators and the Federal Reserve during the consultation period. Moreover, any measures it does recommend will need to be gauged against international efforts as well. For example, President Biden issued an Executive Order in June 2021, asking the Treasury to work with the Financial Stability Oversight Council to assess risks that climate change poses to the financial system in the US.

IV. The US Regulation of the Business of Banks and Safe and Sound Requirements

5.56   The business of banking in the US is primarily interpreted in the light of statute and common law, giving rise to a broad interpretation of its definition. The 'business of banking' articulated in the National Bank Acts of 1863–5 identified some specific bank activities such as acceptance of deposits and note issuance, but with the added proviso 'powers ... necessary to carry on the business of banking'.[165] In common law the traditional business of banks, while considering receiving deposits to be an 'indispensable'[166] and 'unique'[167] part of banking, includes other business that has come to be associated with banking, namely 'discount bills' and 'loan money on mortgage'.[168] The pursuit of either one was considered sufficient for an institution to be deemed to be undertaking banking business.[169]

5.57   The statutory definition of banking at a federal level therefore focuses on 'accepting deposits', but refers to a whole host of activities such as 'discounting and negotiating promissory

---

[161] § 113(a)(1). There is also power to transfer supervision of a foreign non-bank financial company to the Federal Reserve, see § 113(b).
[162] § 113(a)(2).
[163] § 115(d)(1).
[164] § 113(e)(5)(h).
[165] 12 USC § 24 (seventh). For a historical exposition of US banking see *US v Philadelphia National Bank et al*, 374 US 321; 83 S Ct (1963)—see footnote 5 where a list of 'principal banking products' is provided.
[166] *Texas & Pacific Railway Co v Pottorff*, Receiver No 128 291 US 245; 54 S Ct 416; 78 L Ed 777; 1934 US 959, 4.
[167] *US v Philadelphia National Bank*, 374 US 321; 83 S Ct (1963), 44.
[168] *Outlon v Savings Institution*, 84 US 109; 21 L Ed 618 (1873) Lexis 1318; 17 Wall, 109, 620.
[169] Ibid.

notes' and 'buying and selling exchange'. It consequently provides a broad activity-oriented definition that refers to 'all such incidental powers as shall be necessary to carry on the business of banking'.[170] This provides scope to include activities that may or may not be in the traditional domain of banking business but over time are considered appropriate for banks to pursue under this umbrella.[171] The expansion of activities, according to Bernard Shull, 'reflects a culmination of almost 20 years of debate regarding permissible activities of banking firms'.[172] For example, the OCC encourages national banks to undertake other financial services to meet the various needs of their customers provided this does not undermine the safety and soundness of the chartered bank.[173] This has led to the inclusion by the OCC of a whole host of financial services, post-GLB, that banks can pursue, categorized as general banking activities, fiduciary activities, insurance and annuities activities, securities activities, and technology and electronic activities.[174]

A. Volcker Rule

The recent financial crisis has brought to the fore the issue as to what activities banks should be able to pursue in addition to the more traditional forms of banking activities, once again reigniting the debate surrounding the separation of securities business and commercial banking. The key culprit of the crisis is viewed to be the deregulation and dismantlement of the Glass Steagall 1933 provisions separating commercial banking from various forms of securities business, with the enactment of the GLB. This is epitomized by the recommendation by Paul Volcker, former Chairman of the Federal Reserve, for a separation to be put in place once again so there is a separation between commercial banking and what has been referred to as casino banking. However, the culprit is different from the one thought of in 1933—the modern one is considered to be proprietary trading.   **5.58**

The Dodd-Frank Act sets out a number of reforms to the regulation of banks and saving associations. These focus on a range of matters, namely improving the way regulators cooperate with one another to the way examinations are conducted and decisions surrounding enforcement matters. However, it includes a prohibition on banking entities from 'engaging in proprietary trading and acquiring or retaining any equity, partnership, or other ownership interest in or sponsoring a hedge fund or a private equity fund'.[175] The prohibition primarily applies to depository institutions that benefit from FDIC deposit insurance. The scope of the rules applies to banks' domestic and international operations so the impact is far reaching. The Dodd-Frank Act requires the federal bank agencies, the Securities and Exchange Commission, and Commodity Futures Trading Commission to consult with one another to ensure a level of consistency in the application of the prohibition across the various sectors of the financial system. The prohibition is by no means a carte blanche   **5.59**

---

[170] 12 USC § 24 (seventh).

[171] See, eg, *Nations Bank v Variable Annuity Life Insurance Co*, 513 US 251 (1995).

[172] B Shull, 'Financial modernisation legislation in the United States: Background and implications' (2000) UNCTAD Discussion Paper No 151, UNCTAD/OSG/DP/151, 8.

[173] OCC, *A Guide to the National Banking System* (2005) 13. See also OCC, *Activities Permissible for a National Bank* (2005).

[174] Ibid.

[175] § 619.

ban; it does not apply to a whole host of trading activities such as underwriting or market making activities.[176] Moreover, the prohibition does not extend to the sale or securitization of loans. However, banks will be required to maintain 5 per cent of the credit risk associated with these instruments to ensure they have enough skin in the game to incentivize them to monitor quality of the business underlying the financial activities.

5.60   The Economic Growth, Regulatory Relief and Consumer Protection Act 2018 removed the Volcker Rule limitation that prohibited a bank-affiliated investment adviser from using its name on hedge funds and private equity funds, with certain qualifying conditions. The Act also made small banks exempt from the Volcker Rule, where they have less than $10 million in assets and have total trading assets and trading liabilities accounting for 5 per cent or less of total assets. In 2019 the FDIC and the OCC signed the 'Revisions to Prohibitions and Restrictions on Proprietary Trading and Certain Interests in, and Relationships with, Hedge Funds and Private Equity Funds' (2019 Final Rule), which simplified and reduced the compliance requirements of the Volker Rule. The changes include creating a three-tiered approach to apply the programme to banks based on the size of their trading assets.

5.61   The 2020 Final Rule, introduced by the OCC, FDIC, SEC and CFTC modified the Volcker Rule again. These amendments reduce the extraterritorial effects on foreign funds, expands permissible transactions with covered funds and permits banks to engage in certain fund activities.

B. Safety and Soundness

5.62   The Dodd-Frank Act introduces a vast number of reforms to primarily improve the safety and soundness of depository institutions, BHCs, and non-bank financial companies classed as a potential threat to US financial stability. In addition to this, the safety and soundness of banks is now considered from a forward-looking perspective. Each regulatory and supervisory agency has constructed their own forward-looking approach associated with reforms to their supervisory responsibilities and capital and liquidity requirements.[177] Another element to this is the introduction of resolution plans which are addressed in Chapter 6.

5.63   Safety and soundness is a central tenet of US banking regulation, supervision, and enforcement. The provision was first incorporated in US banking regulation with the enactment of the Banking Act of 1933 to act as a benchmark to deal with bank mismanagement.[178] In accordance with USCA 1831 p-1, federal agencies have in place measures to fulfil the standard of safety and soundness. The federal agencies can require banks that do not meet the standard of safety and soundness to correct the 'deficiencies' identified by them. In exceptional circumstances a lack of compliance with the safety and soundness provision can

---

[176] § 619 amended by adding § 13(d)(1)(B)–(J).

[177] Board of Governors of the Federal Reserve System, Federal Deposit Insurance Corporation, Office of the Comptroller of the Currency, Office of Thrift Supervision, 'Agencies to Begin Forward-Looking Economic Assessments' (OCC, 25 February 2009) <http://www.occ.gov/news-issuances/news-releases/2009/nr-ia-2009-14.html>.

[178] Banking Act of 1933, § 30.

give rise to a variety of enforcement sanctions exercised by the federal agencies.[179] The provision is frequently referred to but rarely defined in the statutes, thus reliance is placed on the intent of Congress, the judiciary, and the regulators to provide some clarity as to its meaning.

The principle of safety and soundness is purposefully left in an ambiguous state in the statute books in light of the fact that it needs to evolve with the changing expectations of those at the helm of managing banks and their risks. To assist with its evolving nature, particular responsibility for its scope has traditionally been left to the regulators to articulate acts and omissions considered to threaten the safety and soundness of those institutions they charter or confer membership upon. The statutes have occasionally assisted in clarifying the scope of safety and soundness by prescribing certain acts or omissions considered to be associated with it. But the reason for its first appearance on the statute books seems to be rather unclear. The early rationale of the principle was to enable regulators to remove bank directors who failed to comply with their warnings to avoid 'unsafe and unsound' practices. As Holzman explains, the principle was a tool conferred on regulators by Congress to ensure their decisions and warnings were acted upon with the appropriate level of care and attention.[180] Indeed, the subsequent use of the principle to protect the deposit insurance fund adds further weight to the authority of regulators, with the power to withdraw a bank from the insurance scheme if it failed to comply with their directions. According to Schooner, for instance, the safety and soundness standard is a mechanism to 'guard against the threat of bank insolvency'.[181] In addition to it being a term used to direct bank behaviour, the principle of safety and soundness is considered to be a mechanism to reduce regulatory forbearance by having in place provisions that assist in articulating what is considered to be under the umbrella of 'safety and soundness' and triggers to initiate regulatory intervention, as with the provisions regarding prompt corrective action. According to Baxter, 'safety and soundness has been a principal concern driving a "cradle to the grave" regime of tight regulation' that has underpinned both Federal and State bank regulation.[182] In light of the recent financial crisis it has been necessary for US institutional regulators to take into account the wider macroprudential risks and the risks posed by the financial sectors as a whole or in part when considering the resilience of individual institutions that are part of it. According to a recent GAO report,[183] as a result, staff said they learned that financial stability oversight requires a different perspective and a different, more global approach that considers, among other things, the interconnectedness of financial institutions and their activities. In retrospect, staff noted that stronger bank capital standards—notably those relating to the quality of capital and the amount of capital required for banks' trading book assets—and

5.64

---

[179] For a critical look at the way regulators examine banks in accordance with the 'safety and soundness' standard see GAO, 'Bank examination quality. FRB examinations and inspections do not fully assess bank safety and soundness', Report to Congressional Committees, GAO/AFMD-93-13, February 1993.

[180] TL Holzman, 'Unsafe or Unsound Practices: Is the Current Judicial Interpretation of the Term Unsafe and Unsound?' (2000) 19 *Annual Review of Banking Law* 428.

[181] HM Schooner, 'Fiduciary Duties' Demanding Cousin: Bank Director Liability for Unsafe or Unsound Banking Practices' (1995) 63 *George Washington Law Review* 190.

[182] LG Baxter, 'The Rule of Too Much Law? The New Safety/Soundness Rulemaking: Responsibilities of the Federal Banking Agencies' (1993) 47 *Consumer Finance Law Quarterly Report* 211.

[183] GAO, *Bank Regulation, Lessons Learned and a Framework for Monitoring Emerging Risks and Regulatory Response* (25 June 2015) <http://www.gao.gov/assets/680/670997.pdf>.

more attention to the liquidity risks faced by the largest, most interconnected firms would have made the financial system as a whole more resilient.[184]

5.65   The principle of safety and soundness has not been formally defined in the statutes, as mentioned above, but it has spawned a considerable level of judicial attention as to its scope and meaning.[185] This attention has tended to rely on the interpretation provided by John Horne in his written memorandum during the debate on the Financial Institutions Supervisory Act 1966.[186] This memorandum is cited in a number of cases by various academics as a generic interpretation of safety and soundness. It refers to the lack of clarity over terms such as fraud and negligence as necessary in order to capture the evolving nature of banking business. But more specifically Horne states that 'an "unsafe or unsound practice" embraces any action, or lack of action ... the possible consequences of which, if continued, would be abnormal risk or loss or damage to an institution'.[187] Notwithstanding the definitional challenges, the work of the regulators and the courts has spawned a detailed and complex web of requirements and expectations that give flesh to the idea of safe and sound banking.

5.66   A central plank of the supervisory and examination decision-making process is the CAMELS rating system, known by the acronym for its six key features: Capital, Asset Quality, Management, Earnings, Liquidity, and Sensitivity to Market Risk. In many respects the rating system provides the evidence for the decisions associated with the above discussion of safety and soundness, capital and liquidity shortfalls, and other enforcement actions associated with shortfalls in bank governance and management. The ratings also reflect on these matters relative to the size and complexity of banks' operations. The rating is calibrated between 1 and 5 and determines the intensity of supervisory intervention, with 1 connoting the highest rating and requiring the least supervisory intervention, and 5 the lowest rating and requiring the most supervisory intervention.

5.67   A key determiner of the problems at banks has traditionally been the level of capital they hold at a given point in time as it determines what action the bank and its management are required to take if it is considered a threat to itself and ultimately to the FDIC deposit insurance fund. The regulator under the prompt corrective action (PCA) powers could determine if a bank is either well capitalized, adequately capitalized, undercapitalized, significantly undercapitalized, or critically undercapitalized. The categorization determines how the regulator will intervene and what the banks will be expected to do to improve the capital position. The extensive review of PCA directives during the financial crisis found that a number of bank failures could have been prevented if a more sophisticated set of triggers in addition to capital levels were used, which would have enabled timely intervention in the bank's problems in order to turn its affairs around and improve its capital position.[188] A strategy of aggressive growth and lack of appropriate attention to asset quality, counterparty default risk, and loan concentration were common factors amongst those banks

---

[184] Ibid at 28.

[185] For a jurisprudential analysis of safety and soundness and the policy implications of the various interpretations see Holzman, *supra* n 193.

[186] J Horne, Memorandum submitted to the Chairman of the Senate Committee on Banking and Currency (1996) 112 Congress, Record 26.

[187] Ibid at 474.

[188] GAO, *Bank Regulation: Modified Prompt Corrective Action Framework Would Improve Effectiveness* (23 June 2011) <http://www.gao.gov/assets/330/320102.pdf>.

failing. Moreover, supervisors had already initiated either formal or informal enforcement intervention for reasons associated with their ultimate demise. The recent GAO report[189] has highlighted the complexity and challenges regulators face associated with non-capital triggers, especially the risk of triggering a panic if intervention was disclosed somewhat prematurely by market standards.

C. Capital and Liquidity Requirements

The financial crisis highlighted the immediate limits of capital and liquidity requirements to cushion against potential losses their business activities may give rise to. The reforms referred to as the Collins Amendment were initiated by the FDIC and introduced in phases by the individual regulators before the Basel III reform measures were fully adopted.[190] These reforms to capital requirements and liquidity requirements introduced by the Dodd-Frank Act applied to insured deposit-taking institutions as well as banking holding companies and those non-bank financial companies classed as systemically significant. The US regulators moved towards implementing Basel III in 2013 to ensure their respective depository institutions moved towards compliance with the international minimum standards.[191] The impact of the move towards international standards was not without its criticisms due to the increased compliance costs and the impact of less credit on offer in the economy. Moreover, the impact of Basel III on smaller banks was considerable in comparison to the larger national banks. Nevertheless, the aim of Basel III is to improve the resilience of the banking system as a whole from both a domestic and international perspective by putting in place a more resilient level playing field. Notwithstanding the concerns raised about the impact of Basel III and the cost of compliance, US banks are expected to comply with the new requirements with little problem in the short to medium term. According to research undertaken by the GAO on the impact of Basel III in the US, over '90% of bank holding companies currently meet new requirements and those with insufficient capital would need to raise about $4 billion to $5 billion in capital to cover the capital shortfall and meet the requirements'.[192]

5.68

---

[189] GAO, *Lessons Learned and a Framework for Monitoring Emerging Risks and Regulatory Response* (25 June 2015) 24–31.

[190] The Collins Amendment introduces minimum leverage requirements and risk-based capital requirements for insured depository institutions, bank holding companies, and significant non-bank financial companies. The Amendment means that the capital requirements applied to depository institutions will also apply to the bank holding company. These amendments will eventually mean the leverage requirements and risk-based capital requirements will need to be designed to take into account the various activities undertaken by the above institutions. The minimum risk-based capital ratio is tier 1 capital of 6 per cent total capital ratio of 10 per cent and the minimum leverage ratio of 5 per cent, to be judged as well capitalized. The leverage ratio will attempt to curb the level of exposure recently seen during this period of crisis.

[191] For the Treasury's Office of Comptroller of the Currency and the Federal Reserve Board: Regulatory Capital Rules: Regulatory Capital, Implementation of Basel III, Capital Adequacy, Tradition Provisions, Prompt Corrective Action, Standardized Approach for Risk-weighted Assets, Market Discipline and Disclosure Requirements, Advanced Approaches Risk-Based Capital Rule, and Market Risk Capital Rule; Final Rule, 78 Fed Reg 62018 (11 Oct 2013) and for the Federal Deposit Insurance Corporation: Regulatory Capital Rules: Regulatory Capital, Implementation of Basel III, Capital Adequacy, Tradition Provisions, Prompt Corrective Action, Standardized Approach for Risk-weighted Assets, Market Discipline and Disclosure Requirements, Advanced Approaches Risk-Based Capital Rule, and Market Risk Capital Rule; Interim Final Rule, 78 Fed Reg 55340 (10 Sept 2013). With minor changes, the Federal Deposit Insurance Corporation rule became a final rule in April 2014. See 79 Fed Reg 20754 (14 April 2014).

[192] At p 15.

5.69   The US divides the banking sector into those banks required to comply with either the standardized or the advanced approach. Those banks with assets of $250 billion or more are required to comply with the advanced approach. All banks are required to comply with the minimum capital ratio including the common equity Tier 1 capital ratio to total risk weighted assets; the capital conservation buffer and the leverage ratio. However, only those banks designated as requiring compliance with the advanced approach are required to comply with the countercyclical capital buffer and the supplementary leverage ratio and the full liquidity coverage ratio. As of January 2018, banking organizations and Category III organizations must also maintain a minimum supplementary leverage ratio of 3 per cent, based on the Basel Committee's leverage ratio. The banking agencies have also established enhanced supplementary leverage ratio standards for the eight BHCs identified by the Financial Stability Board as G-SIBs. The US G-SIBs are also subject to a risk-based capital surcharge buffer. In addition to the Basel III requirements, a variety of other requirements are also in place to improve the resilience of the financial system the Comprehensive Capital Analysis and Review (CCAR) for BHCs with assets above $50 billion. For example, to submit to the FRB an annual capital plan to demonstrate how BHCs can maintain capital and liquidity requirements under stress scenarios. The OCC also undertakes a procedure to require its depository institutions to also undertake forward-looking capital planning.[193] The FRB and the OCC are required to review the capital plan to determine whether the arrangements to manage capital are appropriate. The introduction of the capital planning exercise is an example of the supervisor's forward-looking approach in an attempt to get the group entity to assess the future capital needs relative to their respective legal structure and complexity of their business activities. The respective supervisor can also, through the requirement to produce resolution plans, require the institution to increase their capital and liquidity levels if they do not consider them to be 'credible' or satisfy them that resolution is unlikely to be orderly. The FSOC has asked the Federal Reserve and FDIC to continue to implement their authority in a manner that fosters sound resolution planning and better prepares firms and authorities for a rapid and orderly resolution under the Bankruptcy Code.[194]

5.70   A significant component of the wider capital requirements reform has been the focus on funding and liquidity risk management.[195] These elements of prudential supervision are crucial as they equally give rise to insolvency problems. However, in this case the speed with which banks could find themselves in such a position needs managing better which is what the Notice intends to achieve. The Notice highlights the importance of depository institutions managing liquidity risk in a way that is 'commensurate with the institution's complexity, risk profile and scope of operations'.[196] It defines liquidity as 'a financial institution's capacity to meet its cash and collateral obligations at a reasonable cost. Maintaining an adequate level of liquidity depends on the institution's ability to efficiently meet both expected

---

[193] Office of the Comptroller of the Currency, 'Guidance for Evaluating Capital Planning and Adequacy', OCC Bulletin 2012-16 (7 June 2012).

[194] FSOC, 2014 Annual Report, 11 <http://www.treasury.gov/initiatives/fsoc/Documents/FSOC%202014%20Annual%20Report.pdf>.

[195] The Office of the Comptroller of the Currency (OCC), Board of Governors of the Federal Reserve System (FRB), Federal Deposit Insurance Corporation (FDIC), the Office of Thrift Supervision (OTS), the National Credit Union Administration Interagency Policy Statement on Funding and Liquidity Risk Management, 17 March 2010.

[196] Ibid at 1.

and unexpected cash flow and collateral needs without adversely affecting either daily operations or the financial condition of the institution.'[197] The Notice sets out the context to mitigate liquidity risk by referring to effective corporate governance to manage liquidity risk as part of its corporate strategy and the need to assess the extent to which it can access funds from other sources. In the latter case there is a need to assess this on a short, medium, and long-term basis as sources of funds can change over time. In light of this, an unencumbered set of liquid assets to act as a cushion and contingency funding plans for an emergency liquidity event are required.[198] In the latter case the banks will be expected to undertake stress testing to gauge the impact and the way it could cope with it in terms of its liquidity needs and the likelihood of other sources being unavailable. Overall the Notice recommends 'that an independent party regularly reviews and evaluates the various components of the institution's liquidity risk management process.'[199] These measures are a welcome addition as they reinforce the need for more intensive oversight of liquidity in an area which had been neglected in comparison to efforts to improve capital requirements.

D. Stress Testing

Stress testing is a central plan of the US forward-looking approach by which an assessment   **5.71**
can be made of the resilience of banks and their groups to stress situations considered likely presently or in the future both at enterprise and scenario level. As explained by Bernanke:[200]

> First, stress tests complement standard capital ratios by adding a more forward-looking perspective and by being more oriented toward protection against so-called tail risks; by design, stress tests help ensure that banks will have enough capital to keep lending even under highly adverse circumstances. Second, as applied by the Federal Reserve, the stress tests look horizontally across banks rather than at a single bank in isolation. This comparative approach promotes more-consistent supervisory standards. It also provides valuable systemic information by revealing how significant economic or financial shocks would affect the largest banks collectively as well as individually. Third, the disclosures of stress test results promote transparency by providing the public consistent and comparable information about banks' financial conditions.

The FRB, FDIC, and the OCC have incorporated stress testing into their approach to under-   **5.72**
take their respective responsibilities.[201] The stress tests are undertaken on two levels, from a supervisory perspective and by the institutions themselves depending on the size of their balance sheet and with special arrangements for foreign banking organizations depending

---

[197] Ibid at 2.
[198] Ibid at 10.
[199] Ibid at 14.
[200] BS Bernanke, 'Stress Testing Banks: What Have We Learned?', 8 April 2013, Speech at the *Maintaining Financial Stability: Holding a Tiger by the Tail* financial markets conference sponsored by the Federal Reserve Bank of Atlanta, Stone Mountain, Georgia <http://www.federalreserve.gov/newsevents/speech/bernanke201304 08a.htm>.
[201] Annual Stress Test, 77 Fed Reg 62417 (15 Oct 15, 2012) (FDIC) and 77 Fed Reg 61238 (9 Oct 2012) (OCC); Annual Company-Run Stress Test Requirements for Banking Organisations With Total Consolidated Assets Over $10 Billion Other Than Covered Companies, 77 Fed Reg 62396 (12 Oct 2012); OCC, Dodd-Frank Act Stress Testing (DFAST) Reporting Instructions, OCC Reporting Form DFAST-14A, December 2014 <http://www.occ. gov/tools-forms/forms/bank-operations/DFAST-14A-Template-Instructions.pdf>.

on the arrangements of the home regulator.[202] Stress testing is quite possibly the most explicit example of the supervisors' tools to look at depository institutions and groups from a forward-looking perspective and ascertain the extent to which they can manage future risks. The FRB requires bank and non-bank groups that have US$50 billion in consolidated assets to undertake annual stress tests. One aim of the Dodd-Frank Act Stress Testing (DFAST) is to design more tailor-made supervisory examinations for the respective institutions according to the results of the stress testing. Moreover, the outcome of the results provides insights into the institutions' capital positions and the resilience of their capital cushion to emerging shocks. Following President Biden's executive order and the 'whole government' approach to climate change, the Federal Reserve requires banks to measure climate change risk and what steps they are taking to mitigate it. Banks now need to include in their stress tests an understanding of how their portfolios would perform under a range of climate change scenarios, including physical risks such as flooding, drought, and wildfires as well as sector shocks, comparing how oil and gas loans would perform against renewable energy loans. The FRB reported the results from the 2020 stress test, finding that despite suffering substantial losses under a 'severely adverse' scenario, large banks could continue lending to businesses and households. The Federal Reserve's 2021[203] stress test scenario examined by hypothetical scenarios how banks would fare if the economy dipped back into recession during the first three months of the year, nonetheless concluded large banks could continue to maintain lending levels to the real economy.

E. The Directors' Duties

5.73 The federal regulators articulate the practical responsibilities and duties of directors to ensure compliance with their fiduciary duties. The board of directors of a national or state member bank is required to have at least five and no more than 25 members to be properly constituted.[204] A bank director has the responsibility of both directing the bank strategically in its affairs and overseeing its management as they undertake their work. Indeed, the FDIC, for example, contends that the board of directors is 'the source of all authority and responsibility'.[205] It is the board's responsibility to appoint and remove executive officers and managers, and hence it is the board's responsibility to ensure that appointees are suitable for their positions. Therefore, boards of directors have the ultimate responsibility to ensure the bank's safety and soundness. In the execution of these responsibilities the directors are required to exercise diligence and loyalty towards the bank's interests. In order to ascertain whether a director has exercised diligence, a number of factors have been noted as being significant: attending meetings, reviewing information about the bank's activities, acting with independent judgement, and reviewing audit and supervisory reports. These factors

---

[202] § 165(i)(1)–(2).

[203] Board of Governors of the Federal Reserve System (June 2021), *Dodd-Frank Act Stress Test 2021: Supervisory Stress Test Results* < https://www.federalreserve.gov/publications/files/2021-dfast-results-20210624.pdf>, (accessed on March 2022).

[204] Banking Act of 1933, § 31.

[205] FDIC, *Manual of Examination Policies, Management/Administration II, Directors*, available at <https://www.fdic.gov/regulations/safety/manual/Section4-1.html>; FRB, *Commercial Bank Examination Manual*, Section 5000.1, 1; see also *Rankin v Cooper et al*, 149 F 1010; (1907) US App (Circuit Arkansas).

evidence the extent to which a director is actively participating within the decision-making process, and in particular the level of scrutiny a diligent director would show.[206]

F. The Common Law Standard

The US Supreme Court articulated the broad federal common law duty of care owed by bank directors in its decision in *Briggs v Spaulding*.[207] Spaulding and others were directors of the First National Bank of Buffalo, which was placed into receivership after having sustained considerable losses through mismanagement and alleged failure to supervise the bank's activities appropriately. However, it was held that the directors, namely Spaulding, were not liable in negligence for not discovering the losses or preventing their occurrence.[208] The case articulated a standard of care based on what an ordinary prudent and diligent man would exercise under similar circumstances. The decision highlights that the question of negligence is relative, therefore each case needs to be assessed on its own facts.[209] The decision by the court recognized the balance that needs to be struck between an over-stringent standard of care and putting inappropriate individuals off from acting as directors of banks. In the decision of *Washington Bancorporation*[210] the court contended that the simple negligence standard should apply in specific circumstances, whereas the gross negligence standard should apply to more routine 'transactions and actions'.[211] Indeed, the court also contended that the standard of care applied in *Briggs* equated more with a gross negligence standard of care than a simple negligence test.[212] According to Stevens and Neilson, in most cases courts have found directors liable only when there is evidence of a gross dereliction of duty, whether that is evidenced by, inter alia, fraud or a conflict of interest.[213]

5.74

G. The Statutory Position

The liability of bank directors became a particularly prominent issue in the 1980s with the huge number of bank and thrift failures. The savings and loans failures led to the introduction of the Financial Institutions Reform, Recovery, and Enforcement Act of 1989 (FIRREA).[214] The FIRREA gives the bank regulators new powers to 'disapprove' of individuals who seek appointment at a director and senior management level on the basis that they do not have the appropriate 'background, qualifications, experience, and integrity'.[215]

5.75

---

[206] OCC, *The Role of a National Bank Director: The Director's Book* (1997) 69–76.
[207] *Briggs v Spaulding*, 141 US 132 (1891).
[208] Ibid at 163.
[209] Ibid at 152.
[210] *Washington Bancorporation v Wafic R Said*, 812 F Supp 1256 (1993).
[211] Ibid at 1266.
[212] Ibid.
[213] RW Stevens and BH Nielson, 'The standard of care for directors and officers of federally chartered depository institutions: It's gross negligence regardless of whether section 1821 (K) preempts federal common law' (1994) 16 *Annual Review of Banking Law* 169, 186.
[214] Public Law 101-73: Financial Institutions Reform, Recovery, and Enforcement Act of 1989 ('To reform, recapitalize, and consolidate the federal deposit insurance system, to enhance the regulatory and enforcement powers of Federal financial institutions regulatory agencies, and for other purposes').
[215] FIRREA § 914. 'Agency disapproval of directors and senior executive officers of insured financial institutions or financial institution holding companies', see specifically 12 USC § 1831i(e).

Section 212(a) incorporates § 1812(k) of the Federal Deposit Insurance Act (FDIA), which confers a federal statutory standard of care on bank directors and officers. Section 1812(k) enunciates a gross negligence standard as the minimum degree of negligence that needs to be evident before directors and officers of a federally insured depository bank can be held liable for personal damages.[216] The main point of contention with the introduction of the standardized approach in the FIRREA is the position regarding the standard of care prescribed by federal common law and standards espoused by individual states. Section 1812(k) provides a gross negligence ceiling on the matter of the standard of care expected of directors; thus it prevents states from exceeding that with the adoption of standards equivalent to willful neglect.

5.76   This point was articulated in the Supreme Court decision of *Atherton v FDIC.*[217] In this case City Federal Savings Bank was placed into receivership by the Resolution Trust Corporation (RTC), which brought an action against its officers and directors due to various bad loans the bank had made. The court examined the interrelationship of federal and state banking law to determine the scope of § 1812(k) and the applicable standard of care. It held that § 1812(k) provides the minimum level of liability of gross negligence when a state has adopted a more restrictive duty of care. It also held that § 1812(k) does not prevent states from adopting a higher standard of care equivalent to simple negligence. The rationale of the decision was to prevent states adopting a restrictive liability standard by placing a floor on what could be applied to federally chartered banks.[218]

5.77   The Dodd-Frank Act maintains the existing scope for personal liability of directors and officers.[219] The corporation with its powers for an orderly liquidation can pursue for monetary damages in a civil action in its capacity as receiver.[220] The action in civil law would cover actions for gross negligence as well as intentional tortious conduct as defined by state law.[221] The Dodd-Frank Act is silent on cases where a higher standard of care is required to be discharged by directors and officers, adopted in a state as explored as above. What is clear is the *minima* continues to be gross negligence as a floor.

5.78   The financial crisis has led to a number of claims that regulators have not held those deemed responsible for the crisis accountable. It is safe to say it is not without wanting to: from 1 January 2009, through 19 June 2015, the FDIC has authorized suits in connection with 150 failed institutions against 1207 individuals for D&O liability. This includes 107 filed directors and officers liability (D&O) lawsuits (54 of which have fully settled, one of which resulted in a favourable jury verdict, and one of which was dismissed and is on appeal) naming 815 former directors and officers. The FDIC also has authorized 64 other lawsuits

---

[216] J Shepherd, 'The Liability of Officers and Directors Under the Financial Institutions Reform, Recovery and Enforcement Act of 1989' (1992) 90 *Michigan Law Review* 1119; PA Lowry, 'The Director Liability Provision of the Financial Institutions Reform, Recovery and Enforcement Act: What Does it Do?' (1997) 16 *Annual Review of Banking Law* 355; RW Stevens and BH Nielson 'The standard of care for directors and officers of federally chartered depository institutions: It's gross negligence regardless of whether section 1821 (K) pre-empts federal common law' (1994) 16 *Annual Review of Banking Law* 169.

[217] J W *Atherton v FDIC,* 519 US 213 (1997); see also W Plotkin, 'V. Director and officer liability' (1999) 18 *Annual Review of Banking Law* 46.

[218] J W *Atherton v FDIC,* 519 US 213 (1997) at 228–229.

[219] Orderly Liquidation Authority § 210 Powers and Duties of the Corporation (f) Liability of Directors and Officers.

[220] § 210(f)(1)(A)–(C).

[221] § 210.

for RMBS, LIBOR suppression, fidelity bond, insurance, accounting malpractice, appraiser malpractice, and attorney malpractice claims. In addition, 80 residential mortgage malpractice and fraud lawsuits are pending, consisting of lawsuits filed and inherited.[222] A significant challenge to the success of these proceedings against individuals comes partly in the form of the business judgement rule. In the recent decision in *Loudermilk*, 2014 in which the FDIC as receiver initiated proceedings against nine officers and directors of Buckhead Community, the court needed to decide whether the directors could rely on the business judgement rule as a defence against a claim in negligence for the losses sustained by the bank amounting to $22 million.[223] In this decision the business judgement rule protected the directors from liability as they successfully established that while they may have erred in judgement in the decisions they made, they had not engaged in fraud or bad faith in reaching those decisions that ultimately led to the losses sustained by the bank. The decision highlights the importance of officers and bank directors to make sure decisions are made with the appropriate level of due diligence to ascertain the risks posed by them to avoid action in negligence; as it does not absolve them completely in such an action: 'the business judgment rule at common law forecloses claims against officers and directors that sound in ordinary negligence when the alleged negligence concerns only the wisdom of their judgment, but it does not absolutely foreclose such claims to the extent that a business decision did not involve "judgment" because it was made in a way that did not comport with the duty to exercise good faith and ordinary care'. The case went to trial in October 2016, the jury returning a verdict resulting in all the defendants being charged. The final compensatory damages were just under $5 million. It was less than a complete victory for the FDIC, however, who sought over $21 million in damages based on 10 bad loans. In 2019 the Eleventh Circuit dismissed the directors' appeal, rejecting their argument that the district court has abused their discretion in excluding evidence related to the Great Recession as an intervening cause of harm to the bank.

H. Other Enforcement Actions

The federal banking regulators have a number of enforcement options, embracing informal[224] and formal powers.[225] These can be subdivided into enforcement actions that are publicized[226] and those that are not.[227]   **5.79**

Informal actions are used in instances where the act or omission of the bank warrants a less severe sanction: commitments, board resolutions, and memoranda of understanding.   **5.80**

---

[222] FDIC, 'Professional Liability Lawsuits' <https://www.fdic.gov/bank/individual/failed/pls/>.

[223] *FDIC v Loudermilk et al* No S14Q0454, 11 July 2014; see more recently, *FDIC v Richard Allen Rippy; James D Hundley; Frances Peter Fensel, Jr; Horace Thompson King, Iii; Frederick Willets, Iii; Dickson B Bridger; Paul G Burton; Ottis Richard Wright, Jr; Otto C Buddy Burrell, Jr, On Appeal From The United States District Court For The Eastern District Of North Carolina in Case No 7:11-cv-00165-BO. Brief for Amicus Curiae the Chamber of Commerce of The United States of America Urging Affirmance*. Date February 2015.

[224] OCC, *Policies and Procedures Manual, Enforcement Act Policy,* (2001) PPM 5310-3 (Rev), 30 July 2001, 18–21.

[225] Ibid.

[226] For power to publicize enforcement actions see 12 USC § 1818(u); in relation to a prompt corrective action directive the authority to publicize is pursuant to 12 USC § 1831; for safety and soundness orders see 12 USC § 1831 p-1; for a description of publicizing enforcement decisions see OCC, *Policies and Procedures Manual, supra* n 236 at 15; Federal Reserve Bank, *Commercial Bank Examination Manual,* s 5040.1.

[227] See, eg, OCC, *Policies and Procedures Manual, supra* n 236 at 15.

Nevertheless they can vary in their severity depending on, for example, the 'nature, extent, and severity of the bank's problems and weaknesses' and the extent to which the regulator is confident that the bank can rectify the issues.[228] While the respective regulators can initiate these informal sanctions, they are deemed voluntary arrangements with no formal compulsion. However, Jackson and Symons point out that not complying with an informal action would lead to formal supervisory action, as it suggests a lack of commitment on the part of the bank to deal with issues as they arise.[229] A bank board resolution (BBR) is a resolution adopted by the board of directors to implement reforms initiated by the respective regulator.[230] A 'commitment' is a request by the regulators to resolve small issues at the bank.[231] A memorandum of understanding (MoU) builds on the former resolution of an action plan to rectify a number of minor problems at the institution.[232]

5.81   The approach changes with formal enforcement actions, which are publicized.[233] These are used where serious problems exist which affect, for example, the safety and soundness of an institution or a failure of compliance with regulatory rules.[234] The action taken by the regulators centres on whether the bank has acted in an 'unsafe and unsound' way which undermines, for instance, the interests of depositors.[235] The standard of 'unsafe and unsound' is wide, and amenable to various sorts of non-compliance. It refers to a broad range of incidents which are serious acts of imprudence that give rise to abnormal risks to the safety of a bank. The US courts have shed further light on the standard and have not simply accommodated the decision of the regulator. For instance, in a case of simple breach of contract, the court held that it is important to assess how remote the breach is from threatening the existence of the bank, and if it were to continue whether it would result in only a minor financial loss.[236] Written agreements are issued to ensure compliance in a broad range of areas which point to less severe forms of non-compliance.[237]The key sanction is the cease and desist order (C&DO).[238] This can require the institution or its affiliated party to refrain from unsafe or unsound practices, or violating applicable rules and regulations.[239] The order is accepted by the institution or individual before it is formally issued by the regulator; this avoids having to go through a lengthy administrative hearing simply to issue the order, which is already accepted by both sides. The order requires the deficient party to take appropriate action to rectify the problem that resulted in the order being given.[240] Under FIRREA a fine in the region of $1 million per day (although fines can range from $1,000 to $25,000 a day) can be levied on an institution or individual.[241] The maximum penalty for a single violation of the statute, depending on when it occurred and when it is assessed, is currently between $1.1 million and $2 million. Where the Department of Justice (DOJ) is able to

---

[228] Ibid at 7.
[229] HE Jackson and E Symons, *Regulation of financial institutions* (1999) St Paul, West Group, 335.
[230] OCC, *The Role of a National Bank Director: The Director's Book* (1997) 97.
[231] Ibid at 98; see also OCC, *Policies and Procedures Manual, supra* n 236 at 18.
[232] Ibid.
[233] OCC, *Policies and Procedures Manual, supra* n 236 at 4.
[234] Ibid at 7–8.
[235] 12 USC § 1831 p-1.
[236] *Gulf Federal Saving & Loan Association v Federal Home Loan Bank Board*, 651 F 2d 259, 264 (5th Cir 1981).
[237] For written agreements see, eg, 12 USC § 1818(b)(1).
[238] 12 USC § 1818(b).
[239] Ibid.
[240] 12 USC § 1818(b)(6).
[241] 12 USC § 1818(i).

show a continuing violation, the statute permits fines of $1.1 million or $ 2 million per day, or $5.5–$10.2 million per violation, whichever is less. The DOJ under President Biden's administration is expected to increase its focus on white collar enforcement against directors and financial institutions. The FIRREA has already been employed to address misconduct in connection with the government's Paycheck Protection Program (PPP). According to the DOJ, Slide Belts Inc made false statements on its PPP loan application when it omitted that it had filed for chapter 11 bankruptcy. The DOJ argued that the company and their CFO, CEO, and President are liable for just under $5 million as a result of the violations of the FCA and FIRREA. The issue was settled in January 2021. The level of the fine relates to the gravity of the failure, the question of recklessness and/or breach of fiduciary duty, and the benefit accrued by the individuals or institutions.[242] A fine could be levied for violation of a broad range of regulations, or for non-compliance with an existing enforcement order. For example, Credit L Credit Agricole, SA, France and its New York affiliates[243] were fined in total $13 million for not complying with a written agreement and additional 'unsafe and unsound' practices which pointed to poor management supervision of internal controls and risk management techniques in its business operation. The ultimate sanction the regulators can initiate is an order to prohibit or remove authority to conduct 'banking business'.[244] The FRB has initiated a number of prohibition orders in light of the number of banks put in to receivership with the FDIC.[245] In the case of Wells Fargo Financial Inc, a subsidiary of Wells Fargo & Company, a prohibition order has been initiated against a number of former employees for, inter alia, violations of law and unsafe and unsound banking, known to have falsified individuals' income and employment status to secure mortgages with the company.[246] More recently, five senior managers at Credit Suisse North American Offshore Banking business were prohibited from the banking industry indefinitely due to violations of tax law associated with maintaining undeclared accounts in the US.[247]

In March 2021 the FRB issued enforcement action prohibiting two directors from their office as a result of them breaching fiduciary duties and engaging in unsafe or unsound practices. Both were officers of the Central Bank & Trust, Mark Kiolbasa a chief loan officer and President and Frank Smith the CFO. They had attempted to solicit business, contacting Central customers and those employed at Central to persuade them to transfer to their new Farmers State Bank in Wyoming, whilst they were still employed at Central. The FRB also issued a prohibition from banking to Andrea Vella, a senior executive at Goldman Sachs for his role in Goldman's financing of a defrauded Malaysian sovereign wealth fund. He had failed to escalate the involvement of a person of known concern to the bank. He was prohibited from banking and fined $1.42 million. This power can be initiated in circumstances   **5.82**

[242] 12 USC § 1818(i)(2).

[243] Enforcement Action is available at <http://www.federalreserve.gov/boarddocs/press/enforcement/2004/20040310/attachment.pdf>.

[244] 12 USC § 1818(e)(1) and (7).

[245] Type of action: Prohibition from banking: <http://www.federalreserve.gov/apps/enforcementactions/search.aspx>.

[246] James Buckley Saunders, Wells Fargo Financial Inc, Des Moines, Iowa a nonbank subsidiary of Wells Fargo & Company, San Francisco, California, 8/26/2010: <http://www.federalreserve.gov/boarddocs/legaldevelopments/ordersother/section8/2010/20100826.pdf>.

[247] See <http://www.federalreserve.gov/newsevents/press/enforcement/20150511a.htm>; Markus Walder, Marco Parenti Adami, Susanne D Ruegg Meier, Roger Schaerer, and Michele Bergantino Institution-Affiliated Parties of Credit Suisse AG Zurich, Switzerland <http://www.federalreserve.gov/newsevents/press/enforcement/enf20150511a1.pdf>.

similar to a C&DO where there is evidence that an enforcement order has not been complied with, or 'safe and sound' rules and regulations have been violated or depositors' interests are threatened. However, the degree of culpability and knowledge on the part of the institutions or individuals would need to be extensive when exercising the power to prohibit them from operating in the industry.[248] The federal regulator can issue a suspension order with immediate effect if it considers the interests of depositors are under threat. The evidence would need to point to 'continuing disregard' of regulation, which is interpreted to mean 'heedless indifference to the prospective consequences'.[249]

5.83 The above powers are added to by the Dodd-Frank Act by enabling the FRB or the FDIC the discretion to ban Senior Executives and Directors if they have violated any law or regulation; any final C&DO; any written agreement; or another agency agreement; or participated in any unsafe or unsound practice or an act or omission of their fiduciary duties.[250] In such circumstances the individual could be given a written notice prohibiting participation in the company's affairs for two years.[251]

[248] 12 USC § 1818(e)(3).
[249] Docket No FDIC-85-215e, 1986 FDIC Enf Dec (p 14) 5069, 6741.
[250] § 213(b)(1).
[251] § 213(c).

6

BANKS IN DISTRESS

I. Sermons and Burials

The Governor of the Bank of England, Mervyn King, in his speech at the Lord Mayor's ban- **6.01** quet on 17 June 2009, a few months after the Banking Act 2009 ('the Banking Act') came into force, made it clear that he did not consider the present legislation to be sufficient to achieve financial stability; he said:

> The Bank of England has a new statutory responsibility for financial stability … To achieve financial stability the powers of the bank are limited to those of the voice and the new resolution powers. The Bank finds itself in a position rather like that of a church whose congregation attends weddings and burials but ignores the sermons in between. Like the church, we cannot promise that bad things won't happen to our flock—the prevention of all financial crises is in neither our nor anyone else's power, as a study of history or human nature would reveal. And experience suggests that attempts to encourage a better life through the power of the voice is not enough. Warnings are unlikely to be effective when people are being asked to change behaviour which seems to them highly profitable. So it is not entirely clear how the bank will be able to discharge its new statutory responsibility if we can do no more than issue sermons or organize burials.
>
> Whatever the ultimate shape of the structure and regulation of the banking system … change will be necessary.

6.02   The 'new resolution powers' referred to by the Governor are the subject matter of the rest of this Part on bank resolution. It also looks at the new reforms governing investment banks.

II. Northern Rock: The Catalyst for the Banking Legislation

6.03   The government's initial response to the failure of Northern Rock plc was to introduce emergency legislation: the Banking (Special Provisions) Act 2008 (BSPA). The BSPA is described in the preamble to the statute as:

> An Act to make provision to enable the Treasury in certain circumstances to make an order relating to the transfer of securities issued by, or of property, rights or liabilities belonging to, an authorised deposit-taker; to make further provision in relation to building societies; and for connected purposes.

6.04   This statute introduced a measure of 'last resort' for failing banks: public ownership. The legislation was itself a temporary, expedient measure, with a sunset clause after 12 months, to give the Treasury, the Bank of England, and the former Financial Services Authority (FSA) some breathing space in which to devise a more sophisticated process for dealing with failing banks and building societies: that process became law in the Banking Act as part of the Special Resolution Regime (SRR).

6.05   In the meantime, the BSPA was used, through secondary legislation, to deal with the failures of Northern Rock, Bradford & Bingley, Kaupthing Singer & Friedlander Limited ('Kaupthing'), and Heritable Bank.

6.06   The day after the BSPA had received Royal Assent, the government announced that it had acquired all the shares in Northern Rock, thereby bringing it into what was referred to as 'temporary public ownership'. Although the government, at the time when the legislation was enacted, had not intended to bring any other financial institution into public ownership;[1] when, in late September 2008, the former FSA determined that Bradford & Bingley no longer met its threshold conditions for operating as a deposit taker under the FSMA 2000, all that building society's shares were taken into public ownership and in exercise of powers conferred on the Treasury under the BSPA ('the Transfer Order'), the building society's UK and Isle of Man retail deposit business and its branch network were transferred to Abbey National plc by order. Subsequently, pursuant to further Order,[2] an independent valuer was appointed to determine the amount of compensation payable to persons who held Bradford & Bingley shares immediately before the transfer.

6.07   The government, under the Transfer Order, varied the terms of Bradford & Bingley's subordinated debt and, among other things, extinguished existing share options and provided for rights and obligations of lenders, bondholders, swap-counterparties, suppliers, and

---

[1]   Alistair Darling told the House of Commons on the first reading of the Bill: 'The Government has no intention at present to use the Bill to bring any institution other than Northern Rock into temporary public ownership.'

[2]   Bradford & Bingley plc Compensation Scheme Order 2008, SI 2008/3249 as amended by the Bradford & Bingley plc Compensation Scheme (Amendment) Order 2009. The original order provided for an appointment of the valuer, the amendment provided that on an application by the valuer the court may require a person to provide any information that is reasonably required for the purpose of assessing the amount of compensation payable by the Treasury.

other counterparties—which would otherwise be triggered by the transfer—not to be triggered. Like the BSPA, the Banking Act gives the Treasury and the Bank of England sweeping powers to modify contracts and trust arrangements.

In October 2008 when the former FSA determined that Kaupthing no longer met the **6.08** threshold conditions, the Treasury used powers under the BSPA to protect the depositors of that bank and the stability of the financial system. Kaupthing was put into administration in October 2008 pursuant to the provisions of Schedule B1 to the Insolvency Act 1986. A statutory instrument made under the BSPA provided for the transfer of certain rights and liabilities of Kaupthing to ING. This order required the administrators of Kaupthing to perform their functions in accordance with certain objectives overriding those in paragraph 3(1) of Schedule B1 to the 1986 Act. The administrators were required to ensure that Kaupthing provided the services and facilities reasonably required by ING to discharge its obligations in respect of the transferred rights and liabilities and to ensure that Kaupthing performed the other obligations that had been imposed on it under the Transfer Order. The Treasury had the power to ensure that these objectives were either achieved or disapplied.

The Heritable Bank plc was placed into administration on 7 October 2008. The next day the **6.09** retail deposit savings balances were transferred to ING Direct. The transfer was made pursuant to the Heritable Bank plc Transfer of Certain Rights and Liabilities Order 2008[3] made under powers conferred on the Treasury by the BSPA.

The Banking Act received Royal Assent on 12 February 2009, shortly before the temporary **6.10** provisions under the BSPA ceased to have effect. The Banking Act, section 262, gave the Treasury the power to repeal the BSPA by way of order and the substantive provisions of the Banking Act were to come into force by way of Treasury order.

The main provisions of the Banking Act came into force, by order, on 21 February 2009.[4] **6.11** Part 1 of the Banking Act gives the authorities the tools to deal with banking institutions in financial difficulties and replaces the temporary special provisions regime that was provided by the BSPA with a permanent SRR; Part 2 introduces the Bank Insolvency Procedure (BIP) which provides for the winding up of a failed or failing bank; and Part 3 introduces the Bank Administration Procedure (BAP) for use where part of a failing bank's business has been transferred, by means of the SRR, to a private bank or a bridge bank. The transposition of the Bank Recovery and Resolution Directive (BRRD) has extended the resolution regime to investment banks and financial groups. The chapter also explains the objectives to safeguard depositors and client assets and money, as well as resolution techniques to assist the resolution process and the UK's relationship and responsibilities with the European Union in resolution post Brexit.

---

[3] SI 2008/2644. There was a further statutory instrument that made certain amendments to the original order, SI 2009/310.

[4] Banking Act 2009 (Commencement No 1) Order 2009, SI 2009/296. By separate orders that came into effect on the same date, an order modified the provisions of Part 3 of the Banking Act, on administration, the Banking Act (Bank Administration) (Modification for Application to Banks in Temporary Public Ownership) Regulations 2009, SI 2009/312; Banking Act 2009 (Bank Administration) (Modification for Application to Multiple Transfers) Regulations 2009, SI 2009/313; Bank Administration (Sharing Information) Regulations 2009, SI 2009/314; Banking Act 2009 (Parts 2 and 3 Consequential Amendments) Order 2009, SI 2009/317; Banking Act 2009 (Third Party Compensation Arrangements for Partial Property Transfers) Regulations 2009, SI 2009/319; Banking Act 2009 (Restrictions of Partial Property Transfers) Order 2009, SI 2009/322.

III. The Institutions to Which the Banking Act Applies

6.12   The Banking Act has undergone various reforms over the years with the Financial Services Act 2012, the Financial Services (Banking Reform) Act 2013, and the transposition of the BRRD in 2014. In 2016 the Bank Recovery and Resolution Order amended the SRR for banks and investment firms to strengthen and clarify the UK's transposition of the BRRD. In 2019 the EU adopted the BRRD II. The Bank Recovery and Resolution (Amendment) (EU Exit) Regulations 2020 (BRRD SI) seeks to ensure that the regime under the BRRD II continues to work after the UK has left the EU. It implements the BRRD's policy and framework, but it assumes that there will be no cooperation with EU authorities. The Bank Recovery and Resolution and Miscellaneous Provisions (Amendment) (EU Exit) Regulations 2018 also amends the Banking Act so that the SRR functions effectively after Brexit. These reforms, inter alia, put in place an SRR and administration and insolvency procedures in various forms depending on the type of institution regulated by Part 4A of the Financial Services and Markets Act 2000 (FSMA 2000).[5] For the purposes of this chapter reference will be made to 'UK institutions' that have permission under 4A of the FSMA 2000 to carry on regulated activity in the UK and are regulated and supervised by either the Prudential Regulation Authority (PRA), the Financial Conduct Authority (FCA), or the Bank of England. The Bank of England is the designated resolution authority and the Treasury will have responsibility for matters relating to financial assistance that may be provided and/or decisions regarding temporary public ownership as part of the decision-making framework for an orderly resolution or insolvency. While the Banking Act was originally introduced to deal with banks in distress it has been significantly modified to apply to a range of UK institutions[6] such as building societies,[7] investment firms,[8] and central counterparties[9] and banking groups.[10] The Act provides the 'appropriate regulator' and the Bank of England as resolution authority the tools to deal with the UK institution that is experiencing financial difficulties.

6.13   The SRR regime in Part 1 of the Banking Act applies to building societies, investment firms (that hold client assets and or money), and banking groups. Parts 2 and 3 (insolvency and administration) have been applied to building societies and are modified significantly to apply to investment firms and central counterparties by secondary legislation.[11] The reforms to the Banking Act mean the appropriate regulator and the resolution authority have new responsibilities to cooperate and coordinate with their overseas counterparts to assist with cross-border institutions in distress either in the form of a group, branches, or

---

[5]   FSMA 2000, s 55A.

[6]   As a consequence of the insolvency of Lehmans the banking legislation was amended to add provisions to the Banking Act such that the Treasury may, through secondary legislation, make changes to insolvency law governing UK investment banks if that is deemed appropriate following a consultation exercise. A Consultation Document was published in May 2009. As noted in the Bank of England, Financial Stability Paper, July 2009, in practice most of the investment banking business in the UK is carried out by larger financial groups which often also have deposit taking and in some cases insurance businesses and, therefore, there is an issue as to whether an SRR for such complex institutions should be developed and, if so, with what objectives.

[7]   Banking Act 2009, s 84.

[8]   Ibid, s 89A.

[9]   Ibid, s 89B.

[10]   Ibid, s 81B.

[11]   Building Societies (Insolvency and Special Administration) Order 2009, SI 2009/805.

subsidiaries. The appropriate regulator and the Bank of England, as resolution authority, will be expected to work with the UK institutions and their respective overseas regulator, where applicable, via the supervisory-resolution colleges on the crisis prevention and crisis management to work out *ex ante* and *ex post* the most appropriate course of action to safeguard critical functions and minimize market disruption and safeguard financial stability. The Bank Recovery and Resolution (Amendment) (EU Exit) Regulation 2020 implements the regime under the BRRD directives, given that the UK has now left the EU. Member States of the EU no longer receive preferential treatment but are treated in UK legislation in the same way as other third countries. Under the BRRD, UK regulators were required to follow operational and procedural mechanisms to cooperate with other EU authorities, but the BRRD SI removes these mechanisms from the UK regime. Instead, UK authorities will share information with the EU in the same way as with third countries, on a case by case basis. The PRA has confirmed that it will continue to support supervisory cooperation with third countries.

IV. The Role of the Appropriate Regulator, the Bank of England, and the Treasury

The Treasury, the PRA, the FCA, and the Bank of England are required to have regard to specific objectives when using or when considering the use of the stabilization options in the SRR, the BIP, or the BAP. The 'special resolution objectives' are:[12]   **6.14**

(1) ensure the continuity of critical functions;
(2) protect and enhance financial system stability in the UK; an amendment to this objective was made under section 8(2) of The Bank Recovery and Resolution Order 2014. It now states:

Protect and enhance the stability of the financial system of the UK, including in particular by:
  a) Preventing contagion, and
  b) Maintaining market discipline

(3) protect and enhance public confidence in the financial system of the UK;
(4) protect public funds and minimize reliance on extraordinary public financial support;
(5) protect depositors, the deposit guarantee scheme, investors, and the compensation scheme;
(6) protect client assets and money;
(7) avoid interfering with property rights in contravention of a Convention right (within the meaning of the Human Rights Act 1998).

The 'special resolution regime: Code of Practice' ('the Code') was originally published in 2010.[13] It was revised again in 2015 and then 2017 to reflect changes made by the Bank   **6.15**

---

[12] Banking Act 2009, s 4.
[13] HM, Treasury 'Banking Act 2009: Special Resolution Regime: Code of Practice', March 2015. Section 5 of the Banking Act requires the Treasury to issue a code of practice about the use of stabilization powers, BIP, and BAP and specifies the areas on which guidance may be given. The statute requires the authorities to have regard to

Recovery and Resolution Order 2016 and has been revised once again in 2020 following the UK's exit from the EU and the BRRD SI, which implements the BRRD II rules in the UK. The Code makes the point that some of the terms used in the list of objectives are defined by the Banking Act and that the terms are 'context-specific'. The resolution objectives are considered relative to the circumstances and timing as threats to financial stability in terms of severity arise over time. The Code sets out the factors that the Authorities 'may' consider to be relevant.

6.16   The reforms have introduced a new Objective 1 of continuity of critical functions which extends to banking services. This is new in the Code and it refers to ensuring continuity of day-to-day banking services extending beyond just insured deposits. The Code explains: 'The term "critical functions" means activities, services or operations that, if discontinued, would likely lead to disruption of services that are essential to the real economy or disrupt financial stability.' Therefore, those dealing with distressed institutions need to be mindful of this matter both at the prevention and crisis management phases. This can include services provided to other parts of the business that are necessary for the banking activity to be undertaken. The original Objective 1 listed in the 2010 Code of protecting and enhancing stability of the financial system explicitly refers to preventing contagion, with the failure of one institution impacting on the confidence in others but also across investment exchanges and central counterparties. In addition to this, it also refers to maintaining market discipline while safeguarding this objective, in order to ensure that financial market intermediaries act in an efficient and prudent manner. This reflects the Bank of England's responsibility to ensure that resolution decisions reached consider the views of the PRA and FCA—in respect of them being mindful of their own objectives. The reference to 'public confidence' in Objective 3 is highlighted, since a loss of public confidence can be a catalyst for a bank in resolution to reach a point of insolvency. The official 'safety net' players need to ensure matters are communicated clearly and the public are made aware that their deposits are protected and the default of any potential bank will not lead to undue delays in the payout of compensation if that point has arisen. The resolution techniques explained below need to be mindful of the risks posed to public confidence. Objective 4 requires official safety net players to protect public funds. This requires the official safety net players to exercise their powers and use public funds if the need arises but to ensure that the costs of resolution are placed on the shareholders and creditors first and supported by the use of resolution funding arrangements to minimize not only the possible use of public funds but also public losses. Objective 5 highlights how the resolution authority needs to safeguard the interests of depositors and protect client assets. This is undertaken at two levels: at the resolution level with the exercise of the resolution tools to safeguard their interests and also at the insolvency level, with the modified administration and insolvency procedures by conferring on them a higher priority in terms of their claims. The reason for the seventh objective is explained in the Code: the inclusion of this objective acknowledges the importance of ensuring that any interference with the Convention rights is in the public interest

---

the Code. Before issuing the Code, the Treasury was required to consult with the FSA, the Bank of England, and the Financial Services Compensation Scheme (FSCS). See Banking Act, s 6. This was revised and published in December 2020. See <https://assets.publishing.service.gov.uk/government/uploads/system/uploads/attachment_data/file/945165/SRR_CoP_December_2020.pdf>.

and is proportionate.[14] This is intended to ensure that the exercise of powers under the SRR does not deprive a creditor or a shareholder of rights in circumstances that would give rise to a valid claim to compensation under the Human Rights Act.

The statute does not rank the objectives. The weight given to each of them will vary ac- **6.17**
cording to the circumstances of each case, in particular, the circumstances specific to the institution in distress and those relating to the financial system.[15]

The requirement that the Authorities should 'have regard' to these objectives in using or **6.18**
considering the use of the stabilization powers, administration, or winding up, gives the Authorities flexibility but, on the other hand, as Professor Roman Tomasic has written:[16]

> The subjective nature of the phrase, 'to have regard to' makes its effect somewhat uncertain, so that its use does not inspire confidence; it reminds us of other legal uses of this phrase, such as in the director's duties provisions found in s. 172(1) of the Companies Act 2006. Perhaps the SRR objects clause could have been expressed more objectively, as occurs with the goals of insolvency administration under para. 3(1) in Sch. B1 to the Insolvency Act 1986 …

The Bank of England's position on the objectives is that they are:[17] **6.19**

> Exactly in line with the approach taken in other countries whose SRRs are subject to an overarching financial stability remit or public interest test[18] … Indeed the United Kingdom provides more guidance on these issues than most other regimes through the Code of Practice published under section 5 of the Act.

While the Code does outline the factors that the Authorities may consider relevant when **6.20**
having regard to these objectives as explained below,[19] this does not overcome the concern that the goals are highly subjective.

The role of each of the UK Authorities is to determine whether:[20] **6.21**

(1) the institution is failing or likely to fail;
(2) it is not reasonably likely that action will be taken by or in respect of the institution that will prevent the failure of the firm;
(3) the action is necessary in the public interest; and
(4) the SRR objectives would not be met to the same extent by winding up the firm.

The PRA or FCA, as required in Chapter 4, section 7 of the Act (for investment firms solely **6.22**
regulated by it) will be responsible for making the determination that a banking institution or an investment firm is failing, or is likely to fail to satisfy the threshold conditions, and that it is not reasonably likely that action will be taken by or in respect of the institution that will

---

[14] The Code, para 3.25
[15] The Code, para 3.26; Bank of England News Release on Dunfermline Building Society, 20 March 2009.
[16] 'Creating a Template for Banking Insolvency Law Reform After the Collapse of Northern Rock: Part 2' (2009) 22(6) *Insolvency Intelligence*.
[17] The Bank of England's Financial Stability Paper No 5—July 2009, Peter Brierley, 'The UK Special Resolution Regime for failing banks in an international context'.
[18] The paper sets out the tests in certain other jurisdictions.
[19] The Code, paras 3.27–3.33.
[20] Chapter 4 of the Code.

enable the institution to meet those conditions. The Code of Practice has been amended to exclude reference to the threshold conditions, but the Bank of England paper published in 2014 makes explicit reference to the threshold conditions. In some respects the 2015 Code confers on the PRA and the FCA wider discretion to determine whether the institution is failing or likely to fail by eliminating the need to determine it with reference to the threshold conditions. The institution is required to exercise a number of preventative measures, namely utilize options set out in recovery plans and the convert assets and liabilities to restore viability. Moreover, the decisions by the PRA or FCA could involve intense supervision options to prevent payment of dividends or a debt for equity swap, for instance. The Bank of England has explained that the basis for deciding this trigger point is 'reasonably likely' which is not equated to 'certain' to.[21] It is likely to mean the PRA and FCA will intervene a lot earlier for the purposes of resolution, before the threshold conditions are called into question, since the bank or the investment firm will be expected to initiate the conversion or write down of assets and liabilities to restore regulatory capital and liquidity levels. In accordance with sections 6A and 6B, initiatives can be taken to recapitalize the institution by either 'cancelling or transferring common shares (known as Common equity tier 1, 'CET1') away from the original owners so that they bear the first losses, and write down (ie reduce the principal value of) 'relevant capital instruments' or converting them into CET1 when certain conditions are met. Relevant capital instruments are instruments that meet the definition of Additional Tier 1 and Tier 2 instruments under the Capital Requirements Regulation', at the point of non-viability.[22] It is unlikely, however, this on its own is going to restore viability. It is likely to be utilized in conjunction with one of the other resolution options which will be determined by the Bank of England. The Bank of England will need to determine, as the resolution authority, whether the intervention of the institution is likely to prevent the failure, whether the action is in the public interest, and whether SRR objectives are best met by initiating liquidation. The PRA and FCA as the supervisory authorities are in the best place to assist the Bank of England to determine condition 2, that the institution itself is unlikely to prevent its failure so triggering the use of the resolution powers and techniques.

6.23   The PRA or the FCA will also be responsible for the authorization of a bridge bank and ongoing supervision of institutions in the SRR.

6.24   The Bank of England will be responsible for the operation of the SRR, including the decision on which of the SRR tools to use, and its implementation (with the exception of the power to take an institution into public ownership). The Bank of England will also remain responsible for the provision of liquidity support.

6.25   The Treasury will be responsible for decisions with implications for public funds, for ensuring the UK's ongoing compliance with its international obligations, and for matters relating to the wider public interest. The Treasury will also be responsible for implementing any decision to take a bank into public ownership. The Treasury will also exercise a number of the ancillary powers under the SRR (particularly those where Parliamentary

---

[21] *The Bank of England's Approach to Resolution*, October 2014, 10.
[22] The Code, para 5.1.

scrutiny is required), including the power to modify the law and powers in relation to compensation.

The former Governor of the Bank of England, Mervyn King, made it clear that in his view **6.26** the decision to invoke the SRR should not be that of the regulator alone. His argument was that if the Bank of England had the right to trigger the regime in addition to the regulator this could prevent the risk of 'regulatory forbearance'—where banking supervisors delay too long before implementing the regime because of the concern that the need to implement the SRR is seen as a failure on the part of the regulators.[23] The government refused to agree to the dual control of the trigger for implementation of the SRR on the grounds that this would lead to dual regulation of banks which would be wasteful and costly.[24] The reforms meant the prudential supervisor and the Bank of England form the decision, in consultation, to place a firm in resolution.[25] It is then for the Bank of England to decide which resolution tool or tools to utilize to resolve the problems at the institution. The Bank of England will need to work with the Treasury to decide whether to place an institution into temporary public ownership or to utilize other public funds to recapitalize the bank.

A Banking Liaison Panel has been established under section 10 of the Banking Act to advise the Treasury on the effect of, among other things, the SRR and the financial markets. **6.27** The Panel members are participants in the banking and financial sector and representatives from relevant government bodies. The Panel gives formal advice to the Treasury.

While each of the Authorities has a role, the Treasury is clearly the senior partner. The PRA **6.28** and FCA decide whether resolution is required, but do not decide the means by which the bank is resolved. The Bank of England can decide how a bank is resolved, but is unlikely to be able to make such a decision without the consent of the Treasury in most cases because section 9 of the Banking Act prohibits the Bank of England from exercising any powers without the consent of the Treasury where:

(1) The Treasury issues a written notice to the effect that the exercise of the Bank's powers would contravene the international obligations of the UK.

(2) The Bank's proposed actions have 'implications for public funds'.

(3) The Treasury specifies considerations regarding public funds that need to be taken into account by the Bank of England before stabilization powers are exercised.

There are, in reality, unlikely to be many proposed resolutions for failing banks or investment banks. Notwithstanding this, if it is going to exercise either the stabilization powers **6.29** or initiate the bank insolvency procedure in the public interest, the Bank of England is expected to consult with the Treasury, PRA, FCA, and, in the latter case, the Financial Services Compensation Scheme (FSCS).

---

[23] Mervyn King's speech to the BBA on 10 June 2008 and his evidence to the Treasury Select Committee on 22 July 2008.

[24] This view was expressed by Ian Pearson, Economic Secretary to the Treasury, during the House of Commons committee stage debate on s 7 of the legislation on 6 November 2008.

[25] *The Bank of England's Approach to Resolution*, October 2014, 9. The updated version was published in October 2017, with the discussion of the Bank and the PRA's involvement in the resolution process at 7–9: <https://www.bankofengland.co.uk/-/media/boe/files/news/2017/october/the-bank-of-england-approach-to-resolution>.

V. Recovery and Resolution Plans

6.30   The recovery and resolution plans are an integral part of the decision-making process for the Authorities as they decide how best to prepare and resolve an institution in advance.[26] The plans provide an opportunity to the Authorities at the supervisory stages to address impediments that could hinder the resolvability of the institution. The recovery and resolution plans are the outcome of the dialogue associated with 'Living Wills', as it was evident to the authorities at the time that more advance planning would enable both the institutions and the authorities to work out the most orderly ways to address the problems associated with banks and investment banks in distress. The UK Authorities were in many respects first movers on the introduction of recovery and resolution plans and have required its largest banks to complete them, and a number of revisions have been required since then. With the stabilization tools now in place the authorities are better equipped to deal with institutions in distress, at a domestic and cross-border level. In many respects recovery and resolution planning are one of the most crucial parts of the pre-resolution agenda. As noted elsewhere, the recovery and resolution planning process complements the existing supervisory process but with resolution at the forefront of the process rather than at the tail-end. This could lead to a far more nuanced understanding of the risks within an institution than perhaps that which is gained by traditional supervisory returns. Moreover, robust planning at this stage also enables the authorities to work out the likely timing of intervention needed to ensure orderly resolution.

A. Recovery Plans

6.31   The recovery plan is primarily the responsibility of the firm.[27] The institution is responsible for drafting the plan on an institution and/or group level. The institution will need to decide the options it best thinks can address scenarios of distress across the core business lines and critical functions. The institution is expected to decide the options it considers suitable to remedy the scenario identified and the credibility of the option to realistically address the scenario needs to be evaluated. The recovery plan will need to have in place, with the respective external and internal stakeholders, appropriate lines of authority for decision making and communication.

6.32   The PRA expects the recovery option to explain the need to access central bank facilities against the possibility of winding down the business. This information would provide the PRA with an idea of how dependent the institution would be on central bank assistance if normal lines of finance were to seize and the extent to which it would be in the public interest to exercise the stabilization options. It would also require the institution to consider which stabilization options and/or whether the bank insolvency procedure or the bank administration procedure is the appropriate option. Moreover, it would need to consider the

---

[26]   PRA, Policy Statement, *Recovery and Resolution Plans*, PS1/15 January 2015. The policy sets out the final PRA rules on implementing the Bank Recovery and Resolution Directive (BRRD).

[27]   PRA, Recovery Pack, January 2015; *Supervisory Statement, Recovery Planning*, Statement 9/17, July 2020 version: <https://www.bankofengland.co.uk/-/media/boe/files/prudential-regulation/supervisory-statement/2020/ss917update-december-2020.pdf?la=en&hash=7EE218D863A63481884C23BD12C17AA72C147F81>

likely impact of the scenario on the wider market and the likely effectiveness of using a stabilization option. While the institution is expected to draft the plan, it is the PRA or FCA that will need to assess the credibility of the options put forward.

B. Resolution Plans

The resolution plan is primarily the responsibility of the Bank of England as the resolution authority, as to its effectiveness and credibility.[28] However, the institution is required to provide information about its corporate structure and business lines in order to determine the resolution strategy. In particular, the way the business lines are undertaken, namely by branches or subsidiaries will decide whether the resolution authority takes the lead or will need to cooperate to ensure that the resolution is appropriately coordinated and information can be shared. **6.33**

The information needed to complete the resolution plan are matters such as the group structure, the use of branches and subsidiaries, the size of core business lines, the level of capital required to support significant entities, the location and resources of the Treasury function, funding arrangements, intra-group guarantees, access to market infrastructure, and critical shared services. This will require information about back office functions and system and the timeliness of retrieving information. The utility of each stabilization option will need to be reviewed in light of this information and an assessment will need to be taken of the possible impediments to their use. This review should lead to the authorities deciding, with the institution, the stabilization option which is likely to be used in a given scenario. It will also provide the basis for deciding whether business lines and critical functions are transferable in order to reach the appropriate outcome. More importantly, firms are expected to assess the extent to which critical functions can continue uninterrupted if certain transfer orders were initiated. In 2018, the PRA announced that it would delay Resolution Pack Phase 1 submissions under SS19/13 to 2020 for the largest PRA regulated firms. This postponement has been extended to the end of 2022 in order to alleviate operational burden on firms in response to Covid-19. **6.34**

VI. Early Intervention and the PRA Proactive Intervention Framework

In circumstances where a bank is moving towards the point where it no longer has adequate capital or adequate liquidity, the regulatory authority intensifies its monitoring of the bank and makes greater demands that the bank take corrective action to raise capital or increase its liquidity than would have been the case before the recent crisis in the banking system. Thomas Huertas, in a speech to the London Financial Regulation Seminar on 19 January 2009 in which he used Bradford & Bingley as an example of early resolution of a banking institution in distress, said: **6.35**

---

[28] PRA, Part, Resolution Pack, January 2015; *Supervisory Statement, Resolution Planning*, January 2019. <https://www.bankofengland.co.uk/-/media/boe/files/prudential-regulation/supervisory-statement/2018/ss1913-update.pdf?la=en&hash=AF6C017CD36D5EE06321E150441D185252D97065>

Bradford & Bingley is a case in point. As the risk of Bradford & Bingley increased during 2008, the FSA intensified its monitoring of the bank, required the bank to undertake actions to mitigate that risk, including raising new capital. The FSA also worked with private sector investors to find a solution to the bank's problems. In addition, the FSA engaged in extensive contingency planning with the Bank of England, the Treasury and the FSCS so that a resolution (through taking the bank into TPO[29] and transferring its deposits to Abbey) could be effected over a weekend following the FSA's determination that the bank no longer met threshold conditions.[30]

6.36   The powers under the Banking Act can only be exercised where one of the regulators (ie PRA or FCA) has determined that two conditions, set out in section 7, are met, whether the bank or investment bank is to be resolved by stabilization options, by way of bank administration or wound up.

> Condition 1: The bank is failing, or is likely to fail, to satisfy the threshold conditions (within the meaning of section 41(1) of the FSMA); and
> Condition 2: Having regard to timing and other relevant circumstances it is not reasonably likely that (ignoring stabilization powers) action will be taken by or in respect of the bank that will enable the bank to satisfy the threshold conditions.

6.37   The PRA or FCA is not required to have regard to the Special Resolution Objectives when determining whether a bank is failing or has failed.[31]

6.38   In determining whether Conditions 1 and 2 are met, the PRA or FCA is required to ignore the effect of any financial assistance provided to the bank by the Treasury or the Bank of England, although this does not include 'ordinary market assistance' offered by the Bank of England 'on its usual terms'. The Banking Act also provides that the Treasury may, by Order, decide that a specified activity or transaction or class of activity or transaction is not to be treated as financial assistance for a specified purpose of that statute.

6.39   The PRA and FCA publish guidance on the threshold conditions, and how they expect their firms to meet them on a continuous basis.[32] The main conditions are, in brief, that the firm should conduct its business in a prudent manner; that the firm should maintain appropriate financial and non-financial resources, that the firm is fit and proper, and that the firm or its group can be effectively supervised. In addition to the threshold conditions, the PRA or FCA will need to decide whether the potential losses can be minimized or wiped out if it exercises the power to write down or convert existing assets and liabilities. The PRA or FCA will need to appoint an independent body to undertake the valuation to assist with that decision.

6.40   On Condition 2: the PRA and FCA have set out in writing the approach that they take to assessing whether this condition is met.[33] The PRA or FCA is required to ignore the issue

---

[29] Temporary Public Ownership.

[30] Although that speech was delivered shortly before the introduction of the Banking Act, the threshold conditions in the Bill were subsequently enacted.

[31] Banking Act 2009, s 7(6).

[32] See Banking Act 2009, s 7(5D): 'The threshold conditions' means the threshold conditions as defined by subsection (1) of s 55B of the FSMA 2000, for which the PRA is treated as responsible under subsection (2) of that section.

[33] Banking Act 2009.

as to whether the stabilization powers could resolve the situation, because it is considering whether alternative measures might resolve the position and not whether the stabilization powers will work.

The PRA or FCA will need to also address possible impediments to resolvability that could **6.41** create obstacles to the Bank of England exercising the stabilization powers.[34] The PRA or FCA could initiate such actions at the recovery planning stage and the Bank of England could initiate this at the resolution planning stage. The Bank of England published a Statement of Policy to explain how it will exercise the power to deal with possible impediments to resolvability.[35] This explains how the powers of the Bank of England could be exercised and how far-reaching they are, building on the Banking Act requirements: including directing the institution to take certain measures in order to address impediments to the utilization of stabilization powers and giving directions imposing requirements to amend group financial support agreements, limit business large exposures, dispose of assets, cease to carry on activities or observe restrictions on activities, cease new business lines, and ensure that critical functions can be operationally separated. The Bank of England is required to provide reasons for giving the direction, and provide a timeline for the institution to comply with the directions.[36]

The circumstances that the PRA or FCA may take into account depend on the nature of **6.42** their concerns about the bank, in particular whether these concerns relate to adequacy of liquidity, capital adequacy, adequacy of non-financial resources, and the prospects of the bank securing a material and relevant transaction with a third party. The PRA or FCA will also assess the reasons behind any likely or actual failure of compliance. Serious failures of management, systems, or internal controls may call into question the adequacy of the bank's non-financial resources or suitability.

The PRA has introduced the 'Proactive Intervention Framework' (PIF) to explain the struc- **6.43** ture of its supervisory decision-making process as its judgement about a firm changes and it considers the firm to be near 'proximity to failure'. The PIF is set out in five stages: Stage 1—Low risk to viability of firm; Stage 2—Moderate risk to viability of firm; Stage 3—Risk to viability absent action by the firm; Stage 4—Imminent risk to viability of firm; Stage 5— Firm in resolution or being actively wound up.[37]

The PRA will set out how it will intensify supervision and also the types of powers it will **6.44** initiate to move the institution away from the 'proximity of failure'.[38] At Stage 3 the PRA will have identified threats to the firm's safety and soundness and is expected to engage with the board and initiate options set out in the recovery plan. It could also change the firm's management and restrict its business activities. At the resolution level the PRA and the Bank of England are expected to set about putting in place the contingency plans drawn up for the firm. A firm at Stage 4 is considered to be at imminent risk to viability. At this stage the PRA will expect the firm to have initiated recovery options and will need to be satisfied that the

---

[34] Ibid, s 3A.
[35] The Bank of England's power to direct institutions to address impediments to resolvability, December 2015.
[36] Banking Act 2009, s 3B.
[37] PRA, *Approach to Banking Supervision*, October 2018, at 32: <https://www.bankofengland.co.uk/-/media/boe/files/prudential-regulation/approach/banking-approach-2018.pdf>.
[38] Ibid.

options are credible to resolve the problems at the firm. The Bank of England is expected to be in dialogue with the FSCS if the firm is to be wound up or if it is in the public interest to initiate the stabilization options. Finally, at Stage 5, the Bank of England has decided the firm needs to be formally in resolution or wound up. At this point the PRA is expected to decide whether the firm is failing or likely to fail to meet threshold conditions. The Bank of England will have placed the firm in resolution and is expected to be working with the FSCS in order for the FSCS to initiate a depositor payout or to assist with the transfer of depositor funds to either a bridge bank or a private purchaser.

6.45 The breadth of the scope for determining whether the Conditions are satisfied gives the Authorities flexibility, which enables them to react to different circumstances in a pragmatic manner. The rationale for this approach is that the Authorities will take steps to deal with a failing bank or a bank that is likely to fail before it is balance sheet insolvent and they will, therefore, be in a position to resolve the position of the bank quickly and preserve more value than would be the case were action only permitted once a bank was insolvent or on the verge of insolvency. The idea behind this is that the PRA or FCA will be less likely to indulge in 'regulatory forbearance' if, after a period of heightened supervision that has not remedied the problem, it can trigger the resolution of a bank that does not involve, at least at the outset, formal insolvency proceedings.[39]

6.46 The corollary of the appropriate regulator's flexibility in deciding at what stage to step in to resolve a bank is that it is difficult for the institution and financial markets to form any clear idea as to when and in what circumstances the Authorities will invoke any particular resolution procedure.

6.47 Furthermore, the flexible approach to bank resolution goes so far as to give Treasury order-making powers to make orders with retrospective effect. Section 75(3) of the Banking Act provides that:

> in so far as the Treasury consider it necessary or desirable for giving effect to the particular exercise of a power under this Act in connection with which the order is made (but in relying on this subsection) the Treasury shall have regard to the fact that it is in the public interest to avoid retrospective legislation.

6.48 In debates in Parliament the government, at the time, made it clear that this power was to be used to override law that prevented the SRR from operating in a timely fashion. The House of Lords Select Committee on the Constitution expressed the view that 'desirability' should not be a basis on which to allow ministers to change the law retrospectively.[40] The Committee had noted, in correspondence, that there had been no exact precedent for retrospective law-changing powers 'based on a minister's perception of what is desirable rather than what is necessary'. The Committee's report concludes that:

> We note Lord Myners' statement that section 75(3) of the Banking Act 2009 'does not set a precedent for the use of retrospective powers'. The fact of the matter is, however, that a precedent has been set. It is not, in our view, an acceptable precedent.

---

[39] See, eg, Financial Stability Paper No 5—July 2009.
[40] House of Lords Select Committee on the Constitution, 11th Report of Session 2008–09, Banking Act 2009: Supplementary report on retrospective legislation, HL Paper 97.

The government did not change its position; the government remains of the view that the **6.49** flexibility is required to enable the SRR powers to be used effectively in an emergency.

When the PRA or FCA determines that the Conditions are satisfied, the next step for the **6.50** Bank of England is the choice of the appropriate stabilization option.

VII. The Special Resolution Regime: Part 1 of the Banking Act

The purpose of the SRR is to address situations where:[41] **6.51**

> ... all or part of the business of a bank encountered, or is likely to encounter, financial difficulties ...
>
> The special resolution regime includes five stabilization options, the bank insolvency procedure, and the bank administration procedure.[42] For the purposes of this chapter only the five stabilization options will be discussed, along with the tools to ensure the stabilization options can be executed.

The five stabilization options are: **6.52**

(1) transfer to a private sector purchaser;
(2) transfer to a bridge bank;
(3) transfer to an asset management vehicle;
(4) the bail-in technique;
(5) transfer to temporary public ownership.

A banking institution does not have to be insolvent before the Authorities can use the **6.53** powers of the Special Resolution Regime. The Bank of England has explained that 'the regime permits resolution to occur before a firm is "balance sheet insolvent"'.[43] Thomas Huertas, in the same speech to the seminar on 19 January 2009,[44] explained the assessment of threshold conditions in the following terms:

> This is necessarily a judgment rather than a simple quantitative test, but the Bill plainly envisages the possibility that the bank could be put into resolution whilst it still has positive net equity. The resolution regime is very much an early intervention regime to allow the authorities to intervene well in advance of the point at which corporate insolvency procedures would permit intervention. This early intervention feature broadly implements the lessons drawn from the theory of early intervention and the practice of early intervention in other countries, namely that early intervention limits both the losses of the troubled institution in question as well as potentially society at large.

The SRR provides the Authorities with a number of procedures to deal with failing insti- **6.54** tutions if the public interest test is met and to achieve continuity of critical functions and

---

[41] Banking Act 2009, s 1(1).
[42] The latter two are considered in Chapter 7.
[43] *The Bank of England's Approach to Resolution*, October 2017 at 14 states: 'the regime permits resolution to be triggered when there is evidence a bank is failing or likely to fail, this can happen before it is "insolvent"; that is, before it can no longer pay its debts as they fall due or the value of its assets falls below the value of its liabilities'.
[44] In his speech, 'The rationale for and limits of bank supervision'.

maintain franchise value. This averts a crisis in the financial system at an early stage and thereby avoids insolvency and achieves an orderly resolution of the bank or investment bank's problems:

6.55   The stabilization powers could be exercised if the Authorities consider the following general conditions[45] and relevant specific conditions are met: Condition 1, the bank is failing or likely to fail, as set out in section 7(5C); Condition 2,[46] it is not reasonably likely the bank will be able to resolve its problems and avert Condition 1; Condition 3,[47] the stabilization powers need to be exercised in the public interest to achieve one of the resolution objectives; Condition 4[48] the resolution objectives would not be either fully or partially achieved by winding up the bank. The PRA and the Bank of England both need to factor into their decision financial assistance provided by the Treasury, and exclude this to determine whether the conditions are met.[49] The Banking Act also requires the Authorities to take into account specific conditions in respect of the private sector purchaser, bridge bank, or the asset management vehicle. The Bank of England is required to take into account the financial assistance provided by the Treasury and seek the Treasury's approval when deciding on the stabilization option.[50] In respect of an asset management vehicle, the Bank of England is required to satisfy two conditions: Condition A requires the asset management vehicle to be used with one or more of the other stabilization powers. Condition B requires the Bank of England to consider the adverse effect on the market due to the transfer of assets or liabilities and the liquidation of the assets; the transfer is important for the purposes of the bank or bridge bank, and to maximize the proceeds from the distribution. In respect of assessing Conditions A and B, the Bank is required to consult with the PRA, the FCA, and the Treasury since it will either impact on the continuing authorization of the bank or the bridge bank meeting the threshold conditions or the financial assistance provided by the Treasury.[51] Special Conditions are also attached to the use of the temporary public ownership. Condition A is that the exercise of the power is necessary to resolve or reduce a serious threat to the stability of the financial system of the United Kingdom. Condition B is that the exercise of the power is necessary to protect the public interest, where the Treasury has provided financial assistance or the Bank of England has provided extraordinary public support in respect of the bank for the purpose of resolving or reducing a serious threat to the stability of the financial system of the United Kingdom.

6.56   The Bank of England is required to assess the most appropriate stabilization options to utilize to achieve the resolution objectives. This will primarily have in mind the overall stability of the financial system and lead to safeguarding depositors and/or client assets. The stabilization options are likely to be used in conjunction with one another and so it is unlikely that a single stabilization option will resolve the problems at the bank or investment bank. In order to execute the stabilization options the Bank of England will need to execute a range of transfer orders of either shares or liabilities of the business, primarily to optimize

---

[45]   Banking Act 2009, s 7.
[46]   Ibid, s 7(2).
[47]   Ibid, s 7(3).
[48]   Ibid, s 7(4).
[49]   Ibid, s 7(5A)–(5B).
[50]   Ibid, s 8(1)–(3).
[51]   Ibid, s 8ZA(1)–(4).

the best outcomes to either restore insolvency, safeguard critical functions or safeguard depositors or client assets. Resolution needs to be executed by way of transfer tools of either shares, liability, or property—in whole, in part, or temporarily—to be executed at different points in time to achieve the best possible outcomes. These will be discussed later.

The Bank of England has set out the resolution process in three phases. At the stabilization phase, the Bank of England is expected to work out the most appropriate resolution options to utilize. In this phase the Bank of England is likely to utilize the institution's loss-absorbing capacity and/or one or more of the stabilization options. In this phase the Bank will need to assess the access to payment and clearing systems needed to continue in business. The success of executing resolution in many respects is essentially dependent on whether the recovery and resolution planning process is robust enough to ensure the timeliness and efficiency needed to achieve the resolution objectives. It is anticipated the authorities will need approximately 48 hours (the 'resolution weekend') to execute the resolution and transfers.   **6.57**

The second phase of dealing with institutions in distress is the restructuring phase, during which the Bank of England investigates the causes of the problems and attempts to restructure the business to secure critical functions. The stabilization options play a critical role during the restructuring phase. The restructuring phase takes place after the stabilization options have been initiated. The management or administrator of the institution will be expected to put together the reorganization plan, which will consist of a long-term plan of improving the overall viability of the business involving either sale of certain business lines and/or the winding up of loss-making business lines. The aim of the process is to restore or safeguard the franchise value of the business so as to ensure enough value in the business is retained.   **6.58**

The final phase is the exit from resolution. Ultimately, the Bank of England does not want to be burdened with a private institution lingering on its desk, so the assessment of the institution during the stabilization phase and restructuring phase needs to be mindful of the time frame within which the bank will be either wound up or will be in a position where its capital and liquidity position is stabilized so that it is sufficiently capitalized.   **6.59**

The private sector purchaser is quite possibly the option of first choice[52] and in some respects could be an option considered at the pre-resolution stage. To ensure the marketability of the bank that is distressed the option to undertake a full or part sale of the business means that the Bank of England has the discretion to restructure the business to best achieve the sale. The Bank of England can undertake a number of share and property transfers to execute the sale.   **6.60**

The second stabilization option is the bridge bank. The setting up of the bridge bank enables the Bank of England to transfer the critical function or functions to it to ensure their continuity. The new company is expected to be wholly or partly owned by the Bank of England. The Bank of England will transfer, in whole or in part, shares or property to the new bridge bank. This stabilization option enables the Bank of England time to work out the best options for the business and give it time to improve the business for onward sale in the future to a private purchaser. The bridge bank will need to be authorized by the PRA or FCA and   **6.61**

---

[52] Ibid, s 11.

meet authorization criteria. The Code sets out in detail the requirements for the running of the bridge bank and the expectations attached to the management body and strategic business aims.[53] The bridge bank will be wound down once it is either merged with another entity or ceases to meet authorization requirements, or it may be wound up by the Bank of England.

6.62   The third stabilization option is the asset management vehicle.[54] The Bank of England is expected to transfer to the asset management vehicle all or part of the business. The transfer will be primarily of the 'bad' part, in order to shore up the remainder for onward transfer to the bridge bank. Moreover, assets and liabilities from the bridge bank can also be transferred to the asset management vehicle to improve the viability of the bridge bank and its attractiveness for onward sale. The asset management vehicle will be wholly or partly owned by the Bank of England or by the Treasury. The aim of the asset management vehicle is to maximize the return on the distressed debt it has acquired and is likely to acquire during the resolution phase. The Code also sets out how the asset management vehicle is expected to be run and what its objectives will be.

6.63   In the case of using the asset management vehicle for distressed banking groups the PRA or the FCA is required to assess two further conditions to determine whether it should be used as a stabilization option. They need to consider whether the banking group can function properly if the transfer was to be completed and whether the transfer maximizes the proceeds of the distribution.[55]

6.64   The fourth stabilization option is the bail-in tool and it enables the Bank of England to ensure the existing shareholders' and creditors' interests are utilized first to restore viability of the bank or investment firm. The Bank of England is expected to produce a bail-in instrument to initiate the conversion or write down bail in on either a partial or full basis and issue resolution instruments, called 'certificates of entitlement' in the form of securities to the new owner, for instance. In order to ensure that all can be completed over the resolution weekend, the Bank may transfer the new securities to a third party depository bank in the short term on trust for onward transfer.[56] The Bank of England will focus in the first instance on the Tier 1 Common Equity. The Bank of England is able to either cancel, dilute, or transfer existing shareholdings so that they bear the first losses. The Tier 2 instruments are either reduced or converted to restore the level of Common Equity Tier 1 capital. Following this, if a shortfall still remains then the subordinated debt and unsecured senior creditors' debt will either be reduced or converted into shares or other securities in accordance with the hierarchy of claims in normal insolvency proceedings. The Bank of England is required to allocate losses proportionally equally in accordance with the ranking of creditors.

6.65   The Bank of England may appoint a resolution administrator[57] in the context of bank resolutions involving recourse to the bail-in tool.[58] It may do so either through a

---

[53]   Ibid, s 12(3)(a)–(e).
[54]   Ibid, s 12ZA.
[55]   Ibid, s 81ZBA.
[56]   *The Bank of England's Approach to Resolution*, October 2017 at p. 16: <https://www.bankofengland.co.uk/-/media/boe/files/news/2017/october/the-bank-of-england-approach-to-resolution.pdf?la=en&hash=FC806900972DDE7246AD8CD1DF8B8C324BE7652F>. For bail see pp 8 and 16.
[57]   Banking Act 2009, s 62B(1). The resolution administrator can be either an individual or body corporate.
[58]   *The Bank of England's Approach to Resolution*, October 2017 at p. 8 and p. 16.

separate 'appointment instrument'[59] or it may be included in a provision in a 'Part 1 instrument', which may include a mandatory reduction instrument, a share transfer instrument, a property transfer instrument, or a resolution instrument.[60] The institution of the resolution administrator and an outline of its functions have been introduced in the Banking Act in sections 62B to 62C through the Bank Recovery and Resolution Order 2014.[61]

The resolution administrator's main role is to hold any securities transferred or issued to it   **6.66**
in its capacity as resolution administrator.[62] The securities are held according to the terms of a Part 1 instrument,[63] and may provide limitations on the scope of the administrator's discretion in relation to the securities, for example, specifying the resolution administrator's rights and obligations[64] or that certain rights may be exercised only as directed by the Bank of England.[65] The resolution administrator is obliged to take 'all measures necessary to promote the special resolution objectives'[66] and have regard to those that may be contained in a Part 1 instrument or appointment instrument.[67]

Further functions which the resolution administrator may be authorized to perform in ac-   **6.67**
cordance with an appointment instrument or a Part 1 instrument[68] include managing the bank's business (or any power in this respect),[69] exercising any other of the bank's powers[70] or any power the Bank of England considers appropriate.[71] The administrator may also be required to produce reports to the Bank of England on any matter contained in the instrument[72] at the times specified therein.[73] Before exercising specified functions, the instrument may require the resolution administrator to consult specified persons[74] or be prohibited from exercising the former without the latter's consent.[75] Lastly, the resolution administrator 'may do anything necessary or desirable for the purposes of or in connection with the performance of the functions of the office'.[76]

The bail-in tool has a number of benefits which the other stabilization options do not,   **6.68**
such as the ability to resolve the problems without breaking up complex business activities that would take considerable amount of time to execute and last longer than the resolution weekend. There are two possible options of where within the group the bail in could occur. The first is referred to as the Single Point of Entry and the other is the

---

[59] Banking Act 2009, s 62B(2)(a).
[60] Ibid, s 62B(2)(b).
[61] In force: 1 January 2015, SI 2014/3329, art 1(2).
[62] Banking Act 2009, s 62B(4)(a).
[63] Ibid, s 62B(6).
[64] Ibid, s 62B(7)(b).
[65] Ibid, s 62B(7)(a).
[66] Ibid, s 62B(8)(a).
[67] Ibid, s 62B(8)(b).
[68] Ibid, s 62C.
[69] Ibid, s 62C(1)(a).
[70] Ibid, s 62C(1)(b).
[71] Ibid, s 62C(1)(c).
[72] Ibid, s 62C(2)(a).
[73] Ibid, s 62C(2)(b).
[74] Ibid, s 62C(4)(a).
[75] Ibid, s 62C(4)(b).
[76] Ibid, s 62D(1).

Multiple Point of Entry; these are executed either at the parent group level or subgroup level respectively. In the short to medium term, the group and/or subgroups remain intact and retain critical franchise value. It will be for the Bank of England to notify the PRA or FCA.

6.69   The fifth stabilization option that the UK Authorities can consider is temporary public ownership.[77] In this case the Treasury primarily takes the lead in consultation with the Bank of England. This stabilization option in the Code is referred to as a 'last resort' and is expected to be utilized once the other stabilization options have been exhausted. The Treasury in this case makes the transfer order to either the Treasury's nominee or the Treasury's wholly owned company. While not formal temporary public ownership, the BRRD has also introduced the public equity support tool which enables the Treasury to recapitalize the institution.[78]

6.70   The Treasury may bring the holding company of a bank into temporary public ownership.[79] If it is to do so, the Treasury is required to ensure at least 8 per cent of the liabilities are bailed-in to part reduce the losses.[80] A bank holding company may, however, only be taken into temporary public ownership if the PRA or FCA is satisfied that a bank in the group satisfies the general conditions set out in section 7 of the Banking Act. The Treasury is also required to be satisfied that it is necessary to take this action for the purposes specified in the conditions for temporary public ownership in section 9 of the Banking Act, to resolve or reduce a serious threat to the stability of the financial system or to protect the public interest. The Treasury will consider whether action in relation to the bank alone would be sufficient for the purposes of section 9 before taking a bank holding company into temporary public ownership. The Treasury will also balance the interests of relevant parties against the public interest in resolving the financial difficulties caused by the failing bank. The Treasury can initiate a partial transfer of the assets owned by the company's private sector purchasers. The limitations on partial property transfers provided for in sections 47, 48, and 69 of the Banking Act and the secondary legislation apply to these transfers. Where the Treasury takes a bank holding company into temporary public ownership, certain provisions of the Banking Act are also applied to bank holding companies by section 83 of the Banking Act.

6.71   The Code makes it clear that it is highly unlikely that circumstances will arise in which it would be desirable for the Treasury to take a holding company into public ownership where the holding company did not have a close connection with the operation of a bank or where the primary activities of the holding company were not closely related to financial services.[81]

---

[77]   Ibid, s 13.
[78]   *The Bank of England's Approach to Resolution*, October 2017, see p. 17 (para 1.38) and temporary public ownership on p. 13.
[79]   Banking Act 2009, s 82.
[80]   The Code, paras 6.53 and 6.73
[81]   The Code, paras 6.78.

VIII. The Impact of Share Write-down and Conversion, and Share Transfers and Property Transfers

Where the Authorities intervene to resolve a bank that is likely to fail or is failing, it is ex- **6.72** pected shareholders will bear the first losses. As part of the move for banks to have loss absorbing capacity (total loss-absorbing capacity (TLAC) and/or minimum requirement for own funds and eligible liabilities (MREL)) it will be mandatory for regulatory purposes to have capital instruments which will be expected to be written down once the institution reaches the point of non-viability (PONV). It is anticipated that the write-down of loss absorbing capacity up to approximately 8 per cent could significantly assist with turning the affairs of the institution around. During the pre-resolution phase the Bank of England is required to undertake a valuation of the bank's balance sheets and of its assets and liabilities to determine the size of the losses.[82] In the first instance shareholders bear the first losses through the power to write down and convert if: the institution meets (either outside of the formal trigger of stabilization options or part of the stabilization options) resolution conditions; it can only restore viability through a write-down; there is a capital shortfall despite extraordinary public financial support; or the viability of the banking group is called into question and requires the write-down power to be initiated in the interests of the group. The option to write down and convert is also an integral part of the new bail-in stabilization tool. The Bank of England is required in its exercise of the bail-in option to ensure that holders of Common Equity Tier 1 bear the first losses and those holding Additional Tier 1 and Tier 2 instruments are reduced or converted into Common Equity Tier 1 instruments.[83] Moreover, if the Authorities choose to sell the business of the bank to a commercial purchaser then the Bank of England may make a property transfer instrument and/or a share transfer instrument. If the resolution is to be by way of the transfer of all or part of the business to a bridge bank established and controlled by the Bank of England then the Bank of England may make a property transfer instrument. For the purposes of the asset management vehicle the Bank of England makes a transfer order as well as supplemental transfer orders. If the bank is to be taken into temporary public ownership, the Treasury may make a share transfer order. There are different provisions for each type of transfer and safeguards for shareholders and creditors, including provision for compensation.

The new write-down and conversion powers either outside or within the stabilization options **6.73** are set out in sections 6A, 6B, and 6C of the Banking Act. The Banking Act sets out the circumstances in which the powers could be initiated. Case 1:[84] the need for the stabilization option has been met and it has been decided the power should be initiated. Case 2:[85] the PRA establishes that the bank is failing or likely to fail and the Bank of England decides that the bank is unlikely to resolve its own problems. Case 3:[86] the viability of the bank on a consolidated basis is the focus of attention which can be addressed by the instruments held by its subsidiary. Case 4:[87] the viability of the group requires the instruments of the bank's parent undertaking to be

---

[82] Banking Act 2009, s 6E.
[83] Ibid, s 12AA.
[84] Ibid, s 6A(2).
[85] Ibid, s 6A(3).
[86] Ibid, s 6A(4).
[87] Ibid, s 6A(5).

taken into consideration. Case 5:[88] extraordinary public financial support is required by the bank and the relevant capital instruments need to be taken into consideration.

6.74   In these cases the Bank of England is able to draft an instrument which contains a mandatory reduction provision that either cancels, transfers, or dilutes existing Common Equity Tier 1 capital instruments; Additional Tier 1 instruments are reduced and/or converted into Common Equity Tier 1 capital instruments. In these instances the aims are to achieve the resolution objectives and/or meet the requisite Tier 1 capital requirements. The Bank of England can also initiate a mandatory reduction instrument and in such circumstances the reduction is permanent and owes no liability to the holder of the capital instrument. To initiate mandatory reduction instruments, the Bank of England is required to consult the PRA, FCA, or the Treasury when commencing these powers. The Bank of England is also required to report that it has taken such action to the Chancellor of the Exchequer.

6.75   There are two situations in which the Authorities have the power to transfer shares. The first is where the Authorities are able to find a private sector purchaser for the bank and for that purpose the Bank of England may make a share transfer instrument.[89] The second is where the bank is taken into temporary public ownership and for that purpose the Treasury may make a share transfer order.[90]

6.76   When the Bank of England makes a share transfer instrument it is required to send copies, as soon as reasonably practicable, to the banking institution concerned, the Treasury, and the PRA or the FCA. It is also required to publish a copy on its website and in two newspapers chosen by the Bank of England, to maximize the likelihood of the instrument coming to the attention of persons likely to be affected.[91]

6.77   A share transfer order is made by statutory instrument and may be subject to annulment pursuant to a resolution of either House of Parliament. The notice provisions that apply to the Bank of England apply, *mutatis mutandis*, to the Treasury.[92]

6.78   A share transfer instrument[93] and a share transfer order[94] provide for securities issued by a specified bank to be transferred and may relate to either specified securities or securities of a specified description. A transfer takes effect by virtue of the instrument or order and in accordance with the provisions on ancillary matters[95] and can provide for continuity as they can provide for the transferee to be treated for any purpose connected with the transfer as the same person as the transferor.[96]

6.79   For the purpose of share transfers, 'securities' is broadly defined:[97]

(1)   … 'securities' includes anything falling within any of the following classes.
(2)   Class 1: shares and stock.

---

[88]   Ibid, s 6A(6).
[89]   Ibid, s 11.
[90]   Ibid, s 13.
[91]   Ibid, s 24.
[92]   Ibid, s 25.
[93]   Ibid, s 15.
[94]   Ibid, s 16.
[95]   Ibid, s 17.
[96]   Ibid, s 18(1).
[97]   Ibid, s 14.

    (3) Class 2: debentures including
        (a) debenture stock,
        (b) loan stock,
        (c) bonds,
        (d) certificates of deposit,
        (e) any other instrument creating or acknowledging a debt.
    (4) Class 3: warrant and other instruments that entitle a holder to acquire anything in Class 1 or 2.
    (5) Class 4: rights which—
        (a) are granted by a deposit-taker, and
        (b) form part of the deposit-taker's own funds for the purposes of section 1 of Chapter 2 of Title V of Directive 2006/48/EC (on taking up and pursuit of business of credit institutions).

Thus share transfer orders that may be made by the Treasury to take a bank into public ownership and the share transfer instrument by which the Bank of England can sell all or part of a bank's business to a private sector purchaser can have very wide effect, in particular as the orders and instruments are not limited to share transfers but include the transfer of a range of other securities including bonds, loan stock, and warrants.[98] **6.80**

The Banking Act expressly provides that a transfer 'takes effect despite any restriction arising by virtue of contract or legislation or in any other way'. 'Restriction' is defined as follows:[99] **6.81**

    (a) any restriction, inability, or incapacity affecting what can and cannot be assigned or transferred (whether generally or by a particular person), and
    (b) a requirement for consent (by any name).

A share transfer instrument or order may also provide for a transfer to take effect 'free from any trust, liability or other encumbrances (and may include provision about their extinguishment)' and may also extinguish rights to acquire shares, stock, and debentures.[100] **6.82**

Further, the Banking Act expressly provides that a share transfer instrument or order may provide that, for the purpose of determining whether there has been an event of default, the share transfer instrument or order, as the case may be, is to be disregarded.[101] The reason for this is that if a share transfer were to cause an event of default this could seriously damage the value of the bank's assets at a time when the Authorities are intervening to try to protect the value of those assets and stabilize the bank's business. **6.83**

---

[98] The interpretation of 'securities' is widely drawn; ibid, s 14. Share transfer instruments can be made in respect of 'securities' as can share transfer orders; ibid, ss 15 and 16.

[99] Ibid, s 17(4).

[100] Ibid, s 17(3), (5), and (6).

[101] Ibid, s 22. Section 22 was omitted from the Banking Act by The Bank Recovery and Resolution Order 2014, s 28. It has been suggested that this provision also applies to contracts between third parties on the basis that ISDA raised this concern in response to the Treasury's consultation and the matter was raised by Baroness Noakes in the House of Lords, but Lord Myners' response in the debate did not deal with this point; see Miles Bake, Stephen Walsh, and Kevin Hawken, 'The Banking Act: The New "Special Resolution Regime" for Dealing with Failing Banks and its Legal Consequences', *The Banking Law Journal*, April 2009.

IX. Compensation and Valuation

6.84 The Banking Act provides for four different methods for compensating shareholders for loss caused by a share transfer under the statute:[102]

(1) A 'compensation scheme order' which establishes a scheme for determining whether compensation should be paid and for paying any compensation.

(2) A 'bail-in compensation order' with which to compensate those where a transfer has been initiated.

(3) A 'resolution fund order', a scheme pursuant to which the transferors are entitled to the proceeds of the disposal of the securities that have been transferred.

(4) A 'third party compensation order' which is an arrangement to compensate third parties.

6.85 These orders are required to be made by statutory instrument and may not be made unless a draft has been laid before and approved by resolution of each House of Parliament.[103]

6.86 Where the Bank of England makes a share transfer instrument to transfer shares in a bank to a private sector purchaser, the Treasury is required to make a compensation scheme order. Where the Treasury makes a share transfer order to take the bank into temporary public ownership, the Treasury is required to make either a compensation scheme order or a resolution fund order.[104] A compensation scheme order may provide for the appointment of an independent valuer and may specify valuation principles.[105] The statute expressly sets out the following valuation principle: 'In determining an amount of compensation (whether or not in accordance with valuation principles) an independent valuer must disregard actual or potential financial assistance provided by the Bank of England or the Treasury (disregarding ordinary market assistance offered by the Bank on its usual terms).'[106]

6.87 This assumption was also in the BSPA[107] and was challenged by the shareholders of Northern Rock plc who brought proceedings for a declaration under section 4 of the Human Rights Act 1998 that the material terms of the BSPA and the compensation scheme order were incompatible under Article 1 of the First Protocol to the European Convention on Human Rights; *SRM Global Master Fund LP & Ors v Commissioners of Her Majesty's Treasury*.[108] The shareholders' challenge was to the assumptions under section 5(4) of the BSPA determining the amount of compensation payable to them, in particular that the assumptions were that all the financial assistance provided by the Bank of England and the Treasury had been withdrawn and that neither of those institutions would provide further financial assistance to Northern Rock.[109] The shareholders' argument was that the consequence of

---

[102] Banking Act 2009, s 49. There is also provision for compensation to be paid to persons other than the transferors; see also, ibid, ss 59 and 60.

[103] Ibid, s 62.

[104] Ibid, ss 50 and 51.

[105] Ibid, s 57.

[106] Ibid, s 57(3).

[107] Ibid, ss 49–62 set out the provisions on compensation.

[108] [2009] EWCA Civ 788.

[109] See s 57 of the Banking Act: 'In determining the amount of compensation … an independent valuer must disregard actual or potential financial assistance provided by the Bank of England or the Treasury (disregarding ordinary market assistance offered by the Bank on its usual terms).'

the assumptions was that the shares would be valued on a forced sale basis and therefore be valued at nil. The decision of the court was that it would only interfere where the judgement of the state as to what was in the public interest was manifestly without reasonable foundation. The financial assistance had been given to Northern Rock to protect the banking system and the economy, and the purpose of the assumptions was to put the shareholders in the position they would have been in if that assistance had not been provided. The court would not, therefore, interfere in the judgement of the state.

A resolution fund order is required to provide for a determination of who is entitled to the proceeds on disposal of 'things transferred' and the way in which the proceeds and the shares will be calculated.[110] The proceeds are likely to be calculated net of the costs of resolution, which costs could include the costs of financial assistance provided by the Treasury and/or the Bank of England in the course of the resolution.[111]   **6.88**

The sources of compensation where there have been compensation scheme orders or resolution fund orders[112] are the Treasury and the FSCS.[113]   **6.89**

There are provisions for continuity after the transfer of shares which is of particular importance where the banking institution is part of a group. First, the transferee is also 'treated for any purpose connected with the transfer as the same person as the transferor'.[114] Secondly, the former group company must provide services and facilities that are required to enable the transferred bank to operate effectively (the 'continuity obligation') and this obligation may be enforced as if created by contract between the transferred bank and the former group company.[115] The continuity obligation is subject to the right to receive reasonable consideration. The continuity obligation is not limited to the provision of services or facilities to the transferred bank; the 'continuity authority' (the Bank of England where ownership was transferred to a private sector purchaser and the Treasury where the bank has been taken into public ownership) may give notice to the former group company that specific activities are required to be undertaken in accordance with the continuity obligation and on specified terms. The statute also gives the continuity authority the right to cancel or modify any contract or other arrangement between the transferred bank and the former group company and to confer and impose rights and obligations on the former group company which have effect as if created by contract between them. In so doing, the continuity authority 'shall aim, so far as is reasonably practicable' to preserve or include provision for 'reasonable consideration'.[116] The power to cancel, modify, and confer and impose rights and obligations is circumscribed to the extent that it may only be exercised insofar as the 'continuity authority' considers it necessary to ensure the provision of services and facilities to enable the transferred bank to operate effectively. It may be exercised by the Bank   **6.90**

---

[110] Banking Act 2009, s 58.

[111] The Code, para 12.14.

[112] Banking Act 2009, s 61. These sources are also available for third party compensation orders.

[113] The orders may also specify any other person.

[114] Banking Act 2009, s 18. The section also provides that the instrument or order may provide for agreements made or other things done by the transferor to be treated as if they had been done by the transferor, to modify references in an instrument or document to a transferor, and require or permit the transferor and/or transferee to provide information and assistance to the other.

[115] Ibid, ss 66 and 67.

[116] The Treasury may by order specify matters which are to be or which are not to be considered in determining what amounts to reasonable consideration; ibid, s 69(1).

of England only with the consent of the Treasury and must be exercised by way of the share transfer instrument or order or supplemental instrument or order.

6.91   When a bank becomes subject to the SRR the Bank of England has the power to cause a bank's property to be transferred pursuant to a property transfer instrument made under the Banking Act.[117] The transfer instrument may relate to 'all property, rights or liabilities' of the bank; or 'all its property, rights and liabilities subject to specified exemptions'; or 'specified property, rights and liabilities'; or 'property, rights or liabilities of a specified description'.[118] The property that may be transferred includes, 'the rights and liabilities under the law of a country or territory outside the United Kingdom'.[119] The transfer may also make other provisions for the purposes of or in connection with the transfer of property, rights, or liabilities of a banking institution.[120]

6.92   A property transfer or partial property transfer, like share transfers, can include provisions such that any or all of the contractual consequences of a transfer can be disregarded under the terms of the property transfer instrument.[121]

6.93   A property transfer instrument may provide for a transfer to be conditional on a specified event occurring or not occurring or a situation arising or not arising[122] and may make provision for the consequences of a breach of the condition.[123]

6.94   The statutory provisions for continuity where there has been a property transfer are substantially the same as those that provide for continuity in respect of share transfers.[124]

1. Partial property transfers

6.95   The main issue that has caused concern in relation to property transfers is the effect of a partial property transfer,[125] which is the power to split a bank and to make a transfer of a part of the bank's property. The power to make a property transfer instrument in respect of 'some but not all' of the property could have an adverse impact on secured financing, set-off, and netting arrangements. The most likely use of this power is to transfer the valuable part of an institution's business to a private sector bank or a bridge bank, leaving the original bank with poor quality assets and all the liabilities. Although it could be used to transfer the poor quality assets to a bridge bank, leaving the original bank in an improved financial position.[126]

6.96   The statutory provisions on partial property transfers in the Banking Act are:

---

[117]   Ibid, s 33(1).
[118]   Ibid, s 33(2).
[119]   Ibid, s 35(1)(d).
[120]   Ibid, s 33(2).
[121]   Ibid, s 34(3) and (4).
[122]   Ibid, s 34(5).
[123]   Ibid, s 34(6). The consequences may include automatic vesting in the original transferor; or an obligation to effect a transfer back to the original transferor; or, a provision making a transfer or anything done in connection with a transfer void or voidable.
[124]   Ibid, ss 63–65.
[125]   Defined in ibid, s 47(1): 'means a property transfer instrument which provides for the transfer of some, but not all, of the property, rights and liabilities of a bank'.
[126]   The Code, Chapter 8.

(1) Section 47 gives the Treasury the power to make orders restricting the making of partial property transfers, to impose conditions on the making of such transfers, to require such transfers to make provision for specified effect, and/or to provide for a property transfer to be void or voidable if made or purported to be made in contravention of the provisions of the order or any other order under that section.

(2) Section 48 gives the Treasury powers similar to those in section 47 to be used in cases where the making of partial property transfers might affect certain interests,[127] namely, security interests, title transfer collateral arrangements, set-off arrangements, and netting arrangements.

The government, aware of creditor and market issues arising from the provisions governing property transfers, published a consultation document: 'Special resolution regime: safeguards for partial property transfers' in November 2008. In the light of the responses to the consultation and the advice from the Bank of England, the former FSA and an expert liaison group on banking (which included legal, financial, and insolvency experts from the banking sector) the secondary legislation providing safeguards for partial transfers was laid before Parliament on 20 February 2009 and commenced on 21 February 2009, at the same time as the secondary legislation on partial transfers. These orders are the Banking Act 2009 (Restriction of Partial Property Transfers) Order 2009 ('the Safeguards Order') and the Banking Act 2009 (Third Party Compensation Arrangements for Partial Property Transfers) Regulations 2009. The Safeguards Order provides that: **6.97**

> Where a person and a bank have entered into a set-off, netting or title transfer financial collateral arrangement, all rights and liabilities under that arrangement have to be transferred, or none at all.[128]

The Safeguards Order also prevents the termination provisions from being disregarded in respect of set-off, netting, or title transfer of financial collateral arrangements relating to 'relevant financial instruments'.[129]   **6.98**

There was, however, concern among market participants that the Safeguards Order did not go far enough to provide the necessary protection. Lord Myners told the House of Lords on 16 March 2009:   **6.99**

> I am aware that some market participants are concerned that the scope of the safeguards is not wide enough, in particular with regard to the protections provided for set-off and netting. I understand that these concerns are primarily related to technical drafting, rather than the property that the order clearly excludes as a result of government policy, and that there are varied legal interpretations on whether some financial contracts have been excluded … I can review the safeguards order. If changes to the order are necessary and compatible with the authorities' flexibility, the Government will make such changes before the Summer Recess.[130]

---

[127] As defined in the Banking Act 2009, s 48(1)(a)–(d).
[128] Article 3 of the Order.
[129] Clause 9 of the Safeguards Order.
[130] Official Record, 16 March 2009: Column GC2–GC3.

6.100   The issue concerning the scope of the Safeguards Order was considered by the Banking Liaison Panel which provided advice to the Treasury on 17 June 2009.[131] The Panel recommended that the Safeguards Order be amended to cover the full range of transaction types that could be covered by netting arrangements and that it should be extended to include certain financial instruments that were not covered by the definition of 'relevant financial instruments'. The rights that were excluded by the Safeguards Order[132] were defined by reference to the Markets in Financial Instruments Directive (MiFID). The Panel noted that:

> The first problem arises from the extent to which the MiFID definitions of 'financial instrument' do not, or arguably do not, cover a range of transaction types that can be or are typically covered in netting arrangements. Particular transactions include spot and forward FX, commodity/bullion forwards and options, and longevity/mortality derivatives. A related issue is the treatment of banking transactions not currently covered by the relevant financial instruments ('RFI') definition: a range of transactions not least in trade finance is not currently covered.

6.101   The Panel therefore recommended extending the definition of 'relevant financial instruments' to include certain types of additional transactions and certain additional types of banking activities.

6.102   The Panel also advised on certain other amendments to the definition of excluded rights in Article 1 of the Safeguards Order. The issue that had been raised was the wording of the excluded rights that provided for the netting arrangements to be excluded where they relate to a contract 'entered into … in the course of carrying on an activity which relates *solely*[133] to relevant financial instruments'. The concern was that the word 'solely' would be construed to mean that if there were one transaction that fell outside this type of transaction this would invalidate the netting agreement in its entirety, described by the Panel as 'one bad apple spoils the barrel'.[134] The example of the problem caused by the use of the word 'solely' given by the Panel was where a bank entered into a series of cash settled commodity derivatives transactions with a counterparty as a hedge for a purchase of physical commodities. In this case, the Panel stated, it would appear that the transaction would not constitute protected rights and liabilities because they had been entered into in the course of an activity which does not relate *solely* to the relevant financial instruments, as this definition does not include physical commodities. The Panel also noted that similar issues would arise with respect to derivatives entered into by a bank to hedge its loan or mortgage book. The Panel recommended that the word 'solely' be deleted from the clauses in the excluded rights and that a new paragraph be inserted to reinforce the point that the inclusion of an unprotected right or liability under a set-off, netting, or title transfer collateral arrangement would not cause the arrangement to lose the protection provided by the Safeguards Order.

6.103   The Banking Act 2009 (Restriction of Partial Property Transfers) (Amendment) Order 2009, which came into force on 9 July 2009, amends the statutory instrument on partial

---

[131] Banking Liaison Panel, Subgroup on the Banking Act 2009 (Restriction of Partial Property Transfers) Order 2009.

[132] Article 1(3).

[133] Emphasis added.

[134] Paragraph 36 of the Advice.

property transfers[135] in accordance with the recommendations of the Banking Liaison
Panel advice to the Treasury.

In effect, the Bank of England cannot cherry-pick financial contracts with a given party that   **6.104**
are subject to set-off and netting arrangements. Either all such contracts have to be transferred or none of them can be transferred.

Secured creditors are protected by the Safeguards Order in that no partial property transfer   **6.105**
instrument can transfer assets over which a bank has security without also transferring the
relevant liabilities:[136] ie their claims cannot be separated from the assets that secure the liabilities. This protection is in respect of all security interests, including floating charges.

Structured finance arrangements, such as securitizations and covered bond programmes,   **6.106**
are also protected: the liability cannot be separated from the collateralization pool in a partial property transfer and it is not possible to transfer some but not all of the rights and obligations under such arrangements.

The junior creditors are particularly vulnerable in the case of a partial property transfer.   **6.107**
Peter Brierley in a Bank of England paper explained the position of these creditors as
follows:

> ... one of the key advantages of a PPT[137] is that it makes it possible to effect a resolution at a
> lower cost to the taxpayer, for example by allowing a greater proportion of the losses to be
> imposed on junior creditors, such as subordinated debt holders, whose claims may be left
> behind in the rump of the failed bank rather than being transferred to a private sector pur-
> chaser or bridge bank. In current conditions,[138] therefore, the SRR's stabilization powers, if
> they can be deployed, are more likely to be used to effect a PTT rather than a whole-bank
> resolution.

So far as the creditors remain with the residual bank, the Treasury has the power to make   **6.108**
regulations to compensate the creditors of a residual bank[139] and is required to ensure that
these creditors are compensated so that they are no worse off than they would be had the
whole of the bank been in an insolvency proceeding and there had been no PPT and no bank
administration. This is referred to as the 'no creditor worse off' safeguard ('the NCWO').
The NCWO Order[140] provides for the appointment of an independent valuer and sets out
principles for valuing what the creditors would have received in a hypothetical liquidation.

2. Property held on trust

A property transfer instrument may make provision in respect of property held on trust   **6.109**
(however that trust arises) and it may also make provision in respect of the terms on which
the property is to be held after the transfer and how any powers, provisions, and liabilities in

---

[135] Banking Act 2009 (Restriction of Partial Property Transfers) Order 2009.
[136] Article 5.
[137] Partial Property Transfer.
[138] The paper was published in July 2009, but the conditions do not appear to have changed materially since
that date.
[139] Banking Act 2009, s 60.
[140] SI 2009/319.

respect of the property are to be exercised after the transfer or have effect on the instrument coming into effect ('the Trust Issue').

6.110   The Panel also considered whether section 34(7) of the Banking Act extended to trusts where the bank is either the trustee or beneficiary and the trust arrangements for any bond held by a failing bank could be modified or terminated irrespective of the consequences for the transaction, bondholders, or other interested parties. The concern was that this could result in trust business and financial and corporate transactions with a trust element being lost to UK banks. The Panel recommended that the Safeguards Order be amended to reduce the scope of the problem by limiting the power to remove or alter the terms of a trust to circumstances where it was necessary or expedient to do so;[141] where the transferor was the trustee of the trust and its obligations became those of the transferee; and, where the transferor was the beneficiary of the trust, such property interests as it has as a beneficiary.

3. Compensation

6.111   The Banking Act makes provision for compensation orders where the Bank of England has made a property transfer order which is analogous to the orders that may be made for compensation where there has been a share transfer order or instrument: there may be a compensation scheme or a resolution fund order.[142] As with the compensation for share transfers, an independent valuer is appointed by the Treasury to deal with compensation. The valuer is required to adhere to certain assumptions set out in the statute, including a requirement that the valuer must disregard actual or potential financial assistance provided by the Bank of England or the Treasury. This was the assumption that was unsuccessfully challenged in the courts by the shareholders of Northern Rock.

6.112   The reforms introduced by the BRRD mean there are new safeguards that relate to compensation claims regarding the use of the bail-in stabilization option.[143] Again the principle is that 'no person is worse off as a result of the application of the bail-in option than they would have been had the bank gone into insolvency'. The 2014 Regulations require the appointment of an independent valuer; the valuer must assess the creditors' losses had the insolvency occurred rather than bail-in ('the insolvency treatment'); the valuer must assess the actual treatment received or expected to be received if no compensation were paid (actual treatment). If it is different, then the creditors should expect compensation.

X. The Resolution of Dunfermline Building Society

6.113   The first and only use to date of the resolution regime is in relation to the Dunfermline Building Society at the end of March 2009.

6.114   The Authorities subjected all banks and building societies to a severe stress test when assessing whether the institution was eligible to participate in the Credit Guarantee Scheme that was established following the collapse of Lehman Brothers. The result of the test on

---

[141] There is no equivalent safeguard where there is a full property transfer, but these are unlikely to arise in practice and the same principle would be expected to be applied to such transfers.
[142] The statutory provisions that apply are ss 49, 52–66.
[143] The Code, para 12.23.

Dunfermline indicated that it did not have sufficient capital to meet the requirements of the scheme. The former FSA also had doubts about the ability of the building society's management to cope with the turbulent market conditions.[144] The former FSA used its powers to instruct a 'skilled person' to report on the position of Dunfermline. The first report concluded that a specific loan provision should be increased by £3 million and that there should be a general provision of £15 million (an increase of £13 million on the provision at the end of 2007). The second report concluded that while the society could be viable for another 12 months, it faced a number of execution and financial risks to the implementation of its plan. A new Chief Executive was appointed in December 2008. Lord Turner stated in the letter to the Chancellor:[145]

> It is worth noting that in liquidity terms there was no immediate problem: the problems related to future possible solvency under stressed conditions; Dunfermline's situation was therefore different from that faced with Northern Rock or Bradford & Bingley.

The former FSA considered a number of options and as recapitalization was not available, **6.115** the board of the Dunfermline Building Society decided on 28 March 2009 that the society was unable to continue as a going concern. The former FSA then reached the conclusion that the society was likely to fail to satisfy the threshold conditions and that it was not reasonably likely that action would be taken to rectify the situation. This decision triggered the resolution process.

On 30 March 2009 the Chancellor of the Exchequer and the Governor of the Bank of **6.116** England announced a resolution for the Dunfermline Building Society.[146] Under the Banking Act, Dunfermline's retail and wholesale deposits, branches, head office, and residential mortgages (other than social housing loans and related deposits) were transferred to Nationwide Building Society. The sale to Nationwide followed a 'sale process' conducted by the Bank of England under the SRR provisions over the weekend of 28 and 29 March 2009. Dunfermline's social housing loan book was transferred to a bridge bank, wholly owned by the Bank of England. On the same date, and in advance of the announcement, the court made an order putting the remainder of Dunfermline's business, comprising commercial loans, certain residential mortgages, subordinated debts, and most treasury assets, into the Building Society Special Administration Procedure (BSSAP).

The Treasury had concluded that Dunfermline would require substantial future capital **6.117** given the scale of future losses and that it had only a limited capacity to service new capital because of historically low profits. The Treasury concluded that an injection of funds would not be likely to provide value for money and would not provide a sustainable and lasting solution. The announcement states that the Treasury consulted the Bank and the former FSA and concluded that the conditions for entry into the SRR were satisfied and that the Bank of England, following consultations with the Treasury and the former FSA, had concluded that the offer from Nationwide best met the objectives of the SRR.

---

[144] Lord Turner wrote to the Chancellor of the Exchequer on 17 April 2009 setting out the FSA's approach to the Dunfermline Building Society.
[145] Ibid.
[146] See <http://www.bankofengland.co.uk/archive/Documents/historicpubs/news/2009/030.pdf>.

6.118 When the former Tripartite Authorities needed to use the provisions in Parts 2 and 3 of the Banking Act to resolve the Dunfermline Building Society, the provisions of the statute did not apply to building societies at the time when the Treasury concluded that Dunfermline was failing or likely to fail. The Treasury, in the exercise of powers conferred by sections 130, 158, and 259(1) of the Banking Act, made an order that it was necessary to exercise the powers in sections 130 and 158 of the Banking Act without laying a draft order before Parliament, and made an order applying Parts 2 and 3 of the Banking Act to building societies.[147] The Order was laid before Parliament on 30 March 2009, the day after it was made.

6.119 On 22 December 2009 an independent Appointment Panel appointed an independent valuer for the purposes of the compensation arrangements that had been put in place as a consequence of the partial property transfers to Nationwide and to the bridge bank.[148]

6.120 What the authorities did in relation to Dunfermline was, in effect, to use the transfer powers, the administration procedure, and a bridge bank to resolve the problems of that building society.

XI. Bank Insolvency Procedure: Southsea Mortgage & Investment Company Limited

6.121 Southsea, a small bank with just over 250 depositors and around £7.4 million deposits, was established on the South Coast of England.[149] Its main difference from other UK banks was the higher interest rate for depositors due to higher interest charged on loans. The financial crisis led to a sharp decrease in property value, which worsened the financial position of the bank. After a series of discussions with the former FSA, a 'wind-down plan' was decided according to which the bank would stop accepting deposits from new customers and issuing new loans. A strategy was also implemented to maximize recoveries from the outstanding loan book. The bank was nonetheless solvent at the time but its financial projections continued to deteriorate as a result of the crisis.

6.122 As a consequence, the Bank of England and the former FSA at the time began proceedings for a potential insolvency in accordance with the Bank Insolvency Procedure that forms part of the SRR under the Banking Act 2009. Under the Act the bank liquidator has two objectives. Objective 1, which takes precedence over objective 2, is to work with the FSCS to ensure that each depositor has their account transferred to another bank or receives payment from the FSCS as soon as possible.[150] Objective 2 is to wind up the affairs of the bank in order to achieve the best result for the bank's creditors as a whole. The appointment of a bank liquidator can only be made by either the Bank of England, FSA, or HM Treasury via a Court application. Following an application from the Bank of England, the court was satisfied that Southsea was unable, or likely to become unable, to pay its debts, in accordance

---

[147] Building Societies (Insolvency and Special Administration) Order 2009, made on 29 March 2009.

[148] Secondary legislation was used to put the compensation arrangements in place: the Dunfermline Building Society Compensation Scheme, Resolution Fund and Third Party Compensation Order 2009.

[149] Bank of England, Southsea Mortgage and Investment Company Ltd, News Release, 16 June 2011.

[150] *Southsea Mortgage and Investment Company Ltd*, Southsea Mortgage and Investment Company Limited FSCS Accelerated Compensation for Depositors Instrument 2011. <https://www.fscs.org.uk/globalassets/determinations/southsea-mortgage-and-investment-company-ltd-determination.pdf>

with section 96 of the Banking Act 2009. A liquidation committee was established with members from the Bank of England, FSA, and FSCS to devise a liquidation strategy. The bank liquidator pursued a strategy to achieve objective 1 and notified the committee when it had been achieved in order to pass a 'full payment resolution'. In order to achieve objective 1 reliance was placed on the Single Customer View file, which contains the depositor and account information that is used by the FSCS to process compensation payouts.

The Single Customer View file was submitted to the FSCS by close of business on the first **6.123** day of the bank liquidator's appointment. The FSCS was then able to pay compensation to 80 per cent of depositors by close of business the next day. In this way, it managed to minimize disruption and provide access to funds by paying out as quickly as possible. However, 14 depositors (uneligible depositors) with amounts in excess of £85,000 were not eligible for compensation until the winding-up proceedings commenced in June 2011.

XII. Third Country Resolution Actions

A significant weakness identified during the global financial crisis was the lack of appro- **6.124** priate resolution regimes for banks and investment banks in distress. This situation was made more difficult for those jurisdictions with a large number of groups of banks operating cross borders since the lack of a consistent approach meant it led to difficulties cooperating with one another when one institution experienced financial distress.[151] The FSB Cross-Border Cooperation on Crisis Management 2009 and Key Attributes 2011 have played an important role in initiating reforms on two levels: first, setting out the principal features of what an effective resolution regime should consist of; and, secondly, highlighting the importance of cooperation and coordination of resolution of cross-border banks. In 2014 the FSB adopted additional guidance that elaborates specific Key Attributes. This guidance is sector-specific and states how the attributes ought to be applied for insurers, financial market infrastructures, and the protection of client assets in resolution. No changes were made to the text of the 12 Key Attributes. Building on the international initiatives, the adoption of the EU BRRD has put in place a framework for not only cross-border cooperation and coordination at the 'crisis prevention' stage of recovery and resolution planning but also at the 'crisis management' stage to require Member States to recognize one another's resolution decisions and cooperate to secure a more orderly resolution of banks and investment banks that are parts of groups. In addition to those reforms the BRRD also put in place measures to assist Member States to cooperate and coordinate with third countries. The BRRD SI seeks to 'onshore' the BRRD. However, the cross-border cooperation between the UK and EU will not remain the same now that the UK has officially left the EU.

There have been several consequences of Brexit: **6.125**

- EU-led resolutions are no longer automatically recognized by the UK, as the UK has extended its third country recognition framework to include EU resolutions. The EU resolutions will be recognized by the UK unless doing so would be contrary to relevant UK statutory safeguards.

---

[151] For a comprehensive analysis see, RM Lastra (ed), *Cross Border Bank Insolvency* (2011).

- The UK regulators are no longer obligated to follow operational and procedural mechanisms set out in the BRRD to cooperate with other EU authorities. This does not prevent the UK regulators from cooperating with the EU, but they will receive the same treatment as other third countries.
- The Bank of England now has sole responsibility for drawing up resolution plans.

6.126 The UK and the EU have agreed a Memorandum of Understanding, establishing a Framework for Regulatory Cooperation on Financial Services, 31 March 2021.[152] This includes establishing arrangements for 'exchanges of views on regulatory initiatives' and 'enhanced co-operation and co-ordination including in international bodies'.[153] It is hoped that a pragmatic understanding will be reached and maintained. But is yet to be published.

6.127 In respect of the FSB Key Attributes and the BRRD (post Brexit) the Bank of England has the discretion to recognize resolution actions. The success or failure of these reforms is still to be seen. The FSB published a consultation paper setting out proposals on quantitative targets to address the challenges faced by cross-border payments. The consultation covers a description of the principles and targets to be set across four identified challenges for cross-border payments (cost, speed, transparency, and access), to be achieved by 2027.

6.128 A notable challenge with the recent reforms is that they provide a relatively new set of techniques and expectations to deal with banks in distress distinct from the techniques and expectations associated with insolvency proceedings. In respect of the latter, a significant body of law exists relating to section 426 of the Insolvency Act 1986. However, in relation to the Banking Act resolution powers a significant number of provisions of the Act apply to assist with cross-border transfers of assets, liabilities, and property.

6.129 The Bank of England is required to cooperate at both the crisis prevention and crisis management levels with a bank or investment bank from another country including EEA member states. Post Brexit, EEA member states will be treated the same as other third countries. A significant part of the cooperation and coordination is undertaken within the supervisory and resolution colleges for cross-border groups. However, the UK will be given observer status in EU supervisory and resolution colleges rather than the member status it had before Brexit. The principle of mutual recognition requires member states to recognize one another's resolution decisions and take into consideration the impact of the resolution decision on other EEA countries. In this respect the decisions taken by another EEA resolution authority in accordance with the BRRD will not now have automatic effect in the UK. The Bank of England will be expected to cooperate and assist on a case-by-case basis in cross-border resolutions by initiating instruments for the transfer of assets and/or liabilities. Moreover, the UK is expected to cooperate and coordinate efforts.

6.130 In relation to supporting a foreign resolution authority's resolution decisions and actions; the Bank of England undertakes its decisions based on whether the institution is located in the UK and authorized by the PRA or FCA. A different approach is taken if the entity is

---

[152] *HM Treasury*, Technical Negotiations Concluded on UK – EU Memorandum of Understanding, 26 March 2021, <https://www.gov.uk/government/news/technical-negotiations-concluded-on-uk-eu-memorandum-of-understanding>
[153] Ibid.

a branch or subsidiary. In the latter case the UK resolution regime would apply. With regard to the resolution of a foreign parent or a part of the group located in a third country with either a branch or subsidiary located in the UK, the Banking Act requires the Bank of England to follow specific procedures to determine how it should cooperate with its foreign counterparts.

In view of the significant number of branches in the UK banking system it is no surprise **6.131** a separate part of the Banking Act 2009 is devoted to branches.[154] The Act sets out the measures the Bank of England will need to take when it makes a property transfer for a UK branch, namely the need to make a pre-resolution valuation of the business of the UK branch by an independent valuer.[155] In an urgent case the Bank of England does have the discretion to carry out a provisional valuation when making a transfer instrument. As with other valuations in resolution, the Bank of England is required to consider inter alia which stabilization option is likely to be employed, the type of property and liabilities being transferred, and the eligible liabilities expected to be converted in a bail in. The valuation needs inter alia to set out the balance sheet for the business of the UK branch and an analysis of the accounting value of the property of the third country institution.[156] The independent valuer will also need to set out a prudent assumption about the rate of default and losses at the third country institution. The Bank of England is required to have Treasury approval before making the instrument, which is informed by the PRA and FCA assessments in the consultation process, which in turn are closely linked with the third country branch compliance with the PRA and FCA Threshold Conditions. The following conditions need to be met in such decisions:[157]

Condition 1 is that the third-country institution is failing or likely to fail.

Condition 2: is that, having regard to timing and other relevant circumstances, it is not reasonably likely that action will be taken by or in respect of the third-country institution that will result in Condition 1 ceasing to be met.

Condition 3 is that—

(a) the third-country institution is unable or unwilling, or is likely in the near future to be unable or unwilling, to pay its debts or other liabilities owed to [F9UK] creditors or otherwise arising from the business of the UK branch as they fall due, and

(b) no third-country resolution action has been taken, no normal insolvency proceedings have been initiated, and no such action or proceedings are likely in the near future to be taken or initiated, in relation to the institution.

Condition 4 is that making a property transfer instrument is necessary having regard to the public interest in the advancement of one or more of the special resolution objectives.

Condition 5 is that—

(a) third-country resolution action has been taken, or the Bank of England has been notified that such action will be taken, in relation to the third-country institution

---

154 Banking Act 2009, s 89JA.
155 Ibid, s 89JA(4).
156 Ibid, s 89JA(6)–(7).
157 Ibid, s 89JA(7)(1)–(6).

and the Bank has refused or proposes to refuse to recognise such action for one or more of the reasons specified in section 89H(4), or

(b)   third-country resolution action has not been, and is not likely to be, taken in relation to the third-country institution.

6.132   When a third country notifies the Bank of England about a resolution of a third country institution which either has a branch or subsidiary or creditors in the UK, the Bank of England is required, with the approval of the Treasury, to make an instrument either recognizing the action, refusing to recognize the action, or only partially recognizing the action.[158] The Bank of England can refuse to recognize the action if the following circumstances apply: there would be an adverse effect on financial stability in the UK; the action relates to a branch in compliance with the special resolution objectives; creditors located in the UK would not receive the same treatment as creditors located in the third country; the third country resolution action would have material fiscal implications for the UK; or recognition would be unlawful under the Human Rights Act 1998.[159] In this regard, the Bank of England in taking such decisions is required to give due consideration to the interests of the third country where the group entity is located. The legal effect of the recognition of the third country resolution action also needs to be taken into account and the Bank of England is required to determine whether the same legal effects are produced in the UK as they are in the third country. In relation to this the Bank of England is expected to support resolution actions which correspond to the UK resolution objectives.[160] Following this the Bank of England is expected, subject to the above requirements, to cooperate with either the third country resolution actions by assisting with a transfer to a bridge bank.[161]

6.133   The Bank of England recently agreed to the request by the National Bank of Ukraine to resolve the problems at the Ukrainian bank PrivatBank by recognizing the bail-in of four loans made by UK SPV Credit Finance Plc. The Bank of England exercised its powers under section 89H of the Banking Act and recognized the request, having obtained approval from HM Treasury.[162] A Bank of England recognition is formalized by the publication of a 'third country instrument' and comes in force on the time and date indicated in the instrument, referred to as the recognition time.[163]

---

[158] Banking Act 2009, s 89H(1)–(2). Amendments to the Banking Act 2009 have been made in relation to this section. They essentially remove all reference to EEA states following Brexit. These amendments were set out in Schedule 1 para 41 of the Bank Recovery and Resolution and Miscellaneous Provisions (Amendment) (EU Exit) Regulations 2018.

[159] Ibid, s 89H(4)(a)–(e). Again, amendments made by Schedule 1, para 41 of the 2018 Regulations to reflect Brexit and remove reference of EEA states.

[160] Ibid, s 89I(6), amended by Schedule 1, para 41 of the 2018 Regulations. Reference to 'third country' has substituted 'country' for 'territory'.

[161] Ibid, s 89J. Amendments have been made by Chapter 1, regulations 65–66 of the Bank Recovery and Resolution (Amendment) (EU Exit) Regulations 2020, removing references to EEA states and substituting 'central bank' for 'Bank of England'. Similarly, amendments have been made under Schedule 1 of the 2018 Regulations to reflect the UK leaving the EU.

[162] UK Parliament, PrivatBank (Recognition of Third-Country Resolution Action) Instrument 2021, Statement made on 19 May 2021. <https://questions-statements.parliament.uk/written-statements/detail/2021-05-19/hlws38>

[163] Banking Act 89H(2); see The PrivatBank (Recognition of Third-Country Resolution Action) Instrument 2021   <https://www.bankofengland.co.uk/-/media/boe/files/news/2021/may/the-privatbank-recognition-of-third-country-resolution-action-instrument-2021.pdf>.

XIII. Recognized Central Counterparties

The reforms introduced by the Financial Services Act 2012 extended the powers set out in **6.134** the Banking Act to cover central counterparties (CCPs),[164] which are regulated and supervised by the Bank of England and the FCA. The Bank of England is responsible for deciding whether to use the stabilization options, which are determined by applying the following conditions: (1) the CPP is failing or likely to fail to meet its recognition requirements;[165] (2) it is reasonably unlikely for the CCP to take action for it to continue critical clearing services. In deciding whether or not those conditions have been met the Bank of England is required to consult the Treasury, the PRA, and the FCA.

The Bank of England will also act as the resolution authority for CCPs.[166] The Code provides **6.135** the rationale and approach to the resolution of CCPs if one were to experience distress. In light of the fact that CCPs, unlike banks, do not have a coherent capital and liquidity framework to comply with, their exposure to market risk and member counterparty risks, as a result of their default, makes them quite susceptible to failure. A resolution regime is certainly necessary to mitigate the spillover effects and disruption resulting from the failure of a CCP. The Bank of England has the following stabilization powers that have been specifically adapted to apply to CCPs:[167]

(1) Transfer some or part of the business of the CCP or its group undertaking to a commercial purchaser.
(2) Transfer some or all of the business of the CCP or its group undertaking to a bridge CCP.
(3) Transfer the ownership of a CCP to any person.

In making a decision as to which stabilization option to utilize in the circumstances of a CCP experiencing distress, the Bank of England is required to assess the merits of each option and the impact of adopting one of the stabilization options over the other in terms of meeting its resolution objectives.

The Code also sets out the modified special resolution objectives that are to be applied to **6.136** CCPs: Objective 1, protect and enhance UK financial system stability; Objective 2, protect and enhance public confidence in the stability of the financial system; Objective 3, maintain continuity of CCP clearing services; Objective 4, protect public funds; Objective 5, avoid interfering with property rights in accordance with the Human Rights Act 1998. A key focus of the objectives would be to ensure critical functions of the CCP which are acutely interconnected with clearing members are not disrupted, and to utilize stabilization options to

---

[164] Banking Act 2009, s 89B; see specific guidance in the Banking Act 2009: special resolution regime code of practice, December 2020, 88–100: <https://assets.publishing.service.gov.uk/government/uploads/system/uploads/attachment_data/file/945165/SRR_CoP_December_2020.pdf>.

[165] FSMA 2000, ss 285 and 286, respectively. Amendments to s 285 have been made by The Central Counterparties (Amendment and Transitional Provision) (EU Exit) Regulations 2018, The Investment Exchanges, Clearing Houses and Central Securities Depositories (Amendment) (EU Exit) Regulation 2019. Section 286 not amended apart from changes introduced by the Central Securities Depositories Regulations 2017.

[166] Banking Act 2009, s 89B.

[167] Ibid, s 89B(2)–(3).

try and ensure continuity of CCP clearing services. Bail-in is not an option for CPPs because it would result in the termination of the contract and a potential interference with netting and collateral arrangements. In light of such measures, banks would have to calculate their exposure to a CCP on a gross basis and run a risk of running unmatched positions, which would undermine all the post-financial crisis efforts to promote the use of CCPs.

7

BANKING ACT RESTRUCTURING AND INSOLVENCY PROCEDURES

I. Introduction

The general insolvency legislation, contained mainly in the Insolvency Act 1986 and the **7.01** Insolvency Rules 1986, works effectively, for the most part, in the rescue or liquidation of companies. Over the years special insolvency regimes have been put in place for a number of important industries, including certain types of utility[1] and transport companies.[2] The purpose of these special regimes is to meet the situation where the application of the normal corporate insolvency law to a monopoly company causes essential services to be interrupted.

Historically, company insolvency procedures have been used more or less successfully to **7.02** deal with consequences of bank insolvency. In the 1990s, the most notable insolvency proceedings were the provisional liquidation of the Bank of Credit and Commerce International SA (BCCI) in July 1991 and the administration orders made in respect of members of the

---

[1] For example, the Energy Act 2004 created a special administration procedure for companies owning or operating gas and electricity networks with the objective of ensuring a continuity of supply through either the rescue of the company as a going concern or the transfer of the business to another company or companies. There is also a special regime for the water industry. The Water Industry (Special Administration) Rules 2009.

[2] Railway Act 1993; see also Railway Act 2005 for Scottish services.

Barings group in February 1995. Company insolvency procedures were also used more or less satisfactorily for other less high-profile bank insolvencies.[3]

7.03 As no retail bank has a monopoly of the market the government did not respond to the failure of Northern Rock by proposing special insolvency proceedings[4]—the government's focus was on the development of the special resolution regime (SRR).[5] So far as the normal insolvency procedures were concerned according to the first discussion paper *Banking reform—protecting depositors: a discussion paper*, published in October 2007, the Authorities' opinion of the normal insolvency proceedings was:[6]

> Generally, financial firms are subject to normal corporate insolvency procedures, which have a narrow focus on the failing firm and the interests of creditors. In a normal administration, the administrator is able to suspend creditors' (including retail depositors') ability to exercise their contractual rights so that the amount of loss can be established and apportioned among them. This means that firms and individuals may not be able to use their accounts or access their money—possibly for a period of weeks or even months. Any outstanding debts may also be offset against the relevant creditors' claim, in effect recovering those debts before repaying those creditors a proportion of their net claim on the bank. While any difference may be recoverable through the FSCS, this may cause disruption, not only to the customers of the bank, but also to the firms and consumers with whom the customers of the bank interact.

7.04 On 30 January 2008, a further paper, *Financial Stability and Depositor Protection: Strengthening the Framework*, was published by the Authorities.[7] In that paper the government proposed legislation to introduce a modified insolvency process for banks as a 'stand alone insolvency regime for banks based on existing insolvency provisions and practice'.[8] Although the main focus of the paper was the SRR, the extensive list of questions for consultation included the following:[9]

- Should a new bank insolvency procedure be introduced for banks and building societies as an option for the Authorities instead of normal insolvency procedures?
- Do you think that there ought to be provision in the bank insolvency procedure for continued trading of some of the bank's business in the interests of depositors or other creditors? If so, how do you think this might work?
- Should a bank insolvency procedure be a stand-alone regime in which the bank liquidator has the combined powers of an administrator and liquidator? Are any other powers required?

The majority response was that it was unnecessary to make wholesale changes to the normal insolvency provisions to ensure rapid payments to eligible FSCS claimants.[10]

---

[3] For example, Mount Banking plc and Equatorial Corporation plc.
[4] Paragraphs 3.17 and 3.18 of the discussion paper published in October 2007.
[5] The SRR is considered in Chapter 6.
[6] Paragraph 2.7.
[7] Cm 7308.
[8] See paras 4.33–4.35.
[9] Questions 4.14–4.15 and 4.18.
[10] Summary of Consultation Responses, p 137 of the July paper, Cm 7436.

In a subsequent paper presented to Parliament by the Chancellor of the Exchequer in July **7.05** 2008, the purpose of which was to provide more technical detail on the SRR, *Financial Stability and Depositor Protection: Special Resolution Regime*,[11] the Chancellor explained the government's opposition to a special insolvency regime for banks as follows:

> a modified form of insolvency as a first step is unlikely to enhance consumer or market confidence, particularly in the ability of the bank to continue to meet its financial obligations. Further, it puts the bank into a governance framework that is very unlike that of other commercial banks. Taken together, these factors could reduce the likelihood of a private sector solution …[12]

The paper concludes on this point that, for these reasons: **7.06**

> [T]he Authorities do not propose to establish a form of special insolvency regime for UK banks. The Authorities' preferred model is more in line with aspects of the US approach for resolving failing banks. While the United States has a statutory regime for banks that is distinct from that which applies to other companies, it does not use this model. One important US method for resolving failing banks, whereby assets and liabilities are split between a newly created bridge bank and the residual company, is broadly similar to the bridge bank tool proposed for the UK.

The Authorities gave a number of reasons for the need to develop the SRR rather than focus **7.07** on developing a special form of insolvency proceedings. Two of them appear to have been of particular importance. The first reason is the insolvency requirements that must be met under the Insolvency Act 1986.[13] A company in financial difficulties may only be put into administration if the company is or is likely to become unable to pay its debts[14] and a company may only be wound up if it is unable to pay its debts.[15] This precludes early and pre-emptive steps which may be necessary to prevent the financial problems in one bank from causing a run on other banks and more general financial instability.

The second reason was that neither the court nor the insolvency practitioner who has been **7.08** appointed as office holder is required to take any account of the public policy objectives that come into play when a certain course of action may have wider systemic consequences by causing a loss of confidence in the banking system. The course of action that is appropriate to addressing the problems of an individual bank looked at in isolation from the financial system could cause or worsen a crisis in the financial system. Banks are essentially different

---

[11] Cm 7459.

[12] Cm 7459, para 3.6, Box 3.1.

[13] 'Unable to pay its debts' has the meaning given in s 123 of the Insolvency Act 1986; see Sch B1, para 111(1). The meaning in s 123 encompasses 'cash flow' insolvency in the sense of inability to pay debts as they fall due and balance sheet insolvency where the value of the company's assets is less than its liabilities, including contingent liabilities.

[14] 'Likely' in this context means 'more probable than not'; *Re Colt Telecom Group plc* [2002] EWHC 2815 (Ch), BPIR 324. Where, however, a qualifying floating charge holder (as defined in Sch B1, para 14 of the 1986 Act) makes an application to the court for an administration order the court may make an administration order whether or not it is satisfied that the company is or is likely to become unable to pay its debts; see Sch B1, para 35(2). Where the appointment is by the company or the directors the requisite statutory declaration must include a statement that the company is unable or likely to become unable to pay its debts within the meaning of s 123 of the 1986 Act—Sch B1, paras 27(2)(a) and 30(a).

[15] Insolvency Act 1986, ss 122(1)(f) and 123. Companies can, of course, be wound up for reasons other than insolvency, eg, when a company either does not trade for a year or has ceased to trade for a year or on just and equitable grounds. The grounds on which a company may be wound up are listed in s 122(1) of the Insolvency Act 1986.

from commercial firms in that they issue liquid deposits, extend credit, and process payments and their failure is potentially more damaging to economic activity than the failure of other companies. There are also banks that are 'too big to fail'. A sound banking system is essential to the efficient performance of other economic activities. This second issue has not only determined the characteristics of the SRR but, as explained below, is reflected in the modification of the objectives of administration and liquidation as applied to banking institutions.

7.09 This chapter explains the key features of the resolution regime and how it applies to both banks and investment firms. It specifically looks at the reforms introduced by the Financial Services Act 2012, the Financial Services (Banking Reform) Act 2013, and the move to implement the Bank Recovery and Resolution Directive 2015 (as well as The Bank Recovery and Resolution (Amendment) (EU Exit) Regulations 2020, which implement the BRRD and the BRRD II post Brexit) to put in place a special regime for banks and investment banks. This chapter will discuss the specific measures concerning the broader special administration and insolvency arrangements. The chapter will then look at the treatment of depositors and client assets and explain the priority accorded to them during the administration and insolvency procedure.

II. The Administration and Liquidation Regime for Banking Institutions

7.10 The government, having rejected a special insolvency regime for banks, included provisions in the Banking Act 2009 for the administration and liquidation of banking institutions that were based in large part on the procedures set out in the Insolvency Act 1986 and the Insolvency Rules 2016. The bank administration procedure and the bank insolvency procedure exist alongside the normal insolvency procedures. This is to ensure that, in principle, creditors can wind up a bank or building society or put it into administration,[16] or have a provisional liquidator in respect of a bank or building society.[17]

III. The Bank Administration Procedure

7.11 The primary legislation on the bank administration procedure comprises of specific provisions in Part 3 of the Banking Act 2009 ('the Banking Act'), the modified provisions of the Schedule B1 to the Insolvency Act 1986, the modifications to which are set out in Table 1 in Part 3 of the Banking Act ('Table 1'), and the other provisions of the Insolvency Act 1986, also with some modifications, as set out in Table 2 in Part 3 of the Banking Act ('Table 2'). The rules that apply to bank administrations are set out in the Bank Administration (England and Wales) Rules 2009 which apply, with some modifications, the Insolvency Rules 2016.[18]The Bank Administration (England and Wales) (Amendment) Rules

---

[16] HM Treasury—Note to the BLP sub-group on building society insolvency, 8 December 2009, para 2.
[17] Pursuant to s 135 of the Insolvency Act 1986.
[18] There are also a number of other relevant regulations: the Banking Act 2009 (Bank Administration) (Modifications for Application to Banks in Temporary Public Ownership) Regulations 2009; the Banking Act

2010[19] incorporate reforms to the bank administration procedure introduced by the wider reforms introduced by the Insolvency Service.[20] The aim of the reforms is to improve the application of the bank administration procedure.

The paper entitled *Financial stability and depositor protection; special resolution regime* by   **7.12**
the Bank of England, the Treasury, and the former Financial Services Authority (FSA) explained the purpose of the bank administration procedure as follows:[21]

> The Authorities therefore propose the creation of a special bank administration procedure for the residual company which would be modelled on existing insolvency procedures— principally administration under Schedule B1 to the Insolvency Act 1986. It is recognised that given the overall objectives of the SRR, some significant departures from, and modifications to, these ordinary administration provisions will be necessary.

Bank administration is intended to be used where only part of the business of the failing   **7.13**
bank has been or is to be transferred to a private purchaser or resolution company.[22] The part that has not been transferred (the residual bank) is likely to retain property, information, and rights essential to the successful continuation of the business that has been transferred to the private purchaser or to the resolution company. If, as is likely, the residual entity is insolvent, then that entity can be subject to the bank administration procedure.

The first aim of the administration procedure is to ensure that the residual bank supports   **7.14**
the resolution company or the private bank to which the bank's business has been sold or transferred, by providing such services, systems, contracts, and other facilities as may be necessary to ensure the new bank's effective operation.[23] This is intended to assist the resolution company or the private purchaser to operate in circumstances where these services cannot be transferred immediately to the resolution company or private purchaser. Only once this objective has been achieved do the objectives of the bank administration procedure become those of the 'normal' administration. The position was described as follows in the Explanatory Notes to the Banking Bill:

> The bank administrator has specified objectives. First, either to provide support to the bridge bank or private sector purchaser. Once such support is no longer required, the objective is to achieve either of the two principal aims or an ordinary administration; either to rescue the company as a going concern or to achieve a better result for creditors than in an immediate liquidation.[24]

(Bank Administration) (Modifications for Application to Multiple Transfers) Regulations 2009; and the Bank Administration (Sharing Information) Regulations 2009. The Financial Services Act 2012 (Consequential Amendments and Transitional Provisions) Order 2013, replacing reference to the former FSA to reference to the new 'appropriate regulator': FCA or PRA.

[19] Bank Administration (England and Wales) (Amendment) Rules 2010.
[20] 'The amendments to the BAP Rules are required to provide that reference to the 1986 Rules means the 1986 Rules amended up to August 2009 (SI 2009/2472) (this is to enable the BAP Rules to work despite future amendments to the 1986 Rules).'
[21] Cm 7459, para 3.82.
[22] Banking Act 2009, s 136(2)(a), amended slightly by the Bank and Resolution Order 2016, section 12ZA: in s 136(2) 'bridge bank' has been substituted for 'resolution company'.
[23] Ibid, s 136(2)(c).
[24] Para 289 of the Explanatory Notes.

A. The Application for an Administration Order

7.15 Under the Banking Act provisions only the Bank of England can apply for an administration order and must nominate a person to be appointed as the bank administrator.[25] A bank administrator must be a licensed insolvency practitioner and must have consented to act.[26]

7.16 The Bank of England may apply to the court for a bank administration order[27] in respect of a residual bank where: (i) a partial property transfer has occurred or is intended pursuant to the SRR stabilization powers; and (ii) where the Bank of England is satisfied that the residual bank is unable to pay its debts or is likely to become unable to pay its debts as a result of a property transfer that the bank has made or intends to make.[28]

7.17 The content of the application, the statement of the proposed bank administrator, and that of the Bank of England are set out in detail in the Bank Administration (England & Wales) Rules 2009 ('the Administration Rules'),[29] which is a modified form of the rules governing 'normal' administrations in the Insolvency Rules 1986.

7.18 The Bank of England is required to serve the application on the bank, the proposed administrator(s), any holder of a qualifying floating charge[30] who is known to the Bank of England, any person who has given notice to the appropriate regulator of the intention to commence insolvency proceedings against the bank,[31] and transferees of property where the transfer was made pursuant to a property transfer order.[32] The Bank is also required to give notice to the appropriate regulator and to any person known to the Bank of England to be charged with execution against or has distrained against the bank or its property.[33]

7.19 The court, when fixing the venue, is required to have regard to the desirability of having an application heard as soon as reasonably practicable and the need of the bank's representatives to be at the hearing.[34] The Bank of England, the appropriate regulator the bank, a director of the bank, and any person who has given notice to the PRA or Financial Conduct Authority (FCA) of intention to commence insolvency proceedings may appear or be represented at the hearing, together with any person who 'appears to have an interest' and has the court's permission to appear.[35]

---

[25] Banking Act 2009, s 142. The Bank's right to appoint an administrator is described as one of the 'main features of bank administration'; s 136(2)(b), amended slightly by the Bank and Resolution Order 2016—after reference to 'section 12', the order inserts 'section 12ZA'.

[26] Ibid, s 143(2) (this has been amended slightly by the Bank and Resolution Order 2016, inserting grounds for applying a property transfer instrument: 12(2) or s 12ZA(3).

[27] Ibid, s 136(2)(b). Court practice and procedure governing applications in normal insolvency proceedings, rr 7.1–7.10 of the Insolvency Rules 1986 do not apply to bank administrations. The practice and procedure is set out in rr 50–57 of the Bank Administration Rules. The Insolvency Rules 1986 have been replaced by the 2016 Rules. The rules on the appointment of an administrator by the Court are set out in Part 3 Chapter 2.

[28] Banking Act 2009, s 143.

[29] Rules 9, 11, and 12.

[30] As defined in para 14(2) of Sch B1 to the Insolvency Act 1986.

[31] Banking Act 2009, s 120.

[32] Rule 15 of the Administration Rules. The method of service is governed by r 18 and service is required to be verified by witness statement, r 19. The property transfer order is one that is made under s 11(2)(b) of the Banking Act 2009.

[33] Rule 20 of the Administration Rules.

[34] Rule 21 of the Administration Rules.

[35] Rule 22 of the Administration Rules.

B. The Purpose of the Administration

The bank administrator has two objectives:[36] 'Objective 1', the objective of support for the private purchaser of the bank's business or the resolution company by ensuring that the business that has been purchased continues to be supplied with services and facilities that the Bank of England thinks are required for the effective conduct of the business;[37] and 'Objective 2', the objective of standard non-bank company administration, namely, rescue as a going concern or achieving a better result for creditors than an immediate winding up.[38]   **7.20**

The Bank of England has a central role in the administration of the bank until the Bank of England considers that Objective 1 has been achieved.   **7.21**

The bank administrator is required to ensure that the 'non-sold or non-transferred' part of the bank ('the residual bank') provides the services and/or the facilities required to enable the private sector bank or a resolution company to operate effectively[39] and, whether the sale or transfer is to a private sector bank or a residual bank, the bank administrator is required to enter into any agreement, at the request of the Bank of England, for the residual bank to provide services and/or facilities to the residual bank.[40]   **7.22**

Where there has been a transfer or sale to a private sector bank, the administrator in the pursuit of Objective 1 is required to have regard to the terms of agreements made at the request of the Bank of England and any other agreement between the private sector bank and the residual bank.[41] The statute also expressly provides for the administrator, if the administrator is in doubt about the effect of the terms of any agreement made between the residual bank and the private sector bank, to seek the direction of the court under paragraph 63 of Schedule B1 to the Insolvency Act 1986. In addition, the private sector bank may also apply under that provision where there is a dispute about any agreement with a residual bank.[42]   **7.23**

Where the sale is to a resolution company, the administrators must ensure that, so far as is reasonably practicable, an agreement entered into includes provision for consideration at a market rate, although this does not prevent the bank administrator from entering into an agreement on any terms the administrator thinks necessary in pursuit of Objective 1.[43]   **7.24**

Whether the sale or transfer is to a private sector bank or a residual bank, the administrator must avoid action that is likely to prejudice the performance by the residual bank in accordance with those terms.[44]   **7.25**

---

[36] Banking Act 2009, s 137. Amended slightly by the Bank Recovery and Resolution Order 2016, reference to 'bridge bank' has now been substituted for 'resolution company'.

[37] The Bank Administration (Sharing Information) Regulations 2009 set out the mandatory provisions governing information sharing between a bank administrator, the Bank, and, after a partial transfer, to a bridge bank.

[38] See para 7.26.

[39] This is one of the 'main features of bank administration'; ibid, s 136(2)(c).

[40] Ibid, s 138(3) and (4).

[41] Ibid, s 138(3)(a).

[42] Ibid, s 138(2)–(4). Words have been inserted into s 138(2): 'including a bridge bank supplemental property transfer instrument or bridge bank supplementary reverse property transfer instrument' by the 2016 Order. In s 138(4) reference to 'bridge bank' has been replaced with 'resolution company' by the 2016 Order;

[43] Ibid, s 138(4)(b) and (c).

[44] Ibid, s 138(3)(b) and (4)(a).

7.26 Where a bank administrator requires approval of or consent from the Bank of England to any action pursuant to the provisions of the Banking Act on administration, the Bank of England may withhold approval or consent only on the grounds that the action 'might prejudice the achievement of Objective 1'.[45]

7.27 The pursuit of Objective 1 ceases when the Bank of England notifies the administrator that the residual bank is no longer required for the purposes of the private sector purchaser or the residual bank. If the administrator thinks that Objective 1 should cease and the Bank of England has not given notice, the administrator may apply to the court for directions under paragraph 63 of Schedule B1, and the court may direct 'the Bank to consider whether to give notice'.[46] Therefore, as the court's power is limited to directing the Bank of England to consider giving notice, the decision as to whether Objective 1 has been achieved is, in effect, a decision that only the Bank of England can make.

7.28 Objective 2 is described in the statute as 'normal' administration,[47] which is to rescue the bank as a going concern (Objective 2(a)) or achieve a better result for the residual bank's creditors as a whole than would be likely if the residual bank were wound up without first being in bank administration (Objective 2(b)). The administrator is required to aim to achieve Objective 2(a) 'unless of the opinion'[48] either that it is not reasonably practicable to achieve that objective or that Objective 2(b) would achieve a better result for the residual banks' creditors as a whole. These provisions are the same as the first two objectives for 'normal' administrations of non-bank companies at paragraph 3 of Schedule B1 to the Insolvency Act 1986.[49]

C. The Process of Administration

7.29 The bank administrator is deemed to be an officer of the court.[50] The duties and powers of a bank administrator are substantially the same as those of a non-bank administrator[51] and, as in a normal administration, the bank administrator may do 'anything necessary or expedient for the pursuit of the objectives'.[52]

7.30 As in a normal administration, the administrator is required to prepare a statement of proposals for achieving the objectives 'as soon as is reasonably practicable after appointment'.[53] The administrator is required, however, to produce two separate sets of proposals; one for the Objective 1 Stage and the other for the Objective 2 Stage.[54] The administrator is required

---

[45] Ibid, s 138(5).

[46] Ibid, s 139.

[47] Ibid, s 140—the heading to that section.

[48] It is unclear why the change has been made to 'unless of the opinion' in para 3(3) of Sch B1 to the Insolvency Act 1986, which is 'unless he thinks' has not been copied into this provision. In this context there is no material difference between the phrases.

[49] The third objective in 'normal' administration, 'realising the property to make a distribution to one or more secured or preferential creditors'; para 3(1)(c) of Sch B1 to the Insolvency Act 1986 is not included as an objective in the bank administration procedure.

[50] Banking Act 2009, s 146.

[51] Ibid, s 145.

[52] Ibid, s 145(1); the objectives are described in s 137.

[53] Ibid, s 147.

[54] Rules 28 and 29 of the Administration Rules.

to agree the Objective 1 Stage proposals with the Bank of England. If the administrator and the Bank of England are unable to agree, the administrator may apply for directions pursuant to paragraph 63 of Schedule B1 to the Insolvency Act 1986 and the court may make any order, including an order dispensing with the need for the Bank of England's agreement.[55]

The administrator must also send the statement of proposals to the appropriate regulator. **7.31** The administrators' proposals concerning the Objective 1 Stage, notwithstanding that they are made under section 147 of the Banking Act, have the same effect as those produced in a 'normal' administration pursuant to paragraph 49 of Schedule B1 to the Insolvency Act 1986. The Objective 2 Stage proposals are, as is the case with normal administration proposals, made pursuant to paragraph 49 of Schedule B1 to the Insolvency Act 1986.

There is a specific rule governing the contents of the report to creditors during the Objective **7.32** Stage 1 process which requires the report to contain the same information as in a normal administration, but also details of additional information, in particular details of transfers, any requirements that have been imposed on the bank to achieve Objective 1 and arrangements for managing and financing the bank during the Objective 1 Stage.

1. The Objective 1 stage—the Bank of England's control of the administration process

The bank administrator is required to accede to requests made by the Bank of England **7.33** for the residual bank in administration to enter into an agreement for the residual bank to provide services or facilities to achieve the first objective. Further, until this objective is achieved, the administrator is also required to provide such information and records that may be requested by the Bank of England or the resolution company. The Treasury is also empowered to make regulations concerning the information that must be provided to the Bank of England or the resolution company.[56]

The administrator is obliged to pursue the first objective until the Bank of England issues an **7.34** achievement notice signifying that the support of the residual bank or resolution company is no longer required.[57] Until this notice has been issued the interests of creditors other than the depositors are secondary.

A creditors' committee cannot be established until Objective 1 has been completed, this is **7.35** achieved under the legislation by the amendment of the provisions of Schedule B1 to the Insolvency Act 1986 on creditors' meetings such that these provisions do not apply on the company entering into administration but only on the giving of notice of the achievement of Objective 1.[58] Until notice is given the Bank of England has the functions of the creditors' committee.

An administrator may apply to the court for directions before Objective 1 has been achieved, **7.36** but he is required to give notice to the Bank of England and the Bank of England is entitled to participate in the proceedings.[59]

---

[55] Banking Act 2009, s 147.
[56] Ibid, s 148.
[57] Ibid, ss 139 and 153.
[58] The amendments to paras 50–58 of Sch B1 are in Table 1 in the Banking Act 2009.
[59] Schedule B1, para 63 as amended in Table 1.

7.37 Until the Bank of England has given an Objective 1 Achievement Notice, a distribution to creditors may be made only with the Bank of England's consent.[60] Where, however, there has been a transfer to a resolution company and before the Bank of England has given an Objective 1 Achievement Notice, a distribution of the prescribed part may be made with the Bank of England's consent or out of assets which have been designated as realizable by agreement between the bank administrator and the Bank of England.[61]

7.38 The management of the bank's affairs, business, and property must be conducted in accordance with the principles agreed between the bank administrator and the Bank of England.[62] The discretion in managing and distributing the assets are fettered where the bank is in administration under the Banking Act in that, following the transfer to a resolution company, until the Bank of England has given an Objective 1 Achievement Notice distribution may be made by the administrator only with the Bank of England's consent or out of assets which have been designated as realizable by agreement between the bank administrator and the Bank of England.[63]

7.39 The bank administrator can disclaim onerous property only with the consent of the Bank of England following a transfer to a resolution company and before the Bank of England has given an Objective 1 Achievement Notice.[64]

7.40 The administrator may only dispose of or take any action relating to property subject to a floating charge as if it were not subject to a charge and the court may only make an order relating to property subject to a fixed charge if the administrator or the court (as the case may be) is satisfied that the action will not prejudice the pursuit of Objective 1.[65] An application to dispose of goods which are in the possession of the bank under a hire-purchase agreement may only be made with the Bank of England's permission.[66]

7.41 Misfeasance proceedings may be brought by the bank administrator and also by the Bank of England.[67] The Bank of England may also make an application challenging the administrator's conduct of the residual bank on any grounds, not just on grounds of unfair prejudice, and the grounds may include insufficient pursuit of Objective 1.[68]

7.42 Only the Bank of England can apply to replace an administrator during the Objective 1 Stage.[69] The modification to the normal insolvency provision is that until an Objective 1 notice has been given the Bank of England and no other person may make an application to replace the administrator; as in a normal administration an administrator can only be

---

[60] Schedule B1, para 65 as amended in Table 1.
[61] Insolvency Act 1986, s 176A, as amended in Table 2 of the Banking Act 2009.
[62] Schedule B1, para 68 as amended in Table 1.
[63] Insolvency Act 1986, s 168(4) and para 13 of Sch 4, modified in Table 2.
[64] Insolvency Act 1986, ss 178–188, as modified by Table 2.
[65] Schedule B1, paras 70 and 71 as amended in Table 1.
[66] Schedule B1, para 73 as amended by Table 1.
[67] Schedule B1, para 75 as amended by Table 1.
[68] Schedule B1, para 74 as amended by Table 1. A court may only make an order on an application by a creditor under this provision until notice of the achievement of Objective 1 has been served if the court is satisfied that the order would not prejudice the pursuit of Objective 1.
[69] Paragraph 91 of Sch B1 to the Insolvency Act 1986 as modified by the Banking Act 2009 in Table 1, s 145(6). The rules on who is to be served, given notice, and appear are the same as those that apply where there is an application for a bank administration order. In addition the administrator whose removal is sought and the administrator who is to be appointed are entitled to be served. Rule 39 of the Administration Rules.

replaced where he dies, resigns, is removed from office, or where he vacates office because he ceases to be qualified.[70] Where a bank administrator has been appointed on an application to the court made by the Bank of England, he can resign by notice in writing to the court or to the Bank of England.[71] Until Objective 1 Stage has been achieved, an application to remove the administrator may only be made with the consent of the Bank of England.[72]

Where an administrator vacates office before the achievement of Objective 1, the discharge **7.43** of the administrators' liability takes effect at a time determined by the Bank of England.[73] The former administrators' remuneration and expenses that are charged on the property in his custody and control immediately before he ceased to be an administrator, are only payable in accordance with the directions of the Bank of England and if the Bank of England is satisfied that they will not prejudice the achievement of Objective 1.[74]

Applications to vary the time periods in Schedule B1 may only be made with the Bank of **7.44** England's consent until an Achievement Notice has been served and the court is required to have regard to the achievement of Objective 1.[75] The Bank of England's consent is required to vary time for the submission of the administrators' proposals, to vary the time for notice of creditors' meetings, and to vary the date for the initial creditors' meeting.[76]

The administrator's remuneration is fixed by the Bank of England as a percentage of the **7.45** value of the property with which he has to deal or by reference to the time properly given by the administrator and his staff to the matters arising in the administration. The administrator may challenge the remuneration fixed by the Bank of England. Notice of any such application must be given to the appropriate regulator and the appropriate regulator may appear and be heard. The rule permitting a creditor to claim that the remuneration is excessive does not apply in the Objective 1 Stage.[77]

The provisions governing the administration of the residual bank during the Objective 1 **7.46** Stage give the Bank of England extensive and close control over the conduct of the administration. The degree of control over all aspects of the administration is such that, in reality, the administrator during the Objective 1 Stage has very little scope for action without the concurrence of the Bank of England.

The court may appoint a provisional administrator of a bank pursuant to section 135 of **7.47** the Insolvency Act 1986 as modified in Table 2 of the Banking Act. A provisional bank administrator may only pursue Objective 1 and the court may confer on the provisional bank administrator functions in connection with pursuit of Objective 1. An application to terminate the provisional administration may be made by the provisional bank administrator

---

[70] Paragraph 90 of Sch B1 applies to bank administration.
[71] Schedule B1, para 87 as amended by Table 1.
[72] Schedule B1, para 88 as amended by Table 1.
[73] Schedule B1, para 98 as amended by Table 1.
[74] Schedule B1, para 99 as amended by Table 1. The amendment does not expressly state that this restriction on payment only applies until an Objective 1 Achievement Notice has been given by the Bank. It would, however, be contrary to the other provisions of the statute were the Bank to continue to have this control over remuneration and expenses once the Bank had formed the view that Objective 1 had been achieved and given notice of that achievement.
[75] Schedule B1, para 107 as amended by Table 1.
[76] Schedule B1, para 108 as amended by Table 1 substitutes the Bank's consent for the consent of the secured creditor and certain preferential creditors.
[77] Insolvency (Reform) Rules 2010, rules 2.106–2.109.

or the Bank of England. The appointment of a provisional administrator lapses on the appointment of an administrator.[78]

2. The Objective 2 stage

7.48   The modifications to and comments on Schedule B1 in Part 3 of the Banking Act (ie Table 1) are relevant only to the conduct of the administration during the Objective 1 Stage, once the Bank of England has issued an achievement notice in relation to that objective, the administration continues in the same manner as a company administration under Schedule B1 to the Insolvency Act. It is only at this stage that a creditors' committee can be constituted as the Bank of England performs the function of such a committee during the Objective 1 Stage.[79]

7.49   There are, however, some modifications to the Bank Administration Rules that apply to this stage of the administration. The requirements governing the meetings to consider the administrator's proposals apply to the proposals for the Objective 2 Stage and an invitation to the meeting must be sent to the appropriate regulator and to the FSCS. When the administrator fixes a venue for the meeting he is required to have regard not only to the convenience of creditors, as in a normal administration, but also to the convenience of the appropriate regulator and FSCS. The appropriate regulator and FSCS are to be given notice in relation to issues concerning appeals against proofs of debt and distributions to the FSCS.[80]

7.50   The rules on the priority of expenses of a bank administration are the same as those in a normal administration, save that 'super priority' is given to expenses incurred in any provisional bank administration.[81] Remuneration is fixed, at the Objective 2 Stage, in the same way as in a normal administration, subject to any pending application made by the Bank in the Objective 1 Stage.[82]

3. Statutory claims available to bank administrators

7.51   During the administration the provisions in the Insolvency Act 1986 for fraudulent trading, wrongful trading,[83] preferences and transactions at an undervalue, extortionate credit transactions, transactions defrauding creditors, and avoidance of floating charges all apply in bank administrators, with minor modifications.[84] The bank administrator may also use the powers to get in the bank's property, require cooperation, and make inquiries.[85]

4. Termination of the administration

7.52   In circumstances where the Bank of England has served an Objective 1 Achievement Notice and the administrator believes that the residual bank has been rescued as a going concern,

---

[78]   Insolvency Act 1986, s 172(1), (2), and (5).
[79]   Part 3 Insolvency 2016 rules para 3.39.
[80]   The Insolvency Rules 2016, Part 3 Chapter 9.
[81]   Insolvency Rules 2016, Part 3 Chapter 10.
[82]   Insolvency Rules 2016, Schedule 11.
[83]   The Banking Act 2009, s 120(9).
[84]   Insolvency Act 1986, ss 213, 214, 238, 239, 240–246 are applied by Table 2. When making orders under ss 238 (transaction at under value) and 239 (preference), the court when considering making an order is required to have regard to Objective 1.
[85]   Insolvency Act 1986, ss 234–237 are applied by Table 2, unmodified.

the administrator may give notice of the termination of administration and file a notice with the court, the Registrar of Companies, and the appropriate regulator. On filing the notices the administrator's appointment ceases to have effect.[86]

If the Bank of England has given an Objective 1 Achievement Notice and the bank administrators pursue the objective of achieving a better result for the residual bank's creditors as a whole than would be likely to be achieved were the residual bank to be wound up without first being in bank administration, the bank administrator may bring the administration to an end in one of two ways. If there is no property which might permit a distribution to creditors, the administrator may take steps to dissolve the company. Alternatively, the bank administrator may make a proposal for a company voluntary arrangement.[87] The bank administrator may not take either of these steps unless he is satisfied that he has received any funds likely to be received from any scheme under a resolution fund order made under section 52 of the Banking Act.[88] **7.53**

The Banking Act 2009 (Bank Administration) (Modification for Application to Multiple Transfers) Regulations 2009 modify the administration provisions that apply to banks pursuant to Part 3 of the Banking Act where more than one property transfer instrument is made by the Bank of England. This could arise where the property is transferred first to a resolution company and then to an end transferee. **7.54**

The provisions of the Company Directors Disqualification Act 1986 are applied to the new bank administration regime to ensure that appropriate action can be taken against the directors of a failed bank. **7.55**

The provisions of the Banking Act do not preclude a bank administration under the Insolvency Act 1986. On an application for an administration order in respect of a bank the court may, instead, make a bank insolvency order. The appropriate regulator or the Bank of England may apply for such an order.[89] An administrator of a bank may not be appointed unless the appropriate regulator has been notified by the application for the administration order that an application has been made or by the person proposing to appoint an administrator, of the proposed appointment. The appropriate regulator must, therefore, be notified of proposals to appoint an administrator by order of the court and by way of an out-of-court appointment. The appropriate regulator is required to inform the Bank of England. A copy of the notice to the appropriate regulator must be filed with the court. An appointment may not be made until a period of two weeks, which begins with the day on which the notice is received by the appropriate regulator, has ended or the appropriate regulator has informed the proposed appointor that it does not intend to apply for a bank insolvency order and the Bank of England has informed the proposed appointor that it does not intend to apply for **7.56**

---

[86] Banking Act 2009, s 153; para 80 of Sch B1 to the Insolvency Act 1986 and r 48 of the Bank Administration Rules.

[87] Banking Act 2009, s 153. Part 1 of the Insolvency Act 1986 on company voluntary arrangements applies to bank administrators, subject to the modification in s 154(3) that the meeting must be summoned by the administrator as nominee and may not be summoned by any other person. (The Insolvency Act 1986, s 3(2) applies and s 3(1) does not apply.) Rule 49 of the Bank Administration Rules supplements the statutory provision on dissolution at the end of administration.

[88] Banking Act 2009, s 154(6). A resolution fund order is an order under s 52 of the Banking Act 2009. Where the Bank has made a property transfer instrument that transfers all or part of the property owned by the bank to a bridge bank, the Treasury is required to make a resolution fund order making provision for compensation whether by a compensation scheme order or a third party compensation order.

[89] Banking Act 2009, s 117.

a bank insolvency order or exercise a stabilization power under Part 1 of the Banking Act. Finally a 'normal' administration order in respect of a bank cannot be made if a bank insolvency order is pending.[90]

IV. Bank Insolvency Procedures

7.57   Part 2 of the Banking Act is concerned with the winding up of a bank based on the existing compulsory winding-up process for commercial companies and is supplemented by the Bank Insolvency (England & Wales) Rules 2009.[91] The institutions that can be subject to the bank insolvency procedure are institutions approved under Financial Services and Markets Act 2000 (FSMA 2000).[92] The insolvency procedure has been applied to building societies by secondary legislation.[93]

A. The Application for a Bank Winding-Up Order

7.58   To try to deal with the need to avoid a 'run' on a failing bank and to preserve the bank's assets, the process of applying for a bank insolvency order is modified as compared with the rules that apply in the normal procedures so that there can be a court hearing without delay. An application to court under the Banking Act to appoint a person as liquidator can be made by the Bank of England, the appropriate regulator, or the Secretary of State.[94]

7.59   There are three grounds for an application for an insolvency order in respect of a bank:

(1) Ground A: the bank is unable to pay or likely to become unable to pay its debts.[95] In addition it is necessary to show that a bank is in default of an obligation to pay an amount that is due and payable under an agreement.[96]

(2) Ground B: it is in the public interest to wind up the bank.[97]

(3) Ground C: it is fair to wind up the bank. This appears to be intended to be no different from 'just and equitable' that is familiar in the context of the winding up of non-bank companies.[98]

7.60   Where the insolvency order is sought the court may only, in the exercise of its discretion, make an insolvency order in respect of a bank if the court is satisfied that the bank has 'eligible depositors'; ie depositors eligible for compensation under the Financial Services Compensation Scheme (FSCS).[99] On an application by the Bank of England or by the

---

[90]   Ibid, s 120.

[91]   These came into effect on 25 February 2009.

[92]   Banking Act 2009, s 91.

[93]   Building Societies (Insolvency and Special Administration) Order 2009.

[94]   Banking Act 2009, s 95.

[95]   The definition in s 123 of the 1986 Act applies to banks.

[96]   Banking Act 2009, s 93(4).

[97]   Building societies cannot be wound up on grounds of public interest. The government's view is that it is not necessary to make ground B available to the FSA.

[98]   Banking Act 2009, s 93(8). The Act points out that 'fair' has a meaning similar to that of 'just and equitable'. The Explanatory Notes to the Banking Bill explain that 'fair' is used in place of the well-known words 'just and equitable' and that 'fair' has replaced these words because they are 'somewhat antiquarian'.

[99]   Banking Act 2009, s 97(1).

appropriate regulator the court must be satisfied that grounds A or C are satisfied and on application by the Secretary of State the court must be satisfied that grounds B and C are satisfied.

Further, where the Bank of England or the appropriate regulator apply for an insolvency order in respect of a bank there are further requirements. The bank is required to be failing or likely to fail to meet the threshold conditions in section 41(1) of the FSMA 2000 (as amended by the Financial Services Act 2012) and it is not reasonably likely that action will be taken by the bank to satisfy these conditions (in the absence of the use of the stabilization powers under Part 1 of the Banking Act).[100]   **7.61**

B. The Process of the Winding Up

The bank liquidator, who is an officer of the court,[101] has two objectives. Objective 1 is to ensure that each eligible depositor has their account transferred to another financial institution or receives payment from the FSCS as soon as practicable.[102] Objective 2 is to wind up the affairs of the bank so as to achieve the best result for the bank's creditors as a whole. Although the bank liquidator is required to begin working towards both objectives, Objective 1 'takes precedence' over Objective 2.[103] The position is described in the Explanatory Note to the Banking Bill as follows:[104]   **7.62**

> Once objective 1 has been achieved, or has been substantially completed, the process of liquidation will continue in much the same way as a normal winding up with the liquidator calling a meeting of creditors, realising the assets of the failed bank and distributing the proceeds to creditors.

Therefore, as with bank administration, the normal provisions are varied to give priority to the protection of the interests of depositors eligible for compensation under the FSCS. The aim of these provisions is the orderly winding up of a failing bank together with prompt compensation payments from the FSCS to eligible depositors. Alternatively, their deposits are transferred to different, financially sound, institutions.   **7.63**

The general powers and duties of the liquidator are set out in section 103 of the Banking Act which lists, with only minor modifications, the main provisions of the Insolvency Act 1986 that apply to non-banks. In short, most of the standard company insolvency provisions apply equally to banks.   **7.64**

From the commencement of the liquidation the members of the liquidation committee will be nominees of the bank, the appropriate regulator, and the FSCS, and the liquidator is required to report to this committee.[105] A meeting of this committee is only quorate if all members (or their nominated representatives) are present.[106] The liquidator is required to   **7.65**

---

[100] These conditions are conditions 1 and 7 in s 7 of the Banking Act 2009.
[101] Ibid, s 105.
[102] Ibid, s 99.
[103] Ibid, s 99(4).
[104] Paragraph 234.
[105] Banking Act 2009, s 100.
[106] Ibid, s 101(2).

report on the progress concerning the eligible depositors and must recommend to the liquidator the manner in which he should pursue the principal objective of protecting the depositors. When the eligible depositors have been paid by the FSCS or have been transferred to a different bank, the liquidator would then seek to form a new creditors' committee from representatives of creditors who were not 'eligible depositors'.[107] The meeting to convene a new committee may elect '2 or 4 individuals' as new members. Two of these individuals replace the Bank of England and the appropriate regulator. The FSCS may continue on the committee, or may resign from the committee (in which case three or five new members may be elected). If the resulting committee has fewer than three members or an even number of members the liquidation committee ceases to exist at the end of the meeting,[108] although the committee may be reformed at the instigation of the liquidator.[109]

7.66   For the purpose of achieving Objective 1, the FSCS may make or arrange for payments to be made to eligible depositors and may make money available to facilitate the transfer of accounts of eligible depositors. A bank liquidator must comply with a request from the FSCS for information and must provide information to the FSCS which he thinks might be useful for the purpose of cooperating in the pursuit of Objective 1.[110] Where a bank liquidator arranges the transfer of eligible depositors' accounts from the bank to another financial institution, the arrangements may disapply or provide that they shall have effect despite any restriction arising by virtue of contract or legislation or in any other way. For this purpose 'restriction' includes 'any restriction, inability, incapacity affecting what can and cannot be assigned or transferred … and a requirement for consent (by any name)'. The bank liquidator, in making the arrangements, is required to ensure that the eligible depositors will be able to remove money from the transferred accounts as soon as reasonably practicable after the transfer.[111]

7.67   Even after their removal as members of the committee, the Bank of England and the appropriate regulator may attend meetings of the liquidation committee and are entitled to copies of documents relating to the committee's business, may make representations to the committee, and may participate in legal proceedings relating to the committee.

7.68   The liquidation committee is required to recommend to the liquidator whether to pursue the transfer of relevant accounts to another financial institution (Objective 1) or whether to pursue payment of the eligible depositors by the FSCS (Objective 2). The liquidation committee is required to consider the desirability of achieving Objective 1 as soon as possible and Objective 2 which is to wind up the affairs of the bank so as to achieve the best result for the bank's creditors as a whole. Objective 1 takes precedence over Objective 2, but the bank liquidator is obliged to begin working towards both objectives from the commencement of his appointment.[112]

7.69   The provisions of the Insolvency Act are applied with some modifications and comments as set out in the Table of Applied Provisions in Part 2 of the Banking Act. The modifications are

[107]   Ibid, s 100(6).
[108]   Ibid, s 100.
[109]   Ibid, s 101(8).
[110]   Ibid, s 123.
[111]   Ibid, s 124.
[112]   Ibid, ss 102 and 99.

for the most part not substantial. The general functions of a winding up, to secure that the assets of the company are got in, realized, and distributed to the company's creditors are also the general function of a bank liquidator, save that these functions are subject to Objective 1, the transfer or payment of eligible depositors.[113]

The general powers of the liquidator in a bank liquidation are those of a liquidator in a normal liquidation, save that in the former neither a creditor nor a contributory may apply to the court with respect to the exercise of the liquidator's powers unless the liquidation committee has passed a full payment resolution,[114] although a person aggrieved by an action of the liquidation committee before it has passed such a resolution may apply to the court.[115] A 'full payment resolution' is a resolution by the liquidation committee that Objective 1, the transfer of eligible deposits to a private bank or payment by the FSCS, has been achieved entirely or so far as reasonably practicable.[116]   **7.70**

Further, in exercising the liquidator's powers under Schedule 4 to the Insolvency Act 1986, the bank liquidator is required to have regard to Objective 1. In addition, the power to bring or defend any action or legal proceedings has been varied to expressly include the power to submit matters to arbitration. The Banking Act also confers some additional express powers on the bank liquidator: the power to insure the business and property of the bank, the power to do all such things (including the carrying out of works) as may be necessary for the realization of the property of the bank, and the power to make any payment which is necessary or incidental to the performance of the liquidator's business.[117] The implication of the addition of these express powers is that the legislature has taken the view that these powers do not fall within the liquidator's general powers, in a normal liquidation, to carry on the business of a company so far as may be necessary for its beneficial winding up or the power to do all such things as may be necessary for winding up the company's affairs and distributing its assets.[118]   **7.71**

The bank liquidator may not apply to the court for directions in relation to any particular matter arising in the winding up and a person aggrieved by an act or decision of the bank liquidator may not apply to the court unless the liquidation committee has passed a full payment resolution, ie until the committee has resolved that Objective 1 has been achieved insofar as is reasonably practicable.   **7.72**

The bank liquidator remains in office until he vacates that office by resigning (which requires that he gives notice to the court), on removal on disqualification, on appointment of a replacement, or because the bank has been put into voluntary arrangement, administration, or has been dissolved.[119]   **7.73**

---

[113] Insolvency Act 1986, s 143 as modified by the Table of Applied Provisions in Part 2 of the Banking Act.
[114] Ibid, s 167 as modified by the Table of Applied Provisions in Part 2 of the Banking Act.
[115] Banking Act 2009, s 101(3).
[116] Ibid, s 100(5)(a).
[117] Ibid, s 104.
[118] Insolvency Act 1986, Sch 4, paras 5 and 13.
[119] Banking Act 2009, ss 106–116.

1. Claims for Misfeasance, Misconduct, and Adjustment of Prior Transactions

7.74 The provisions on misfeasance, fraudulent trading, wrongful trading, restriction on reuse of company names, transactions at an undervalue, preferences, the avoidance of floating charges, transactions defrauding creditors, and other claims available to a liquidator in a normal liquidation are available to the bank liquidator. There are a few modifications, most notably the provision that anything done by the bank in connection with the exercise of a stabilization power under Part 1 of the Banking Act is not a transaction at an undervalue for the purposes of sections 238 and 423 and does not amount to giving a preference under section 239.[120]

2. Termination of the liquidation

7.75 The liquidator can bring the liquidation to an end by proposing a company voluntary arrangement pursuant to section 1 of the Insolvency Act[121] or may apply for the appointment of an administrator pursuant to Schedule B1, paragraph 38 of that statute.[122] On the completion of the liquidation, the bank liquidator is required to hold a meeting of the liquidation committee to report to the committee on the conducted insolvency. He is also required to send a copy of the report to the appropriate regulator, the FSCS, the Bank of England, the Treasury, and the Registrar of Companies.[123]

7.76 A petition for a winding-up order may be presented against a bank under the Insolvency Act 1986. The same conditions apply to the presentation of a winding-up petition as to the appointment of an administrator of a bank under the Insolvency Act 1986.[124] A resolution for voluntary winding up of a bank may not be made unless those conditions are satisfied.[125]

7.77 On 18 January 2010, the Banking Liaison Panel (BLP) advised that provision should be made in the legislation for the building society administrator to have the power to change the name of the residual society so that it is distinguished from the business of the society that has been transferred. In the administration of the residual company of Dunfermline, the BLP noted that building societies may only change their name by special resolution and must notify the appropriate regulator.[126] So far as banks are concerned, Companies House takes the view that the administrator has the power to change the name of the company and will register changes made by the administrator.

V. Building Societies

7.78 The Building Societies Act 1986, as amended by the Building Societies Act 1997, applied UK insolvency legislation to building societies.[127] The Insolvency Rules 1986 were not directly applied to building societies with the consequence that the mandatory set-off rules therein do not apply.

---

[120] Insolvency Act 1986, ss 238, 239, and 423.
[121] Insolvency Act 1986, s 1.
[122] Pursuant to Sch B1 to the Insolvency Act 1986.
[123] Banking Act 2009, s 115(2)(b).
[124] See para 7.55.
[125] Banking Act 2009, s 120.
[126] The procedure is set out in the Building Societies Act, Sch 2, para 9.
[127] Sections 86–92 and Schs 15 and 15A of the 1986 Act.

As explained above, the bank administration procedure and bank insolvency procedure are **7.79** applied to building societies by secondary legislation.[128] The Banking Liaison Panel (BLP) Sub-group on building society insolvency and special administration[129] provided advice to the Treasury on 18 January 2010 on the following issues:

(1) the application of the Insolvency Rules 1986 to building societies and set-off;
(2) the building societies' special administration procedure (BSSAP); and
(3) the building societies' insolvency procedure (BSIP).

On the first issue, the BLP was concerned that the Insolvency Rules 1986 did not apply to **7.80** building societies and that, although the Building Societies Act 1986 provides that rules may be made under the Insolvency Act 1986 to give effect, in relation to building societies, to the provisions of the applicable winding-up legislation, no such rules had been made. The BLP agreed with the principles outlined in the consultation document, but was concerned to ensure that there was equal treatment of banks and building societies in the administration and insolvency procedures. The draft rules for building societies insolvency included provision for set-off, by contrast if 'normal' insolvency proceedings were commenced by 'ordinary creditors' there were no rules on set-off and these should be made under the Building Societies Act 1986.

The BLP also noted that the draft BSIP rules provide that sums owed to building society **7.81** members are carved out of the set-off provisions because the members are 'technically shareholders' and rank below creditors in insolvency. In this respect the 2009 Order enables the administrator to make a distribution to shareholder members and creditors in line with Objective 2. In this respect a reference to depositors includes holders of shares in the society.

VI. The Treatment of Creditors in Bank Insolvencies

The new feature of the insolvency regime as it applies to banks is the focus on the eligible **7.82** depositors and the objective of prompt payment to this class of creditors, whether in administration or liquidation. This first objective, putting payment of depositors ahead of all else, means that the rights of other creditors, including secured creditors, have a lower priority in the process, albeit not in the distribution because the depositors' claims are paid by the FSCS which becomes subrogated to their claims;[130] the FSCS will now be a preferential creditor of the bank.

The court has been asked to consider the set-off provisions of the insolvency rules as they **7.83** apply to bank deposits. Kaupthing Singer & Friedlander Limited (KSF), an Icelandic bank with branches in the UK, went into administration on 8 October 2008 and on the same day certain deposits ('the Edge Accounts') were transferred from KSF to ING Direct NV.[131] In

---

[128] Building Societies (Insolvency and Special Administration) Order 2009; Building Society Special Administration (England and Wales) Rules 2010.

[129] The remit of the subgroup is to provide advice to the Treasury on behalf of the Banking Liaison Panel under s 10 of the Banking Act 2009.

[130] PRA, *Depositor Protection*, Subrogation, 28.2, December 2020: <https://www.prarulebook.co.uk/rulebook/Content/Part/213751/15-06-2021#213751>.

[131] Under the Banking (Special Provisions) Act 2008.

administration KSF's creditors were the FSCS for sums paid by the FSCS to ING so that FSCS would take over liability to the Edge depositors for deposits of £2.6 billion; the Non-Edge Deposit with deposits of about the same value (ie £2.6 billion), and trade and other creditors who ranked equally with the FSCS and the Non-Edge Depositors. Some creditors of KSF also owed money to KSF. In *Kaupthing Singer & Friedlander Limited (in administration)*[132] the court was asked to give directions concerning four issues arising from the rules governing set-off. The judge held that for the purposes of set-off in administration a 'future debt' is a debt that is not due for payment at the date of notice of intention to make a distribution; the same valuation principles applied to sums owed to the creditor and sums owed by the creditor; a creditor could not claim post-administration interest but the company could do so; set-off for debts falling due before the distribution date should be given full value while set-off for debts falling due after the distribution date should be discounted; in applying insolvency set-off to interest bearing debts that were future debts the discount should apply at the date of the notice of distribution and the company cannot add on interest arising between that date and the date on which the loan matures.

7.84   Rule 72 of the Bank Insolvency (England & Wales) Rules 2009 provides for the mandatory set-off of mutual credits and debits, similar to rule 14.24 of the Insolvency Rules 2016. Rule 73 of the Bank Insolvency Rules 2009 provides that, with regard to eligible depositors, set-off will only apply to any balance exceeding the compensation limit. The appropriate regulator has consulted about this and these rules may be amended to make compensation payments to eligible depositors on a 'gross basis' with no set-off of any debts owed by the eligible depositor to the failed bank.

7.85   The Companies Act requirement to register a charge is disapplied by section 252 of the Banking Act where a charge is given by a bank to the Bank of England, the European Central Bank, or any other central bank. The purpose of this provision is to ensure that banks are not discouraged from taking advances from these institutions when they are in need of liquidity by the disclosure of a charge given in respect of advances from these institutions where the advances can include emergency funding. This provision appears to undermine one of the objectives of the statutory requirements for the registration of charges under the Companies Act: the provision of information to prospective lenders as to the company's general financial position and the extent to which the company's assets are charged.

VII. Deposit Protection

7.86   The FSCS was set up under the FSMA 2000 as the UK's compensation fund of last resort for customers of financial services firms. The FSCS is a non-profit-making body with an independent board. The appropriate regulator sets the framework within which the FSCS operates. In particular, the appropriate regulator is responsible for setting the eligibility and compensation limits that apply to the FSCS. The scheme covers eligible deposits held by a firm authorized by the appropriate regulator and depositors with the UK branches of

---

[132] [2009] EWCA 2308.

credit institutions from other EEA states. This has changed since Brexit.[133] FSCS protection may change if a customer or their firm is based in the EEA. FSCS protection will depend on where the firm is authorized and in which jurisdiction the firm holds the deposits. UK branches of EEA-authorized deposit-taking firms will become UK authorized and members of the FSCS—if these firms hold their customer's deposits in the UK then they will still be protected by the FSCS. Deposits held in EEA branches of UK firms will cease to be protected by the FSCS but should be protected by an EEA deposit guarantee scheme instead. Certain deposits are not eligible, such as those of another bank or investment bank or deposit by a public authority with the exception of small local authorities. The FSCS is a key facilitator in the insolvency procedure and can assist the procedure provided that it is using its resources in an efficient and economic manner.

The FSCS only pays compensation for financial loss.   **7.87**

The FSCS provides compensation for bank deposits and other financial products.[134] It will   **7.88**
pay compensation when a member is in default and the appropriate regulator has decided it can no longer comply with the part 4 permission to undertake deposit-taking business. The maximum compensation payable from January 2017 to each depositor is £85,000, with up to £170,000 for joint accounts. A new category of depositor with a temporary high balance of £1 million, from the sale of a house, for instance, has been created. Compensation will be calculated based on eligible deposits on the compensation date. In the case of joint accounts each depositor is considered separately and compensated equally.

The time it takes to pay compensation for eligible deposits has been an area of considerable   **7.89**
concern given the importance and reliance individuals placed on their bank accounts. The FSCS is required to pay compensation as soon as reasonably practicable, with the requirement that by 2024 it must be able to make a payout in seven business days. The current practice is seven working days, but fifteen working days for the more complex issues In order to expedite such rapid payouts firms are required to mark eligible deposits so that they are identifiable. The firm is required to be in a position to be able to provide the FSCS with the aggregate amount of eligible deposits and other information to enable the FSCS to pay compensation as rapidly as possible. The firm is required to provide the PRA or FSCS all single customer views and exclusions within 24 hours. The firm is required to be able to automatically identify eligible depositors and the amount covered and ensure that this is accurate. The automation of this information provides the basis for the firm to be able to transfer eligible deposits in order to achieve the desired stabilization option or administration.

When a bank (including a building society) goes into an insolvency procedure: **7.90**

The bank liquidator or building society liquidator will have specific statutory objectives:

- to work with the FSCS to enable prompt payouts to eligible depositors or to facilitate the bulk transfer of accounts to another institution; and
- to wind up the affairs of the failed bank in the interests of creditors as a whole.

---

[133] FSCS, Brexit and FSCS protection, <https://www.fscs.org.uk/about-us/brexit/>
[134] Long-term insurance, insurance brokering, investment business, and mortgage advice and arranging mortgages.

The first objective has precedence over the second.

7.91   In achieving these statutory objectives the FSCS will need to work with the liquidation committee to decide whether it would be more suitable to undertake a bulk transfer or to take a more incremental approach, where the liquidator works with the FSCS to pay eligible depositors.

7.92   In a building society insolvency, the FSCS takes over two types of claims. This arises because building society customers can hold their account in one of two ways: as members of the society, in which event they are members not creditors; or as non-members, for example, current account holders, in which event they are creditors. The FSCS holds rights equivalent to the members whom it has paid and will be a creditor in respect of monies it has paid to non-members. Therefore, the FSCS could be owed a substantial sum of money by the building society, but will only be a creditor in respect of the sums paid to creditors.[135]

7.93   The FSCS has, therefore, been given particular rights in a building society liquidation: it is a member of the liquidation committee as of right; it will have a right to apply to court to challenge the liquidator's remuneration even if it is a creditor for less than 25 per cent of the total value of claims in the liquidation;[136] it will have the right to call a meeting of the liquidation committee;[137] and it will have the right of a creditor who is a member of the liquidation committee to stop a resolution by post.[138]

7.94   The FSCS also becomes subrogated to the rights of members that have been paid by the FSCS.[139] On payment the FSCS is:

> immediately and automatically subrogated, subject to such conditions as the FSCS determines are appropriate, to all or any part … of the rights and claims … of the claimant against the relevant person.

The effect of subrogation is that the FSCS has the right to participate in the distribution of the surplus after the distribution to ordinary creditors and enables the FSCS to attend meetings of contributories.

7.95   The BLP agreed with the Treasury that the following rights should be given to the FSCS:

(1) the right of creditors that are owed at least 25 per cent of the total in value to apply to the court claiming that the liquidator's remuneration is excessive; the right of the FSCS should not be dependent on the extent to which they are a creditor or on the value of members' claims subrogated;

(2) the right of a creditor who is a member of the liquidation committee to call a meeting of the liquidation committee; and

(3) the right of a creditor who is a member of the liquidation committee to stop a resolution by post.

---

[135] Banking Liaison Panel (BLP), Subgroup on building society insolvency and special administration, Advice to HM Treasury, 18 January 2010 <https://www.gov.uk/government/uploads/system/uploads/attachment_data/file/210282/bankingliaisonpanel_advice180110.pdf>.

[136] Ibid, at 19.

[137] Ibid.

[138] Ibid.

[139] See COMP 7.3.8, FCA Handbook <https://www.handbook.fca.org.uk/handbook/COMP/7/3.html?date=2015-12-21>.

The BLP was also concerned that where members' rights are transferred to the FSCS, it is important that these rights should revert to the members after the FSCS has ceased to be involved in the insolvency process.   **7.96**

The Financial Services Act 2010 provides for an expansion of the role of the FSCS to act as paying agent for other compensation schemes or arrangements.[140] This legislation was introduced because in 2008 the FSCS went beyond its remit to ensure that eligible claimants in failed banks were fully compensated for their deposits, including those in the UK branch (Icesave) of Landsbanki, by paying compensation due from the Icelandic deposit-guarantee scheme to ensure that eligible depositors were fully compensated for their deposits. This was done by private agreement.   **7.97**

The Financial Services Act 2012 makes provision for the cost of funding the exercise of the SRR powers to be recovered from the FSCS up to the net costs that the FSCS would have incurred had the bank gone into default and FSCS compensation been paid in the normal way (subject to a cap). There is provision in the FSMA 2000, section 214B[141] for the FSCS to contribute to the cost of the use of SRR powers, but it did not take into account the actual costs (if money were to be borrowed) or opportunity costs (because money could have been used elsewhere).   **7.98**

The Banks and Building Societies (Depositor Preference and Priorities) Order 2014[142] sets out the implementation of the depositor preference rule, in line with the Bank Recovery and Resolution Directive 2015.[143] The introduction of the BRRD has reformed the hierarchy of creditors in an insolvency so leading to amendments to the Insolvency Act 1986 and the respective priority of debts set out therein. The reforms move the implicit priority and protection to safeguard depositors with deposit protection to an explicit safeguard to set out the priority of eligible deposits and other deposits. The order sets out the reforms to introduce 'ordinary preferential debts' and 'secondary preferential debts'.   **7.99**

The category of ordinary preferential debts includes the FSCS giving it the status of 'super preferred' which will implicitly include eligible depositors protected up to the limit of £85,000. The category of secondary preferential debts is new and includes 'other deposits', which refers to deposits other than those protected by (and exceeding) the compensation limit, or micro, small, or medium-size businesses' deposits. This category also includes the deposits of a branch of a credit institution located outside the EEA. Post Brexit this may include deposits of a branch located within the EEA. A deposit held with an EEA branch of a UK firm is no longer covered by the FSCS. The secondary preferential debt category is therefore new and will rank behind the ordinary preferential debt category. These will rank ahead of unsecured senior creditors and unsecured subordinated creditors. As a consequence of   **7.100**

---

[140] FSMA 2000, s 224C.
[141] This was implemented in the FSMA 2000 and in the FSMA (Contribution to Costs of Special Resolution Regime) Regulations 2009.
[142] Banks and Building Societies (Depositor Preference and Priorities) Order 2014.
[143] Directive 2014/59/EU establishing a framework for the recovery and resolution of credit institutions and investment firms and amending Council Directive 82/891/EEC, and Directives 2001/24/EC, 2002/47/EC, 2004/25/EC, 2005/56/EC, 2007/36/EC, 2011/35/EU, 2012/30/EU, and 2013/36/EU, and Regulations (EU) No 1093/2010 and (EU) No 648/2012 of the European Parliament and of the Council. The Bank Recovery and Resolution (Amendment) (EU Exit) Regulations 2020 (BRRD SI), following Brexit, 'onshores' the BRRD and ensure the continued function of the regime.

these reforms, some deposits that do not fall in to the category of eligible deposits and other deposits will be exposed to significantly more risk.

7.101 The Bank Code of Practice 2020 explains how the Bank will have to reconcile the competing demands posed by the different resolution tools, including the bank insolvency procedure or the bank administration procedure. It will entail assessing how efficiently the covered deposits will be best safeguarded. Therefore, it may lead to a situation where the latter may be the appropriate first option rather than a last resort so that covered deposits are paid out efficiently and promptly using FSCS funds. This decision-making process will also have to assess whether a delay in a payout to covered deposits in the interests of depositors as a whole is a risk necessary to take to satisfy the resolution objectives. The code explains:

> In assessing the degree of continuity required to protect depositors, the Bank will take into account the diverse nature of deposits as a liability class. That is to say, different types of deposit liabilities require a greater or lesser degree of continuity of access in resolution or to avoid depositor hardship due to lack of access to their funds.

VIII. Cross-Border Bank Insolvency

7.102 The Reorganisation and Winding-up of Credit Institutions Directive[144] was introduced in the wake of the failure of BCCI and was implemented in the UK by the Credit Institutions (Reorganisation and Winding Up) Regulations 2004. The Regulations have been amended by The Credit Institutions and Insurance Undertakings Reorganisation and Winding Up (Amendment) (EU Exit) Regulations 2019 and The Bank Recovery and Resolution (Amendment) (EU Exit) Regulations 2020 to reflect the UK's exit from the EU. This, in the context of cross-border bank failures, provides for a single set of proceedings in the home country and for an equal treatment of creditors.[145] The Directive did not, however, harmonize national bank insolvency procedures.

7.103 The absence of harmonization means that the basis of insolvency law in different jurisdictions can be incompatible. Some countries adopt the 'universal' approach in which a home country will seek to resolve a locally incorporated international bank as a single entity, applying a single proceeding to the bank and its branches worldwide and treating creditors equitably regardless of their location. Others use a 'territorial' approach such that the international activities of a bank are resolved through separate entity resolutions applied by the host countries to the local entities, including branches and subsidiaries of the bank completely separately from the main proceedings applied to the parent bank by the authorities in the home country.

7.104 The Directive is based on a form of universality; it applies the universal approach to the resolution of a bank and its branches abroad, but preserves the ability of the host countries

---

[144] Directive 01/24/EC, 4 April 2001.

[145] The City of London Law Society's response of 17 September 2008 to the consultation document dated July 2008 entitled *Financial Stability and Depositor Protection: Special Resolution Regime* made the point that it was unclear whether bank administration proceedings would be an 'insolvency proceeding' for the purpose of this Directive so as to be recognized in the EEA because the primary purpose of the procedure is to support the bridge bank rather than the procedure being a collective procedure for the creditors.

to apply territorial approaches to locally incorporated subsidiaries. The combination can become a problem if the authorities in the host country ring-fence assets attributable to the local branch of a foreign bank and use them to pay the claims of creditors of that branch. The Bank of England is concerned that this could be adopted by any country in respect of local branch activities of a UK bank and undermine the administration procedure. Post Brexit, the provisions in UK law that conferred exclusive jurisdiction for an automatic recognition of EEA insolvencies are removed.

IX. The Investment Bank Special Administration Regime

In 2009 the Treasury commenced consultation on new measures to deal with failed investment banks in accordance with section 223 of the Banking Act 2009, to enable the authorities to manage in an orderly manner the failure of an investment bank and minimize the chances of a catastrophic fallout in terms of delays experienced with the administration of Lehman Bros International (Europe) Limited (LBIE). The reforms have led to a reform of the administration and parts of the insolvency regime, in particular ensuring that client assets are returned as efficiently as possible to minimize disruption to the financial activities of the clients. The rationale of a special administration regime (SAR) and insolvency regime for investment banks enables the authorities to deal with the fallout of a financial conglomerate. The latter consists of a variety of entities, both deposit-taking and investment banks, operating in accordance with Part IV Permission under the FSMA 2000. This can take the form of safeguarding and administering investments, dealing in investment (either as a principal or agent), or holding client assets. In the latter respect 'client assets' is interpreted to also mean 'client money'. The administrator will have special objectives which it will need to comply with to satisfy the requirements set out on the Regulations. **7.105**

After a period of consultation, on 16 December 2009, the Treasury published proposals to strengthen the Authorities' ability to deal with any future failure of an investment bank, 'Establishing resolution arrangements for investment banks'.[146] **7.106**

The aim was to develop a resolution regime that would enable a more effective management of the failure of an investment bank than was achieved with Lehman Brothers International Europe (LBIE). Insolvency proceedings in respect of Lehman Brothers were commenced in more than 20 countries. Moreover, Lehman Brothers operated a centralized cash management system to collect funds from and transfer funds to different parts of its organization. A cross-border insolvency protocol and guidelines were developed to promote information sharing among the officeholders. The US courts approved the arrangements, although the officeholders in some jurisdictions did not sign up to the arrangements (France, Japan, and the UK). **7.107**

---

[146] This was the second consultation paper on this issue and sets out detailed proposals for effective resolution of a failed investment firm. The first paper, published in May 2008, was titled, 'Developing effective resolution arrangements for investment banks'. Both consultation papers were developed with input from the Bank and the FSA and the advice of industry experts.

A. Lehman Brothers

7.108   Just as the Lehman Brothers insolvency resulted in over 75 separate bankruptcy proceedings, the administration of Lehman Brothers International (Europe) (LBIE), the UK and EU trading company of the Lehman Brothers group, provides a range of lessons post the global financial crisis for regulators and central banks in terms of how best to manage a liquidity crisis.[147] Following the full payout of subordinated creditors, it was apparent to the administrators (PwC) that there was an estimated £5 billion distributable cash surplus. This prompted a series of hearings in UK courts regarding potential repayments for unsecured creditors in order of priority in insolvency proceedings. The latter is known as an insolvency 'waterfall'.[148]

7.109   *Joint administrators of LB Holdings Intermediate 2 Ltd and Others v Lomas and Others* ('the Waterfall I case'), heard in the UK Court of Appeal (CA) in May 2015 concerned the right of unsecured creditors to recover statutory interest accrued during LBIE's administration (stage 6 in Lord Neuberger's order of priority in insolvency). It also clarified the scope of non-provable liabilities (stage 7) in relation to currency conversion claims and shareholders' contributions with respect to the waterfall (stage 8). In spite of the subordinated creditors' arguments that statutory interest was not a liability of the company in liquidation as per rule 2.88(2) corroborated with section 189 of the Insolvency Act 1986,[149] the Court of Appeal held that unsecured creditors had the right to statutory interest as the latter survived the transition from administration to liquidation.[150]

7.110   With regard to stage 7 of the insolvency waterfall, it was agreed by the majority in the CA that creditors who suffered a shortfall as a result of the depreciation of the sterling against the contractual currency[151] following the insolvency process would be able to recover it as a non-provable liability.[152] On the other hand, as to whether LBIE's shareholder Lehman Brothers Holding Intermediate Ltd (LBHI2), likewise a subordinated creditor of LBIE, was entitled to be paid at the below stages of the waterfall, the court decided that the debt was to be subordinated until stage 7 creditors are paid out.[153] In connection to this, section 71(1) of the Insolvency Rules 1986 provides that, when a company is in liquidation, shareholders are obliged to contribute to its assets in order to pay for its debts and liabilities.[154] However, LBIE was an unlimited company, previously chosen as such for tax reasons,[155] and its shareholders LBHI1 and Lehman Brothers Ltd (LBL) were limited companies facing administration.[156] The shareholders argued that the meaning of 'liabilities' under section 74 was solely

---

[147] *Joint administrators of LB Holdings Intermediate 2 Ltd and Others v Lomas and Others* [2014] EWHC 704 (Ch); [2015] EWCA Civ 485 (14 May 2015) ('Waterfall I') and *Re Lehman Brothers International (Europe) (In Administration)* [2015] EWHC 2269; [2015] EWHC 2270 (Ch) ('Waterfall II').

[148] *Joint administrators of LB Holdings Intermediate 2 Ltd and Others v Lomas and Others* [2015] EWCA Civ 485 at 19.

[149] Ibid at 190.

[150] Ibid at 111.

[151] Ibid at 159.

[152] Ibid at 166.

[153] Ibid; 'Lehman Brothers "waterfall application" in the Court of Appeal', 26 June 2015.

[154] *Joint administrators of LB Holdings Intermediate 2 Ltd and Others v Lomas and Others* [2015] EWCA Civ 485 at 172.

[155] Ibid at 2.

[156] 'Lehman Brothers "waterfall application" in the Court of Appeal', 26 June 2015.

comprised of proven liabilities, and therefore they were not obliged to contribute statutory interest and non-proven liabilities.[157]

Nevertheless, the Court of Appeal rejected this interpretation on the grounds that, inter alia, **7.111** it would be irrational if contributories 'were liable in relation to the lowest item in the waterfall, namely the adjustment of contributories' rights among themselves, yet not liable for the two items above it, namely statutory interest and non-provable liabilities'.[158] Furthermore, liquidators, if so required, were obliged to pay a company's non-provable liabilities.[159] It was ultimately decided that the distribution would take place in the following order: first, statutory interest payable under rule 2.88 of the Insolvency Rules 1986; secondly, creditors' non-provable claims, including those regarding currency exchange losses due to the sterling's depreciation against the currency in which their contractual claims were payable 'between the commencement of the administration and the date on which dividends were paid on such claims'; and, thirdly, the subordinated debt totalling $2.27 billion.[160]

The outcome of 'Waterfall I' has received mixed reactions from practitioners. The circum-   **7.112** stances are extremely rare, with the failure of Lehman being viewed as a tipping point during the global financial crisis, yet its corporate form as an unlimited liability entity and a considerable surplus being encountered by the administration is not the expected situation. The novelty of the issues and the considerable amounts at stake might prompt an appeal of the decision to the UK Supreme Court.[161] On the other hand, it has been argued that closing the legislative gap between contractual and statutory interest 'will be seized on' by practitioners and that it would be relevant to consider the latter for the purposes of modernizing the 1986 Insolvency Rules going forward.[162] Likewise, the decision as regards the applicability of the contributory rule solely in liquidation as opposed to in administration,[163] has been welcomed.[164]

The 'Waterfall II' application considers outstanding issues raised by LBIE's administra-   **7.113** tors before proceeding with distributing the £7.39 billion surplus.[165] The hearings have been divided into three: 'Waterfall IIA'[166] mainly addresses unsecured creditors' entitlement to statutory interest on their proved debts,[167] and 'Waterfall IIB'[168] deals with the impact of post-administration agreements, namely the multilateral Claims Resolution Agreement (CRA) and the Claims Determination Deeds (CDD). 'Waterfall IIC', scheduled for later hearing, is set to address the ISDA Master Agreement and other market standard contracts.[169]

---

[157] *Joint administrators of LB Holdings Intermediate 2 Ltd and Others v Lomas and Others* [2015] EWCA Civ 485 at 173.

[158] Ibid at 202.

[159] Ibid at 50–51.

[160] *Re Lehman Brothers International (Europe) (In Administration)* [2015] EWHC 2270 (Ch) at 4.

[161] Ibid.

[162] Ibid.

[163] According to which 'a party that is both a creditor of a company and a contributory cannot recover anything in its capacity as creditor until it has discharged in full its liability as a contributory', as discussed in E Holland and N van den Berg, 'Seniority of Debts Flushed out in Waterfall Application' (2014) *Corporate Rescue and Insolvency* 99–102 at 101. See also *Cherry v Boultbee* (1838) 2 Keen 319, (1839) 4 My&Co 442.

[164] *Re Lehman Brothers International (Europe) (In Administration)* [2015] EWHC 2270 (Ch) at 4.

[165] Ibid at 6.

[166] *Re Lehman Brothers International (Europe) (In Administration)* [2015] EWHC 2269.

[167] *Re Lehman Brothers International (Europe) (In Administration)* [2015] EWHC 2270 (Ch) at 6.

[168] Ibid.

[169] Ibid.

7.114   In brief, the High Court in 'Waterfall IIA' considered whether, on the basis of *Bower v Marris*,[170] the calculating and paying of the post-insolvency interest should be 'treated as appropriated first to any interest outstanding at the date of distribution, and only then in reduction to the principal amount of debt'.[171] This argument was advanced by the senior credit group (SCG) holding unsecured debts of £2.75 billion and York, on behalf of four co-participants in unsecured $676.25 million claims. Interpreting rule 2.88(7) of the Insolvency Rules, the court clarified that the relevant period from which interest would need to be paid started from the administration and ended on the distribution date, and thus interest would not be paid after the relevant distribution, as *Bower* might suggest.[172] The latter case is inapplicable[173] as in respect of statutory interest, dividends would discharge the outstanding principal before interest comes into play.[174]

7.115   It was added that statutory interest, calculated at the judgment rate of 8 per cent is payable on a simple, as opposed to compound, basis.[175] Further, rule 2.88 concerns only the payment of interest on proved debts, at the exclusion of non-provable claims and, if a proved debt consists of several separate debts, it should be disaggregated so as to calculate the statutory interest for each part.[176] As regards rule 2.88(9), apart from the administration date, it was held that the rate applicable to the debt would not include a foreign judgment date, save where the latter was already available at the administration date.[177] Interest in respect of future and contingent debts would likewise be payable from the administration date, as opposed to any set date on which the debt fell due, according to rule 2.88(7).[178] Finally, a currency conversion claim should be calculated disregarding the statutory interest paid to the creditor.[179]

7.116   'Waterfall IIB' made several findings on whether the post-administration contracts had any effect on the unsecured creditors' claims, more specifically if they released or modified their rights to statutory interest on their proved debts or to currency conversion claims.[180] The main purpose of the agreements was to 'simplify and accelerate the ascertainment of claims to trust assets and unsecured claims' and to 'accelerate the return of trust assets and distributions among unsecured creditors'.[181] Concerning statutory interest claims under rule 2.88, it was concluded that the CRA does not limit the latter to the 8 per cent judgment rate, meaning that signatories to the CRA may claim the interest in question at a higher contractual rate.[182] Moreover, the CRA would release non-provable interest claims should they be found to exist[183] but would not do so with regard to currency conversion claims, nor would it create these.[184] Thus, 'for the purposes of admission to proof, all such claims must

---

[170] 41 ER 525.
[171] *Re Lehman Brothers International (Europe) (In Administration)* [2015] EWHC 2269 at 35.
[172] Ibid at 134–135.
[173] Ibid at 155.
[174] Ibid at 149.
[175] Ibid at 8, 28.
[176] Ibid at 29.
[177] Ibid at 183.
[178] Ibid at 225.
[179] Ibid at 231.
[180] *Re Lehman Brothers International (Europe) (In Administration)* [2015] EWHC 2270 (Ch) at 5.
[181] Ibid at 3.
[182] Ibid at 114.
[183] Ibid at 116.
[184] Ibid at 135.

be converted into sterling in accordance with rule 2.86.[185] However, to the extent of the sterling's depreciation against the relevant currency after the administration date, 'the unsatisfied balance of the foreign currency obligation remains outstanding as a debt and can be claimed out of the surplus after the payment of proved debts and statutory interest'.[186]

Similarly, 'Agreed Claims CDDs', the first type of CDDs expressed in the currency of the underlying contract,[187] had no effect on claims to statutory interest pursuant to rule 2.88.[188] However, in case of non-provable claims, 'it would be difficult to argue that such claims survived the express release in clause 2.1.1 of the Agreed Claims CDD'.[189] Agreed Claims CDDs also do not release currency conversion claims.[190] The same treatment for statutory interest and currency conversion claims (including the exception provided for non-provable claims) is applied under Admitted CDDs; the latter are later-developed CDDs, invariably expressed in sterling.[191] Richards J concluded that it would have been an unfair outcome, in accordance with *Ex parte James*[192] or paragraph 74 of Schedule B1 for the CRA or any of the CDDs to have the effect of releasing currency conversion claims. In such a situation, the administrators would have been directed not to enforce the releases.[193]   **7.117**

B. Investment Bank Special Administration Regulations 2011

The Banking Act 2009 provides the basis for the authorities to formulate an SAR for investment banks.[194] The relevant regulation is the Investment Bank Special Administration Regulations 2011. This Regulation complements the regime discussed above when an investment bank is a deposit-taking institution and has eligible deposits.[195] However, where, inter alia, it does not have eligible deposits, the 2011 Regulation regime applies a separate special administration. In this respect, the investment bank can be put into Special Administration (Bank Administration) or Special Administration. The application to the court for a special administration order can be made by the investment bank, the directors of the investment bank, creditors, the Secretary of State, or the appropriate regulator. The appropriate regulator has a right to be heard by the court if an application for an order is made to the court. The following grounds form the basis of applying to the court for such an order: **7.118**

> 6.—(1) In this regulation—
>> (a) Ground A is that the investment bank is, or is likely to become, unable to pay its debts;
>> (b) Ground B is that it would be fair to put the investment bank into special administration; and

[185] Ibid.
[186] Ibid.
[187] Ibid at 137–138.
[188] Ibid at 146.
[189] Ibid at 147.
[190] Ibid at 154.
[191] Ibid, at 155.
[192] (1874) LR 9 Ch App 609.
[193] *Re Lehman Brothers International (Europe) (In Administration)* [2015] EWHC 2270 (Ch) at 183–189.
[194] See Banking Act 2009, ss 233, 234, 235(3), 259(1).
[195] See Banking Act 2009, s 97(1).

(c) Ground C is that it is expedient in the public interest to put the investment bank into special administration.

(2) The [appropriate regulator] or the persons listed in regulation 5(1)(a) to (e) may apply for a special administration order only if they consider that Ground A or Ground B is met.

(3) The Secretary of State may apply for a special administration order only if it appears to the Secretary of State that Grounds B and C are met.

(4) The sources of information on the basis of which the Secretary of State may reach a decision on Ground C include those listed in section 124A(1)(a) of the Insolvency Act (petition for winding up on grounds of public interest).

C. Review of the Investment Bank Special Administration Regime

7.119   The SAR for investment banks was set up with an obligation on the Treasury to undertake a review of its effectiveness after two years of it coming into force. The final report by Peter Bloxham was published in January 2014. This report led to the reforms introduced in the Investment Bank (Amendment of Definition) and Special Administration (Amendment) Regulations 2017. While it is beyond the scope of this work to undertake a thorough analysis of the report and its recommendations, the report highlights the importance of working out a number of areas that have posed challenges to administrators when dealing with client assets and money, especially improving the synergy between Client Assets Sourcebook (CASS) rules on a going concern basis and the SAR when dealing with client assets during the gone concern phase. It once again stresses the importance of improving supervisory, resolution, and administration and insolvency law to ensure the interests of wider stakeholders in financial regulation are effectively safeguarded as much as possible during those phases. It highlights how the CASS rules to safeguard client assets need to be reviewed to ensure as far as possible they are 'resolution proof' so that client assets and money can be transferred as efficiently as possible with minimal delay during the gone concern phase. The report particularly highlights the challenges posed when clients have assets with the investment bank in administration and are creditors of the investment bank as well. This set of circumstances was prevalent in the second high-profile investment bank failure after Lehman, that of MF Global.

7.120   On 16 December 2011 MF Global was the first investment bank to enter the SAR and so offers considerable insights into the challenges posed by the regime.

7.121   As explained in the Bloxham Report:[196]

> Cases in the UK MF Global SAR have highlighted the potentially complex interplay between a client's entitlements to the Client Money Pool (CMP) under the CASS statutory trust and their claims as a creditor of the failed firm. The starting point is that a client of a failed firm in SAR has a dual status:

---

[196] Peter Bloxham, *Final Review of the Investment Bank Special Administration Regulations 2011*, January 2014.

1. one, pursuant to and calculated in accordance with CASS, to a share of the CMP, as a beneficiary of the statutory trust established pursuant to CASS (CMP Entitlement), together with an unsecured claim on the general estate for any breach of trust which results in a shortfall in distributions from the CMP (Shortfall Claim); and

2. a 'parallel' claim under contract (or for breach of contract) on the general estate (Parallel Claim), as an ordinary unsecured creditor of the failed firm.

These claims will overlap. A further complication is that these two rights are valued on different bases, as follows:

1. The CMP Entitlement is based on a notional calculation carried out as at the date of the Primary Pooling Event, assuming a close out of client positions on or very close to that date.

2. The Parallel Claim will be computed in accordance with general insolvency principles, including application of the 'Hindsight' Principle.[197]

The Bloxham review highlights the challenges of calculating what clients are entitled to and this is dependent on the investment bank having accurate and up-to-date records so that the administrator can determine the clients' interests. The case of *MF Global* highlighted the need for judicial intervention to bridge the gaps exposed by the CASS rules and the administration of a large complex investment bank, rather than using the administrative procedures, resulting in its clients not receiving their assets as expeditiously as previously hoped with the introduction of the SAR. The Bloxham Report supports the CMP approach as it leads to a speedier return of client assets, albeit with the risk of a shortfall, which could be made up at a later point. The Treasury published their 'reforms to the investment bank special administration regime' paper in March 2016, which considers the issues raised in the Bloxham Report. Many of the suggestions in the Report were adopted in the 2017 Regulations. The Treasury commented on both the *Lehman Brothers* and *MF Global* cases, and promised to adopt certain policies which would improve the SAR, especially when it comes to the distribution process of client money. **7.122**

The administrator under the SAR is required to comply with the following objectives in no particular order of importance to achieve in their view the best results for clients and creditors. Moreover the appropriate regulator can provide directions to the administrator to prioritize the objectives set out in the special administration and be mindful of the stability of the UK financial system or maintain confidence in the stability of the UK financial system. **7.123**

Objective 1 is to return client assets within a reasonably practicable time period and in the order of priority that the administrator considers appropriate to achieve Objective 1.[198] In this respect the administrator is required to return client assets with the result that the investment bank relinquishes control over them. The administrator will be required to put in place a time frame to manage claims (a 'bar date') and a reasonable period of time after notice has been provided so that the claimants can calculate the size of the entitlement. This means the administration of the investment bank needs to make a public announcement so **7.124**

---

[197] See *Lehman Brothers International (Europe) v CRC Credit Fund Ltd* [1212] Bus LR 667; see also *Joint administrators of MF Global UK Limited v Attestor Value Master Fund LP and Scheider Trading Associates Limited and the Financial Services Authority* [2013] EWHC 92.

[198] Regulation 11-12.

as to provide notice to clients of the investment bank. In respect to the distribution of client assets such as securities, the administrator will be required to return those securities at the market price calculated by the investment bank at the time when the investment bank was about to enter special administration, or, alternatively, the administrator will be required to exercise his discretion and offer a fair and reasonable price. The rationale behind the introduction of a bar date also means it improves the timeliness and efficiency of the distribution of client assets in accordance with the Distribution Plan agreed to by the Creditors Committee. For example, with MF Global the administrators decided to put in place a bar date for the submission of claims to client assets.[199] The FSCS has also played a significant role in assisting with compensating eligible claims in its role as the single compensation fund of last resort for customers of authorized financial services firms.[200] It has assisted private customers with individual accounts held with MF Global. In this respect the FSCS must pay up to £50,000 in compensation per claim once it has received the account balance information from the administrator. An objective has also been added after Regulation 10 of the 2011 Regulations, which is set out in Regulation 7 of the 2017 reforms. This sets out the duty of the administrator to work with the FSCS, and details the expected cooperation with the FSCS which should begin 'as soon as reasonably practicable after appointment as the administrator'. For example, the FSCS will cover the shortfall for those eligible to receive FSCS compensation as a result of applying the agreed costs when distributing client assets.[201] In view of this the FSCS would need to work closely with the administrator when such matters are worked out in the distribution plan.

7.125   Objective 2 requires the administrator to work with market infrastructure bodies so as to comply with the bodies' default rules and facilitate the settlement or prompt cancellation of non-settled market contracts.[202] This will require the administrator to work with the body and share appropriate information and share documents to minimize disruption to the market. Moreover, the market infrastructure body is required to provide the administrator with any information that the administrator may reasonably require to comply with Objective 2.

7.126   The recent case related to the administration of MF Global provides some insights into the challenges administrators can face when attempting to ask for disclosure of documents and information associated with MF Global's broker dealer business on LCH.Clearnet, in particular, LCH.Clearnet France.[203] The request for the information related to the extent of the losses it incurred once its positions were closed out, so as to investigate and ascertain whether LCH closed those positions with the appropriate duty of care. When the positions in MF Global's positions in Spanish and Italian governments bonds were closed out, it was claimed by the administrators that the positions appeared to have been closed out at a lower

[199] *In the Matter of MF Global UK Limited; In the Matter of The Investment Bank Special Administration Regulations 2011*, No 9527 of 2011. The Investment Bank (Amendment of Definition) and Special Administration (Amendment) Regulations 2017, 12A—F: <http://www.kpmg.com/UK/en/IssuesAndInsights/ArticlesPublicati ons/Documents/PDF/Advisory/MF-Global-UK-Notice-of-Client-Asset-Bar%20Date.pdf>.

[200] FSCS, Update for Customers of MF Global UK Limited, 9 December 2011 <http://www.fscs.org.uk/news/ 2011/december/update-for-customers-of-mf-glob-94jtb5vy/>   <http://www.kpmg.com/UK/en/IssuesAndInsig hts/ArticlesPublications/Pages/MF-Global-Client-Creditor-claims-forms.aspx>.

[201] *Re Reyker Securities Plc* (in Special Administration) [2020] EWHC 3286.

[202] Regulation 13. No amendments made to regulation 13 in the 2017 reforms.

[203] *MF Global UK Limited (in special administration) v LCH Clearnet Limited and LCH Clearnet SA* [2015] EWHC 2319.

rate than the market rate indicated on the Bloomberg screens. Its primary focus was on the extent to which section 236 of the Insolvency Act 1986 had extraterritorial application to seek the necessary information and documents that the administrators sought. The order was rejected on a number of grounds, primarily that section 236 does not have extraterritorial reach and the fact that the application was time barred. More interestingly, it was decided that the application by the administrators did not relate to a matter that required investigating. The latter decision was based on the surrounding circumstances, notably the European Sovereign Debt crisis which was unfolding at the time during which the positions were closed out. In this respect, David Richards J decided, based on the sheer size of the positions taken by MF Global and the market information being used most notably the price of smaller positions, that this indicated that:

> the resulting difference in price is simply not of itself sufficient to justify the far-reaching order for the production of information, documents and tape recordings sought by the administrators in this case ... Dealing prices on one day are often not a good guide to dealing prices on another day and, having regard to the extraordinary events on those two days, I am satisfied that the differences in prices achieved for the Italian government bonds are not such as to warrant the banking of the order sought under s 236.

Objective 3 requires the administrator to either rescue the investment bank as a going concern or wind it up in the best interests of the creditors. This objective has also given raise to judicial reasoning in yet another MF Global[204] application to the courts to ascertain whether the appointed administrators in light of this objective are appointed analogous to a liquidator therefore giving rise to a complete event of default. The primary focus of the first part of Objective 3 indicates how the administrator in light of this purpose is realizing the assets and planning the distribution of the proceeds among the creditors mindful of the circumstances that the company is possibly rescuable as a going concern. Whereas in the latter part of Objective 3, the company ceases to trade and the sole objective is the realization of assets and the distribution of assets among creditors. In these circumstances, the policy context of the provision is such that the likelihood of a turn around of the investment bank's affairs once client money and positions are closed out is small. The only likely outcome for such an investment bank is closure and liquidation. In the reasoning of the decision it was explained that the possibility of rescue is only likely before the investment bank goes into special administration. **7.127**

The administrator is able to ensure continuity of supply of services and facilities such as hardware and software or financial data, data processing, or security for the data to the investment bank to ensure within the parameter of the special administration that it can continue supplying its investment services, such as safeguarding or the administration of client assets, in as orderly a manner as possible.[205] This means the administrator can prevent the termination of a supply unless payment for those supplies has either lapsed for more than 28 days, or the administrator decides to terminate the supply or the supplier can demonstrate they are suffering hardship to a court and the court orders the termination due to the hardship suffered by the supplier. **7.128**

---

[204] *Richard Heis, Michael Robert Pink and Richard Dixon Fleming v MF Global Inc* [2012] EWHC 3068.
[205] Regulation 14.

7.129 A number of decisions assist in our understanding of the application of the Investment Bank Administration Regulation and the role of the appointed administrator.[206] In *Strand Capital Ltd* the court explained how client assets and client money is expected to be distributed in line with the SAR.[207] In *Strand Capital Ltd*, the court approved of Arnold J's decision in *Beaufort*,[208] setting out the distribution plan that can be executed, if the court approve the distribution plan, the necessary notifications have been made, and the creditors' committee have either approved or been given the opportunity to explain why they do not approve the distribution plan. This therefore ensures, as explained in the decision of the High Court in *Hume Capital Securities* that the court is:[209]

> satisfied that all relevant interests and persons have been given the proper opportunity to make representations on the proposals and have either specifically agreed to them or at least not objected to them and that the plan proposed by the administrators has been approved by the creditors' committee, the court is very likely to be slow to withhold approval or to substitute its own assessment of what is just and reasonable for that of the persons whose interests are affected.

7.130 In the 2020 decision in *Beaufort* the court explained some of the issues for not returning client assets and managing them when the work of the administrator has to all intents and purposes been completed in accordance with the approved Distribution Plan but some clients remain distributable.[210] The reasons could be that the client assets are considered non-returnable by the administrator and so the administrator is discharged from complying with the Distribution Plan; or where the client has not completed the necessary application and so the administrator can exercise the right to liquidate the client assets and return the proceeds to the client net of costs and deductions; or when the administrator considers the clients assets as Tainted Client Assets in the Distribution Plan. Those actions are an attempt to demonstrate to the court that the administrator has made all reasonable efforts in terms of due diligence to discharge their responsibilities in accordance with Objective 1 and so draw to a conclusion the special administration by applying to the court for a petition to liquidate the firm. It would then be up to a late claimant to liaise with the official receiver to recover the assets subject to the costs of holding such assets after the administration. The administrator is not expected to remain in office and incur costs of the residual assets in custody. Further details about potential claimants is provided in Regulation 12. However, the fact that clients remain undistributed was not envisaged when the SAR was first drafted so significant reliance is placed on the courts to assist. In view of this it falls on the court to make an order for the winding up of the company despite client assets remaining undistributed and bring to an end the special administration once the objectives have been reasonably fulfilled.

---

[206] *Hartmann Capital Ltd & Ors, Re Investment Bank Special Administration Regulations 2011* [2015] EWHC 1514; *Strand Capital Ltd, Re The Investment Bank Special Administration Regulations 2011* [2019] EWHC 1449; *SVS Securities Plc, Re The Investment Bank Special Administration Regulations 2011* [2020] EWHC 1501; *Pritchard Stockbrokers Ltd, Re* [2019] EWHC 137; *Worldspreads Ltd, Re Investment Bank Special Administration Regulations 2011* [2015] EWHC 1719; *Beaufort Asset Clearing Services Ltd, Re* [2020] EWHC 3627; *Heis & Ors v Financial Services Compensation Scheme Ltd & Anor* [2018] EWCA Civ 1327

[207] *Strand Capital Ltd, Re The Investment Bank Special Administration Regulations 2011* [2019] EWHC 1449 (Ch)

[208] *In the matter of Beaufort Asset Clearing Services Ltd* [2018] EWHC 2287.

[209] *Hume Capital Securities Plc* [2015] EWHC 3717 at [11].

[210] *Beaufort Asset Clearing Services Ltd, Re* [2020] EWHC 3627 (Ch).

D. Special Administration (Bank Insolvency) Procedure

The Special Administration (Bank Insolvency) Procedure is set out in Schedule 1 of the   **7.131**
Investment Bank Order. In the circumstances explained above, where the investment bank
holds client assets and eligible deposits, then the investment bank could be put in to special administration (bank administration) or special administration (bank insolvency). In
those circumstances the administrator is faced with a dilemma as to whether to place priority of the client assets over the eligible deposits and vice versa.

In such circumstances the administrator is explicitly required to give priority to the interests   **7.132**
of eligible depositors. The administrator is required to transfer the relevant account within
a reasonable time period so that eligible deposits are either transferred or paid out as soon
as reasonably practicable. The administrator is directed to place precedence of Objective
A over the special administration objectives set out in the Statutory Order 'until full payment resolution is passed'. Notwithstanding the priority given to Objective A in Schedule
1, the administrator is nevertheless required to initiate work on the special administration
objectives set out above.

E. Special Administration (Bank Administration) Procedure

The Special Administration (Bank Administration) Procedure is set out in Schedule 2 of   **7.133**
the Investment Bank Order. This procedure is used where the investment bank has a deposit-taking bank as well and to ensure the deposit-taking part is transferred to a private
purchaser or a resolution company. In compliance with this procedure the administrator
is required, according to Objective A, to provide support to a private sector purchaser or
resolution company. The administrator is required to place priority on meeting Objective A
over the special administration objectives until the administrator is notified by the Bank of
England with an 'Objective A Achievement Notice' that the residual part of the bank is no
longer needed and will be likely to be placed in a winding-up procedure. The administrator
is required to work closely with the appropriate regulator and the Bank of England, with the
latter required to liaise with the administrator to realize listed assets to ensure the transfer of
assets and liabilities to the newly set up resolution company.

8

RESOLUTION OF US BANKS AND OTHER FINANCIAL INSTITUTIONS

I. Introduction

'Resolution', as understood in the United States, refers to a particular way of dealing with bank failures or the failures of other financial institutions.[1] Like the traditional bankruptcy model,[2] two of the principal goals of resolution have been to maximize the value and minimize the losses of an institution for the benefit of its depositors and other stakeholders as a group (including any deposit insurance fund) and, at least in a receivership, to determine who receives the residual value of the institution, in what amounts, in what order of priority, in satisfaction of their claims.[3] But resolution is also designed to promote a third set of

8.01

---

[1] The authors Randall D Guynn and Eric McLaughlin acknowledge the superb contributions of John Douglas, former General Counsel of the US Federal Deposit Insurance Corporation, widely recognized bank resolution expert and co-author of prior versions of this chapter. The authors also express their deep gratitude to Luigi L DeGhengi, Mary Jane Dumankaya, Eric B Lewin, Daniel E Newman, Russell Quarles, Andrew Rohrkemper, Gabriel D Rosenberg, Andrew B Samuel, Margaret E Tahyar, Erika D White, and Andrew Xiang in the preparation of this chapter, as well as Reuben Grinberg, Jacob Herz, Jared Kaplan, Nancy Lee, David Miller, Arthi Sridharan, Andrew Terjesen, and Danielle Unterschutz in the preparation of previous versions of this chapter. Unless otherwise noted, this chapter reflects legislative and regulatory developments as of 31 August 2021.
[2] Thomas H Jackson, *The Logic and Limits of Bankruptcy Law* (2001) ('Bankruptcy Law') 10–17, 20.
[3] Federal Deposit Insurance Act (FDIA), §§ 11(d)(3)–(11), (d)(13)(F)(i) and (ii), 12 USC §§ 1821(d)(3)–(11), (d)(13)(F)(i) and (ii); Housing Economic Recovery Act (HERA), § 1145(a), 12 USC §§ 4617(b), 4617(c)(1);

goals: to deal with a failed institution in a manner that reduces the risk of contagion,[4] to preserve or restore public confidence in the banking or wider financial system, and otherwise
to promote financial stability.[5]

8.02   Resolution authority was first introduced in the United States in 1933 as part of the deposit insurance programme for banks.[6] As originally enacted, it was little more than the
method by which the Federal Deposit Insurance Corporation (FDIC) honoured its obligations to insured depositors.[7] It evolved over time into a complementary method of reducing
contagion, preserving and restoring public confidence in the banking system and otherwise promoting financial stability—the fundamental purposes of deposit insurance[8]—as
well as minimizing the cost to the banking system of providing deposit insurance.[9] The
most significant revision to the FDIC's bank resolution powers was made by the Financial
Institutions Reform, Recovery and Enforcement Act of 1989 (FIRREA).[10] The US bank
resolution statute is contained within the Federal Deposit Insurance Act (FDIA).[11] It operates like a special type of insolvency code for US insured depository institutions (IDIs)
administered by the FDIC.

8.03   Congress subsequently created a resolution law modelled on the bank resolution statute
for Fannie Mae and Freddie Mac,[12] the large government-sponsored enterprises (GSEs)
that provide financial support to the US residential mortgage market,[13] as well as for the
Federal Home Loan Bank System. The GSE resolution statute is administered by the Federal
Housing Finance Agency (FHFA), rather than the FDIC. It was used by FHFA to put Fannie

---

Dodd-Frank Wall Street Reform and Consumer Protection Act (the 'Dodd-Frank Act'), §§ 210(a)(2)–(7), 210(a)
(9)(e)(i) and (ii), 210(b)(1), 12 USC §§ 5390(a)(2)–(7), 5390(a)(9)(E)(i) and (ii), 5390(b)(1).

[4]   Douglas Diamond and Phillip H Dybvig, 'Bank Runs, Deposit Insurance, and Liquidity' (1983) 91 *J Pol Econ*
401 ('Diamond and Dybvig'); Hal S Scott, *Interconnectedness and Contagion* (2012) ('Contagion').
  [5]   Federal Deposit Insurance Corporation (FDIC), *Resolutions Handbook* (15 January 2019) 1, 2, 5–6, 23, 25.
  [6]   Federal Reserve Act of 1913, §12B(l)–(n), as added by the Banking Act of 1933, Pub L No 73-66, § 8, 48 Stat
162, 172–77. The Bank Conservation Act was also enacted in 1933 as part of the Emergency Banking Relief Act
of 1933. It permitted the Comptroller of the Currency to appoint conservators for national banks '[w]henever he
shall deem it necessary in order to conserve the assets of any bank for the benefit of the depositors and other creditors thereof...' Pub L No 73-1, tit II, 48 Stat 1, 2–5. Previously, bank insolvencies had been handled under a variety
of state statutes and common law receivership proceedings. FDIC, *Resolutions Handbook, supra* n 5, 24–25.
  [7]   Federal Reserve Act of 1913, §12B(l), as added by the Banking Act of 1933, Pub L No 73-66, § 8, 48 Stat
162, 172–77 (resolution power limited to transferring insured deposits to a depository institution national bank
(DINB)); FDIC, *The First Fifty Years: A History of the FDIC 1933–1983* (1984) 81.
  [8]   Diamond and Dybvig, *supra* n 4; Milton Friedman and Anna Jacobsen Schwartz, *A Monetary History of the
United States, 1867–1960* (National Bureau of Economic Research 1963) 434–37, 440–42 ('Monetary History');
James R Barth, Cindy Lee, and Triphon Phumiswasana, 'Deposit Insurance Schemes' in Cheng-Few Lee and Alice
C Lee (eds), *Encyclopedia of Finance* (2nd edn, 2013) 208.
  [9]   FDIA, § 13(c)(4)(A), (d)(3)(D)(ii), 12 USC 1823(c)(4)(A), (d)(3)(D)(i) and (ii).
  [10]   Pub L No 101-73, 103 Stat 183.
  [11]   The bank resolution statute consists of §§ 11–15 of the FDIA, 12 USC §§ 1821–1825, plus certain definitions
and other supplementary provisions scattered throughout the FDIA, but the most important provisions for purposes of this chapter are §§ 11 and 13, 12 USC §§ 1821 and 1823.
  [12]   12 USC §4617. Fannie Mae is the common name for the Federal National Mortgage Association and Freddie
Mac is the common name for the Federal Home Loan Mortgage Corporation.
  [13]   Fannie Mae and Freddie Mac had assets and liabilities of approximately US$4.0 trillion and US $2.6 trillion,
respectively, with very little stockholders' equity, at 31 December 2020. Fannie Mae, 'Annual Report on Form 10-K
for the Year Ended December 31, 2020'; Freddie Mac, 'Annual Report on Form 10-K for the Year Ended December
31, 2020.'

Mae and Freddie Mac into conservatorship one week before Lehman Brothers failed in September 2008.[14] They remain in conservatorship as of the cut-off date for this chapter.[15]

As a result of the global financial panic of 2008, a strong interest in creating or expanding **8.04** resolution authority arose in the United States and around the world. The US enacted Title II of the Dodd-Frank Wall Street Reform and Consumer Protection Act ('the Dodd-Frank Act'),[16] which expanded resolution authority to apply to bank holding companies (BHCs) and most other nonbank financial companies when certain conditions are satisfied.[17] The most important conditions are that the liquidation, recapitalization, or reorganization of a particular financial company under otherwise applicable insolvency law, principally the US Bankruptcy Code, 'would have serious adverse effects on financial stability in the United States'[18] and that any action under Title II of the Dodd-Frank Act 'would avoid or mitigate such adverse effects'.[19] If a financial institution that becomes insolvent or reaches the point of non-viability can be resolved under the US Bankruptcy Code in a manner that stems contagion, preserves or restores public confidence in the US financial system, or otherwise promotes financial stability in the US as effectively as Title II, then Title II cannot be lawfully invoked. Seizing on this implication from the conditions for invoking Title II, the Bipartisan Policy Center, a private-sector think tank, published a report explaining how the existing US Bankruptcy Code could be used in a manner that would promote the financial stability goal as effectively as Title II under most circumstances, therefore reducing the need for Title II and the likelihood that it can be lawfully invoked.[20] The Hoover Institution, another private-sector think tank affiliated with Stanford University, proposed a new chapter 14 to the US Bankruptcy Code that would include tools designed to help the US Bankruptcy Code resolve large financial companies in a manner that would promote financial stability.[21]

During the same period, the Financial Stability Board issued a series of reports, including **8.05** a report identifying the Key Attributes of effective resolution regimes and recommending that every country enact such a regime.[22] The UK enacted the Banking Act 2009, which gave the Bank of England and HM Treasury resolution authority over banks. In 2013, the UK enacted the Financial Services (Banking Reform) Act 2013, which expanded the Bank of England's resolution authority to include authority over building societies, investment firms, and certain banking group companies, and included a direct bail-in and a bridge

---

[14] Press Release, Fed Housing Fin Agency, Statement of FHFA Director James B Lockhart at News Conference Announcing Conservatorship of Fannie Mae and Freddie Mac (7 September 2008).

[15] See *supra* n 1.

[16] Pub L No 111-203, tit II, 124 Stat 1326 (2010).

[17] Dodd-Frank Act, § 203(b), 12 USC § 5383(b).

[18] Dodd-Frank Act, § 203(b)(2), 12 USC § 5383(b)(2).

[19] Dodd-Frank Act, § 203(b)(5), 12 USC § 5383(b)(5).

[20] John F Bovenzi, Randall D Guynn, and Thomas H Jackson, *Too Big to Fail: The Path to a Solution*, A Report of the Failure Resolution Task Force of the Financial Regulatory Reform Initiative of the Bipartisan Policy Center (May 2013) ('BPC Report').

[21] Thomas H Jackson, 'Bankruptcy Code Chapter 14: A Proposal' in Kenneth E Scott and John B Taylor (eds), *Bankruptcy Not Bailout: A Special Chapter 14* (2012) ('Original Ch 14').

[22] Financial Stability Board, *Key Attributes of Effective Resolution Regimes* (4 November 2011) ('Key Attributes I'); Financial Stability Board, *Thematic Review of Resolution Regimes: Peer Review Report* (11 April 2013); Financial Stability Board, *Key Attributes of Effective Resolution Regimes* (15 October 2014) ('Key Attributes II'). See also Basel Committee on Banking Supervision, *Report and Recommendations of the Cross-border Bank Resolution Group* (September 2009).

bail-in tool.[23] Germany and Switzerland enacted similar statutes.[24] The European Union (EU) adopted the Bank Recovery and Resolution Directive (BRRD), which established a framework for the enactment of special resolution regimes in all EU Member States.[25]

8.06   In addition, a consensus developed around the world that the most promising way to resolve most global systemically important banking groups (G-SIBs)—and thus to provide a last-resort solution to the 'too big to fail' problem if increased capital and liquidity requirements are not entirely successful—is to use resolution authority in a manner that has come to be known as the single-point-of-entry (SPOE) recapitalization ('bail-in') within resolution strategy.[26] The SPOE strategy was first publicly announced by then-acting FDIC Chairman Martin Gruenberg in May 2012.[27] It is a variation on a number of bail-in strategies that had been discussed most actively in Europe at least since 2010.[28] The Bank of England and the FDIC published a joint paper describing and endorsing the SPOE strategy as the most promising strategy for resolving most G-SIBs, while recognizing that a multiple-point-of-entry (MPE) strategy may be more appropriate for others.[29] The Bipartisan Policy Center issued a report explaining how the SPOE strategy could be carried out under either Title II of the Dodd-Frank Act or the US Bankruptcy Code,[30] and the Hoover Institution developed a revised chapter 14 proposal, called chapter 14 2.0, a portion of which was specifically designed to facilitate an SPOE strategy under the US Bankruptcy Code.[31] The US House of Representatives passed a bill in December 2014 that would have implemented the SPOE portion of chapter 14 2.0 and a nearly identical version of the bill was introduced in 2015,[32]

---

[23]   Financial Services (Banking Reform) Act 2013, Schedule 2, 121–123.

[24]   German Banking Act of 1998 (*Kreditwesengesetz*) ('German Banking Act') (as amended in 2011 to include a resolution regime with a transfer order (bridge bail-in) tool); German Recovery and Resolution Act (*Sanierungs- und Abwicklungsgesetz*) (effective 1 January 2015) ('German Resolution Act') (new resolution regime that replaced the resolution provisions of the German Banking Act and includes both a direct and bridge bail-in tool); Swiss Federal Law on Banks and Savings Banks (8 November 1934) (*Bundesgesetz über die Banken und Sparkassen*; SR 952.0) ('Swiss Banking Law'), as implemented by Ordinance of the Swiss Financial Market Supervisory Authority on the Insolvency of Banks and Securities Dealers (30 August 2012) (*Verordnung der Eidgenössischen Finanzmarktaufsicht über die Insolvenz von Banken und Effektenhandlern*; SR 952.05) ('Swiss Resolution Ordinance').

[25]   Directive 2014/59/EU of the European Parliament and of the Council of 15 May 2014 establishing a framework for the recovery and resolution of credit institutions and investment firms and amending Council Directive 82/891/EEC, and Directives 2001/24/EC, 2002/47/EC, 2004/25/EC, 2005/56/EC, 2007/36/EC, 2011/35/EU, 2012/30/EU, and 2013/36/EU, and Regulations (EU) No 1093/2010 and (EU) No 648/2012, of the European Parliament and of the Council (EU BRRD).

[26]   Randall D Guynn, 'Framing the TBTF Problem: The Path to a Solution' in Martin Neil Baily and John B Taylor (eds), *Across the Divide: New Perspectives on the Financial Crisis* (2014).

[27]   Remarks by Martin J Gruenberg, Acting Chairman, FDIC, to the Federal Reserve Bank of Chicago Bank Structure Conference (10 May 2012).

[28]   See, eg, Wilson Ervin and Paul Calello, 'From Bail-out to Bail-in', *The Economist* (28 January 2010); Thomas F Heurtas, 'The Road to Better Resolution: From Bail Out to Bail In', *LSE Financial Markets Group Paper Series*, Special Paper 195 (December 2010). A bail-in strategy is simply a way of recapitalizing a financial institution by converting certain types of debt to equity. Paul Tucker, Deputy Governor for Financial Stability at the Bank of England, was also an early proponent of bail-in.

[29]   Bank of England and FDIC, Joint Paper, *Resolving Globally Active, Systemically Important, Financial Institutions* (10 December 2012); Martin Gruenberg and Paul Tucker, 'When Global Banks Fail, Resolve Them Globally', *Financial Times* (10 December 2012).

[30]   BPC Report, *supra* n 20, at 33–35.

[31]   Thomas H Jackson, 'Building on Bankruptcy: A Revised Chapter 14 Proposal for the Recapitalization, Reorganization, or Liquidation of Large Financial Institutions' in Kenneth E Scott, Thomas H Jackson, and John B Taylor (eds), *Making Failure Feasible: How Bankruptcy Reform Can End 'Too Big to Fail'* (2015).

[32]   Financial Institution Bankruptcy Act of 2014, HR 5421, 113th Cong, 1st Sess (2014); Financial Institution Bankruptcy Act of 2015, HR 2947, 114th Cong, 1st Sess (2015).

and similar bills were introduced in the US Senate in 2013 and 2015.[33] The US Treasury issued a report in 2018, recommending adoption of a new chapter 14 to the Bankruptcy Code and certain amendments to Title II of the Dodd-Frank Act to constrain the FDIC's discretion and make it more consistent with the rule of law.[34] Finally, the US and other countries required systemically important financial institutions (SIFIs) to prepare or participate in the preparation of recovery and resolution plans (otherwise known as 'living wills'), describing how a particular SIFI could be resolved under the applicable resolution regime or ordinary bankruptcy laws without destabilizing the financial system or the need for taxpayer-funded bailouts.

This chapter first describes the fundamentals of resolution authority as conceived in the US.   **8.07**
It then discusses the US bank resolution statute and how it has been used to resolve failed banks in the US, and outlines the GSE resolution statute that applies to Fannie Mae, Freddie Mac, and the Federal Home Loan Bank System, which was based on the US bank resolution model. It describes the new resolution authority in Title II of the Dodd-Frank Act, which applies to all BHCs and most other nonbank financial institutions if certain conditions are satisfied. It also describes how the SPOE strategy works and how the SPOE strategy could be implemented under either Title II or the US Bankruptcy Code. It concludes with a summary of the international initiatives to expand and coordinate the use of resolution authority across borders.

II. Fundamentals of Resolution Authority

Resolution authority has two principal components. The first—the core resolution   **8.08**
powers—provides a designated administrative agency or bankruptcy court with the authority to take control of a bank or other financial institution that has reached the point of non-viability. These powers enable an administrative agency or bankruptcy court to maximize the residual value and minimize the losses of the failed institution, preserve its critical operations, stem contagion, preserve or restore public confidence in the banking or wider financial system and otherwise promote financial stability. There are at least two ways of accomplishing these goals:

1. *Receivership or Bankruptcy.* Placing the financial institution in a receivership or bankruptcy proceeding and quickly separating its equity and loss-absorbing liabilities from the viable parts of its business, including any critical operations, and either:
   a. quickly selling those viable parts of its business to a third party for 'fair value';
   b. transferring them to a bridge entity while leaving the equity interests and loss-absorbing liabilities behind in the receivership or bankruptcy proceeding and either selling or liquidating those viable parts of its business in an orderly manner or effecting a bridge bail-in.[35]

---

[33] Taxpayer Protection and Responsible Resolution Act of 2013, S 1861, 113th Cong, 1st Sess (2013): Taxpayer Protection and Responsible Resolution Act of 2015, S 1840, 114th Cong, 1st Sess (2015).

[34] US Department of the Treasury, 'Report to the President of the United States, Orderly Liquidation Authority and Bankruptcy Reform' (21 February 2018).

[35] A bridge bail-in refers to the exchange of a failed legal entity's unsecured debt for the equity or other residual value of a bridge legal entity to which all or any portion of the failed legal entity's assets and liabilities have been transferred.

In order to effect either strategy, the receiver must temporarily stay the holders of the failed institution's equity interests and loss-absorbing liabilities from enforcing their rights in order to effect the sale, reorganization, or bridge bail-in.[36]

2. *Conservatorship.* Solely in the case of the FDIC or FHFA, placing a failed bank, GSE, or Federal Home Loan Bank into a conservatorship and operating it as a going concern until it can be rehabilitated for the benefit of its stakeholders,[37] or converted into a receivership to be liquidated in an orderly manner. While a conservatorship is possible for an insured bank, the FDIC typically does not use conservatorship as a resolution tool.

8.09   A critical part of the resolution process of banking organizations is the protection of insured deposits. The US, similar to most countries, protects depositors up to a stated limit. The underlying theory is that smaller depositors are not in a position to judge the financial condition of a bank, and should not be expected to bear losses when a bank fails. The FDIC, in its role as receiver for a failed bank, will if at all possible transfer the insured deposits to a viable third party institution or to a bridge bank. If it is unable to do so, it will make arrangements to pay the insured depositors immediately. Taking immediate steps to protect insured depositors is a critical element of the US resolution process and is viewed as critical to the maintenance of financial stability and the avoidance of contagion.

8.10   The second component of resolution authority is a claims process for claims either left behind or otherwise separated from the continuing parts of the business in a receivership or bankruptcy proceeding. The claims process includes the determination of the validity, amount, and holders of the claims in the receivership or bankruptcy proceeding. The entity conducting the claims process is charged with distributing the residual value of the failed institution or the bridge institution to the creditors and other stakeholders either left behind or otherwise separated from the continuing parts of the business in the receivership or bankruptcy proceeding in accordance with the priority of their claims and in satisfaction of their claims.[38] Note that the conservatorship provisions of the resolution statutes for insured banks, the GSEs and the Federal Home Loan banks do not include a claims process. The reason is simple. If a conservatorship is successful and the company is rehabilitated, no

---

[36] A direct bail-in refers to the exchange of a failed legal entity's unsecured debt for equity in the same legal entity, including a write-down of the debt to reflect any shortfall in the value of the equity. The power to do a direct bail-in in the US currently exists only under chapter 11 of the US Bankruptcy Code and not under Title II of the Dodd-Frank Act, the bank resolution provisions in the FDIA or the resolution provisions that govern Fannie Mae, Freddie Mac, or the Federal Home Loan Banks. In contrast, the EU BRRD and the UK, German, and Swiss resolution statutes all include the power to effect either a direct bail-in or a bridge bail-in. See *supra* nn 23–25.

[37] At least in the case of Fannie Mae or Freddie Mac, these stakeholders include the public. Indeed, in *Collins v Yellen*, No. 19-422, slip op. (594 US ___ (2021)), the US Supreme Court construed the incidental powers clause in 12 USC § 4617(b)(2)(J)(ii) to authorize the FHFA to take any actions it reasonably determines to be in the best interests of the public, even if they would not be in the 'best interests of the companies or their shareholders', or presumably their creditors or counterparties. The Court therefore upheld the FHFA's actions in agreeing to the so-called net worth sweep amendment to their Senior Preferred Stock Purchase Agreements with the US Treasury. That amendment obligated Fannie Mae and Freddie Mac to pay dividends to the US Treasury equal to their entire net worth minus a small specified capital reserve rather than at the rate agreed in the original agreements. According to the Court, the FHFA could have reasonably determined that the net worth sweep amendment was in the best interests of the public, even though several shareholders challenged the action in court, arguing that it was inconsistent with the FHFA's statutory duty to preserve and conserve the assets of Fannie Mae and Freddie Mac for their benefit.

[38] FDIA, § 11(d)(11)(A), 12 USC § 1821(d)(11)(A); HERA, § 1145(a), 12 USC § 4617(c)(1); Dodd-Frank Act, § 210(b)(1), 12 USC § 5390(b)(1).

such process is needed. If a conservatorship is unsuccessful, then the expectation is that the conservatorship would be converted into a receivership.

In order for the core resolution powers to achieve their value maximization and finan- **8.11** cial stability goals, the essential elements of placing a failed institution into conservatorship, or placing it into a receivership or bankruptcy proceeding and separating its equity interests and loss-absorbing liabilities from the viable parts of its business, must be completed quickly, if possible over a weekend (commonly referred to as a 'resolution weekend'). Otherwise, the residual value of the failed institution can dissipate rapidly, like a melting ice cube on a hot summer day, especially during a financial crisis. Allowing that value to dissipate will not only harm the failed institution's stakeholders, but it could also foster contagion, undermine confidence in the financial system, and otherwise destabilize the financial system.

The urgency for swift action that exists in exercising the core resolution powers does not **8.12** exist for the claims process. The speed with which the remaining value is divided up among the non-insured deposit claimants generally does not affect confidence in the financial system or financial stability, as long as any claims against the receivership or bankruptcy estate are tradable, and the process is carried out within a reasonable period of time in an otherwise fair and equitable manner. The third party, bridge, or recapitalized firm, which succeeds to the failed institution's operations through the exercise of core resolution powers, can continue to perform the failed firm's critical operations and maximize its residual value and minimize its losses for the benefit of the claimants in the resolution or bankruptcy proceeding. Indeed, the agency or bankruptcy court needs enough time to identify, validate, and determine the amount of any claims and to determine the residual value of the failed institution, without having to determine that value based on fire-sale prices, especially during a financial crisis. Requiring the claims process to be completed too quickly, such as by Monday morning following resolution weekend, could undermine the financial stability goals that the core resolution powers are trying to achieve by undermining the public's confidence in the fairness of the claims process for the claims either left behind or otherwise separated from the continuing parts of the business in the receivership or bankruptcy proceeding.

The core resolution powers are designed to overcome what has traditionally been viewed **8.13** as the weaknesses of the traditional bankruptcy model during a financial panic.[39] The two main goals of the bankruptcy model are to maximize the value of an insolvent company for the benefit of its creditors as a group and to determine who gets what value, in what order.[40] The goals of bankruptcy have not traditionally been viewed as including the preservation or restoration of public confidence in the financial system during a financial panic or of financial stability. Nor have bankruptcy judges traditionally been viewed as having the requisite experience or tools to achieve that objective.

What is needed to achieve the financial stability goal are core resolution powers that enable **8.14** experienced financial regulatory agencies or bankruptcy judges to move quickly to protect insured depositors and to preserve the franchise value and critical operations of a failing

---

[39] Randall D Guynn, 'Are Bailouts Inevitable?' (2012) 29 *Yale J on Reg* 121, 135–140.
[40] Bankruptcy Law, *supra* n 2 at 10–17, 20.

financial institution. These steps will maximize the institution's residual value and minimize its losses for the benefit of its stakeholders and will promote financial stability. During a financial panic, credit dries up, financial assets become illiquid, and the perceived value of financial assets drops to exaggerated levels with extraordinary speed. The disorderly failure of a large financial institution or a large number of smaller financial institutions can result in a contagious panic that can destabilize the financial system. The core resolution powers are designed to preserve value, minimize losses, and stem panics until the markets recover, credit again flows freely, and asset prices become more easily determinable.

8.15 An essential element of the core resolution powers is the power to subordinate the claims of long-term unsecured debt to those of short-term unsecured debt. All of the US resolution laws include this power in the form of a general power to discriminate among creditors within the same class retrospectively,[41] if necessary to achieve certain value maximization, loss minimization, financial stability, or other goals.[42] This general power to discriminate among similarly situated creditors retrospectively includes, but is not limited to, the authority to subordinate the claims of the holders of long-term unsecured debt to those of the holders of short-term unsecured debt. This power is subject, however, to the condition that the disfavoured creditors receive at least as much value in satisfaction of their claims as they would have received in a hypothetical liquidation of the failed institution.[43] This condition has become widely known as the no-creditor-worse-off-than-in-liquidation (NCWOL) principle.[44]

8.16 The purpose of the power to subordinate long-term unsecured debt to short-term unsecured debt is to reduce the incentive of depositors and other short-term debt holders to run, reduce the risk of contagion, and promote financial stability. The holders of short-term unsecured debt have the legal right to run when they believe their bank or other financial institution is insolvent or might become insolvent. The long-term unsecured debt holders do not.

8.17 The power to discriminate between long-term and short-term unsecured claims retrospectively has been roundly criticized, however, for essentially using long-term unsecured debt to bail out short-term unsecured debt.[45] Such retroactive discrimination has been criticized as being unfair to long-term unsecured debt holders because they may not have been fully compensated for the risk of being subordinated to the claims of short-term unsecured debt holders. It has also been criticized for creating moral hazard because the short-term unsecured debt holders may not have internalized the costs of being ranked senior to long-term unsecured debt holders.

---

[41]   FDIA, § 11(i)(2) and (3), 12 USC § 1821(i)(2) and (3); HERA, § 1145(a), 12 USC § 4617(c)(2), (i)(7)(A)(iv); Dodd-Frank Act, § 210(b)(4)(A), (h)(5)(E)(i), 12 USC § 5390(b)(4)(A), (h)(5)(E)(i).

[42]   FDIA, §§ 11(d)(2)(B)(iv), (D) and (E), (d)(4)(B)(i), (d)(13)(E)(i), 12 USC § 1821(d)(2)(B)(iv), (D), (E), (d)(4)(B)(i), (d)(13)(E)(i); HERA, § 1145(a), 12 USC § 4617(b)(2)(B)(iv) and (D), (b)(11)(E)(i), (c)(2)(A), (i)(7)(A)(iv)(I); Dodd-Frank Act, § 210(a)(9)(E), (b)(2), (b)(4)(A)(i) and (iii), (h)(5)(E)(i)(I) and (II), 12 USC § 5390(a)(9)(E), (b)(2), (b)(4)(A)(i) and (iii), (h)(5)(E)(i)(I) and (II). FDIC, *Resolutions Handbook, supra* n 5 at 2, 5, 25.

[43]   FDIA, § 11(i)(2) and (3), 12 USC § 1821(i)(2) and (3); HERA, § 1145(a), 12 USC § 4617(c)(2), (i)(7)(A)(iv); Dodd-Frank Act, § 210(a)(7)(B), (b)(4)(B), and (h)(5)(E)(ii), 12 USC § 5390(a)(7)(B), (b)(4)(B), and (h)(5)(E)(ii).

[44]   Key Attributes I, *supra* n 22, § 5.2; Key Attributes II, *supra* n 22, § 5.2.

[45]   Kenneth E Scott, 'A Guide to the Resolution of Failed Financial Institutions: Dodd-Frank Title II and Proposed Chapter 14' in Kenneth E Scott and John B Taylor (eds), *Bankruptcy Not Bailout: A Special Chapter 14* (Hoover Institution 2012).

The principal response to these criticisms has been to require long-term unsecured debt to   **8.18** be legally, contractually, or structurally subordinated to short-term unsecured debt in advance of any receivership or bankruptcy proceeding, rather than doing so retrospectively as a matter of administrative discretion. By subordinating long-term unsecured debt to short-term unsecured debt in advance instead of retrospectively, the market should respond by causing the interest payable on long-term unsecured debt to rise in order to compensate the holders of long-term unsecured debt for the risk of being subordinated to short-term unsecured debt. The market should also respond by causing the interest payable on short-term unsecured debt to fall, thus requiring investors in short-term debt to internalize the costs of their preferred status.[46]

The goal of subordinating long-term unsecured debt to short-term unsecured debt in advance   **8.19** of receivership or bankruptcy proceedings has been accomplished in the US in several ways without amending any unsecured debt instruments or enacting any statutes. First, most US banking and other financial groups are headed by a parent holding company. US banking groups have long issued virtually all of their long-term unsecured debt at the top-tier parent level. They have long issued virtually all of their deposits and most other short-term unsecured debt at the operating subsidiary level. Unsecured debt issued at the parent level is considered to be structurally subordinated to unsecured debt at the operating subsidiary level in a bankruptcy or receivership proceeding.

The Board of Governors of the Federal Reserve System (Federal Reserve) has reinforced this   **8.20** structural subordination in the case of US G-SIBs in two ways. First, it promulgated a regulation requiring the top-tier parents of US G-SIB groups to issue and maintain a minimum level of total loss absorbing capacity (TLAC) in the form of long-term debt and equity, including regulatory capital.[47] The clean holding company provisions of that regulation effectively required the top-tier parents to move virtually all of their short-term liabilities and qualified financial contracts with third parties to their operating subsidiaries. Second, the Federal Reserve and the FDIC jointly required the US G-SIBs to enter into secured support agreements that effectively subordinated the claims of the long-term debtholders of the top-tier parent of a US G-SIB group to the claims of creditors of the operating subsidiaries of the US G-SIB group with respect to virtually all of the financial assets of the top-tier parent, an intermediate holding company, or a funding vehicle, or all of them. The Federal Reserve also participated in developing the Financial Stability Board's proposal for TLAC.[48]

Another essential element of core resolution powers is the ability to prevent the mass ter-   **8.21** minations of qualified financial contracts (QFCs) of otherwise solvent, performing entities based solely on the commencement of a receivership or conservatorship, or a cross-default triggered by the insolvency of the top-tier parent or another affiliate of the entity. Preventing such terminations allows the solvent, performing entity to continue as a going concern and to meet its obligations rather than default, which is a critically important benefit in and of

---

[46] BPC Report, *supra* n 20 at 31.

[47] Board of Governors of the Federal Reserve System, 'Total Loss-Absorbing Capacity, Long Term Debt, and Clean Holding Company Requirements for Systemically Important U.S. Bank Holding Companies and Intermediate Holding Companies of Systemically Important Foreign Banking Organizations', 82 Fed Reg 8266 (17 January 2017) ('TLAC Rule').

[48] Financial Stability Board, *Adequacy of Loss-Absorbing Capacity of Global Systemically Important Banks in Resolution* (10 November 2014).

itself, and also prevents fire sales of collateral held by counterparties. The US bank resolution statute, Title II of the Dodd-Frank Act and the GSE resolution statute all give the FDIC or the FHFA the authority to stay the termination of QFCs of an entity in receivership or conservatorship, if certain conditions are satisfied. In addition, Title II of the Dodd-Frank Act gives the FDIC the authority to stay the termination of QFCs of affiliates of the entity in liquidation, if certain conditions are satisfied. To mitigate the risk of cross-defaults triggered by insolvency proceedings in respect of a parent or other affiliate under the Bankruptcy Code, the banking regulators' 'QFC Stay Rules' require US G-SIBs and the US operations of foreign G-SIBs to amend their QFCs to prohibit the exercise of default rights against them based directly or indirectly on an affiliate becoming subject to insolvency proceedings under relevant insolvency regimes, subject to certain creditor protections. In addition, the 'clean holding company requirements' included in the Federal Reserve's TLAC Rule[49] prohibit US G-SIB top-tier parents and top-tier US IHCs of non-US G-SIBs from entering into third-party QFCs (other than guarantees). This is meant to decrease the market impact of termination of QFCs and fire sales of collateral upon the insolvency of such an entity, including as would occur in a resolution utilizing an SPOE strategy.

III. Resolution of US Insured Depository Institutions

8.22   The resolution of US IDIs (including insured banks and savings associations) is governed primarily by sections 11 and 13 of the FDIA. The 2008 global financial panic marked the largest wave of bank and savings association (commonly referred to as thrifts) failures in the United States since the US savings and loan crisis ended in the early 1990s.[50] The FDIC resolved 25 failed institutions in 2008, 140 in 2009, 157 in 2010, 92 in 2011, and 51 in 2012.[51] As of 31 March 2021, the FDIC had 55 insured institutions on its 'problem list', with approximately $50 billion in assets.[52] For tabular and graphical representations of the three principal waves of bank or IDI failures during the past hundred years, see Table 8.1 and Figures 8.1 to 8.5. For a comparison between the US Bankruptcy Code and the US bank resolution statute, see the Annex to this book.

8.23   In this section III on bank resolutions, we begin with certain background issues designed to illustrate the peculiar nature of banking organizations in the United States, particularly including deposit insurance. As the government has a direct financial interest whenever a bank fails, we discuss the role, responsibility, and organization of the FDIC. We next describe the steps that have been taken to prevent failures, followed by a discussion of how the FDIC deals with a failed bank. This discussion includes a review of the statutory powers of the FDIC, the claims process, and other specific provisions designed to enhance the resolvability of failed institutions. Finally, we discuss the developments in failure resolution for the largest banks following the global financial crisis of 2008.

---

[49] See *supra* n 47.
[50] FDIC, 2008 Annual Report 5.
[51] FDIC, 2014 Annual Report 126.
[52] FDIC, Quarterly Banking Profile (First Quarter 2021) chart 9.

Table 8.1 Waves of Major IDI Failures Beginning with the Great Depression

	Number of Failed IDIs	% of Total IDIs that Failed (1)	Deposits of Failed IDIs (billions) (A)	Total Domestic Deposits of All IDIs (billions) (2)(A)	Deposits of Failed IDIs as % of Total Domestic Deposits (2)	Estimated Losses (billions) (3)(A)	Estimated Losses as % of Total Domestic Deposits (2)(3)
Roaring 20s and Great Depression (1921–1939)	15,119	49.0%	$156.5	$669.8	23.4%	$32.9	4.9%
Savings and Loan Crisis (1982–1992)	2,275	12.8%	$1,072.9	$5,388.3	19.9%	$210.4	3.9%
2008 Global Financial Crisis (2008–2012)	465	5.6%	$589.0	$9,693.0	6.1%	$81.9	0.8%

(A) Stated in 2020 dollars

(1) Number of failed IDIs/total number of IDIs in first available year of period.

(2) Average of total domestic deposits of all IDIs over the years of the period.

(3) Data missing estimated losses for 1982–1985.

Sources: FDIC Annual Report (2020), available at: <https://www.fdic.gov/about/financial-reports/reports/2020a nnualreport/2020ar-final.pdf>; FDIC, Failures and Assistance Transactions Database, available at: <https://banks. data.fdic.gov/bankfind-suite/failures>; FDIC, The First Fifty Years, Chapter 3: 'Establishment of the FDIC', at 36, available at: <https://www.fdic.gov/bank/historical/firstfifty/chapter3.pdf>; FDIC, *Annual Historical Bank Data, Commercial Banks—Structure Report and Savings Institutions—Structure Report*, available at <https://banks.data.fdic. gov/explore/historical/>; Bureau of Labor Statistics, *CPI Inflation Calculator*, available at: <https://www.bls.gov/data/ inflation_calculator.htm>; OCC Annual Reports 1921–1933, available at: <https://fraser.stlouisfed.org/title/?id= 56#!19155>; Milton Friedman and Anna Jacobson Schwartz, A Monetary History of the United States 1867–1960 (National Bureau of Economic Research 1963), Table 16.

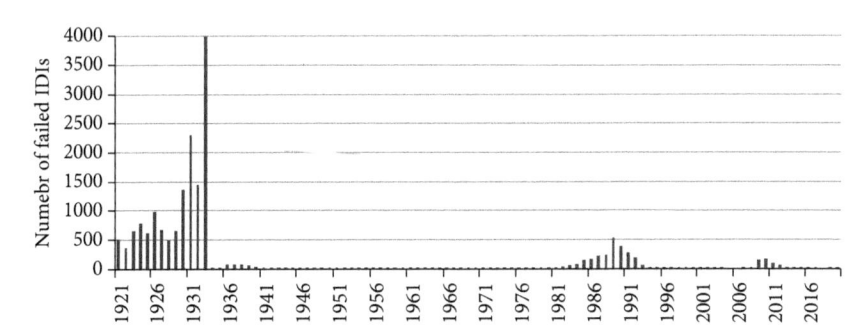

Figure 8.1 Waves of Major US IDI Failures

Sources: FDIC, *Failures and Assistance Transactions Database*, available at: <https://banks.data.fdic.gov/explore/ failures>; FDIC, *The First Fifty Years*, Chapter 3: 'Establishment of the FDIC', at 36, available at: <https://www.fdic. gov/bank/historical/firstfifty/chapter3.pdf>.

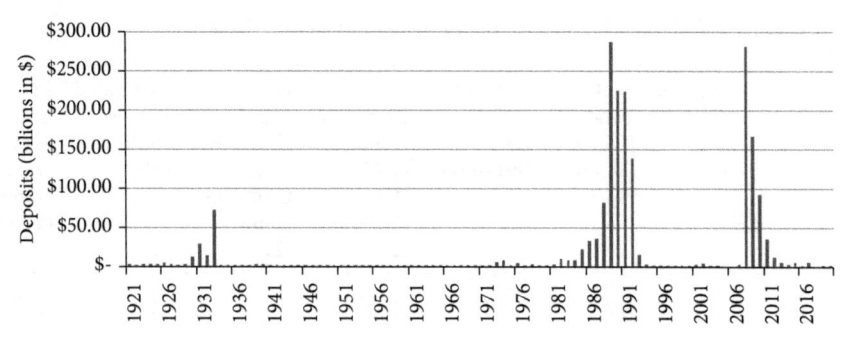

Figure 8.2 Deposits in Failed US IDIs (in 2020 Dollars)

Sources: FDIC, *The First Fifty Years*, Chapter 3: 'Establishment of the FDIC', at 36, available at: <https://www.fdic.gov/bank/historical/firstfifty/chapter3.pdf>; FDIC, *Failures and Assistance Transactions Database*, available at: <https://banks.data.fdic.gov/explore/failures>; Bureau of Labor Statistics, *CPI Inflation Calculator*, available at: <https://www.bls.gov/data/inflation_calculator.htm>.

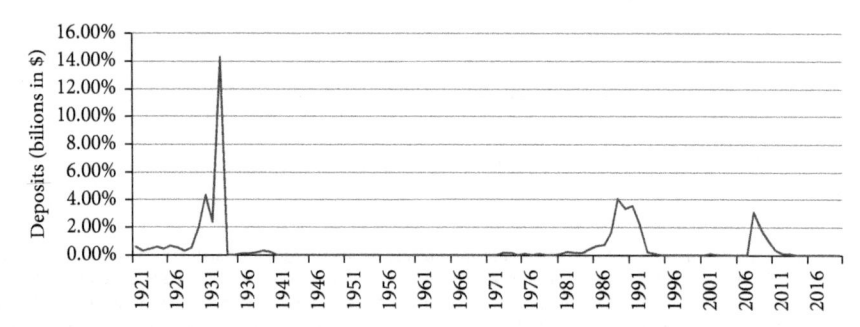

Figure 8.3 Deposits in Failed US IDIs as Percentage of Total Domestic Deposits

Sources: FDIC, *Annual Report* (2020), available at: <https://www.fdic.gov/about/financial-reports/reports/2020annualreport/index.html>; FDIC, *Failures and Assistance Transactions Database*, available at: <https://banks.data.fdic.gov/explore/failures>; FDIC, *The First Fifty Years*, Chapter 3: 'Establishment of the FDIC', at 36, available at: <https://www.fdic.gov/bank/historical/firstfifty/chapter3.pdf>; Bureau of Labor Statistics, *CPI Inflation Calculator*, available at: <https://www.bls.gov/data/inflation_calculator.htm>.

A. Background

1. Chartering authorities and primary regulators

8.24   The US is unique, both in the number of banking organizations (nearly 5,000 as at 31 March 2021)[53] and in the chartering process. Banking organizations may be chartered either under US federal law or under the laws of any state. For federally chartered institutions, the primary regulator is the Office of the Comptroller of the Currency (OCC), a division of the US Treasury.[54] The OCC is also the primary regulatory authority for federal branches and agencies of foreign banks. For state-chartered banks and savings associations, and

---

[53] FDIC, Statistics at a Glance—Historical Trends, row 1, column 1 (as of 31 March 2021).
[54] The primary federal banking supervisor for federally chartered savings associations and thrift holding companies used to be the Office of Thrift Supervision (OTS), but the Dodd-Frank Act closed the OTS and divided its supervisory functions among the OCC (federal-chartered savings associations), the FDIC (state-chartered savings associations), and the Federal Reserve (savings and loan holding companies). Dodd-Frank Act, § 312(b)(1), 12 USC § 5412(b)(1).

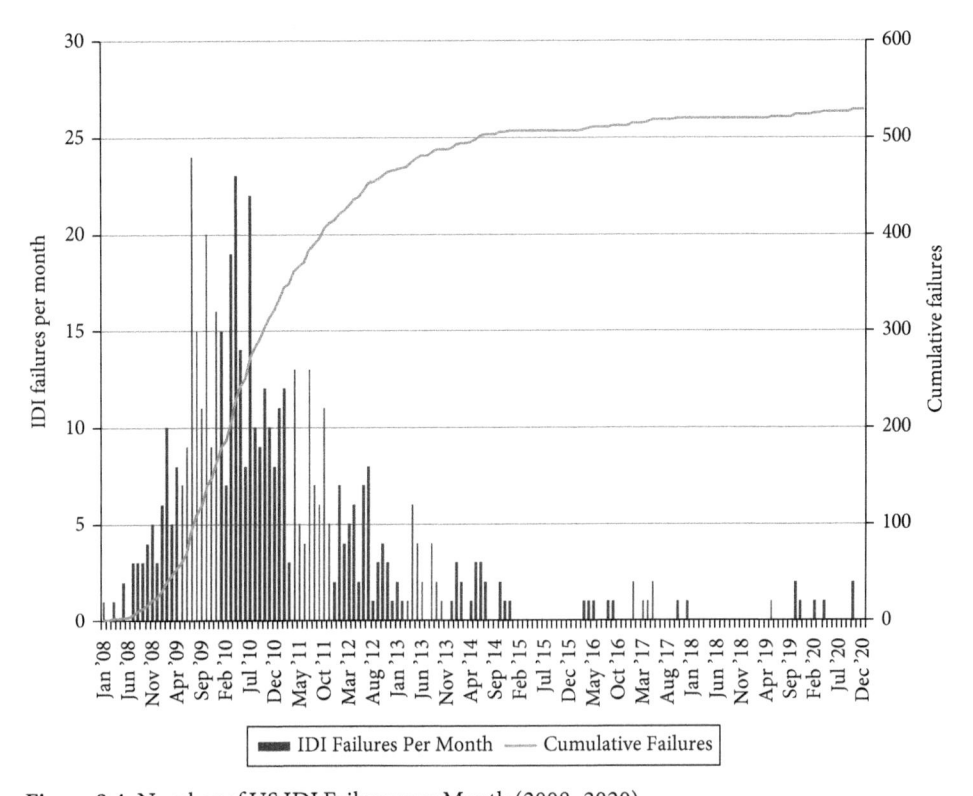

Figure 8.4 Number of US IDI Failures per Month (2008–2020)

Source: FDIC, *Failures and Assistance Transactions Database*, available at: <https://banks.data.fdic.gov/explore/failures>.

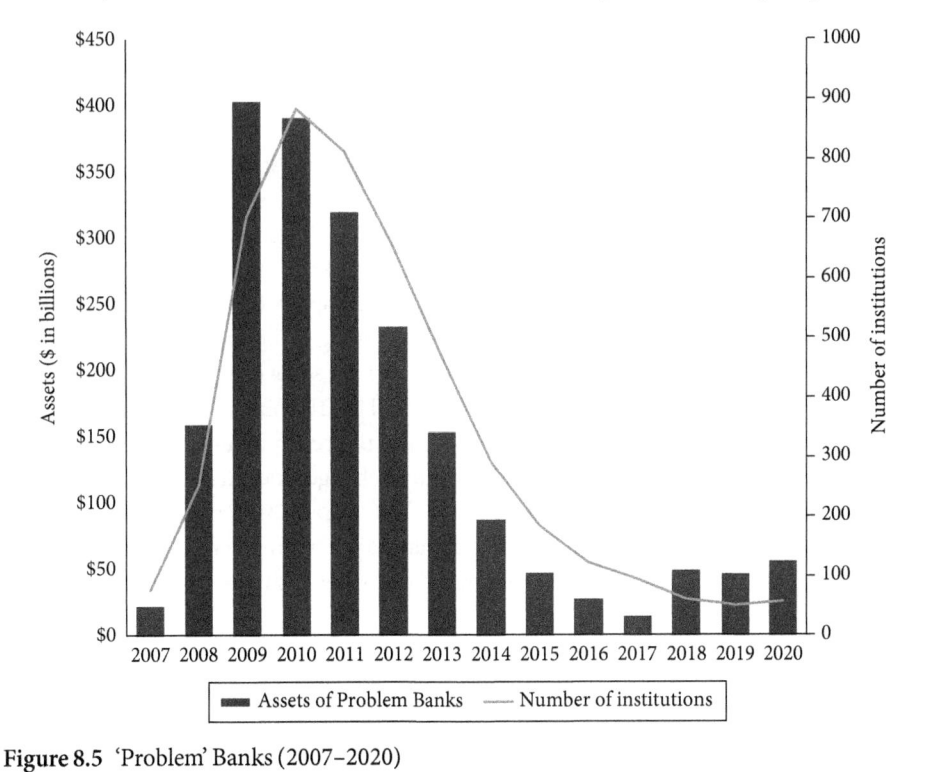

Figure 8.5 'Problem' Banks (2007–2020)

Source: FDIC, Quarterly Banking Profile, First Quarter 2010, available at: https://www.fdic.gov/analysis/quarterly-banking-profile/fdic-quarterly/2010-vol4-2/fdic-quarterly-vol4no2.pdf; FDIC, Quarterly Banking Profile, First Quarter 2021, available at: https://www.fdic.gov/analysis/quarterly-banking-profile/qbp/2021mar/.

state-licensed branches and agencies of foreign banks, the primary supervisor is typically the banking supervisor of the chartering or licensing state. However, state-chartered banks are also regulated by one of two federal regulators. If a state-chartered bank is a member of the Federal Reserve System, its primary federal regulator will be the Federal Reserve; if not, its primary federal regulator will be the FDIC. Generally a state-chartered bank will have the right to decide whether or not it obtains Federal Reserve membership.

8.25   In addition to the regulation of state-chartered, Federal Reserve member banks, the Federal Reserve also regulates companies that control banks, either BHCs or savings and loan holding companies (SLHCs).

8.26   It is the chartering authority of a particular banking institution that determines whether the banking institution is to be placed into receivership. As a practical matter, this decision is taken in close consultation with the FDIC. Under certain limited circumstances, the FDIC has the power to appoint itself receiver for a financial institution. We are unaware of the FDIC ever exercising this power.

8.27   The FDIC had no resolution authority over BHCs, SLHCs, or the nonbank affiliates of an IDI prior to the enactment of the Dodd-Frank Act. Instead, when a bank failed, the holding companies were typically liquidated under the normal bankruptcy laws, although on occasion, if there were viable assets, the holding companies could be reorganized or recapitalized. Other nonbank affiliates of the failed depository institution were also traditionally subject only to liquidation, recapitalization, or reorganization under normal bankruptcy laws, the Securities Investor Protection Act (SIPA), or some other US or non-US insolvency law that was not under the FDIC's jurisdiction.

8.28   Prior to the 2008 financial crisis, holding companies of failed banks rarely engaged in significant activities other than through their IDI subsidiaries. There was little systemic impact resulting from the bankruptcies of these holding companies or other nonbank affiliates. However, the global financial crisis of 2008 highlighted that most of the largest, most global BHCs and SLHCs engage in a broad range of activities either directly or indirectly through nonbank subsidiaries. As a result, Title II of the Dodd-Frank Act granted the FDIC the authority to serve as the receiver of BHCs, SLHCs, and any of their nonbank financial subsidiaries under certain limited conditions. If the holding company or the particular nonbank financial subsidiary is insolvent or in danger of becoming insolvent, and if its resolution under the ordinary bankruptcy laws 'would have serious adverse effects on financial stability in the United States' and if its resolution under Title II would avoid or mitigate those adverse effects, the Secretary of the Treasury, upon the recommendation of the Federal Reserve and either the FDIC or the Securities and Exchange Commission (SEC), and after consultation with the president, may appoint the FDIC as receiver.[55] Only systemically important financial institutions that fail during a financial crisis are likely to be subject to this authority, but the breadth of the authority means that receivership is theoretically possible

---

[55]   Dodd-Frank Act, § 203(b)(2) and (5), 12 USC § 5383(b)(2) and (5). For more details, see section V.A.

with respect to virtually any nonbank financial institution, small or large, at any time. The FDIC's power to resolve holding companies under such circumstances is substantially similar to its resolution authority over FDIC-insured banks.

2. Deposit insurance

The US has an explicit, well-developed deposit insurance framework. Virtually all feder-   **8.29**
ally and state-chartered depository institutions have the option to be FDIC insured, upon application to and approval by the FDIC.[56] Deposits are generally insured up to $250,000 per person, per insured account ownership capacity, per institution.[57] The FDIC, an independent government agency, collects deposit insurance premiums (generally called assessments) from insured institutions based upon their assets and riskiness, and maintains a deposit insurance fund ('the DIF') to hold those assessments.[58]

Whenever an insured financial institution fails, the FDIC assures that depositors are pro-   **8.30**
tected up to the full amount of the deposit insurance. It generally accomplishes this goal by assuring that the deposits are transferred and assumed by another strong financial institution, although on occasion it is required to pay out the depositor claims by cheque.

Were the deposit insurance fund to be inadequate to honour claims or meet other obliga-   **8.31**
tions, the FDIC has a line of credit from the Treasury.[59] Congress has periodically stated that the insurance obligations of the FDIC are backed by the 'full faith and credit' of the US, even though as a technical matter funds would need to be appropriated to meet the obligations if the deposit insurance fund or other resources at the disposal of the FDIC were insufficient.[60]

3. Structure of the FDIC, and the FDIC's resolution unit

The FDIC was created by the Banking Act of 1933.[61] It is governed by a board of directors   **8.32**
composed of five members. There are three public members, one of whom is designated chairman and one vice chairman, and two governmental members—the Comptroller of the Currency (the head of the OCC and the federal regulator of US national banks) and the Director of the Consumer Financial Protection Bureau. One of the three public members

---

[56] FDIA, § 5(a), 12 USC § 1815(a). There are a limited number of small banking organizations with only state deposit insurance. State deposit insurance schemes were once commonplace, but have been supplanted by FDIC insurance. Both private and state-based insurance used to exist for credit unions, which are bank-like organizations with limited powers, but now credit union deposit insurance is largely provided by the federal government and, in a relatively small number of cases, is provided by a private insurer. US Government Accountability Office, *Report to Congressional Committees, Private Deposit Insurance: Credit Unions Largely Complied with Disclosure Rules, but Rules Should be Clarified*, at 1 n 2, 4 n 11 (March 2017), available at: <https://www.gao.gov/assets/gao-17-259.pdf>. Depository institutions, including credit unions, that do not provide federal deposit insurance are required to disclose this fact. 12 U.S.C. § 1831t(b).

[57] Dodd-Frank Act, § 335, 12 USC § 1821(a)(1)(E); FDIC, 'Understanding Deposit Insurance' (2019), available at: <https://www.fdic.gov/deposit/deposits/>.

[58] FDIA, § 11(a), 12 USC § 1821(a).

[59] FDIA, § 14(a), 12 USC § 1824(a).

[60] Full Faith and Credit of US Government Behind the FDIC Deposit Insurance Fund, FDIC Advisory Op, No 36 (9 November 1987); FDIC, *Frequently Asked Questions: Temporary Liquidity Guarantee Program* (2009).

[61] Banking Act of 1933, Pub L No 73-66, § 8, 48 Stat 162, 168–80 (adding §12B to the Federal Reserve Act of 1913).

must have state bank supervisory experience, and not more than three of the five members may be from the same political party.[62]

8.33   The FDIC has a permanent staff organized into divisions and offices. The Division of Resolutions and Receiverships is the division principally responsible for the resolution of most insured banks and thrifts, although the Division of Risk Management Supervision, the Division of Depositor and Consumer Protection, and the Legal Division also play important roles. The Division of Complex Financial Institution Supervision and Resolution is responsible for the FDIC's resolution authority over the largest, most complex IDIs and foreign banking organizations in the US and their nonbank financial affiliates.

8.34   The FDIC operates primarily through regional offices. It carries out its supervisory functions through the Division of Risk Management Supervision and the Division of Depositor and Consumer Protection, and the bulk of the staff of these divisions is primarily located within these regional offices. The regional offices have established local field offices to facilitate the examination process. The FDIC carries out its resolution function through the Division of Resolutions and Receiverships, which operates primarily though the FDIC's main office in Washington DC. The Division has a large regional office in Dallas, Texas, and will establish smaller offices where necessary.

4. Nature of the resolution process

8.35   An insured financial institution may be placed into receivership by its chartering authority. Grounds are generally liquidity insolvency (insufficient liquid assets to meet the claims of creditors when due) or balance sheet insolvency (assets insufficient to cover liabilities), although the statutes governing bank failures may specify a broad number of grounds for the appointment of a receiver. Under federal law, grounds for appointing a receiver include operating in an unsafe or unsound condition, failure to meet certain capital requirements, and violations of certain laws, regulations, or orders. Normally the chartering authority will consult with the FDIC as to the timing of the appointment of a receiver. Under certain circumstances, the FDIC may appoint itself receiver of an insured depository institution. We are unaware of the FDIC ever exercising this power.

8.36   In contrast to a bankruptcy proceeding under the US Bankruptcy Code, which is a judicial process, a proceeding under the bank resolution statute is fundamentally an administrative proceeding conducted by the FDIC. There is little input from creditors or other claimants and virtually no judicial review. As conservator or receiver, the FDIC succeeds by operation of law to all of the rights, powers, and interests of the failed depository institution, its officers, directors, and shareholders, and is given plenary power to administer its affairs.[63] Unlike a proceeding under the US Bankruptcy Code, no creditors' committees or trustees exist, and no court oversees the FDIC's activities. Any claims against the failed institution must first be submitted to the FDIC for its own administrative determination, and only after the FDIC considers the claim will a claimant be permitted to assert its claim before a court for *de novo* review.[64]

---

[62]   FDIA, § 2(a)(1), (b), 12 USC § 1812(a)(1), (b).
[63]   FDIA, § 11(d)(2)(A)–(D), 12 USC § 1821(d)(2)(A)–(D).
[64]   FDIA, § 11(d)(6)(A), 12 USC § 1821(d)(6)(A).

One potential justification for the FDIC's dominant role in bank failures is that in virtually   **8.37**
every failure it is the largest single creditor. For most banks, deposits are the largest single
class of liabilities, and insured deposits are the largest category of deposits. When a bank
fails and the FDIC must use its resources to protect the insured depositors,[65] it becomes
subrogated to the claims of those depositors.[66] Further, as deposit claims have a priority
over other general unsecured creditor claims, in many failures the assets of the failed bank
are insufficient to cover general creditor claims. Accordingly, the FDIC in the typical failure
has the most at stake as a creditor of the failed bank's estate.

The administrative nature of the proceedings, and the FDIC's manner of carrying out its   **8.38**
authority, often create substantial frustrations for creditors and other parties affected by
the failure. In one sense, everyone other than the FDIC is a passive observer, without direct
access or input to the FDIC as it performs its functions. As noted, there is no creditors' committee or other method to provide input to the FDIC as it carries out its functions. Indeed,
it is said that the only rights of creditors are to submit a claim, participate in the claims process, appeal from the FDIC's claims determination if not satisfied, receive whatever distribution to which entitled, and review the FDIC's accounting of its receivership.

Although as conservator or receiver the FDIC is supposed to function as the neutral arbiter   **8.39**
of the claims process, its interest as the largest creditor is often pitted against the interests
of competing creditors. It has a strong incentive to use its extraordinary powers to deny,
avoid, or set aside conflicting creditor claims. In addition, the statutory framework gives the
FDIC's subrogated deposit claims priority over the claims of general creditors.[67]

5. Limited legal guidance

There is very limited legal guidance as to the contours of the FDIC's powers and authorities   **8.40**
under the FDIA. This is to be contrasted with the extensive body of case law, legal commentary, and other guidelines that exists with respect to reorganizations and liquidations under
the US Bankruptcy Code. As described by two former general counsels to the FDIC and the
Federal Home Loan Bank Board (a US government agency that formerly had resolution
authority over savings associations), respectively, this is 'a confusing area'. They continued:

> The challenge arises less because of the complexity of the rules than because of their am-
> biguity and obscurity. The US Bankruptcy Code generally constitutes the starting point
> for rules governing the financial failure of companies in the United States. It contains
> a detailed set of rules that fill three volumes of US Code Annotated, volumes of West's
> Bankruptcy Reporter, and over four linear feet of Collier's [on Bankruptcy]. But the stat-
> utes governing conservatorships and receiverships of federally insured banks and thrifts
> fill, at most, about 111 pages of the US Code Annotated. Moreover, those 111 pages were
> fundamentally changed less than 18 months ago in the Financial Institutions Reform,
> Recovery and Enforcement Act of 1989 ('FIRREA').[68]

---

[65] FDIA, § 11(a), 12 USC § 1821(a).
[66] FDIA, § 11(g), 12 USC § 1821(g).
[67] FDIA, § 11(d)(11), 12 USC § 1821(d)(11).
[68] John L Douglas, Jordan Luke, and Rex R Veal, 'Introduction', *Counselling Creditors of Banks and Thrifts: Dealing with the FDIC and RTC*, PLI Order No A4-4323 (14 January 1991).

8.41   The FDIC has promulgated few regulations to implement the resolution statutes[69] and has issued only a relatively small number of advisory opinions, policy statements, and other guidelines to supplement them. Even these advisory opinions are of limited value, as the FDIC takes the position that advisory opinions issued by its staff, including its general counsel, are not binding on it.[70] Further, the FDIC reserves the right to withdraw any of its policy statements at any time,[71] potentially with retroactive effect. As a result, there is no clarity surrounding how various issues would be resolved in the conservatorship or receivership of an insured institution.

8.42   In addition, there is very little case law or legal commentary clarifying the resolution statutes. Depository institution failures tend to occur in waves with much lower frequency than insolvencies governed by the US Bankruptcy Code, which are routine. There have, since the creation of the FDIC, been essentially only three groups of failures: the first, during the Great Depression, the second, during the US savings and loan crisis of the 1980s, and finally, the wave of failures during the global financial panic of 2008. See Table 8.1 and Figures 8.1 to 8.5 for tabular and graphical illustrations of how US bank failures have occurred in three principal waves, with almost no failures between each wave. With few failures, there are few cases, and with few cases, little in the way of legal commentary.

B. Supervisory and Other Tools to Prevent Failure

8.43   Bank regulation in the United States has two principal purposes: to protect depositors and customers, and to ensure the safety and soundness of individual banks. However, with the global financial crisis of 2008, prudential regulation and supervision of individual banks has been supplemented by macro-prudential, or systemic, regulation and supervision that focuses on promoting the stability of the overall US banking system. By focusing on capital, liquidity, lender-of-last-resort, and other tools, the objective is to assure a resilient banking system that both minimizes the risk of failure and attempts to mitigate against contagion that could result from the failure of a large institution. During the 2008 global financial crisis, these tools were supplemented by a variety of extraordinary measures, including the Troubled Asset Relief Program (TARP), open-bank assistance, and the Temporary Liquidity Guarantee Program (TLGP).

1. Capital and liquidity regulation

8.44   The 2008 financial crisis highlighted the importance of capital and liquidity requirements. Properly calibrated capital and liquidity requirements can make banks resilient against failure under severely adverse economic scenarios. These requirements also give banks sufficient room to engage in the sort of liquidity transformation that is their core function and contribution to market efficiency.[72]

---

[69]   12 CFR Part 360.

[70]   See, eg, FDIC Advisory Op, No 1 (6 January 1997).

[71]   Statement of Policy on the Development and Review of Regulations, 63 Fed Reg 25157 (7 May 1998).

[72]   Diamond and Dybvig, *supra* n 4 (banks increase the efficiency of markets by transforming long-term loans and other illiquid assets into demand deposits and other liquid claims against them). During the nineteenth century, this core function of US banks was more obvious since the liquid claims that the US banks created were principally banknotes, or 'paper money', which was desperately needed as an efficient means of exchange and store of

US IDIs are subject to both risk-based and leverage capital requirements that are consistent   **8.45**
with the Basel III framework.[73] Capital regulations require a bank's assets (or risk-weighted
assets) be worth more than its liabilities by a specified percentage, and further define the
type of instruments that count as capital. As discussed more fully in section III.B.6 on enhanced prudential standards, US BHCs that are identified as G-SIBs and their IDI subsidiaries are subject to higher capital requirements than other US banking organizations.
G-SIBs and other large BHCs are also subject to supervisory stress testing and capital planning exercises that require them to meet certain capital requirements even after suffering
the sort of losses that would be expected to occur in a severely adverse economic scenario.[74]
Smaller banking organizations are not subject to stress testing or are only required to conduct company-run stress tests on their capital adequacy.[75]

In addition to maintaining capital, the US G-SIBs are required under the TLAC rule to   **8.46**
maintain an additional cushion protecting against insolvency in the form of long-term
debt. This requirement will be discussed further below, but the objective is to assure that
in the event of failure, there is sufficient long-term unsecured debt that can be converted to
equity so that the institution can be recapitalized.

Historically, reserve requirements were the only form of liquidity regulation applicable to   **8.47**
all US IDIs. Reserve requirements mandate that an IDI hold cash or other forms of central bank money equal to a fraction of its deposits and certain other liabilities.[76] Certain
large US BHCs are also subject to Basel III liquidity requirements, including the liquidity
coverage ratio, which requires that a certain percentage of their assets consist of cash and
other high quality liquid assets (HQLAs) such as US government securities.[77]

2. Prompt corrective action

Following the savings and loan crisis in the 1980s, Congress enacted a scheme of prompt   **8.48**
corrective action based upon the capital condition of the bank. A bank is either well

---

value because of a chronic shortage of gold, silver, and other commodity money in the US. Bray Hammond, *Banks and Politics in America from the Revolution to the Civil War* (1957) 95–99.

[73] OCC, Regulatory Capital Rules: Regulatory Capital, Implementation of Basel III, Capital Adequacy, Transition Provisions, Prompt Corrective Action, Standardized Approach for Risk-weighted Assets, Market Discipline and Disclosure Requirements, Advanced Approaches Risk-Based Capital Rule, and Market Risk Capital Rule, 78 Fed Reg 62018 (11 October 2013); Davis Polk, Client Memorandum, *US Basel III Final Rule: Visual Memorandum* (30 April 2015) 21–22.

[74] Board of Governors of the Federal Reserve System, 'Dodd-Frank Act Stress Test 2021: Supervisory Stress Test Results' (June 2021), available at: <https://www.federalreserve.gov/publications/files/2021-dfast-results-20210 624.pdf>.

[75] Ibid.

[76] 12 CFR § 204.5(a)(1) (requiring IDIs to hold cash reserves equal to a maximum of 10 per cent of the amount of their deposits over a certain threshold). During the eighteenth and nineteenth centuries, US banks were subject to reserve requirements by charter, contract, or state or federal regulation. These sources of authority required banks to hold gold, silver, or other commodity money equal to a fraction of their banknotes in circulation (ie, paper currency) or, less frequently, their deposit obligations. Bray Hammond, *Banks and Politics in America: From the Revolution to the Civil War* (1957) 137–38, 142–43; William Graham Sumner, *A History of Banking in the United States* (1896) 22; Joshua N Feinman, 'Reserve Requirements: History, Current Practice, and Potential Reform', 79 Federal Reserve Bulletin 569, 572 (1993).

[77] Liquidity Coverage Ratio: Liquidity Risk Measurement Standards: Final Rule, 79 Fed Reg 61440 (10 October 2014); Davis Polk, Client Memorandum, *US Basel III Liquidity Coverage Ratio Final Rule: Visual Memorandum* (23 September 2014); Davis Polk, Client Memorandum, *Final Tailoring Rule for US Banking Organizations* (19 November 2019).

capitalized, adequately capitalized, undercapitalized, significantly undercapitalized, or critically undercapitalized depending upon its capital level. As a bank deteriorates and moves from one level to another, the regulators must impose greater and greater restrictions on the activities of the institution.

8.49 Even an institution that falls from well capitalized to adequately capitalized may be subjected to restrictions on dividends and distributions and limitations on its ability to accept, renew, or roll-over insured deposits. When an insured institution becomes undercapitalized, is found to be in an unsafe or unsound condition, or is found to be engaging in an unsafe or unsound practice,[78] the institution's federal banking supervisor has the authority to take a number of actions in response to a triggering event, including:

- requiring the insured institution to adopt a capital restoration plan. This plan, in order to be acceptable, must be guaranteed by its parent (up to a maximum exposure of 5 per cent of the insured institution's total assets);
- imposing restrictions on dividends by the insured institution or its parent;
- restricting the insured institution's growth or requiring it to terminate certain activities or sell certain assets;
- requiring the insured institution or any affiliate to be divested;
- imposing limits on the interest rates payable on deposits; or
- imposing limits on executive compensation or requiring the insured institution's board or senior management to be replaced.[79]

8.50 If an institution becomes critically undercapitalized, there is a strong regulatory presumption that the institution will be placed in receivership within 90 days.[80]

8.51 These prompt corrective action tools are designed to force an insured institution and its owners to take remedial action to rehabilitate a weakened institution before it becomes insolvent. It is unclear whether these provisions actually prevent failures since the capital measurements that trigger the prompt corrective action restrictions are largely based on historical cost rather than current mark-to-market balance sheets. Historic values simply do not adequately capture the rapid deterioration of asset values and thus are often lagging indicators of the true health of an institution.

3. Discount window and other lender-of-last-resort facilities

8.52 There is a great difference between a capital insolvency and a liquidity failure. A bank may have plenty of capital, yet lack sufficient liquid assets to meet the claims of its depositors and other creditors if they lose confidence in the institution.[81] Indeed, one of the fundamental causes of the 2008 global financial crisis was the lack of confidence in the value of various classes of assets on the balance sheets of major financial institutions. A fundamental function of a central bank is to act as the lender of last resort, allowing a bank to convert its illiquid assets into cash at a fair price. Absent such a lender, the bank would be forced to sell its illiquid assets at fire-sale prices in order to meet the demands of its short-term creditors

---

[78] FDIA, § 38(e)–(i), 12 USC § 1831o(e)–(i).
[79] Ibid.
[80] FDIA, § 38(h)(3), 12 USC § 1831o(h)(2).
[81] Diamond and Dybvig, *supra* n 4.

to withdraw cash. In short, the lack of confidence in the bank's solvency or liquidity would become a self-fulfilling prophesy. Further, as the institution sold assets at depressed prices, it would affect the market prices of those assets and thus the balance sheets of other financial institutions, spreading the contagion.

To mitigate against such liquidity risks, Congress empowered the Federal Reserve to provide solvent banks with a means of converting their illiquid assets into cash by selling them at a discount to the Federal Reserve or pledging them to the Federal Reserve at an appropriate haircut to secure a loan of cash through the Federal Reserve's discount window.[82] It is interesting to note that Milton Friedman and Anna Schwartz argued in their classic book that the Federal Reserve's reluctance to use its discount window aggressively during the 1930s helped to trigger or deepen the Great Depression by allowing thousands of otherwise solvent banks to fail because of a lack of liquidity, which resulted in what they termed 'The Great Contraction' in the money supply.[83] Historically, the Federal Reserve discouraged the use of the discount window by stigmatizing and imposing a penalty rate on its use.[84] However, fully aware of the Friedman and Schwartz thesis, the Federal Reserve took several steps during the period leading up to and after the global financial panic of 2008 to eliminate the stigma and encourage insured institutions to borrow from the discount window as needed during the financial crisis, and it did so again during the COVID-19 pandemic.[85] In March 2020, the Federal Reserve and other banking agencies issued a joint statement encouraging banks to use the discount window.[86] In the following days, all eight of the US G-SIBs announced that they were accessing funding from the discount window at that time, and the Federal Reserve subsequently stated that it was 'encouraged by the notable increase in discount window borrowing' and welcomed its continued use.[87]   **8.53**

Section 13(3) of the Federal Reserve Act gives the Federal Reserve authority to provide emergency secured liquidity to a wide range of market participants under 'unusual and exigent circumstances'.[88] Although enacted in 1932 and invoked twice during the twentieth century, no actual lending took place under this authority prior to the global financial panic   **8.54**

---

[82] Federal Reserve Act, § 10B, 12 USC § 347b(b); 12 CFR Part 201 (Regulation A).

[83] Friedman and Schwartz, *Monetary History, supra* n 8 at 10, 299–305, Chapter 1 (Introduction) and Chapter 7 (The Great Contraction). They also blamed the Federal Reserve's doubling of reserve requirements in 1936 for a contraction in the money supply that resulted in a sharp recession in 1937–38.

[84] Board of Governors of the Federal Reserve System, 'Extensions of Credit by Federal Reserve Banks; Reserve Requirements of Depository Institutions', 12 CFR Part 201, Federal Reserve Docket No R-1123, 67 Fed Reg 67777, 67782 (7 November 2002); Furfine, *The Fed's New Discount Window and Interbank Borrowing* (13 May 2003).

[85] See, eg, Madigan, Director, Federal Reserve's Division of Monetary Affairs, 'Bagehot's Dictum in Practice: Formulating and Implementing Policies to Combat the Financial Crisis'. Speech at the Federal Reserve Bank of Kansas City's Annual Economic Symposium, Jackson Hole, Wyoming (21 August 2009); Bernanke, 'The Federal Reserve's Balance Sheet'. Speech at the Federal Reserve Bank of Richmond's 2009 Credit Markets Symposium (3 April 2009).

[86] Board of Governors of the Federal Reserve System, 'Federal Banking Agencies Encourage Banks to Use Federal Reserve Discount Window' (16 March 2021), available at: <https://www.federalrese rve.gov/newsevents/pressreleases/bcreg20200316a.htm>. See also Bill Nelson, 'Discount Window Stigma: We Have Met the Enemy, and He Is Us' (10 August 2021), available at: <https://bpi.com/discount-window-stigma-we-have-met-the-enemy-and-he-is-us>.

[87] Financial Services Forum, 'Financial Services Forum Statement on the Discount Window' (16 March 2020), available at: <https://www.fsforum.com/types/press/releases/financial-services-forum-statement-on-the-discount-window/>; Board of Governors of the Federal Reserve System, 'Federal Reserve Board Encouraged by Increase in Discount Window Borrowing To Support the Flow of Credit to Households and Businesses' (19 March 2020), available at: <https://www.federalreserve.gov/newsevents/pressreleases/monetary20200319c.htm>.

[88] Federal Reserve Act, § 13(3), 12 USC 343.

of 2008.[89] Section 13(3) was the foundation for almost all of the Federal Reserve's emergency assistance programmes during the 2008 financial crisis, including its rescue of AIG, its Primary Dealer Credit Facility, and its Term Asset-Backed Securities Loan Facility.[90] Congress later determined that the Federal Reserve should not have used its power under section 13(3) to bail out individual firms during the 2008 financial crisis and imposed limitations on its future use.[91] As a result, section 13(3) may only be invoked by the Federal Reserve with the consent of the Secretary of the Treasury and only to implement a programme or facility with broad-based eligibility.[92] It remains an open question whether these restrictions may hamper the Federal Reserve's assistance of solvent, but temporarily illiquid, firms during the next financial crisis, but they posed no impediment to the extensive emergency lending undertaken by the Federal Reserve during the pandemic.

8.55   The Federal Reserve's response to the COVID-19 pandemic included the establishment of a number of emergency lending programmes, some of which were reprised from the financial crisis and others that were newly developed. Many of these lending programmes had a similar structure, wherein the Federal Reserve created a special purpose vehicle (SPV) in which the US Treasury made an initial equity investment. The SPV could use its initial funding to lend to or purchase assets from participants in the programme and subsequently pledge such loans or assets to the Federal Reserve as collateral for additional funding to make more loans or purchase more assets.

8.56   In addition to its emergency lending programmes, the Federal Reserve also exercised its authority over monetary policy in a manner that complemented its role as the lender of last resort. Major dislocation in the market for US Treasury securities in March 2020 compelled the Federal Reserve to respond by effectively offering an unlimited amount of liquidity to backstop the Treasury repo market.[93] In July 2021, the Group of Thirty (G30) published a report identifying certain weaknesses in the Treasury market and making recommendations to improve its resilience.[94] Among other changes, the G30 recommended the establishment of a domestic Standing Repo Facility, through which the Federal Reserve could guarantee the availability of repo financing for Treasury securities to a broad range of market participants without having to depend on the willingness and ability of primary dealers to serve as intermediaries.[95] The G30 report also recommended that the similar Foreign and International Monetary Authority repo facilities that the Federal Reserve had established as an emergency measure in March 2020 be made permanent.[96] Within hours of the G30 report's release, the Federal Reserve announced the establishment of a permanent Standing Repo Facility and Foreign and International Monetary Authority facilities.[97] Although these facilities were established under the Federal Reserve's monetary policy authority

[89] David Fettig, 'The History of a Powerful Paragraph: Section 13(3) Enacted Fed Business Loans 76 Years Ago', *The Region* (June 2008) 34.

[90] Davis Polk, *Financial Crisis Manual* (2009) 144–80.

[91] Dodd-Frank Act, § 1101, 12 USC § 4511, amending § 13(3) of the Federal Reserve Act, 12 USC § 343.

[92] Federal Reserve Act, § 13(3)(A) and (B)(iv), 12 USC § 343(3)(A) and (B)(iv).

[93] G30 Working Group, 'U.S. Treasury Markets: Steps Toward Increased Resilience' (July 2021), available at: <https://group30.org/images/uploads/publications/G30_U.S_._Treasury_Markets-_Steps_Toward_Increased_Resilience__1.pdf.>.

[94] Ibid. See also Davis Polk, 'G30 Publishes Report on Recommendations for Treasury Market Reform' (17 August 2021), available at: <https://www.davispolk.com/insights/client-update/g30-publishes-report-recommendations-treasury-market-reform>.

[95] G30 Working Group, *supra* n 93.

[96] Ibid.

[97] Board of Governors of the Federal Reserve System, 'Statement Regarding Repurchase Agreement Arrangements' (28 July 2021), available at: <https://www.federalreserve.gov/newsevents/pressreleases/monetary20210728b.htm>.

rather than its emergency lending authority, their purpose fully accords with Bagehot's classic guidelines for central banks in their role as lenders of last resort, which state that in times of financial stress central banks should 'lend to merchants, to minor bankers, to "this man and that man," whenever the security is good'.[98]

4. Deposit insurance

While deposit insurance creates a governmental obligation when a bank fails, deposit in-   **8.57**
surance also serves as an important source of liquidity for banks. It reduces the risk of runs by protecting insured depositors against losses up to a statutory maximum and relieves insured depositors from any risks associated with the financial condition of the bank. Dodd-Frank raised the deposit insurance limits to $250,000 per person per certain account capacities per bank.[99] Deposit insurance is provided by the FDIC and paid for directly by the banking industry and indirectly by insured depositors based on insurance premium assessments imposed on US IDIs.[100] During the 2008 financial crisis, the FDIC took additional steps to extend deposit insurance to certain forms of bank obligations in an attempt to avoid liquidity insolvencies.

5. Supervision, examination, and enforcement

The legal and regulatory framework surrounding banks is designed to protect depositors   **8.58**
and customers and to assure that the institutions operate safely and soundly. The state and federal regulators are granted wide powers to regulate, supervise, and examine the institutions. The supervisory powers include both on-site and off-site examination and evaluation of the institution to assure compliance as well as safety and soundness.

To ensure compliance with laws, rules, and regulations, and to ensure that a bank is operating   **8.59**
in a safe and sound fashion, the regulators have been granted a variety of enforcement tools.[101] Many of these tools are quite informal and are part of the normal examination and supervisory process, including simple discussions between the institution and its regulator, commitment letters, board resolutions, or memoranda of understanding. The FDIA also sets forth a variety of other formal enforcement tools, such as written agreements, cease and desist orders, civil financial penalties, removal and prohibition orders, and, in extreme cases, the authority to remove deposit insurance from an institution.[102] For a graphical representation of this continuum, see Figure 8.6. These tools are available against not only the institution, but also individuals and entities participating in the affairs of the institution, known as 'institution-affiliated parties'.[103] Cease and desist orders are available not only to prohibit certain actions, but also to mandate corrective action or even restitution.[104] Civil money penalties can run to over $2 million per day per violation under certain circumstances.[105] The removal and prohibition powers can preclude an individual from participating in the affairs of any insured depository institution.[106]

---

[98] Walter Bagehot, Lombard Street: A Description of the Money Market (John Murray 1873) 51.

[99] Dodd-Frank Act, § 335, 12 USC § 1821(a)(1)(E). See FDIC, 'Understanding Deposit Insurance' (2019), available at: <https://www.fdic.gov/deposit/deposits/>.

[100] Prior to the Dodd-Frank Act, the assessments were calculated as a percentage of insured deposits. After Dodd-Frank, assessments are calculated as a percentage of assets. Dodd-Frank Act, § 331(b), amending § 7(b)(2) of the FDIA, 12 USC § 1817(b)(2).

[101] FDIA, § 8, 12 USC § 1818.

[102] FDIA, § 8, 12 USC § 1818(a).

[103] FDIA, § 3(u), 12 USC § 1813(u).

[104] FDIA, § 8(b)(1), 12 USC § 1818(b)(1).

[105] FIDA, § 8(i), 12 USC § 1818(i); 12 CFR § 263.65(b) (increasing maximum statutory amount for knowing or reckless violations to $2.073 million per day to adjust for inflation).

[106] FIDA, § 8(e), 12 USC § 1818(e).

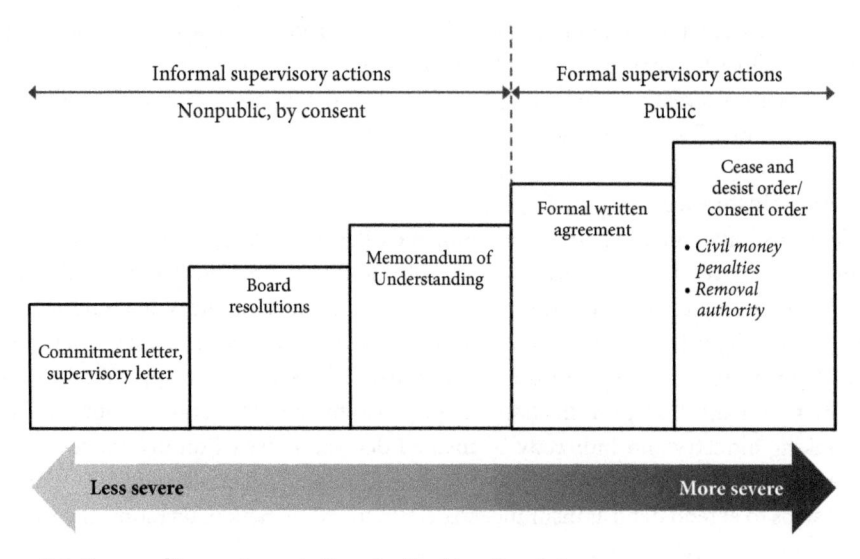

Figure 8.6 Range of Supervisory Actions by Banking Regulators

6. Enhanced prudential standards

8.60   As a result of the financial crisis, and in order to prevent the systemic effects resulting from failures of large banking organizations, Congress mandated that systemically important financial institutions become subject to enhanced prudential standards. These enhanced standards include more stringent capital and liquidity requirements, risk management requirements, single counterparty credit limits, and stress test requirements.[107] While all BHCs and covered SLHCs with assets of $100 billion or more are subject to enhanced prudential standards, firms are generally organized into four tiers, from Category I to Category IV firms, with a different scope of enhanced prudential standards applying to each Category. The most stringent enhanced standards are reserved for Category I firms, which are US G-SIBs. Category II firms include BHCs and covered SLHCs with assets of $700 billion or more and those with $100 billion or more of assets and $75 billion or more in cross-jurisdictional activity. Category III firms include BHCs and covered SLHCs with assets of $250 billion or more and those with $100 billion or more of assets and $75 billion or more of any of three additional indicators of systemic risks, such as short-term wholesale funding, non-bank assets, or off-balance sheet exposures. Category IV firms include all other BHCs and covered SLHCs with $100 billion or more of assets. See Figure 8.7 for a graphical illustration of some of the most important enhanced prudential standards and how they relate to certain ordinary prudential standards.

---

[107] Davis Polk, Client Memorandum, *US Bank Holding Companies: Overview of Dodd-Frank Enhanced Prudential Standards Final Rule* (24 February 2014); Davis Polk, Client Memorandum, *Final Tailoring Rules for US Banking Organizations* (21 November 2019).

Enhanced Prudential Standards	Asset Size of BHC or G-SIB Status			
	Category IV	Category III	Category II	Category I U.S. G-SIBs
TLAC Requirement				✓
G-SIB Surcharge				✓
Enhanced Supplementary Leverage Ratio				✓
Advanced approaches risk weights			✓	✓
Accumulated Other Comprehensive Income recognized in capital	May opt out	May opt out	✓	✓
Simplified approach for minority interests and certain capital deductions	✓	✓	Ineligible	Ineligible
Countercyclical Capital Buffer (if deployed)		✓	✓	✓
Supplementary Leverage Ratio		✓	✓	✓
Company-run Stress Test		Biennial (even years)[1]	Annual	Annual
Single-counterparty credit limits		✓	✓	✓
Liquidity Coverage Ratio	Reduced monthly (70%)/None[2]	Full/Reduced daily (85%)[3]	Full	Full
Net Stable Funding Ratio	Reduced (70%) /None[2]	Full/Reduced (85%)[3]	Full	Full
Stress capital buffer	✓	✓	✓	✓
Supervisory Stress Test	Biennial (even years)	Annual	Annual	Annual
Internal liquidity stress testing	Quarterly	Monthly	Monthly	Monthly
Liquidity risk management	Slightly tailored	✓	✓	✓
Risk committee and risk management	✓	✓	✓	✓

Figure 8.7 Enhanced Prudential Standards

(1) A Category III firm is required to submit internal stress test results to the Federal Reserve as part of its annual capital plan submission, but is required to publicly disclose its company-run stress test results only once every two even years.

(2) A reduced monthly Liquidity Coverage Ratio and Net Stable Funding Ratio of 70% of the relevant full requirement applies to a Category IV firm with ≥ $50 billion of weighted short-term wholesale funding.

(3) A reduced daily Liquidity Coverage Ratio and Net Stable Funding Ratio of 85% of the relevant full requirement applies to a Category III firm with < $75 billion of weighted short-term wholesale funding.

8.61   In addition to the company-run and supervisory stress testing mandated by the Dodd-Frank Act, the Federal Reserve performs additional periodic supervisory stress testing procedures, both as a prudential supervisory tool (referred to as the Comprehensive Capital Analysis and Review (CCAR)) and to calibrate firm-specific stress based capital buffer requirements for large BHCs (referred to as the stress capital buffer (SCB)). Under the CCAR stress testing, the Federal Reserve compares its own model for testing the capital adequacy of a US bank holding company against the company's own model under various economic scenarios, including a severely adverse economic scenario defined by the Federal Reserve. Under the SCB, the Federal Reserve uses the results of its own stress testing models to calibrate firm-specific capital buffer requirements for each large BHC. Each firm's SCB, which is recalibrated periodically (annually, for the largest BHCs) based on the Federal Reserve's severely adverse economic scenario and subject to a 2.5 per cent floor, is added to the firm's other capital buffer requirements to arrive at a total firm-specific capital buffer requirement. If a BHC fails to maintain its firm-specific capital buffer above this requirement, it will face a graduated set of limitations on its ability to make capital distributions (eg pay dividends or repurchase shares) or discretionary bonus payments. In practice, the stress testing results have become an additional tool to assure that important financial institutions maintain adequate capital even in the most adverse circumstances.

8.62   In addition to stress testing, the Federal Reserve requires each G-SIB to maintain a specified level of TLAC sufficient to recapitalize the organization were it to otherwise fail. The TLAC requirements generally require the top-tier parent BHC of each US G-SIB to maintain a combination of Tier 1 regulatory capital and additional qualifying debt that can be 'bailed in' or converted to equity if other capital has been exhausted due to losses. There is a separate independent requirement that the parent maintain a specified level of long-term unsecured debt, and a 'clean holding company' framework that imposes severe restrictions on the other debt obligations of the top-tier parent bank holding company. The purpose is to enhance resilience and resolvability of the US G-SIBs. The required minimum level of TLAC is 18 per cent of risk-weighted assets, plus certain adjustments that can raise the minimum substantially. Similar requirements apply to the US intermediate holding companies of foreign G-SIBs with at least $50 billion in US non-branch assets.[108]

7. Recovery and resolution plans

8.63   To further protect against failure, the Federal Reserve has required certain large, domestic US BHCs to prepare recovery plans. Implemented following the 2008 financial crisis, recovery plans are different from and in addition to resolution plans, and set forth the actions firms must take to return to a position of financial stability once it is experiencing or is likely to encounter serious financial distress short of insolvency or other failure. Recovery plans are designed to identify a range of options that must be taken to restore or enhance capital and liquidity levels to maintain the confidence of market participants during a range of

---

[108]   TLAC Rule, *supra* n 47 at 8311.

stress scenarios, including the possible sale of valuable assets.[109] They require US G-SIBs to address financial weaknesses well before the point of non-viability, with the goal of substantially reducing the risk of insolvency or other failure. Recovery plans thus act as a buffer against loss of public confidence in individual firms or the broader financial system. The Federal Reserve has continued to test and require improvements in recovery plans, and expanded the range of BHCs required to develop them. Additionally, the OCC requires national banks with $250 billion or more in assets to prepare recovery plans.[110]

The Dodd-Frank Act, as amended, requires BHCs with $250 billion or more in assets to prepare resolution plans, setting forth how they would be resolved under the US Bankruptcy Code or other normally applicable insolvency laws without relying on the resolution powers granted to the FDIC under Title II of Dodd-Frank.[111] To the extent that these resolution plans are deemed by the regulators to be 'not credible' or otherwise 'would not facilitate an orderly resolution of the company under the [Bankruptcy Code]', the institution may be required to take additional steps to improve resolvability, which could include divestitures, ceasing certain activities, or implementing other measures. While the ostensible purpose of these resolution plans is to assure that in the event of failure, the organization is capable of being resolved without adverse systemic impact or taxpayer capital support, the underlying thesis is that by improving resolvability, the institution will also improve resilience and avoid failure in the first instance. **8.64**

The FDIC has also required banks with $50 billion or more in assets—now, as a practical matter, $100 billion or more in assets—to prepare their own resolution plans.[112] The FDIC has provided extensive guidance to the affected institutions as to the assumptions it must incorporate into their plans and the types of resolution strategies they must address.[113] Again, the expectation is that these resolution plans will also enhance the resiliency of the banks. **8.65**

8. Source of strength obligations

The Federal Reserve has long maintained that BHCs must serve as a 'source of strength' to their subsidiary banks.[114] The Federal Reserve has stated that it would be an unsafe or unsound practice for a bank holding company parent to fail to serve as a source of financial **8.66**

---

[109] 'Consolidated Recovery Planning for Certain Large Domestic Bank Holding Companies', Federal Reserve Supervision and Regulation Letter, SR 14-8 (25 September 2015); 'Heightened Supervisory Expectations for Recovery and Resolution Preparedness for Certain Large Bank Holding Companies—Supplemental Guidance on Consolidated Supervision Framework for Large Financial Institutions (SR letter 12-17/CA letter 12-14)', Federal Reserve Supervision and Regulation Letter, SR 14-1 (24 January 2014).

[110] OCC, Guidelines Establishing Standards for Recovery Planning by Certain Large Insured National Banks, Insured Federal Savings Associations, and Insured Federal Branches; Technical Amendments, 83 Fed Reg 66604 (27 December 2018).

[111] Dodd-Frank Act, § 165(d), 12 USC § 5365(d), as amended by the Economic Growth, Regulatory Relief, and Consumer Protection Act of 2018, § 401, Pub L No 115-174, 132 Stat 1296.

[112] The FDIC's regulation requiring these resolution plans establishes this $50 billion threshold. See 12 CFR § 360.10(a). However, in practice for the near future, the threshold is $100 billion. In November 2018, the FDIC announced a moratorium on bank resolution plans as it considered revisions to its regulations; that moratorium was lifted in January 2021 for banks with $100 billion or more in assets. See FDIC, 'FDIC Announces Lifting IDI Plan Moratorium' (19 January 2021) available at: <https://www.fdic.gov/resauthority/idi-statement-01-19-2021.pdf>.

[113] 12 CFR § 360.10; see also FDIC, 'Statement on Resolution Plans for Insured Depository Institutions' (25 June 2021), available at: <https://www.fdic.gov/resauthority/idi-statement-06-25-2021.pdf> (discussing scope, timing, and content of resolution plans).

[114] 12 CFR § 225.4(a).

and managerial strength to a subsidiary bank, including failing to inject additional capital into the bank to address any capital deficiency.[115] Notwithstanding the potential breadth of the doctrine, it is unclear whether a court would require a holding company to inject capital into a troubled subsidiary absent a specific legally binding agreement to do so, and thus the doctrine has become more a matter of discussion between the Federal Reserve and the holding company when there is financial stress at a subsidiary bank.

8.67   The source of strength doctrine does arise in connection with applications before the Federal Reserve, and the Federal Reserve has often denied applications where it views the parent holding company as lacking sufficient financial resources to support its subsidiary banks.

8.68   Congress codified the Federal Reserve's source of strength doctrine in the Dodd-Frank Act and extended it to all depository institution holding companies.[116] Notwithstanding the codification, it remains unclear whether the source of strength doctrine creates a legal obligation on the part of parent holding companies to inject capital into insolvent bank subsidiaries.[117]

8.69   Since the Federal Reserve has become the supervisory agency for all SLHCs, the Federal Reserve issued final rules that extend the source of strength doctrine to all SLHCs.[118] In addition, the rule specifies that if the Federal Reserve believes that an activity of the SLHC or a nonbank subsidiary constitutes a serious risk to the financial safety, soundness, or stability of a subsidiary savings association and is inconsistent with the principles of sound banking, the Federal Reserve may require the SLHC to terminate the activity or divest control of the nonbanking subsidiary.[119]

8.70   While neither the OCC nor the FDIC historically imposed source of strength obligations on other depository institution holding companies, they typically imposed them contractually on owners of depository institutions that were not otherwise subject to the Bank Holding Company Act.[120] They typically did so as a condition to certain regulatory action in connection with chartering or the acquisition of specialized institutions, such as trust companies, credit card banks, or industrial banks, where the owner may not be subject to the Federal Reserve's oversight. They have continued to impose source of strength

---

[115] Policy Statement on the Responsibility of Bank Holding Companies to Act as Sources of Strength to Their Subsidiary Banks, 52 Fed Reg 15707 (30 April 1987).

[116] Dodd-Frank Act, § 616(d), adding new § 38A to the FDIA, 12 USC § 1831o-1.

[117] *MCorp Fin Inc v Bd of the Governors of the Fed Reserve Sys*, 900 F 2d 852 (5th Cir 1990), *rev'd* in part on procedural grounds, 502 US 32 (1991); Miller, 'Bankruptcy Code FDIC/RTC Interplay: Holding Company vs. Subsidiary/Affiliates Interplay' in *Counselling Creditors of Banks and Thrifts: Dealing with the FDIC and RTC*, PLI Order No A4-4323 (Practising Law Institute, 14–15 January 1991).

[118] 12 CFR § 238.8; see also preamble to Regulation LL, 76 Fed Reg 56508, 56514 (13 September 2011).

[119] 76 Fed Reg 56508, 56514 (13 September 2011).

[120] See, eg, OCC, 'Preliminary Conditional Approval to Charter Paxos National Trust, New York, New York' (2021), 5 (as a condition of approval, requiring entry into written Capital and Liquidity Support Agreement with parent company and OCC setting forth parent company's obligation to provide capital and liquidity support); 'Capital and Liquidity Maintenance Agreement By and Among the FDIC, Square, Inc., Jack Dorsey and Square Financial Services, Inc.' (2020), 2 (draft agreement required by the Order approving Square Financial Services Inc.'s deposit insurance application to be entered into prior to the effective date of FDIC insurance); 'Capital Maintenance Agreement By and Among the FDIC, GMAC LLC, IB Finance Holding Company LLC and GMAC Bank 2-3 (2006). Operating Agreement Between Direct Merchants Credit Card Bank NA, Metris Companies Inc and the OCC' (2003), 7–8.

obligations through capital and liquidity management agreements (CALMAs) since the Dodd-Frank Act extended the source of strength doctrine to all depository institution holding companies.[121]

Further, as noted above, the prompt corrective action provisions require a bank that be-   **8.71** comes undercapitalized to submit a capital restoration plan that, in order to be acceptable, must include a limited guarantee by its parent holding company.[122]

9. Government assistance to open financial institutions

Until 2010, the FDIC had the authority, under the systemic risk exception to the least-cost   **8.72** requirement in section 13(c) of the FDIA, to provide financial assistance to troubled banks or thrifts prior to failure to avoid contagion or other systemic risk.[123] This type of assistance, referred to as open-bank assistance, was provided before an institution was closed. Such assistance could take a variety of forms, including equity infusions, guarantees, or loss-sharing arrangements on troubled assets. The FDIC used open-bank assistance to rescue Continental Illinois and a small number of other troubled banks during the savings and loan crisis of the late 1980s and early 1990s.[124] During the global financial panic of 2008, the FDIC used this authority under the systemic risk exception in connection with the pro-posed Citigroup/Wachovia transaction (which was not consummated), where the FDIC agreed to provide Citigroup with protection against certain potential losses on a portfolio of troubled Wachovia assets.[125] The FDIC also used this authority for its Temporary Liquidity Guarantee Program (TLGP),[126] its participation in the asset guarantee programmes for Citigroup and Bank of America,[127] and the legacy loan portion of the Public-Private Investment Programme.[128]

Open-bank assistance transactions have become politically controversial in the United   **8.73** States and many other countries. Nevertheless, when faced with a choice between a taxpayer-funded rescue and allowing one or more systemically important banking entities to fail in a way that could result in a destabilization or collapse of the financial system, the US and most governments around the world have chosen rescue as the lesser of two evils.[129]

---

[121] Dodd-Frank Act, § 616(d), adding new § 38A to the FDIA, 12 USC § 1831o-1.

[122] FDIA, § 38(e)(2)(C), 12 USC § 1831o(e)(2)(C).

[123] FDIA, § 13(c), 12 USC § 1823(c).

[124] For resource materials on the FDIC's policies and practices with respect to open bank assistance prior to 1991, see Murphy, 'FDIC Assistance', *The Thrift Industry Restructured: The New Regulators and Opportunities for the Future*, PLI Order No A4-4264 (Practising Law Institute, 1989). See also *Inquiry into Continental Illinois Corp. and Continental Illinois National Bank: Hearings before the Subcomm on Financial Institutions Supervision, Regulation and Insurance of the H Comm. on Banking, Finance and Urban Affairs*, 98th Cong, (1984); 'Continental Illinois and "Too Big to Fail"' in *An Examination of the Banking Crises of the 1980s and Early 1990s* (1997) 236.

[125] Press Release, FDIC, 'Citigroup Inc. to Acquire Banking Operations of Wachovia: FDIC, Federal Reserve and Treasury Agree to Provide Open Bank Assistance to Protect Depositors' (29 September 2008). See also Dealbook, 'Wells Fargo to Buy Wachovia in $15 Billion Deal', *New York Times* (3 October 2008).

[126] FDIC, 2008 Annual Report 100–101. Temporary Liquidity Guarantee Program, 73 Fed Reg 72244 (26 November 2008).

[127] FDIC, 2008 Annual Report 100–01. See also Press Release, FDIC, 'Joint Statement by Treasury, Federal Reserve and the FDIC on Citigroup (23 November 2008); Press Release, FDIC, Treasury, Federal Reserve and the FDIC Provide Assistance to Bank of America' (16 January 2009).

[128] FDIC, 2008 Annual Report 100–01; Press Release, FDIC, 'Joint Statement by Secretary of the Treasury Timothy F. Geithner, Chairman of the Board of Governors of the Federal Reserve System Ben S. Bernanke, and Chairman of the Federal Deposit Insurance Corporation Sheila Bair' (8 July 2009).

[129] Guynn, *supra* n 39 at 122.

These rescue operations have undeniably been successful in avoiding meltdowns of various financial systems in the past. The massive amount of capital and liquidity provided to individual US banks and the US banking system by the Treasury, the Federal Reserve, and the FDIC during the 2008 financial crisis stopped runs throughout the US and global financial systems that could have resulted in a collapse of those systems. As a result, notwithstanding the statutory limitation imposed on the FDIC, open-bank assistance is likely to remain an option of last resort, especially if none of the other techniques used by the FDIC or the Federal Reserve are likely to be successful in a particular situation.

8.74 The TLGP was a critical part of the effort by the FDIC, the Treasury, and the Federal Reserve to stabilize the US financial system during the fourth quarter of 2008.[130] Through the TLGP, the FDIC guaranteed certain senior unsecured debt issued by participating insured depository institutions, their holding companies, or their affiliates. The TLGP was highly attractive to participating entities, particularly the larger BHCs, because it provided access to funding at relatively low cost at a time when funding was quite difficult to obtain. Regardless of the participating entity's credit rating, the three major credit rating agencies rated debt issued under the TLGP with their highest ratings based on the FDIC guarantee. Most fixed-rate debt issued under the TLGP bore an annual interest rate between 1.5 per cent and 3 per cent.

8.75 The Dodd-Frank Act repealed the FDIC's authority to provide open-bank assistance.[131] At the same time, it provided express authority for the FDIC to establish liability guarantee programmes like the TLGP, but subjected that authority to certain substantive and procedural hurdles. The programmes must be widely available, may only be provided during times of severe economic distress to provide credit support to the liabilities of depository institutions, depository institution holding companies, or their affiliates that are solvent, and may not include investments in equity in any form.[132] In order for the FDIC to have the power to establish such a programme, both the Federal Reserve and two-thirds of the FDIC board must have determined that a 'liquidity event' has occurred and that a failure to establish the programme would have serious adverse effects on financial stability or economic conditions in the US. The FDIC must also obtain a joint resolution of Congress approving the programme and establishing the maximum amount of debt that can be guaranteed. It is somewhat surprising that some of the most effective programmes used by the regulators during the 2008 crisis have been subjected to restrictions that could handicap the ability of the regulators to respond to future crises.

8.76 The US Treasury does not have general statutory authority to provide financial assistance to troubled banks and thrifts to help prevent them from failing. However, during the 2008 global financial panic, the US Congress gave the US Treasury temporary authority to invest up to $700 billion in certain assets and instruments of financial institutions pursuant to the Emergency Economic Stabilization Act of 2008, otherwise known as the Troubled Asset Relief Program, or TARP.[133] The Treasury used this authority for various financial assistance programmes during the financial crisis, including its programme to provide capital

---

[130] See Davis Polk, *Financial Crisis Manual* (2009) 116–43.
[131] Dodd-Frank Act, § 1106, 12 USC § 5613.
[132] Dodd-Frank Act, §§ 1105–1106, 12 USC §§ 5612–5613.
[133] Emergency Economic Stabilization Act, 12 USC § 5205(5). See also Davis Polk, *Financial Crisis Manual* (2009) 41–66.

to various BHCs and SLHCs and its Public-Private Investment Program (PPIP), which fo-cused on purchasing legacy loans and securities held by depository institutions.[134] This au-thority has expired.

In response to the COVID-19 pandemic, the US Congress in March 2020 gave the US Treasury **8.77** the authority to provide up to $500 billion of loans, guarantees and other investments in support of eligible businesses, states and municipalities. The Treasury used this authority to provide fi-nancial support to, and thereby increase the lending power of, various loan facility programmes administered by the Federal Reserve. Each of these programmes targeted different funding markets, ranging from primary and secondary commercial credit markets, commercial paper, small- to medium-sized business loans (so-called "Main Street" facilities), asset-backed secur-ities, and money market mutual funds. Collectively, these facilities enhanced the availability of credit to a wide range of institutions and borrowers, including private financial and commer-cial companies as well as public-sector borrowers such as municipalities.

C. Resolution Process

If, notwithstanding all efforts, an institution becomes balance-sheet insolvent or otherwise **8.78** fails, its chartering authority will revoke its charter to conduct business.[135] If the insured institution is a national bank or federally chartered savings association and a receiver is appointed, the FDIC must be appointed as its receiver.[136] Although this requirement does not extend to state-chartered banks and savings associations, the FDIC has the power to appoint itself as the conservator or receiver of any FDIC-insured state institution, which overrides or pre-empts the appointment of any state or other federal agency.[137] Accordingly, for FDIC-insured institutions, the FDIC will almost certainly act as receiver.

1. Grounds for closing an institution
The grounds for closing an insured institution and appointing the FDIC as its receiver or **8.79** conservator are extremely open-ended and include:

- the institution being unable to pay its obligations in the normal course of business;
- the institution being in an unsafe or unsound condition;
- the board or shareholders consenting;
- the institution being critically undercapitalized;
- the institution engaging in an unsafe or unsound practice likely to weaken its condition;
- the institution wilfully violating a cease and desist order;
- books, papers, records, or assets being concealed; or
- the institution being found guilty of a federal criminal anti-money laundering offence.[138]

---

[134] Press Release, US Department of the Treasury, *Treasury Department Releases Details on Public Private Partnership Investment Program* (23 March 2009); US Department of the Treasury, *White Paper: Public-Private Investment Program* (2009); Press Release, US Department of the Treasury, *Treasury Announces TARP Capital Purchase Program* (14 October 2008). See also Davis Polk, *Financial Crisis Manual* (2009) 181–205.

[135] FDIC, *Resolutions Handbook, supra* n 5 at 2, 5–6.

[136] FDIA, § 11(c)(2), 12 USC § 1821(c)(2).

[137] FDIA, § 11(c)(4), 12 USC § 1821(c)(4).

[138] FDIA, § 11(c)(5), 12 USC § 1821(c)(5).

8.80   Note that these grounds grant wide discretion to the chartering authority, and many of these conditions may occur well before balance-sheet insolvency.

8.81   Notwithstanding the wide range of the grounds for closing an institution and putting it into an FDIC receivership, the chartering authorities have traditionally relied on balance-sheet insolvency as the primary basis for determining closure. Occasionally, for larger institutions, the charterer will close a bank owing to a lack of liquidity (the inability of the institution to pay its obligations when due in the ordinary course of business).

8.82   The FDIC can serve as either conservator or receiver of an insured institution, although it has historically been reluctant to act as conservator. A conservator takes control of an insured institution with the intent and ability to operate the institution as a going concern until it is rehabilitated for the benefit of its stakeholders. The conservator generally does not engage in wholesale liquidation of the business, although it may sell assets, cease lines of business, or take other similar actions that would be consistent with restoring the institution to a 'sound and solvent condition', or to 'preserve and conserve' the value of the institution, in each case for the benefit of its stakeholders.[139] One factor making the FDIC reluctant to serve as conservator is that there are no provisions in the conservatorship section of the bank resolution statute dealing with claims against an institution in conservatorship. Further, the FDIC has traditionally worried about how having a government-controlled institution operating in the market might affect other private institutions. If a conservatorship is successful in restoring the insured institution to a healthy condition, it will be terminated. If it is unsuccessful, it will be converted into a receivership and the institution will be sold or its assets will be liquidated in an orderly manner.

8.83   Conservatorships have been extremely rare, and have occurred only when the FDIC was unable to find a ready buyer for a failed institution and determined that if operated for a short period of time, a buyer could be found. Most historical examples of conservatorships have been limited to so-called 'pass-through' conservatorships (occasionally referred to as 'pass-through receiverships'), where the institution fails and is placed into receivership; a new institution is chartered, and the assets and most liabilities of the failed bank are passed to the new institution; and the FDIC will then immediately be appointed conservator for the new institution.[140] Many of the savings and loan associations handled by the Resolution Trust Corporation (the specialized agency established during the savings and loan crisis of the late 1980s to handle failed thrifts) were pass-through receiverships and were operated as conservatorships for a period of time, until the Resolution Trust Corporation was prepared to commence sale or liquidation of the failed institution.[141] IndyMac, which failed in 2008, also involved a pass-through receivership and conservatorship. Before the assets of this new institution were sold to an investor group, it was placed into receivership and the FDIC effected the resolution transaction.[142]

---

[139]   FDIA, § 11(d)(2)(C), 12 USC § 1821(d)(2)(C).

[140]   FDIC, *Resolutions Handbook: Methods for Resolving Troubled Financial Institutions in the United States*, 96 (2003) (superseded by 2019 edition).

[141]   See, eg, FDIC, 1998 Annual Report (2000), available at: <https://www.fdic.gov/about/strategic/report/98Annual/failed.html>.

[142]   FDIC, 'Failed Bank Information, Information for IndyMac Bank, F.S.B., and IndyMac Federal Bank, F.S.B., Pasadena, CA' (2015), available at: <https://www.fdic.gov/bank/individual/failed/IndyMac.html>.

The conservatorships of Freddie Mac and Fannie Mae are possibly the only genuine   **8.84**
conservatorships, and their conservatorships were effected under the Housing and
Economic Recovery Act of 2008 (HERA), which was based on the bank resolution model.[143]
It is conceivable that the FDIC might use a genuine conservatorship in the case of a systemically important bank, although with the bridge bank authority, it is more likely that the
FDIC would continue to place the insolvent institution into receivership and charter a new
bridge bank to continue its operations under FDIC control.

While the distinction between conservatorships and receiverships can appear fuzzy, the   **8.85**
FDIC would typically use a conservatorship to operate institutions until it is prepared to effect a resolution transaction. The receivership is typically used by the FDIC to effect a resolution transaction, either the sale of the assets of the failed institution to a third party, or to
effect a liquidation or both.

2. Effect of appointment

When the FDIC is appointed as conservator or receiver of an institution, it steps into the   **8.86**
shoes of the failed institution.[144] It succeeds by operation of law to all of the rights, titles,
powers, and privileges of the insured institution and its stockholders, members, directors,
officers, account holders, and depositors, subject to the provisions of the FDIA.[145]

3. Timing of appointment

To minimize disruption to its customers, an insured institution is typically closed and the   **8.87**
FDIC is appointed as receiver after the close of business on a Friday, although in emergency
cases a closing can occur during other days of the week. The Friday closing facilitates the
transfer of assets and liabilities to a new acquirer and gives the new acquirer the weekend
to prepare for a Monday reopening. The acquirer must also be prepared to operate ATMs
and facilitate consumer access to accounts over the weekend, even prior to the Monday
opening. In the case of a systemically important institution with an international business,
the acquirer must be ready to operate upon the opening of the Asian markets on Monday
morning (ie Sunday evening in the US).

Upon closing, the FDIC attempts to engage in a transaction that will transfer assets and   **8.88**
liabilities to another healthy privately owned banking organization. On rare occasions, a
suitable acquirer cannot be found and the FDIC may elect to operate the failed institution
through a conservatorship (typically a pass-through receivership as noted above) or use its
bridge bank authority. For small institutions where no buyer can be found, it may be forced
to conduct a pay-off of the depositors and liquidate the assets.

4. FDIC's duties

The FDIC does not have unlimited flexibility in resolving failed banking institutions. It has   **8.89**
a statutory duty to resolve all insured institutions in a manner that is 'least costly to the
deposit insurance fund of all possible methods',[146] and that both maximizes the residual

---

[143] See, eg, FHFA, 'FHFA as Conservator of Fannie Mae and Freddie Mac', available at: <http://www.fhfa.gov/
Conservatorship/Pages/History-of-Fannie-Mae--Freddie-Conservatorships.aspx>.
[144] See, eg, *O'Melveny & Meyers v FDIC*, 512 US 79, 80 (1994).
[145] FDIA, § 11(d)(2), 12 USC § 1821(d)(2).
[146] FDIA, § 13(c)(4), 12 USC § 1823(c)(4).

value of the institutions and minimizes their losses for the benefit of their depositors and other stakeholders.[147] It is also generally precluded from using the deposit insurance fund to benefit existing shareholders.[148] The 'least-cost resolution' and 'no shareholder benefit' duties limit the flexibility of the FDIC in carrying out resolutions. These restrictions were added in 1991 and 1993, respectively, in reaction to the perceived tendency by the FDIC and other responsible federal agencies at the time to rescue or otherwise provide 'open-bank assistance' to troubled IDIs during the savings and loan crisis of the 1980s. The least-cost test was also added to impose some discipline on the FDIC, which had developed a tendency to do a whole-bank or near whole-bank purchase and assumption sales transaction (see section III.C.5), even if there were other less costly resolution transactions available. The FDIC also has a policy to resolve failed institutions in a manner that avoids contagion, maintains public confidence in the US financial system, and otherwise promotes financial stability.[149]

8.90 Prior to enactment of the Dodd-Frank Act, the FDIC's least-cost test contained a 'systemic risk' exception that permitted it to provide open-bank assistance to individual IDIs if necessary to avoid 'serious adverse effects on economic conditions or financial stability' during a financial emergency.[150] The Dodd-Frank Act amended this exception, and now precludes the FDIC from providing open-bank assistance to any individual institution.[151] It now provides an exception from the least-cost test only with respect to IDIs in receivership. If invoked, which still must be for systemic reasons, the FDIC may provide financial assistance to facilitate the resolution of an IDI in receivership even if such assistance would not be consistent with the least-cost test.

5. Purchase-and-assumption sale transactions

8.91 Clearly the FDIC's preferred resolution strategy is a transaction that permits another institution to assume some portion of the liabilities of the failed institution and acquire some or all of the assets of the failed institution.[152] Known as a 'purchase and assumption' (P&A) transaction, the FDIC may engage in such a transaction with a third party without obtaining consent or approval of any person.[153] The purchaser must have a bank or thrift charter, although on occasion the acquirer may obtain a charter from a chartering authority at the time of the P&A transaction.

8.92 The FDIC has discretion to determine which assets are sold to the acquirer. Since it remains subject to the least-cost resolution test as receiver, it selects the assets to sell based upon its analysis of whether the deposit insurance fund is better off transferring the assets to the acquiring institution as part of the P&A transaction or whether it should sell the assets separately. The assets sold as part of the P&A transaction can include any or all of the assets of

---

[147] FDIA, § 11(d)(13)(E)(i) and (ii), 12 USC 1821(d)(13)(E)(i) and (ii).
[148] FDIA, § 11(a)(4)(C), 12 USC § 1821(a)(4)(C).
[149] FDIC, *Resolutions Handbook, supra* n 5, 1.
[150] 12 United States Code Annotated § 1823(c)(4)(G) (West Publishing 2009).
[151] Dodd-Frank Act, § 1106(b), 12 USC § 5613(b).
[152] FDIC, *Resolutions Handbook, supra* n 5, 16–19.
[153] FDIA, § 11(d)(2)(G)(i)(II), 12 USC § 1821(d)(2)(G)(i)(II). At least one court—the US Court of Appeals for the Ninth Circuit—has ruled that when the FDIC engages in a P&A without obtaining consents or approvals that are required under contracts, it must pay damages to the aggrieved party. *Bank of Manhattan, N.A. v FDIC*, 778 F 3d 1133 (9th Cir 2015).

the failed bank—cash and securities, performing loans, non-performing loans, buildings, furniture, fixtures, and equipment, or any combination thereof. To facilitate the sale, the FDIC can offer loss-sharing or other forms of protection to the purchaser.[154] Any assets not sold as part of the P&A transaction will be sold later to other parties.

The acquiring institution will assume the insured deposits and may elect to assume uninsured deposits as well. On occasion, the acquiring institution will assume certain secured liabilities such as Federal Home Loan Bank advances. It is the rare P&A transaction where the acquirer will assume general unsecured creditor obligations. **8.93**

Any assets not purchased by the acquiring institution, and any liabilities not assumed, will be left with the FDIC as receiver, which will liquidate the assets over time. The proceeds of the asset sales, including the proceeds of the sale to the acquiring bank under the P&A transaction, will be used to satisfy the claims of creditors of the failed institution in accordance with the statutory priorities.[155] In general, following the satisfaction of secured creditor claims, the FDIC will recover its administrative expenses. The remaining priorities are first, claims on deposits payable in the US (domestic deposits), second, general unsecured creditor claims (including claims on deposits payable solely outside the US (foreign deposits)), third, subordinated creditor claims, and finally claims of equity holders. **8.94**

6. Bridge banks

If the FDIC is unable to find a financial institution to assume the deposit liabilities of the failed bank when it is closed, the FDIC may request the OCC to charter a new national bank or federal savings association to operate as a 'bridge bank'.[156] A bridge bank is an entity used by the FDIC to assume all or any portion of a failed institution's business, and thereby continue to operate the business as a going concern without interruption. The FDIC's board selects a CEO and board of directors for the bridge bank, generally consisting of senior FDIC personnel, retired FDIC executives, and experienced bankers. Once the FDIC has stabilized the bank, it will seek an acquirer. An acquirer can then make a bid for all or any portion of the assets and liabilities of the bridge bank, or for the bridge bank as a whole. The FDIC generally uses this option if it believes that the temporary operation and subsequent sale of the institution would be more financially attractive to the FDIC than an immediate liquidation, or if it determines that temporarily operating the business through a bridge bank will facilitate financial stability. **8.95**

The FDIC has the authority to transfer any assets or liabilities from the closed bank to the bridge bank without the need for consent or approval from any party, just as it does in a P&A transaction.[157] The closed bank together with assets and liabilities not transferred to the bridge bank, remains in receivership, and the left-behind assets will be liquidated and the proceeds will be used to satisfy unpaid claims. The FDIC must merge, transfer, or terminate and dissolve the bridge bank within two years of its organization, with the option of three additional one-year periods at the FDIC's discretion.[158] This period is designed to give **8.96**

---

[154] FDIA, § 13(c)(2)(A), 12 USC § 1823(c)(2)(A).
[155] FDIA, § 11(d)(11), 12 USC § 1821(d)(11).
[156] FDIA, § 11(n)(1)(A), 12 USC § 1821(n)(1)(A).
[157] FDIA, § 11(d)(2)(G), 12 USC §1821(d)(2)(G).
[158] FDIA, § 11(n)(9), 12 USC § 1821(n)(9).

the FDIC time to find one or more third party acquirers for all or part of the bridge bank's assets and liabilities, or for the bridge bank itself. To facilitate the sale of the bridge bank, and to maximize the recoveries, the FDIC will often enter into loss-sharing agreements or provide other financial assistance to an acquirer.

7. Recapitalization (bail-in) within resolution

8.97 In resolving small, mid-size, and regional banks the FDIC has typically engaged in a P&A sale transaction, with or without loss-sharing, as discussed more fully in section III.C.5. While the FDIC is likely to continue resolving such institutions with this strategy, it is unlikely to use this strategy to resolve the largest, most systemically important US banks. First, the strategy is unlikely to be the least-cost to the deposit insurance fund or maximize the residual value of the institution or minimize its losses for the benefit of its stakeholders. Secondly, and perhaps just as important, such a transaction would result in an even larger, more systemically important bank. Instead, the FDIC is likely to use some other technique for systemically important banks such as a recapitalization (bail-in) within resolution strategy or a multi-acquirer or orderly wind-down strategy.

8.98 A recapitalization (bail-in) within resolution strategy involves the conversion of external long-term unsecured debt or intercompany unsecured debt into equity interests. Since by statute insured deposits, uninsured deposits that are solely payable in the US and uninsured deposits that are dually payable at a foreign branch or in the US (collectively, domestic deposits) rank senior to the general liabilities of a US bank (including uninsured deposits that are payable solely at a foreign branch of a US bank),[159] it should be possible to convert long-term unsecured debt or intercompany liabilities into equity interests without fostering a run by the holders of domestic deposits. Assuming a large IDI has sufficient long-term unsecured debt and intercompany liabilities to result in the IDI being fully recapitalized if they are converted to equity interests, and only an immaterial amount of short-term non-deposit liabilities, it should be possible for the FDIC to use this strategy to recapitalize the failed IDI without fostering a contagious run on demand deposits or other short-term unsecured liabilities throughout the US banking system.

8.99 Several of the US G-SIBs have proposed recapitalization within resolution strategies in their IDI resolution plans filed with the FDIC. They believe that the strategy is least-cost to the deposit insurance fund of all possible alternatives and the one that is most likely to maximize its residual value and minimize its losses for the benefit of its stakeholders.[160] Further, they believe that it minimizes systemic disruption, and avoids the creation of larger, more systemic banks. Under this method, the FDIC would establish a bridge bank and transfer

---

[159] FDIA, § 11(d)(11), 12 CFR § 1821(d)(11). Three US law firms—Cleary Gottlieb, Davis Polk, and Sullivan & Cromwell—jointly published a paper in which they argued that the term 'deposit liability' includes foreign branch deposits for purposes of § 11(d)(11). Cleary Gottlieb, Davis Polk, and Sullivan & Cromwell, *The Status of Foreign Branch Deposits under the Depositor Preference Rule* (2 January 2013). The FDIC rejected that view, however, based on an opinion by a then acting general counsel of the FDIC in 1994. FDIC, Deposit Insurance Regulations; Definition of Insured Deposit, 78 Fed Reg 56583 (13 September 2013); FDIC Advisory Opinion, 'Deposit Liability' for Purposes of National Depositor Preference Includes Only Deposits Payable in the US, FDIC 94-1 (28 February 1994). According to the FDIC, a foreign branch deposit must be dually payable at both the foreign branch and in the US to be included in the term 'deposit liability', 78 Fed Reg 56583, 56586 (13 September 2013).

[160] This is a reference to the statutory requirement imposed on the FDIC to utilize the resolution method that results in the least cost to the DIF. See FDIC, 'Title I and IDI Resolution Plans' (2021), available at: <https://www.fdic.gov/regulations/reform/resplans/>.

all of the failed IDI's assets to the bridge bank and cause the bridge bank to assume all of the IDI's insured deposits and uninsured domestic deposits as well as other short-term debt. The rest of the IDI's liabilities, including external senior unsecured debt and intercompany debt would be left behind in the IDI's receivership. By leaving these and other liabilities behind in the receivership, the FDIC will have effectively recapitalized the business transferred to the bridge bank.

After the bridge bank's operations have been stabilized and the bridge bank is able to pre-   **8.100** pare reliable financial statements, the FDIC would transfer the bridge bank to a newly created holding company ('New Holdco') owned by a trust in exchange for the trust's promise to return the value of the bridge bank to the FDIC as receiver. The plan would be to dispose of assets or lines of business as appropriate, and to sell all or a portion of New Holdco's equity to the public through private sales, an initial public offering (IPO), or one or more follow-on public offerings. The net proceeds from such sales and any unsold equity in New Holdco to the IDI's receivership would be distributed to the holders of claims against the IDI in accordance with the priority of their claims and in satisfaction of their claims.

To facilitate the recapitalization within resolution strategy, the Federal Reserve has adopted   **8.101** regulations requiring the top-tier parent BHCs of the US G-SIBs to maintain sufficient external third-party unsecured debt so that if the equity of the parent is exhausted, the debt can be converted into equity and the US G-SIB can be recapitalized.

8. Break-up and sell strategy

Although the IDI that emerges from a recapitalization within resolution strategy is inevit-   **8.102** ably smaller than the IDI that entered the process, and sometimes significantly so,[161] each US G-SIB was required to include a break-up and sell strategy (which the FDIC called a 'multiple acquirer strategy') in their 2015 IDI resolution plans.[162] The FDIC described a break-up and sell strategy as a technique that 'primarily involves the separation and sale of the [IDI]'s deposit franchise, core business lines, and/or major assets to multiple acquirers'. The FDIC stated that a break-up and sell strategy 'may be accomplished through a combination of transactions, including purchase-and-assumption transactions, initial public offering of securities ("IPO"), and liquidation'. The FDIC specifically noted that it expected 'at least one [break-up and sell] strategy [to] involve the recapitalization of a portion of the [IDI] through single or multiple IPO transactions'. As any break-up and sell strategy would necessarily take some period of time to accomplish, the FDIC indicated that it expected IDIs to use a bridge bank to hold the assets until the assets could be sold.[163] In its most recent guidance on IDI resolution plans, the FDIC requires IDIs to present a sale strategy that contemplates the sale of different franchise components of the IDI,[164] which would facilitate a multiple acquirer strategy.

---

[161] Statement of Randall D Guynn, Partner, Davis Polk, Hearing before the Subcommittee on Financial Institutions and Consumer Protection, Senate Committee on Banking, Finance and Urban Affairs (29 June 2015) 7–8 (discussing the reduced footprint principle that is an inevitable by-product of the SPOE and other recapitalization within resolution strategies).

[162] FDIC, *Guidance for Covered Insured Depository Institution Resolution Plan Submissions* (December 2014).

[163] Ibid.

[164] FDIC, 'Statement on Resolution Plans for Insured Depository Institutions' (June 2021), 5–6.

9. Orderly wind-down strategy

8.103 An orderly wind-down strategy involves the creation of a bridge bank and the transfer of all or a portion of the failed bank's assets and liabilities to the bridge bank. The FDIC then causes the bridge bank to sell any businesses and assets transferred to it in an orderly manner over an extended period of time. The bridge bank permits the FDIC to maintain franchise value and maximize the value realized from the sale of the bridge bank's assets, with the net proceeds being turned over to the FDIC receivership to be distributed to the holders of any claims left behind in the receivership in accordance with the priority of claims and in satisfaction of such claims.

10. Liquidation strategy

8.104 The FDIC also required the US G-SIBs to include a liquidation strategy in their 2015 IDI resolution plans.[165] Liquidation of a G-SIB would be costly and disruptive, and the FDIC indicated that it did not expect a liquidation strategy to be least-cost to the deposit insurance fund of all possible alternative strategies or otherwise maximize the residual value of the bank or minimize its losses. Rather, the FDIC mandated that a liquidation strategy be included in the 2015 plans in order to establish a baseline against which other strategies could be compared for purposes of the least-cost test.

D. FDIC-Assisted Purchase-and-Assumption Sale Transactions

8.105 As noted, the FDIC uses P&A transactions as it resolves failed community, mid-size, and regional banks. Invariably, the FDIC has provided some form of financial assistance in the form of cash or other value to the acquiring institution as the insured deposit liabilities assumed have usually exceeded the value of the assets transferred (even when the FDIC provided additional protection in the form of loss sharing). Because of the importance of these assisted transactions both to the FDIC and to potential bidders, this section provides more detail about P&A sale transactions with FDIC assistance.

1. Initiation of the process

8.106 The process for an FDIC-assisted transaction begins when the FDIC or an insured institution's chartering authority has determined that the institution has exhausted its capital or is rapidly running out of sufficient liquidity to operate its business in the ordinary course. As noted, under the prompt corrective action provisions, a bank that is 'critically undercapitalized'—that is, one where its tangible equity, which is defined as Tier 1 capital plus non-Tier 1 perpetual preferred stock, is at or below 2 per cent of total assets[166]—generally must be closed within 90 days unless it has been able to recapitalize itself.[167]

8.107 The decision whether to close the institution is reached by the institution's chartering authority, generally in consultation with the FDIC.

---

[165] Ibid.
[166] 12 CFR § 325.103(b)(5).
[167] FDIA, § 38(h), 12 USC § 1831o(h).

When the chartering authority or the FDIC believes an insured institution is in danger of failing, the FDIC has typically sent a resolution team to the failing bank or thrift to obtain the necessary data to conduct an auction process. The resolution team will prepare an information package for potential bidders, perform an asset valuation, determine the appropriate resolution structure, and conduct an on-site analysis to prepare for the closing. The time between the FDIC's determination that an institution is running out of liquidity or receipt of a prompt corrective action notice and the closing of an assisted transaction has generally been about 90 days, although it has been longer or shorter depending upon the facts and circumstances surrounding the institution.   **8.108**

2. The bidding process

The FDIC will invite qualified bidders to participate in an auction for the assets and liabilities of the failed bank. Qualified bidders will generally be strong financial institutions with good management and the financial capacity to absorb the assets and liabilities of the failed bank. The FDIC will determine the specific assets to be offered as part of the package. The bidder will be expected to assume the insured deposits (although brokered deposits are often excluded from the transaction). The bidder will be offered the opportunity to assume the uninsured deposits as well.   **8.109**

As part of the bidding process, the FDIC has typically established a reserve price for the failing institution, by estimating the fair market value of the institution's assets and then deducting any estimated costs of disposition and direct marketing, arriving at a net figure that is known as the liquidation value of the assets. The estimated liquidation value of the assets is part of the FDIC's evaluation of the least-cost test for the resolution of the institution. For a brief period of time in the early 1990s, the FDIC attempted to increase the volume of assets sold at resolution by revealing its reserve price for asset pools. The FDIC observed that revealing the reserve price has advantages and disadvantages, but noted that in circumstances where few bids are submitted, disclosing the reserve price tended to bias the bidding towards that price.[168] The FDIC does not currently reveal its reserve price, primarily to reduce the risk of receiving bids that are lower than a bidder's maximum willingness to pay.   **8.110**

To maximize the number of bidders and foster competition, the FDIC also does not currently disclose the names or number of bidders for a particular failing institution during the bidding process. After the transaction has closed, however, the FDIC publishes on its website certain details about the bidders and bids received, including the winning bidder and bid and, after one year, the second-place bid. It has also revealed, at the same time as the winning bid, the names of all bidders and bids, but has not associated each bidder with a particular bid.[169]   **8.111**

The FDIC has multiple goals in resolving a failed bank. It attempts to sell as much of the bank as possible to the highest bidder in a manner that maintains public confidence in   **8.112**

---

[168] FDIC, *Resolutions Handbook: Methods for Resolving Troubled Financial Institutions in the United States* (2003) 10–11 (superseded by 2019 edition).

[169] 5 USC § 552. The FDIC's policy on releasing bidding information in response to requests is set out in FDIC, 'Failed Financial Institution Bid Disclosure Policy', available at: <https://www.fdic.gov/resources/resolutions/bank-failures/failed-bank-list/biddocs.html>.

the US financial system and results in the least disruption to insured depositors and other stakeholders of the bank, consistent with the FDIC's statutory obligation to resolve the bank in a manner that is least costly to the deposit insurance fund. The least-cost test requires the FDIC to adopt the resolution method that 'is the least costly to the Deposit Insurance Fund of all possible methods' of meeting its obligations with respect to the failed institution. In practical terms, the least-cost test means that the FDIC may not accept a bid if (i) there is another bid that is less costly to the deposit insurance fund or (ii) it would result in a more costly resolution of the institution than a deposit pay-off and liquidation of the assets. If the FDIC receives at least one bid that would result in lower losses to the deposit insurance fund than a deposit pay-off and liquidation of the institution, normally the FDIC would accept the highest such bid it receives. However, the requirement of the least-cost test may lead it to use another technique such as a bridge bank or recapitalization within resolution that would be less costly to the deposit insurance fund.

8.113 The FDIC determines the mix of assets and liabilities it will offer potential bidders in a P&A transaction. Considerations include the following:

- Should it offer the bank in whole or in parts? The FDIC has found that it is sometimes easier to sell certain parts of a bank separately, such as a trust business, a credit card operation, or branches. Occasionally, the FDIC has divided a bank into geographic regions if it believed doing so would facilitate the sale.
- Which types of assets should it offer to bidders?
- How should it package saleable assets? Should they be sold with or without loss sharing?
- How should the value of the assets be determined?

8.114 After the FDIC has completed its initial work on the failing institution, the Franchise and Asset Marketing Branch of the FDIC's Division of Resolutions and Receiverships has typically sent a notice of the opportunity to bid on the failing institution to approved bidders through a secure website. These bidders must register as such on the FDIC's secure internet channel, designate two contacts, and provide the email addresses and phone numbers of the two contacts. They have also been invited to indicate their geographic preferences for future acquisitions and whether they were interested in purchasing deposit franchises or asset portfolios, or both. There is strict confidentiality, as the FDIC seeks to avoid causing a 'run' on the institutions before it can be resolved in an orderly fashion.

8.115 In general, approved bidders have been limited to banks, thrifts, BHCs, or SLHCs that are 'well capitalized' and in satisfactory condition. Generally only banks, thrifts, BHCs, or SLHCs are permitted to participate in the bidding process, although nonbanking institutions have been permitted to participate in special situations.[170] The FDIC has tended to permit institutions to bid on institutions in their geographic areas, but has made exceptions for strong management teams. It has generally permitted an institution to bid on another institution that is smaller, not larger, in size, but has made exceptions for strongly capitalized banks with strong management teams.

---

[170] FDIC, *Resolutions Handbook, supra* n 5, 11.

It has been possible for other bidders to participate in the auction if they obtain what has   **8.116**
become known as a 'shelf' charter. That is, the party undertakes all the necessary steps to
obtain a charter by satisfying all of the financial, management and business conditions such
that the regulators have indicated a willingness to activate a charter, with deposit insurance, if and when a bid from the proponents for a failed bank is accepted. The FDIC has
permitted generally potential investors without an active charter (but with a 'shelf' charter)
to participate in the bidding process when few other feasible purchasers exist. Examples
include the IndyMac, BankUnited, Silverton, and Nexity transactions. On occasion these
nonbank bidders have entered into agreements with the FDIC to purchase a bridge bank
that will have assumed some or all of the assets and liabilities of the failed bank. The FDIC
has the statutory authority to establish and sell a bridge bank in order to facilitate a transaction, but the FDIC has rarely used this transaction structure with a small, mid-size, or even
regional bank.

In the past, the FDIC invited approved bidders that indicated an interest in bidding on a par-   **8.117**
ticular failing institution to an information meeting. Only at the meeting and after signing a
confidentiality agreement would the potential buyers receive hard-copy documents from the
FDIC. Since 2000, the FDIC has marketed banks using secure online data rooms and these in-
person meetings have ceased.

Under the more modern procedures, the FDIC has contacted approved acquirers to inform   **8.118**
them of a potential FDIC transaction and to provide general information about the offering.
The offering will not name the failing bank, but has generally revealed the state or region in
which the bank resides and its size. Interested potential bidders have been permitted to view
an executive summary with more specific information about the failing bank on the FDIC's
secured website. Interested qualified bidders have then notified the FDIC of their desire to proceed, and thereby obtained full access to all available information provided through the FDIC's
online data room following execution of an appropriate confidentiality agreement. The information provided has included detailed financial data on the failing institution, the assets and
liabilities being offered, descriptions of the resolution methods being offered, the legal documents, including any proposed P&A or loss-sharing agreements, details on the due diligence
process, and the bidding procedures.

A potential bidder has been required to have received assurance from its primary federal regulator   **8.119**
that it would be permitted to acquire the failed institution in order to participate in the bidding
process. It has also been required to satisfy a number of other conditions, including the following:

- The bidder must have contacted all appropriate state and federal regulators and arranged
  to receive all necessary regulatory approvals for the transaction before the FDIC's proposed closing of the failed bank transaction.
- The institution resulting from the transaction would need to be 'well capitalized' and have
  a fully funded allowance for loan losses as of closing.
- If a bidder was a *de novo* institution, the resulting institution would also have been required to satisfy any additional conditions imposed by the chartering authority of the *de
  novo* institution, such as super capital requirements imposed on *de novo* institutions (eg a
  10 per cent Tier 1 risk-based capital ratio for the first three years of operation), a comprehensive business plan, and qualified directors and senior executive officers.

- In the case of a bidder that is a 'private capital investor', the FDIC has proposed additional requirements.[171]

8.120   If a prospective bidder failed any of these conditions, the FDIC reserved the right to reject the bid.

8.121   If there is time, each approved bidder has been permitted to conduct limited on-site due diligence on the bank. The FDIC has tightly controlled the due diligence process, ensuring that all bidders have had equal access to information. Potential acquirers have occasionally been given the opportunity to speak with management of the bank, but access to information may be limited by the FDIC. For instance, the FDIC generally has taken the position that bidders should not have access to the target's examination reports or other supervisory information.

8.122   There is some debate as to whether the various restrictions imposed by the FDIC on bidder qualifications, access to information, and special requirements for private equity and other types of financial bidders, depress the prices that qualified bidders are required to bid, or discourage certain qualified bidders from bidding at all. To some degree, these restrictions are arguably balanced, at least in part, by loss-sharing protection and other incentives designed to encourage robust bidding when asset values are highly uncertain, such as during a financial crisis. Nevertheless, some are concerned that the FDIC's process is subject to being exploited by the relatively small number of experienced bidders or bidders advised by the relatively small number of experienced advisers. In other words, they believe that these procedures and special requirements on private equity bidders may inhibit the FDIC's ability to receive the highest price for a failed insured institution, which raises questions about whether the FDIC is fully compliant with the least-cost test. They believe that the FDIC, the deposit insurance fund, and other creditors of a failed insured institution might receive better value and otherwise be better off if the FDIC adopted a more open and transparent bidding process.

8.123   In contrast, the FDIC believes that its procedures are appropriately calibrated to satisfy the least-cost test. In a 2009 study, the FDIC determined that immediate disclosure of losing bids, particularly the cover bid, was having an adverse effect on the FDIC's ability to minimize costs to the deposit insurance fund.[172] The study included data suggesting that immediate or full disclosure of losing bids was reducing the incentive of bidders to offer their highest bid based on analysis of previous competitions. The FDIC was concerned that disclosing winning bids well above second bids might be viewed as outliers and discounted by some as anomalies. The FDIC believes that its current procedures reduce the possibility of the FDIC being exploited by experienced or well-advised bidders as described above.

3. The transaction structure

8.124   All FDIC-assisted transactions have revolved around the assumption of liabilities and the purchase of assets. The transaction structures have included the following options:

---

[171] FDIC, Final Statement of Policy on Qualifications for Failed Bank Acquisitions, 74 Fed Reg 45440 (2 September 2009).
[172] Rosalind L Bennett and Haluk Unal, *The Effects of Resolution Methods and Industry Stress on the Loss on Assets from Bank Failures* (2009).

- On the liability side of the balance sheet:
- insured deposits only;
- potentially adding uninsured deposits;
- potentially adding certain secured liabilities such as Federal Home Loan Bank advances and covered bonds; or
- potentially adding certain other debt obligations.
- On the asset side of the balance sheet:
- cash and readily marketable securities;
- performing assets, with or without loss sharing;
- non-performing assets, with or without loss sharing; and
- premises and equipment.

Based upon its analysis of the appropriate method to maximize values, the FDIC may include intellectual property, employee relationships, equity in subsidiaries, and joint ventures as part of the assets offered. **8.125**

In a so-called 'whole bank' transaction, virtually all the bank's assets are purchased and all or certain of its liabilities assumed pursuant to a P&A agreement. As described above, the parent holding company and its nonbank subsidiaries have been excluded from the FDIC's resolution process. Subsidiaries of the failed institution have not been placed into receivership when the FDIC deals with the failed institution. However, because the equity of a subsidiary of the bank is as an asset of the receivership estate of the failed institution, these subsidiaries can be included in whole-bank transactions. **8.126**

In addressing the liabilities that might be assumed, the FDIC will often exclude brokered deposits and Home Loan Bank advances, paying those obligations off rather than passing them to the assuming institution. Further, a bidder that wishes to assume uninsured deposits or other unsecured liabilities must carefully consider how such assumption affects the FDIC's calculation of the least-cost test. In essence, the bid involving assumption of uninsured liabilities must be more advantageous to the FDIC (or, in other words, less costly to the FDIC) than a bid that does not assume uninsured deposits. **8.127**

The FDIC decides whether it needed to offer loss-sharing or other financial assistance to make the structure marketable. The FDIC will sell or liquidate any assets that have not been purchased, and will address the rights of unassumed liabilities as part of its receivership duties. **8.128**

The FDIC has normally provided a cash payment to the acquirer that has approximated the difference in the value of assets and liabilities. As the other structures imply, they have involved the purchase of only part of the assets or liabilities of the failed institution. In essence, one can think of the bid as being how much assistance the assuming bank will require in order to acquire the assets offered and assume the liabilities of the failed bank that must be assumed in the P&A transaction. **8.129**

As noted, the FDIC has offered additional financial assistance to facilitate the transaction in the form of the FDIC's standard loss-sharing arrangements.[173] These arrangements are **8.130**

---

[173] FDIC, *Resolutions Handbook, supra* n 5, 18.

typically offered for assets that are difficult to value. The FDIC has had two types of loss-sharing arrangements, one with two tranches and the other with three tranches. The three-tranche loss-sharing arrangement has generally been reserved for banks with assets above $500 million. In those arrangements, the assuming bank has typically borne 100 per cent of the losses on an amount called the 'first-loss tranche'. This tranche can be a positive amount of assets or zero. If zero, loss sharing has started immediately upon any losses. Losses incurred in excess of the first loss tranche and up to an amount called the 'stated threshold' have typically been shared 80 per cent by the FDIC and 20 per cent by the assuming bank although in certain situations the parties have been permitted to bid on the percentage of sharing. The stated threshold has generally represented the FDIC's estimate of the maximum amount of expected losses. Any losses above the stated threshold are shared 95 per cent by the FDIC and 5 per cent by the assuming bank, although again on occasion the percentages can vary.

8.131   Two-tranche loss-sharing arrangements have generally been used for smaller banks with less than $500 million in assets. The first tranche has covered losses up to the intrinsic loss estimate, which is the FDIC's estimate of embedded credit losses in the assets offered. Loss incurred in excess of the intrinsic loss estimate has been referred to as the second tranche. Again, the first tranche loss is typically 80 per cent–20 per cent, with the buyer assuming 80 per cent of the first tranche loss, and the FDIC assuming 80 per cent of the second tranche loss. If potential bidders are willing to share a greater portion of the loss, bidders have been able to change this loss-share percentage by submitting a bid to lower the FDIC's loss-share percentage in each tranche. On occasion, the FDIC has experimented with creating a middle tranche between the two where there would be no loss sharing, with the intent of incentivizing the acquirer to minimize losses before passing to the lower tranche where the FDIC will be assuming a greater portion of the losses.

8.132   Generally consumer loans and government guaranteed loans have not been covered by FDIC loss-share agreements, and often neither have single-family residential mortgage loans. In addition, the FDIC has maintained the right to claw back some upside from the assuming bank when the actual losses have been significantly less than estimated. The FDIC has on occasion imposed specific obligations on assuming banks in dealing with single-family mortgages in default.

8.133   The FDIC used a variety of different assisted transaction structures during the savings and loan crisis of the 1980s and early 1990s. But a major study of these structures after the savings and loan crisis persuaded the FDIC that whole-bank or asset pool transactions, with loss sharing, were the most effective structure in producing the least-cost result for the FDIC in most closed-bank transactions.[174] As a result, the FDIC has been exceedingly resistant to any asset structure other than whole-bank or asset pool transactions, with its standard loss-sharing provisions.[175]

---

[174]   FDIC, *Managing the Crisis: The FDIC and RTC Experience 1980–1994*, Vol 1 (1998).
[175]   For a discussion of some of the other structures, which the FDIC now strongly resists, see FDIC, *Resolutions Handbook: Methods for Resolving Troubled Financial Institutions in the United States* (2003) 19–40 (superseded by 2019 edition).

FDIC-assisted transactions have proven to be quite attractive to potential bidders for a **8.134** number of reasons. First, the FDIC process gives purchasers the option to avoid assuming certain types of liabilities. Thus, any unsecured senior or subordinated debt and obligations to shareholders can remain behind in the receivership, relieving the acquirer of substantial liabilities and claims. For example, in the JPMorgan Chase acquisition of Washington Mutual, the largest failed bank in the history of the United States, the acquirer was able to avoid approximately $10 billion in unsecured debt of the failed bank, and assumed no obligations to shareholders.

Secondly, as a general proposition, contingent claims, including litigation exposure, can be **8.135** left behind in the receivership. Accordingly, the assuming bank generally has not had to worry about past actions of the institution and its management.

Thirdly, the acquirer has been able to piggyback off the FDIC's 'repudiation power'. As **8.136** explained more fully in section III.F.5 below, the FDIC has the power to repudiate any contract that it finds 'burdensome' within a reasonable period of time after the institution is closed or where repudiation would facilitate the administration of the receivership estate. This repudiation power is not limited to executory contracts, although as a practical matter, the FDIC has not repudiated contracts that have been fully executed. The FDIC has exercised the repudiation power where it determines that some performance obligation remains on the part of the failed bank that satisfies the statutory test of being burdensome. The FDIC also has the power to 'cherry-pick' the contracts it will repudiate, unless the contract is a special type of contract called a 'qualified financial contract' (QFC). QFCs include securities contracts, commodities contracts, forward contracts, repurchase agreements, swap agreements, and master agreements for any of the foregoing. In the case of QFCs, the FDIC must repudiate all or none of the QFCs with a particular counterparty and its affiliates.[176]

When the FDIC repudiates a contract, it must pay the counterparty damages. Damages **8.137** are limited to 'actual direct compensatory damages', determined as of the date the FDIC was appointed as conservator or receiver.[177] This damages formula excludes punitive or exemplary damages, damages for lost profits, or opportunity or damages for pain and suffering.[178] Special rules exist for leases, which require the FDIC to pay accrued and unpaid rent through the date of repudiation of the lease.[179]

As noted, an exception is made for QFCs, where damages are measured as of the date of repudiation and damages may include the cost of cover and are calculated in light of industry practices.[180] However, damage claims arising from repudiation are generally unsecured claims against the receivership estate. They are treated as 'general creditor' claims, subordinate in priority to the claims of depositors. Due to the statutory priority of claims in a receivership, general unsecured creditor claims have rarely been paid in full following a receivership, and in many instances receive no recovery at all.

---

[176] FDIA, § 11(e)(11), 12 USC § 1821(e)(11).
[177] FDIA, § 11(e)(3)(A), 12 USC § 1821(e)(3)(A).
[178] FDIA, § 11(e)(3)(B), 12 USC § 1821(e)(3)(B).
[179] FDIA, § 11(e)(4)–(5), 12 USC § 1821(e)(4)–(5).
[180] FDIA, § 11(e)(3)(C), 12 USC § 1821(e)(3)(C).

8.139 The FDIC effectively allows the winning bidder to take advantage of its repudiation power by giving the winner the option for up to 90 days or more to assume certain contracts, including leases for bank premises or data processing facilities and other contracts providing for services to or by the failed bank. Because the FDIC will generally repudiate any contract or lease for which the option to assume has not been exercised by the winning bidder, the counterparty on any such contract or lease has a powerful financial incentive to renegotiate the terms of any contract or lease that has terms that are above market at the time of the closed-bank transaction in order to induce the bidder to continue the contract. If a bidder exercises the option to assume any leases for bank premises, the bidder has been required to purchase the related furniture, fixtures, and equipment at fair market value. The FDIC has also typically given the winning bidder the option for up to 90 days or more to purchase any owned bank premises, and the related furniture, fixtures, and equipment, at fair market value.

8.140 Closely related to the repudiation power is the ability of the FDIC to avoid termination of any contract solely as a result of the institution's insolvency.[181] See sections III.F.4 and 6 below. Thus, the FDIC and the acquirer have had the ability to keep in effect those contracts for the services needed for the operation of the institution. Interestingly, a service provider may not be able to terminate the contract as a result of the FDIC's power, but may still be subject to a later, timely repudiation by the FDIC if they are no longer necessary.

4. Marketing the failed or failing bank

8.141 The FDIC generally decides—without any input from potential bidders—which transaction structures to offer bidders, based on what it believes to be the options most likely to produce the least-cost result for the deposit insurance fund. It alone determines the structure of any assistance, such as loss sharing. It provides its standard form P&A agreement, modified to reflect the selected structure, and then instructs bidders to bid on that structure on a 'take it or leave it' basis. In other words, the FDIC generally has not permitted any negotiation of the legal documentation it has proposed. Instead, it has purported to require bidders simply to increase or decrease their bids to reflect any perceived flaws in the non-financial terms of the proposed legal documentation, rather than to negotiate the non-financial terms.

8.142 Although the FDIC's standard forms are not publicly available, examples of executed P&A agreements have been available on the FDIC's website, including those with loss sharing (eg Downey Savings) and those without loss sharing (eg Washington Mutual). Most posted forms have followed a common pattern, but a few appear to have been highly negotiated (eg IndyMac and BankUnited) probably because bidding was less competitive.

8.143 The FDIC has been successful in enforcing this marketing strategy in a competitive bidding situation. Instances have arisen where strategic buyers (ie other financial institutions) have been unable or unwilling to bid on a particular institution. In those cases, the FDIC has shown a willingness to consider modifications proposed by potential bidders. Notwithstanding the willingness to consider modifications, the FDIC has nonetheless unilaterally determined the legal form of documentation and the required bidding

---

[181] FDIA, § 11(e)(13), 12 USC § 1821(e)(13).

format. It has reserved the right to reject, and has generally rejected, any bid that it has considered to be 'non-conforming'—that is, a bid that has reflected a modification of the legal documentation—because that modification would introduce a variable that the FDIC has found hard to compare with those that bid in accordance with the predetermined format. Moreover, accepting a non-conforming bid may conflict with the statutory requirement that the FDIC conduct its operations in a manner that 'ensures adequate competition and fair and consistent treatment of offerors' and prohibits discrimination.[182]

In situations where the FDIC has been faced with a single serious bidder or liquidation, **8.144** it has shown far more flexibility in negotiating both financial and non-financial terms.[183] Even in such extreme situations, a bidder would find the FDIC to be far less willing to negotiate terms than a typical private counterparty in a merger or acquisition transaction. Bidders have therefore needed to be sparing in the changes they have proposed to the FDIC's standard documentation in order to avoid having their bid rejected by the FDIC staff. While the FDIC's rigidity can be extremely frustrating to many bidders, it can work to a well-advised bidder's advantage by providing it with opportunities to make lower bids and therefore real opportunities for enhanced value.

Bank failures have tended to come in waves, and a backlog of insolvent or near insolvent **8.145** banks has often developed. See Table 8.1 and Figures 8.1 to 8.5 for tabular and graphical illustrations of the three principal waves that occurred during the past century. Several reasons can account for this condition. First, the FDIC typically has become overworked and understaffed, placing limits on its ability to process failures through its pipeline.[184] Secondly, some strategic buyers have had their own problems or otherwise have had limited capacity to absorb all the failed banks. The FDIC has also created disincentives for private capital investors to bid on failed banks.[185] These factors, in turn, have discouraged early intervention, resulting in greater deterioration in asset values before a failed bank has been closed and lower bids from approved bidders. This, in turn, may have resulted in increased cost to the deposit insurance fund of resolving failed banks. These conditions have created two potential opportunities for bidders—greater leeway on legal documentation and the ability to make a least-cost bid closer to the FDIC's actual cost of liquidation.

As noted above, the FDIC is required to accept the bid that results in the 'least cost' to the **8.146** FDIC.[186] If a particular bidder is the only bidder for a particular institution and the bid does not satisfy the least-cost test, the FDIC's only other options are to liquidate the bank or transfer its assets and liabilities to a bridge bank to wait for better market conditions. The FDIC calculates its net liquidation cost based upon its experience as liquidator with the type of assets it will be required to dispose of. Bids are evaluated against this net liquidation cost.

---

[182] FDIA, § 11(d)(13)(E), 12 USC § 1821(d)(13)(E).

[183] The transactions involving BankUnited and Indymac reflected substantial deviations from the FDIC's standard forms. See, eg, *Master Purchase Agreement by and Among The Federal Deposit Insurance Corporation as Conservator for IndyMac Federal Bank, FSB, IMB Holdco LLC and Onewest Bank Group LLC* (18 March 2009), available at: <https://www.fdic.gov/foia/files/indymacmasterpurchaseagrmt.pdf>.

[184] Testimony of Mitchell L Glassman, Director, Division of Resolutions and Receiverships, Federal Deposit Insurance Corporation, at 9, in *Hearing before the Subcomm. on Financial Institutions and Consumer Credit, H. Comm. on Financial Servs* (21 January 2010).

[185] FDIC, Final Statement of Policy on Qualifications for Failed Bank Acquisitions, 74 Fed Reg 45440 (2 September 2009).

[186] FDIA, § 13(c)(4), 12 USC § 1823(c)(4).

The winning bid will be the one that ultimately costs the FDIC the least amount of money. If no bid results in a cost to the FDIC that is less than its net liquidation cost, the FDIC will refuse to sell the institution and proceed with other alternatives, which will generally result in the liquidation of the bank. It would normally be only a larger institution or specific, peculiar circumstances that would lead the FDIC to attempt to operate the bank for an extended period of time in order to sell the institution at a later date.

8.147 If a bidder can accurately estimate the FDIC's net liquidation cost and there are no other bidders, it can bid $1 above that amount and qualify as the least-cost bid. For example, assume that the FDIC is selling an institution with $100 of insured deposit liabilities and assets with a net liquidation value of $75. In this example, the FDIC's loss as a result of liquidation would be $25. Assuming the FDIC is not confident that its costs would fall if it transferred the institution's assets and liabilities to a bridge bank, a single bidder would be able to be the least-cost bid by submitting a negative bid of $24, meaning that the FDIC will, upon the bidder's assumption of the deposit liabilities and purchase of the assets, pay the bidder $24 in cash to entice the bidder to purchase the institution.

8.148 Bids are generally submitted several days before the bank is anticipated to close. After the FDIC has accepted one or more bids in a closed-bank auction, has determined which bid satisfies the least-cost test, cleared the bid with the other relevant regulators, and notified the winning bidder, it will then sign the appropriate legal documentation. The chartering authority will then close the bank, typically on Friday after the close of business, and the FDIC will simultaneously announce the agreement with the winning bidder. The failed institution will then reopen for business as a subsidiary or part of the new owner the next business day (and will be expected to assure customer access to ATMs and other electronic banking channels over the weekend). This is an important aspect of the FDIC process. The winning bidder must be prepared to operate the bank immediately. No extended period will be provided to prepare for the process of assuming operational control of the failed institution.

8.149 The FDIC's resolution handbook contains further details on assisted transactions.[187] Most of the material in the current edition reflects the FDIC's policies, but the current edition is woefully lacking in details compared to the prior edition. The prior edition, which the FDIC no longer makes available online, included many more details about assisted transactions, although many of the earlier transactions no longer reflect current FDIC policies.[188] Similarly, the FDIC's review of the savings and loan crisis—Managing the Crisis[189]— also includes some material that generally reflects current FDIC policies and practices (eg chapter 2), but other parts are historical and do not reflect its current practices. The FDIC staff has made certain PowerPoint presentations available that reflect the FDIC's current closed-bank bidding process.[190] In addition, the FDIC provides a Failing Bank

---

[187] FDIC, *Resolutions Handbook, supra* n 5.

[188] FDIC, *Resolutions Handbook: Methods for Resolving Troubled Financial Institutions in the United States* (2003) (superseded by 2019 edition) (current policies largely reflected only in overview, chapter 2, sections 3–6, chapter 8, and glossary).

[189] FDIC, *Managing the Crisis: The FDIC and RTC Experience 1980–1994* (1998).

[190] FDIC Staff Presentation, *The Failing Bank Marketing Process: Whole Bank Transactions and Loss Share Transactions* (American Bankers Association, 2 September 2009); FDIC Staff Presentation, *Resolutions: The Process of Bidding on Distressed Banks in the New Millennium* (18 July 2008).

Acquisitions web page on its website, which contains information that allows institutions to better understand FDIC-assisted transactions and how the FDIC markets failing financial institutions.[191]

E. Claims Process

In order to assure that claims against the failed bank are properly evaluated, the FDIC con-   **8.150**
ducts a claims process and distributes the residual value of the failed bank, including the net proceeds from any sale or liquidation of the failed bank's assets, to the proven depositor, general creditor, and other claims left behind in the receivership in accordance with the priority of their claims. The FDIC administers the claims process, sorting out valid from invalid claims, determining priorities, and administering distributions from the receivership estate, which it refers to as dividends.[192] When the various claims and priorities are sorted out, the FDIC uses the institution's assets to satisfy accepted claims to the extent of such assets in accordance with the statutory priorities.[193] Section 11 authorizes the FDIC to conduct the claims process without any court supervision.[194] Although the FDIC's decision to disallow a claim is not reviewable by a court, any claimant not satisfied by the FDIC's determination is permitted to initiate a *de novo* judicial consideration of the claim following completion of the administrative claims process.[195]

Once an institution is closed and the FDIC is appointed receiver, the FDIC is required to   **8.151**
notify potential claimants of the failure and advise them of the process by which they are to submit potential claims. Claimants have 90 days in which to submit a claim and the FDIC has 180 days to consider the claim. If the FDIC denies the claim, or if the 180-day consideration period lapses without a determination, only then can the claimant obtain judicial consideration of the claim, but the litigation must be filed within 60 days of the denial or the lapse of the period, whichever occurs earlier. Failure to abide by these time limits will result in a bar of further prosecution of the claim.[196]

F. FDIC Super Powers

In addition to the power to repudiate or enforce contracts briefly discussed above, the FDIC   **8.152**
has a variety of 'super powers' that allow it to avoid, set aside, or otherwise limit the claims of creditors and other stakeholders.[197] By far the most important legislative development that advantages the FDIC and adversely impacts creditors of the failed institution is the domestic depositor preference rule, which was the latest of these 'super powers' to be enacted. There are various other super powers, discussed below, that limit the ability of claimants to

---

[191] See FDIC, *Failing Bank Acquisitions* (last updated 3 March 2021), available at: <https://www.fdic.gov/buying/FranchiseMarketing/>.
[192] FDIA, § 11(d), 12 USC 1821(d); FDIC, *Resolutions Handbook, supra* n 5, 27–28.
[193] FDIA, § 11(d)(11), 12 USC § 1821(d)(11).
[194] FDIA, §11(d)(5)(E), 12 USC § 1821(d)(5)(E).
[195] FDIA, § 11(d)(6), 12 USC 1821(d)(6).
[196] FDIA, § 11(d)(6)(B), 12 USC 1821(d)(6)(B).
[197] Douglas, Luke, and Veal, *supra* n 68.

assert and recover on their claims. With only a few important differences, the FDIC's super powers are the same whether it acts as a receiver or conservator.

1. Domestic depositor preference rule

8.153   The FDIC's most important 'super power' is simply the statutory priority that was given to domestic deposit claims in 1993 by the National Depositor Preference Law.[198] Section 11(d)(11) of the FDIA now gives deposits payable in the US (domestic deposits, either insured or uninsured) priority over all other unsecured claims, including those of depositors whose claims are payable solely outside the US (foreign branch deposits) and general unsecured creditors. In summary, section 11(d)(11) contains the following priority of claims:

- administrative expenses of the receiver;
- any deposit liability (other than foreign branch deposits payable solely outside the US);[199]
- any other general or senior liability (including foreign branch deposits);
- any obligation subordinated to depositors or general creditors; and
- any obligation to shareholders or members.[200]

8.154   The reason this 'super power' has been so important is that most insured institutions have domestic deposit liabilities that constitute the overwhelming bulk of their total liabilities. Further, at the time of failure, the value of the assets of a failed institution has typically been insufficient to satisfy the claims of domestic depositors. For example, based on our review of 10 of the largest institutions to fail in 2008 and 2009, domestic deposits generally accounted for at least 97 per cent of the failed institution's liabilities,[201] and the value of each institution's assets averaged just 65 per cent of total liabilities.[202] Under these conditions, the assets will be insufficient to satisfy the claims on all domestic deposit liabilities; as a result, nothing will be left for general unsecured claims or any other claims junior to domestic deposits.

8.155   On those relatively rare occasions where there are sufficient assets to pay the depositor claims, the other 'super powers' become extremely relevant. And because the IDI subsidiaries of US G-SIBs are substantially funded by non-deposit liabilities, these 'super powers' are likely to be far more important in resolving those IDIs. There are at least two reasons for

---

[198] See FDIC, *Failing Bank Acquisitions* (last updated 3 March 2021), available at: <https://www.fdic.gov/buying/FranchiseMarketing/>.

[199] FDIA, §11(d)(5)(E), 12 USC § 1821(d)(5)(E).

[200] FDIA, § 11(d)(11), 12 USC § 1821(d)(11).

[201] Our review was based on data contained in the closed institution's call report as of the quarter ended immediately before it was closed. See ANB Financial, NA (closed 9 May 2008) (98 per cent); BankUnited (closed 21 May 2009) (95.5 per cent); Colonial Bank (closed 14 August 2009) (98 per cent); Corus Bank, NA (closed 11 September 2009) (99 per cent); Downey Savings and Loan, FA (closed 21 November 2008) (99.5 per cent); First National Bank of Nevada (closed 25 July 2008) (95 per cent); Georgian Bank (closed 25 September 2009) (99 per cent); Guaranty Bank (closed 21 August 2009) (98 per cent); Indymac FSB (closed 11 July 2008) (98 per cent); Silver State Bank (closed 5 September 2008) (95 per cent); Washington Mutual Bank (closed 25 September 2008) (89 per cent).

[202] See ANB Financial, NA (closed 9 May 2008) (79 per cent); BankUnited (closed 21 May 2009) (56 per cent); Colonial Bank (closed 14 August 2009) (76 per cent); Corus Bank, NA (closed 11 September 2009) (65 per cent); Downey Savings and Loan, FA (closed 21 November 2008) (81 per cent); First National Bank of Nevada (closed 25 July 2008) (60 per cent); Georgian Bank (closed 25 September 2009) (49 per cent); Guaranty Bank (closed 21 August 2009) (63 per cent); Indymac, FSB (closed 11 July 2008) (57 per cent); Silver State Bank (closed 5 September 2008) (63 per cent).

this prediction. First, the FDIC is likely to put such IDIs into receivership when they run out of liquidity long before they are balance sheet insolvent. Secondly, the domestic deposit liabilities of such IDIs (except for Morgan Stanley Bank, NA) account for a smaller—and in many cases, a substantially smaller—percentage of their total liabilities compared to most US IDIs.[203] All of the IDI subsidiaries of US G-SIBs (except for Morgan Stanley Bank, NA) have significant amounts of liabilities that are subordinate to domestic deposit liabilities, including foreign branch deposits, federal funds liabilities, trading liabilities, other borrowed money, subordinated debt, and other liabilities.[204] As a result, the value of the assets of such an IDI in receivership is far more likely to be sufficient to satisfy all the claims on domestic deposits, thus resulting in no loss to the deposit insurance fund.[205] This means that an IDI subsidiary of a US G-SIB is likely to have excess assets for the junior creditors to fight over. Thus, the FDIC's other 'super powers' will be relevant because the domestic depositor preference rule will not have decided the whole game.

2. Contingent claims not provable

Although it has no statutory basis for doing so, the FDIC has long taken the position that   **8.156**
claims against an insured institution for contingent obligations are not provable in a conservatorship or a receivership.[206] Thus, the beneficiary of an undrawn line of credit, standby letter of credit, or guarantee may have no provable claim to draw down additional amounts or to exercise its indemnification or guarantee rights once the FDIC has been appointed receiver or conservator. Alternatively, the FDIC has taken the position that contracts for contingent obligations can be repudiated as 'burdensome', and that damages for such repudiation will be zero as they must be determined as of the date of the receivership.[207]

On rare occasions, the FDIC may include contingent obligations in any assets or liabilities   **8.157**
transferred to a third party bank in a P&A agreement. If they are transferred, the beneficiaries may enforce their rights against the third party bank. For example, the FDIC transferred certain contingent obligations in both the JP Morgan/WaMu and the US Bank/Downey Savings transactions.[208] Whether the FDIC would do so in other bank failures is uncertain, although we could envision the FDIC doing so in connection with resolving a US G-SIB if it believed that doing so would promote financial stability and be consistent with the least-cost test.

---

[203] Our data are based on the figures provided by the US G-SIBs in their call reports dated 31 March 2021: Bank of America, NA, 88 per cent; The Bank of New York Mellon, 61 per cent; Citibank, NA, 44 per cent; Goldman Sachs Bank USA, 87 per cent; JPMorgan Chase Bank, NA, 68 per cent; Morgan Stanley Bank, NA, 99 per cent; State Street Bank & Trust, 59 per cent; and Wells Fargo Bank, NA, 91 per cent.

[204] These data are based on the figures provided by the US G-SIBs in their call reports dated 31 March 2021: Bank of America, NA, 12 per cent; Bank of New York Mellon, 39 per cent; Citibank, NA, 56 per cent; Goldman Sachs Bank USA, 13 per cent; JPMorgan Chase Bank, NA, 32 per cent; Morgan Stanley Bank, NA, 1 per cent; State Street Bank & Trust, 41 per cent; and Wells Fargo Bank, NA, 9 per cent.

[205] This conclusion is consistent with the public summaries of the 2021 Title I and 2018 IDI resolution plans filed by the US G-SIBs, many of which concluded they could be resolved under a severely adverse economic scenario without any loss to the deposit insurance fund. See FDIC, Title I and IDI Resolution Plans, available at: < https://www.fdic.gov/regulations/reform/resplans/>.

[206] Courts have not always agreed that contingent claims are not provable in a receivership. See, eg, *McMillian v FDIC*, 81 F 3d 1041(11th Cir 1996).

[207] FDIA, § 11(e), 12 USC 1821(e).

[208] See, eg, *Purchase and Assumption Agreement, Whole Bank, Among Federal Deposit Insurance Corporation, Receiver of Washington Mutual Bank, Henderson Nevada, Federal Deposit Insurance Corporation and JPMorgan Chase Bank, National Association* (25 September 2008), available at: <https://www.fdic.gov/foia/files/washington_mutual_p_and_a.pdf>.

3. High bar to enforceability of contracts

8.158   The FDIC has the right to avoid any secret or side agreement that is not reflected on the books and records of the failed bank, although the statute imposes several additional restrictions that can frustrate enforceability of legitimate contracts. Section 13(e) of the FDIA provides that any agreement with an insured institution that tends to 'diminish or defeat the interest of the [FDIC] in any asset acquired by it [as receiver or conservator under the FDIA], either as security for a loan or by purchase or as receiver' is not enforceable against the institution or the FDIC, and may not form the basis of a claim against the institution, unless the agreement:

- is in writing;
- was executed by the insured institution and any person claiming an interest under it contemporaneously with the acquisition of the asset by the institution;
- was approved by the board of directors of the insured institution or its loan committee and the approval is reflected in the minutes of the board; and
- has continuously been an official record of the insured institution.[209]

8.159   Section 13(e) has been one of the most litigated provisions, because it goes so far beyond the normal enforceability requirements under otherwise applicable non-insolvency law. Further, because it is so specific, it can be difficult as a practical matter to satisfy each of the conditions.

8.160   These requirements were added to the FDIA in 1950 to codify and expand the Supreme Court's decision in *D'Oench Duhme & Co v FDIC*.[210] They defeat the enforceability against an insured institution in receivership or conservatorship of any otherwise enforceable oral contracts and create a substantial risk that many otherwise enforceable written contracts will not be enforceable against an insured institution in receivership or conservatorship for failure to satisfy the technical requirements of the statute.

8.161   For example, if a creditor had an otherwise enforceable and perfected security interest in certain assets, but the security agreement failed to satisfy one of the requirements in section 13(e) (for example, was not created contemporaneously with the underlying obligation or not properly approved by the board or committee), the security interest could be unenforceable against the FDIC and could not form the basis of a claim against the institution. While these provisions were designed to protect the FDIC against 'secret' or 'side' agreements not reflected on the records of the institution (eg a guarantor that a loan officer supposedly promised would never be called upon or a note executed solely as an accommodation), in practice the breadth of the provisions can be traps for the unwary.

8.162   The contemporaneous execution requirement is particularly difficult to satisfy in the context of contractual arrangements that purport to govern a series of transactions over a long period of time before or after the contract is executed, such as a revolving line of credit or a security agreement that grants a security interest in previously or subsequently acquired collateral. The statute contains an exception for agreements for revolving lines of credit from

---

[209]   FDIA, § 13(e), 12 USC § 1823(e).
[210]   315 US 447 (1942).

the Federal Reserve or any Federal Home Loan Bank.[211] Such lines of credit agreement are deemed to have been executed contemporaneously with any drawdown. The FDIC has also issued a policy statement on security interests to the effect that the FDIC 'will not seek to avoid otherwise legally enforceable and perfected security interests solely because the security agreement granting or creating such security interest does not meet the "contemporaneous" requirement of [the Federal Deposit Insurance Act]'.[212] Of course, the FDIC has the right to withdraw its policy statements at any time, potentially with retroactive effect.[213]

4. Power to enforce contracts despite ipso facto clauses

The FDIC has the power to 'enforce any contract ... entered into by the depository institution notwithstanding any provision of the contract providing for termination, default, acceleration, or exercise of rights upon, or solely by reason of, insolvency or the appointment of or the exercise of rights or powers by a conservator or receiver'.[214]   **8.163**

This means that contractual counterparties are prohibited from accelerating, terminating, or otherwise exercising any rights under any contract against the insured institution solely as a result of the appointment of a receiver or conservator for the institution, thus defeating any claim for damages that might otherwise be asserted.   **8.164**

Two exceptions to this rule exist. First, the rule does not apply to QFCs in receivership (as distinguished from conservatorship) after a one business day cooling-off period unless transferred to another solvent institution within that one-day period.[215] Secondly, the rule does not apply to directors' or officers' liability insurance contracts or depository institution bonds in either conservatorship or receivership.[216] Counterparties to such contracts may accelerate, terminate, or otherwise exercise the rights solely because of the insolvency or the appointment of a conservator or receiver.   **8.165**

5. Repudiation of contracts

The FDIC also has the power to disaffirm or repudiate any contract or lease, including QFCs, to which the insured institution is a party if the FDIC determines within a reasonable period of time that: **8.166**

- the contract would be burdensome; and
- the repudiation or disaffirmance of the contract would promote the orderly administration of the institution's affairs.[217]

This repudiation power was added to the FDIC's toolkit by section 212(e) of the Financial Institutions Reform, Recovery and Enforcement Act of 1989 (FIRREA). Prior to FIRREA, the FDIC tended to rely on the common-law right of an equity receiver to disaffirm executory contracts.[218]   **8.167**

---

[211] FDIA, § 13(e)(2), 12 USC 1823(e)(2).
[212] Statement of Policy Regarding Treatment of Security Interests After Appointment of the FDIC as Conservator or Receiver, 58 Fed Reg 16833, 16834 (31 March 1993).
[213] Statement of Policy on the Development and Review of Regulations, 63 Fed Reg 25157 (7 May 1998).
[214] FDIA, § 11(e)(12)(A), 12 USC § 1821(e)(12)(A).
[215] FDIA, § 11(e)(8)(G)(ii), 12 USC § 1821(e)(8)(G)(ii).
[216] FDIA, § 11(e)(13)(A), 12 USC § 1821(e)(13)(A).
[217] FDIA, § 11(e)(1)(C), 12 USC § 1821(e)(1)(C).
[218] See, eg, *Resolution Trust Company v Camp*, 965 F 2d 25, 31 (5th Cir 1992).

8.168   Under the US Bankruptcy Code, executory contracts and unexpired leases must either be assumed and performed, or assigned or rejected, with the approval of the bankruptcy court.[219] In contrast, the FDIC's repudiation power contains no such limitation, and theoretically applies to both executory and non-executory contracts, although repudiation of a contact that has been fully executed presents substantial difficulties and to our knowledge has not been attempted by the FDIC. The FDIC may cherry-pick among contracts in exercising this power, even among similar contracts involving the same parties, except in the case of QFCs, where if it elects to repudiate, it must repudiate all or none of the contracts with a particular counterparty and its affiliates.[220]

8.169   The statute itself does not define what constitutes a 'reasonable' period of time. The FDIC has indicated, however, in the context of security interests, that a reasonable period of time would generally be no more than 180 days after the FDIC's appointment as receiver or conservator,[221] and in its standard P&A agreement, appears to operate under the six-month guideline. While courts have allowed longer periods under certain circumstances, at least one court has indicated that approximately six months to one year should generally qualify as a reasonable period of time.[222] However, a more recent decision states that the amount of time that is 'reasonable' must be determined according to the circumstances of each case.[223] The statute also contains no definition of the term 'burdensome', so the FDIC has wide latitude to interpret that standard, provided that its interpretation is reasonable. One court has held that the FDIC is not required to make a formal finding as to why a contract is burdensome.[224]

8.170   If the FDIC disaffirms or repudiates a contract, it must pay the counterparty damages.[225] The FDIA provides that the damages resulting from repudiation are generally limited to 'actual direct compensatory damages; and determined as of the date of the appointment of the conservator or receiver'.[226] The damages formula in the FDIA excludes punitive or exemplary damages, damages for lost profits or opportunity, or damages for pain and suffering. This very narrow definition of damages was added by section 212(a) of the FIRREA. In contrast, under the US Bankruptcy Code, breach of contract damages are generally allowed for rejected contracts, and administrative expense claims are often allowed to the extent that the debtor accepted benefits under the contract after the petition date. The FDIA contains a special rule for QFCs, under which damages include the cost of cover and are determined based on industry standards.[227]

8.171   As noted, damages are generally measured as of the date the FDIC was appointed as conservator or receiver.[228] This means that the FDIC is not required to pay interest for the period

[219] 11 USC § 365(a).

[220] FDIA, § 11(e)(11), 12 USC § 1821(e)(11).

[221] Statement of Policy Regarding Treatment of Security Interests After Appointment of the FDIC as Conservator or Receiver, 58 Fed Reg 16833 (31 March 1993).

[222] See *Texas Co v Chicago & AR Co*, 36 F Supp 62, 65 (D Ill 1940), reversed on other grounds, 126 F 2d 83, 89–90 (7th Cir 1942).

[223] *Resolution Trust Corp v CedarMinn Bldg Ltd P'ship*, 956 F 2d 1446, 1455 (8th Cir 1992).

[224] *1185 Ave of Americas Assoc v Resolution Trust Corp*, 22 F 3d 494, 498 (2nd Cir 1994).

[225] FDIA, § 11(e)(3), 12 USC § 1821(e)(3).

[226] FDIA, § 11(e)(3)(A), 12 USC § 1821(e)(3)(A).

[227] FDIA, § 11(e)(3)(C), 12 USC § 1821(e)(3)(C).

[228] FDIA, § 11(e)(3)(A)(ii)(I), 12 USC § 1821(e)(3)(A)(ii)(I).

between appointment and repudiation. Thus, for instance, if the FDIC repudiated a debt obligation, the institution would be required to pay the counterparty damages in the form of principal plus accrued interest until the date of appointment, but not until the date of repudiation or the original maturity date of the debt obligation or, indeed, for that matter, from repudiation until actual payment. In the case of QFCs, damages are measured as of the date of disaffirmance or repudiation, which eliminates the post-appointment interest issue through the later date; however, this additional interest does not necessarily preserve the benefit of the original bargain.

The statute contains special rules for leases, governing both cases where the failed institution is the lessor and cases where it is the lessee.[229] In general, when the institution is the lessee the FDIC will pay rent until the effective date of repudiation.[230] This is particularly important for leased bank premises, where the FDIC or third party acquirer will take a period of time to determine whether it wishes to continue use of the property. Generally, if repudiated, the FDIC will not be obligated to pay future rent or be subject to acceleration or other penalties associated with unpaid future rent.   **8.172**

6. Special treatment for qualified financial contracts

QFCs include securities contracts, commodities contracts, forward contracts, repurchase agreements, swap agreements, and master agreements for any of the foregoing.[231] QFCs receive preferential treatment in receivership and, to a far lesser extent, in conservatorship. They are basically the same as the list of protected contracts under the US Bankruptcy Code.[232]   **8.173**

The enforceability of *ipso facto* clauses in QFCs is different depending on whether the institution is in receivership or conservatorship. If in receivership, counterparties have the right to exercise any contractual rights to terminate, liquidate, close-out, net, or resort to security arrangements upon the appointment of the FDIC as receiver, subject to a one business day cooling-off period,[233] unless the FDIC elects to transfer all, but not less than all, of the QFCs with a particular counterparty to a single third party financial institution.   **8.174**

In a conservatorship, the general rule against the enforceability of *ipso facto* clauses applies. Counterparties may not terminate, close out, or net QFCs solely on account of the insolvency, financial condition, or appointment of the conservator.[234] This, in effect, continues all relationships under their existing contractual provisions.   **8.175**

The FDIC is not permitted to cherry-pick with respect to QFCs with a particular counterparty and its affiliates. It must either transfer all of the QFCs with a single counterparty and its affiliates to a new institution, or must leave all such QFCs with the receivership.[235] Damages for repudiated QFCs are determined as of the date of repudiation, and may include the cost of cover, and are calculated in light of industry practices.[236]   **8.176**

---

[229] FDIA, §§ 11(e)(4)–(5), 12 USC §§ 1821(e)(4)–(5).
[230] FDIA, § 11(e)(4)(B), 12 USC § 1821(e)(4)(B).
[231] FDIA, § 11(e)(8)(D)(i), 12 USC § 1821(e)(8)(D)(i).
[232] 11 USC § 362(b)(6).
[233] FDIA, § 11(e)(10)(B)(i), 12 USC § 1821(e)(10)(B)(i).
[234] FDIA, § 11(e)(10)(B)(ii), 12 USC § 1821(e)(10)(B)(ii).
[235] FDIA, § 11(e)(11), 12 USC § 1821(e)(11).
[236] FDIA, § 11(e)(3)(C), 12 USC § 1821(e)(3)(C).

8.177   The FDIA prohibits the enforceability of walkaway clauses in QFCs in both conservatorship and receivership.[237]

8.178   Many QFCs contain cross-default provisions permitting acceleration in the event of insolvency or financial distress of affiliates. The FDIA does not grant the FDIC authority to override such cross-defaults. Note, however, that section 210(c)(16) of the Dodd-Frank Act[238] gives the FDIC the power to override cross-defaults in QFCs that are tied to the insolvency or financial distress of the insured institution's parent or other affiliate if certain conditions are satisfied. Instead, if they are overridden at all, such cross-defaults would be overridden pursuant to section 2 of the International Swaps and Derivatives Association (ISDA) 2015 Universal Resolution Stay Protocol ('the ISDA Universal Protocol') or section 2 of the ISDA 2018 US Resolution Stay Protocol (the 'ISDA US Protocol' and, together with the ISDA Universal Protocol, the 'ISDA Protocols') if contained in an agreement between counterparties that have agreed to be bound by the ISDA Protocols.[239]

7. Security interests

8.179   Notwithstanding the FDIC's general repudiation power, the FDIA protects legally enforceable and perfected security interests from being avoided for any reason, unless:

- the underlying security agreement does not satisfy the requirements of section 13(e);
- the security interest was taken in contemplation of the institution's insolvency; or
- the security interest was taken with the intent to hinder, delay, or defraud the institution or its creditors.[240]

8.180   The FDIC may not exercise its avoidance powers with respect to any extension of credit from any Federal Home Loan Bank or any Federal Reserve Bank, and for any security interest in assets securing such an extension of credit.[241]

8.181   In the case of national banks and possibly federally chartered savings associations, the FDIC is also permitted to rely on the preference avoidance powers contained in 12 USC § 91 to set aside security interests that amount to preferential transfers. By contrast, under the US Bankruptcy Code, preferential transfers made on account of antecedent debt, within 90 days of bankruptcy while the debtor was insolvent, and which allow the creditor to receive more than the creditor would receive in liquidation, may be avoided, subject to defences if the transfer was for 'new value' or outside the 90-day preference period.[242] Notwithstanding, the FDIC has not attempted to exercise the right to avoid preferential transfers solely because they occur within 90 days of failure; rather, the FDIC has used other bases for avoidance, such as fraud or failure to satisfy the requirements of section 13(e) of the FDIA.

8.182   Because all security interests are in some sense taken 'in contemplation of an institution's insolvency', depending on how it is interpreted this exception could swallow the rule. The

---

[237] FDIA, § 11(e)(8)(G)(i), 12 USC § 1821(e)(8)(G)(i).

[238] Dodd-Frank Act, § 210(c)(16), 12 USC § 5390(c)(16).

[239] ISDA 2015 Universal Resolution Stay Protocol, available at: http://www2.isda.org/functional-areas/protocol-management/protocol/22; ISDA 2018 US Resolution Stay Protocol, available at: <https://www.isda.org/protocol/isda-2018-us-resolution-stay-protocol/>.

[240] FDIA, § 11(e)(12), 12 USC § 1821(e)(12).

[241] FDIA, § 11(e)(14), 12 USC § 1821(e)(14).

[242] 11 USC § 547.

FDIC has provided no guidance on how 'in contemplation of insolvency' would be interpreted generally, but has not attempted to avoid security interests taken in the normal course of business. In 2005, the FDIA was amended to delete the 'in contemplation of insolvency' exception for collateral securing QFCs.[243] Such security interests are avoidable only if taken with the actual intent to defraud, and not merely because they were taken in contemplation of an institution's insolvency.[244]

8. Discretion to discriminate among similarly situated creditors

Section 11(i)(2) of the FDIA provides that the maximum liability of the FDIC to a person having a claim against an insured institution is the amount the claimant would have received if the FDIC had liquidated the assets and liabilities of the institution.[245] It was added by section 212(a) of FIRREA in reaction to *First Empire Bank v FDIC*,[246] which had held that the FDIC was required to comply with the pro rata distribution rules in the National Bank Act in resolving a national bank.[247] The pro rata distribution rules required the FDIC to treat similarly situated creditors equally.[248]   **8.183**

If section 11(i)(2) is read solely as a maximum liability provision, it would seem to permit the FDIC to keep the difference between the value it would have realized on a hypothetical liquidation of the institution's assets and liabilities and any greater amount the FDIC actually realizes by resolving the institution in a manner that maximizes its residual value.   **8.184**

However, treating the provision as establishing the FDIC's maximum liability to a creditor is inconsistent with the way the provision has generally been understood. Instead, it has generally been understood by both the FDIC and most commentators to permit the FDIC to treat similarly situated creditors unequally—to award some creditors more than their pro rata share of the residual value of the institution and some less than their pro rata share—provided that each creditor receive at least as much value as it would have received in a hypothetical liquidation of the assets and liabilities of the failed institution.[249] In other words, it has been construed to impose a ceiling on the FDIC's liability if it exercises its discretion to favour some creditors over others and a floor on the recovery by any disfavoured creditors. Thus, it becomes a 'minimum liability' amount. This reading is consistent with section 210 of the Dodd-Frank Act, which contains an express minimum recovery right for disfavoured creditors tied to the amount they would have recovered in a liquidation.[250] In contrast, chapter 11 of the US Bankruptcy Code requires equal treatment within classes of creditors, unless it can be shown that favouring certain creditors, such as critical vendors, over others will maximize the residual value of the estate for the benefit of all creditors.[251]   **8.185**

---

[243] Bankruptcy Abuse Prevention and Consumer Protection Act of 2005, Pub L No 109-8 § 903, 119 Stat 23, 160–65. See also FDIA, § 11(e)(8)(C)(ii), 12 USC § 1821(e)(8)(C)(ii).

[244] Michael Krimminger, *Adjusting the Rules: What Bankruptcy Will Mean for Financial Markets Contracts* (2005) 4 and n 9.

[245] FDIA, § 11(i)(2), 12 USC § 1821(i)(2).

[246] *First Empire Bank v FDIC*, 572 F 2d 1361 (9th Cir 1978).

[247] 12 USC §§ 91, 194.

[248] *First Empire Bank v FDIC*, 572 F 2d 1361, 1371 (9th Cir 1978).

[249] See, eg, FDIC, 'Treatment of Uninsured Depositors and Other Receivership Creditors' in *Managing the Crisis: The FDIC and RTC Experience 1980–1994*, vol 1, part 1 (August 1998).

[250] Dodd-Frank Act, § 210(a)(7)(B), (b)(4)(B), and (h)(5)(E)(ii), 12 USC § 5390(a)(7)(B), (b)(4)(B), and (h)(5)(E)(ii).

[251] Douglas Baird, *The Elements of Bankruptcy* (6th edn, 2014), 229–230, 261.

8.186   As the FDIA does not contain a priority rule that subordinates long-term unsecured debt to other short-term unsecured debt, the FDIC probably needs this discretionary authority in order to favour short-term unsecured creditors over long-term unsecured creditors in order to stem runs and otherwise promote financial stability in the course of resolving a failed bank.

8.187   Section 11(i)(3) of the FDIA also permits the FDIC to use its own resources (or theoretically other resources of the receivership) to make additional payments to certain claimants if it believes that it would help minimize its losses. If it elects to do so, it is not obligated to make such payments to any other claimant or category of claimant, even if of the same type. As an example, the FDIC may determine that unpaid utility bills should be paid in full in order to assure uninterrupted service. The payment of a utility bill, which is a general unsecured claim, does not, for example, require the FDIC to pay an unpaid bill for legal services.

9. Super-priority over fraudulent transfers by insider or debtor

8.188   As conservator or receiver of an insured institution, the FDIC has the right to avoid and recover any fraudulent transfer by an insider or debtor of the insured institution to a third party that occurs within five years of appointment if such transfer was made with the intent to hinder, delay, or defraud the insured institution or the receiver or conservator.[252] The FDIC's claim is senior to any claim by a trustee in bankruptcy or other person (except another federal agency) in a proceeding under the US Bankruptcy Code.[253] The FDIC may recover from any immediate or intermediate transferee, except for a transferee who took as a good-faith purchaser for value.[254]

10. Cross-guarantees

8.189   The FDIC has the right to recover any losses incurred in assisting or resolving any insured institution from any other insured institution under common control with the failed institution.[255] The FDIC's claim may be estimated and assessed in advance of any expenditure of funds and is subordinated to general creditors and depositors, but senior to the claims of shareholders and affiliates.[256] The cross-guarantee provision has been used by the FDIC to prevent a bank holding company from allowing one of its subsidiary banks to fail yet retaining other solvent bank subsidiaries.

11. Statute of limitations, tolling, and removal powers

8.190   The FDIC enjoys special powers with respect to litigation and claims involving failed institutions designed to facilitate its administration of the failed bank's estate.

8.191   First, any ongoing litigation against the failed institution will be stayed. The FDIC would like to drive all potential claimants through the administrative claims process; however, the stay will only last 45 days in the case of a conservatorship and 90 days in the case of a receivership.[257]

---

[252] FDIA, § 11(d)(17)(A), 12 USC § 1821(d)(17)(A).
[253] FDIA, § 11(d)(17)(D), 12 USC § 1821(d)(17)(D).
[254] FDIA, § 11(d)(17)(B)–(C), 12 USC § 1821(d)(17)(B)–(C).
[255] FDIA, § 5(e)(1), 12 USC § 1815(e)(1).
[256] FDIA, § 5(e)(2)(A)–(C), 12 USC § 1815(e)(2)(A)–(C).
[257] FDIA, § 11(d)(12)(A), 12 USC § 1821(d)(12)(A).

Courts are required to grant the stay upon the request of the FDIC.[258] Note that the filing of a claim with the receiver (which many claimants often do in order to preserve all remedies) does not affect the ability of the claimant to continue any action that was filed before the appointment of the FDIC as receiver.[259]

Secondly, claimants (unless they had previously commenced litigation) will be required to file an administrative claim that will be handled by the FDIC.[260] When a claimant files an administrative claim under the claims procedure, it will be deemed to have commenced an action for applicable statute of limitations purposes, even though the plaintiff may be precluded from actually commencing litigation in court until the administrative process concludes.[261]   **8.192**

Thirdly, the FDIC will have the power to remove most actions filed in state court to federal court.[262]   **8.193**

Fourthly, with respect to claims that the FDIC might wish to assert as receiver, the FDIC enjoys a special statute of limitations of six years for contract claims and three years for tort claims or, if longer, the statute provided by state law.[263] The statute of limitations does not begin to run until the date of the FDIC's appointment as conservator or receiver or, if later, the date the cause of action accrues.[264] This extended statute of limitations will not, however, revive claims that expired prior to the date of receivership. Thus, the FDIC has the benefit of an entirely new statutory period within which to bring claims. Indeed, for claims of fraud or intentional misconduct resulting in unjust enrichment or substantial loss to the institution, unless the cause of action accrued more than five years from the date of appointment, the FDIC is entitled to take advantage of the special statute of limitations.   **8.194**

These litigation powers are extremely important. In addition to having to address litigation to which the failed institution was a party, as receiver the FDIC will both initiate and be subject to multiple claims. Following a failure, the FDIC routinely investigates director and officer liability and professional malpractice claims. The extended statute of limitations provides ample opportunity for the FDIC to conduct investigations and bring claims without having to worry about rapidly expiring state statutes of limitation.   **8.195**

IV. Resolution Authority over Fannie Mae, Freddie Mac, and the Federal Home Loan Banks

A. Background

1. Fannie Mae and Freddie Mac

Fannie Mae, the common name for the Federal National Mortgage Association, was originally chartered in 1938 to provide liquidity and stability to the US secondary mortgage   **8.196**

---

[258] FDIA, § 11(d)(12)(B), 12 USC § 1821(d)(12)(B).
[259] FDIA, § 11(d)(6)(A), 12 USC § 1821(d)(6)(A).
[260] FDIA, § 11(d)(12), 12 USC § 1821(d)(12). See also Self-Help Liquidation of Collateral by Second Claimants in Insured Depository Receiverships, FDIC Advisory Op, No 49 (15 December 1989).
[261] FDIA, § 11(d)(5)(F)(i), 12 USC § 1821(d)(5)(F)(i).
[262] FDIA, § 11(d)(13)(B), 12 USC § 1821(d)(13)(B).
[263] FDIA, § 11(d)(14)(A), 12 USC § 1821(d)(14)(A).
[264] FDIA, § 11(d)(14)(B), 12 USC § 1821(d)(14)(B).

market.[265] Fannie Mae's charter was amended in 1968 to make it a congressionally chartered, privately owned corporation.[266] Fannie Mae does not make direct loans to borrowers. Rather, it purchases residential mortgages and mortgage-related securities in the secondary mortgage market, packages these instruments into pools, issues interests in the pools called mortgage-backed securities (MBS), guarantees the MBSs, and sells the guaranteed MBSs into the secondary market. Fannie Mae also purchases and retains some mortgages for its own investment portfolio.[267]

8.197 Freddie Mac, officially known as the Federal Home Loan Mortgage Corporation, was chartered by the US Congress in 1970 to provide further stability, liquidity, and affordability to the US housing market.[268] Freddie Mac has a similar congressional mandate to Fannie Mae.[269] As a result of their public charter and private ownership, Fannie Mae and Freddie Mac are referred to as 'government-sponsored enterprises' or GSEs.

8.198 In 1992, the Federal Housing Enterprises Financial Safety and Soundness Act ('the Safety and Soundness Act') created the Office of Federal Housing Enterprise Oversight (OFHEO) as a regulatory office within the Department of Housing and Urban Development (HUD) with oversight over Fannie Mae and Freddie Mac.[270] HUD was responsible for overseeing that Fannie Mae and Freddie Mac accomplished the purposes articulated in their charters, including the promotion of home ownership in the US, while OFHEO was responsible for overseeing the safety and soundness of the organizations.[271]

8.199 As of 31 December 2020, Fannie Mae and Freddie Mac held mortgage loans (including MBS) of approximately $3.7 trillion and $2.4 trillion, respectively.[272]

2. Federal Home Loan Bank System

8.200 The Federal Home Loan Bank Act was passed by Congress in 1932, and established the Federal Home Loan Bank System.[273] The System was created to provide liquidity to the housing finance market, which had been severely affected by the Great Depression.[274] The Federal Home Loan Bank Act created 12 Federal Home Loan Banks, which functioned as regional cooperatives.[275] All federally chartered thrifts were required to become members of the Federal Home Loan Bank in their district, and to invest capital in the bank.[276] The

---

[265] Federal National Mortgage Association, 'Annual Report on Form 10-K' for the fiscal year ended 31 December 2020.

[266] Housing and Urban Development Act of 1968, Pub L No 90-448, tit VIII, 82 Stat 476, 536, 12 USC § 1717.

[267] Federal National Mortgage Association, *supra* n 265, 80–81.

[268] Federal Home Loan Mortgage Corporation Act, Pub L No 91-351, § 301, 84 Stat 451 (1970), codified at 12 USC § 1451.

[269] Federal National Mortgage Association Charter Act, § 301, 12 USC § 1716.

[270] Federal Housing Enterprises Financial Safety and Soundness Act of 1992, Pub L No 102-550, § 1311, 106 Stat 3941, 3944.

[271] Ibid, § 1321, 106 Stat at 3952.

[272] Federal National Mortgage Association, 'Annual Report on Form 10-K' for the fiscal year ended 31 December 2020, F-4; Federal Home Loan Mortgage Corporation, 'Annual Report on Form 10-K' for the fiscal year ended 31 December 2020, 176.

[273] Federal Home Loan Bank Act, Pub L No 72-304, 47 Stat 725 (1932).

[274] US Gov't Accountability Office, *Testimony Before the Committee on Banking, Housing and Urban Affairs, U.S. Senate, Federal Home Loan Bank System: An Overview of Changes and Current Issues Affecting the System* (13 April 2005) 5.

[275] Federal Home Loan Bank Act, Pub L No 72-304, § 3, 47 Stat 725, 726 (1932).

[276] Home Owners' Loan Act, Pub L No 73-43, § 5(f), 48 Stat 128, 133 (1933).

System acted as a central credit facility that made advances to thrifts, which used the liquidity to make mortgage loans to home-buyers.[277] The thrifts were required to secure their advances by granting security interests to the Federal Home Loan Banks in high-quality assets in excess of the value of their advances.[278]

The Federal Home Loan Bank Act also created the Federal Home Loan Bank Board **8.201** to oversee the safety and soundness regulation of the Federal Home Loan Banks and of thrifts.[279] In the 1980s, the Board delegated its oversight responsibility over thrifts to each of the Federal Home Loan Banks.[280] Also, in the 1980s, a large number of thrifts failed, forcing Congress to appropriate billions of dollars to cover the costs associated with ensuring the payment of insured thrift deposits.[281]

In 1992, Congress passed FIRREA, which abolished the Federal Home Loan Bank Board **8.202** and established the Federal Housing Finance Board to oversee the Federal Home Loan Banks.[282] Oversight over thrifts was transferred to the Office of Thrift Supervision.[283] FIRREA also opened up the Federal Home Loan Bank System to commercial banks and credit unions engaged in mortgage activities.[284] In 1999, with the passage of the Gramm-Leach-Bliley Act, thrifts were no longer required to become members of the Federal Home Loan Bank System.[285]

As of 31 December 2020, the Federal Home Loan Bank System consisted of 11 coopera- **8.203** tively owned banks, which acted as a general source of liquidity to approximately 6,700 member financial institutions, which include commercial banks, thrifts, community banks, credit unions, community development financial companies, insurance companies, and state housing finance agencies.[286] At year-end 2020, Federal Home Loan Banks had approximately $423 billion in outstanding secured advances.[287]

B. Resolution Authority

1. Housing and Economic Recovery Act of 2008

In response to widespread concern that Fannie, Freddie, and the Federal Home Loan Banks **8.204** were in troubled financial condition just before the global financial panic of 2008,[288] the US

---

[277] US Gov't Accountability Office, *Testimony Before the Committee on Banking, Housing and Urban Affairs, U.S. Senate, Federal Home Loan Bank System: An Overview of Changes and Current Issues Affecting the System* (13 April 2005) 5.

[278] Federal Home Loan Bank Act, Pub L No 72-304, § 10, 47 Stat 725, 731–732 (1932).

[279] Ibid, § 17, 47 Stat at 736; Home Owners' Loan Act, Pub L No 73-43, § 5, 48 Stat 128, 132 (1933).

[280] US Gov't Accountability Office, *Testimony Before the Committee on Banking, Housing and Urban Affairs, U.S. Senate, Federal Home Loan Bank System: An Overview of Changes and Current Issues Affecting the System* (13 April 2003) 5.

[281] Ibid, 6.

[282] FIRREA, Pub L No 101-73, §§ 401, 702, 103 Stat 183, 354, 413.

[283] Ibid, § 301, 103 Stat at 278.

[284] Ibid, § 702, 103 Stat at 413.

[285] Financial Services Modernization Act of 1999, Pub L No 106-102, § 603, 113 Stat 1338, 1450–51.

[286] FHFA, 'Annual Report to Congress 2020' (15 June 2021), 1, 45.

[287] Ibid, 41.

[288] The publicly traded shares of Fannie and Freddie dropped by more than 60 per cent during the first half of July 2008 alone.

Congress passed the Housing and Economic Recovery Act of 2008 (HERA).[289] HERA consolidated the federal regulatory oversight of Fannie, Freddie, and the Federal Home Loan Banks into a single new agency called the Federal Housing Finance Agency (FHFA). FHFA replaced both OFHEO and HUD as Fannie and Freddie's safety and soundness and mission regulator.[290] FHFA replaced the Federal Housing Finance Board as the federal supervisor of the Federal Home Loan Banks.

2. New resolution authority

8.205   Prior to the passage of HERA, the resolution authority over Fannie Mae and Freddie Mac was limited to the appointment of a conservator, with no statutory authority for placing either of them into receivership.[291] In addition, the grounds for placing them into conservatorship were quite limited.[292] The conservator also had few express statutory powers.[293]

8.206   HERA created a much more detailed resolution scheme for Fannie Mae, Freddie Mac, and the Federal Home Loan Banks based on the US bank resolution model.[294] It also gave FHFA prompt corrective action powers similar to those enjoyed by the federal banking regulators under the FDIA.[295] Finally, it gave the Secretary of the Treasury temporary authority to provide unlimited financial assistance to Fannie, Freddie, and the Federal Home Loan Bank System.[296]

8.207   The new resolution authority gave FHFA the authority to appoint itself as conservator or receiver of any of the covered entities. The grounds for putting any of them into conservatorship or receivership were expanded to mirror the grounds set forth in the FDIA.[297] The effect of conservatorship or receivership was the same: FHFA would succeed by operation of law to the rights, titles, powers, and privileges of the entity, and its officers, directors, and stockholders.[298] FHFA could also prescribe regulations regarding the conduct of conservatorships or receiverships.[299]

8.208   The statute gave FHFA core resolution powers, including the power to establish temporary bridge companies to facilitate orderly resolution.[300] In exercising any power as conservator or receiver to sell or dispose of any assets, the statute requires FHFA to maximize the net present value return from the sale or disposition, minimize the losses realized in the resolution, and ensure adequate competition and fair and consistent treatment of offerors.[301]

---

[289]   HERA, Pub L No 110-289, 122 Stat 2654.

[290]   Ibid, §§ 1101, 1102(a), 12 USC §§ 4511, 4513(a).

[291]   Federal Housing Enterprises Financial Safety and Soundness Act, Pub L No 102-550, § 1367, 106 Stat 3941, 3980 (1992).

[292]   Ibid, § 1369, 106 Stat at 3981–3982.

[293]   Ibid, § 1369A, 106 Stat at 3983–3984. The powers of a conservator included the power to avoid a security interest taken by a creditor with the intent to hinder, delay, or defraud the enterprise or creditors; and the ability to enforce a contract notwithstanding an *ipso facto* clause.

[294]   HERA, §§ 1002(a)(3), 1145(a), 12 USC §§ 4502(20), 4617.

[295]   HERA, § 1361, 12 USC §§ 4611–4616.

[296]   HERA, § 1117(a), 12 USC § 1719(g).

[297]   12 USC § 4617(a)(3).

[298]   12 USC § 4617(b)(2).

[299]   12 USC § 4617(b)(1).

[300]   12 USC § 4617(b)(2)(E) and (i).

[301]   12 USC § 4617(b)(11)(E).

At the same time, the incidental powers clause in 12 USC § 4617(b)(2)(J)(ii) authorizes   **8.209**
FHFA to 'take any action authorized by this section, which the Agency determines is in the
best interests of the regulated entity or the Agency'. In *Collins v Yellen*,[302] the US Supreme
Court broadly construed the incidental powers clause to authorize FHFA, as conservator of
Fannie Mae or Freddie Mac, 'to act in what it determines is "in the best interests of … *the
Agency*" … and, by extension, the public it serves',[303] even if that action is inconsistent with
'the best interests of the companies or their shareholders', or presumably their creditors or
counterparties.[304] Based on this construction of the incidental powers clause, the Court
held that FHFA had the statutory authority to enter into the net worth sweep amendment
to the Senior Preferred Stock Purchase Agreements with the US Treasury. The net worth
sweep amendment obligated Fannie and Freddie to pay the US Treasury dividends equal to
their entire net worth minus a small, specified capital reserve rather than at the rates specified in the original agreements.

HERA also gave FHFA the authority to liquidate covered companies and conduct an ad-   **8.210**
ministrative claims process,[305] with the same sort of limited judicial oversight over FHFA as
exists over the FDIC in section 11 of the FDIA.[306] It further gave FHFA many of the 'super
powers' enjoyed by the FDIC to set aside, avoid, or otherwise limit otherwise enforceable
claims of creditors. For example, FHFA has the power to treat similarly situated creditors
differently in its exercise of core resolution powers if certain conditions are satisfied, including that each creditor receives what it would have received in a hypothetical liquidation
proceeding as if such core resolution powers had not been exercised.[307] It also has the power
to enforce contracts despite *ipso facto* clauses that would otherwise give the counterparty
rights to accelerate performance upon the appointment of a conservator or receiver or the
insolvency of the institution, with similar exceptions for the close-out of QFCs.[308] In addition, the statute authorizes FHFA to repudiate any 'burdensome' contracts within a 'reasonable' period of time,[309] with damages for repudiation calculated in the same limited way
as under the bank resolution statute,[310] with similar exceptions for QFCs. But because these

---

[302] *Collins v Yellen*, No. 19-422, slip op. (594 US ___ (2021)).
[303] Ibid, 13–14 (emphasis in original).
[304] As explained by the Court, ibid, 13–15:

> Instead of mandating that the FHFA always act in the best interests of the regulated entity, the Recovery
> Act authorizes the Agency to act in what it determines is 'in the best interests of the regulated entity *or
> the Agency*'. §4617(b)(2)(J)(ii) (emphasis added). Thus, when the FHFA acts as a conservator, it may
> aim to rehabilitate the regulated entity in a way that, while not in the best interests of the regulated
> entity, is beneficial to the Agency, and, by extension, the public it serves. This distinctive feature of an
> FHFA conservatorship is fatal to the shareholders' statutory claim.
>
> …
>
> … [Thus, w]hether or not this new arrangement [the net worth sweep amendment] was in the best
> interests of the companies or their shareholders, the FHFA could have reasonably concluded that it was
> in the best interests of members of the public who rely on a stable secondary mortgage market. The
> Recovery Act therefore authorized the Agency to choose this option.

[305] 12 USC § 4617(b)(3).
[306] 12 USC § 4617(b)(5)(E).
[307] 12 USC § 4617(c)(2).
[308] 12 USC § 4617(d)(8), (d)(13).
[309] 12 USC § 4617(d).
[310] 12 USC § 4617(d)(3).

entities do not take deposits, no depositor preference or 'least cost' resolution requirement is imposed, as is contained in the FDIA.

8.211   Finally, HERA provides that 'no court may take any action to restrain or affect the exercise of powers or functions of [FHFA] as a conservator or a receiver'. This provision is virtually identical to a provision in the FDIA.[311] The provision in the FDIA has long been referred to as the anti-injunction provision,[312] and understood to be limited to preventing injunctive relief against the FDIC that would interfere with its ability to prevent the value of a failing bank from melting like an ice cube during a financial emergency.[313] Yet, in *Collins v Yellen*,[314] the US Supreme Court construed the identical language in HERA as barring judicial review of any action taken by FHFA within its statutory authority as conservator or receiver, including any action pursuant to the incidental powers clause in 12 USC § 4617(b)(2)(J)(ii). As noted above, the Court broadly construed the incidental powers clause as authorizing FHFA to take any action it reasonably determines to be in the best interests of the public, even if that action is inconsistent with 'the best interests of the companies or their shareholders', or presumably their creditors or counterparties.[315] Accordingly, when acting as conservator or receiver, FHFA is subject to virtually no judicial review of any actions that it reasonably determines to be in the public interest.

C. Exercise of New Resolution Authority

8.212   On 7 September 2008, less than six weeks after Congress provided the newly created FHFA with a full array of resolution powers and the Secretary of the Treasury with his temporary financial assistance powers, FHFA put Fannie Mae and Freddie Mac into conservatorship with the consent of their respective boards of directors.[316] At the same time, the Treasury Secretary announced a programme to provide financial assistance of up to $200 billion to these two institutions ($100 billion each), in return for senior preferred stock with a 10 per cent annual dividend and warrants for 79.9 per cent of the common stock of each institution.[317] In effect, the US Treasury guaranteed approximately $5.5 trillion of Fannie Mae's and Freddie Mac's combined debt and guarantee liabilities. The US Treasury also created a temporary backstop lending facility for the Federal Home Loan Banks, which expired at the end of 2009.[318]

---

[311]   Compare 12 USC § 4617(f) with FDIC, § 11(j), 12 USC 1821(j) (providing that '[e]xcept as provided in this section, no court may take any action, except at the request of the Board of Directors by regulation or order, to restrain or affect the exercise of powers or functions as a conservator or a receiver').

[312]   See, eg, *Bank of Am. Nat. Ass'n v Colonial Bank*, 604 F.3d 1239, 1244 (11th Cir 2010) (describing 12 USC § 1821(j) as 'what is commonly referred to as [the FDIA's] "anti-injunction" provision'); see also *Robinson v RTC (In re Landmark Land)*, 1997 U.S. App. LEXIS 6476 (4th Cir 1997).

[313]   See, eg, *Telematics Int'l v NEMLC Leasing Corp.*, 967 F.2d 703, 705 (1st Cir 1992) (noting that, '[t]o enable the FDIC to move quickly and without undue interruption to preserve and consolidate the assets of the failed institution, Congress enacted a broad limit on the power of courts to interfere with the FDIC's efforts', before going on to describe the anti-injunction provision in 12 USC § 1821(j)).

[314]   *Collins v Yellen*, No. 19-422, slip op. at 13–15 (594 US ___ (2021).

[315]   See *supra* n 304.

[316]   Press Release, Fed Housing Fin Agency, *Statement of Federal Housing Finance Agency Director James B. Lockhart at News Conference Announcing Conservatorship of Fannie Mae and Freddie Mac* (7 September 2008); Press Release, Fed Housing Fin Agency, *Fact Sheet: Questions and Answers on Conservatorship* (7 September 2008).

[317]   Press Release, Fed Housing Fin Agency, *Fact Sheet: Questions and Answers on Conservatorship* (7 September 2008).

[318]   Press Release, US Treasury Dep't, *Fact Sheet: Government Sponsored Enterprise Credit Facility* (7 September 2008); US Treasury Dep't, *Lending Agreement* §§ 1.0, 17.1 (September 2008).

The articulated purpose of these actions was to stabilize the US financial markets.[319] As the   **8.213**
failure of Lehman Brothers and the rescue of AIG one week later demonstrate, this exercise
of resolution authority over Fannie and Freddie did not stabilize the financial markets. On
the contrary, these actions may have further spooked the markets because they may have
signalled that the US financial system was in worse financial condition than the markets
had previously assumed.

D. Recent Developments

When Fannie Mae and Freddie Mac were both placed into conservatorship in 2008, almost   **8.214**
no one would have expected that the conservatorships would still be in place nearly thirteen
years later, with no end in sight. Conservatorship had always been understood to be a temporary mechanism to rehabilitate the institution in conservatorship.[320] If the rehabilitation
was successful, the conservatorship was terminated. If it was unsuccessful, it was converted
into a receivership and the institution was liquidated in an orderly manner.[321] Indeed, when
FHFA first placed Fannie Mae and Freddie Mac into conservatorship, it tried to preserve
the private-sector corporate governance structures of those firms and their New York Stock
Exchange (NYSE) listings in anticipation of a prompt and successful rehabilitation. But
eventually the common stock of both institutions fell to below $1 per share and they were
de-listed from the NYSE.[322]

Perhaps the most significant event that sidetracked this normal procedure of terminating   **8.215**
the conservatorships if rehabilitation was successful, or converting the conservatorships
into receiverships if rehabilitation was unsuccessful, was the adoption in 2012 of the net
worth sweep amendment to the original 2008 agreements that govern Treasury's investment and recoveries from the conservatorships. The net worth sweep amendment replaced
the 10 per cent dividend payments made to Treasury on its preferred stock investments
in Fannie Mae and Freddie Mac with a 'quarterly sweep' of every dollar of profit each firm
earns going forward.[323] The net worth sweep amendment was adopted by agreement between FHFA and Treasury, without the consent of the holders of common stock or junior
preferred stock of Fannie Mae or Freddie Mac. It was adopted just before the firms started
generating substantial profits.

The net worth sweep amendment had the practical effect of preventing the firms from   **8.216**
building up a capital buffer against future losses.[324] Without such a capital buffer, they would
not be able to meet the condition for terminating the conservatorships—rehabilitation.
Nor would the creditors or other stakeholders have any crystallized claims against the

---

[319] Press Release, US Treasury Dep't, *Statement by Secretary Henry M. Paulsen, Jr. on Treasury and Federal Housing Finance Agency Action to Protect Financial Markets and Taxpayers* (7 September 2008); US Treasury Dep't, *Fact Sheet: Treasury Senior Preferred Stock Purchase Agreement* (7 September 2008).

[320] Michael Krimminger and Mark A Calabria, 'The Conservatorships of Fannie Mae and Freddie Mac: Actions Violate HERA and Established Insolvency Principles', Cato Working Paper No 26 (9 February 2015) 43.

[321] Ibid.

[322] See, eg, Julianne Pepitone, 'Fannie Mae and Freddie Mac delist from NYSE', *CNNMoney.com* (7 July 2010), available at: <http://money.cnn.com/2010/07/07/markets/fannie_freddie_tickers/>.

[323] Press Release, Treasury Department Announces Further Steps to Expedite Wind Down of Fannie Mae and Freddie Mac (17 August 2012).

[324] Krimminger and Calabria, *supra* n 320 at 16.

residual value of the firms, unless the Director of FHFA converts the conservatorships into receiverships.

8.217   Several shareholders filed suit against the US Treasury and FHFA. One set of lawsuits alleged that the FHFA's agreement to the net worth sweep amendment violated its fiduciary duties, as conservator, to the non-governmental stakeholders in Fannie Mae and Freddie Mac, and therefore exceeded its statutory authority. It also alleged that the FHFA's single director structure imposed an unconstitutional for-cause limitation on the President's authority to remove the Director. The District Court dismissed the statutory claim for failure to state a claim and granted summary judgment on the constitutional claim.[325] The Fifth Circuit affirmed the District Court's decision on the statutory claim, but reversed it on the constitutional claim.[326] The Fifth Circuit, sitting en banc, vacated the three-judge panel's decision on the statutory claim, holding that the statutory claim should have survived the government's motion to dismiss under Rule 12(b)(6) of the Federal Rules of Civil Procedure.[327] But it agreed that FHFA was unconstitutionally structured.[328] As described more fully below, the US Supreme Court reversed the en banc Fifth Circuit on the statutory claim, but affirmed it on the constitutional claim.

8.218   A second set of lawsuits, filed in the US Court of Federal Claims, alleged, among other things, that the net worth sweep amendment was a taking of private property for public use without just compensation, in violation of the Takings Clause of the Fifth Amendment to the US Constitution.[329] In an opinion issued in December 2019 and reissued in March 2020, the Court of Federal Claims dismissed these plaintiffs' direct takings claims (ie, the claims arising from the plaintiffs' losses as shareholders of the GSEs), for lack of standing.[330] The Court of Federal Claims ruled against the government's motion to dismiss with respect to the plaintiffs' indirect takings claims, which are rooted in the rights of the GSEs themselves.[331] That opinion is subject to an ongoing interlocutory appeal in the US Court of Appeals for the Federal Circuit, for which oral argument took place on 4 August 2021.

8.219   In 2015, during the pendency of this litigation, Michael Krimminger, former General Counsel to the FDIC and one of the leading US experts on the FDIC's bank resolution powers, and Mark Calabria of the Cato Institute, who served as Director of FHFA from 2018 to 2021, wrote an important article.[332] In it, they argued that FHFA, as conservator, has a duty to return Fannie Mae and Freddie Mac to 'sound and solvent' operations meeting all regulatory capital, liquidity, and other prudential requirements.[333] If it is unable to do

---

[325] *Collins v FHFA*, 254 F. Supp. 3d 841 (SD Tex. 2017).

[326] *Collins v Mnuchin*, 896 F. 3d 640 (5th Cir 2018) (per curiam). See Davis Polk & Wardwell, 'Fifth Circuit Holds that FHFA is Unconstitutionally Structured' (18 July 2019), available at: <Fifth Circuit Holds That FHFA is Unconstitutionally Structured | Davis Polk>.

[327] *Collins v Mnuchin*, 938 F. 3d 553 (5th Cir 2019) (en banc).

[328] Ibid.

[329] See, eg, Complaint, *Fairholme Funds, Inc v United States*, No 13-465C (United States Court of Fed. Cl., 9 July 2013) 8–9, 25–27.

[330] Opinion and Order, *Fairholme Funds, Inc. v United States*, No 13-465C (US Court of Fed. Cl., filed under seal 6 December 2019, reissued for publication 13 December 2019, reissued following motion to certify interlocutory appeal 9 March 2020) 38–41.

[331] Ibid, 41–45.

[332] Krimminger and Calabria, *supra* n 320.

[333] Ibid, 16.

so, then it has a duty to convert the conservatorships into receiverships and liquidate the assets of the GSEs in an orderly manner for the benefit of all their stakeholders, not just the US.[334] Alternatively, if the GSEs are returned to sound and solvent operations, the conservatorships must be terminated.[335]

Krimminger and Calabria also argued that FHFA is required to carry on the businesses of   **8.220**
Fannie Mae and Freddie Mac to 'preserve and conserve the assets and property' of the institutions under conservatorship.[336] Instead, under the net worth sweep arrangement, Fannie Mae and Freddie Mac had paid the US government $228 billion, or $40 billion more than they borrowed from Treasury, as of year-end 2014.[337] Because the firms had not been allowed to accumulate capital, Krimminger and Calabria argued that US taxpayers may be on the hook if the firms fail again.[338] They concluded by arguing that if the net worth sweep amendment is allowed to stand, it may adversely affect public confidence in the fairness and predictability of the US government's participation in resolution proceedings of all types, including those under the FDIA or Title II of the Dodd-Frank Act.[339]

Mark Calabria was subsequently appointed Director of FHFA in December 2018. Under his   **8.221**
leadership, FHFA and the Treasury amended the Senior Preferred Purchase Agreements to allow Fannie Mae and Freddie Mac to build up capital by suspending their obligations to pay cash dividends to the US Treasury and instead allowing them to retain earnings until they had built up $25 billion and $20 billion, respectively, in capital.[340] FHFA also issued a final rule imposing minimum capital requirements on Fannie Mae and Freddie Mac, which required them to build up common equity tier 1 and total capital ratios similar to those required of the US G-SIBs.[341] FHFA announced its strategic plan to prepare Fannie and Freddie to exit conservatorship once they had sufficient capital and liquidity to operate as viable entities outside conservatorship.[342] Finally, FHFA issued a final rule on resolution planning, which required Fannie Mae and Freddie Mac to prepare and submit resolution plans showing how they could be resolved in a manner that imposed all of their losses on shareholders and bondholders, without destabilizing the US mortgage market and without requiring any extraordinary government assistance.[343]

---

[334] Ibid, 6.

[335] Ibid, 43.

[336] Ibid, 42.

[337] Joe Light, 'Treasury Department: Fannie, Freddie Bailout Wasn't a Loan', Wall S J (21 April 2015); Rodney Johnson, 'The Real Reason Why the US Treasury Took Over Fannie and Freddie', Forbes (29 July 2015).

[338] Krimminger and Calabria, supra n 320 at 7 ('because the Third Amendment deprives Fannie and Freddie of 100 per cent of their net worth, it means that no capital is accumulated against future losses. That leaves the taxpayers on the hook once again').

[339] Ibid, 7. See also Randall D Guynn, 'Background and Perspectives on Fannie and Freddie Conservatorships', 12, The Future of Fannie and Freddie Conservatorship and the Takings Clause, The Classical Liberal Institute & NYU Journal of Law & Business (30 September 2013) ('if the government gets away with the dividend sweep of Fannie and Freddie, it will establish a dangerous precedent for the rights of analogous stakeholders of failed banks and systemically important financial institutions under the [FDIA] and [Title II of the Dodd-Frank Act]'), video of proceedings available at: <http://www.law.nyu.edu/news/Fannie-Freddie-conference-CLI>.

[340] 'Letter Agreement between US Department of the Treasury and Federal Housing Finance Agency' (27 September 2019), available at: <https://home.treasury.gov/system/files/136/9-27-19%20_FNMA%20Capital%20Agreement_0.pdf>.

[341] FHFA, 'Enterprise Regulatory Capital Framework', 85 Fed Reg 82150 (17 December 2020).

[342] FHFA, '2019 Strategic Plan for the Conservatorships of Fannie Mae and Freddie Mac' (October 2019).

[343] FHFA, 'Resolution Planning', 86 Fed Reg 23577 (4 May 2021).

8.222   The question whether the net worth sweep exceeded FHFA's statutory authority was resolved by the US Supreme Court in *Collins v Yellen*.[344] The Court concluded that it did not. It broadly construed the incidental powers clause in 12 USC § 4617(b)(2)(J)(ii) as authorizing FHFA to take any actions as conservator that it reasonably determines to be in the best interests of the public, even if that action is inconsistent with 'the best interests of the companies or their shareholders', or presumably the creditors or counterparties of Fannie Mae and Freddie Mac.[345] Because FHFA could have reasonably determined that the net worth sweep was in the public interest, the Court concluded that FHFA was acting within the scope of its statutory authority when it agreed to the net worth sweep amendment. The Court also broadly construed 12 USC § 4617(f) to bar judicial review over any action taken by FHFA that was within its statutory authority. Accordingly, the Court held that the courts were barred from reviewing any action by FHFA, except to the extent that it acts outside its statutory authority.

8.223   The Court in *Collins* also held that the single director structure of FHFA was unconstitutional to the extent that the Director was not removable by the President except for cause. The Court held that under the US Constitution, the President had the authority to remove the Director at will. On the same day as the Court's decision, President Biden removed Director Calabria from office and replaced him with Acting Director Sandra Thompson.

8.224   While FHFA has for the time being allowed Fannie Mae and Freddie Mac to continue building up capital, it is not clear how long that policy will last or whether FHFA and the Treasury will reinstitute the net worth sweep. It is also uncertain whether FHFA will continue or reverse Director Calabria's strategic plan to terminate the conservatorships.

V. Resolution Authority over Systemically Important Financial Institutions

8.225   With some notable dissenters,[346] a consensus developed in the US after the financial panic of 2008 that some form of resolution authority based on the bank resolution model should be extended to most nonbank financial institutions under certain circumstances. Proponents argued that resolution authority is essential to ending bailouts. They argued that because ordinary bankruptcy proceedings have the potential to trigger a chain reaction of failures throughout the financial system during a financial panic, such proceedings produce an irresistible temptation to bail out financial institutions that are considered to be 'too big or interconnected to fail' during such a panic.[347] Opponents countered that far from being a solution to bailouts, resolution authority actually institutionalizes bailouts.[348]

---

[344] *Collins v Yellen*, No. 19-422, slip op. at 13–15 (594 US ___ (2021)).

[345] See *supra* n 304.

[346] See, eg, Paul Mahoney and Steven Walt, 'Viewpoint: Treasury Resolution Plan Solves Nothing', *Am Banker* (20 November 2009); Peter J Wallison and David Skeel, Op-Ed: 'The Dodd Bill: Bailouts Forever', *Wall St J* (7 April 2010); John B Taylor, Op-Ed: 'How to Avoid a "Bailout Bill"', *Wall St J* (3 May 2010).

[347] See *Too Big to Fail: The Role of Bankruptcy and Antitrust Law in Financial Regulation Reform: Hearing Before the Subcomm. on Commercial and Administrative law, H. Comm. on the Judiciary*, 111th Cong (2009) (testimony of Michael S Barr, Assistant Secretary of the Treasury).

[348] See, eg, Hearings Before the House Financial Services Committee (29 October 2009) (remarks of Rep Hensarling).

The Obama Administration released its original proposal on 25 March 2009 and a revised **8.226** version on 23 July 2009.[349] The US House of Representatives passed an amended version of the Administration's proposal as part of the Wall Street Reform and Consumer Protection Act of 2009 ('the House Bill').[350] The Senate passed a different version as part of the Restoring American Financial Stability Act of 2010 ('the Senate Bill'), and previous versions of the Senate Bill included other versions of the resolution authority proposal.[351] The House and Senate Conference Committee used the version contained in the Senate Bill, after reflecting certain technical amendments, as its base text ('the Conference Base Text').[352] On 21 July 2010, the US passed the final version as Title II of the Dodd-Frank Act.[353] The purpose of this chapter is to summarize the key elements of the new resolution authority in Title II, identify the main policy issues raised in the debate over the various proposals, and summarize certain alternative proposals that were made based on the bankruptcy model.

A. Orderly Liquidation Authority Framework

The Orderly Liquidation Authority in Title II of the Dodd-Frank Act is modelled largely on **8.227** sections 11 and 13 of the FDIA, but with several significant differences. These differences were designed to harmonize the rules defining creditors' rights with those contained in the US Bankruptcy Code, discourage bailouts, and reduce the moral hazard that could result if shareholders or unsecured creditors are insulated from the losses they would have suffered in a liquidation or reorganization under the US Bankruptcy Code. Thus, section III of this chapter provides a good summary of the basic framework of Title II, except for the following key differences:

- *Orderly liquidation authority.* The resolution authority provided for in Title II has been named the 'orderly liquidation authority' to emphasize that it does not include a conservatorship option or permit bailouts of failed institutions. This does not mean that the statute requires or even authorizes the FDIC to do a fire-sale liquidation of a failed institution. Instead, the statute includes a duty to maximize the value of the failed institution and minimize losses for the benefit of its stakeholders[354] and includes the

---

[349] See Davis Polk, 'Client Memorandum', *Treasury's Proposed Resolution Authority for Systemically Significant Financial Companies* (30 March 2009); Davis Polk, 'Client Memorandum', *The Regulatory Reform Marathon* (28 July 2009).

[350] Wall Street Reform and Consumer Protection Act of 2009, HR 4173, 111th Cong, 1st Sess § 1601 et seq (2009).

[351] Restoring American Financial Stability Act of 2010, Senate Substitute Amendment for HR 4173, 111th Cong, 2nd Sess, §§ 201–214 (20 May 2010). See also Staff of S Comm on Banking, Housing, and Urban Affairs, 111th Cong, 1st Sess, Restoring American Financial Stability Act of 2009 §§ 201–210 (Comm Print 10 November 2009); Staff of S Comm on Banking, Housing, and Urban Affairs, 111th Cong, 2nd Sess, Restoring American Financial Stability Act of 2010 §§ 201–211 (Comm Print 20 March 2010). See Davis Polk, Client Memorandum, *House and Senate Debate Resolution Authority* (12 November 2009); Davis Polk, Client Memorandum, *Summary of the Wall Street Reform and Consumer Protection Act Passed by the House of Representatives, December 11, 2009, Resolution Authority* (15 December 2009); Davis Polk, Client Memorandum, *Summary of the Restoring American Financial Stability Act, Passed by the Senate on May 20, 2010, Resolution (Orderly Liquidation) Authority* (22 May 2010).

[352] Restoring American Financial Stability Act of 2010, Conference Base Text for HR 4173, 111th Cong, 2nd Sess, Title II (10 June 2010).

[353] Dodd-Frank Act, Title II (21 July 2010).

[354] Dodd-Frank Act, § 210(b)(9)(E)(i) and (ii), 12 USC § 5390(b)(9)(E)(i) and (ii).

ability to transfer all or any part of the assets and liabilities of the failed institution to a bridge financial company. While the FDIC is required to liquidate any bridge within two years, with possible extensions of up to a total of five years, the bridge option provides the FDIC with the power to preserve the firm's franchise value and critical operations so that it can be liquidated in an orderly manner or recapitalized pursuant to a bridge bail-in.

- *Covered companies*. Unlike almost any other statute, the orderly liquidation authority is not limited to a fixed category of persons, determinable in advance, such as all systemically important financial companies. Instead, it could apply to any 'financial company'[355] if certain determinations are made. The required determinations depend as much on general market conditions as they do on the systemic importance of a particular firm in a vacuum. The conditions for coverage are more likely to be satisfied during a financial panic. They are less likely to be satisfied during periods of relative calm.
- Subject to the exceptions described below for broker-dealers or insurance companies, a financial company will be designated as a covered financial company, and the FDIC will be appointed as its receiver, if at any time (including on the eve of bankruptcy) the Treasury Secretary makes certain financial distress[356] and systemic risk determinations,[357] upon the recommendation of two-thirds of the Federal Reserve and

---

[355] Subject to the exclusions and qualifications, the term 'financial company' is defined as any company that is incorporated or organized under US Federal or State law that is: (i) a bank holding company, as defined by the Bank Holding Company Act; (ii) a nonbank financial company (including an insurance company or a securities broker-dealer) that has been determined by the Council to be systemically important and therefore subject to supervision by the Federal Reserve; (iii) any company that is predominantly engaged in activities that are financial in nature or incidental to a financial activity under § 4(k) of the Bank Holding Company Act (including an insurance company or securities broker-dealer); and (iv) any subsidiary of any of the foregoing that is predominantly engaged in activities that are financial in nature or incidental to a financial activity under § 4(k) of the Bank Holding Company Act (other than a subsidiary that is an insured depository institution or an insurance company). The following companies are excluded from the term financial company for purposes of the orderly liquidation authority: Fannie Mae, Freddie Mac, any Federal Home Loan Bank, any Farm Credit System institution and any government entity. No company may be deemed to be predominantly engaged in activities that are financial in nature or incidental to a financial activity unless the consolidated revenues of such company from such activities constitute at least 85 per cent of the total consolidated revenues of such company (including any revenues attributable to a depository institution investment or subsidiary). Dodd-Frank Act, § 201(a)(11), 12 USC § 5381(a)(11).

[356] The financial distress condition for putting a financial company in receivership under the new orderly liquidation authority is effectively limited to balance-sheet insolvency or illiquidity, and does not extend to the pre-insolvency conditions described in section III.C.1 for closing an insured depository institution. Dodd-Frank Act, § 203(b)(4), 12 USC § 5383(b)(4). Indeed, unless the board of directors or shareholders of a financial company consent to the company's receivership, the Secretary of the Treasury is required to obtain an order from the US Federal District Court for the District of Columbia to the effect that the Secretary's determination that the company is insolvent was not arbitrary or capricious. Dodd-Frank Act, § 202, 12 USC § 5382.

[357] The required determinations include: (i) the financial company is 'in default or in danger of default'; (ii) the failure of the financial company and its resolution under otherwise applicable insolvency law would have serious adverse effects on financial stability in the US; (iii) no viable private sector alternative is available to prevent the default of the financial company; (iv) any effect of using the orderly liquidation authority on the claims or interests of creditors, counterparties, and shareholders of the financial company and other market participants would be appropriate given the beneficial impact of using the orderly liquidation authority on US financial stability; (v) the use of the orderly liquidation authority would avoid or mitigate the adverse effects that would result from resolving the financial company under otherwise applicable insolvency law; (vi) a Federal regulatory agency has ordered the financial company to convert all of its convertible debt instruments that are subject to being converted by regulatory order; and (vii) the company satisfies the definition of 'financial company' contained in the statute. Dodd-Frank Act, § 203(b), 12 USC § 5383(b).

two-thirds of the FDIC Board, and in consultation with the President.[358] Title II applies to all financial subsidiaries of a covered financial company other than IDIs (which continue to be covered by the FDIA's resolution provisions). Systemically important insurance companies could be covered financial companies, but they would be resolved by state insurance authorities under otherwise applicable state insurance insolvency laws, rather than by the FDIC under the substantive provisions of the new resolution authority.[359] Insurance company subsidiaries, however, would not be covered financial companies merely because they are subsidiaries of a covered financial company.[360]

- *Harmonized with the US Bankruptcy Code.* The final law reflects a substantial harmonization of the rules defining creditors' rights with those contained in the US Bankruptcy Code, thus narrowing the gap between these two laws on this important issue. The rules are therefore very different from the FDIC's super powers discussed in section III.F, which remain in place without substantial modification only for the resolution of IDIs under the FDIA. Important differences include:

- *No depositor preference rule.* Since the covered financial companies are not authorized to take deposits, the statute does not include a depositor preference rule.

- *Key contingent claims are provable.* Contingent claims in the form of guarantees, letters of credit, lines of credit, and other similar claims are recognized as provable claims equal to their estimated value as of the date of the FDIC's appointment as receiver, which is essentially the same as under the US Bankruptcy Code.[361]

- *Special enforceability requirements.* Although agreements against the interest of the receiver or a bridge financial company must be in writing and meet certain other special enforceability requirements as required by the bank resolution statute (but not the US Bankruptcy Code), any written agreement that is duly executed or confirmed in the ordinary course of business that the counterparty can prove to the satisfaction of the receiver is enforceable (closer to the US Bankruptcy Code).[362]

- *Damages for a repudiated debt obligation.* Damages for the repudiation of such obligations are calculated as the face amount of the obligation plus accrued interest and accreted original issue discount, determined as of the date of the receiver's appointment.[363]

---

[358] If the financial company is a securities broker-dealer or its largest US subsidiary is a securities broker-dealer, the designation must be approved by two-thirds of the Securities and Exchange Commission and two-thirds of the Federal Reserve Board, provided that the FDIC is consulted. If the financial company is an insurance company or its largest US subsidiary is an insurance company, the designation must be approved by the Director of the new Federal Insurance Office and two-thirds of the Federal Reserve Board, provided that the FDIC is consulted. Dodd-Frank Act, § 203(a), 12 USC § 5383(a).

[359] The Dodd-Frank Act provides that the FDIC has backup authority over insurance companies under applicable state insurance insolvency law, if the appropriate state regulatory agency has not filed the appropriate judicial action to place the company in liquidation under state law within 60 days of a determination by the US District Court for the District of Columbia to authorize the Treasury Secretary to appoint the FDIC as receiver for such company. Dodd-Frank Act, § 203(e), 12 USC § 5383(e).

[360] Insurance company subsidiaries are carved out of the definition of 'covered subsidiaries'. Dodd-Frank Act, § 201(a)(9), 12 USC § 5381(a)(9).

[361] Dodd-Frank Act, § 210(c)(3)(E), 12 USC § 5390(c)(3)(E).

[362] Dodd-Frank Act, § 210(a)(6), 12 USC § 5390(a)(6).

[363] Dodd-Frank Act, § 210(c)(3)(D), 12 USC § 5390(c)(3)(D).

- *Limited right to 'post-appointment' interest.* Similar to the 'post-petition' interest provisions of the US Bankruptcy Code for a secured claim, any accrued interest is calculated through the date of repudiation, to the extent that such allowed secured claim is secured by property worth more than the amount of such claim.
- *Security interests and security entitlements.* Legally enforceable or perfected security interests and legally enforceable security entitlements in respect of assets held by the covered financial company must be respected as property rights.[364]
- *Preferential or fraudulent transfers.* Legally enforceable or perfected security interests and other transfers of property are not avoidable if 'taken in contemplation of the company's insolvency' as the FDIC has consistently asserted under the FDIA. Instead, they are avoidable only if they amount to preferential or fraudulent transfers under language that was lifted directly from sections 546, 547, and 548 of the US Bankruptcy Code.[365]
- *Set-off rights.* Set-off rights must be respected as under the US Bankruptcy Code, with some qualifications to permit the receiver to transfer liabilities to a third party or bridge financial company even if the transfer destroys the mutuality of offsetting claims.[366]
- *Choice-of-law rules.* Non-insolvency choice-of-law rules determine the applicable non-insolvency law governing the perfection of security interests and the creation and enforcement of security entitlements.[367]
- *Additional due process.* This narrows the gap between the due process protections of the US Bankruptcy Code and those provided under the bank resolution statute, including the gatekeeping role of the US Federal District Court for the District of Columbia discussed above, additional opportunity for judicial review of the claims process, and certain notice and hearing rights.[368]
- *Minimum recovery right.* To ensure minimum due process, all creditors are entitled to receive at least what they would have received in a liquidation of the covered financial company under chapter 7 of the US Bankruptcy Code, at least if the FDIC exercises its power to favour some creditors over others within the same class.[369] A creditor's maximum entitlement is both its maximum and minimum entitlements.[370] This minimum recovery right is analogous to the no-creditor-worse-off-than-in-liquidation (NCWOL) principle described in the Financial Stability Board's Key Attributes document.[371]
- *Mandatory rule-making.* The FDIC is required to promulgate rules to implement the orderly liquidation authority in a manner that further reduces the gap between how creditors are treated in a liquidation under the US Bankruptcy Code and how they are treated under the orderly liquidation authority.[372]

---

[364] Dodd-Frank Act, § 210(c)(12), 12 USC § 5390(c)(12).
[365] Dodd-Frank Act, § 210(a)(11), 12 USC § 5390(a)(11).
[366] Dodd-Frank Act, § 210(a)(12), 12 USC § 5390(a)(12).
[367] Dodd-Frank Act, § 210(a)(1)(I), 12 USC § 5390(a)(1)(I).
[368] Dodd-Frank Act, § 202, 12 USC § 5382.
[369] Dodd-Frank Act, § 210(a)(7)(B), (b)(4)(B), and (h)(5)(E)(ii), 12 USC § 5390(a)(7)(B), (b)(4)(B), and (h)(5)(E)(ii).
[370] Dodd-Frank Act, § 210(b)(4), (d)(4) and (h)(5)(E), 12 USC § 5390(b)(4), (d)(4) and (h)(5)(E).
[371] Financial Stability Board, *Key Attributes of Effective Resolution Regimes for Financial Institutions* (updated version, 15 October 2014) 11.
[372] Dodd-Frank Act, § 209, 12 USC § 5389.

Despite these important differences, Title II is still modelled on the bank resolution authority and therefore shares most of its features, including some of the 'super powers' given to the FDIC. The FDIC is the resolving authority. It has the power to take control of certain troubled or failing financial institutions, if certain financial distress and systemic risk determinations are made. It may transfer any part of a covered institution's business to a third party at fair value. If a third party buyer cannot be found at fair value, the FDIC may establish a 'bridge' financial company to hold the part of the business worth preserving until it can be sold to a third party at fair value, liquidated in an orderly fashion or recapitalized pursuant to a bridge bail-in.   **8.228**

The FDIC has the power to provide a wide range of financial assistance, including loss-sharing arrangements, to facilitate the transfer of assets and liabilities to a third party in connection with the liquidation of a covered institution.[373] But certain limitations are imposed on the FDIC's discretion that do not apply when it resolves IDIs under the FDIA, including that:[374]   **8.229**

- unsecured creditors must bear losses (up to the amount they would have suffered in a liquidation under chapter 7 of the US Bankruptcy Code); and
- the management and board members responsible for the failed condition must be removed.

The FDIC is generally responsible for liquidating the covered institution left behind in receivership (after transferring all or any portion of its assets and liabilities to a bridge financial company) and conducting an administrative claims process for claims left behind in the receivership with very limited judicial oversight.[375] In both its exercise of core resolution powers and its administration of the claims process, the FDIC has some of the 'super powers' that it has under the bank resolution provisions of the FDIA. For example, it has the power to treat similarly situated creditors differently by 'cherry-picking' which assets and liabilities to transfer to a third party or bridge financial company, provided that each creditor left behind in the receivership receives no less for its claims than the value it would have received in a hypothetical liquidation under chapter 7 of the US Bankruptcy Code as if no such transfer had taken place.[376] The FDIC has the power to treat all oral and some written contracts as unenforceable, even if they would be enforceable under applicable state or other non-insolvency law. It has the power to enforce contracts despite any so-called *ipso facto* clauses that purport to accelerate the contracts upon the commencement of a resolution or insolvency proceeding, subject to the same exceptions for qualified financial contracts as in the bank resolution statute.[377] The FDIC also has the discretion to repudiate any 'burdensome' contract within a 'reasonable' period of time, and limit the amount of any claim for damages as a result of repudiation to 'actual direct compensatory damages', subject   **8.230**

---

[373] Dodd-Frank Act, § 204(d), 12 USC § 5384(d).
[374] Dodd-Frank Act, § 206, 12 USC § 5386.
[375] Dodd-Frank Act, § 210(a), 12 USC § 5390(a).
[376] Dodd-Frank Act, § 210(a)(7)(B), (b)(4)(B), and (h)(5)(E)(ii), 12 USC § 5390(a)(7)(B), (b)(4)(B), and (h)(5)(E)(ii).
[377] Dodd-Frank Act, § 210(c)(13), 12 USC § 5390(c)(13).

to the same exceptions for QFCs and to certain new exceptions for contingent claims and debt obligations.[378] And it enjoys the same special powers with respect to litigation.[379]

8.231   Because Title II could apply to securities broker-dealers that are members of the Securities Investment Protection Corporation (SIPC), the statute includes provisions that are intended to provide customers with the same level of protection for customer property as would be provided in a normal SIPC proceeding under the SIPA.[380] If the FDIC were appointed receiver of a systemically important or other covered broker-dealer that is a member of SIPC, the FDIC would be required to appoint SIPC as trustee for the liquidation of the broker-dealer. Effectively, the FDIC would exercise the core resolution powers and SIPC would conduct the claims process for left-behind claims and assets, including left-behind customer claims and customer property. The FDIC would have the power to transfer any assets and liabilities of a covered broker-dealer (including any customer claims and corresponding customer property held by the covered broker-dealer) to a bridge financial company, and SIPC would be required to satisfy any left-behind customer claims 'in the same manner and amount' as if the FDIC had not been involved in the receivership and no transfer of assets or liabilities to a bridge financial company had taken place.

8.232   Title II also contains certain provisions designed to reduce the moral hazard potentially caused by allowing the FDIC to transfer certain 'cherry-picked' liabilities to a third party or bridge financial company, while preserving the FDIC's authority to use its 'cherry-picking' power to preserve, promote, or restore financial stability during a financial panic. The new resolution authority attempts to strike an appropriate balance between these anti-moral-hazard, anti-bailout, and pro-financial-stability goals by requiring the FDIC to recover any costs incurred in resolving a covered financial company from any of the company's creditors who received 'excess benefits' in the resolution proceeding, but only to the extent of such excess benefits and over an extended period of time.[381]

8.233   The FDIC may incur costs in a resolution proceeding in a variety of ways, including by being required to top up any left-behind creditors for any *shortfall* between what the creditors would have received in a hypothetical liquidation under chapter 7 of the US Bankruptcy Code and any lesser amount they actually received in the resolution proceeding. Transferred creditors could receive an 'excess benefit' to the extent they received more on their claims as a result of the transfer than they would have received in a hypothetical liquidation under chapter 7 of the US Bankruptcy Code. The FDIC would have the power to finance any costs it incurs by borrowing from the Treasury, but would be required to repay such borrowed funds within five years, first, by recovering any 'excess benefits' from any creditors and, second, by imposing assessments on financial companies with assets of $50 billion or more.[382] Because the FDIC could take up to five years to complete the resolution of a covered company, it could conceivably allow transferred creditors to use their 'excess benefits' for up to 10 years from the time the institution is first put into receivership (if the cost and the borrowing were incurred at the end of the receivership).

---

[378]   Dodd-Frank Act, § 210(c)(1)–(3), (c)(8)–(12), 12 USC § 5390(c)(1)–(3), (c)(8)–(12).
[379]   Dodd-Frank Act, § 210(a)(8)–(10), 12 USC § 5390(a)(8)–(10).
[380]   Dodd-Frank Act, § 205, 12 USC § 5385.
[381]   Dodd-Frank Act, § 210(o)(1), 12 USC § 5390(o)(1).
[382]   Dodd-Frank Act, § 210(o)(1), 12 USC § 5390(o)(1).

Unlike the proposed resolution authority in the House Bill, the final resolution authority in the Dodd-Frank Act does not include a pre-funded orderly liquidation fund or a provision allowing the FDIC to impose haircuts on secured creditors. The House Bill would have required the creation of a pre-paid systemic dissolution fund of at least $150 billion, which would have been funded through assessments on all financial companies with assets of $50 billion or more and all financial companies that manage a hedge fund with assets under management of $10 billion or more.[383] The House Bill also would have allowed the FDIC to recover some of its losses by imposing a 10 per cent haircut on the claims of certain secured creditors.[384] This provision would essentially have allowed the FDIC to convert up to 10 per cent of a secured claim into an unsecured claim. It was aimed primarily at short-term financing in the form of repurchase agreements based on non-US government security collateral.

8.234

Title II gives the FDIC one business day to decide whether to transfer or repudiate QFCs.[385] This is the same as the bank resolution statute. The original Senate proposals would have given the FDIC a longer period of time, such as three or five business days, to make this decision. The FDIC argued that it needed this extra time to make the required determination with systemically important financial companies because they generally have more complex QFC portfolios than the type of IDIs that the FDIC has experience resolving. Critics argued that three or five days was too long during a financial crisis when asset and collateral values can be extremely volatile.

8.235

B. Key Policy Issues

The debate over the treatment of systemically important nonbank financial companies following their insolvency is extremely important, for the debate frames the key policy issues that must be addressed before any new insolvency framework is introduced. The insolvencies of AIG and Lehman Brothers convinced the Obama administration and Congress that new powers were needed, but there was vigorous debate over the proper approach. This section outlines the key policy issues that were debated.

8.236

1. Why not apply the US Bankruptcy Code?

In the absence of the required financial distress and systemic risk determinations under the new resolution authority, the US Bankruptcy Code would govern the liquidation, recapitalization, or reorganization of a financial company other than an IDI or insurance company. Even broker-dealers that are members of the Securities Investor Protection Corporation are resolved under the US Bankruptcy Code, with SIPA supplementing its provisions with respect to customer property. The US Bankruptcy Code prevents moral hazard—that is, the incentive to take excessive risks if investors are entitled to the upside from their investments but are protected from the downside—by ensuring that shareholders, creditors, and counterparties of covered financial companies suffer appropriate losses if such companies

8.237

---

[383] Wall Street Reform and Consumer Protection Act of 2009, HR 4173, 111th Cong, § 1609(n)(6) (2009).
[384] Wall Street Reform and Consumer Protection Act of 2009, HR 4173, 111th Cong, § 1609(a)(4)(D)(iv) (2009).
[385] Dodd-Frank Act, § 210(c)(10), 12 USC § 5390(c)(10).

are insolvent. The US bankruptcy process is generally considered to be transparent and consistent with due process. It has rules governing creditors' rights that are widely understood and considered to be neutral among similarly situated classes of creditors.

8.238 Unless harmonized with the US Bankruptcy Code or other applicable insolvency laws, any new resolution authority would change the 'rules of the game' for creditors and counterparties on the eve of bankruptcy, and thereby disrupt their reasonable expectations with little or no prior notice. Creditors, counterparties, customers, and other stakeholders have very different rights depending on whether their claims are governed by the US Bankruptcy Code or the FDIA, and changing the rules of the game on the eve of bankruptcy could itself create systemic risk. This problem was addressed in the Dodd-Frank Act by largely harmonizing the rules that define creditors' rights in Title II with their counterparts under the US Bankruptcy Code. This approach leaves a federal agency in charge of the process, with the bridge financial company option, but otherwise requires it to apply the substantive rules defining creditors' rights as they currently exist in the US Bankruptcy Code, with only a few exceptions.

8.239 While there remain substantial procedural differences in the way failures are handled under the US Bankruptcy Code and the new orderly liquidation authority under Title II of the Dodd-Frank Act (primarily in the judicial oversight and relative transparency of US bankruptcy proceedings), Congress attempted to strike a reasonable balance between the desired need for government control over how these systemically important institutions should be addressed and the expectations of creditors.

2. The 'too big to fail'/moral hazard debate

8.240 The US Treasury and other proponents of the new resolution authority argued that some form of resolution authority was necessary to eliminate taxpayer-funded bailouts of financial companies that are perceived to be 'too big to fail', and the moral hazard that such bailouts produce, in a way that does not destabilize the financial system.[386] These proponents noted that a resolution authority would combat the notion that certain firms are 'too big to fail' by providing a mechanism to allow them to be liquidated in an orderly fashion. For example, Federal Reserve Chairman Bernanke stated that establishing a credible process for imposing such losses is essential to restoring a meaningful degree of market discipline and addressing the 'too big to fail' problem.[387] According to resolution authority proponents, the only alternatives to resolution authority were to allow these companies to fail in a disorderly fashion the way Lehman Brothers was or to rescue them in an ad hoc fashion the way AIG was.

8.241 No one understood at the time that it was possible to do an SPOE recapitalization of a failed bank holding company under chapter 11 of the US Bankruptcy Code, using the authority for quick sales under section 363 of the US Bankruptcy Code. When Professor Thomas Jackson, one of the leading bankruptcy scholars in the country and the principal author

---

[386] See *Too Big to Fail: The Role of Bankruptcy and Antitrust Law in Financial Regulation Reform: Hearing Before the Subcomm. on Commercial and Administrative law, H. Comm. on the Judiciary*, 111th Cong (2009) (testimony of Michael S Barr, Assistant Secretary of the Treasury).

[387] *Regulatory Reform: Hearing before the H. Comm. on Financial Servs.*, 111th Cong (2009) (testimony of Ben Bernanke, Chairman, Board of Governors of the Federal Reserve System).

of the original chapter 14 proposal, first heard about SPOE under chapter 11, he called it a genuine break through and immediately suggested how the proposed new chapter 14 might be revised to facilitate the successful use of SPOE under the US Bankruptcy Code.

Critics asserted that the new resolution authority in Title II would not end 'too big to fail' or reduce moral hazard, but would rather institutionalize them.[388] These commentators expressed a concern that having a resolution authority under which certain creditors could be protected against losses by having their claims assumed by third parties or a bridge financial company would create moral hazard by insulating the claims against losses they would have suffered in a bankruptcy proceeding. **8.242**

These critics pointed to the financial assistance provided to Freddie Mac and Fannie Mae in connection with their conservatorships as examples, and argued that the new resolution authority would create 20 new Fannie Maes and Freddie Macs.[389] They asserted that the institutionalization of such bailouts would increase moral hazard and give potentially covered companies a funding advantage over their competitors. Such critics would leave the US Bankruptcy Code in place to ensure that shareholders, creditors, and counterparties of non-depository institution financial companies suffer appropriate losses if such companies fail. **8.243**

The Dodd-Frank Act attempted to strike an appropriate balance between the anti-moral-hazard, anti-bailout, and pro-financial-stability goals by: **8.244**

- prohibiting the Federal Reserve or the FDIC from providing any financial assistance to a financial company unless the assistance is part of a market-wide programme or unless, in the case of the FDIC, the company is being liquidated in an FDIC receivership;[390] and
- requiring the FDIC to recoup any costs incurred in the receivership of a systemically important financial company by clawing back any 'excess benefits' received by any of its creditors whose claims are transferred to a third party or bridge financial company in the receivership proceeding, while giving the FDIC an extended period of time (up to five to ten years) to recoup such excess benefits.[391]

3. The proper procedure for handling creditor claims

Some proponents of the general concept of resolution authority strongly supported giving a federal agency 'core resolution powers' modelled on the FDIA. But they believed that the FDIA was the wrong model for the claims process for left-behind claims, as applied to non-depository institution financial companies. They argued that an administrative claims process modelled on the FDIA is too opaque and does not provide the same level of due process and judicial review as the US Bankruptcy Code. They also argued that the rules defining creditors' rights in the FDIA should not be used for the resolution of non-depository **8.245**

---

[388] See *supra* n 346.

[389] *On Systemic Regulation, Prudential Matters, Resolution Authority, and Securitization: Hearing before the H. Comm. on Financial Servs*, 111th Cong (2009) (testimony of Peter J Wallison, Arthur F Burns Fellow in Financial Policy Studies, American Enterprise Institute). See also Jonathan GS Koppell, Op-Ed: 'The Cloning of Fannie and Freddie', *Wall St J* (28 December 2009).

[390] Dodd-Frank Act, §§ 1101–1106.

[391] Dodd-Frank Act, § 210(o), 12 USC § 5390(o).

financial companies.[392] They asserted that using such rules would be inconsistent with provisions in the resolution authority statute which guarantee all creditors that they will receive the same recovery as they would have received in a liquidation under the US Bankruptcy Code.

8.246   In addition, critics asserted that the FDIA rules are deliberately designed to reinforce the priority of deposit creditors—a class of creditors that does not exist for non-depository institutions—over unsecured non-deposit creditors—a class of creditors that account for only a tiny portion of the balance sheets of most depository institutions. The rule allowing the FDIC to set aside security interests if they were taken 'in contemplation of insolvency' would also create a serious risk that otherwise perfected security interests may be set aside when applied to nonbank financial companies, thus causing secured credit to dry up during times of financial stress.

8.247   Instead, they argued that the resolution authority needed to be adapted so that it provides a more transparent claims process, additional judicial review, neutral rules governing creditors' rights, and protection of secured creditors rights modelled on the US Bankruptcy Code.[393]

8.248   Finally, they argued that unless the proposed resolution authority reflected a compromise between the FDIA and bankruptcy or other applicable insolvency models, it would have the unintended consequence of making our credit markets inefficient—creating uncertainty as to creditor treatment; increasing the cost and reducing the availability of credit to these financial companies, consumers, small businesses, and others in the system; slowing jobs growth; increasing unemployment; and causing liquidity to dry up during times of financial stress.[394]

8.249   Defenders of the bank resolution model for both the core resolution powers and the ancillary claims process countered that the right of *de novo* judicial review after the administrative claims process has been completed would provide adequate due process for creditor claims.[395] They argued that no significant difference in outcomes would arise between the FDIC's application of the rules defining creditors' rights in the FDIA and a typical bankruptcy court's application of the rules in the US Bankruptcy Code. As a result, they asserted that the unintended consequences are more feared than real.

8.250   Proponents of the bankruptcy model for the ancillary claims process had responses to each of these defences. First, they asserted that the administrative claims process under the FDIA was in fact more opaque and would provide far less due process and judicial review than a

---

[392] *Systemic Regulation, Prudential Matters, Resolution Authority and Securitization: Hearing before the H. Comm. on Financial Servs,* 111th Cong 21 (2009) (testimony of Scott Talbot, Senior Vice President for Government Affairs, Financial Services Roundtable).

[393] *Systemic Regulation, Prudential Matters, Resolution Authority and Securitization: Hearing before the H. Comm. on Financial Servs,* 111th Cong 2 (2009) (testimony of Philip L Swagel, Visiting Professor, McDonough School of Business).

[394] *Systemic Regulation, Prudential Matters, Resolution Authority and Securitization: Hearing before the H. Comm. on Financial Servs,* 111th Cong 4 (2009) (testimony of Scott Talbot, Senior Vice President for Government Affairs, Financial Services Roundtable).

[395] See *Too Big to Fail: The Role of Bankruptcy and Antitrust Law in Financial Regulation Reform: Hearing Before the Subcomm. on Commercial and Administrative law, H. Comm. on the Judiciary,* 111th Cong (2009) (testimony of Michael H Krimminger, Special Advisor for Policy, Federal Deposit Insurance Corporation).

bankruptcy process. Second, significant differences in outcomes would arise between the two sets of rules. Moreover, if no significant differences in outcomes really would arise, the FDIC should be required to apply the rules under the US Bankruptcy Code to avoid creating any legal uncertainty about the matter and to avoid any inconsistencies between the applicable rules and the minimum recovery guarantees in both the House and Senate versions.

Other defenders of the bank resolution model for both the core resolution powers and the ancillary claims process argued that if the rules governing creditors' rights in the proposed resolution authority would impose greater losses on creditors or subject them to greater legal uncertainty of recovery than the Bankruptcy Code, the rules would serve the important public policy purpose of further enhancing market discipline and reducing moral hazard.[396]   **8.251**

Proponents of the bankruptcy model argued that this argument seemed overwrought and ill-conceived, and was inconsistent with numerous provisions in Title II that were designed to ensure that creditors and other stakeholders would never fare worse in a Title II proceeding than they would in a bankruptcy proceeding.[397] For example, Title II cannot even be lawfully invoked unless resolution of the company under the US Bankruptcy Code would result in serious adverse effects on financial stability in the US *and* Title II would mitigate or avoid such adverse effects.[398] There is perhaps no better way to foster contagion and cause serious adverse effects on financial stability in the US than to use Title II in a manner that treats creditors and other stakeholders worse than they would have been treated in a bankruptcy proceeding. Thus, if Title II were used in this manner, the FDIC would have violated a fundamental condition for invoking it in the first place.[399]   **8.252**

They also argued that imposing greater losses on creditors than they would have suffered in a liquidation under the Bankruptcy Code is inconsistent with the minimum recovery provisions of Title II.[400] Moreover, the public policy goals in favour of market discipline and reducing moral hazard must be balanced against the important public policy goals of due process and fundamental fairness, and encouraging a healthy level of credit during normal times. Otherwise, Congress could deny all recovery to creditors even if some assets were available to satisfy all or part of their claims.   **8.253**

4. Funding

A significant policy discussion arose over who should bear the costs of failure of a systemically important financial company and whether an *ex ante* resolution fund should be   **8.254**

---

[396] *Systemic Regulation, Prudential Matters, Resolution Authority and Securitization: Hearing before the H. Comm. on Financial Servs*, 111th Cong 4–5 (2009) (testimony of Sheila Bair, Chairman, Federal Deposit Insurance Corporation).

[397] Dodd-Frank Act, § 210(a)(7)(B), (b)(4)(B), (d)(2)–(3), (h)(5)(E), 12 USC § 5390(a)(7)(B), (b)(4)(B), (d)(2)–(3), (h)(5)(E).

[398] Dodd-Frank Act, § 203(b)(2), (5), 12 USC § 5383(b)(2), (5).

[399] Comment Letter from the Securities Industry Association to the FDIC in Response to the FDIC's Notice of Proposed Rulemaking Implementing Certain Orderly Liquidation Authority Provisions of the Dodd-Frank Act (18 November 2010); Comment Letter from the Securities Industry Association to the FDIC in Response to the FDIC's Interim Final Rule Implementing Certain Orderly Liquidation Authority Provisions of the Dodd-Frank Act (24 February 2011).

[400] Dodd-Frank Act, § 210(a)(7)(B), (b)(4)(B), and (h)(5)(E)(ii), 12 USC § 5390(a)(7)(B), (b)(4)(B), and (h)(5)(E)(ii).

established to address future failures of systemically important institutions, or whether *ex post* funding would be more appropriate. While under the Dodd-Frank Act, Congress adopted an *ex post* funding model that attempts to impose the costs first on creditors of the failed institution and, to the extent of any shortfall, other large financial institutions, the debate over the proper approach for funding these liquidations is likely to continue.

8.255   As adopted, the Dodd-Frank Act gives the FDIC the power to recover liquidation costs, first, by clawing back any 'excess benefits' received by any claimants that received more in the resolution of a covered company than they would have received in a liquidation of the company under chapter 7 of the Bankruptcy Code.[401] To prevent this power from being destabilizing, the FDIC has the discretion to recoup any excess benefits over an extended period of time, instead of imposing immediate haircuts on creditors. If the FDIC is not able to recover all of its costs in this manner, it may recover any shortfall by imposing assessments on certain large US financial companies. To meet short-term funding needs in connection with a resolution, the FDIC is empowered to borrow from the US Treasury.[402]

8.256   The first aspect of this debate is who should bear the costs of failure. Many argued that the costs should be imposed on the large, complex financial institutions that ultimately might have to be resolved under the new authority. Critics questioned whether it was appropriate to impose the cost of the new resolution authority on the targeted pool of large companies. The direct beneficiaries of the financial assistance would not be these companies, except to the extent that they were among the creditors or counterparties whose claims are assumed by a third party or bridge financial company pursuant to the FDIC's exercise of its core resolution powers. Instead, the direct beneficiaries would be the creditors and counterparties whose claims are assumed. To the extent the transfer of these claims helps to stabilize the financial system, the indirect beneficiaries would be everyone who benefits from financial stability.

8.257   Critics also argued that unless the creditors and counterparties whose claims would be assumed bear the cost of the financial assistance, they would in fact be insulated from losses, undermining market discipline and creating a degree of moral hazard that would not exist if all US financial companies were resolved under the Bankruptcy Code or other applicable insolvency law.[403] On the other hand, if there were to be some form of clawback from these creditors and counterparties equal to the difference between what they would have received in a bankruptcy liquidation and what they actually received because of the third party assumption of liabilities, it might undo the stabilization benefits of giving the FDIC the power to transfer the claims.

8.258   As noted, the Dodd-Frank Act attempted to resolve this policy issue by giving the FDIC power to recover its costs, first, by recouping any 'excess benefits' from any claimants who received more in the resolution than they would have received in a liquidation under chapter 7 of the Bankruptcy Code and, secondly, from large financial companies.[404] Only

---

[401] Dodd-Frank Act, § 210(o), 12 USC § 5390(o).

[402] Dodd-Frank Act, § 210(n), 12 USC § 5390(n).

[403] Peter J Wallison, Task Force Report, Financial Reform Project, Pew Economic Policy Group, Briefing Paper No 4: *The Argument Against a Government Resolution Authority* (2009) 8–9.

[404] Dodd-Frank Act, § 210(o), 12 USC § 5390(o).

time will tell whether such a clawback power can be exercised in a way that is consistent with promoting financial stability or whether it will have a destabilizing effect by creating an incentive for short-term creditors to 'run' at the slightest hint of financial trouble.

A vigorous debate has also arisen over whether the tax to recover these costs should be **8.259** imposed before or after the resolution authority is exercised. The principal argument advanced in favour of an *ex ante* tax is that an *ex post* tax would allow the companies that are resolved to escape bearing any of the cost of their own resolution. The principal arguments advanced against an *ex ante* tax and in favour of an *ex post* tax are (i) it is impossible to know whether the resolution authority will ever be used or how much it will cost if used, and (ii) the creation of a fund makes it more likely the fund will be put to use by placing an entity into resolution under this authority, and creating an incentive on the part of the government to bail out creditors and counterparties rather than using the claw-back procedure to impose the costs of failure on those creditors and counterparties.

5. Who should be the resolving agency?

Under the Dodd-Frank Act, the FDIC must be appointed as the receiver for all covered **8.260** financial companies, except for insurance companies. The FDIC would be required to consult with the state or federal regulators of a covered financial company in carrying out its functions as receiver.[405] The FDIC is required to prepare an orderly liquidation plan acceptable to the Treasury Secretary before it could borrow any funds to cover its resolution costs.[406] It would not be permitted to take any action inconsistent with this plan without the Treasury Secretary's consent. But otherwise, nothing would require the FDIC to follow the direction of any other regulator.

Until recently, the FDIC had little to no experience with the type of large, complex, and **8.261** global financial institutions that would be the subject of the new resolution authority. Its supervisory experience was limited to community banks and other relatively small IDIs. Although the FDIC had resolved at least one relatively large savings association (Washington Mutual),[407] that savings association had relatively simple and purely US domestic activities compared to the more complex, cross-border operations of the core targets of the new resolution authority, and that institution was resolved in such a way as to minimize FDIC involvement as essentially all assets were transferred to a single institution buyer.

Given the FDIC's lack of experience, a debate ensued over the degree of autonomy the **8.262** FDIC should be granted as it handled the resolution of a large, complex financial institution. Many argued that some form of oversight board should be formed, consisting of the Treasury Secretary, the Chairman of the Federal Reserve, the Chairperson of the FDIC, and the primary federal regulator of the company being resolved.[408] The FDIC would carry out the resolution powers under the new authority, subject to the direction of this

---

[405] Dodd-Frank Act, § 204(c), 12 USC § 5384(c).

[406] Dodd-Frank Act, § 210(n)(9), 12 USC § 5390(n)(9).

[407] Washington Mutual had total assets of US $309 billion as of 30 June 2008. See Washington Mutual, Inc, Quarterly Report on Form 10-K for quarterly period ended 30 June 2008.

[408] See *Systemic Regulation, Prudential Matters, Resolution Authority and Securitization: Hearing before the H Comm. on Financial Servs*, 111th Cong (2009) (testimony of T Timothy Ryan, Jr, President and CEO, Securities Industry and Financial Markets Association).

oversight board. They proposed that the oversight board would also be the rule-making authority under the proposed resolution authority and be responsible for international coordination.

8.263 In the end, none of these proposals was enacted. After the passage of Title II, the FDIC made substantial efforts to increase its experience with G-SIBs. It established a new Office of Complex Financial Institutions. It reviewed comment letters from the private sector,[409] and participated in a series of public/private workshops about how to use its new authority to resolve G-SIBs. As a product of these comment letters and workshops, it developed its SPOE recapitalization within resolution strategy for resolving US G-SIBs under Title II. The SPOE strategy has since been widely praised or endorsed as the most promising strategy for resolving G-SIBs in a manner that will promote financial stability without the need for taxpayer-funded bailouts.[410] The FDIC has now had several years to review dozens of resolution plans submitted by some of the largest and most complex G-SIBs under section 165(d) of the Dodd-Frank Act and the FDIC's rules for IDIs.[411]

6. Mandatory rule making

8.264 The FDIC does not have a history of transparency in providing *ex ante* legal certainty on how ambiguities in the FDIA are to be resolved. Although it has permissive rule-making authority under the FDIA, it has rarely exercised that authority. It has also been very sparing in providing other forms of legal guidance, including policy statements, general counsel opinions, and other interpretations. In addition, all of these sources of legal guidance may be withdrawn by the FDIC at any time with, or in some cases without, notice.

8.265 Further, FDIC receiverships are handled primarily within the FDIC, with little judicial oversight or review. This is to be contrasted with the US Bankruptcy Code, where there are extensive statutes, rules, and procedures, and a well-developed body of case law. Further, in a bankruptcy proceeding, the judge is directly involved, providing significant and substantial oversight.

8.266 To counter this culture and tradition, the Dodd-Frank Act includes mandatory rule-making authority, with the requirement that the FDIC use its authority to further harmonize the rules governing creditors' rights with those in the Bankruptcy Code.[412]

7. Valuation issues

8.267 Neither the new resolution authority nor any of its earlier versions has included any specific procedures for ensuring that the FDIC obtains the highest possible price for any assets and liabilities sold or transferred pursuant to its exercise of core resolution powers, or assigns

---

[409] Joint Comment Letter from the Securities Industry and Financial Markets Association and The Clearing House Association in Response to FDIC's Second Notice of Proposed Rulemaking under Title II of the Dodd-Frank Act (23 May 2011) (advocating recapitalization within resolution under Title II); Certain Orderly Liquidation Authority Provisions under Title II of the Dodd-Frank Wall Street Reform and Consumer Protection Act (Final Rule), 76 Fed Reg 41626, 41634–41635 (15 July 2011) (FDIC praising the joint comment letter from SIFMA and TCH 'as an example of the value generated by constructive dialogue between the private financial markets and the federal government on topics such as this one').

[410] Guynn, *supra* n 26.

[411] See Title I and IDI Resolution Plans, available at: <https://www.fdic.gov/regulations/reform/resplans/>.

[412] Dodd-Frank Act, § 209, 12 USC § 5389.

a fair value to what the assets would have been worth in a liquidation under chapter 7 of the Bankruptcy Code. Because the amount received for such assets and liabilities, and the value placed on those assets as if they had been liquidated under the Bankruptcy Code, has a direct relationship to the size of the minimum recovery rights of left-behind claimants, the law may eventually need to be amended to include some incentives and procedures, as well as judicial review, to ensure that the FDIC does not sell any assets or liabilities at below the maximum value possible over some reasonable time period or assigns an artificially low value to what the assets would have been worth in a hypothetical liquidation under the Bankruptcy Code.

8. Practical remedy for minimum recovery rights?

The Dodd-Frank Act also lacks a clear and practical remedy for left-behind claimants **8.268** who believe they did not receive their minimum recovery entitlement in a resolution proceeding (ie the amount they would have received in a liquidation under chapter 7 of the US Bankruptcy Code, at least if they were treated differently from similarly situated creditors). Each such claimant has the implied right to bring a separate proceeding in federal court to recover the shortfall from the FDIC. But the cost of such individual proceedings could be prohibitive and exceed the shortfall amount. The policy issue is whether to provide aggrieved parties with an express right to a collective proceeding in a single federal district court after the termination of the receivership. Proponents argued that such a collective proceeding, or just the threat of such a proceeding, would 'keep the FDIC honest' in carrying out its duty to make sure all left-behind claimants receive what they would have received in a liquidation under chapter 7 of the Bankruptcy Code. It would also give them a practical remedy if the FDIC violated its trust. Critics argued that the FDIC is a federal agency that can be trusted to carry out its statutory duties responsibly, and that a collective proceeding could subject the FDIC to unnecessary litigation costs.

9. Haircuts on secured claims?

Early in the process of considering the new resolution authority, the FDIC argued for a **8.269** provision that would have given the FDIC the discretionary authority to impose a 10 per cent haircut on certain secured claims (other than those of certain favoured creditors like the Federal Reserve), effectively turning 10 per cent of an otherwise secured claim into an unsecured claim. While incorporated into the House Bill, neither the Senate Bill nor the final legislation included such a provision. Proponents argued that such a haircutting power would be an appropriate way to help the FDIC recoup its resolution costs. Perhaps more importantly, they argued that exposing a portion of a secured claim to unsecured risk would increase the incentive of the secured creditor to monitor its debtor and create greater market discipline. In the absence of such risk, proponents argued, secured creditors would not adequately monitor their debtors. Critics of the proposal vigorously argued that this power would reduce the supply of secured credit and increase its cost. Secured creditors would respond by exiting the market or reducing the term of their credit to overnight or intraday periods in order to be able to 'run' at the slightest sign of trouble. It would also make secured creditors unwilling to provide credit during a financial crisis, at the very time when any liquidity—even secured liquidity—is most needed from the private sector. It could transform central banks from lenders of last resort during a financial crisis to the only willing lenders during a financial crisis.

8.270   As noted, the final legislation did not incorporate the haircut provision. However, it required the Financial Stability Oversight Council to prepare a report for Congress on whether haircuts 'could improve market discipline and protect taxpayers'.[413] The Financial Stability Oversight Council submitted its report to Congress in July of 2011.[414] The report concluded that haircuts on secured credit were unnecessary.

10. Extend automatic stay to QFCs

8.271   A final policy issue is whether to impose a stay on the ability of counterparties on QFCs to exercise their close-out rights (liquidate collateral, etc) upon the insolvency of a covered financial company. Such counterparties are exempt from the automatic stay under the US Bankruptcy Code. They are subject to a one-business-day stay under the FDIA and the new resolution authority.[415] This one-business-day stay is designed to give the FDIC time to decide whether to repudiate or transfer a failed institution's QFCs to a third party or bridge bank, or simply to allow the counterparties to exercise their close-out rights. The Conference Base Text would have imposed a three-business-day stay, and earlier versions of the Senate Bill would have imposed a five-business-day stay. The House Bill would have imposed only a one-business-day stay.

8.272   Some commentators argued for an indefinite stay. They contended that the exemption of QFCs from an automatic stay is a major source of instability when a financial institution fails.[416] During the debate of the Senate Bill, Senator Nelson proposed an amendment that would have eliminated the exemption for QFCs from the automatic stay under the Bankruptcy Code and subject them to a 90-day stay under the new resolution authority.

8.273   Critics countered that such a rule would be far from stabilizing when looked at from an *ex ante* point of view, rather than *ex post*. They argued that the prospect of an automatic stay would destabilize the derivatives markets, reduce the supply of credit including repurchase agreement credit, and increase its cost. QFC counterparties would seek to protect themselves from such a rule by reducing the term of their QFCs to the shortest term possible (including overnight or even intraday) in order to facilitate a 'run' at the slightest hint of financial trouble.[417]

---

[413] Dodd-Frank Act, § 216.

[414] Report to the Congress on Secured Creditor Haircuts (July 2011).

[415] Dodd-Frank Act, § 210(c)(10), 12 USC § 5390(c)(10).

[416] See, eg, Thomas Jackson and David Skeel, Op-Ed: 'Bankruptcy Reform Will Limit Bailouts', *Wall St J* (21 April 2010).

[417] Professors Mark Roe and Stephen Adams also argued that both the current safe harbours in the US Bankruptcy Code and their outright repeal would result in value destruction and thus be suboptimal from a public policy perspective. In contrast, they argued that a temporary stay of 10 days (with a possible extension of another 10 days) on the right to close out QFCs, together with the express authority to break up a derivatives book and sell it along product lines (eg, interest rate swaps, foreign currency swaps, etc), would maximize the value of a failed institution's derivatives book. Mark J Roe and Stephen D Adams, 'Restructuring Failed Financial Firms in Bankruptcy: Selling Lehman's Derivatives Portfolio' (2015) 32 *Yale J on Reg* 363. The authors do not provide a persuasive reason, however, why a derivatives book could not be broken up and sold along product lines pursuant to an SPOE recapitalization within resolution strategy under the US Bankruptcy Code or Title II of the Dodd-Frank Act where the operating subsidiaries (which are the counterparties on virtually all QFCs) remain open and operating.

C. Single-Point-of-Entry Strategy

The most significant development since the enactment of Title II has been the FDIC's de-   **8.274**
velopment of its SPOE recapitalization within resolution strategy for resolving US G-SIBs
under Title II.[418] The strategy has also been proposed for resolutions of US G-SIBs under
the US Bankruptcy Code outside Title II, as discussed in section V.D. The SPOE strategy
has been widely recognized as the most promising solution to the 'too big to fail' problem[419]
since it was first publicly announced by then-acting FDIC Chairman Martin Gruenberg in
May 2012.[420]

Under the SPOE strategy, the FDIC would put the top-tier parent of a failing US G-SIB into   **8.275**
a receivership under Title II.[421] It would immediately set up a bridge financial company and
transfer all of the parent's assets, including its operating subsidiaries, to the bridge. It would
leave behind in the parent's receivership all of the equity interests in and long-term unsecured debt and other unsecured liabilities of the parent, except for an immaterial amount
of essential operating liabilities. Essential operating liabilities assumed by the bridge would
include obligations to pay rent and utilities, guarantees of operating subsidiary liabilities,
and derivatives used to hedge the bridge's ongoing treasury operations. The FDIC would
keep the parent's operating subsidiaries open and operating, and out of insolvency or other
resolution proceedings. A step-by-step graphical illustration of how the SPOE strategy
works is contained in a report by the Failure Resolution Taskforce of the Bipartisan Policy
Center.[422]

The FDIC would recapitalize the business transferred to the bridge by leaving behind in the   **8.276**
parent's receivership enough long-term unsecured debt and other unsecured liabilities to
ensure that the bridge is well capitalized. It would recapitalize any undercapitalized operating subsidiaries by forgiving any of their intercompany debt liabilities to the parent, including deposit liabilities, or contributing parent assets to the operating subsidiaries where
needed. It would borrow whatever it needed from the US Treasury to provide the bridge
and its operating subsidiaries with sufficient liquidity to convert their illiquid assets into
cash. It would provide liquidity in accordance with the classic principles established by
Walter Bagehot, namely only to solvent entities on a fully secured basis at above-market
interest rates. The bridge and its operating subsidiaries would be more than solvent—they
would all be well capitalized as a result of implementing the recapitalization within resolution strategy.

Because US G-SIBs are required by the Federal Reserve's TLAC Rule to maintain minimum   **8.277**
levels of TLAC in the form of regulatory capital and long-term unsecured debt at their top-
tier holding companies and hold virtually all of their demand deposit liabilities and other
short-term unsecured debt at their operating subsidiaries, their long-term unsecured debt

---

[418] See FDIC, Public Notice and Request for Comments, 'Resolution of Systemically Important Financial
Institutions: The Single Point of Entry Strategy', 78 Fed Reg 76614 (8 December 2013).
[419] Guynn, *supra* n 26 at 282.
[420] Remarks by Martin J Gruenberg, Acting Chairman, FDIC, to the Federal Reserve Bank of Chicago Bank
Structure Conference (10 May 2012).
[421] See FDIC, Public Notice, *supra* n 418.
[422] BPC Report, *supra* n 20, at 23–31.

will be structurally subordinate to their demand deposits and other short-term unsecured debt. This structural subordination has been reinforced by secured support agreements that all of the US G-SIBs have entered into as part of their resolution planning processes. These secured support agreements pledge virtually all of the financial assets of their top-tier parent holding companies, intermediate holding companies or funding vehicles to secure the obligations of their operating subsidiaries.

8.278   Because of the Federal Reserve's TLAC Rule, the US G-SIBs should have enough regulatory capital and long-term unsecured debt to be recapitalized at fully phased in Basel III levels if they run out of all their required regulatory capital,[423] and there is very little risk that demand deposits or other short-term unsecured debt would suffer any losses. As a result, the FDIC should be able to use the SPOE strategy to resolve US G-SIBs in a manner that will maximize the residual value of the US G-SIB for the benefit of its stakeholders yet should stem runs and contagion[424] and otherwise preserve financial stability without the need for a taxpayer-funded bailout.

8.279   The FDIC would then conduct a claims process for the equity interests, long-term unsecured debt, and other liabilities left behind in the parent's receivership. After it had identified, validated, and determined the amount of all allowed claims after a six- to nine-month process, and the value of the bridge and its operating subsidiaries will have stabilized and they could satisfy all of their liquidity needs from the private sector, the FDIC would distribute the residual value of the bridge to the claims left behind in the parent's receivership in accordance with the priority of their claims and in satisfaction of their claims. The FDIC has various options as far as the form of value it could distribute. It could do a public offering of the bridge's equity and distribute the net proceeds to the receivership. It could distribute shares in the bridge to the receivership. Or it could distribute a combination of shares and the net proceeds from a partial public offering of the bridge's shares. Once a majority of the bridge's shares are sold to a trust in return for a promise to sell the shares to the public and distribute the net proceeds of the shares to the parent's receivership, the bridge should cease to be a bridge and its charter should be converted to that of an ordinary private-sector entity.[425]

8.280   The overarching benefit of the SPOE method is that only the parent holding company is put into a receivership; the operating subsidiaries remain open and operating. This is important for several reasons. If the financial institution in question has cross-border operations, including foreign branches, the transfer of any assets of the branches is generally unenforceable or prohibited without the consent of foreign counterparties, foreign regulators, or foreign courts. SPOE avoids the need for those consents. It reduces or eliminates the incentive for foreign regulators to ring-fence the foreign branches of operating subsidiaries, which are kept open and operating, and reduces the need for the FDIC to rely on cooperation from foreign authorities.

---

[423] Statement of Randall D Guynn, Hearing Before the Subcomm on Fin Inst and Consumer Protection, S Comm on Banking, Fin and Urban Affairs (29 June 2015) Exhibit F.
[424] Contagion, *supra* n 4.
[425] Dodd-Frank Act, § 210(h)(13) and (14), 12 USC § 5390(h)(13) and (14).

Another benefit is that by taking advantage of the structural subordination of long-term **8.281** unsecured debt to short-term unsecured debt and exercising its authority to stay the termination of QFCs with performing counterparties, the SPOE strategy reduces or eliminates the incentive of demand depositors or other short-term creditors to run and the right of derivatives counterparties to terminate. This reduces or eliminates the likelihood of contagious panic throughout the financial system. Meanwhile, the orderly liquidation fund ensures that the bridge financial company will have access to sufficient secured liquidity to preserve going-concern value and prevent value destruction of valuable but illiquid assets.

D. Resolution Under the US Bankruptcy Code

Despite the enactment of Title II of the Dodd-Frank Act, the US Bankruptcy Code remains **8.282** the principal law under which nonbank financial companies are to be liquidated, recapitalized, or reorganized when they fail. Title II is only lawfully permitted to be invoked if resolution of a covered company would result in serious adverse effects to financial stability in the United States and Title II would avoid or mitigate those adverse effects.[426]

1. Existing US Bankruptcy Code
The US G-SIBs recently submitted their Title I resolution plans for 2021. All of them in- **8.283** dicated in the public summaries of their plans that they believed they could be resolved under chapter 11 of the existing US Bankruptcy Code pursuant to an SPOE recapitalization strategy.[427] They identified the strategy as the one most likely to enable them to be resolved in a rapid and orderly manner without extraordinary government support and without imposing serious adverse effects on financial stability in the US. Under this strategy, only the top-tier parent would be put into a bankruptcy proceeding. Most of the assets of the parent, including its ownership interests in all of its operating subsidiaries, would be transferred to a newly formed bridge company pursuant to section 363 of the US Bankruptcy Code. The failed parent's long-term unsecured debt would be left behind in the bankruptcy estate. The largely debt-free bridge holding company would be held by a trust for the benefit of the bankruptcy estate. Its shares would be sold in public or private sales or transferred to the parent's bankruptcy estate for distribution under a plan of reorganization in accordance with the priority of claims and interests in the bankruptcy case. Some or all of the operating subsidiaries would be recapitalized and remain open and operating, though they would shrink by more than half as a by-product of the SPOE strategy.[428] Others would be sold or wound down in an orderly fashion outside insolvency proceedings (ie, a solvent wind-down).[429]

---

[426] Dodd-Frank Act, § 203(b)(2) and (5), 12 USC § 5383(b)(2).
[427] Board of Governors of the Federal Reserve System, 'Living Wills (or Resolution Plans)' (2021), available at: <http://www.federalreserve.gov/bankinforeg/resolution-plans.htm>.
[428] See, eg, JP Morgan Chase & Co., '2021 Targeted Resolution Plan Public Filing' (2021), 22–24, available at: <https://www.jpmorganchase.com/content/dam/jpmc/jpmorgan-chase-and-co/investor-relations/documents/events/2021/resolution-plan-2021/resolution-plan-2021.pdf>.
[429] See, eg, Citigroup Inc., '2021 Resolution Plan: Public Section' (1 July 2021), 6–7, available at: <https://www.federalreserve.gov/supervisionreg/resolution-plans/citigroup-1g-20210701.pdf>.

8.284   The Failure Resolution Taskforce of the Bipartisan Policy Center issued a report showing how an SPOE recapitalization strategy could be carried out under chapter 11 of the existing US Bankruptcy Code.[430] But it also argued in favour of a proposed new chapter 14 in order to make that outcome more legally certain and to minimize the need to use Title II of the Dodd-Frank Act in order to avoid or mitigate serious adverse effects on financial stability in the US.[431]

2. Proposed new chapter 14

8.285   In 2012, a working group at Stanford University's Hoover Institute proposed a new chapter 14 of the US Bankruptcy Code.[432] The purpose of new chapter 14 was either to replace Title II of the Dodd-Frank Act or minimize the circumstances under which Title II could be lawfully invoked.[433] As noted above, Title II may only be lawfully invoked if the resolution of a particular nonbank financial company under the US Bankruptcy Code would result in serious adverse effects to financial stability in the United States and the use of Title II would avoid or mitigate those effects.[434] The proponents of new chapter 14 believed that it would be more consistent with the rule of law than the Orderly Liquidation Authority in Title II of the Dodd-Frank Act and more likely to result in losses being imposed on the private sector instead of taxpayers.

8.286   The original version of proposed chapter 14 defined 'financial institution' as any institution, including any subsidiaries, with $100 billion or more in assets 'that is substantially engaged in providing financial services or financial products'.[435] However, while the original version of chapter 14 would apply to insurance companies, stock brokers, and commodity brokers, it would not extend to IDIs.[436]

8.287   The proposal greatly expanded the role of the failed institution's primary regulator. It granted the primary regulator standing to be heard as a party or to raise motions relevant to its regulations in any chapter 14 proceeding.[437] Moreover, to address potential systemic consequences from the failure, the primary regulator would be empowered to commence an involuntary case against the institution, including on the grounds of mark-to-market balance sheet insolvency or 'unreasonably small capital'.[438] The primary regulator would also have standing to file motions for a quick sale of the failed company or any of its assets under section 363 of the Bankruptcy Code subject to court review.[439] Finally, the primary regulator would be empowered to file a plan of reorganization for the institution at any time after the order for relief.[440]

---

[430] BPC Report, *supra* n 20, at 33–35 (describing how an SPOE recapitalization strategy could be carried out under Chapter 11 of the existing US Bankruptcy Code).

[431] Ibid, 80, 87.

[432] Original Ch 14, *supra* n 21.

[433] Scott, *supra* n 45 at 23.

[434] Dodd-Frank Act, § 203(b)(2) and (5), 12 USC § 5383(b)(2) and (5).

[435] Original Ch 14, *supra* n 21 at 4.

[436] Ibid, 10–13.

[437] Ibid, 13–15.

[438] Ibid.

[439] Ibid, 16–17.

[440] The order for relief occurs upon filing in a voluntary case and after a court order in a contested involuntary petition. Ibid, 21–22.

Another major element of the original proposal would be to permit the debtor-in-posses- **8.288**
sion (DIP), through DIP financing provided by the government or the private sector, to
'advance' a partial or complete payout to certain liquidity-sensitive creditors before final
distribution. These payouts would be subject to court approval and several burden of proof
requirements, including showing that the payout is necessary either for liquidity or systemic reasons, that the payout is less than a conservative estimate of the creditors' likely
eventual payout, and that such prepayment is not likely to favour particular creditors. If the
government provides the funding, the petitioners for such funding must show that no private funding on reasonably comparable terms is available.[441]

The proposal also directly addressed longstanding concerns over a lack of judicial experi- **8.289**
ence and political pressure in bankruptcy proceedings, specifically those involving large
financial institutions. Here, the proposal required chapter 14 cases to be heard by a panel
of Article III district court judges in the Second and DC Circuits who have been selected
by the Chief Justice of the United States.[442] The idea is that the quality of US Article III
judges would, on average, be higher than that of US bankruptcy judges and that Article III
judges would be more resistant to political pressure because unlike bankruptcy judges they
have life tenure.[443] These Article III judges would have exclusive jurisdiction along with the
power to appoint a special master from a pre-designated panel to hear the case and all proceedings under it that could normally have been heard by a bankruptcy judge.[444]

3. Proposed chapter 14 2.0

Largely in response to the development of the SPOE recapitalization within resolution **8.290**
strategy under Title II of the Dodd-Frank Act, the Hoover group updated and expanded
its original chapter 14 proposal to include provisions that would facilitate an SPOE strategy
under the US Bankruptcy Code, calling this updated version chapter 14 2.0.[445]

The most significant change in chapter 14 2.0 is the 'section 1405 transfer' provision that **8.291**
would expressly authorize the 'quick sale' of a covered company's assets to a newly created
bridge financial company, while leaving behind in the bankruptcy estate all or any portion
of the covered company's liabilities.[446] By leaving enough liabilities behind in the bankruptcy estate, such a quick sale to a bridge financial company would result in the recapitalization of the business transferred to the bridge financial company. Professor Jackson, the
author of chapter 14 2.0, calls this technique the 'two-entity' recapitalization strategy, but he
notes that it is substantially identical to the FDIC's SPOE strategy.[447] At the core of this two-
entity recapitalization technique lie two principles: (i) that sufficient long-term unsecured
debt must exist to be 'left behind' in the bankruptcy estate; and (ii) that the bridge company
otherwise owns the assets, rights, and liabilities of the former holding company.[448]

---

[441] Ibid, 47–48.
[442] Article III judges are those who have been appointed under Article III of the US Constitution. District court
judges are appointed under Article III. Bankruptcy judges are not.
[443] Bankruptcy judges are appointed for 14-year terms. 28 USC § 152.
[444] Original Ch 14, *supra* n 21 at 7–10.
[445] See Jackson, *supra* n 31.
[446] Jackson, *supra* n 31 at 30–31.
[447] Ibid, 19–20, 23.
[448] Ibid, 39.

8.292   The section 1405 transfer allows either the institution or the Federal Reserve to make a motion to transfer the estate's property, contracts, and liabilities other than capital structure debt[449] to the newly created bridge company. The section 1405 transfer motion must be heard no sooner than 24 hours after its filing, and the court must rule within 48 hours after its filing. The court may approve the section 1405 transfer only upon finding (or the Federal Reserve certifying that it found) that 'the bridge company adequately provides assurance of future performance of any executory contract, unexpired lease, or debt agreement being transferred'.[450] Although the bridge company is not generally subject to the jurisdiction of the chapter 14 judge subsequent to the transfer, upon application by the bridge company, the judge does retain jurisdiction for up to six months to award financing on terms applicable to DIP financing in section 1413.[451]

8.293   The SPOE provisions of chapter 14 2.0 contain rules applicable to debts, executory contracts, and unexpired leases—including QFCs. Thus, these assets and liabilities may successfully be transferred to or assumed by the bridge company within the 48-hour window and remain there so 'business as usual' is taken over by the bridge company upon assumption.[452] Specifically, this requires overriding certain contractual provisions regarding change of control, as well as 'ipso facto' clauses allowing the termination or modification of contracts based on the commencement of a bankruptcy proceeding or a deterioration in the financial condition of the covered company, including ratings downgrades.[453] Chapter 14 2.0 would also modify the 'safe harbors' for QFCs that would otherwise allow the immediate termination of QFCs of the covered company. These modifications and overrides would allow a bridge company to assume debt, executory contracts (including QFCs), and unexpired leases 'as if nothing happened' as opposed to it having been breached and accelerated. Importantly, they would apply equally with respect to contracts held by subsidiaries that are transferred to the bridge company.[454] As the newly created bridge company will by definition have no long-term unsecured debt, chapter 14 2.0 provides the bridge company a window during which it need not be in compliance with certain long-term unsecured debt requirements, such as those included in the Federal Reserve's TLAC Rule.[455] This window terminates at the earlier of either: (i) confirmation of the debtor's plan of reorganization that involves the distribution of securities (or proceeds from sales) of the bridge company; or (ii) one year from the section 1405 transfer.[456]

8.294   In addition to the section 1405 transfer provision, chapter 14 2.0 would make other significant changes to the initial chapter 14 proposal. The definition of 'covered financial corporation' is revised to include institutions with consolidated assets of more than $50 billion, other than bank (subject to FDIC resolution), stockbroker, or commodity broker subsidiaries. The definition expressly excludes 'financial market infrastructure corporations' such

---

[449] Ibid, 43.
[450] Ibid, 32–33.
[451] Ibid, 33.
[452] Ibid, 39.
[453] Ibid, 39–40. Note that this goes further than the existing US Bankruptcy Code under § 365, which lacks any provisions expressly allowing for the transfer of debt or the override of change of control provisions.
[454] Ibid, 42–43.
[455] Financial Stability Board, *Consultative Document, Adequacy of loss-absorbing capacity of global systemically important banks in resolution* (10 November 2014).
[456] Jackson, *supra* n 31 at 43–44.

as central counterparty clearinghouses.[457] Also, the new version of chapter 14 would require at least one district court judge in each circuit to be selected by the Chief Justice of the United States for chapter 14 cases. Those cases that involve a section 1405 transfer need only be handled by the designated judge up to the point of transfer, and the designated judge may appoint a bankruptcy judge to assist as special master.[458]

The role of the regulators would differ significantly in chapter 14 2.0. If the Federal Reserve   **8.295** determines, after consultation with the Secretary of the Treasury and the FDIC, that commencement of a chapter 14 case is 'necessary to avoid serious adverse effects on the financial stability of the United States', it may file a petition on behalf of the company that is equivalent to a voluntary petition. The Federal Reserve and the primary regulator would retain their standing from the initial proposal to be heard on any issue relevant to the regulation of the institution and the Federal Reserve also has standing to be heard on any issue affecting 'the financial stability of the United States'. The FDIC is granted more limited standing, relating solely to the opportunity to be heard in a section 1405 transfer.[459]

4. Financial Institutions Bankruptcy Act

On 1 December 2014, the US House of Representatives passed the Financial Institutions   **8.296** Bankruptcy Act (FIBA), which would add a new subchapter V to existing chapter 11 of the US Bankruptcy Code.[460] FIBA resembles in many ways the SPOE provisions of chapter 14 2.0. The House introduced a new bill in 2015 that is substantially identical to the 2014 bill.[461] Like the SPOE portion of chapter 14 2.0, this bill was designed primarily to facilitate an SPOE resolution strategy under the US Bankruptcy Code. In particular, it would expressly authorize the transfer of all or substantially all of the assets of a covered company to a new bridge company, while leaving all capital structure liabilities behind in the bankruptcy case.[462] In exchange, the debtor institution would retain a beneficial interest in the new bridge company through a private trust that holds the bridge company's equity, or sale proceeds thereof, for the benefit of the bankruptcy estate.[463]

FIBA applies to 'covered financial corporations', which mirror the 'covered financial com-   **8.297** panies' definition in Title II of the Dodd-Frank Act, and would include: (i) BHCs; and (ii) corporations that have total consolidated assets greater than $50 billion and are primarily engaged in financial activities, other than stockbrokers, commodity brokers, or institutions such as banks, insurance companies, and similar institutions that are not eligible to be debtors under the Bankruptcy Code.[464]

[457] Ibid, 44.

[458] Ibid, 46–47.

[459] Ibid, 38–39.

[460] Financial Institutions Bankruptcy Act of 2014, HR 5421, 113th Cong (2014) (as passed by the House on 8 December 2014). Statement of Donald S Bernstein, Partner, Davis Polk, in *Hearing Before The Subcomm on Regulatory Reform, Commercial and Antitrust Law, H. Comm. On Judiciary* (15 July 2014).

[461] Financial Institutions Bankruptcy Act of 2015, HR 2947, 114th Cong (2015) (as introduced in the House on 7 July 2015). Statements of Donald S Bernstein and Richard Levin, *Hearing Before Subcomm on Regulatory Reform, Commercial and Antitrust Law, H Comm On Judiciary* (9 July 2015).

[462] HR 2947, 114th Cong § 3 (2015) (§ 1185).

[463] HR 2947, 114th Cong § 3 (2015) (§ 1186).

[464] HR 2947, 114th Cong § 2(a) (2015).

8.298   Taken together, FIBA's provisions would accomplish four things: (i) expressly permit a quick transfer of a covered company's assets to a new bridge company; (ii) facilitate the recapitalization of the business transferred to the bridge by permitting the covered company to leave behind in the bankruptcy estate all capital structure debt;[465] (iii) impose certain restrictions on creditors' rights; and (iv) amend the 'safe harbors' for QFCs to impose a temporary 48-hour stay on the exercise of close-out rights and a permanent override of any cross-defaults based on the parent's or another affiliate's failure or financial condition, if certain conditions are satisfied.[466]

8.299   As proposed, FIBA authorizes the Federal Reserve to file an involuntarily case against a covered company if it shows that the commencement of the case and the transfer to a bridge company is necessary to prevent imminent substantial harm to financial stability in the United States.[467] Any dispute over an involuntary filing must be resolved within 24 hours after the petition is filed. Regulators, including the Federal Reserve, the SEC, the OCC, and the FDIC each have standing to appear and be heard on any issue in the case.[468] Finally, FIBA mandates that the Chief Justice of the Supreme Court designate at least 10 bankruptcy and at least 12 appellate court judges, three in each of four districts, to be available to hear cases under subchapter V.[469]

5. Taxpayer Protection and Responsible Resolution Act

8.300   The Taxpayer Protection and Responsible Resolution Act (TPRRA) was introduced in the Senate in December 2013.[470] A substantially revised version of TPRRA was reintroduced in 2015.[471] The new version is substantially similar to FIBA, except that it would add a new chapter 14 to the US Bankruptcy Code instead of a new subchapter V of chapter 11, repeal Title II of the Dodd-Frank Act, and impose restrictions on the Federal Reserve's authority to provide DIP financing to the covered company or the bankruptcy estate.[472] It also would not give the Federal Reserve a right to initiate an involuntary petition and would not impose a minimum dollar threshold on the definition of 'covered financial corporation'.

6. National Bankruptcy Conference

8.301   The National Bankruptcy Conference (NBC), a voluntary, non-partisan, not-for-profit organization composed of about 60 of the leading bankruptcy judges, professors, and practitioners in the US, wrote a letter commenting on FIBA and TPRRA.[473] While commending

---

[465] Defined as 'all unsecured debt of the debtor for borrowed money, other than a QFC, for which the debtor is the primary obligor ...'. See HR 2947, 114th Cong (2014) (§ 1182(3)).

[466] HR 2947, 114th Cong § 3 (2015) (§§ 1182(2), 1185, 1189, 1191).

[467] HR 2947, 114th Cong § 3 (2015) (§ 1183).

[468] HR 2947, 114th Cong § 3 (2015) (§ 1184).

[469] HR 2947, 114th Cong § 4 (2015).

[470] Taxpayer Protection and Responsible Resolution Act, S 1861, 113th Cong (2013).

[471] Taxpayer Protection and Responsible Resolution Act, S 1840, 114th Cong, 1st Sess (2015). Statements of Thomas H Jackson, Randall D Guynn, and John B Taylor, Hearing before the Subcomm on Fin Inst and Consumer Protection, S Comm on Banking, Fin and Urban Affairs (29 June 2015).

[472] S 1840, 114th Cong § 3, § 5, § 6 (2015).

[473] Letter dated 18 June 2015 from the NBC to the Honorable Tom Marino, Chairman, House Subcommittee on Regulatory Reform, Commercial and Antitrust Law; the Honorable Hank Johnson, Ranking Member, House Subcommittee on Regulatory Reform, Commercial and Antitrust Law; the Honorable Chuck Grassley, Chairman, Senate Committee on the Judiciary; and the Honorable Patrick J Leahy, Ranking Member, Senate Committee on the Judiciary.

both bills for facilitating the SPOE resolution strategy under the Bankruptcy Code, the NBC provided five comments:

- Title II of the Dodd-Frank Act should not be repealed.
- Regulators should have the power to continue supervising the operations of a systemically important financial institution (SIFI) being resolved in a bankruptcy case.
- Regulators should not be given the power to commence a bankruptcy case against a covered company.
- The legislation should not impose any limitations on the power of the Federal Reserve to provide lender-of-last-resort liquidity to a recapitalized firm.
- Bankruptcy judges should not be replaced by Article III district judges in bankruptcy cases for resolving SIFIs.

7. Treasury Report

In 2018, the US Treasury submitted a report to the President on Title II of the Dodd-Frank **8.302** Act and bankruptcy reform.[474] It concluded that Title II should not be repealed. Instead, it recommended that Title II be retained but amended to limit the FDIC's discretion in certain respects and make it more consistent with the rule of law. Treasury also recommended that Congress enact a new chapter 14 along the lines of the Hoover Institution's proposed chapter 14 2.0.

E. Resolution Planning

A resolution plan is a plan for liquidating, reorganizing, or otherwise resolving a systemic- **8.303** ally important financial institution (SIFI) that has reached the point of insolvency, non-viability, or failure. It is the last stage along the full continuum of contingency planning from risk management to early remediation to recovery planning to resolution planning that is sometimes referred to as a 'living will'.[475] Activating the resolution plan would be a last resort, when various *ex ante* solutions designed to reduce the likelihood of failure have been unsuccessful. Section 165(d) under Title I of the Dodd-Frank Act, as amended, requires all BHCs and foreign banking organizations with assets of $250 billion or more, as well as any nonbank financial institution that has been designated as systemically important, to prepare and regularly update a resolution plan (Title I Resolution Plan).[476] The amendments to section 165(d) under Title I of the Dodd-Frank Act also provided the Federal Reserve with the discretionary authority to apply the Title I Resolution Plan requirements to firms with $100 billion or more and less than $250 billion in total assets. In amending the rule implementing the Title I Resolution Plan requirements, the Federal Reserve exercised that discretion to also apply the Title I Resolution Plan requirements to BHCs and foreign

---

[474] US Treasury, Report to the President of the United States, 'Orderly Liquidation Authority and Bankruptcy Reform' (21 February 2018).

[475] The Federal Reserve and the FDIC have used the term 'living will' interchangeably with 'resolution plan'. See 76 US Fed Reg 67323, 67323 (1 November 2011).

[476] Dodd-Frank Act, § 165(d), 12 USC § 5365(d), as amended by the Economic Growth, Regulatory Relief, and Consumer Protection Act of 2018, § 401, Pub L No 115-174, 132 Stat 1296.

banking organizations that are Category II or Category III banking organizations under the Federal Reserve's Regulation YY.

8.304   The FDIC separately subjects all US IDIs with assets of $50 billion or more to a separate resolution plan (IDI Resolution Plan) requirement specific to resolving the IDI under the FDIA.[477] Although the two processes were designed to complement each other and the requirements for both have been substantially similar, there is a growing divergence between the two types of resolution plan.[478] In June 2021 the FDIC announced a modified approach to implementing its IDI Resolution Plan rule requirements that the FDIC characterized as 'an effort to provide greater utility in planning for a resolution' and 'focus[ed] on obtaining information necessary to inform [the FDIC's] ability to resolve [an IDI subject to the requirements] and on confirming that the [IDI] has the capability to provide the information and analyses required by the [IDI Resolution Plan rule]'.[479] As part of this focus on information and capabilities, the FDIC streamlined the content requirements and stated that it may require IDIs to undertake capabilities testing.[480]

8.305   The Title I Resolution Plans are required to be divided into a public section and a confidential section. The confidential section is more extensive than the public section and must include an executive summary, detailed information about organizational structure, resolution strategies, corporate governance, management information systems, interconnections and interdependencies, supervisory and regulatory issues, and contact information.[481] The public section is similar, but the description is meant to be significantly less detailed so that financial institutions can protect confidential proprietary and supervisory information.[482]

8.306   Most importantly, the Title I Resolution Plan must include specific information about the financial institution's resolution strategies, which is its plan for 'rapid and orderly resolution'.[483] This is defined as 'a reorganization or liquidation of the covered company ... under the Bankruptcy Code that can be accomplished within a reasonable period of time and in a manner that substantially mitigates the risk that the failure of the covered company would have serious adverse effects on financial stability in the United States'.[484] Under the implementing regulations, these resolution plans must assume that the covered company is resolved under the US Bankruptcy Code or other applicable insolvency law, and that no 'extraordinary support' from the US or any other government would be available. Each Title I Resolution Plan is also required to explain how it would work under the most recent 'baseline', 'adverse', and 'severely adverse' macroeconomic scenarios provided to the financial

---

[477]   12 CFR § 360.10. Although the rule applies to IDIs with at least $50 billion on in assets, on 25 June 2021 the FDIC announced a modified approach to how it would implement the IDI Resolution Plan rule which included a moratorium on IDI Resolution Plan submissions for IDIs with more than $50 billion but less than $100 billion in assets. FDIC, 'Statement on Resolution Plans for Insured Depository Institutions' (25 June 2021), available at: <https://www.fdic.gov/resauthority/idi-statement-06-25-2021.pdf>.

[478]   Randall D Guynn, 'Resolution Planning in the United States' in Patrick S Kenadjian (ed), *The Bank Recovery and Resolution Directive—Europe's Solution for 'Too Big to Fail'*? (2013).

[479]   FDIC, 'Statement on Resolution Plans for Insured Depository Institutions' (25 June 2021).

[480]   Ibid.

[481]   12 CFR § 243.5.

[482]   12 CFR § 243.11.

[483]   12 CFR § 243.5(c).

[484]   12 CFR § 243.2.

institution by the Federal Reserve in connection with the CCAR stress testing and capital planning process.[485]

Domestic financial institutions must include information for their worldwide operations, including material entities, critical operations, and core business lines.[486] 'Material entity' refers to a subsidiary or foreign office of the financial institution that is significant to the activities of a critical operation or core business line.[487] 'Critical operations' are the operations of the financial institution and its material entities, including associated services, functions and support, the failure or discontinuation of which, in the view of the financial institution or as jointly directed by the Federal Reserve and the FDIC, would pose a threat to the financial stability of the US.[488] 'Core business lines' means the business lines of the financial institution and its material entities, including associated operations, services, functions and support, that, in the view of the financial institution, upon failure would result in a material loss of revenue, profit, or franchise value.[489] For foreign banking organizations, the information is only required with respect to their operations that are domiciled or conducted in whole or in part in the US, along with information about any interconnections or interdependencies between the US and foreign operations, and how the US resolution plan is integrated into the organization's overall resolution or contingency planning process.   **8.307**

The IDI resolution plans have substantially similar requirements as Title I Plans, including a requirement to file public and confidential portions of the plans.[490] There are, however, important differences between the two types of plans, the most important of which relates to their objectives. The FDIC has indicated that the Title I Plans focus principally on financial stability, whereas the IDI Plans may focus on other objectives. In order to facilitate review of a financial institution's Title I Resolution Plan, the institution must provide the Federal Reserve and the FDIC with such information and access to personnel as the Federal Reserve and the FDIC jointly determine is necessary to assess the credibility of the plan and the ability of the financial institution to implement it. If the Federal Reserve and the FDIC jointly determine that the plan has one or more deficiencies, the financial institution must submit a revised resolution plan that addresses the deficiency no later than 90 days after receiving notice, unless the Federal Reserve and the FDIC jointly determine otherwise. If the regulators both decide that a Title I Resolution Plan is not credible, they must jointly notify the financial institution in writing of such a determination no later than 12 months after the plan was required to be submitted. Neither agency may unilaterally give such notice of deficiencies without the consent of the other.[491]   **8.308**

If the financial institution fails to cure the deficiency in its Title I Resolution Plan, the Federal Reserve and the FDIC may jointly impose on the institution, or any of its subsidiaries, more   **8.309**

---

[485]   12 CFR § 243.4(h)(1). See also Dodd-Frank Act, § 165(i)(1), 12 USC § 5365(i)(1); Board of Governors of the Federal Reserve System, '2021 Stress Test Scenarios' (February 2021).

[486]   12 CFR § 243.5(a)(1).

[487]   12 CFR § 243.2.

[488]   12 CFR § 243.2. Critical operations may be identified jointly by the Federal Reserve and FDIC or be self-identified by the institution. Each firm subject to the Title I Resolution Plan rule must have a process and methodology to identify each of its critical operations. 12 CFR § 243.3.

[489]   12 CFR § 243.2.

[490]   The FDIC has, however, streamlined the requirements for the confidential portions of the IDI Resolution Plans under the FDIC's modified approach to implementing the IDI Resolution Plan Rule.

[491]   12 CFR § 243.8(b).

stringent capital, leverage, or liquidity requirements or restrictions on growth, activities, or operations.[492] Any requirements or restrictions imposed in response to a failure to cure resolution plan deficiencies would apply until the date when the Federal Reserve and the FDIC jointly determine that the financial institution has submitted a revised resolution plan that adequately remedies the deficiencies.[493] If the financial institution fails to do so within the first two years following the imposition of such requirements, the financial institution would face the further threat of mandated divestitures (ie break-up).[494] There are conditions and procedures that the Federal Reserve and the FDIC must follow prior to making such determinations and neither agency may unilaterally act without the consent of the other. The regulations for the IDI Resolution Plan are not so specific in detailing the possible list of consequences for non-compliance.

8.310   Since 2015, the Federal Reserve and FDIC have jointly issued public feedback letters to institutions that submit Title I Resolution Plans, in which they identify progress that an institution has made since its prior submission and any shortcomings, deficiencies, or other areas for improvement that may not rise to the level of a shortcoming or deficiency.[495] In the feedback letters to the eight US G-SIBs on their 2019 Title I Resolution Plans, the Federal Reserve and FDIC determined that six of the plans contained shortcomings (generally related to governance mechanisms) and two did not; and no deficiencies were identified.[496] In 2018, the Federal Reserve and FDIC identified shortcomings in the resolution plan submissions of four large foreign banking organizations.[497]

8.311   The Federal Reserve and FDIC in 2019 amended the Title I Resolution Plan rule and issued new guidance for the resolution plans of the eight US G-SIBs, updating and superseding all prior guidance.[498] The Federal Reserve and FDIC also indicated that additional guidance on resolution capital and liquidity may be forthcoming. Similarly, in 2021 the FDIC announced a modified approach to implementing its IDI Resolution Plan rule.[499] The resolution planning guidelines and expectations of the Federal Reserve and FDIC will probably continue to evolve over time.

8.312   One of the key updates to both the Title I Resolution Plans and IDI Resolution Plans has been the formalization of an extended submission cycle as compared to the original rules. When the rules were initially adopted, annual submissions were required; however, an annual process was found to be impractical owing to the time needed to review the plans. As a

---

[492] 12 CFR § 243.9(a).

[493] 12 CFR § 243.9(b).

[494] 12 CFR § 243.9(c).

[495] These letters are available at: <https://www.federalreserve.gov/supervisionreg/agency-feedback-letters-index.htm>.

[496] Federal Reserve, FDIC, 'Agencies Find No Deficiencies in Resolution Plans from the Largest Banks; Find Shortcomings for Several Firms' (17 December 2019), available at: <https://www.federalreserve.gov/newsevents/pressreleases/bcreg20191217a.htm>.

[497] Federal Reserve, FDIC, 'Federal Reserve and FDIC Announce Resolution Plan Determinations for Four Foreign-Based Banks and Finalize Guidance for Eight Domestic Banks' (20 December 2018), available at: <https://www.federalreserve.gov/newsevents/pressreleases/bcreg20181220c.htm>.

[498] Federal Reserve and FDIC, 'Guidance for 2019 165(d) Resolution Plan Submissions by Domestic Covered Companies that Submitted Resolution Plans in July 2017', 84 Fed. Reg. 1438 (4 February 2019); Federal Reserve and FDIC, 'Resolution Plans Required' (1 November 2019), available at: <https://www.federalregister.gov/documents/2019/11/01/2019-23967/resolution-plans-required>.

[499] FDIC, *supra* n 479.

consequence, the amended Title I Resolution Plan rule has adopted a two-year submission cycle for the US G-SIBs and a three-year submission cycle for other institutions subject to the rule. The submissions alternate between full resolution plans and what are called 'targeted' resolution plans that contain a subset of the content of a full resolution plan, along with information responsive to any targeted information requests issued by the Federal Reserve and the FDIC.[500] As part of the FDIC's modified approach, it has divided the IDIs subject to the IDI Resolution Plan rule into two groups based on size and made each subject to a three-year cycle.[501]

VI. International Coordination of Cross-Border Resolutions

Many large US financial companies have international operations outside the US through a network of branches, offices, and subsidiaries. These branches, offices, and subsidiaries are generally subject to different insolvency laws or special resolution regimes in different jurisdictions. For a long time, there were no international agreements or arrangements that provided any overarching coordination if a major cross-border financial firm failed. Following the global financial panic of 2008, regulatory agencies in many jurisdictions turned their attention to making arrangements for a potential cross-border failure. If such arrangements are not put into place or turn out to be unsatisfactory, there is a fear that each jurisdiction will attempt to grab assets and control as much of the process as possible in order to protect its own citizens—perhaps beneficial for the residents of the country fortunate enough to have substantial assets within its boundaries, but perhaps not helpful in promoting global financial stability.

8.313

Under the Dodd-Frank Act, the FDIC is required to consult with the state and federal regulators of each covered financial company in exercising its powers as receiver.[502] The FDIC is also required to consult with the primary regulators for non-US subsidiaries and coordinate with them regarding the resolution of those entities.[503]

8.314

As part of its efforts to improve cross-border coordination of resolutions, the FDIC has contacted regulators in a number of foreign jurisdictions on an individual basis. In 2012, the FDIC released a joint paper with the Bank of England, 'Resolving Globally Active, Systemically Important, Financial Institutions'.[504] In the paper, the FDIC and the Bank of England expressed a commitment to developing an SPOE resolution strategy in both jurisdictions. As the paper notes, one advantage of the SPOE resolution strategy for cross-border coordination is that it does not require the commencement of separate territorial or entity-focused insolvency proceedings.[505] The financial firm's home jurisdiction would oversee a resolution of the top entity while its foreign subsidiaries and branches largely

8.315

---

[500] 12 CFR § 243.4.
[501] FDIC, *supra* n 479, at 2.
[502] Dodd-Frank Act, § 204(c), 12 USC § 5384(c).
[503] Dodd-Frank Act, § 210(a)(1)(N), 12 USC §5390(a)(1)(N).
[504] FDIC and Bank of England, Joint Paper, 'Resolving Globally Active, Systemically Important, Financial Institutions' (10 December 2012).
[505] Ibid, 11.

continue to operate as they did before. The paper was an outgrowth of a Memorandum of Understanding (MOU) entered into in 2010 by the FDIC and the Bank of England.[506] The FDIC has pursued MOUs with a number of regulators around the world in an effort to secure similar commitments to cross-border cooperation.[507] Regulators from other countries have also sought to negotiate MOUs with each other to enhance cross-border resolution.[508] Concerns have been raised about the efficacy of MOUs in a crisis situation since they are not legally binding.[509]

8.316   In 2011, the Financial Stability Board (FSB) adopted the *Key Attributes of Effective Resolution Regimes for Financial Institutions* ('Key Attributes').[510] The Key Attributes identified the core elements that the FSB considered necessary for a resolution framework to enable authorities to resolve financial institutions in an orderly manner, without taxpayers being exposed to loss while maintaining continuity of critical economic function. A revised draft of the Key Attributes was adopted by the G20 in 2014 that retained the original 12 Key Attributes and added appendices to deal with financial market infrastructure, insurers, and the treatment of client assets.[511]

8.317   The Key Attributes provided a common foundation for the development of cross-border cooperation in resolution. Several of the Key Attributes promote the establishment of specialized resolution authorities that are designed to facilitate cross-border cooperation. At the most basic level, this takes the form of promoting resolution regimes that are predisposed to a cross-border perspective. For example, the Key Attributes call for specialized resolution regimes to be enacted with one of their statutory objectives being that the resolution authorities duly consider the potential impact of their resolution actions on the financial stability of other jurisdictions.[512] Another of the Key Attributes is that part of the statutory mandate of a resolution authority should be to strongly encourage a cooperative solution with foreign resolution authorities whenever possible.[513]

---

[506] FDIC and Bank of England, Memorandum of Understanding Concerning Consultation, Cooperation and the Exchange of Information Related to the Resolution of Insured Depository Institutions with Cross-Border Operations in the United States and the United Kingdom (22 January 2010).

[507] FDIC and China Banking Regulatory Commission, Appendix to Memorandum of Understanding between the China Banking Regulatory Commission and the Federal Deposit Insurance Corporation to Address Cross-Border Resolutions (26 May 2010); FDIC and Canadian Deposit Insurance Corporation, Memorandum of Understanding Concerning the Resolution of Insured Depository Institutions and Certain Other Financial Companies with Cross-Border Operations in the United States and Canada (12 June 2013); and FDIC and People's Bank of China, Memorandum of Understanding between Federal Deposit Insurance Corporation and People's Bank of China Regarding Cooperation, Technical Assistance and Cross Border Resolutions (24 October 2013).

[508] Memorandum of Understanding on Cooperation Between the Financial Supervisory Authorities, Central Banks and Finance Ministries of the European Union on Cross-Border Financial Stability (1 June 2008); and Cooperation agreement on cross-border financial stability, crisis management and resolution between relevant Ministries, Central Banks and Financial Supervisory Authorities of Denmark, Estonia, Finland, Iceland, Latvia, Lithuania, Norway and Sweden (17 August 2010).

[509] See Basel Committee on Banking Supervision, *Report and Recommendations of the Cross-border Bank Resolution Group* (2010) at 35–36. For example, there was a precursor to the current EU MOU in effect in 2008, Memorandum of Understanding on Cooperation Between the Banking Supervisors, Central Banks and Finance Ministries of the European Union in Financial Crisis Situations (18 May 2005), and it did not prevent ring-fencing at that time. The Cross-border Resolution Group report also notes that the longstanding relationship between Dutch and Belgian regulators did not prevent an uncoordinated response to Fortis.

[510] Key Attributes I, *supra* n 22.

[511] Key Attributes II, *supra* n 22.

[512] Ibid, 6.

[513] Ibid, 12.

One of the Key Attributes' recommendations, which has been implemented in the years **8.318**
since they were adopted, is the creation of Crisis Management Groups (CMGs).[514] A CMG
is focused on the orderly resolution of a specific financial institution and includes the supervisory authorities, central banks, resolution authorities, and finance ministries from that financial institution's home jurisdiction and from any jurisdiction that is host to subsidiaries
or branches of that institution that are material to its resolution. Each CMG is responsible
for the coordination and information sharing between the authorities in whose jurisdictions a financial institution has a systemic presence, as well as reviewing the recovery and
resolution planning process for that financial institution. By the autumn of 2014, CMGs
were in place for all banking groups designated as G-SIBs by the Financial Stability Board.[515]

Crisis Management Groups also facilitate the creation and implementation of institution-   **8.319**
specific cross-border cooperation agreements among all of the authorities who are members of a particular institution's CMG. In Annex I of the 2014 Key Attributes, the Financial
Stability Board provides some guidance on the elements of a cross-border cooperation
agreement. Such agreements should include a commitment by all members of the CMG
to conduct periodic scenario simulations to test the viability of the institution's resolution
plan. The agreement should also include a commitment by the institution's home authority
to coordinate the assessment of its resolvability, as well as any efforts to enhance resolvability of the institution.[516] According to the Key Attributes, the cross-border cooperation
agreements should also identify the members of the institution's CMG both before and
during a crisis and set out the procedures for information sharing within the CMG.[517]

The Key Attributes also identify certain resolution powers as important elements in an ef-   **8.320**
fective resolution regime. One of these powers is the bail-in within resolution tool.[518] The
power should be flexible enough that the resolution authority can convert or write down
claims while still respecting the hierarchy of claims in liquidation, including, once the bank
has entered resolution, contingent convertible instruments. A resolution authority should
also have the power to impose a temporary stay of up to 48 hours on early termination
rights in financial contracts.[519]

All FSB members made commitments to implement the Key Attributes by the end of 2015.   **8.321**
A major step in their implementation was the adoption of the EU BRRD,[520] which was expressly designed to bring European national resolution frameworks into line with the Key
Attributes. According to the FSB's April 2021 report on progress in the implementation
of these Key Attributes, almost all home jurisdictions of G-SIBs, as well as key host jurisdictions, have in place comprehensive resolution regimes that give them the option of resolving a failing G-SIB, and a significant number of them have produced resolution plans
for these G-SIBs.[521] Crisis Management Groups have been established for all G-SIBs, and

---

[514] Ibid, 14.
[515] Financial Stability Board, *Towards Full Implementation of the FSB Key Attributes of Effective Resolution Regimes for Financial Institution* (updated, 12 November 2014), 11.
[516] Key Attributes II, *supra* n 22.
[517] Ibid, 22, 24.
[518] Ibid, 9.
[519] Ibid, 10–11.
[520] EU BRRD, *supra* n 25.
[521] FSB, 'Evaluation of the Effects of Too-Big-To-Fail Reforms, Final Report' (1 April 2021), 3, available at: <https://www.fsb.org/wp-content/uploads/P010421-1.pdf>.

home and host authorities have signed institution-specific cross-border cooperation agreements for most G-SIBs.[522] Altogether, the report concluded that too-big-to-fail reforms have 'reduced systemic risks, enhanced the credibility of resolution and market discipline and ultimately produced net benefits for society'.[523] Most G-SIBs already meet their final requirements for TLAC and the market has absorbed these issuances without difficulty, with no material effect on the supply of credit from these changes in market structure.[524] Nonetheless, the FSB's April 2021 report determined that there are still a number of gaps that need to be addressed, including: obstacles to resolvability, such as clarity on resolution funding mechanisms, the valuation of bank assets in resolution, and operational continuity; the fact that public funds continue to be used to support small or medium-sized banks, even in jurisdictions with well-developed resolution frameworks; and opportunities to improve the provision and availability of data so that market participants and public authorities have better transparency.

8.322   In implementing the Key Attributes, the Financial Stability Board has identified two main approaches that a jurisdiction might follow: a recognition regime or a regime based on supportive measures.[525] Under a recognition regime, a jurisdiction would, at the request of a foreign party, accept the commencement of a foreign resolution proceeding by that jurisdiction's courts or administrative agency, so that the relevant domestic authority would enforce the foreign resolution measure or grant other forms of domestic relief.[526] In a regime based on supportive measures, the jurisdiction would take action that would produce the effect of or support the actions taken by a resolution authority in a foreign jurisdiction.[527] Although the ultimate objective according to these principles should be statutory frameworks that give prompt effect to foreign resolution actions, the principles also recognize that elements of these regimes can be enacted by contractual measures agreed to by the parties involved.[528]

8.323   The Key Attributes provide a set of core elements for resolution authorities, but they are designed to operate at a high level and do not always provide practical guidance for effective implementation. The appendices added to the Key Attributes in 2014 were meant to address the request for more practical guidance with respect to some aspects of the Key Attributes. The IMF has studied the characteristics of national resolution regimes and identified the following issues that still need to be addressed in order to implement the Key Attributes in a manner that creates effective cross-border resolution: (i) how losses are to

---

[522] Ibid.

[523] Ibid, 1.

[524] Ibid, 3, 6.

[525] Financial Stability Board, *Principles for Cross-border Effectiveness of Resolution Actions* (updated, 3 November 2015). Although the Principles for Cross-border Effectiveness are focused on the resolution of banks, they provide guidance for other financial institutions as well. The Financial Stability Board recognizes that each regime might be better suited to certain resolution actions and existing cross-border frameworks have adopted a combination of both approaches.

[526] Ibid, 5–6. Recognition can occur without the exercise of resolution powers in the jurisdiction of the foreign party requesting domestic proceedings, but it would not extend to the application of foreign law inconsistent with the domestic framework of the jurisdiction enacting the proceedings.

[527] Ibid, 6.

[528] Ibid, 8. The principles highlight contractual measures with respect to restrictions on early termination rights and recognition of the write-down, cancellation, or conversion of debt instruments by relevant resolution authorities (Principles 8 and 9). For an example of these contractual measures being implemented, see the discussion below of the 2014 ISDA Resolution Stay Protocol.

be allocated among private sector stakeholders in a resolution; and (ii) how to manage the risk that public funds will be needed to effect an orderly resolution.[529] These issues must be addressed in a way that removes the temptation for resolution authorities to act unilaterally in the interests of their home jurisdictions.

The ISDA Universal Protocol[530] and the FSB's proposed and final international standard on **8.324** TLAC[531] represent two of the most important accomplishments or near accomplishments in cross-border cooperation.[532] Among other things, the ISDA Universal Protocol requires adhering parties to give extraterritorial effect to provisions in special resolution regimes that would impose temporary stays on the exercise of remedies in ISDA Master Agreements and certain other financial contracts or would override cross-defaults in those agreements based on a parent or other affiliate's failure or financial distress, as well as agree to contractual limitations on the exercise of cross-defaults to a parent or other affiliate becoming subject to proceedings under relevant insolvency regimes. The ISDA US Protocol[533] accomplishes the same for the US resolution regimes and extends the scope of agreements covered to all QFCs. Other jurisdictions have adopted rules similar to the US QFC Stay Rules, and ISDA has promulgated an 'ISDA Resolution Stay Jurisdictional Modular Protocol' intended to provide an industry-wide mechanism to comply with these rules.[534] In addition, many jurisdictions, including the United States, have adopted rules implementing the FSB's TLAC standard.[535] The TLAC requirement seeks to ensure the availability of sufficient amounts of loss-absorbing capacity at the right location within a G-SIB's group structure so as to provide home and host authorities and the market with confidence that G-SIBs can be resolved in an orderly manner that maintains the continuity of critical economic functions and diminishes any incentives to ring-fence additional assets domestically *ex ante* or during resolution.[536]

VII. Conclusion

In response to the global financial panic of 2008, a strong interest in creating or expanding **8.325** resolution authority took root in the US and around the world. This chapter has described

---

[529] IMF, *Cross-Border Bank Resolution: Recent Development* (2 June 2014) 11.

[530] International Swaps and Derivatives Association, Inc (ISDA), ISDA 2014 Resolution Stay Protocol.

[531] Financial Stability Board, *Adequacy of Loss-Absorbing Capacity of Global Systemically Important Banks in resolution* (10 November 2014); Financial Stability Board, *Total Loss-Absorbing Capacity (TLAC) Principles and Term Sheet* (9 November 2015).

[532] Financial Stability Board, Press Release, *FSB Welcomes Industry Initiative to Remove Cross-Border Close-out Risk* (October 2014); Federal Reserve Board and FDIC Joint Press Release, *Federal Reserve Board and FDIC Welcome ISDA Announcement* (October 2014).

[533] ISDA, 'ISDA 2018 US Resolution Stay Protocol' (22 August 2018), available at: <https://www.isda.org/protocol/isda-2018-us-resolution-stay-protocol/>.

[534] ISDA, 'ISDA Jurisdictional Modular Protocol' (3 May 2016), available at: <https://www.isda.org/protocol/isda-resolution-stay-jurisdictional-modular-protocol/>. At the time of writing, jurisdictional modules have been published and are in effect for Italy, Japan, Switzerland, and the United Kingdom. In addition, the following jurisdictions are covered under the ISDA BRRD II Omnibus Jurisdictional Module to the ISDA 2018 Jurisdictional Modular Protocol: Austria, Belgium, Denmark, Finland, France, Germany, Greece, Ireland, Luxembourg, Spain, and Sweden.

[535] See FSB, 'Review of the Technical Implementation of the Total Loss-Absorbing Capacity (TLAC) Standard' (July 2019).

[536] Ibid, 6.

the fundamental characteristics of resolution authority as conceived and implemented in the US. The US has long had a workable model for resolving community banks, mid-size banks, and even some regional banks. It has adapted that model to larger and more complex financial institutions, including the US G-SIBs and the US GSEs. The FDIC has developed an SPOE recapitalization within resolution framework that is widely viewed as the most promising model for resolving the US G-SIBs in a manner that maximizes the value of the enterprise for the benefit of its stakeholders, preserves critical operations, and promotes financial stability without the need for any taxpayer-funded bailouts. Various bankruptcy lawyers have also developed ways to implement that strategy under either Title II of the Dodd-Frank Act or chapter 11 of the US Bankruptcy Code. The US is also examining various proposals to add a new chapter 14 to the US Bankruptcy Code in order to facilitate the successful implementation of an SPOE strategy under the US Bankruptcy Code.

8.326   This progress in the US is paralleled by similar progress in Europe and other parts of the world. The FSB has issued a report on the Key Attributes of effective resolution regimes and urged all countries to enact one. The UK, Germany, and Switzerland have enacted special resolution regimes that reflect the Key Attributes. The EU has adopted the BRRD, which requires EU Member States to enact special resolution regimes consistent with the BRRD's framework. The UK, Germany, Switzerland, and other European jurisdictions have identified the SPOE bail-in within resolution strategy as their preferred strategies for resolving most G-SIBs. There is also increasing international coordination of cross-border resolution through the CMGs and the FSB. Since 2014, senior officials from the US, UK, and the European Union have met regularly for planned exercises to enhance understanding of one another's resolution regimes and strengthen coordination on cross-border resolution.[537]

---

[537] FDIC, 'US, European Banking Union, and UK Officials Meet for Planned Coordination Exercise on Cross-Border Resolution Planning' (9 April 2019), available at: <https://www.fdic.gov/news/press-releases/2019/pr19 033.html>; Single Resolution Board, 'US, European Officials to Hold Planned Coordination Exercise on Cross-Border Resolution Planning' (23 April 2019), available at: <https://www.srb.europa.eu/en/content/us-european-officials-hold-planned-coordination-exercise-cross-border-resolution-planning-1>.

9

EUROPEAN BANK RESOLUTION REGIME

I. Introduction

The response to the European banking and sovereign debt crisis has resulted in the introduction of the Bank Recovery and Resolution Directive 2015 (BRRD).[1] Lessons learnt resulted in revisions (as part of the European Banking Package 2021)[2] introduced by the Directive amending Directive 2014/59 regarding loss absorbing and recapitalization capacity (BRRD II), adopted in 2019.[3] A Single Supervisory Mechanism[4] (SSM) and a Single Resolution Mechanism[5] (SRM) have also been established to facilitate the supervision and resolution, respectively, of significant banks and banking groups participating in the Banking Union. This has led to a significant overhaul of the micro-prudential and macro-prudential

9.01

---

[1] Directive 2014/59/EU establishing a framework for the recovery and resolution of credit institutions and investment firms and amending Council Directive 82/891/EEC, and Directives 2001/24/EC, 2002/47/EC, 2004/25/EC, 2005/56/EC, 2007/36/EC, 2011/35/EU, 2012/30/EU, and 2013/36/EU, and Regulations (EU) No 1093/2010 and (EU) No 648/2012, of the European Parliament and of the Council. Amended by several Directives (Directive 2017/1132, Directive 2017/2399, Directive 2019/879, Directive 2019/2162).

[2] European Council, 'Banking Union: Council Adopts Measures to Reduce Risk in the Banking System' (14 May 2019) <https://www.consilium.europa.eu/en/press/press-releases/2019/05/14/banking-union-council-adopts-measures-to-reduce-risk-in-the-banking-system/>.

[3] Directive (EU) 2019/879 of the European Parliament and of the Council of 20 May 2019 amending Directive 2014/59/EU as regards the loss-absorbing and recapitalization capacity of credit institutions and investment firms and Directive 98/26/EC.

[4] Regulation No 1024/2013 conferring specific tasks on the European Central Bank concerning policies relating to the prudential supervision of credit institutions.

[5] Regulation No 806/2014 establishing uniform rules and a uniform procedure for the resolution of credit institutions and certain investment firms in the framework of a Single Resolution Mechanism and a Single Resolution Fund and amending Regulation (EU) No 1093/2010. Amended by Regulation 2019/877 which came into force May 2019.

oversight of the European financial and economic system to improve, inter alia, the way financial crises are managed and to maintain financial stability. The European agenda of reform has also led to a major overhaul of the micro-prudential regulatory and supervisory techniques and tools to improve the general safety and soundness of banks and financial firms. This was considered necessary due to the lack of a common approach to the supervision and resolution of banks and investment firms, leading to situations where Member States primarily acted in their own interest rather than in a coordinated way with commonly understood outcomes for the European Union as a whole. With a significant role for the regulator as supervisor to play in the proceedings, a particular concern was the overreliance on corporate insolvency procedures which were not considered fit for purpose to deal with the wider stakeholder concerns arising from a bank failure. In part, the reforms of both macro-prudential and micro-prudential oversight include a more coherent approach to improvements to resolution of banks in distress. The key policy objective of those reforms is to minimize both the possibility of taxpayer bail-outs and spill-over effects of the failure of banks and financial firms and replace it with a resolution regime that places the primary burden on its shareholders and particular creditors, and introduces new techniques to resolve problems experienced by them. However, the experience so far would indicate significant amounts of discretion have led to assistance for banks near to insolvency and eligible for recapitalization or liquidity assistance that have ultimately needed additional support and or indeed dismantlement for private purchase, as is proposed with Monte dei Paschi di Siena, because the problems were far bigger than originally thought. Moreover, it aims to provide a structure to ensure cooperation and coordination between regulators and resolution authorities of Member States and third countries to manage those in distress with a potential cross-border failure.

9.02   The BRRD forms a central foundation stone of the new regime to deal with distressed banks in as orderly a manner as possible. The European response has been very much part of the international initiatives by the Basel Committee on Banking Supervision (BCBS)[6] and the Financial Stability Board (FSB)[7] to introduce a more robust and responsive approach to resolving banks in distress.

9.03   This chapter will explain the salient features of the European framework of supervision and resolution. It will also explain separately the European Banking Authority (EBA) technical standards and/or guidance where necessary to assist the interpretation of the provisions in the directive.

II. The Pillars of the Banking Union

9.04   The depth of the European financial crisis highlighted a number of structural weaknesses at the macro-prudential and micro-prudential level. The initial objective has been to improve the safety and soundness of banks with significant reforms introduced by the Capital

---

[6] Basel Committee on Banking Supervision, *Report and Recommendations of the Cross-border Bank Resolution Group* (March 2010).

[7] Financial Stability Board, *Key Attributes of Effective Resolution Regimes for Financial Institutions* (October 2011) and amended and updated Financial Stability Board, *Key Attributes of Effective Resolution Regimes for Financial Institutions* (October 2014).

Requirements Directive IV (CRD IV)[8] and Capital Requirements Regulation (CRR).[9] Since then CRR II and CRD V have introduced improve focus on liquidity regulation with the Leverage Coverage Ratio and the Net Stable Funding Ratio. In addition to improving regulation, significant reform has occurred at the wider EU level with the creation of new supervisory authorities: the European Banking Authority;[10] the European Securities and Markets Authority;[11] and the European Insurance and Occupational Pensions Authority.[12] The primary purpose of these new authorities is to improve rule and guidance formation so that their application and compliance in the European Union is more consistent than was the case in the past; partly forming what is generally referred to as the 'Single Rulebook'.

The Banking Union consists of two primary pillars—supervision and resolution—with the **9.05** authority of early intervention as the link connecting the two broad SSM and SRM decision-making processes and a deposit guarantee scheme. The former mechanisms are equally important and necessary to address the divergences between Member States with respect to supervision and resolution, whereas the latter serves a pivotal ancillary function. The SSM consists of the European Central Bank (ECB) with responsibility to exercise bank supervision of banks considered 'significant' at the supranational level with support from the national supervisory authorities in the Eurozone countries.[13] The non-Eurozone countries can enter into a close cooperation agreement with the ECB to confer on it responsibility for bank supervision for its significant banks. In this respective, Croatia and Bulgaria, as part of their commitment to adopt the euro, are participating in the exchange rate mechanism (ERM II) and Banking Union.

The Banking Union primarily forms a dual supervisory system determined by size since **9.06** those banks not considered significant in the Member State remain supervised by the national authorities. The primary aim of the SSM, with the ECB at its helm as supervisor, is to improve the quality of supervision of those banks and their group entities that could pose a threat to the financial stability of the Member State and the wider EU, by applying a single approach to the application of the prudential rulebook on those institutions considered significant. The second pillar of the Banking Union establishes a supranational

---

[8] Directive 2013/36/EU on access to the activity of credit institutions and the prudential supervision of credit institutions and investment firms, amending Directive 2002/87/EC and repealing Directives 2006/48/EC and 2006/49/EC. Directive (EU) 2019/878 of the European Parliament and of the Council of 20 May 2019 amending Directive 2013/36/EU as regards exempted entities, financial holding companies, mixed financial holding companies, remuneration, supervisory measures and powers, and capital conservation measures (Hereinafter CRD V); Regulation (EU) 2019/876 of the European Parliament and of the Council of 20 May 2019 amending Regulation (EU) No 575/2013 as regards the leverage ratio, the net stable funding ratio, requirements for own funds and eligible liabilities, counterparty credit risk, market risk, exposures to central counterparties, exposures to collective investment undertakings, large exposures, reporting and disclosure requirements, and Regulation (EU) No 648/2012 (Hereinafter CRR II)

[9] Regulation No 575/2013 on prudential requirements for credit institutions and investment firms and amending Regulation (EU) No 648/2012. Amended by Regulation 2018/405, Regulation 2017/2401, Regulation 2017/2188, Regulation 2019/630, Regulation 2019/876, Regulation 2019/2033, Regulation 2020/873.

[10] Regulation No 1093/2010 establishing a European Supervisory Authority (European Banking Authority), amending Decision No 716/2009/EC and repealing Commission Decision 2009/78/EC.

[11] Regulation No 1095/2010 establishing a European Supervisory Authority (European Securities and Markets Authority), amending Decision No 716/2009/EC and repealing Commission Decision 2009/77/EC.

[12] Regulation No 1094/2010 establishing a European Supervisory Authority (European Insurance and Occupational Pensions Authority), amending Decision No 716/2009/EC and repealing Commission Decision 2009/79/EC. Amendments introduced by the Regulation 2019/2175.

[13] Regulation No 1024/2013 conferring specific tasks on the European Central Bank concerning policies relating to the prudential supervision of credit institutions.

administrative arrangement, the Single Resolution Mechanism (SRM) and a Single Resolution Body (SRB).[14] The SRMR II Regulation introduces similar amendments to the SRM Regulation as introduced by the BRRD II to its counterpart but applicable to significant banks of participating Member States.[15] The SRB as resolution authority for such banks is responsible for individual banks' total loss-absorbing capacity (TLAC) requirements and minimum requirement for own funds and eligible liabilities (MREL) to ensure they have sufficient loss-absorbing capacity for the purposes of recapitalization in resolution or to restore viability. In respect of MREL requirements, there is a wide margin of administrative discretion to decide the sufficient level of loss absorbing capacity on a case-by-case basis. With the SRB as the single resolution authority responsible for setting such requirements there is a greater likelihood of consistency across the participating Member States rather than setting MREL requirements in line with national interpretations, which would lead to different levels. The SRB utilizes the text of the SRM Regulation, which mirrors in most parts the text of the BRRD, to develop a unified administrative regime to govern resolution decision making and decide resolution schemes. Those schemes are to be executed by the national resolution authorities. The SRM applies primarily to the following: the participating significant banks and some smaller cross-border banks; banks for which the ECB is the supervisory authority; and banks with subsidiaries or significant branches in other Member States. Member States that are not part of the Eurozone can voluntarily opt in and enter into cooperation arrangements with the ECB for the purposes of supervision. Non-Eurozone Member States with sole responsibility for supervision are required to put in place their own resolution measures.

9.07   In line with the financial arrangements introduced in the BRRD, in participating non-Eurozone Member States and Eurozone Member States, the SRM establishes a Single Resolution Fund for participating Member States to assist with financial support to bank resolution. This approach is advocated to break to some extent the doom loop noted above between sovereigns and banks that was so prevalent during the European experience of the recent banking crisis. This is premised on the fundamental principle in resolution that the first losses are to be borne by shareholders and creditors. Since insolvency is prevented, it needs to be ensured that the shareholders and creditors in resolution are no worse off than in a hypothetical insolvency proceeding. It is anticipated that the application of this principle will minimize potential reliance on the resolution fund. Therefore, resolution is essentially financed by the private sector. However, in exceptional cases the extraordinary public funding facilities can be relied on in wider market-based systemic crises.

9.08   The European Stability Mechanism (ESM) introduced the backstop to the Single Resolution Fund in 2022.[16] This will be an additional emergency fund that can be called upon and doubles the size of the Single Resolution Fund. The backstop is provided through public money

---

[14] Regulation No 806/2014 of the European Parliament and the Council, 15 July 2014, establishing uniform rules and a uniform procedure for the resolution of credit institutions and certain investment firms in the framework of a Single Resolution Mechanism and a Single Resolution Fund and amending Regulation (EU) No 1093/2010. Amended by the Regulation 2019/877, which came into force May 2019.

[15] Regulation (EU) 2019/877 of European Parliament and of the Council of 20 May 2019 amending Regulation (EU) No 806/2014 as regards the loss-absorbing and recapitalization capacity of credit institutions and investment firms.

[16] ESM, 'How Much Could the ESM Lend to the Single Resolution Fund?' <https://www.esm.europa.eu/content/how-much-could-esm-lend-single-resolution-fund>.

to provide immediate support and confidence to the market. This will be a publicly funded backstop that has to be paid back in the years after its use by all of the banks in the Banking Union. This ensures that the taxpayer will be fully reimbursed.

A. The Rationale for the BRRD

The BRRD and the recent reforms put in place a complex administrative procedure to re-   **9.09** solve banks and investment firms in distress, either as single institutions or as parts of a group. The new measures regarding resolution attempt to address some of the fundamental weaknesses of the previous divergent regimes and, regardless of the form the legal entity takes, by introducing a common approach in the European Union and, indeed, a more centralized supranational approach for those participating in the Banking Union. Moreover, BRRD and the wider reforms put in place measures more akin to a universalist aspiration and approach to resolution with the attempts to address cross-border issues on the European level and cooperation initiatives with third countries; and so minimizing Member State discretion. The measures explained above attempt in many ways to address failing institutions and groups, and the impact of their failure or risk of failure on market confidence and the impact on wider financial and economic stability. Those wider concerns need to safeguard specific stakeholders such as depositors and investment clients' assets and money and require particular 'carve-outs' of general insolvency laws to ensure that their interests are sufficiently protected and spill-overs are minimized. The BRRD starts off on the premise that failing institutions should be dealt with through general insolvency and liquidation proceedings. In this respect, a difference of treatment appears to be emerging between Member States and the SRB decisions relating to banks in resolution that do not meet the public interest threshold of providing critical functions in the real economy and so are resolved through national insolvency proceedings. The important factor in respect of the SRB position is whether national insolvency proceedings can provide a suitable outcome for depositors and minimize any potential disruption locally. The BRRD leaves the insolvency winding-up and liquidation process within the parameters of the Member State's discretion. No assistance is provided in the BRRD to ensure a consistent approach amongst Member States, so leading to questions about the outcomes of different national proceedings. However, many of the interventions explained do not provide a true demarcation line between recovery and resolution on the one hand and insolvency and winding up on the other hand. This is because of the practical consequences of the use of resolution tools and the reforms to the hierarchy of priority of claims. The safeguarding principle that no shareholder or creditor will be worse off than in insolvency proceedings attempts to mitigate the broader impact and minimize the need for a bailout.

The focus of the reforms has placed particular attention on the recoverability and resolv-   **9.10** ability of banks and financial firms from endogenous and exogenous shocks, from both an *ex ante* and *ex post* supervisory perspective. A primary aim of the BRRD is to safeguard critical financial functions by putting in place a consistent set of tools to deal with banks at the wide spectrum of impending insolvency or actual insolvency. The need for a coherent framework was evident for not only deposit-taking banks but also investment firms and both of their group and parent level entities. The rationale of the toolkit for early intervention and resolution is not premised to save individual firms per se. This is not a guarantee but should, rather, ensure orderly resolution in order to minimize disruption to the marketplace and to the wider financial system. While the early premise of the European regime was to almost eliminate any possibility of government assistance to minimize the risk of moral hazard, the directive takes a rather pragmatic view that there certainly will be cases where government support will be required to enable the resolution process to be undertaken in a more orderly manner if the institution is still a going concern. Thereby, the interests of depositors and clients are not placed at unnecessary risk. The toolkit, however, is expected to provide the competent and resolution authorities the equipment to deal with either large or small banks, but most notably those designated as Global Systemic Financial Institutions (G-SIFI) and those considered Domestic Systemic Financial Institutions (D-SIFI), which in the latter case would not pose a direct cross-border threat but certainly a domestic threat to financial stability that could culminate into a global threat. Nonetheless, more clarity is provided in CRD V and the CRR II package that requires non-EU G-SIBs with two or more EU firms to establish an EU intermediate parent undertaking to better 'ring fence' the European entity for the purposes of resolution so that the European part of the resolution satisfies the aims of its resolution scheme. There are also technical lines of communication and accountability that need to be worked out in advance to manage the resolution process between, for instance, the ministry of finance, central bank, the competent authority, and the resolution authority. These will also be managed within the respective supervisory college and resolution college for those groups with significant cross-border operations; requiring home and host states at multiple levels to cooperate and coordinate their resolution plans.

9.11   The European Resolution Framework puts in place a more coherent approach, dealing not only with commercial bank failures, which has been the traditional focus of special resolution regimes, but also dealing with investment firms as separate standalone entities. In addition to those firms that undertake those regulated activities the directive also applies at the wider group and parent level, thereby capturing financial holding companies[17] and mixed financial holding companies.[18]

9.12   The directive does not put in place a particular form that the architecture of the official safety net should take. Moreover, it does not stipulate the form the competent and resolution authorities should take.[19] It does, however, require the resolution authority to be a public administrative authority with operational independence from the competent authority. What operational independence amounts to is possibly debatable, since the two authorities could co-exist within the same public administrative body and be functionally independent. One cannot assume there will be one competent authority, as it may be the case that regulation and supervision is shared amongst a multiple set of authorities, and so the Member State will need to decide that those other authorities will have powers conferred for the purposes of preparation and crisis prevention. It is likely that those regulating commercial and investment businesses will need these powers to ensure compliance with the BRRD. In some jurisdictions it will mean the setting up of a new department within the competent authority or a separate resolution authority. With the wider mandate to have in place a system

---

[17]   BRRD, Art 1(1)(c)–(d).
[18]   Ibid.
[19]   Ibid, Art 3.

of resolution for both commercial and investment banking with market experience, a significant amount of capacity building is also necessary to develop the appropriate expertise. This primarily means that those responsible for the day-to-day supervision and those responsible for exercising resolution decisions and tools respectively have separate reporting lines within the official safety net to the central bank, and the ministry of finance.[20] Despite the administrative separation of the responsibilities, the directive does recognize that both the competent authority and the resolution authority will need to work closely in areas such as recovery and resolution plans and determining resolvability, for instance. The directive also instructs the Member State to limit the liability of both the competent and resolution authorities in accordance with the limits of national law.[21] The extensive powers of those authorities and the impact on a wide range of stakeholders of their acts or omissions requires them to undertake those decisions unfettered by the threat of legal action.

The important synergies between supervision and resolution on a going concern and gone concern basis are set out in the context of preparation for resolution of distressed institutions and groups.[22] The intensity of the level of supervision will increase as matters escalate. The powers of early intervention in this respect are therefore similarly interlinked to the relationship between supervision and resolution. This is a critical phase, in that the more work undertaken at this point the more efficient the competent and resolution authorities are likely to be in achieving the resolution objectives and minimizing spill-over effects from the institution in the resolution or in the nearing resolution phase.   **9.13**

B. Recovery and Resolution Plans

The BRRD first of all provides the basis for the competent authority to understand better the size and complexity of the institutions and groups it is responsible for overseeing on a solo or consolidated supervisory level and their respective resolution entity and resolution group level.[23] This forms the basis of the requirements to request certain institutions or groups to prepare recovery and resolution plans to enable the competent and resolution authorities to work out *ex ante* the areas of risk in terms of their critical functions[24] and core business lines[25] and possible resolution tools likely to be used to deal with banks in distress. The directive does not elaborate on what a critical function or business line is, but leaves it to the discretion of the competent authority, and possibly the resolution authority, to work this out with the institution and group. The directive is assisted by the technical standards,   **9.14**

---

[20] Ibid, Art 3(3).
[21] Ibid, Art 3(12).
[22] Title II Preparation, Recovery and Resolution Planning.
[23] Ibid, Art 4(1).
[24] Ibid, Art 2(1) (35): ' "critical functions" means activities, services or operations the discontinuance of which is likely in one or more Member States, to lead to the disruption of services that are essential to the real economy or to disrupt financial stability due to the size, market share, external and internal interconnectedness, complexity or cross-border activities of an institution or group, with particular regard to the substitutability of those activities, services or operations'.
[25] Ibid, Art 2(1) (36): ' "core business lines" means business lines and associated services which represent material sources of revenue, profit or franchise value for an institution or for a group of which an institution forms part'.

guidelines, and reports by the EBA in this respect.[26] The directive refers to 'critical functions' in the context of a whole manner of areas and is interlinked with the recovery and resolution planning process and assessing the utility of resolution tools. The term critical functions is given a wide interpretation covering business activities, internal and external services, and operations in the form of back office or front office support either to the firm itself or to a third party, business units, and legal entities. The impact of not providing a critical function needs to be assessed as part of the recovery and resolution, which needs to include the possible impact of the disruption or loss of the critical function to itself and third parties. Moreover, the institution or group will need to assess the substitutability of the critical function in the impact assessment.

9.15 The competent authority and the resolution authority have the discretion to decide whether an institution or group is required to prepare a recovery and resolution plan.[27] Those institutions considered to have a relatively complex business model and risk profile that incorporates a significant level of interconnection with the wider financial system will be required to produce a recovery plan which would form the basis of the resolution plan. Notwithstanding the discretion of the competent authorities to request such plans, it is not a barrier to taking the necessary action to prevent resolution tools being exercised to safeguard an institution's critical financial functions. The requirement to produce a recovery plan applies to both individual institutions and groups. The primary aim of the recovery plan is for the institution to explain how it will 'restore its financial position following a significant deterioration of its financial situation'.[28] The plan cannot assume in the risk assessment of the business activities and financing arrangements that the authorities will provide extraordinary public financial support.[29] However, what is considered extraordinary during stable times may form part of ordinary financial support offered by a ministry of finance or central bank. This is captured by the need to explain how the institution would access central bank facilities in circumstances where it can provide the appropriate assets as collateral in the normal course of its daily business.

9.16 The key features of recovery planning operate at a high level of the firm, with responsibility for completing and approving it resting at the board level.[30] The management body will need to set out in a systemic manner the steps and actions the institution will take within the time frame it sets itself to fulfil its options. The plans require the institution to explain how in various scenarios it will attempt to remedy problems it faces either at the international, national, sector, or institutional level. The information that needs to be included in the recovery plan is set out in the Annex to the BRRD, section A. The list is quite large and significantly it includes, inter alia: the capital and liquidity actions it would need to take; impediments to being able to implement the planned actions; identifying critical functions; the marketability of core business areas; identifying areas of risk and leverage within the business; and arrangements to restructure liabilities and business lines.

---

[26] EBA, Recovery, Resolution, and DGS <https://www.eba.europa.eu/regulation-and-policy/recovery-and-res olution>. Technical advice on the delegated acts on critical functions and core business lines, EBA/Op/2015/05, March 2015.
[27] BRRD, art 4(1).
[28] Ibid, Art 5(1).
[29] Ibid, Art 5(3).
[30] Ibid, Art 5(9).

The responsibility of reviewing the recovery plan falls on the competent authority in ac-   **9.17**
cordance with the aims of the directive and technical standards and guidance provided by
the EBA.[31] The competent authority is required to assess the plan according to whether it is
'reasonably likely to maintain or restore the viability and financial position of the institution
or of the group, taking into account the preparatory measures that the institution has taken
or has planned to take';[32] in accordance with the requirements set out in the Annex to the
BRRD. The competent authority can require the institution to resubmit the plan if it is of the
view that there is a 'material deficiency' or 'material impediment' that would prevent the institution from implementing the options that it sets out to be utilized in a given scenario.[33]
The EBA, in light of its review and assessments through various surveys have proposed revisions to the guidelines on recovery indicators to ensure banks place more attention on its
loss absorbing capacity, the amount of unencumbered assets to improve access to central
bank facilities and its liquidity position.[34]

Recovery plans need to be produced by institutions and groups rather than individuals.[35]   **9.18**
In this respect, the group-parent undertaking is required to produce a plan for the whole
group capturing the issues identified above, and also intra-group support arrangements.[36]
The management body of the group entity is required to assume responsibility for drawing
the plan. The group recovery plan will need to include subsidiaries and significant branches
in Member States.[37] In some cases the group entity will likely include subsidiaries that are
required to produce a recovery plan in their own right if the home state so decides.[38] In circumstances where Member States cannot agree on the group plan and its more important
constituent parts then the EBA is required to intervene and decide or, alternatively, the decision of the consolidated supervisor will be given precedence.[39] The group entity will need
to coordinate in those circumstances so that there are minimal impediments. Moreover,
the group entity would also, on a practical level, ensure that its group recovery plan has appropriate synergies with other recovery and resolution plans in other third countries. As
with the individual recovery plans, the group recovery plans are also assessed to ensure that
obstacles to resolution are minimized.[40] In many respects the likely cross-border nature of
group activities will mean that considerably more effort is needed to coordinate with other
competent and resolution authorities to ensure there is sufficient understanding of how best
to coordinate efforts. In this respect the supervisory college and resolution college will take
an important role to assist the process.[41] The EBA guidelines 2015 elaborate on the recovery

---

[31] EBA, Guidelines on the minimum list of qualitative and quantitative recovery plan indicators, EBA-GL-2015-02, July 2015; <http://www.eba.europa.eu/documents/10180/ 1147256/EBA-GL-2015-02_EN+Guidelines+on+recovery+plan+indicators.pdf/485181d4-f8f1-4604-9a78-17a12164e793>.

[32] BRRD, Art 6(2)(a).

[33] Ibid, Art 6(5) see also recital 24 and the wide implications of the discretion of the competent authority.

[34] EBA, Consultation Paper, Draft Revised Guidelines on recovery plan indicators under Article 9 of Directive 2014/59/EU, March 2021

[35] Ibid, Art 7.

[36] Commission Implementing Regulation (EU) 2016/911 of 9 June 2016 laying down implementing technical standards with regard to the form and the content of the description of group financial support agreements in ac-cordance with Directive 2014/59/EU of the European Parliament and of the Council establishing a framework for the recovery and resolution of credit institutions and investment firms.

[37] Ibid, Art 7(1)–(3).

[38] Ibid, Art 7(2).

[39] Ibid, Art 7(3)–(4).

[40] Ibid, Art 9.

[41] Ibid, Art 8, albeit Directive 2019/879 limited changes to its substance; recital 96: 'Resolution colleges should be established around the core of the existing supervisory colleges through the inclusion of resolution authorities

plan indicators; explaining how it is important that the recovery plans assess areas such as capital, liquidity, asset quality, market-based information, macroeconomic information, and profit levels. It is evident that the EBA expects institutions and groups to comply with these minimum indicators but it important to note that competent authorities can request additional indicators and further detail to be provided relative to the complexity of the business and risks associated with the institution or group.[42] A particular challenge is likely to be coordinating the different indicators across the group and its subgroups in other third countries.

9.19   In addition to drawing up the group-wide recovery plan, as mentioned above, the group-parent undertaking is also responsible for intra-group financial support arrangements where applicable.[43] The purpose of intra-group financial support is to ensure the financial stability of the group as a whole, mindful also of the solvency and liquidity of the group undertaking providing the support.[44] This is intended to be voluntary and subject to appropriate safeguards; equally, it is not purported to affect contractual or statutory liability arrangements through, for instance, cross-guarantees protecting the participating institutions.[45]

9.20   Intra-group financial support arrangements must be adopted pursuant to an agreement entered into in accordance with Chapter III of BRRD.[46] The other party to the agreement must satisfy the conditions therein[47] as well as the conditions for early intervention.[48] The group financial support agreement can only be concluded if none of the parties meets the conditions for early intervention at the time that it is made, as decided by their respective competent authorities.[49] In addition, Member States are required to remove impediments to the application of the agreement in national laws, provided that Chapter III provisions do not prevent Member States from imposing intra-group transaction limitations in relation to national laws as per Regulation (EU) No 575/2013,[50] transposing Directive 2013/36/EU,[51]

and the involvement of competent ministries, central banks, EBA and, where appropriate, authorities responsible for the deposit guarantee schemes. In the event of a crisis, the resolution college should provide a forum for the exchange of information and the coordination of resolution actions.' For further details about the role of Resolution Colleges see ibid, Art 88, explained in section VI.A below.

[42] EBA, on the minimum list of qualitative and quantitative recovery plan indicators, EBA-GL-2015-02, July 2015.
[43] BRRD, Art 7(5).
[44] Ibid, recital 38.
[45] Ibid.
[46] Ibid, Art 7(5).
[47] Ibid, Art 19(1).
[48] See ibid, Art 27.
[49] Ibid, Art 19(8).
[50] Regulation (EU) No 575/2013 of the European Parliament and of the Council of 26 June 2013 on prudential requirements for credit institutions and investment firms and amending Regulation (EU) No 648/2012, OJ L 176, 27.6.2013, pp 1–337.
[51] Directive 2013/36/EU is amended by: Directive 2018/843, Directive 2019/878, Directive 2021/338. The 2021 directive was introduced as a response to the Coronavirus pandemic and only amend Article 94(2). The 2019 Directive amends areas of the 2013 Directive that are not sufficiently clear and have been subject to divergent interpretations or are over burdensome for certain institutions. Directive 2013/36/EU of the European Parliament and of the Council of 26 June 2013 on access to the activity of credit institutions and the prudential supervision of credit institutions and investment firms, amending Directive 2002/87/EC and repealing Directives 2006/48/EC and 2006/49/EC, OJ L 176, 27.6.2013, pp 338–436.

or from requiring parts or activities within a group to be separated for financial stability reasons.[52]

The agreement may provide for financial support to one or more subsidiaries in any com- **9.21**
bination of entities within the group, such as from the parent to the subsidiaries or vice versa, or between subsidiaries.[53] The support may include, inter alia, loans, guarantees, or assets to be used as collateral, in different transactions including as between the benefi-ciary and a third party.[54] For any transaction made in pursuance to it, the group financial support agreement will need to specify the calculation principles of the relevant consider-ation.[55] Third parties are precluded from exercising any right, claim, or action arising from the agreement.[56]

Several conditions must be met in order to provide group financial support. Notably, there **9.22**
needs to be 'reasonable prospect' that the support will significantly redress the financial dif-ficulties of the group entity;[57] the support must have the objective of 'preserving or restoring the financial stability of the group as a whole or any of the entities of the group' and be 'in the interests of the group entity providing the support';[58] there must also be reasonable pro-spect that the consideration for the support will be paid and that, for instance, the loan will be reimbursed (if a loan was made).[59] Further, the support must not jeopardize the liquidity or solvency of the group entity providing it[60] or its resolvability,[61] and it must not create a threat to financial stability, particularly in the group entity's Member State.[62] The EBA has developed technical standards in relation to some of the conditions,[63] submitted to the European Commission in July 2015.[64]

The Resolution Plan, on the other hand, is primarily the responsibility of the resolution **9.23**
authority to produce once the recovery plan is drafted with the firm.[65] BRRD II requires resolution authorities to designate resolution entities for the purposes of resolution plan-ning.[66] Another legal form is also introduced: the resolution group, consisting of entities and subsidiaries that on their own are not classed as resolution entities but as a group form a resolution group.[67]

The resolution plan will include the possible resolution tools likely to be utilized for a **9.24**
given core business line or critical function. The resolution authority will assess the likely

---

[52] BRRD, Art 19(4).
[53] Ibid, Art 19(5)(a).
[54] Ibid, Art 19(5)(b).
[55] Ibid, Art 19(7).
[56] Ibid, Art 19(9).
[57] Ibid, Art 23(1)(a).
[58] Ibid, Art 23(1)(b).
[59] Ibid, Art 23(1)(d).
[60] Ibid, Art 23(1)(e).
[61] Ibid, Art 23(1)(i).
[62] Ibid, Art 23(1)(f).
[63] See EBA, 'Guidelines specifying the conditions for group financial support under Article 23 of Directive 2014/59/EU', EBA/GL/2015/17, 9 July 2015 <https://www.eba.europa.eu/documents/10180/1137032/EBA-GL-2015-17+Guidelines+on+group+financial+support.pdf>.
[64] BRRD, Art 23(2).
[65] Ibid, Art 10 has been revised so that the review is carried out after the resolution actions or the exercise of powers referred to in Directive 2019/879, Art 59.
[66] Inserted in Art 2(1)(e) by Directive 2019/879, Art 83a. See also SRMR II Art 1 which includes Art 3(1)(24a).
[67] Inserted in Art 2(1)(e) by Directive 2019/879, Art 83b. See also SRMR II Art 1 which includes Art 3(1)(24b).

impediments that could arise in a potential scenario and assess the credibility of the options set out in the recovery plan to achieve its proposed responses.[68] As with the recovery plan, the resolution plan is premised on the assumption, in part, that there is no extraordinary public funding available or central bank emergency liquidity assistance or liquidity assistance based on non-standardized collateral or interest rate.[69] Notwithstanding the limits placed on such assistance the resolution plan can include the possibility of such assistance being offered, provided the appropriate assets can be set aside to use as collateral. The resolution plan requires coordination and cooperation with the resolution authority's counterparts and competent authorities to ensure that the information they need about other parts of the institution or group is readily available.[70] However, in the absence of a joint decision for the execution of the group resolution plan between resolution authorities a resolution authority in a Member State can decide its own resolution strategy and provide a detailed explanation as to why it is taking a separate decision to the members of the resolution college.[71] In respect of third country subsidiaries, the resolution authority needs to decide whether to include it or not by agreeing to include the subsidiary with the Union parent undertaking and so provide support to that subsidiary. Alternatively, the subsidiary can remain the responsibility of the third country and its resolution authority to determine whether it has the requisite loss-absorbing capacity at the entity level.

9.25   The specific requirements are set out in the BRRD Annex, Section B. The arrangements will need to include coordination and cooperation arrangements at the Union level and with third countries where the group may have legal entities.[72] BRRD II expects resolution authorities to work out the level of MREL for the proposed resolution strategy provided for in the resolution plan for both those designated for resolution and those designated for winding up under national law. The BRRD II also recognizes that resolution authorities may have additional powers that are not prescribed in the BRRD and enable such resolution the right to incorporate them for resolution groups as well.[73]

C. Resolvability

9.26   The focus on resolvability of the institution or group is very much tied to the process of supervision and resolution in a continuum.[74] In this respect BRRD II provides the resolution authorities the discretion to be able to impose and indeed take action for a breach or impediment relating to levels of funds and eligible liabilities for resolution entities at the subsidiary and group level.[75] The resolution authority is conferred the discretion to decide the evidentiary nature of the impediment and whether the actions by the entity or group has addressed it. If it has not then the resolution authority can exercise enforcement sanctions

---

[68] Ibid, Art 10(1)–(3).
[69] Ibid, Art 10(3)(a)–(c).
[70] Ibid, Art 11.
[71] Ibid, Art 16.
[72] Ibid, Arts 12–13.
[73] Ibid, Art 12(3)(e).
[74] Ibid, Art 15. See EBA, Consultation Paper, Guidelines for Institutions and Resolution Authorities on Improving Resolvability, March 2021.
[75] Recitals 17 and 24; Arts 17 and 18 of Directive 2019/879. See also SRMR II recital 21; Art 12j.

but the BRRD is silent on the punitive nature of such sanctions and leaves such decisions to the resolution authority rather than prescribe a set of enforcement sanctions to potentially take.[76] The benefit for the Banking Union is that the new enforcement powers for the SRB enable it over time to develop consistency of practice and improve bank compliance when it comes to decisions relating to removing impediments to resolvability. The assessment of resolvability needs to incorporate specifically the extent to which such institutions can be effectively supervised as well as the credibility of the resolution plans and assessing the likely impediments that could hinder the process. The general question posed is to what extent is the institution or group resolvable either by using 'normal' insolvency proceedings and winding up group entities under normal insolvency proceedings, or by applying resolution tools? In this assessment consideration needs to be given to the spill-over effects on the wider financial system and its stability, and continuity of critical economic functions.

The assessment of resolvability needs to be made based on the criteria set out in the Annex   **9.27**
to the BRRD, section C. The assumption that there is no extraordinary support, central bank emergency liquidity assistance, or liquidity assistance on the basis of non-standard forms of collateral, is incorporated in evaluating whether the institution or group is resolvable.[77] BRRD II puts greater emphasis on deciding when a group shall be deemed to be resolvable. It also explains that group-level resolution authorities must notify the EBA in a timely manner whenever a group is deemed not to be resolvable.[78] In the context of groups, the supervisory college and the resolution college play a crucial role in determining how best to overcome the impediments at a cross-border level.[79] BRRD II and SRMR II include powers to prohibit certain distributions between parts of the group.[80] The extent to which supervisors and resolution authorities can require changes in the business organization of an institution or group is quite extensive, as indicated in just some of the actions requested to be taken to resolve impediments, such as addressing the level of large exposures and divesture of assets or business lines, new or old.[81] Moreover, the competent authority or resolution authority could require the institution or group to make changes to its own funds and/or liabilities to improve the level of eligible instruments for conversion or write-down.[82] In this respect MREL instruments held by retail investors could be considered an impediment to resolvability, a matter specifically addressed in BRRD II. Equally, a high concentration of investors holding the requisite MREL can also be considered an impediment to resolvability.

D. Loss-Absorbing Capacity

The options for resolution require resolution authorities to give close attention to the loss-   **9.28**
absorbing capacity of the bank in line with the potential impact on financial stability. The responsibility to ensure the minimum amount of loss-absorbing capacity requires continuous monitoring, in contrast to resolution planning, which is broadly speaking an

---

[76] Art 17(3).
[77] Ibid, Arts 15(1)(a)–(c) and 16(a)–(c).
[78] Directive 2019/879.
[79] Ibid, Art 16(2), Art 16a (which covers the power to prohibit certain distributions), and Art 17.
[80] BRRD II, Art 16a; SRMR II Art 10a.
[81] Ibid, Art 18 as amended by Directive 2019/879.
[82] Ibid, Arts 17 and 18.

annual process. In this respect the international and regional focus needs to be on creating a level playing field and ensuring the rules associated with loss-absorbing capacity are proportionate between large 'complex' and small 'narrow' banks, but equally important for those included in the single-point-of-entry (SPOE) and multiple-point-of-entry (MPE) resolution strategies. In this respect, capital requirements are outward facing and do form the basis of the external cushion for absorbing losses, whereas the MREL is seen as inward facing (albeit externally issued) and forms the basis of an internal cushion for absorbing losses by utilizing funds for recapitalization. The level of loss absorption is likely to lead to a position where the bank is compliant with regulatory capital levels at the minimum, or even above, but that does not necessarily imply it will be recapitalized to the same level as before to maintain, in this way, its position as a global systemically important institution (G-SII) or other systemically important institution (O-SII). For it to retain such a position the level of loss-absorbing capacity is likely to be extremely high, which is not likely to be the aim of the resolution authority. The decision to set the MREL by the resolution authority will differ on whether it is the group-wide resolution authority or the resolution authority of an individual subsidiary; more specifically, whether the resolution strategy is likely to be a SPOE or an MPE during resolution. In the former the parent entity is expected to be put in resolution to recapitalize the operating subsidiaries, whereas in the latter individual subsidiaries are placed in resolution. In this scenario, the group-wide decision on recapitalization is likely to lead to greater economies of scale and, therefore, lower levels of loss-absorbing funds, whereas the alternative is likely to mean higher or even no loss-absorbing funds at the local level. The advantage the SRB has in this respect, and indeed the Banking Union, is the ability to address differences across the group and respective entities between the home and host participating Member States.

9.29   The BRRD II and SRMR II formally introduce the FSB TLAC term sheet to stand alongside the MREL requirements in EU law. The TLAC term sheet attempts to provide a level playing field for G-SIIs. The consistency of approach attempts to reduce the potential competitive advantage that could exist if countries sought to apply different standards and so pose different business costs to the requisite parts of the G-SII. The complementarity of TLAC and MREL means they provide the ingredients for potential recapitalization of systemic and non-systemic institutions to either ensure continuity of critical functions or an orderly insolvency to minimize reliance on public funds. BRRD II takes a more explicit approach on eligible liabilities for the purpose of dealing with resolution entities and for entities that are subsidiaries of resolution entities.[83] In the latter case the resolution authority is conferred considerable discretion for MREL where the subsidiaries are designated for insolvency and winding-up proceedings and are able to set MREL above the loss absorption amount.[84]

9.30   The BRRD II provides that MREL is based on own funds and eligible liabilities from a proportion of subordinated and unsubordinated debt instruments depending on which category the entity falls within. In this respect, BRRD II refers to subordinated eligible instruments, which is wider than its predecessor, which refers to subordinated eligible liabilities, since it includes Tier 2 instruments as well.[85] The more technical approach to working

---

[83]   Art 45b(1)–(3).
[84]   Art 45c(3)(a)(i).
[85]   Art 44a, defined in Art 2(1)(71b).

out a bank's MREL is based on risk-weighted assets so it is aligned with the calculation of capital requirements. The entities are placed in to the following categories: those designated as G-SIIs, so falling within the requirements of TLAC plus the potential for more if the resolution authority considers it necessary; the new top-tier banks with assets over EUR 100 billion; and those remaining, which fall within the discretion of the resolution authority to work out their loss-absorbing capacity.[86] In all three instances there are administrative discretion factors, in that all three can pose a systemic risk or a risk of contagion even for those entities designated for insolvency and winding-up proceedings. In the latter category are essentially narrow banks that are reliant on deposits as their primary or sole source of funding.[87]

III. Early Intervention

9.31 The power of early intervention is an integral part of supervision.[88] However, the decision-making powers surrounding the decision-making process has required a structure to enable the competent authority or the resolution authority and the institution and group to understand how it is likely to be decided and what actions are likely to be taken. The trigger for early intervention can be pulled when 'an institution infringes or, due, inter alia, to a rapidly deteriorating financial condition, including deteriorating liquidity situation, increasing level of leverage, non-performing loans, or concentration of exposures, as assessed on the basis of a set of triggers, which may include the institution's own funds requirement, is likely in the near future to infringe prudential capital requirements.[89] In this respect, early intervention measures are just some of the actions that could be taken, which also include private sector measures or other supervisory actions that could prevent the failure of the institution.[90] BRRD II extends the early intervention powers to enable resolution authorities to introduce a moratorium—to suspend payments or delivery obligations for a maximum of two days once the entity is, inter alia, considered to be failing or likely to fail.[91] It can equally limit payouts to depositors to a daily amount. For example, in Malta in the decision regarding Nemea Bank plc, after its licence was withdrawn for failure to comply with its directions on regulatory requirements and as part of the process of protecting depositors, depositors were limited to withdrawals of between EUR 250–2,500 per depositor.[92] This provided the time to the Maltese authorities to protect the depositor base and determine the bank's assets and liabilities.

9.32 The infringements emphasize the balance sheet; and the competent authority and resolution authority will need to be mindful of the fact that such risks to balance sheet insolvency are

---

[86] Art 45d–f; Art 12e–g SRMR II.
[87] Art 45c(5).
[88] Ibid, Art 27. See also supervisory powers in association with CRD Directive 2014/65/EU and CRR to address actual or likely infringements of supervisory requirements: Arts 104–105 CRD. See EBA Report on the Application of Early Intervention Measures in the European Union in Accordance with Articles 27–29 of the BRRD, 2021.
[89] Ibid, Art 27(1).
[90] Art 32(1)(b).
[91] Art 33a.
[92] EBA, Notification from Malta Depositor Compensation Scheme on Unavailability of Deposits at Nemea Bank plc <https://www.eba.europa.eu/regulation-and-policy/recovery-and-resolution/notifications-on-resolut ion-cases-and-use-of-dgs-funds/malta>.

a time lag indicator of ensuing problems, and once they materialize it could be too late. Certainly the recent EBA 2015 guidelines rightly place appropriate emphasis on a broader range of significant events as well, including conduct of business failures, conduct failures, and prudential failures.[93] It may be argued that the introduction of infringement limits the discretion of the competent authority. Evidence of one of those infringements may result in their being little time to resolve the matter. In light of this, a range of other indicators such management behaviour and culture could be factored into the decision-making process as precursors to the explicit infringements indicated above. When it is evident that an infringement has occurred, the competent authority can require the institution or group management body to initiate measures set out in the recovery plan or take alternative actions within the decided time frame to resolve the infringement.[94] The competent authority or the resolution authority could, inter alia, ask the management to restructure its debt or find a private sector purchaser, for instance. In circumstances where there is personal culpability of management, the competent authority should have the power to be able to remove them and appoint new management or a temporary administrator.[95] The EBA guidelines unfortunately leave to the competent authority the discretion to determine when a trigger is expected to be pulled, as it does not explain what level of evidence it needs to exercise the trigger, should it 'reasonably likely' or 'highly likely' to infringe the requirements. The evidentiary burden for the administrative decision will determine how much time the competent and resolution authority will need to allow the institution to work out its position. Moreover, the guidelines will implicitly require the competent authority for resolution and prudential purposes to cooperate and coordinate with the markets and conduct of business regulator since some of the significant events as possible trigger events are market-based, linked to rogue trading or fraud.[96] This is necessary; however, it will mean cooperation agreements will need to be in place to ensure that this type of information is shared in a timely manner.

9.33   The competent authority can appoint a temporary administrator not with the remit to decide in lieu of them but primarily for the purpose of identifying the financial position and putting in place proposals to either preserve or restore the institution's or group's financial position.[97] In the case of groups, early intervention powers require a lot more coordination since a decision like that will have an impact on the confidence in other parts of the group.[98] In this scenario, the consolidated supervisor is responsible for notifying the other competent authorities and resolution authorities. The competent authorities in a group scenario may face the challenge and indeed criticism of either not intervening early enough or intervening too late, and so prematurely giving rise to conflicts. Moreover, where multiple administrators are appointed by competent authorities there is the risk that the powers and

---

[93]   EBA, Guidelines on triggers for use of early intervention measures pursuant to Article 27(4) of Directive 2014/59/EU, July 2015, para 24: <http://www.kpmg.com/UK/en/IssuesAndInsights/ArticlesPublications/Pages/MF-Global-Client-Creditor-claims-forms.aspx>.

[94]   BRRD, Art 27(1)(a)–(h).

[95]   Ibid, Art 28; see also Art 110 relating to 'Administrative penalties and other administrative measures'.

[96]   EBA, Guidelines on triggers for use of early intervention measures pursuant to Article 27(4) of Directive 2014/59/EU, July 2015, para 24.

[97]   BRRD, Art 29.

[98]   Ibid, Art 30.

authority of temporary administrators could differ, giving rise to an inconsistent approach across the European Union for single entities or groups.

The regulatory space of supervision and early intervention is a continuum. It is evident in the directive that supervision interventions such as a management intervention to restructure its debts in the first instance and then possibly directions to write-down or convert capital instruments or initiate a firm-led private purchase, as explained above, can be and are likely to be taken pre-emptively of pulling the trigger on early intervention powers to move the bank into resolution. In light of this scenario, Article 68 requires the competent and resolution authorities to ensure that contracts are drafted in the future so that the triggering of the early intervention power does not amount to an event of default—an enforcement event or an event classed as insolvency. BRRD II provides more specificity to Article 68 of the BRRD by explaining that a crisis prevention or crisis management measure does not constitute non-performance of a contractual obligation. BRRD II also emphasizes the importance of the continuity of contracts, by providing that substantive obligations in contracts for payments or delivery obligations and provision of collateral continue to be performed despite such measures being taken. **9.34**

IV. Resolution Objectives, Conditions, and Principles

The core within the BRRD are the introduction of a comprehensive framework for a toolkit to resolve banks in distress in Europe.[99] The framework builds on the regulatory and supervisory reforms explained above in the form of 'preparation' and 'early intervention' powers. The limits of regulation and supervision mean banks can experience periods of distress through risks materializing either endogenously or exogenously. The resolution toolkit set out in the BRRD provides the techniques to try to resolve banks in distress, either to ensure that they continue as a going concern, or to restore them as a going concern or place a part or the whole institution or group into insolvency proceedings so that they can be put into winding-up proceedings, in an orderly manner.[100] The directive introduces a number of tools in the lexicon of bank resolution which are well established or relatively new in the formal sense when it comes to thinking about a special resolution regime for banks and investment firms. It is important to note, however, that one tool is unlikely to be used on its own to resolve a bank in distress. Resolution schemes will consist, rather, of a combination of tools. This section will explain the role and purpose of each tool. **9.35**

The use of resolution tools exists within the context of a set of objectives, conditions, and principles that the competent and resolution authorities will need to be mindful of to determine the best options to deal with the bank in distress. It is important for the institution or group and the competent authorities at the recovery planning stage understand the utility of the resolution tools when assessing how to deal with significant risks that could arise within their business lines and critical functions. The resolution authority will need to be mindful of those objectives when assessing the 'resolution plans' and deciding which tool or set of tools will best address the various scenarios. **9.36**

---

[99] Ibid, Art 31.
[100] See ibid, recitals 5–14.

9.37   The resolution objectives are to ensure continuity of critical functions; avoid significant adverse effects on financial stability; protect public funds; protect covered depositors and investors; and protect client funds and client assets.[101] While regulation and supervision of financial services is implicitly mindful of these objectives, it is important to emphasize the importance of putting them in an explicit setting; coinciding with the wider concerns of financial stability, since it provides a clear expression of whose interests competent and resolution authorities are primarily concerned about. Notwithstanding the hierarchy of interests the resolution authority is required to evaluate the use of the resolution tools, keeping in mind the importance of minimizing the costs of resolution and maintaining value within the institution or group to minimize unnecessary losses to shareholders and creditors, despite the fact that it does not explicitly make reference to those respective groups at this point.

9.38   The decision to take an institution or group into resolution is based on a set of conditions, namely whether it is failing or is likely fail.[102] This decision is likely to be taken by the competent authority but in light of the authority of competent authorities in Member States the BRRD indicates it can be a joint decision with the resolution authority. The point at which the decision is taken certainly resides within a time frame, which is primarily within the discretion of the competent authority or resolution authority to determine. The BRRD leaves the method to determine whether an institution or group is failing or likely to fail within the discretion of the Member State. It does not set down a criteria to decide, which in some respects means Member States could differ on when the decision is made, and so some could take the decision earlier than others, significantly impacting the period in which early intervention can be applied. Determining whether an institution is failing or likely to fail is quite possibly the most intrusive decision in the autonomy of the institution that a competent or resolution authority can take.[103] The directive also provides a rather catch-all provision, namely that the decision to place the institution into resolution has to be in the public interest.[104] The Directive 2019/879 inserts Article 32b, which covers the insolvency proceedings for institutions that are not subject to resolution action, cases where a resolution action would not be in the public interest but need to be wound up. Article 32b continues to allow Member States to exercise their own national approach to such cases as part of their normal insolvency proceedings that lead to the winding up of the entity. Equally, it will remain in the discretion of the Member State to decide how the decision in Article 32b influences their decision about the authorization of the entity. The provision protects the competent and resolution authorities while making it necessary for the resolution authority to be able to present sufficient and compelling evidence to stand up to any potential judicial review to determine whether the decision is proportionate in light of competing interests. For instance, the resolution authorities will need to have in place a credible procedure for the valuation of assets and liabilities which will need to be carried out within a specific time frame by an independent valuation. The due process will need to be credible to mitigate some of the challenges associated with resolution and provide that the decision ultimately results in the shareholders or creditors in a position of being no worse off than they would be in a hypothetical insolvency proceeding. Moreover, the ability to undertake

---

[101]   Ibid, Art 31(2)(a)–(e).
[102]   Ibid, Art 32 as amended by Directive 2019/879.
[103]   Ibid, Art 32(1)(a)–(c) as amended by Directive 2019/879.
[104]   Ibid, Art 32(1)(c).

an independent valuation within an appropriate time frame will need to be explained to minimize the expectations gap associated with the process of valuation.

The directive leaves some ambiguity with respect to the order of decisions. Since it builds **9.39** the possibility of the competent authority into this part of the decision-making process, it has to look for options such as a private sector solution *ex ante* rather than to take the decision as to whether the institution is failing or likely to fail *ex post*. The write-down or conversion of capital instruments to reduce the risk of the institution failing seems to imply that write-down and conversion and possibly a private takeover, which the institution could orchestrate, are likely to be pre-early intervention supervisory decisions rather than strictly resolution measures, *ex post*.[105] The triggers to assess whether an institution is failing are stated to be based on objective criteria but on what basis it is to be determined is not spelt out in any satisfactory detail. It is inevitable that the objective criteria will consist of a significant amount of supervisory judgement and experience, rather than simply being based on quantitative measures. For instance, is a threshold of *'reasonably'* likely or *'highly'* likely necessary for the likely to fail or failing trigger?[106] It could place significant evidentiary burden on the competent and resolution authorities to come to a decision to exercise resolution powers. It primarily focuses on infringements of the authorization criteria, which is quite wide as it could refer to qualitative and quantitative aspects of authorization such as conduct of business risk, conduct risk, and prudential risks. The directive however, refers to the level of own funds, deterioration of assets, the level of asset to liabilities, and cash flow insolvency. However, the resolution authority will primarily need to determine whether or not the institution or group has reached a point of non-viability. After exhausting its powers, the competent authority has then to decide at the supervisory level, once the write-down and conversion of capital instruments has been completed, which resolution tool to utilize either separately or jointly.[107]

In addition to criteria associated with authorization, and other criteria of individual institu- **9.40** tions, it also sets out responses to more market-wide sector-based issues for which extraordinary public financial support is needed to stabilize the markets and circumvent instability in the wider economy.[108] This can take the form of a state guarantee, asset purchase schemes of capital instruments for the purposes of capital shortfalls found to exist after a market-wide stress test or asset quality review has been undertaken by the competent authority and has identified the need for such measures to be taken.[109] The directive therefore leaves the option for states to utilize techniques deployed during the global financial crisis to address technically solvent institutions that nevertheless pose market-wide risks. These measures will also require the authorities to seek approval for the purposes of state aid rules before they can be deployed.

The disciplining effects of the resolution process are set out in the principles of resolution.[110] **9.41** These explain who bears the losses and in what order: shareholders are required to bear the

---

[105] Ibid, Art 32(1)(c).
[106] It is worthy to recall the European nature of this regime subject to translation (mistakes) and differing connotations to the words 'reasonably' and 'highly'.
[107] BRRD, Art 59(4). The title of Article 59 has been replaced and is now 'Requirement to write down or convert relevant capital instruments and eligible liabilities'; Art 21 SRMR II
[108] Ibid, Art 32(4)(a)–(d)(i)–(iii).
[109] Ibid, Art 32(4).
[110] Ibid, Art 34.

first losses, then the unsecured creditors, and finally uninsured depositors in order of priority. In this respect covered deposits under the Deposit Guarantee Schemes Directive are fully protected.[111] The competent authorities and resolution authorities will need to assess the culpability of management in the demise of the institution or group and either replace them immediately or retain them until an orderly resolution can be worked out in light of the fact that the existing management will have full institutional knowledge of the business lines and critical functions that the institution or group undertakes.[112]

9.42   Valuation of assets and liabilities will play a critical role in the resolution process, since it will determine its success in terms of contributing to the decision regarding which resolution tool will achieve the resolution objective, conditions, and principles.[113] The process of valuation is not a perfect science and is primarily determined by the quality and accuracy of the information the institution holds and the timeliness of the information given to them. While considering the conditions for resolution the independent valuation will include the following matters: whether the conditions for write-down and conversation of capital have been achieved and the impact on the dilution of shares; the eligible debtholders of the outcome of the bail-in; which assets and liabilities are to be transferred to the bridge bank; and the decision on which assets and liabilities will be included in the sale of business tool.[114]

9.43   A key factor in the success of the independent valuation will be the timing of intervention to safeguard and ascertain value within the institution to minimize losses. In this respect the principle 'no creditor worse off' will apply. The valuation will need to be structured according to the priority of claims on the assets in the institution.[115] If the valuation cannot be done on time, then a provisional valuation is possible. This is perhaps the most critical aspect of the resolution process to ensure that value is retained. The competent and resolution authorities will need to ensure that they act within the remit of their administrative duties to avoid potential judicial review or actions in torts. It is evident the valuation process will be the basis to decide the resolution tool and the transfers or retransfers of assets and liabilities between the various parts of the restructured bank. These issues will be explored in the next section.

V. Resolution Tools

9.44   The directive requires the resolution authority to be given a range of tools and powers to exercise and manage the resolution process.[116] While the resolution authority is required to take 'ownership and control' for the purposes of resolution, the exercise of its powers do not equate to it acting in the capacity of director or shadow director of the institution or group in resolution. Once the resolution authority determines that the objectives and conditions

---

[111]   Ibid, Art 34(1)(a)–(i).
[112]   Ibid, Art 35.
[113]   Ibid, Art 36.
[114]   Ibid, Art 36(4)(a)–(g) as amended by Art 59 of Directive 2019/879 to now refer to capital instruments and eligible liabilities in accordance.
[115]   Ibid, Art 36(8).
[116]   Ibid, Art 37(1)–(3) see also Art 72.

of resolution are threatened or met, the resolution authority needs to decide which resolution tool or tools to initiate either individually or in combination with one another.[117] The directive is silent on the use of insolvency procedures to deal with the residual bank, which are also an integral part of the process of dealing with banks in distress. This matter essentially remains in the discretion of the existing insolvency laws of each Member State. The resolution tools are the sale of business tool, the bridge institution tool, the asset separation tool, and the bail-in tool. A number of these have been in place for a significant length of time and there is a considerable level of institutional experience connected to them when it comes to their use, apart from the bail-in tool which constitutes a true innovation.

A. The Sale of Business Tool

The resolution authority is required to have in place the power to be able to transfer ownership and the assets and liabilities of the institution to a private purchaser.[118] The directive requires the resolution authority to follow a number of measures. The resolution authority will be required to take reasonable steps to get commercial terms and put in place a process of marketing the assets, rights, and liabilities.[119] The latter is limited in terms of disclosure if it poses material risks to financial stability. The transfer or re-transfer of shares, assets, and liabilities will enable the resolution authority to assist with ensuring the commercial terms of the business. A particular issue associated with regulation and supervision of the purchaser is to ensure that the acquirer has the appropriate authorization to undertake the business acquired.[120] This will require involvement of the competent authority to assess whether the acquirer is indeed fit and proper to undertake the acquired business. This is likely to be considered at the point of initiating interest in the acquisition. The directive does recognize that the need for speedy and orderly resolution may mean that the due diligence to gauge whether the acquirers' authorization criteria is met runs the risk of the competent authority not agreeing with the authorization. In some respects it forms a kind of cooling-off period for all parties involved. It is therefore important for the competent and resolution authorities to work closely together at the point of assessing which resolution tool or combination of tools is the most appropriate to resolve the problems at the institution in distress. This would avoid circumstances where the resolution authority has to ask the acquirer to divest its ownership within the divestment period.[121] The new acquirer will need to be assessed for the purposes of membership of payment systems and clearing and settlement systems, and compensation schemes.[122] The competent and resolution authorities will also need to minimize the risk of conflicts of interest in the way that it evaluates the commercial terms between private sector bidders during the process of executing the sale and transfer of assets and liabilities.[123]

9.45

---

[117] Ibid, Art 37(4)–(5).
[118] Ibid, Art 38(1).
[119] Ibid, Art 38(2)–(3).
[120] Ibid, Art 38(7).
[121] Ibid, Art 38(9)(a)–(f).
[122] Ibid, Art 38(12)(a)–(b).
[123] Ibid, Art 39.

B. The Bridge Institution Tool

9.46   The bridge bank tool has been an important tool in the resolution toolkit in a number of jurisdictions.[124] The bridge bank is expected to take responsibility of the critical function.[125] It will take responsibility by either a transfer of shares or instrument of ownership or assets and liabilities to the bridge bank.[126] The initiation of the bridge bank can be undertaken at the initiative of the resolution authority and does not require shareholder agreement.[127] This avoids the resolution authority seeking approval of the shareholders, which may not always be forthcoming, and enables the resolution authority to undertake the set-up of the bridge bank to achieve the resolution objectives and principles. The bridge bank will either be owned by a public authority or the resolution authority.[128] The bridge bank is not expected to be the 'bad bank'. In the balance sheet of the newly created bank, the liabilities cannot be greater than the assets after the transfer and/or part and reverse transfer of assets and liabilities.[129] The resolution authority has the discretion to initiate transfers and reverse transfers to improve the balance sheet of the bridge bank and ensure that it is a going concern. Since the bridge bank is publicly owned such transfers can be undertaken during the life of the bridge bank. The bridge bank will undertake the business of the authorization of the bank in resolution and so the new institution benefits from the franchise value of the business.

9.47   Once the assets are transferred the shareholders or creditors have no further rights to the transferred assets.[130] The management of the bridge bank can have their liability configured so that it can be limited to an extent where they are exempted from liability unless the act or omission is one of gross negligence.[131] The resolution authority will set out the constitution of the bridge bank and it will craft out its commercial strategy and its appetite to risk. However, the bridge bank is expected to cease to exist when it merges with another bank by way of sale of the business to a third party.[132] The directive provides a time frame for the life of the bridge bank of up to two years, with the option for the resolution authority to extend the period in extraordinary circumstances.[133]

C. Asset Separation Tool

9.48   The asset separation tool provides the mechanism to transfer and carve out rights, assets, and liabilities to the asset management vehicle.[134] This approach has gained significant prominence during the financial crisis, and became known as the 'bad bank' approach. The main difference to the financial crisis, however, and the other resolution tools, is that it

---

[124] Ibid, Art 40.
[125] Ibid, Art 40(1).
[126] Ibid, Art 40(1)(a)–(b).
[127] Ibid, Art 40(1).
[128] Ibid, Art 40(2)(a)–(b).
[129] Ibid, Art 49(3).
[130] Ibid, Art 40(12).
[131] Ibid, Art 40(13).
[132] Ibid, Art 41(3)(a)–(e)
[133] Ibid, Art 41(5)–(6).
[134] Ibid, Art 42.

cannot be applied alone but in conjunction with other resolution tools—most notably the bail-in tool. Once the institution is in resolution the resolution authorities will need to work out how to improve the viability of the bridge bank and ensure that the resolution object-ives are complied with. The asset management vehicle contributes significantly to achieving that purpose. The asset management company will be separately incorporated but either partially or wholly owned as a public authority.[135] The assets and liabilities transferred to the asset management vehicle are more likely to be those deemed bad assets and liabilities, so essentially non-performing, but attempting to execute the sale to maximize the value or ensure orderly liquidation.[136] This will place the asset management vehicle at arm's-length and enable them to manage the winding down of bad assets without institutional and polit-ical interference. The resolution authority is required to ensure that the asset management vehicle is separately constituted but has the authority to appoint management and approve remuneration policy.[137] The resolution authority will need to work with the asset arrange-ment vehicle to work out its strategy and appetite for risk. More importantly, the resolution authority has the authority to limit the liability of the asset management vehicle to the shareholders or creditors of the rights, assets, or liabilities transferred to it,[138] unless the asset management vehicle acts with gross negligence in the discharge of its responsibilities. The process of resolution is not static but a fluid relationship and it will involve the various stakeholders in resolution to ensure that assets and liabilities are transferred or re-trans-ferred fully and/or partially from the various parts of the institution in resolution, from the institution itself, the bridge bank, and the asset management vehicle to ensure that the ob-jectives and principles of resolution are complied with.

D. The Bail-in Tool

The bail-in tool is the newest tool in the lexicon of bank resolution tools and is perhaps the most controversial given the purpose of the tool.[139] The bail-in power is primarily aimed at recapitalizing the bank and possibly turning its affairs around so that it complies with au-thorization requirements and can continue to undertake regulated activities or fund reso-lution measures. The bail-in tool allows write-down of equity and certain debt instruments as well as converting debt instruments into equity.[140] However, it is important to note this needs to be assessed to ensure subordinated debt holding is not the result of criminal ac-tivities. If it is the case, then bail-in of such instruments is likely to be denied. This was the case in the SRB resolution decision to place the Latvian bank AS PNB Banka into national insolvency proceedings, when the potential for conversion of subordinated debt into equity to recapitalize the bank was not implemented as per the recovery plan.[141]

9.49

---

[135] Ibid, Art 42(2)(a)–(b).
[136] Ibid, Art 42(3).
[137] Ibid, Art 42(4)(a)–(d).
[138] Ibid, Art 42(13).
[139] Ibid, Art 43.
[140] Ibid, Art 43(2)(a)–(b).
[141] Decision of the Single Resolution Board of 15 August 2019 concerning the assessment of the conditions for resolution in respect of AS PNB Banka (SRB/EES/2019/131), 8: <https://www.srb.europa.eu/system/files/media/document/non-confidential_version_of_the_resolution_decision_in_relation_to_as_pnb_banka.pdf>.

9.50   The aim of BRRD II in respect of the loss-absorbing capacity of a bank is to improve consistency across the Member States and in respect of bail-in to improve its application for groups operating across borders.[142] BRRD II amends the requirement for contractual recognition of bail-in. There is now an exemption to the requirement where it would be legally or otherwise impracticable to include a contractual recognition of bail-in in a contract. The exemption does not apply to an Additional Tier 1 instrument, Tier 2 instrument, or unsecured debt instrument, the aim of which is to improve the process for bail-in in a resolution.

9.51   The Member State is required to work out in advance with the institution or group which liabilities are eligible for bail-in.[143] However, the resolution authority is prohibited from bailing-in a number of liabilities[144] such as deposits covered by the deposit guarantee scheme (DGS), secured liabilities, any liabilities held for a client that qualify as either client assets or client money, liabilities that arise from a fiduciary relationship, liabilities (to other institutions) with an original (or in certain cases remaining) maturity of less than seven days, liabilities with a maturity of less than seven days, employee remunerations and salaries with the exception of material risk takers, commercial trade creditors, tax and social security authorities, and the deposit guarantee scheme. The resolution authority nevertheless does have some discretion to decide which debt instruments are eligible for bail-in when considering the available time, market conditions, and the implications for financial stability.[145] However, the exclusion of otherwise eligible bail-in liabilities has to be proportionate and should not undermine the safeguarding of critical functions or business lines. The assessment of included and excluded liabilities in a write-down or conversion needs to be mindful of the principle that no shareholder or creditor is to be worse off than in a hypothetical insolvency proceeding.[146] If only certain creditors within a creditors' class are subject to the bail-in, affected creditors should be compensated.

9.52   A more pressing issue exposed by a number of Italian banks has been the sale of subordinated debt instruments to retail investors. Unknown to retail investors prior to the sale their life savings, in some cases, were exposed to bail-in to recapitalize the bank. In order to address this risk BRRD II requires banks to undertake due diligence to determine their exposures to retail investors.[147] But more importantly, the banks need have in place suitability tests to advise retail clients of their risk exposure to bail-in by limiting such instruments to 10 per cent and a minimum of at least EUR 10,000 in their portfolio, for example. From the perspective of MREL the size of retail investor holding of such liabilities could be considered by the resolution authority as an impediment to resolvability because of the political implications of bailing in such retail investors who are not necessarily aware of the risk.

9.53   The write-down and conversion of capital instruments needs to comply with the priority of claims set out in insolvency proceedings so that Common Equity Tier 1 instruments are written down in proportion to the losses incurred; and if necessary the Additional Tier 1 and Tier 2 instruments are either written down or converted into Common Equity Tier

---

[142]   BRRD II, recital 8.

[143]   Ibid, Art 44 as amended by Directive 2019/879 (BRRD II); SRMR Art 12b to include exemption to the contractual recognition of bail-in.

[144]   Ibid, Art 44(2)(a)–(g).

[145]   Ibid, Art 44(3)(a)–(d) as amended by BRRD II.

[146]   Ibid, Art 44(4).as amended by BRRD II in order to reflect the ability to exclude bail-in liability.

[147]   Art 44a; SRMR II, recital 14.

1 instruments.[148] Nevertheless, the resolution financing arrangement can be expected to make a contribution of up to 5 per cent to the resolution of the institution provided that at least 8 per cent has been bailed-in by shareholders and those with eligible liabilities.[149] The level of equity and liabilities bailed-in needs to be proportionate so that the institution continues to meet the authorization criteria.

The bail-in tool requires institutions to have in place own funds and eligible liabilities as a percentage of total liabilities and own funds of the institution.[150] The BRRD II extends the discretion of the Member State to allow banks to use any part of their own funds including in excess of the required level for the purpose of MREL. In part this means the banks own funds are utilized to the extent possible before losses fall on creditors as would be the case in normal insolvency proceedings. In this respect, eligible liabilities need to be fully paid up; unsecured; with a maturity of at least one year; should not arise from a derivative; or should not be a publicly insured deposit. However, BRRD II enables Member States to exercise their discretion to allow some structured loan notes with embedded derivatives to be used for the purpose of bail-in.[151] The resolution authority and the competent authority are expected to work together to ensure that the institution has appropriate liabilities for bail-in to ensure resolution.[152] This is likely to form part of the assessment to produce recovery and resolution plans, at the preparation stage. In addition to the expectation to report to the competent and resolution authorities, banks are expected to disclose the levels and maturity profiles of eligible liabilities and bail-in liabilities to the public. The resolution authority and the competent authority will need to work together to work out the minimum requirement that institutions will need to hold at an institutional and group level. This also requires them to assess whether the DGS could contribute to the financing of the resolution. The move towards ensuring that institutions meet minimum requirements will then form the basis of data submitted to the EBA so that it can report on the move towards compliance with these requirements to the European Commission. **9.54**

The resolution authority will need to assess the amount of eligible bail-in liabilities to determine whether there is enough to convert into Common Equity Tier 1 capital.[153] The resolution authority needs to keep this under review to determine whether or not there is enough for the institution in resolution or a bridge institution. The resolution authority will also need to assess whether there are enough bail-in liabilities to meet the needs of the asset management vehicle, if that resolution tool is utilized in conjunction with bail-in. The level of bailed-in liabilities varies considerably in light of the business and financing model of institutions which means the institutions will need to change them to ensure that they have enough. **9.55**

The resolution authority will also need to set out their treatment of shareholders so that they are informed about how their rights and interests will be impacted by the write-down **9.56**

---

[148] Ibid, Art 60(1) as amended by BRRD II to include a new title 'provisions concerning the write down or conversion of relevant capital instruments and eligible liabilities.

[149] Ibid, Art 44(5)(a)–(b).

[150] Ibid, Art 45.

[151] Art 45b; SRMR II Art 72c.

[152] Ibid, Art 46 as amended by BRRD II to now refer to 'bail-inable liabilities' which is also replaced in SRMR II Art 3(1)(48).

[153] Ibid, Art 46(2).

and bail-in policy.[154] The directive requires shareholders to be aware that the resolution authority can either cancel or transfer existing shares or other instruments to bailed-in creditors. This will comply with the principle that shareholders will bear the first losses in a resolution, and then creditors. The resolution authority during the process of write-down and transfer needs to review whether it is sufficient or not, as it could mean they will have to compensate or re-transfer. The resolution authority will need to value the shares and liabilities to determine the possible rate of conversion and write-down depending on the class of instruments and in accordance with the predetermined sequence according to the Member State's insolvency law. Moreover, in circumstances where the resolution authority decides to exercise its resolution powers and only partly bail-in equity and liabilities, then the original shareholder and creditors will need to be compensated based on an estimation of the recovery rate in a hypothetical insolvency proceeding under normal insolvency law.[155]

9.57   The resolution authority will need to ensure that all administrative requirements such as registers and listing of shares for instance are amended and changed to ensure application of bail-in. It will also need to ensure that all procedural impediments to conversion are removed. The designated liabilities will require amendment to include a contractual provision to recognize bail-in. Thereby, liabilities governed or being otherwise subject to the laws of a third country become bail-in eligible. In this respect the contractual parties agree to abide by the write-down or conversion. The move towards complying with the provision is an onerous one and will require the EBA to assist with technical guidance to assist resolution authorities with devising a list of liabilities included and excluded from bail-in.

9.58   The power to write down or convert capital instruments can be taken at two points in time, either before, or in conjunction with resolution tools when the conditions for resolution are considered to exist.[156] In light of the fact that this power of intervention interferes with private law rights the Member State has to ensure the resolution authority has the powers to exercise that decision. The competent and resolution authorities will need to ensure that they know where those capital instruments are located and the amount, especially when the competent and resolution authorities are responsible for a group resolution; it could be located either at the entity-subsidiary or parent level. In fact, in order to make liabilities 'bail-inable', the obligations need to be subordinated in order not to infringe the creditor hierarchy.

9.59   The approach of such subordination varies among Member States. For instance, Germany proposes a subordination of certain liabilities upon insolvency (statutory subordination). The Italian authorities proposed a statutory subordination approach which seeks to make certain liabilities more senior if insolvency proceedings are commenced. A third approach, suggested for instance by Spain, includes issuing a new form of Tier 3 liabilities. The English approach is to require financial institutions to issue sufficient liabilities at holding level (structural subordination), thereby subordinating them in relation to the liabilities of the operating entities. If the structure of the bank group does not allow debt to be issued at holding level, the terms of the liability should contain provisions causing the subordination (contractual subordination).

---

[154]   Ibid, Art 47 as amended by BRRD II.
[155]   See also, ibid, Art 74.
[156]   Ibid, Art 48 as amended by BRRD II.

The stabilization tools explained above provide the first line of defence when it comes to **9.60** dealing with banks in distress either individually and/or in combination with one another. The directive sets out the resolution tools but does not imply that one resolution tool or another is likely to take a dominant role, albeit the institution will need a sufficient amount of capital instruments that can be written down or converted so as to recapitalize the bank or fund the resolution measure. The more likely scenario is this power will be exercised in conjunction with other resolution tools. Moreover, when there is a wider market-based situation of distress, governments may utilize market-wide tools so that critical functions and business lines can continue and a sufficient amount of value can be retained to ensure creditors are not in a position where they are worse off than in a hypothetical insolvency proceeding. Notwithstanding the utility of the resolution tools and the central bank facilities and extraordinary facilities to resolve distress banks, they on their own may not be a complete panacea. The directive takes a rather pragmatic view and incorporates the need for Member States to work out *ex ante* when and how government assistance may be provided in the last resort. This is explored in the following section.

E. Government Financial Stabilization Fund

The political rationale for the directive was primarily driven to eradicate the moral hazard **9.61** problem arising from government bail-outs with taxpayers' funds. However, the likelihood of that occurring in a climate where there is limited *ex ante* privately funded schemes to ensure that means a total private sector resolution to provide an orderly resolution for distressed institutions is quite remote. The government stabilization tool is expected to assist in circumstances where resolution tools on their own will not achieve the objectives of resolution, the risk is systemic, and there is a necessity for government-funded support to be provided to minimize the risk to financial stability and protect the public interest.[157] The directive sets out two options: the public equity support tool and the temporary public ownership tool, both of which have been utilized to deal with banks in distress.[158] In the latter case, the recapitalization by the public means it is required to be managed on commercial terms and the bank is expected to be sold back to the private sector when the financial position allows. In the former, the Member State is required to transfer ownership to a newly established corporation which is expected to be wholly owned by the state. In this case, the newly owned institution is also expected to be run on commercial terms and returned to the private sector when it is commercially and financially expedient to do so.

F. Resolution Powers of the Resolution Authority: Administrative and Procedural

The resolution authority requires a considerable range of powers to execute its responsibil- **9.62** ities set out in the directive.[159] The resolution authority and competent authority will need

---

[157] Ibid, Art 56.
[158] Ibid, Arts 57 and 58.
[159] Ibid, Art 63; see also Arts 81–82.

to plan administratively how they will work together both at the crisis prevention and crisis management stage. They will also need to work out lines of communication and formal notification of their decisions for internal purposes and public purposes. These processes of decision making and communication will need to comply with professional secrecy laws to safeguard and manage the resolution process as orderly as possible.[160] However, more widely than that, both authorities will need to vary levels, work out lines of communication, notification of decisions and orders with the central bank, the deposit guarantee scheme, ministry of finance, and the designated body responsible for resolution financing arrangements. The procedural arrangements for resolution will require the resolution authority and the competent authority to put in place mechanisms for cooperation and coordination with their counterparts in third countries. In this case, a significant amount of that work will be undertaken within the supervisory and resolution colleges.

9.63   The resolution authority is expected to have a range of powers and responsibilities to ensure that it can undertake its role in resolution.[161] The resolution authority will require powers to request information and oversee the completion of the resolution plan at the preparation stages. The resolution authority will also have its own powers to undertake on-site inspections. While the authority likely to trigger early intervention is the competent authority which will be the supervisory authority, the resolution authority will also need to be able to exercise such a power, as well as having powers to initiate resolution, namely the authority to seize control of an organization and exercise those rights normally administrated by shareholders and the management body. The resolution authority is required to have all the powers to fully execute resolution. A central plank to the success of cross-border resolution of institutions and groups is appropriate cooperation between the Member States and their authorities. The directive requires Member States to give effect to transfer orders relating to instruments of ownership, assets, rights, and liabilities from other Member States.[162]

9.64   Member States are required to provide all reasonable assistance to ensure compliance with such orders. Moreover, Member States 'are not entitled to prevent, challenge, or set aside the transfer under any provision of the law of the member state where the assets are located or of the law governing the shares, other instruments of ownership, rights or liabilities'.[163] In other instances, where Member States exercise either their write-down or conversion powers other Member States cannot permit those affected to challenge that decision, under any provision of law. The directive requires resolution authorities to work in conjunction with the administrator with their third-country counterparts to take 'all necessary steps' to ensure compliance with their orders relating to transfers of shares, assets, rights, or liabilities.[164] In instances where there is no cooperation from a third country the resolution authority should have the authority not to proceed with a requested transfer order or exercise conversion powers relating to shares, assets, liabilities, or rights.[165]

[160] Ibid, Art 84.
[161] Ibid, Art 63(1)(a)–(m). The words 'eligible liabilities' are replaced with 'bail-inable liabilities' by the BRRD II.
[162] Ibid, Art 64(1)(a)–(f).
[163] Ibid, Art 66(3).
[164] Ibid, Art 67(1)(a)–(c).
[165] Ibid, Art 67(2).

The resolution authority and the competent authority need to ensure that the powers of **9.65** crisis prevention and crisis management are clearly delineated in the Member State and work out the extent to which there is likely to be impediments to cooperation and coordination with third countries. A particular challenge that the directive identifies is the recognition of crisis management measures and distinguishing between crisis prevention measures namely early intervention powers and insolvency powers, in particular the impact of such decisions on contractual enforcement provisions. While this may be less of a challenge in the European Union with the efforts going into resolving and recognizing resolution orders, such impediments may act as an obstacle regarding third countries in terms of coordination and cooperation.

The decisions of the competent and resolution authority are far-reaching and in normal cir- **9.66** cumstances would be subject to judicial review. However, in circumstances where those decisions are in the context of crisis prevention and crisis management, then a right to appeal against such decisions needs to be managed to minimize delays to the crisis prevention or resolution proceedings.[166] Therefore, the directive requires courts to review such matters in light of the economic case made by the competent or resolution authorities. However, this right to an appeal cannot act as a suspension of the recovery and resolution proceedings, which will be expected to be applied without delay against the distressed bank or group.

The resolution authority essentially leads the resolution and is conferred responsibility to **9.67** decide whether normal insolvency proceedings should be initiated.[167] Moreover, where a resolution authority in another Member State decides to initiate insolvency proceedings against the same institution or entity, it needs to acquire the consent of the resolution authority and notify the competent authority. The Member State and the resolution authority can apply for a stay against judicial proceedings against a claim addressed to either the resolution authority or the institution or group in resolution.[168]

1. *Goldman Sachs International v Novo Banco SA*

Goldman Sachs International v Novo Banco SA[169] (hereinafter 'Novo Banco') and *Bayerische* **9.68** *Landesbank v Hypo Alpe Adria Bank International AG (now HETA Asset Resolution AG)*[170] ('Heta') are the first judicial interpretations to date in relation to BRRD provisions, specifically Articles 66 and 86 regarding the mutual recognition of Member State resolution proceedings and the resolution authority's request for a stay of proceedings. It will be noted that both decisions take a narrow view in this respect.[171] For this reason, resolution authorities are advised to adhere strictly to the BRRD's terms going forward.[172]

The *Novo Banco* case was heard in the UK courts pursuant to a facility agreement entered **9.69** into by the parties.[173] The facts concerned the resolution of distressed Portuguese bank

---

[166] Ibid, Art 85(1)–(4).
[167] Ibid, Art 86.
[168] Ibid, Art 86(3).
[169] [2015] EWHC 2371 (Comm), 07 August 2015.
[170] Az 32 0 26502/12, 8 May 2015.
[171] C Mecklenburg, 'EU Cross-Border Bank Resolution Challenges Remain Severe Despite the Common Framework' (2015) *Financial Regulation International*, Issue 18.8 at 9.
[172] Ibid at 8.
[173] The agreement contained an express choice for English law in settling any disputes. *Goldman Sachs International v Novo Banco SA* [2015] EWHC 2371 (Comm) at 7.

Banco Espírito Santo SA (BES) through operating a bridge bank, 'Novo Banco', created by the Bank of Portugal in its capacity as resolution authority as per the BRRD.[174] As a resolution measure, the assets and liabilities of BES were transferred onto Novo Banco, with the exception of certain 'excluded liabilities'.[175] The point of contention was whether the liabilities arising out of the facility agreement (consisting of a $835 million loan granted to BES by a Luxembourg entity[176]) were to be considered in this category as well. The Bank of Portugal issued a ruling in December 2014 according to which the loan in question was not an 'excluded liability' and therefore remained in the residual bank, effectively negating the transfer.[177] However, the claimants, which included Goldman Sachs, pursued Novo Banco as the defendant borrower, arguing that it had replaced BES via a statutory transfer.[178]

9.70 Novo Banco applied to set aside the proceedings as well as to obtain a stay of the proceedings in accordance with Articles 86 and 66(3) of the BRRD. The latter provides, inter alia, that creditors and third parties affected by the transfer of assets or liabilities are not entitled to prevent, challenge, or set aside the transfer 'under any provision of law of the Member State where the assets are located or of the law governing the shares, other instruments of ownership, rights or liabilities'. Novo Banco contended that the UK courts had no jurisdiction under Regulation (EU) 1215/2012[179] to hear the claims. Instead, it should be recognized that there had been no transfer of the liability according to the Bank of Portugal's ruling. Under Portuguese law, the latter was regarded as an administrative act which may only be reviewed by administrative courts.[180] On the contrary, the claimants argued that the ruling had no effect in English law, under which the facility agreement was concluded. They deemed irrelevant the Bank of Portugal's ruling status as a matter of Portuguese law.[181]

9.71 The UK court dismissed Novo Banco's application for three reasons. Firstly, Regulation (EU) 1215/2012 applied to civil and commercial matters, at the exclusion of administrative ones.[182] The court was persuaded by the claimants' argument that theirs was a private law (debt) claim based on rights contained in the facility agreement,[183] and therefore fell under the material scope of the Regulation,[184] as opposed to Novo Banco's interpretation.[185] Moreover, the defendant was not a public body, nor it did it exercise public powers.[186] Thus, the court held that it did indeed have jurisdiction to decide the matter. Secondly, the court stated that it would not pronounce on the validity of the Bank of Portugal's ruling, but rather on its effect in English law.[187] The non-justiciability or act of state doctrine[188] was

---

[174] *Goldman Sachs International v Novo Banco SA* [2015] EWHC 2371 (Comm).
[175] Mecklenburg, *supra* n 145 at 10.
[176] Ibid.
[177] Arguing instead, inter alia, a re-transfer to BES under BRRD, Art 40(7). Ibid at 34.
[178] Ibid.
[179] Regulation (EU) 1215/2012 of the European Parliament and of the Council on jurisdiction and the recognition and enforcement of judgments in civil and commercial matters (recast) ('Recast Brussels Regulation').
[180] *Goldman Sachs International v Novo Banco SA* [2015] EWHC 2371 (Comm) at 53(6).
[181] Ibid at 61.
[182] Recast Brussels Regulation, Art 1(1).
[183] *Goldman Sachs International v Novo Banco SA* [2015] EWHC 2371 (Comm) at 71.
[184] Recast Brussels Regulation, Art 25.
[185] *Goldman Sachs International v Novo Banco SA* [2015] EWHC 2371 (Comm) at 73.
[186] Ibid at 72.
[187] Ibid at 109.
[188] According to which adjudication on the 'validity, legality, lawfulness, acceptability or motives of state actors' is prohibited. Ibid at 110.

further inapplicable due to the Bank of Portugal acting as a resolution authority for BRRD purposes, as opposed to being an emanation of the Portuguese state.[189] Thirdly, the court clarified that a stay of proceedings would only be enforced in 'rare and compelling' circumstances,[190] which was not the case in Novo Banco.

There have been two appeals of this case since then. First, Nova Banco appealed the High Court's decision and on 4 November 2016 the Court of Appeal overturned the High Court's decision, therefore reinstating the principle of mutual recognition set out in the EBRRD and Reorganisation Directive. **9.72**

Goldman Sachs appealed the Court of Appeal's decision. The Supreme Court unanimously agreed with the Court of Appeal. The August and December decisions were both valid administrative acts that had effect in Portuguese law, and as such should be recognized by the English courts in the UK. This meant that the effect of the December decision was to cancel the transfer of the Oak liability to Novo Banco. The Supreme Court held that Novo Banco was therefore never party to the jurisdiction clause in the facility agreement. Lord Sumption held that the Reorganisation Directive's purpose was to ensure that all assets and liabilities of an institution, regardless of the country in which they are situated, are dealt with in a single process in the home Member State. To do so, it needed to be fully effective, so it could not make sense for other provisions to affect its operation. The Court held that there was no basis for referral to the ECJ as the relevant provision of EU law was beyond serious argument. **9.73**

2. Bayerische Landesbank v Hypo Alpe Adria Bank International AG (now HETA Asset Resolution AG)

The facts in *Heta* related to the resolution of distressed financial institution Hypo Alpe Adria International AG ('Hypo').[191] This consisted of establishing a bridge bank, namely Heta Asset Resolution AG ('Heta') to which Hypo's assets and liabilities were transferred, save for 'excluded liabilities'.[192] In addition, the March 2015 administrative measure to initiate Heta's resolution was supported by a 15-month moratorium on its liabilities, issued by the Austrian Financial Market Authority (FMA). Acting as the resolution authority for the purposes of the BRRD and the Federal Act on the Recovery and Resolution of Banks (BaSAG),[193] FMA considered the temporary moratorium necessary to prevent Heta's insolvency.[194] **9.74**

The administrative decision taken by the FMA was contested by certain creditors as it deferred the maturity of some of Heta's eligible liabilities, thereby postponing the payment due date (until 31 May 2016).[195] Bayerische Landesbank ('BayernLB') challenged the moratorium on the grounds of insufficient legal basis as well as its qualification as a BRRD **9.75**

---

[189] Ibid at 111.
[190] Ibid at 118.
[191] *Bayerische Landesbank v Hypo Alpe Adria Bank International AG (now HETA Asset Resolution AG)* (Az 32 0 26502/12) (8 May 2015).
[192] Ibid.
[193] The relevant legislation through which BRRD was transposed in Austrian law.
[194] DC Bauer, 'Resolving Austria's HETA—major milestone for the European bank resolution regime', 6 September 2015 <https://www.dlapiper.com/en/uk/insights/publications/2015/10/global-insight-15/resolving-austrias-heta/>.
[195] Ibid.

measure.[196] In this sense, BayernLB argued that the objective of the Recovery Measures for Hypo Alpe Adria Bank International AG ('HaaSanG') and its Regulation on the Application of the Measures ('HaaSanV') were different as compared to those under the BRRD: whereas the former intended to terminate Heta's banking activities, the latter sought to ensure their continuation. Furthermore, the moratorium cannot be qualified as a resolution regime for the purposes of Article 66 of the BRRD corroborated with Article 2 because the measures are applied against a bad bank (ie Heta) as opposed to a credit institution as required.[197] Heta's licence had been revoked and it was subsequently converted into an asset management firm.[198] Notwithstanding Heta being explicitly made subject to the BaSAG, the Munich court refused to recognize the moratorium, deciding that its application to Heta was outside the scope of the BRRD.[199] Consequently, German courts were not obliged to give effect to other resolution authorities' measures and Heta was ordered to pay Bayern around €2.3 billion.[200] Heta appealed against this decision; the European Commission also initiated proceedings against the Republic of Austria for its failure to transpose the BRRD in an adequate manner. Therefore, highlighting the importance of the competent and resolution authorities to think through the implications of terminating authorization when the continuity of authorization is crucial for an orderly resolution. Moreover, the competent and resolution authorities need to clearly understand that resolution is not a catch-all term to also include bank and insolvency administration. The directive is quite clear on this matter, in particular what is a resolution tool and what is an insolvency tool for the purposes of managing the resolution process, and the residual bank for the purposes of winding up and liquidation of assets and liabilities.

VI. Cross-Border Group Resolution

9.76 The cross-border resolution of institutions and groups requires a significant degree of timely cooperation and coordination between the home and host Member State or between Banking Union participating and non-participating Member States. The SRB mitigates significant impediments to cross-border resolution for those banks considered significant in participating Member States. Insolvency proceedings remain the responsibility of the participating Member States.[201] An equally important dimension is cooperation and coordination with third countries, either in the capacity as home state or host state supervisor, in a timely and efficient manner.

9.77 The directive requires Member States to work out in advance the role and responsibilities of competent and resolution authorities.[202] The process of cooperation and coordination between the various parties across borders will be partly assisted by the forward planning undertaken at the preparation stage with the recovery and resolution plans. But these plans

---

[196] See Regulation (EU) No 575/2013, Art 4(1); Directive 2013/36/EU, Art 2(5); *Bayerische Landesbank v Hypo Alpe Adria Bank International AG (now HETA Asset Resolution AG)* (Az 32 0 26502/12) (8 May 2015).
[197] Ibid.
[198] Ibid.
[199] Ibid.
[200] Ibid.
[201] SRB, Cases <https://www.srb.europa.eu/en/cases>.
[202] BRRD, Art 87(a)–(l).

will form only a starting point and the catalyst for early intervention and resolution may not necessarily arise from a scenario captured by the plans, although they will provide the authorities with a very good idea of the critical functions and business lines which will need to be considered during the resolution phase, and will decide which tools best address the problems experienced at the institution or group.

In this respect, the directive identifies the broader hurdles relating to subsidiaries and **9.78** branches located in other Member States, but more broadly than that it seeks to minimize the adverse effects on financial stability in the EU and Member States.[203] Thus, 'due consideration is given to the objectives of balancing the interests of the various Member States involved and of avoiding unfairly prejudicing or unfairly protecting the interests of particular Member States, including avoiding unfair burden allocation across Member States'. As noted earlier, the advance planning is likely to enable authorities to work out burden allocation rather than equal burden sharing, notwithstanding the uneven form it may take both from a supervisory, resolution, and liquidation perspective. In many respects, while the directive provides a legal framework to mandate cooperation it primarily takes one Member State or third-country resolution authority to act in its own public interest and initiate insolvency proceedings to undermine the purpose of the directive. The broad powers and purposes of the resolution authority may resonate with other competent and resolution authorities but may not readily fit with the narrow approach taken by the courts. This is perhaps frustrating from the perspective of the resolution authority given that the purpose of the directive is to put in place a resolution process that minimizes costs based on the resolution authorities' economic assessment, with the principle that shareholders and creditors take the first losses but no shareholder or creditor will be worse off than liquidation with the application of the resolution tools.

VII. The Resolution Colleges

The directive requires the establishment of resolution colleges for groups that operate within **9.79** the EU.[204] The rationale of such colleges is necessary to ensure an appropriate platform for consultation between the respective authorities both at the crisis prevention level and crisis management level. The consideration of the recovery and resolution plans is the first matter. Those plans will be an important basis for the assessment of the resolvability of groups and possible impediments to orderly resolution. The selection of competent and resolution authorities members of resolution colleges is perhaps a rather contentious matter with the resolution authority for the group taking a lead role and other members selected where subsidiaries and significant branches are located. The level of cooperation and coordination required seeks to minimize the impact of such decisions on the markets and wider financial and economic stability. While the written arrangements within the European Union provide the basis for an *ex ante* understanding of how the resolution of the group is likely to be executed with the objectives, conditions, and principles in mind, who is and who is not

---

[203] Ibid, Art 34(2).
[204] Ibid, Art 88(1)(a)–(i) as amended by BRRD II to expect the group-level resolution authorities to establish resolution colleges to carry out the tasks referred to in Arts 12, 13, 16, 18, 45h, 91, and 92. Reference to Art 45 has been replaced with Articles 45–45h.

a member of the resolution college could pose challenges in terms of the timing of decision making and whether those outside the resolution college respect the decisions of the lead resolution authority for the purposes of leading the resolution for the group. Despite the fact that the membership criteria are indicated, the directive leaves it to the lead resolution authority to decide which members to invite to attend a given meeting.

9.80   A special regime applies to cross-border groups with principal business activities in a third country and with a European presence in the form of a subsidiary or significant branches.[205] In this type of case, the competent authority and resolution authority for those entities will need to set up a European Resolution College. The authority of the host Member State where a subsidiary or group holding company is located will take responsibility for it as consolidated supervisor. However, if those institutions are located by way of branches then it is likely that the competent authority of the significant branch will take responsibility and coordinate the organizing of the European Resolution College.

9.81   A crucial element in the cooperation between Member States themselves as well as third countries is information exchange.[206] In this respect the institution's or group's consolidated supervisor and the resolution authority are responsible for ensuring relevant information is exchanged between the respective authorities. In order to prevent the creation of panic amongst the Member States, resulting in disjointed responses, the information exchange needs to be timely. In this respect, consent is required for the onward sharing of information. In such cases resolution authorities will be expected to provide their EU counterparts with 'all the relevant information in a timely manner'; and in respect to third countries, the resolution authority must seek the consent of the third-country resolution authority for the onward transmission of that information.[207]

9.82   The existence of Member States with different levels of exposure and interests located within them brings about considerable challenges for the lead resolution authority in terms of managing the expectations of their counterparts. This risk could arise where a subsidiary of the group is placed in resolution by its resolution authority. In this case, the relevant resolution will be required to notify the group-level resolution authority and the members of the resolution college. In such a case the group resolution authority is expected to assess the impact of the decision on the group as a whole.[208] After the assessment at the group level, the resolution authority will be expected to provide a group resolution scheme and share it with the resolution members within 24 hours or a longer period, depending on what was agreed. If the group-level resolution authority has not initiated a resolution scheme within that time frame, then the resolution authority for the subsidiary can continue with its resolution actions. In such circumstances, the EBA is expected to mediate in order for national resolution authorities to come to a joint decision. Irrespective of the consensus-based approach, the directive does envisage disagreements amongst Member States. In those cases the dissenting resolution authority needs to identify the reasons for not following the group-level resolution authority and the resolution plan, which it must then circulate amongst the other resolution authorities.[209] The resolution authorities in such circumstances are still required

---

[205]   Ibid, Art 89.
[206]   Ibid, Art 90.
[207]   Ibid, Art 90(3).
[208]   Ibid, Art 91.
[209]   Ibid, Art 91(8).

to cooperate closely and inform the resolution college about the measures they are taking to coordinate their efforts at the group level.[210] A number of similar measures apply to the group-level resolution authority responsible for the parent undertaking of the group. However, the extent to which the group resolution scheme includes all parts of the group and the parent essentially depends on the extent of the problem and whether it is likely to impact other parts of the group after determining whether the parent and/or other parts of the group are failing or likely to fail. However, the resolution authorities responsible for the different parts of the group will need to determine whether to follow the resolution scheme and so act jointly, or whether to act separately but still informing the other resolution authorities of the actions taken.[211] The directive requires that a resolution authority which decides to act independently must notify the group-level resolution authority and other resolution authorities and provide reasons for the departure.

The experience so far shows that while the regulatory authorities and resolution authorities are likely to cooperate and coordinate their decisions at a broad administrative level they also need to be mindful, in light of the recent cases explored in the previous section, that the detail also needs to be considered, since the courts can take a different view from the aspirations of the regulatory and resolution authorities. **9.83**

VIII. Relations with Third Countries

A considerable amount of cross-border banking and finance exists within the EU and a proportion of it has significant origins in third countries. The directive attempts to put in place a framework of cooperation and coordination between EU Member State competent and resolution authorities and their third-country counterparts so that the level of disruption to markets and impact on financial stability is minimized. The directive provides a broad context for cooperation linked to crisis prevention and crisis management arrangements.[212] The crisis prevention tools such as information sharing to complete recovery resolution plans will involve the competent and resolution authorities separately. However, while the EU resolution framework advocates a separation of roles of supervision and resolution, their third-country counterparts may only consist of one authority that is both supervisor and resolution authority. In many respects the requests for information in the context of resolution exist within the broader supervisory mandates associated with techniques such as consolidation, supervision, and arrangements for information sharing in relation to financial conglomerates. **9.84**

The directive sets out the expected approach for those institutions or groups that have a parent located in a third country, a significant branch or a subsidiary in a Member State.[213] In relation to these entities, the directive anticipates cooperation to inform the resolution process and sets out *ex ante* the expected role of the EU competent and resolution authorities. The directive encourages Member States to enter into bilateral agreements with third **9.85**

---

[210] Ibid, Art 91(12).
[211] Ibid, Art 92.
[212] Ibid, Art 93.
[213] Ibid, Art 93(1)(a)–(c).

countries to work out how they will attempt to work with one another in resolution. As a stop-gap measure, the directive provides an interim measure to recognize and enforce third-country resolution proceedings until such agreements are made. The European Resolution Colleges are expected to play an important role in this regard, to provide a platform for coordination and recognition of proceedings emanating from a third country.

9.86 The directive offers limited assurance of third-country cooperation and coordination for resolution. It provides a number of eventualities that primarily mean at best that the resolution authorities will commit to a number of *ex ante* arrangements to recognize and enforce third-country resolution proceedings which will be dependent on Member States' own discretion. It could result in one Member State recognizing and cooperating with a third-country resolution authority and possibly other Member States' resolution authorities not cooperating to the same extent.[214] In this respect the directive expects Member States to give due consideration to such matters and the financial stability in those Member States. As a minimum the Member States are required to be in a position where they can exercise their powers of resolution regarding: assets of third-country institutions in a Member State or governed by Member State law; rights and liabilities booked in a branch located in a Member State; transfer of shares; exercising contractual powers to support third-country resolution proceedings; and rendering enforceable rights to terminate, liquidate, or accelerate contractual rights that arise from resolution actions that relate to third-country resolution proceedings.[215]

9.87 The directive does provide a basis for Member States to act in their own public interest when considering whether or not to recognize third-country resolution proceedings.[216] For example, this may apply if the third-country proceedings would have an adverse impact on financial stability in the Member State; independent resolution of the branch is necessary; the third country would not confer the same treatment of creditors and depositors with similar legal rights; there would be material fiscal implications for the Member State; or it would be contrary in light of national law.

9.88 In relationship to third-country branches located in a Member State, the authorities will need to decide whether third-country resolution proceedings or Member State resolution proceedings are to apply.[217] When the circumstances listed in Article 95 are present, the Member State acting in the public interest or where the third country is unable or unwilling to act in the wider interest, will need to be in a position to exercise resolution proceedings in accordance with the resolution objectives, conditions, and principles.

9.89 The directive also requires the EBA to consider entering into non-binding cooperation agreements with third countries to put in place their intentions *ex ante* to organize resolution of entities set up in the European Union. However, the cooperation agreements should be general and not made in reference to a particular third-country entity in the Member State. The directive explicitly provides they are not legally binding on the Member State. Notwithstanding the non-binding nature of the agreements, they are expected to

---

[214] Ibid, Art 94.
[215] Ibid, Art 94(4)(a)–(d).
[216] Ibid, Art 95(a)–(e).
[217] Ibid, Art 96.

assist with: recovery and resolution plans; assessment of resolvability impediments to resolution; early intervention measures; and the resolution powers and tools. Moreover, the cooperation arrangements could include arrangements for sharing information, forming separate recovery and resolution plans, and the possible resolution tools to be expected to be used.

A particular problem identified by the global financial crisis was the lack of a coherent cross-   **9.90**
border resolution regime which primarily led to Member States taking action in their own public interest: taking a territorial rather than a universalist approach. The extent to which the directive remedies this is debatable. The directive certainly enables the competent and resolution authorities to *ex ante* work out the possible options they are likely to initiate in resolution and to enter into non-binding cooperation arrangements. In some instances, the directive limits the Member State's authority when it sets out options for resolution of third-country entities—for example, when it requires two or more entities to be operating in the EU when it could be the case that an individual subsidiary or indeed significant branch could well pose risks to markets functioning efficiently and financial stability in the respective Member State and more widely.

IX. Contractual Recognition of Bail-in

The introduction of contractual recognition of bail-in is an attempt to improve the ef-   **9.91**
ficiency of executing a resolution in the EU that involves third country creditor interests either through a contractual or non-contractual liability.[218] In view of this, liabilities in a particular class governed by a third country are expected to include a contractual clause to the effect that the counterparty recognizes the liabilities may be subject to a bail-in, namely a write-down and conversion of the liabilities in to equity by the resolution authority in a EU Member State. This exercise requires an assessment to make sure the third country allows for such recognition or whether the firm has capacity to comply with such contractual terms. The international standard terms used in markets play a vital role to ensure consistency of practice and these have been embedded since 2016.[219]

The resolution authority will need to assess on a case-by-case basis the use of contractual   **9.92**
recognition of bail-in during the resolvability assessment to ensure there are no impediments to executing the proposed resolution strategy. In this respect BRRD II introduces an exemption where it could be legally or otherwise impracticable for the parties to agree to a contractual recognition of bail-in clause in a contract. The EBA is mandated to prepare standards to govern the use of contractual recognition of bail-in and the 'conditions of impracticability'. The 'conditions of impracticability' include: it is prohibited by law or by an instruction of the relevant third country authority; or by a non-negotiable international standard term(s) apply; or standard terms in trade finance apply.[220] In view of these

---

[218] Art 55.

[219] LMA, 'The Recommended Form of Bail-In Clause and Users Guide', 15 April 2021: <https://www.lma. eu.com/application/files/4216/1848/7274/MARKUP_the_recommended_form_of_Bail-In_Clause_and_Users_ Guide.pdf>.

[220] EBA, Final Report, Draft regulatory technical standards on impracticability of contractual recognition of the bail-in clause under Article 55(6) of Directive 2014/59/EU and Draft implementing standards for the notification of impracticability of contractual recognition of the bail-in clause under Article 55(8) of Directive 2014/59/EU.

complexities it is incumbent on banks in practice to seek legal opinions from respective third country law firms to ascertain whether it is impossible or impracticable for such contractual terms to be included.

9.93   The resolution authority could include liabilities that do not have the contractual recognition clause in excluded liabilities and if it is more than 10 per cent of that class then the resolution authority is likely to assess the implications as part of the resolvability assessment to determine whether it is an impediment to resolution.[221] If impediments do exist then the resolution authority could exclude the liabilities from the firm's MREL requirement. The resolution authority could also make an exception when the bank has not included such liabilities in their MREL because there is sufficient loss-absorbing capacity in the other classes of liabilities. The assessment of contractual recognition of bail-in is a dialogue between the resolution authority and the firm. The firm is required to comply with the resolution authority's notification requirements. The resolution authority needs to assess the implications of the impracticalities of contractual bail-in and feed back to the bank in a reasonable time frame their assessment on the potential impediment to resolvability. While what is reasonable time is not defined it will be necessary within the time to readjust to offset any potential shortfall.

X. The Financing Arrangements

9.94   The financing arrangements in Title VII are designed in accordance with the respective resolution objectives, conditions, and principles set out in Articles 31 and 34 of the BRRD.

9.95   The first part of the financing arrangements focuses on Member States' abilities to raise funds and set up lines of finance to support a resolution process.[222] The standard expected to be achieved by a Member State is one of adequate financial resources, rather than what would be envisaged to be appropriate financial recourses.[223] The latter would obviously place a greater burden on the resolution authority to raise greater amounts of funds. The BRRD expects a Member State to raise those financial resources via levies *ex ante* to enable the development of a common resolution fund.[224]

9.96   An important point to remember is that a fund of this nature is not necessarily going to be the same as the DGS fund, if one exists, but the chances of this not being the case is likely to be remote. This is because funding for most DGSs will be burdensome on its own, let alone adding the need to raise an additional pool of funds for other parts of the resolution process.[225] The fact that the DGS fund and the resolution fund are not necessarily the same fund means that a Member State may want to change its funding and financing arrangements so that it is one fund, which will make it easier to raise and manage resources.

9.97   The BRRD allows a Member State to 'top up' the fund by exercising its right to levy *ex post* extraordinary levies.[226] It would appear that Member States that currently raise

---

[221] Art 55(2)(4)–(5).
[222] Ibid, Arts 99 and 100.
[223] Ibid, Art 100(3).
[224] Ibid, Art 100(4)(a), (b), and (c).
[225] Ibid, Art 109.
[226] Ibid, Art 104.

contributions solely *ex post* for their DGS will face the biggest hurdles and require significant reforms. Such a move, as discussed below, will take a considerable length of time and pose significant short to medium-term burdens on banks and the state to build up the DGS at a time when private and public resources are limited. The question here is: will the markets act with restraint in such circumstances when banks and the state are facing an expectation to move to adopt such requirements and equally face the pressure of raising higher levels of capital? In addition, what will be the means of building a fund for the DGS part of the resolution authority? The resolution authority is also given the power to raise finance through the state channels, either from the treasury or central bank.[227]

9.98 Article 101 of the BRRD provides a transparent framework to understand when and what financing arrangements will be expected to be utilized during a resolution process. The resolution authorities are expected to raise funds for the purposes of resolving distressed banks. The resolution authority is able to utilize the financing arrangements for a variety of purposes, from putting in place a guarantee, providing loans or purchasing assets, or making contributions to the bank in resolution, a bank subsidiary, a bridge bank, or an asset management vehicle; either individually or in combination with one another.

9.99 However, Article 101 implies quite clearly that the resolution tools and responsibilities may be placed in various parts of the official safety net and so this aspect raises a concern as to what role the DGS will play in the resolution process. The requirements set out in Article 92 of the BRRD seem to imply that the resolution authorities will be working towards utilizing the financing arrangements to restructure the banks prior to an insolvency rather than utilizing the DGS fund to simply compensate depositors. It implies that the resolution authorities will, more than likely, not close failing banks but, instead, will seek to restructure them. In addition, the resolution authorities and the placement of these tools in different parts of the safety net will require close coordination and indeed collaboration to ensure all the parts come together to achieve the resolution objectives and principles set out above and it also means that they all must share the same objective. As indicated in Article 101, potential losses to the fund raised in conformity with Article 100 are required to conform to the resolution objective and principles.[228]

9.100 A significant burden on the Member States and their banks will be to raise an adequate fund to assist with resolutions.[229] This is because Member States will be required to build up a fund that represents as a minimum 1 per cent of the amount of the guaranteed deposits of all the credit institutions in their territory. The resolution authorities are required to achieve this level within 10 years and can seek an extension of a further four years if they are within that period required to make a disbursement higher than 0.5 per cent of the covered deposits.[230] The funding level is expected to be built up by contributions by members of the DGS by annual contributions.[231] The level of contribution to the financial

---

[227] Ibid, Art 105.
[228] Ibid, Art 101(2).
[229] Ibid, Art 102.
[230] Ibid, Art 102(2).
[231] Ibid, Arts 103(1) and 104; See also European Commission, Proposal for a Directive of the European Parliament and of the Council establishing a framework for the recovery and resolution of credit institutions and investment firms and amending Council Directives 77/91/EEC and 82/891/EC, Directives 2001/24/EC, 2002/47/EC, 2004/25/EC, 2005/56/EC, 2007/36/EC, and 2011/35/EC and Regulation (EU) No 1093/2010, COM(2012) 280

arrangements is determined by whether or not the DGS is either part of the financial arrangements.[232]

9.101   The important feature of the calculation is that it is not a flat-rate contribution system but it is expected that Member States will adjust the contributions in accordance with the risk profile of the institution. The premiums will be adjusted in accordance with a bank's risk exposure which will include its trading, off-balance-sheet situation, and leverage; sources of funds; financial condition of the institution; probability of the bank entering resolution; complexity and the resolvability of the bank; and its systemic importance.[233]

9.102   The move to a risk-based contribution system is laudable and far more equitable than a flat-rate contribution system as it will need to be adjusted according to the risk profile of the bank, which should mean that less risky banks pay lower premiums. The BRRD provides a significant amount of discretion in many respects, as it will be the Member State that determines how the adjustment is calculated rather than a 'one size fits all' approach. Moreover, the burden of including a risk-adjusted premium system will be more onerous in a jurisdiction with a highly concentrated banking system as it will fall on a few very large players that may not necessarily be in the best of shape. Consider the UK situation, where eight of the 10 largest retail banks and building societies have either been taken over or are currently supported by state means. Moreover, the move in some jurisdictions to ring-fence commercial and retail banking from investment firm activities implies that the way a Member State calculates risks will need further thought as the off-balance-sheet and trading activities deemed high risk will be separated. In addition to this, it has been noted in a number of places that retail banks tend to rely on retail deposits for finance and lack the wide creditor base generally envisaged and so the level of risk-adjusted premiums generated by those banks may not perhaps be as significant as one would expect.

9.103   A rather unique feature of the European financing arrangements is the extension of the burden sharing principle for group resolutions by requiring the resolution authorities to assist one another in the task of financing a group resolution.[234] In this scenario, the national financing arrangements are expected to assist one another by 'supporting' their respective individual institution. However, those Member States that have a significant number of overseas banks will more than likely find it politically necessary to negotiate such arrangements with third countries, albeit recovery and resolution plans envisage cooperation.

---

final, Brussels, 6.6.2012, Art 94(2): (a) if a Member State has availed itself of the option provided for in Article 99(5) of this Directive to use the funds of Deposit Guarantee Scheme for the purposes of Article 92 of this Directive, the contribution from each institution shall be *pro-rata* to the amount of its liabilities excluding own funds and deposits guaranteed under Directive 94/19/EC with respect to the total liabilities, excluding own funds and deposits guaranteed under Directive 94/19/EC, of all the institutions authorized in the territory of the Member State. (b) if a Member State has not availed itself of the option provided for in Article 109 to use the funds of the Deposit Guarantee Scheme for the purposes of Article 92, the contribution from each institution shall be pro-rata to the total amount of its liabilities, excluding own funds, with respect to the total liabilities, excluding own funds, of all the institutions authorized in the territory of the Member State.

[232]   If the DGS is part of the financial arrangements then the contribution from the bank is expected to be pro rata to the amount of its liabilities, excluding own funds and deposits guaranteed with respect to the total liabilities. If the Member State has not opted to use the funds of the DGS then the contribution by the bank is expected to be pro rata to the total amount of its liabilities, excluding own funds and total deposits guaranteed.

[233]   BRRD, Art 103(7).

[234]   Ibid, Art 107.

PART III
SOVEREIGN DEBT RESTRUCTURING

10

AN INTRODUCTION TO SOVEREIGN DEBT RESTRUCTURING

I. Introduction

Sovereign debt restructuring comprises multilateral, bilateral, and private debt instruments **10.01** (mainly commercial loans and global bonds[1]). The first two have their own set of policies and rules on how to perform a restructuring. However, the latter lacks a structured or institutional approach. Therefore, the focus of this Part of the book will be on private sovereign debt restructuring with particular emphasis on bonded debt.[2]

In recent times, the last wave of bond financing resulted from the 'Brady Plan'. The Brady **10.02** Plan was a plan articulated in 1989 by US Treasury Secretary Nicholas F Brady to address

---

[1] Different terminology is usually used when dealing with the bonds issued by a sovereign. The most common term is 'Eurobonds' which refers to bonds issued in a currency other than that of the issuer. 'Single Jurisdiction Registered Bonds' can refer to a type of Eurobond but registered in a single jurisdiction and therefore with a more specific name linked to the jurisdiction in which they were issued (eg Yankee, Panda or Samurai bonds, etc). This terminology is also sometimes seen just as a particular common type of Eurobond based on the currency and jurisdictions involved. 'Foreign bonds' in turn refers to a bond issued by a foreign issuer and registered for sale to investors in the country where it is being issued and in the currency of legal tender in that jurisdiction. 'Global bonds' are like Eurobonds but can also be issued simultaneously in the country of the issuer. Finally, another possible term used in the context of debt issuance is 'international bonds', which covers both Eurobonds and global bonds. Since sovereigns usually issue global bonds, this chapter will favour this terminology.

[2] The author of this Part of the book, Rodrigo Olivares-Caminal, has written extensively about the legal framework applicable in sovereign debt restructurings and this chapter incorporates and/or adapts some of his earlier work, including among others: *Legal Aspects of Sovereign Debt Restructuring* (2009); 'Understanding the Pari Passu Clause in Sovereign Debt Instruments: A Complex Quest' (2009) 43(3) .*The International Lawyer*; 'Is There a Need for an International Insolvency Regime in the Context of Sovereign Debt? A Case for the Use of Corporate Debt Restructuring Techniques' (2009) 24(1). *Journal of International Banking Law & Regulation*; 'The Use of Corporate Debt Restructuring Techniques in the Context of Sovereign Debt' (2005) 2(5). *International Corporate Rescue*; 'Rethinking Sovereign Debt Restructuring Mechanisms' (2003) 9(4). *Law & Business Review of the Americas*; 'The Definition of Indebtedness and the Consequent Imperilling of the Pari Passu, Negative Pledge and Cross-Default Clauses in Sovereign Debt Instruments', *Oxford Capital Markets Law Journal*, April 2017; 'Improving Transparency of Lending to Sovereign Governments', The Overseas Development Institute Working Paper No. 583, July 2020; 'Venezuela: A War of Principles or Just a Matter of Semantics?' (2020) 17(1) *International Corporate Rescue* ; and 'Sovereign Debt Litigation', in Max Plank Encyclopaedia of International Procedural Law (Oxford University Press 2020).

the debt crises that had occurred in the developing countries during the 1980s. The debt crises originated in the amounts of unsustainable debt amassed over several years and to which loans granted by commercial banks to sovereigns in order to refinance previous loans contributed significantly. The main objective of the commercial bank re-finance was to maintain the service of interests to keep the loans as performing in their financial statements—otherwise, they would have had to write them off. By injecting fresh money to restructure principal and keep interests performing, debtors entered into a debt trap that were not able to escape until the Brady Plan was put into place. Although the Brady Plan evolved on a case-by-case basis, its main features were: (1) adjustment programmes; (2) menus of debt restructuring options assuring the collection of the credit and that the new debt would be traded in order to diversify risks; and (3) additional financing.[3]

10.03   Since the outset of the Brady Plan in 1989, Argentina, Brazil, Bulgaria, Costa Rica, the Dominican Republic, Ecuador, Ivory Coast (Côte d'Ivoire), Jordan, Mexico, Nigeria, Panama, Peru, the Philippines, Poland, Russia, Uruguay, Venezuela, and Vietnam have been able to restructure their unsustainable debt—mostly in syndicated loans—by the issuance of 'Brady Bonds'. As result of the Brady Plan, sovereigns were able to swap commercial non-performing loans for capital markets tradable global bonds (ie Brady Bonds) with a longer maturity profile. The commercial banks, who were the creditors holding the non-performing loans, swapped their loans for tradable debt instruments that they off-loaded in the capital markets.

10.04   As a result, most of the emerging market debt held by private investors is now in the form of global bonds, not in commercial bank loans.[4] The countries that participated in the Brady Plan as well as others that did not default during the 1980s and early 1990s continued issuing global bonds on a regular basis to cover their primary budget deficits or simply to raise money from the capital markets. This resulted in some countries amassing enormous amounts of debt—in some cases unsustainable.

10.05   As noted by Krueger, since 1980, emerging market bond issues have grown four times as quickly as syndicated bank loans.[5] It is broadly estimated that the total global bond market almost reaches US$3 trillion.[6] As a result of the rapid increase of global bond issuance, 'together with the increased frequency of virulent financial crises, bond restructuring has gained in importance, particularly for sovereign borrowers'.[7]

---

[3] See Emerging Markets Trading Association, The Brady Plan, available at <http://www.emta.org/templ ate.aspx?id=35>. For an enlargement on the Brady Plan (and its predecessor, the 'Baker Plan') see Lex Rieffel, *Restructuring Sovereign Debt: The Case for Ad Hoc Machinery* (2003) 149–177; and Ross P Buckley, *Emerging Markets Debt: An Analysis of the Secondary Market* (1999).

[4] Lee C Buchheit, Unitar Training Programs on Foreign Economic Relations, Doc No 1, 'Sovereign Debtors and Their Bondholders' (2000) at 4.

[5] Anne Krueger, *International Financial Architecture for 2002: A New Approach to Sovereign Debt Restructuring*, address at the National Economists' Club Annual Members' Dinner American Enterprise Institute (26 November 2001), available at <http://www.imf.org/external/np/speeches/2001/112601.htm>.

[6] See Bank for International Settlements, Debt Securities statistics, available at <https://www.bis.org/statistics/secstats.htm?m=6%7C33%7C615>.

[7] Report by the secretariat of the United Nations Conference on Trade and Development, New York and Geneva 2001, p 143, available at <http://www.unctad.org/en/docs/tdr2001_en.pdf> (Trade and Development).

In retrospective, debts documented in syndicated loans were relatively easy to restructure   **10.06**
within the framework of the 'London Club'.[8] The London Club is an informal group of commercial banks gathering together to negotiate their claims against a sovereign debtor.[9]

II. The Collective Will Problem

As result of the use of global bonds to finance sovereign needs, capital markets have become   **10.07**
more efficient and diversified. However, there are a number of serious downsides when a
country faces unsustainable debt. These include: (1) creditors who have become increasingly numerous, anonymous, and difficult to coordinate; (2) the variety of debt instruments
involved and the range of legal jurisdictions in which debt is issued, with no single, statutory
legal framework applicable (enabling creditors to holdout or litigate for better terms).[10] In
addition, recent sovereign debt crises or episodes have shown a higher degree of aggressive-
ness from either creditors (eg some of the Argentine creditors after the debt crisis of 2001–
2002[11]) or debtors (eg Ecuador in its 2009 default[12] or Argentina in 2016[13] and 2020[14]).

---

[8] The first meeting of the London Club took place in 1976 in response to Zaire's debt payment problems.
Further negotiations between 1976 and 1981 with Peru, Turkey, Sudan, and Poland were instrumental in coining
what would be known as the 'London Approach'. The 'London Approach' is based on the following principles: (1)
if a corporation is in trouble, banks should maintain the credit facilities in place and not press for insolvency;
(2) banks should work together to reach a solution; (3) decisions about the debtor's future are made only on the
basis of comprehensive information shared among all banks and parties; and (4) seniority of claims is recognized but there is an element of shared burden. See Lex Rieffel, *Restructuring Sovereign Debt: The Case for Ad Hoc
Machinery* (2003); see John Flood, Robert Abbey, Eleni Skordaki, and Paul Aber, *The Professional Restructuring
of Corporate Rescue: Company Voluntary Arrangements and the London Approach*, The Chartered Association of
Certified Accountants, Research Report No 45, 1995, p ii; and also see John Armour and Simon Deakin, 'Norms in
Private Insolvency: The "London Approach" to the Resolution of Financial Distress' (2001) 1 *Journal of Corporate
Law Studies* 33–34.

[9] See IMF, *A Guide to Committees, Groups and Clubs: A Factsheet*, September 2015, available at <http://www.
imf.org>.

[10] See IMF, *Proposals for a Sovereign Debt Restructuring Mechanism (SDRM): A Factsheet*, January 2003, available at <http://www.imf.org/external/np/exr/facts/sdrm.htm>.

[11] Some creditors have resorted to litigation in different jurisdictions including, inter alia, France, Germany,
Ghana, Italy, Switzerland, the UK, and the US to collect on the monies owed by Argentina as result of its default. There have been several attempts to attach different types of assets, for example revenues of state-owned
enterprises, military assets, exchanged bonds, central bank reserves, payments to multilateral organizations, satellites, etc.

[12] Ecuador allegedly engaged in an aggressive secondary repurchase through intermediaries when the price
for the defaulted 2012 and 2030 bonds hit rock-bottom but before an official moratorium was announced or a
default actually occurred. As Porzecanski argues, there are clear links between the drop in Ecuadorian central
bank reserves and the purchase of debt in the secondary market during the default period. It is also alleged that
the vehicle used was Banco del Pacifico, acting through a broker and that it managed to acquire about half of the
total outstanding debt in each series in the secondary market, which could have distorted the readings from the
outcome of the buyback exercise. See Arturo Porzecanski, 'When Bad Things Happen to Good Sovereign Debt
Contracts: The Case of Ecuador' 73 *Duke Law and Contemporary Problems* 251. Also see Ben Miller, 'Ecuador
Restructuring: Inside Job' (2009) *Latin Finance* 1 July.

[13] In 2016, Argentina had recourse to the use of the statute of limitations—a defence not used by debtors as they
will be seeking additional financing in the near future—in order to disavow certain stale claims.

[14] In 2020, Argentina was again faced with the need to restructure its debt. Argentina made an aggressive financial offer including substantial haircuts but also the legal terms included the possibility of redesignation of eligible
claims. This would have allowed Argentina to redesignate the perimeter of the debt and create a smaller group in
which the required contractual majority to force an amendment would have been reached and then perform successive exchanges until all bonds were restructured (also known as the 'pac-man' technique since as in the video
game, you start eating others until you have done with all of them). See Brad W Setser, 'The State of Argentina's
Debt Restructuring … ', Council on Foreign Relations, 24 June 2020, available at <https://www.cfr.org/blog/state-
argentinas-debt-restructuring>.

10.08   Substantially, what had been the conventional remedy of providing debt service relief through a combination of rescheduling the principal and compulsory new money infusions has been virtually exhausted for many debtor countries.[15] A sovereign bond restructuring is usually performed by means of contractual amendments through the use of collective action clauses (CACs) or an exchange offer. An exchange offer can be understood as an offer to voluntarily exchange the 'original' debt instruments for a 'new' debt instrument with different financial and legal terms. Usually, the new terms of the bonds entail an extension in the maturity, a par value reduction, and/or a lower interest rate in order to let the debtor gain some breathing space. There is no set rule to determine which terms should be amended during an exchange offer, and this may also include an amendment to other non-financial terms as well, for example legal covenants, governing law, etc.[16]

10.09   In this context, debtors and creditors need to: (1) obtain debt sustainability by reducing debt burden in an orderly manner; (2) protect the value of the assets and the rights of the creditors to avoid litigation; (3) achieve the restructuring over a short period of time to reduce disruptions and regain access to capital markets; (4) share a common effort; and (5) avoid moral hazard to shun market distortions. Not only debtors and creditors would benefit from this but also the international capital markets as a whole.

10.10   A series of new developments have taken place in the area of sovereign debt restructuring, namely: (1) the EU sovereign debt crisis and (2) the Argentine litigation in New York;[17] and (3) the emergence of a new framework within the international architecture to address the financial constraints triggered by the COVID-19 pandemic.

10.11   The former is a debt crisis that originated in Greece in late 2009 and that has extended to other Euro-area Member States ever since, affecting Portugal, Ireland, Spain, and Cyprus. These Euro-area Member States (EAMS) have experienced financial difficulties and have either been unable to repay or refinance their debt, or to provide financial assistance to their over-indebted banking sector. This has been as result of primary budget deficits and accelerating debt levels that spiked as a result of a rise in the interest rate spreads for government bonds. The need to assist these troubled economies prompted an institutional reaction that resulted in the incorporation of the European Financial Stability Facility (EFSF)[18] and the establishment of the European Stability Mechanism (ESM).[19]

10.12   Also, as part of the assistance provided to Greece, there was a need to restructure its private sector debt in 2012.[20] The Greek government managed to reduce 53.5 per cent of the face

---

[15] Lee C Buchheit, 'Alternative Techniques in Sovereign Debt Restructuring' (1988) *University of Illinois Law Review* 371, 374.

[16] It is also worth noting that there have been cases where only one of the so-called financial terms (ie maturity, interest rate, or par value) was amended.

[17] See *NML Capital Ltd v Republic of Argentina*, No 08 Civ 6978 (TPG), 2011 WL 9522565, at 2 (SDNY Dec 7, 2011); *NML Capital Ltd v Republic of Argentina*, 699 F 3d 246, 264 (2d Cir 2012); and *NML Capital Ltd v Republic of Argentina*, 727 F 3d 230 (2d Cir 2013), *cert denied*, 134 S Ct 2819 (2014).

[18] The EFSF is a temporary credit-enhanced special purpose vehicle (SPV), with minimal capitalization, created to raise funds from capital markets on its investment grade rating, with the objective of providing financial assistance to distressed EAMSs at lower interest rates than otherwise would be available to them.

[19] The ESM is an intergovernmental organization under international public law that will mobilize funding and provide financial assistance, under strict economic policy conditionality, to its members, when they are threatened or experiencing severe financing problems. Its underlying *raison d'être* is to help to assure Euro-area financial stability, in the context of macro-economic adjustment programmes, taking into account the severity of the economic and financial imbalances of the Euro-area Member States.

[20] This restructuring was known as private sector involvement or PSI.

value of its Greek law governed bonds by retrofitting collective action clauses (CACs).[21] Since 93 per cent of the total outstanding bonds issued by Greece were governed by Greek law, the Greek government passed a law unilaterally introducing a CAC in selected Greek governed bonds that did not contain this clause at the moment of their issuance. Then, through an exchange offer, once the necessary majorities to trigger the CAC were achieved, it was used to cramdown the dissenting minority and obtain a high degree of participation. In the English-governed instruments, there was no need to retrofit CACs since these instruments already had CACs, however, the use of the CAC was blocked on certain instruments and therefore it was not possible for the clause to be used on all of the instruments. The overall bondholder participation in the Greek private sector involvement (PSI) was of approximately 97 per cent of the total outstanding bonds. The high degree of participation has been achieved not only because of the use of CACs but also because of a 'reverse' exit consent,[22] since creditors were instructed that most likely there would be a need to restructure further (in the future) the Greek debt. Therefore, the Greek PSI resulted in two private sector developments, ie the retrofitting of CACs and the development of what is known as a reverse exit consent.

The Argentine litigation in New York relates to a claim initiated by a hedge fund to collect **10.13** on defaulted debt obligations issued by Argentina, based on the breach of the *pari passu* clause.[23] This litigation has had several instances and gave rise to additional claims in the US and abroad. As result of these multiple claims there has been a number of interesting developments: (1) the interpretation of the *pari passu* clause in sovereign debt instruments for the first time by the Second Circuit Court of Appeals; (2) the 'realization' that US courts can grant equitable remedies to obtain specific performance in cases where the debtor can shield behind the sovereign personality; (3) the policy reaction that prompted in the adoption of

---

[21] CACs are clauses whereby, if they are included in the prospectus of the bonds, the interaction of the bondholders is required to take certain actions. There are four different types of CACs. These are: (1) collective representation clauses; (2) majority action clauses; (3) sharing clauses; and (4) acceleration clauses. Within CACs, majority action clauses are the type of clauses that have been strongly pursued by the official sector and many academics, and they were effectively incorporated in bond issuances. Majority action clauses enable the amendment of any of the terms and conditions of the bonds, including the payment terms, if the required majority therein established is obtained. The retrofitting of CACs in the Greek restructuring resulted from the enactment by the Greek Parliament of the Bondholders Act 4050/12 that resolved the unilateral amendment of certain debt obligations to include CACs. See Article 1 of the Greek Bondholders Act 4050/12 (an English version is available at <http://andreaskoutras.blogspot.co.uk/2012/03/better-tarnslation-of-bondholders-act.html>).

[22] 'Exit consent' is the technique by which holders of defaulted bonds which have accepted an exchange offer—at the moment of accepting said offer—grant their consent to amend certain terms of the bonds to be restructured. By using the exit consent technique, the exchange offer is conditioned to a minimum threshold of creditors' acceptance and the amendments to the terms are performed once the required majority has been obtained forcing those creditors that do not want to participate in the exchange offer to take part. Otherwise, they will be left with a depreciated bond that does not have its original features and can be difficult to enforce or sell in the secondary market. A 'reverse' exit consent can be understood as a situation where in the exchange offer you offer better contractual terms (not necessarily financial terms but legal terms) to creditors to entice their participation. Although this can be seen as contractual enhancements or 'sweeteners' it is referred to as 'reverse' exit consent because rather than diminishing the rights of creditors you enhance their rights when exiting their old bonds.

[23] The *pari passu* clause is a standard clause in public or private international unsecured debt obligations. The *pari passu* clause is commonly included in debt obligations to protect the lender from being subordinated either because of other concealed debt obligations that were not disclosed or because of the creation of a legally senior class of creditors (which will amount to a subordination or relegation in their ranking). The *pari passu* clause has elements of a representation and warranty (the debt obligation ranks equally with the borrowers' other unsubordinated indebtedness) and a covenant (a promise that this status will be retained in the future). From a close reading of the clause, it can be argued that it has two elements: (1) an internal limb, ie that [the bonds] will rank *pari passu* with each other; and (2) an external limb, ie that [the bonds] will rank *pari passu* with other unsubordinated or unsecured (present or future) indebtedness of the issuer.

single-limb CACs,[24] *pari passu* clauses that expressly disavow a ratable payment interpretation and creditor engagement clauses;[25] and (4) a revival of the discussion of whether there is a need for a statutory approach to deal with sovereign debt crises.[26]

III. Recent Challenges Posed by COVID-19

10.14   The recent financial constraints triggered by the COVID-19 pandemic have pushed again for revisiting the status quo of the international architecture to deal with sovereign debt crises. In response to the impending difficulties being faced by certain economies which would be faced with massive additional fiscal spending to face the health crisis caused by COVID-19, two initiatives were unveiled to avert instances where servicing existing debt would compound and constrain those countries' response to the crisis. The G20 devised the Debt Service Suspension Initiative (DSSI), an initiative by which bilateral official creditors could, upon request, suspend debt payment obligations from 73 low- and lower-middle-income economies. This initiative was supported by the IMF and the World Bank, which helped in monitoring the use of the resources to address the pandemic shock.[27] The aim of the DSSI was to temporarily free liquidity so that these countries could use available cash to mitigate the impact of the COVID-19 crisis on their population. The G20 agreed to extend the initial debt service suspension twice, first until the end of June 2021 and then was rolled over for other six months until the end of 2021. The DSSI, however, covered just a small portion of the total indebtedness of sovereigns and for a limited period and had conceptual flaws.

10.15   The shortcomings of the DSSI have been officially recognized by the G20 which endorsed the 'Common Framework for Debt Treatments beyond the DSSI' (the Common Framework) as a complementary and superseding arrangement to deal with the impending debt issues.[28] Under the Common Framework, eligibility is based on the IMF-WBG debt sustainability analysis (DSA). The Common Framework requires the applicant to disclose the necessary public sector information on financial commitments (debt) but respecting commercially sensitive information (without clarifying what this comprises). The Common Framework also requires the participating debtors to seek treatment on a comparable basis from other creditors, including the private sector, and brings on board official creditors previously unaffected, such as China.[29] The new framework proposes the signing of legally non-binding Memoranda of Understandings (MoUs) by all participating creditors and by the debtor,

---

[24] A single limb-CAC is a collective action clause that allows the aggregation of different bond series and which can then be restructured with a single majority requirement.

[25] The first two have been endorsed by the official sector. The single-limb CAC has also been developed, based on what happened in the Greek Private Sector Involvement (PSI) where certain bondholders were able to obtain blocking holdings due to small bond issuances.

[26] The revival of the statutory approach is also shared with the EU sovereign debt crises, as can be evidenced by the following quote: '[t]he Greek and Argentine sagas have revived interest in a dormant IMF proposal for a sovereign-debt restructuring mechanism (SDRM)'. See *The Economist*, 'An illusory haven: What lessons should investors learn from the Argentine and Greek restructurings?', 20 April 2013.

[27] IMF, 'Questions and Answers on Sovereign Debt Issues', 12 February 2021. The IMF is also providing debt relief through grants to the 29 poorest countries under the Catastrophe Containment and Relief Trust amounting to approx. US$500 million.

[28] G20 Statement, Extraordinary G20 Finance Ministers and Central Bank Governors' Meeting, 13 November 2020.

[29] Kristalina Georgieva, Remarks by IMF Managing Director Kristalina Georgieva During a Virtual Extraordinary Meeting of G20 Finance Ministers and Central Bank Governors, 13 November 2020.

stating the key parameters of the agreement, later to be implemented through bilateral agreements.

IV. Some General Considerations

Although each sovereign debt restructuring episode is unique, there are certain similarities   **10.16**
that can be recognized, with the aim of establishing common elements involved in previous debt restructuring episodes and the roles played by each party in these processes to provide a basis for understanding their different interests in a restructuring. Sovereign debt restructuring has an important degree of complexity because it merges the perspectives of the debtor, creditors, and international financial institutions. However, it is worth noticing that the perspective of creditors involved in a sovereign debt restructuring episode has different shades since retail and sophisticated creditors do not share the same interests. In addition, even within the same type of creditors, such as sophisticated creditors, for example, a hedge fund and an investment bank do not necessarily share the same interest either.

The main issue in sovereign debt restructuring since the late 1990s has been tackling   **10.17**
holdout creditors.[30] In this regard two main approaches to deal with this issue have been developed: (1) the possibility of adopting a statutory sovereign debt resolution mechanism (in the vein of that proposed by the International Monetary Fund (IMF) in 2001 known as Sovereign Debt Restructuring Mechanism commonly known by its acronym SDRM[31]); and, (2) a contractual approach by the use of CACs or exchange offers coupled with exit consents[32] and contractual 'sweeteners'.[33]

As evidence demonstrates, episodes of sovereign bond restructuring have been resolved   **10.18**
quickly, without severe creditor coordination problems, and involving little litigation—the only significant exception being Argentina, a 'serial defaulter' and a 'rogue debtor'. So why mend something that is not broken? The exchange offers of Pakistan (1999), Ukraine (1999), Ecuador (2000, 2009, and 2020), Uruguay (2003), Argentina (2005–10 and 2020), Belize (2006), and Greece (2012), simply to name a few and these being amongst the most complex, can be used to demonstrate that exchange offers or the use of contractual provisions (CACs) work. In all of these cases, the degree of creditors' participation has been above 90 per cent. Of the 34 sovereign bond exchanges since 1997, only two have been affected by holdout creditors.[34]

The   ad   hoc   market-centred   voluntary   approach   of   exchange   offers   **10.19**
(prospectus'   terms   enhancement,[35]   trust   indentures,[36]   advisory

---

[30] Those creditors who do not take part in the debt exchange are usually referred to as 'holdouts'.

[31] See IMF, *supra* n 8.

[32] Lee Buchheit and G Mitu Gulati, 'Exit Consents in Sovereign Bond Exchanges' (2001) 48 *UCLA Law Review* 59–84.

[33] A contractual sweetener can be understood as better contractual terms, usually granting additional legal protection to creditors that might assist in convincing creditors to participate in an exchange offer.

[34] Elena Duggar, Richard Cantor, and Bar Oosterveld, *The Role of Holdouts Creditors and CACs in Sovereign Debt Restructuring*, Moody's Investors Service Sovereign Default Series (10 April 2013), available online at <https://www.moodys.com/Pages/Sovereign-Default-Research.aspx>.

[35] For example the 'mandatory pre-payment clause' or the 'mandatory re-instatement of principal clause' used in Ecuador sovereign debt restructuring in 2000.

[36] In the US and the UK, the common practice is to issue bonds under a trust indenture. This implies the appointment of a trustee in respect of the bonds to represent the bondholders. The appointment of a trustee benefits the bondholders in many aspects, inter alia: (1) sophisticated monitoring; (2) unified enforcement; (3) pro rata

committees,[37] etc) and use of contractual features (CACs, creditor committees, etc) should be endorsed. However, it can benefit from complementary contractual sweeteners (to entice creditors to participate) and the use—if required—of exit consents (to increase the degree of participation of those creditors that were not convinced by the contractual sweeteners). If CACs are already included in the debt instruments, the debt instruments can simply be amended by the required contractual majority (without attempting to distort the collective will).

10.20   Both alternatives within the contractual approach either have flaws (eg CACs are not included in all bonds, only in most of those issued as of late 2003, and even if they are included they do not always allow aggregation and/or might have certain limitations as a double limb in a small value issuance where a holder of a small claim can block the whole restructuring) or can be improved (eg by using them combined or with special features[38]).

10.21   Additionally, the role of the IMF should be redefined since it has been drifting from one extreme (international lender of last resort for, eg, Mexico in 1995) to another (no involvement in the debt crisis, eg Argentina in 2001 and 2020)—and, in between, lending to a developed country like Greece, which falls into arrears[39]—without being exempt from criticisms. The IMF should play an active role in the restructuring procedures, similar to its role during the implementation of the Brady Plan but without overexposing itself. In extreme cases, the IMF can even endorse a sovereign's request before the United Nations to prevent creditors from seizing assets during a short restructuring period, as occurred in the case of Iraq.[40] Within an ad hoc legal framework, this can be an ad hoc 'SDRM-like' restructuring mechanism.

V. Concluding Remarks

10.22   Finally, it is worth stressing that every episode of sovereign debt restructuring includes a heavy influence of politics and the need for additional financing in order to keep the economy running. The role played by economic sanctions which are instruments of foreign policy transposed into law (eg those imposed by the Office of Foreign Assets Control

payment, etc. It also benefits the issuer as well since namely: (1) it protects it against 'rogue' creditors; (2) provides greater flexibility for waivers and modifications; (3) the issuer only has to deal with one single representative of all the creditors; etc. See Philip Wood, 'International Loans, Bonds and Securities Regulation', *Law and Practice of International Finance* (1995) 164–166.

[37] The advisory committees are committees comprising representative creditors that interact with the sovereign in trying to find a workable proposal for both parties, debtor and creditors. They were used many times during the Brady Plan era.

[38] It can be argued that in the restructuring of Uruguay sovereign debt in 2003 various techniques were used together (ie 'tick-the-box' exit consents, the adoption of CACs with the possibility of aggregation, and term enhancements). However, it is worth noticing that in the case of Uruguay there was no default and the restructuring was launched to prevent a moratorium on the outstanding debt. In addition, the latest draft of the model CACs adopted ex-post Uruguay 2003 allows for a single-limb voting mechanism (see <http://www.icmagroup.org/Regulatory-Policy-and-Market-Practice/Primary-Markets/collective-action>).

[39] On 30 June 2015 Greece became the first developed country to fall into arrears with the IMF. See IMF Press Release No 15/310 dated 30 June 2015. On 20 July 2015 Greece repaid the totality of its arrears to the IMF. See IMF Press Release No 15/344 dated 20 July 2015.

[40] UN Res No 1483/03.

of the US Treasury Department)[41] are becoming an issue of greater concern.[42] As Gelpern has clearly stated, 'it is impossible to separate politics and finance in sovereign workouts'.[43] Despite the impossibility of separating politics from sovereign debt restructuring, the primary focus in the final chapters of this book will be on the legal issues.

Upon an event of default, a creditor is faced with two alternatives: (1) pursue remedies against the debtor in a court of law trying to collect the full par value of the credit; or (2) enter into negotiations with the debtor to reach a restructuring agreement, which usually implies worsening the original terms of the credit. Chapter 11 will address the different issues that need to be considered before initiating litigation against a sovereign, with particular emphasis on the enforceability of a favourable ruling. Then, an analysis of the current status quo of the ad hoc market-centred sovereign debt restructuring framework is provided in Chapter 12. Particular emphasis will be put on the techniques and mechanisms developed to tackle the holdout problem in view of the lack of a universal insolvency regime applicable to sovereigns.   **10.23**

---

[41] The Office of Foreign Assets Control of the US Treasury Department administers and enforces economic and trade sanctions based on US foreign policy and national security goals against targeted foreign countries and regimes, terrorists, international narcotics traffickers, those engaged in activities related to the proliferation of weapons of mass destruction, and other threats to national security, foreign policy, or the economy of the US. See US Department of the Treasury: <https://home.treasury.gov/policy-issues/office-of-foreign-assets-control-sancti ons-programs-and-information>.

[42] See Thomas Laryea, 'Why it's Time to Lift the Trading Ban on Venezuela's Debt', *FT Alphaville* (19 February 2021) <https://www.ft.com/content/ade67fa7-0d56-4c21-9f58-a78ba4387cc5>.

[43] Anna Gelpern, 'What Iraq and Argentina Might Learn from Each Other' (2005) 6(1) *Chicago Journal of International Law* 414.

11

LITIGATION ASPECTS OF SOVEREIGN DEBT

I. Sovereign Debt Litigation

A disruption in the economy of a country might trigger a crisis of considerable magnitude, forcing creditors to examine their legal options for recovery.[1] **11.01**

In debt documented in tradable instruments (ie global bonds), this disruption would be evidenced by an 'event of default'. The following are considered standard 'events of default' in a bond prospectus: (1) non-payment (non-payment of principal or interest for a period of 30 consecutive days); (2) breach of other obligations (breach of other obligations over the grace period following written notice to remedy the failure); (3) cross default; (4) moratorium; (5) contestation (contest the validity of the debt securities); (6) failure authorizations (failure or modifications—in a manner that adversely affects the performance of the material obligations—of the authorizations necessary to perform); (7) monetary judgment (any monetary judgment exceeding an amount agreed in the prospectus and it is not adequately satisfied, bonded, contested in good faith, or receives a stay of execution in respect of, such judgment within a grace period); (8) illegality (the adoption of any applicable law, rule, or regulation which would make it unlawful to comply with the obligations agreed); and (9) International Monetary Fund (IMF) membership cessation.[2] **11.02**

---

[1] See Paul L Lee, 'Central Banks and Sovereign Immunity' (2003) 41 *Columbia Journal of Transnational Law* 327 at 394.

[2] See, for example, Prospectus of the República Oriental del Uruguay to issue debt securities and/or warrants to purchase debt securities up to $3,000,000,000 (reflecting additional filings made with the SEC pursuant to Rule 424(b)(3) on 15 April 2003 and 9 May 2003), pp 73–74 and Prospectus, dated 27 December 2004, of the Republic of Argentina exchange offer to exchange eligible securities for Par Bonds due 2038, Discount Bonds due December

11.03   Upon a default scenario, sovereign states usually establish that the situation is of public emergency by means of passing a law or enacting an executive order or decree.[3] Then, it is likely that local courts will not rule against the default and extraordinary emergency situation instituted by the sovereign's government due to the situation of emergency that the country is facing.[4] Even if this type of norm is not in place when the claim is initiated, the affected government might resort to any recourse to impede a favourable ruling or its enforcement. As stated by Wood, a state is in charge of its own law-making machinery and can therefore change its laws and compel its courts to give effect to changes.[5] This is the reason why creditors are left with almost only one choice: to pursue their credit in a country different from that of the debtor. Otherwise, they have to face the uncertainty of litigating in an unpredictable and unfriendly jurisdiction where the legislative machinery can change the rules.

11.04   In pursuit of fairness and neutrality, creditors will prefer to sue in the courts of their own country or in the courts of the applicable law of the debt instruments, which is usually other than that of the debtor's country.

11.05   Usually, in bond issuances, there would be a choice of law clause. Thereafter, the court would apply its own choice of law rules to decide whether the contractual choice made by the parties can be upheld. This will imply that a court might have to apply a law with which it has no familiarity. Therefore, in global bond issuances, this uncertainty has been resolved by the sovereign borrower's submission to a perceived fair, neutral, and expert forum in the jurisdiction of the selected governing law which in most cases results in the application of either English or New York state law.[6]

11.06   It is also arguable that a creditor would prefer to sue in a jurisdiction where it can execute—if it succeeds—a favourable judgment. However, the fact that the sovereign has assets in any given jurisdiction does not imply that those assets will remain there until a judgment is rendered or even an interim measure is granted. This evaluation should be performed together with deciding on the most favourable jurisdiction to sue, considering whether there would be assets to execute, and collecting on the judgment.

2033, Quasi-Par Bonds due December 2045, and GDP-linked Securities that expire in December 2035; and the Prospectus dated 27 December 2004, pp 204–205. For example: (1) the grace period for 'breach of other obligations' is 60 days in the case of Uruguay and 90 in the case of Argentina; and (2) the agreed amount in the 'monetary judgment' is $60 million in the case of Uruguay and $90 million in the case of Argentina.

   [3] For example, upon the Argentine crisis of 2001 the Congress passed law 25,561 declaring a public emergency of Argentina, particularly in the social, economic, administrative, financial, and currency exchange areas. More recently, the Greek Bondholders Act 4050/12, Article 1(11) states that '[t]he provisions of this Article aim to protect the supreme (overriding) public interest, are mandatory rules effective immediately, prevail any contrary legislation of general or special provisions or regulations issued by the administration or agreements ...'.
   [4] Even in some cases where the sovereign immunity has been waived by the debtor, that immunity is limited within its own territory. For example in the Prospectus of the República Oriental del Uruguay to issue debt securities and/or warrants to purchase debt securities up to $3,000,000,000 (reflecting additional filings made with the SEC pursuant to Rule 424(b)(3) on 15 April 2003 and 9 May 2003), on p 87, the sovereign immunity clause reads as follows: 'Uruguay will waive that immunity in respect of any claims or actions regarding its obligations under the securities, except that Uruguay will not waive immunity from attachment prior to judgment and attachment in aid of execution under Uruguayan law.'
   [5] Phillip R Wood, *Project Finance, Subordinated Debt and State Loans* (1995) 99.
   [6] As will be analysed below, the applicable law is relevant when a sovereign is under distress because the alternatives of the debtor would be different depending on the applicable law.

It can be said that it is highly probable that the creditor would prefer to sue the sovereign **11.07** debtor either in England and Wales or the State of New York. These two jurisdictions will provide the certainty and predictability that a creditor requires. In addition, they provide a certain level of insulation to avoid the interference of other legal systems, conceptual sophistication, and the fact that both are English-speaking jurisdictions, English being the language of the international financial markets. Therefore, most sovereign debt issuances are subject either to English or New York state law.

After having preliminarily decided where to sue, the creditor is faced with another dilemma. **11.08** Is the debtor entitled to sovereign immunity or state immunity, as referred under New York and English law, respectively? Both under New York law and English law[7] there are certain situations in which the sovereign is entitled to sovereign/state immunity from jurisdiction or adjudication as well as from attachment and execution.[8]

In addition to proving the effectiveness of a waiver of immunity or an immunity exception from **11.09** jurisdiction, a bondholder has to demonstrate that the court has personal jurisdiction over the sovereign as well as subject matter jurisdiction over the suit to be able to sue a sovereign.

Once a creditor has decided where to sue and after going through the issues of: (1) having **11.10** to determine if the foreign state has sovereign immunity; and (2) establishing whether the court has personal jurisdiction over the foreign state and subject matter jurisdiction over the case, the intervening court may not be in a position to adjudicate the merits of the claim against a sovereign based on the fact that the foreign sovereign's act is subject to the application of the act of state and comity doctrines.

A common practice in sovereign debt financing is the submission to jurisdiction, ie that the **11.11** sovereign has: (1) submitted to the court; (2) appointed a process agent; and (3) expressly waived immunity from suit. Even, if this is not the case, obtaining a favourable judgment to collect on defaulted debt instruments issued by a sovereign under New York and English law is relatively straightforward. Since issuing a bond is a commercial activity, the sovereign issuer submits himself to the jurisdiction as a private party subject to the courts of law.

If there were any doubts in this respect, in 1992 the Supreme Court of the United States had **11.12** to resolve a case involving the rescheduling of sovereign bonds, which became a landmark case in sovereign immunity. In *Republic of Argentina v Weltover, Inc*,[9] bondholders brought a breach of contract action against Argentina and its central bank pleading that the issuance of bonds and Argentina's unilateral extension of its payment date fell within the Foreign Sovereign Immunity Act 1976[10] (FSIA) immunity exception because it is 'a commercial activity of the foreign state' that has 'a direct effect in the United States'. The Supreme Court held that: (1) '[w]hen a foreign government acts, not as a regulator of a market, but in the

---

[7] Focus is given to US and English law, this notwithstanding it is worth noting that other countries or regions have enacted Acts de-immunizing state immunity (eg the Singaporean State Immunity Act 1979; the Pakistani State Immunities Ordinance 1981; the South African Foreign States Immunity Act 1981; the Canadian State Immunity Act 1982; the Australian Immunities Act 1982; or the European Convention on State Immunity 1972 (Cmnd 7742)).

[8] For general background on the topic, its history, and evolution see Gamal Moursi Badr, *State Immunity: An Analytical and Prognostic View* (1984), or Charles J Lewis, 'State and Diplomatic Immunity' (2nd edn, 1985).

[9] *Republic of Argentina v Weltover, Inc*, 504 US 607, 112 S Ct 2160, USNY, 1992.

[10] Title 28, §§ 1330, 1332, 1391(f), 1441(d), and 1602–1611 of the United States Code.

manner of a private player within it, the foreign sovereign's actions are "commercial" within the meaning of the Foreign Sovereign Immunities Act';[11] and (2) a unilateral rescheduling of the bond payments has a 'direct effect' in the United States, which was designated as the place of performance for Argentina's ultimate contractual obligations even though the bondholders were foreign corporations.[12] As noted by Lee, the decision in the *Weltover* case removed any lingering doubts as to whether the issuing of debt instruments by a government constitutes a commercial activity under the FSIA.[13]

11.13   Therefore, New York and English courts normally have personal and subject matter jurisdiction. In addition, issuing a bond is neither protected by sovereign immunity nor an act of state. State immunity will bar the court from hearing the case and passing judgment. An act of state will bar the court from reopening or questioning an act of a foreign state—it assumes the lawfulness of the act. In any of these two situations—whether the sovereign has submitted to jurisdiction or not—the creditor would be able to bring a suit and, if it is successful, will be entitled to a court judgment for the payment of money. Upon obtaining a favourable judgment, the creditor would have different alternatives to enforce the money judgment. However, the basic enforcement device is property execution. Here creditors are faced with two alternatives: (1) execute property within the debtors' territory by means of recognition of a foreign court decision; or (2) try to execute property abroad. These two alternatives have pros and cons.

11.14   Executing property in the sovereign state faces the creditor with the issue that it would be highly probable that due to *public ordre*, the judgment would not be enforced or if enforced it would be payable with other debt instruments with very unattractive financial terms (long-term maturity and trading in a secondary market at steep discount). The pros are that there would be assets to enforce the money judgment forcing the sovereign to settle or be condemned to pay *in specie* (with *new* bonds). The cons are that the execution process would be completely uncertain.

11.15   On the other hand, if the creditor tries to execute the money judgment abroad, for example in New York or England and Wales, the pros are that the whole process is clearly determined and even an outcome can be easily predicted because there have been many cases where sovereigns have been sued as a result of their default (in opposition to suing in the sovereign's own courts where the process will be characterized by its uncertainty).[14] However, the cons are that it would be very difficult to find assets to enforce the money judgment. The basic enforcement device is execution of property. The key element is to be able to attach property to execute.[15]

---

[11]   In this regard, the Supreme Court added that 'under § 1603(d), it is irrelevant why Argentina participated in the bond market in the manner of a private actor ... [i]t matters only that it did so'.

[12]   In *Verlinden BV v Central Bank of Nigeria* (461 US, at 489, 103 S Ct 1969), the US Supreme Court expressly stated that the FSIA permits 'a foreign plaintiff to sue a foreign sovereign in the courts of the United States, provided the substantive requirements of the Act are satisfied'.

[13]   Lee, *supra* n 1.

[14]   See, eg, *Pravin Bankers Associates Ltd v Banco Popular del Perú* 165 BR 379, SDNY (1994); 895 F Supp 660, SDNY (1995); 912 F Supp 77, SDNY (1996); 109 F 3d 850 (1997); 9 F Supp 2d 300, SDNY (1998); *Elliott Associates LP v Banco de la Nación y República del Perú*, 948 F Supp 1203, SDNY (1996); 961 F Supp 83, SDNY (1997); 12 F Supp 2d 328, SDNY (1998); 194 F 3d 363, 2nd Cir (NY) (1999); 194 FDR 116, 54 Fed R Evid Serv 1023, SDNY (2000); *Lightwater Corp Ltd v República Argentina*, 2003 WL 21146665, SDNY (2003); *EM Ltd v República Argentina*, 2003 WL 22120745, SDNY (2003); *LNC Investments, Inc v The Republic of Nicaragua*, No 96 Civ 6360, SDNY (2 Apr 1999).

[15]   For example, certain debtor countries like Argentina will do everything that is within its reach to avoid the attachment of assets abroad, even before the default (eg Central Bank reserves that were deposited in New York

Sovereign states usually do not have many assets located abroad and if they do, not all of **11.16** them are capable of being attached because some of them enjoy statutory immunity[16] from the processes of execution (injunctive relief and execution). The United States restricted sovereign immunity through its FSIA and the UK through its State Immunity Act 1978 (SIA).[17]

As noted by Schreuer, a distinction should be made between property intended for com- **11.17** mercial purposes and that designated for sovereign or official functions.[18] However, to make a distinction on the functionality of the property is not new since it had already been carried out in 1891 by the Institut de Droit International.[19] The distinction between sovereign or official property and commercial property does not always provide a clear answer and it is here where a deeper analysis is required.

Hence, it is relevant to analyse which are the assets that a sovereign state usually has or **11.18** might have abroad and if those assets can be attached as a means to levy the execution of a money judgment. For example, as noted by Lee, the accounts of a foreign central bank in the United States will be a natural target for creditors holding dollar claims against a foreign government.[20]

If prior to the judgment the debtor transfers all its property from the jurisdiction the judg- **11.19** ment execution will not be able to be levied, deceiving the creditor.[21] Thus, New York law[22] provides for an order of attachment with notice[23] or without notice[24] to be granted before a New York judgment against property of the debtor when: (1) the defendant is a non-domiciliary residing outside the state, or is a foreign corporation not qualified to do business in the state; (2) the defendant resides or is domiciled in the state and cannot be personally served despite diligent efforts to do so; (3) the defendant, with intent to defraud his creditors or frustrate the enforcement of a judgment that might be rendered in the plaintiff's favour, has assigned, disposed of, encumbered, or secreted property, or has removed it from the state or is about to do any of these acts; or (4) the cause of action is based on a judgment, decree, or order of a court of the United States or of any other court which is entitled to

---

banks were withdrawn; funds of the *Banco Nación*—the national bank—that were in their New York branch were repatriated; salaries of government employees abroad were paid into deposit accounts in Argentina or the money was sent via the so-called diplomatic pouch, which enjoys immunity; the presidential airplane avoided landing in countries where bondholders had asked for garnishments, such as Germany; and the frigate *Libertad*, also avoided certain ports). See Alejandro Rebossio, 'El gobierno se protege de los embargos', *La Nación*, 5 February 2004.

[16] Due to the increase of commercial affairs between countries, a distinction between acts of government (*acta jure imperii*) and acts of a commercial matter (*acta jure gestionis*) was developed and the principle became restrictive. The sovereign immunity principle not only applies to the state itself but also to the sovereign of the state in his public capacity, to the government of the state, and any department of its government. The immunity protects a foreign state not only in direct proceedings against it *in personam* but also in indirect proceedings against property which is in its possession or control or in which it claims an interest.

[17] Also, there is a European Convention on State Immunity 1972 (Cmnd 7742).

[18] Christoph H Schreuer, *State Immunity: Some Recent Developments* (1998) 145.

[19] See Article 2 of the *Projet de Règlement International Sur la Compétence des Tribunaux dans les Procès Contre les Etats, Souverains ou Chefs d'Etat étrangers* adopted by the Institut de Droit International, 1891.

[20] Lee, *supra* n 1, 394.

[21] See Reade H Ryan Jr, 'Mitigation of Loss: Remedies in the Event of Debtor Non-Performance' in Michael Gruson and Ralph Reisner (eds), *Sovereign Lending: Managing Legal Risk* (1984) 178.

[22] § 6201 of the New York Civil Practice Law & Rules.

[23] § 6210 of the New York Civil Practice Law & Rules.

[24] According to § 6211(b) of the New York Civil Practice Law & Rules, if the order of attachment is granted without notice to the debtor, it requires a subsequent motion by the plaintiff for the court to confirm the order on notice to the debtor for a period not exceeding five days after the levy of attachment.

full faith and credit, or on a judgment which qualifies for recognition under the Uniform Foreign Money-Judgments Recognition Act.[25]

11.20   Figure 11.1 summarizes the main issues related to the litigation aspects of sovereign debt.

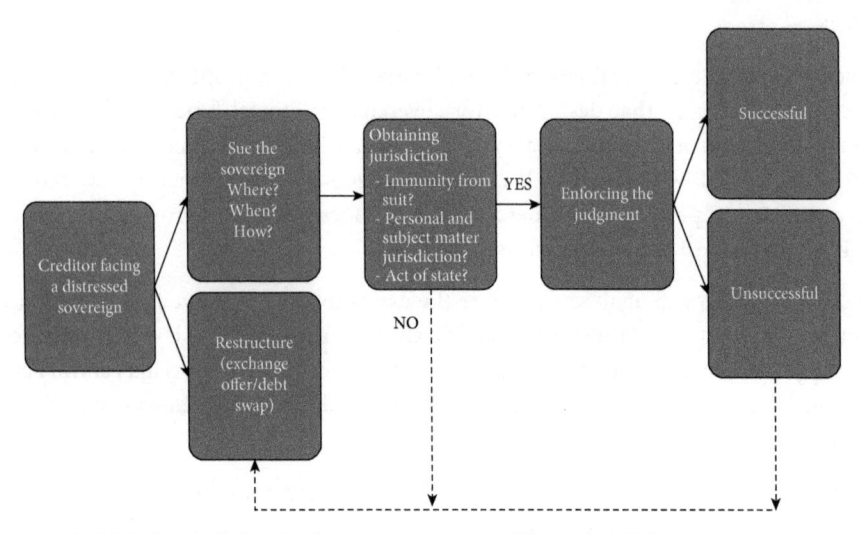

Figure 11.1 Main Issues Related to Litigation Aspects of Sovereign Debt

11.21   Although it is fairly straightforward to obtain a favourable judgment, enforcing it is a completely different story. Although the litigator's imagination has no boundaries, a sovereign usually does not have many attachable assets abroad. Even those few assets that are located abroad, ie diplomatic missions, central bank reserves, payments to and from multilateral organizations (eg IMF), military assets, etc, usually enjoy a certain level of immunity. Therefore, unless there are certain exceptional circumstances, a creditor of a sovereign state should be better off participating in a restructuring arrangement where it can have certain leverage as a group.

11.22   However, there is an additional important financial aspect that needs to be considered, ie the interest rates that will apply on any claim, be it contractual, pre judgment, and post judgment. The currency denomination and the court imposing the applicable interest rate can also have relevance. Throughout the last decade during litigation against Argentina in New York, it has become evident that interest accrues at a different rate depending on whether the creditor has accelerated but not sued or whether there is a court order against the debtor.[26] Sovereign debt financing documents normally specify that interest will accrue at the contractual rate until principal is paid in full (this applies in both scenarios, post maturity and/or acceleration). On the contrary, if the creditor decides to sue, interest will accrue (post maturity and acceleration) at the New York statutory rate of 9 per cent until judgment (according to section 5004 of the New York Civil Practice Law and Rules) and

---

[25] The Uniform Foreign Money-Judgments Recognition Act 1962 has been codified in New York Civil Practice Law, article 53.

[26] See Mitu Gulati and Mark Weidemaier, 'Venezuelan Debt: Further Thoughts on Why not Accelerate and Sue Venezuela now?', *Credit Slips* (12 March 2018).

then at the Federal Statutory rate of approximately 3 per cent until payment (according to section 1961 28 of the United States Code). The rate of interest used in calculating the amount of post-judgment interest is the weekly average one-year constant maturity (nominal) US Treasury yield, as published by the Federal Reserve System. Table 11.1 summarizes the pros and cons of suing versus not suing or delaying suit.

Table 11.1 Pros & Cons of Suing v. Not Suing (or Delaying Litigation)

Suing		Not Suing/Delaying Litigation
UK	US	
The rate of interest from judgment and until enforcement is fixed at 8%	Low accrual of interest from judgment and until enforcement (after judgment interest will be calculated at a floating rate based on one-year US Treasury rates)	Interest will accrue on principal (post maturity or acceleration) at contractual rates (under New York law, interest on unpaid interests will accrue at the New York statutory rate of 9% until judgment)
Interruption of the limitations period		Risk that the sovereign might use the limitation period as a defence
Prevent the use of CACs and Exit Consents		If CACs are used the bondholders can impose the will of the majority on a minority (and use exit consents to force the hand of holdout creditors)

In the UK, the English courts derive statutory power to award pre-judgment interest under the Late Payment of Commercial Debts (Interests) Act of 1998 and section 35A of the Senior Courts Act of 1981, which confers discretion on the court to award simple interest at such rates as it thinks fit. It is usually awarded at 1 per cent over the base rate. However, the 'presumption' is rebuttable if evidence to the contrary is available. Post-judgment debts on sterling sums accrue simple interest at a rate of 8 per cent per annum until payment, unless rules of court provide otherwise.[27] The rate is fixed and can only be altered by statutory instrument.[28] Where a judgment debt is in a currency other than sterling, the rate of interest shall be such rate as the court thinks fit.[29] This discretion allows the court to award interest at the rate appropriate to the currency in question and was prompted by the decision of the House of Lords in *Miliangos v George Frank (Textiles) Ltd*,[30] (the 'Miliangos principle') where it was recognized that the courts could pronounce judgments in currencies other than sterling. In *Novoship (UK) Limited v Nikitin and Others*,[31] the court held that the 8 per cent figure under the Judgments Act of 1838 could not be regarded as the default rate for foreign currency debts, nor did it represent the prevailing rate for borrowing in dollars. It is worth noticing that the post-judgment applicable rate for debts in a currency other than sterling can change from time to time.

11.23

---

[27] See s 17 of the Judgments Act 1838.
[28] See *Thomas v Bunn* [1991] 1 AC 36u.
[29] See s 44A, Administration of Justice Act 1970.
[30] [1976] A.C. 443.
[31] [2015] 2 WLR

II. Required Pre-Action Analysis

A. Where to Sue and under What Law?

11.24   This section will focus on jurisdiction considerations and analyse the application of any exceptions—ie sovereign immunity (or state immunity, as referred to under English law) and the act of state doctrine. State immunity will bar a court from hearing a case and passing judgment.[32] An act of state will bar a court from reopening for questioning an act of a foreign state—it assumes the lawfulness of the act. Finally, it is worth mentioning that it is common practice in sovereign debt documents to include a waiver of immunity, a choice of foreign jurisdiction, and enforcement of the proceedings.[33]

1. The sovereign's own courts

11.25   Upon the occurrence of an event of default (assuming that there is no grace period or if there is, that it has elapsed) a sovereign could pass or enact a law or issue an executive order declaring the situation a public emergency.[34] These acts or orders are unlikely to be justiciable so local courts are unlikely to rule against either the default or the legislative measure, given their political nature.[35] The possibility of biased domestic courts means that suing a sovereign in its own courts is not a viable option.

2. Foreign courts (courts other than those of the defaulting sovereign)

11.26   To resolve uncertainty, international loans and bond issuances usually provide for choice of law and for the sovereign borrower's submission to a perceived fair, neutral, and expert forum in the jurisdiction of the selected governing law. Most often this results in the application of either English or New York state law due to the conceptual sophistication of financial law in these jurisdictions. According to Tennekoon, there are many issues that should be considered in order to decide which should be the proper law. These are: (1) the level of insulation (ie how effective the system is at rejecting the interference of other systems); (2) the certainty and result predictability in applying the chosen law; (3) the degree of party autonomy in avoiding judicial interference; (4) conceptual sophistication; (5) market familiarity; (6) language (the language of the financial markets is English); and (7) legal limitations on the choice of law.[36] Therefore, most sovereign debt issuances are subject either to

---

[32]   In some cases, in order to decide if one of the parties has state immunity, a court will hear the case and only rule upon this issue.

[33]   See Report of the International Monetary Law Committee, International Law Association (MOCOMILA), Berlin Conference (2004), 6, available at <http://www.ila-hq.org/pdf/monetary%20Law/2004%20Berlin%20report.pdf>.

[34]   For example, upon the Argentine crisis, Congress passed law 25,561 declaring the public emergency of Argentina, particularly in the social, economic, administrative, financial, and currency exchange areas. Greece, although a default was prevented, passed Greek Act no. 4050/2012 of 23 February 2012 with a similar provision (Article 1 para 11).

[35]   Even in some cases where sovereign immunity has been waived by the debtor, that immunity is limited in its own country. For example, in the Prospectus of the República Oriental del Uruguay issuing debt securities and/or warrants to purchase debt securities up to US$3 billion (reflecting additional filings made with the SEC pursuant to r 424(b)(3) of the Securities Act 1933 on 15 April 2003 and 9 May 2003), 87, the sovereign immunity clause reads as follows: '... Uruguay will waive that immunity in respect of any claims or actions regarding its obligations under the securities, except that Uruguay will not waive immunity from attachment prior to judgment and attachment in aid of execution under Uruguayan law'.

[36]   Ravi C Tennekoon, *The Law and Regulation of International Finance* (Butterworths 1991).

New York State law or English law. As analysed below, the applicable law is relevant when a sovereign is under distress because depending on the applicable law the debtor would have different options.

Note that personal and subject matter jurisdiction as well as the acting jurisdiction's limits **11.27** on choice of law may occasionally restrict its assumption of jurisdiction, notwithstanding the specification of the acting jurisdiction's law in the bond contract.

B. Can the Debtor Sovereign Claim Immunity from Suit?

Both US law[37] and English law[38] allow sovereign or state immunity from jurisdiction or **11.28** adjudication and thereby from attachment and execution[39] in some circumstances. English law uses the term 'state immunity' for sovereign immunity, and 'immunity from jurisdiction' for immunity from adjudication, but this article will follow the American conventions.

Ever since the full entry into force of the FSIA,[40] US law has required sovereigns to specially **11.29** plead their immunity as an affirmative defence.[41] Sovereigns, their political subdivisions, and their instrumentalities who successfully plead immunity are granted blanket immunity from US court jurisdiction and from attachment and execution of US court judgments[42] with few exceptions.[43]

Sections 1605 to 1607 of the FSIA list two exceptions to immunity from the jurisdiction of **11.30** the US courts which are of particular relevance to loan and bond issuances: (1) waiver of immunity;[44] and (2) acts performed in connection with commercial activities. The waiver can be explicit, such as through friendship, commerce, or navigation treaties,[45] or through agreements between the parties. The waiver can even be by implication, which is interpreted in light of the circumstances.[46] Courts have found implied waivers where: (1) a foreign state has agreed to arbitration in another country; (2) a foreign state has agreed that the law of a particular country should govern a contract; or (3) a foreign state has filed a responsive pleading in an action without raising the defence of sovereign immunity.[47]

---

[37] Reference is made to US law rather than New York law because the Foreign Sovereign Immunity Act 1976 is a federal law.

[38] Although the focus is on New York (US, if the legislation is of a federal nature) and English law, other countries have enacted acts de-immunizing state immunity (eg the Singaporean State Immunity Act 1979; the Pakistani State Immunities Ordinance 1981; the South African Foreign States Immunity Act 1981; the Canadian State Immunity Act 1982; or the Australian Immunities Act 1982).

[39] For general background on the topic, its history and evolution, see Gamal Moursi Badr, *State Immunity: An Analytical and Prognostic View* (Martinus Nijhoff Publishers 1984); or Charles J Lewis, State and Diplomatic Immunity, 2nd edn (Lloyd's of London Press Ltd 1985).

[40] 28 U.S.C § 1602 et seq.

[41] House Report No. 94-1487, p 17, 9 September 1976.

[42] FSIA, §§ 1604 and 1609.

[43] FSIA, §§ 1605 through 1607, 1610, and 1611.

[44] 28 U.S.C § 1605(a)(1).

[45] See House Report No. 94-1487 *supra* n 41. The fact that a treaty exists does not mean that it can be invoked by an individual unless it has been incorporated into domestic law.

[46] See eg *Creighton Ltd. v Government of State of Qatar*, 181 F.3d 118, 122 (D.C. Cir 1999); *Maritime International Nominees Establishment v Republic of Guinea*, 693 F.2d 1094, 1102 n13 (DC Cir 1982); *Marlowe v Argentine Naval Commission*, 604 F. Supp. 703, 709 (D.D.C. 1985); *Eaglet Corp. v Banco Central de Nicaragua*, 839 F. Supp. 232, 236 (S.D.N.Y. 1993) (per curiam).

[47] See House Report No. 94-1487 *supra* n 41, 6617.

11.31   Generally, obtaining a loan or issuing a bond is not protected by sovereign immunity under the second exception from immunity for claims arising out of the sovereign's commercial activities.[48] While the applicability of the commercial activities exception is generally contingent on the existence of a nexus connecting the activity to US territory,[49] the US Supreme Court ruled in *Republic of Argentina v Weltover, Inc.*[50] that Argentina's bond issuance and unilateral extension of its payment date fell within the FSIA immunity exception (section 1605(a)(2)) because (1) such bond rescheduling was primarily a private commercial activity of a foreign state;[51] and (2) such activity had 'a direct effect in the United States', given that the US was designated as the place of performance for Argentina's ultimate contractual obligations despite the bondholders' citizenship as foreign corporations.[52]

11.32   Under the UK's State Immunity Act 1978 (SIA), the immunity of a state refers to immunity from jurisdiction but also to immunity from enforcement and other procedural privileges[53] and the courts must give effect to the immunity conferred even if the state does not appear in the proceedings in question.[54] Only foreign states, heads of state, governments, and government departments are eligible for state immunity.[55] The relevant exceptions under the SIA mirror those available under US law: the foreign state is not immune (1) if it has submitted to UK court jurisdiction;[56] or (2) if the proceedings relate to commercial activities or consequences of a contract linked to the UK. However, Mann[57] and Wood[58] note that under the SIA, the objective test relating to the commercial nature of the transaction[59] includes acts of sovereignty such as buying shoes for the army. In other words, states are not entitled to immunity in cases where the breach of contract arises from an act done in exercise of its sovereign authority[60].

C. Personal and Subject Matter Jurisdiction

11.33   After overcoming the hurdle of sovereign immunity, creditors must demonstrate that the court has personal jurisdiction (or power over the sovereign), and subject matter jurisdiction (or power over the claim) when a sovereign is sued.

---

[48] FSIA, § 1603(d).

[49] 28 U.S.C § 1605(a)(2): Where the action is based upon (1) commercial activity carried on in the US by the foreign state, (2) an act performed in the US in connection with a commercial activity of the foreign state elsewhere; or (3) an act outside the territory of the US in connection with a commercial activity of the foreign state elsewhere in circumstances where that act causes a direct effect in the US, a foreign state is not immune from the jurisdiction of US courts.

[50] *Republic of Argentina v Weltover, Inc.*, 504 U.S. 607, 112 S.Ct. 2160, U.S.N.Y., 1992.

[51] In this regard, the Supreme Court added that 'under § 1603(d), it is irrelevant why Argentina participated in the bond market in the manner of a private actor ... [i]t matters only that it did so'.

[52] In *Verlinden B.V. v Central Bank of Nigeria* (461 U.S., at 489, 103 S.Ct. at 1969), the US Supreme Court expressly stated that the FSIA permits 'a foreign plaintiff to sue a foreign sovereign in the courts of the United States, provided the substantive requirements of the Act are satisfied'.

[53] State Immunity Act 1978, §13.

[54] Ibid, §1(2).

[55] Ibid, §14(1).

[56] Ibid, §2(1); §2(2). Unlike the FSIA, the SIA does not allow immunity to be waived by implication, ie it has to be expressly waived; §2(3)(a)–(b).

[57] See Frederick A Mann, 'Sovereign Immunity under English Law' in Michael Gruson and Ralph Reisner (eds), *Sovereign Lending: Managing Legal Risk* (Euromoney Publications 1984) 109.

[58] Phillip Wood, Law and Practice of International Finance (Sweet & Maxwell 1980) 100.

[59] See Mann *supra* n 57.

[60] Ibid.

1. Personal jurisdiction

Statutory and constitutional limits on personal jurisdiction must be met to support per-   **11.34**
sonal jurisdiction over a defendant in a US court. US case law on personal jurisdiction is
derived from the due process requirements of the Fourteenth Amendment to the constitution.[61] US courts hold that personal jurisdiction is proper only if 'sufficient minimum contacts so as not to offend due process and substantial justice' exist between the defendant and
the state of the forum court.[62] Extensive contact with a state will generally lead to personal
jurisdiction. Since most US states in their long-arm statutes assume the full extent of jurisdiction available to them under federal law, personal jurisdiction analysis under federal law
generally yields the same result under state law.[63]

However, if extensive contacts supporting such broad adjudicative authority are lacking,   **11.35**
courts may still possess specific jurisdiction, provided that the defendant has sufficient minimum contact with the forum state.[64] The defendant purposefully availed itself of the forum
state,[65] and that suit in that forum is reasonably foreseeable to the defendant given its contact with the forum.[66] Sufficient minimum contact with the forum includes the situation in
which a US state is the place of performance specified in a contract and when the US forum
is designated in a contract's choice of law clause. For an act to suggest that a defendant state
has purposefully availed itself of a forum, evidence is needed that the defendant directed
some intentional act towards that forum state. It includes the conduct of business within
a state[67] because by the act of conducting this business a defendant state derives benefits
from the law of that state.[68] Personal jurisdiction over the defendant must be fair without
imposing the unreasonable burdens of litigation in an inconvenient forum,[69] given due process concerns.

When an action arises out of sovereign debt issuance, specific personal jurisdiction over   **11.36**
that sovereign state is likely to exist (subject to the existence of sovereign immunity). In a
case against Argentina decided in 1986, the US Supreme Court recognized that 'by issuing
negotiable debt instruments denominated in United States dollars and payable in New York
and by appointing a financial agent in that city, Argentina purposefully availed itself of the
privilege of conducting activities within the United States'.[70] Note that exercise of personal
jurisdiction is authorized by proper service in the US and in England and Wales,[71] and that
it is common for sovereign debtors to appoint a service agent in the jurisdiction of the loan
or bond contract's governing law.

---

[61]   U.S.C.A. Const. Amend. XIV.
[62]   *International Shoe Co. v Washington*, 326 U.S. 310 (1945).
[63]   According to New York Civil Practice Law, §302(a)1, a court may exercise personal (long-arm) jurisdiction
over any non-domiciliary, who in person or through an agent 'transacts any business within the state'.
[64]   See *Elkin v Austral Am. Trading Corp.*, 10 Misc. 2d 879, 170 NYS 2d 131 (Sup. Ct. 1957); *National Equipment
Rental, Ltd. v Szukhent*, 375 US 311 (1964); *World-Wide Volkswagen Corp. v Woodson* 444 US 286 (1980); or, *Asahi
Metal Industry Co. Ltd. v Superior Court of California*, 480 U.S. 102 (1987).
[65]   *International Shoe Co. v Washington*, 326 U.S. 310 (1945); *World-Wide Volkswagen Corp. v Woodson* 444 US
286 (1980); *Hanson v Denckla*, 357 U.S. 235, 253, 78 S. Ct. 1228, 1240, 2 L. Ed. 2d 1283 (1958).
[66]   *Asahi Metal Industry Co. Ltd. v Superior Court of California*, 480 U.S. 102 (1987).
[67]   *Hanson v Denckla*, 357 U.S. 235, 253, 78 S. Ct. 1228, 1240, 2 L. Ed. 2d 1283 (1958); *World-Wide Volkswagen
Corp. v Woodson* 444 US 286 (1980).
[68]   *J. McIntyre Mach., Ltd. v Nicastro*, 564 U.S. 873, 131 S. Ct. 2780, 180 L. Ed. 2d 765 (2011).
[69]   *World-Wide Volkswagen Corp. v Woodson* 444 U.S. 286 (1980).
[70]   *Rep. of Arg. v Weltover*, 504 U.S. 607, 619, 119 L. Ed. 2d 394, 112 S. Ct. 2160–20 (1992).
[71]   In the US, service of process is governed by Rule 4 of the Federal Rules of Civil Procedure (FRCP) and in
England and Wales in Part 6 of the Civil Procedure Rules (CPR).

2. Subject matter jurisdiction

11.37   With respect to subject matter jurisdiction, the US federal courts have limited jurisdiction. They can only hear cases within the narrow areas bestowed upon them by the Constitution[72] and Congress. Two paths to federal subject matter jurisdiction include diversity jurisdiction[73] and federal question jurisdiction.[74] Diversity jurisdiction exists where claims are between parties with different citizenships, meaning that all defendants must be from different states or countries to all plaintiffs in the case;[75] the matter in dispute exceeds the sum or value of US$75,000 (exclusive of interest and costs). The diversity jurisdiction treats all non-US parties as if they possessed the same citizenship, and it cannot entitle courts to hear actions by foreign plaintiffs against another foreign state.[76] The federal question jurisdiction covers matters 'arising under' the Constitution, treaties, or other federal laws,[77] such as the FSIA, which codifies the standards governing foreign sovereign immunity as an aspect of substantive federal law.[78] Section 1330(b) of the FSIA provides for personal jurisdiction[79] over sovereigns and, in most instances, this will grant federal subject matter jurisdiction over suits against sovereigns.

11.38   In contrast, US state courts are courts of general subject matter jurisdiction. They can hear all claims excepting most tax, bankruptcy, and trademark matters, provided they possess personal jurisdiction.[80] New York statutes specifically grant state court subject matter jurisdiction over (1) foreign corporations in actions brought by New York residents (including New York corporations[81]); (2) in actions brought by non-New York residents (including foreign corporations, if claims relate to breach of contracts made or performed in New York[82]); or, (3) if the defendant is a foreign corporation doing business or authorized to do business in New York.[83] New York state courts assert subject matter jurisdiction over foreign states in actions arising out of contracts valued at US$1 million or more, provided the sovereign has submitted to New York jurisdiction.[84] No New York statute expressly limits the subject matter jurisdiction over foreign states (as distinct from foreign governmental corporations).[85] However, given that claims against sovereigns are unavailable unless sovereign immunity is waived, and given that the FSIA provides for federal jurisdiction where sovereign immunity is waived, even when such claims are filed in state courts, parties may

---

[72]   US Constitution, Article III, section 2.

[73]   The foreign diversity clause provides that the judicial power extends 'to Controversies ... between a State, or the Citizens thereof, and foreign States, Citizens or Subjects'. See US Constitution Article III, Clause 2.

[74]   The so-called 'arising under' clause provides: 'The judicial Power [of the United States] shall extend to all Cases ... arising under this Constitution, the Laws of the United States, and Treaties made, or which shall be made, under their Authority'. See US Constitution Article III, Clause 2.

[75]   28 USC §1332.

[76]   See *Mossman v Higginson*, 4 Dall. US 12 (1800).

[77]   28 USC §1331.

[78]   See *Verlinden B.V. v Central Bank of Nigeria*, 461 US 480 (1983).

[79]   28 U.S.C. §1330(b); *Shapiro v Republic of Bolivia*, C.A.2 (N.Y.) 1991, 930 F.2d 1013; *Texas Trading & Mill. Corp. v Federal Republic of Nigeria*, C.A.2 (N.Y.) 1981, 647 F.2d 300.

[80]   New York Business Corporation Law, §1314(b)(4). The statute also provides for subject matter jurisdiction over claims by non-residents where 'a non-domiciliary would be subject to personal jurisdiction of the courts of this state'.

[81]   Ibid, §1314(a).

[82]   Ibid, §1314(b)(1).

[83]   Ibid, §1314(b)(5).

[84]   New York General Obligations Law, §5-1402.

[85]   Ryan *supra* n 21, 176.

remove the case to the nearest federal court sitting in the same state because the claims arise under federal law.

Under English law, if a defendant is domiciled in England, which is common practice in **11.39** sovereign financing as sovereign issuers usually appoint an agent for service of process in the jurisdiction, English courts will have jurisdiction over the dispute, and it will not be open to the defendant to argue that the case should be determined by the courts of a different jurisdiction.

However, it is also relevant to assess whether it is a non-EU or an EU defendant. Regarding **11.40** the former, and assuming that there is no agent for service in the jurisdiction, English courts would have jurisdiction over a defendant who is domiciled outside the EU if the defendant can be served with the claim form (while) in England, even if only visiting (eg doing a bond issuance roadshow or simply meeting with creditors).[86] If the defendant cannot be served while in England, the claimant can still obtain permission from the English courts to serve notice outside the jurisdiction. Regarding the latter, under the Recast Brussels Regulation, English courts have jurisdiction to determine a dispute involving a defendant that is domiciled in an EU Member State if: (1) the parties have entered into an agreement conferring exclusive jurisdiction to the English courts; and (2) the obligation which is the subject of the dispute was to be performed in England and Wales.

D. Are There Other Defences to Suit? The Doctrines of Act of State and Comity

1. Act of state doctrine

The act of state doctrine precludes the courts of the US and UK from inquiring into the val- **11.41** idity of the public acts of a recognized foreign sovereign power which have been committed within its own territory.[87] The application of the act of state doctrine necessitates a case-by-case analysis. This is based on the sensitivity of foreign policy given the legal and political issues involved.[88] Generally, there are two prerequisites: (1) that the sovereign's action is taken within its own territory; and (2) that the application takes place within the sovereign's own territory.[89] Typically, illegality of a sovereign's act under its own law does not prevent application of the act of state doctrine.[90]

---

[86] A possible defence is to argue that the court should not exercise its jurisdiction if there is a more appropriate forum (doctrine of 'forum non conveniens').

[87] See *Underhill v Hernandez*, 168 U.S. 250, 252, 18 S.Ct. 83, 42 L.Ed. 456 (1897); Banco Nacional de Cuba v Sabbatino, 376 U.S. 398, 401, 84 S.Ct. 923, 11 L.Ed.2d 804 (1964); M. Salimoff & Co. v Standard Oil Co. of New York, 186 N.E. 679 N.Y.,1933; Frazier v Foreign Bondholders Protective Council, Inc., 125 N.Y.S.2d 900 N.Y.A.D. 1 Dept.,1953; Holzer v Deutsche Reichsbahn-Gesellschaft, 14 N.E.2d 798 N.Y.,1938.

[88] The US Supreme Court argued in *Sabbatino* that: 'If the act of state doctrine is a principle of decision binding on federal and state courts alike but compelled by neither international law nor the Constitution, its continuing vitality depends on its capacity to reflect the proper distribution of functions between the judicial and political branches of the Government on matters bearing upon foreign affairs. ... It is also evident that some aspects of international law touch much more sharply on national nerves than do others; the less important the implications of an issue are for our foreign relations, the weaker the justification for exclusivity in the political branches.' *Banco Nacional de Cuba v Sabbatino*, 376 U.S. 398, 401, 84 S.Ct. 923, 11 L.Ed.2d 804 (1964).

[89] See Restatement (Second) Foreign Relations Law of the United States § 41 (1965).

[90] See *Banco de España v Federal Reserve Bank of New York*, 114 F.2d 438, C.A.2 1940.

11.42   In *Alfred Dunhill of London Inc. v Republic of Cuba*, the US Supreme Court held that purely commercial acts of sovereigns would not be afforded act of state doctrine protection.[91] Consequently, the act of state doctrine will rarely prevent courts from inquiring into the validity of a sovereign's attempts to force refinancing of its obligations to sovereign bondholders. In *Libra Bank Ltd. v Banco Nacional de Costa Rica*, the New York federal appeals court considered whether the act of state doctrine required recognition of a Costa Rican Central Bank resolution restraining external payments in foreign currencies, and thus whether the resolution would protect a Costa Rican bank subject to the resolution from an action to collect brought by an English corporation as agent for 16 banks.[92] The appeals court rejected the act of state doctrine defence, holding that the *situs* of the debt owed was the US, given that (1) Banco Nacional had consented to jurisdiction in New York; (2) the loan agreement was construed under New York law; (3) payments were due at a New York bank; and, (4) Banco Nacional had US$2.5 million in various New York bank accounts at the time the decrees were entered.[93]

11.43   In the UK, the position with respect to the act of state doctrine is similar to that in the US. Fox notes that the main difference is that in the UK the act of state doctrine operates as a defence to litigation, while in the US, it operates as a defence but may also be used as a 'basis for a substantive remedy'.[94]

2. Comity

11.44   Comity can be understood as the courteous mutual recognition by nations of the laws and customs of other nations. It is important to stress that in both the US and UK, the legal doctrine of comity recognizes and enforces other jurisdictions' legal decisions as a matter of courtesy, or based on the need for reciprocity, but not as a matter of law.

11.45   Comity is similar to the act of state doctrine in that it recognizes the legislative, judicial, and executive actions of foreign sovereigns.[95] However, while act of state doctrine extends recognition of foreign sovereign actions even when such recognition may conflict with US or UK law and public policy, comity only selectively extends recognition to those legislative, judicial, and executive actions of sovereigns that conform to current US and UK law and policy.[96]

11.46   In the Libra Bank Ltd. v Banco Nacional de Costa Rica case,[97] Banco Nacional raised comity as a defence, but the New York federal appeals court rejected it on the grounds that the Costa Rican Central Bank resolution ordered the confiscation of property without compensation, and such an action is repugnant to the spirit and letter of the US Constitution.[98]

---

[91]   425 US 682 (1976).

[92]   *Libra Bank Ltd. v Banco Nacional de Costa Rica* 570 F. Supp. 870 (SDNY 1981); *Libra Bank Ltd. v Banco Nacional de Costa Rica*, 676 F.2d 47, C.A.2 (N.Y.) (1983).

[93]   570 F.Supp. 870, 881–882.

[94]   Hazel Fox, *The Law of State Immunity* (Oxford University Press 2002), 484. Also see *Banco Nacional de Cuba v Sabbatino*, 376 U.S. 398.

[95]   *Hilton v Guyot*, 159 U.S. 113, 163-164 (1895).

[96]   See Restatement (Second) Foreign Relations Law of the United States § 43 (1965).

[97]   Libra Bank Ltd. v Banco Nacional de Costa Rica, 570 F. Supp. 870 (SDNY 1981); Libra Bank Ltd. v Banco Nacional de Costa Rica, 676 F.2d 47, C.A.2 (N.Y.) (1983).

[98]   Libra Bank Ltd. v Banco Nacional de Costa Rica, 570 F. Supp. 870 (SDNY 1981); Libra Bank Ltd. v Banco Nacional de Costa Rica, 676 F.2d 47, C.A.2 (N.Y.) (1983).

Note that in *Allied Bank International v Banco Credito Agricola de Cartago*,[99] a case similarly based on Costa Rican payment restraints, comity and act of state protection were similarly denied. Buchheit notes that the comity defence may still be available in US court actions to recover on debt obligations whose payment has been interrupted by a foreign government moratorium or standstill.[100]

III. Legal Precedents

A. Cases Being Analysed

Some litigation cases will be analysed to illustrate certain aspects of sovereign debt litiga-   **11.47**
tion and since important conclusions can be drawn from these cases. The cases chosen for the analysis highlight the impact that litigation can have in the outcome of a whole restructuring. First, a series of cases related to the breach of a *pari passu* clause will be analysed to illustrate how this could lead to the default of the newly issued debt instruments resulting from an exchange offer.[101]

Secondly, two cases where the creditor managed to temporarily block the settlement of an   **11.48**
exchange offer which could have had serious implications for the debtor and all those creditors that accepted the exchange offer will be discussed.[102]

---

[99] Allied Bank International v Banco Credito Agricola de Cartago No. 83-7714, slip op. (2d Cir 23 April 1984).
[100] Lee Buchheit, 'Act of State and Comity: Recent Developments' in David Sassoon and Daniel Bradlow (eds), *Judicial Enforcement of International Debt Obligations* (*International Law Institute* 1987) 103.
[101] These cases include: (1) *Pravin Banker Associates v Banco Popular del Peru* cases (165 BR 379, SDNY (24 February 1994); 1995 WL 102840, SDNY (8 March 1995); 895 F Supp 660, SDNY (24 August 1995); 912 F Supp 77, SDNY (19 January 1996); 1996 WL 734887, SDNY (24 December 1996); 109 F 3d 850, 65 USLW 2640, 2nd Cir (NY) (25 March 1997); and 9 F Supp 2d 300, SDNY (15 June 1998)); (2) *Elliott Associates LP v Republic of Peru and Banco de la Nación del Peru* cases (948 F Supp 1203, SDNY (13 December 1996); 961 F Supp 83, SDNY (28 April 1997); 12 F Supp 2d 328, SDNY (6 August 1998); 194 F 3d 363, 2nd Cir (NY) (30 October 1999); 194 FDR 116, 54 Fed R Evid Serv 1023, SDNY (1 June 2000); and *Elliott Assocs LP*, General Docket No 2000/QR/92, Court of Appeals of Brussels, 8th Chamber, 26 September 2000 (not reported, on file with the author)); (3) *Red Mountain Financial, Inc v Democratic Republic of Congo and National Bank of Congo* (No CV 00-0164 R (CD Cal, 29 May 2001)); (4) *Kensington International Ltd v Republic of Congo* (16 April 2003, unreported) (approved by the Court of Appeals [2003] EWCA Civ 709); (5) *Kensington International Ltd v BNP Paribas SA*, No 03602569 (NY Sup Ct, 13 August 2003); (6) *LNC Investments v Nicaragua* case (*LNC Investments, Inc v The Republic of Nicaragua*, No 96 Civ 6360, 2000 US Dist LEXIS 7738, at 1 (SDNY, 6 June 2000), unilateral order granted by the Vice-President of the Commercial Tribunal of Brussels (Tribunal de commerce de Bruxelles) (RR 101/03) dated 25 July 2003 in *Re La Republique du Nicaragua v LNC Investments LLC et Euroclear Bank SA* (not reported, on file with the author); *Republique Du Nicaragua v LNC Invs. LLC et Euroclear Bank*, No RK 240/03 (Tribunal de Commerce de Bruxelles) 2003 (Belg) (not reported, on file with author); and *Republique du Nicaragua v LNC Invs LLC*, No 2003/KR/334, at 2 (Cour D'Appeal de Bruselas, Neuvieme Chambre (Ct App Brussels, 9th Chamber) 2004) (on file with author)); (7) *Macrotecnic International Corp v Republic of Argentina and EM Ltd v Republic of Argentina* (SDNY, 12 Jan 2004) (No 02 CV 5932 (TPG), No 03 CV 2507 (TPG)); and (8) *NML Capital, Ltd v Republic of Argentina* (No 08 Civ 6978 (TPG), 2011 WL 9522565, at 2 (SDNY Dec 7, 2011); 699 F 3d 246, 264 (2d Cir 2012); 727 F 3d 230 (2d Cir 2013); 134 S Ct 2819 (2014)).
[102] These cases are *EM Ltd v Argentina* (restraining notice) and *NML Ltd v Argentina* (attachment) cases. The analysis provided is based on (1) *EM Ltd et al v The Republic of Argentina*, summary order, 13 May 2005, United States Court of Appeals for the Second Circuit, New York; (2) *Amicus Curiae* brief by the Clearing House Association on behalf of Argentina in connection with the *EM Ltd* case; (3) *Amicus Curiae* brief by the Clearing House Association on behalf of Argentina in connection with the *NML Ltd* case; (4) *Amicus Curiae* brief by the Pension Fund Union (*Asociación de Fondos de Jubilaciones y Pensiones*) on behalf of Argentina; (5) *Amicus Curiae* brief by Fintech Advisory Inc on behalf of Argentina in connection with the *EM Ltd* case; (6) *Amicus Curiae* brief

B. Some Preliminary Distinctions: Using a Fiscal Agent and
a Trust Structure

11.49   When issuing debt, the sovereign has to choose between using either a fiscal agent or a trust structure. A brief comment on the use of trust deeds and fiscal agreements is required since they represent an important aspect in structuring sovereign debt issues, particularly in the case of potential litigation as is evidenced in the case of *Elliott Associates, L.P. v the Republic of Peru and Banco de la Nación del Peru*,[103] which is analysed in section III.C.2 below.

11.50   Under a fiscal agent agreement, a fiscal agent is appointed to handle the 'fiscal'[104] matters of the issuer (eg redeeming bonds and coupons at maturity). Under a trust structure (indenture or deed, depending if it is under New York or English law), a trustee is appointed as a fiduciary managing the matters related to the issuance to ensure that the issuer meets all the terms and conditions of the issuance. The main difference between these two structures used in bond issuances is that the fiscal agent acts as a representative and agent of the issuer while the trustee is a fiduciary representing the bondholders. The fiscal agent structure has been the prevailing practice in international bond issuances, recent bond issuances have shifted to the use of trust structures (eg Argentina on its bonds subject to English and New York law, Belize, Dominica, Ecuador, Grenada, Uruguay, and Mexico).[105]

11.51   The distinction between the fiscal agent and the trustee is not a minor issue. The difference is that payments made through a trustee cannot be attached because as soon as the funds are deposited in the trustee's account they are no longer the sovereign's funds, on the contrary, they are held by the trustee acting on behalf of the bondholders. The case of the fiscal agent is different since the funds held on a fiscal agent account are funds of the sovereign until those funds are deposited in each bondholder's account.

11.52   However, until the funds have been deposited in the trust account they are in transit and subject to attachments (they still are funds of the sovereign). This is the reason why the place of payment is so relevant if they are going to be deposited in the fiscal agent or the trustee's account. There are two possible scenarios, ie that the fiscal agent or the trustee has an account outside or inside the sovereign's jurisdiction. If the account is held outside the sovereign's jurisdiction, the funds can be threatened with an attachment. The second scenario, ie accounts held within the sovereign's jurisdiction, requires a twofold analysis: the case of the fiscal agent and the case of the trustee. In the case of the fiscal agent with an account within the jurisdiction of the sovereign, the situation would be the same as in the case of an account outside the jurisdiction because the fiscal agent will have to repatriate the funds to arrange the payments to the sovereign's international bondholders (ie the

by the Emerging Markets Creditor Association (EMCA) in connection with the *NML Ltd* case; (7) Appellants' Brief and Appendix due on 6 April 2005; Appellee's Brief in Opposition due on 13 April 2005; Reply Brief due on 20 April 2005; (8) *NML Capital Ltd et al v Republic of Argentina* unreported opinion dated 31 March 2005; (9) *NML Capital Ltd et al v Republic of Argentina*, hearing transcript, 29 March 2005, United States District Court for the Southern District of New York; and (10) *NML Capital Ltd v Republic of Argentina*, ex parte motion, 21 March 2005, United States District Court for the Southern District of New York and the Memorandums of Law filed.

[103] 12 F Supp 2d 328, SDNY (6 August 1998).
[104] Fiscal is used in a monetary sense as involving financial matters rather than taxes only.
[105] See Lee C Buchheit, 'Supermajority Control Wins Out', *International Financial Law Review*, April 2007.

creditors). The case of the trustee is different because funds can be safely deposited in the trustee's account within the sovereign's jurisdiction (probably even shielded by a law passed by the sovereign debtor) and then be transferred abroad. Once the funds have safely reached the trustee's account, the ownership over those funds is transferred to the creditors via the fiduciary duty of the trustee.

Finally, it is worth mentioning that the 'safety' of the governmental funds within its own **11.53** jurisdiction is so because it will arbitrate the required mechanisms to shield or insulate said funds from potential attachments. It could be either by passing or enacting emergency laws, decrees, or resorting to the legislative branch.

C. The *Pari Passu* Cases

1. *Pravin Banker Associates v Banco Popular del Peru*

Pravin Banker Associates (Pravin) invested in debt issued by Banco Popular del Peru **11.54** (Banco Popular).[106] Banco Popular's main shareholder, Republic of Peru (Peru), collateralized the debt.[107] Due to Peru's financial crisis, Banco Popular defaulted on the repayment of principal.[108] Pravin, after sending notice to the debtor, claimed the repayment for the total outstanding debt from Banco Popular.[109] Peru appointed a liquidation committee to restructure Banco Popular's debt.[110] Pravin refused to participate in Peru's liquidation process, and filed a claim against Banco Popular and Peru for the full repayment of the nominal value of its claim.[111]

In the proceedings, Peru stated that Pravin had bought the debt at discount and that a total **11.55** recovery at face value could not be considered by any party. In addition, Peru claimed that a full face value recovery would have resulted in an illegal enrichment by Pravin who would have obtained an unexpected gain at Peru's disgrace. In *Pravin Banker Associates v Banco Popular del Peru*,[112] the Court of Appeals for the Second Circuit had to balance two conflicting principles to determine if international comity should be extended to the defendant: (1) the success of sovereign debt restructuring, including the IMF's involvement under the Brady Plan, which was part of US foreign policy, and (2) the sanctity of contracts and consequently the repayment of the owed debt at face value, preserving the status of New York as an international financial centre.[113]

After having granted two waiting periods (six months and two months, respectively), the **11.56** Court of Appeals held that Pravin was not obligated to abide by the Brady Plan since the

---

[106] See *Pravin Banker Assocs v Banco Popular del Peru*, 109 F 3d 850 at 852, 2nd Cir (1997).
[107] Ibid.
[108] Ibid.
[109] Ibid at 853.
[110] Ibid.
[111] Ibid.
[112] 165 BR 379, SDNY (24 February 1994); 1995 WL 102840, SDNY (8 March 1995); 895 F Supp 660, SDNY (24 August 1995); 912 F Supp 77, SDNY (19 January 1996); 1996 WL 734887, SDNY (24 December 1996); 109 F 3d 850, 65 USLW 2640, 2nd Cir (NY) (25 March 1997); and 9 F Supp 2d 300, SDNY (15 June 1998).
[113] *Pravin Banker Assocs v Banco Popular del Peru*, 109 F 3d 850 at 855, 2nd Cir (1997).

participation of creditors in such type of restructuring processes was strictly voluntarily.[114] In addition, the Court of Appeals considered that an undefined suspension of the proceedings would affect US interests (the respect of the terms and conditions of valid contracts executed under New York law).[115]

2. Elliott Associates, LP v Banco de la Nación

11.57   After the *Pravin* case, Peru found itself in court again in *Elliott Associates, LP v the Republic of Peru and Banco de la Nación del Peru*.[116] Elliott, a distressed fund, acquired $20.7 million of defaulted bonds in the secondary market at discount ($11.4 million).[117]

11.58   The District Court entertaining the claim ruled in favour of Peru.[118] However, the Second Circuit Court of Appeals reversed the decision on the basis that Elliott's purchase of Peru's distressed sovereign debt was not in violation of section 489 of New York Judiciary Law.[119] Section 489 prohibits the purchase of a claim 'with the intent and for the purpose of bringing an action or proceeding thereon'.[120] The Court of Appeals held that the investor did not violate the law since the debt instrument was acquired for the primary purpose of enforcing it, with the intent to resort to litigation only if necessary to accomplish the enforcement.[121] The decision to file a claim was as a consequence of Peru's failure to perform its obligation.[122]

11.59   As in the *Pravin* case, the Court of Appeals balanced two aspects: (1) granting the possibility to US citizen bondholders to claim the payment of their credit, which limited the chances of achieving a debt restructuring under the IMF's umbrella; and (2) not allowing the claim because it would affect New York as a financial world centre.[123] Needless to say, both issues were important for US foreign affairs policy.[124] The Court of Appeals was of the opinion that the protection of investors was a priority.

11.60   Attachment orders were obtained in Florida, Maryland, New York, and Washington DC which interfered with the payments to be performed by the fiscal agent. Therefore, Peru arranged for the creation of a trust to make twice-yearly interest payments due on the Brady bonds on its behalf.[125]

11.61   The peculiarity of this case, although similar to the *Pravin* case, was the lack of assets to attach in the United States, which forced the claimant to resort to the courts of Belgium,

---

[114] Ibid at 855. Also see International Debt Management Act of 1988, 22 USC § 5331(b)(4).
[115] See ibid at 853.
[116] 12 F Supp 2d 328, SDNY (6 August 1998).
[117] Ministry of Economy and Finance of Peru, Final Report on the Settlement Agreement with Elliott Associates LP, September 2000 (on file with the author).
[118] 12 F Supp 2d 328, SDNY (6 August 1998).
[119] See 194 F 3d 363 at 372, 2nd Cir (1999).
[120] NY [Jud] § 489 (Consol 1983).
[121] See 194 F 3d 363 at 372, 2nd Cir (1999).
[122] 194 F 3d 363 at 379, 2nd Cir (1999).
[123] John Nolan, *Special Policy Report 3: Emerging Market Debt & Vulture Hedge Funds: Free-Ridership, Legal & Market Remedies*, Financial Policy Forum, at <http://www.financialpolicy.org/DSCNolan.htm>.
[124] See Samuel E Goldman, Comment, 'Mavericks in the Market: The Emerging Problem of Hold-Outs in Sovereign Debt Restructurings' (2000) 5 *UCLA Journal of International Law & Foreign Affairs* 159, 196.
[125] See Ministry of Economy and Finance of Peru, Final Report on the Settlement Agreement with Elliott Associates LP, *supra* n 41. In relation to the trust structure, see Resolution No 140-2000-EF/75 of the Ministry of Economy and Finance of Peru.

Canada, England, Germany, Luxembourg, and the Netherlands to seek enforcement of the decision.[126]

Elliott's attempt to enforce the judgment in Belgium was reversed on first instance. **11.62** However, on 26 September 2000, Elliott obtained a restraining order from the Brussels' Court of Appeals[127] prohibiting Chase Manhattan (financial agent) and Euroclear (clearing house) to pay interest on Peru's Brady Plan bonds (approximately $80 million, due on 6 October 2000).[128] The Brussels' Court of Appeals resolution stated that '[i]t ... appears from the basic agreement that governs the repayment of the foreign debt of Peru that the various creditors benefit from a *pari passu* clause that in effect provides that the debt must be repaid pro rata among all creditors'.[129]

Peru's Brady bonds were issued as result of a sovereign debt restructuring in which Elliott **11.63** voluntarily decided not to take part. With the Brussels' Court of Appeals resolution preventing the payment of interests without also paying Elliott on a pro rata basis, Peru was facing the possibility of defaulting again, on the recently restructured bonds which totalled $3,837 million.[130] Although Peru did not make the payment of interest on the due date, it technically had a 30-day grace period to fulfil the payment before entering into default. As noted by López-Sandoval, Elliott's strategy was twofold: (1) trying to attach the funds at the level of the fiscal agent; and (2) capturing funds at the level of the clearing houses.[131]

Facing this situation, Peru desisted in implementing the trust structure to circumvent **11.64** the attachment orders obtained in the United States (which curtailed payments through the Depositary Trust Company (DTC) because the Brussels' Court of Appeals resolution also made it impossible to make payments through Euroclear). The only window that was left open—although temporarily—was to perform the payments through Clearstream (Luxembourg). Performing the interest payments through Clearstream would have implied that only those bondholders holding an account with Clearstream would be paid or that bondholders not holding an account with Clearstream should open an account there (which implied a further delay and eventually an additional cost to Peru).[132] In addition, it was only a matter of time before Elliott would obtain a restraining order in Luxembourg, where the main offices of Clearstream are located.

This scenario forced Peru to reach an agreement with Elliott in order to avoid a default on **11.65** its recently restructured debt under the auspices of the Brady Plan. On 28 September 2000, Peru enacted 'Urgent' Decree No 083-2000 and Resolution No 143-2000-EF of the Ministry of Economy and Finance of Peru to negotiate and settle Elliott's claim. These norms were complemented by 'Urgent' Decree No 084-2000 that authorized a loan granted by the

---

[126] See Eduardo Luis López Sandoval, 'Sovereign Debt Restructuring: Should We Be Worried About Elliott?', Harvard Law School, Seminar on International Financial Law, May 2002, p 12.

[127] Elliott Associates, LP, General Docket No 2000/QR/92 (Court of Appeals of Brussels, 8th Chamber, 26 September 2000) (not reported, on file with the author).

[128] Ibid. These payments were going to be made by the Fiscal Agent (Chase Manhattan Bank) through Depository Trust Company (DTC) in New York, Euroclear in Brussels, and Clearstream in Luxembourg.

[129] Ibid.

[130] See Ministry of Economy and Finance of Peru, Final Report on the Settlement Agreement with Elliott Associates LP, *supra* n 41.

[131] López Sandoval, *supra* n 50 at 13.

[132] See Ministry of Economy and Finance of Peru, Final Report on the Settlement Agreement with Elliott Associates LP, *supra* n 41.

National Bank to the Ministry of Economy and Finance to procure the required funds to settle Elliott's claim.

11.66   The total debt calculated as of 30 September 2000 was $57.47 million plus $9 million to cover legal expenses. The final settlement agreement included a payment for all concepts in the total amount of $58.45 million. It was executed on 29 September 2000 and ratified by 'Supreme' Decree No 106-2000-EF. General releases were executed together with the settlement. Finally, Peru was able to pay the due interest in time to avoid incurring a new default. By means of this agreement, Elliott obtained a gain worth 400 per cent of the purchase value of the defaulted bonds.[133]

11.67   The decision of the Brussels Court of Appeals was based on the violation of the equal treatment of creditors under the *pari passu* clause. The *pari passu* clause, as noted by Buchheit 'is short, obscure and sports a bit of Latin; all characteristics that lawyers find endearing'.[134] An analysis of the scope, possible interpretation, and judicial views on this clause follows.

3. The *pari passu* clause in sovereign debt instruments

11.68   As a result of the ruling in the *Elliott* case by a Brussels' Court of Appeals, various creditors in different jurisdictions (Belgium, California, England, and New York) have argued that as a result of the *pari passu* clause sovereigns should be prevented from making payments to other creditors without paying creditors on a pro rata basis.[135]

11.69   *Pari passu* literally means 'with equal step', from the Latin *pari*, ablative of *par*, 'equal' and *passu*, ablative of *passus*, 'step'. That is to say, that *pari passu* refers to things that are in equal step, things that rank equally. In 1900 Palmer expressed that '[t]here is no special virtue in the words "*pari passu*", "equally" would have the same effect, or any other words showing that the [bonds] were intended to stand on the same level footing without preference or priority among themselves'.[136]

11.70   A *pari passu* clause is a standard clause included in public or private international unsecured debt obligations (syndicated loan agreements and bond issuances). Buchheit and Pam traced the modern origins of this clause and discovered that it was used in unsecured cross-border debt instruments in the early 1970s.[137] In the case of bond issuances, it reads, for example, as follows (emphasis added):

> The Securities are general, direct, unconditional, unsubordinated and unsecured obligations of [Country XYZ] for the payment and performance of which the full faith and credit of [Country XYZ] has been pledged and [Country XYZ] shall ensure that its obligations

---

[133] See John Nolan, *supra* n 47.

[134] Lee Buchheit, *How to Negotiate Eurocurrency Loan Agreements* (2nd edn, 2000) 82–83.

[135] Financial Market Law Committee, *Pari Passu* Clauses, Issue 79, March 2005, p 3, available at <http://www.fmlc.org >.

[136] Francis B Palmer, *Company Precedents* (8th edn, 1900) 109–110.

[137] See Lee Buchheit and Jeremiah Pam, 'The *Pari Passu* Clause in Sovereign Debt Instruments' (2004) 53 *Emory Law Journal* 869, 902. Chabot and Gulati claim that the clause was used for the very first time in Mexico's 1843 General Santa Anna's Black Eagle bond. See Benjamin Chabot and Mitu Gulati, 'Santa Anna and his Black Eagle: the Origins of Pari Passu?' (2014) 9(3) *Capital Markets Law Journal*, July.

hereunder shall *rank pari passu* among themselves and with all of its other present and future unsecured and unsubordinated Public Debt.[138]

From a close reading of the clause, it can be argued that it has two limbs: (1) an internal **11.71** limb, ie that the bonds will rank *pari passu* with each other; and (2) an external limb, ie that the bonds will rank *pari passu* with other unsecured (present or future) indebtedness of the issuer.

However, not all *pari passu* clauses are drafted in the same way. They vary according to the **11.72** drafter, denoting diversity in the language of the clause which might derive in different interpretations. Therefore, a *pari passu* clause can also read as follows (emphasis added):

> The Notes and Coupons of all Series constitute direct, unconditional, unsecured and unsubordinated obligations of [Country XYZ] and shall at all times *rank pari passu* and without any preference among themselves... *The payment obligations of the [Country XYZ] under the Notes and the Coupons shall at all times rank at least equally with all its other present and future unsecured and unsubordinated External Indebtedness.*[139,140]

This second type of *pari passu* clause complicates things since it opens two possible inter- **11.73** pretations. These possible interpretations are: (1) the narrow or 'ranking' interpretation, where obligations of the debtor rank and will rank *pari passu* with all other unsecured debt obligations; and (2) the broad or 'payment' interpretation, that when the debtor is unable to pay all its obligations, they will be paid on a pro rata basis. Wood is of the opinion that the key word is 'rank' and that 'rank' means 'rank', not 'will pay' or 'will give equal treatment'.[141]

According to Buchheit and Pam, the broad or 'payment' interpretation has four practical **11.74** implications: (1) it may provide a legal basis for a creditor to seek specific performance of the covenant (ie a court order directing the debtor not to pay other debts of equal rank without making a ratable payment under the debt benefiting from the clause); (2) it may provide a legal basis for a judicial order directed to a third-party creditor instructing that creditor not to accept a payment from the debtor unless the *pari passu*-protected lender receives a ratable payment; (3) it may provide a legal basis for a court order directing a third-party financial intermediary such as a fiscal agent or a bond clearing system to freeze any non-ratable payment received from the debtor and to turn over to the *pari passu*-protected creditor its ratable share of the funds; and (4) it may make a third-party creditor that has knowingly received and accepted a non-ratable payment answerable to the *pari passu*-protected creditor for a ratable share of the funds.[142]

---

[138] Offering Memorandum of the Government of Belize dated 18 December 2006, for the exchange of US Dollar Bonds due 2029, p 142.

[139] Clause included in the Information Memorandum of the Republic of Argentina of a Medium Term Note Programme of $15,000,000,000 dated 31 October 2000.

[140] According to Wood, the statement that bonds are direct, unconditional, and other such adjectives does not add anything and could safely be omitted (see Philip Wood, 'Pari Passu Clauses—What Do They Mean?' (2003) 18(10) *Butterworths Journal of International Banking and Financial Law* 371, 373 (November 2003).

[141] Ibid at 372.

[142] Buchheit and Pam, *supra* n 61 at 880.

11.75   In this regard, the *Elliott* case[143] worked as a benchmark that sets an *ex ante* and *ex post* scenario in relation to the interpretation of the *pari passu* clause. The *ex ante* situation was that the only possible interpretation of the clause was the narrow or ranking interpretation and that it was included to avoid the creation of preferences either by the sovereign (paying one or some creditors in detriment to others) or by creditors (following a procedure available in certain jurisdictions—like Spain and the Philippines—that allows creditors to obtain a priority without requiring the other party's agreement). This is the reason why commercial banks in the early 1970s started using the clause in unsecured debt instruments.[144]

11.76   Articles 913(4) and 1924(3)(a) of the Spanish Commercial and Civil Code, respectively, refer to the preference of creditors whose credit is instrumented by means of a public deed (notarized by a Notary Public).[145] This type of credit had a preference over those—although of the same type—not instrumented in a public deed.[146] The Philippines—strongly influenced by the Spanish Civil Code—has a norm similar to the one of Spain. Article 2244(14) of the Philippines Civil Code grants priority to those credits that appear in a public instrument or a final judgment.[147] These two countries are the main reason for the emergence and broad spread of the *pari passu* clause in sovereign bonds.[148]

11.77   After the decision of the Belgian court in the *Elliott* case, other cases followed. Creditors were willing to benefit from the broad or 'payment' interpretation. The analysis of these cases follows.

4. The *Red Mountain* case (California)

11.78   On 29 May 2001, in *Red Mountain Financial, Inc v Democratic Republic of Congo and National Bank of Congo*,[149] the court was requested to enforce different provisions of a credit agreement between the plaintiff and defendants. Among the provisions was a *pari passu* clause from a 1980 credit agreement. The District Court expressly denied the performance of the *pari passu* clause but nonetheless enjoined Congo from making any payments

---

[143] See Elliott Associates, LP, General Docket No 2000/QR/92 (Court of Appeals of Brussels, 8th Chamber, 26 September 2000) (not reported, on file with the author).

[144] See Buchheit and Pam, *supra* n 61 at 903.

[145] The Spanish Insolvency Law 22/2003 of 9 July 2003 amended section 1924 of the Spanish Civil Code. Although under section 91 of the new insolvency law a whole new ranking of preferences not including credits instrumented through public deeds is included, subsection (3)(a) of s 1924 of the Spanish Civil Code has not been amended. Therefore, in the event of sovereign issuances—not subject to insolvency laws—the unamended section 1924(3)(a) of the Civil Code still applies.

[146] See Philip Wood, *International Loans, Bonds and Securities Regulation: Law and Practice of International Finance* (1995) 41.

[147] Section 2244(14) of the Philippines Civil Code (Republic Act No 386) reads as follows: 'Credits which, without special privilege, appear in (a) a public instrument; or (b) in a final judgment, if they have been the subject of litigation. These credits shall have preference among themselves in the order of priority of the dates of the instruments and of the judgments, respectively' (the full text of the Philippines Civil Code is available at <http://www.chanrobles.com/civilcodeofthephilippinesbook4.htm>).

[148] Buchheit and Pam also consider Argentina as a country that forced the inclusion of the *pari passu* clause since in 1972 it re-enacted a practice dating back to 1862 where foreign creditors were subordinated to local creditors in the bankruptcy of an Argentine debtor (see Buchheit and Pam, *supra* n 61 at 905, quoting Emilio J Cardenas, 'International Lending: Subordination of Foreign Claims Under Argentine Bankruptcy Law', in David Suratgar (ed), *Default and Rescheduling* (1984) 63).

[149] *Red Mountain Financial, Inc v Democratic Republic of Congo*, No CV 00-0164 R (CD Cal, 29 May 2001).

in relation to its external indebtedness without making a proportionate payment to Red Mountain.[150] The case was settled by the parties.

5. The *Kensington International* case (England)

On 20 December 2002, in *Kensington International Ltd v Republic of Congo*,[151] the *pari passu*   **11.79**
clause was again under scrutiny. This is an English case where the plaintiff was trying to recover defaulted debt[152] governed by a loan agreement subject to English law; and, to prevent Congo from making payments to other creditors on, inter alia, a *pari passu* clause.[153] The intervening judge denied the plaintiff's request[154] on grounds unrelated to the *pari passu* clause and the decision was upheld by the Court of Appeal.[155] The views on the *pari passu* clause in this case 'are of persuasive authority only'.[156]

6. The *Kensington International II* case (against BNP) (New York)

The Kensington saga had a second part in New York. This case is interesting because it gave   **11.80**
the *pari passu* clause a new twist, taking it to another level after the new reading of the *pari passu* in the *Elliott* case.[157] A claim was filed in a New York state court in 2003, *Kensington International Ltd v BNP Paribas SA*.[158] One of the arguments of this claim was that BNP tortuously interfered with Kensington's rights to collect the monies owed by the Republic of Congo on the basis of a ratable payment right due to the *pari passu* clause included in the 1984 loan agreement giving rise to the plaintiff's credit against Congo. This resulted from the fact that according to the plaintiff's line of argument, BNP had received payments from new financings entered into between the defendant and Congo after 1985. In other words, from the fact that BNP collected payments without distributing them on a pro rata basis with Kensington, which should have occurred as a result of the broad or 'payment' interpretation of the *pari passu* clause.

7. The *LNC* case (Belgium)

In 1999, the New York courts rendered *LNC Investments, Inc* a decision by which Nicaragua   **11.81**
was obligated to pay $87 million resulting from defaulted commercial loans granted in the 1980s.[159] LNC Investments preferred to file a claim rather than participate in the sovereign

---

[150] Congo and its Central Bank were 'enjoined from making any payments to be made on their behalves with respect to any External Indebtedness ... unless and until Congo and its [central bank] (or each one of them) make or cause to made a proportionate payment to Red Mountain at the same time'. (See *Red Mountain Financial, Inc v Democratic Republic of Congo*, No CV 00-0164 R (CD Cal, 29 May 2001).)
[151] 16 April 2003, unreported. Approved by the Court of Appeals [2003] EWCA Civ 709.
[152] The debt was acquired after Congo defaulted on the loan agreement.
[153] The relevant part of the *pari passu* clause reads as follows: 'the claims of all other parties under [the loan] agreement will rank as general obligations of the People's Republic of the Congo, at least pari passu in right and priority of payment with the claims of all other creditors of the People's Republic of the Congo'.
[154] 2002 No 1088 at 6:13–16 (Commercial Ct, 16 April 2003).
[155] 16 April 2003, unreported. Approved by the Court of Appeals [2003] EWCA Civ 709.
[156] Financial Market Law Committee, *supra* n 59 at 12.
[157] An example of a case of tortuous liability for breach of contractual provision prior to the *Elliott* interpretation is *Citibank NA v Export-Import Bank of the United States*, No 76 Civ 3514 (CBM) (SDNY, 9 August 1976).
[158] See *Kensington International Ltd v BNP Paribas SA*, No 03602569 (NY Sup Ct, 13 August 2003).
[159] *LNC Investments, Inc v The Republic of Nicaragua*, No 96 Civ 6360, 2000 US Dist LEXIS 7738, at 1 (SDNY, 6 June 2000).

debt restructuring procedure.[160] LNC Investments enforced the decision—following the precedent of *Elliott*—in a Brussels Court.[161]

11.82   As in *Elliott*, LNC Investments obtained a judicial order that prohibited interest payments of restructured bonds.[162] The order was directed to both Deustche Bank AG as fiscal agent, and Euroclear as the clearing house.[163]

11.83   The decision was appealed by Nicaragua, and the Brussels' Court of Appeals reversed the decision.[164] Even though it might seem that the Brussels courts reversed the criteria set forth in the *Elliott* case, it is difficult to determine so because the Court of Appeals did not directly consider the *pari passu* clause as it did in *Elliott*. The case was resolved on procedural grounds—the Court of Appeals reversed the decision because Euroclear was not a proper party to the litigation.[165]

8. A new legislative development to curtail the applicability of the *pari passu* clause

11.84   Finally, to provide a comprehensive coverage of the *pari passu* clause reference should be made to a legislative development in Belgium. Law 4765 (C-2004/03482) was passed in November 2004 reinforcing Article 9 of the Belgian Law of 28 April 1999 that implemented the EU Directive of the European Parliament and of the Council of 19 May 1998 on settlement finality in payment and securities settlement systems ('the EU Settlement Finality Directive').[166]

11.85   Although the EU Settlement Finality Directive does not prevent attachments, the objective by reinforcing the law implementing this directive was to shield the flow of funds through Euroclear. The text of the reformed norm reads as follows (emphasis added):

> No cash settlement account with a settlement system operator or agent, *nor any transfer of money to be credited to such cash settlement account, via a Belgian or foreign credit institution*, may in any manner whatsoever be attached, put under trusteeship or blocked by a participant (other than the settlement system operator or agent), a counterparty or a third party.[167]

11.86   According to the explanatory memorandum that accompanied the new law (ie Law 4765 (C-2004/03482)), the aim is to avoid disruptive actions by creditors by attaching cash accounts held with Belgian clearing systems or obtaining injunctions such as the ones obtained by Elliott and LNC.[168]

---

[160] Ibid at 13.
[161] *Republique Du Nicaragua v LNC Invs LLC*, No 2003/KR/334, at 2 (Cour D'Appeal de Bruselas, Neuvieme Chambre (Ct App Brussels, 9th Chamber) 2004) (on file with author).
[162] Ibid at 7.
[163] Ibid.
[164] Ibid at 19.
[165] See William W Bratton, '*Pari Passu* and A Distressed Sovereign's Rational Choices', 53 *Emory Law Journal* 823, footnote 10.
[166] 98/26/EC, OJ L166 published on 11 June 1998, p 45 as amended by Directive 2009/44/EC of 6 May 2009.
[167] The text emphasized corresponds to the amendment introduced in November 2004.
[168] See DOC 51 1157/011 of the Belgium Parliament (*Chambres des Représentants de Belgique*) dated 25 May 2004, p 64 (on file with the author).

9. *Applestein, Macrotecnic International Corporation and EM Ltd v Argentina*

In January 2004, upon the memorandum of law of Argentina and the plaintiffs, the US **11.87** Statement of Interest[169] and the *amicus curiae* briefs filed by the Federal Reserve Bank of New York[170] and the New York Clearing House,[171] a New York District Court was asked to consider whether the *pari passu* covenant in Argentina's bonds could be used by judgment creditors as a legal basis to interfere with Argentina's payment of its other indebtedness (should the Argentine government continue paying international organizations such as the IMF or other non-defaulted unsecured creditors as the holders of domestic bonds). Although the court did not address the *pari passu* issue, the plaintiffs had to sign an agreement giving the court a 30-day notice before filing any request intended to stop payments under the *pari passu* clause.[172] Although the substantive matter was not resolved, an order was issued by the court ordering Argentina to divulge information about government property outside the country that is used for commercial purposes: a discovery measure.

10. *NML Capital Limited (and Others) v Argentina*: the latest, and most important, chapter in the *pari passu* saga

This is the latest and most important chapter in the *pari passu* saga, since it is the first time **11.88** that New York courts interpreted the clause in sovereign debt instruments governed by New York law.[173] This litigation, *NML Capital Limited (and Others) v Argentina*,[174] resulted from Argentina's moratorium on its external debt in December 2001 and technical default in January 2002. In 2005, Argentina launched an exchange offer in an attempt to cure its default on its external debt obligations and obtained a 76.15 per cent degree of participation.[175]

NML Capital Limited (and others) decided to holdout in the exchange offer launched by **11.89** Argentina and brought suit for breach of the *pari passu* clause included in a 1994 Fiscal

---

[169] In the US statement of interests, it was stressed that '[a] novel reading of *the pari passu* clause, however, that would prohibit sovereign debtors from making payments to third party creditors or require sovereign debtors to make simultaneous, ratable payments to all creditors would undermine [a] well understood established framework...' (see Statement of Interest of the United States at 14, *Macrotecnic Int'l Corp v Republic of Argentina and EM Ltd v Republic of Argentina* (SDNY, 12 Jan 2004) (No 02 CV 5932 (TPG), No 03 CV 2507 (TPG)).

[170] The Federal Reserve Bank of New York urged the court to interpret the *pari passu* clause narrowly 'so as to discourage the terrorism of payments and settlement systems, and to encourage parties to compromise in sovereign debt restructurings' (see Memorandum of Law of Amicus Curiae Federal Reserve Bank of New York in Support of Defendant's Motion for an Order Pursuant to CPLR § 5240 Denying Plaintiffs the Use of Injunctive Relief to Prevent Payments to Other Creditors at 13, *Macrotecnic Int'l Corp v Republic of Argentina and EM Ltd v Republic of Argentina* (SDNY, 12 Jan 2004) (No 02 CV 5932 (TPG), No 03 CV 2507 (TPG)).

[171] The New York Clearing House Association LLC stated that its members 'have long understood [the pari passu] clause ... to prohibit a debtor from creating unsecured debt that ranks senior in legal rights of payment to the payment obligations the debtor has'. See Memorandum of Amicus Curiae the New York Clearing House Association LLC in Support of Motion Pursuant to CPLR § 5240 to Preclude Plaintiff Judgment Creditors from Interfering with Payments to Other Creditors at p 2, *Macrotecnic International Corp v Republic of Argentina and EM Ltd v Republic of Argentina* (SDNY, 12 Jan 2004) (No 02 CV 5932 (TPG), No 03 CV 2507 (TPG)).

[172] Transcript of Conference before Judge Thomas P Griesa at 9, *Applestein v Republic of Argentina and Province of Buenos Aires* (SDNY, 15 Jan 2004) (No 02 CV-1773 (TPG)).

[173] In the *Elliott* litigation, the interpretation of the clause included in a New York law governed debt instrument was conducted by a Belgian court.

[174] *NML Capital Ltd v Republic of Argentina* (No 08 Civ 6978 (TPG), 2011 WL 9522565, at 2 (SDNY, 7 Dec 2011); 699 F 3d 246, 264 (2d Cir 2012); 727 F 3d 230 (2d Cir 2013); 134 S Ct 2819 (2014)).

[175] For a detailed analysis of Argentina's exchange offer see Rodrigo Olivares-Caminal, 'Sovereign Bonds: A Critical Analysis of Argentina's Debt Exchange Offer' 10(1) *Journal of Banking Regulation*, November 2008. The exchange offer was reopened in 2010 to reduce the number of holdout creditors and an additional participation of 16.25 per cent was achieved, an aggregated total between both exchange offers of 92.4 per cent. See Press Release issued by the Argentine Ministry of Economy and Public Finances dated 23 June 2010.

Agency Agreement governed by New York law.[176] The US District Court[177] and the Court of Appeal for the Second Circuit[178] ruled that no payment of interest may be made on the exchange bonds (all those that accepted the exchange offers) without making a *ratable* payment of the amount due on the holdouts (ie the full amount of principal and accrued unpaid interest). Ratable was construed in a way that if Argentina paid the outstanding interests on the exchange bonds (which were due every six months) *in full* it had to pay *in full* the totality of monies due to the holdout creditors. Later, the US Supreme Court declined to hear a petition for a writ of certiorari.[179]

11.90   In January 2012, the District Court issued a temporary restraining order enjoining Argentina from altering the payment process (including the use of different firms or other vehicles).[180] In addition, in February 2012 the District Court issued an injunctive relief enjoining Argentina each time that a payment was done to the exchange bondholders the same fraction of the amount due to them had to be paid to holdouts.[181] The justification for this exceptional measure was equitable relief since Argentina made clear (even by a formal act, ie the Lock Law[182]) its intention not to pay any money judgment. Since Argentina might

---

[176] The *pari passu* clause included in paragraph 1(c) of the 1994 Fiscal Agency Agreement reads: 'The Securities will constitute (except as provided in Section 11 below) direct, unconditional, unsecured and unsubordinated obligations of the Republic and shall at all times rank pari passu and without any preference among themselves. The payment obligations of the Republic under the Securities shall at all times rank at least equally with all its other present and future unsecured and unsubordinated External Indebtedness (as defined in this Agreement).'

[177] *NML Capital Ltd et al v Republic of Argentina*, United States District Court, Southern District of New York, New York, 7 December 2011.

[178] *NML Capital Ltd et al v Republic of Argentina* (Docket No 12-105(L)) (2d Cir, 26 Oct 2012).

[179] *NML Capital Ltd et al v Republic of Argentina*, 2014 WL 655502 (US 16 Jun 2014) (No 13-990). Certiorari is usually seen as the writ that the US Supreme Court issues to a lower court to review its judgment for legal error (reversible error) and review where no appeal is available as a matter of right.

[180] *NML Capital Ltd v Republic of Argentina*, No 08 Civ 6978 (TPG), United States District Court, Southern District of New York (3 January 2012).

[181] *NML Capital Ltd et al v Republic of Argentina*, United States District Court Southern District of New York, New York, 23 February 2012.

[182] In 2005, in order to exert additional pressure on bondholders to accept the exchange offer, the Argentine legislature passed the Lock Law (Law 26,017) on 9 February 2005, which was promulgated the following day. The Lock Law provides that Argentina is prohibited from offering holdout bondholders who may have initiated judicial, administrative, arbitration, or any other type of action to enforce their rights, a more favourable treatment than that which was offered to those that accepted the exchange offer. The following is a free translation of the Lock Law: 'ARTICLE 1— Notwithstanding the validity of other applicable norms, the sovereign bonds eligible for the exchange offer established by Decree No. 1735 dated 9 December 2004, that were not tendered according to what has been established in said decree will be subject to the provisions of this law. ARTICLE 2— The national Executive Branch shall not re-open the exchange offer established under Decree 1735/04, in relation to the bonds referred in article 1 hereof. ARTICLE 3— The National Government is prohibited from performing any type of judicial, extra-judicial or private transaction in relation to the bonds referred in article 1 of this law. ARTICLE 4— The National Executive Branch shall, according to the terms of the issuance of the bonds and the applicable norms in each jurisdiction, pass the required administrative acts and adopt the required measures to de-list from all stock exchanges—local or foreign—the bonds mentioned in the previous article. ARTICLE 5— The National Executive Branch will send a report to the honourable National Congress reflecting the effects of the exchange offer and the new levels of debt and its decrease. ARTICLE 6— Notwithstanding what has previously been established, eligible sovereign bonds as established by Decree No. 1735/04 that were deposited under any cause or title under the name of any instance, type or jurisdiction's court, whose legally owners had not adhered to the exchange offer referred by the previously mentioned decree nor had expressly stated their will of not taking part in the exchange offer on the judicial file, before the closing date according to what has been established in the timetable of the referred decree No. 1735/04, will be replaced as a matter of law by "STEP UP PAR BONDS 2038 of the ARGENTINE REPUBLIC" according to the conditions set forth for the allocation, settlement and issuance of said bonds by means of Decree No. 1735/04 and its complementary norms. The Ministry of Economy and Production has the right to pass the required complementary norms to implement the exchange ordered by this article. ARTICLE 7— Decree No. 1733 dated 9 December 2004 is hereby ratified. ARTICLE 8— Inform the National Executive Branch.' For an enlargement on the Lock Law see Rodrigo Olivares-Caminal, 'To Rank Pari Passu or Not to Rank Pari Passu: That is the

refuse to comply with the injunction order (under US Rule 65(d)(2)) the District Court stated that the parties, their officers, agents, servants employees, attorneys as well as other persons who were in active concert or participation with them were bound by the injunctions. The injunctions expressly prohibited Argentina's agents from aiding and abetting any further violation of the order by the court. The temporary restraining order and the injunctive relief were issued by the District Court while the Court of Appeals for the Second Circuit and the Supreme Court were deciding on the issues appealed by Argentina. The injunctive relief issued in February 2012 was subject to a stay pending an appeal, which was affirmed by the Court of Appeals for the Second Circuit on 23 August 2013,[183] and a writ of certiorari was denied by the US Supreme Court on 16 June 2014, thus lifting the previously ordered stay on the injunction.[184]

Most practitioners and legal scholars thought that it would be just a matter of time until a **11.91** New York court would pass an interpretation of the *pari passu* clause to interpret correctly the *pari passu* clause and revert the position adopted by the Belgian court in the *Elliott* case. In *NML, Ltd v Republic of Argentina*, the first great surprise occurred when the District Court ruled that 'it is declared, adjudged and decreed that the Republic [of Argentina] violates Paragraph 1(c) of the FAA whenever it lowers the rank of its payment obligations ... including (and without limitation) by relegating NML's bonds to a non-paying class ...'.[185] The salient point here is to understand why NML's bonds had been relegated to a non-paying class. The answer to this is the so called 'Lock Law'.[186] This is why the District Court found that there had been a form of subordination. It said '... that the Republic lowered the rank of NML's bonds in violation of Paragraph 1(c) of the FAA when it enacted [the Lock Law]'.[187]

In the Argentine restructuring case, the bonds that were restructured did not include col- **11.92** lective action clauses (CACs). Argentina was unable to use exit consents because, in one of the bond series, bondholders managed to get a blocking holding curtailing any possible amendments to the non-payment terms. Therefore, Argentina had to resort to contractual 'sweeteners' in order to make the exchange offer more appealing to creditors. One of these contractual 'sweeteners' was the rights upon future offers (RUFO) clause that is used to guarantee that if a debtor decides to enter into a repurchase, a new exchange offer, or to enter into a settlement on better terms than the exchange offer made to the original bondholders, same favourable terms will be offered to them as well. In other words this means that if 'more beneficial' terms are subsequently offered they will also be extended to those that that accepted the initial exchange offer, ie that nobody would be better off for holding out. This is usually intended to show that an exchange offer is definitive and, in the event that there is a holdout creditor, the sovereign is not willing to enter into any kind of settlement agreement

Question in Sovereign Bonds after the Latest Episode of the Argentine Saga' (2009) 15(4) *Law & Business Review of the Americas*.

[183] *NML Capital Ltd v Republic of Argentina*, No 12-105, United States Court of Appeals for the Second Circuit, 23 August 2013.

[184] *NML Capital Ltd et al v Republic of Argentina*, Supreme Court of the United States No 13-990, 16 June 2014.

[185] *NML Capital Ltd v Republic of Argentina*, No 08 Civ 6978 (TPG), 2011 WL 9522565, at 2 (SDNY, 7 December 2011).

[186] The 'Lock Law' is a law passed by the Argentine legislature preventing the Argentine government from reopening the exchange process or making any kind of court, out-of-court, or private transaction or settlement with respect to the bonds that were subject to the exchange offer.

[187] Ibid.

with more beneficial terms. If it enters into a settlement to put an end to ongoing litigation and pays the holdouts 100 per cent of the value of the claim, then bondholders who accepted a reduction in the face value of the original or old bonds will be entitled to that same treatment. When Argentina included the RUFO clause in the prospectus with a view to enhancing the degree of investor participation, it forgot to include the word 'settlement', rendering it inadequate since it failed to protect bondholders who accepted the 2005 exchange offer from the possibility that a separate settlement might be reached with a holdout creditor. As a result of this gaffe, Argentina passed what is known as the 'Lock Law' which prevented the Argentine government from reopening the exchange process or making any kind of court, out-of-court, or private transaction or settlement with respect to the bonds that were subject to the exchange offer. However, it was the Lock Law that provided a basis for judging that there had been an alteration in the legal ranking. For, by means of the Lock Law, Argentina opened the way for an interpretation of the *pari passu* clause in the narrow or payment interpretation and not in the broad payment interpretation as in the Belgian case since it provides the basis for subordination. It can be argued that Argentina formally subordinated a class of creditors lowering holdouts to a non-performing class by means of the Lock Law. In addition, in its US Securities and Exchange Commission annual report filings (Form 18K), Argentina stated that holdouts are a category separate from its regular debt-holders and that since 2005 it has 'not [been] in a legal ... position to pay' that category. Emphasis should be put on the 'legal position', which can be read as an indirect acknowledgement by Argentina that holdout creditors are a different category created by law. In this line of thinking, Buchheit noted that 'you can do pretty much whatever you want in discriminating among creditors (in terms of who gets paid and who does not) but do not try to justify your behavior by taking steps that purport to establish a legal basis for discrimination'.[188] This is precisely what happened in the case of Argentina.

11.93   More worrying is that when the New York court was faced with the need to interpret the *pari passu* clause, it found itself in the same position as in the year 2000 with the Belgian courts. The District Court found that 'Argentina lowered the rank of the plaintiff bonds in two ways: when it made payments currently due under the exchange bonds while persisting in its refusal to satisfy its payment obligations currently due under the bonds; and when it enacted the Lock Law'.[189] This clearly denoted that it was not just the actual subordination but something else. The decision of the District Court was appealed to the US Court of Appeals for the Second Circuit. Surprisingly, the Court of Appeals understood that '... in pairing the two sentences of its Pari Passu Clause, the FAA manifested an intention to protect bondholders from more than just formal subordination'.[190] Again, as the District Court found, it seems that it was not just the actual subordination (which took place as result of the Lock Law) but something else.

11.94   According to the Court of Appeals, the *pari passu* clause protects against: (1) 'the issuance of other superior debt (first sentence)';[191] and (2) 'the giving of priority to other payment

---

[188]   Lee Buchheit, 'The Pari Passu Clause Sub Specie Aeternitatis' (1991) *International Financial Law Review*.

[189]   *NML Capital Ltd v Republic of Argentina*, No 08 Civ 6978 (TPG), 2011 WL 9522565, at 2 (SDNY 7 Dec 2011).

[190]   *NML Capital Ltd v Republic of Argentina*, 699 F 3d 246, 264 (2d Cir 2012).

[191]   The first sentence of the *pari passu* clause included in the Argentine bonds reads: '... shall at all times rank *pari passu* and without any preference among themselves'.

obligations (second sentence)'.[192] *Prima facie* this seems to confirm the broad interpretation of the *pari passu* clause; however, that is not the case. The Second Circuit Court of Appeals intervened on two occasions, (1) in October 2012 when it unanimously affirmed the orders of the District Court and remanded the case to the District Court for clarification of 'ratable payment' and the application of injunctions on third-party intermediaries;[193] and, (2) in August 2013 when it affirmed the amended District Court's orders (after the 'ratable payment' and third-party injunctions clarifications).[194]

On this second intervention by the Court of Appeals, it 'clarified' its previous decision by **11.95** stating that '[a]s we explicitly stated in our last opinion, we have not held that a sovereign debtor breaches its pari passu clause every time it pays one creditor and not another, or even every time it enacts a law disparately affecting a creditor's rights ... [w]e simply affirm the district court's conclusion that Argentina's extraordinary behavior was a violation of the particular *pari passu* clause found in the [Fiscal Agency Agreement]'.[195] This closed the door to a broad interpretation of the clause by expressly stating that Argentina's facts are quite unusual and that the Lock Law played a central role in it.

Table 11.2 summarizes the similarities and differences regarding the *pari passu* clause inter- **11.96** pretation in the *Elliott* and *NML* cases, the two main judicial precedents on the interpretation of the *pari passu* clause in sovereign debt instruments.

Table 11.2 *Pari Passu* Clause Interpretation in the *Elliott* and *NML* Cases

Pari passu litigation	*Elliott*	*NML*
Ranking	Unaltered	Altered
Type of interpretation	Broad or payment	Narrow or ranking
Outcome of the interpretation	Incorrect	Correct
Remedy	Ratable payment as a result of the interpretation of the clause	Ratable payment as a result of the equitable remedies granted by the court

Another important clarification included in the second intervention by the Court of **11.97** Appeals was the interplay between the *pari passu* clause and payments of multilateral debt obligations. This analysis follows in the next section.

D. The *Pari Passu* Clause and Multilateral Debt Payments

The Financial Markets Law Committee noted that in the event that a sovereign is not able **11.98** to service its debt as result of the broad or 'payment' interpretation, it will not be allowed to pay either the IMF, World Bank, or other multilateral organizations or its government

---

[192] The second sentence of the *pari passu* clause included in the Argentine bonds reads: '... shall at all times rank at least equally with all its other present and future unsecured and unsubordinated [e]xternal [i]ndebtedness'.
[193] *NML Capital Ltd v Republic of Argentina*, 699 F 3d 246, 264 (2d Cir 2012).
[194] *NML Capital Ltd v Republic of Argentina*, 727 F 3d 230 (2d Cir 2013).
[195] Ibid, p 23, paras 11–15.

ministers, civil servants, police force, armed forces, judges, and state teachers.[196] Since a sovereign cannot bring its essential services to a halt (even upon an event of default), the broad or 'payment' interpretation seems to require a carve-out for essential functions and/ or not to be the correct one.

11.99   The IMF and other multilateral organizations enjoy a preferred status. Until very recently, this priority did not emanate from any norm. It was a general understanding that has only been challenged in court—albeit without success—by means of the *pari passu* clause. As noted by the IMF, the preferred creditor status is fundamental to its financial responsibilities and its financing mechanism.[197] In addition, a President of the World Bank stated that '[t]he pari passu clause, for example, does not prevent a debtor from, as a matter of practice, discriminating in favour of international financial institutions such as the [World] Bank and the IMF in making debt service payments'.[198] Duvall has noticed that many developing countries have continued to make payments to multilateral financial institutions even when they were unable to service commercial bank loans.[199] He also argues that the so-called 'preferred creditor status' of the World Bank rests on practical considerations rather than legal grounds and, thus, is not thought to violate such countries' *pari passu* undertakings. But, most importantly, the preferred status emanates from the international lender of last resort (ILOLR) role of the IMF and other multilateral organizations. This role not only benefits the IMF (and its members) but also other creditors (bilateral and private) that end in a better position by the assistance provided by the IMF to the sovereign to regain sustainability and therefore an orderly restructuring. The ILOLR is performed by the IMF when other credit providers are not willing to lend as a result of the deteriorating situation of the country.

11.100   In 2012, in the context of the EU sovereign debt crisis, the Euro-area Member States (EAMS) adopted the Treaty Establishing the European Stability Mechanism. This treaty became the first official document that formally acknowledged the super-priority enjoyed by the IMF by means of Recital No. 13, which reads: '... the ESM loans will enjoy preferred creditor status in a similar fashion to those of the IMF, while accepting preferred creditor status of the IMF over the ESM'.[200]

11.101   The Second Circuit Court of Appeals intervening in the Argentine *pari passu* litigation indicated that 'subordination of obligations to commercial unsecured creditors beneath obligations to multilateral institutions like the IMF would not violate the Equal Treatment Provision for the simple reason that commercial creditors never were nor could be on equal footing with the multilateral organizations'.[201]

---

[196] Financial Market Law Committee, *supra* n 59 at 14.

[197] IMF, 'Financial Risk in the Fund and the Level of Precautionary Balances', prepared by the Finance Department (in consultation with other departments), approved by Eduard Brau, 3 February 2004, available at <http://www.imf.org/external/np/tre/risk/2004/020304.pdf>.

[198] *Review of IBRD's Negative Pledge Policy with Respect to Debt and Debt Service Reduction Operations*, Memorandum from Barber B Conable, President, World Bank, to Executive Directors (dated 19 July 1990).

[199] Thomas A Duvall, 'Legal Aspects of Sovereign Lending' in Thomas M Klein (ed), *External Debt Management: An Introduction*, World Bank Technical Paper No 245 (1994) 43–44.

[200] See <http://europa.eu/rapid/press-release_DOC-12-3_en.htm>.

[201] *NML Capital Ltd v Republic of Argentina*, 727 F 3d 230 (2d Cir 2013), p 22, paras 12–18 citing *NML Capital Ltd v Republic of Argentina*, 699 F 3d 246, 264 (2d Cir 2012).

E. The Attachment of the Tendered Bonds (Future Rights)

1. General aspects

Another relevant case to analyse in the sovereign debt context is *NML Capital Ltd v the* **11.102**
Republic of Argentina.[202] This case is relevant since, as in the *Elliott* case, the creditors were
able to pose a threat to the whole restructuring process. Also, the arguments of the claimants
were novel and very ingenious, opening a new possibility to future sovereign debt litigation.

NML Capital Ltd (NML) had initiated two legal actions against Argentina that were **11.103**
awaiting resolution.[203] Both actions had been initiated for contractual breach and derived
damages as the result of the failure to meet contractually mandated principal and interest
payments to NML according to the debt instruments issued by the Republic of Argentina by
means of the Fiscal Agency Agreement dated 19 October 1994 executed between Argentina
and the Bankers Trust Company.

The instruments that gave origin to the two legal actions are the following: **11.104**

(1) *First Case* (03 Civ 8845 (SDNY) (TPG)): was initiated on 7 November 2003 by the
breach in the payment of:
  (a) 12 per cent Global Bonds issued by Argentina and maturing on 1 February 2020.
  NML is the holder of $60,244,000 of these bonds. It is worth noting that 92 per
  cent of the paramount was acquired by NML or its affiliates before 29 November
  2001 at an average of 55 per cent of its par value.
  (b) 10.25 per cent Global Bonds issued by Argentina and maturing on 21 July 2030.
  NML is the holder of $111,909,000. It is worth noting that over 97 per cent of the
  par value was acquired by NML or its affiliates before 28 November 2001 at an
  average of 62 per cent of its par value.
(2) *Second Case* (05 Civ 2434 (SDNY) (TPG)): was initiated on 28 February 2005 by
the breach of payment of the 'Floating Rate Accrual Note' or 'FRANs' issued by
Argentina, maturing on 10 April 2005. NML is the holder of FRANs in a total amount
of $32,000,000.

2. Request of attachment

None of the cases was resolved on substance, aiming to obtain a pre-judgment attachment **11.105**
to protect their interests and prevent Argentina from disposing of the assets.

In requesting this preventive measure, NML argued that the same District Court had pre- **11.106**
viously granted a summary judgment[204] in *Lightwater Corporation Ltd, Old Castle Holdings
Ltd and Macrotecnic International Corp;*[205] *EM Ltd;*[206] and in *Allan Applestein TTEE FBO*

---

[202] The analysis provided is based on the cases listed *supra* n 27.
[203] *NML Capital Ltd v The Republic of Argentina*, 03 Civ 8845 (SDNY) (TPG); and *NML Capital Ltd v The
Republic of Argentina* 05 Civ 2434 (SDNY) (TPG).
[204] According to Hazard Jr and Taruffo, in a summary judgment the motion contends that the evidence clearly
establishes the facts and that the moving party is entitled to judgment on those facts (G Hazard Jr and M Taruffo,
American Civil Procedure: An Introduction (1993) 113).
[205] 2003 WL 1878420.
[206] 2003 WL 22110745.

DCA.[207] In these cases the court resolved that: (1) the obligation of Argentina was unconditional; (2) sovereign immunity had been waived; and (3) Argentina was in default. Hence,
NML argued that there were sufficient elements to show that there was no genuine issue as
to any material fact and that the moving party was entitled to a judgment as a matter of law
(Rule 56 of the US Federal Rules of Civil Procedure).

11.107 Likewise, referring to an article published in an Argentine newspaper, NML argued that the
Argentine government was carrying out everything that was within its reach to avoid the
attachment of assets abroad way before the default.[208]

11.108 According to Rule 64 of the US Federal Rules of Civil Procedure, a court can order pre-
judgment attachment 'under the circumstances and in the manner provided by the law of
the state in which the district court is held, existing at the time the remedy is sought'. Under
the law of the State of New York, the plaintiff may obtain an *ex parte* pre-judgment attachment of the interests of the defendant if:[209] (1) it has stated a money judgment claim; (2) it
has a probability of success on the merits; (3) the existence of one of more grounds enumerated in § 6201 of the Civil Procedure Laws and Rules of New York;[210] and (4) the amount
claimed exceeds all counterclaims known to the plaintiff.

11.109 The intervening court understood that these four prongs were established, and on 21 March
2005 ordered an *ex parte* pre-judgment attachment on:[211]

(1) the bonds tendered by the bondholders of Argentina that decided to participate in
the exchange offer launched by Argentina in January 2005 and that were received
by the Bank of New York in its capacity of Exchange Agent in descending order of
interest yield up to a total principal value of $7 billion; and

(2) the assets of Argentina, and any interest of Argentina in personal property, and any
debt due or to become due to Argentina within the State of New York, which are
used for a commercial activity in the US, and other property otherwise subject to
pre-judgment attachment as a result of the existence of an express waiver of immunity therefrom, but not of (a) property belonging to any consulate, embassy, or
permanent UN mission of Argentina and/or; (b) any property that is, or is intended
to be, used in connection with a military activity and is of a military character or is
under the control of a military authority or defence agency, as will satisfy the sum of
$366,481,703 million and the fees and expenses of the Marshal.

11.110 According to an estimation made by NML representatives, faced value bonds in the amount
of $7 billion would be needed to satisfy its credit. They arrived at this figure based on a cal-
culation of the value at which these bonds were traded in the secondary market (30 per cent
of their par value). Although $1.2 billion would be sufficient to satisfy the claimant's credit,
considering that the value in the secondary market can diminish, NML representatives

---

[207] 2003 WL 22743762.

[208] Rebossio, *supra* n 15.

[209] According to NY CPLR §§ 6201, 6211, and 6212(a).

[210] CPLR is the acronym used for the civil practice law and rules that shall govern the procedure in civil judicial
proceedings in all courts of the state of New York and before all judges, except where the procedure is regulated by
inconsistent statute. Section 6201 establishes the grounds for attachment.

[211] *NML Capital, Ltd v Republic of Argentina*, *ex parte* motion, 21 March 2005, United States District Court for
the Southern District of New York.

requested an enlargement of that sum to a total of $7 billion. The District Court endorsed this amount. This amount would allow NML's claim to be covered even if the bonds were sold at 5 per cent of their par value. As a side note, it is worth stressing that the bonds being attached were defaulted bonds that were tendered in an exchange offer.

3. *Vacatur* of the attachment and the restraining notices

After granting the *ex parte* pre-judgment attachment, the court signed other similar orders **11.111** and also approved certain applications relating to restraining notices[212] under New York state law. As stated by the court, restraining notices under state law are different from attachments in that they can have prospective effect, whereas an attachment is only valid as to property which is subject to attachment at the time of the service of the order of attachment on the party holding the property or supposedly holding the property.[213]

The court summoned all the parties involved to a hearing in March 2005 based on the fact **11.112** that Argentina brought on a motion to vacate the original order of attachment and provided enough documentation to raise an issue about the validity of all orders of attachment and the validity of the restraining notices or applications relating to the restraining notices. Besides Argentina and NML, the other parties involved—either due to an attachment order or a restraining notice—were, inter alia, EM Ltd, Lightwater Corporation Ltd, and Old Castle Holdings Ltd.

As stated by the District judge, 'there [were] merits to the arguments of both sides and **11.113** there [were] difficulties to the arguments on both sides'.[214] This notwithstanding, after considering the arguments of the plaintiffs and the defendant, the District judge resolved to vacate the attachment and to vacate and deny the applications with regard to the restraining notices.[215]

In order to arrive at this conclusion, there were two main arguments to be analysed. First, **11.114** it was considered whether the bonds tendered at the exchange offer were the property of Argentina or not. In this respect, it was resolved that the bonds still were the property of its holders and not of Argentina. The bonds could only become the property of Argentina after the exchange offer was settled, which was originally scheduled to happen in April 2005.[216] Secondly, it was considered what had really been attached prior to the *vacatur* decision. In other words, over which assets were the restraining notices granted? It was resolved that it was over the contractual (future) right of Argentina to receive the tendered bonds on the date of the settlement.

One of the central arguments of the plaintiffs was that upon the acceptance of the exchange **11.115** offers, Argentina had an irrevocable obligation to exchange the bonds.

---

[212] The restraining notices were issued pursuant to Federal Rules of Civil Procedure 69 which authorizes the process to enforce judgments in accordance with 'the practice and procedure of the state in which the district court is held'. Additionally, § 5222 of the Civil Procedure Laws and Rules of New York specifically addresses issues related to restraining notices.

[213] *NML Capital Ltd v Republic of Argentina*, not reported in F Supp 2d, 2005 WL 743086 (SDNY).

[214] Ibid.

[215] According to *Black's Law Dictionary*, 'vacate' is to nullify or cancel, to make void or invalidate. *Vacatur* is one of the mechanisms of annulling a judicial decision to restore the status quo prior to the enactment of the judicial decision that is vacated. A vacated decision has no precedential value (see Bryan A Garner (ed), *Black's Law Dictionary* (7th edn, 1999) 1546).

[216] Argentina, *supra* n 2, Prospectus Supplement S-2.

11.116   In this regard, the Prospectus Supplement states that '[o]nce the [e]ligible [s]ecurities have been tendered pursuant to the [o]ffer, tendering holders may not withdraw their tenders except under certain limited circumstances'.[217] Prior to that, within the 'Risk Factors' listed in the Prospectus Supplement, Argentina warned the bondholders that 'holders should be aware that the terms of the offer allow Argentina to terminate or extend the offer, to withdraw or amend the offer in one or more jurisdictions, and to reject valid tenders of eligible securities, in each case at Argentina's sole discretion ... [a]ccordingly, there can be no assurance that the exchange of eligible securities for new securities pursuant to the offer will be completed (in any particular jurisdiction or at all)'.[218]

11.117   However, the Prospectus Supplement states that '[o]nce Argentina has announced the acceptance of tenders on the [a]nnouncement [d]ate ... Argentina's acceptance will be irrevocable [and] [t]enders, as so accepted, shall constitute binding obligations of the submitting holders and Argentina to settle the exchange'.[219]

11.118   Although Argentina had not subjected the acceptance or consummation of the exchange offer to any minimum level of participation,[220] it took into consideration the outstanding claims[221] and expressly stated that 'there can be no assurance that it will be completed in accordance with the schedule and terms set forth in [the] prospectus supplement'.[222]

11.119   Summing up, if the wording of the Prospectus Supplement is carefully followed, it can be argued that: (1) until Argentina accepts the tendered bonds it has the right to reject them—individually or collectively—at its sole discretion;[223] (2) on 18 March 2005 Argentina announced the acceptance of all the tendered bonds,[224] which made the acceptance irrevocable as per the wording stated in the Prospectus Supplement;[225] (3) on the same date, ie 18 March 2005, upon the acceptance of the tendered bonds, Argentina acquired the (future) contractual right on the bonds that were going to be settled in the near future.

11.120   Returning to the analysis of the District Court resolution, the judge understood that there was a contractual obligation on Argentina to accept or reject the tendered bonds. Upon acceptance, bonds will be settled and upon settlement the tendered bonds will become the property of Argentina. In this scenario, the judge considered that an exchange offer implies an 'exchange'—like its name indicates—and it is because of it that Argentina has the right to cancel the bonds tendered in the exchange offer. Hence, under the exchange offer, Argentina does not only have the right to receive the bonds but also to cancel them. Likewise, the judge understood that the plaintiffs not only do not have faculties to cancel the tendered bonds but, besides, that they do not intend to do so because they consider that there is a secondary market for them (a value or at least an interest by Argentina to cancel them, which results

---

[217]   Ibid S-29.

[218]   Ibid S-29. The capital letters of the terms 'Offer', 'Eligible Securities', and 'New Securities' as defined in the Prospectus Supplement have been omitted.

[219]   Ibid S-48.

[220]   Ibid S-47.

[221]   Ibid S-30 and S-31.

[222]   Ibid S-20.

[223]   Ibid S-47.

[224]   See the document issued by the Ministry of Economy on 18 March 2005 titled 'Oferta de Canje—Anuncio Final', p 5.

[225]   'Once Argentina has announced the acceptance of the tenders ... Argentina's acceptance will be irrevocable'. Argentina, *supra* n 2, Prospectus Supplement S-48.

in a quantifiable value or otherwise an un-cancelled outstanding obligation). In the judge's own words: (1) 'upon acceptance of the exchange offer, the bondholders have an irrevocable obligation to tender their bonds'; (2) '[t]he terms of the exchange offer also express the idea that [Argentina] will have an obligation to issue the new bonds in place of the old ones which have been tendered and which would be surrendered at the time of the closing'; (3) 'an essential part of the contractual right of [Argentina] is the right to cancel [the] bonds which it receives at the closing'; (4) 'the foundation of the exchange offer is to do what the name states, to have an exchange'; (5) '[Argentina's] contractual rights under the exchange offer are not merely to receive the bonds but to receive the bonds and to cancel those bonds'; (6) '[t]he attaching plaintiffs have no power to cancel the bonds and, of course, no intention [since] [t]hey contemplate the idea that the bonds would remain in effect and would have a market value'.[226]

A key element in the District judge's argumentative line and, as he stated, 'one flaw in the   **11.121**
position of the attaching plaintiffs'[227] is that there is a contractual right of cancellation that would have been affected in case of not ordering the *vacatur* of the attachments and the restraining notices.[228] Thus, the District judge argued that the exchange offer could not be performed since it would lack one of its fundamental elements.[229] It is worth noting that the Financial Representative in the US for the Republic of Argentina stated in a 'declaration in support of Argentina's application for an order to show cause why the Court should not vacate its order of 21 March 2005' that if the attachments and restraining notices were not vacated the exchange offer would not be carried out.[230] Therefore, the judge resolved that:

(1) 'There is no realistic basis ... to assume that there is some ironclad contractual right of [Argentina] to receive the bonds on the closing date if these attachments are in effect.'

(2) 'Consequently ... the existence of the attachments would, if allowed to stand, negate the very contractual obligations which are cited as a basis for the attachments, and I am granting the motion to vacate the attachments.'

(3) '... the restraining notices have the same problems as the attachments in effectively frustrating the carrying out of the exchange offer, [t]herefore, for basically the same reasons that I gave in dealing with the attachments, it is my ruling that there is not, and it is not foreseeable in the future that there will be, property in the form of bonds to be subject to restraining notices.'

There is an important issue that seems to have been overlooked or misapprehended by the   **11.122**
District judge. According to the contractual terms, upon the acceptance of the tendered bonds—which occurred on 18 March 2005—the bondholders have an irrevocable obligation to tender their bonds.[231] This is so because: (1) Argentina made an offer to the bondholders, an offer to exchange their bonds in default for new bonds; (2) the bondholders

---

[226] See *supra* n 136.
[227] Ibid.
[228] Ibid.
[229] Ibid.
[230] See para 13 of the Declaration of Federico C Molina, Financial Representative in the United States of America for the Republic of Argentina, dated 24 March 2005 filed in *NML Capital Ltd v The Republic of Argentina*, 03 Civ 8845 (TPG) and 05 Civ 2434 (TPG).
[231] Argentina, *supra* n 2, Prospectus Supplement, S-48.

accepted this offer, expressing their consent by tendering the bonds which would be cancelled and replaced by the new bonds on the settlement date; and (3) according to the contractual terms of the Prospectus Supplement, '[o]nce Argentina has announced the acceptance of the tenders ... Argentina's acceptance will be irrevocable'. Having stated clearly the irrevocable character of the Argentine obligation to settle the bonds, which implies the cancellation of the tendered bonds and their replacement with the new bonds to be issued, a different issue to consider is the order of rights or obligations. It is true that if Argentina does not settle the bonds, the future contractual right of Argentina on the bonds that would emerge upon settlement will not exist. But also a new and different obligation emerged on 18 March 2005, ie to settle the tendered bonds. After that, on 21 March 2005, the attachment was ordered on the future right that Argentina would have on the settled bonds. Although, as previously mentioned, this future contractual right would not emerge as the result of the attachment, Argentina, due to the acceptance of the tendered bonds on 18 March 2005, had the obligation to settle the bonds. After the acceptance on 18 March 2005, Argentina did not have the *right* to settle, it had the *obligation* to settle. If Argentina did not perform the settlement, it would be liable for breach of the contractual obligation originated on 18 March 2005. Therefore, the argument of the District judge regarding there being no realistic basis to assume that there was some ironclad contractual right of Argentina to receive the bonds on the closing date if these attachments were in effect is not entirely correct. Therefore (1) above can be rebutted.

11.123 As regards the second issue listed in (2) above, that the existence of the attachments would—if allowed to stand—negate the very contractual obligations which were cited as a basis for the attachments (the emergence of the contractual right over the tendered bonds upon settlement), is not entirely correct either. This is so because the attachment over a total principal value of $7 billion of tendered bonds is not applicable over all the tendered bonds, which totalled $62.3 billion. That amount of the attachment is only 11.2 per cent of the total tendered debt. Besides the fact that it would only partially negate the contractual obligation, Argentina still had the chance to satisfy the contractual obligation to settle despite the attachment (in the event that it would have not been vacated). If Argentina had issued an additional amount of $7 billion in bonds—to tender the bonds of those creditors who had tendered their bonds as result of the exchange offer but had been subject to the attachment—this would not result in an impossibility to perform on behalf of Argentina. It would have only resulted in an increase in the economic costs of the whole exchange offer process, or rephrased in a different way, it would have been a less economically beneficial exchange offer for Argentina. However, instead of increasing the whole cost of the restructuring in $7 billion, Argentina could have opted to settle the claims with NML and the other creditors that enjoined. Settling would have resulted in at least a 70 per cent reduction of the cost.[232] In summary, these are the costs that a sovereign has to bear as a result of not honouring its outstanding contractual obligations and not engaging in meaningful settlement discussions.

---

[232] The lawyers of NML argued that bonds should be valued at 30 per cent of their par value for a calculation on the amount necessary to satisfy their claim. Therefore, it can be said that only 30 per cent of the $7 billion (which anyway has been increased to play on the safe side) is the real claim of the plaintiffs.

As regards the third issue listed in (3) above, reference should be made to the two previous   **11.124**
paragraphs because the arguments applied in the analysis of the viability of the attachment
are applicable to the restraining notices.

Finally, a brief comment should be made to what has been held in three previous sov-   **11.125**
ereign debt restructuring cases, ie *Allied Bank International v Banco Credito Agricola de
Cartago*;[233] *Pravin Banker Assocs v Banco Popular del Peru*;[234] and *National Union Fire Ins
Co of Pittsburgh, Pa v People's Republic of the Congo*.[235]

In the *Allied* case, the Court of Appeals held that allowing the foreign sovereign to refuse   **11.126**
payment of financial obligations 'would vitiate an express provision of the contracts between the parties' something the Court of Appeals concluded would be 'inconsistent with
the law and policy of the United States'.[236] Thus, the Court of Appeals found that any 'co-
operative adjustments' of sovereign debt were 'grounded in the understanding that, while
parties may agree to renegotiate conditions of payment, the underlying obligations to pay
nevertheless remain valid and enforceable'.[237]

In the *Pravin* case, the court held that the 'United States policy under Brady Plan was essen-   **11.127**
tially call for voluntary participation by creditor banks in negotiations with foreign debtor
nations to restructure their debt, and Plan did not abrogate contractual rights of creditor
banks nor compel creditors to forbear from enforcing those rights while debt structuring
negotiations were ongoing, or prohibit them from "opting out" of settlements resulting
from such negotiations'.[238]

In the *National Union Fire Insurance* case, the court considered that if it were to refuse to   **11.128**
enforce this default judgment on the ground that to do so would interfere with the Congo
making payments pursuant to a debt rescheduling agreement entered into with other creditors, it would have the effect of depriving a creditor of its right to choose whether to reschedule a debt or to enforce the underlying obligation to pay, which would be contrary to
the US policy as articulated in the *Allied* case.[239]

(a) Stay order in the vacatur
In the hearing where the judge resolved to vacate the attachments and to vacate and stay the   **11.129**
restraining notices, the representative of one of the plaintiffs argued that if Argentina went
forward with the settlement of the exchange offer and settled (cancelled the tendered bonds
and issued the new bonds in their place) the plaintiffs would not have an opportunity to
appeal.[240]

Therefore, in order to maintain the status quo as it existed as of the date of the judge's reso-   **11.130**
lution to vacate the attachments and to vacate and stay the restraining notices, the plaintiffs'

---

[233] 757 F 2d 516 (2d Cir 1985).
[234] 895 F Supp 660 (SDNY 1995).
[235] 729 F Supp 936 (SDNY 1989).
[236] This is taken from the reference to the *Allied* case in *Elliott Associates, LP v Republic of Peru*, 948 F Supp 1203 (SDNY 1996).
[237] Ibid.
[238] 895 F Supp 660 (1995).
[239] See *National Union Fire Ins Co of Pittsburgh, Pa v People's Republic of the Congo*, 729 F Supp 936 (SDNY 1989).
[240] See *supra* n 136.

representative requested a stay on the effect of the order to vacate until the Second Circuit Court of Appeals resolved the issue.[241] The motion was made pursuant to US Federal Rule of Civil Procedure 7(b)(1)[242] and granted it not only in regard to the motioning plaintiff but extended it to all the plaintiffs (ie to all the judicial proceedings in which it had been put into effect).

(b) Resolution of the Court of Appeals

11.131 On 13 May 2005, the US Court of Appeals for the Second Circuit unanimously granted a Summary Order affirming the District Court's order vacating the *ex parte* attachment and the restraining and execution orders in the two main procedures,[243] ie *EM Ltd v Republic of Argentina* (restraining notice) and *NML Ltd v Republic of Argentina* (attachment). This also applies in the other enjoining related matters.

11.132 In order to reach this resolution, the Court of Appeals acknowledged that the reason for the District Court to vacate the restraint and attachment is that if these measures were still in effect, the conclusion of the exchange offer was in doubt. The Court of Appeals expressly endorsed the argument of the District Court stating that it 'acted well within its authority to vacate the remedies in order to avoid a substantial risk to the successful conclusion of the debt restructuring'.[244] Moreover, the Court of Appeals stated '[t]hat restructuring is obviously of critical importance to the economic health of a nation'.[245] This notwithstanding, the court also acknowledged that the parties disputed a number of issues including: (1) whether the tendered bonds could be regarded as assets or debts of Argentina; and (2) whether Argentina was impermissibly trying to defeat the collection efforts of the plaintiffs/appellants by using the threat of a failure of the debt restructuring to fend off the restraint and attachment remedies.[246]

11.133 The Court of Appeals considered that it was not necessary to rule definitively on any of the substantive law issues disputed by the parties—even if the District Court view on some of the issues was wrong—and therefore it did not find any issue in the decision of the District Court that was arguably incorrect in the view of procedural law. As previously mentioned, the Court of Appeals considered that the District Court acted within its authority. The issue under analysis was the exercise of discretion of the District Court.

11.134 As stated in a previous sovereign restructuring case, '[u]nder New York law, granting of pre-judgment attachments is discretionary with trial court, and even when statutory requisites are met, attachment may be denied'.[247] A plaintiff is never entitled to attachment as a matter of right, it is discretionary for the court and the practice is that it should be used sparingly.[248] Additionally, in many cases of the forum it has also been ruled that an attachment is a harsh remedy and should be construed strictly against the moving party.[249]

---

[241] Ibid.
[242] Rule 7 of the Rules of FRCP deals with pleadings and the form of motions.
[243] 131 Fed Appx 745 CA 2 (NY), 2005.
[244] Ibid.
[245] Ibid.
[246] Ibid.
[247] *Elliott Associates LP v Republic of Peru*, 948 F Supp 1203 (SDNY 1996). Also see *Filmtrucks, Inc v Earls*, 635 F Supp 1158, 1162 (SDNY 1986); *Trigo Hnos Inc v Premium Wholesale Groceries Inc*, 424 F Supp 1125, 1133 (SDNY 1976).
[248] See *Katz Agency Inc v Evening News Ass'n*, 514 F Supp 423 (DCNY 1981).
[249] See *Sidwell & Co Ltd v Kamchatimpex*, 632 NYS 2d 455 (NY Sup 1995).

A final comment in regard to this case is that both the District Court and the Court of **11.135** Appeals were concerned about the viability of the exchange offer. Although the analysis is based on a procedural aspect where the District Court exercised its discretion, which according to the Court of Appeals was subject to law, upon an analysis of the substantive issues the outcome might have been different. It seems that since it was not a substantive issue affecting US foreign policy, the court used its discretion with a utilitarian focus to avoid a major harm.

IV. Conclusion

These cases are useful to illustrate the difficulties and complexities in suing a sovereign state. **11.136** The difficulties are evidenced by the enforcing tactics required in the *Elliott* case where attachment orders were obtained in four different US states—Florida, Maryland, New York, and Washington DC—plus the need to resort to the courts of Belgium, Canada, England, Germany, Luxembourg, and the Netherlands to seek enforcement of the decision or the length and several procedural instances undergone in the *NML v Argentina pari passu* litigation. The complexities are evidenced in the *EM/NML Ltd* cases where the lack of assets forced the creditors to attempt to attach an intangible right over a future asset of the debtor.

Successful cases such as *Elliott* or the *NML pari passu* litigation are rarely seen in sovereign **11.137** debt restructuring, as most divergences are settled rather than litigated. Moreover, several sovereign states attempt to challenge all aspects—even if they know that the law does not support their position—as a way to delay things (in the hope that it will become the problem of the next administration) and also to frustrate and increase the litigation expenses in the hope that the case will become economically inefficient and/or the counterparty will run out of resources.

As a result of cases like *Elliott* and in an attempt to create a more orderly restructuring **11.138** framework, in 2001 the IMF proposed a structured restructuring approach based on US chapter 11 which is known as the Sovereign Debt Restructuring Mechanism (SDRM). The market rejected the IMF proposal of an orderly structured approach and developed other techniques, ie the use of contractual provisions such as credit enhancement terms, collective action clauses, or the use of exit consent. All these techniques are used to enhance exchange offers. These structured market-oriented approaches, as well as the SDRM proposed by the IMF, are analysed in the following chapter.

12

TRANSACTIONAL ASPECTS OF SOVEREIGN DEBT RESTRUCTURING

I. Transactional Aspects of Sovereign Debt Restructuring

A. Introduction

12.01 The amount of accumulated debt and its progressive increase have led to repayment problems and, in some cases, default. Thus, as countries amass unsustainable debt burdens (ie when the ratio of debt to gross domestic product rises to such an extent that the application of policies cannot revert the situation), they have an increasing need to restructure their sovereign debt.[1]

12.02 Broadly speaking, sovereign debt restructuring can be understood as the technique used by sovereign states to prevent or resolve financial and economic crises and to achieve or regain debt sustainability levels. The International Monetary Fund (IMF) has recently reviewed its lending framework in the context of sovereign debt vulnerabilities aiming at introducing greater flexibility and allowing them to be able to provide exceptional access to funding on the base of a debt operation that involves an extension of maturities.[2] However, there have been significant developments in sovereign debt restructuring involving private sector creditors since the IMF's last stocktaking exercise in 2014. The main conclusion is that while the current contractual approach has been largely effective in resolving sovereign debt cases, it has gaps that could pose challenges in future restructurings.[3]

---

[1] See IMF, 'Proposals for a Sovereign Debt Restructuring Mechanism (SDRM): A Factsheet', January 2003, available at <http://www.imf.org/external/np/exr/facts/sdrm.htm>.

[2] See IMF, 'The Fund's Lending Framework and Sovereign Debt—Preliminary Considerations', June 2014, available at <http://www.imf.org/external/np/pp/eng/2014/052214.pdf>.

[3] See IMF, 'The International Architecture for Resolving Sovereign Debt Involving Private-Sector Creditors—Recent Developments, Challenges, and Reform Options', October 2020, available at <https://www.imf.org/-/media/Files/Publications/PP/2020/English/PPEA2020043.ashx>.

12.03   Sovereign debt restructuring has two aspects: procedural and substantial. While the procedural aspect focuses on the way in which the restructuring should be performed (eg using collective action clauses (CACs) or via a voluntary exchange offer sometimes enhanced by the use of other techniques), the substantial aspect involves the actual restructuring of debt, which is characterized by rescheduling amortization schedules as well as the possibility of reducing interest rates and/or principal. The substantial aspect can be carried preemptively (debt reprofiling) or after the default has taken place (restructuring).

12.04   A debt reprofiling is a voluntary extension of maturities prior to an event of default. Usually it does not involve a reduction of principal or interest. In other words, the main difference between a debt reprofiling and a debt restructuring is the time when it is performed. Jamaica is an excellent example, where interest costs and principal repayments exceeded the country's revenues and through a voluntarily pre-emptive domestic debt exchange offer performed in early 2010, it managed to ease its servicing debt burden.[4]

12.05   In a restructuring, by using CACs, you can bind all creditors (in the series or across series, depending on whether the aggregation feature has been contemplated in the CAC included in the debt instrument). CACs might not always be available or, even if they are, it may not be possible to use them as the required threshold might not be reached, in which case a voluntary exchange offer could be used. As a result of the use of voluntary exchange offers as the mechanism to restructure sovereign debt, almost invariably there would be outstanding bondholders that held out and did not take part in the exchange offer.[5] Due to the existence of holdouts, the dynamics in the relationship of the parties involved change. The parties usually involved are:

(1)   the sovereign, debtor of the so-called 'old bonds' and the 'new bonds'. The 'old bonds' are those held by the holdouts that did not participate in the exchange offer. The 'new bonds' are those that were issued to creditors by the sovereign debtor as a result of the exchange offer, ie as a result of the tender of their old bonds in exchange for new bonds;

(2)   the bondholders who hold the 'old bonds', ie the holdouts;

(3)   the bondholders who hold the 'new bonds', ie the creditors that entered the exchange offer, also referred to as the 'exchange bondholders'.

12.06   Bondholders, the holdouts, and the exchange bondholders would like to collect on their bonds. The holders of the old bonds (the holdouts) would like to collect principal and accrued past due interest by trying to attach any possible assets of the sovereign, adopting an active litigation role.[6] A different role would be performed by the holders of the new bonds, ie the exchange bondholders, who would have a passive investor role waiting for

---

[4] See Joel Chiedu Okwuokei and Bert van Selm, 'Debt Restructuring in the Caribbean—The Recent Experience' in Krishna Srinivasan, Inci Otker, Uma Ramakrishnan, and Trevor Coleridge Alleyne (eds), *Unleashing Growth and Strengthening Resilience in the Caribbean* (International Monetary Fund November 2017), available at <https://www.elibrary.imf.org/view/books/071/24291-9781484315194-en/ch08.xml>

[5] The non-participation of bondholders does not necessarily mean that they decided to holdout, it can just be the case that bondholders were not aware of the exchange offer. It is not uncommon that when trying to delist a company to find that some stockholders are not able to be traced. This problem is amplified in the case of a sovereign, where the bondholding is atomized around the globe.

[6] The perils of litigation have been analysed in the previous chapter.

their interest payments to become due (usually every six months) and collecting the principal upon maturity (or simply offloading the 'new bonds' in the secondary market at any point in time). With these scenarios, the sovereign debtor does not have many options left. The sovereign debtor would have to pay the holders of the new bonds regularly because otherwise it would be in default again, while at the same time trying to avoid an attachment on its assets that will disrupt the flow of payments. Or even, an injunctive relief as happened in *NML v Argentina*.[7] Another example is the ongoing situation in Venezuela, who entered in default in 2017 and has faced multiple litigation cases where there have been several attempts to attach both the government and assets of its state-owned oil company (PdVSA).

The priority of the sovereign debtor should be to maintain the flow of payments to its majority creditors unaltered, while sorting out how to deal with the holdout minority in a way that will not imply a breach of the contractual rights of the exchange bondholders. **12.07**

With many banks and retail bondholders now involved, private creditors have become increasingly numerous, anonymous, and difficult to coordinate in absence of CACs. The variety of debt instruments and derivatives in use has also added to the complexity to be faced. As the IMF stated: **12.08**

> Bondholders are more diverse than banks, and so too are the goals with which they approach a restructuring. Some are interested in a rapid and orderly restructuring that will preserve the value of their claims. Others, which buy debt on the secondary market in hope of profiting through litigation, prefer a disorderly process allowing them to buy distressed debt more cheaply. Individual bondholders also have more legal leverage than banks and are less vulnerable to arm-twisting by regulators.[8]

The goal of debt restructuring should be a better and more timely handling of unsustainable sovereign debts, while at the same time protecting asset value and creditors' rights.[9] This in turn, will allow the sovereign to maintain the provision of essential services to its population (education, health, justice, security, etc). **12.09**

The next section will consider the different techniques used to facilitate debt restructuring. It will also refer to the positions held by the different parties (ie the official and the private sector actors) involved in the development and/or use of these techniques. **12.10**

B. Current Debate on Sovereign Debt Restructuring: Procedures and Methods

Transactions are typically regulated by the law chosen by the parties. In the case of a bond issuance or other debt obligations, it is the issuer (bearing in mind the interests of the **12.11**

---

[7] See Chapter 11, section III.C.10.
[8] Anne Krueger, *International Financial Architecture for 2002: A New Approach to Sovereign Debt Restructuring*, address at the National Economists' Club Annual Members' Dinner American Enterprise Institute (26 November 2001), available at <http://www.imf.org/external/np/speeches/2001/112601.htm>.
[9] Ibid.

investors/lenders) or the lender in other debt obligations who decides which will be the applicable law. According to Tennekoon,[10] there are many issues that should be considered in order to decide which should be the proper law that will govern the debt obligation. These are: (1) the level of insulation (ie how effective is the system to reject the interference of other systems); (2) the certainty and result predictability in applying the chosen law; (3) the degree of party autonomy to avoid judicial interference; (4) conceptual sophistication; (5) market familiarity; (6) language (English is the language of the financial markets); and (7) legal limitations on the choice of law. Therefore, most sovereign debt obligations are subject either to New York law or English law. As analysed below, the applicable law is relevant when a sovereign is under distress because the alternatives available to the debtor are different depending on the applicable law. These alternatives not only refer to litigation, but also refer to the transactional aspects of a debt restructuring.

12.12   While there is widespread agreement for a revamped sovereign debt restructuring process, there is also disagreement over what the actual process should be.[11] As Buchheit and Gulati have observed, 'a sovereign bond issuer of the early twenty-first century is much in the same spot as a distressed corporate or railroad bond issuer of the early twentieth century'.[12] They contend that the financial community is again confronted with the same three options: (1) an insolvency reorganization procedure (Sovereign Debt Restructuring Mechanism, SDRM); (2) the inclusion of contractual provisions in the bonds that would allow a restructuring of those instruments with the consent of the required majority of the bondholders (CACs); or (3) the pursuit of a court-supervised debt restructuring, engaging the equitable powers of the civil courts to oversee such a process (class actions)[13] or an injunctive relief as seen in the Argentine *pari passu* litigation. As noted by Roubini, the question is: when sovereign debt restructuring or reprofiling and a face value reduction become necessary and unavoidable, what will be the appropriate regime that will provide an orderly mechanism while safeguarding the balance of rights, both of creditors and the debtor?[14]

12.13   Miller is of the opinion that Buchheit and Gulati, taking historical experience with corporate debt into consideration, are suggesting two ways to move forward: the New York court-ordered approach (either the equitable powers of the civil courts to oversee such a process or a SDRM-like statutory approach) and/or the London-style solution of self-organizing creditors.[15]

---

[10] See Ravi C Tennekoon, *The Law and Regulation of International Finance* (1991) 16–24.

[11] See Randall Dodd, 'Sovereign Debt Restructuring' (2002) 9(1–4) *Financier*, available at <http://people.umass.edu/econ797f/Syllabus%20and%20Readings/Readings/doddsovdebt.pdf>.

[12] Lee C Buchheit and G Mitu Gulati, 'Sovereign Bonds and the Collective Will' (2002) 51(4) *Emory Law Journal* 1317–1363.

[13] Ibid. An attempt to use a class action in sovereign restructuring was tested in three cases. In the first two, no class was certified because the parties settled the case prior to any further development. These where: (1) *Hirshon v Republic of Bolivia*, 979 F. Supp. 908 (D.D.C. 1997); and, (2) *Carl Marks & Co., Inc. v Union of Soviet Socialist Republics*, 665 F. Supp. 323 (S.D.N.Y. 1987). In the context of one of Argentina's defaults, a class was certified for the first time (*H.W. Urban GmbH v Republic of Argentina*, No. 02 Civ. 5699 (TPG), 2003 U.S. Dist. LEXIS 23363 (S.D.N.Y. Dec. 30, 2003).

[14] See Nouriel Roubini, 'Private Sector Involvement in Crisis Resolution and Mechanisms for Dealing with Sovereign Debt Problems', paper prepared for the Bank of England Conference on the Role of the Official Sector and Private Sector in Resolving International Financial Crises, 23–24 July 2002.

[15] See Marcus Miller, 'Sovereign Debt Restructuring: New Articles, New Contracts—or No Change?', International Economic Policy Briefs, No PB02-3 (April 2002), available at <http://www.iie.com/publications/pb/pb02-3.pdf>.

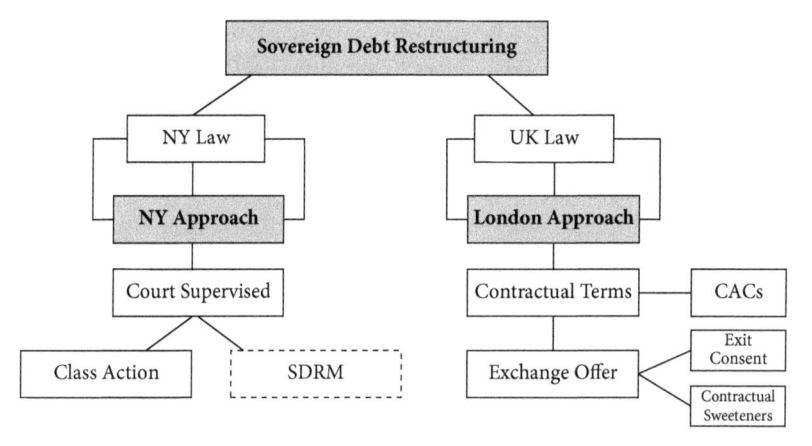

Figure 12.1 The Ad Hoc Legal Framework of Sovereign Debt Restructuring

Figure 12.1 summarizes this ad hoc legal framework applicable to sovereign debt restructuring (mainly bonds). **12.14**

In order to understand the ad hoc legal framework applicable to sovereign debt restructuring, Figure 12.1 has simplified the choice of law in sovereign bonds issuances. It focuses on New York and English law, which account for most of the issuances. Other laws, in regard to bonds' contractual rights, are assimilable to these two (eg bonds issued under German law are comparable to those issued under New York law, and bonds issued under Japanese and Luxembourg law are comparable to those issued under English law). **12.15**

So far, in the sovereign debt restructuring episodes of the 1990s and 2000s, the major issue of concern has been the holdout problem, ie creditors holding out in the hope of obtaining a better deal. In light of this situation, the IMF in the early 2000s had come with a statutory approach proposing the SDRM, based on chapter 11 of the US Bankruptcy Code for corporations.[16] More recently, and on the backdrop of the health crisis triggered by the COVID-19 pandemic, the official sector has come up with two initiatives: the Debt Service Suspension Initiative (DSSI) and the Common Framework. The market itself came up with two techniques to deal with the same issue: (1) voluntary exchange offers combined (or not) with exit consents or exit amendments; and (2) the use of CACs. In addition, enhanced contractual arrangements that are used to make the exchange offer more attractive can also be included under the market initiative. Among the proponents of the decentralized market-centred approach—as opposed to the centralized, non-market approach of the SDRM[17]—are the G10[18] **12.16**

---

[16] See 11 USC §§ 1121–1141. Chapter 11 is a court-supervised reorganization of an insolvent or near insolvent business while continuing with its day-to-day operations.

[17] See Dodd, *supra* n 10 at 3.

[18] The G10 Rey Report was issued in May 1996 and recommends the adoption of CACs as a measure to facilitate debt restructuring. The Group of 10 (G10) refers to the group of countries that have agreed to participate in the General Arrangements to Borrow (GAB). The GAB was established in 1962, when the governors of eight IMF members—Belgium, Canada, France, Italy, Japan, the Netherlands, the UK, and the US—and the central banks of two others—Germany and Sweden—agreed to make resources available to the IMF for drawings by participants, and under certain circumstances, for drawings by non-participants. The GAB was strengthened in 1964 by the association of Switzerland, then a non-member of the IMF, but the name of the G10 remained the same. The following international organizations are official observers of the activities of the G10: Bank of International Settlements, European Commission, IMF, and OECD (see <http://www.imf.org/external/np/exr/facts/groups. htm#G10>).

members; US Treasury;[19] INSOL International (an association of international insolvency practitioners);[20] Emerging Markets Creditors Association (EMCA); Emerging Markets Trade Association (EMTA); Institute of International Finance (IIF);[21] and the International Capital Market Association (ICMA).[22]

12.17   Since the holdout problem has been the major concern in sovereign debt restructuring, the IMF came up with the statutory approach proposal of a SDRM. The main features of the proposed SDRM are: (1) a stay upon the decision of a super-majority vote of creditors; (2) preferred creditor status for new money upon the decision of a super-majority of creditors (similar to debtor-in-possession financing, ie 11 USC § 364); (3) negotiations with creditors and a programme supported by the IMF; and (4) super-majority voting across all classes.[23] The SDRM never managed to gain enough support and it still has to overcome political resistance towards it and to resolve some shortcomings.[24] This notwithstanding, at the EU level a statutory vehicle has been established, ie the European Stability Mechanism (ESM), which is designed to safeguard financial stability within the euro area.[25] However, the IMF published a paper in 2014 where it supports the idea of contractual enhancement to address collective action problems and seems—although they are not mutually exclusive— to have departed from the idea of establishing a statutory approach like the SDRM.[26] In the same vein, the DSSI and Common Framework operate as an ad hoc solution aimed at bringing the different players around a table to find a mutually convenient solution.

12.18   The sections below analyse the statutory arrangement of the SDRM proposed by the IMF due to its historical value and—to certain extent—its contribution to the development of other alternatives or techniques. This analysis will be followed by consideration of the statutory developments in the EU a result of the sovereign debt crisis in Greece and other

---

[19]   John B Taylor, 'Sovereign Debt Restructuring: A U.S. Perspective', remarks at the conference on Sovereign Debt Workouts: Hopes and Hazards? at the Institute for International Economics, 1–2 April 2002, Washington DC, available at <http://www.iie.com/publications/papers/paper.cfm?ResearchID=455>.

[20]   INSOL International, 'Statement of Principles for a Global Approach to Multi-Creditor Workouts', available at <http://www.insol.org/pdf/Lenders.pdf>.

[21]   The IIF produced the Principles for Stable Capital Flows and Fair Debt Restructuring. These principles were conceived in the aftermath of the sovereign debt crises in the 1990s and they constitute a voluntary code of conduct between sovereign debt issuers and their private sector creditors that was agreed in the early 2000s and endorsed by the G20 Ministerial Meeting in Berlin in 2004. The principles are based on voluntary, market-based, flexible guidelines aiming at shaping sovereign debtors' behaviour and their private creditors with a view to promoting and maintaining stable capital flows and supporting financial stability and sustainable growth. The principles have four pillars, these are: (1) data and policy transparency; (2) open dialogue and cooperation; (3) good-faith negotiations; and (4) fair treatment (avoidance of discrimination) of all creditors. See <https://www.iif.com/topics/principles-stable-capital-flows-and-fair-debt-restructuring>.

[22]   ICMA has been actively working and collaborating with several international institutions and has published model collective action clauses, *pari passu* and creditor engagement provisions for inclusion in the terms and conditions of sovereign debt securities. The aim is to standardize the use of these terms in sovereign debt instruments aiming at facilitating future sovereign debt restructurings or avoiding misconstrued interpretations of certain contractual provisions. See <http://www.icmagroup.org/resources/Sovereign-Debt-Information>.

[23]   See IMF, *supra* n 1.

[24]   Among other things, one of the main questions regarding the SDRM is what would happen if a sovereign state obtained an agreement with its creditors through a SDRM and thereafter defaults again? A twice-defaulting country would show that the SDRM is not a panacea, and it would question the IMF's ability to oversee the implementation of measures and assess debt sustainability. It is worth bearing in mind that the administration of a country cannot be replaced or intervened in, nor the assets sold to the highest bidder. See Alina Arora and Rodrigo Olivares-Caminal, 'Rethinking the Sovereign Debt Restructuring Approach' (2003) Law & Bus Rev Am 636.

[25]   See Treaty establishing the European Stability Mechanism (ESM) 2012.

[26]   See IMF, 'Strengthening the Contractual Framework to Address Collective Action Problems in Sovereign Debt Restructuring', October 2014, available at <https://www.imf.org/external/pp/longres.aspx?id=4911>.

peripheral countries and the more recent pandemic developments (ie DSSI and the Common Framework). Some other initiatives, also developed further in this chapter, suggest the use of a domestic statute to shield enforcement actions. In addition, further detail is provided on the status quo of the decentralized, market-oriented approach and the use of CACs, exit consents, and contractual term enhancements. The analysis on these issues will follow.

C. The SDRM Proposed by the IMF

Recently, the debate on the reform of the international financial architecture has been centred on how to ensure orderly sovereign debt restructuring.[27] This is a recurrent theme that came to the fore after Argentina's default in 2002, once more with the EU sovereign debt crisis in 2007–2009 and the recurrent situation of Greece, and more recently as a result of the health crisis triggered by the COVID-19 pandemic. In this sense, the IMF believes that incentives are lacking to help countries with unsustainable debt resolve the problem promptly and in an orderly fashion.[28] This drives up the cost of default, ie it is harmful to the country, its citizens, and the international community.[29] Sovereigns sometimes unnecessarily delay decisions (and actually actions), trying to avoid the unavoidable because they fear the effect that this will have on their reputation, which will be translated into higher interest rates.   **12.19**

Therefore, since domestic insolvency law serves as a useful model in the distressed/insolvency context, the IMF started considering a sovereign debt restructuring mechanism for sovereign debt in 2001. However, UNCTAD (United Nations Conference on Trade and Development) was the first international organization to call for an orderly workout procedure for external debt of developing countries drawing on national insolvency laws, notably chapters 9 and 11 of the United States bankruptcy law.[30] It is also fair to stress that it was Sachs[31] who reignited the discussion in 1995 with an influential paper on international bankruptcy procedures for sovereigns.[32] Moreover, Schwarcz[33] in 2000 elaborated on the idea and proposed a convention to avoid reliance on the IMF.   **12.20**

The IMF proposed a 'twin-track' mechanism known as 'SDRM', which was based on two complementary approaches to create a more orderly and predictable process for sovereign   **12.21**

---

[27] See IMF, *supra* n 1.

[28] Krueger, *supra* n 7 at 1.

[29] See IMF, *supra* n 1.

[30] See UNCTAD, Trade and Development Report, 1986.

[31] Jeffrey Sachs stated that '[t]here is considerable confusion as to how the principles of bankruptcy should translate to the case of sovereign borrowers, ie governments. In the international context there is little formal law covering state insolvency, and certainly no bankruptcy code. Therefore, the question is mostly a normative one—how should international practice, and specifically IMF practice, be arranged in view of the lessons of bankruptcy law?' (See Jeffrey Sachs, 'Do We Need an International Lender of Last Resort?', Frank D Graham Lecture, Princeton University, 1995, available at <http://www.earth.columbia.edu/sitefiles/file/about/director/pubs/intllr.pdf>.)

[32] According to Kenneth Rogoff and Jeromin Zettelmeyer (*Early Ideas on Sovereign Bankruptcy Reorganization: A Survey*, IMF, March 2002, WP 02/57) the idea of a bankruptcy procedure for sovereigns can be traced back—at least—to 1776 when Adam Smith stated '[w]hen it becomes necessary for a State to declare itself bankrupt, in the same manner as when it becomes necessary for an individual to do so, a fair, open and avowed bankruptcy is always the measure which is both least dishonorable to the debtor, and least harmful for the creditor' (Adam Smith, *An Inquiry into the Nature and Causes of the Wealth of the Nations*).

[33] Steven L Schwarcz, 'Sovereign Debt Restructuring: A Bankruptcy Reorganization Approach' (2000) 85 Cornell Law Review 956.

debt restructuring. First, the contractual approach in which debt restructuring would be facilitated by enhanced use of certain contractual provisions in sovereign debt contracts.[34] Secondly, the establishment of a universal statutory framework would create a legal framework for collective decisions by debtors and a super-majority of its creditors.[35] As explained by the IMF, the central objective was to put countries and their creditors in a better position to restructure unsustainable sovereign debt in an orderly and timely manner.[36] Although a country could access the SDRM after default, ideally the SDRM would encourage a country with unsustainable debt and its creditors to restructure before default becomes the only option.[37] It is worth stressing that the SDRM would have only applied to sovereign debt governed by foreign law or debt subject to the jurisdiction of foreign courts.[38]

12.22 According to the IMF, the objectives of the SDRM would be:[39]

(1) to put countries and their creditors in a better position to restructure unsustainable sovereign debts in an orderly and timely manner;

(2) to benefit citizens of the countries whose debts were being restructured because the period of economic dislocation would be reduced and to benefit creditors since their asset values would be preserved;

(3) to increase the efficiency and stability of the global financial system by creating a more predictable environment for workouts in cases of unsustainable debt burdens, which would result in a reduction of the overall risk of lending to emerging-market countries.

12.23 A formal SDRM would need to be built on the following four key issues to achieve its objectives:[40]

(1) *Deterring disruptive litigation*: preventing creditors from obtaining relief through national courts. For example, granting a legal stay or a standstill to avoid holdouts, rogue creditors, free riders, and vulture funds from disrupting negotiations that could lead to a restructuring agreement.

(2) *Protecting creditor interests*: providing a guarantee that the debtor country would act responsibly during the course of any standstill.

(3) *Priority financing*: encouraging private lenders to provide fresh money during the restructuring procedure to facilitate ongoing economic activity.

(4) *Majority restructuring*: restructuring agreements reached by the parties should be binding to all of them, and not only on the majority who have agreed to them.

---

[34] IMF, 'IMF Board Discusses Possible Features of a Sovereign Debt Restructuring Mechanism' (7 January 2003), available at <http://www.imf.org/external/np/sec/pn/2003/pn0306.htm>.

[35] Ibid.

[36] See IMF, *supra* n 1, at A.2.

[37] Ibid at 8.

[38] See Report of the International Monetary Law Committee, International Law Association (MOCOMILA), Berlin Conference (2004), p 6, available at <http://www.mocomila.org/publication/2004-mocomila-berlin-rep ort.pdf>.

[39] See IMF, *supra* n 1.

[40] Krueger, *supra* n 7.

In order to achieve these objectives, the IMF proposed an SDRM with the following features: **12.24**

    (1) super-majority voting;[41]
    (2) a mechanism that would deter disruptive litigation;[42]
    (3) good faith negotiations;[43]
    (4) transparency requirements;[44]
    (5) grant of seniority to new lenders;[45] and
    (6) the establishment of a dispute resolution forum.[46]

The SDRM was designed only to help sovereign states whose debts are unsustainable. The   **12.25**
process would allow states to reorganize their finances and activities to restore debt payments. The SDRM would allow creditors to decide collectively on a restructuring, though ultimately a debtor could not use the SDRM without the consent of a super-majority of its creditors.[47]

In April 2002, the International Monetary and Financial Committee (IMFC)[48] endorsed   **12.26**
the work performed in the elaboration of the SDRM and encouraged the IMF to continue to examine the legal, institutional, and procedural aspects of two approaches, which could be complementary and self-reinforcing: (1) a statutory approach, which would enable a sovereign debtor and a super-majority of its creditors to reach an agreement binding all creditors; and (2) an approach, based on contract, which would incorporate comprehensive restructuring clauses in debt instruments.[49]

---

[41] Super-majority voting will resolve the new terms of the restructuring agreement and prevent minority creditors from blocking an agreement or enforcing the terms of the original debt contracts. See IMF *supra* n 1.

[42] In the 2003 version of the SDRM, the IMF replaced the original idea of an automatic stay by a mechanism to deter disruptive litigation by creditors during the debt restructuring negotiations. This notwithstanding, no further specification has been made (IMF *supra* n 1).

[43] See IMF, *supra* n 1. Creditors would have assurance that the debtor will negotiate in good faith and will pursue policies—most likely designed in conjunction with financial support from the IMF—that will help protect the value of creditor claims and limit dislocations in the economy.

[44] See IMF, *supra* n 1. The SDRM would establish transparency requirements that would, among other things, enable creditors to have information about how other creditors are being treated during the restructuring process.

[45] See IMF, *supra* n 1. Creditors could agree to give seniority and protection from restructuring to fresh private lending, in order to facilitate ongoing economic activity through the continued provision of trade and other types of credit.

[46] See IMF, *supra* n 1. A dispute resolution forum would be established to resolve disputes that may arise during the voting process or when claims are being verified.

[47] See IMF, *supra* n 1 at questions D.3 and D.4.

[48] The IMFC was established on 30 September 1999, by a resolution of the IMF Board of Governors, to replace the Interim Committee of the Board of Governors on the International Monetary System (usually known simply as the Interim Committee), which had been established in 1974. The change signified a strengthening of the role of the primary advisory committee of the Board of Governors. The IMFC usually meets twice a year, in September or October before the Bank-Fund Annual Meetings, and in March or April at what are referred to as the Spring Meetings. Like the Interim Committee, the IMFC has the responsibility of advising, and reporting to, the Board of Governors on matters relating to the Board of Governors' functions in supervising the management and adaptation of the international monetary and financial system, including the operation of the adjustment process, and in this connection reviewing developments in global liquidity and the transfer of resources to developing countries; considering proposals by the Executive Board to amend the Articles of Agreement; and dealing with disturbances that might threaten the system. The IMFC has 24 members who are Governors of the IMF (generally ministers of finance or central bank governors). See IMF, 'A Guide to Committees, Groups and Clubs: A Factsheet', August 2015, available at <http://www.imf.org/external/np/exr/facts/groups.htm>.

[49] See IMF, Communiqué of the International Monetary and Financial Committee of the Board of Governors of the International Monetary Fund, 20 April 2002, available at <http://www.imf.org/external/np/sec/pr/2002/pr0222.htm>.

1. The interaction of the SDRM with other creditors, preferred status of the IMF, and special treatment of HIPCs

12.27   Other relevant matters under the umbrella of the SDRM are the treatment to be given to other debt, ie domestic debt, Paris Club debt, and other multilateral institutions' debt (including the IMF).

12.28   According to the IMF, the inclusion of domestic debt in the SDRM should be considered on a case-by-case basis since foreign or non-resident investors may only be willing to provide substantial debt reduction if they know that domestic creditors are shouldering a fair share of the burden too.[50]

12.29   With regard to Paris Club debt, there has been some inclination by the IMF to exclude these claims from the formal framework of the SDRM. This notwithstanding, it should be borne in mind that Paris Club minutes of agreements usually include a 'comparability of treatment provision' and could also include a 'pull-back clause' to ensure that the debtor will not agree better terms with its private creditors and if it does, then it will be entitled to exit the agreement reached with the debtor. These two clauses, using the Paris Club and Antigua and Barbuda's agreed minutes on 19 September 2010 and Pakistan's agreed minutes on 30 January 1999, as an example, read as follows:

> *Comparability Treatment Provision*: '[i]n order to secure comparable treatment of its debt due to all its external public or private creditors, the Government of Antigua and Barbuda commits to seek promptly from all its external creditors debt reorganisation arrangements on terms comparable to those set forth in the [minutes], while trying to avoid discrimination among different categories of creditors. Consequently, the Government of Antigua and Barbuda commits to accord all categories of creditors ... a treatment not more favourable than that accorded to the [Paris Club] Participating Creditor Countries.'
> *Pullback Clause*: '[t]he participating Creditor Countries will review the implementation of the conditions stated ... for the comparability of treatment between all external creditors; if the Participating Creditor Countries determine that these conditions are not substantially fulfilled, they will declare the provisions set forth [in the minutes] null and void.'

12.30   As widely known, the 'lender of last resort' (LOLR) role of the central bank remains the major rationale for most central banks around the world, both in developed and developing countries as witnessed during the US subprime mortgage crises and the 'credit crunch'. The LOLR role is to provide credit in emergency situations. This role of the LOLR has been adopted by the IMF in the international level (ILOLR), in favour of its member states during economic and/or financial crises (eg the IMF's massive financial interventions in Mexico in 1994, Russia in 1994, South East Asia in 1997, and more recently in Greece and Argentina).

12.31   Since the IMF is not a commercial organization seeking profitable lending opportunities and often lends at a time when other creditors are reluctant to do so—and at interest rates that are below those that would be charged at that juncture by the private sector[51]—preferred creditor status is assigned to this lending. The IMF has clearly explained that the ILOLR role

---

[50]   IMF, *supra* n 1.
[51]   Ibid.

benefits not just its members but official and private creditors alike by allowing the Fund to assist member countries in regaining a sustainable financial path and helping to promote orderly resolutions to debt problems, when necessary.[52] As noted by Lastra, the IMF plays different roles by wearing different 'hats'. Among these are: (1) that of an 'honest broker' or arbiter between creditors and debtors; (2) a primary lender by means of providing financial assistance to countries experiencing balance of payment needs; (3) a preferred creditor with an interest at stake; (4) an ILOLR; (5) a crisis manager; and (6) a standard setter.[53] Therefore, putting the IMF claims together with commercial claims in a workout would fundamentally undermine the Fund's capacity to play those vital roles in future.[54]

The reasons outlined in the previous paragraph, are the rationale for the de facto priority   **12.32** claimed by and implicitly assigned to the IMF, International Bank for Reconstruction and Development (World Bank), and other regional developing banks.[55] This de facto priority has been recognized in an official document for the first time under Recital 13 of the European Stability Mechanism Treaty, which states that the ESM will enjoy preferred creditor status in a similar fashion to the IMF, while accepting the preferred creditor status of the IMF over the ESM.[56] More recently, this status has also been acknowledge by the US courts.[57] However, Bolton and Skeel Jr[58] contend that this de facto priority is partly an illusion because the IMF has generally agreed to roll over its loans when the sovereign is unable or unwilling to pay since the rolling-over of the debt amounts to a net-present value reduction on the stock of debt.

The possibility of obtaining debtor-in-possession (DIP) financing is a feasible alternative to   **12.33** financing restructurings in replacement of the ILOLR. It is an alternative in terms of privatizing the source of money, ie shifting the source of funds from international organizations to private lenders. It should be pointed out as an example that, in 1992, Macy's (a US department store) obtained new working capital in a $600 million loan through DIP financing only three weeks after filing its petition under chapter 11 of the US Bankruptcy Code, while Russia had to wait more than a year.[59] Shifting the source of funding from the ILOLR to the capital markets will foster inter-creditor coordination and would reduce moral hazard. This change of source of credit for the sovereign will not diminish current creditors' status since the IMF, World Bank, or other regional developing banks' already have de facto priority over non-secured creditors. However, the importance of their role as ILOLR can be reduced for funds as debtors would be able to tap to the capital markets.

---

[52] IMF, 'Financial Risk in the Fund and the Level of Precautionary Balances', Prepared by the Finance Department (in consultation with other departments), approved by Eduard Brau, 3 February 2004, available at <http://www.imf.org/external/np/tre/risk/2004/020304.pdf>.

[53] See Rosa M Lastra, *Legal Foundations of International Monetary Law* (2006) 499.

[54] IMF, *supra* n 1.

[55] See Nouriel Roubini and Brad Setser, 'The Reform of the Sovereign Debt Restructuring Process: Problems, Proposed Solutions and the Argentine Episode' paper prepared for the conference on 'Improving the Sovereign Debt Restructuring Process' co-hosted by the Institute for International Economics and Institut Francais des Relations Internationales, Paris, 9 March 2003, p 4; Lastra *supra* n 52 at 486; Schwarcz, *supra* n 32 at 956–1034 and 'Idiot's Guide to Sovereign Debt Restructuring' (2004) 53 *Emory Law Journal* 1189–1218; IMF, *supra* nn 1 and 51.

[56] See Recital 13 ESM Treaty.

[57] 12-105(L), *NML Capital, Ltd. v Republic of Argentina*.

[58] Patrick Bolton and David Skeel Jr, 'Redesigning the International Lender of Last Resort' (2005) 6 *U Chicago Journal of International Law* 177.

[59] See Jeffrey D Sachs, 'IMF, Reform Thyself', *Wall St J*, 21 July 1994.

12.34   Schwarcz points out that permitting debtors to grant priority in order to attract new money credits tends to create value for the unsecured creditors, even though those creditors' claims are subordinated to the new money.[60] The availability of new money credit increases a debtor's liquidity, thereby reducing the risk of failure and increasing the expected value of unsecured claims. Likewise, permitting a sovereign debtor to grant priority in order to increase liquidity will reduce the risk of economic failure to some extent.[61]

12.35   Debtor-in-possession financing can be in the form of syndicated loans (eg the first Greek bailout which was an ad hoc syndicated loan granted by other euro area Member States) or may be raised again from the capital markets (eg the European Financial Stability Facility (EFSF)/ESM). It has been proposed that this funding may be raised from the capital markets by the IMF acting as an intermediary rather than involving itself directly.[62] Accordingly, the IMF would borrow funds from the capital markets on a non-recourse basis and re-lend those funds to the debtor state. The debtor state's priority loan would be given as collateral for the capital borrowed by the IMF from the market. Schwarcz considers that the lenders thus would be in the same position as if they had made the loan directly to the state. Further, because the borrowing would be on a non-recourse basis, the IMF would avoid liability for the debtor state's potential default and thereby reduce moral hazard given that the capital market lenders could look only to their collateral (the debtor state's assigned loan) for repayment. Moreover, the intermediary funding approach would enable the IMF to continue its current practice of imposing conditionality on funding.

12.36   Schwarcz's proposal has been based on the basic premise that the IMF can act as an 'intermediary funding source' and issue collateralized securities. It is highly improbable that the articles of the IMF, unless they are amended, would be interpreted to permit the IMF to act as an intermediary funding source and to issue securities.[63] However, instead of the IMF, other multilateral organizations such as the World Bank or International Finance Corporation (IFC) may act as the intermediary funding source, as has already been done in the past. Securitization (eg collateralized loan obligations or collateralized debt obligations) may be used for a variety of reasons, including a desire for liquidity, reducing financing costs or mismatches between assets and liabilities, and managing balance sheets better.[64]

12.37   In the light of the remote possibility of an IMF bailout or funding for restructuring, a sovereign would be required to arrange financing for restructuring through a mechanism similar to DIP financing. What would be the financial price of the DIP financing for the sovereign country? Although it may seem at first sight to be very expensive and difficult due to the distressed situation, financing is not impossible and in fact may prove to be financially more viable. This DIP financing could be raised by the World Bank or the IFC (or other third party), acting as an intermediary financing fund to borrow funds from the capital markets by securitization of the asset pool of receivables from the sovereign debtor and simultaneously re-lend those funds back to the sovereign debtor. The asset pool of receivables from

---

[60]   Schwarcz, *supra* n 32.
[61]   Ibid.
[62]   Ibid.
[63]   IMF, Article V: Operations and Transactions of the Fund § 2.
[64]   Hal S Scott and Philip A Wellons, *International Finance: Transactions, Policy, and Regulations* (8th edn, 2001) 759.

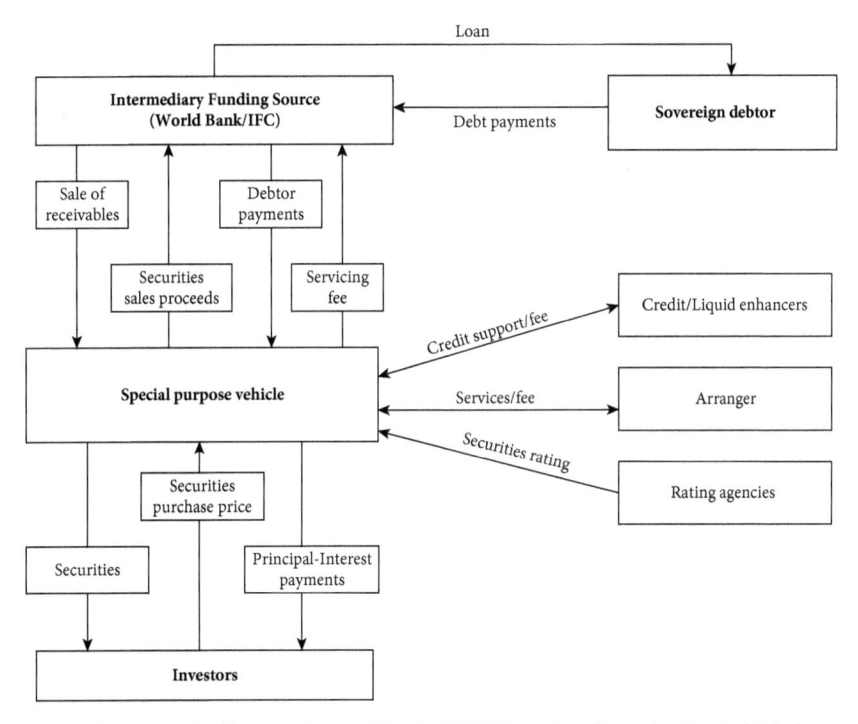

Figure 12.2 Structure for Transaction to Obtain DIP Financing from the Capital Markets through Securitization

Figure 12.2 is a simplified structure for sovereign DIP financing based on Scott and Wellons' securitization structure (Hal S Scott and Philip A Wellons, *International Finance: Transactions, Policy, and Regulations* (8th edn, 2001) at 760, Exhibit 1).

the sovereign debtor on these loans would be the collateral for the capital raised by World Bank or the IFC from the market. Figure 12.2 illustrates how to structure such a transaction.

To ensure that the investors do not have recourse to the World Bank or the IFC and to avoid **12.38** any liability for the sovereign debtor's potential default, the World Bank or the IFC would have to set up a special purpose vehicle (SPV) and transfer all the assets (the receivables) to it. The investors would only have recourse to the assets of the SPV (the asset pool of receivables from the sovereign debtor), which would also be the collateral for the securities. Such a financing plan could be a workable solution in cases where the number of series or the total outstanding amount is limited. Nevertheless, the possibility of the World Bank or the IFC agreeing to issue the securities backed by the right to collect the amount due by the sovereign rests on a political issue.

This idea of using an intermediary financing fund is what the ESM (and its predecessor, the **12.39** EFSF) has been doing at the EU level during the EU Sovereign Debt Crisis that started in 2010. There are certain particularities regarding the use of a guarantee which is explained in more detail below.[65]

---

[65] See below at section D.

12.40 It is worth stressing, however, that the IMF's proposal of a SDRM is not based on the notion of insolvency for countries because countries cannot become insolvent.[66] The IMF was promoting a mechanism to facilitate debt workout negotiations which differed from insolvency laws because: (1) it did not include an automatic stay on the enforcement of creditors' rights; (2) there was no ultimate sanction of liquidation; (3) policies were not supervised by an insolvency court; and (4) creditors could not insist on a change in management.[67]

12.41 Finally, the debt problems of low-income countries are dealt with under the Highly Indebted Poor Country (HIPC) initiative.[68] Debt relief under the HIPC initiative was launched jointly by the IMF and the World Bank in 1996.[69] In 1997, this initiative was linked to the Poverty Reduction and Growth Facility (PRGF) and a trust administered by the IMF was set up, ie the HIPC-PRGF Trust.[70] In 1999, the international community recognized the need for a concerted effort to deal with the external debt problem of certain countries (mostly African) and revamped the HIPC initiative to provide faster and deeper debt relief to allow HIPC to reach a level of sustainability.[71] On 8 December 2005, the IMF's Executive Board approved the Multilateral Debt Relief Initiative (MDRI) involving a total debt relief of HIPC and those countries with per capita income below $380 and outstanding debt to the IMF at end-2004.[72] On the same date, the Exogenous Shocks Facility was also approved as part of the PRGF Trust to support HIPCs in the event of economic shocks caused by rising oil prices, natural disasters, contagion of conflicts, or crisis in neighbouring countries, etc.

12.42 Since the SDRM deals with issues concerning sovereign debt to private sector creditors, it is more relevant to those countries that have borrowed on international capital markets, which is usually not the case with HIPC countries.[73]

2. Disadvantages of the SDRM

12.43 Under the SDRM, a super-majority of creditors, regardless of the bond issue or loan obligations held, would be able to vote to accept new terms of payment under a restructuring

---

[66] Lex Rieffel, *Restructuring Sovereign Debt: The Case for Ad-hoc Machinery* (2003) 289.

[67] IMF, *supra* n 1.

[68] According to the IMF's glossary of selected financial terms, the HIPC Initiative was adopted in 1996 and provides exceptional assistance to eligible countries to reduce their external debt burdens to sustainable levels, thereby enabling them to service their external debt without the need for further debt relief and without compromising growth. It involves multilateral, Paris Club, and other official and bilateral creditors. To be eligible for the HIPC, countries must: (1) have established a strong track record of performance under programmes supported by the IMF's Poverty Reduction and Growth Facility (PRGF) and the International Development Association (IDA); (2) be IDA-only and PRGF-eligible; (3) face an unsustainable debt burden; and (4) have developed a Poverty Reduction Strategy Paper. In 2005, the HIPC Initiative was supplemented by the Multilateral Debt Relief Initiative (MDRI) which allows for 100 per cent relief on eligible debts of countries completing the HIPC Initiative process. See <http://www.imf.org>.

[69] See IMF, 'Debt Relief under the Heavily Indebted Poor Countries (HIPC) Initiative: A Factsheet', available at <http://www.imf.org/external/np/exr/facts/hipc.htm>.

[70] Instrument to establish—under Article V, Section 2(b)—the Poverty Reduction and Growth Facility Trust, decision No 8759—(87/176) ESAF 18 December 1987 as amended.

[71] The HIPC include: Afghanistan, Benin, Bolivia, Burkina Faso, Burundi, Cameroon, Central African Republic, Chad, Comoros, Côte d'Ivoire, Eritrea, Ethiopia, Ghana, Guinea, Guinea-Bissau, Guyana, Haiti, Honduras, Liberia, Madagascar, Malawi, Mali, Mauritania, Mozambique, Nicaragua, Niger, Republic of Congo, Rwanda, São Tomé & Príncipe, Senegal, Sierra Leone, Somalia, Sudan, Tanzania, The Gambia, Togo, Uganda, and Zambia.

[72] See IMF, 'IMF Executive Board Agrees on Implementation Modalities for the Multilateral Debt Relief Initiative', Public Information Notice (PIN) No 05/164, 8 December 2005, available at <http://www.imf.org/external/np/sec/pn/2005/pn05164.htm>; and 'The Multilateral Debt Relief Initiative (MDRI): A Factsheet', April 2007, available at <http://www.imf.org/external/np/exr/facts/mdri.htm>.

[73] IMF, *supra* n 1.

agreement and minority creditors would be bound by the decision of the majority.[74] Consequently, a dispute resolution forum would be created for different purposes, such as verifying claims, guaranteeing the integrity of the voting process that led to the restructuring, and adjudicating disputes among creditors. Thus, to grant a legal stay binding on all parties, the mechanism must have the force of universal law.[75] Otherwise, creditors would be able to sue the debtor state in their own jurisdiction, in the jurisdiction regulating the bond issuance, or in the jurisdiction of the debtor state. Obtaining a convention or a treaty binding all countries would be likely to take a very long time. In 2002, an IMF official stated that 'even with unanimous political support this approach could not be in place for at least two or three years'.[76] Two years later, due to the criticism and scepticism towards the SDRM, another IMF officer expressly stated that '[t]he debate on the Sovereign Debt Restructuring Mechanism [SDRM] has been shelved for the time being'.[77] Some critics believe the process could take decades 'and could end up being ineffective if too many nations refuse to join [in]'.[78] Since the IMF initiative was shelved, more than 10 years have passed. However, the idea of a statutory approach is far from defunct, and there is strong support in certain academic circles and even at the policy level.[79]

The imposition of standstills and the use of majority voting in debt restructuring agreements binding on a dissenting minority require an amendment to the IMF's Articles of Agreement; or a new treaty. In order to amend the Articles of Agreement of the IMF, two criteria have to be met: (1) the amendment is supported by a two-thirds majority of members (numerosity); and (2) the members voting for the amendment hold at least 85 per cent of the voting power.[80] The United States has a decisive vote in amending the IMF's Articles of Agreement since its quota,[81] ie the country's economic position relative to other members, entitles it to 16.5 per cent of the total members' voting rights. Therefore, if the US does not vote in favour of the amendment, the second criteria cannot be attained. In order to vote in favour of the amendment, the US Congress must approve the change. There is no indication, however, that there would be sufficient political support for the SDRM in the   **12.44**

---

[74] Barry Eichengreen and Ashoka Mody, *Is Aggregation a Problem for Sovereign Debt Restructuring?* (January 2003), available at <http://emlab.berkeley.edu/users/eichengr/research/aeapapers&proceedings5jan15-03.pdf>.

[75] Krueger, *supra* n 7.

[76] Ibid.

[77] IMF, Interview with Mark Allen: IMF needs to do far more to help countries learn from each other's successes and failures, IMF Survey, Vol 33, No 7, 12 April 2004, p 99, available at <http://www.imf.org/external/pubs/ft/survey/2004/041204.pdf>. In the same vein, see international press articles (*The Economist*, 'Dealing with Default', Washington DC, 8 May 2003; Paul Blustein, '"Bankruptcy" System for Nations Fail to Draw Support', *Washington Post*, 2 April 2003; Alan Beattie, 'Brown Plan to Reform Global Financial System Meets Opposition', *Financial Times*, 14 April 2003).

[78] Owen C Pell, 'Nations Need Bankruptcy Process, Outside the Box', 8 February 2002, available at <http://jp.whitecase.com/files/Publication/03e66ae8-3c8c-4a4b-8d01-a8e3f92b6266/Presentation/PublicationAttachment/26fe173a-d3ac-417d-a874-adce8d10058f/article_nations_need_bankruptcy_process_pell.pdf>.

[79] The UN General Assembly adopted a resolution in August 2014 on sovereign debt restructuring that would establish an intergovernmental negotiation process aimed at increasing the efficiency, stability, and predictability of the international financial system by establishing a multilateral legal framework for sovereign debt restructuring. The resolution was passed with 124 votes in favour, 11 votes against, and 41 abstentions. See UN Resolution 'Towards the establishment of a multilateral legal framework for sovereign debt restructuring processes' (document A/68/L.57/Rev.1).

[80] See Art XXVIII(a) of the Articles of Agreement of the IMF.

[81] As of 31 July 2015, the US quota was SDR 42,122.4 million (16.77%). SDR stands for 'special drawing rights', an international reserve asset created by the IMF in 1969 as a supplement to existing reserve assets. See <http://www.imf.org/external/np/exr/facts/quotas.htm>.

US Congress,[82] which was recently confirmed when the United States voted against the UN Resolution 'Towards the establishment of a multilateral legal framework for sovereign debt restructuring processes'.[83]

12.45   If a treaty were to be adopted, it has to emanate from an international body, which would take several years of political negotiations and several more (in the event that it was finally agreed) for ratification.[84]

12.46   Even if a binding treaty were adopted, other issues that would need to be considered are whether the treaty would be binding to pre-existing debt obligations (ie retroactive effect)? This requires a twofold analysis: (1) on one hand, it can be easily argued that the default and the need to use the SDRM occurred after the adoption of the treaty; but (2) on the other hand, the terms and conditions of the debt instruments giving rise to the rights of the bondholders would have been 'agreed' prior to the adoption of the treaty. Regarding the latter, it is worth mentioning that Article 28 of the 1969 Vienna Convention on the Law of Treaties sets the non-retroactivity of treaties as the general rule, unless otherwise established.

12.47   Notwithstanding the aforementioned practical difficulties in implementing the SDRM, due to a greater predictability in the restructuring progress afforded by the adoption of the SDRM, an improvement in the functioning of international capital markets should be expected.[85] However, while an SDRM would make the process of restructuring easier and faster, this may create an environment where governments do not try their hardest to avoid defaults in the first place.[86] As sovereign debt always has the potential to lead to 'opportunistic defaults' (unwillingness to pay as opposed to inability to pay) as evidenced in 2009 by Ecuador,[87] a restructuring that is too 'easy' may poison the functioning of the markets.

12.48   Krueger stated:

> [T]he Fund's involvement would be essential to the success of such a system [referring to the SDRM]. We are the most effective channel through which the international community can reach a judgment on the sustainability of a country's debt and of its economic policies, and whether it is doing what is necessary to get its balance of payments back into shape and to avoid future debt problems.[88]

12.49   What would happen if a sovereign state obtained an agreement with its creditors through an SDRM and thereafter defaulted again? It should be noted that although the SDRM is based

---

[82] Patrick Bolton, *Toward a Statutory Approach to Sovereign Debt Restructuring: Lessons from Corporate Bankruptcy Practice Around the World*, at 27–28, available at <http://204.180.229.21/external/pubs/ft/staffp/2002/00-00/pdf/bolton.pdf>.

[83] Doc A/68/L.57/Rev.1.

[84] For example, the 1983 'Vienna Convention on Succession of States in Respect of State Property, Archives and Debts' has not yet entered into force. See <http://legal.un.org/avl/ha/ vcssrspad/vcssrspad.html>.

[85] IMF, *supra* n 1.

[86] Michael Heise, 'An Improved International Finance Architecture Contributions from the Official and Private Sector, Speech at the Conference for New Sovereign Debt Restructuring Mechanisms: Challenges and Opportunities' (21–22 February 2003).

[87] See Lee Buchheit and Mitu Gulati, 'The Coroner's Inquest' (2009) *International Financial Law Review* 3; Arturo C Porzecanski, 'When Bad Things Happen to Good Sovereign Debt Contracts: The Case of Ecuador', 73 *Law and Contemporary Problems* 251–271 (Fall 2010) and Ben Miller, 'Ecuador Restructuring: Inside Job', *Latin Finance*, 1 July 2009.

[88] Krueger, *supra* n 7.

on the US chapter 11, there is no ultimate sanction of liquidation and creditors cannot insist on a change in management as happens in the case of corporations. The lack of sanctions alters the whole rationale of the system and therefore the dynamics are different from those of an insolvency regime. A twice-defaulting country would demonstrate that the SDRM is not a panacea, and it would question the IMF's ability to oversee the implementation of agreed policies and design an adequate economic and financial plan (see eg Argentina or Belize).

Further, establishing a quasi-judicial entity under the IMF would likely be a time-consuming and difficult process.[89] In addition, many countries fear that the introduction of statutory and even contractual mechanisms for debt restructuring would impair their access to international capital markets and discourage capital flows.[90]   **12.50**

Thus, it is apparent that the SDRM has some shortcomings and many enemies. Its enemies include the private financial sector, especially representatives of different actors in the international bond market, and developing countries who feel no ownership of the proposal and express even less enthusiasm for it. In addition, it is unclear where developed countries stand, or if they stand together.[91] The question then is whether an institutional change in the international financial system providing for orderly sovereign debt restructuring is needed.[92]   **12.51**

Despite its shortcomings, the SDRM does provide some benefits. It is innovative in bringing debtors and creditors together (irrespective of the use of CACs). It is also innovative because it secures greater transparency and provides a mechanism for dispute resolution.[93] The gap between a SDRM statutory approach and CACs has narrowed due to the more recent development of single-limb CACs whereby a single vote can be tendered to restructure multiple debt instruments. The aggregate voting mechanism in single-limb CACs allows the debtor and its creditors to act as if all of the debt was governed by a single CAC, as stressed by the IMF's SDRM as one of its main features.[94] This aggregation mechanism was used in Uruguay's 2003 debt reprofiling and now has become a recommended feature under ICMA's standard draft model CACs.[95] Therefore, the wide spread of CACs and the possibility of series aggregation can replicate some of the envisaged advantages of the SDRM.   **12.52**

Although the adoption of the SDRM could be considered as a positive step in debt restructuring, the effects of the SDRM could also be achieved through the broader use of CACs in a decentralized market-oriented approach as proposed by Taylor[96] ('using the tools we already have'), or perhaps using them more creatively and more confidently to promote   **12.53**

---

[89] Mark Jewett, 'Legal Approaches and Procedures', Speech at the Conference for New Sovereign Debt Restructuring Mechanisms: Challenges and Opportunities (21–22 February 2003).

[90] Yilmaz Akyüz, 'Some Reflections on SDRM', Speech at the Conference for New Sovereign Debt Restructuring Mechanisms: Challenges and Opportunities (21–22 February 2003), available at <http://www.networkideas.org/alt/feb2003/alt27_SDRM.htm>.

[91] See Barry Herman, 'The International Community Should Continue Work on a Mechanism for Restructuring Sovereign Debt', Speech at the Conference for New Sovereign Debt Restructuring Mechanisms: Challenges and Opportunities (21–22 February 2003).

[92] See Roubini, *supra* n 13.

[93] See Akyüz, *supra* n 88.

[94] See IMF, *supra* n 1.

[95] See ICMA Standard CACs, August 2014, available at <http://www.icmagroup.org/Regulatory-Policy-and-Market-Practice/Primary-Markets/collective-action>.

[96] See Taylor, *supra* n 18.

orderly workouts, as proposed by Buchheit and Gulati.[97] It is important to note that the sovereign debt restructuring regime proposed by the IMF would not be substantially different from a contractual approach; mainly it would be 'creditor-centred' rather than 'IMF-centred'.[98] There are other proponents that criticize the IMF SDRM for lacking objective independence.[99]

12.54   According to Cohen and Portes,[100] the SDRM proposal was shelved because it would have required an amendment to the Articles of Agreement. However, Lastra contends that a more modest alternative could be a 'creative' interpretation of Article VIII, Section 2(b) of the IMF Articles of Agreement as a means to impose a stay on creditors.[101] This position is also supported by Francotte[102] and Gianvitti.[103] The latter also argues that an interpretation under Article XXIX of the Articles of Agreement can be reached to create uniformity of interpretation within the courts of IMF members.[104]

12.55   This notwithstanding, the SDRM (or some form of statutory approach) remains a live issue. Moreover, the recent financial crises have reignited the discussion of a structured approach to deal with sovereign debt issues. Yet, as Sgard stated, the fact that the SDRM proposal was eventually shelved does not imply it has lost any political or historical significance since it highlights the range of possible solutions which dominant states are ready to consider.[105]

12.56   Although a market-oriented approach has worked in the restructuring cases of Russia, Ukraine, Ecuador, Pakistan, Uruguay, Belize, Grenada, Argentina, Ecuador, etc, the view of the IMF is that the costs at present are too high and too disruptive to the international community as a whole.[106] The IMF has reviewed its sovereign debt policy in 2014 and has published two papers endorsing pre-emptive reprofiling[107] and the strengthening of the sovereign contractual features.[108] This was followed by a policy paper in 2020 assessing the need to involve private sector creditors as part of the necessary architecture for resolving sovereign debt.[109] As previously discussed, Buchheit and Gulati contend that the existing collective decision-making provisions in sovereign bonds can—if used more confidently and creatively—replicate certain features of domestic corporate bankruptcy, ie automatic

---

[97]   Buchheit and Mitu Gulati, *supra* n 11.

[98]   See Roubini, *supra* n 13.

[99]   See, eg, Christoph G Paulus and Steven T Kargman, 'Reforming the Process of Sovereign Debt Restructuring: A Proposal for a Sovereign Debt Tribunal', paper presented at the UN workshop on 'Debt, Finance and Emerging Issues in Financial Integration', 8–9 April 2008.

[100]   Daniel Cohen and Richard Portes, 'Dealing with Destabilizing "Market Discipline"', paper prepared for the conference on 'Market Discipline: the Evidence across Countries and Industries', organized by the Bank for International Settlements and the Federal Reserve Bank of Chicago, 30 October–1 November 2003, p 5, available at <http://faculty.london.edu/rportes/research/FRBC-BIS220104.pdf>.

[101]   Lastra, *supra* n 52 at 481.

[102]   See Pierre Francote, 'The Fund Agreement in the Courts' in Robert Effros (ed), *Current Legal Issues Affecting Central Banks*, Vol 1 (1992).

[103]   See François Gianvitti, 'The Reform of the International Monetary Fund' in Rosa M Lastra (ed), *The Reform of the International Financial Architecture* (2001) 102.

[104]   Ibid.

[105]   Jérôme Sgard, 'The Renegotiation of Sovereign Debts and the Future of Financial Multilateralism', paper presented at the Fifth Pan-European Conference of the Standing Group on International Relations, The Hague, 9–11 September 2004.

[106]   IMF, *supra* n 1.

[107]   IMF, The Fund's Lending Framework and Sovereign Debt—Preliminary Considerations, June 2014, available at <http://www.imf.org/external/np/pp/eng/2014/052214.pdf>.

[108]   See *supra* n 25.

[109]   See *supra* n 3.

stays; cramdowns; and DIP financing, but not its coordination feature. Coordination among different series of bonds was resolved in Uruguay's debt reprofiling by the aggregation mechanism in which amendments to any terms (including payment terms) were incorporated into one or more series of bonds simultaneously[110] and recently perfected by ICMA's single-limb CAC. More importantly, the proposed SDRM: (1) excludes the debt obligations of the IMF as well as other multilateral organizations; and (2) is inclined to exclude the Paris Club and domestic creditors. In other words, it coordinates private creditors, which can also be achieved by the use of CACs. Another feature that needs to be addressed is the possibility of a stay, a feature of SDRM that can also be addressed contractually— although not much progress has been made.

3. An alternative SDRM

The recent case of Iraq's restructuring highlighted the possibility of using a different alter-   **12.57**
native to achieve the same outcome as an SDRM, without the need for a formal statutory regime to be put in place for that specific purpose. This section will analyse the mechanisms and types of resolutions adopted by the UN in the case of Iraq and will also illustrate how they can be used to recreate an SDRM.

(a) UN resolutions

A UN Resolution is a formal text adopted by a UN body. Although any UN body can issue   **12.58**
resolutions, in practice most resolutions are issued by the Security Council or the General Assembly. There are two types of UN resolutions, ie substantive or procedural resolutions. In addition, resolutions can be classified by the organ that takes the decision, eg UN General Assembly resolutions or UN Security Council resolutions. The UN General Assembly consists of all the members of the United Nations.[111] Each member of the General Assembly shall have one vote.[112] Decisions of the General Assembly on what have been referred as 'important questions' shall be made by a two-thirds majority of the members present and voting. Decisions on other questions, including the determination of additional categories of questions to be decided by a two-thirds majority, shall be made by a majority of the members present and voting.

The UN Security Council has 15 members, out of which five are permanent members   **12.59**
(China, France, Russia, UK, and the US).[113] Resolutions on procedural matters shall be made by an affirmative vote of nine members. Decisions on all other matters shall be made by an affirmative vote of nine members including the concurring votes of the permanent members.

Most General Assembly resolutions are considered non-binding. Articles 10 and 14 of the   **12.60**
UN Charter refer to General Assembly as 'recommendations'. The International Court of Justice, ie the principal judicial organ of the UN,[114] has reiterated the recommendatory nature of General Assembly resolutions. However, some General Assembly resolutions

---

[110] In order to approve the amendment, a double majority is required: (1) 85 per cent of the aggregate principal amount of all affected series; and (2) 66⅔ per cent of each specific series.
[111] See Art 9 of the UN Charter.
[112] See Art 18 of the UN Charter.
[113] See Art 23 of the UN Charter.
[114] See Art 92 of the UN Charter and Art 1 of the Statute of the International Court of Justice.

dealing with matters internal to the UN, such as budgetary decisions or instructions to lower-ranking organs, are binding on their addressees. Resolutions adopted under Chapter VII of the UN Charter (ie 'Action with Respect to Threats to the Peace, Breaches of the Peace, and Acts of Aggression') are adopted by the Security Council. Under Article 25 of the UN Charter, UN member states are bound to carry out 'decisions of the Security Council in accordance with the present Charter'.

12.61   Resolutions made under Chapter VII are considered binding because there is an enforcement mechanism under Articles 41, 42, and 43, but resolutions under Chapter VI (Pacific Settlement of Disputes) have no enforcement mechanisms and are generally considered to have no binding force under international law.

12.62   In 1971, the majority of the members of the International Court of Justice (ICJ) stated in a (non-binding) Namibia advisory opinion that all UN Security Council resolutions are legally binding.[115] This is based on Article 25 of the UN Charter that states that '[t]he Members of the United Nations agree to accept and carry out the decisions of the Security Council in accordance with the present Charter'. Moreover, the ICJ argued that Article 25 of the UN Charter has no limitation as to which type of decisions (ie Chapter VI or Chapter VII) and that Article 25 is immediately after Article 24 in the part of the Charter which deals with the functions and powers of the Security Council. The ICJ stated that '[i]f Article 25 had reference solely to decisions of the Security Council concerning enforcement action under Articles 41 and 42 of the Charter, that is to say, if it were only such decisions which had binding effect, then Article 25 would be superfluous, since this effect is secured by Articles 48 and 49 of the Charter'.

12.63   In May 2003, the UN Security Council adopted Resolution No 1483/03 shielding Iraq from possible seizures or attachments of its oil reserves. The effects of this resolution can be assimilated to those of a standstill as proposed by the SDRM without the need to reform the IMF's articles of association or without the need to adopt an international treaty. The effects of this resolution are considered in the next section.

(b) The Iraqi case and the use of UN resolutions

12.64   The UN Security Council adopted Resolution No 1483/03 in May 2003. This resolution shielded Iraq from possible seizures or attachments of its oil reserves until 31 December 2007. Security Council Resolution No 1546/04 dated 8 June 2004 decided that the provisions of paragraph 22 of Resolution No 1483/03 shall continue to apply, with the exception that the privileges and immunities provided in that paragraph shall not apply with respect to any final judgment arising out of a contractual obligation entered into by Iraq after 30 June 2004.[116] In extreme cases, the IMF can even endorse a sovereign's request before the UN to prevent creditors from seizing assets during a short restructuring period, as occurred in the recent case of Iraq.

---

[115] See International Court of Justice, Legal Consequences for States of the Continued Presence of South Africa in Namibia (South West Africa) notwithstanding Security Council Resolution 276 (1970), Advisory Opinion of 21 June 1971.

[116] The rationale behind this resolution is to extend immunity to Iraqi obligations with the exception of those entered into by the new government. 30 June 2004 was the date of the transfer of sovereignty back to the Iraqi citizens.

Since UN Security Council resolutions are not self-executing and do not confer rights on US **12.65** citizens which are judicially enforceable in US domestic courts in the absence of implementing legislation,[117] the US President enacted Executive Order No 13,303.[118] Executive Order No 13,303 was enacted on the same date as the UN's Security Council Resolution No 1483/03. The substantial difference between both pieces of legislation is that the US Executive Order does not have an expiration date regarding the shielding of Iraqi assets. On 29 November 2004, Executive Order No 13,364 was enacted to protect central bank assets.[119]

As noted by Gelpern, the 'great powers' stand ready to give less fortunate governments **12.66** extraordinary legal protections in extreme legal circumstances.[120] It is very important to trace a timeline between what has been happening in the SDRM arena and the adoption of UN Security Council Resolution No 1483/03 in order to stress the real importance of the latter. As previously explained, various scholars agree that the SDRM proposal has been shelved and it has been pinpointed that the reason behind this decision is that the 'IMF Board officially shelved the proposal as politically unfeasible'[121] as evidenced in the Report of the Managing Director to the International Monetary and Financial Committee on the IMF's Policy Agenda from April 2003.[122] It can be argued that only 40 days after the SDRM was shelved, an ad hoc SDRM was adopted by UN Security Council Resolution No 1483/03 of 22 May 2003, shielding Iraq's oil reserves from creditors. Although creditors can obtain final judgments they are not able to enforce them against oil reserves (or central bank reserves). In the informal sovereign debt restructuring framework, the adoption of a UN Security Council Resolution can work as a soft-touch alternative approach to the IMF's idea of an SDRM. It is worthy of note that oil reserves—the main asset targeted by UN resolutions—account for more than 75 per cent of Iraqi's total sources of income.[123]

(c) Domestic legislative initiatives

In the absence of a cross-border statutory multilateral solution, and to an extent inspired by **12.67** the shielding of assets in Iraq, some countries have enacted (or are considering enacting) domestic legislation to assist sovereign debtors in regaining sustainability. These initiatives are summarized in Table 12.1. Regrettably, the drafters of these laws do not seem to fully grasp the dynamics of sovereign debts and the way in which the market operates, nor the

---

[117] See *Diggs v Richardson*, 555 F 2d 848 (DC Cir 1976).

[118] Executive Order 13,303 Protecting the Development Fund for Iraq and Certain Other Property in Which Iraq Has an Interest, 68 Fed Reg 31931 (28 May 2003).

[119] Executive Order No 13,364 Modifying the Protection Granted to the Development Fund for Iraq and Certain Property in Which Iraq Has an Interest and Protecting the Central Bank of Iraq, 69 Fed Reg 70177 (29 November 2004). Other relevant Executive Orders regarding the protection of assets in the US include: (1) Executive Order 13,315 dated 28 August 2003; and (2) Executive Order 13,350 dated 29 July 2004. Finally on 22 May 2006, in accordance with section 202(d) of the National Emergencies Act (50 USC 1622(d)), the US President decided to extend the national emergency protecting the Development Fund for Iraq and certain other property in which Iraq has an interest for a year.

[120] Anna Gelpern, 'What Iraq and Argentina Might Learn from Each Other' (2005) 6(1) *Chicago Journal of International Law* 391, 414.

[121] Ibid at 399.

[122] See Report of the Managing Director to the International Monetary and Financial Committee on the IMF's Policy Agenda, available at <http://www.imf.org/external/np/omd/2003/041103.htm>.

[123] See Iraq—Letter of Intent, Memorandum of Economic and Financial Policies, and Technical Memorandum of Understanding, Baghdad, 24 September 2004, available at <http://www.imf.org/external/np/loi/2004/irq/01/index.htm>.

Table 12.1 Domestic Legislative Initiatives to Protect Sovereign Debtors

Legislative Piece	Scope/Coverage	Remedy	Status
Belgian Vulture Fund Act 2008	Shield any sums and goods under Belgian official development assistance or international cooperation.[a]	Are exempt from creditor seizure.[b]	In force
UK Debt Relief (Developing Countries) Act 2010	A 'qualifying debt' is a debt incurred before the commencement of the Act that: (1) is public or publicly guaranteed, (2) is external, (3) is a debt of a country to which the HIPC initiative applies or a potentially eligible HIPC country, and (4) in the case of a debt of a country to which the HIPC initiative applies, is incurred before a decision point is reached in respect of the country.[c]	There is a limited amount that can be recovered, which is the relevant proportion of the amount that would otherwise be recoverable in respect of the qualifying debt (or cause of action).[d] The relevant proportion is defined in Article 4 as: (a) the amount of the debt if it were reduced in accordance with the HIPC initiative (on the assumption, if it is not the case, that completion point has been reached) OVER (b) the amount of the debt without it having been so reduced.[e] Where the qualifying debt is a debt of a potentially eligible HIPC initiative country, the relevant proportion is 33%.[f]	In force
Belgian Vulture Fund Act 2015	Any repurchased loan or claim against a state when a creditor pursues an illegitimate advantage (ie a manifest disproportion between the repurchase value and its face value). In addition, one of the following criteria must be met: (1) the debtor state was in a state of insolvency or proven or imminent default at the time of the purchase of the claim; (2) the creditor has its registered office in a tax haven; (3) the creditor makes systematic use of legal proceedings to obtain a repayment on its claim; (4) the debtor state has conducted a restructuring in which the creditor has refused to participate; (5) the creditor abused the weak position of the debtor state to negotiate a manifestly unbalanced repayment agreement; and/or, (6) the full repayment of the sums claimed by the creditor would have an identifiable adverse impact on the public finances of the debtor state and is likely to jeopardize the socio-economic development of its population.	No more than the purchase price.[g] In addition, whatever the law applicable to the legal relationship between the creditor and the debtor state, no enforceable title can be obtained, and no conservatory measure or execution can be taken in Belgium.	In force
French SAPIN II 2016	Financial sovereign instruments (debt securities and contracts) if: (1) the foreign state appeared on the list of beneficiaries of official development assistance established by the development assistance committee of OECD at the time of issuance of the debt; (2) the holder of the debt acquired it while the state was in default or had proposed change to the terms of the debt (if not more than 48 months); and (3) a proposed modification, applicable to the debt obligation, has been accepted by creditors representing at least 66% of the principal amount, regardless of the threshold required, if any, for it to be valid.[h]	No precautionary measure and no enforcement measure targeting property belonging to a foreign state may be authorized by a judge at the request of the holder of a debt instrument.[i]	In force

New York Senate Bill 6627 (2021)[j]	To add Article 7 to the existing New York Banking Law to provide effective mechanisms for restructuring unsustainable sovereign and subnational debt claims (ie payment claims against a state for monies borrowed; or for the state's guarantee of, or other contingent obligation on monies borrowed).[k]	A state may invoke application of Article 7 of the NY Banking Law by filing a voluntary petition for relief with an independent body referred by the New York state senate finance committee. Within 30 days after filing its petition for relief the state shall notify all of its known creditors of its intention to negotiate a plan under this article.[l] A comprehensive audit shall be conducted by an independent body appointed by the supervisory authority.[m] The state may submit a plan to its creditors at any time, and may submit alternative plans from time to time.[n] The plan shall become effective and binding on the state and its creditors when it has been agreed by each class of creditors.[o] A class of claims has agreed to a plan if creditors holding at least 66% in amount and more than 50% in number of the claims of such class.[p]	Bill

[a] Law to prevent the seizure or transfer of public funds intended for international cooperation, in particular by the vulture fund technique, Art 2, dated 6 April 2008, available at <http://www.ejustice.just.fgov.be/mopdf/2008/05/16_1.pdf#Page8>, p. 8.

[b] See Article 2 of the Law to prevent the seizure or transfer of public funds intended for international cooperation, in particular by the vulture fund technique, dated 6 April 2008, available at <http://www.ejustice.just.fgov.be/mopdf/2008/05/16_1.pdf#Page8>, p 8.

[c] UK Debt Relief (Developing Countries) Act 2010, Art 1, available at <https://www.legislation.gov.uk/ukpga/2010/22/section/1/enacted>.

[d] Ibid, Art 3, available at <https://www.legislation.gov.uk/ukpga/2010/22/section/3/enacted>.

[e] Ibid, Art 4, available at <https://www.legislation.gov.uk/ukpga/2010/22/section/4/enacted>.

[f] Ibid.

[g] Law on the fight against the activities of vulture funds, Art 2, dated 12 July 2015, available at <http://www.ejustice.just.fgov.be/cgi_loi/change_lg.pl?language=fr&la=F&cn=2015071205&table_name=loi>.

[h] See Article L211-1 and L211-41 of the French Monetary and Financial Code, available at < https://www.legifrance.gouv.fr/codes/article_lc/LEGIARTI000032469968/>

[i] See Article 60 of Law Sapin II, available at <https://www.legifrance.gouv.fr/jorf/id/JORFTEXT000033558528>.

[j] Alexander Gladstone, 'New York Lawmakers Float Crackdown on Hedge Funds' Sovereign-Debt Tactics' (Wall Street Journal, 8 February 2021) <https://www.wsj.com/articles/new-york-lawmakers-float-crackdown-on-hedge-funds-sovereign-debt-tactics-11612780201?mod=searchresults_pos12&page=1>

[k] See §301 of New York Senate Bill S6627, available at <https://www.nysenate.gov/legislation/bills/2021/S6627>

[l] See §303 of New York Senate Bill S6627, available at <https://www.nysenate.gov/legislation/bills/2021/S6627>

[m] New York Senate Bill S6627, §304(1), available at <https://www.nysenate.gov/legislation/bills/2021/S6627>.

[n] Ibid, §305(1).

[o] Ibid, §305(4).

[p] Ibid, §305(5).

way in which restructurings are conducted. These laws fall far short of achieving the desired outcome as they are full of loopholes and/or produce some undesired effects (eg an increased funding cost or a shift in players).

(d) Voluntary principles

12.68   UNCTAD has launched a project aiming at promoting responsible sovereign lending and borrowing.[124] These voluntary principles are intended to establish clear responsibilities on both the borrower's and the lender's sides with the aim of reducing the prevalence of sovereign debt crises and promoting sustained economic growth. In the event that disputes and/or defaults occur, negotiations will be facilitated if lenders and borrowers can refer to an agreed set of standards during the negotiation phase. The parties would then not only be encouraged to follow generally accepted principles that enhance responsible practices but they would also have a common reference point in the case of a dispute. A distinctive element of these draft principles is their focus on the fiduciary duty of governments which emphasizes that sovereign borrowing and lending to sovereigns involves diverse interests, including future generations of citizens, and a wide range of public and private, domestic, and international claimants on state resources. Other issues addressed by the draft principles include: transparency and accountability, due diligence, audits, country ownership, and social responsibility. It seems that UNCTAD has given in to the original apolitical nature of these principles and lately has moved towards a more ideologically driven agenda. In some of the latest UNCTAD documents a clear push for a statutory approach and debt forgiveness can be observed, even questioning the role of the long-established multilateral bodies.[125] Part of this deviation was triggered by the UN Resolution passed '[t]owards the establishment of a multilateral legal framework for sovereign debt restructuring processes'[126] but mainly was the result of the imbalanced advisory assistance requested by UNCTAD, where the private sector is not properly represented.

12.69   The UN Ad hoc Committee on Sovereign Debt Restructuring Processes published a list of nine principles after its Third Working Session in July 2015.[127] These principles are: (1) auto-determination; (2) good faith; (3) transparency; (4) impartiality; (5) equitable treatment; (6) sovereign immunity; (7) legitimacy; (8) sustainability; and (9) majority restructuring.[128] On 10 September 2015, the UN adopted a draft resolution setting out the nine basic principles on sovereign debt restructuring published by the UN Ad hoc Committee

---

[124] In 2009 UNCTAD launched the Project to Promote Responsible Sovereign Lending and Borrowing aimed at developing a compendium of internationally recognized principles that promote and reinforce responsible sovereign lending and borrowing practices. The Principles on Promoting Responsible Sovereign Lending and Borrowing were published in 2012. See UNCTAD, Principles on Promoting Responsible Sovereign Lending and Borrowing (PRSLAB), available at <http://unctad.org/en/PublicationsLibrary/gdsddf2012misc1_en.pdf>.

[125] See UNCTAD, Sovereign Debt Workouts: Going Forward—Roadmap and Guide, April 2015, available at <http://unctad.org/en/PublicationsLibrary/gdsddf2015misc1_en.pdf>.

[126] Document A/68/L.57/Rev.1.

[127] See Press Release by the Ad hoc Committee on Sovereign Debt Restructuring Processes, available at <http://www.un.org/pga/ad-hoc-committee-on-sovereign-debt-restructuring-processes>. The Chair's report with the list of principles is available at <http://www.jubileeusa.org/fileadmin/user_upload/Resources/Policy_Archive/AHC_on_SDRP_Final_Chairs_Summary_July_24__6PM.pdf>.

[128] See *supra* n 127.

on Sovereign Debt Restructuring Processes.[129] Although not directly binding, the UN has invited all member and observer states, competent international organizations, and other relevant stakeholders to support and promote these basic principles.

A precursor of this voluntary set of commonly accepted principles are those of the IIF that launched the Principles for Stable Capital Flows and Fair Debt Restructuring (the 'IIF Principles') in 2004. The IIF Principles incorporate voluntary, market-based, flexible guidelines for the behaviour of sovereign debtors and private creditors with the aim of promoting and maintaining stable capital flows, financial stability, and sustainable growth. The IIF Principles promote crisis prevention through the pursuit of strong policies, data and policy transparency, and open communication and dialogue with creditors and investors. The IIF Principles strive for effective crisis resolution through, inter alia, good-faith negotiations with representative groups of creditors and the non-discriminatory treatment of all creditors. The IIF Principles were endorsed by the G20 Ministerial Meeting in Berlin in November 2004. The IIF Principles were then complemented in 2012 by the Addendum to the Principles for Stable Capital Flows and Fair Debt Restructuring (the 'IIF Addendum'). The IIF Addendum outlines the recommendation to assess the recent experience with sovereign debt crisis prevention, management, and resolution in the Euro Area and elsewhere; draw appropriate lessons; and make recommendations for the strengthening of the existing framework for sovereign debt crisis prevention and resolution.   **12.70**

Probably the most difficult aspect of the SDRM, which is also applicable to the initiatives of the UN and UNCTAD is not a technical one, but the political one. The next section analyses what has been done in the EU to address the Euro Area sovereign debt crisis.   **12.71**

D. The ESM: An Institution Designed to Avert Financial Crises

The severe international financial crisis and economic downturn that was sparked by problems in the US subprime mortgage market and compounded by the failure of Lehman Brothers led to a widening in budget deficits and ratios of higher public debt to gross domestic product (GDP) in many countries. This was reflected in lower public sector revenues and increased expenditures to shore up aggregate demand, and also led to a need to lend support to troubled financial institutions and to create measures to check the risk of financial panic.   **12.72**

As the financial and economic situation worsened, investors became increasingly risk-adverse and risk evaluation became very difficult. In a number of countries, the turmoil in the banking sector seems to have been tempered only by large infusions of government financial intervention that, in turn, aggravated the sovereign debt picture. For some European countries, the deterioration in borrowing conditions seemed to go beyond what underlying economic fundamentals might have called for in more normal times.   **12.73**

The Euro Area Member States (EAMSs) are of particular interest, because they have been at the epicentre of the EU sovereign debt crisis and there have been important spillover effects from   **12.74**

---

[129] See draft resolution on '*Basic Principles on Sovereign Debt Restructuring Processes*' (A/69/L.84), adopted by the UN General Assembly in New York at its Sixty-Ninth Session on 10 September 2015, with 136 Member States voting for, six against, and 41 abstentions.

one EAMS to another, to the point at which the stability of the euro area as a whole has been called into question. Greece, Ireland, Portugal, Spain (for the banking sector), and Cyprus, for example, have had to seek financial assistance from the European Commission (EC), other EAMSs, the IMF, the European Central Bank (ECB), and non-EAMSs countries in attempts to rectify public sector finances and to reduce their debt burden in an orderly manner.

12.75   The introduction of the euro was accompanied by increased intra-eurozone financial interdependence and, as it has turned out, some financial fragility and risks that have become apparent only under crisis conditions. Thus a euro-area-specific issue seems to have emerged as a component of the broader evolving international state of affairs.

12.76   The EU institutional reaction to recent European financial distress scenarios in the sovereign context is addressed in the following paragraphs. In particular, it will focus on providing a critical analysis of the treaty that created the European Stability Mechanism (ESM), an intergovernmental organization under international public law, and some suggestions regarding the challenges going forward.

1. Initial responses

12.77   In early May 2010, Greece and the European Commission (acting on behalf of the EAMSs) entered into a memorandum of understanding (MOU) for a programme to correct fiscal and external imbalances, and to restore confidence.[130] The programme's financing requirements would be covered by the EAMSs and the IMF to facilitate Greece's re-access to capital markets. The estimated 'public financing gap' for the entire length of the programme was €110 billion,[131] to be covered by means of an intergovernmental framework involving pooled matching bilateral loans provided by the EAMSs in the amount of €80 billion,[132] and an IMF Standby Arrangement in the amount of €30 billion.[133] Greece would draw on these resources throughout the programme period on an eight-to-three ratio for each disbursement.[134] The coordination and management procedures were set out in an inter-creditor agreement.[135]

---

[130] See section 5 of the MOU between the European Commission, acting on behalf of the EAMS and the Hellenic Republic, dated 3 May 2010 (unpublished, on file with the author).

[131] See section 23 of the MOU, *supra* n 128.

[132] The Loan Facility Agreement was entered into on 8 May 2010 by the Kingdom of Belgium, Ireland, Kingdom of Spain, French Republic, Italian Republic, Republic of Cyprus, Grand Duchy of Luxembourg, Republic of Malta, Kingdom of the Netherlands, Republic of Austria, Portuguese Republic, Republic of Slovenia, Slovak Republic, Republic of Finland, and the bank KfW (acting on behalf of the Federal Republic of Germany), as lenders, and the Hellenic Republic as borrower (and the bank of Greece as the agent of the borrower). The lenders, in all of their functions, rights, and obligations under the Loan Facility Agreement, act through and are represented by the EC, and have agreed to act in a coordinated manner and to channel communications (to the EC) through the Euro Working Group Chairman. The release of subsequent loans is conditioned upon the EAMS (except Greece) deciding favourably, after consultation with the ECB on the basis of the findings of verification by the EC, that the implementation of the economic policy of Greece accords with the adjustment programme or any other conditions laid down in the Council Decision on the basis of Articles 126(9) (EU Council Recommendations in re Budget Deficits) and 136 (Specific Provisions for Member States whose Currency is the Euro) TFEU and the MOU.

[133] Greece requested a Standby Arrangement in an amount equivalent to SDR26, 432.9 million (€30 billion) for a period from 9 May 2010 to 8 May 2013, which was approved on 9 May 2010.

[134] See *supra* n 128. The eight-to-three ratio has to do with the contribution ratio of the programme to which the EAMSs contributed €80 billion and the IMF, €30 billion.

[135] The intercreditor agreement was entered into on 8 May 2010 between the Kingdom of Belgium, Federal Republic of Germany, Ireland, Kingdom of Spain, French Republic, Italian Republic, Republic of Cyprus, Grand Duchy of Luxembourg, Republic of Malta, Kingdom of the Netherlands, Republic of Austria, Portuguese Republic, Republic of Slovenia, Slovak Republic, and Republic of Finland (unpublished, on file with the author).

Following the execution of these agreements, the Economic and Financial Affairs Council **12.78** (Ecofin)[136] met to address the Greek situation, which had broader eurozone implications. The Council decided to adopt a comprehensive package of measures directed at preserving financial stability in Europe.[137] These measures included the establishment of two additional sources of financial assistance to complement the initial ad hoc loan facility agreed with Greece, as follows.

- The European Financial Stabilization Mechanism (EFSM) is a mechanism based on Article 122(2) of the Treaty on the Functioning of the European Union (TFEU), which foresees financial support for Member States in difficulty resulting from factors beyond their control.[138] It consists of an intergovernmental agreement to provide financial assistance of up to €60 billion, subject to terms and conditions similar to those mandated by the IMF in the context of a joint EU–IMF support package. The EFSM was to operate independently of the facility providing medium-term financial assistance for non-euro EAMS balance-of-payments disequilibria.
- The European Financial Stability Facility (EFSF) is a temporary credit-enhanced SPV, with minimal capitalization, created to raise funds from capital markets on its investment grade rating, with the objective of providing financial assistance to distressed EAMSs at lower interest rates than otherwise would be available to them. On 26 October 2011, heads of state or government of the EAMSs agreed to enlarge the capacity of EFSF based on two approaches: partial credit enhancement to primary sovereign bonds issued by an EAMS; and the creation of one or more co-investment funds (CIFs) to allow the combination of public and private funding to enlarge the resources available to the EFSF's financial assistance instruments.[139] Financial support to EAMSs through the EFSF would be on comparable terms to the stability support loans that were advanced by EAMSs to Greece on an ad hoc basis prior to the establishment of the EFSF.

In October 2010 (after financial assistance had been provided to Greece, and while eco- **12.79** nomic and financial conditions continued to deteriorate), the EU Council agreed on the need for a permanent crisis prevention mechanism to help to safeguard the financial stability of the euro area as a whole.[140] It was resolved that consultations should be undertaken towards a limited Treaty amendment for this purpose, but not for modifying the so-called

---

[136] The Economic and Financial Affairs Council is commonly known as 'Ecofin' and is composed of the economics and finance ministers of the EU Member States, as well as budget ministers when budgetary issues are discussed. It meets once a month and covers EU policy in areas such as economic policy coordination, economic surveillance, monitoring of EU Member States' budgetary policy and public finances, the euro (legal, practical, and international aspects), financial markets and capital movements, and economic relations with third countries. One of the most important tasks of Ecofin (jointly with the European Parliament) is to prepare and adopt the budget of the European Union on a yearly basis. See <http://www.consilium.europa.eu/en/topics/budget>.

[137] See Council of the European Union, 'Extraordinary Council Meeting: Economic and Financial Affairs, Brussels, 9–10 May 2010', Press Release No 9596/10 (Presse 108) (May 2010), available at: <http://www.consilium. europa.eu/uedocs/cms_data/docs/pressdata/en/ecofin/114324.pdf>.

[138] As noted in Council Regulation (EU) No 407/2010, these difficulties may be caused by a serious deterioration in the international economic and financial environment. See Council Regulation (EU) No 407/2010 (OJ L118/1).

[139] See *Euro Summit Statement*, Brussels, 26 October 2011, available at: <http://www.consilium.europa.eu/ued ocs/cms_data/docs/pressdata/en/ec/125644.pdf>, 6, para 19.

[140] European Council, *Conclusions of the European Council, 28–29 October 2010*, EUCO 25/1/10 (REV 1), CO EUR 18 (CONCL 4), 30 November 2010, available at <http://www.consilium.europa.eu/uedocs/cms_data/docs/ pressdata/en/ec/117496.pdf>.

'no bailout' clause included in Article 125 TFEU.[141] In December 2010, the EU Council agreed that there was a need for EAMSs to establish a permanent stability mechanism—that is, the ESM. Under the Conclusions of the European Council[142] and EU Council Decision 2011/199/EU, it was resolved to add a paragraph to Article 136 TFEU to establish a permanent stability mechanism for EAMSs,[143] which is looked at next.

2. The ESM

12.80   The Treaty establishing the features of the ESM was finalized in February 2012 and came into force in October 2012, when instruments of ratification, approval, or acceptance were deposited by EAMS signatories whose initial subscriptions represented no less than 90 per cent of the total capital subscriptions.[144]

12.81   The ESM is to be an international financial institution[145] based in Luxembourg.[146] It will mobilize funding and provide financial assistance, under strict economic policy conditionality, to its members, when they are threatened or experiencing severe financing problems.[147] Its underlying *raison d'être* is to help to assure euro area financial stability, in the context of macro-economic adjustment programmes, taking into account the severity of the economic and financial imbalances of the EAMSs.[148]

12.82   The Treaty begins by restating the importance of the EU framework and its economic governance rules (eg the Stability Growth Pact (SGP),[149] and the macro-economic imbalances framework and economic governance rules of Europe, including the Treaty on Stability, Coordination and Governance[150]), whereby the ESM is to be seen as a backstop mechanism to help safeguard the financial stability of the euro area as a whole.

---

[141] See *supra* n 135.

[142] European Council, *Conclusions of the European Council, 24–25 March 2011*, EUCO 10/1/11 (REV 1), CO EUR 6 (CONCL 3), 10 January 2011, available at <http://www.consilium.europa.eu/uedocs/cms_data/docs/pressdata/en/ec/120296.pdf>.

[143] See European Council Decision 2011/199/EU of 25 March 2011 amending Article 136 of the Treaty on the Functioning of the European Union with regard to a stability mechanism for Member States whose currency is the euro, 6 April 2011 (OJ L91/1), available at <http://eur-lex.europa.eu/LexUriServ/LexUriServ.do?uri=OJ:L:2011:09 1:0001:0002:EN:PDF>. The following paragraph has been added to Article 136 TFEU: 'The Member States whose currency is the euro may establish a stability mechanism to be activated if indispensable to safeguard the stability of the euro area as a whole. The granting of any required financial assistance under the mechanism will be made subject to strict conditionality.'

[144] See Art 48 of the ESM Treaty.

[145] See Art 1(1) of the ESM Treaty.

[146] See Art 31(1) of the ESM Treaty.

[147] See Arts 3 and 12 of the ESM Treaty.

[148] See Art 12 of the ESM Treaty.

[149] The Stability and Growth Pact (SGP) is a set of rules designed to ensure that countries in the EU pursue sound public finances and coordinate their fiscal policies by enforcing fiscal responsibility. It is based primarily on Articles 121 and 126 TFEU. Specifically, each country must maintain an annual budget deficit that is no greater than 3 per cent of GDP and the national debt must be lower than 60 per cent of its GDP.

[150] These include: (1) the 'Six Pack'; (2) the Treaty on Stability, Coordination and Governance (TSCG) or 'Fiscal Compact'; and (3) the 'Two Pack'. The Six Pack is made up of five Regulations and one directive, ie EU secondary law, which entered into force on 13 December 2011. It applies to all 27 Member States. The Six Pack addresses fiscal surveillance and macro-economic surveillance under the 'Macroeconomic Imbalance Procedure' (Regulation (EU) No 1174/2011 and 1176/2011). The TSCG is an intergovernmental agreement (not EU law) signed by all EU Member States except Croatia, the Czech Republic, and the UK on 2 March 2012. The fiscal part of the TSCG is referred to as the 'Fiscal Compact' and works as a stricter version of the Stability and Growth Pact. The 'Two Pack' is made up of two regulations, EU Regulations 472/2013 and 473/2013, which are applicable to EAMSs only (based on Art 136 TFEU) aiming at further strengthening the surveillance mechanisms in the euro area.

Use of the ESM is to be limited to extreme circumstances; access to financial assistance is **12.83** subject to strict economic policy conditionality, accompanied by a macro-economic adjustment programme, and a rigorous analysis of public debt sustainability is mandatory. Like the EFSM and EFSF, the ESM will call for active participation of the IMF on both technical and financial aspects. It is important to stress that one of the Recitals of the Treaty states that financial assistance to the Treaty's contracting parties (ESM members) will be limited to cases in which regular access to market financing is impaired.[151] Thus lending is restricted to circumstances in which no conventional party would be willing to lend[152]— that is, the ESM will be acting as ILOLR. The role of ILOLR is usually played by the IMF,[153] but the Recital states that the ESM will enjoy preferred creditor status in a similar fashion to the IMF, while accepting the preferred creditor status of the IMF over the ESM.[154] It is worth noticing that IMF creditor priority has not been formally established anywhere and is de facto. The Treaty is the first formal document in which it has been officially acknowledged. Therefore, the treaty has created a second super-priority creditor, although one that is subordinate to the IMF.

The required funding is obtained either by issuing financial instruments, by entering into **12.84** financial or other agreements with third parties, and/or by means of arrangements with ESM members.[155] The ESM will use risk management tools to minimize potential adverse outcomes.[156]

The ESM has an authorized capital stock of €700 billion[157] divided into paid-in shares (€80 **12.85** billion)[158] and callable shares (€620 billion).[159] If an ESM member fails to meet the required payment under a capital call,[160] an appeal will be made to all other ESM members to cover the shortfall,[161] thereby ensuring that the ESM receives the total amount of required paid-in capital. Experience with the EFSF, which has required a capital increase and the use of leverage to increase its financing capacity as the crisis worsened, suggests that, to reassure

---

[151] See Recital 13 of the ESM Treaty.

[152] It is worth noting that, theoretically speaking, there could always be someone willing to lend if the associated risk is properly priced. So far, during the EU sovereign debt crisis, when financing rates have gone above a 7 per cent return (and have remained at such rate or increased), official financial assistance has been provided.

[153] Regarding the ILOLR role of the IMF, see Sachs, *supra* n 30; Charles W Calomiris, 'The IMF's Imprudent Role as Lender of Last Resort' (1998) 17(3) *Cato Journal* 275; Stanley Fischer, 'On the Need for an International Lender of Last Resort' (1999) 13 *Journal of Economic Perspectives* 85; Adam Lerrick and Allan H Meltzer, 'Blueprint for an International Lender of Last Resort' (2003) 50 *JME* 289; Giancarlo Corsetti, Bernardo Guimarães, and Nouriel Roubini, *The Tradeoff between an International Lender of Last Resort to Deal with Liquidity Crisis and Moral Hazard Distortions: A Model of the IMF's Catalytic Finance Approach*, IMF Seminar Series Research Paper 03/149 (June 2003).

[154] See Recital 13 ESM Treaty. Note that the decision to forgo the preferred creditor status in the Financial Assistance Facility Agreement (FAFA) for the recapitalization of the Spanish banks was the results of negotiations conducted by the EFSF which has a *pari passu* status and was envisaging an assignment to ESM.

[155] See Art 3 of the ESM Treaty.

[156] See Art 21(3) of the ESM Treaty.

[157] See Art 8(1) of the ESM Treaty.

[158] See Art 8(2) of the ESM Treaty. The paid-in capital can be used to purchase top-rated liquid sovereign bonds for investment purposes but not for the purchase of sovereign bonds under ESM primary and/or secondary market intervention. See ESM FAQ, 23 March 2015, available at <http://www.esm.europa.eu>.

[159] See Art 25(2) of the ESM Treaty.

[160] See Arts 8(4) and 9 of the ESM Treaty.

[161] See Art 25(2) of the ESM Treaty.

markets, it would have been prudent to have provided the ESM with a more substantial capital base and/or allowed a more flexible approach.

12.86   The capital participation of ESM members is based on their central banks' subscription to the ECB's capital, pursuant to Article 29 of Protocol (No 4) of the Statute of the European System of Central Banks (ESCB) and the ECB.[162] The ESM will assume tasks that would have been previously performed by the EFSM and EFSF.[163] Total lending outstanding will have an initial ceiling of €500 billion.

12.87   The governance structure of the ESM is complicated because it comprises a board of governors, a board of directors, and also establishes the position of a managing director with specific tasks. The board of governors is in charge of setting the guidelines and policies of the ESM, while the board of directors is entrusted with the day-to-day operations of the ESM in accordance with the Treaty and its by-laws.[164] Considering the division of responsibilities, an analogy can be made with the governance structure of a company regarding shareholders' meetings and their role, as well as board of directors' meetings and their agenda. However, each ESM member, irrespective of its percentage participation, has only one vote. Each ESM participant appoints one member to the board of governors,[165] while, in turn, each governor appoints a member to the board of directors;[166] board appointments are revocable at any time.[167] Appointments to both boards also include the appointments of alternates, in case of absence of the principal or impossibility to participate. Both the board of governors and the board of directors require a double threshold quorum of two-thirds of the members, with voting rights representing at least two-thirds of the voting rights.[168] Decisions made by the board of governors can be adopted either by mutual agreement (that is, unanimity, although abstentions do not prevent a mutual agreement decision)[169] or an 80 per cent qualified majority.[170] It is worth stressing that the Treaty contemplates an emergency voting proceeding for situations in which the EU Commission and the ECB conclude that a failure to urgently adopt a decision to grant or implement financial assistance can threaten the economic and financial sustainability of the euro area. In these cases (that is, under an emergency voting proceeding), the grant of financial assistance, the economic policy conditionality, and the choice of instruments has to be adopted by unanimity, meeting the requirement of a qualified majority of 85 per cent of the votes cast.[171] Decisions

---

[162]   OJ C115, 9 May 2008, 230.

[163]   There was a transitional period between the establishment of the ESM and until the phasing out of the EFSF. During this time, the consolidated ESM and EFSF lending was not to exceed €500 billion (see Art 39 of the ESM Treaty), also subject to the authorization of the board of governors in assuming the rights and obligations of the EFSF (Art 40 of the ESM Treaty). As of 1 July 2013 the EFSF may no longer engage in new financing programmes or enter into new loan facility agreements, being the ESM the sole and permanent mechanism to deal with new requests for financial assistance by EAMS. The EFSF will remain active rolling-over bonds issued to finance the loans for the three EFSF programme countries (Ireland, Portugal, and Greece).

[164]   The ESM by-laws are going to be adopted by the board of governors (see Art 5(7)(c) of the ESM Treaty). The first by-laws were adopted on 8 October 2012.

[165]   See Art 5(1) of the ESM Treaty.

[166]   See Art 6(1) of the ESM Treaty.

[167]   See Arts 5(1) and 6(1) of the ESM Treaty.

[168]   See Art 4(2) of the ESM Treaty.

[169]   See Art 4(3) of the ESM Treaty.

[170]   See Art 4(5) of the ESM Treaty.

[171]   See Art 4(4) of the ESM Treaty.

of the board of directors can be adopted by mutual agreement, qualified majority, and/or simple majority.[172]

Any ESM member who fails to comply with its financial obligations (eg paid-in shares, calls of capital, or reimbursement of the financial assistance) will not be able to exercise its voting rights until the situation is rectified.[173]   **12.88**

The managing director is the legal representative of the ESM, and will chair the meetings of the board of directors and shall participate in the meetings of the board of governors.[174]   **12.89**

There will be an auditing board comprising five independent members not taking instructions from the ESM governing bodies, the ESM members, or any other public or private body.[175] The accounts will be subject to external audit.[176] The members of the auditing board are appointed by the board of governors, and shall include two members from the supreme audit institutions of the ESM members and one from the European Court of Auditors.[177]   **12.90**

ESM financial assistance for stability support can consist of: precautionary financial assistance;[178] financial assistance for the recapitalization of financial institutions of an ESM member;[179] loans;[180] a primary[181] and/or secondary market support facility.[182] All these types of stability support are subject to strict conditionality, which may range from a macro-economic adjustment programme to a continuous respect of pre-established eligibility conditions.[183]   **12.91**

ESM members undertook an irrevocable and unconditional obligation to provide their respective contributions to the authorized capital stock,[184] which also is the limit of their liability.[185] The board of governors has the mandate to establish a reserve[186] fund and, if required, other funds.[187] In the event of ESM losses, these will be covered by (in order of priority): (i) the reserve fund; (ii) the paid-in capital; and (iii) the appropriate amount of the authorized unpaid capital, which will be called in if needed[188] to cover a shortfall between the paid-in capital and the total subscribed capital.[189]   **12.92**

---

[172] See Art 4(2) of the ESM Treaty.
[173] See Art 4(8) of the ESM Treaty.
[174] See Art 7 of the ESM Treaty.
[175] See Art 30(1) and (2) of the ESM Treaty.
[176] See Art 29 of the ESM Treaty.
[177] See Art 30(1) of the ESM Treaty.
[178] See Art 14 of the ESM Treaty.
[179] See Art 15 of the ESM Treaty. This can be done through loans to governments or directly recapitalizing the financial institutions. On 8 December 2014 the ESM Board of Governors adopted the ESM direct recapitalization instrument (DRI) which has been introduced to support the euro area's banking union and may be used in very specific circumstances to recapitalize euro area financial institutions as a last resort when other instruments (including the bail-in mechanism) have been exhausted.
[180] See Art 16 of the ESM Treaty.
[181] See Art 17 of the ESM Treaty.
[182] See Art 18 of the ESM Treaty.
[183] See Arts 12(1) and 13(3) of the ESM Treaty.
[184] See Art 8(4) of the ESM Treaty.
[185] See Art 8(5) of the ESM Treaty.
[186] The board of governors created the reserve fund with the net income generated by ESM operations and the proceeds of the financial sanctions received from ESM members under the multilateral surveillance procedure, the excessive deficit procedure, and the macro-economic imbalances procedure established under the TFEU.
[187] See Art 24(1) of the ESM Treaty
[188] See Art 25(1) of the ESM Treaty.
[189] See Art 9(3) of the ESM Treaty.

12.93   Any new Member State adopting the euro will become an ESM member with full rights and obligations as from the entry into force of a decision of the EU Council taken in accordance with Article 140(2) TFEU.[190] New ESM members will be admitted on the same terms and conditions as existing ESM members,[191] and will receive shares in the ESM in exchange for their capital contributions.[192]

12.94   The Treaty encourages EU Member States, EAMSs, and non-EAMSs to provide financial assistance on an ad hoc basis (eg Denmark, Sweden, and the UK provided bilateral assistance to Ireland to complement the EFSM–EFSF–IMF programme).[193] In such cases, the EAMSs (ie ESM members) will grant equivalent creditor status to those involved in bilateral lending alongside the ESM.[194] Recital 14 of the Treaty reads: '[EAMSs] will support equivalent creditor status of the ESM and that of other States lending bilaterally in coordination with the ESM'. The wording is not very clear and it can lead to conflicting views regarding the creditor status of other bilateral lenders. However, it can be understood that third parties (eg a non-EAMS or even a non-European state) lending on a bilateral basis will have a status equal to the preferred creditor status of the ESM.

12.95   Non-EAMSs providing financial assistance on an ad hoc basis will participate as observers in the ESM meetings when financial assistance and monitoring are discussed, and will have access to all available information in this respect.[195]

12.96   The 28 EU Member States have authorized the EAMS to request the EU Commission and the ECB to perform the tasks required by the Treaty.[196] The Commission and the European Council are entrusted with post-programme surveillance within the framework established by Articles 121 and 136 TFEU.[197]

12.97   Any disputes concerning the interpretation and application of the Treaty arising among the ESM members, or between them and the ESM, should be submitted to the board of governors.[198] If the decision of the board of governors is contested, the dispute will be submitted to the jurisdiction of the Court of Justice of the European Union (CJEU), following the criteria set forth in Article 273 TFEU.[199]

12.98   The procedure for the granting of the financial assistance is as follows.[200]

(a)   An ESM member makes a formal request for financial assistance to the chairperson of the board of governors.

(b)   Upon receipt of a request, the chairperson will request the European Commission (in liaison with the ECB) to:

---

[190]   See Art 2(1) of the ESM Treaty. This was the case with the accession of Latvia and Lithuania.
[191]   See Arts 2(2) and 44 of the ESM Treaty.
[192]   See Art 2(3) of the ESM Treaty.
[193]   See Recital 9 of the ESM Treaty.
[194]   See Recital 14 of the ESM Treaty.
[195]   See Arts 5(4), 6(3), and 38 of the ESM Treaty.
[196]   See Recital 10 of the ESM Treaty.
[197]   See Recital 17 of the ESM Treaty.
[198]   See Art 37(2) of the ESM Treaty.
[199]   See Art 37(3) of the ESM Treaty.
[200]   See Art 13 of the ESM Treaty.

(i) assess the existence of a risk to the financial stability of the euro area as a whole;[201]

(ii) undertake (jointly with the IMF) a debt sustainability analysis (DSA) of the ESM member in distress;[202] and

(iii) assess the financing needs of the ESM member[203] and the type of private sector involvement required (that is, maintenance of exposure or a reprofiling/ restructuring).[204]

(c) Based on the Commission's assessment, the board of governors may decide to grant—in principle—financial assistance to the ESM member.[205]

(d) If the decision of the board of governors is favourable, the Commission (jointly with the IMF and in liaison with the ECB) will negotiate with the ESM member an MOU detailing the economic policy conditionality, contained in a macro-economic adjustment programme, to be attached to the financial assistance.[206]

(e) The draft MOU will be considered by the board of governors and, subject to its approval, the Commission will sign the MOU on behalf of the ESM.[207]

(f) The board of directors will approve the financial assistance agreement drafted by the managing director, detailing the technical aspects of the financial assistance and the disbursement of the first tranche.[208]

(g) A warning system will be put in place by the ESM to ensure that it receives the repayments due under financial assistance in a timely manner.[209]

(h) The Commission (jointly with the IMF and in liaison with the ECB) will be entrusted with monitoring the compliance with the economic policy conditionality attached to the financial assistance.[210] A mutual agreement decision by the board of directors, based on the monitoring performed by the European Commission, is required prior to any further tranche disbursement in the case of financial assistance for the recapitalization of financial institutions or loans.[211]

An additional feature, as a complementary measure to safeguard the stability of the euro, is the mandatory inclusion of standardized and identical CACs as of July 2013 in the terms and conditions of all new euro area government securities with maturities of more than one year.[212] This measure was brought forward and came into force on 1 January 2013. It is ironic that a treaty was required to do this, despite the April 2003 statement by EU Member States of their intention to lead by example.[213] That same year, the Ecofin Chairman (a

12.99

---

[201] See Art 13(1)(a) of the ESM Treaty.
[202] See Art 13(1)(b) of the ESM Treaty.
[203] See Art 13(1)(c) of the ESM Treaty.
[204] See Recital 12 of the ESM Treaty.
[205] See Art 13(2) of the ESM Treaty.
[206] See Art 13(3) of the ESM Treaty.
[207] See Art 13(4) of the ESM Treaty.
[208] See Art 13(3) and (5) of the ESM Treaty.
[209] See Art 13(6) of the ESM Treaty.
[210] See Art 13(7) of the ESM Treaty.
[211] See Arts 15(5) and 16(5) of the ESM Treaty.
[212] See Art 12(3) of the ESM Treaty.
[213] See Ecofin, *Implementation of the EU Commitment on Collective Action Clauses in Documentation of International Debt Issuance*, ECFIN/CEFCPE(2004)REP/50483, Brussels, 12 November 2004, available at <http://europa.eu/efc/sub_committee/pdf/cacs_en.pdf>.

former Minister of Economy and Finance of Greece) stated that 'EU Member States will no longer issue such bonds without any CACs'.[214] It may be that the Treaty is not the most suitable place for the inclusion of such a provision. The inclusion of CACs is something on which the EU, as a whole, has been working since 2003 and it may be that the requirement would be more appropriately included elsewhere, where it would have broader application ie to all EU Member States and not just EAMS. Nevertheless, such an initiative should be welcomed, although extended to non-EAMSs.

3. A critical analysis of the ESM

12.100   The ESM is another step in strengthening the economic aspect of the union and should be welcomed as the latest edifice in the international architecture to prevent and/or minimize the effects of financial crises. However, the foregoing analysis suggests that considerable room for improvement remains. The new mechanism does not significantly change what the IMF could do, except that it creates a European-centred institution. The latest draft of the ESM Treaty has reduced the private sector involvement. In addition, the granting of preferred creditor status can produce a crowding-out effect.

12.101   The financing capacity of the ESM clearly seems to be at odds with a realistic appraisal of potential requirements. The different pools of financial assistance that have been temporary created until the ESM became operative collectively exceed the ESM's financing capacity. Additionally, some observers have estimated that, in a scenario of distress involving countries such as Italy or Spain, the €700 billion maximum capacity of the ESM would be insufficient to calm financial markets if others were to join in turmoil.[215] It has been suggested that at least €1 trillion may be required.[216]

12.102   The ESM's scope for action may be too restrictive. The EFSF, the temporary SPV created to provide liquidity assistance, potentially has greater capacity owing to its maximizing lending techniques (that is, partial credit enhancement to primary sovereign bonds issued by an EAMS in the form of partial protection certificates and the creation of one or more CIFs).[217] However, it is worthy of note that the Treaty authorizes the ESM board of governors to reassess and eventually increase the authorized capital stock.[218]

12.103   It should also be kept in mind that extensive financial assistance from the ESM could inadvertently reduce the supply of funds from private lenders, since their claims would be subordinate to those of the ESM, as an ILOLR. So far, the ILOLR role has been fulfilled by the IMF. On the other hand, bilateral and private creditors may see their positions enhanced,

---

[214] Statement by Mr Christodoulakis, Minister of Economy and Finance of Greece, in his capacity as Chairman of the EU Council of Economic and Finance Ministers, to the International Monetary and Financial Committee, 12 April 2003. Ironically, perhaps, not all post-2003 Greek government bonds included a CAC.

[215] Adrian Blundell-Wignall, 'Solving the Financial and Sovereign Debt Crisis in Europe' (2011) 2 OECD Journal of Financial Market Trends 1, available at <http://www.oecd.org/dataoecd/14/25/49481502.pdf>.

[216] John McDermott, 'China to Europe: That's Sure a Nice EFSF that You Have There', *FT Alphaville blog*, 28 October 2011, available online at <http://ftalphaville.ft.com//2011/10/28/715586/china-to-europe-thats-a-sure-nice-efsf-you-have-there>.

[217] Technical work is under way to be submitted to the ESM governing bodies in view of extending to the ESM the partial protection certificates and the co-investment funds to support market access for countries within a full or precautionary programme. See ESM FAQ, 2 September 2015, available at <http://www.esm.europa.eu>.

[218] See Art 10 of the ESM Treaty.

by virtue of the assistance provided by the ESM to the EAMSs and the associated policy conditionality. While the ESM will be providing ILOLR lending and therefore should be granted priority, its priority will not be exempt from challenges in courts of law, since it is not pre-established, but rather imposed by the Treaty (particularly in instances of pre-incurred debts). On a more practical note, to the extent that it diminishes perceived repayment prospects, the preferred creditor status assigned to the ESM (jointly with, although inferior to, that of the IMF) may reduce the private sector demand for sovereign debt and thereby increase public sector financing costs.

The role of the ESM vis-à-vis that of the IMF raises some questions. The ESM has been **12.104** designed to work very closely with the IMF. For example, upon the request for ESM stability support by a distressed EAMS, the European Commission, together with the IMF and in liaison with the ECB, will assess the actual financing needs of the EAMS. Then, the Commission and the IMF (jointly with the ECB) will negotiate an MOU with the EAMS, outlining a macro-economic adjustment programme. The Commission and the IMF (jointly with the ECB) will be responsible for monitoring compliance with policy conditionality. Thus there is a close relationship between the ESM (and the EU institutions) and the IMF. In common with the IMF, the ESM will be providing financial assistance in exchange for conditionality. In conclusion, one might ask whether it is appropriate to create another international organization, under public international law with super-priority, which will replicate some of the functions of the IMF, but lack its experience, credibility, resources, and long-established ad hoc super-priority.

4. An ESM add-on

With the continuous deterioration of the sovereign debt portfolio of the EAMSs, it is not **12.105** impossible that the 'unique and exceptional' nature of the Greek restructuring[219] in relation to the private sector involvement might need to be repeated. The differentiating element is that the debt instruments of other EAMS are not majorly governed by their own domestic laws, as was the case in Greece and which facilitated the retrofitting of CACs.[220] Therefore constraining holdout creditors might not be a simple task.

Buchheit et al[221] argue that EAMSs can immunize the assets of an EAMS (held within the **12.106** EU) in a similar fashion to what was done in the Iraqi case[222] by means of a simple addition to the ESM Treaty—that is, the inclusion of an additional Article to the text of the Treaty granting immunity from judicial process to the assets and revenue streams of any EAMS who is receiving stability support from the ESM. The aim of this provision would be to prevent any form of attachment, garnishment, execution, injunctive relief, or similar forms of

---

[219] See Council of the European Union, Statement by the Heads of State or Government of the Euro Area and EU Institutions, Brussels, 21 July 2011, available at <http://www.consilium.europa.eu/uedocs/cms_data/docs/pressd ata/en/ec/123978.pdf>, para 6; Euro Summit Statement, Brussels, 26 October 2011, available at <http://www. consilium.europa.eu/uedocs/cms_data/docs/pressdata/en/ec/125644.pdf>, para 15.

[220] In the case of the Greek restructuring, the Greek Parliament passed Act 4050/12 which resolved to retrofit CACs in the bonds governed by Greek law. Therefore, all Greek law governed bonds could be restructured by the will of the majority using the newly introduced CACs.

[221] Lee Buchheit, Mitu Gulati, and Ignacio Tirado, *The Problem of Holdout Creditors in Eurozone Sovereign Debt Restructurings*, Duke Law School Working Papers (January 2013), available at <http://scholarship.law.duke.edu/ faculty_scholarship/2808>.

[222] See section I.C.3.b.

judicial process by any claimant who was eligible to participate in a restructuring exercise under a 'private sector involvement' initiative as part of an ESM provision of financial assistance. The authors also explain that such immunity from process would protect the provision of financial support for the restabilization of the economy, but shall automatically expire when all amounts due to the ESM have been repaid in full.

12.107   Another important element highlighted by Buchheit et al[223] is that such a measure would not be effective if it were not replicated by other EU Member States (although non-EAMS), such as the UK. In this sense, the authors argue that the UK might wish to incorporate such immunities into its own law to prevent driving financial transactions away from London. However, this might not be a simple task, since it might have a retroactive effect on previous debt obligations, and would clash with party autonomy, the sanctity of contracts and the respect for the rule of law, long-established principles under English law. The UK supreme Court has noted that '[d]espite statutory inroads, party autonomy is at the heart of English commercial law'.[224] Lord Neuberger had previously stressed that it is desirable that, so far as possible, the courts give effect to contractual terms which parties have agreed. And there is a particularly strong case for autonomy in cases of complex financial instruments.[225]

E. The Use of CACs, Exit Consent, and Term Enhancements

12.108   The use of CACs and exit consents in the sovereign debt context are two market-oriented techniques that migrated from corporate bond practice and were developed as a response to the holdout problem and the IMF's proposal of a statutory approach. These two are complemented by the use of contractual term enhancements. The analysis of these two techniques, jointly with the contractual term enhancers will follow.

1. Collective action clauses

12.109   Collective action clauses are clauses that sometimes are included in the prospectus of a bond issuance and require the interaction of bondholders to perform an action provided for in said clause. Nowadays, the inclusion of CACs in sovereign bond issuances has become an industry standard. Issuers follow the standardized ICMA model CACs. There are four different types of CACs. These are:[226] (1) collective representation clauses;[227] (2) majority action clauses;[228] (3) sharing clauses;[229] and (4) acceleration clauses.[230]

12.110   Since CACs is the 'genus' that comprises different 'species' which entail a 'collective action' (including particularly majority action clauses, which are the most developed in the area of

---

[223] Buchheit et al, *supra* n 219.

[224] *Belmont Park Investments PTY Limited v BNY Corporate Trustee Services Limited and Lehman Brothers Special Financing Inc*, [2011] UKSC 38, para 103.

[225] *Perpetual Trustee Company Ltd and Another v BNY Corporate Trustee Services Ltd and Others*, [2010] Ch 347.

[226] See Liz Dixon and David Wall, 'Collection Action Problems and Collective Action Clauses', *Financial Stability Review*, June 2000.

[227] Collective representation clauses are intended to coordinate representation of the bondholders as a group.

[228] Majority action clauses are clauses that provide for an action to be taken or adopted by a majority decision.

[229] These clauses provide that any proceeds obtained from the debtor would be shared among all the creditors on a pro rata basis.

[230] These are common clauses included in US bonds issued through a fiscal agent agreement which require 25 per cent of the outstanding bonds to accelerate un-matured principal upon an event of default.

sovereign debt); the widely used terms 'collective action clauses' or 'CACs' are used interchangeably with 'majority action clauses', unless otherwise specified.

Majority action clauses have been the focus of the international financial architecture since **12.111** the endorsement of the G10 Rey Report in 1996.[231] Former US Under Secretary John B Taylor was the father of this approach.[232] Since the Rey Report, majority action clauses were promoted by the official sector and many academics and have been effectively incorporated in bond issuances. As a result of the Greek sovereign debt crisis, on 26 July 2011, the Economic and Financial Committee (EFC) Sub-Committee on EU Sovereign Debt Markets distributed for comment by market participants and other stakeholders a draft model CAC to be included in all euro-area sovereign debt aiming at facilitating future restructuring processes. After the consultation process, the EFC Sub-Committee approved a model CAC. On 2 February 2012, the Treaty Establishing the European Stability Mechanism was signed stating that '[c]ollective action clauses shall be included, as of 1 January 2013, in all new euro area government securities, with maturity above one year, in a way which ensures that their legal impact is identical'.[233] As a consequence, the model CAC has become mandatory in all new euro-area sovereign debt issued on or after 1 January 2013. In addition to this, the ICMA has worked with its members and other public sector and private sector representatives on a revised and updated CAC and a new standard *pari passu* clause for inclusion in the terms and conditions of sovereign debt. The IMF in October 2014 has strongly endorsed the use of CACs.[234] Therefore, special focus will be provided on CACs.[235]

CACs enable the amendment of any of the terms and conditions of the bonds—including **12.112** the payment terms—if the required majority therein established is obtained. The use of CACs proposes that the sovereign borrowers and their creditors put a package of new collective action clauses in the bonds that describe as precisely as possible what happens if a country decides that it has to restructure its debt.[236] This would 'prevent a minority of creditors from blocking negotiations with the debtor'[237] and create a more orderly and predictable workout process.[238] These clauses would represent a decentralized, market-centred approach because the debtor and creditors would have determined both the contracts and

---

[231] See the 'Resolution of Sovereign Liquidity Crises' (May 1996) drafted by a working group under the auspices of the G10 Deputies—commonly referred to as the 'G10 Report' or the 'Rey Report' (named after Jean-Jacques Rey).

[232] Taylor, *supra* n 18.

[233] See para 3 of Art 12 of the ESM Treaty.

[234] See IMF, 'Strengthening the Contractual Framework to Address Collective Action Problems in Sovereign Debt Restructuring', *supra* n 25.

[235] For an elaboration of CACs see G10, 'Report of the G10 Working Group on Contractual Clauses', 26 September 2002; IMF, 'Collective Action Clauses in Sovereign Bond Contracts—Encouraging Greater Use' (prepared by the Policy Development and Review, International Capital Markets and Legal Departments in consultation with other Departments), 6 June 2002 and 'The Design and Effectiveness of Collective Action Clauses' (prepared by the Legal Department in consultation with the Policy Development and Review and the International Capital Markets Departments), 6 June 2002, both available at <http://www.imf.org>; Mark Gugiatti and Anthony Richards, 'Do Collective Action Clauses Influence Bond Yields? New Evidence from Emerging Markets', Reserve Bank of Australia, Research Discussion Paper 2003-02, March 2003; Anna Gelpern, 'How Collective Action is Changing Sovereign Debt', IFLR, May 2003, at 19–23; Stephen Choy and Mitu G Gulati, 'Innovation in Boilerplate Contracts: The Case of Sovereign Bonds' (2004) 53 Emory L J 929; Michael Bradley and Mitu Gulati, *Collective Action Clauses for the Eurozone, Review of Finance* (2013); Lee Buchheit and Mitu Gulati, 'Drafting a Model Collective Action Clause for Eurozone Sovereign Bonds' (2011) 6(3) *Capital Markets Law Journal*; Mark Weidemaier and Mitu Gulati, 'A People's History of Collective Action Clauses' (2013) 54(1) *Virginia Journal of International Law*.

[236] Taylor, *supra* n 18.

[237] Dodd, *supra* n 10 at 3.

[238] Taylor, *supra* n 18.

the workout process contained in the contracts on their own terms[239] at the moment of issuance of the debt.

12.113   The origin of these clauses under English law can be traced back to 1879, when debtors facing liquidity problems were faced with no alternative but liquidation, which they wanted to avoid.[240] In the United States, the use of CACs in the sovereign debt context was not widely accepted as in English law due to section 316(b) of the Trust Indenture Act of 1939 (TIA)[241] that expressly states that the amount due under a publicly issued corporate bond cannot be affected without the consent of each bondholder and provides that a deferment of a maximum of three years is acceptable upon the approval of 75 per cent of the bondholders. As noted by Buchheit and Gulati, although the TIA is not applicable to foreign sovereign bonds issued in the US, the amendment clauses included in such sovereign bonds have almost invariably followed the TIA-driven approach to amendments (ie unanimity for payment terms).[242] This practice changed after 2003 when Mexico and Brazil issued bonds governed by New York law including CACs.

12.114   Currently, the inclusion of these clauses in sovereign bonds is optional (except for euro-area Member States) and often depends on the market convention.[243] While bonds issued under trust deeds and fiscal agency agreements governed by English law contain CACs (customary practice), they are not included in bonds governed by New York law issued before 2003, including Brady bonds.[244] These clauses, however, have been excluded from bonds issued under New York law as a matter of practice and not due to any legal impediment. However, as of 2003 there has been a widespread use of CACs in bond issuances including those issued under New York law.

12.115   CACs found in international sovereign bonds that have been restructured consist only of: (1) majority action (restructuring) provisions, which enable a qualified majority to bind a minority to a restructuring plan (including payment terms) either before or after default; and (2) majority enforcement provisions, which enable a qualified majority to limit the ability of a minority to enforce their rights following a default.[245]

12.116   In 2002 Taylor proposed the inclusion of a new package of clauses based on the following template of CACs:[246]

> (1) *Majority Action Clauses*: designed to empower a super-majority (often 75 per cent) of bondholders to agree to a change in payment terms in a manner that is binding on all bondholders, thereby preventing holdouts.

---

[239] Ibid.

[240] See Sir Francis B Palmer, *Company Precedents for Use in Relation to Companies Subject to the Companies Acts 1862 to 1900: With Copious Notes* (9th edn, 1903).

[241] USC 15 § 77 et seq.

[242] Buchheit and Gulati, *supra* n 11 at 1329.

[243] Report by the Secretariat of the United Nations Conference on Trade and Development, New York and Geneva 2001, p 144, available at <http://www.unctad.org/en/docs/tdr2001_en.pdf> (Trade and Development).

[244] IMF, 'Involving the Private Sector in the Resolution of Financial Crisis—Restructuring International Sovereign Bonds' (prepared by the Policy Development and Review and Legal Departments) p 4, available at <http://www.imf.org/external/pubs/ft/series/03/IPS.pdf>.

[245] Ibid at 4 and 9.

[246] Taylor, *supra* n 18 at 3.

(2) *Collective Representation Clauses*: designed to establish a representative forum (such as a trustee or committee) for coordinating negotiations between the issuer and the bondholders and to empower it to initiate litigation, at the behest of a specified majority of bondholders.

(3) *'Cooling-off' Period Clauses*: designed to provide a cooling-off period between the date when the sovereign notifies its creditors that it wants to restructure and the date that the representative is chosen, setting a fixed time limit. During this temporary suspension, a deferral of payments might be necessary and the possibility of such suspension or deferral should be incorporated in the clause along with appropriate penalties. During the cooling-off period, bondholders would be prevented from initiating litigation.

The official sector, however, in addition to the Taylor proposals, supports the inclusion of **12.117** the standard 'sharing clause' as in syndicated loans agreements (along with representation clauses and majority action clauses) because this ensures that all payments made by the debtor are shared among the creditors on a pro rata basis.[247] The official sector also believes that if such a clause is included in bonds, it would help to prevent maverick litigation, rogue creditors, and vultures—even after the cooling-off period proposed by Taylor.[248] Orderly restructuring would then result. Moreover, some speculate that the absence of the 'sharing clause' in the Brady bonds has made litigation a more attractive option for the new class of creditors.[249]

On practical grounds, it is very difficult to enforce a sharing clause in a bond issuance. It **12.118** should be borne in mind that there is a shift of responsibility (and liability) to the creditor that successfully collects. This type of clause will not be effective in fiscal agency structures due to practical reasons.

Since the Mexican debt crisis in 1998, the official sector has been urging emerging-market **12.119** borrowers to include the aforementioned CACs in bond contracts in efforts to improve communication with bondholders and to facilitate bond restructuring.[250] The G10 agreed to work with emerging-market countries and creditors to incorporate standardized contingency clauses[251] into debt contracts, and to simultaneously coordinate with the IMF to provide incentives for the adoption of these clauses.[252] The IMF has noted that debt instruments governed by UK and Japanese law have traditionally included CACs and that 75 per cent of the debt instruments issued under New York law nowadays also include CACs.[253]

---

[247] For a detailed description of the object and purpose of this clause as well as the differences between the US and UK in the use of this clause, see Lee Buchheit, *How to Negotiate Eurocurrency Loan Agreements* (IFLR, 2nd edn) 82–83.

[248] Trade and Development, *supra* n 239 at 143.

[249] See Philip J Power, 'Sovereign Debt: The Rise of the Secondary Market and its Implications for Future Restructurings' (1996) 64 *Fordham Law Review* 2701.

[250] Trade and Development, *supra* n 239 at 143.

[251] These include majority action clauses, engagement clauses, and clauses regulating the conditions under which a rescheduling or a restructuring would be initiated.

[252] See Richard H Clarida, 'Remarks at the Conference on The Role of the Official and Private Sectors in Resolving International Financial Crises' (23–24 July 2002).

[253] See IMF, 'Strengthening the Contractual Framework to Address Collective Action Problems in Sovereign Debt Restructuring', supra n 25 at 17.

Unfortunately, some sovereign borrowers may exclude CACs deliberately to demonstrate to the market that there is no possibility of restructuring.[254]

12.120 Further discussion is required regarding pricing, costs, and yields of bonds with CACs. Gugiatti and Richards provide empirical evidence that the inclusion of CACs has not influenced borrowing costs over the past decade and they have also made a comparison between bonds issued in Europe with CACs and bonds issued in the US and Europe without CACs, concluding that the inclusion of CACs does not impact secondary market yields.[255] In addition, two other empirical studies have demonstrated that—historically—the market does not pay attention to the inclusion of CACs[256] and neither has the inclusion of CACs been an important variable in the decision of borrowers or investors.[257]

12.121 Taylor has also suggested that the inclusion of CACs could be encouraged by making them a requirement for every country that has or is seeking IMF funding.[258] Alternatively, it could serve as the basis for lower borrowing costs on loans from the IMF.[259] In the words of Eichengreen and Mody, a combination of moral suasion, regulatory, and financial incentives would be used to encourage lenders and borrowers to adopt these provisions.[260] As explained below, there would be no need to use a 'carrot or stick' approach as they have become widely accepted since 2003.

12.122 In 2003, with bond issuances by Mexico and Brazil, majority action clauses were incorporated in sovereign bonds issued under New York law. The path set by Mexico and Brazil was rapidly followed by Belize, Chile, Colombia, Costa Rica, Egypt, Guatemala, Indonesia, Israel, Korea, Lebanon, Panama, Peru, the Philippines, Poland, Qatar, South Africa, Turkey, Uruguay, Venezuela, and many more thereafter. Before 2003, only bonds subject to English law included majority action clauses allowing for the amendment of any term, even payment terms, because of the misconception about the applicability of section 316(b) of the TIA.

12.123 So far, the required threshold to amend the terms of the bonds containing majority action clauses has been 75 per cent in aggregate principal amount of the outstanding bonds (eg Egypt, Lebanon, Mexico, Qatar, Uruguay, etc) for the so-called 'Reserve Matters'. Brazil has been the only case where, in 2003, 85 per cent was required, although it then moved to the standard practice of 75 per cent.

12.124 Payment terms are the quintessential aspect that creditors tend to protect in a bond issuance and therefore require a qualified majority for their amendment. The payment terms as such constitute the backbone of the 'Reserve Matters' but other issues such as governing law,

---

[254] Buchheit and Gulati, *supra* n 11.

[255] Gugiatti and Richards, *supra* n 231.

[256] Torbjorn Becker, Anthony Richards, and Yunyong Thaicharoen, 'Bond Restructuring and Moral Hazard: Are Collective Action Clauses Costly?' (2003) 61(1) *Journal of International Economics* 127–161.

[257] Clifford R Dammers, remarks in a Panel Discussion at Reinventing Bretton Woods Committee Conference, 'New Rules of the Game in Global Finance: An International Bankruptcy Procedure for Sovereign Debtors?', New York, 28–29 May 2002; and Peter Petas and Rashique Rahman, 'Sovereign Bonds—Legal Aspects that Affect Default and Recovery', Deutsche Bank Global Emerging Markets—Debt Strategy, May 1999 at 59–78.

[258] Taylor, *supra* n 18.

[259] Ibid.

[260] Eichengreen and Mody, *supra* n 72.

submission to jurisdiction, or immunity can also be included. The following are examples of what are usually included under the 'Reserve Matters': (1) changing the date on which any amount is payable; (2) reducing the principal amount (other than in accordance with the express terms of the debt securities; (3) reducing the interest rate; (4) changing the method used to calculate any amount payable; (4) changing the currency or place of payment of any amount payable; (5) modifying the obligation to make any payments (including any redemption price therefor); (6) changing the identity of the obligor; (7) changing the definition of 'outstanding debt securities' or the percentage of affirmative votes or written consents, as the case may be, required to make a 'reserve matter modification'; (8) changing the definition of 'uniformly applicable' or 'reserve matter modification'; (9) authorizing a third party to exchange or substitute all the debt securities for, or convert all the debt securities into, other obligations or securities; (10) changing the legal ranking, governing law, submission to jurisdiction, or waiver of immunities provisions of the terms of such debt securities; and (11) increasing the percentage of the aggregate principal amount then outstanding required to be held by holders to declare the debt securities of such series due and payable immediately, or reducing the percentage of the aggregate principal amount then outstanding required to be held by holders to waive any existing defaults or rescind or annul any notice of acceleration and its consequences.

Uruguay is a particular case since by an aggregation mechanism, amendments to any terms **12.125** (including payment terms) can be incorporated into two or more series of bonds simultaneously (aggregation). In order to approve the amendment applicable to two or more bond series, a double majority is required: (1) 85 per cent of the aggregate principal amount of all affected series; and (2) 66⅔ per cent of each specific series.[261]

2003 was the year that defined the discussion of whether the inclusion of CACs in sovereign **12.126** bonds is convenient and/or if it would impact on the bond prices. A clear example that the inclusion of these clauses would not affect the price of the bond was that Brazil's issuance— including CACs—was oversubscribed by 700 per cent. Moreover, in the same year, Uruguay closed a comprehensive reprofiling of its foreign currency bonds—including CACs and an aggregation mechanism—with 93 per cent participation. However, not everything is a bed of roses in the international financial markets, as there are some allegations that the inclusion of CACs in Chilean bonds 'means that the Chilean authorities are bowing to pressure from the US Treasury, which has been pushing for all emerging-market issuers to include such clauses'.[262]

Finally, a remark on Belize should be made. In 2006, it became the first sovereign after more **12.127** than 70 years to restructure bonds subject to New York law using CACs. Of the total $1.1 billion outstanding debt, 50 per cent approximately was deposited in five different bonds placed in the Caribbean region,[263] three bonds were subject to English law with CACs, and the other two bonds were subject to New York law—one with CACs and the other without

---

[261] See Prospectus of the República Oriental del Uruguay to issue debt securities and/or warrants to purchase debt securities up to $3,000,000,000 reflecting additional filings made with the SEC pursuant to Rule 424(b)(3) on 15 April 2003 and 9 May 2003, S-39 to S-41.

[262] Nick Ashwell, 'Chile Places First Sovereign Bond with Collective Action Clause', World Markets Research Centre (Global Insight), 27 January 2004.

[263] See Joanna Chung and Richard Beales, 'Belize Blazes a Trail with Sovereign Debt', *Financial Times*, 12 February 2007.

(therefore requiring unanimous consent to reform payment terms).[264] The bonds under New York law with CACs had a threshold of 85 per cent to amend their terms. Belize requested bondholders of this bond issue to tender their bonds in an exchange offer and to, simultaneously, consent in writing to amend the payment terms of this bond to match the terms of the new bonds. Tenders representing 96.8 per cent of the aggregate principal amount of the eligible claims were received into the exchange, resulting in 98.1 per cent of the total eligible claims stemming from the use of the CACs feature.[265] The percentage of acceptance within the New York bonds with CACs was 87.3 per cent. After Belize, the Seychelles in 2010, St Kitts and Nevis and Belize again in 2013 have used CACs.[266]

12.128   Collective action clauses have evolved as a result of the lessons learnt through recent debt crisis episodes in order to address the issues of coordination and preventing disruptive holdout positions. Originally, CACs were included on single bond issuances and aggregation was not a common feature. Following Uruguay's debt reprofiling in 2003, aggregation has become a feature available in the sovereign debt toolkit but subject to an increased double threshold (two-limb voting). Then and as a result of what happened when Greece tried to use its CACs on the English law governed debt instruments, it was discovered that 25 per cent in a small debt issuance can become a blocking holding of the whole restructuring exercise and that a new twist was required, that is, a single vote across different series (ie a single-limb vote in aggregated debt instruments). Table 12.2 summarizes the current status quo in the CAC menu.

2. Recent developments undermining the spirit of CACs: Re-designation and Pac-Man

12.129   The recent Argentine and Ecuadorian debt restructurings of 2020 put to the test the ICMA model CACs. These restructurings are useful case studies to illustrate two controversial legal techniques that challenged the use of CACs and were employed by the sovereigns to deal with the creditor coordination issue, generally the prime obstacle in a composite restructuring situation. These are the 'Re-designation' and 'Pac-Man' techniques.[267]

12.130   Despite an initial firm resistance from the creditor community, in September 2020, Argentina restructured almost $65 billion and Ecuador $17.4 billion of bonds with over 90 per cent support from its bondholders, garnering an 'unprecedented' creditor support.[268] However, critical concessions were sought by the bondholders to accept these strategies and successfully go ahead with the restructuring proposals.

---

[264] See Lee C Buchheit, 'Supermajority Control Wins Out' (April 2007) *International Financial Law Review* 2.

[265] See Government of Belize, 'Belize Closes Exchange Offer: 98.1% Commercial External Debt Restructured', Press Release dated 20 February 2007.

[266] See IMF, *A Survey of Experiences with Emerging Market Sovereign Debt Restructurings* (2012), available at <https://www.imf.org/external/np/pp/eng/2012/060512.pdf>.

[267] The author would like to thank Gunjit Dinesh Madra for valuable research assistance in this section of the chapter.

[268] Regarding Argentina, see Argentine Government, 'The Argentine Republic Announces the Results of the Exchange of External Public Debt under Foreign Law', 31 August 2020, available at <https://www.economia.gob.ar/en/the-argentine-republic-announces-the-results-of-the-exchange-of-external-public-debt-under-foreign-law/>. Regarding Ecuador, see Cleary Gottlieb, Ecuador's Successful $17.4 Billion Sovereign Debt Restructuring, available at <https://www.clearygottlieb.com/news-and-insights/news-listing/ecuadors-successful-17-4-billion-sovereign-debt-restructuring>.

Table 12.2 The CAC Menu

CAC Menu		
Key Features	Voting Procedure and Specific Possibilities		
	Single Series Voting	Aggregated Voting	
		Two Limb	Single Limb
Voting Threshold	75% per series	66⅔% aggregate + 50% per series	75% in aggregate
Uniform applicability requirement	No	No	Yes
Sub- aggregation	No	Yes	Yes
Pros	Provides a contractual restructuring feature.	Provides greater creditors' protection.	Allows cross- series restricting through a single vote.
Cons	Limited to a single series (a vote is required for each series).	A minority in a small series can block the whole restructuring.	Might cramdown the will of an entire series (or more than one).
Example	Non- aggregateable CAC[1]	EU Model CAC[2]	ICMA Model CAC[3]

1 For example most CACs issued prior to 2003.

2 See Euro area model CAC 2012 available at <http:// europa.eu/ efc/ sub_ committee/ pdf/ cac_ - _ text_ model_ cac.pdf>.

3 See ICMA Standard CACs (August 2014) available at <http:// www.icmagroup.org/ resources/ Sovereign- Debt- Information>.

Source: Author's own based on IMF's figure 1, included in IMF, 'Strengthening the Contractual Framework to Address Collective Action Problems in Sovereign Debt Restructuring', October 2014, p 23, available at <https:// www.imf.org/ external/ pp/ longres.aspx?id=4911>.

In the Argentine debt restructuring, the universe of bonds comprised instruments issued   **12.131**
under two different indentures. As a result, different CAC majority thresholds applied to
alter the terms of the original bonds, thereby adding an additional layer of complexity:

- The 2005 indenture bonds (the so-called Kirchner bonds as they were issued under the
  Presidency of Nestor Kirchner and his wife who succeeded him in power): these were
  bonds issued as part of the previous restructuring carried out in 2005 and others issued in 2010, governed by the Trust Indenture of 2005 (12 series, with a total principal
  amount of circa $22 billion) containing a double limb, ie 'Second Generation CAC'
  with a high voting threshold of 85 per cent in aggregate and 66 per cent per individual
  series.
- The 2016 indenture bonds (the so-called Macri bonds): bonds issued in 2016 under
  the Presidentship of Mauricio Macri, governed by the Trust Indenture of 2016 (17
  series with a total principal amount of circa $40 billion), with acceptance thresholds
  of 66 per cent in aggregate and 50 per cent per individual series (ie lower than the 2005
  Indenture threshold of 85 per cent in aggregate and 66 per cent per individual series).
  These bonds incorporated the Third Generation ICMA model CACs ('single-limb

voting'). The voting process for bonds issued under both indentures would be staggered, where the Kircher bonds would tender their vote first and then the Macri bonds. Therefore, for calculation purposes, if the modifications were accepted in the Kirchner bonds, the total amount of the Kirchner bonds and their approval would be aggregated to the total number used to calculate the percentage acceptance required under the Macri bonds.

- The carved-out 2005 or 2016 indenture bonds (if any): If a series (or more than one) in either of the two bonds (the 2005 or 2016 bonds), is excluded or carved out of the original perimeter of 'eligible debt', the majority requirement for that series will be not less than 75 per cent of the aggregate principal amount of such excluded series.

12.132   This notwithstanding, in the proposed exchange, Argentina sought to restructure all series of the 2016 Indenture bonds (the Macri bonds) by employing the two-limb voting option under the ICMA CACs 'menu' of options. Citing a strategic rationale pertaining to economics of the deal, the sovereign chose against employing the ICMA's 'Uniformly Applicable' single-limb voting mechanism.[269]

(a) The 'Re-designation amendment'

12.133   Further, owing to the strong possibility of not meeting the 50 per cent minimum voting threshold as required per series of the 2016 Indenture bonds (the Macri bonds) forming part of the aggregated voting pool, Argentina sought bondholders' consent to amend the 'Finality' condition also known as the 'All or Nothing' condition of the ICMA two-tier voting mechanism. The 'Finality' or 'All or Nothing' feature means that if an issuer, after launching the deal, wished to exclude any series of bonds, notice to all bondholders would be necessary and either: (1) the participating bondholders be given a time frame during which they could reconsider their decision if they felt that the alteration could have a deleterious impact on their decision to participate; or, (2) initiate another exchange proposal with a reorganized (or re-designated) voting group. Therefore, by removing the 'Finality' condition, Argentina will be able to re-designate the pool of eligible claims being considered for the purpose of voting, that is, re-designate the affected pool, and this is referred as the 'Re-designation Amendment'.

12.134   As part of the strategy, Argentina sought to have the possibility to reconfigure, at its sole discretion, the series of 'eligible bonds' that were identified at the beginning of the voting exercise. The bonds included within the pool of bonds being restructured could be re-designated or changed even after the completion of the voting process. This re-designation required the approval of holders of 50 per cent of the outstanding principal of each series (the 'Non-Reserve Matter' voting threshold) as the designation of investors into classes, for voting purposes, was not considered a 'Reserve Matter' that mandated a qualified majority support. This undermined the collective will or spirit of these type of clause and was seen as an exploitation of loopholes in the debt documentation undermining investor rights.

12.135   The two characteristics of the ICMA model CACs at the epicentre of controversy were:

---

[269] See Lee C Buchheit and Mitu Gulati, 'The Argentine Collective Action Clause Controversy' (October 2020) 15(4) *Capital Markets Law Journal* 470.

- The two-tier aggregated voting structure: The structure required the consent of 66 per cent of all aggregated bondholders and a simple majority, ie 50 per cent, of individual series of bonds forming a part of the designated voting pool; and
- The Finality condition: Once the groups of bonds to be aggregated had been identified, the decision was 'final' (therefore an 'all or nothing' situation) with respect to that particular offer.

In practice, in a simplified hypothetical scenario, if series I, II, III, IV, and V were elected to be aggregated for a two-tier vote (the universe of bonds or the 'eligible bonds') and, after closing of the offer and counting of votes, series V failed to attain the 50 per cent voting mark required for each series, the offer would have failed in its entirety.   **12.136**

In essence, with the re-designation feature, the issuer has complete discretion to select the bonds to be aggregated for voting even after the vote has been tendered and the sovereign knows whether the required majority has been achieved. In the hypothetical scenario of series I, II, III, IV, and V, series V could be removed ex-post as the required double threshold has not been met. However, after deciding which bonds constitute the eligible bonds and communicating this to the investors, the classification is deemed a material term of the proposal and cannot be tweaked without giving a fresh chance to the investors to reassess their decision to participate and how they will tender their vote.   **12.137**

Argentina intended to eliminate the 'Finality' or 'All or Nothing' condition, this being the biggest innovation of the restructuring.[270] Section 11.3 of the 2016 Argentine Indenture (which draws from the standard ICMA language) states: '[t]he Republic shall have the discretion to ... designate which Series of Debt Securities will be included in the aggregated voting ...; provided however that once the Republic ... designates the Series of debt securities that [will be subject to the aggregated vote] those elections will be final for purposes of that vote or consent solicitation'.   **12.138**

Argentina contended that it retained the ability to 're-designate' the series of eligible bonds by removing those series that voted against the restructuring as if they had not been included in the voting process in the first place. To borrow a commentator's analogy, it was like 'a president holding elections and then afterward invaliding certain votes to make sure he wins'.[271] Accordingly, the sovereign could 'manipulate' the voting pools by means of re-defining the pool of eligible bonds to surpass the required threshold mark in the series referred to as the 'affected series'. This would allow Argentina, after the votes had been cast and counted, to achieve the simple majority to modify or entirely waive the 'finality' restriction.   **12.139**

However, the sovereign's ability to alter the voting framework (ie 're-designate' the voting pools) without notifying and/or giving revocation rights to investors, especially when the proposal does not have the backing of a qualified supermajority, raises substantive and procedural concerns pertaining to voting integrity, transparency, and procedural fairness of an exchange. Bondholders are entitled to know how their own votes (and those of their   **12.140**

---

[270] See Argentina's exchange offer dated 17 August 2020. Also see Guido Demarco, 'Restructuracion de Deuda Soberana: Aspectos Legales' Editorial (2021) *Abaco*.

[271] See Mitu Gulati and Mark Weidemaier, The Argentine Re-Designation Drama: Notes from Two Frustrated Readers, *Credit Slips*, referring to Anna Gelpern's quote. available at <https://www.creditslips.org/creditslips/2020/06/the-argentine-re-designation-drama-notes-from-two-frustrated-readers.html>

brethren) will be calculated as this can condition the way in which they will vote. Moreover, transparency is critical in assessing the range of potential restructuring outcomes. In a complex, cross-series debt restructuring where voting decisions are based on the bondholders' economic inclinations and their speculation as to the demeanour or treatment of other bondholders, free flow of information amongst all parties is *sine qua non*. Re-designation, as contained in the Argentine proposal, was perceived as impacting the voting results in a manner that could affect bondholders' genuine intentions and affect their recoveries. The primary objective of the ICMA framework is to frustrate holdouts that can thwart a restructuring proposal that has not garnered the mandated support of a majority of investors. Re-designation, on the other hand, holds the potential of altering that result by allowing a restructuring without the mandated qualified majorities. The other undesired potential consequence of the re-designation is that it will in turn leave behind the excluded/unrestructured series that may be susceptible to subsequent 'Uniformly Applicable' exchange proposals through the use of single-limb CACs.

12.141   Coincidentally, around the same time of the Argentine restructuring, Ecuador also set forth a re-designation strategy. Its biggest investor cohort (comprising almost the same actors involved in Argentina's restructuring) did not retaliate in this case. This can be the result for two reasons:

1. The bonds did not restrict the possibility of re-designation despite being subjected to New York law because the indentures that were also governed by New York law included the ICMA CACs modelled under English law that does not impose the same 'Finality or All or Nothing' limitation as its New York law counterpart; and
2. The restructuring proposal followed a negotiation process with the sovereign's largest investor class and was tailored to garner broad approval from a supermajority of the country's creditors in a two-limb CAC mechanism.

12.142   Therefore, Ecuador's strategy to re-designate was perceived by the bondholder groups as assisting the country to implement an agreed upon/deliberated restructuring that had supermajority support, instead of forcing an exchange offer that commanded only minority support, as in Argentina's case. Evidently and unsurprisingly, context mattered.

(b) The Pac-Man technique

12.143   Further exacerbating the atmosphere surrounding the Argentine deal was another development—a technique named 'Pac-Man' (invoking a computer game wherein one character ruthlessly guzzles others). The strategy supposed that Argentina, at any time after the initial restructuring terminated (ie Restructuring 1), could launch subsequent 'sequential' aggregated restructurings (ie Restructurings 2, 3, 4, and so on) for the 2016 Indenture bonds (the Macri bonds), and incorporate any series that either declined to participate in Restructuring 1 or were left out as part of the re-designation strategy, thereby 'ganging up' those that accepted against one or more of the bonds that were left out. Noteworthily, in subsequent restructurings, Argentina would have employed the 'Uniformly Applicable' single-limb voting mechanism. As a result, the subsequent restructurings (Restructurings 2, 3, 4, and so forth) would have had the potential of eliminating any holdouts as the majority was bestowed with the power of cramming down the dissenting minorities. Therefore, through the Pac-Man technique, the creditors of Restructuring 1, a minority of the total universe of bonds, could bind some of the dissenting/non-participating creditors in subsequent sequential restructurings by aggregating small portions of dissenting/non-participating creditors with the assenting ones. These are aggregated in tandem so as not to outnumber the favourable votes in the required 75 per cent supermajority under the 'Uniformly Applicable' single limb.

12.144 Accordingly, via the Pac-Man technique, the cumulative voting strength of the participating or amended bondholders—in Restructuring 1—can be leveraged to coerce the holdouts from that particular round, in successive 'sequential' restructuring rounds, to concede to the same (or ever-so-slightly improved) commercial terms. The proposed restructuring can put forward commercial terms that are, on the one hand, slightly better for the already restructured creditors, but, on the other, materially worse for other excluded/un-restructured bondholders (the proposal is technically 'Uniformly Applicable' as it advances the same terms to all bondholders constituting the voting group, notwithstanding the divergent incentives of the two opposing bondholder pools). To reiterate, the single-limb or third-generation CACs require the support of 75 per cent of bonds computed in an aggregated manner, provided the offer is 'Uniformly Applicable' to all 'affected' creditors. The ICMA CACs mandate no constraint on the pooling together of bonds, provided they are issued under the same indenture or under indentures containing similar aggregation provisions.[272]

12.145 This exercise can, in theory, be successfully repeated (Restructurings 2, 3, 4, and so forth), each time cramming down an additional series of originally unrestructured bonds. It implies that the original conceding minority investors (as the threshold would not have been achieved and there would have been a need to re-designate)—by successive restructurings and aggregation— would be in a position to gobble the original holding out majority, achieving a result that would not have been otherwise possible in a single attempt.

12.146 To summarize, a sovereign can restructure remaining bonds with less than supermajority support (maybe even with a minority) by sequentially proceeding to aggregate, via the single-limb or third-generation CACs, the restructured bonds with a 'portion' of the 'unaffected' bonds. As a result, Argentina's tactics, though arguably within the ambit of 2014 CACs, caused mayhem in the global investor community due to their forceful undermining of the voluntary spirit of majority voting.

12.147 Following with a hypothetical example, there are five series of bonds, I, II, III, IV, and V, individually representing an outstanding principal of $100 million, for a total of $500 million issued under a double-limb CAC with acceptance thresholds of 66 per cent in aggregate and 50 per cent per individual series (ie like Argentina's 2016 Indenture bonds). They are all pooled together for a restructuring vote. For a 66 per cent approval, a positive vote from holders of over $333.3 million in aggregate principal amount is required (Table 12.3).

12.148 Continuing with our example, series II and IV rejected the proposal, which would jeopardize the entire restructuring (the 'All or Nothing' feature as explained above). However, if the voting pool is re-designated to incorporate just series I, III, and V—commanding over 66 per cent support in aggregate and 50 per cent individually—in the re-designated group,

[272] Ian Clark and Dimitrios Lyratzakis, 'Towards a More Robust Sovereign Debt Restructuring Architecture: Innovations from Ecuador and Argentina', (January 2021) 16(1) *Capital Markets Law Journal* 42..

Table 12.3 Hypothetical Example of a Vote Tender in a Restructuring Scenario

Series	Voting result per series	Individual series requirement (>50%)
I	94%	YES
II	49%	NO
III	95%	YES
IV	47%	NO
V	69%	YES
TOTAL AGGREGATE	$354 of a required aggregate total of $333	

we can restructure those three series of bonds (into, say, series I*, III*, and V*), while series II and IV remain as 'unaffected series'. Therefore, if the sovereign does not pay, bondholders of series II and IV can sue to enforce their claims. Further, assume that the sovereign puts forward another restructuring proposal (Restructuring 2) where the aggregation of series I*, III*, and V* (the recently restructured series) with series II is proposed. As a condition precedent, the proposal must extend the same terms to all bondholders constituting the voting group (ie the 'Uniformly Applicable' condition). Since I*, III*, and V* have materially worse terms than II and IV because they have already been restructured (and most likely suffered a face value reduction and/or an interest reduction), ever-so-slightly better terms in the new proposal than those previously offered (eg an annual interest payment of 3.50% rather than 3.25%) would provide an incentive for them to participate. Garnering the support of more than 75 per cent of those three series (I*, III*, and V*) should be easily achievable since for them it would be like 'free money'. If the sovereign garners 100 per cent approval from those series and the same level of support from series II (ie 49 per cent as in Restructuring 1), that puts the acceptance rate already at above 75 per cent. Why 75 per cent and not 66 per cent as in the first vote tender? Because series I*, III*, and V* would have been issued under the ICMA third-generation CAC menu that allows for aggregation across series. Therefore, in order to aggregate different series (ie II and IV with I*, II*, and III*) and approve the restructuring an aggregate 75 per cent would be required. As a result of the Pac-Man technique, by garnering 100 per cent support from series I*, III*, and V*, the 75 per cent threshold of the entire voting pool can be easily achieved even if the 100 per cent of series I*, III*, and V* is not achieved, thereby dragging in the previously unrestructured series (in our example II). Whereas in Restructuring 1, the dissenting series II and IV with more than a 50 per cent holdout rate could have halted the restructuring, after Restructuring 2 they would have been crammed down. Depending on the numbers and individual scenarios, sequential rounds of re-designation and voting can be imagined using some series to bind all (eg Restructuring 3 bringing in series IV jointly with series I*, III*, and V* from Restructuring 1 and series II* from Restructuring 2), something that could be contrary to the spirit of the collective envisaged in the use of CACs.

(c) The proposed fixes: a way forward

12.149 Argentina's restructuring offer of April 2020 contained the above-mentioned controversial move of combining re-designation with the Pac-Man technique, thereby raising concerns.

The investor community at large shared the perspective that these mechanisms did violate the intent of the ICMA framework but were not contractually prohibited. Ecuador, which was conducting a restructuring simultaneously with Argentina, was the first to provide a solution towards fixing the gap exploited through the re-designation and Pac-Man techniques. To address the resentment around the re-designation, Ecuador's proposal (released on 19 July 2020) permitted the debtor to re-designate the series of bonds forming the aggregated voting pool *only if*: (1) five business days were given to the holders to reconsider their participation after the decision to re-designate was communicated; or, (2) the offer obtained the support of holders of more than 66 per cent of the principal of the initially allotted voting group (rather than the reduced threshold of 50 per cent for 'Non-Reserved' matters).

This implies that where a supermajority of bondholders concedes to an alteration of the voting pool structure, after the voting process has taken place, the proposed readjustment of the voting structure is immaterial to their determination of whether to approve or stay away from the restructuring. However, the threshold of 66 per cent as the minimum participation mark is up for debate between the debtor and the investor community. Other transactions could set a different threshold.   **12.150**

Similar logic was followed while addressing the Pac-Man technique, meaning that thereby a supermajority of bondholders, in the debtor's original exchange proposal, could legitimize or concede to a subsequent Pac-Man transaction, thereby eliminating any dissenting creditors from round one. The strategy by no means provides a free pass to gang up on the minority and coerce a disadvantageous offer upon it as the subsequent Pac-Man-style exchanges must uphold the 'Uniformly Applicable' criterion, and each bondholder must receive a similar deal.   **12.151**

Accordingly, it was suggested that where the initial restructuring exercise attracts more than 75 per cent of the outstanding principal of all bonds constituting the aggregated voting pool, the issuer could initiate a subsequent, 'Uniformly Applicable', proposal to gobble up any dissenting or excluded creditors from the first round. It seems logical as surpassing the 75 per cent voting threshold would anyway assist in concluding a single-limb 'Uniformly Applicable' restructuring in round one so the net impact on dissenting creditors would be identical. Alternatively, if the debtor does not attain a 75 per cent voting threshold in the first round, it must refrain for at least 36 months from employing a Pac-Man restructuring to cramdown or drag along the dissenting creditors from the first restructuring.   **12.152**

The Argentine authorities accepted the solutions proposed by Ecuador to resolve the controversy and a consensus was reached to grant similar protections to the Argentine creditor groups as well. In the end, Argentina reported that it kept one series of bonds outside the restructuring wherein CACs could not be triggered in order to cram down all bondholders constituting that series.[273]   **12.153**

Improving these shortcomings in the ICMA model CAC framework through limited restraints on the mechanisms perceived as 'controversial' fosters productive engagement with investors by the sovereign issuers.   **12.154**

---

[273] Argentine Government, *supra* n 289.

12.155   The 're-designation' and 'Pac-Man' techniques sought to circumvent the 'Finality or All-or-Nothing' condition under New York law, a requirement which is not present in the ICMA-recommended language for bonds governed by English law and it does not seem readily apparent why the recommended provisions for bonds governed by New York law are more restrictive.[274]

12.156   A related topic to CACs is how to deal with those bonds that were issued under New York law prior to 2003 and that do not include CACs, those that intentionally do not include CACs, or simply where that, despite the fact that they include CACs, the required majority cannot be obtained. The next section will address: (1) the use of exit consents and the interrelated topic of how to perform amendments to the terms of the bonds issued under New York and English law; and (2) the use of contractual sweeteners to enhance the degree of creditor participation.

12.157   So far, in the sovereign debt restructuring episodes, the major issue of concern has been the issue of holdout creditors. As noted in the 2004 MOCOMILA report, it is relevant to stress that CACs (and exit consents) appear to have no effect on bondholders that have obtained a court judgment prior to the exchange offer.[275] However, these only represent a very small percentage of the total outstanding debt obligations. A recent study suggests that the problem of holdouts has been overestimated, since of the 34 sovereign bond exchanges since 1997, only two have been affected by holdout creditors.[276]

3. The use of exit consents and amendments to the terms of the bonds under New York and English law

12.158   Exit consent is a technique by which holders of bonds in default which have accepted an exchange offer—at the moment of accepting said offer—grant their consent to amend certain terms of the bonds being exchanged. By using the exit consent technique, the exchange offer is conditioned on a minimum threshold of creditors' acceptance and the amendments to the terms are performed once the required majority has been obtained.

12.159   By means of performing certain amendments to the terms and conditions of the bonds in default, which compared to the exchange offer are less attractive (mostly in legal although also probably in financial terms), forcing a greater number of bondholders to accept the exchange offer. Otherwise, if bondholders do not accept the exchange offer they will be holding an impaired bond, not featuring some of the original contractual term features.

12.160   In order to amend the bonds subject to New York law (and not including CACs), their terms and conditions can be divided into three categories:[277]

    (1) *Category I*: these clauses are those that expressly require unanimous amendment (100 per cent of the bondholders) and are related to payment terms. Examples of

---

[274] See Clark and Lyratzakis, *supra* n 293.

[275] See MOCOMILA, *supra* n 37 at 6.

[276] Elena Duggar, Richard Cantor, and Bar Oosterveld, 'The Role of Holdouts Creditors and CACs in Sovereign Debt Restructuring', *Moody's Investors Service Sovereign Default Series* (10 April 2013), available at <http://www.moodys.com/research/Sovereign-Defaults-Series-The-Role-of-Holdout-Creditors-and-CACs--PBC_150162>.

[277] Lee Buchheit and G Mitu Gulati, 'Exit Consents in Sovereign Bond Exchanges' (2001) 48 *UCLA Law Review* 59–84. In the same sense, Michael M Chamberlin, 'At the Frontier of Exit Consents', at the Bear Stearns & EMCA Sovereign Creditors Rights Conference on 8 November 2001, available at <http://www.emta.org/privateAssets/0/113/1806/2a8b0d38-3474-459d-8bab-79e962e0b3a0.pdf>.

these clauses include: the amount of debt or par value of the bond, the maturity date, the issuance currency, and the conditions for amending the bond's terms.

(2) *Category II:* these are the set of clauses that if modified, produce an effect on the clauses related to the payment terms mentioned above (eg applicable law, events of default and acceleration rights).

(3) *Category III:* these are all the remaining clauses that are not included under Category I or II (eg financial covenants, listing requirements, *pari passu* clause, etc).

In the absence of CACs, amendments clauses are still included in the debt instruments to remedy mistakes or overcome unforeseen circumstances. Under New York law, in order to amend the clauses under Category I, the affirmative vote of 100 per cent of the bondholders is required—a threshold almost impossible in international issuances. Category II—as noted by Buchheit and Gulati—is a grey area that has not been tested yet. Finally, Category III includes bond clauses that can usually be amended by the favourable vote of a 66⅔ per cent in aggregate principal amount of the outstanding bonds.[278]   **12.161**

On the other hand, under English law, although the requirements are more flexible than under New York law, it varies according to the conditions established at the moment of the issuance. They usually vary from a simple majority with an aggravated quorum to 75 per cent in aggregate principal amount of the outstanding bonds. For example, under an Argentine bond issuance subject to English law, in order to amend the payment terms (Category I under New York law) a quorum of two or more persons holding or representing not less than 75 per cent (or, at any adjourned such meeting not less than 25 per cent) is required and the amendment can be resolved by a simple majority.[279] In this sense, it is worth   **12.162**

---

[278] 66⅔ is the percentage usually required to amend Category III clauses. See, eg, Republic of Argentina Amendment No 3 to Registration Statement Under Schedule B No 333-117111, Fed Sec L Rep 201 (4 September 2004). The following is an example of an amendment clause from the Republic of Argentina under Registration Number 333-117111 sovereign debt prospectus under New York law: 'Modifications: ... Any modification, amendment, supplement or waiver to the terms and conditions of the debt securities of a single series, or to the indenture insofar as it affects the debt securities of a single series, may generally be made, and future compliance therewith may be waived, with the consent of Argentina and the holders of not less than 66⅔% in aggregate principal amount of the debt securities of such series at the time outstanding. However, special requirements apply with respect to any modification, amendment, supplement or waiver that would: (i) change the due date for the payment for the principal of (or premium, if any) or any instalment of interest on the debt securities of a series; (ii) reduce the principal amount of the debt securities of a series, the portion of the principal amount which is payable upon acceleration of the maturity of the debt securities of a series, the interest rate of the debt securities of a series, or the premium payable upon redemption of the debt securities of a series; (iii) change the coin or currency of payment of any amount payable under the debt securities of a series; (iv) shorten the period during which Argentina is not permitted to redeem the debt securities of a series, or permit Argentina to redeem the debt securities of a series if Argentina had been permitted to do so prior; (v) change the definition of outstanding or the percentage of votes required for the taking of any action pursuant to the modification provisions of the indenture (and the corresponding provisions of the terms and conditions of the debt securities) in respect of the debt securities of a series; (vi) change the obligation of Argentina to pay additional amounts; (vii) change the governing law provision ...'

[279] The following is a sample clause according to these specifications: 'Meetings of Noteholders, Modification and Waiver: (a) Meetings of Noteholders: ... [T]he quorum for any meeting to consider an Extraordinary Resolution will be two or more persons holding or representing a clear majority in nominal amount of the Notes of the relevant Series for the time being outstanding, or at any adjourned meeting two or more persons holding or representing holders of Notes of the relevant Series whatever the nominal amount of the Notes of the relevant Series held or represented, unless the business of such meeting includes consideration of proposals, inter alia, (i) to amend the dates of maturity or redemption of the Notes of any Series or any date for payment of interest thereon, (ii) to reduce or cancel the nominal amount of the Notes of any Series, (iii) to reduce the rate or rates of interest in respect of the Notes of any Series or to vary the method or basis of calculating the rate or rates or amount of interest, (iv) if there is shown on the face of the Notes of any Series a Final Redemption Amount, Early Redemption Amount, Optional Redemption Amount, Minimum Rate of Interest and/or a Maximum Rate of Interest, to reduce

noting that in an issuance by the Republic of Moldova—also subject to English law—the required quorum is two or more persons holding or representing not less than 75 per cent (or, at any adjourned such meeting, not less than 25 per cent) and the resolution shall be adopted by a majority consisting of not less than 75 per cent in aggregate principal amount of the outstanding bonds.[280]

12.163   To summarize, in the absence of CACs:

(1) the terms and conditions usually required to amend a sovereign bond issued under New York law are: (a) a 51 per cent nominal value quorum in the first meeting or a 25 per cent quorum on any subsequent adjourned meeting; (b) unanimity (100 per cent of the nominal value of the series) to amend the payment terms (Categories I and II); and/or (c) a 66⅔ per cent of the nominal value of the series to amend any other term (Category III) which does not imply amending the clauses included under Categories I and II;

(2) the terms and conditions usually required to amend a sovereign bond issued under English law are: (a) simple majority of the nominal value of each series to adopt resolutions; (b) the quorum required to amend the payment terms or other clauses that may affect the payment terms (Categories I and II) will be two or more persons holding or representing not less than 75 per cent, or at any adjourned meeting

---

such Redemption Amount, Minimum Rate of Interest and/or such Maximum Rate of Interest, (v) to change the method of calculating the Final Redemption Amount, the Early Redemption Amount, the Optional Redemption Amount or the Amortised Face Amount, as the case may be, in respect of the Notes of any Series, (vi) to change the currency or currencies of payment of the Notes of any Series or (vii) to modify the provisions concerning the quorum required at any meeting of Noteholders of any Series or the majority required to pass the Extraordinary Resolution, in which case the necessary quorum will be two or more persons holding or representing not less than 75 per cent., or at any adjourned meeting not less than 25 per cent., in nominal amount of the Notes of the relevant Series for the time being outstanding ... In the Trust Deed, "Extraordinary Resolution" is defined to mean a resolution passed at a meeting of holders of Notes of a Series, which meeting was duly convened and held in accordance with the provisions of the Trust Deed, by a majority consisting of not less than 50 per cent of the votes cast.' Information Memorandum from the Republic of Argentina, $20,000,000,000, Medium-Term Note Programme for the Issuance of Notes due from 30 days to 30 years from the Date of Issue 34-35 (2001).

[280] This clause reads as follows: '12. Meetings of Noteholders, Modification and Waiver: (a) Meetings of Noteholders. The Agency Agreement contains provisions for convening meetings of Noteholders to consider matters relating to the Notes, including the modification of any provision of these Conditions or the Deed of Covenant. Any such modification may be made if sanctioned by an Extraordinary Resolution (as defined below). The quorum at any such meeting for passing an Extraordinary Resolution shall be two or more persons holding or representing a clear majority of the principal amount of the Notes for the time being outstanding, or at any adjourned meeting two or more persons being or representing Noteholders whatever the principal amount of the Notes for the time being outstanding so held or represented, except that at any meeting the business of which includes consideration of proposals, inter alia, (i) to modify the maturity of the Notes or the dates on which interest is payable in respect of the Notes, (ii) to reduce or cancel the principal amount of, or interest on, the Notes, (iii) to change the currency of payment of the Notes, or (iv) to modify the provisions concerning the quorum required at any meeting of Noteholders or the majority required to pass an Extraordinary Resolution, the necessary quorum for passing an Extraordinary Resolution shall be two or more persons holding or representing not less than 75 per cent., or at any adjourned such meeting not less than 25 per cent., of the principal amount of the Notes for the time being outstanding. As used in this Condition 12, "Extraordinary Resolution" means a resolution passed at a meeting of the Noteholders duly convened and held in accordance with the provisions contained in these Conditions and the Agency Agreement by a majority consisting of not less than 75 per cent of the persons voting thereat upon a show of hands or if a poll shall be duly demanded then by a majority consisting of not less than 75 per cent of the votes given on the poll. An Extraordinary Resolution passed at any meeting of Noteholders will be binding on all Noteholders, whether or not they are present at the meeting.' Republic of Moldova, 9.875% Notes due 2002, $75,000,000 (see Buchheit and Gulati, *supra* n 8, annex).

not less than 25 per cent of the nominal value of the series; and (c) the quorum required to amend any other terms of the bond that does not affect the payment terms (Category III) will be two or more persons holding or representing not less than 50 per cent of the nominal value of the series.

Collective action clauses and exit consents are two collective decision-making techniques used in the sovereign context. On the one hand, CACs are used to facilitate the restructuring by avoiding disturbances and reducing costs. As previously discussed, this type of clause is available in bonds issued under English law and in most bonds issued under New York law since 2003, probably a must after the 2014 ICMA draft 'menu' clause and the endorsement of the IMF.[281] On the other hand, exit consents are primarily used in bonds issued under New York law that do not include CACs to 'force' a majority of bondholders to participate in an exchange offer.[282] This notwithstanding, it may be the case that even if the bonds include CACs, the threshold to amend the payment terms (a super-majority) cannot be achieved while the percentage to amend other terms can (more than 66⅔ per cent and less than 75 per cent). Finally, in general terms and with regard to the use of CACs, bonds subject to German law are comparable to bonds issued under New York law. In the same manner, bonds issued under Japanese and Luxembourg law are comparable to bonds issued under English law.   **12.164**

The following section will deal with the evolution of these techniques and how they have been used in actual sovereign debt restructuring episodes besides the recent episodes of Argentina and Ecuador 2020 already addressed.   **12.165**

---

[281] For the draft models of standard CACs, see: (1) ICMA Standard CACs (August 2014) available at <http://www.icmagroup.org/resources/Sovereign-Debt-Information>; and (2) Euro area model CAC 2012 available at <http://europa.eu/efc/sub_committee/pdf/cac_-_text_model_cac.pdf>.

[282] In 1986, in *Katz v Oak Industries* (508 A 2d 873 (Del Ch 1986)), a New York court recognized the validity and legitimacy of using the 'exit consents' technique in the corporate context. In 1993, in *Unigard Security Ins Co v North River Ins Co* (4 F 3d 1049 (2d Cir 1993)), the court recognized the argument that the use of exit consents is legitimate because the drafters of the terms and conditions of the bonds issued after the *Oak Industries* case did not make any amendments to the contractual terms of the bonds to limit the use of exit consents. On the other hand, *Assenagon Asset Management SA v Irish Bank Resolution Incorporation Limited (formerly Anglo Irish Bank Corporation Limited)*, is an English case where exit consent was used in an share burden attempt on subordinated floating rate notes due in 2017 issued by Anglo Irish Bank on 15 June 2007. The rationale was to reduce the costs to the Irish taxpayer resultant from the nationalization of Anglo Irish Bank in September 2010. Under the terms of the subordinated floating rate notes, 75 per cent of the noteholders could 'assent to any modification of the provisions'. The offer extended to the noteholders consisted of the issuance of €0.20 of new notes in exchange for every €1 of the existing notes, subject to the condition that the noteholders would vote at a meeting to be conveyed in favour of a resolution allowing the redemption of the existing notes for €0.01 per €1,000 of existing notes. The meeting was held and 92 per cent of the noteholders voted in favour. Assenagon, who held €17 million of notes, did not agree to the exchange offer and as result of the majority decision, its €17 million notes were redeemed for €170 (€17,000,000 / €1,000 = €17,000 ⇨ €17,000 x €0.01 = €170). Assenagon filed a claim on three main heads: (1) that the resolution was ultra vires because the terms of the notes did not confer the power to destroy their value; (2) that there was a conflict of interest under the terms of the existing bonds by those who tendered the votes (had already agreed to exchange and were holding the bonds for the beneficiary) and that their votes should have been disregarded; and (3) that the resolution was an abuse of power by the voting majority because it conferred no benefit on the noteholders as a class. The High Court ruled in favour of Assenagon. Following the three main heads of Assenagon, the High Court resolved: (1) the complete extinguishment of the bondholders' rights was within the powers conferred by the terms of the notes; (2) that the votes of the bondholders who had agreed to the exchange should have been disregarded based on the terms included in the notes dealing with conflict of interest; and (3) it was unlawful for the majority noteholders to assist the issuer/debtor in coercing the minority by voting for a resolution that would destroy the minority's economic rights. See *Assenagon Asset Management SA v Irish Bank Resolution Incorporation Limited (formerly Anglo Irish Bank Corporation Limited)* [2012] WLR(D) 243, [2012] EWHC 2090 (Ch) at [82] to [83].

4. CACs, exit consents, and term enhancements in practice

12.166 Restructurings by Ukraine (1999) and Ecuador (2000) clearly established that restructuring is possible within the given parameters and limitations by the tactical and often complementary use of exchange offers and collective decision-making provisions. The terms of the bonds in each of these cases had determined the restructuring technique that was to be adopted, ie exchange offers and amendments. These restructurings involved sovereign bonds that were governed both by English law[283] (issued under trust deeds and fiscal agency agreements and included CACs), as well as bonds governed by New York law (including Brady bonds, that did not contain such clauses). As previously noted, the vast majority of bonds issued by emerging-market sovereigns are governed either by New York law or English law. Unlike sovereign bonds issued under English law, payment terms for bonds issued under the New York law can be restructured only by unanimous consent of the bondholders unless they include CACs. Therefore, the technique of exchange offers is the only available option to amend bonds issued under New York law that do not contain CACs.[284]

12.167 In the cases of Ukraine and Ecuador:

> ... each of the restructuring involved an exchange offer in which bondholders were invited to exchange their instruments for new longer maturity instruments. In each case, it was possible to secure agreement on comprehensive restructurings that both provided immediate cash-flow relief and contributed toward putting the members' debt onto a basis consistent with a return to medium-term viability. In each case, participation rates were high, and there was no creditor litigation.[285]

12.168 In addition, the Ukrainian bonds were restructured using an innovative hybrid mechanism that combined an exchange offer for all of the instruments with the use of collective action provisions in three of the instruments.[286] Of the four outstanding bonds, one series of bonds was governed by German law and did not contain CACs and was therefore restructured by a one-step exchange offer for the new bonds. Bondholders of the other three bonds, which contained CACs and were governed by Luxembourg law, were invited to tender their old bonds and, at the same time, to grant an irrevocable proxy vote to the exchange agent. The vote would be cast at a subsequent bondholders' meeting and would favour modifications to the old bonds that would bring them in line with the payment terms of the new bonds being offered in exchange. As opposed to the Pakistani bond restructuring in 1999, Ukraine made an innovative use of the CACs. Pakistan's bonds were governed by English law, but due to the uncertainty of the outcome of the bondholders' meetings, the use of CACs was not triggered.

12.169 To overcome this uncertainty, Ukraine predicated the calling of the bondholders' meeting for the proposed amendments to the payment terms, subject to the receipt of sufficient

---

[283] The governing law in the Ukraine restructuring was Luxembourg law, which, for the purpose of CACs and amendment terms, is the same as English law.

[284] Lee C Buchheit, 'Unitar Training Programs on Foreign Economic Relations', Doc No 1, Sovereign Debtors and Their Bondholders, p 4 (2000).

[285] IMF, *supra* n 240. Also see Duggar, Cantor, and Oosterveld *supra* n 266.

[286] IMF, *supra* n 240 at 6.

irrevocable proxies in favour of the proposed amendments. Upon the receipt of sufficient proxies to amend the payment terms of the original bonds, a meeting was called, the proxies voted, and the amendments were adopted, thereby making them binding on all the bondholders of the three series. Subsequent to the meetings, the bondholders participated in the exchange by tendering the modified bonds for new bonds containing the amended payment terms. As noted by the IMF, using a tender process permitted numerous additional modifications of non-payment terms to be adopted without bondholders formally having to accept each as an amendment to the old bond and ensured that the four original issues were merged into two relatively large issues which differed only in terms of the currency of denomination and the associated coupons.[287]

All participating creditors, irrespective of their roles and responsibilities, share a basic **12.170** interest to prevent and resolve crises and promote greater financial stability. As such, they would be willing to expedite restructuring by participating in debtor-creditor consultations. The Ukrainian case is an illustration of how the common inter-creditor interests and market mechanics could facilitate coordination. The restructuring of the bonds through an exchange offer was made in the context of an arrangement under the IMF's Extended Fund Facility, and a request for a debt restructuring by Paris Club creditors (although at the time of the exchange offer, the Ukraine's right to draw under the arrangement had been temporarily suspended).[288]

This ground-breaking technique of using CACs with the predicated requirement of a ma- **12.171** jority of irrevocable proxies, the breach of which entailed substantial civil liabilities, not only provided certainty that bondholders who had tendered proxies would not backtrack and reject the proposed amendments at the meetings, but also solved the holdout problem feared by Pakistan. Even if dissenting bondholders refused to participate in the exchange, they were still bound to the payment terms adopted by the qualified majority. Thus, Buchheit and Gulati argue that holdouts were faced with the prospect of being left with an amended illiquid old bond that paid out no earlier than the very liquid new bond offered in the exchange.[289]

The Ecuadorian debt restructuring performed in 2000 led to the creation of another innova- **12.172** tive technique, called exit consents (also known as exit amendments). This innovation was the result of the limitations involved in restructuring Brady bonds and eurobonds governed by New York law, which require the unanimous consent of the bondholders for the amendment of payment terms. Unlike the Ukrainian restructuring, where the CACs permitted the majority to amend all the terms of the bonds (payment and non-payment) and make them binding on the minority, Ecuador did not have such an option and therefore would have had to resort primarily to the exchange offer technique. Although the Ecuadorian bonds did not contain CACs to amend payment terms, they did contain amendment clauses permitting a simple majority to amend all other terms, such as waivers of sovereign immunity, submissions to jurisdiction, and financial covenants. Ecuador was the first sovereign to use the amendment clauses through exit consents to deal with the potential holdout problem in

---

[287] Ibid at 33.
[288] Ibid.
[289] See Buchheit and Gulati, *supra* n 11 at 24.

the restructuring of international sovereign bonds that do not contain CACs applicable to payment terms.[290]

12.173　As Buchheit and Gulati have explained, through an exit amendment the specified majority or super-majority of bondholders can exercise their power to amend the old bond—just before they exit the old bond—as an incentive for all other holders to come along with them.[291] To address this 'potential holdout problem, Ecuador used exit consents to modify certain non-payment terms in order to make the old bonds less attractive, thereby creating incentives for bondholders to participate in the exchange.[292] Bondholders who tendered instruments under the exchange offer automatically voted in favour of a list of amendments to the non-payment terms in the instruments that they were about to leave. The amendments they consented to involved the deletion of some of the non-payment terms such as: (1) the requirement that all payment defaults must be cleared as a condition for any rescission of acceleration; (2) the provision restricting Ecuador from purchasing any of the Brady bonds while a payment default is continuing; (3) the covenant prohibiting Ecuador from seeking a further restructuring of Brady bonds; (4) the cross-default clause; (5) the negative pledge covenant; and (6) the covenant to maintain the listing of the defaulted instruments on the Luxembourg stock exchange.[293] Following the example of Ukraine, each tender for exchange was made irrevocable and the completion of the exchange was made subject to bondholders holding the requisite majority consenting to the amendments.[294]

12.174　Aside from the use of exit consents to weaken the legal rights of bondholders who decided not to participate in the exchange, the Ecuadorian government made some additional commitments to enhance the exchange offer. For example, the Ecuadorian government included the following clauses in the bonds:

(1) *Mandatory pre-payment arrangement*: this required the retirement of an aggregate outstanding amount of each type of bond by a specified percentage each year starting after 11 and six years for the 2030 and 2012 bonds, respectively, through purchases in the secondary market, debt-equity swaps, or by any other means. As Ecuador could purchase the bonds on the secondary market, it would provide the liquidity that investors wanted.[295] According to the IMF: '[t]his feature is intended to give bondholders some assurance that the aggregate amount of the new bonds would be reduced to a manageable size prior to their maturity dates while giving Ecuador flexibility to manage its debt profile.[296] If Ecuador failed to meet the reduction target, a mandatory partial redemption of the relevant bond would be triggered in an amount equal to the shortfall.[297]

(2) *Mandatory 'reinstatement' of principal clause*: this obliged Ecuador to issue additional bonds in the same amount of the debt reduction obtained through the exchange offer in the event that an interest default occurs during the first 10 years of the

---

[290]　See IMF, *supra* n 240 at 29.
[291]　Buchheit and Mitu Gulati, *supra* n 267.
[292]　See IMF, *supra* n 240 at 29.
[293]　Ibid at 8 and 35.
[294]　Ibid at 35.
[295]　Scott and Wellons, *supra* n 62 at 1304.
[296]　See IMF, *supra* n 240 at 33.
[297]　Ibid at 33–34.

new issuance, and if this default continues for a period of 12 months. This clause was also introduced to discourage casual defaults on the new bonds by giving the government an incentive to make payments.[298]

Thus, the novel use of exit consents, combined with the above described incentive clauses in the Ecuador debt restructuring, proved effective in ensuring that by the expiry of the exchange offer, 97 per cent of its bondholders agreed to participate.[299] Exit consents were criticized at the time, as well as later, by some of Ecuador's creditors as being more coercive than encouraging.[300]   **12.175**

The Ecuadorean case involved—for the first time in sovereign bond restructurings—a pure and simple use of the exit consents technique. The case of Ukraine represented a mixed technique, in the sense that it combined both exit consents and the use of majority action clauses. In the Ukrainian case, a proxy was granted to use the majority action clause to amend the terms of the old bonds to make them equal in terms to the new bonds offered.   **12.176**

Prior to the Ecuadorian restructuring, an article by Buchheit and Gulati argued that in comparison with other proposals for addressing the holdout creditor problem—such as international insolvency codes, IMF-administered stays on creditor remedies, and generally applicable legal defences for sovereign debtors—exit consents, assuming they can be made to work, would do far less violence to the existing fabric of international financial and legal relationships.[301] The case of Ecuador proves that exit consents can be made to work. Chamberlin, however, believes that sovereigns attempting to push the exit consents frontier too far will someday be challenged in court by holdout creditors.[302]   **12.177**

In 2003, it was the turn of Uruguay to reprofile its debt. To achieve this, Uruguay organized a series of meetings with its creditors, enabling it to be aware of the degree to which its offer was acceptable. Therefore, Uruguay sought the consent of the bondholders to amend three clauses of the old bonds: (1) removal of the cross-default clause; (2) delisting of the bonds requiring stock exchange listing; and (3) amendment of the waiver immunity clause. The amendment of the cross-default clause and the delisting of bonds were previously used in the case of Ecuador. This notwithstanding, in the case of Uruguay it was the first time that the waiver immunity clause was amended. The aim in amending this clause was to reinstate the immunity that sovereigns enjoy in the US by means of the Foreign Sovereign Immunity Act 1976 (FSIA) and in the UK by means of the State Immunity Act 1978 (SIA) only with regard to the payment streams due under Uruguay's new bonds. The rationale behind this was to avoid the seizure of interest payments by creditors who had not participated in the restructuring as had occurred in the *Elliott* case with respect to Peru's Brady bonds.[303]   **12.178**

Following the Ecuadorian path, Uruguay used exit consents in 2003. Uruguay's exchange offer included 'check-the-box' exit consents to amend the waiver of immunity among   **12.179**

---

[298] Ibid.

[299] Ibid at 35.

[300] See Chamberlin, *supra* n 267.

[301] Buchheit, *supra* n 274 at 25.

[302] See Chamberlin, *supra* n 267 at 4.

[303] See Elliott Associates, LP, General Docket No 2000/QR/92 (Court of Appeals of Brussels, 8th Chamber, 26 September 2000) (unreported, on file with the author).

other features.[304] In contrast to the Ecuadorian case, the use of exit consents in the case of Uruguay was consensual. This means that creditors were able to choose if they wanted to grant their exit consents aside from accepting the commercial terms of the offer. The means by which creditors consented to the use of exit consents was through the ticking of a box, giving rise to the term 'check-the-box' exit consents. The use of exit consents through this innovative way of obtaining creditors' approval was widely accepted in all the bond series, save for one where it was rejected by 13 per cent of its holders.[305]

12.180   In contrast to the cases of Ecuador and Uruguay, the use of exit consents was not available in the case of Argentina's sovereign exchange offer in 2005. This technique was not available because of the time lapse between the announcement of the moratorium and the date at which the exchange offer to amend the terms of the bonds was made effective. The time lapse permitted creditors to organize themselves. Consequently, Argentina feared the risk of having to face a blockade by holdout creditors representing more than 33⅓ per cent. Therefore, Argentina decided not to use the exit consents technique[306] due to the possibility of blocked holdings that would have prevented reaching the required 66⅔ per cent needed to amend the terms of the bonds.

12.181   Greece is another interesting case that indirectly relates to exit consent. Although, technically, the exit consent technique has not been used, it can be argued that a variation of exit consent has developed. Again, technically it does not tick all the boxes but in some informal discussions people have referred to a 'reverse' exit consent since creditors were 'connived' to exit their old bonds and accept new bonds being convinced that a new bond restructuring would be required at some point in the future and they would be better placed because of the 'stronger' legal terms inserted in the new bonds. Therefore, it is referred as a 'reverse' exit consent because rather than worsening the terms of the old bond, there is a betterment of the terms of the new bond (not economically but forward looking in the event of another restructuring). There is a creation of value for creditors, in better legal terms in the event of a future restructuring.

12.182   On the use of CACs, Greece also provided a very interesting lesson (or new tool) with the retrofitting of CACs in non-bearing CAC debt instruments. Greece's restructuring is an example that the market-centred approach works. Without the need of an international statutory process for sovereigns (eg SDRM) Greece managed to restructure its debts by reducing 53.5 per cent of the face value of its Greek governed bonds by retrofitting CACs. Since 93 per cent of the total outstanding bonds issued by Greece were governed by Greek law, the Greek government passed a law (the Bondholders Act 4050/12[307]) unilaterally introducing

---

[304] Lee Buchheit and Jeremiah Pam, 'Uruguay's Innovations' (2004) 19(1) *JIBLR* 28–31.

[305] Ibid.

[306] On 15 November 2004 Argentina filed a Memorandum of Law with the District Court of the Southern District of New York in opposition to plaintiffs' motion for a preliminary injunction in the case *Silvia Seijas, Heather M. Munton and Thomas L Pico Estrada v The Republic of Argentina* (04 Civ 400) in which Argentina confirmed that it would not use exit consents in their exchange offer. The relevant part of this Memorandum reads as follows: '... Plaintiffs' ex parte motion for a preliminary injunction is based on their incorrect speculation that the Republic's as-yet unannounced Exchange Offer will contain "exit consents" that will somehow inflict irreparable harm upon them. Of course had plaintiffs simply waited until the November 29 launch of the Exchange Offer (which is not scheduled to close until 2005) they would have learned what the Republic has publicly confirmed: the Exchange Offer will not include exit consents ...'.

[307] For an unofficial English translation see <http://andreaskoutras.blogspot.co.uk/2012/03/better-tarnslation-of-bondholders-act.html>.

a CAC clause in those bonds that did not contain this clause. Then, in the process of an exchange offer, once the necessary majorities to trigger the CAC were achieved, it was used to cramdown the dissenting minority and obtain a great degree of participation. In the English governed instruments it was not necessary to retrofit CACs because these instruments already contained CACs; however, the use of the CAC was blocked on certain instruments and therefore the clause was not able to be used on all of them, giving rise to the single-limb CAC proposed by the ICMA in 2014. The overall bondholder participation was of approximately 97 per cent of the total outstanding bonds.

Since the development of the use of exit consents in the sovereign context in 2000, there **12.183** have been three cases in which this technique was considered as an option. Ecuador and Uruguay were able to use exit consents to obtain an overwhelming degree of creditors' participation in their exchange offers—97 per cent and 93 per cent, respectively.[308] On the other hand, Argentina, without using exit consents, obtained 76.17 per cent participation. There is a 17–21 per cent gap between the Argentinian creditors' rate of participation in the exchange offer and those of other sovereigns which used exit consents.

Argentina's 2005 case was much more complex due to the number of bond series (152), the **12.184** number of applicable laws (eight), the number of creditors spread around the world (over 700,000), and the haircut proposed (75 per cent of the par value). Future restructurings with similar characteristics to that of the Argentine case would be needed to determine whether the use of exit consents is a panacea or not.

The fact that Argentina achieved a 76.17 per cent participation does not necessarily mean **12.185** that it would have been able to restructure the terms of the bonds using exit consents (66⅔ per cent) or CACs (75 per cent in the case of per series and/or single-limb CACs). There is a mathematical chance that although Argentina exceeded the 66⅔ per cent in aggregate principal amount of the outstanding bonds (being 66⅔ per cent in aggregate principal amount the threshold requirement under New York law to restructure the terms of the bonds), at the moment of de-aggregation of each series, the required percentage might have not been achieved. If, back then, the latest single-limb draft CACs had been available, Argentina would have probably been able to achieve a successful restructuring.

Argentina launched a second exchange offer in 2010 to the creditors that did not partici- **12.186** pate in the previous exchange offer launched in 2005, aiming at reducing the percentage of holdout creditors. This second exchange offer was carefully drafted not to trigger the most favoured creditor clause that would have given the option to those that participated in the first exchange offer to exchange their debt instruments. Argentina managed to reduce the number of outstanding creditors achieving an aggregate acceptance between both exchange offers of 93 per cent.

Unforeseen sovereign risk needs to be taken into consideration when managing sovereign **12.187** debt portfolios to avoid a predictable need to restructure. Countries in disaster-prone areas have often had to restructure their debt repeatedly in a relatively short amount of time due to the proliferation of tragedies striking their territory and population. Thus, a recent innovation in the sovereign debt space has been the inclusion of 'hurricane clauses' in sovereign

---

[308] It is worth noting that Uruguay's debt reprofiling took place without it having defaulted.

debt instruments. These clauses contractually allow for a moratorium on debt payments in the case of a predefined event occurring in the country. The provision is structured as follows: (1) there is a definition of what an Eligible Event is, taking into account the natural disaster risks for the country; (2) the clauses establish that if an Eligible Event occurs, the sovereign debtor will not incur a default for failing to make payments on the debt; (3) it establishes a predetermined schedule for resuming payments; and (4) missed interest payments are added to due principal.

12.188   Grenada, the sovereign nation located in the Caribbean, has included this provision in their debt instruments, allowing Grenada—if hit by a hurricane and depending on its severity—to stop servicing its interest payment for a pre-agreed period of time until the economy recovers. The interests are not forgone but will be capitalized into the principal amount. It provides the sovereign debtor with breathing space to regularize its finances and resume payments without major disruption. In late 2019, Barbados closed a comprehensive debt restructuring, resulting in all its debt instruments being climate resilient.

12.189   The aforementioned restructuring cases are a clear illustration of Buchheit and Gulati's arguments that the existing collective decision-making provisions in sovereign bonds, even within their given parameters and limitations, can, if used more confidently and creatively, mimic most of the features of domestic corporate insolvency to varying degrees, such as automatic stays, cramdowns, and, eventually, DIP financing.[309]

12.190   The coordination features among bondholders and other types of creditor, ie bilaterals, multilaterals, and trade creditors. Buchheit and Gulati point out that the existing CACs have one serious limitation—since they operate within the four corners of the bonds containing the clauses, CACs cannot be used to deal with the coordination problem outside the bonds.[310] According to the two authors, some other method, yet undiscovered or unused, will have to be used to encourage closer coordination among the various creditors, such as the Paris Club, trade creditors, and multilateral creditors.[311]

12.191   With regard to the issue of intra-coordination in the absence of single-limb CACs (coordination within similarly situated creditors such as different series of bonds), there are two alternatives: (1) aggregation, as in the case of Uruguay (but unfortunately this feature is only available to future bond issuances); or (2) as suggested by Buchheit and Gulati, in cases where the majority of the bonds are issued and governed by New York law—to engage in the equity powers of the US federal courts under Rule 23 of the Federal Rules of Civil Procedure (FRCP 23) where bondholders can be homogenized into a single voting class and any court-approved compromise of the action would bind all members of the class.[312] The exchange offers of Pakistan (1999), Ukraine (1999), Ecuador (2000 and 2020), Uruguay (2003), Argentina (2005–2010 and 2020), Belize (2006 and 2013), and Greece (2012) can be used to consider whether the use of market-oriented mechanisms, mainly exchange offers coupled with other participation enhancement techniques, work. These seven different countries

---

[309] See Buchheit and Gulati, *supra* n 11.
[310] Ibid at 21–22.
[311] Ibid at 22.
[312] Ibid at 30.

have been selected because they serve as a wide sample of different types of restructuring episode, including pre-emptive debt reprofiling, default (with and without nominal value reductions), and the use of CACs (with the re-designation and Pac-Man technique attempts) and exit consents. In all these cases, the degree of participation in the exchange offer, which means the rate of acceptance, has been above 90 per cent (Pakistan 99 per cent, Ukraine 95 per cent, Ecuador 97 and 98 per cent, Uruguay 93 per cent, Argentina 93 per cent after two rounds of exchanges and 99 per cent, Belize 97 per cent, and Greece 97 per cent).[313] Despite the fact that none of these exchange offers have achieved 100 per cent, it can be claimed they have been successful for the high degree of participation—in all of them well above 90 per cent. This is the result of contractual creativeness in a scenario where the dynamics are different due to the lack of, and impossibility of having, an insolvency regime.

F. Case Study: Uruguay's Debt Reprofiling—How to Perform a Successful Exchange Offer

1. Introduction

In this section, the case of Uruguay's debt reprofiling in 2003 is used to illustrate how an exchange offer can be carried out in a successful manner. By means of an exchange offer, Uruguay extended the maturity of its debt obligations and reduced interest rates (in some series) averting default. Usually, countries try to delay the unavoidable (ie default) so that markets do not financially punish the sovereign with high interest rates once a restructuring has been carried out and it tries to re-access the capital markets. Uruguay did exactly the opposite: a fast and smooth pre-emptive voluntary exchange offer that permitted its re-access to the markets within a month of the restructuring and without being penalized with a high interest rate.   **12.192**

This restructuring is also of paramount significance because it is the first time that a sovereign has replaced all its outstanding bonds with new ones with CACs.[314]   **12.193**

2 A success story in debt reprofiling

First, a brief analysis of the economic situation of Uruguay will be rendered. Secondly, an analysis of the legal techniques used is also provided.   **12.194**

Uruguay's economy suffered a vast deterioration during 2002 and the beginning of 2003 due to the 2001–2002 Argentine crisis. The Argentine upheaval severely impacted Uruguay due to the number of Argentine depositors in the Uruguayan banking system. Uruguay portrayed its sovereign debt restructuring offer as a pre-emptive step to deal with a serious liquidity problem before the situation would deteriorate into a full-fledged default.[315] Uruguay's restructuring has been described by Beattie[316] as one that is almost straight out of the US Treasury Wall Street Rulebook of 'voluntary market-based' solutions. This   **12.195**

---

[313] See Rodrigo Olivares-Caminal, *Legal Aspects of Sovereign Debt Restructuring* (2009) and recent developments.

[314] John Barham, 'Cooking Up a New Solution', *Latin Finance*, June 2003 at 12.

[315] See Buchheit and Pam, *supra* n 294 at 28–31.

[316] See Alan Beattie, 'Uruguay Provides Test Case for Merits of Voluntary Debt Exchange', *Financial Times*, 23 April 2003, available at <http://www.globalpolicy.org>.

notwithstanding, the bond market rapidly reacted to the Uruguayan strategy and the value of the bonds reached default levels. Uruguay's total outstanding amount of debt was approximately $5.3 billion. The outstanding international debt totalled $3.8 billion, including $400 million of Brady bonds and $200 million of Samurai bonds.[317] The international bonds were 19 series subject to English and New York law and were denominated in USD, EUR, JPY, GBP, and Chilean Pesos (CLP).[318] Approximately 50 per cent of the outstanding debt was held by retail investors and the same percentage was held by domestic investors.

12.196   The offer was preceded by extensive consultations with bondholders in several financial centres. In public announcements, Atchugarry—Uruguay's former Minister of Economy and Finance—stated that the terms and conditions of the offer reflected the negotiations held with the bondholders. In part, the success of the reprofiling is attributable to the continuous interaction between the Uruguayan government and its creditors.

12.197   The debt reprofiling consisted of: (1) an exchange offer to restructure all the outstanding domestic and international debt; and (2) amendment to the terms and conditions of the Samurai bond using CACs. The offer was announced on 10 April 2003, and completed on 29 May 2003, resulting in a successful restructuring with a bondholders' acceptance of 93 per cent. The transaction thus challenged the widely held view that investors will refuse to take seriously a proposal to restructure sovereign bonds unless they are forced to confront an open payment default.[319]

12.198   Two types of bonds were offered to the bondholders:

> (1) the so-called *Bonos Extensión*, which were new bonds in the same currency of origin, bearing the same interest rate, with a five-year deferral on the original maturity date of the old bond; and,
> (2) the so-called *Bonos Liquidez*, which offered greater liquidity than the old bonds since they are expected to be traded in the secondary debt market and they would provide a benchmark for future issues.

12.199   In separate but cross-conditioned transactions, Uruguay conducted a domestic exchange offer on terms similar to the international offer and asked holders of Uruguay's Samurai bond, which contained a CAC allowing changes to payment terms with the consent of 66⅔ per cent of holders voting at a meeting with a 50 per cent quorum, to amend its payment terms to extend the maturity date.[320] Both the legal analysis underlying the use of the CAC, and the procedures for that use, were untested in Japan at the time Uruguay sought a five-year deferral of the maturity date of its Samurai bond.[321] The clauses were successfully used to extend the maturity from 2006 to 2011, and to raise the interest rate from 2.2 per cent to 2.5 per cent.[322]

---

[317] A Samurai bond is a yen-denominated bond issued by a non-Japanese borrower mainly targeting the Japanese market.

[318] See Buchheit and Pam, *supra* n 294 at 28–31.

[319] Ibid.

[320] See Puhan Chunam and Federico Sturzenegger, 'Default Episodes in the 1980s and 1990s: What Have We Learned?' in J Aizenman and B Pinto, *Managing Volatility Crises: A Practitioners' Guide* (2011) and Cleary, Gotlieb, Stean, and Hamilton, 'Uruguay in Groundbreaking $5.2 Billion Debt Restructuring', Press Release, 29 May 2003.

[321] See Buchheit and Pam, *supra* n 294 at 28–31.

[322] See Chunam and Sturzenegger, *supra* n 310.

According to Buchheit and Pam,[323] Uruguay's exchange offer included several innovative   **12.200**
legal techniques, some of them are: (1) 'check-the-box' exit consents (including the use of
exit consents to amend the waiver of immunity); (2) incorporation of CACs in all the new
bonds, including special features such as aggregation vote packing and, disenfranchisement; and (3) prohibition of the use of exit consents coercively.

These techniques are analysed below.   **12.201**

(a) 'Check-the-box' exit consents

As previously mentioned, exit consents were used for the first time in the debt restruc-   **12.202**
turing of Ecuador in 2000. In that opportunity, by accepting the terms and conditions of
the new bonds that were offered creditors were also granting their consent for the use of
exit consents. As opposed to the 2000 Ecuadorian case, by accepting the exchange offer
bondholders were obliged to grant their exit consent. The use of exit consents in the case
of Uruguay was consensual. This meant that creditors were able to choose if they wanted
to grant their exit consents besides accepting the commercial terms of the offer. The way by
which creditors gave their consent to the use of exit consents was by the sole fact of ticking
a box, thereby it was so-called 'check-the-box' exit consents. The use of exit consents by this
innovative mechanism of getting the consent of creditors was widely accepted in all the
series except in one where it was rejected by 13 per cent of its holders.

(b) The use of exit consents to amend the waiver of immunity

As a result of various meetings held between the government and its creditors, Uruguay was   **12.203**
aware of the degree of acceptance of its offer among creditors. Therefore, Uruguay sought
the consent of the bondholders to amend three clauses of the old bonds: (1) to remove the
cross-default clause; (2) to de-list the bonds that require to be listed on a stock exchange;
and (3) to amend the waiver immunity clause.

The amendment of the cross-default clause and the de-listing of the bonds were previously   **12.204**
used in the case of Ecuador. This notwithstanding, in the case of Uruguay it was the first
time that the waiver immunity clause was amended. The aim in amending this clause—only
in regard to the payment streams due under Uruguay's new bonds—was to reinstate the
immunity that sovereigns have in the US and the UK by means of the Foreign Sovereign
Immunity Act of 1976 and State Immunity Act of 1978, respectively. The rationale behind
this was to avoid the seizure of interest payments by creditors that had not participated in
the restructuring as happened to Peru's Brady bonds in the *Elliott* case.[324]

(c) Incorporation of CACs in all the new bonds

Uruguay included CACs in all its new bonds issued as a result of the exchange offer.   **12.205**
Uruguay followed the proposed CAC by the G10 working group in 2002. This means that
in the hypothetical case that Uruguay needs to restructure its bonds again, any term of the
bonds (including the payment terms) can be amended with the consent of holders of 75 per

---

[323] See Buchheit and Pam, *supra* n 294 at 28–31.
[324] Elliott Associates, LP, *supra* n 324.

cent of the aggregate principal amount of each series. It is worth mentioning that Uruguay bonds are subject to New York law.

(d) Aggregation

12.206 This is one of the most innovative features of Uruguay's debt reprofiling. By the aggregation mechanism, amendments to any terms (including payment terms) can be incorporated into one or more series of bonds simultaneously. In order to approve the amendment, a double majority is required: (1) 85 per cent of the aggregate principal amount of all affected series; and (2) 66⅔ per cent of each specific series.

(e) Vote packing

12.207 Uruguay included a covenant in the new bonds to guarantee the bondholders that new bonds would not be issued nor any existing series of bonds would be re-opened. The aim of this covenant was to avoid the new bonds being placed in the hands of investors that would vote in favour of a proposed amendment, thereby diluting the bondholders' holding.

12.208 This clause reads as follows: 'Uruguay agrees that it will not issue new debt securities or re-open any existing series of debt securities with the intention of placing such debt securities with holders expected to support any modification proposed by Uruguay (or that Uruguay plans to propose) for approval pursuant to the modification provisions of the indenture or the terms and conditions of any series of debt securities'.[325]

(f) Disenfranchisement

12.209 The 'disenfranchisement' feature means that bonds owned or controlled by Uruguay or any public sector instrumentality of Uruguay are to be disregarded in a vote on a modification to the terms of the bonds. Prior to any vote, Uruguay shall deliver to the trustee a certificate signed by an authorized representative of Uruguay specifying any debt securities that are owned or controlled by Uruguay or any public sector instrumentality.[326]

12.210 The importance of the inclusion of a disfranchisement clause came to the forefront a few years later when Ecuador defaulted on its external debt. Ecuador decided to stop servicing a subset of its external bonds because these bonds were found to be illegitimate or illegal by the debt audit commission (Comisión para la Auditoría Integral del Crédito Público (CAIC)) mandated by a Presidential decree in 2006.[327] The audit report produced by the CAIC found several cases in which Ecuador's debt was incurred by illegal and/or illegitimate means. Following the recommendation of the audit commission, on November 2008

---

[325] See Uruguay, *supra* n 259.

[326] Ibid. 'Public sector instrumentality' means Banco Central, any department, ministry, or agency of the government of Uruguay or any corporation, trust, financial institution, or other entity owned or controlled by the government of Uruguay or any of the foregoing, and 'control' means the power, directly or indirectly, through the ownership of voting securities or other ownership interests or otherwise, to direct the management of or elect or appoint a majority of the board of directors or other persons performing similar functions in lieu of, or in addition to, the board of directors of a corporation, trust, financial institution, or other entity.

[327] The objective of CAIC is to audit the processes by which public debt has been incurred to determine its legitimacy, legality, transparency, quality, efficacy, and efficiency, considering legal and financial aspects, the economical, social, gender, and environmental impacts, and the impact on nationalities and people. The scope of the audit comprised agreements, contracts, and other forms of public financing between 1976 and 2006. Although the CAIC concluded that several debt instruments were either illegal and/or illegitimate, Ecuador only defaulted on the 2012 and 2030 bonds.

Ecuador suspended interest payment on the 2012 global bonds deemed to be illegitimate and, after a 30-day grace period, it formally entered in default on 15 December 2008. At the moment of the default, Ecuador had three outstanding series of bonds: (1) 12 per cent USD Global Bonds due 2012; (2) USD Step-up Global Bonds due 2030; and (3) USD Global Bonds due 2015.

The 2012 and 2030 bonds were issued in 2000 to restructure the Brady bonds. The 2015   **12.211** bonds were issued to purchase some of the 2012 bonds in accordance with the issuance terms of the latter (Mandatory Pre-payment Arrangement). Although the CAIC concluded that several debt instruments (the three bonds and other debt instruments) were illegal and/or illegitimate, it was decided to default only on the 2012 and 2030 bonds.

On 20 April 2009, Ecuador launched a cash buyback offer to repurchase the 2012 and 2030   **12.212** bonds. The buyback offer expired on 15 May 2009. The final buyback price was USD 35 cents per dollar of outstanding principal, which was accepted by 91 per cent of the bond-holders.[328] The Ecuadorian default is a landmark case because it is the first default in modern history in which ability to pay played almost no role.[329]

One important issue is that Ecuador allegedly performed an aggressive secondary repur-   **12.213** chase via intermediaries when the price for the 2012 and 2030 bonds hit rock bottom but before an official moratorium was announced or a default actually occurred.[330]

The 2012 and 2030 Ecuadorian bonds included a debt purchase provision, ie a 'manda-   **12.214** tory prepayment arrangement'. This contractual arrangement required the retirement of an aggregate outstanding amount for each type of bond by a specified percentage each year starting after six and 11 years for the 2012 and 2030 bonds, respectively, through purchases in the secondary market, debt-equity swaps or by any other means.[331] This contractual pro-vision included in the Ecuadorian bonds clearly denotes that the purchase in the secondary market of a debtor's own debt not only is legal but also desired since it can contribute to reduce the amount of outstanding debt to make it more manageable. However, Ecuador's repurchase took place after certain events that could have affected the trading price of the debt instruments.[332] This put in evidence a systemic failure affecting market integrity, since Ecuador could have been in a position to perform a disclosure of market manipulative

---

[328] Republic of Ecuador Press Release, dated 12 June 2009.

[329] In the Ecuadorian Noteholder Circular dated 20 April 2009 to submit in a modified Dutch auction to sell Bonds for Cash it was stated that as of 31 December 2008 the total internal and external debt represented 26.12 per-cent of GDP, which was totally manageable. A 2008 financial report stated that '... it is still difficult to argue that Ecuador's debt faces a sustainability problem ... the current situation is triggered by a lack of willingness to pay (rather than a lack of ability to pay) ...' Deutsche Bank, Ecuador: On the Likelihood of Debt Restructuring, EM Special Publication, Global Markets Research, 17 November 2008.

[330] See Miller and Porzecanski, *supra* n 85.

[331] According to an IMF publication: '[t]his feature is intended to give bondholders some assurance that the ag-gregate amount of the new bonds would be reduced to a manageable size prior to their maturity dates while giving Ecuador flexibility to manage its debt profile'. See IMF, 'Involving the Private Sector in the Resolution of Financial Crisis—Restructuring International Sovereign Bonds' 2001. If Ecuador failed to meet the reduction target, a man-datory partial redemption of the relevant bond would be triggered in an amount equal to the shortfall.

[332] These include, announcements on the delay of interest payments, videos of meetings among the minister of finance and other individuals discussing, etc. (See *The Economist*, 'Caught on Camera: A Setback for Rafael Correa', 26 July 2007.)

information and at the same time decide how to proceed (ie default or not).[333] Therefore, even if the ties between the secondary actors and the Ecuadorian government were to be proven, the actual default made it very difficult to demonstrate an undesired behaviour since the default occurred and therefore the possible allegations of deliberate market manipulation ceased to exist.[334]

(g) Prohibition of the use of exit consents coercively

12.215   In order to avoid the use of exit consents in future potential restructuring in a coercive way, Uruguay's new debt instruments foreclose any possibility of mischief in this regard. To achieve this, the terms of the bonds require that any modifications to the payment terms of the bonds proposed in the context of a future exchange offer cannot make the terms of that exchange offer less favourable than the current terms.

12.216   Uruguay's prospectus reads as follows:

> If any ... modification is sought in the context of a simultaneous offer to exchange the debt securities of one or more series for new debt instruments of Uruguay ..., Uruguay shall ensure that the relevant provisions of the affected debt securities, ... are no less favourable to the holders thereof than the provisions of the new instrument being offered in the exchange, or, if more than one debt instrument is so offered, no less favourable than the new debt instrument issued having the largest aggregate principal amount.[335]

3. Some concluding remarks on Uruguay's exchange offer

12.217   Uruguay's debt swap was successful and ground-breaking because it avoided default, obtaining the desired maturity stretch and the inclusion of CACs in all its new bonds which will facilitate any future potential debt restructuring. In order to make the proposal more attractive, an incentive was tendered to sweeten the terms of the exchange offer (ie upfront cash to international debt maturing in the near to medium term; and, upfront cash to the domestic debt maturing in 2003[336]). In 2003, after the debt exchange, the economy resumed growth with a 2.5 per cent rise in GDP.

G. COVID-19-Triggered Initiatives[337]

12.218   Since the outbreak of the COVID-19 pandemic on 11 March 2020,[338] low- and middle-income countries (LMICs)[339] entered the pandemic with weaker structural

---

[333] As argued by Porzecanski there are clear links between the decrease of Ecuadorian Central bank reserves and the purchase of debt in the secondary market during the default period. Also, it is alleged that the vehicle used was Banco del Pacifico acting through a broker. See Porzecanski, *supra* n 85.

[334] Ecuador allegedly managed to acquire a substantial percentage of debt in the secondary market which could have distorted the readings from the outcome of the buyback exercise given that it allegedly acquired around 50 per cent of the total outstanding debt in each series.

[335] Uruguay, *supra* n 259.

[336] Chunam and Sturzenegger, *supra* n 310 at 55.

[337] The author would like to thank Dagmara Joanna Hanyz for valuable research assistance in this section of the chapter.

[338] WHO, 'WHO Director-General's Opening Remarks at the Media Briefing on Covid-19' (11 March 2020) <https://www.who.int/director-general/speeches/detail/who-director-general-s-opening-remarks-at-the-media-briefing-on-covid-19---11-march-2020>.

[339] As defined by World Bank, 'World Bank Country and Lending Groups' <https://datahelpdesk.worldbank.org/knowledgebase/articles/906519>.

conditions,[340] disproportionately vis-à-vis high-income economies. According to the World Bank, the COVID-19 pandemic pushed 92 million more people into extreme poverty in 2020, in particular across Sub-Saharan Africa and South Asia, marking the first net rise in global poverty in more than 20 years.[341] As a result of the deterioration in economic conditions and the urgent need to increase public expenditure to counteract the effects of the pandemic, the World Bank and the IMF urged the G20 countries to establish the DSSI. Due to its limitations, it was shortly followed by its successor, the Common Framework for Debt Treatments Beyond the DSSI (Common Framework). These are the two recent official developments to assist in coping with the growing debt burden aggravated as result of the COVID-19 pandemic.

1. Historical context

The public debt situation in many LMICs was already precarious prior to the COVID-19 pandemic. These countries had accumulated more debt than ever before since the global financial crisis of 2008. The single most prominent feature of this debt accumulation had been an extraordinary rise in external indebtedness,[342] which outpaced more traditional forms of financing such as multilateral and bilateral debt. The increase in external indebtedness was driven by the need to finance domestic investment-savings gaps.[343] It was also encouraged by international investors' search for higher yields in the context of the long period of low international interest rates in high-income economies and unprecedented levels of global liquidity associated with quantitative easing in the aftermath of the financial crisis of 2008. By February 2020, the IMF Executive Board was already expressing concerns at the continued high levels of public debt in many low-income countries (LICs), which could constrain fiscal space, ultimately leading to lower investment and economic growth, in particular if global risks materialize,[344] as was the case since the start of the pandemic.

12.219

According to UNCTAD, total external debts of developing countries and economies in transition (developing countries)[345] reached $10 trillion in 2019, more than doubling from 2009.[346] This increase further fragmented the creditor composition of emerging market debt. At the end of 2018, 62 per cent of developing countries' debt was held by private creditors, compared to 46 per cent at end-2009, and the share of this debt owed to foreign bondholders rose from 60 per cent to 76 per cent.[347] The steep increase in foreign-currency denominated bonds was particularly pronounced in LICs[348] and UN least-developed

12.220

---

[340] Akihiko Nishio, 'Covid-19 Is Hitting Poor Countries the Hardest. Here's How World Bank's IDA Is Stepping Up Support' (28 January 2021) <https://blogs.worldbank.org/voices/covid-19-hitting-poor-countries-hardest-heres-how-world-banks-ida-stepping-support>.

[341] World Bank, <https://blogs.worldbank.org/opendata/updated-estimates-impact-covid-19-global-poverty-turning-corner-pandemic-2021>

[342] Portion of a country's debt that is borrowed from foreign lenders as opposed to domestic lenders.

[343] Refers to the deficit between current aggregate savings and the level of savings required to provide funds for business investment. https://archive.unescwa.org/investment-savings-gap

[344] IMF, 'The Evolution of Public Debt Vulnerabilities in Lower Income Economies' (2020) IMF Press Release No. 20/33.

[345] There is no established convention for the designation of 'developing', 'transition', and 'developed' countries. UNCTAD follows the classification as defined in the UNCTAD 'Handbook of Statistics 2019' for these three major country groupings, available at <https://unctad.org/en/PublicationsLibrary/tdstat44_en.pdf>.

[346] UNCTAD, Trade and Development Report 2020, 8.

[347] Ibid.

[348] See World Bank, Debt & Fiscal Risk Toolkit, available at <https://www.worldbank.org/en/programs/debt-toolkit/dsa>.

countries (LDCs),[349] with several countries becoming new issuers.[350] For example, at the beginning of 2020, a total of 21 African countries had outstanding global bonds amounting to $115 billion.[351]

12.221 This rise in external indebtedness has increased debt vulnerabilities. Funding from international capital markets involves higher financing costs, variable maturities, and higher exposure to interest rates, exchange rates, and roll-over risks than the more traditional multilateral or bilateral financing.[352] The reliance on the global bond markets also weakens countries' ability to 'self-insure' against exogenous shocks and increased market risk, as demonstrated by the decrease in the ratio of short-term external debt-to-reserves from its peak in 2009 at 544 per cent to 279 per cent in 2019. In the context of the COVID-19 crisis, this was a severe limitation on the ability of developing countries to bridge liquidity crises arising from this shock.

12.222 Rising external debt burdens continued to absorb a growing share of LMICs' resources. In 2019, developing countries spent 14.6 per cent of their export revenues (up from 7.8 per cent in 2011) and 4.7 per cent of government revenues (up from 2.7 per cent in 2012) on the costs of servicing public debt.[353] However, the situation is much more acute in many developing countries that rely on commodity exports, and in middle-income countries with high debt burdens where debt servicing costs consume more than a quarter of government revenues.[354]

12.223 The COVID-19 pandemic exposed existing debt vulnerabilities of LMICs,[355] pushing many countries to the brink of default and some even into actual default. In March 2020, the IMF[356] and World Bank[357] warned that the COVID-19 pandemic could prompt a protracted debt crisis for many developing countries.[358] A record number of six countries across Latin America (Argentina, Belize, Ecuador, Suriname), the Middle East (Lebanon), and Africa (Zambia) defaulted on their bonds in 2020. Over 30 countries had their credit ratings downgraded throughout 2020,[359] and some were even downgraded more than twice.[360] According to the IMF, in June 2021 seven LICs were in debt distress, 29 were at high risk, and 24 at medium risk of debt distress.[361]

---

[349] See UNCTAD, List of UN's Least Developed Countries, available at <https://unctad.org/topic/least-develo ped-countries/list>.

[350] IMF, 'The Evolution of Public Debt Vulnerabilities in Lower Income Economies' (2020) IMF Policy Paper, 17.

[351] UNCTAD, Trade and Development Report 2020, 8.

[352] Ibid.

[353] Ibid, 7.

[354] Ibid.

[355] IMF, 'The Evolution of Public Debt Vulnerabilities in Lower Income Economies' (2020) IMF Policy Paper, 10.

[356] Chris Giles, 'Prepare for Emerging Markets Debt Crisis, Warns IMF Head', *Financial Times* (30 March 2021) <https://www.ft.com/content/487c30f4-7f21-4787-b519-dde52264d141>.

[357] Jonathan Wheatley, 'UN Chief Warns of Coming Debt Crisis for Developing World', *Financial Times* (29 March 2021) <https://www.ft.com/content/abcd97d3-fb65-47e5-973a-598514f1fd5a>.

[358] UNDESA, 'Covid-19 and Sovereign Debt' (United Nations, Policy Brief #72) May 2020, 1.

[359] Fitch Ratings, 'Sovereign Defaults Hit Record in 2020; More Are Possible' (8 June 2021) <https://www.fitch ratings.com/research/sovereigns/sovereign-defaults-hit-record-in-2020-more-are-possible-08-06-2021#:~:text= Fitch's%20recent%20Sovereign%202020%20Transition,in%20both%202016%20and%202017>.

[360] OECD, 'Sovereign Borrowing Outlook 2021' <https://www.oecd-ilibrary.org/sites/0bac8d21-en/index. html?itemId=/content/component/0bac8d21-en#back-endnotea3z3>.

[361] IMF, 'List of LIC DSAs for PRGT-Eligible Countries', <https://www.imf.org/external/pubs/ft/dsa/dsalist. pdf>. Also see the World Bank's latest publicly available Debt Sustainability Analyses under the Joint Bank-Fund Debt Sustainability Framework for Low Income Countries (LIC-DSF), available at <https://www.worldbank.org/ en/programs/debt-toolkit/dsa>.

The outbreak of the pandemic led to a sudden stop in capital flows to LICs in 2020 as investors raced to pull funds out of what was perceived as high-risk markets, fearing sovereign defaults given the limited fiscal space of many of these LMICs. According to estimates by the IIF, international investor outflows from emerging market countries amounted to nearly $100 billion over a period of 45 days starting in late February 2020, which represents a far greater scale than in any previous crisis.[362] Although the emerging markets have calmed since April 2020, the UNCTAD warned that without a 'concerted international action to reduce the debt overhang in developing countries the return of stormier conditions is an ever-present threat to their chances of recovery'.[363]   **12.224**

Since its outbreak, COVID-19 has induced a contraction in global economic activity that has knocked more economies into simultaneous recession than at any time since 1870. The IMF projected global growth at −4.4 per cent in 2020[364] compared with +2.9 per cent in 2019.[365] The World Bank estimates economies eligible for International Development Association (IDA) funds and UN LDCs have contracted by about 2.8 per cent in 2020 compared with average growth of 3.6 per cent in the previous five years. The Sub-Saharan African countries look particularly vulnerable.[366]   **12.225**

The COVID-19 debt triggered a conundrum that can be seen as a 'high-debt, low-growth trap'.[367] The slowing down of global economic activity has reduced inflows of foreign investments and tax revenues to LMICs' economies. By straining LMICs' budgets, COVID-19 weakens their ability to finance the health response and support their populations and economies. Therefore, COVID-19 (and the need to finance the health response) has led to a surge in additional public expenditure, which has been covered through additional borrowing in many of the LMICs.[368] Just to illustrate this point, the IMF estimates that sub-Saharan Africa's LICs face additional external funding needs of $245 billion to help strengthen the pandemic response over 2021–2025. The corresponding figure for all sub-Saharan Africa is $425 billion.[369] The IMF expects fiscal balances to turn sharply negative to −10.3/−9.1 per cent of GDP in emerging market and middle-income economies, and −5.5 per cent of GDP in LICs.[370] With this negative outlook, the World Bank and the IMF were fearing a systemic crisis—one that did not materialize[371]—and asked the G20 countries for a concerted initiative to deal with the impending debt crisis.   **12.226**

---

[362] UNCTAD, Trade and Development Report 2020, 6.

[363] Ibid, 7.

[364] IMF, 'World Economic Outlook: A Long and Difficult Ascent' (October 2020) <https://www.imf.org/en/Publications/WEO/Issues/2020/09/30/world-economic-outlook-october-2020>.

[365] IMF, 'World Economic Outlook: Tentative Stabilization, Sluggish Recovery?' (January 2020) <https://www.imf.org/en/Publications/WEO/Issues/2020/01/20/weo-update-january2020>.

[366] IMF, 'Regional Economic Outlook: Sub-Saharan Africa Navigating a Long Pandemic' (April 2021)

[367] UN DESA, 'Public Finances After Covid-19: Is a High-Debt, Low-Growth Trap Looming for Developing Countries?' (2020) Briefing No. 142 <https://www.un.org/development/desa/dpad/publication/world-economic-situation-and-prospects-october-2020-briefing-no-142/>.

[368] United Nations Department of Economic and Social Affairs, 'Covid-19 and Sovereign Debt', United Nations, Policy Brief #72, May 2020.

[369] IMF, 'Regional Economic Outlook: Sub-Saharan Africa Navigating a Long Pandemic', April 2021, VI.

[370] IMF, 'Fiscal Monitor Update', January 2021, 1.

[371] At the time this section was being drafted, the systemic crisis has not materialized as foreseen.

2. Debt Service Suspension Initiative (DSSI)

12.227   On 15 April 2020, the G20 member countries endorsed a coordinated approach to provide a Debt Service Suspension Initiative (DSSI) for the world's poorest countries,[372] whereby bilateral creditors would commit to a temporary suspension of debt service payments. The DSSI aims to ease financing constraints on eligible countries and free up scarce resources to manage the severe impact of the COVID-19 pandemic.

12.228   Countries that are eligible for the DSSI are all active IDA countries and all UN LDCs that are current on any debt service to the IMF and the World Bank. Eligible countries must also be benefiting from or have made a request for IMF financing including emergency facilities. This amounts to a total of 76 countries of which 65 per cent are on the African continent.[373] Middle-income countries are excluded from the DSSI despite the fact that several of them have experienced equally devastating COVID-19-induced shocks on their economic and fiscal positions. According to the World Bank, 80 per cent of the 124 million people estimated to have been pushed into extreme poverty in 2020 because of the pandemic were in middle-income countries.[374]

12.229   By requesting a debt service suspension, the beneficiary country commits to using the created fiscal space to increase social, health, or economic spending in response to the COVID-19 pandemic. The requesting countries are also required to disclose all public sector financial debts (respecting confidentiality) and not to contract any new non-concessional debt during the suspension period other than in compliance with limits agreed under the IMF's Debt Limit Policy or the World Bank's policy on non-concessional borrowing.

12.230   The suspension covers principal and interest repayments for debts entered into before 24 March 2020. The payments are suspended on a net present value (NPV) neutral basis, meaning that they are not forgiven or reduced but simply delayed. Therefore, the DSSI is not intended to address the pre-existing problems of debt unsustainability in several of the LMICs (as many entered the pandemic with pre-existing structural problems and already evident unsustainable balance of payments). Although the suspension period was originally agreed to last until the end of 2020, it was extended twice by six months each time (in October 2020 and April 2021) until the end of 2021 because of the continuing COVID-19 crisis.

12.231   Payments suspended between May and December 2020 are due for repayment after a one-year grace period with payments spread over three years. The grace period for payments suspended during the first six months of the DSSI extension running through to June 2021 remains the same, but the repayments are spread over five years to avoid overlaps and clustering of debt service payments.[375] By providing rapid liquidity support for LICs, the DSSI improves their capacity to cope with the immediate liquidity challenges that arose from

---

[372] G20, 'Communiqué of the Virtual Meeting of the G20 Finance Ministers and Central Bank Governors', Riyadh, Saudi Arabia, 15 April 2020 <http://www.g20.utoronto.ca/2020/2020-g20-finance-0415.html#a2>

[373] See World Bank, 'Covid-19 Debt Service Suspension Initiative Brief', 24 September 2021, available at <https://www.worldbank.org/en/topic/debt/brief/covid-19-debt-service-suspension-initiative>.

[374] See World Bank, 'Covid-19 to Add as Many as 150 Million Extreme Poor by 2021', Press Release 7 October 2020, available at <https://www.worldbank.org/en/news/press-release/2020/10/07/covid-19-to-add-as-many-as-150-million-extreme-poor-by-2021>.

[375] Daniel Munevar, 'The G20 "Common Framework for Debt Treatments beyond the DSSI": Is It Bound To Fail?' (Eurodad Briefing, 2020) 1.

the crisis, while safeguarding access to external sources of financing.[376] As of 13 November 2020, 46 countries requested debt service suspension,[377] benefiting from \$5.7 billion debt service deferral.[378] The IMF estimates that the first six-month DSSI extension through June 2021 could provide an additional \$7.3 billion of debt service suspension for the participating countries.[379]

The DSSI called upon commercial creditors to participate in the initiative on comparable **12.232** terms when requested by eligible countries. A commitment was made by the IIF to support the DSSI,[380] and terms of reference for voluntary private sector participation were published on 28 May 2020.[381] This notwithstanding, private creditors have not been consulted nor are part of the debt relief conversations and as a result the DSSI has failed to commit commercial creditors to debt suspension on a voluntary basis.[382] Consequently, LICs continued to service \$13 billion of private debts throughout 2020,[383] partially as a result of their increased repayment capacity generated by the bilateral debt suspensions under the DSSI.[384] For most IDA borrowers, private creditors account for a relatively small share of the countries' external public debt. However, they account for a significant share in some countries (eg, Côte d'Ivoire (60 per cent), Ghana (58 per cent), and Chad, St. Lucia, and Zambia (all 50 per cent)).

The lack of involvement or consultation with private creditors on the design of the DSSI or **12.233** when deciding on each arrangement by the G20 whilst demanding a voluntary participation of the private creditors is the main reason behind the failure of the initiative as it is presented as a 'fait accompli' after dictating what the private sector face value reduction should be.[385] It has been argued that the decision to restrict the DSSI to bilateral official creditors reflected the priority at the outset of the crisis to provide immediate support. However, involving private creditors could have resulted in higher private creditor participation, which could have increased the revenues available to eligible countries by \$8.8 billion in 2020 alone.[386]

---

[376] Paris Club, 2020 Annual Report, 17, available at <https://clubdeparis.org/en/communications/press-release/publication-of-the-2020-annual-report-of-the-paris-club-15-07-2021>.

[377] Ibid.

[378] See G20 Leaders' Declaration, 21 November 2020, available at <http://www.g20.utoronto.ca/2020/2020-g20-leaders-declaration-1121.html>.

[379] IMF, 'Questions and Answers on Sovereign Debt Issues', 8 April 2021, available at <https://www.imf.org/en/About/FAQ/sovereign-debt#s2q2>.

[380] Paris Club and IIF (2020), 'Collaboration between the Paris Club and the IIF to Support the DSSI', 30 April 2020, available at <https://clubdeparis.org/en/communications/press-release/collaboration-between-the-paris-club-and-the-iif-to-support-the-dssi-30>.

[381] IIF, 'IIIF Releases New Framework to Facilitate Voluntary Private Sector Involvement in the G20/Paris Club Debt Service Suspension Initiative', 28 May 2020, available at <https://www.iif.com/Press/View/ID/3918/IIF-Releases-New-Framework-to-Facilitate-Voluntary-Private-Sector-Involvement-inthe-G20Paris-Club-Debt-Service-Suspension-Initiative>.

[382] Myriam Vander Stichele, 'Will the G20 let private finance escape debt relief once again?' <https://www.somo.nl/will-the-g20-let-private-finance-escape-debt-relief-once-again/> accessed 25 August 2021.

[383] IIF, 'G20 DSSI: What's Owed to Private Creditors?', IIF Weekly Insight (7 May 2020).

[384] Stephen Connelly, Celine Tan, Karina Patricio Ferreira Lima, and Chris Tassis, 'The G20 Debt Service Suspension Initiative: What of Commercial Creditors?' (December 2020) Butterworths Journal of International Banking and Financial Law 742..

[385] Laura Gardner-Cuesta, 'Unpacking the G20's Common Framework for Sovereign Debt Restructuring', Debtwire, 10 February 2021.

[386] Paul Steele and Sejal Patel, Tackling the Triple Crisis: Using Debt Swaps to Address Debt, Climate and Nature Loss Post-Covid-19 (IIED 2020) 17.

12.234 Like private creditors, multilateral development banks have not suspended their debt claims under the DSSI either. They have, however, supported the DSSI through providing net-positive flows to DSSI-eligible countries during the suspension period while maintaining their current rating and low cost of funding. Both the IMF and the World Bank have substantially increased their overall lending beyond that which their member countries can typically request through the concessional financing facilities. As of early April 2021, the IMF had approved emergency financing of about $12 billion to 51 LICs. The IMF is also providing debt service relief through the Catastrophe Containment and Relief Trust (CCRT)[387] to 29 of its poorest and most vulnerable member countries, including 22 sub-Saharan African countries, covering these countries' eligible debt falling due to the IMF for the period between April 2020 and mid-October 2021. The IMF is working with the CCRT donors to extend the duration of grant-based debt relief to April 2022.

12.235 The DSSI was ill-fated due to the limited number of participants (eg multilaterals, China, and the private sector were not bound) and firepower (only able to postpone debt payments despite the fact that several countries needed more than just a 'breathing space' due to severe underlying structural problems). This in turn gave rise to the Common Framework, as explained in section 3 below.

3. Common Framework for Debt Treatments beyond the DSSI

12.236 As the eligible countries' ability to request suspension under the DSSI ended in December 2021, at the G20 Riyadh Summit, rather than extending the already twice-extended DSSI, the G20 countries endorsed a more comprehensive debt resolution framework: the Common Framework for Debt Treatments Beyond the DSSI (Common Framework). The Common Framework aims to facilitate on a case-by-case basis the debt restructurings of DSSI-eligible countries in order to provide a long-term and sustainable response to debt vulnerabilities aggravated by the depth and duration of the COVID-19 pandemic.[388]

12.237 The scope of the Common Framework is much broader than that of the DSSI as it can offer a tailor-made debt treatment to address both liquidity and solvency challenges of the requesting country. In the case of unsustainable debts, the Common Framework can provide a debt restructuring, for example, with a sufficient reduction in the NPV of debt to restore sustainability and/or help the country meet the debt sustainability requirements necessary to enable the IMF to lend.

12.238 The Common Framework can also be used by countries with continuing liquidity issues post-DSSI by providing a deferral of a portion of debt service payments (a reprofiling or rescheduling) for a number of years to ease financing pressures. In contrast to the DSSI, which applied uniform debt suspension to all eligible countries, the liquidity relief provided through the Common Framework is tailored to the requesting country's specific needs. The terms of repayment, including the grace period, are adjusted to meet the duration and

---

[387] In the context of the COVID-19 crisis, the CCRT aims to cover two years' worth of debt service to the IMF and has been funded by donor contributions, including from the European Union, Japan, and the United Kingdom.

[388] See G20 Leaders' Declaration, 21 November 2020, available at <http://www.g20.utoronto.ca/2020/2020-g20-leaders-declaration-1121.html>.

depth of the liquidity pressures faced by the country in question, which is a major advantage over the DSSI.

The Common Framework also seeks to address the lack of private sector participation in the DSSI. Unlike the DSSI, countries requesting a debt workout under the Common Framework are required to seek a treatment at least as favourable as the one agreed under the Common Framework with the G20 countries to ensure fair burden sharing from all creditors, including commercial creditors. However, it remains untested how the 'comparability of treatment' principle will be implemented in relation to commercial creditors under the Common Framework. It is difficult to understand why the private sector will agree on a haircut imposed by the official sector without even being heard. The same issue of lack of consultation remains, notwithstanding the non-binding nature of the arrangement. The agreed debt treatment arrangement between the debtor and its bilateral creditors under the Common Framework is to be recorded in a memorandum of understanding (MoU). To become effective, the MoU must be implemented by the participating creditors through bilateral agreements individually signed with the debtor country. As such, MoUs do not have a legal binding foundation that would be directly enforceable against third parties (ie the private creditors).[389]   **12.239**

In the absence of a legally binding mechanism to enforce comparability of treatment,[390] moral suasion of the G20/Paris Club countries may again be the method by which private creditors will be encouraged to participate. This may be particularly important in the context of the Sub-Saharan bonds that fall due over the next decade,[391] with a spike of maturities in 2024 and 2025.[392] If debt workouts under the Common Framework fail to involve bondholders this spike may overwhelm the sovereigns' ability to refinance their bonds.   **12.240**

As of September 2021, only three countries (Chad, Ethiopia, and Zambia) have requested debt treatments under the Framework.[393] Each has different characteristics and is moving at different speeds. Whereas Chad and Zambia look more like solvency candidates, Ethiopia looks more like a liquidity issue. The treatment of these cases could set a precedent for how the Framework will be operationalized. Chad could emerge as the first successful case of debt treatment under it,[394] sending a positive signal to other countries to seek help through the Framework. However, Chad has no bonds or publicly traded debts, and only one major commercial, external oil-backed loan. As such, it is not going to be a helpful precedent to showcase how the Common Framework might be applied in other countries, like Zambia, where global bonds represent a material portion of the defaulted debt. Therefore, uncertainty remains over how the Framework will apply to private creditors. It is not clear if a   **12.241**

---

[389] See International Development Agency and IMF, 'Heavily Indebted Poor Countries (HIPC) Initiative and Multilateral Debt Relief Initiative (MDRI)—Status of Implementation' (2009).

[390] Laura Gardner Cuesta, 'Unpacking the G20's Common Framework for Sovereign Debt Restructuring', *Debtwire* (10 February 2021).

[391] Anna Gross, African Countries Face 'Wall' of Sovereign Debt Repayments (10 February 2020), available at <https://www.ft.com/content/8c232df6-4451-11ea-abea-0c7a29cd66fe>.

[392] Gregory Smith, Can Africa's Wall of Eurobond Repayments Be Dismantled? (29 January 2020), available at <https://www.bondvigilantes.com/insights/2020/01/can-africas-wall-of-eurobond-repayments-be-dismantled>.

[393] Patrick Curran, 'DSSI Provides Limited Relief', *Tellimer* (19 July 2021).

[394] Paris Club, 4th Meeting of the Creditor Committee for Chad under the Common Framework (11 June 2021), available at <https://clubdeparis.org/en/communications/communique-presse/4th-meeting-of-the-creditor-committee-for-chad-under-the-common>.

restructuring of Ethiopia's bilateral debt under the Framework will extend to the country's sole issued bond, under the principle of comparability of treatment. The Ethiopian government has already indicated that it wants to exclude the bond, despite the comparable treatment clause because it consists of only 4 per cent of the total debt. But it remains to be seen whether the official bilateral creditors will agree in the light of criticisms of the DSSI over the lack of private sector participation. If Ethiopia is forced to include its bond debt, it risks losing market access. This may work as a disincentive to other countries from joining the Common Framework.

12.242   The Common Framework has, again, been criticized for its limited scope to DSSI eligible countries only. For example, the UN urged international organizations to choose beneficiary countries for any future debt relief initiatives based on the level of vulnerability rather than on income.[395] All countries facing liquidity and/or solvency issues aggravated by the pandemic should be able to request relief. For example, had the Common Framework existed in 2020, only one (Zambia) out of six defaulting countries in 2020 would have been eligible for the Common Framework. International bond financing comprises a larger proportion of middle-income countries' overall debt financing than DSSI-eligible countries. Whilst only 22 out of the 73 DSSI-eligible countries have international bonds,[396] most middle-income countries have several issued series of global bonds.

12.243   Table 12.4 summarizes the main features of the G20 DSSI and Common Framework Initiatives.

12.244   In summary, these two initiatives represent a historic achievement as it is the first time that Paris Club creditors and non-Paris Club G20 creditors have come together to agree on a

Table 12.4 Main Features of the G20 DSSI and Common Framework Initiatives

Main Features	DSSI	Common Framework
Beneficiary countries	73 low income/IDA-only countries	73 low income/IDA-only countries
Participating creditors	G20 countries	G20 countries
Purpose	Liquidity relief	Solvency or liquidity relief depending on individual circumstances of the beneficiary country that is requesting debt treatment
Available debt treatment	Temporary suspension of debt servicing payments of debts entered into before 24 March 2020	Restructuring; reprofiling; and/or rescheduling of any debts
Duration of the initiative	Beneficiary countries may request suspension between 1 May 2020 and 31 December 2021	No fixed end date

---

[395] United Nations, 'Debt and Covid-19: A Global Response in Solidarity' (17 April 2020) 7.
[396] Stuart Culverhouse, 'The G20's Common Framework six months on' (Tellimer, 30 July 2021).

common debt treatment framework in consultation with the IMF and World Bank. In addition to 22 Paris Club creditors, five non-Paris Club G20 members (China, India, Saudi Arabia, South Africa, and Turkey), and two non-Paris Club and non-G20 countries (Kuwait and the UAE) implemented the DSSI in 2020.[397] This is evidence that multilateral cooperation on debt issues can deliver concrete and meaningful results. However, the 'elephant in the room' is the non-involvement of the private sector, which has been presented with a fait accompli by the official sector where they are challenged with a take it 'as it is' or 'we will blame you' situation.

II. Conclusion

To sue or not to sue? That is the question. It is very likely that a creditor will be able to obtain a favourable ruling in a New York or an English court to collect the monies owed by a sovereign resulting from a debt obligation.   **12.245**

Enforcing a ruling is a completely different story. The creditor will have to face two different issues. On the one hand, sovereign immunity granted either by the FSIA or the SIA. And, on the other, to be able to find attachable assets.   **12.246**

The first issue does not present much uncertainty since the US Supreme Court has cleared any discussion by means of the *Weltover* case.[398] In that case it was stated that when a sovereign performs commercial activities in the manner of a private player within the market, its actions should be considered as 'commercial' according to the scope of the FSIA. Therefore, it will not be protected by sovereign immunity. The same is the case with the law in England.   **12.247**

The second issue, ie to find attachable assets, is one of great difficulty. Usually, assets located beyond the sovereign's own jurisdiction are not attachable (eg diplomatic missions, military assets, payments to or from multilateral organizations, etc). In addition: (1) central bank reserves enjoy a sovereign immunity that goes beyond the normal standard of immunity (ie pre-judgment attachment is forbidden in the US and subject to an express waiver in England; in addition, there is an overwhelming care in regard to the nature of said reserves under both regimes); and (2) payments of other debt instruments (mainly those resulting from a restructuring exercise) have been shielded either by an increase in the use of trust structures (the trustee acting as an agent of the bondholders) or as a result of norms as the one adopted in Belgium to protect payments made through clearing and settlement systems. Moreover, a sovereign in distress will repatriate attachable assets and/or avoid exposing them in other jurisdictions (eg national planes or vessels).[399]   **12.248**

There is some scope for litigation for those that make a living out of trading and investing in distressed debt—sophisticated investors that are familiar with the risks and can cope with   **12.249**

---

[397] Paris Club, 2020 Annual Report, p. 17, available at <https://clubdeparis.org/en/communications/press-release/publication-of-the-2020-annual-report-of-the-paris-club-15-07-2021>.

[398] *Republic of Argentina v Weltover, Inc*, 504 US 607 (1992).

[399] On 11 October 2012, the High Court of Ghana gave an interlocutory ruling which prevented a naval ship belonging to the Republic of Argentina from departing the shores of Ghana until the final determination of a substantive suit that NML Capital Limited, a New York-based entity, had commenced against Argentina in Ghana.

the costs of several years of litigation, usually in different jurisdictions.[400] The sovereign will play the long game and challenge any possible aspect, even knowing that most likely they will lose hope that either the creditor will run out of money and/or that another administration will be in office to foot the bill resulting from an adverse course order.

12.250   This leads to the fact that it is more likely that creditors will participate in an exchange offer—a call to voluntary tender the old bonds in exchange for new bonds—to restructure the non-performing/defaulted bonds. Exchange offers have been successful to restructure the outstanding bonds of a sovereign, eg Belize, Greece, Grenada, Ecuador, Pakistan, Russia, Ukraine, Uruguay, and even Argentina. Distressed investors and holdouts will continue trying to collect their monies. However, this is not detrimental to the capital markets since they are necessary to provide liquidity. In addition, distressed investors and holdouts can be discouraged by the inclusion and use of CACs and therefore the degree of participation can be increased by means of certain techniques (eg exit consents or enhancement of contractual provisions).

12.251   Therefore, if exchange offers are the way forward to restructure sovereign debt, the question to be faced is: which is the applicable legal framework, if there is one? The answer is that there is an informal ad hoc legal framework built on contractual law, previous restructuring experiences, and mainly New York and English case law.

12.252   The current ad hoc legal framework has two perspectives. One from the standpoint of the sovereign and one from the standpoint of the creditors. The path to be followed by the sovereign is either an exchange offer or—in most of the cases with bonds issued as of 2003—to use the collective will of bondholders in the event that the bonds contain CACs. The path to be followed by the creditors is either entering into an exchange offer (voluntary or through the use of CACs) or suing (collectively as a group or class or individually to collect on their claim).

12.253   Would the SDRM proposal be a solution to deal with rogue debtors? Not necessarily. The IMF should perform on the one hand, a discretionary role similar to that performed by central banks when they provide emergency liquidity assistance. On the other hand, it should develop a consistent policy in its dealing with member countries when experiencing balance-of-payments problems. With the benefit of hindsight, neither the bailouts of Mexico (1995), South East Asia (1997–1998), and Russia (1998) nor the lack of intervention as in the case of Argentina (2001–2002) are desired. Recent over-lending and/or roll-overs (Greece 2012 and Argentina 2020) also raise several questions. The involvement of the IMF in the restructuring negotiations as an uninterested third party to provide a critical analysis to the fiscal and budgetary projections (ie repayment capacity) can enhance creditor participation (in certain ways similar to that performed during the Brady plan). This is not something different from the current IMF's surveillance duty. It will only imply more proactivity. Conditionality also plays an important role in ascertaining political conscience, something which sometimes developing countries lack.

---

[400] In the still ongoing Argentine saga, there have been more than 30 attempts to attach assets—eg central bank reserves, payments to international organizations, military assets, satellites, etc—which have taken place all over the world, including among others France, Germany, Ghana, Italy, Switzerland, the UK, and several states within the US.

The IMF's SDRM proposal created a big intellectual debate but this initiative has been **12.254** shelved due to lack of support. Its occurrence is not foreseen in the near future and we may wonder if it will ever happen. Bonds are instruments of the financial markets and financial markets are neither keen on major changes nor on the introduction of third parties to regulate their functioning or a part of it (its restructuring) unless there is a real need.

The new additions to the international financial architecture, ie DSSI and the Common **12.255** Framework, were ill conceived as they do not involve the private creditors but hope to drag them along despite the fact that they are not consulted nor heard during the decision point.

In summary, the endorsement of the 'decentralized market-centred' approach vis-à-vis the **12.256** 'centralized statutorily non-market-oriented' approach is the best alternative to address sovereign debt restructuring. Within the decentralized market-centred approach, CACs have been useful to re-draft the whole scenario facilitating further restructurings and discouraging holdouts (the dissenting minority can be crammed down by the agreeing majority). Exit consents (despite the criticism after the Ecuadorian restructuring)[401] and the enhancement of contractual terms are useful techniques to augment the participation percentage.

As evidence demonstrates, previous episodes of sovereign bond restructuring have been **12.257** resolved quickly, without severe creditor coordination problems, and involving little litigation—the only significant exception being Argentina. So why mend something that is not broken? The exchange offers of Pakistan (1999), Ukraine (1999), Ecuador (2000 and 2020), Uruguay (2003), Argentina (2005–2010 and 2020), Belize (2006 and 2013), and Greece (2012) can be used to demonstrate that exchange offers work. In all of these cases, the degree of creditors' participation in the exchange offers has been above 90 per cent. Of the 34 sovereign bond exchanges since 1997, only two have been affected by holdout creditors.[402]

Different cases have demonstrated that litigation is not necessarily a solution. Therefore, **12.258** the use of trust structures should also be favoured as in the case of Uruguay and partially Argentina. Trust structures not only simplify dealings with creditors but also discourage litigation. In addition, they curtail attempts to freeze payments of the debtor, as payments are no longer in the hands of the sovereign.

---

[401] In addition, the criticism has become unfounded as a result of the use of voluntary 'tick-the-box' exit consents in the Uruguayan debt reprofiling of the year 2003.
[402] Duggar, Cantor, and Oosterveld, *supra* n 266.

ANNEX

Certain Key Differences Between the US Bankruptcy Code and the US Bank Resolution Statute (Sections 11 and 13 of the Federal Deposit Insurance Act)

Topic	Bankruptcy Code	Bank Resolution Statute
Applicability	Most individuals and business entities with specified connections to the United States are eligible; exceptions include most banks, credit unions, insurance companies, and insured depository institutions (IDIs).	All US state or federally chartered banks or savings associations whose deposits are insured by the FDIC.
Commencement of Proceedings	By debtor (voluntarily) or creditors (involuntarily).	By the institution's chartering authority or the FDIC.
Control of Business	Debtor in possession or bankruptcy trustee.	The FDIC, as receiver or conservator. Upon appointment as such, the FDIC automatically succeeds by operation of law to all of the rights, titles, powers, and privileges of any stockholder, member, officer, or director of the IDI.
Stay of Litigation	Automatic stay during the proceedings. Creditors may not prosecute litigation that was or could have been commenced before the filing of the petition; remedies against property (like foreclosure) also generally stayed.	No automatic stay in the case of receivership, except for automatic temporary one-business-day stay of the exercise of close-out rights on qualified financial contracts (QFCs). In the case of conservatorships, there is an automatic stay of the enforceability of all contractual rights and remedies (including in QFCs) that arise solely by virtue of appointment of conservator or insolvency of the institution, except in the case of D&O insurance policies or depository institution bonds (see enforceability of *ipso facto* clauses below). The FDIC as receiver or conservator may request a stay of litigation not to exceed 90 days or 45 days, respectively.
Close-Out of Certain Financial Contracts by Counterparties[1]	Protected financial contracts can be closed-out/netted immediately, and remedies against collateral can be exercised under exceptions to the automatic stay.	In the case of receivership, close-out/netting of QFCs by counterparties temporarily stayed for one business day in the case of a receivership (otherwise same as Bankruptcy Code) to allow receiver to determine which QFCs to transfer (all-or-none with a particular counterparty and its affiliates). In the case of conservatorship, close-out/netting of QFCs not permitted if triggered by appointment of conservator or insolvency (see enforceability of *ipso facto* clauses below).

[1] See sections 8.21 and 8.178 of Chapter 8 for further information regarding contractual limitations on qualified financial contract (QFC) cross-default rights required under the QFC Stay Rules and the implementation of these limitations through the ISDA Protocols.

Topic	Bankruptcy Code	Bank Resolution Statute
Customer Property	Customer property held by stockbrokers and commodity brokers is treated separately and specific rules govern its distribution. Customer name securities to be delivered to customers, with certain exceptions in the case of negative net equity.	No express provisions protecting customer property, although in practice property held in trust is unaffected by insolvency of the depository institution (although if the funds have been deposited in a bank that is placed in receivership, such funds are treated similarly with all other deposits of such bank). Under very old case law, customer property rights are respected only if properly segregated from bank's assets. Substantial legal uncertainty under that case law regarding what is required to satisfy segregation requirements short of physical segregation given the dematerialization of securities and other assets since those cases were decided.
Financial Assistance	Subject to the requirement of 'adequate protection' of existing lien holders, the debtor can obtain post-bankruptcy (DIP) financing and lenders can receive priming liens and super-priority claims (subject to Bankruptcy Court approval). Such financing can be provided by any source, including the federal government.	*Emergency Open Assistance:* upon a systemic risk determination by the FDIC, the Fed and the Treasury Secretary in consultation with the President, the FDIC may provide wide range of financial assistance to prevent financial instability, subject to specified limitations. *Closed Assistance:* as receiver, the FDIC may provide a wide range of financial assistance to assist in the resolution of the covered financial company.
Bridge Company	No concept of a bridge company, but nothing prevents the debtor-in-possession from setting up a company and seeking an order from the bankruptcy court to transfer all or any part of its assets and liabilities to the new company under Section 363 of the US Bankruptcy Code and appointing a trustee to manage the affairs of the new company for the benefit of the bankruptcy estate.	The FDIC can organize a bridge bank to assume liabilities or purchase assets of the failed institution, and such liabilities and assets can be quickly transferred to such entity.
Prompt Transfer of Assets and Liabilities to Buyer	A quick sale of assets to a third party can be done with the approval of the bankruptcy court under Section 363 of the US Bankruptcy Code.	The FDIC has broad discretion to sell or transfer assets and liabilities to a third party, notwithstanding any otherwise applicable consent requirements, subject to certain limitations in the statute but no meaningful judicial review.

Topic	Bankruptcy Code	Bank Resolution Statute
Cherry-Picking Powers	Select assets can be sold free and clear of claims and liens, subject to court approval of the transfer, but limited by close-outs of protected financial contracts and subject to providing for the value of existing liens. Selected liabilities may be assumed by a buyer.	The FDIC has broad discretion to cherry-pick which assets or liabilities to transfer even among the same class of creditors, subject to three limits: (i) any left-behind claimants would be entitled to a minimum distribution equal to what they would have received in a liquidation as if no such transfer took place; (ii) if the FDIC transfers any QFCs with a particular counterparty, it must transfer all QFCs with that counterparty; and (iii) all assets are transferred subject to pre-existing liens unless the FDIC is able to invalidate the lien pursuant to one of its 'super powers' discussed below.
Assumption or Rejection of Executory Contracts and Leases	Executory contracts or leases must either be assumed and performed/assigned or rejected upon approval of the Bankruptcy Court.	The FDIC has broad discretion to repudiate or disaffirm any contract or lease (not merely executory contracts) within a reasonable period of time (not defined) after its appointment as receiver.
Damages for Rejected or Repudiated Contracts	Breach of contract damages generally allowed for rejected contracts. Administrative expense claims generally allowed to the extent the debtor accepted benefits under the contract after the petition date.	Damages for repudiation or disaffirmance are limited to 'actual direct compensatory damages' (resulting in smaller damages claims than for identical contracts rejected under the Bankruptcy Code) determined as of the date of the appointment of the receiver, with the exception of QFCs, for which damages are calculated as of the date of disaffirmance or repudiation and are measured in accordance with market custom (cost of cover included).
Enforceability of *Ipso Facto* Clauses	Generally unenforceable, with exceptions for financing contracts, protected financial contracts, and other protected agreements.	Unenforceable in any contracts (other than QFCs in receivership, D&O insurance policies, or depository institution bonds).
Oral Contracts	In some cases, oral agreements can form the basis of a claim.	Only written contracts approved by the board or loan committee of the failed institution contemporaneously with acquisition of any related asset and continuously maintained as an official record of the failed institution will be recognized under the statute.
Definition of a 'Claim'; Contingent Claims	A right to payment, including a contingent or unliquidated right. Generally speaking, contingent claims, such as under undrawn guarantees or letters of credit, loan commitments, or unused portions of committed lines of credit, are provable and estimated by the Bankruptcy Court.	Not defined. Generally speaking, the amount of an allowed claim is determined by applicable non-insolvency law. The FDIC takes the position that contingent claims, such as under undrawn guarantees or letters of credit, unused loan commitments, or unused portions of committed lines of credit, are not provable claims or can be repudiated without creating any claim for damages.

Topic	Bankruptcy Code	Bank Resolution Statute
Partially Secured Creditors	Partially secured claims are divided into secured and un-secured portions based on the value of the collateral. The secured portion gener-ally must receive the value of the collateral; the unsecured portion receives distributions comparable to other general unsecured claims.	Portion of claim that exceeds the value of the collateral considered unsecured. No payments may be made with respect to un-secured claims other than in connection with the disposition of all unsecured claims.
Post-Insolvency Interest	Generally disallowed, except (i) where the debtor is solvent and (ii) to the extent the value of a secured creditor's col-lateral exceeds its principal claim.	Generally not payable, with exceptions for QFCs or as the FDIC may provide by regula-tion, policy statement, or staff interpretation.
Unequal Treatment of Similarly Situated Creditors	Generally, similarly situ-ated creditors are required to receive similar treatment in a reorganization under chapter 11 or a liquidation under chapter 7, although favoured treatment for selected creditors can be au-thorised by the bankruptcy court if such treatment is found to preserve or en-hance the value of the estate for remaining creditors. For example, critical vendors payments may be approved by the bankruptcy court, and selected liabilities may be assumed by a buyer in a bank-ruptcy court approved sale, subject to the good business reason test described above.	The FDIC has broad authority to take actions that result in unequal treatment of similarly situated creditors (cherry-picking liabilities to be assumed by third party or bridge com-pany, as described above). While the statute requires left-behind creditors to receive at least as much as they would have received in a liquidation as if no unequal treatment took place, it is unclear who makes this determin-ation, the degree to which judicial review is available, and the remedy for failure to meet this standard after transfer of assets to a bridge company or third party.
Priority of Unsecured Claims	Tax claims and certain al-lowed unsecured claims (including those based upon any commitment by the debtor to a federal deposi-tory institution's regulatory agency, or the predecessor to such agency, to maintain the capital of an IDI) have pri-ority junior to administrative expenses, but senior to other unsecured creditors.	The Federal Deposit Insurance Act provides a hierarchy of recoveries: first are the FDIC's administrative expenses; second, deposit claims (both insured and uninsured); third, general unsecured creditors; fourth, subor-dinated claims; and finally shareholder claims, in order of rank.

Topic	Bankruptcy Code	Bank Resolution Statute
Avoidability of Perfected Security Interests	'Preferential' transfers made on account of antecedent debt within 90 days before bankruptcy (or one year for insiders) while debtor was insolvent may be avoided under Section 547, but defences include transfers for 'new value' and transfers made in the ordinary course of business. Certain protected financial contracts are exempt from preference risk.	The FDIC interprets the statute to give it the power to avoid any security interest (unless securing a QFC) if taken 'in contemplation of the company's insolvency.' No insolvency requirement or new value exception. On its face, substantial legal uncertainty about scope of this avoidance power. But old case law has effectively limited this avoidance power to security interests taken within days of conservatorship or receivership after the board of the insured institution became aware the institution would be closed because of the role of banks in processing huge volumes of payments and transfers for others. Security interests taken to secure QFCs are avoidable only if taken with 'actual intent' to hinder, delay, or defraud.
Fraudulent Transfer	Pre-bankruptcy transfers made or obligations incurred on or within two years prior to the petition date (i) with actual intent to hinder, delay or defraud creditors or (ii) for less than 'reasonably equivalent value' and while the debtor was insolvent or that rendered the debtor insolvent, are generally voidable, subject to certain defences. State law fraudulent conveyance laws also apply. Certain protected financial contracts are exempt from constructive fraudulent transfer risk.	The FDIC has the power to set aside fraudulent transfers based on applicable state fraudulent transfer law. In addition, the FDIC has the power to set aside transfers by certain insiders or debtors of the financial company if made within five years of the receivership with the intent to hinder, delay, or defraud. The FDIC's power under this special provision is superior to that of a trustee in bankruptcy. Certain defences are available.
Judicial Supervision of Claims Process	Yes, by the Bankruptcy Court.	No, the FDIC has broad authority to conduct the administrative claims process, subject only to after-the-fact *de novo* judicial review.
Rule-making and Legal Guidance	There are statutory requirements of notice and hearing for most substantive actions, as well as procedural rules, case law, and legal commentary interpreting the Bankruptcy Code. The Federal Rules of Bankruptcy Procedure are prescribed by the federal judiciary, subject to the right of Congress to reject or modify such Rules. The various Bankruptcy Courts may enact their own Local Rules.	The FDIC has the right but not the duty to make any rules or regulations implementing the bank resolution statute. The FDIC has issued only a few regulations (see 12 CFR Part 360). Other guidance is limited to policy statements (which can be withdrawn at any time, possibly with retroactive effect) and staff opinions (which are invariably expressly stated not to be binding on the FDIC).

Topic	Bankruptcy Code	Bank Resolution Statute
Assessments	Administrative creditors of the debtor are granted priority over pre-bankruptcy creditors with respect to estate assets, and trustees and professionals receive compensation subject to approval of the Bankruptcy Court.	The FDIC would has the power to recoup its costs, if any, of resolving a covered financial company from the deposit insurance fund and by making assessments against commonly controlled IDIs (cross-guarantee liability).

Name Index

Subject Index